THE OXFORD HANDBOOK OF

DIGITAL DIPLOMACY

THE OXFORD HANDBOOK OF

DIGITAL DIPLOMACY

Edited by
CORNELIU BJOLA
and
ILAN MANOR

OXFORD
UNIVERSITY PRESS

Great Clarendon Street, Oxford, OX2 6DP,
United Kingdom

Oxford University Press is a department of the University of Oxford.
It furthers the University's objective of excellence in research, scholarship,
and education by publishing worldwide. Oxford is a registered trade mark of
Oxford University Press in the UK and in certain other countries

© Oxford University Press 2024

The moral rights of the authors have been asserted

First Edition published in 2024

All rights reserved. No part of this publication may be reproduced, stored in
a retrieval system, or transmitted, in any form or by any means, without the
prior permission in writing of Oxford University Press, or as expressly permitted
by law, by licence or under terms agreed with the appropriate reprographics
rights organization. Enquiries concerning reproduction outside the scope of the
above should be sent to the Rights Department, Oxford University Press, at the
address above

You must not circulate this work in any other form
and you must impose this same condition on any acquirer

Published in the United States of America by Oxford University Press
198 Madison Avenue, New York, NY 10016, United States of America

British Library Cataloguing in Publication Data
Data available

Library of Congress Control Number: 2023944918

ISBN 978–0–19–285919–8

DOI: 10.1093/oxfordhb/9780192859198.001.0001

Printed and bound by
CPI Group (UK) Ltd, Croydon, CR0 4YY

Links to third party websites are provided by Oxford in good faith and
for information only. Oxford disclaims any responsibility for the materials
contained in any third party website referenced in this work.

CONTENTS

List of Figures and Tables   ix
List of Contributors   xiii

PART I   CONCEPTS AND THEORIES

1. Introduction: Understanding Digital Diplomacy—The Grammar
   Rules and Patterns of Digital Disruption   3
   CORNELIU BJOLA AND ILAN MANOR

2. Digital Diplomacy: Projection and Retrieval of Images
   and Identities   29
   MARCUS HOLMES

3. From Micro to Macro Digital Disruptions: A New Prism for
   Investigating Digital Diplomacy   45
   ILAN MANOR AND JAMES PAMMENT

4. Soft Power in the Digital Space   63
   GARY D. RAWNSLEY

5. Researching Influence Operations: 'Dark Arts' Mercenaries
   and the Digital Influence Industry   80
   EMMA L. BRIANT

PART II   DIPLOMATIC PRACTICES

6. Diplomatic Negotiations in the Digital Context: Key Issues,
   Emerging Trends, and Procedural Changes   103
   KRISTIN ANABEL EGGELING AND REBECCA ADLER-NISSEN

7. Digital Diplomacy and Cyber Defence   121
   LUCAS KELLO

vi CONTENTS

8. Digital Nuclear Diplomacy 138
RHYS CRILLEY

9. Digital Feminist Foreign Policy 157
JENNIFER A. CASSIDY

10. History and Digital Public Diplomacy: Media Disruption and Global Public Engagement Online in Historical Perspective 177
NICHOLAS J. CULL

11. Digital Cultural Diplomacy: From Content Providers to Opinion Makers 194
NATALIA GRINCHEVA

12. Digital Propaganda and Diplomacy 212
PAWEŁ SUROWIEC-CAPELL

13. Ethical Challenges in the Digitalization of Public Diplomacy 232
ZHAO ALEXANDRE HUANG AND PHILLIP ARCENEAUX

14. Transforming International Development: Navigating the Shift towards Digital Cooperation 250
LUCIANA ALEXANDRA GHICA

15. New Trends in Digital Diplomacy: The Rise of TikTok and the Geopolitics of Algorithmic Governance 269
ALICIA FJÄLLHED, MATTHIAS LÜFKENS, AND ANDREAS SANDRE

PART III DIPLOMATIC INSTITUTIONS

16. The Digital Hybridization of Ministries of Foreign Affairs: The Case of the Nordic and Baltic States 291
CORNELIU BJOLA AND DIDZIS KĻAVIŅŠ

17. Digital Diplomatic Cultures 311
GEOFFREY WISEMAN

18. The Digitalization of Permanent Missions to International Organizations 330
CAROLINE BOUCHARD

19. The Digital Adaptation of International Bureaucracies 348
MATTHIAS ECKER-EHRHARDT

CONTENTS   vii

20. Virtual Diplomatic Summitry   367
    ELSA HEDLING

21. Digital Diplomacy and Non-Governmental and Transnational
    Organizations   383
    FIONA MCCONNELL AND ALEX MANBY

22. Digitalization of Diplomacy: Implications for Cities   401
    EFE SEVIN

23. Digital Diplomatic Representation: The Rise of Tech
    Ambassadors   420
    ANNE MARIE ENGTOFT MELDGAARD AND TOM FLETCHER

24. International Law, Big Tech Regulation, and Digital Diplomatic
    Practice   437
    VICTORIA BAINES

PART IV DIPLOMATIC RELATIONS

25. The European Union and Digital Diplomacy: Projecting Global
    Europe in the Social Media Era   457
    RUBEN ZAIOTTI

26. NATO's Digital Diplomacy   475
    KATHARINE A. M. WRIGHT

27. Digital Diplomacy of the Central Asian Countries   491
    ALISHER FAIZULLAEV

28. Chinese Wolf-Warrior Diplomacy: Motivations, Modalities, and
    Sites of Practice   511
    ANDREW F. COOPER AND JEFF HAI-CHI LOO

29. Diversities and Developments in Asia Pacific Digital Diplomacy   528
    DAMIEN SPRY

30. Digital Diplomacy in Latin America: Among Early Adopters and
    Latecomers   546
    DANIEL AGUIRRE AND ALEJANDRO RAMOS

31. Diplomacy in Times of Crisis in the GCC: The Blockade and the
    Pandemic   564
    BANU AKDENIZLI

32. The North–South Divide, the Digital Agenda, and Digital Diplomacy 582
JORGE HEINE AND JUAN PABLO PRADO LALLANDE

33. International Geopolitics and Digital Games in the Nationalist Agenda of Great Powers 600
ANTONIO CÉSAR MORENO CANTANO

34. Digital Diplomacy during Wars and Conflicts 619
MORAN YARCHI

Index 637

LIST OF FIGURES AND TABLES

FIGURES

1.1	Visual simplicity in action: tweets with asymmetrical quality of information	9
1.2	Emotional framing in action: tweets with contrasting emotional valence	10
1.3	Computational personalisation in action: tweets with contrasting connective action	12
1.4	Hybridity complementing face-to-face diplomacy	14
6.1	Exemplary COREPER I meeting agenda posted on Twitter on 22 December 2021	111
8.1	US Strategic Command tweet	148
8.2	ICAN's Instagram	149
8.3	Rafael Mariano Grossi and the IAEA head to Ukraine	151
8.4	NAFO and 'the superbonker 9000'	152
9.1	Soft power 'resources'	162
9.2	@SweMFA coded tweets online (2021)	167
9.3	Sweden's soft power 'resources' online (2021)	167
9.4	@SRE_mx coded tweets online (2021)	170
9.5	Mexico's soft power 'resources' online (2021)	171
9.6	Comparative context soft power 'resources' online (2021)	173
16.1	Digital hybridization as assemblage formation	296
19.1	Types of Facebook pages and Twitter accounts across time	353
28.1	An analytical framework to explain China's wolf-warrior diplomacy	516
30.1	Years Latin American MFAs joined Twitter (2009-2020)	548
30.2	Ranking of Latin American presence on social media platforms	552
33.1	The Uncensored Library in *Minecraft*	601
33.2	An *H1Z1* player waves the Taiwanese flag in protest against the Chinese majority group Red Army	604
33.3	Screenshot of the video game *FAU-G* celebrating the Indian Army in its fight to defend territorial integrity against China	612

TABLES

12.1	Key differentiators between digital propaganda and digital diplomacy	218
14.1	UN Roadmap for digital cooperation (2020)	258
16.1	The digital presence of Baltic and Nordic MFAs	298
16.2	Common themes of digital hybridization across Baltic and Nordic MFAs	299
16.3	Distribution of digital hybridization themes by country (number of references per topic)	300
16.4	Distribution of the intensity of digital hybridization by country (number of references per category)	301
16.5	Distribution of digital hybridization themes and intensity by region	302
16.6	Key features of the three models of digital assemblages	305
22.1	Case selection	407
22.2	Data gathered per case	408
22.3	Logic of practice	408
22.4	Summary of diplomatic activities	410
22.5	Summary of branding activities	412
22.6	Descriptive information on tweets	413
22.7	Summary of digitization	414
27.1	Population, spread of the Internet, social media, and mobile connection in CAC as of early 2022	493
27.2	Social media accounts of CAC presidents as of 01 August 2023	498
27.3	Social media accounts and Telegram channels of CAC foreign ministries as of 01 August 2023 (with percentage of followers' growth compared to 01 January 2022)	499
27.4	The Twitter accounts of the foreign ministries of CAC as of 01 January 2022 and 01 June 2022	500
27.5	Posts on the Facebook accounts of the MFAs of CAC for the period from 01 October 2021 to 25 December 2021	501
27.6	Social media accounts of the permanent missions of CAC to the UN as of 01 August 2023 (with the percentage of growth in the number of followers since 01 October 2021)	502
27.7	The Twitter activity of the permanent missions of CAC to the UN from 01 October 2021 to 01 June 2022 (data from 06 June 2022)	502
27.8	The use of Twitter by Permanent Representatives of CAC to the UN as of 01 October 2022	503

27.9	Social media accounts of the embassies of CAC in Washington, DC, as of 01 August 2023 (with percentage of growth in the number of followers since 01 January 2022)	504
27.10	Social media accounts of the embassies of CAC in Moscow, Russia as of 01 August 2023 (with percentage of growth or decline in the number of followers since 01 October 2021)	504
30.1	A Latin American conceptual mosaic of a decade of digital diplomacy	550
30.2	Twitter follower count of MFA institutions vs. president and FA minister	551
30.3	Latin American ranking of the most followed leaders and foreign ministers on Twitter	556

Contributors

Rebecca Adler-Nissen, Professor, Department of Political Science, University of Copenhagen

Banu Akdenizli, Associate Professor of Communication, Northwestern University Qatar

Phillip Arceneaux, Assistant Professor of Strategic Communication, Miami University of Ohio

Daniel Aguirre, Senior Global Futures Scientist, Arizona State University.

Victoria Baines, IT Livery Company Professor of Information Technology at Gresham College, London

Corneliu Bjola, Associate Professor, Diplomatic Studies, University of Oxford

Emma L. Briant, Associate Professor of News and Political Communication, Monash University

Caroline Bouchard, Associate Professor Department of Social and Public Communication, Université du Québec à Montréal, Québec

Antonio César Moreno Cantano, Associate Professor, Department of International Relations and Global History, Universidad Complutense Madrid

Jennifer A. Cassidy, Department Lecturer Diplomatic Studies Program, University of Oxford

Andrew F. Cooper, University Research Chair, Department of Political Science, and Professor, the Balsillie School of International Affairs, University of Waterloo.

Nicholas J. Cull, Professor of Public Diplomacy, University of Southern California

Rhys Crilley, Lecturer in International Relations, Department of Politics and International Relations, University of Glasgow

Matthias Ecker-Ehrhardt, Senior Researcher, Centre for Global Cooperation Research, Universität Duisburg-Essen

Kristin Anabel Eggeling, Assistant Professor, Department of Political Science, University of Copenhagen

Anne Marie Engtoft Meldgaard., Tech Ambassador, Ministry of Foreign Affairs of Denmark

Alisher Faizullaev, D.Sc. and Ph.D., Adjunct Professor, Webster University in Tashkent.

Alicia Fjällhed, PhD-student at the Department of Strategic Communication, Lund University

Tom Fletcher, Principal of Hertford College, University of Oxford

Luciana Alexandra Ghica, Associate Professor, Department of Comparative Governance and European Studies, University of Bucharest

Natalia Grincheva, Programme Leader, BA Arts Management, LASALLE College of the Arts Singapore, University of the Arts Singapore Senior Research Fellow (Honorary), Digital Studio, The University of Melbourne

Elsa Hedling, Associate Senior Lecturer, European Studies, Centre for Languages and Literature, Lund University

Jorge Heine, Research Professor, Frederick S. Pardee School of Global Studies, Boston University

Marcus Holmes, Professor, Department of Government, William & Mary

Zhao Alexandre Huang, Associate Professor in Information and Communication Sciences, Université Paris Nanterre

Lucas Kello, Associate Professor and Departmental Lecturer, Department of Politics and International Relations, University of Oxford

Didzis Kļaviņš, Senior Researcher, University of Latvia, Faculty of Social Sciences

Juan Pablo Prado Lallande, Associate Professor, Faculty of Law and Social Sciences, University of Puebla

Jeff Hai-chi Loo, PhD student in the Global Governance program at Balsillie School of International Affairs, University of Waterloo

Matthias Lüfkens, Founder of DigiTips, Geneva-Based digital advisory firm, Founder of Twiplomacy

Alex Manby, PhD Student, School of Geography and the Environment, University of Oxford

Ilan Manor, Senior Lecturer, Department of Communication Studies, Ben Gurion University of the Negev

Fiona McConnell, Professor of Political Geography, School of Geography and the Environment, University of Oxford

James Pamment, Associate Professor, Department of Strategic Communication, Lund University

Alejandro Ramos, Deputy Head of Mission, Embassy of Mexico in New Zealand, Ministry of Foreign Affairs of Mexico

Gary D. Rawnsley, Head of the School of Social & Political Sciences, University Professor of Public Diplomacy of Lincoln, University of Lincoln

Andreas Sandre, Press and Public Affairs Officer, The Embassy of Italy to the United States in Washington

Efe Sevin, Assistant Professor, Department of Mass Communication, Towson University

Damien Spry, Adjunct Research Fellow, University of South Australia

Paweł Surowiec-Capell, Senior Lecturer in Public Relations and Strategic Communication, Department of Journalism Studies, University of Sheffield

Geoffrey Wiseman, Professor and Endowed Chair in Applied Diplomacy, Grace School of Applied Diplomacy, DePaul University, Chicago.

Katharine A. M. Wright, Senior Lecturer in International Politics, Newcastle University

Moran Yarchi, Professor, Sammy Ofer School of Communications, Reichman University

Ruben Zaiotti, Associate Professor, Director of Jean Monnet European Union Centre of Excellence, Dalhousie University

PART I

CONCEPTS AND THEORIES

CHAPTER 1

INTRODUCTION: UNDERSTANDING DIGITAL DIPLOMACY—THE GRAMMAR RULES AND PATTERNS OF DIGITAL DISRUPTION

CORNELIU BJOLA AND ILAN MANOR

INTRODUCTION

As Machiavelli reminds us, innovation is not easy to implement: 'it ought to be remembered that there is nothing more difficult to take in hand, more perilous to conduct, or more uncertain in its success, than to take the lead in the introduction of a new order of things' (Machiavelli, 2000: 10). The case of the digital disruption of diplomacy supports Machiavelli's insight. Etymologically, the term disruption originates from the past-participle stem of Latin disrumpere 'break apart, split, shatter, break to pieces', where dis- stands for 'apart' + rumpere for 'to break' (Hoad, 2003). Its meaning is thus epistemically infused with negative connotations of discontinuity, fragmentation, and destruction. However, the context in which it is mostly discussed exudes optimistic aspirations of technological progress, political emancipation, and economic development. As discussed in more detail elsewhere (Bjola, 2018), the most fascinating aspect of technological disruption is its remarkable capacity for both destruction and creation. On the one hand, by laying the groundwork for new economic or social opportunities, new technologies stimulate new thinking and innovative practices that reinforce and sustain them in the long term. On the other hand, by disrupting traditional ways in which people work, collaborate, and research, they also create pervasive conditions for active and enduring resistance against them.

Digital diplomacy is a good example of how disruption applies to international affairs. In simple terms, *digital diplomacy refers to the use of digital technologies, such as social media and other online platforms, including virtual communication channels and the metaverse, by ministries of foreign affairs (MFAs) and international organizations (IOs) to communicate with each other and the general public, conduct diplomacy, and advance their foreign policy goals.* It includes activities such as sending and receiving official statements, exchanging informal diplomatic signals, participating in virtual conferences and meetings, and engaging with the public through social media and other online platforms to explain and promote their policies and positions. Digital diplomacy is thus seen by governments and IOs as a way to reach a wider audience and connect with people in different parts of the world in real-time. It also allows these organizations to be more transparent and accountable to the public, as well as to respond more quickly to events and issues that arise.

Therein lies the potential of digital technologies to disrupt traditional diplomacy and international relations, primarily by influencing how diplomacy is conducted. By making it possible for MFAs and IOs to communicate and collaborate in real-time, digital diplomacy enables decision-makers to be more efficient and effective in their bilateral and multilateral relations. This may be particularly relevant in the case of international crises as direct communication between parties in conflict can help de-escalate tensions and facilitate the resolution of disputes (Cassidy and Manor, 2016). However, it can also create new challenges, such as the potential for the spread of misinformation and propaganda, which can further inflame tensions (Bjola, 2020). Digital diplomacy may also affect the balance of power between different countries, as it allows smaller and less powerful actors to have a greater voice and influence in international affairs. Furthermore, non-state actors such as civil society organizations and NGOs can also use digital tools to advocate for their causes and to challenge the policies of larger and more powerful actors (Hall, Schmitz, and Dedmon, 2019).

The increasing use of virtual diplomacy, which the Covid-19 pandemic has accelerated, may lead to a decline in the role of physical embassies and diplomatic missions, as governments and IOs rely more on digital channels to communicate and collaborate (Bjola and Manor, 2022). This could have implications for the ability of governments and organizations to build and maintain relationships with other countries and international organizations, which face-to-face diplomacy is supposed to foster (Holmes and Wheeler, 2020). Digital diplomacy has also disrupted the way that public opinion is shaped and influenced, as it allows MFAs and IOs to communicate directly with the public through social media and other online platforms (Manor, 2019). This gives them greater control over the information that is shared, but it also allows for greater transparency and accountability, as digital tools can be used to share information and engage with the domestic and international public more directly.

It is also important to note that while the terms *digitized* and *digital diplomacy* will be used interchangeably in this volume, they bear slightly different meanings. Digitization primarily refers to the technical aspect underlying the adoption of digital technologies by MFAs in their work, as when conventional means of diplomatic engagement are improved and streamlined with the assistance of digital technologies. From this perspective, the digitization of diplomacy represents the process of conducting traditional diplomacy in a digital context through the use of online platforms, training management systems, and bespoke software to deliver content and facilitate communication and collaboration between diplomats and their partners. In contrast, the term 'digital diplomacy' calls attention to a broader perspective of the role of digital technology in diplomacy, not only as an instrument or medium of communication and collaboration but also as a different mode of thinking about and practising diplomacy. From this perspective, digital diplomacy encompasses the process of upgrading, augmenting, and rewiring diplomacy in a digital context.[1]

Upgrading refers to the incorporation of digital formats into existing diplomatic tasks and activities, such as the use of social media platforms like Facebook and Twitter (now X) for public diplomacy, in addition to traditional print media and television. *Augmenting* goes beyond upgrading by expanding the field of diplomacy to previously inaccessible areas, such as the appointment of tech ambassadors or the establishment of virtual embassies. *Rewiring* fundamentally alters the way diplomacy is conducted by blurring or even eliminating the distinction between offline and online diplomacy, as the process of hybridization has just begun to do. It is crucial to understand the technical aspects of the technological revolution that is disrupting diplomacy, but at the same time, we should not overlook the broader and deeper impact that digital technologies have had on the conduct of diplomacy. To truly grasp the implications and opportunities of the digital age for diplomacy, we need to consider all three dimensions—upgrading, augmenting, and rewiring. They serve to enhance our understanding and ability to navigate the ongoing transformations within the field of diplomacy, as well as the challenges it faces in its endeavour to maintain relevance and effectiveness in the international arena in the digital age.

The purpose of this handbook is to provide an authoritative account of the disruptive role of digital diplomacy as an instrument of foreign policy. To this end, the handbook brings together a wide range of contributions to engage in theoretical reflections and case study discussions of the processes by which digital technologies have disrupted diplomatic theory, practices, institutions, and relations. It pursues four key objectives. First, the volume aims to provide a comprehensive understanding of the concepts and theories related to digital diplomacy. The first thematic section thus focuses on the dynamics of technological disruption, power, identity, and influence among key players such as MFAs, embassies, private actors, and social media platforms. It endeavours to understand when, why, and how these actors exert their influence in the digital age, and how the digital transformation affects diplomatic practice and international relations. Second, the handbook offers a thematic overview of the study of digital diplomacy practices, encompassing traditional themes such as public diplomacy, negotiation, and international development, as well as emerging themes such as cyber defence, feminist foreign policy, tech regulation, ethics, and more. It engages with dominant understandings and practices of digital diplomacy reflectively and analytically,

---

[1] This metaphor is inspired by a similar argument put forth by Bjola and Kornprobst (2023) regarding the progression of international relations theory in the digital age.

exploring the intersections of issues such as media, gender, ethics, and algorithmic governance with the theory and practice of digital diplomacy.

Third, the handbook explores how diplomatic institutions have adjusted their internal structures and cultures to stay current with digital advancements and how they are addressing regulatory challenges. It also investigates how diplomatic institutions are adapting their approach to forms and mechanisms of bilateral and multilateral representation and how digital technologies are affecting the way diplomatic organizations interact with each other and non-state actors. The fourth section of this volume provides an in-depth examination of the current state of digital diplomacy within ministries of foreign affairs and regional organizations around the world, and its impact on their operations and effectiveness in the global arena. Through an analysis of case studies and data from a diverse range of countries, including Europe, Asia Pacific, South America, the Middle East, and more, this section explores the various approaches and strategies adopted by these institutions to integrate digital diplomacy into their operations. It also examines the challenges and barriers faced by these institutions in the adoption and implementation of digital diplomacy, and how they have been overcome.

The starting point of our discussion in this introductory chapter is the digital medium, more specifically the 'grammar rules' that control the logic of interaction in the digital space: visual simplicity, emotional framing, computational personalization, and engagement hybridization. We argue that these rules reflect how digital technologies have disrupted the space in which diplomacy operates. In so doing, they have challenged MFAs and IOs to adapt so that they can maintain their ability to meaningfully influence policy outcomes in the international arena. In the second part of the chapter, we examine five patterns of disruption of diplomacy under the impact of digital technologies (from below, from above, from aside, through diffusion, and through crisis) and explain how the contributions to this volume analytically illuminate each category.

THE DIGITAL MEDIUM IS THE MESSAGE

The Canadian communication theorist Marshall McLuhan once famously remarked that 'the medium is the message' (McLuhan, 2012), a phrase that has since become emblematic for describing the social role and political influence of media technologies in contemporary societies. What McLuhan suggested was that the medium of communication is just as significant, if not more so, than the message being conveyed. This is mainly because the medium affects both how we craft the message that we seek to deliver to our intended audiences and how the message is received by the public. McLuhan's observation was made, of course, in a particular historical context, the 1960s, when television surpassed print newspapers and radio as the main public sources of information. One could similarly argue that its meaning remains relevant today as well, in the digital age. Surveys show, for instance, that social media platforms such as Facebook, Twitter, and Instagram have outpaced print newspapers as the public's most-frequented medium in

Western countries and they might be able to close the gap with television soon enough (Shearer, 2018; Ofcom, 2019).

That being said, in what way can we actually claim that the digital medium is indeed the message, as McLuhan might suggest? What is specific about the digital medium to make it stand distinct compared with other forms of communication and to what extent does its distinctiveness have any bearing on how the message is crafted, delivered, and received? We argue in this section that the distinctiveness of the digital medium is shaped by four dominant mechanisms that control the logic of message design and communication: visual simplicity, emotional framing, computational personalization, and engagement hybridization. These four mechanisms are not entirely novel, but their combination generates patterns of digital engagement that are distinctly different from those promoted by previous mediums and channels of communication. Similarly to how grammar rules govern how we communicate verbally, these mechanisms govern how we communicate digitally. Visual simplicity affects the format and texture of the information to be transmitted, emotional framing informs the style and form of messaging, computational personalization shifts the focus of communication from macro- to micro-level alignment, while engagement hybridization allows for physical and virtual environments to integrate, complement, and empower each other.

Digital grammar rules

The main source of influence of the digital medium is data.[2] This influence stems from how data is generated, stored, accessed, analysed, and used. Statistics show that 60% of the world's population is now online and each person generates around 1.7 MB of data every second. In 2021, the total amount of data created by all digital users was about 74 zettabytes (one ZB is the equivalent of one trillion GBs), but the digital universe is expected to grow to 149 zettabytes by the end of 2024 (Andre, no date). Qualitatively, 80–90% of the overall digital data universe is made of unstructured data (i.e., information that comes in different formats that are not easily searchable and storable), out of which only 0.5% is analysed and used today (Dialani, 2020). Furthermore, new formats of data are also emerging on top of the data produced by real-world events. For example, synthetic data, that is, data artificially generated using mathematical models or algorithms, as opposed to real data, which is directly observed from the real world, is estimated to completely overshadow real data in AI models by 2030 (Goasduff, 2022).

> **Rule #1:** *Visual simplicity: visual messages with low-quality information content travel faster and further.*

---

[2] This section draws on a distinct examination of the authenticity criteria for digital diplomacy (Bjola, 2022).

The information glut brought about by the 'data revolution' (Kitchin, 2014) has important implications for how people communicate online and interact socially, which in turn engenders new opportunities but also challenges for digital diplomacy. First and foremost is the growing role of visual over text-based messaging in political communication (Muñoz and Towner, 2017; Lalancette and Raynauld, 2019). As Crilley et al. point out, the visual power of digital images comes from their ability to project themselves into the symbolic universe of understandings, emotions, and purposes that inform people's political behaviour (Crilley, Manor, and Bjola, 2020). As discussed elsewhere, diplomatic communication has traditionally been embedded in a textual-oriented culture that has favoured verbal refinement over precision (Bjola, Cassidy, and Manor, 2019: 85–86). The digital medium has, in turn, shifted attention from textual interpretations and verbal subtleties to the role of images and visual narratives in shaping people's understanding of world events.

Weng et al. (2012) have shown that the combination of social network structure and competition for finite user attention provides a sufficient condition for the emergence of a broad diversity of viral content. However, out of the 'soup' of contending viral messages, those that come on top contain low-quality information, as both the information load and the limited attention of the users lead to low discriminative power (Qiu et al., 2017). In other words, the intrinsic features of social media platforms favour the formation of viral content, but the attention deficit of the users fuelled by ever-increasing information abundance acts as a filter for the quality of the viral content. *Visual simplicity*, that is, the prevalence of visual messages with low-quality content, has thus become the first 'grammar rule' of digital engagement. It encourages diplomats to communicate in an accessible manner, using visual cues and plain language. Otherwise, they risk their message going unnoticed by the target audience.

Figure 1.1 offers two examples of how effective visual simplicity could be in practice. The tweet (see Figure 1.1a) posted by the UN Secretary-General, Antonio Guterres, inviting Arnold Schwarzenegger to attend the Climate Action Summit in September 2019 went quickly viral (United Nations, 2019). It has reached roughly three times the average of Likes and RTs received by the UN account, despite the scarcity of the information provided, except for a brief reference to the actor's famous 'I'll be back' line. By contrast, the information-rich tweet posted by the European External Action Service (EEAS) outlining European Union (EU)–Asia security priorities (see Figure 1.1b), an important topic in the evolving geopolitical context, has been hardly noticed by the online public (European External Action Service—EEAS EU, 2019). Visual simplicity enables diplomats to engage with larger audiences, but at the same time, their message still needs to pack high-quality info in a visually appealing manner in order to make a significant qualitative difference for the audience.

Rule #2: *Emotional framing: messages that evoke intense emotions stand out.*

A second important 'grammar rule' introduced by the digital medium refers to the dominant role that emotions play in the dissemination and reception of digital messages.

FIGURE 1.1 Visual simplicity in action: tweets with asymmetrical quality of information

Source: United Nations (2019). Available at: https://twitter.com/UN/status/1142372405345751040 (accessed 28 January 2023); European External Action Service (2019). Available at: https://twitter.com/eu_eeas/status/1134384253192593408 (accessed 28 January 2023).

Studies show that messages that are more emotion-expressing are significantly more likely to be shared on social media (Chen, Yan, and Leach, 2022). Emotionally charged Twitter messages are also likely to be retweeted more often and more quickly compared to neutral ones (Stieglitz and Dang-Xuan, 2013). Part of the explanation for this trend relates to the emotional affordances made available by social media platforms, which encourage users to express, share, consume, and evaluate emotional content (Steinert and Dennis, 2022). Importantly, the valence of emotions (positive vs negative) matters as well. Positive (joy) as well as negative (contempt, guilt, or distress) emotions allow online messages to diffuse faster and stronger, while tweets infused with primary emotions like anger or fear have led to a lower yet significant impact on information diffusion (Chawla and Mehrotra, 2021). Kramer et al. (2014) also demonstrated that emotional states could be transferred to others via emotional contagion, leading people to experience the same emotions without even their awareness.

Similar to the first 'grammar rule', *emotional framing* encourages diplomats to alter their neutral and formal style of offline communication and frame their online statements and declarations in more emotional and informal terms. Due to the nature of their profession, diplomats cannot cross certain lines of sobriety without incurring reputational costs, but conventional manners of digital interaction are unlikely to attract the attention of the online public. At the same time, they need to bear in mind that emotional framing has a constitutive effect on online audiences. Emotions not only influence how the message is diffused, but also help build cognitively consonant communities. For this reason, it makes a significant difference for a diplomatic account to be followed by an online public that is habituated to expect emotionally intense messages, positive or negative. The short-term gain that may follow from intense emotional framing may entail long-term path dependencies that eventually may undermine the strategic objectives set for digital diplomacy.

The influence of emotional framing on message dissemination and reception is well illustrated by the two tweets in Figure 1.2, posted by the former Iranian Foreign Minister, Javad Zarif (see Figure 1.2a), and the Permanent Representative of Ukraine to the United Nations, Sergiy Kyslytsya (see Figure 1.2b), in two different situations. Mr Zarif was reacting to a statement made by the former US President Donald Trump threatening military action against Iran (Al Jazeera, 2019), while Ambassador Kyslytsya indirectly questioned the justification of allowing the Russian Permanent Representative to the UN to speak to the UN Security Council, amid Russia's invasion of Ukraine (Charles, Ryder, and Earl, no date). Mr Zarif's tweet (2019) conveyed a pugnacious expression of angry defiance, while Amb. Kyslytsya (2022) relied on sarcasm, as a contrast between a positive sentiment and a negative situation, to establish a connection with the viewer. Both messages enjoyed high levels of reception by the audience (several times the average of RTs and Likes normally received by the two diplomats) largely due to their effective emotional framing.

Rule #3: <u>Computational personalization</u>: *online engagement is a function of algorithmic alignment with digital profiles.*

In a seminal article, later expanded in a book, Bennett and Segerberg (2012) made the argument that social networking relied on co-production and co-distribution based on personalized expressions, a process which they called 'the logic of connective action'.

FIGURE 1.2 Emotional framing in action: tweets with contrasting emotional valence

Source: Zarif, J. (2019). Available at: https://twitter.com/JZarif/status/1130419673756049410 (accessed 28 January 2023); Kyslytsya, S. (2022). Available at: https://twitter.com/SergiyKyslytsya/status/1509560144757207044 (accessed 28 January 2023).

Taking public action thus becomes less an issue of demonstrating support for some generic goals, and more an act of personal expression and self-validation achieved by sharing ideas online, negotiating meanings, and structuring trusted relationships. For example, the personalized action frame 'we are the 99 per cent' that emerged from the US occupy protests in 2011, or the more recent 'MeToo' movement, travelled the world via personal stories, images, and videos shared on social networks such as Twitter, Facebook, and Instagram. While the logic of connective action describes the process by which the online public becomes involved in social networking, *computational personalization*, the third grammar rule of digital engagement, speaks to the condition by which connective actions are enabled, calibrated, and amplified through computational means.

Computational communication bridges the fields of computer science, sociology, psychology, and communication studies. It involves the study of large and complex data sets, consisting of digital traces and other 'naturally occurring' data, requiring algorithmic solutions for analysis and prediction, and allowing the study of human communication by applying and testing communication theory (van Atteveldt and Peng, 2018: 82). Algorithms are now routinely used for a variety of purposes to influence the choices of digital users through processes that seek to enable connective actions: to recommend products on e-commerce websites to increase the likelihood of purchasing a product, to show a sponsored political post on social media to increase the likelihood of voting for a political party, or to recommend news article to increase the likelihood of spending more time on a news platform to increase revenues (Zarouali et al., 2022: 3).

For MFAs and embassies, computational personalization is not necessarily an easy task, as often their online activities are primarily about projecting and emphasizing their own set of policy priorities, approaches, and strategies to address various issues on the global agenda. Personalization would imply exactly the opposite: removing oneself from the 'digital spotlight' and identifying themes that can connect with as many individuals as possible via personal appeals to recognition and self-validation. The lower the barriers for individual identification with social or political goals, the more opportunities for horizontal engagement, and by extension, the more likely for such content to be absorbed, reflected upon, and disseminated through social networks. The goal of computational personalization is therefore to facilitate connective actions via co-participation in the production of stories and narratives that are strategically relevant to the MFA's diplomatic agenda by tailoring them as closely as possible to the digital profile of the online users.

Computational personalization is also related to 'algorithmic diplomacy' (Cocking, 2016) by which diplomats attempt to burst their algorithmic confines. Indeed, embassies, MFAs, and IOs are all engulfed by algorithmic filter bubbles that determine who will be able to view their online content. Thus, diplomats often personalize content to shatter their filter bubbles or penetrate users' filter bubbles by creating content that may obtain virality. The two examples below demonstrate such attempts. The tweet in Figure 1.3 was published by Ukraine's ambassador to the United States on 4 July 2022 (Markarova,

FIGURE 1.3 Computational personalisation in action: tweets with contrasting connective action

Source: Markarova, O. (2022). Available at: https://twitter.com/omarkarova/status/1543921360996540418 (accessed 28 January 2023); Russian Embassy, UK (2018). Available at: https://twitter.com/russianembassy/status/975309334191230977 (accessed 28 January 2023).

2022). This tweet is personalized as it consists of a message that would be relevant to American Twitter users as the ambassador links Ukraine's struggle for democracy and independence with America's historic battle for independence and democratic rule. This tweet would not be relevant to Brazilian or Chilean Twitter users. Moreover, the ambassador suggests that the same values that underpinned America's struggle for independence also underpin Ukraine's struggle against Russia, and thus America must support Ukraine's war effort. By using the hashtag #4thOfJuly the ambassador also 'piggybacked' on a trending hashtag potentially increasing the reach of her tweet and breaking her algorithmic confines.

The second tweet in Figure 1.3 was published by the Russian embassy to the UK (2018). In this case, personalization was achieved by referencing a staple of British culture, the legendary detective Hercule Poirot created by Agatha Christie and portrayed on British television by the actor David Suchet. The tweet suggests that the British government's investigation into the alleged Russian attempt to kill a former spy in Salisbury was so inept that the UK required the help of the fictitious Poirot. Yet through the use of humour, the tweet also suggests that the UK's allegations against Russia are as fanciful as Poirot himself. Notably, non-British Twitter users would likely resonate less with these messages. Thanks to the invocation of a cultural icon, and the employment of a humorous tone, the Russian tweet breached its algorithmic confines, as the tweet was shared widely and even garnered attention from traditional British media outlets.

Rule #4: *Engagement hybridization: physical and virtual engagements integrate, complement, and empower each other.*

The Covid-19 pandemic has led to an acceleration of the process of hybridization of diplomacy. According to Bjola and Manor (2022), hybrid diplomacy combines face-to-face, physical diplomacy with virtual engagement via video-conferencing technologies such as Zoom or Microsoft Teams. The pandemic necessitated a swift migration to video-conferencing technologies as embassies, MFAs, and IOs all lay dormant with diplomats across the world entering quarantines, lockdowns, and self-isolation. At times, hybrid diplomacy was used to maintain the day-to-day functions of diplomacy, such as when embassies and MFAs held operational meetings on Zoom, but also for managing the pandemic, facilitating international collaboration, ensuring foreign policy continuity, countering disinformation, or experimenting with digital innovation (Bjola and Coplen, 2022a). However, hybrid diplomacy was also used to continue negotiations that began offline, before the pandemic struck (Bjola and Coplen, 2022b).

As is often the case with digitization, hybrid diplomacy remained an integral part of diplomacy even once the Covid-19 pandemic subsided. Nowadays, hybridity is often used to complement face-to-face diplomacy. For instance, throughout the Russia–Ukraine war, North Atlantic Treaty Organization (NATO) ministers have met both in person and through virtual platforms to better coordinate the Alliance's response to Russia's actions and respond in real time to security threats. Similarly, G7 leaders held a virtual summit (see Figure 1.4a) in which they discussed a possible solution to the Russia-Ukraine War (von der Leyen, 2022). In another instance (see Figure 1.4b), Ukraine's foreign minister remotely joined a meeting of the EU Foreign Affairs Council (Kuleba, 2022). In these instances, hybridity complemented offline diplomacy but did not replace it entirely.

However, studies suggest that the efficacy of hybrid diplomacy may be limited. For instance, Bjola and Manor (2022) found that diplomats cannot develop trust within virtual settings. The development of trust, a key component of negotiations, requires face-to-face meetings in which body language, non-verbal cues, and rapport allow diplomats to establish personal ties. Hybridity also requires that diplomats develop new skills. This is especially true of moderators who must ensure that all virtual participants remain engaged in meetings or conferences. Finally, the duration of virtual meetings is crucial as long meetings can lead to a form of 'Zoom fatigue' that prevents diplomats from obtaining shared goals.

Adler-Nissen and Eggeling (2022) prefer to use the term 'blended diplomacy' when investigating virtual diplomacy. They argue that digital technologies have become entangled as one can no longer separate analogue and digital diplomacy. The smartphone is now the digital extension of the physical diplomat. And yet, blended diplomacy also takes note of resistance to digital technologies. Indeed, diplomats may resist using new technologies either because these are seen as distracting from diplomacy's core function or because they disrupt well-established working routines. Indeed, there is a great difference between a face-to-face gathering of ambassadors, in which pre-existing

FIGURE 1.4 Hybridity complementing face-to-face diplomacy

Source: von der Leyen, U. (2022). Available at: https://twitter.com/vonderleyen/status/1602364234796601354 (accessed 28 January 2023); Available at: https://twitter.com/DmytroKuleba/status/1602330251450892290 (accessed 28 January 2023).

protocols govern interactions, and digital interactions between ambassadors in a WhatsApp group, which include improvisation and a collective struggle to define new protocols (Cornut, Manor, and Blumenthal, 2022).

It is also important to note that the four grammar rules outlined in this section can be used for both constructive and destructive purposes in the realm of diplomatic relations. The visual simplicity of the information being transmitted, the emotional framing of messaging, the use of computational personalization, and the integration of physical and virtual environments through engagement hybridization all have the potential to both advance and undermine diplomatic efforts. The 'dark side of digital diplomacy' involving the use of provocative, easily accessible, emotionally charged, and algorithmically tailored messaging delivered through both online and offline channels to advance foreign policy objectives is well documented in academic literature (Benkler, Farris, and Roberts, 2018; Bjola and Pamment, 2018; Tabatabai, 2018). These uses are not accidental byproducts of digital disruption, but rather conscious adaptations to specific foreign policy objectives. As such, diplomats must be aware of the potential consequences of utilizing these grammar rules in both positive and negative ways.

MAPPING DIGITAL DISRUPTION

While the four grammar rules of digital engagement set out the broader constraints within which digital diplomacy operates, the specific pattern by which the combination of these rules influences MFAs and IOs' strategies remains indeterminate. According to the social construction of technology (SCOT) theory, technology design is an open process marked by an alternation of variation and selection, which can produce different outcomes depending on the social circumstances of development, the degree to which relevant social groups share the same set of meanings attached to the technology, and the level of consensus regarding the technological frame used to inspire action such as goals, key problems, current theories, rules of thumb, or testing procedures (Klein and Kleinman, 2016: 29–31). Critical to understanding the capacity of a novel technology to go mainstream is how successfully meaning is negotiated between different relevant social groups (producers, advocates, users, and bystanders) and how well the resulting interpretation is attached to the technology to induce closure and stabilization (Humphreys, 2005). Applied to digital diplomacy, this means that different MFAs may interpret the four grammar rules and by extension the use of social media and digital services in different ways, leading to a range of policy outcomes, depending on how relevant and useful they are perceived by stakeholders.

We identify five distinct mechanisms through which the implementation of 'grammar rules' in digital diplomacy may lead to disruption. These include *disruption from below*, in which the impact of the grammar rules on personal conduct among diplomats subsequently permeates the work of MFAs or IOs. *Disruption from above* is instigated by digital-savvy leaders who encourage subordinates to adopt these rules. *Disruption from aside* arises from pressure laterally generated by diaspora and civil society groups. *Disruption through diffusion* occurs when MFAs adopt the rules in an effort to emulate the success of their competitors and partners. Finally, *disruption through crises* occurs when MFAs are forced to improvise and adapt in the face of challenging circumstances. Each of these forms of disruption presents unique opportunities for the advancement of digital diplomacy.

Disruption from below

Digital disruption can be a bottom-up process in which individual diplomats begin experimenting with digital technologies. If successful, these patterns of use then permeate into MFAs and IOs. One notable example of engagement hybridization is diplomats' use of WhatsApp groups to manage negotiations in IOs. Cornut, Manor, and Blumenthal (2022) found that EU ambassadors to the UN in Geneva are all members of a WhatsApp group. This group is used to negotiate texts, such as UN resolutions, to coordinate votes at different UN forums, and to ensure that the EU votes as a single block.

The WhatsApp group has proven disruptive as it has reduced the time required to negotiate and agree on texts and has also increased social ties between EU ambassadors transforming them into a more unified political block in Geneva.

Notably, this WhatsApp group was launched by a former EU ambassador to Geneva who had first experimented with WhatsApp groups when planning a family vacation. Indeed, studies have shown that diplomats' use of technology is often shaped by personal experiences with different technologies be it social media or blog sites (Manor, 2019). The Geneva WhatsApp group was not the result of an institutional desire to leverage a new digital technology nor was it mandated by the EU's External Action Service. However, the use of WhatsApp groups has since become more common among EU nations, many of which used WhatsApp groups to manage embassy activities remotely during Covid-19 lockdowns and quarantines (Bjola & Manor, 2022).

Another example of disruption from below can be found in the use of Twitter by the UK's former ambassador to Lebanon, Tom Fletcher. Unlike many of his peers, Fletcher used Twitter to comment on both political issues or bilateral ties between the UK and Lebanon, while also documenting his personal experiences as a foreigner living in Lebanon and commenting on daily life in Lebanon. One of the most salient features of the ambassador's approach was the utilization of a conversational tone with positive emotional framing, accompanied by the integration of vibrant visuals, in order to establish and strengthen digital connections with Lebanese Twitter users (Fletcher, 2016). By the end of his tenure, Fletcher boasted a Twitter following of tens of thousands of users.

Importantly, Fletcher's approach to Twitter was soon integrated into the UK FCO's approach to digital diplomacy. The FCO adopted a risk-prone attitude to social media encouraging diplomats and ambassadors to use Twitter in a personable way, to comment on personal experiences, to share their private lives with followers, and to adopt a conversational tone striking a balance between an official representative and a globetrotting tourist. In one instance, the head of the FCO's Diplomatic Academy urged British diplomats to improve their social media presence by making their messages more visually and emotionally appealing to their target audiences (Manor, 2019).

The concept of 'disruption from below' is extensively discussed throughout the volume. Manor and Pamment examine the interplay between macro- and micro-level disruptions and how they shape the emergence of new professional norms, values, and routines in the context of digital technologies. They argue that these disruptions have a significant impact on how digital technologies are integrated into professional practice. Eggeling and Adler-Nissen examine how the use of digital technologies, including diplomats' phones, individual digital competencies, and shared institutional norms, co-constitute diplomatic negotiations in the digital age. They argue that these factors are closely intertwined and shape the way diplomatic negotiations are conducted in the digital context. Huang and Arceneaux's chapter discusses the professionalization of digital diplomacy practices and the ethical challenges practitioners face in shaping the image and reputation of their government. They explore how digital technologies have led to new ethical considerations in diplomacy and how practitioners navigate these challenges.

Grincheva examines how traditional government actors of cultural diplomacy in the digital realm are becoming increasingly dependent on cultural institutions and communities that serve as key content providers, thus increasing the complexity of global cross-cultural communications. She argues that this dependence has significant implications for cultural diplomacy in the digital age. Bjola and Kļaviņš propose a theory of digital hybridization to explain how new structures, known as digital assemblages, are formed through the co-junction and co-evolution of digital and diplomatic components. They argue that these digital assemblages are formed as foreign ministry actors pursue their foreign policy objectives. Baines' chapter examines the roles and relationships of key actors, identifies emerging trends, and speculates on future changes to public and customary international law in the context of digital diplomacy. She argues that digital technologies have significant implications for the field of diplomacy and international law.

Disruption from above

Digital disruption may also be a bottom-down process. This occurs when senior policymakers display a zeal for digital technologies. For example, the US State Department's embrace of digital technologies in general, and social media in particular, was facilitated by the endorsement of Secretary of State Hillary Clinton and the digital enthusiasm of her two digital advisors, Jared Cohen and Alec Ross (Hayden, 2012). They argued that online interactions between diplomats and digital publics should be a permanent fixture of diplomacy. The two also lobbied for greater transparency in American diplomacy, advocating the sharing of reports, analyses, and processes via digital technologies. When describing diplomacy in the twenty-first century, Alec Ross told American diplomats that 'open was good, closed was bad, and authenticity is key' (Manor, 2019). In this comment, Ross emphasized diplomacy's need to become more open and more inviting. Yet, once transparency is adopted by diplomats, digital publics come to expect transparency to become the norm both online and offline. Failure to meet these expectations can lead to increased mistrust and suspicion among digital publics, which can have significant negative implications for diplomatic relations.

Another notable example of disruption from above can be found in Carl Bildt, former Swedish prime minister and foreign minister. As soon as Bildt took on the role of foreign minister he advocated the rapid adoption of digital technologies. He launched one of the world's first blog sites operated by a foreign minister, which was closely followed by Swedish and foreign ambassadors to keep themselves abreast with Sweden's foreign policy priorities (Manor, 2019). Bildt also oversaw an ambitious project, the launching of Sweden's embassy in the virtual world of Second Life, which was the world's first virtual embassy accessible to anyone with an Internet connection (Bengtsson, 1970). Most importantly, Bildt used social media to both narrate Sweden's foreign policy, and reach out and interact with other world leaders in a public way (Kļaviņš, 2021). Bildt's ambitious attitude towards digital technologies shaped the Swedish MFA's approach to digital technologies, one marked by a desire for experimentation and embracing a wide range of digital technologies spanning from social media and blogs to virtual worlds.

The integration of digital technologies in statecraft and diplomacy 'from above' is the subject of various chapters in the handbook. Rawnsley, for example, examines the case of China and how it has employed digital technologies to present itself as a 'soft power' externally, while also using these same technologies to control society and limit political accountability, transparency, and the autonomy of civil society. Cassidy investigates how Sweden and Canada have employed and continue to employ the adoption and promotion of a feminist foreign policy as a digital tool of attraction. The author argues that tools of attraction have become a key factor in building reputation and influence on the global stage, with digital diplomacy serving as a crucial medium in this regard. Ghica looks at how the agenda on digital development cooperation has emerged from a multistakeholder dialogue led by the United Nations. She argues that digital technologies and international development cooperation are now at the forefront of the global strategic framework for managing current and future challenges, and for ensuring social and economic progress worldwide. Bouchard examines how digital technologies have influenced behaviours, patterns of use, procedures, and norms in the diplomatic activities (negotiations, networking, public diplomacy) of the permanent missions to the United Nations.

Ecker-Ehrhardt provides an in-depth analysis of the motivational factors and conducive conditions that explain why international bureaucracies have turned to and increasingly employ digital diplomacy. Zaiotti elaborates on the challenges and opportunities in EU digital diplomacy by providing empirical examples of EU efforts in this domain, such as the 2017 'European Way' social media campaign and the EU's communication strategy during the Iran nuclear deal negotiations. Wright, on the other hand, examines the digital diplomacy efforts of NATO. She argues that in recent years, NATO has taken a range of approaches to expand its presence and become more involved in shaping, engaging, and innovating digital diplomatic narratives. The author also notes that NATO's digital diplomacy during normal circumstances differs from its response during crisis situations, where significant silences limit its efficacy in response to hybrid warfare.

Disruption from aside

Scholars have argued that one cannot examine the digitization of diplomacy without understanding how digital technologies have shaped other fields that orbit the world of diplomats. Disruption from the side has also been facilitated through the digital activities of non-state actors including diasporas. Some countries have prioritized the creation of digital ties with diasporas. The Kenyan and Rwandan MFAs have allocated, for instance, substantial digital resources towards digital diaspora engagement given diasporas' contribution to national GDPs (Bjola, Manor and Adiku, 2021a). These MFAs have formulated digital diaspora policies and have even invested in technologies that can enhance ties between diasporas and their origin countries, such as smartphone applications for sending remittances to families and friends (Bjola, Manor and Adiku 2021a).

It is also important to note that diaspora engagement could be challenging for MFAs, as diaspora groups tend to assert themselves in unpredictable ways. When states use digital technologies to reach out to diasporas, the borders of the nation-state extend virtually and also come to include diasporas in their 'imagined community'. Yet states may also boycott diasporas if these become too vocal or critical, leading to a contraction of the state's borders (Bernal, 2014). Diplomats from many countries have to contend with vocal diasporas that criticize their former countries and lambast their former governments. Organized, digital diasporas can harm a nation's image and impede its bilateral or multilateral activities.

Disruption from the side may also arise from civil society groups. The increased transparency demanded of all social media users has led to normative pressure on diplomats and IOs to become more transparent themselves. As a result, climate summits, multilateral negotiations, and UN deliberations have started to be broadcasted live through tweets and live streams (Wichowski, 2013). Some have argued that this is merely the façade of transparency as much of diplomacy still takes shape behind closed doors, and far from preying eyes (Duncombe, 2017). Others have suggested that transparency might actually prove counterproductive as when live-streamed, diplomats merely reiterate national narratives rather than formulate responses to challenges and crises. Climate negotiations, for instance, have been disrupted by networks of digital publics who use social media to exert pressure on diplomats and impact the agenda of climate discussions (Hopke and Hestres, 2018).

The concept of 'disruption from aside' is examined by the contributors to this volume from a variety of perspectives. Briant argues that the rise of social media platforms has created a 'wild west' in which disinformation can be distributed with algorithmic precision to influence individuals' minds and behaviours. She introduces the concept of the 'digital influence industry', distinguishing it from other actors and analysing its role and importance in understanding how influence operations and propaganda may affect states' international positions. Cull identifies a three-phase pattern in the introduction of new technology to public diplomacy: a period of symbolic use, early application, and mature application. This pattern allows for an understanding of the micro-processes at work within foreign ministries and the macro-trends unleashed in wider society, which in turn shape the wider landscape of foreign policy.

McConnell and Manby examine how digital diplomacy is being reworked by three types of 'new' diplomatic actors: non-governmental organizations (NGOs), transnational advocacy networks (TANs), and diaspora organizations. The chapter by Engtoft and Fletcher explores the evolving role of technology companies in diplomacy, as they not only design but also own the platforms through which diplomacy is conducted. The authors then analyse the implications of this development on the function of diplomatic representation. Sevin contends that cities use digital platforms to engage with audiences beyond their traditional jurisdictions, and proposes the idea of international activities of cities by merging city branding and city diplomacy. Finally, Moreno Cantano examines how countries such as China, India, and Pakistan are leveraging the widespread popularity of video games as a means of promoting digital cultural diplomacy and technonationalist projections of power.

Disruption through diffusion

Studies also suggest that digital disruption occurs through diffusion, as MFAs often mimic their peers and adopt similar digital strategies. For example, Russia and Ukraine were both among the first MFAs to employ humour in their digital communications (Chernobrov, 2021; Budnitsky, 2022). Yet in recent years the MFAs of Israel, France, the UK, and Canada have all used humour when commenting on contentious issues. This phenomenon is representative of the fact that the logic of digital technologies shapes diplomats' digital activities, as on social media all users become brands that compete for the attention of all other users. Social media brands are marked by adopting a unique tone and appearance using tailored forms of visual representation and emotional framing. This logic has permeated into MFAs, giving rise to new practices. Indeed, some MFAs use humour, sarcasm, and cynicism to develop a distinct online brand, while others adopt a unique visual style. The Ukrainian MFA routinely uses memes to comment on international affairs to counter Russian propaganda and protect its reputational security (Cull, 2022; Serafin, 2022). The logic of digital technologies therefore also shapes digital practices and leads to a certain standardization of digital practices across MFAs.

Disruption through diffusion has also been evident in MFAs' emphasis on consular affairs. Scholars have suggested that much of digital diplomacy is actually domestic diplomacy. Faced with budget cuts and a narrowing remit within governments, MFAs use social media to communicate with domestic audiences and the national citizenry. Some MFAs use Twitter to 'sell' foreign policies to sceptic local audiences (Bjola and Manor, 2018). Others have turned to digital technologies to offer better consular aid (Melissen and Caesar-Gordon, 2016). The MFAs of Poland, Canada, and Israel have developed consular smartphone applications while the UK FCO and the US State Department manage a consular Twitter page (Manor, 2019). Recent studies have found that MFAs targeted the national citizenry during the early stages of the Covid-19 pandemic, publishing travel warnings, updating citizens on specially charted flights, and documenting the consular achievements of diplomats and embassies across the world (Bjola and Coplen, 2022a; Manor and Yrachi, 2023). In this fashion, diplomats demonstrated their worth to the national citizenry. This was true of numerous MFA including Austria, Denmark, France, Germany, Israel, New Zealand, Sweden, and the UK.

Several contributions in this volume thoroughly discuss the opportunities and challenges presented by the process of 'disruption through diffusion' for digital diplomacy. In his chapter, Kello examines the emergence, expansion, and evolution of cyber issues within the realm of diplomacy and international relations. The author evaluates the successes and failures of institutional efforts to regulate interstate cyber conduct and analyses the persistent challenges that impede meaningful diplomatic agreement. Fjällhed, Sandre, and Lüfkens focus on TikTok as a case study where the international geopolitics of algorithmic governance has become a prominent topic in public discourse. This requires a geopolitical analysis in digital diplomacy as it opens up the possibility of critically reviewing how diplomatic actors may implicitly or explicitly shape the algorithmic structures of other platforms.

Wiseman examines the impact of digital technologies on four main types of diplomacy: bilateral, multilateral, polylateral, and omnilateral. The author suggests that all four dimensions of diplomacy are developing their unique blend of analogue and digital practices, resulting in a wide variety of digital diplomatic cultures. Spry provides an overview of the practices and contexts of digital diplomacy in the Asia Pacific and analyses the diffusion of emergent practices such as coercive diplomacy and foreign interference, the increasing role of digital networks that facilitate diplomacy, and the evolving information disorder that problematizes diplomatic practice. Aguirre and Ramos review how the Latin American experiences provide insight into how different countries have recognized the importance of developing a strong online presence and a digital diplomacy strategy that is in step with the times. Heine and Lallande examine how shared objectives and challenges inform the issue of Internet governance and related digital matters from the perspective of the North–South divide.

Disruption through crises

The trajectory of diplomacy's digitalization has always been impacted by crises, be it wars, terrorism, or pandemics. Following the Russian intervention in the 2016 US elections (Bjola and Manor, 2021b) and the growing use of social media to spread misinformation and conspiracy theories, some MFAs now view social media with suspicion. Diplomats have even adopted new approaches to social media dedicating digital resources to identifying and blocking fake social media accounts that spread false information. To this end, the Israeli MFA has created a code-writing unit, while the UK Foreign Office has established a big data unit. Similarly, the Lithuanian MFA has created a monitoring unit tasked with identifying and countering Russian narratives spread online (Manor, 2019). The use of digital technologies for strategic communications has thus taken centre stage.

Russia's war of aggression against Ukraine has seen a host of digital innovations, especially from the Ukrainian government. Since the war started, the Ukrainian Ministry of Digital Transformation has exerted online pressure on big tech companies to exit the Russian market. This often took the form of tweeting open letters to tech CEOs. Additionally, the Ukrainian government has utilized digital platforms to gather financial support, specifically for buying weapons and medical equipment. They have also employed social media to recruit an IT Army to protect themselves but also to carry on cyber-attacks against Russia (Soesanto, 2022). Finally, Ukraine has also launched a new nation branding campaign called 'Brave Ukraine' highlighting the nation's determined stand against Russian aggression (Kaneva, 2022).

While wars and invasion facilitate digital disruption so do pandemics. As previously noted, the Covid-19 pandemic led to the mass adoption of virtual meetings software, such as Zoom, as a new form of engagement hybridization. Yet the pandemic also disrupted diplomacy as it changed the MFAs' approach to social media. One important example is China's new assertive and even abrasive tone on social media. Known as 'Wolf Warrior' diplomacy (Huang, 2022), Chinese diplomats used social media to negate accusations that the Covid-19 pandemic originated in a Chinese lab, to lambast the West for their poor management of the pandemic, and to accuse world governments and IOs of being too lax on Covid-19 regulations as opposed to China's stringent restrictions on its citizens. What began during the pandemic has continued in its wake with some scholars suggesting that China's new online rhetoric is meant to signal its new great power status.

The current volume discusses the issue of 'disruption through crises' from multiple perspectives. Holmes examines the interactions between the United States, Russia, and Ukraine surrounding the 2022 invasion of Ukraine to understand how the relationship between states and digital audiences creates a feedback loop, which empowers audiences to shape and reshape the way states present themselves online. Crilley, on the other hand, investigates how digital communication technologies have changed essential elements of diplomacy related to nuclear weapons, crisis management, arms control, and disarmament. Surowiec-Capell highlights the reinvention of propaganda in the digital era, and how it has become a crucial topic to study in the field of diplomacy. This is demonstrated through case studies of Russia's intervention in the 2016 US presidential elections, the EU membership referendum in the UK, and the 'LGBT-free zones' in Poland.

Hedling explains how virtualization has been utilized to sustain institutionalized routines of summitry in the face of multiple crises and disruptions. Cooper and Hai-chi Loo investigate the shift in diplomacy that occurred due to perceived strategic necessity, as seen in President Xi Jinping's belief in the importance of 'wolf-warrior diplomacy' for maintaining the privileged position of the Chinese Communist Party and consolidating his personal support. Akdenizli contends that the GCC's digital diplomacy is driven by power and competition, as illustrated by the cases of the 2017–2021 Blockade and the 2019–2021 Covid-19 pandemic. Yarchi insists that the battle of ideas and perceptions in times of war and conflict plays a critical role in the ability of political actors to achieve their goals. This leads countries and other political actors to invest time and resources in an attempt to influence public perceptions in their favour, using all available tools, many of which are centred around digital platforms.

In conclusion, the handbook offers a thematically comprehensive, theoretically enlightening, and empirically rich examination of the processes by which digital technology is fundamentally changing the way diplomacy is conducted. As the 'grammar rules' of the diplomatic space are being rewritten, MFAs and IOs are forced to adapt to this change, but they do so at different paces depending on the type of disruptive pressure they face: from below, from above, from aside, through diffusion, or through crises. As the advent of Artificial Intelligence and the emergence of the metaverse precipitate rapid developments in international politics, this volume also endeavours to catalyse further academic discussion on the manner in which technology is upgrading, augmenting, and reconfiguring the conduct of diplomacy. It is therefore our aspiration that the handbook will incite further scholarly inquiry on the future of digital diplomacy from an interdisciplinary perspective, including but not limited to diplomatic studies, communication studies, data science, sociology, and international relations. As technology continues to evolve and reshape our global landscape, it is imperative that we comprehend and prepare ourselves for the ways in which diplomacy will continue to evolve in the next phase of the Digital Revolution.

SUGGESTED READINGS

Bjola, C. and Holmes M. (2015) *Digital Diplomacy: Theory and Practice.* Routledge.
Gkeredakis, M., Lifshitz-Assaf, H., and Barrett, M. (2021) "Crisis as Opportunity, Disruption and Exposure: Exploring Emergent Responses to Crisis through Digital Technology," *Information and Organization,* 31(1): 100344.
Manor, I. (2019) *The Digitalization of Public Diplomacy.* Cham: Palgrave Macmillan.
Owen, T. (2015) *Disruptive Power: The Crisis of the State in the Digital Age.* Oxford: Oxford University Press.
Renieris, E. M. (2023) *Beyond Data: Reclaiming Human Rights at the Dawn of the Metaverse.* MIT Press.

BIBLIOGRAPHY

Adler-Nissen, R. and Eggeling, K. A. (2022) "Blended Diplomacy: The Entanglement and Contestation of Digital Technologies in Everyday Diplomatic Practice," *European Journal of International Relations,* 28(3), pp. 640–666. doi: 10.1177/13540661221107837.
Al Jazeera (2019) *Trump Threatens Iran's 'End' If It Seeks Fight with the US.* Available at: https://www.aljazeera.com/news/2019/5/20/trump-threatens-irans-end-if-it-seeks-fight-with-the-us (Accessed: 28 January 2023).
Andre, L. (no date) *53 Important Statistics About How Much Data Is Created Every Day.* Available at: https://financesonline.com/how-much-data-is-created-every-day/ (Accessed: 28 January 2023).
van Atteveldt, W. and Peng, T. Q. (2018) "When Communication Meets Computation: Opportunities, Challenges, and Pitfalls in Computational Communication Science," *Communication Methods and Measures,* 12(2–3), pp. 81–92. doi: 10.1080/19312458.2018.1458084.
Bengtsson, S. (1970) "Virtual Nation Branding: The Swedish Embassy in Second Life," *Journal For Virtual Worlds Research,* 4(2). pp. 1–26. doi: 10.4101/jvwr.v4i2.2111.
Benkler, Y., Farris, R., and Roberts, H. (2018) *Network Propaganda.* Oxford University Press. doi: 10.1093/oso/9780190923624.001.0001.
Bennett, W. L. and Segerberg, A. (2012) "The Logic of Connective Action," *Information, Communication and Society,* 15(5), pp. 739–768. doi: 10.1080/1369118X.2012.670661.

Bernal, V. (2014) *Nation as Network: Diaspora, Cyberspace, and Citizenship*. University of Chicago Press. Available at: https://play.google.com/store/books/details?id=TC2OBAAAQBAJ.

Bjola, C. (2018) "Diplomacia digital 2.0: tendencias y resistencias," *Revista Mexicana de Política Exterior*, 113(113), pp. 35–52. Available at: https://revistadigital.sre.gob.mx/index.php/rmpe/article/view/233.

Bjola, C. (2020) "Coping with Digital Disinformation in Multilateral Contexts: The Case of the UN Global Compact for Migration," in Ruben, B. C. Z. (ed.) *Digital Diplomacy and International Organisations*. Abingdon, Oxon; New York, NY: Routledge, 2021, pp. 267–286. doi: 10.4324/9781003032724-15.

Bjola, C. (2022) "In Virality we Trust – Quest for Authenticity in Digital Diplomacy," in Omahna, I. and Ilc, M. (eds.) *Be a Digital Diplomat: Guide for Digital Diplomacy Practitioners*. Center za evropsko prihodnost (CEP), pp. 43–53. Available at: https://play.google.com/store/books/details?id=rE-YzwEACAAJ.

Bjola, C., Cassidy, J., and Manor, I. (2019) "Public Diplomacy in the Digital Age," *The Hague Journal of Diplomacy*, 14(1–2), pp. 83–101. doi: 10.1163/1871191X-14011032.

Bjola, C. and Coplen, M. (2022a) "Digital Diplomacy in the Time of the Coronavirus Pandemic: Lessons And Recommendations," in Hare, P. W., Manfredi-Sánchez, J. L., and Weisbrode, K. (eds.) *Handbook of Diplomatic Reform and Innovation*. Palgrave Macmillan. pp. 323–342.

Bjola, C. and Coplen, M. (2022b) "Virtual Venues and International Negotiations: Lessons from the COVID-19 Pandemic," *International Negotiation*. Brill Nijhoff, 1(aop), pp. 1–25. doi: 10.1163/15718069-bja10060.

Bjola, C. and Kornprobst, M. (eds.) (2023) *Digital International Relations.*. Abingdon, Oxon; New York, NY: Routledge.

Bjola, C. and Manor, I. (2018) "Revisiting Putnam's Two-Level Game Theory in the Digital Age: Domestic Digital Diplomacy and the Iran Nuclear Deal," *Cambridge Review of International Affairs*, 31(1), pp. 3–32. doi: 10.1080/09557571.2018.1476836.

Bjola, C., Manor I, and Adiku G.A. (2021a). "Diaspora Diplomacy in the Digital Age," in Kennedy, Liam (ed.) *Routledge International Handbook of Diaspora Diplomacy*. New York: Routledge, pp. 334–346.

Bjola, C. and Manor, I. (2021b) "Digital Propaganda as Symbolic Convergence: The Case of Russian Ads During the 2016 US Presidential Election," in Rawnsley, Gary D., Yiben Ma, and Kruakae Pothong (eds.) *Research Handbook on Political Propaganda*. Edward Elgar Publishing, pp. 80–97. doi: 10.4337/9781789906424.00013.

Bjola, C. and Manor, I. (2022) "The Rise of Hybrid Diplomacy: From Digital Adaptation to Digital Adoption," *International Affairs*, 98(2), pp. 471–491. doi: 10.1093/IA/IIAC005.

Bjola, C. and Pamment, J. (2018) *Countering Online Propaganda and Extremism: The Dark Side of Digital Diplomacy*. Abingdon and New York: Routledge.

Budnitsky, S. (2022) "Global Disengagement: Public Diplomacy Humor in the Russian–Ukrainian War," *Place Branding and Public Diplomacy*, 19, pp. 211–217. doi: 10.1057/s41254-022-00291-1.

Cassidy, J. and Manor, I. (2016) "Crafting Strategic MFA Communication Policies During Times of Political Crisis: A Note to MFA Policy Makers," *Global Affairs*, 2(3), pp. 331–343. doi: 10.1080/23340460.2016.1239377.

Charles, P. T., Ryder, H., and Earl, G. (no date) *War Represents a Failure of Diplomacy. It Pays to Read Past Page One*. Available at: https://www.lowyinstitute.org/the-interpreter/war-represents-failure-diplomacy-it-pays-read-past-page-one (Accessed: 28 January 2023).

Chawla, S. and Mehrotra, M. (2021) "Impact of Emotions in Social Media Content Diffusion," *Lithuanian Academy of Sciences. Informatica*, 45(6), pp. 11–28. doi: 10.31449/INF.V45I6.3575.

Chen, J., Yan, Y., and Leach, J. (2022) "Are Emotion-Expressing Messages More Shared on Social Media? A Meta-Analytic Review," *Review of Communication Research*, 10, pp. 1–45. doi: 10.12840/ISSN.2255-4165.034.

Chernobrov, D. (2021) "Strategic Humour: Public Diplomacy and Comic Framing of Foreign Policy Issues," *British Journal of Politics and International Relations*, 24(2), pp. 207–400. doi: 10.1177/13691481211023958.

Cocking, S. (2016) *Using Algorithms to Achieve Digital Diplomacy. A Conversation with Elad Ratson, Director of R&D at Ministry of Foreign Affairs*. Available at: https://irishtechnews.ie/using-algorithms-to-achieve-digital-diplomacy-a-conversation-with-elad-ratson-director-of-rd-at-ministry-of-foreign-affairs/ (Accessed: 28 January 2023).

Cornut, J., Manor, I., and Blumenthal, C. (2022) "WhatsApp with Diplomatic Practices in Geneva? Diplomats, Digital Technologies, and Adaptation in Practice," *International Studies Review*, 24(4). Available at: https://academic.oup.com/isr/article-pdf/doi/10.1093/isr/viac047/47901538/viac047.pdf.

Crilley, R., Manor, I., and Bjola, C. (2020) "Visual Narratives of Global Politics in the Digital Age: An Introduction," *Cambridge Review of International Affairs*, 33(5), pp. 628–637. doi: 10.1080/09557571.2020.1813465.

Cull, N. J. (2022) "The War for Ukraine: Reputational Security and Media Disruption," *Place Branding and Public Diplomacy*, 19, pp. 195–199. doi: 10.1057/s41254-022-00281-3.

Dialani, P. (2020) *The Future of Data Revolution will be Unstructured Data*. Available at: https://www.analyticsinsight.net/the-future-of-data-revolution-will-be-unstructured-data/ (Accessed: 28 January 2023).

Duncombe, C. (2017) "Twitter and Transformative Diplomacy: Social Media And Iran–US Relations," *International affairs*, 93(3), pp. 545–562. doi: 10.1093/ia/iix048.

European External Action Service - EEAS EU (2019) "With European prosperity and Asian peace and security closely connected, the EU has decided to strengthen its security cooperation in and with Asia. Check out the factsheet https://t.co/FYCF9g1t5W pic.twitter.com/vcx21n5tuv" [Twitter post]. Available at: https://twitter.com/eu_eeas/status/1134384253192593408 (Accessed: 28 January 2023).

Fletcher, T. (2016) *Naked Diplomacy: Power and Statecraft in the Digital Age*. UK ed. London: William Collins. Available at: https://www.gartner.com/en/newsroom/press-releases/2022-06-22-is-synthetic-data-the-future-of-ai

Goasduff, L. (2022) "Is Synthetic Data the Future of AI?," *Gartner*. Available at: https://www.gartner.com/en/newsroom/press-releases/2022-06-22-is-synthetic-data-the-future-of-ai (Accessed: 28 January 2023).

Hall, N., Schmitz, H. P. and Dedmon, J. M. (2019) "Transnational Advocacy and NGOs in the Digital Era: New Forms of Networked Power," *International Studies Quarterly*, 64(1), pp. 159–167. doi: 10.1093/isq/sqz052.

Hayden, C. (2012). "Social Media at State: Power, Practice, and Conceptual Limits for US Public Diplomacy," *Global Media Journal*, 12, pp. 1–21.

Hoad, T. (2003) *The Concise Oxford Dictionary of English Etymology*. Oxford: Oxford University Press, p. 552

Holmes, M. and Wheeler, N. J. (2020) "Social Bonding in Diplomacy," *International Theory*, 12(1), pp. 133–161. doi: 10.1017/S1752971919000162.

Hopke, J. E. and Hestres, L. E. (2018) "Visualizing the Paris Climate Talks on Twitter: Media and Climate Stakeholder Visual Social Media During COP21," *Social Media + Society*, 4(3), p. 2056305118782687. doi: 10.1177/2056305118782687.

Huang, Z. A. (2022) "'Wolf Warrior' and China's Digital Public Diplomacy During the COVID-19 Crisis," *Place Branding and Public Diplomacy*, 18(1), pp. 37–40. doi: 10.1057/s41254-021-00241-3.

Humphreys, L. (2005) "Reframing Social Groups, Closure, and Stabilization in the Social Construction of Technology," *Social Epistemology*, 19(2–3), pp. 231–253. doi: 10.1080/02691720500145449.

Kaneva, N. (2022) "'Brave Like Ukraine': A Critical Discourse Perspective on Ukraine's Wartime Brand," *Place Branding and Public Diplomacy*. LLC. 19, pp. 232–236. doi: 10.1057/s41254-022-00273-3.

Kitchin, R. (2014) "Big Data, New Epistemologies and Paradigm Shifts," *Big Data and Society*, 1(1). pp. 1–12. doi: 10.1177/2053951714528481.

Kļaviņš, D. (2021) "Mapping Innovation Diplomacy in Denmark and Sweden," *The Hague Journal of Diplomacy*, 16(4), pp. 565–596. doi: 10.1163/1871191X-bja10078.

Klein, H. K. and Kleinman, D. L. (2016) "The Social Construction of Technology: Structural Considerations," *Science, Technology, & Human Values*, 27(1), pp. 28–52. doi: 10.1177/016224390202700102.

Kramer, A. D. I., Guillory, J. E., and Hancock, J. T. (2014) "Experimental Evidence of Massive-Scale Emotional Contagion through Social Networks," *Proceedings of the National Academy of Sciences of the United States of America*. National Academy of Sciences, 111(24), pp. 8788–8790. doi: 10.1073/pnas.1320040111.

Kuleba, D. (2022) "Grateful to @JosepBorrellF for inviting me to today's EU Foreign Affairs Council. My message was simple: No Step Back in supporting Ukraine until Russian aggression is defeated. Sanctions on Russia and military assistance to Ukraine should be significantly stepped up. pic.twitter.com/bnzstrotga" [Twitter post]. Available at: https://twitter.com/DmytroKuleba/status/1602330251450892290 (Accessed: 28 January 2023).

Kyslytsya, S. (2022) "Dear @Bkerrychina it's not a prop. To the contrary it's a re-reading of the book I enjoyed some years ago; and reading it is a much healthier alternative to putin's amb's malarkey. Per 'War represents a failure of diplomacy. It pays to read past page one.' https://t.co/b68CoCuyjV" [Twitter post]. Available at: https://twitter.com/SergiyKyslytsya/status/1509560144757207044 (Accessed: 28 January 2023).

Lalancette, M. and Raynauld, V. (2019) "The Power of Political Image: Justin Trudeau, Instagram, and Celebrity Politics," *The American Behavioral Scientist*, 63(7), pp. 888–924. doi: 10.1177/0002764217744838.

von der Leyen, U. (2022) "Today with our @G7 partners we paid tribute to the determination and strength of Ukrainian people and reiterated our unwavering support to Ukraine. We stand ready to support with repairs now and with reconstruction, later. pic.twitter.com/en7r7rtdri" [Twitter post]. Available at: https://twitter.com/vonderleyen/status/1602364234796601354 (Accessed: 28 January 2023).

Machiavelli, N. (2000) *The Prince,*. South Bend, US: Infomotions, Inc. Available at: http://ebookcentral.proquest.com/lib/oxford/detail.action?docID=3314652.

Manor, I. (2019) *The Digitalization of Public Diplomacy*. Cham: Palgrave Macmillan. doi: 10.1007/978-3-030-04405-3.

Manor, I. and Yrachi, M. (2023) "From the Global to the Local and Back Again: MFAs' Digital Communications During COVID-19," *International Journal of Communication Systems*,

17(0), p. 22. Available at: https://ijoc.org/index.php/ijoc/article/view/19447 (Accessed: 28 January 2023).

Markarova, O. (2022) "#4thOfJuly Happy Independence Day to free and brave people of USA from free and brave people of Ukraine! UA💚💙US Our nations are united by love to democracy&independence and willingness to defend it. Thank you for standing with UA in this civilizational battle! God bless America! pic.twitter.com/evydnujoen" [Twitter post]. Available at: https://twitter.com/omarkarova/status/1543921360996540418 (Accessed: 28 January 2023).

McLuhan, M. (2012) "The Medium is the Message," in McLuhan, M. (ed.) *Media and Cultural Studies: Keyworks.* John Wiley & Sons, pp. 100–107.

Melissen, J. and Caesar-Gordon, M. (2016) "'Digital Diplomacy' and the Securing of Nationals in a Citizen-Centric World," *Global Affairs*, 2(3), pp. 321–330. doi: 10.1080/23340460.2016.1239381.

Muñoz, C. L. and Towner, T. L. (2017) "The Image is the Message: Instagram Marketing and the 2016 Presidential Primary Season," *Journal of Political Marketing*, 16(3–4), pp. 290–318. doi: 10.1080/15377857.2017.1334254.

Ofcom (2019) "Half of People Now Get Their News from Social Media". Available at: https://www.ofcom.org.uk/about-ofcom/latest/features-and-news/half-of-people-get-news-from-social-media (Accessed: 28 January 2023).

Qiu, X. et al. (2017) "Limited Individual Attention and Online Virality of Low-Quality Information," *Nature Human Behaviour*, 1(7), p. 0132. doi: 10.1038/s41562-017-0132.

Russian Embassy, UK (2018) "In absence of evidence, we definitely need Poirot in Salisbury! pic.twitter.com/ehtleqmcpp" [Twitter post]. Available at: https://twitter.com/russianembassy/status/975309334191230977 (Accessed: 28 January 2023).

Serafin, T. (2022) "Ukraine's President Zelensky Takes the Russia/Ukraine War Viral," *Orbis*, 66(4), pp. 460–476. doi: 10.1016/j.orbis.2022.08.002.

Shearer, E. (2018) "Social Media Outpaces Print Newspapers in the U.S. as a News Source," *Pew Research Center.* Available at: https://www.pewresearch.org/fact-tank/2018/12/10/social-media-outpaces-print-newspapers-in-the-u-s-as-a-news-source/ (Accessed: 28 January 2023).

Soesanto, S. (2022) "The IT Army of Ukraine: Structure, Tasking, and Eco-System," CSS Cyberdefense Reports. ETH Zurich. doi: 10.3929/ETHZ-B-000552293.

Steinert, S. and Dennis, M. J. (2022) "Emotions and Digital Well-Being: on Social Media's Emotional Affordances," *Philosophy and Technology*, 35(2), pp. 1–21. doi: 10.1007/S13347-022-00530-6/METRICS.

Stieglitz, S. and Dang-Xuan, L. (2013) "Emotions and Information Diffusion in Social Media—Sentiment of Microblogs and Sharing Behavior," *Journal of Management Information Systems*, 29(4), pp. 217–248. doi: 10.2753/MIS0742-1222290408.

Tabatabai, A. M. (2018) "A Brief History of Iranian Fake News: How Disinformation Campaigns Shaped the Islamic Republic," *Foreign affairs*, 97(4). Available at: https://www.foreignaffairs.com/articles/middle-east/2018-08-24/brief-history-iranian-fake-news.

United Nations (2019) "'Normally I say "I'll be back", but now I say: "I'll be there"' -- Arnold @Schwarzenegger accepts invitation from @antonioguterres to the UN #ClimateAction Summit in September. https://t.co/yAXgSbKnOU pic.twitter.com/damfafhdfp" [Twitter post]. Available at: https://twitter.com/UN/status/1142372405345751040 (Accessed: 28 January 2023).

Weng, L. et al. (2012) "Competition Among Memes in a World with Limited Attention," *Scientific Reports.* Nature Publishing Group, 2(1), p. 335. doi: 10.1038/srep00335.

Wichowski, A. (2013) "Social Diplomacy: Or How Diplomats Learned to Stop Worrying and Love the Tweet," *Foreign Affairs*, 92(2). Available at: http://www.foreignaffairs.com/articles/139134/alexis-wichowski/social-diplomacy.

Zarif, J. (2019) "Goaded by #B_Team, @realdonaldTrump hopes to achieve what Alexander, Genghis & other aggressors failed to do. Iranians have stood tall for millennia while aggressors all gone. #EconomicTerrorism & genocidal taunts won't "end Iran". #NeverThreatenAnIranian. Try respect—it works!" [Twitter post]. Available at: https://twitter.com/JZarif/status/1130419673756049410 (Accessed: 28 January 2023).

Zarouali, B. et al. (2022) "The Algorithmic Persuasion Framework in Online Communication: Conceptualization and a Future Research Agenda," *Internet Research*. Emerald, 32(4), pp. 1076–1096. doi: 10.1108/intr-01-2021-0049.

CHAPTER 2

DIGITAL DIPLOMACY: PROJECTION AND RETRIEVAL OF IMAGES AND IDENTITIES

MARCUS HOLMES

THE PUZZLE OF DIGITAL DIPLOMACY

WHAT are states doing when they pursue diplomacy digitally?[1] While US President Donald Trump made 'Twitter diplomacy' a common, often daily, phenomenon, the practice of using social media to engage publicly with other states, their leaders, and their publics through social media has been occurring for some time. Often this engagement has significant political ramifications. In August 2014, the President of Azerbaijan, Ilham Aliyev, engaged in a polemic via Twitter. The substantive topic involved Nagorno-Karabakh, disputed territory both Azerbaijan and Armenia lay claim to. In these tweets Aliyev proclaimed, 'We will restore our territorial integrity either by peaceful or military means. We are ready for both options. . . We are not living in peace, we are living in a state of war. The war is not over. Only the first stage of it is. But the second stage may start too. No-one can rule that out. We don't want war, we want peace. But at the same time, we want our lands back.' Aliyev was responding to recent clashes in the region and took to Twitter to, in part, attempt to manage the dynamic situation on the ground through deterrence. Pundits and foreign policy officials alike interpreted the tweets as a threat toward Armenia and worried that increased violence might soon ensue. Some also asked a legitimate question: why would a head of state deliver such a threat over

---

[1] The author would like to thank Corneliu Bjola, Graham Lampa, Ilan Manor, and two anonymous reviewers for excellent feedback and suggestions. The author would also like to thank Mason Liddell, who provided tremendous expertise and inspiration as a dutiful research assistant.

social media?[2] More recently, US President Joe Biden has utilized the same tool for re-assurance rather than threat, signalling support for allies during particularly dangerous geopolitical moments.[3]

The development and widespread adoption of digital technologies by individual diplomats, foreign ministries, and heads of state has had substantial ramifications for the way diplomacy is conducted and, to a certain extent, has changed the meaning of diplomacy itself. As I previously argued (2015; see also Bjola and Holmes 2015), one way to understand digital diplomacy is to conceive of it as a form of change management in the international system. That is, practitioners of digital diplomacy, from leaders such as Aliyev and Biden, to social media technologists working in back rooms of foreign ministries and embassies, and everyone in between, attempt to observe, and respond to, changes occurring in the international system. These changes include both quotidian incremental adjustments to the system, as a consequence of everyday political and so-cial processes, as well as transformational shocks to the system, such as the threat of war or pandemics. This model of digital diplomacy highlights the dyadic interaction between the state or international organization (IO) and its constituents and salient others. Rather than simply *projecting* a message, brand, or image digitally, digital diplo-macy also crucially concerns observation, listening, and data gathering. This acquired information is then used to further refine the image or identity projected. *Retrieval*, in other words, informs projection. From this perspective, digital diplomacy is not just a form of public diplomacy, which implies discursive engagement with others, but also represents an exercise of data analysis and response, understood in the broadest sense, and information gathering and processing. As such, digital diplomacy dovetails with a wide array of statecraft activities, including intelligence gathering and grand strategy creation.

In this chapter I develop these two aspects of digital diplomacy, projection and re-trieval, and theorize their interconnections. In particular, I focus on how the medium itself, digital technology, allows states and international organizations to manage change in ways that, in previous epochs of history, were unavailable. At least since Marshall McLuhan's dictum, 'the medium is the message', media scholars have turned their attention towards the ways in which message delivery mechanisms affect both the reception of the message and structure available information within a society. As print and analogue media began to give way to digital media, the dynamics of that in-formation dissemination changed. Hierarchical models of corporate control gradually gave way to more heterarchical models where distinctions between interpersonal con-nectivity, mass communication, public, and private began to blur. The result is a model of communication where geographic separations mean little, the potential volume of

---

[2] It should be noted that Aliyev's threats were not solely delivered on Twitter, though these received the most attention.

[3] See, for example, tweets supporting Ukraine and NATO allies in an effort 'to deter further Russian aggression' in January 2022.

communication is incredibly high, communication is largely instantaneous from a time latency perspective, and interaction between actors across traditionally bounded domains is possible and often routine. Put simply, if the medium is the message, then digital represents a new way of thinking about communication, specifically the ways in which actors interact with others.[4] New media theory suggests that digitization enables reciprocal processes of projection and retrieval at scale that are difficult to achieve at best, and unavailable at worst, in traditional media forms. This is what makes digital technology unique.

Projection is complex and has been used in a variety of ways, from the physical tone of voice used such that another can hear what is being said, to the use of empathy in order to place the self onto another in order to understand them. Here I refer to the ability of actors to interact with each other in such a way that actors form, and manage, identities and impressions in the digital domain and may crossover to the kinetic domain. Drawing from the dramaturgical symbolic interactionist work of Erving Goffman,[5] this perspective argues that digital media allows actors to cultivate a digital 'front-stage' identity through the projection of information, images, and signals across geographic, social, and political boundaries. From this perspective, to project is to set forth a particular impression that one wants to convey and make that impression available to wide audiences.[6] The use of social media as part of a nation-branding campaign, for example, utilizes projection to form an impression on a foreign audience. Digital technologies create a '"de-spatialized visibility," allowing for an intimate form of self-presentation freed from the constraints of co-presence'.[7] Actors are able to project a particular identity diffusely and are not limited by physical constraints. As with Goffman's original metaphor of the actor on a stage projecting to an audience, slip-ups may provide glimpses to the 'back-stage', or kinetic, domain. Such a mistake could expose the kinetic identity of an actor as well as its digital identity.[8]

The second way that digital media transforms the interactions actors have with each other is through a reciprocal process of information, image, and signal gathering. This process is called 'retrieval' and, in media terms, refers to the ability of actors to access content within a given structure (defined broadly). In the Goffman framework, the actors on stage require an audience if an impression is to be formed; audiences are able

---

[4] Media theory with regard to digital technology is vast. Price, Jewitt, and Brown (2013), Berry (2014), and Papacharissi (2015) provide excellent overviews.

[5] Goffman (1959).

[6] 'Impression' here captures a wide range of terms that are often found in the literature, including branding, which has become something of a cottage industry with respect to digital diplomacy. I use the broad term impression to refer to generally to an ideational construct that represents a feeling or opinion about projecting actor.

[7] Thompson (2005: 38).

[8] In fact, something of a cottage industry has sprouted to track such slip-ups. Politwoops, a product of the Sunlight Foundation, is an archive of tweets by politicians that have subsequently been deleted and often provide insight into the 'back-stage' of the politicians' thinking at a moment in time. Available at: http://politwoops.sunlightfoundation.com/.

to retrieve both the intended and unintended information projected from the stage. The same is true with digital media and it takes place at multiple scales. An individual diplomat may monitor the reaction to a particular image-projecting tweet, and ministries of foreign affairs (MFAs) mine social media platforms to gauge broad public sentiment in response to image projection.[9]

These two processes of projection and retrieval are both necessary and useful because of the dynamism of the social world.[10] As symbolic interactionists point out, identities and impressions are in flux because they are a product of interaction. As long as interaction remains part of the system, then identities and impressions will be continually changing in response to the other's changes. Practice theorists have identified two ideal-types of change that form a continuum and capture the types of change states encounter in the system. *Endogenous* change refers to the slow day-to-day quotidian bottom-up small factors that might not be perceptual as change itself in any one occurrence but result in meaningful changes to prevailing structures over time. On the other end of the continuum, *exogenous* change refers to the big transformational transitions that occur rarely: hegemonic transitions, pandemics, world wars, cold wars, major alliance formations, and so forth. Exogenous shocks are akin to what Emmanuel Adler (1991) has termed 'cognitive punch[es]' where old ways of thinking need to be re-evaluated and updated.

In what follows, I develop a dramaturgical theory of projection and retrieval as well as the interconnection between these two processes of managing change in the international system. States may project a particular image, such as a preferred branding message, while monitoring and retrieving responses to, and engagement with, that image. In making this argument, I will briefly introduce the Goffman framework and apply it to digital diplomacy in order to theorize how states (and international organizations) and audiences relate and interact with one another. Just like actors on a stage, in a symbolic interactionist framework the 'audience' may play multiple roles, from passive receiver of information to antagonist or challenger. Actors adjust to the audience's advances, potentially changing strategies or, in some cases, as a result of the interaction with the audience, their own identities as well. In this way, digital diplomacy projection and retrieval represent a feedback loop. I illustrate the argument with examples drawn from the Russian invasion of Ukraine in the spring of 2022.

---

[9] It should be noted that other actors, such as intelligence agencies, engage in similar types of data mining and visualization of social media platforms, either to verify specific data on individuals or broader trends relevant to intelligence. Neither is the focus of this chapter, however, which highlights retrieval for diplomatic purposes.

[10] Dynamism is not new and efforts to manage that dynamism are not new either, though the speed and efficiency of digital projection/retrieval makes them saliently unlike prior iterations of these strategies.

Managing Change: A Digital Approach

The Front-Stage and Back-Stage

Among the various activities in which states engage with social media—from culling perspectives and emotions of foreign publics from Twitter discussion, to blasting emergency information to citizens abroad in a crisis situation—the presentation of the 'self' has received comparatively little attention, which is surprising given its importance in both creating and managing a particular impression the state wishes to express (see Holmes, 2015; Manor and Holmes, 2022). In this section, I develop the dramaturgical perspective to digital diplomacy, that is one that utilizes a theatrical metaphor, and argue that, like individuals, states attempt to actively create and manage the impressions that are formed about them, as if they were on a stage in front of an audience, through social media. Erving Goffman's 1959 *The Presentation of the Self in Everyday Life* ushered in a dramaturgical to the micro-sociological study of face-to-face interactions in everyday encounters.[11] The logic has since been applied to states in a variety of settings (see Carson, 2018 for a recent review), though it is only recently that scholars have begun to understand the importance of digital technology in managing these impressions (though see Manor and Holmes, 2022).

Erving Goffman's social theory (1956/1959) emphasizes the importance of self-presentation in everyday life. Goffman argues that much of what occurs in micro-level social interactions, such as face-to-face interactions, represents the active attempt at trying to maintain a particular appearance in front of others. Goffman begins with an assumption: 'when an individual appears before others he will have many motives for trying to control the impression they receive of the situation' (Goffman, 1959: 15). These motives can be fairly innocuous, such as the proprietors of a hotel motivated to maintain a certain image of quality service (1959: 20), or restaurant employees purposefully acting professionally and courteously in front of customers while acting informally when not in their view (1959: 116–117). More generally, psychologists and sociologists have noted the need for individuals to have a presentation that matches their own self-image, as well as a presentation that is meant to match the preferences and expectations of the audience(s). Such attempts to cultivate and maintain a particular image are therefore ubiquitous within social establishments. While a Twitter account would not be on the mind of Goffman in the 1950s, social media contains the essence of what Goffman considers in such a concept: regular interaction between performers and audiences.

As if they were on a stage, individuals use what is available to them, including clothing, words, movements, actions, posture, speech patterns, facial expressions, etc., to convey a particular meaning to the audience (1959: 24). Goffman's theatrical

---

[11] There is now a vast literature applying Goffman's framework to social media, exemplars include: Hogan (2010).

metaphor is organized into three stages: the front-stage, the back-stage, and the outside. The front-stage is where the situation framing and definition occur. The back-stage is where performers are able to retreat to and the impression 'fostered by the performance is knowingly contradicted as a matter of course' (1959: 112). It is, as in a staged theatrical production, where the performers can stop performing and be 'themselves' relative to the main performance. Side or secondary performances may arise, however, since the 'back-stage' is also a place of regularized social interaction.[12] The outside or off-stage is an area where individuals who are not part of the performance and may interact with the audience members in a non-performance manner. Finally, in addition to the boundaries of various stages, social interaction is also bounded and enhanced by the work of teams. Goffman notes that performers will cooperate with each other, share information, help and trust each other, and, quite importantly, share 'the party line', forming a team (1959: 85). Teams are how a group of individuals can manage a central impression through cooperation. Importantly, a team may have internal disputes that are voiced and deliberated in the back-stage, but when on the front-stage, a single unified group should always exist.

We can begin to see how this dramaturgical perspective might apply to diplomacy conducted through the social establishment of social media. Individuals or teams of performers use what is available to them—including text, graphics, video, and imagery—to produce a performance that is then viewed, and responded to, by an audience. Sometimes these performances are highly scripted, for example in the posting of a press release on Twitter or responding to a practical question regarding a passport application. Other times, however, the performers have quite a bit of agency to construct the performance to their liking. The performance, such as a tweet, is only as meaningful as its reception, and response, by the audience. While the performers create the performance, the audience has a reciprocal power to accept or reject the projection. Put another way, the performers act and the audience accepts, but only because it chooses to do so.

The Power of the Audience and the Power of the Performer

This means that power to manage impressions exists both in the performer and in the audience. In any given performance on the front-stage, the team of performers is limited by the capacity of the audience. As Goffman notes, 'whether an honest performer wishes to convey the truth or whether a dishonest performer wishes to convey a falsehood, both must take care to enliven their performances with appropriate expressions, exclude

---

[12] While it is out of the scope for this chapter, there is an interesting question that arises with respect to the front-stage and back-stage 'melting' together. If the back-stage can become a front-stage, due to the regularized activity where performers will put on acts for each other, this suggests at some point in time performers are in a liminal space where they are at once performers and audience.

from their performances expressions that might discredit the impression being fostered, and take care lest the audience impute unintended meanings' (1959: 66). The care taken to create 'appropriate expressions' and not to 'impute unintended meanings' is a consequence of the audience inferring from the performance a particular reality. The limit on the performers' expression is the ability, or desire, of the audience to understand and accept the (intended) meaning of the message. For instance, the cues that Goffman discusses, such as furniture, may have cultural connotations that limit the effectiveness of the message: what works for one audience, in one culture, may not work for another.

Crucially, there is nothing in the stage metaphor to suggest that the audience must passively accept what goes on stage. To be sure, audiences do this routinely. They will, as Samuel Taylor Coleridge put it in the nineteenth century, 'suspend disbelief', in order to play the game of drama and presentation. For instance, if an actor falls on stage or makes a mistake with lines, audiences will typically look beyond the mistake to continue the game. But there is nothing to suggest that they must accept the manipulation. As Goffman points out:

> We have then, a basic social coin. With awe on one side and shame on the other. The audience senses secret mysteries and powers behind the performance, and the performer senses that his chief secrets are petty ones. As countless folk tales and initiation rites show, often the real secret behind the mystery is that there really is no mystery; the real problem is to prevent the audience from learning this too
>
> (1959: 70).

The performers will attempt to manipulate the audience into thinking that there is something magical occurring in the performance, but they cannot *prevent* the audience from not buying it. In this way, the performers are *always* constrained at a basic level by the audience because the audience represents the final arbiter of whether or not the manipulation is successful.

Perhaps more subtly, however, power can also be placed *with* the audience. The first way this might happen is when the audience becomes aware of the attempt to control impressions and does not respond favourably. If, for example, individuals in the audience recognize the attempts to control impressions and do not want to be controlled, they might speak out against the performers and alert others to what is occurring. In such an instance, the performers will lose the ability to control their impression upon the audience and threaten their future ability to do so. Similarly, if individuals create a conflicting impression in two separate audiences, then each audience will be unlikely to accept future performances. The statesman that tells one country that war is not imminent, but another country that war is certainly imminent, will have a credibility problem if the audience happens to overlap.

More fundamentally, even if the performer is successful in managing a particular impression, it is not necessarily the case that power has been exerted in all cases. As Goffman notes, often in social interaction the result is not real consensus, but a *veneer of consensus* (1959: 9). Put simply, sometimes the audience accepts what the performer is projecting, at a surface level, but changes nothing about themselves. This distinction is also made in the IR literature on rhetoric and persuasion. Some scholars have noted that 'agreement' or 'consensus' need not be a Habermasian moment where both parties change their opinions and come to an agreement (Krebs and Jackson, 2007). Sometimes consensus is reached for more superficial reasons (such as saving face or being forced into a particular argument through rhetorical action). Perhaps in these cases, the impression has not been managed at all, but the audience has accepted its role in the game. In this instance, it is unclear where power should be placed, if anywhere. Thus, as with the tension between structure and agent, so too is there a tension in Goffman's work between whether we should view impression management power residing with the performer, the audience, somewhere in between, or nowhere.

These intricacies of the dramaturgical theory have been developed in some depth because they are particularly acute when it comes to applying Goffman to a state or IO attempting to manage change in the international system digitally. In particular, they combine to illustrate the tricky tightrope states and IOs must walk in order to create, and maintain, their desired impression. On the one hand, states, but more specifically those charged with portraying the state through social media, have tremendous flexibility, and agency, in their ability to project an image of their choosing and significant power in the ability to convey that image to an extremely broad and diverse audience. On the other hand, they are constrained by the audience's ability, and desire, to accept that impression. Indeed, in the case of social media, the audience has the agency to actively engage with the projection, questioning, pushing back, or even retaliating against it. This duality of projection and retrieval is particularly important because on the audience end it may be the sole way that individuals or groups have meaningful interaction with a foreign state.

Projection and Retrieval: States on a Digital Stage

Goffman's theory of impression management is ultimately a theory of human identity performance and response. By producing and maintaining a particular impression in front of others, individuals are producing a particular relational identity performance; if accepted, these performances are constitutive of identity. Crucially, feedback is provided by the audience, which, in turn, informs further projection. In this way, projection of an identity and retrieval of response to that projection represent a feedback loop. In digital diplomacy, this occurs through social media. Social media enables diplomats to function as if they were an individual in Goffman's world: they might comment on events dominating the news cycle, offer insight into national and international crises, celebrate holidays, and even partake in online traditions such as #ThrowBackThursday. Through these online activities, a foreign nation state comes to life, projecting an identity image that may or may not be accepted by others but that will be responded to in some way. Engagement with the audience is key. As the US Department of State's social media strategy makes clear, the value of social media for diplomacy is in the two-way nature of the medium:

> Many organizations use social media primarily as a broadcast mechanism to distribute traditional content via new channels. When used in this limited way, social media can be 'low impact' for an organization's resources, but will also likely be low impact when it comes to advancing an organization's goals. Organizations that predominantly use social media to move traditional content online end up forgoing the benefits that accrue to those that take full advantage of the two-way nature of the medium.[13]

Or, as Graham Lampa, lead author of the strategy puts it, 'Diplomats that do social media well are *listening* and *responding* to what they hear'.[14]

Crucially, digital national impression management is just as strategic as that of an individual in the Goffmanian framework. Scholars suggest that diplomats can manage national impression, or develop a national 'brand', by highlighting certain policies, linking foreign policies to desirable norms and values, promoting cultural achievements, and demonstrating global leadership. For example, Manor and Segev (2015) trace how the Obama administration in the United States sought to brand itself as a friend of the Arab and Muslim world, following the Afghanistan and Iraq wars started under the previous administration. In doing so, the administration was attempting to manage challenging relationships in the Middle East, most notably in Syria, while demonstrating a commitment, at least rhetorically, to values of 'mutual interest and mutual respect' between 'the US and Muslims around the world'. This projection of identity and commitment to values was not uniformly accepted by the audience, and many argued that the effort was not specific enough and successful engagement required targeted engagement with country-specific plans for identity projection (Satloff, 2009). The US State Department was keenly aware of the power to listen to audiences and change tact, when necessary. For example, a memo drafted by Graham Lampa, former Special Advisor for Digital Diplomacy, and approved by Richard Stengel, former Under Secretary of State for Public Diplomacy and Public Affairs of United States at the time, argues, 'News stories come together in minutes, not hours or days. We have to be in that global conversation: it is a two-way street that allows us to talk, listen, and interact with audiences we seek to influence.'[15] What followed was a specific and targeted campaign to project an image that US identity had changed and that the social relationship between the US and key Arab and Muslim countries had also consequently changed. The broad

---

[13] "Social Media Guidance Cable #5: Social Media Strategy Framework for Overseas Missions," US Department of State, October 18, 2013. Case No. F-2015-04681. Doc No. C06107215.

[14] Interview with Graham Lampa, former Special Advisor for Digital Diplomacy, July 2022.

[15] Unclassified US Department of State memo, Case No. F-2015-04681 Doc No. C06107220.

language of mutual interests and respect evolved into specific projections regarding free public speech in Egypt, the Peace Process, and Syria's chemical weapons programme (Manor and Segev, 2015). The feedback loop of projection and retrieval of reaction and response from the audience, informing subsequent projection, is apparent.

In some cases, retrieval processes represent qualitative assessments of whether the audience is accepting and engaging with the projected image, though increasingly states are relying on quantitative or 'Big Data' indicators or automated analyses. The Swedish MFA, for example, utilizes a real-time 'dashboard' to aggregate data across social media platforms to provide instantaneous retrieval of impressions, followers, and other forms of engagement, complete with a ranking of which messages are working well and which are not, allowing diplomats to amend future projections (United States Advisory Commission on Public Diplomacy, 2018: 88). Under the Obama administration, the US Department of State recognized the need for more automated assessment in helping social media content providers to listen and respond to audiences. The rollout of the Hootsuite social media dashboard app during this period was aimed at facilitating social media listening to inform, and refine, US identity projection.[16] The concept of using feedback from social media to help refine the strategic projection is built into the US' overall digital diplomacy strategy.[17]

While the social media site is thus the stage on which nations manage their impressions overtly, the back-stage is the room in which content is planned and created. As Dinnie (2015) has argued, the creators of identity or nation-branding projection strategies range from government officials to marketing professionals. A nation's projected image may be constructed by a team or teams of content creators, which include subject matter experts working in collaboration with new media specialists. 'Brand Norway', a large effort to give Norway a 'new visual identity to strengthen Norway's position as a clear and effective nation brand', utilized private firms (such as Scandinavian Design Group) and policy officials to leverage Norway's soft power and project an image of desirability for investment. As audiences for these images become increasingly diverse, states and IOs are seeking to target them with 'greater precision and profiling' (United States Advisory Commission on Public Diplomacy, 2018). This often requires combining subject and area experts, with deep knowledge of the specific audience, with trained professionals, such as those in marketing firms, to craft a particular projection image.

One of the challenges of moving strategy from the back-stage to the front-stage is the problem of multiple audiences. As discussed above, in the dramaturgical framework the audience has the power to accept or reject a particular projection. Digital diplomacy is challenging, in part, because any projection is, in principle, made in front of multiple audiences. In some instances, this is known beforehand and anticipated. In August 2014, the Canada at NATO Twitter account posted a sarcastic response to perceived Russian aggression against Crimea in Ukraine. The tweet projected 'Geography can be tough.

---

[16] Interview with Graham Lampa, former Special Advisor for Digital Diplomacy, July 2022.
[17] Ibid.

Here's a guide for Russian soldiers who keep getting lost & "accidentally" entering #Ukraine', with a map displaying 'Russia' and 'Not Russia'. The aim of the tweet was to project solidarity with Ukraine and an identity that was firmly connected to the state of Ukraine. The reactions were easily anticipated, as the projection clearly took a side in the conflict. Many individuals in the West saw the snarky message to be effective and in keeping with their own understanding of the situation, while audiences in Russia were not amused, leading to counter-snarky projections and calls for more professionalism from Canada at NATO.

In some cases, however, the response is not anticipated and audiences may force-fully reject a projection, leading what was a sound back-stage strategy to fail on the front-stage. In May 2014, Michelle Obama tweeted a photo of herself holding a sign that read '#BringBackOurGirls', a projection that referenced the recent abduction of 250 Nigerian girls by Boko Haram. The projection here was solidarity with the affected Nigerian families. While many audiences accepted the projection and engaged posi-tively with it, this response was far from universal. As Manor describes (2016), the tweet led to 'a counter social media campaign' that not only rejected the projection, but also included graphical projections of '#BringBackYourDrones', referencing the use of drones by the Obama administration. Subsequent counter-projections included imagery of '#WeCantBringBackOurDead'. As Manor notes, the effect of this rejec-tion and counter-projection was the reignition of debates regarding the US war on terror, rather than the intended humanitarian effect (Manor, 2016). In refining the strategy, subsequent tweets from the First Lady continued to engage with the topic, and the hashtag, but without the easily manipulated imagery that could be used for counter-projection.

In attempting to manage change in the international system with digital tools, states and IOs are thus involved in complicated dramaturgical production of various stages, scripts, audiences, and feedback loops. Like actors on a stage, states and IOs enjoy significant power to project, while the audience enjoys the power to accept, reject, or counter.

Tracing Projection and Retrieval During War: Ukraine in 2022

Well before the Russian invasion of Ukraine in 2022, Ukraine, Russia, and the United States were all engaged in long-term impression projection, involving management of day-to-day changes in the system. As the US Department of State argued intern-ally, after the annexation of Crimea in 2014, 'the ongoing crisis in Ukraine highlighted the fact that a new approach to digital communications is necessary. . . '. Messaging was coordinated on an 'hour-by-hour' basis with the aim of responding to, and countering, Russia's image projection: 'The Ukraine Communications Team – which debunked

Russia's misinformation in real time, created positive story lines, and coordinated across government – is a model for this new kind of communication.'[18]

For its part, Ukraine has repeatedly pressed that Crimea will return to them. On 27 February 2021, @MFA_Ukraine wrote, 'But rest assured that one day, #Crimea will be UA once again' in English. On 11 January 2021, they projected that they 'will return Crimea and we should not question this fact for a moment' in Ukrainian. On 28 December 2020, they said that they will 'never give up Crimea and Donbas' in German. These tweets were generally supported by their audience, but saw relatively little engagement, with twenty-one, forty-six, and fifteen retweets respectively and few replies. These are not isolated examples. On 11 October 2020, @MFA_Ukraine began to use the '#CrimeaPlatform' hashtag to very little fanfare. They continued using this hashtag semi-regularly to push Crimea's return until 23 August 2021. Again, responses were positive but relatively few. Their most replied-to message using #CrimeaPlatform garnered only eight replies, while their most retweeted tweet with that hashtag got 125 retweets. After the 2022 invasion the hashtag returned; their 26 February 2022 revival received fifty-one replies and 279 retweets while proclaiming '#CrimeaPlatform We condemn in the strongest possible terms the unprovoked invasion of Ukraine by armed forces of [Russia]'. This tweet, again, is broadly filled with supportive replies. In general, across late 2020 and early 2021, there are dozens of examples of Ukraine discussing Crimea on Twitter. Sometimes it is an outright statement that they will not give it up, other times a sorrowful article featuring Crimean natives, or a subtle implication that Crimea is still part of Ukraine. References to Crimea are often bureaucratic in nature. There are references to 'temporary [Russian] occupation', 'breaching [Russian] obligations under international law', and 'political prisoners'. During this period, Ukraine's image projection strategy is one that is consistent with the notion of slow, incremental, (little) endogenous change: Crimea is part of Ukraine and should be returned.

During the same late-2020–early-2021 time period, Russia's preferred method of engaging with Ukraine online was by tying Ukraine to Nazism. Sometimes these tweets draw historical ties between Ukraine and Nazis, though more often they are contemporary accusations. On 23 November 2021, @mfa_russia tweeted 'the #UN General Assembly approved a #Russia-sponsored resolution on Combatting glorification of Nazism. It was opposed by only two countries – the #US and #Ukraine.' Russia's intention appears to be to project Russia, and Russians living in Ukraine, as potential victims of Nazism while simultaneously projecting Ukraine as the aggressor. Consider a 13 November 2021 tweet where Russia accuses Ukraine of 'absurd discriminatory laws on forced Ukrainisation' as an example. In Russia's narrative, Ukraine is supporting discrimination and hurting its citizens. This building of an impression of victimhood supports Russia's claims on 24 February 2022 that the people of the Donbas region 'have asked Russia for help'.

---

[18] Unclassified US Department of State memo, Case No. F-2015-04681 Doc No. C06107220.

Despite their frequency and consistency in projecting an image of victimhood and laying the groundwork for the 2022 invasion, Russia's messaging was not particularly well received by its Twitter audience. These tweets, like Ukraine's during this period, were not terribly popular. Most have a few dozen retweets and ten or fewer replies. However, unlike Ukraine, Russia's replies are much more split. Though there are often some supportive messages, there is far more pro-Ukraine sentiment voiced. For example, on 21 January 2021, @mfa_russia wrote that they hope 'the bigotry of Ukrainisation sinks into oblivion' as a response to what Russia perceives as cultural genocide. Some examples of responses include an infographic fact-check of the Ukrainian language law, the claim that 'Russia needs to respect it's [sic] Older neighbor, Ukraine and not meddle in their country', and that one replier 'thought [Ukraine] had a warm relationship with #Russia. But the #Kremlin initiated warfare against them in 2014.' These types of replies are typical for the time period.

Immediately prior to the 24 February 2022 invasion, Russia ramped up the image projection and began crafting a slightly altered narrative to justify the war, projecting an image of a state that would be acting in self-defence, thereby countering and attempting to reject competing narratives by the United States and its allies. On 17 February, @mfa_russia tweeted a quote from Sergey Lavrov, Russia's minister of foreign affairs: 'This entire situation is not developing here in Russia but in the minds & media of the West, above all the #USA and #GreatBritain.' He accused the 'West' of drumming up delusions of Russian aggression. Simultaneously, @mfa_russia supported 'strengthening the common defence space of Russia & Belarus [. . .] in the light of the growing military activity of @NATO'. In the days before the invasion, Russia was projecting an image that not only denied that it was behaving aggressively, but that its main concern was security. This image projection as the defensive actor would continue as the invasion began.

In order to reconcile self-defence with invasion, Russia turned to a victimhood image. On 24 February, @mfa_russia wrote that 'the People's Republics of Donbass have asked Russia for help' and that their military operation is to protect those who have been 'facing genocide'. This is subsequently linked explicitly to self-defence. On 24 February, they stated that the US 'policy of containing Russia [. . .] is not only a threat to our interests but to the very existence of our state'. Russia is, in its projection, the victim. Russia's diplomats, according to Russia, 'have come under repeated attack'. The next day, @mfa_russia announced a special military operation 'to demilitarize and denazify Ukraine'. The juxtaposition of self-defence—removing diplomats in harm's way—with aggressive acts creates a tension that is pointed out by observers. They use self-defence to justify removing their diplomats, but the next day announce an offensive attack against the country from which their diplomats were just removed.

Ukraine, for its part, in response attempted to project strength and unity. On 15 February, prior to the invasion, @MFA_Ukraine wrote that support from Ukrainian partners allowed Ukraine to be 'in a strong position and prepared for any scenario'. On 17 February, they affirmed that Poland, the UK, and Ukraine had joined together 'to safeguard stability and build resilience in Ukraine'. Later, they thanked Norway for its aid. In doing so, @MFA_Ukraine said, 'together with our partners, we continue strengthening

Ukraine's resilience'. Ukrainian leadership projected messages of unity between allies, creating a strong impression of unity against Russia. They also emphasized unity between Ukrainians. On 16 February, @MFA_Ukraine wrote that 'We are strong when we are united, we are strong when we are together'. Rhetoric about the strength of Ukrainians is a common projection of @MFA_Ukraine. On 26 February, they announced the birth of the first baby born in the shelters of Kyiv: 'Under the ground, next to the burning buildings and Russian tanks. . . We shall call her Freedom!' This is a clear example of Ukraine projecting resilience. The message is, essentially, life is still flourishing under Russian attacks.

Ukraine was simultaneously trying to interact with its audience, retrieving responses, and addressing them. On the day of the invasion, they began a 'Twitter-storm'. The goal was to tag users and governments to spread the message that '#RussiaInvadedUkraine' and '#StopRussianAggression'. After the invasion began, Ukraine's messages were spread further. They occasionally repeated strategies that successfully engaged their audience. For example, on 27 February, @MFA_Ukraine tweeted out an infographic of Russian losses in Ukraine. Measured by likes, it was their second most popular post in the two weeks surrounding the invasion. The next day, they tweeted out an updated but otherwise identical infographic and again engendered significant audience engagement. Based on the success of these initiatives, the infographics continued.

CONCLUSION: PROJECTION AND RETRIEVAL IN A DYNAMIC WORLD

If states are on a stage, then performance, and perceptions of that performance, matters. As I have argued, a dramaturgical approach to understanding digital diplomacy centres the audience in the performance: it has the power to accept, reject, or suggest refinement of the message. While public diplomacy has long been centred on projection, or talking, states that do not listen to this audience feedback are missing an important opportunity to refine their projection. As the Obama administration's efforts to foreground retrieval in the 2010s and the Ukraine case examples illustrate, social media strategists intuit the importance of this feedback loop and often take steps to systematically implement it. Put simply, one way states attempt to manage change in the international system is by projecting images and identities while refining those projections through audience retrieval.

This dramaturgical approach to understanding digital diplomacy has important ramifications for policymakers, including the diplomats who engage with social media. With the ability to immediately respond to events in the system, and gather near instantaneous feedback in the process, diplomats are in a position to be at the forefront of change management during major shocks to the system. The 2022 Ukraine crisis illustrates the ways in which diplomats and MFAs quickly responded to events and changed projection during the lead-up and into the invasion. At the same time, however, just as actors on a stage may hone their craft through time, digital diplomacy also affords states the ability to monitor audience reaction over longer time horizons, testing the reaction of subtle changes to their projections. Finally, it is important to note that like an audience in a theatrical performance, it may be the case that in many or most instances an audience's only interaction with a particular state will be as that audience. One might imagine the number of individuals whose only interaction with Ukraine or Russia will take place digitally. Or as Holmes and Manor put it, digital diplomacy has a way of bringing the state into existence in everyday life for many audience groups. As such, when a state engages in digital diplomacy on stage it is coming to life, taking an agentic form that interacts with those around it.

By way of conclusion, it is worth considering the need for future research to investigate how performer and audience characteristics, including competence, affect the feedback loop. Just as no two performances of Hamlet may be exactly the same, states vary in their digital diplomacy performances as well, with important variation in willingness to engage, utilization of humour, and competence with respect to learning from audience reactions to their projections. Similarly, as anyone who has utilized social media can attest, the quality of audience engagement, particularly anonymous engagement, can vary considerably. For example, while one particular projection may have the desired intended effect with one audience, it may not for a different audience. It can be difficult to differentiate signals from noise. Understanding the characteristics that make audiences likely to respond to projections in particular ways is critical to being able to craft a projection and refinement strategy. Understanding which types of audience feedback are worth incorporating into one's projection may be even more important.

Further Reading

Bjola, Corneliu, and Marcus Holmes (eds.). 2015. *Digital Diplomacy: Theory and Practice.* Routledge.
Bjola, Corneliu and Ruben Zaiotti (eds.). 2021. *Digital Diplomacy and International Organisations: Autonomy, Legitimacy and Contestation.* Abingdon: Routledge.
Dinnie, Keith. 2015. *Nation Branding: Concepts, Issues, Practice.* Abingdon: Routledge.
Goffman, Erving. 1959. *The Presentation of Self in Everyday Life.* Anchor.
Manor, Ilan. 2016. *Are We There Yet: Have MFAs Realized the Potential of Digital Diplomacy?* Brill Research Perspectives.

Works Cited

Adler, Emanuel, and Beverly Crawford. 1991. *Progress in Postwar International Relations.* New York: Columbia University Press.
Berry, David M. 2015. *Critical Theory and the Digital.* New York and London: Bloomsbury Academic.

Bjola, Corneliu, and Marcus Holmes. 2015. *Digital Diplomacy: Theory and Practice*. Abingdon: Routledge.

Carson, Austin. 2018. *Secret Wars: Covert Conflict in International Politics*. Princeton: Princeton University Press.

Dinnie, Keith. 2015. *Nation Branding: Concepts, Issues, Practice*. Abingdon: Routledge.

Goffman, Erving. 1959. *The Presentation of Self in Everyday Life*. Anchor.

Hogan, Bernie. 2010. "The Presentation of Self in the Age of Social Media: Distinguishing Performances and Exhibitions Online." *Bulletin of Science, Technology & Society* 30 (6): 377–386.

Holmes, Marcus. 2015. Digital Diplomacy and International Change Management. In *Digital Diplomacy: Theory and Practice*, edited by Corneliu Bjola and Marcus Holmes, 13–32. Abingdon: Routledge.

Krebs, Ronald R. and Jackson, Patrick Thaddeus. 2007. "Twisting Tongues and Twisting Arms: The Power of Political Rhetoric." *European Journal of International Relations* 13(1): 35–66.

Manor, Ilan. 2016. *Are We There Yet: Have MFAs Realized the Potential of Digital Diplomacy?*, Leiden, The Netherlands: Brill.

Manor, Ilan and Holmes, Marcus. 2022. "The State in Everyday Life." *International Studies Association Conference Paper*.

Manor and Ilan and Segev, Elad. 2015. America's selfie: How the US portrays itself on its social media accounts. In *Digital Diplomacy: Theory and Practice*, edited by Corneliu Bjola and Marcus Holmes, 89–108. Abingdon: Routledge.

Papacharissi, Zizi. 2015. *Affective Publics: Sentiment, Technology, and Politics*. Oxford, UK: Oxford University Press.

Price, Sara, Carey Jewitt, and Barry Brown. 2013. *The SAGE Handbook of Digital Technology Research*. SAGE.

Satloff, Robert. 2009. Mutual Interest and Mutual Respect: Ideas for U.S. Public Diplomacy toward the 'Muslim World.' Policy Analysis. The Washington Institute for Near East Policy. Available: https://www.washingtoninstitute.org/policy-analysis/mutual-interest-and-mutual-respect-ideas-us-public-diplomacy-toward-muslim-world. Last accessed July 28, 2023.

Thompson, John B. 2005. The New Visibility. *Theory, Culture & Society* 22 (6): 31–51.

United States Advisory Commission on Public Diplomacy. Optimizing Engagement: Research, Evaluation and Learning in Public Diplomacy. Available: https://www.state.gov/wp-content/uploads/2019/06/ACPD-Optimizing-Engagement.pdf. Last accessed July 28, 2023.

CHAPTER 3

....

FROM MICRO TO MACRO DIGITAL DISRUPTIONS: A NEW PRISM FOR INVESTIGATING DIGITAL DIPLOMACY

....

ILAN MANOR AND JAMES PAMMENT

DESPITE the recent growth of the digital diplomacy research corpus, few studies have employed the theoretical framework of digital disruption. We contend that digital disruption may help to explain how and why diplomats adopt digital technologies. Moreover, a theory of digital disruption may help to examine the consequences of diplomats' use of digital technologies at a national or societal level. Notably, disruption differs from technological change. Throughout history, technological innovations have reshaped societies and impacted international relations. Innovations altered power relations among states, reshaped national interests, and created new norms to which international actors adhere (Drezner, 2019).

Drezner (2019) describes the transformative power of technological innovation on international relations through three arguments. First, technological innovation creates new power dynamics. A state may obtain hegemony by being an early adopter of technological innovations. Other nations which are late adopters may suddenly find themselves facing a new balance of power while trying to 'catch up' with the hegemon. Second, innovation may increase the prestige of a state, as was the case during the Space Race of the 1960s. Finally, domestic factors might stifle a state's desire to embrace innovation as political actors favour the status quo. This, in turn, limits the financial and military power of a state as technological innovations drive both.

Technological disruption is a specific form of change, one which, according to Boucher at al. (2020), occurs relatively quickly or dramatically. Disruption breeds tensions at different scales as rapid technological advancements reshape daily life or society. Moreover, the impact of technological disruption ripples across different social realms. Technology can disrupt industries by creating new business models or it can disrupt military action by transforming logistics. Similarly, technology can disrupt societies by altering how democratic debates take place or it can disrupt international relations through new alliances as states join to regulate the use of new technologies. To summarize, digital disruption may be viewed as a digital technology-induced turbulence which produces industry- or society-wide upheaval (Skog, Wimelius, and Sandberg, 2018). But the term also relates to disorder or the interruption of the normal course of unity (Skog, Wimelius, and Sandberg, 2018). In this sense, an industry or a profession may be disrupted due to the introduction of new digital technologies. We adopt this latter definition to explore how digital technologies have disrupted the profession of diplomacy.

To date, digital diplomacy scholars have focused on analysing how digital technologies impact the working routines and procedures of diplomats (Hedling and Bremberg, 2021; Danielson and Hedling, 2022). We conceptualize such studies as focusing on micro-level digital disruption as they illustrate how digital technologies give rise to new professional norms, values, and routines. Some scholars have asserted that digital technologies increase the speed of diplomacy as diplomats now comment on world events as they unfold. This form of 'real-time diplomacy' (Seib, 2012) was most evident during the Covid-19 pandemic as diplomats commented on news reports in near-real time hoping to manage global perceptions of national health policies (Huang, 2022). Others have argued that diplomacy has become more transparent given that social media sites are predicated on users' sharing their personal lives online (Manor, 2019). Still other scholars have argued that digital technologies limit diplomats' ability to craft coherent foreign policy narratives as non-state actors such as rebel groups or diasporas can counter diplomats' narratives (Bernal, 2014; Bos and Melissen, 2019). More recently scholars have argued that the digital technologies have impacted the very language of diplomacy as diplomats increasingly use humour and memes when responding to world events (Chernobrov, 2022, Manor, 2021). Others have noted that digital technologies have impacted international negotiations, which now also take place on Zoom. These changes have been conceptualized as hybrid or virtual diplomacy (Bjola and Coplen, 2022; Bjola and Manor, 2022).

In this chapter we argue that micro-level analyses do not fully capture the dynamics of digital disruption. This is because micro-level digital disruption often stems from macro-level disruptions. By macro-level disruption we refer to digital technologies' impact on governments or societies as a whole. We contend that digital disruption at the macro level is what motivates digital disruption at the micro level, or the level of diplomats' working routines. Such is the case with 'real-time diplomacy', which was born out of necessity. In the wake of the Arab Spring, traditional media institutions migrated to social media sites. Forced to compete over the attention of social media users with bloggers and citizen journalists, who all framed events in near-real time, traditional media institutions also increased the speed of their coverage of world events (Causey and Howard, 2013; Pamment, 2014). As the speed of journalism accelerated, so did the speed of diplomacy. For if diplomats wished to impact the media's depiction of events, they too had to narrate events in 'real time'. In 2016, diplomats denounced a coup in Turkey on Twitter without being certain that such a coup was even underway (Sevin, 2018). Thus, macro-level disruption at the societal level compelled micro-level disruption to digital diplomacy practices.

However, we also contend that micro-level disruptions reverberate and contribute to additional disruptions at the macro level. In the case of memes, diplomats' new language reduces the complexity of international affairs, promising easy fixes to complex crises. One recent example is diplomats' use of memes to glorify Ukraine's President, Volodymyr Zelenskyy, and portray him as a Marvel superhero fighting a real-world super villain, Vladimir Putin. Yet such depictions simplify the 2022 Russia–Ukraine war, a complex international crisis that affects the interests of many states as well as many areas of diplomacy, including national security, trade, and energy. The simplification of complex crises leads to false expectations of what diplomacy can achieve. When such solutions fail to appear, publics lose trust in the international system (Surowiec and Manor, 2021). Thus, micro-level digital disruption, or diplomats' growing use of humour, potentially contributes to macro-level disruption, or public disillusionment with global leadership. To demonstrate the interaction between micro- and macro-level digital disruptions, this chapter focuses on three case studies: the emergence of domestic digital diplomacy, the increased transparency of diplomacy, and the use of nostalgia in diplomatic discourse.

The key point for this chapter is that disruption in digital diplomacy is not simply about controversial tweets or ambassadors' changing social media habits, but is rather the result of a complex interplay between systemic, cultural, and professional practices. We identify three areas in which this interplay is visible. The declining monopoly over international relations has forced ministries of foreign affairs (MFAs) into a more pronounced role in earning domestic support and shaping their citizens' understandings of foreign policy issues. Changing digital diplomacy practices at the micro level respond and further contribute to this trend, re-envisioning the diplomat as lobbyist and facilitator within his own capital. Second, increasing emphasis on transparency about diplomatic issues interacts with an apparent macro-level decline in trust and credibility toward government and experts, in which disinformation finds fertile ground. Strategic use of transparency (Pamment, 2018) helps to minimize the absences and gaps that enable misleading speculation and conspiracies about the intentions of a country's foreign policy. Third, the complexity of interests in contemporary geopolitics begs for historical parallels to simplify and explain, the result of which appears to be a reliance on nostalgic tropes that all too often veer dangerously close to nationalism. While using historical examples, diplomats risk valorizing history in ways that ultimately run contrary to their present diplomatic goals. While these three trends are far from conclusive, we argue that they demonstrate the importance of shifting focus from micro-level analyses of digital disruption to research that attempts to place professional practices within their broader societal context, in order to deepen the theoretical understanding of digital diplomacy.

On Domestic Digital Diplomacy

Recently, scholars have asserted that much digital diplomacy is actually domestic diplomacy, as diplomats use digital technologies to communicate with domestic publics (Adesina, 2017; Bjola and Manor, 2018). This micro-level disruption, or new diplomatic practice, constitutes a shift in diplomacy as MFAs have traditionally faced the world with their back to the nation (Copeland, 2013). Since its inception, diplomacy has been tasked with managing relations with foreign states while interacting with foreign populations (Roberts, 2007). MFAs' previous focus on domestic publics was limited to dealing with stakeholders, dealing with scandals, or providing consular aid.

Domestic digital diplomacy takes many forms. Some MFAs have launched social media accounts that directly target the national citizenry. In 2015, the Obama administration launched the Twitter account @TheIranDeal in hopes of 'selling' the Iran Nuclear Accord to sceptic American publics (Bjola and Manor, 2018). The Twitter account outlined how the Iran deal would prevent the Islamic Republic from developing nuclear weapons while framing the deal as a milestone in America's attempt to mend its relationship with the Muslim world. Similarly, the UK Foreign and Commonwealth Office (FCO), which helped manage the Twitter account of the Global Coalition Against Daesh, used the account to positively portray the war on Daesh by focusing on refugees returning home and rebuilding their communities (Manor and Crilley, 2019). British diplomats demonstrated that the UK's foreign policy was bearing fruit and that UK tax payer money had led to tangible results on the battlefield. In both cases, social media was used by diplomats not just to promote foreign policy achievements among citizens, but to build public consent for major policy initiatives.

In some countries domestic diplomacy predates the advent of digital technologies. The UK's FCO began engaging with local Muslim communities in 2009 as a means of combating Islamic radicalization and terrorism. For instance, the FCO facilitated communication between Muslim scholars and young Muslim audiences in an effort to counter extremist ideology (Curtis and Jaine, 2012). Yet as we argue below, digital technologies reshape domestic diplomacy in three ways. First, they reduce the costs of domestic diplomacy as launching a Twitter account is far more economical than off-line outreach programmes. Second, digital technologies broaden the audience that diplomats can engage with. In many states, digital technologies are used to engage with all citizens, not just specific groups (i.e. young Muslims). Third, through digital technologies, diplomats interact with citizens on a daily basis. As such, domestic diplomacy is not limited to a small number of events. Rather, the diplomat and the citizen interact daily and the citizen is provided with a national prism through which global events may be understood.

Domestic digital diplomacy also takes the form of blog sites. The FCO manages an extensive blogosphere where diplomats offer insight into world events including the Syrian Civil War, the 2014 Crimean invasion, and the refugee crises in Europe (Manor,

2019). In these posts, senior diplomats create a national prism through which world affairs may be understood. For instance, British diplomats have blogged that the UK's staunch opposition to the rule of Syrian President Assad was in keeping with the UK's historic opposition to tyranny.

Elsewhere, digital diplomacy has resulted in the creation of smartphone applications. The Canadian and Polish MFAs have each created smartphone applications focusing on providing digital consular aid (Melissen and Caesar-Gordon, 2016). When explaining the rationale behind these applications, a Canadian diplomat stated that MFAs should view themselves as 'service providers' who must meet their citizens' needs (Manor, 2019). Notably, during the Covid-19 pandemic many MFAs used social media to publicize consular achievements amongst the national citizenry. Images shared online by Israeli, British, and German diplomats depicted ambassadors leading citizens to specially chartered flights and trains.

We assert that in order to understand how this micro-level digital disruption came about, one must focus on macro-level disruption. In this instance, domestic digital diplomacy is a response to digital disruptions at the level of governments. In a digitally connected world, which faces global challenges, a growing number of government ministries collaborate with their foreign peers. Ministries of trade, agriculture, and the environment all face the world and interact with their counterparts overseas. This process has been expedited thanks to whole-of-government approaches to diplomacy (Golberg and Kaduck, 2014) and increased activity in multilateral institutions. Indeed, the multilateral system has led to the internationalization of governments as trade ministries send delegations to the World Trade Organization and health ministries shape efforts in the World Health Organization.

As government ministries faced outwards, MFAs lost their monopoly on managing a state's external affairs. Faced with a narrowing remit within governments, and subsequent budget cuts, MFAs turned inwards with the hope of developing a domestic constituency. By using digital technologies to meet the needs of citizens, diplomats could develop such a constituency and safeguard their remaining territory in governments. The conceptualization of MFAs as service providers (and team players within government) was thus a micro-level response to macro-level digital disruption.

As noted above, different MFAs practice domestic digital diplomacy in different ways suggesting that there are variations in diplomats' micro-level responses to macro-level disruptions. We assert that several factors may account for such variations. The first is institutional mentalities as some MFAs are risk averse and others are risk prone. Risk prone MFAs may seek to leverage new technologies (e.g., smartphone applications) for domestic digital diplomacy while risk averse MFA may use familiar technologies (e.g., Twitter). Moreover, MFAs may differ in their communicative cultures (McNutt, 2014). Some MFAs may embrace the affordance of Web 2.0 applications and seek to converse with domestic publics through social media. Other MFAs may prefer to talk *at* audiences fearing the agency of digital publics that can attack diplomats and nation states (Haynal, 2011).

The structure of MFAs may also shape micro-level responses to macro-level disruption. Those MFAs with dedicated digital departments may embrace new technologies, such as smartphone applications, as they have the resources necessary to master new technologies. Finally, an MFA's goals may lead to variation in responses to macro-level disruptions. In 2015, the UK FCO prioritized communication with British taxpayers, while in Canada and India diplomats prioritized consular aid over audience engagement. Different goals can lead to the adoption of different working routines and different technologies.

Domestic digital diplomacy is far more comprehensive than consular aid, as made evident in the use of Twitter to 'sell' foreign policies to citizens, or blogospheres that help citizens make sense of global events. Yet these micro-level disruptions have resulted in another macro-level or societal disruption as diplomats can now actively shape national perceptions of actors, events, and policies. Diplomats do more than narrate events; they frame events or create a prism through which events and actors can be understood (Manor and Crilley, 2018). Consequently, diplomats may shape the beliefs and worldviews of their citizens. The Obama White House crafted a worldview according to which tensions with other countries could be best resolved through diplomacy rather than force. The British FCO crafted a worldview that rejected any compromise with tyrants.

Through the practice of domestic digital diplomacy, diplomats are transformed into important societal actors able to mould public opinion. Like journalists and politicians, digital disruption has transformed diplomats into powerful discursive agents who can shape public perceptions and, even more importantly, rally support in favour of or against government policies. Diplomats' new societal role is amplified by MFAs' use of digital technologies to communicate with their citizens. The phenomenon of domestic digital diplomacy thus captures the dynamic of macro-micro-macro-level disruptions. Macro-level digital disruption (government ministries encroach on diplomats' domain) leads to micro-level disruption (new diplomatic practice of domestic digital diplomacy) which results in another macro-level disruption (diplomats' role as powerful discursive agents). This dynamic is also present when examining diplomacy's increased transparency.

A More Transparent Diplomacy

Early digital diplomacy studies questioned diplomats' ability to utilize digital technologies. Scholars argued that MFAs' communicative cultures favoured information keeping over information sharing (Copeland, 2013). Indeed, for centuries diplomacy was shrouded by an aurora of discretion, while diplomats viewed information as the currency of diplomacy. As such, information was to be preserved and used strategically to obtain foreign policy goals (Hocking, 2020). By the mid-2000s, MFAs' discrete communicative culture clashed with the sharing culture of the internet. However, time has shown that diplomats are adept at conforming to the norms and logics that govern digital technologies and over the past decade diplomacy has become increasingly more transparent.

One of the first examples of transparent diplomacy was the 2014 Geneva 2 conference, co-hosted by Russia and the US, which sought to end the Syrian Civil War. Diplomats live-tweeted the conference by uploading images of the various delegations and quoting statements made by senior diplomats (Manor, 2019). This was followed by the full publication of the 2015 Iran Deal by the US State Department. Social media users across the world could review the Iran Deal after having followed the long negotiation process on Twitter (Duncombe, 2017).

Nowadays diplomacy's public profile is more apparent. UN Security Council sessions are broadcast live on YouTube; global summits are accompanied with a windfall of 'behind the scenes' images of world leaders; directors of Big Data units give press interviews outlining how nations use data analysis to counter disinformation (Rohaidi, 2019); and UN ambassadors share press releases through their smartphones ensuring that digital publics are as informed as journalists (Manor, 2019), while votes for the UN Security Council are shared by dozens of diplomats in 'real time'.

Almost paradoxically, even intelligence agencies have migrated to social media, sharing daily updates with their followers. The Chief of MI6, Richard Moore, is an avid Twitter user who shares pictures from his family life such as taking a stroll with his wife's guide dog. Reflecting on the possible tension between intelligence gathering and information sharing, the CIA's first tweet stated that 'We can neither confirm nor deny that this is our first tweet'.[1]

The increased transparency of diplomacy was especially evident during the 2022 Russia–Ukraine war. Meetings between Ukrainian diplomats and their foreign counterparts were all shared online while visits by world leaders to Kyiv were accompanied by videos captured on smartphones. Ukraine's minister of digital transformation used Twitter to call on Big Tech CEOs to exit the Russian market. The war also demonstrated how ambassadors employ Twitter or Facebook to share their assessments of world affairs and explain the importance of various diplomatic measures (e.g., financial sanctions) to digital publics. The UK's defence ministry took to publishing daily intelligence briefings assessing Russia's gains or losses and analysing Ukraine's ability to counter Russian advances.[2]

To summarize, the adoption of social media sites by diplomats has seen another micro-level digital disruption as MFAs and their staff have embraced new norms and working routines. The veil of secrecy that accompanied diplomatic activity has been partially lifted. Yet here again we contend that diplomats' new working routines were a response to macro- or societal-level digital disruption, namely the emergence of a sharing society.

[1] See https://twitter.com/cia/status/474971393852182528?lang=en
[2] See https://twitter.com/DefenceHQ/status/1544546167115202560

Bauman and Lyon (2013) argue that in the sharing society, transparency is transformed into a virtue. On social media, everything once done in private must be done in public and for public consumption. As many scholars have noted, all Big Tech companies now rely on users' data to generate profit (Lupton, 2015). The more one tweets and comments, the more information flows to social media algorithms, which can then tailor advertisements to each user. Big Tech's reliance on users' data has created a sharing culture in which individuals are encouraged to embrace the norm of leading public lives. Users are asked to share all aspects of daily life. The norm of information sharing is strengthened by the 'like' and 're-tweet' features (Storr, 2015). As studies have shown, the more one bares his or her soul on social media, the more revealing a Facebook post, the more 'likes' one receives (Richey, Gonibeed, and Ravishankar, 2018). As such, 'likes' enable the sharing society to enforce its norms and preferred behaviours (Manor, 2019).

Social media and Big Tech companies have thus brought about a societal- or macro-level disruption. Digital individuals are now forced to lead transparent lives while privacy is viewed with suspicion and derision. The extent to which individuals have committed to sharing public lives is manifest in the mass number of selfies published daily. Through selfies, individuals document their daily lives sharing their commute to work, their family/work balance, and even marital spats. Popular selfies now consist of images of couples getting a divorce or attending a funeral.

In a society where transparency has been transformed into a virtue, diplomats can no longer operate in the shadows. Digital publics, ordered to lead public lives, also expect their diplomats to lead public lives, to Facebook their daily activities. When diplomats wish to once again draw a veil around their activities, digital publics can respond with suspicion as secrets are forbidden in the sharing society (Bauman and Lyon, 2013). Yet even more fundamentally, diplomats migrated to social media to converse with digital publics and shape how users understand world events (Mazumdar, 2021). To this end, diplomats have sought to cultivate a large social media following, a goal that cannot be achieved without the constant sharing of information. MFAs that share the least information experience 'Social Death'—they are ignored (Lupton, 2015). MFAs that share the most reach the largest numbers of users and are rewarded with virality (Manor and Pamment, 2019). Thus, once again, macro-level digital disruption (the emergence of the sharing society) has led to micro-level disruption (transparent diplomacy).

Critics may argue that the sharing society merely led to the veneer of transparency. Like digital individuals, diplomats perform on the stage of social media but actual diplomacy still takes place in the back-stage, an area reserved for policy makers (Goffman, 1974). Discretion has remained integral to diplomacy and secret negotiations still take place. In 2015, the Iran nuclear negotiations featured a host of images of various diplomats assembled in hotels on Lake Geneva. Yet digital publics were not privy to actual deliberations, nor were they aware of the concessions considered by each side. Some might even argue that discretion remains key to successful diplomacy, especially surrounding sensitive issues. We do not reject such criticism yet point out that performing acts of transparency is in itself a micro-level digital disruption brought about by the foundation of the sharing society. Diplomats know that, at some point, deliberations and negotiations will have to be made public and marketed for public consumption.

The question that follows is whether the increased transparency of diplomacy reverberates and leads to macro-level digital disruptions. The answer to this question is twofold. First, the growing transparency of diplomacy re-enforces the norms of the sharing society. Ambassadors and intelligence chiefs' tweets increase the pressure placed on individuals to lead transparent lives. For if diplomats who historically lurked in the shadows now share their professional and private lives, how can regular individuals refuse to do so?

Second, the expectation of transparent diplomacy may be one of the factors contributing to the popularity of conspiracy theories and the virality of disinformation. For when diplomats do engage in private deliberation, digital publics respond with suspicion. That which is negotiated in secret, or behind closed doors, may soon become a powerful trope used to sow mistrust and doubt. For instance, the 2015 Iran Deal was accompanied by allegations that secret addendums, negotiated behind the scenes, were not made public and even concealed from the US Congress. Whenever EU leaders meet in private they are accused of nefarious activities. The Council of the EU, whose meetings are not made public, has often been described online as a secret apparatus where secret deals are made with powerful lobbyists (Investigate Europe, 2020). A similar trend was observed during the Covid-19 pandemic. Diplomats' unwillingness to comment on unfolding events, or openly confront allegations of wrong-doing, spur conspiracy theories. When Chinese officials failed to comment online on China's handling of the pandemic, it was soon assumed that Covid-19 originated from a Chinese secret lab. Closed door deliberations by the World Health Organization gave way to other conspiracy theories, including that the pandemic was engineered by world governments or was actually created by Big Pharma.

Thus, a lack of diplomatic transparency can translate into suspicion, which may then generate rumours and conspiracy theories. These undermine the credibility of governments and further the belief that there is no truth, only narrative. In this way, micro-level digital disruption, or diplomacy's increased transparency, leads to macro-level disruption as individuals are more willing to entertain or share conspiracy theories that all have one common feature: sowing a deep mistrust of governments who under-share. This is perhaps most evident in the surge in popularity of populist movements who regularly make use of conspiracy theories to 'uncover' the ways in which elites seek to control societies and inhibit free thought (Oliver and Rahn, 2016; Castanho, Vegetti, and Littvay, 2017).

When discussing the issue of transparency, it is important to add three caveats. First, we draw a distinction between actual transparency, in which diplomatic institutions wish to interact with stakeholders or democratize foreign policy formulation (Curtis and Jaine, 2012), and the veneer of transparency. We assert that diplomatic actors, ranging from diplomats to national leaders, may turn transparency into a performance. They pretend to embrace transparency and even seem transparent yet this is but a carefully crafted illusion. One might argue that Donald Trump was the most transparent US President, sharing every thought with his Twitter followers. Yet many of Trump's tweets were used to distract publics or flood journalists with information thus limiting their ability to make sense of policies and decisions. Trump did not share information. He bombarded Twitter with Too Much Information, threatening nuclear war in one tweet then sharing his love of Big Macs in another (Cornut, Rimmer, and Choi, 2022).

There is also a distinction between transparency and the truth. Since it invaded Ukraine in February of 2022, the Russian state has performed acts of transparency. Twitter users have been granted access to meetings at the Kremlin in the form of short videos; they have viewed security briefings in near-real time and have even received daily updates on Russian humanitarian efforts in Ukraine. Yet this is a strategic manipulation of transparency, a performance meant to portray Russia as open and honest. Twitter users are not privy to those meetings in which officials offer an accurate assessment of Russia's activities in Ukraine, which are anything but humanitarian.

Finally, transparency does not magically protect diplomats from conspiracy theories and allegations of misconduct. This is evident in malinformation, in which facts, data, and public statements are used to mislead publics and attack institutions. Unlike disinformation, malinformation is not the circulation of false information with the intent to deceive. Rather, it is the use of truth and facts in a misleading way, such as taking facts and statements out of context and using these facts to discredit an institution. While the WHO may have used digital technologies to increase the transparency of its handling of Covid-19, this did not defend it against conspiracy theories, which often took the shape of malinformation.

NOSTALGIC TROPES IN DIPLOMACY

Diplomats increasingly employ nostalgic tropes in their online communications (Manor and Pamment, 2022). By nostalgia we do not refer merely to posts or tweets that deal with the past but rather with content that re-interprets the past and portrays an idyllic version of it. One notable example was Russia's celebration of Yuri Gagarin's historic journey to outer space. In 2021, the Russian MFA launched a dedicated social media campaign to denote the fifty-year anniversary of Gagarin's flight. Importantly, images of Gagarin seldom featured the cosmonaut in military uniform or even in space suits bearing the emblems of the USSR. Rather, Russia featured Gagarin in civilian clothes while highlighting his warm reception by crowds across the world and images taken from his personal life. Through these nostalgic tropes, present-day Russia sought to associate itself with the scientific and cultural achievements of the USSR. On Twitter, Gagarin was transformed from a Soviet hero to a global hero that allowed humanity to reach beyond the stars. This specific campaign was complemented by an additional campaign that marketed Russia's Covid-19 vaccine, aptly called Sputnik. Here again there was a possible attempt to link Russia's current scientific achievements with those of the USSR, arguing that the same Russian minds that defied the earth's gravity developed the Covid-19 vaccine.

These nostalgic tropes are important as they re-imagine an idyllic past. Gagarin and Sputnik are no longer part of the Space Race or the Cold War, and these images do not conjure fear of the logic of Mutually Assured Destruction. Rather, both Gagarin's flight and the Covid-19 vaccine can be portrayed as disassociated from their geopolitical imperatives: as Russian gifts to mankind.

President Kennedy offered an important analysis of the role that science played in the Cold War, stating 'I don't think that we can exaggerate the great advantage which the Soviet Union secured in the fifties by being first in space. They were able to give prestige to their system; they were able to give force to their argument that they were an advancing society and that we were on the decline' (Kennedy, 1962). Put differently, the Space Race and its related scientific accomplishments were integral to geopolitical competition.

Yet there is no mention of this in Russia's Gagarin campaign. The past is re-imagined and re-interpreted. Gagarin and Sputnik are removed from the context of the Cold War and introduced to a world facing shared global challenges, including pandemics and environmental degradation. These two Cold War icons come to symbolize humanity's ability to rise to any challenge. For if humans could land a man on the moon, they can overcome a virus or face climate change.

Nostalgic tropes were also evident in a British social media campaign following the death of Prince Philip, the Duke of Edinburgh, in April of 2021. Tweets published by the royal family, and re-tweeted by UK embassies the world over, consisted mainly of black and white photos from Britain's history. One tweet commemorated the prince's 1956 visit to Antarctica. This image harkens back to a simpler time. For when the prince visited Antarctica, Britain was still an empire, the British Navy still partially ruled the waves, and Britain was an important member of 'the West'. This was a simpler time compared to the fog that surrounds Britain's future in the post-Brexit haze. In 1956, Britons knew what their country stood for and what role it played in the world.

Another series of tweets celebrated Prince Philip's long career in the Royal Navy. This is yet another nostalgic trope given the unique role that the Royal Navy played in Britain's history. It was the Royal Navy that propelled British power, having laid the first telegraph cables and charted the world's maps. The navy is therefore associated with the zenith of British power. And yet, the images of the prince merely depict a handsome young man in navy uniforms. There are no images of warships or weapons or of war. So, once again the past is re-imagined in a highly selective way. The Royal Navy is transformed from a military force to a traditional institution, closely associated with the institution of the monarchy. These images suggest that the same institutions that helped Britain chart its course post-WW2 may help Britain chart an independent course following Brexit. Nostalgic tropes were used by British diplomats to offer a sense of continuity in the face of a rapidly changing world.

Lastly, nostalgic tropes played a central role in the Israeli MFA's 2017 Twitter campaign, 'Tweeting67', which marked fifty years since the 1967 Six-Day War. As part of the campaign, the MFA launched several fictitious accounts that live-tweeted the War. A fictitious journalist tweeted about heavy fighting along the border with Syria and Egypt.[3] An Israeli diplomat live-tweeted UN deliberations, while Moshe Dayan announced that Israel had successfully struck the Egyptian air force and that he ordered paratroopers to attack Jordan and retake the Eastern part of Jerusalem.[45] The fictitious accounts were all accompanied by black and white images of fighting along the Golan Heights or historic battle plans.

The Israeli tweets recall a simpler time. In 1967, Israeli society was far more uniform in its approach to the Arab World, which was seen as an existential threat. The notion of peace with Arab States was almost unthinkable; Israeli military operations were far less contentious while the debate surrounding the future of occupied Palestinian territories had yet to emerge. At a deeper level, Israelis were joined by a simple vision: securing the borders of Israel and further developing the state, which at the time was a developing country with a poor infrastructure. The world of 1967, brought back to life through MFA tweets, was one of clear dichotomies, of 'us' versus 'them' and of 'good' versus 'bad'. This, we argue, is the allure of nostalgia. Nostalgia's bitter-sweet relationship with the past produces a yearning for simpler times while offering only the most basic layers of sensemaking. Nostalgic tropes are, of course, used by other diplomatic actors. NASA images of present-day space missions resonate with historic images of the Apollo space capsule.[6] The BBC Archive Twitter account transports users to a time when car phones captured people's imagination or when British punk bands dared sing 'God Save the Queen'.

Importantly, digital technologies such as social media facilitate the use of nostalgic tropes given that diplomats use these technologies to renegotiate their nation's past. The past is always present in diplomacy as historical moral blemishes may limit the attractiveness of a state in the present (Quelch and Jocz, 2009). Yet through social media the meaning of the past is renegotiated given that diplomats comment on daily occurrences and use these occurrences to tie the past to the present. A prime example is a series of tweets published in 2022 by Israeli Prime-Minster Yair Lapid and German Chancellor Olaf Scholz, when both visited the Wannsee Villa where the Nazis' Final Solution to the Jewish question was discussed. Both leaders published images of their tour of the Wannsee Villa accompanied by Israeli Holocaust survivors and both tweeted that current ties between Germany and Israel were ironclad because of their shared history, and not in spite of it. The past was thus summoned to the present with Germany no longer depicted as the arch-enemy of the Jewish people but as Israel's closest friend. In this way, German and Israeli digital diplomacy was used to comment on a daily occurrence while renegotiating Germany's past in the present.

---

[3] See https://twitter.com/MEjournalist67/status/873256317149949952
[4] See https://twitter.com/YosiBenZion/status/873381710242512896
[5] See https://twitter.com/MosheDayan67/status/871713222038081536
[6] See https://www.instagram.com/p/CeBofTHuBXi/?hl=en

Crucially, it is the visual nature of social media that leads diplomats to employ nostalgic tropes when commenting on the present. In their desire to appeal to diverse and wide audiences, diplomats often use images that resonate with iconic images of the past. Iconic images are those frequently used in reference to historical events to the degree that they become visual clichés (Hansen, 2015). They are recognized at once, as is the case with the American flag hoisted in Iwo Jima. Manor (2022) found that diplomats often use images that resonate visually with iconic images or that diplomats use iconic images directly on social media. These images are employed as they are intelligible to diverse audiences. They are clichés whose meaning is almost universal. Yet iconic images by nature are nostalgic as they reference events that societies and peoples relive time and again, be it the Blitz or the invasion on D-Day.

Once again, we trace the micro-level digital disruption of using nostalgic tropes with broader societal level digital disruption, namely the contestation of tradition and the global rise of uncertainty. Digitalization by nature blurs national borders as information passes from one country to another bringing with it revolutionary spirits. New ideas challenge tradition, be it by reimaging the role of women in public life or advocating in favour of LGBTQ+ rights. In this sense, digitalization breeds a sense of threat in many societies.

But digitalization also breeds feelings of uncertainty. In a world woven together by digital technologies, no nation is an island and no nation can close itself off to the rest of the world. In such a world, national borders exist but they cannot be fully closed, enabling pandemics to migrate from state to state. In this world, no economy is independent and so sanctioning one national economy leads to costs in all other economies. Superpowers still exist but in the digital world they cannot simply flex their super muscles. The US alone cannot undo environmental harm or end Russia's assault on Ukraine. Even more profoundly, in a digital world truth is easily contested while governments create diverging narratives of world events. According to some social media channels, Russia is responsible for committing war crimes while according to other channels Ukraine is responsible for war crimes.

A world in which borders both exist and do not exist, in which national economies cannot be managed, and in which power cannot be wielded is one marked by uncertainty and threat. Nostalgia is a remedy for such feelings. Nostalgia recreates a world that makes sense, a world marked by simple distinctions and simple challenges such as a confrontation between two distinct and opposing ideologies. Nostalgia also brings comfort as it shines a light on the best aspects of the past. Nostalgia emphasizes social cohesiveness, political unity, and shared fates. The present 'age of rage' makes way for the age of sage leaders and a golden age of national achievements. The ambiguities of the past are brushed aside. For these reasons, nostalgia is now a dominant emotion across the world as apparent in popular culture where films such *Dunkirk* and *Darkest Hour* revisit the moral certitude of WW2.

We therefore argue that nostalgic tropes are a micro-level response to the macro-level disruption of uncertainty. Diplomats increasingly use nostalgic tropes to help audiences make sense of an uncertain and complex world that no longer makes sense. The use of nostalgic tropes is made possible thanks to the visual nature of social media sites. Through visuals, the past can be summoned to the present while the present can once again make sense.

And yet here again we maintain that diplomats' new working routines impact the macro level, specifically that of the nation-state. The reason being that nostalgia is a central theme in nationalist rhetoric. Virdee and McGeever (2018) assert that in the wake of the 2008 financial crisis, a wave of reactionary right-wing politics swept through Europe, calling for the 'restoration of a mythical golden age of sovereign nation-states defined by cultural and racial hegemony'. Virdee and McGeever (2018) state that the Brexit campaign was crafted by nostalgics in search of a lost empire. By using nostalgic tropes diplomats may inadvertently amplify nostalgic sentiments empowering nationalists. This, in turn, complicates the practice of diplomacy as nationalists favour narrow national interests over shared responses to mutual challenges. A disdain for multilateralism and supposed international bureaucracy underpins the worldviews of many nationalist leaders including Donald Trump, Boris Johnson, and Vladimir Putin. This is one possible macro-level reverberation of diplomats' micro-level use of nostalgic tropes, which may be considered alongside dangerous habits of nostalgia such as false equivalency between past and present (as in Russia's justification for war against Ukrainian Nazis) and oversimplification of complex geopolitics (such as reduction of wars into good versus evil).

It should be noted that nostalgia is not limited to Russia or China, nations who are engrossed in the task of bettering their global image. Studies have found that the MFAs of Poland, Lithuania, Israel, the UK, Norway, and the US all use nostalgic tropes and images in their digital communications and have all sought to renegotiate their past (Manor, 2022).

Conclusions

In this chapter we have sought to demonstrate that the theoretical framework of digital disruption may be of use to scholars examining diplomats' use of digital technologies. We assert that the current digital diplomacy research corpus limits itself to investigating micro-level digital disruptions or the level of diplomats' working routines. Yet as has been argued, micro-level disruption actually originates at macro-level disruption, or the digital disruption of society. Moreover, micro-level disruption of diplomacy reverberates generating additional disruption at the macro level.

An important question is what factors might facilitate, or impede, interactions between macro- and micro-level disruption. We contend that micro- and macro-level interactions occur once digital technologies disrupt societies, and not just specific industries. For instance, a new technology may disrupt automobile assembly lines, reducing costs and increasing output. This disruption would have societal implications.

If the cost of automobiles is reduced then more individuals may purchase cars, further increasing environmental degradation. This disruption would necessitate action from diplomats such as new climate accords. Yet it would not necessarily lead to micro-level disruptions or diplomats' adoption of new working routines. Existing routines such as multilateral negotiations would remain in place.

Micro-level disruption is likely to stem from macro-level disruption that reshapes society in some fundamental way. Following Drezner's work (2019) we too place an emphasis on digital disruptions that lead to the adoption of new societal norms (e.g., transparency as a virtue), that reshape societal power dynamics (e.g., the global orientation of government ministries), or that impact the interests of societal actors (e.g., the need to make sense of an uncertain world). Digital disruptions that reshape societal norms, power dynamics, and interests are those most likely to facilitate micro-level disruption, or changes to diplomats' working routines and new uses of digital technologies.

While the three case studies discussed in this chapter do not offer a definitive analysis of micro- and macro-level disruption, we assert that they demonstrate the importance of shifting focus from micro-level analyses to research that attempts to situate digital diplomacy practices within their broader societal context. Specifically, we assert that the relationship between society and diplomacy is reciprocal. Changes in society lead to new diplomatic norms and practices which, in turn, lead to important and substantial societal changes. We thus conclude by stating that digital diplomacy scholars must broaden their horizons and explore the full interplay between society and diplomacy. Disruption theory can aid scholars in broadening their horizons and this chapter is but a stepping stone in this new and important research direction.

ADDITIONAL READING

Adler-Nissen, Rebecca, and Alexei Tsinovoi. 2019. 'International misrecognition: The politics of humour and national identity in Israel's public diplomacy'. *European Journal of International Relations* 25 (1): pp. 3–29. doi: 10.1177/1354066117745365.

Bjola, Corneliu, and Ruben Zaiotti. 2021. *Digital Diplomacy and International Organisations: Autonomy, Legitimacy and Contestation.* Oxon: Routledge.

Ittefaq, Muhammad, and Shafiq Ahmad Kamboh. 2022. 'COVID-19 and national images: The case of #ResignModi'. *Place Branding and Public Diplomacy* 18 (1): pp. 15–17.

Pamment, James. 2022. 'Does public diplomacy need a theory of disruption?'. *Journal of Public Diplomacy* 1 (1): pp. 80–110.

Seib, Philip. 2016. *The Future of Diplomacy.* Cambridge: Polity Press.

REFERENCES

Adesina, Olubukola S. 2017. 'Foreign policy in an era of digital diplomacy'. *Cogent Social Sciences* 3 (1): pp. 1–13. doi: 10.1080/23311886.2017.1297175.

Bauman, Zygmunt, and David Lyon. 2013. *Liquid Surveillance.* Cambridge: Polity Press.

Europe Investigates. 2020. 'Behind closed doors: Secret deals in the Council of the EU', December. https://www.investigate-europe.eu/en/2020/behind-closed-doors-secrets-in-the-council/.

Bernal, Victoria. 2014. *Nation as Network: Diaspora, Cyberspace & Citizenship*. Chicago: The University of Chicago Press.

Bjola, Corneliu, and Ilan Manor. 2018. 'Revisiting Putnam's two-level game theory in the digital age: Domestic digital diplomacy and the Iran nuclear deal'. *Cambridge Review of International Affairs* 31 (1): pp. 3–32. doi: 10.1080/09557571.2018.1476836.

Bjola, Corneliu, and Ilan Manor. 2022. 'The rise of hybrid diplomacy: From digital adaptation to digital adoption'. *International Affairs* 98 (2): pp. 471–491. doi: 10.1093/ia/iiac005.

Bjola, Corneliu, and Michaela Coplen. 2022. 'Virtual venues and international negotiations: Lessons from the COVID-19 pandemic'. *International Negotiation* 28 (1): pp. 1–25. 0.1163/15718069-bja10060.

Bos, Michèle, and Jan Melissen. 2019. 'Rebel diplomacy and digital communication: Public diplomacy in the Sahel'. *International Affairs* 95 (6): pp. 1331–1348. doi: 10.1093/ia/iiz195.

Boucher, Philip et al. 2020. 'Disruption by technology: Impacts on politics, economics and society'. European Parliamentary Research Service. 21/09/2020. https://www.europarl.europa.eu/thinktank/en/document/EPRS_IDA(2020)652079.

Castanho Silva, Bruno, Federico Vegetti, and Levente Littvay. 2017. 'The elite is up to something: Exploring the relation between populism and belief in conspiracy theories'. *Swiss Political Science Review* 23 (4): pp. 423–443. doi: https://onlinelibrary.wiley.com/doi/full/10.1111/spsr.12270.

Causey, Charles, and Philip N Howard. 2013. 'Delivering Digital Public Diplomacy: Information Technologies and the Changing Business of Diplomacy'. In *Relational, Networked and Collaborative Approaches to Public Diplomacy*, edited by R.S. Zaharna, Amelia Arsenault, and Ali Fisher, pp. 144–156. New York: Routledge.

Chernobrov, Dmitry. 2022. 'Strategic humour: Public diplomacy and comic framing of foreign policy issues'. *The British Journal of Politics and International Relations* 24 (2): pp. 277–296. doi: 10.1177/13691481211023958.

Copeland, Daryl. 2013. 'Taking Diplomacy Public: Science, Technology and Foreign Ministries in a Heteropolar World'. In *Relational, Networked and Collaborative Approaches to Public Diplomacy*, edited by R.S. Zaharna, Amelia Arsenault, and Ali Fisher, pp. 56–69. New York: Routledge.

Cornut, Jérémie, Susan Gail Harris Rimmer, and Ivy Choi. 2022. 'The liquidification of international politics and Trump's (un) diplomacy on Twitter'. *International Politics* 59 (2): pp. 367–382. doi: 10.1057/s41311-021-00309-0.

Curtis, Steven, and Caroline Jaine. 2012. 'Public diplomacy at home in the UK: Engaging diasporas and preventing terrorism'. *The Hague Journal of Diplomacy* 7 (4): pp. 369–394.

Danielson, August, and Elsa Hedling. 2022. 'Visual diplomacy in virtual summitry: Status signalling during the coronavirus crisis'. *Review of International Studies* 48 (2): pp. 243–261. doi: 10.1017/S0260210521000607.

Drezner, Daniel W. 2019. 'Technological change and international relations'. *International Relations* 33 (2), pp. 286–303. doi: 10.1177/0047117819834629.

Duncombe, Constance. 2017. 'Twitter and transformative diplomacy: Social media and Iran–US relations'. *International Affairs* 93 (3): pp. 545–562. doi: 10.1093/ia/iix048.

GovInsider. 2019. 'Exclusive: Meet the UK's "Data Diplomat"', March. https://govinsider.asia/innovation/uk-foreign-office-open-source-unit-data-diplomat-graham-nelson/.

Goffman, Erving. 1974. *The Presentation of Self in Everyday Life*. New York: Doubleday.

Golberg, Elissa and Michael Kaduck. 2014. 'Where is Headquarters: Diplomacy, Development and Defence'. In *Diplomacy in the Digital Age*, edited by Janice Gross Stein, pp. 125–140. New York: McClelland & Stewart Ltd.

Haynal, George. 2014. 'Corporate Diplomacy in the Information Age: Catching Up to the Dispersal of Power'. In *Diplomacy in the Digital Age*, edited by Janice Gross Stein, pp. 209–224. New York: McClelland & Stewart Ltd.

Hedling, Elsa, and Niklas Bremberg. 2021. 'Practice approaches to the digital transformations of diplomacy: Toward a new research agenda'. *International Studies Review* 23 (4): pp. 1595–1618. doi: 10.1093/isr/viab027.

Hansen, Lene. 2015. 'How images make world politics: International icons and the case of Abu Ghraib' *Review of International Studies* 41 (2): pp. 263–288. doi: 10.1017/S0260210514000199.

Hocking, Brian. 2020. 'Communication and Diplomacy: Change and Continuity'. In *Global Diplomacy*, edited by Thierry Balzacq, Frédéric Charillon, and Frédéric Ramel, pp. 79–96. Cham: Palgrave Macmillan.

Huang, Zhao Alexandre. 2002. '"Wolf Warrior" and China's digital public diplomacy during the COVID-19 crisis'. *Place Branding and Public Diplomacy* 18 (1): pp. 37–40.

Kennedy, John. F. Remarks to the Staff at the NASA Launch Operations Center. The American Presidency Project. https://www.presidency.ucsb.edu/documents/remarks-the-staff-the-nasa-launch-operations-center-cape-canaveral.

Lupton, Deborah. 2015. *Digital Sociology*. New York: Routledge.

Manor, Ilan. 2019. *The Digitalization of Public Diplomacy*. Cham: Palgrave Macmillan.

Manor, Ilan. 2021. 'The Russians are laughing! The Russians are laughing! How Russian diplomats employ humour in online public diplomacy'. *Global Society* 35 (1): pp. 61–83. doi: 10.1080/13600826.2020.1828299.

Manor, Ilan. 2022. 'Exploring the semiotics of public diplomacy'. *CPD Perspectives of Public Diplomacy* (April): pp. 1–60.https://uscpublicdiplomacy.org/research_project/exploring-semiotics-public-diplomacy.

Manor, Ilan, and Rhys Crilley. 2018. 'Visually framing the Gaza War of 2014: The Israel ministry of foreign affairs on Twitter'. *Media, War & Conflict* 11 (4): pp. 369–391. doi: 10.1177/1750635218780564.Manor, Ilan, and Rhys Crilley. 2019. 'The Aesthetics of Violent Extremist and Counter-Violent Extremist Communication'. In *Countering Online Propaganda and Extremism: The Dark Side of Digital Diplomacy,* edited by Corneliu Bjola and James Pamment, pp. 121–139. Oxon: Routledge.

Manor, Ilan, and James Pamment. 2019. 'Towards prestige mobility? Diplomatic prestige and digital diplomacy'. *Cambridge Review of International Affairs* 32 (2): pp. 93–131. doi: 10.1080/09557571.2019.1577801.Manor, Ilan, and James Pamment. 2022. 'From Gagarin to Sputnik: The role of nostalgia in Russian public diplomacy'. *Place Branding and Public Diplomacy* 18 (1): pp. 44–48. doi: doi.org/10.1057/s41254-021-00233-3.

McNutt, Kathleen. 2014. 'Public engagement in the Web 2.0 era: Social collaborative technologies in a public sector context'. *Canadian Public Administration* 57 (1): 49–70. doi: 10.1111/capa.12058.

Melissen, Jan, and Matthew Caesar-Gordon. 2016. 'Digital diplomacy and the securing of nationals in a citizen-centric world'. *Global Affairs* 2 (93): pp. 321–330. doi: 10.1080/23340460.2016.1239381.

Mazumdar, Theo. B. 2021. 'Digital diplomacy: Internet-based public diplomacy activities or novel forms of public engagement?'. *Place Branding and Public Diplomacy* 667 (1): pp. 1–20. doi: doi.org/10.1057/s41254-021-00208-4.

Oliver, Eric J., and Wendy M. Rahn. 2016. 'Rise of the Trumpenvolk: Populism in the 2016 election'. *The ANNALS of the American Academy of Political and Social Science* 667 (1): pp. 189–206. doi: 10.1177/0002716216662639.

Pamment, James. 2014. 'The mediatization of diplomacy'. *The Hague Journal of Diplomacy* 9 (3): pp. 253–280.

Pamment, James. 2018. 'Accountability as strategic transparency: Making sense of organisational responses to the International Aid Transparency Initiative'. *Development Policy Review* 37 (5): pp. 657–671.

Quelch, John A., and Katherine E. Jocz. 2009. 'Can brand Obama rescue brand America?'. *The Brown Journal of World Affairs* 16 (1): pp. 163–178.

Richey, Michelle, Aparna Gonibeed, and M. N. Ravishankar. 2018. 'The perils and promises of self-disclosure on social media'. *Information Systems Frontiers* 20 (3): pp. 425–437.

Roberts, Walter R. 2007. 'What is public diplomacy? Past practices, present conduct, possible future'. *Mediterranean Quarterly* 18 (4): pp. 36–52.

Rohaidi, Nurfilzah. 2019. 'Exclusive: meet the UK's data diplomat'. Gov Insider, 12 March. https://govinsider.asia/innov ation/uk-foreign-office-open-source-unit-data-diplomat-graha m-nelson/.

Sevin, Efe. 2018. 'Digital diplomacy as crisis communication: Turkish digital outreach after July 15'. *Revista Mexicana de Política Exterior* 113: pp. 1–21.

Seib, Philip. 2012. *Real Time Diplomacy: Politics and Power in the Social Media Era*. Cambridge: Polity Press.

Skog, Daniel A., Wimelius, Henrik, and Johan Sandberg. 2018. 'Digital disruption'. *Business & Information Systems Engineering* 60 (5): pp. 431–437. doi 10.1007/s12599-018-0550-4.

Storr, Will. 2015. *Selfie: How the World Became Self-Obsessed*. London: Picador.

Surowiec, Pawel, and Ilan Manor. 2021. 'Certainty of Uncertainty and Public Diplomacy'. In *Public Diplomacy and the Politics of Uncertainty*, edited by Pawel Surowiec and Ilan Manor, pp. 10–27. Cham: Palgrave Macmillan.

Virdee, Satnam, and Brendan McGeever. 2018. 'Racism, crisis, Brexit'. *Ethnic and Racial Studies* 41 (10): pp. 1802–1819. doi: 10.1080/01419870.2017.1361544.

CHAPTER 4

SOFT POWER IN THE DIGITAL SPACE

GARY D. RAWNSLEY

INTRODUCTION

AHMED Zewail's article, 'The soft power of science', published in *The American Interest*, is a compelling call for greater appreciation of the potential benefits of international collaboration in scientific endeavours. 'The soft power of science', he wrote, 'has the potential to reshape global diplomacy' (Zewail, 2010). A Nobel Laureate from Egypt, Zewail infers that science reflects the deeper understanding of soft power that informs this chapter: the open society, the free flow of ideas and interaction, and the levels of cooperation that have nurtured the essential conditions for scientific progress.

> What I as a young foreign student in the 1970s found most dynamic, exciting and impressive about the United States is what much of the world continues to value about America today: its open intellectual culture, its great universities, its capacity for discovery and innovation (Zewail, 2010).

Meanwhile, the opening ceremony of the 2012 London Olympics—defined as the first 'social media Games'—led audiences on a journey from the Industrial Revolution to the Information Revolution, celebrating the contributions and accomplishments of Britain's scientists, engineers, and innovators. During the ceremony the founder of the World Wide Web, Tim Berners-Lee, tweeted, 'This is for everyone', a message that was then re-tweeted more than 10,000 times. Berners-Lee told CNN:

> The Web is about connecting people through technology, not about documents. ... The Olympics are about connecting people too. It would be nice if the Olympics bring people to use the Web to understand each other, break down

national and cultural barriers and look at each other from a more beautiful point of view (Thompson, 2012).

Both Ahmed Zewail and Tim Berners-Lee reflect this chapter's approach to soft power, which considers specifically how soft power is generated in the digital space and how new technologies communicate a soft power narrative of what the digital space represents. Thus, the digital environment is simultaneously facilitator or creator of soft power, an eloquent message of soft power capacity, and a space through which soft power narratives can flow and be shared.

These ideas are captured by both Zewail and Berners-Lee. Zewail's 'soft power of science' provided the context in which Berners-Lee could progress his ideas; while Berners-Lee's soft power is the 'power of example', revealing what is achievable in an 'enabling environment'—an environment that is characterized by a set of empowering social, cultural, educational, and political structures. America's 'open intellectual culture, its great universities', and 'its capacity for discovery and innovation' that attracted Zewail *is* soft power. Berners-Lee's accomplishments not only reflect this soft power foundation, but also the communication tools he developed advance the further transmission and exchange of soft power that is generated elsewhere. Hence, a central argument of this chapter is that digital space is not separate from physical space: that what transpires offline affects the online environment, and vice versa. The so-called Arab Spring, the war against Islamic State, Donald Trump's presidency, the chaos in the UK around Brexit, the success of nationalist politics across the world, attempts to manage effectively the Covid-19 pandemic, and Russia's invasion of Ukraine in 2022—in all these cases offline and online spaces have intersected and collided, often forming a symbiotic relationship. This is not a revelation, and I have argued this elsewhere to evaluate how political activists have used digital platforms to communicate and mobilize offline (Rawnsley and Ma, 2017; Voltmer and Rawnsley, 2018). The digital environment has not only multiplied the number of actors involved in generating and communicating soft power, but has also opened space to people from diverse backgrounds and with shared interests to organize politically within and across national borders. Especially important is how civil society is an indicator of group autonomy within a political culture that accepts, tolerates, and expects criticism and dissent.

However, this paper is concerned mainly with how states and governments have used the digital landscape to generate and communicate soft power. The political consequences of their dominating the digital space are considerable and far-reaching, as my examples illustrate. Although this chapter could discuss a range of case studies representing populist or authoritarian political systems, including Russia (Pomerantsev, 2014, 2019; Seib, 2021), Poland, Hungary (Applebaum, 2020), and the autocratic regimes in the Middle East (Jones, 2022), I draw attention especially to China, a country and political system I know well and have researched over several decades. The expansion of China's soft power into the digital space has provided a broader picture of China's modernization and provided a new channel through which to communicate its public and cultural diplomacy. At the same time the China case study is a stark reminder that political power offline shapes the online environment; and that how governments organize their online presence and activities can have a profound influence offline.

China's digital soft power also points to the darker character of the modern information landscape that is also discovered in other political societies, including (consolidating and consolidated) democracies. Digital platforms are not the first technologies to reflect soft power and redefine communicative activities. The development of the printing press, the telegraph, telephone, radio, and television have all unveiled the capacity for discovery and innovation, while projecting soft power and influence. Tom Standage (1998) even went as far as labelling the invention of the telegraph in the mid-nineteenth century the 'Victorian internet'. However, digital platforms communicate soft power, propaganda, mis- and disinformation more effectively and efficiently than any other media in history. Their speed, global reach, and relative low cost have expanded the range of voices creating, communicating, and consuming soft power narratives. Anne Applebaum describes 'False, partisan, and often deliberately misleading narratives now spread in digital wildfires, cascades of falsehoods that move too fast for fact checkers to keep up' (Applebaum, 2020: 113).

At the same time digital platforms offer governments, including those that call themselves democratic, greater capacity for more targeted surveillance (Morozov, 2011, 2013; Applebaum, 2020). Hence, the digital space has become another environment in which states seek to exercise power, control political agendas and narratives, and manage popular dissent—offering a 'soft' method of reinforcing their offline 'hard' power. Therefore, I argue that the digital space has not transformed how soft power is generated and has not disrupted our understanding of what soft power is and how it works. Rather, it adds a new dimension to what we already understand about soft power and provides further confirmation of the intersection of 'hard' and soft power.

Before considering the specifics of soft power in the digital space, it is necessary to first address what soft power is and, perhaps most importantly, what it is not.

WHAT IS SOFT POWER?

We should not judge too harshly Donald Rumsfeld, the former US Secretary of Defense, for allegedly confessing he did not know what soft power is (Nye, 2004). Soft power has become not only one of the most familiar, but also perhaps one of the most misunderstood concepts in international relations with as many definitions as there are scholars writing about it. Many sceptics have focused on how soft power has become a convenient catch-all term: in 2009, Leslie Gelb said, 'Soft power now seems to mean almost everything' (Gelb, 2009: 69), while in 2011 Kostas Ifantis noted, 'There seems to be a tendency to call anything attractive "soft power"' (Ifantis, 2011: 45. See also Layne 2010; Isar, 2017; Jaishankar, 2018). Others define it simply as the reverse of hard power. Matthew Fraser observed that 'hard power threatens; soft power seduces. Hard power dissuades; soft power persuades' (Fraser, 2003: 10); and Terry Flew described soft power as a 'synonym for all state-led activities in the international realm that do not involve military force' (Flew, 2016: 290).

However, defining soft power by the fact that it is not hard power is not only tautological, but it also does not get us very far in understanding the value of the concept. Neither does using soft power as an alternative way of describing communicative acts, such as public and cultural diplomacy, public relations, nation branding, or even propaganda. And now, of course we must add to the mix 'smart power', defined as 'the capacity of an actor to combine elements of hard power and soft power in ways that are mutually reinforcing such that the actor's purposes are advanced effectively and efficiently' (Wilson, 2008: 115); and even 'sharp power', defined by Walker thus: 'Today's authoritarian states—notably China and Russia—are using 'sharp power' to project their influence internationally, with the objectives of limiting free expression, spreading confusion, and distorting the political environment within democracies. Sharp power ... typically involves efforts at censorship or the use of manipulation to sap the integrity of independent institutions' (Walker, 2018: 9).

In his excellent and comprehensive analysis of soft power, Hendrick Ohnesorge provides a valuable discussion of the soft power–hard power spectrum, highlighting how the distinction between the two is often opaque (Ohnesorge, 2020: 52–5); and perhaps the conclusion to be drawn from this confusion may be that the label is not so important after all. Former British Ambassador Tom Fletcher advised that 'it matters less whether you call it soft, smart, new, or whatever the next catchy moniker is. What matters is that you call it power. And that you get out there and use it' (Fletcher, 2016: 148). Reflecting on his own contribution to discussions of soft power, Joseph Nye addresses the confusion that has arisen around the term and considers explicitly the problem with trying too hard to differentiate hard and soft power:

> Some resources that are commonly associated with hard power in most contexts can also produce soft power in another context. For example when US naval ships provided tsunami relief to Indonesia in 2004, polls showed a rise of attraction to the US in that country. Some resources can produce hard and soft power simultaneously: witness the Marshall Plan in 1948 or China's Belt and Road Initiative aid program today (Nye, 2021: 201).

Accepting a broad definition of soft power as the power of attraction (but avoiding moral judgements as to *what* or *whom* audiences are attracted—see Nye, 2011, 2021), I prefer to discuss how soft power is generated and then communicated, rather than assuming that soft power can be 'wielded', 'exercised', or even 'strategized'. My understanding is based on the premise that soft power is created by actors working within social and political institutions, processes, and cultures. Moreover, it is most attractive when generated from inside civil society, as detachment from government agendas and behaviours offers soft power a level of credibility that may be otherwise absent. Soft power is determined by:

- The legitimacy and credibility of institutions, actors, and processes
- The behaviour of actors at home and abroad, and the company they choose to keep
- The levels of transparency and accountability, and the capacity for correction
- The free flow of ideas, genuine dialogue, and discussion
- The capacity to build networks for collaboration, especially within civil society

In short, political actors and institutions generate soft power capacity and leverage as a by-product of their positive behaviour, as well as the legitimacy and credibility of the political culture in which they operate. In his 2009 book subtitled *Adventures in British Democracy*, Patrick Hannan reported on a decision in 2008 by Wales's seat of devolved government, the Senedd, to 'restore' free healthcare to 'failed' asylum seekers. Hannan concluded, 'The message' of this decision 'is clear, we are good people' (Hannan, 2009: 130). The image is not constructed and the decision to restore health care was not made because it would make Wales or the Senedd look better. Simply, it was the right thing to do. *This is soft power*. Similarly soft power capacity can be diminished by inappropriate or misguided policies, such as the decision in 2022 of the UK's Boris Johnson government to deport refugees to Rwanda. Both examples highlight that the way we treat the most vulnerable in society is a marker of soft power.

Admiral Mike Mullen of the US Navy has offered a valuable summary, one that governments around the world would benefit from hearing:

> To put it simply, we need to worry a lot less about how we communicate our acts and much more about what our actions communicate. Each time we fail to live up to our values or don't follow up on a promise, we look more and more like the arrogant Americans the enemy claims we are (Mullen, 2012: 4).

In 2004, almost in anticipation of Trump's presidency, Joseph Nye warned that the US could 'squander' its soft power 'by heavy-handed unilateralism' (Nye, 2004: 8). Although Trump's so-called Muslim Ban—an Executive Order preventing travel to the US from seven predominantly Muslim countries—was challenged by America's resurgent civil society and was overturned within days by the judiciary, it still projected a disturbing message about America closing its doors; while in January 2018 the president's description of several African nations, Haiti, and El Salvador as 'shithole countries' provoked a global response that challenged such racist comments as antithetical to American values and the core of soft power. Mexico's former president, Vincente Fox, tweeted in response: 'America's greatness was built on diversity ... or have you forgotten your migration background, Donald?' So, while it is most ironic that the credibility gap actually narrowed during Trump's residency in the White House—he and his administration performed exactly as promised—the damage to US soft power was almost palpable (Manor, 2019; Pitney, 2020; Rawnsley, 2021).

In politics, soft power cannot remedy problems in the hard power domain, and governments soon discover the folly of trying to communicate or spin their way out of misjudged, unethical, or poorly designed and executed policies. Governments must focus on governing, and if they do so for the right reasons, then the soft power follows. The question is not 'How can we make them like us more?' but rather 'How can we govern better?'

Transparency and accountability are indicators of a political culture's soft power. Creating a safe and open environment in which policy and behaviour can be identified, questioned, scrutinized, and, when possible, adjusted is an attractive soft power asset. As George Orwell wrote in his preface to *Animal Farm*, 'If liberty means anything at all, it means the right to tell people things they do not want to hear'. Finding 'the courage to confront the stains', not just of the past as Sophia Gaston (2020) has demanded but to demonstrate daily a 'willingness to confront contentious issues' (Sir Martin Gilbert, quoted in Becket, 2016), adds moral authority, legitimacy, and credibility.

Another dimension to a nation's soft power is the relationship it builds internationally with others in pursuit of its foreign policy objectives. Governments that care about soft power must choose their friends carefully. Claims to champion freedom, democracy, liberty, and human rights ring hollow when the same governments decide to partner with political regimes that deny those same rights to their own citizens. 'My enemy's enemy is my friend', the classic Realist mantra, has driven the US into supporting some very questionable regimes, especially in the Cold War—Iran under the Shah, South Vietnam in the early 1960s, and Chile under Pinochet, to name but a few. What are we to make of the UK's value-driven soft power when the chief Foreign and Commonwealth Office (FCO, now the Foreign, Commonwealth and Development Office, FCDO) mandarin, Sir Simon McDonald, told the House of Commons Foreign Affairs Select Committee in 2015 that human rights are no longer a 'top priority' and that 'prosperity was further up the list' (*Independent*, 2015)? In an essay for *The Conversation*, Armida L.M. van Rij questioned the idea that by trading with Saudi Arabia the UK can exert influence over Riyadh and export British democratic values. She concludes: 'This is a case-study in what happens when a country's supposed economic interests come into conflict with its stated norms and values and its international obligations' (van Rij, 2018). Baroness Warsi has suggested that the FCO 'blind test' countries 'against our stated values and principles', believing that '[M]any a current foreign ally, friend and special relationship would fail such scrutiny' (Warsi, 2017: 195). In her book, *The Enemy Within* (2017), Warsi contends that claims of commitment to an ethical foreign policy by successive UK governments ring hollow. From the Iraq war to Libya, Saudi Arabia, Syria, and Yemen, and even the UK's relationship with the US under President Donald Trump, actions have not matched official rhetoric.

While it is difficult to qualitatively measure the impact of soft power, we can find evidence that the chaos in British politics following the Brexit referendum in 2016 damaged the UK's reputation abroad. For example, journalist Anne Applebaum reported on her conversation with a Spanish politician in March 2019: ' "England, the mother of Parliaments," he said, shaking his head. "We've looked up to them for so long." ' An Italian politician told her: 'We think our democracies are weak, elsewhere in Europe. But even if you took a bunch of Italians, Poles, and Hungarians, kept them up all night and got them drunk, they still wouldn't come up with anything as disastrous as what we are seeing in the House of Commons' (Applebaum, 2019). Describing Brexit as a 'political farce', Thomas Friedman wrote in the *New York Times*: 'Seriously, the United Kingdom, the world's fifth largest economy—a country whose elites created modern parliamentary democracy, modern banking and finance, the Industrial Revolution, and the whole concept of globalization—seems dead-set on quitting the European Union ... without a well conceived plan or maybe without a plan at all' (Friedman, 2019).

The CNN commentator, Fareed Zakaria, titled his essay in the *Washington Post*, 'Brexit will mark the end of Britain's role as a great power'. Zakaria lamented how the UK, 'famous for its prudence, propriety and punctuality, is suddenly looking like a banana republic' and concluded that 'One of the great strengths of democracy is that bad policies are often reversed' (Zakaria, 2019). I would add that in soft power terms, one of the great strengths of democracy is that bad policies *are seen* reversed and that there is no shame in admitting mistakes. And finally, J. Brooks Spector, writing for the South African news website Daily Maverick, published the following in March 2019:

> Yes, the credibility and continuity of Theresa May as party leader and Prime Minister seem at a virtual end, *but Britain's reputation is not coming out much better*. As a separate entity outside of the EU, Great Britain shrinks to a sort of economic 'Middling Britain', useful for some great shopping and often great theatre, but not seen as a serious global player. ... the reputation of the country's prowess as a negotiator would seem to be fatally compromised (Spector, 2019).

As I write this chapter in Spring 2022, the global news agenda is dominated by Russia's invasion (or, in Kremlin speak, 'special military operations') in Ukraine. The war may suggest that hard power does indeed prevail in international politics. And yet ... As the events unfold, we observe how hard power and soft power blur and coalesce. Certainly, the war has clear soft power dimensions. It is possible to argue that one of the drivers of the conflict is Ukraine's long-standing attraction to a political culture and set of values represented by NATO and the EU, which erupted into the so-called Maidan Uprising in 2013. Moreover, Ukraine and Russia have engaged in a vicious information war, with competing narratives circulating mainly through digital media.[1] Joseph Nye noted that 'in the information age, success is not merely the result of whose army wins, but also whose story wins' (Nye, 2010: 8), and in another essay he concluded that 'Narratives become the currency of soft power' (Nye, 2011: 104). The Ukraine war of 2022 confirms that it is still too early to accept Eytan Gilboa's claim that 'Favourable image and reputation around the world, achieved through attraction and persuasion, *have become more important* than territory, access, and raw materials traditionally acquired through military and economic measures' (emphasis added; Gilboa, 2008: 56). As Russia's war

---

[1] David Sanger has noted that 'every technique Americans soon worried about began in Ukraine: manipulated information results, fictional online personas who widen social divisions and stoke ethnic fears, and what was called "fake news" before the phrase was twisted into a new meaning by an American president' (Sanger, 2019: 159).

against Ukraine indicates, the traditional markers of power endure as the foremost cause of international conflict, if not the driver of foreign policy. However, in the social media—in the age of digital soft power—we can see how states face escalating soft power (reputational) costs when they resort to hard power.

Furthermore, the creation of soft power is a long-term process because it depends on developing and deepening relationships, as well as building levels of credibility to amplify and justify attraction; and soft power requires being comfortable with the truth that 'actions always speak louder than words'. What one does will always reveal a far more commanding narrative than what one says, hence my approach to soft power as the 'power of example'. These challenges are difficult to manage at the best of times; for political actors operating in an environment defined by digital soft power, they can be overwhelming.

In his 2002 book, *The Shield of Achilles*, Philip Bobbitt described how the modern state is mutating into a 'market' state 'that is largely indifferent to the claims of justice, or for that matter any particular set of moral values' (Bobbitt, 2002) P 24. I challenge this statement as inaccurate and unduly pessimistic if we look through the lens of soft power. The modern state can exercise a tremendous capacity to undertake moral responsibilities inside and outside its borders; whether it chooses to do so is the true measure of its soft power.

In 1964 at the height of the first Cold War, Senator William J. Fulbright anticipated the introduction of soft power into international relations discourse. In his Foreword to *The Fourth Dimension of Foreign Policy* by P.H. Coombs, Fulbright wrote: 'Foreign policy cannot be based on military posture and diplomatic activities alone in today's world. The shape of the world *a generation from now* will be influenced far more by how well we communicate the values of our society to others than by our military or diplomatic superiority' (emphasis added; Coombs, 1964: ix). Rarely do we find such prescience in academic writing. Indeed, the generation now turning its attention to soft power must confront not only the uncertainties associated with an unstable world, characterized by populist politics, transforming alliances, climate change, and a global pandemic and economic recession, but also the complications of a new digital media environment that has transformed how we produce, consume, and curate news, information, and ideas. How is soft power created and communicated in the digital space? What are the interactions between online and offline environments? And have digital technologies transformed our understanding of soft power and how it is generated, or is it simply a case of new wine in old bottles?

SOFT POWER IN THE DIGITAL SPACE

While sensitive to the need to avoid technological determinism, it is beyond doubt that soft power has been reshaped by the rapid development and proliferation of digital Information Communications Technologies (ICTs). Digital media and platforms have accelerated the flow of communications, interactions, and information between connected institutions and individuals regardless of both their physical location and their wealth or power. As multiple states, substate, and non-state actors discover their voice and influence in the digital landscape, increasingly political competition is a contest both for attention and over the integrity of narratives. The de-territorialization and re-territorialization that occurs in the digital landscape has shaken political power, with transborder civil society groups, mobilized and dispersed as issues come and go, competing with states and nations for allegiance and influence in a less hierarchical distribution of power. The development of ICTs has coincided with transformative shifts in global geopolitics that have created new issues, crises, and challenges; climate change and environmental security; mass migration for political and economic motives; international terrorism; and a global pandemic—all require more collaborative and inclusive responses at both state and non-state levels across national boundaries. Governments have become just one voice, one source of influence, one force of popular mobilization among many, 'promoting and participating in, rather than controlling ... networks across borders' (Nye, 2011).

Meanwhile, digital platforms blur source, content provider, mediator, and consumer as smart phones persuade us to 'upload' and 'download', edit, re-edit, re-frame, discuss, and comment on news stories and information before we pass them along our own networks. Hence, the plurality of voices flowing through networks in an overcrowded information space can constrain the state's power to manage and restrict narratives ... though it can be difficult to secure the free movement of information and prevent government interference, as I will soon discuss.

In this way the digital landscape reflects the soft power generated offline. First, the very development of digital technologies and platforms requires investment in education and research that is pledged to innovation. This also demands commitment to the values that underpin scientific endeavour—the free flow of ideas, dialogue and discussion, and collaboration that first attracted Ahmed Zewail to the United States. It indicates a political culture that respects and values the contribution of unfettered communication, opinions, and information. In his discussion in *The Digitalization of Public Diplomacy*, Ilan Manor describes the messages posted on Twitter by Javed Zarif, Iran's Foreign Minister, in 2013 during negotiations about his country's nuclear ambitions. Manor connects Zarif's use of Twitter to a wider understanding of Iran's soft power:

> By turning to Twitter, the Iranian diplomat was also forging a new image for his nation. In 2013, social media sites ... were still regarded as positive forces in society and the weapon de jour of democratic revolutionaries.... By employing social media, Zarif associated Iran with democracy and the hopeful spirit of the Arab Spring, as opposed to religious zeal and weapons of mass destruction (Manor, 2019: 4).

We could add that Zarif's use of Twitter projected an image of Iran's modernity and, by using English, showcasing his country's awareness of how to participate in the global information marketplace. This too is soft power.

Of course, we must acknowledge that there is a danger in subscribing to the idea that using social media or digital platforms reflects a wider offline soft power capacity. Some political systems embrace fully the digital space without also welcoming such markers of soft power as the free flow of information, accountability and transparency, and autonomous and networked civil societies. I have argued elsewhere (Rawnsley, 2012, 2020) that China is deficient in soft power, even though that country is today a world leader in digital communications and the digitalization of service provision and transactions, such as payment for goods bought offline, calling 'didi' taxi services, and managing compliance of Covid-19 restrictions. The number of Chinese accessing the digital space on mobile devices increased from 50.4 million in 2007 (accounting for just 24% of the total population accessing the internet) to 788 million in 2018 (98% of the total. Chen, 2021). But as Titus Chen (2021) has noted, this increase in use has provided the state with both motivation for and the means of redefining propaganda for the digital age. One reason that this cannot translate into soft power is the absence in China of a vibrant and autonomous civil society, as Joseph Nye recognized in 2021. 'China', he wrote, 'should realize that most of a country's soft power comes from its civil society rather than from its government ... China needs to give more leeway to the talents of its civil society' (Nye, 2021: 205–206).

Another concern that undermines China's soft power is the state's use of digital platforms for surveillance. This takes two forms: one is that the technology lends itself to monitoring users' activities and travel offline; while the other is that the state has access to people's messaging and communications online. Thus, users are denied the freedom to engage in the dialogue and collaboration that the technology promises. All this means that China faces challenges in being recognized for its soft power. Polling undertaken by the Pew organization shows repeatedly that many people in North America, Asia, and Europe continue to have negative opinions about China, based mainly on the Chinese government's record on human rights, its curtailment of political and social freedom, and allegations about China's responsibility for the Covid-19 pandemic (Moncus and Silver, 2021; Silver, Devlin, and Huang, 2021); and these static or even declining opinions about China are recorded *despite* China's escalating investment in soft power programmes, public diplomacy, and cultural relations.

At the same time, alternative narratives are promoted. Wang Yin's research has examined how Chinese responded to content posted on social media such as Weibo by the British embassy in Beijing. Many comments were negative towards the more political content posted, but Wang demonstrates her understanding of soft power when she described why the British embassy left such negative comments online: 'allowing critical and even nationalist comments to be shown to everyone establishes an image of credibility, transparency, and tolerance of the UK. ... Britain appears as a credible country that supports speech freedom and tolerance of different opinions' (Wang, 2020).

The China case study reinforces the idea that access to the digital space alone does not generate soft power, for the offline political culture can either support or restrict online engagement. However, it is useful to acknowledge that all of us living and working in 'digital societies'—in democratic as well as non-democratic political systems—are complicit in and willingly compliant with different levels and forms of surveillance. Ilan Manor has written: 'Even those who wish to remain hidden from the digital world have been digitalized as they are tagged in images shared on social media, while their personal details are digitally embedded into their passports.' Increasingly, we all lead 'digital lives' (Manor, 2019: 36).[2]

We could go one step further and contest the idea that in the digital space soft power is always attractive. A state can exercise soft power if it maintains the capacity to shape narratives, influence opinions, and change attitudes and behaviours without having to resort to coercive methods. Christopher Walker's work on so-called 'sharp power' warns us of the influence exercised by authoritarian states, especially China and Russia (Walker, 2018; Kalathil, Ludwig, and Walker, 2020), while Anne Applebaum's *Twilight of Democracy* is subtitled *The Seductive Lure of Authoritarianism* (Applebaum, 2020). Applebaum chronicles the growth of illiberalism on both the political left and the political right and documents its influence in consolidating and (most worrying) consolidated democracies. Revelations linking Facebook to Cambridge Analytica and dubious practices such as data mining have aroused legal, political, and above all ethical concerns about the role and influence of digital communications (Carroll, 2021), while 'hacking', 'phishing', computer viruses, and other modern forms of information warfare continue to pose serious security threats, online and offline. All these examples indicate not only the use of the digital space to exercise power in new ways, but also how the failure of democratic societies to both confront and manage problems in the digital environment undermines the soft power that is generated around the efficacy of institutions and processes. At the same time, democratic governments must confront the dilemma that if they decide to impose new regulatory processes on media to frustrate the spread of false information, this too undermines soft power: is the flow of erroneous information the price democracies pay for avoiding censorship and upholding free speech—themselves markers of soft power capacity?

As Anne Applebaum has argued, the online environment has unsettled soft power—the 'power of example'—because digital media have encouraged increasing levels of polarization and 'hyperpartisanship' that in turn encourage mistrust in political and social institutions (Appelbaum, 2020: 114). This is demonstrated in the case studies Appelbaum examines, especially Poland and Hungary, but also including the UK and US (particularly in Donald Trump's America) via the creation of new scapegoats for real fears and anxieties, and the advocacy of simple solutions to complex problems (Applebaum, 2020; Rawnsley, 2021).

The proliferation of information, news, and opinions, together with twenty-four-hour access to sources literally (via smart phones) at our fingertips, and our rapidly

---

[2] 'Before the advent of social media, it took a lot of effort for repressive governments to learn about the people dissidents are associated with … creating a comprehensive list … was extremely expensive. In the past, the KGB resorted to torture to learn of connections between activists; today they simply need to get on Facebook' (Morozov, 2011: 156).

deteriorating attention spans[3] create their own problems. This cup-half-full-half-empty situation drives us to identify and adopt strategies to mitigate against information overload. We may either limit the sources we access, avoid those sources with which we disagree, or invest in developing media literacy skills to understand how to use and evaluate the sources and their messages. This has clear soft power implications as soft power is built on credibility, and our verdict on the credibility of information is more important than ever: think of 'fake news' and 'alternative facts'. In a time when we are asked to accept claims that we live in a 'post-truth' world, trust and discourses about trust are themselves currencies of modern power.

So, the digital space expands not just the number of people in the room, but the very room itself—the cup is half full and soft power capacity grows. At the same time, the proliferation of information can create new 'ideological silos' (Ott, 2017: 64) where all opinions are considered equal and whoever shouts the loudest attracts the most attention—the cup is half empty. Rather than providing a platform for genuine dialogue and discussion (conditions for soft power in the digital space), platforms encourage pithy and often brusque responses to news stories and to others' opinions, forcing users to retreat behind their own constricted beliefs, and generating online constraints on meaningful and rational political debate: I am right, you are wrong; and if you do not agree with me, then your opinion does not count and you are not 'one of us'. (On the simplicity encouraged by Twitter, see Kapko, 2016.)

Finally, digital platforms expose the 'credibility gap' between words and actions with more devastating consequences for soft power than other media. When the distinction between content creator, platform, and audience becomes blurred; when news is uploaded and transmitted instantly to anyone with a smart phone; and when narratives emerge as a significant fault line in international politics, it is more important than ever to maintain consistency between what you say and what you do. In the so-called War on Terror the global circulation of what became known as 'trophy photos' of soldiers posing with prisoners prompted Joseph Nye to comment that 'Presidential rhetoric about promoting democracy is less convincing than pictures of Abu Ghraib' (Nye, 2010: 8). It is worthwhile noting that these abuses were openly criticized in the American media. Officials testified before Congress, and the US Supreme Court ruled that detainees at Guantanamo Bay had a legal right to representation. Transparency, accountability, and correction remain the cornerstones of soft power, even in the digital space. What Manor and Segev (2015) termed 'the national selfie' determines the image that countries present and whether they reflect the national values they wish to represent. The connection with soft power is clear, for the national selfie may undermine soft power, as the US discovered in both the War on Terror and during the presidency of Donald Trump. Perhaps the lesson is this: users must remember that the way they *wish* to be seen in the digital space is not necessarily the way they *are* seen, especially if their actions do not

---

[3] Nye (2011) noted that in the modern communications environment, 'Attention, rather than information, becomes the scarce resource'.

match their rhetoric or claims about 'values'. Social media can destroy credibility, and therefore soft power, in an instant.

Conclusions

I opened this chapter on an optimistic note, suggesting Ahmed Zewail and Tim Berners-Lee epitomized the widespread confidence in the digital space as a land of possibility: it both *reflects* and *communicates* soft power capacity. The development of digital platforms represents broad social, political, and cultural values that encourage innovation and collaboration; while their potential for dialogue, discussion, and the free flow of opinions and information indicates a commitment to liberal-democratic values. The digital space can strengthen civil society, help speak truth to power, and mobilize people and politicians across the world to confront and manage together new cross-border challenges.

However, there are reasons to be cautious in ascribing to the digital landscape too much responsibility for generating soft power. One reason is that many political cultures maintain a firm grip on the digital space that undermines the more normative dimension of soft power there. Moreover, the power of soft power lies ultimately with those who consume information in the digital space, for they decide how to interpret or whether to accept particular narratives and the values communicated. So, for example, China's management of the Covid-19 pandemic using digital technology, apps, and codes displayed on smart phones could reflect technical innovation and scientific discovery; it could be a point for aspiration by countries and people struggling to manage their own Covid-19 outbreaks; or it may be confirmation of the growing power of the surveillance society, giving the Chinese government even more means and reason to monitor its citizens. All three are a form of soft power in the digital space.

While Applebaum (2020) and Jones (2022) have indicated that soft power in the digital space is a concern for both democratic and non-democratic societies (Jones provides a comprehensive analysis of 'digital media power' in the Middle East), the example of China demonstrates the limitations of soft power in the digital space: Chinese embassies, ambassadors, and media are extremely active on social media, especially Twitter, even though it is impossible to use Twitter inside China without a VPN.[4] This presence requires openness and therefore an implicit acceptance that being part of the global conversation also means one may attract a level of global criticism. However, it does not provide evidence of commitment to transparency, accountability, and

---

[4] In 2010, just one Chinese diplomat used Twitter. As of July 2020, there were 151 Twitter accounts associated with Chinese diplomats, with 113 having been created since July 2019, and sixty-one since January 2020. By 2019, thirteen Chinese embassies were present on Twitter. 'By 2018, 93 per cent of heads of government and MFAs around the world had social media accounts along with over 4,000 embassies and 1,400 ambassadors' (Bjola and Manor, 2022: 475–476).

correction, suggesting a disconnect between China's presence in the global digital space and the absence of its soft power offline. In fact, online censorship works alongside off-line repression, thereby conflicting with the soft power narratives decided in Beijing. This is lost upon China's current leaders who are convinced that all a country must do is 'tell China's story well' to increase its soft power capacity. Few Chinese inside the country have watched the videos of growing popular unrest that circulated on Twitter during the Spring 2022 lockdown of 26 million people in Shanghai or the outbreak of violence in Zhengzhou when banks froze millions of accounts in Summer 2022. The Chinese government may continue to control the soft power narrative within its own borders, even in the digital space, but it is unable to influence how China's story is narrated and consumed outside the country.

Digital platforms may have expanded the number of voices in a global conversation, alluding to their contribution to a broader understanding of soft power, but at what cost? Are all opinions equal? If living in the post-truth age has taught us any-thing, it is that while everyone has a right to their own opinion, everyone does not have the right to their own facts. And how do we account for the fact that many voices remain marginalized, both online and offline, even in democratic political cultures? From the Uighurs in Xinjiang to the Black Lives Matter movement and the struggle by the transgender community for recognition and equality, many groups across the world feel alienated and lacking influence to change their situation for the better— regardless of claims about soft power. So, to appreciate soft power in the digital do-main it is essential to understand that this landscape affects and is affected by power and the distribution of power offline. Digital platforms have reshaped how we think about and generate soft power, but changes are still made possible by those who de-cide to participate in the real world. The ability to mobilize, collaborate, and exchange news, information, and opinions outside the digital landscape is where soft power is really located.

SUGGESTED READING

Applebaum, Ann (2020), *Twilight of Democracy: The Seductive Lure of Authoritarianism* (New York: Doubleday).

Chitty, Naren, Li Ji, Gary Rawnsley, (eds.) (2024), *The Routledge Handbook of Soft Power*, 2nd edn. (Abindgon: Routledge).

Cull, Nicholas J. (2019), *Public Diplomacy: Foundations for Global Engagement in the Digital Age* (London: Polity).

Manor, Ilan (2019), *The Digitalization of Public Diplomacy* (London: Palgrave Macmillan).

Morozov, Evgeny (2011), *The Net Delusion: How Not to Liberate the World* (London: Allen Lane).

Nye, Joseph S. (2011), *The Future of Power* (New York: PublicAffairs).

Nye, Joseph S. (2021), 'Soft power: The evolution of a concept', *Journal of Political Power*, 14(1): 196–208.

Ohnesorge, Hendrik W. (2020), *Soft Power: The Forces of Attraction in International Relations* (Place: Springer).

References

Applebaum, Anne (2019), 'Brexit has devastated Britain's international reputation—and respect for its democracy', *The Washington Post*, 12 March, https://www.washingtonpost.com/opinions/2019/03/13/brexit-has-devastated-britains-international-reputation-respect-its-democracy/?noredirect=on%utm_term=e.5988685711d

Applebaum, Ann (2020), *Twilight of Democracy: The Seductive Lure of Authoritarianism* (New York: Doubleday).

Becket, Andy (2016), 'Revelation or whitewash – what can we expect from the Chilcot Inquiry?', *The Guardian*, 4 July.

Bjola, Corneliu and Ilan Manor (2022), 'The rise of hybrid diplomacy: From digital adaption to digital adoption', *International Affairs*, 98(2): 471–491.

Bobbitt, Phillip (2002), *The Shield of Achilles* (New York: Alfred A. Knopf).

Carroll, David (2021), 'Cambridge Analytica', in Gary D. Rawnsley, Yiben Ma, and Kruakae Pothong (eds.), *The Research Handbook on Political Propaganda* (London: Edward Elgar), 41–50.

Chen, Titus C. (2021), 'Xi Jinping's grand strategy for digital propaganda', in Gary D. Rawnsley, Yiben Ma, and Kruakae Pothong (eds.), *The Research Handbook on Political Propaganda* (London: Edward Elgar), 127–142.

Coombs, Philip H. (1964), *The Fourth Dimension of Foreign Policy: Educational and Cultural Affairs* (New York: Harper & Row).

Fletcher, Tom (2016), *Naked Diplomacy: Power and Statecraft in the Digital Age* (London: William Collins).

Flew, Terry (2016), 'Entertainment media, cultural power, and post-globalization: The case of China's international media expansion and the discourse of soft power', *Global Media and China*, 1(4): 278–294.

Fraser, Matthew (2003), *Weapons of Mass Distraction: Soft Power and American Empire* (New York: St Martin's Press).

Friedman, Thomas (2019), 'The United Kingdom has gone mad', *New York Times*, 2 April.

Gelb, Leslie H. (2009), *Power Rules: How Common Sense Can Rescue American Foreign Policy* (New York: HarperCollins).

Gilboa, Eytan (2008), 'Searching for a theory of public diplomacy', *Annals of the American Academy of Political and Social Science*, 616: 55–77.

Hannan, Patrick (2009), *A Useful Fiction: Adventures in British Democracy* (Bridgend: Seren).

Ifantis, Kostas (2011), 'Soft power: Overcoming the limits of a concept', in B.J.C. McKercher (ed.), *Routledge Handbook of Diplomacy and Statecraft* (Abingdon: Routledge), 441–452.

Independent (2015), 'Human rights are no longer a "top priority" for the government, says Foreign Office Chief', 2 October.

Isar, Yudhishthir Raj (2017), 'Cultural diplomacy: India does it differently', *International Journal of Cultural Policy*, 21(4): 419–432.

Jaishankar, Dhruva (2018), 'India rising: Soft power and the world's largest democracy', in *The Soft Power 30: A Global Ranking of Soft Power 2018* (Portland: Portland), 62–65.

Jones, Marc Owen (2022), *Digital Authoritarianism in the Middle East: Deception, Disinformation and Social Media* (London: Hurst & Company).

Kalathil, Shanthi, Jessica Ludwig and Christopher Walker (2020), 'The cutting edge of soft power', *Journal of Democracy*, 31(1): 124–137.

Kapko, M. (2016), 'Twitter's impact on 2016 presidential election is unmistakable', 3 November, https://www.sherbornma.org/sites/g/files/vyhlif1201/f/uploads/twitters_impact.pdf

Layne, Christopher (2010), 'The unbearable lightness of soft power', in Inderjeet Parmar and Michael Cox (eds.), *Soft Power and US Foreign Policy: Theoretical, Historical and Contemporary Perspectives* (Abingdon: Routledge), 51–82.

Manor, Ilan (2019), *The Digitalization of Public Diplomacy* (London: Palgrave Macmillan).

Manor, Ilan and Elad Segev (2015), 'America's selfie: How the US portrays itself on its social media accounts', in Corneliu Bjola and Marcus Holmes (eds.), *Digital Diplomacy: Theory and Practice* (Abingdon: Routledge), 89–108.

Moncus, J.J. and Laura Silver (2021), 'Americans' views of Asia-Pacific nations have not changed since 2018 – with the exception of China', Pew Research, 12 April, https://www.pewr esearch.org/fact-tank/2021/04/12/americans-views-of-asia-pacific-nations-have-not-chan ged-since-2018-with-the-exception-of-china/

Morozov, Evgeny (2011), *The Net Delusion: How Not to Liberate the World* (London: Allen Lane).

Morozov, Evgeny (2013), *To Save Everything, Click Here* (New York: PublicAffairs).

Mullen, Mike (2012), 'Getting back to basics', *Joint Forces Quarterly*, (55), 2–4.

Nye, Joseph S. (2004) *Power in the Global Information Age: From Realism to Globalization* (Abingdon: Routledge).

Nye, Joseph S. (2010), 'Responding to my critics and concluding thoughts', in Inderjeet Parmar and Michael Cox (eds.), *Soft Power and US Foreign Policy: Theoretical, Historical and Contemporary Perspectives* (Abingdon: Routledge), 215–227.

Nye, Joseph S. (2011), *The Future of Power* (New York: PublicAffairs).

Nye, Joseph S. (2021), 'Soft power: The evolution of a concept', *Journal of Political Power*, 14(1): 196–208.

Ohnesorge, Hendrik W. (2020), *Soft Power: The Forces of Attraction in International Relations* (Place: Springer).

Ott, Brian L. (2017), 'The age of Twitter: Donald J. Trump and the politics of debasement', *Critical Studies in Media Communication*, 34(1): 59–68.

Pitney, John J. (2020), *Un-American: The Fake Patriotism of Donald J. Trump* (New York: Rowman & Littlefield).

Pomerantsev, Peter (2014), *Nothing is True and Everything is Possible: The Surreal Heart of the New Russia* (London: PublicAffairs).

Pomerantsev, Peter (2019), *This is Not Propaganda: Adventures in the War Against Reality* (London: PublicAffairs).

Rawnsley, Gary D. (2012), 'Approaches to soft power and public diplomacy in China and Taiwan', *The Journal of International Communication*, 18(2): 121–135.

Rawnsley, Gary D. (2020), 'Communicating confidence: China's public diplomacy', in Nancy Snow and Nicholas J. Cull (eds.), *Routledge Handbook of Public Diplomacy*, 2nd edn. (Abingdon: Routledge), 284–300.

Rawnsley, Gary D. (2021), '"Believe me": Political propaganda in the age of Trump', in Gary D. Rawnsley, Yiben Ma, and Kruakae Pothong (eds.), *Research Handbook on Political Propaganda* (Cheltenham: Edward Elgar), 51–66.

Rawnsley, Gary D. and Yiben Ma (2017), '"New media" and democratisation in East Asia', in Tun-chen Cheng and Yun-han Chu (eds.), *Routledge Handbook of Democratization in East Asia* (Abingdon: Routledge), 314–326.

Sanger, David E. (2019), *The Perfect Weapon* (New York: Broadway Books).

Silver, Laura, Kat Devlin, and Christine Huang (2021), 'Large majorities say China does not respect the personal freedom of its people', Pew Research, 30 June, https://www.pewresearch.org/global/2021/06/30/large-majorities-say-china-does-not-respect-the-personal-freedoms-of-its-people/

Sophia Gaston, 'Global Britain and reimagining our relationship to the past', The British Foreign Policy Group, 12 June 2020, https://bfpg.co.uk/2020/06/global-britain-history/

Spector, J. Brooks (2019), 'An un-United Kingdom confronts the Brexit dragon 4.0', *Daily Maverick*, 25 March, https://www.dailymaverick.co.za/article/2019-03-25-an-un-united-kingdom-confronts-the-brexit-dragon-4-0/

Standage, Tom (1998), *The Victorian Internet* (London: W&N).

Thompson, Nick (2012), 'Inventor of Web hopes Olympics can lead to 'beautiful understanding', CNN.com, 3 August, https://edition.cnn.com/2012/08/03/world/europe/tim-berners-lee-olympics-interview/index.html

Seib, Philip (2021), *Information at War: Journalism, Disinformation and Modern Warfare* (Cambridge: Polity Press).

van Rij, Armida L.M. (2018), 'Britain's relationship with Saudi Arabia does far more damage than it's worth', *The Conversation*, 4 September, http://theconversation.com/britains-relationship-with-saudi-arabia-does-far-more-damage-than-its-worth-102619

Voltmer, Katrin and Gary D. Rawnsley (2018), 'The media', in Christian W. Haerpfer, Patrick Bernhagen, Christian Welzel, and Ronald Inglehart (eds.), *Democratization*, 2nd edn. (Oxford: Oxford University Press), 239–252.

Walker, Christopher (2018), 'What is "sharp power"?', *Journal of Democracy*, 29(3): 9–23.

Wang Yin, *Weibo Diplomacy: Management, Measurement and Challenges*, unpublished PhD thesis submitted to Kings College London, February 2020.

Warsi, Sayeeda (2017), *The Enemy within: A Tale of Muslim Britain* (London: Allen Lane).

Wilson, Ernest J. (2008), 'Hard power, soft power, smart power', *The Annals of the American Academy of Political and Social Science*, 616(1): 110–124.

Zakaria, Fareed (2019), 'Brexit will mark the end of Britain's role as a great power', *Washington Post*, 14 March.

Zewail, Ahmed (2010), 'The soft power of science', *The American Interest*, 5(6), 1 July, https://www.the-american-interest.com/2010/07/01/the-soft-power-of-science/

CHAPTER 5

RESEARCHING INFLUENCE OPERATIONS: 'DARK ARTS' MERCENARIES AND THE DIGITAL INFLUENCE INDUSTRY

EMMA L. BRIANT

INTRODUCTION

SINCE 2016's UK Brexit referendum and the US presidential election, concern about influence operations has dominated media coverage, scholarship, and policy debates. The rights, roles, and responsibilities of a range of actors frequently make headlines as journalists, researchers, and policymakers seek to explain falsehoods spreading online. Social media platforms (Benckler et al., 2018; Vaidhyanathan, 2018) enabled a Wild West where disinformation (deliberately false or 'black' propaganda) can be distributed with algorithmic precision in an advertising economy arguably 'enabling and profiting from information warfare being waged' (Dawson, 2021). Some scholars identify the significant role of a digital influence industry (DII) (Bradshaw and Howard, 2018, 2021; Briant, 2018, 2021; Forest, 2022; Hankey, 2018) a concept I develop and analyse here. This chapter advocates for renewed focus on actors behind influence operations (IO), a contested term I define as: coordinated attempts employing information collection and analysis with organized distribution of propaganda, deception, or other forms of information advantage, to achieve an actor's objective. The chapter examines the DII's role in IO, shaping ideas, emotions, and behaviours for governments, politicians, and other actors. It argues a deeper scholarly examination of its relationship to other actors and infrastructure is essential to understanding and addressing IO within a democracy.

Understanding Influence Actors

Classic propaganda theorists like Jacques Ellul centralized the study of the organization and processes of deliberate actors: 'A set of methods *employed by an organized group* that wants to bring about the active or passive participation *in its actions* of a mass of individuals, psychologically unified *through physical manipulations* and *incorporated in an organization*' (1965: 61). Disinformation studies reoriented us away from this traditionally important focus; ignoring Ellul's injunction that 'to study propaganda, we must turn ... to the propagandist' (Ellul, 1965: XII). Instead current trends focus problem construction around the *presence of falsehood*: largely abandoning actors as a category of analysis. In the process, unintentional 'misinformation' has been confusingly discussed in the same breath as deliberate operations (e.g. Marwick and Lewis, 2018). This is impacting on policy. US Government responses focus on sharing of falsehood by 'threat actors' conceived to include misinformation (that not intended to be harmful) alongside deliberate IO (Homeland Security 2022). While a comprehensive survey of the actors who participate in propaganda is beyond the scope of this chapter, I argue that developing concepts which enable a richer understanding of actors is an art we must renew.

Where current IO scholarship focuses on actors this is at the point of 'attribution' i.e. identification of the source of a campaign, using methods derived from cyber security (Pamment and Smith, 2022). As Wanless and Pamment (2019) suggest, '[a]ttribution is often the last piece of the puzzle in analysing how the information environment is shaped'. Yet attribution methods are highly problematic, leaving researchers overly dependent on governments and profit-driven companies. Public pressure has prompted Facebook to produce useful attribution data and analysis (e.g. Gleicher et al., 2021), but tools like Ad Library are underused for examining wrongdoing (Leerson et al., 2021) and access to data remains inadequate (Edelson and McCoy, 2021). Amid efforts to throw sunshine in Big Tech's black boxes (Smith, 2022), those of the influence industry remain an afterthought, the naïve assumption being perhaps that this will 'trickle down' and reveal enough to understand these actors.

Platforms cannot be trusted not to systematically prioritize their business interests, as successive Facebook whistleblowers showed (O'Sullivan, 2021). Platforms know more about actors than they reveal (Francois, 2019), giving limited detail when attributing IO and often not providing the evidence decisions are based on (Pamment and Smith 2022, 8). I would argue that efforts in Congress to force more access to data should extend to a FOIA-style process for social media platforms' internal research and policy documents. Presently, innovations aiming to automatically detect IO actors (Smith, 2021), AI driven disinformation and counter- operations (e.g. GCHQ, 2021) risk making us more reliant on industry. We must also demand access for ethical AI audits that platforms are unlikely to grant of their own accord.

Pamment and Smith (2022) offer a strong framework for improving attribution but the standard process *follows* identification of IO output, then draws on a platform's technical, intelligence, behavioural, or contextual analysis.[1] These identification processes can be abused within deliberate campaigns by those seeking to demoralize, as François and Douek argue occurred in the 2018 US elections (2021: 17). While attribution is vital in identifying the source of a case study, it remains an insufficient evidential basis for us to understand IO strategy, or inform wider policy. Without researching actors in their own right, those running successful covert campaigns that *avoid* this online detection process escape study completely.

A renewal of propaganda studies' focus on actors, infrastructure, process, and organization, conceptually, would also reverse an asymmetry of data power, with sousveillant research putting information in public hands. Social science must examine actors as a research problem extending to closed industries, helping us understand, for example: how industry avoids detection; coordinated actors; funding; and data practices that occur off-platform. Research best practice is collaborative and may include leaks, whistleblowing, transparency data, and investigatory methods including Open Source Intelligence (OSINT) research (Waters, 2016), network analysis, digital forensics,[2] and interviews (Briant, 2015, April 2018). Investigations should consider parallel DII digital transformation and the involvement of related industry including expansive and heterogenous networks of companies strategically deployed together in coordinated IO, from lobbying firms to PR and hacking-for-hire (Corporate Europe Observatory, 2020).

Failing to research IO actors seriously weakens the study of propaganda, as it makes it more difficult to judge motivations and the organization of a campaign. Attribution difficulties led Wanless and Pamment to argue we must abandon the 'line in the sand' distinguishing domestic and foreign actors when determining what is acceptable or not (2019). Similarly, Hao (2021), drawing on François and Douek's research (2018), has argued that, with the difficulties determining this, the distinction of 'intent' doesn't really matter because 'in their tactics and impact, they often look the same'. Yet, propaganda is the '*deliberate*, systematic attempt to shape perceptions, manipulate cognitions, and direct behavior to achieve a response that furthers the desired intent of the propagandist' (Jowett and O'Donnell, 2015: 7). To illustrate why actors matter: a researcher comparing two Facebook pages may find both drive a similar message. One page may be created by Russia's Internet Research Agency (IRA), the other by a citizen group, both may contain falsehoods, and both have harmful effects. Yet there is a big difference between the intentions and organizational structures utilized by an actor such as Russia's IRA, and those of a US citizen expressing ideas within public debate. This further illustrates how intent and organization are related to significantly different judgements we might make about relative acceptability and responses.

---

[1] For example: Stanford Internet Observatory (2019); Nimmo et al. (2019); and Jones (2019).
[2] Such as by the organization Forensic Architecture, see: https://forensic-architecture.org

While citizenship considerations have certainly become more complex (Orden and Pamment, 2021), they still matter. Foreign and domestic actors have a very different relationship to the US Government; citizens have free speech expectations under the constitution. Foreign status in no way should be simplistically equated to illegitimacy or hostility, any more than domestic citizens can be assumed to be benign, but this complexity makes it *more* critical to research and theorize actors.

Actors are key to establishing motive, identifying wider strategies, connected operations, and beneficiaries; all of which are important to considering how originating actors, audiences, and other participants will anticipate and respond to possible interventions. They must not be an afterthought.

This means renewing propaganda studies' traditional focus on actors. Departure from this must be recognized as radical. Abandoning the importance of actors and their motives due to our access issues is unacceptable as a solution, and darkly transformative for democratic propaganda norms. Understanding propaganda as a product of process for which actors are responsible is essential for developing solutions that respect speech online.

RECLAIMING ACTOR-CENTRIC ANALYSIS

Orientation away from actor-centric research has been justified on the basis that early propaganda studies was deterministic. The advent of social media enables greater involvement of audiences in the propaganda process, leading some to propose focus on 'participatory propaganda' (Wanless and Berk, 2018, 2020; Asmolov, 2019). On this basis Wanless and Berk (2018, 2020) generalize and dismiss the value of pre-digital propaganda studies: 'In this top-down communications model, the sender-receiver roles were typically static with the propagandist (government, corporate, military, political) issuing persuasive messaging aimed at achieving a specific outcome among the target audience (general public). This classic understanding of propaganda, however, must be adapted in a Digital Age' (Wanless and Berk, 2018: 5). Yet the deterministic model of propaganda was discredited long before the internet age (Katz and Lazarsfeld, 1955), acknowledging there has always been complexity in audience effects.[3] Even Ellul accounted for what he called 'horizontal propaganda' emanating from 'inside the group' (1965), and in Soviet and Nazi-controlled societies, social networks were built to enable surveillance and nurture 'active' participation in mutual propaganda (McDonough, 2015; Oltermann, 2022). Social media today *accelerate, incentivize, and monetize* social network affordances, a process Gehl and Lawson have termed 'masspersonal social engineering' (2022).

Starbird et al. recognized this history in their analysis of propagandist-participatory interaction in President Donald Trump's 2020 election campaign. They found

---

[3] See for example, Philo (2008).

influencers amplified stories and passed content to political elites, acknowledging how different 'participants' may differ greatly in relative power (2023). History warns against overly expansive definitions of 'participation' that centralize propagandists' *targets* as 'enemies within' without discerning intent (Rosenau, 2014). Problematizing ordinary people as 'participants' in propaganda because they're most 'visible' could lead us further away from accountability for deliberate manipulation by profiting industries or governments.

If one takes an actor-centric perspective, what is today described as 'new' participatory propaganda might be apparent as 'digital-age subversion': deliberate use of clandestine or covert activities aimed at co-opting and infiltrating groups then manipulating tensions in order to destabilize and influence. Indeed these are tactics the DII has honed.

The Digital Influence Industry

Among the many deliberate actors involved in IO, some scholars have identified the rapid transformation of the DII as requiring greater consideration in international politics. To address inconsistencies and imprecision in terminology, I define DII as:

> Private firms for hire as a service in deliberate and often coordinated or synchronized attempts, by employing information collection and analysis with organized distribution of propaganda, deception, or other forms of information advantage, to achieve a client actor's objectives.

Information collection and analysis may include mass surveillance, hacking and spyware, use of data brokers, data-driven profiling and analytics, or even simple surveys and polling. Propaganda technologies include microtargeted advertising,[4] botnets,[5] troll farms,[6] sock-puppets and astroturfing[7] (Kao, 2021), 'hack and leak' campaigns (Scott-Railton et al., 2020; Briant and Wanless, 2018), online influencers,[8] selling 'likes' and high follower count pages, deceptive design and deep fakes,[9] and dark or misleading

[4] Dawson defines microtargeting as 'data informed individualized targeted advertising' (2021).

[5] According to Bhuyan (2006) a 'botnet is a network of compromised computers that can be remotely controlled by an attacker through a predefined communication channel'.

[6] Troll farms are 'professionalized groups that work in a coordinated fashion to post provocative content, often propaganda, to social networks' according to Hao (2021).

[7] Astroturfing is 'the strategy by which established, politically motivated groups (such as corporations, interest groups, political campaigns, etc.) impersonate grassroots activist movements for political gain' (Donovan, date unknown).

[8] Influencers are 'individuals who have a large number of followers on social media platforms' and 'represent or recommend brands on various social media platforms' (Chopra et al., 2021).

[9] Deep fakes are 'synthetic videos that closely resemble real videos' often using advanced graphics to manipulate images of real people (Vaccari and Chadwick, 2020).

high-engagement provocative articles, ads, or posts. Much scholarship focuses on these technologies and platforms, comparatively neglecting a diverse industry and its business models, political economy, and infrastructure.

Forest distinguishes the DII from 'vigilantes or other provocateurs who use their technical skills and tools to manipulate perceptions on behalf of a political or ideological agenda but not for monetary benefit' (2022). Ong and Cabañes' study helpfully distinguishes organizational models of 'disinformation production' as the in-house staff model, advertising and PR model, clickbait model, and state-sponsored model (2019). Only the second of these would constitute the DII, as defined in this chapter, excluding actors such as military personnel, in-house campaign staff, or media systems not providing a for-hire service.

The term 'influence industry' was periodically used by journalists previously as an informal euphemism for lobbying[10] when practitioners do not meet the technical definition of a 'lobbyist' (Firestone, 2011). The answer to this of course is not hedging language but updating lobbying registration rules. So, what do we mean by the DII here: how can it be understood, revisited, and revised through different theoretical approaches and analyses?

As IO are coordinated and organized, the term 'digital influence industry' helps us to talk about how influence companies and their persuasive practices, including disinformation, have rapidly evolved in response to the affordances of changing media systems and the rise of social media, often bringing together data-driven, digital, and non-digital methods. This creates a challenge for definition, let alone regulation and policy. As Forest notes, the DII is far from homogeneous; it 'encompasses firms of various sizes as well as individual freelancers' (2022). Hankey first used 'influence industry' after the Cambridge Analytica scandal to describe such firms as a feature of the movement of commercial methods into politics (2018). Yet the implications of DII straddle national security. At that time, concern was expressed about conflicts of interest that may be prompted as a result of the opacity of DII practices and lack of regulation and oversight including in defence (Briant, 2018b, September 2018). This was prompted by the case of the Trump campaign, the firm Cambridge Analytica, and SCL (its defence contractor parent), when reporting and whistleblower testimonies revealed ties to Russia and concerns over data sharing with a pro-Putin oligarch (US Senate Select Committee on Intelligence, 2020). The case raised potential risks in how firms organize their relationships with external partners and clients.

In defence, the private sector is increasingly central to what some term hybrid threats, which 'exploit all modes of war simultaneously by using advanced conventional weapons, irregular tactics, terrorism, and disruptive technologies or criminality to destabilize an existing order' (Wilkie, 2009). Influence operations may be combined with corruption, funding organizations, funding political parties, other forms of economic

---

[10] See for example Holyoke (2015).

leverage, lawfare, cyber attacks, espionage, and manipulation, as well as paramilitary activities and proxy wars (Treverton et al., 2018).

Digital influence mercenaries (DIM) can be considered a *coercive subset*[11] of DII, characterized by:

1. Coercive Clients: Offering any influence services, without discernment, to state or non-state clients who are backed by force and coercion; especially authoritarian clients, those violating human rights or using aggressive censorship, or those engaged in organized criminal activities.
2. Coercive Methods: Offering or working with partners to enable, for any client, aggressive methods such as sourcing and using information obtained via hacking, spyware, and surveillance; black ops; blackmail, threats, or incitement; and deception. This might include leading, developing, or implementing state-backed destabilization within civilian communities and falsely deflecting blame for such abuses onto another target.

Business models and incentives are both critical to understanding the respective roles of DII and other subsets of the influence economy. On both levels clickbait actors (profit-driven entities that exploit high-engagement falsehood for ad revenue) should be distinguished from DII firms, which Ong and Cabañes' (2019) hesitate to do. Likewise, Forest considers clickbait actors mercenaries 'in that the profit models they pursue have no relation to any particular belief in why they are doing it or whom they are doing it for' (6). Clickbait actors do not meet this chapter's definition of DII as they are not hired by a client to support their agenda. Further, given mercenaries' violent reputational legacy (Isenberg, 2008), DIM must imply coercive intent. Clickbait actors may be a problem of our information environment with manipulative and political *effects*, but are not engaged in coercive IO. If we are to better understand and tackle both economic opportunists and deliberate IO-for-sale we must not define the DII by apparently similar effects. We must distinguish between actors with different primary business models and histories, considering how differing incentive structures interact with the influence economy.

DEVELOPMENT OF DII

The DII concept helps us explain how datafication, unique digital practices, and increasing profitability of influence has been used to transform existing industries; their practices; and their relationships to digital platforms, to each other, and to specialized

---

[11] In this context Bakir et al. have defined coercion as 'an act of persuasion that compels an individual to act against their will through the threat or infliction of costs including, but not limited to, physical force' (2018) p. 14.

technology industries. Together this produced 'complex multi-layered adaptive manipulation', engaging tiers of government, non-profit, digital media industry, and DII involvement (Briant, September 2018). The DII thus developed through interaction between governments, 'Big Tech', and legacy industries.

Particularly post-9/11, the US government seized on the promise of private industry in cyber, intelligence, and IO (Briant, 2015; Helmus et al., 2007) including 'digital infrastructure and a corresponding influence industry', which extended their range of action at home and abroad (Briant, September 2018). The DII grew off military investment in the behavioural, data-driven, and cyber operations that 'Big Tech' platforms made possible (Briant, September 2018; Ongowesi, 2021; Levine, 2018; Perlroth, 2021; Zuboff, 2019). Zuboff suggests industry players capitalized on the collection, analysis, and monetization of our physical and digital behaviours, driving the economy of 'surveillance capitalism' (2019). This transformed legacy media systems into an architecture of surveillant influence in which Big Tech largely aligned its priorities with US national security. Yet as Nicole Perlroth has noted, this did not make the US more secure; 'our own cyberweapons were coming for us' (2021: xxvii).

As Dawson (2021) notes, by 2011 the US Defense Advanced Research Projects Agency (DARPA) was studying social 'media information-sharing patterns and social media psychological profiling'. Their experiments extended to measuring the neurobiological impact of narratives and emotion-cognition interaction, and they aimed to develop models and simulations of narrative influence and its impact on behaviour (DARPA, 2011). Private sector defense contractors in this area included Cambridge Analytica's parent firm SCL, and their prime Archimedes Global, whose projects included early innovations in neuroscience to measure influence effects, using censors to measure brain responses to messaging stimuli to more effectively influence people for counterextremism and counter-terrorism (Interview: Former SCL Employee, 2019; Report on Project Tamburlaine—Target Audience Analysis Among Young Males in Peshawar, Pakistan Behavioral Diagnostics and Neurological Communication Analyses, 2010). Similar methods have now flourished into a widely deployed commercial practice called 'neuromarketing'.[12] This illustrates the revolving door of expertise flowing between Big Tech, national security agencies, and the influence industry (Briant, 2015; Glaser, 2020; Ongowesi, 2021). Counter-terrorism accelerated industry insights and innovations, which were repurposed commercially (Briant, April 2018; Behar, 2016; Entous and Farrow, 2019), the DII flourishing as an export industry consulting for political leaders seeking to retain power (Briant, September 2018; Ackerman, 2021).

Legacy industries like lobbying, private intelligence, political consulting and strategic communications, advertising, marketing, and public relations all transformed to exploit the online environment for a wide range of clients in this time period. A 1992 report surveying the 'torturer's lobby' showed US firms' long history contracting with

---

[12] Current companies using neuromarketing techniques commercially include Buyology, Mindlab, and Sensory Logic.

human rights abusers abroad, including Russia (Brogan, 1992). It revealed millions of dollars being made by the worst actors, many of whom continue today, including Paul Manafort, who set up a DII firm helping Kremlin-backed politicians in Ukraine, before becoming chairman of Trump's 2016 campaign now famous for data misuse. Incoming President Bill Clinton decreed a lifetime ban on his staff working for foreign governments, but rescinded this before leaving office in 2001 (Packenpaugh, 2001). While lobbying still happens in traditional ways, this era saw a 'digital torture lobby' in DIM emerge, as social media entered public affairs (e.g. Tanielian and Ackil, 2014). In 2007, digital lobbying activities were already raising concerns that technologies such as 'astroturfing' to influence congress raised ethical and definitional challenges for lobbying (Public Citizen, 2007).

Legacy industries became less distinct and transformed as specialized data analytics, microtargeted advertising, and intelligence industries such as spyware grew, forming a more cohesive surveillant influence infrastructure—built both to exploit emerging platforms and to be the market incentivizing their growth. Recent industry data shows the dark analytics market size is projected to grow to $1,776 million by 2026 (Research & Markets, 2021).

With little regulation, accelerating datafication poured rocket fuel on unaddressed ethical problems that had smouldered for years within legacy industries. While the Public Relations Society of America calls PR 'a strategic communication process that builds mutually beneficial relationships between organizations and their publics' (PRSA, 2022), emergent practices were far from mutually beneficial (Verwey and Muir, 2019). Terminology like 'Dark PR' (Silverman et al., 2020) and 'Disinformation-for-Hire' implied unethical sub-industries, deflecting pressure off the mainstream. Yet Edwards demonstrates that unethical work was not an outlying dysfunctional off-shoot of mainstream PR (2021). The nature of how this unethical behaviour manifests today is inseparable from wider DII transformation.

A central problem is how opaque networks of companies can obscure activities from authorities, clients, and even staff. Companies also adjust their activities to avoid regulation, for example, Cambridge Analytica planned to relocate their data storage to the Caribbean after the EU General Data Protection Regulation came into effect (Denham, 2021). The Cambridge Analytica scandal also revealed how relationships between companies across related industries are central to understanding coordinated activities, conflicts of interest, and other ethical problems, which may pose vulnerabilities in a hybrid war. Following the inquiry of the UK parliamentary Digital, Media, Culture and Sport Committee into 'fake news', its 'Disinformation Final Report' echoed recommendations for 'stricter regulation of strategic communications companies, with the establishment of professional licensing that can be revoked if necessary' (House of Commons, February 2019). Weak regulation of DII, including firms working in defence, has created conditions for firms like Cambridge Analytica to work in opaque ways that raise risks for national security and it remains 'important to ensure potential vulnerabilities that might have contributed to the crisis are addressed' (Briant, September 2018).

Amid ongoing war with Russia, Western governments continue to fuel a data-driven influence arms race (Heikkilä, 2022). In hybrid conflicts, assemblages of private industry can be central to operations which coordinate cyber and informational activities with coercion, force, or legal and economic levers. Yet in IO scholarship 'strategies of incentivization and coercion are rarely addressed' in how they operate 'in relation to physical, socio-political and economic contexts where incentives and threats are part of persuasive communication activities' (Bakir et al., 2018). Compound pressures may be applied to make hybrid attacks more difficult to resolve, for example they target 'the vulnerabilities of a society and system while deliberately exploiting ambiguity to avoid detection' (Qureshi, 2020: 174). A focus not only on who actors are, but also on how they interact with one another, is essential in understanding the nature of such destabilization operations.

SURVEYING THE DII IS A PRIORITY

Journalists and researchers have taken the lead in exposing many newsworthy DII cases, such as the divisive communications of Bell Pottinger in South Africa (Verwey and Muir, 2019), data-driven 'psychographic' campaigns in the US and UK (Briant 2019, April 2018), astroturfing by China (Kao, 2021), or influencers in the Philippines (Ong and Cabañes, 2019). These tell us little about how typical practices are. We lack a reliable survey of the extent of such unethical practices across the DII. The Oxford Internet Institute attempted to survey the extent of what they called 'cyber troop' activity, noting income and services offered to political and government actors in worldwide IO (Bradshaw and Howard, 2021). The study however, excluded important campaigns in the global south, exaggerated disinformation as 'new', while *underestimating* the number of influence firms and financial turnover (Briant, 2021). NATO StratCom COE's study concluded there is no 'shadowy underworld' involved in manipulation, just an immense 'black market' for 'tools', social manipulation software, fictitious accounts, DDOS attacks, and mobile proxies, which is easily accessed (Bay et al., 2018, 2020).

NATO's survey, conducted by a Ukrainian company called Singularity,[13] asserts most companies offering social media manipulation are based in Russia (Bay, 2018). This may be true but it is hard to independently evaluate this claim and those beyond Russia remain significant. Russia, like many other authoritarian states, in addition to operating state-funded media organizations, has a long history of subcontracting IO to commercial providers, the most well known being its IRA, but also DII outside Russia (Brogan, 1992; Rid, 2021). According to Open Secrets, in this market, Russian outlets

---

[13] Singularity itself claims a unique ability to 'retrieve data from any source and any social network' via their social media API for 'social listening' and studied 315,000 Ukrainian VK user profiles for NATO (VK or VKontakte is a Russian social media service based in Saint Petersburg). For more information See: https://www.singularex.com/cases

have spent 'more than $146 million on foreign influence operations and propaganda in the U.S. since 2016' (Massoglia, 2022).

NATO's study described a 'black market' for campaign management and technology in Russia (Bay, 2018) but neglects Western service providers working for clients that conflict with Western security and human rights standards. This is a notable oversight given its publication in the wake of the Cambridge Analytica scandal. By 2018, whistleblower testimony, research, and reporting had revealed Cambridge Analytica's links to Russia and unethical election campaigns (Cadwalladr and Graham-Harrison, 2018; Confessore, 2018), raising potential conflicts of interest for a network of apparently 'normal' campaign firms regularly hired by Western militaries (including NATO StratCom COE in 2015) (Briant, September 2018). To explore 'dark' sectors of the DII, and hidden segments of the more 'visible' industry, we need independent research on how this 'underworld' operates internationally for a range of clients.

Researching opaque services is challenging, as obscuring activities beneath a 'normal' industry veneer is commonplace. A flashy website may not list all services or partners. How 'shadowy' infrastructure is may well depend on how much a firm has to lose, how deeply we investigate, improvements in country specific transparency and reporting regulations, and strength of local journalism. Solutions are not necessarily 'technical';[14] measures that address 'dark money' often face resistance from politicians whose campaigns benefit from opaque funding.

Grey Propaganda Goes Digital

The 'grey' in grey propaganda is organized into IO by actors and process, it is not simply the lack of identifier on a message. Private industry can be a useful method of distancing activities (Briant, 2015) and Facebook acknowledges DII entities are 'used by sophisticated actors to hide their involvement', which makes attributing IO to state actors challenging (Gleicher et al., 2021). Recently, for example, Russia reportedly paid Ukrainian citizens for social media accounts, to circumvent new Facebook rules (Schwirtz and Frenkel, 2019).

Faced with Russian IO utilizing dark architecture for spreading uncertainty and paranoia (Elswah and Howard, 2020), Western democracies increasingly also adopt 'grey' propaganda, to get a truthful message to audiences where distrust exists. Western tactics recently hit the headlines though when a Pentagon review was launched following Twitter and Facebook's mass removal of pro-US fake accounts (Washington Post, 2022), finally acting on a use of fake accounts by the US that has a long history (Briant 2018a). In 2013, for example, UK former Assistant Head of Defence Media and

---

[14] The UK's new equivalent of, for example, the US Foreign Agents Registration Act (Foreign Influence Registration Scheme), or US legislation such as the DISCLOSE Act (2021).

Communications Operations Plans, Col. Ralph Arundell, pointed me to this development, saying 'increasingly we're going to shift' to 'messaging an audience directly', but this needs to be credible. With social media this meant using other actors to communicate a message, not attributing it to a military source. He said, 'Nobody looks at a viral video on YouTube... and goes who planted that?' (Briant 2015, 176). In a kaleidoscopic media, ensuring that a message sticks requires a source trusted by the audience, and this is where industry flourishes or where cut-outs and proxies may be utilized. For example influencers may give credibility where acknowledging the true source would undermine a message (Forest, 2022).

In an interview (2021), the founding director of the communications division at SHAPE, Mark Laity, commented on the rise of non-attribution[15] by Western governments. He explained, 'grey is honest, truthful [messaging], but you may not say who, where it's coming from' and 'to some degree, the whole of the communications arena now is grey'. He said, the ethical question becomes 'how light is your grey?'

Grey propaganda by proxies raises ethical conundrums not only with respect to truth—contractors may go to lengths to find local civil society organizations, artists, or media to build local 'credible' and more culturally appropriate voices with supportive messaging. This is more truthful and authentic but creates substantial risks for local subcontractors who must be protected, while large contractors who hire them may take on less risk.

As DII actors obscure activities and networks, infrastructure used to defend Western democracy in the shadows can become vulnerable to being turned back on Western populations and can pose regulatory challenges. 'Reflexive control'[16] and masspersonal social engineering might be used to ensure participation of individuals with or without their awareness as in the 2016 US election, when Russia deployed digital subversion operations to polarize the 'Black Lives Matter' and 'Blue Lives Matter' movements using falsely attributed Facebook posts (Arif et al., 2018; Gunther et al., 2019). Unwitting influencers are referred to in Cold War parlance as 'useful idiots' (Safire, 1987). Orden and Pamment note the difficulties of attributing the activities of such citizens to a foreign state (2021). Yet groups may well be targeted in IO due to particular attributes, such as credibility or value for an 'initiating set' enabling influence of a wider group. For example, US military veterans both hold specialized skills and experience, and are highly respected, making them targets for foreign or domestic radicalization (House of Representatives, 2020) including during 6 January 2021. Former senior military personnel became significant influencers alleging Election 2020 was rigged (Dreisback and Anderson, 2021; Rondeaux, 2021; Bender, 2021). Research shows how Facebook's algorithms further incentivize the worst abuse by witting and unwitting actors online, creating influential 'super-users', which Hindman et al. indicate played an outsized role on 6 January (2021).

---

[15] The practice of obscuring the authorship or producer of propaganda, usually where there is a credibility gap.

[16] Reflexive control 'seeks to affect the decision-making process of targeted individuals by manipulating their perception of reality' (Till, 2021).

Conclusions

Concepts that don't centralize *relative power* shift the problem focus away from actors, motives, and responsibilities, and onto content-driven solutions. If we are to hold powerful industry responsible and develop more appropriate responses for IO, we must remember why propaganda studies centralized studying actors, their processes, and their organization. The use of social networks or audience participation is not new, and we must not forget a long literature exploring how actors develop 'top down' strategies to *use* participatory dynamics. In the conceptual tug-of-war between propagandist-centric and audience-centric analysis, it is essential for both to reconcile and concede territory to collaborate on understanding IO.

The DII and DIM concepts which this chapter introduced call for the study of industry-led campaigns and raise unique challenges for research and governance given their opacity and complex relationships to governments, Big Tech, and media companies. Researching actors is the most difficult contemporary challenge in propaganda studies and will require new approaches that aid an understanding of a complex and opaque architecture that's been largely ignored by social science. Public scholarship actively *challenging* such systems requires vital institutional support given risks faced by researchers (McNeil and Briant, 2021). Yet, without this serious and systematic inquiry into its powerful actors, DII will continue to largely escape regulatory response.

Suggested Reading

Briant, E. L. September 2018. 'Building a stronger and more secure democracy in a digital age: A Response to Recent Interim Reports and Proposals'. *Digital, Culture, Media and Sport Select Committee Inquiry into Fake News.* UK Parliament, pp1–6. Date Accessed: 26 July 2022: http://data.parliament.uk/writtenevidence/committeeevidence.svc/evidencedocum ent/digital-culture-media-and-sport-committee/fake-news/written/88559.pdf

Edwards, L. 2021. 'Organised lying and professional legitimacy: Public relations' accountability in the disinformation debate' *European Journal of Communication*, Vol 36, No. 2, pp168–182.

Forest, J. 2022. *Digital Influence Mercenaries: Profits and Power Through Information Warfare.* Naval Institute Press.

François, C and Douek, E. 2021. 'The Accidental Origins, Underappreciated Limits, and Enduring Promises of Platform Transparency Reporting about Information Operations' *Journal of Online Trust and Safety*, Vol 1, No. 1, pp 1–30. Date Accessed: 26 July 2022: https://tsjournal.org/index.php/jots/article/view/17/8

Ong, J C and Cabañes, J, V, A. 2019. 'Four Work Models of Political Trolling in the Philippines' in *NATO StratcomCOE*, pp 1–27. Date Accessed: 26 July 2022: https://stratcomcoe.org/publi cations/four-work-models-of-political-trolling-in-the-philippines/40

Pamment, J and Smith, V. 2022. 'Attributing Information Influence Operations: Identifying those Responsible for Malicious Behaviour Online' *NATO StratcomCOE*, pp1–41. Date Accessed: 26 July 2022: https://stratcomcoe.org/publications/attributing-information-influence-operations-identifying-those-responsible-for-malicious-behaviour-online/244

BIBLIOGRAPHY

Ackerman, S. 2021. *Reign of Terror: How the 9/11 Era Destabilized America and Produced Trump*. New York: Viking.

Asmolov, G. 2019. 'The Effects of Participatory Propaganda: From Socialization to Internalization of Conflicts'. *Journal of Design and Science*. Vol 6: https://jods.mitpress.mit.edu/pub/jyzg7j6x/release/2

Arif, A, Stewart, L. G, and Starbird, K. 2018. 'Acting the Part: Examining Information Operations Within #BlackLivesMatter Discourse'. *Proceedings of the ACM on Human-Computer Interaction*, Vol. 2, CSCW, Article 20, New York, NY, pp1–27. Doi: https://doi.org/10.1145/3274289

Bakir, V, Herring, E, Miller, D, and Rbayobinson, P. 2018. 'Organized Persuasive Communication: A New Conceptual Framework for Research on Public Relations, Propaganda and Promotional Culture'. *Critical Sociology*. Vol 45, No. 3, pp311–328. Doi: https://doi.org/10.1177/0896920518764586

Bay, S. 2018. 'The Black Market for Social Media Manipulation'. NATO Strategic Communication Center of Excellence. Date Accessed: 26 July 2022: https://stratcomcoe.org/publications/the-black-market-for-social-media-manipulation/103

Bay, S, Dek, A, Dek, I, and Fredheim, R. 2020. 'Social Media Manipulation 2020'. NATO Strategic Communication Center of Excellence. Date Accessed: 26 July 2022: https://stratcomcoe.org/cuploads/pfiles/social_media_manipulation_2020_stratcom_coe_21-12-2020_v2-1.pdf

Behar, R. 2016. 'Inside Israel's Secret Startup Machine'. *Forbes*. Date Accessed: 26 July 2022: https://www.forbes.com/sites/richardbehar/2016/05/11/inside-israels-secret-startup-machine/?sh=6c46ae331a51

Bender, B. 2021. ''Disturbing and Reckless': Retired Brass Spread Election Lie in Attack on Biden, Democrats'. *Politico*. Date Accessed: 26 July 2022: https://www.politico.com/news/2021/05/11/retired-brass-biden-election-487374

Benkler, Y, Farris, R, and Roberts, H. 2018. *Network Propaganda: Manipulation, Disinformation, and Radicalization in American Politics*. Oxford: Oxford University Press.

Bhuyan, D. 2006. 'Using Honeynets for Discovering and Disrupting IRC-Based Botnets'. *Journal of Information Warfare*, Vol. 5, No. 1, pp10–18.

Bradshaw, S and Howard, P. 2018. 'Challenging Truth and Trust: A Global Inventory of Organized Social Media Manipulation, Computational Propaganda Project'. Oxford Internet Institute. Date Accessed: 26 July 2022: https://demtech.oii.ox.ac.uk/wp-content/uploads/sites/93/2018/07/ct2018.pdf

Bradshaw, S and Howard, P. 2021. 'Industrialized Disinformation: 2020 Global Inventory of Organized Social Media Manipulation'. Oxford Internet Institute. Date Accessed: 26 July 2022: https://demtech.oii.ox.ac.uk/research/posts/industrialized-disinformation/

Briant, E L. 2015. *Propaganda and Counter-terrorism: Strategies for Global Change*. Manchester: Manchester University Press.

Briant, E L. 2018a. 'Pentagon Ju-Jitsu – Reshaping the Field of Propaganda'. *Critical Sociology*, Vol. 45, No. 3, pp361–378.

Briant, E L. 2018b. 'Our Go1vernments Share Responsibility for the Cambridge Analytica Crisis. . . and Here's How They Should Fix It'. *Open Democracy*. Date Accessed: 26 July 2022: https://www.opendemocracy.net/en/dark-money-investigations/our-governments-share-responsibility-for-cambridge-analytica-crisis-and-her/

Briant, E L. April 2018. 'Three Explanatory Essays Giving Context and Analysis to Submitted Evidence on Leave.EU and Cambridge Analytica strategy'. *Digital, Culture, Media and Sport Committee Inquiry into Fake News.* UK Parliament. Date Accessed: 26 July 2022: https://old.parliament.uk/business/committees/committees-a-z/commons-select/digital-culture-media-and-sport-committee/ne2018cws/fake-news-briant-evidence-17-19/

Briant, E L. September 2018. 'Building a stronger and More Secure Democracy in a Digital Age: A Response to Recent Interim Reports and Proposals'. *Digital, Culture, Media and Sport Select Committee Inquiry into Fake News:* UK Parliament. Date Accessed: 26 July 2022: http://data.parliament.uk/writtenevidence/committeeevidence.svc/evidencedocument/digital-culture-media-and-sport-committee/fake-news/written/88559.pdf

Briant, E L. 2019. 'LeaveEU: Dark Money, Dark Ads and Data Crimes'. In *SAGE Handbook of Propaganda.* Edited by Baines, P, Snow, N, and O'Shaughnessy, N. London: Sage. pp532–549.

Briant, E. 2021. 'The Grim Consequences of a Misleading Study on Disinformation'. 18 February. *Wired.* Date Accessed: 26 July 2022: https://www.wired.com/story/opinion-the-grim-consequences-of-a-misleading-study-on-disinformation/

Briant, E L and Wanless, A. December 2018. 'A Digital Ménage à Trois: Strategic Leaks, Propaganda and Journalism: Strategic Leaks, Propaganda and Journalism'. In *Countering Online Propaganda and Violent Extremism: The Dark Side of Digital Diplomacy.* Edited by Corneliu, B. and Pamment J. London: Routledge. pp 48–64.Brogan, P. 1992. 'The Torturers' Lobby'. *Center for Public Integrity*, pp1–78. Date Accessed: 26 July 2022: https://cloudfront-files-1.publicintegrity.org/legacy_projects/pdf_reports/THETORTURERSLOBBY.pdf

Cadwalladr, C and Graham-Harrison, E. 2018. 'Cambridge Analytica: Links to Moscow Oil Firm and St Petersburg University'. *The Guardian.* Date Accessed: 26 July 2022: https://www.theguardian.com/news/2018/mar/17/cambridge-academic-trawling-facebook-had-links-to-russian-university

Chopra, A, Avhad, V, and Jaju, S. 2021. 'Influencer Marketing: An Exploratory Study to Identify Antecedents of Consumer Behavior of Millennial'. *Business Perspectives and Research*, Vol. 9, No., 1, pp77–91. Doi: https://journals.sagepub.com/doi/10.1177/2278533720923486

Confessore, N. 2018. 'Cambridge Analytica and Facebook: The Scandal and the Fallout So Far'. 4 April. *New York Times.* Date Accessed: 26 July 2022: https://www.nytimes.com/2018/04/04/us/politics/cambridge-analytica-scandal-fallout.html

Corporate Europe Observatory. 2020. 'United Arab Emirates' growing legion of lobbyists support its "soft superpower" ambitions in Brussels'. *Corporate Europe Observatory.* Date Accessed: 26 July 2022: https://corporateeurope.org/en/2020/12/united-arab-emirates-growing-legion-lobbyists-support-its-soft-superpower-ambitions

DARPA. 2011. 'Narrative Networks'. *Defense Advanced Research Projects Agency.* Date Accessed: 26 July 2022: https://www.darpa.mil/program/ narrative-networks

Dawson, J. 2021. 'Microtargeting as Information Warfare'. *The Cyber Defense Review*, Vol. 6, No. 1, pp63–80.

Denham, E. 2021. 'Episode 39: Elizabeth Denham, Emma Briant, David Carroll and Chris Vickery'. *The Infotagion Podcast with Damian Collins MP.* Date Accessed: 26 July 2022: https://infotagion.libsyn.com/elizabeth-denham

DISCLOSE Act of 2021. 117th Congress (2021–2022). Date Accessed: 26 July 2022: https://www.congress.gov/bill/117th-congress/senate-bill/443/text

Donovan, J. Date unknown. 'Definition of Astroturfing in The Media Manipulation Casebook'. *Technology and Social Change Project, Harvard University.* Date Accessed: 26 July 2022: https://mediamanipulation.org/definitions/astroturfing

Dreisback, T and Anderson, M. 2021. 'Nearly 1 In 5 Defendants In Capitol Riot Cases Served In The Military'. *21 January. NPR All Things Considered.* Date Accessed: 26 July 2022: https://www.npr.org/2021/01/21/958915267/nearly-one-in-five-defendants-in-capitol-riot-cases-served-in-the-military

Edelson, L and McCoy, D. 2021. 'How Facebook Hinders Misinformation Research'. 22 September. *Scientific American.* Date Accessed: 26 July 2022: https://www.scientificamerican.com/article/how-facebook-hinders-misinformation-research/

Edwards, L. 2021. 'Organised Lying and Professional Legitimacy: Public Relations' Accountability in the Disinformation Debate'. *European Journal of Communication.* Vol. 36, No. 2, pp168–182.

Elswah, M and Howard, P. 2020. ' "Anything that Causes Chaos": The Organizational Behavior of Russia Today (RT)'. *Journal of Communication,* Vol. 70, No. 5, pp623–645.

Ellul, J. 1965. *Propaganda: The Formation of Men's Attitudes.* Vintage Books. NY.

Entous, A and Farrow, R. 2019. 'Private Mossad for Hire'. 18 February. *The New Yorker.* Date Accessed: 26 July 2022: https://www.newyorker.com/magazine/2019/02/18/private-mossad-for-hire

Farrow, R. 2019. 'The Black Cube Chronicles: The Private Investigators'. 7 October. *The New Yorker.* Date Accessed: 26 July 2022: https://www.newyorker.com/news/annals-of-espionage/the-black-cube-chronicles-the-private-investigators

Firestone, D. 2011. 'Taking Note: Not-Lobbyists in Name Only'. 30 November. *New York Times.* Date Accessed: 26 July 2022: https://takingnote.blogs.nytimes.com/2011/11/30/not-lobbyists-in-name-only/

Forest, J. 2022. *Digital Influence Mercenaries: Profits and Power Through Information Warfare.* Naval Institute Press.

Former SCL Employee, 2019. Interview and related Report on Project Tamburlaine—Target Audience Analysis Among Young Males in Peshawar, Pakistan Behavioral Diagnostics and Neurological Communication Analyses, 2010.

Francois, C. 2019. 'Actors, Behaviors, Content: A Disinformation ABC'. *Transatlantic High Level Working Group on Content Moderation Online and Freedom of Expression,* pp1–12. Date Accessed: 26 July 2022: https://cdn.annenbergpublicpolicycenter.org/wp-content/uploads/2020/05/ABC_Framework_TWG_Francois_Sept_2019.pdf

François, C and Douek, E. 2021. 'The Accidental Origins, Underappreciated Limits, and Enduring Promises of Platform Transparency Reporting about Information Operations'. *Journal of Online Trust and Safety,* Vol. 1, No. 1, pp1–30. Date Accessed: 26 July 2022: https://tsjournal.org/index.php/jots/article/view/17/8

GCHQ. 2021. *GCHQ to Use AI to Tackle Child Sex Abuse, Disinformation and Trafficking.* Date Accessed: 26 July 2022: https://www.gchq.gov.uk/news/artificial-intelligence

Gehl, R and Lawson, S. 2022. *Social Engineering: How Crowdmasters, Phreaks, Hackers and Trolls Created a New Form of Manipulative Communication.* Massachusetts: MIT Press.

Glaser, A. 2020. 'Thousands of Contracts Highlight Quiet Ties Between Big Tech and U.S. Military'. 8 July. *NBC News.* Date Accessed: 26 July 2022: https://www.nbcnews.com/tech/tech-news/thousands-contracts-highlight-quiet-ties-between-big-tech-u-s-n1233171

Gleicher, N, Franklin, M, Agranovich, D, Nimmo, B, Belogolova, O, and Torrey, M. 2021. 'Threat Report: The State of Influence Operations 2017-2020'. Facebook. Date Accessed: 26 July 2022: https://about.fb.com/wp-content/uploads/2021/05/IO-Threat-Report-May-20-2021.pdf

Gunther, R, Beck, P A, and Nisbet, E C. 2019. ' "Fake News" and the Defection of 2012 Obama Voters in the 2016 Presidential Election'. *Electoral Studies,* Vol. 61, pp1–8. Doi: https://doi.org/10.1016/j.electstud.2019.03.006

Hankey, S. 2018. 'The Influence Industry: The Global Business of Using Your Data in Elections'. *Tactical Tech*. Date Accessed: 26 July 2022: https://ourdataourselves.tacticaltech.org/posts/influence-industry/

Hao, K. 2021. 'Troll Farms Reached 140 Million Americans a Month on Facebook Before 2020 Election, Internal Report Shows'. 16 September. *MIT Technology Review*. Date Accessed: 26 July 2022: https://www.technologyreview.com/2021/09/16/1035851/facebook-troll-farms-report-us-2020-election/

Hao, K. 2021. 'How Facebook and Google Fund Global Misinformation'. 20 November. *MIT Technology Review*. Date Accessed: 26 July 2022: https://www.technologyreview.com/2021/11/20/1039076/facebook-google-disinformation-clickbait/

Heikkilä, M. 2022. 'Why Business is Booming for Military AI Startups'. 7 July. *MIT Technology Review*. Date Accessed: 26 July 2022: https://www.technologyreview.com/2022/07/07/1055526/why-business-is-booming-for-military-ai-startups/

Helmus, T, Paul, C, and Glenn, R. 2007. *Enlisting Madison Avenue*. Santa Monica: Rand Corporation.

Hindman, M, Lubin, N, and Davis, T. 2022. 'Facebook Has a Superuser-Supremacy Problem'. 10 February. *The Atlantic*. Date Accessed: 26 July 2022: https://www.theatlantic.com/technology/archive/2022/02/facebook-hate-speech-misinformation-superusers/621617/

Holyoke, T. 2015. *The Ethical Lobbyist: Reforming Washington's Influence Industry*. Washington: Georgetown University Press.

Homeland Security. 2022. 'Summary of Terrorism Threat to the U.S. Homeland'. *National Terrorism Advisory System*. Date Accessed: 26 July 2022: https://www.dhs.gov/ntas/advisory/national-terrorism-advisory-system-bulletin-february-07-2022

House of Commons. February 2019. *Digital, Culture, Media and Sport Committee Disinformation and 'fake news': Final Report*. Date Accessed: 26 July 2022: https://publications.parliament.uk/pa/cm201719/cmselect/cmcumeds/1791/1791.pdf

House of Representatives. 2020. 'Hijacking our Heroes'. *House Report 116-657*. Date Accessed: 26 July 2022: https://www.govinfo.gov/content/pkg/CRPT-116hrpt657/html/CRPT-116hrpt657.htm

Isenberg, D. 2008. 'The Founding Contractors'. Cato Institute. Date Accessed: 26 July 2022: https://www.cato.org/publications/commentary/founding-contractors

Jones, M O. 2019. 'Propaganda, Fake News, and Fake Trends: The Weaponization of Twitter Bots in the Gulf Crisis'. *International Journal of Communication*, Vol. 13, pp1389–1415: https://ijoc.org/index.php/ijoc/article/viewFile/8994/2604

Jowett, G, and O'Donnell, V. 2015. *Propaganda & Persuasion*. Sage: Los Angeles.

Kao, J. 2021. 'Astroturfing: How Hijacked Accounts and Dark Public Relations Faked Support for China's Response to Covid 19'. *Media Manipulation Project*. Date Accessed: 26 July 2022: https://mediamanipulation.org/case-studies/astroturfing-how-hijacked-accounts-and-dark-public-relations-faked-support-chinas

Katz, E and Lazarsfeld, P F. 1955. *Personal Influence: The Part Played by People in the Flow of Mass Communication*. Glencoe, Ill.: The Free Press of Glencoe.

Mark Laity, Former Director of the Communications Division at NATO SHAPE, 2021. Interview.

Leerson, P, Dobber, T, Helberger, N, and de Vreese, C. 2021. 'News from the Ad Archive: How Journalists Use the Facebook Ad Library to Hold Online Advertising Accountable'. *Information, Communication & Society*, Vol. 26, No. 7, pp1381–1400. Doi: https://www.tandfonline.com/doi/full/10.1080/1369118X.2021.2009002

Levine, Y. 2018. *Surveillance Valley: The Secret Military History of the Internet*. New York: Public Affairs.

Marwick, A and Lewis, R. 2018. 'Media Manipulation and Disinformation Online'. *Data and Society*. Date Accessed: 26 July 2022: https://datasociety.net/pubs/oh/DataAndSociety_MediaManipulationAndDisinformationOnline.pdf

Massoglia, A. 2022. 'Russia Pouring Millions Into Foreign Influence and Lobbying Targeting the U.S. Amid Escalating Ukraine Conflict'. *Open Secrets*. Date Accessed: 26 July 2022: https://www.opensecrets.org/news/2022/02/russia-pouring-millions-into-foreign-influence-and-lobbying-targeting-the-u-s-amid-escalating-ukraine-conflict/

McDonough, F. 2015. 'Careless Whispers: How the German Public Used and Abused the Gestapo'. 28 September. *Irish Times*. Date Accessed: 26 July 2022: https://www.irishtimes.com/culture/books/careless-whispers-how-the-german-public-used-and-abused-the-gestapo-1.2369837

McNeil, K and Briant, E. 2021. 'Modern Propaganda: Researching Cambridge Analytica'. *Partnership for Conflict, Crime and Security Research*. Date Accessed: 26 July 2022: https://www.paccsresearch.org.uk/blog/modern-propaganda-researching-cambridge-analytica/

Nimmo, B, Francois, C, Eib, C S, Ronzaud, L, Ferreira, R, Hernon, C, and Kostelancik, T. 2019. *Secondary Infektion*, Graphika. Date Accessed: 26 July 2022: https://secondaryinfektion.org/report/secondary-infektion-at-a-glance/

O'Sullivan, D. 2021. 'Another Facebook Whistleblower Says She is Willing to Testify Before Congress'. 11 October. *CNN*. Date Accessed: 26 July 2022: https://edition.cnn.com/2021/10/11/tech/facebook-whistleblower-sophie-zhang-congress/index.html

Oltermann, P. 2022. 'Red Poets' Society: the Secret History of the Stasi's Book Club for Spies'. 5 February. *The Guardian*. Date Accessed: 26 July 2022: https://www.theguardian.com/world/2022/feb/05/red-poets-society-the-secret-history-of-the-stasis-book-club-for-spies

Ong, J C and Cabañes, J V A. 2019. 'Four Work Models of Political Trolling in the Philippines'. NATO StratcomCOE. Date Accessed: 26 July 2022: https://stratcomcoe.org/publications/four-work-models-of-political-trolling-in-the-philippines/40

Ongowesi, E. 2021. 'Big Tech Has Made Billions Off the 20-Year War on Terror'. 9 September. *Vice*. Date Accessed: 26 July 2022: https://www.vice.com/en/article/4aveeq/big-tech-has-made-billions-off-the-20-year-war-on-terror

Orden, H and Pamment, J. 2021. 'What Is So Foreign About Foreign Influence Operations?'. Carnegie Endowment for International Peace. Date Accessed: 26 July 2022: https://carnegieendowment.org/2021/01/26/what-is-so-foreign-about-foreign-influence-operations-pub-83706

Packenpaugh, J. 2001. 'Clinton Lifts Lobbying Restrictions on Appointees'. *Government Executive*. Date Accessed: 26 July 2022: https://www.govexec.com/federal-news/2001/01/clinton-lifts-lobbying-restrictions-on-appointees/8217/

Pamment, J and Smith, V. 2022. 'Attributing Information Influence Operations: Identifying those Responsible for Malicious Behaviour Online'. NATO StratcomCOE. Date Accessed: 26 July 2022: https://stratcomcoe.org/publications/attributing-information-influence-operations-identifying-those-responsible-for-malicious-behaviour-online/244

Perlroth, N. 2021. *This is How They Tell Me the World Ends*. New York: Bloomsbury.

Philo, G. 2008. 'Active Audiences and the Construction of Public Knowledge'. *Journalism Studies*, Vol. 9, No. 4, pp535–544.

PRSA. 2022. About Public Relations. Date Accessed: 26 July 2022: https://www.prsa.org/about/all-about-pr

Public Citizen. 2007. 'Organizing Astroturf: Evidence Shows Bogus Grassroots Groups Hijack the Political Debate; Need for Grassroots Lobbying Disclosure Requirements'. *Public Citizen*. Date Accessed: 26 July 2022: https://www.citizen.org/wp-content/uploads/organiz ing-astroturf.pdf

Qureshi, Waseem Ahmad. 2020. 'The Rise of Hybrid Warfare'. *Notre Dame Journal of International & Comparative Law*, Vol. 10, No. 2, Article 5. Date Accessed: 10 August 2023: https://scholarship.law.nd.edu/ndjicl/vol10/iss2/5

Rid, T. 2021. *Active Measures: The Secret History of Disinformation and Political Warfare*. New York: Picador.

Research & Markets. 2021. 'Global Dark Analytics Market Report 2021-2026 Rise in Data-driven Marketing / Increased Focus on Data Security / North America to Hold a Significant Market Share'. 21 December. *PR Newswire*. Date Accessed: 26 July 2022: https://www.prn ewswire.com/news-releases/global-dark-analytics-market-report-2021-2026---rise-in-data-driven-marketing--increased-focus-on-data-security--north-america-to-hold-a-sign ificant-market-share-301448854.html

Rondeaux, C. 2021. 'The Digital General'. 27 June. *The Intercept*. Date Accessed: 26 July 2022: https://theintercept.com/2021/06/27/qanon-michael-flynn-digital-soldiers/

Rosenau, W. 2014. 'Subversion Old and New'. 24 April. *War on the Rocks*. Date Accessed: 26 July 2022: https://warontherocks.com/2014/04/subversion-old-and-new/

Safire, W. 1987. 'On Language: Useful Idiots Of the West'. 12 April. *New York Times*. Date Accessed: 26 July 2022: https://www.nytimes.com/1987/04/12/magazine/on-language.html

Schwirtz, M and Frenkel, S. 2019. 'In Ukraine, Russia Tests a New Facebook Tactic in Election Tampering'. 29 March. *New York Times*. Date Accessed: 26 July 2022: https://www.nytimes. com/2019/03/29/world/europe/ukraine-russia-election-tampering-propaganda.html

Scott-Railton, J, Hulcoop, A, Razzak, B A, Marczak, B, Anstis, S, and Diebert, R. 2020. 'Dark Basin Uncovering a Massive Hack-For-Hire Operation'. *The Citizen Lab*. Date Accessed: 26 July 2022: https://citizenlab.ca/2020/06/dark-basin-uncovering-a-massive-hack-for-hire-operation/

Silverman, C, Mac, R, and Dixit, P. 2020. '"I have blood on my hands": A Whistleblower Says Facebook Ignored Global Political Manipulation'. 14 September. *Buzzfeed*. Date Accessed: 26 July 2022: https://www.buzzfeednews.com/article/craigsilverman/facebook-ignore-politi cal-manipulation-whistleblower-memo

Smith, S, Kao, E, Mackin, E, and Rubin, D. 2021. 'Automatic Detection of Influential Actors in Disinformation Networks'. *Proceedings of the National Academy of Sciences*, Vol. 118, No. 4. Doi: https://doi.org/10.1073/pnas.2011216118

Smith, B. 2022. 'A Former Facebook Executive Pushes to Open Social Media's "Black Boxes"'. 2 January. *New York Times*. Date Accessed: 26 July 2022: https://www.nytimes.com/2022/01/ 02/business/media/crowdtangle-facebook-brandon-silverman.html?referringSource=artic leShare

Stanford Internet Observatory. 2019. 'Analyzing a Twitter Takedown Originating in Saudi Arabia'. *Cyber Policy Center*. Date Accessed: 26 July 2022: https://cyber.fsi.stanford.edu/io/ news/smaat-twitter-takedown

Starbird, K., DiResta, R., & DeButts, M. 2023. Influence and Improvisation: Participatory Disinformation during the 2020 US Election. Social Media + Society, 9(2). https://doi. org/10.1177/20563051231177943

Tanielian, M and Ackil, J. 1 June 2014. 'The New Landscape of Lobbying'. *The Washington Post*. Date Accessed: 26 July 2022: https://www.washingtonpost.com/business/capitalbusiness/

the-new-landscape-of-lobbying/2014/06/01/0c3d35b8-e67a-11e3-afc6-a1dd9407abcf_st
ory.html

Till, C. 2021. 'Propaganda through "Reflexive Control" and the Mediated Construction of Reality'. *New Media & Society*, Vol. 23, No. 6, pp1362–1378. https://journals.sagepub.com/doi/pdf/10.1177/1461444820902446

Treverton, G, Threvdt, A, Chen, A, Lee, K, and McCue, M. 2018. *Addressing Hybrid Threats*. Bromma: Swedish Defence University

US Senate Select Committee on Intelligence. 2020. 'Report on Russian Active Measures Campaigns and Interference in the 2016 U.S. Election Vol:5'. *116th Congress Report 116-XX* Date Accessed: 26 July 2022: https://www.intelligence.senate.gov/sites/default/files/docume nts/report_volume5.pdf

Vaccari, C and Chadwick, A. 2020. 'Deepfakes and Disinformation: Exploring the Impact of Synthetic Political Video on Deception, Uncertainty, and Trust in News'. *Social Media and Society*, Vol. 6, No. 1. Doi: https://doi.org/10.1177/2056305120903408

Vaidhyanathan, Siva. 2018. *Antisocial Media How Facebook Disconnects Us and Undermines Democracy*. Oxford: Oxford University Press.

Verwey, S and Muir, C. 2019. 'Bell Pottinger and the Dark Art of Public Relations: Ethics of Individuality Versus Ethics of Communality'. *Journal for Communication Sciences in Southern Africa*, Vol. 38, No. 1, pp96–116. Doi: https://journals.co.za/doi/abs/10.10520/EJC-173da3f023

Wanless, A and Berk, M. 2018. 'Participatory Propaganda: The Engagement of Audiences in the Spread of Persuasive Communications'. Paper presented at the "Social Media & Social Order, Culture Conflict 2.0" conference organized by Cultural Conflict 2.0 and sponsored by the Research Council of Norway on 1 December 2017, Oslo: https://lageneralista.com/wp-content/uploads/2018/03/A-Participatory-Propaganda-Model-.pdf

Wanless, A and Berk, M. 2020. 'The Audience is the Amplifier: Participatory Propaganda'. In *The SAGE Handbook of propaganda*. Edited by Baines, P, O'Shaughnessy, N, and Snow, N. SAGE Publications. pp85–104. Doi: https://dx.doi.org/10.4135/9781526477170.n7

Wanless, A and Pamment, J. 2019. 'How Do You Define a Problem Like Influence?'. *Journal of Information Warfare*, Vol. 18, No. 3, pp1–14: https://carnegieendowment.org/files/2020-How_do_you_define_a_problem_like_influence.pdf

Washington Post. 20 September 2022. 'Opinion: The Pentagon's Alleged Secret Social Media Operations Demand a Reckoning'. *Washington Post*. Date Accessed: 15 October 2022: https://www.washingtonpost.com/opinions/2022/09/20/military-pentagon-fake-social-media/

Waters, N. 2016. 'The Importance of OSINT: Misinformation and Verification of Conflict Media'. 3 March. *Bellingcat*. Date Accessed: 26 July 2022: https://www.bellingcat.com/resour ces/articles/2016/05/03/the-importance-of-osint-misinformation-and-verification-of-conflict-media/

Wilkie, R. 2009. 'Hybrid Warfare – Something Old, Not Something New'. *Air & Space Power Journal*, Vol. 23, No. 4, pp13–18.

Zuboff, S. 2019. *The Age of Surveillance Capitalism*. New York: Public Affairs.

PART II

DIPLOMATIC PRACTICES

CHAPTER 6

DIPLOMATIC NEGOTIATIONS IN THE DIGITAL CONTEXT: KEY ISSUES, EMERGING TRENDS, AND PROCEDURAL CHANGES

KRISTIN ANABEL EGGELING AND
REBECCA ADLER-NISSEN

INTRODUCTION

DIPLOMACY has long been imagined as taking place in confidential closed-door meetings. In these meetings, negotiation happens: the careful pushing and pulling of political agendas while seeking to avoid revealing or crossing the capital's red lines. Scholars and practitioners of diplomacy agree that negotiation is an intimate affair, which requires not only substantial political knowledge, but also professional competencies and an environment of confidentiality, tact, and trust.

This chapter considers how diplomatic negotiations unfold in digital—or *digitalizing*—contexts in today's digitally mediated work environments that shape how diplomats interact, meet, and negotiate. Such settings are today not only historically and locally constituted, but also formed by digital technologies and 'scopic media', i.e., screen-based technologies of observation and projection, which render distant phenomena situationally present (Eggeling and Adler-Nissen, 2021; Knorr-Cetina, 2014). Digitalization, like other technological transformations before it, is said to alter diplomacy's conduct fundamentally. Some observers see a break between 'classic' negotiation rituals and protocols (Holmes, 2022) and 'the latest information and communication technologies' (Balzaqc et al., 2020: 14); others see diplomacy facing 'an existential challenge in the digital space' (Owen, 2016: 302). Others again argue that 'hierarchical communication flows are replaced by multidirectional flows'

(Hocking, 2020: 83) as digital information and communication technologies create new affordances for everyday diplomacy (Adler-Nissen and Drieschova, 2019). In the context of the move of diplomatic communication online due to the Covid-19 pandemic, moreover, work on virtual negotiations has pointed to its 'dramatically altered rhythm and flow' (Maurer and Wright, 2020); 'hollowed out' summits due to the 'elimination of the performative and interpersonal dimension' (Naylor, 2020); and a 'missing sense of togetherness and trust' when negotiations go online (Bramsen and Hagemann, 2021). This chapter further explores such optimistic, pessimistic, and pragmatic arguments.

Given the situated nature of diplomatic negotiations, we work throughout the chapter with empirical illustrations from an active diplomatic site: the European Union. We draw on ethnographic and interview material with diplomatic actors in the EU generated between 2018 and 2023. We explore how digital devices such as mobile phones, screens, or social media apps in the negotiation room support or challenge core diplomatic norms, protocols, and procedures. We also consider, more radically, what happens to diplomatic negotiations when digital environments become the foreground of the interaction itself and negotiations are conducted virtually or in hybrid formats. Through our case, we discuss critical issues, emerging trends, and procedural changes in the practice of diplomatic negotiations spurred by digitalization. Our chapter begins with a brief overview of the different theoretical positions on how digitalization shapes negotiation: facilitating, undermining, or changing it. In the second part, we move on to our explorations of how digital technologies from smartphones to video conferencing have begun to co-constitute diplomatic negotiations and how the increasing presence of digital technologies have made negotiation a 'blended practice' (Adler-Nissen and Eggeling, 2022).

Conceptualizing How Digitalization Shapes Diplomatic Negotiations

Scholars of different persuasions and research styles view the meeting of digitalization and diplomatic negotiations differently.[1] This has to do both with their understanding of digital technology and their conception of how diplomatic negotiations ideally should work. While we cannot do justice to all perspectives and authors, we can identify three broad interpretations of how digitalization shapes diplomatic negotiations: facilitating, challenging, or renegotiating.

---

[1] See Hedling and Bremberg (2021), Bjola and Zaiotti (2020) and Bjola (2015) for useful overviews of this literature.

Facilitating Negotiations

The first and perhaps dominant interpretation in the debate sees digital technologies as facilitating (better) diplomatic negotiations. From former American President Woodrow Wilson to the co-founder of Microsoft Bill Gates, there have been calls for using technology to open international negotiations up to the public. Multilateral institutions and democratization have made diplomacy a more public affair, and today, digital communication technology is central in this endeavour to create more transparency and publicity. The information revolution has transformed how state officials work and how citizens, organizations, and private companies are employed for diplomatic purposes. Diplomacy scholars agree that one of the most transformative aspects of digital information technologies is 'the direct involvement of publics in transnational engagement' (Cross and Melissen, 2013: xviii). Whereas social media enables a more public display of diplomacy, video conferencing and real-time text messaging enable more private and discrete communication between closed circles during negotiations. In both its public and private forms, digitalization is a potential game-changer for pursuing international relations as it enables coordinating interactions and information flows on a global scale. These new possibilities enable more direct forms of engagement between diplomats and with publics, and they are assumed to increase the authenticity and effectiveness of messages (Sotiriu, 2015: 37, 41; Bjola and Jiang, 2015), create more genuine relationships with foreign audiences (Bjola and Jiang, 2015; Arsenault, 2009), and may also facilitate direct communication between not just state executives and representatives, but also individuals not physically present at the negotiation table, which was previously technically impossible. As such, digitalization might make negotiations more inclusive and democratically responsive. However, it may also make them more hidden or less easy to trace when private messaging such as WhatsApp or Telegram are used.

Challenging Negotiations

The second position sees digital technologies as primarily a *threat* to diplomatic negotiations, to their quality and security. The most common argument is that confidentiality, a well-entrenched norm in diplomatic negotiations, is challenged by digitalization. It is not merely weak spots in IT infrastructure that threaten confidentiality. It is also diplomats themselves who actively use digital technologies in ways that undermine trust and confidentiality. Most diplomats and scholars see diplomacy as a professional culture of discretion that needs confidential spaces to negotiate successfully (Sharp, 2009; Berridge, 2002). This 'ethos of confidentiality' (Weiler, 2000) is evidenced in the unwillingness of executives and diplomats to disclose their views during negotiations and in the refusal of governments to release information provided in confidence even if this information is entirely innocuous. From this perspective, digital technologies, particularly social media, can be seen as a threat. Of course, leaking was widespread in international negotiations before digital technology (Castle and Pelc, 2019). Yet, leaking via social media is seen as an increasing problem. The use of social media from inside the negotiation room is different from previous forms of public engagement by diplomats. It happens simultaneously with the diplomatic process and appears to be less controllable and more dramatic. Disinformation/misinformation propagation on social media might also lead to negotiation difficulties if the greater public believes a particular narrative about reality on the ground.

Digitalization also appears to undermine diplomatic negotiations by reducing diplomats' patience and tact, mainly because of the rise of fast paced digital communication and public posts on social media (Hocking, 2020; Bjola and Manor, 2022). The speed of digital communication and the immediacy of the social media arguably leaves little room for patience and 'careful consideration' during negotiations (Cornut et al., 2021). Unlike before, the digital context does not reward the patient diplomat, the one who can resist the urge to respond immediately. This argument sees successful negotiations as depending on pragmatism and a sense of timing, knowing when views have matured enough for agreements to be made. Digital technologies moreover seem to infringe on the diplomatic need for a 'space to think and interact courteously and civilly' (Hillebrandt and Novak, 2016). Most scholarly conceptions of diplomatic negotiations include the principle of tact. Satow defined diplomacy as 'the application of intelligence and tact to the conduct of official relations' (1922: 1). The endurance of this virtue in the diplomatic (self-)imagination is illustrated by the continued emphasis placed on 'the procedural dos and don'ts' (Bjola and Kornprobst, 2013: 70). It involves the careful consideration of the other to reduce the potential for conflict and advises diplomats to use 'polysemantic communication' to avoid direct confrontation (Faizullaev, 2017: 2). Finally, one of the difficulties with digital interaction is that the serendipitous meeting is less likely to occur, which may mean fewer opportunities to read the temperature among negotiation partners as well as less intelligence gathering among interlocutors.

Renegotiating Negotiations

The third position sees digital technologies as neither inherent facilitators nor an inherent threat but as something negotiated, more gradually and incongruently transforming the conditions and dynamics of diplomatic work. While the mere presence of digital technologies in negotiation rooms may change how diplomats express their positions, this change is neither one-directional nor inevitable. It is both reflexively assessed and also resisted. The meaning of the digital context, in other words, is highly situated. From this perspective, like other technologies before it (on the telegraph, for instance, see Kurbalija, 2013), the meaning of digital technology in diplomacy is neither given nor 'transparent' (Grint and Woolgar, 1997: 10). The characteristics of 'the digital' are not linked to an independent essence but to the nexus of social actions of which they are part. The underlying idea here is the simple but crucial point that technologies do not influence social practice independent of human appropriation and interpretation. While often implicitly present, such social dynamics are still relatively little explored in the 'digital diplomacy' literature. So far, this interpretation, seeing the digital as socially negotiated, has led to two different types of studies. First, those primarily interested in the affordances of digital technologies, for example, ask how the presence of digital tools changes who gets to participate in diplomatic negotiations and how. As part of this research agenda, scholars have looked at how digitally modified documents feature as a central site of diplomatic negotiations (see Adler-Nissen and Drieschova, 2019), how diplomats use messenger apps to test the waters for their negotiation position, or how new spaces for negotiation open when different digital channels (e.g., Zoom, text, and WhatsApp) can be used in tandem. The second type of studies are those more interested in exploring the change in procedure and 'rules of the game' following technological change. If diplomatic negotiations are held in hybrid, synthetic, or entirely virtual settings (Eggeling and Adler-Nissen, 2021; Kuus, 2021), do traditional procedures of meeting agendas, designated speaking times, simultaneous interpretation, entrenched hierarchies, and performances of diplomatic decorum still hold?

Asking such questions, scholars inspired by sociological and practice-oriented theories are occupied with how what is considered 'correct behaviour' by diplomats themselves changes if diplomatic negotiations take in digitalizing contexts. In his analysis of the Wikileaks revelations, Murray (2016) showed that diplomats continue to refer to a confidentiality principle. As he concludes: 'To argue, therefore, that revolutions in ICT [Information Communication Technology] have fundamentally changed the game of diplomacy is problematic ...' (Murray, 2016: 28). Considerations of when and how digital communication should or should not be used are paralleled by another, more basic set of concerns about whether they should be used at all. What is at stake is more than a question of who has the most 'reach' on social media. Rather than 'automation' or 'disruption', digitalization hits deeper and has conjured negotiation of the nature of diplomatic work itself (Adler-Nissen and Eggeling, 2022). In the second half of the chapter, we consider these three positions in the context of multilateral diplomatic negotiations in the EU.

DIGITALLY MEDIATED NEGOTIATIONS IN PRACTICE: INSIGHTS FROM THE EUROPEAN UNION

Brussels is a global diplomatic hub like New York, Jakarta, and Nairobi. In the early 2020s, the Belgian capital hosts more than 180 diplomatic missions and the headquarters of multiple multilateral organizations, including NATO and, our focus in this chapter, the EU. There are two levels of diplomatic relations in the EU: one concerned with the

Union's *external affairs* with third countries, institutionalized in the European External Action Service (EEAS) and the presidents of the EU's three principal institutions (the Parliament, the Commission, and the Council); and another concerned with the Union's *internal affairs* of its twenty-seven member states, institutionalized in individual permanent representations (PERMREPs) and their collective interactions in the EU Council. In this chapter, we focus on internal EU negotiations among the Councils of Permanent Representatives (COREPER) and their preparatory bodies. Each member state sends three ambassadors to the EU: one permanent representative who joins COREPER II, the diplomatic body concerned with economic, financial, foreign, general, and justice and home affairs; one deputy representative who joins COREPER I, the diplomatic body concerned with agriculture and fisheries, competitiveness, education, employment, environment, and transport; and a third ambassador who joins the Political and Security Committee (PSC). The ambassadors are supported by diplomatic advisors, attachés, and support staff, and EU bureaucrats and civil servants. Currently, more than 40,000 people are employed by EU institutions. All of them experience changes to their jobs in the context of societal digitalization.

Over the last two decades and with increasing speed, electronic and digital devices, digital services, and online forms of information exchange and interaction have become commonplace in the diplomatic scene in Brussels. Like in other professional settings, most documents are now created and worked on digitally, digital repositories have replaced wooden filing cabinets, and diplomatic information is shared in face-to-face encounters and via digital channels like text messages, emails, intranets, and social media platforms. In the context of the Covid-19 pandemic, moreover, digital devices further moved into the foreground of diplomatic working methods, when tools like video-conferencing systems started being used not only for long-distance communication or exchanges with external partners but became a de facto site of EU diplomacy itself (see Eggeling and Adler-Nissen, 2021; Kuus, 2021). These developments have given rise to commentary that diplomatic work is fundamentally changing when it is digitally mediated, a statement we probe in the sections below by zooming in on how negotiations are affected when they (partly) 'go online'. However, it is worth considering that changes to the practice of negotiating happen within broader technological transformations in the diplomatic field. While recent changes to diplomatic practice seemed abrupt and radical, diplomacy remains, in general and in the EU, a cautious profession. As one employee of the General Secretariat of the EU Council put it in an interview in 2021:

> [With digitalization,] more will change in the next ten years than in the 30 before that. When I first started here [in the early 1990s], we used typewriters and stencils. Electronic typewriters, at least that much, but typewriters. There will be constant renewal in this field, but the [EU] institutions will never be the first movers ... it is also not our job to be on the technological cutting edge. We are a cautious institution; there are established norms and rules for a reason ... [and] careful with how we grow and develop. (I:1)

As this long-term Brussels professional put it, much is at stake with digitalization in diplomacy, not only its practical working methods but also its 'norms and rules'. After a year and half of mainly working virtually, another Brussels diplomat reports a similar impression at the end of 2021:

> Beyond questions about the specifics of our work—*how may negotiations work virtually?*—there is also a much broader debate if digitalisation will be an existential threat to diplomacy and whether we could now close all of our embassies and just meet online. Of all the places I have been sent, Brussels would be the one [place] where this would at least be somewhat possible because the institutions have been here for a while and the internet connection generally works. But I think it will even not happen here because of cultural differences, communicative differences, and different technological development statuses across countries. If it would work anywhere, it would work here. Still, even here, there are so many files that go into so much technical detail or that are politically so touchy that we still need the physical representations. (I:2)

These statements signal that even in a technologically comfortable environment like Brussels, diplomatic actors are cautious about the character digitalization may have for their work. While we see no revolution or 'existential threat', we can identify three broad understandings among practitioners of how diplomatic work, particularly negotiations, unfolds in digitalizing contexts. Moreover, we will see that the same tool (e.g., a digital messaging service like WhatsApp) can be seen as either beneficial, threatening, or producing change in negotiation procedures. From this perspective, and following the third position above, digital tools have neither a prescribed meaning nor an inherent function but are always tied to situated performances and interpretations.

Digitalization as Facilitator

The first view is optimistic, highlighting digital technology's ability to flatten hierarchies and connect diplomatic actors in new, faster, cheaper, and more convenient ways with each other and with external players like technical experts, journalists, lobbyists, or national constituencies. As outlined above, many argue that diplomatic negotiation becomes more transparent and democratically accountable when it has a digital element. Especially to outsiders of the diplomatic elite, the online publication of meeting room agendas or the live-tweeting of ambassadors from inside the negotiation room look like possibilities for direct insight into the ordinarily blocked-off engine rooms of international relations. The Secretariat of the European Council itself used a version of this argument when it introduced *Council Live* for the partial live-streaming of Council and ministerial meetings on the internet in 2009 (Article 7(3), EU Council, 2009), and set up an 'open data' portal containing meta-data of voting patterns and meeting agendas in 2015 (EU Council, 2022). These are two examples of techno-optimistic measures against mounting criticisms of limited accountability and intransparent 'closed door' deals (Naurin, 2007). Concerning the live streams, one Council employee explained:

> There is a rule in the Council now that all legislative deliberations on topics that will have a direct impact on citizens' lives need to be live-streamed ... the point of this is to add visibility to the work we do. It is sometimes hard to understand what the Council does, and there have also been issues and calls for more transparency in the last years. This is why we stream live from the meeting room now. (I:3)

In addition to making internal deliberations more public and thus bolstering the democratic legitimacy of the institution as a whole, digital tools are also lauded by negotiators themselves for improving or enabling their work. While diplomacy is sometimes considered a stuffy and old-school profession, EU diplomats across ranks integrate new communication tools into everyday tasks. For instance, numerous text messaging channels have become part of Brussels' communication environment. Apps such as WhatsApp, Signal, or Telegram are in continuous use, yet for different purposes and in different ways. They can be used 'bilaterally' to arrange meetings, share information and news, or signal support to a colleague during a negotiation; as well as 'multilaterally' to 'test the waters' for negotiation positions and agenda items or ask colleagues about their perceptions of a statement or event. The importance of such exchanges grew during the Covid-19 pandemic when EU diplomats deliberately set up additional group chats to keep the informal part of their work going during lockdowns. Yet, these exchanges are limited neither to the EU nor to pandemic times. Jones and Clark (2019: 1275) report from the UN General Assembly in 2017 that diplomats use 'WhatsApp a lot ... [and] often send a photo through mobile phones saying "Saw you speaking that was a great statement ... thanks for mentioning our country"'. Next to a convenient, fast, and low-cost way to communicate, texting can thus also serve as a channel to share subtle negotiation signals like trust, agreement, or appreciation that could otherwise only be picked up via body language or facial expressions in the negotiation room.

The presence and use of digital tools like video streaming, digital publication of negotiation files, and smartphones in the room impact diplomatic negotiations in multiple ways. The decision on which parts of the ministerial meetings are streamed online, for instance, is taken by majority vote in COREPER and is then arranged as a 'public' item by the member state holding the rotating Council presidency (I:3). Which items are publicly streamed indicates the EU political priorities of that member state and can signal both to voters at home and to the community in Brussels. The same logic applies to the setting and digital publication of meeting agendas—a popular thing to do, for example, via Council presidency social media accounts. In recent years, Twitter followers have been informed about the items on the agendas of the week's COREPER II, COREPER I, and PSC meetings. Figure 6.1 provides an illustrative example.

One diplomat responsible for such and similar posts during the 2021 Slovenian Council presidency explained the relation between digital communication and diplomatic negotiations with an example from a recent EU summit on enlargement:

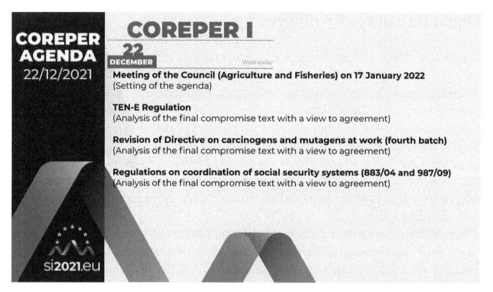

FIGURE 6.1 Exemplary COREPER I meeting agenda posted on Twitter on 22 December 2021
Source: https://twitter.com/SLOtoEU/status/1473574439111507970/photo/1 (accessed 19 January 2022).

'To set the stage for the discussion and to signal early on to both the European people and the other negotiation parties that Slovenia and the Presidency are pro-enlargement, we were publishing positive, pre-planned posts on Twitter using memorable quotes from the Slovenian President on past enlargement questions' (I:4). These posts were designed to 'frame the conversation from the beginning, to manage expectations and to set the tone around what Slovenia's ambitions, red lines and desired outcomes would be' (I:4). The quotes, moreover, were 'picked in a way that whatever the outcome of the meeting will be, it can be framed as a success back to national audiences' (I:4). Public social media posts may thus have multiple audiences and purposes in the context of ongoing negotiations, helping diplomatic actors set the tone, manage expectations, and signal convictions as well as red lines.

The internal use of digital communication also impacts ongoing negotiations. One clear implication of text messaging, for example, is the establishment of parallel informal communication loops that can be both in- and exclusionary. As one ambassador explained, 'we have various WhatsApp groups: There is an official [ambassadors] group, then there is a more leisure-oriented group, one for smaller countries, the Nordic-Baltics, I think the Benelux have one, the Visegrad, and so on' (I:5). While, on the one hand, allowing more accessible communication among 'like-minded' member states, the reproduction of such digital fault lines also reproduces regional and political differences in the EU. Enhancing exchange and transparency among members of one chat group always also means less communication with those belonging to another group. This point exemplifies the Janus-faced character of digital tools and foreshadows the second, more pessimistic view of digitalization as a challenge to diplomatic negotiations.

Digitalization as a Challenge

The second view is a more pessimistic one that points to issues of limited trust in the safety of digital communication channels and the disruptions of diplomatic norms as digital devices become commonplace. When diplomats rely on tools like laptops, smartphones, and digital communication platforms, possibilities for espionage, hacks, and leaks arise that may threaten the integrity of their work. At the same time, practitioners may struggle to uphold long-term characteristics of their profession. Tact or patience may suffer when diplomats are prompted to reply or provide statements for fast-paced email or social media communication, and they may struggle to respect confidentiality when handling restricted information digitally or exchanging virtually via teleconference systems.

Critical voices grew louder during Covid-19 about the challenges of a missing sense of purpose, togetherness, and trust when negotiations moved online (Holmes et al., 2021; Naylor, 2020; Bramsen and Hagemann, 2021). While the pandemic heightened such worries, they were already present in the diplomatic field before. For instance, it was already a common practice in Brussels pre-2020 to limit use of digital devices in meeting rooms; jam 4G signals at high-level meetings; or negotiate restricted files in secure rooms only. The pandemic, nevertheless, pushed questions of secure digital communication to the top of the working methods agenda. One trigger event was the hack of a Dutch journalist into a video-conference negotiation of the EU twenty-seven Defence Ministers in November 2020. Following a tweet by the Dutch defence minister that displayed the meeting link and a partial access code, a journalist managed to access the confidential meeting. Following the incident, a Council official stated that 'we have all the time been conscious of, and have warned that, videoconferences ... are vulnerable from a security point of view', saying that this was one reason why they are 'not formal Council meetings and no classified matters can be discussed' (cited in Cerulus, 2020). Reflecting on the same incident, one EU diplomat stated: 'If you think about it, this is the best thing that could have happened ... the question how we can securely communicate via virtual tools ... [is] experiencing a sort of revival now' (I:6). Another worry that has been discussed in the field is the loss of informality and the difficulties of 'new colleagues to join the professional networks of the town' (I:2). 'I have still not met most of the colleagues that started during the pandemic in person', one diplomat reports, 'so here we needed to make an extra effort to draw them in' (I:2).

In Brussels, both technical and social 'extra efforts' were made by single diplomats and the EU institutions to alleviate the challenges and risks of virtual negotiations. Technological strategies have focused on the EU's own digital communication platforms, particularly the 'Interactio' platform used by the EU Commission and 'Pexit', the platform used by the EU Council. 'We set up Pexit during the pandemic', a senior Council official explained, and 'we have tried to secure it in every way possible. No platform is 200% secure, but this is the best there is. We use it because we have control over it and can offer assistance if something goes wrong. Next to security problems, this is another reason why we don't use Zoom or WebEx, because if there are technical problems, we cannot do anything' (I:7). This last point may sound purely service-oriented, but outages in corporate software can seriously impact diplomatic negotiations. As one diplomat noted following a two-day global outage of Facebook and WhatsApp in October 2021, 'we are currently lacking behind and remain dependent on private company products. This is a problem. We saw what happened with Facebook the other week: all of the sudden we could not communicate anymore' (I:8). These examples illustrate how different digital tools influence the negotiation meeting and the leg work done by diplomatic attachés beforehand. In addition, the rise of virtual negotiation meetings has led to the drawing of new boundaries in the EU decision-making process regarding what counts as a formal negotiation—and what does not. Following the rules for internal working methods set in the 2009 Lisbon Treaty, the Council stipulated that virtual meetings cannot be considered formal meetings and thus have no formal decision-making power (I:1). This is where politics enters the relation between digitalization and diplomatic negotiations, and new hierarchies emerged in the EU between physical in-person and virtual or hybrid negotiations as their decisions carry different amounts of political weight.

Socially, the possibility and, at times, unavoidability of virtual negotiations has cemented the role of the COREPER as the critical diplomatic body in the EU. Throughout the pandemic—even in times of 'hard' lockdowns in Belgium—COREPER I and II ambassadors kept on meeting in person (Maurer and Wright, 2020; Eggeling and Adler-Nissen, 2021). 'The ambassadors felt cut off during the first virtual summit when they could not be in the room with their leaders', a Commission staff member often present at COREPER meetings explained, which is why they 'insisted on having physical meetings from the very beginning' (I:9). 'We talk about many difficult things in these meetings', one ambassador further explained, 'it may be possible to talk about single-issue files in virtual meetings, but our problems are the difficult things. For those we have to talk together. We need spontaneity and exchange to generate ideas, paths forward and find compromises' (I:10). One effect of the COREPER meeting being in person was that contentious negotiation files were either escalated up from the technical level or escalated down from the political level to the diplomatic level, thus directly impacting the negotiation procedure and upping the social prestige and standing of the diplomats (I:2). After some time, working groups working on key files were also allowed to take up in-person meetings sooner and more regularly than those groups whose files were deemed less essential. 'The rotating presidency gained a lot of power here', according to one diplomat, 'as they could decide which meetings to hold in-person and which ones online' (I: 2). Similar to the example of pre-planned Twitter posts discussed above, differentiated uses of digital tools can thus be used in negotiations to signal intent and political priority.

Yet, finally, even if negotiations happen in person, not all digital challenges and vulnerabilities can be suspended. The weakest point may in fact not be IT security risks but a situated use of technology that goes against socially accepted negotiation norms. In COREPER, 'we meet with phones and such things all the time because we meet for long hours, so people are reading their mails [or] giving instructions to their staff on other issues', one ambassador explains (I:11). But there is a shared understanding that

> these meetings should take place in an atmosphere of certain confidentiality. So one should not tweet what somebody else is saying ... the most harmful consequence of such a 'false transparency', as I would call it, is that people would no longer be prepared to say openly what they think or what their government position is in such a setting ... if a colleague of mine would be tweeting what I am saying at the COREPER meeting, next meeting I would no longer be saying that (I:11).

Tweeting from the negotiation room, what some tech-optimistic observers may consider a sign of more transparency, thus has a different meaning for the diplomatic practitioners themselves. 'What would happen then?', the ambassador continued,

> The discussions would move into a much more closed setting ... and the true work would move elsewhere behind some closed-door not necessarily including all the member states, so member state like Slovenia or Denmark would be the first to fall out and be excluded, only the big guys would get invited ... so one has to be careful. Greater transparency may, if it is applied wrong ... actually lead to much less transparency ... less consensus and less decisions (I:11).

In the EU, one of the core tensions that digitalization has brought to the fore is the tension between transparency for democratic legitimacy and internal restraint among the negotiating partners for the sake of confidentiality. As this ambassador and other diplomats put it, the risk of social media leaking is a fundamental challenge to the integrity of diplomatic negotiations.

Digitalization as Negotiated

Notwithstanding the advantages and risks, digitalization is here to stay. While it is unlikely that digital interactions will fully replace physical representation and face-to-face meetings (consider I:1 and I:2 again), there is also no going back to a romanticized ideal of 'naked' traditional diplomacy without any element of syntheticism (Eggeling and Adler-Nissen, 2021). With technological advancement, there moreover is a real possibility that virtual/augmented reality could make the distance between 'physical representation' and 'digital representation' much smaller over time (Holmes, 2022). Instead, what we see, at least in the context of Brussels' internal negotiations, is the emergence of a 'blended' form of diplomacy (Adler-Nissen and Eggeling, 2022) that comes with the invention and negotiation of new rules, procedures, and norm(al)s as to how diplomatic work is and ought to be done.

In this third view, digitalization is a development that—like other technological innovations before it—will alter some established ways of doing things and the institutionalization of new working methods. Seen through this lens, digitalization is but the latest step in the dynamic history of an international profession that has always been characterized by and subject to technological change. Take the invention of the tele-graph in the mid-nineteenth century. When in the 1840s the first telegraph landed on the desk of the British foreign minister John Henry Temple, now also known as Lord Palmerston, he reportedly declared 'My God, this is the end of diplomacy' (Dizard, 2001 cited in Adler-Nissen, 2016: 97). And indeed, the telegraph went on to change diplo-matic practice by increasing capital control, rearranging communication monopolies, demanding concision and shorter messages, opening possibilities for tapping and espi-onage, as well as centralizing, and upping the overall speed of diplomatic communica-tion, 'but it did not make the diplomat-as-communicator obsolete' per se (Adler-Nissen, 2016; see also Hamilton and Langhorne, 1995: 190–196; Kurbalija, 1996: 1–2).

Similar dynamics can be observed in Brussels, where negotiations happen in increas-ingly digitalizing contexts. In recent years, scholars working with performative or practice-oriented approaches have made many valuable contributions to our understanding of diplomatic practice in the digital age. Particularly scholarship with roots in Science and Technology Studies (STS) has become prominent in this regard, as it does not merely take technological tools—like smartphones or software—as a passive means to an end or as purely mechanical elements of social practice, but as containing a specific agency them-selves that makes them active participants in the socio-material world. An illustrative ex-ample is Adler-Nissen and Drieschova's (2019) work on 'track change diplomacy'. Arguing more generally that 'each technological innovation has helped determine what kind of diplomacy can take place', the authors argue that international negotiation has primarily become 'a mediated struggle for semantic control over [digital] documents' (2019: 531–132). When files are negotiated in the EU Council, the working file is sent around as a .docx Microsoft Word file that the different negotiation parties can alter as per the affordances of this software, including **bolding**, <u>underlining</u>, *italicizing*, and inserting, commenting on, or deleting text and comments through the 'track change' function. The practical effects of this way of working, Adler-Nissen and Drieschova argue, are the normalization of shared authorship; the streamlining of a particular aesthetic of the produced negoti-ation artefacts; and, as with other technologies before, the general increase in speed with which texts are produced and circulated and hence negotiations conducted. Some parts of this may be construed as an advantage. Still, digital tools show their indeterminacy, as negotiators report more easily losing oversight and that 'the process of negotiating tends to gain a life of its own' (Adler-Nissen and Drieschova, 2019: 532). Capital instructions and red negotiation lines may look blurrier when they are added to the margins of a document, where they can be moved, edited, replaced, or deleted without a trace.

Indeed, losing oversight and a grasp of what is essential is a pressing concern among Brussels diplomats today. One ambassador, for example, told the following story about how the simultaneous ubiquity and elusiveness of emails are upsetting his ability to do 'real work':

> In August, everything shuts down. There are no emails, no messages, but the sun still rises and the world still turns. But then, in the last week in August, a time starts that I find even physically painful: thousands of people come back from their summer

holiday and start deleting, sending and forwarding [emails] in an unbelievable swirl ... When we had the presidency last year, I spent a lot of time sorting senseless – and I really mean superfluous – information and I have this issue; I assume others have it, too. This begs the question: Who really has the time to think about politics? (I:12)

In this example, two extraordinary moments are singled out as being overburdening due to unmanageable information flows: the return from the summer holiday and holding the Council presidency. The latter feeling has been shared by other EU diplomats, who broadly agree that the six months of the presidency are a 'completely different game' in terms of workload and constantly having to 'be on' (I:4). Yet, the presence and flow of ubiquitous digital information also affects everyday diplomatic work and reaches into the negotiation room. The same ambassador continued his reflections:

we [diplomats] are no different from other people ... when something is not particularly interesting, we get our smartphones out and start reading the newspaper or else. This is not great, of course. People get distracted and may lose the moment when they have to say something ... we also have these discussions now about banning phones from the room, but this has more to do with confidentiality, classified documents and security than with concern for our attention. I am worried about the latter: there is endless possibility with these technologies, but there is also the problem of constantly getting buried under too much information. We have to watch out that our jobs don't turn into superficial information management. (I:12).

In the last quote, we see a deeper form of reflection beyond concerns about how to do diplomatic work virtually, digitally, or online, moving deeper into the territory of professional self-understanding. In the digital context, what is the core of the diplomatic profession if its core practices—including negotiation and information-sharing, relationship building, and analysing situations—are becoming digitally mediated? Diplomats raise these questions in the field at the time of writing, and tracing them will be an empirical task in the future. What we can already see is that conducting negotiations in increasingly digital contexts impacts how negotiations take place, who is involved, and what negotiators think about their work. In Brussels, this has so far included the deepening of existing regional and ideological fault lines (consider like-minded WhatsApp groups), the crystallization of local professional hierarchies (think which diplomats meet how), and new ways to signal political interests and priorities (think what is put on public agendas or which files are considered essential to be negotiated in in-person formats). These changes cannot be reduced to threats or advantages of certain technological tools but are linked to situated performances and interpretations.

Conclusion

How have diplomatic negotiations evolved in the digital context, and what are key issues, emerging trends, and procedural changes in the meeting of diplomacy and digitalization more generally? In this chapter, we have outlined three different positions in the literature on this question: there are those scholars who view digital technologies, including social media, as facilitating better and transparent negotiations, where the process becomes more involving and transparent, and the outcome may be seen as more legitimate. The second position takes the opposite view, seeing digitalization as a threat to negotiations' security and quality, pointing out the problems with breach of confidentiality, undermining tact and patience. The third position perceives more continuity than change. It is interested in the fine-grained modifications that happen to both the material and social dimensions of negotiations, from how information flows to how norms may be renegotiated. The attention-grabbing aspect of digital communication now challenges patience. Tact is challenged by the characteristic speed and crudeness of viral online interactions. Yet, the partial defence of the diplomatic scripts and norms from within indicates that diplomats are not ready to let go of long-proven professional standards. At stake in the debate on what digitalization does to diplomacy is not just how we might measure digital transformation but also how we see negotiations in the first place and which kinds of ideals we have of diplomacy.

Moving on from our illustrations of what digitalization does to negotiations, digitalization is an increasingly contested issue within international diplomacy. Next to tools for diplomatic conduct, digital technologies and questions concerning regulation, management, and democratic limits are also becoming important themes in international diplomacy. At the time of writing, these multiple dimensions of 'digital diplomacy' meet when EU officials rely on digital tools to negotiate proposals about platform regulation and market access (the so-called Digital Services Act and Digital Markets Act). While officials and diplomats defined red lines for how much data social media platforms may collect about their users, they posted negotiation updates on platforms like Instagram or Twitter. As one of the ambassadors mentioned above, the meeting between digitalization and diplomatic activity often produces an 'unbelievable swirl'. More research is needed on the intersection of digital working methods in diplomacy and the increasingly digitally mediated geopolitical playing field in which diplomacy happens. Today, the digital has become both a tool and a theme in diplomatic negotiations.

Suggested reading

Adler-Nissen, R., and A. Drieschova. 2019. 'Track-Change Diplomacy: Technology, Affordances, and the Practice of International Negotiations'. *International Studies Quarterly* 63(3): pp. 531–545.

Adler-Nissen, R., and K.A. Eggeling. 2022. 'Blended Diplomacy: The Entanglement and Contestation of Digital Technologies in Everyday Diplomatic Practice'. *European Journal of International Relations* 28(3): pp. 640–666.

Bjola, C., and I. Manor 2022. 'The Rise of Hybrid Diplomacy: From Digital Adaption to Adoption'. *International Affairs* 98(2): pp. 471–491.

Eggeling, K.A., and R. Adler-Nissen. 2021. 'The Synthetic Situation in Diplomacy: Scopic Media and the Digital Mediation of Estrangement'. *Global Studies Quarterly* 1(2): pp. 1–14.

Hedling, E., and N. Bremberg. 2021. 'Practice Approaches to the Digital Transformations of Diplomacy: Toward a New Research Agenda'. *International Studies Review* 23(4): pp. 1595–1618.

Kuus, M., 2023. 'Bureaucratic Sociability, or the Missing Eighty Percent of Effectiveness: The Case of Diplomacy'. *Geopolitics* 28(1): pp. 174–195.

REFERENCES

Adler-Nissen, R. 2016. 'Diplomatic Agency'. In *The SAGE Handbook of Diplomacy*, edited by Costas Constantinou, Pauline Kerr, and Paul Sharp, pp. 92–103. 1st ed. Los Angeles: Sage.

Adler-Nissen, R. and A. Drieschova. 2019. 'Track-Change Diplomacy: Technology, Affordances, and the Practice of International Negotiations'. *International Studies Quarterly* 63(3): pp. 531–545.

Adler-Nissen, R., and K.A. Eggeling. 2022. 'Blended Diplomacy: The Entanglement and Contestation of Digital Technologies in Everyday Diplomatic Practice'. *European Journal of International Relations* 28(3): pp. 640–666.

Arsenault, A. 2009. 'Public Diplomacy 2.0'. In *Toward a New Public Diplomacy: Redirecting U.S. Foreign Policy*, edited by Philip Seib, pp. 135–153. Palgrave Macmillan Series in Global Public Diplomacy, 1st ed. New York: Palgrave Macmillan US.

Balzaqc, T., F. Charilon, and F. Ramel. 2020. 'Introduction: History and Theories of Diplomacy'. In *Global Diplomacy*, edited by Thierry Balzaqc, Frédéric Charilon, and Frédéric Ramel, pp. 1–16. Cham: Palgrave Macmillan.

Berridge, G. 2002. *Diplomacy: Theory and Practice*, 5th ed. New York: Palgrave.

Bjola, C. 2015. 'Introduction: Making Sense of Digital Diplomacy'. In *Digital Diplomacy*, edited by Bjola Corneliu and Marcus Holmes, pp. 1–9. 1st ed. London: Routledge.

Bjola, C. and M. Kornprobst. 2013. *Understanding International Diplomacy: Theory, Practice and Ethics*, 1st ed. London: Routledge.

Bjola, C. and L. Jiang. 2015. *Social Media and Public Diplomacy: A Comparative Analysis of the Digital Diplomatic Strategies of the EU, US and Japan in China*, Palgrave Macmillan Series in Global Public Diplomacy, 1st ed. New York: Palgrave Macmillan US.

Bjola, C., and I. Manor. 2022. 'The Rise of Hybrid Diplomacy: From Digital Adaption to Adoption'. *International Affairs* 98(2): pp. 471–491.

Bjola, C., and R. Zaiotti. 2020. *Digital Diplomacy and International Organisations*, 1st ed. London: Routledge.

Bramsen, I., and A. Hagemann. 2021. 'The Missing Sense of Peace: Diplomatic Approachment and Virtualization During the COVID-19 Lockdown'. *International Affairs* 2: pp. 539–560.

Castle, M., and K. Pelc. 2019. 'The Causes and Effects of Leaks in International Negotiations'. *International Studies Quarterly* 63(4): pp. 1147–1162.

Cerulus, L., 2020. 'A Reporter Hacked an EU Council Meeting. Here's Why He Did It'. *Politico*. November 23. Available at: https://www.politico.eu/article/dutch-reporter-hacked-eu-council-interview/#:~:text=Using%20login%20information%20shared%20on,EU%20was%20on%20the%20agenda. (Accessed: 4 August 2023).

Cornut, J., S. Rimmer, and I. Choi. 2021. 'The Liquidification of International Politics and Trump's (Un)Diplomacy on Twitter'. *International Politics* 59: pp. 367–382.

Cross, M., and J. Melissen. 2013. *European Public Diplomacy: Soft Power at Digital Diplomacy*, Palgrave Macmillan Series in Global Public Diplomacy, 1st ed. New York: Palgrave Macmillan US.

Eggeling, K.A., and R. Adler-Nissen. 2021. 'The Synthetic Situation in Diplomacy: Scopic Media and the Digital Mediation of Estrangement'. *Global Studies Quarterly* 1(2): pp. 1–14.

EU Council, 2009. 'Acts whose Publication is not Obligatory', Council's Rules of Procedure. Available at:https://eurlex.europa.eu/legal-content/EN/TXT/PDF/?uri=CELEX:32009D0 937&from=EN (Accessed: 19 January 2022).

EU Council, 2022. 'Transparency and Access to Documents', Consilium, EU Council Website. Available at: www.consilium.europa.eu/en/general-secretariat/corporate-policies/trans parency (Accessed: 19 January 2022).

Faizullaev, A. 2017. 'Symbolic Insult in Diplomacy: A Subtle Game of Diplomatic Slap'. *Brill Research Perspectives in Diplomacy and Foreign Policy* 2(4): pp. 1–116.

Grint, K., and S. Woolgar. 1997. *The Machine at Work: Technology, Work and Organization*, 1st ed. Cambridge: Polity Press.

Jones, A., and Clark, J. 2019. 'Performance, Emotions, and Diplomacy in the United Nations Assemblage in New York'. *Annals of the American Association of Geographers* 109(4): pp. 1262–1278.

Knorr Cetina, K. 2014. 'Scopic Media and Global Coordination: the Mediatization of Face-to-Face Encounters'. In *Mediatization of Communication*, edited by Knut Lundby, pp. 39–62. 1st ed. Berlin: De Gruyter Mouton.

Hamilton, K. and R. Langhorne. 1995. *The Practice of Diplomacy: Its Evolution, Theory and Administration*, 2nd ed. London and New York: Routledge.

Hillebrandt, M. and S. Novak. 2016. 'Integration without Transparency? Reliance on the Space to Think in the European Council and Council'. *Journal of European Integration* 38(5): pp. 527–540.

Hocking, B. 2020. 'Communication and Diplomacy: Change and Continuity'. In *Global Diplomacy*, edited by Thierry Balzaqc, Frédéric Charilon, and Frédéric Ramel, pp. 79–96. Cham: Palgrave Macmillan.

Holmes, M. 2022. 'Diplomacy in the Rearview Mirror: Implications of Face-to-Face Diplomacy Ritual Disruption for Ministries of Foreign Affairs'. In: *Ministries of Foreign Affairs in the World*, edited by Christian Lequesne, pp. 352–368, 1st ed. Leiden: Brill.

Holmes, M., N.K. Saunders, and N.J. Wheeler. 2021. 'UN General Assembly: Why Virtual Meetings Make It Hard for Diplomats to Trust Each Other'. The Conversation. Available at: https://theconversation.com/un-general-assembly-why-virtual-meetings-make-it-hard-for-diplomats-to-trust-each-other-146508 (Accessed: 19 January 2022).

Kurbalija, J. 1996. 'Information Technology and Diplomacy in A Changing Environment'. *Diplomatic Studies Programme*, Discussion Papers (No. 20), pp. 1–42. Available at: https://issuu.com/diplo/docs/dsp_information_technology_diplomacy_changing_envi (Accessed: 4 August 2023).

Kurbalija, J. 2013. 'The Impact of the Internet and ICT on Contemporary Diplomacy'. In *Diplomacy in a Globalizing World: Theories and Practices*, edited by Pauline Kerr and Geoffrey Wiseman, pp. 141–150. 1st ed. Oxford: Oxford University Press.

Kuus, M., 2023. 'Bureaucratic Sociability, or the Missing Eighty Percent of Effectiveness: The Case of Diplomacy'. *Geopolitics* 28(1): pp. 174–195.

Maurer, H. and N. Wright. 2020. 'A New Paradigm for EU Diplomacy? EU Council Negotiations in a Time of Physical Restrictions'. *The Hague Journal of Diplomacy* 15(4), pp. 556–568.

Murray, S. 2016. 'Secret "Versus" Open Diplomacy Across the Ages'. In *Secret Diplomacy: Concepts, Contexts and Cases*, edited by Corneliu Bjola and Stuart Murray, pp. 29–45. 1st ed. New York: Routledge.

Naylor, T. 2020. 'All That's Lost: The Hollowing of Summit Diplomacy in A Socially Distanced World'. *The Hague Journal of Diplomacy* 15(4): pp. 583–598.

Naurin, D. 2007. *Deliberating behind Closed Doors: Transparency and Lobbying in the European Union*. Colchester: ECPR Press.

Owen, T. 2016. 'The Networked State and the End of 20th Century Diplomacy'. *Global Affairs* 2(3): pp. 301–307.

Satow, E. 1922. *A Guide to Diplomatic Practice*. London: Longmans.

Sharp, P. 2009. *Diplomatic Theory of International Relations*, 1st ed. Cambridge: Cambridge University Press.

Sotiriu, S. 2015. 'Digital Diplomacy: Between Promises and Reality'. In *Digital Diplomacy*, edited by Bjola Corneliu and Marcus Holmes, pp. 33–51. 1st ed. London: Routledge.

Weiler, J. 2000. 'The Rule of Lawyers and the Ethos of Diplomats: Reflections on the Internal and External Legitimacy of WTO Dispute Settlement'. *Journal of World Trade* 35(2): pp. 191–207.

Cited interviews

I:1—In-person interview with senior official in the General Secretariat of the EU Council; 18 October 2021 in Brussels, Belgium

I:2—In-person interview with senior diplomat of a member state PERMREP; 29 September 2021 in Brussels, Belgium

I:3—In-person interview with senior press and spokesperson in the General Secretariat of the Council of the European Union; 12 December 2019 in Brussels, Belgium

I:4—In-person interview with an EU diplomat and spokesperson of a member state PERMREP; 13 October 2021 in Brussels, Belgium

I:5—In-person interview with an EU ambassador; 27 March 2019 in Brussels, Belgium

I:6—Statement by EU diplomat in a Webinar on diplomatic work during the Covid-19 pandemic; 15 December 2020

I:7—In-person interview with senior staff in the General Secretariat of the EU Council; 20 October 2021 in Brussels, Belgium

I:8—In-person interview with a diplomat of a member state PERMREP; 15 October 2021 in Brussels, Belgium

I:9—Phone interview with a senior EU Commission staff member; 16 April 2020

I:10—Phone interview with an EU ambassador of a member state PERMREP; 4 May 2020

I:11—In-person interview with an ambassador of a member state PERMREP; 26 March 2019 in Brussels, Belgium

I:12—In-person interview with an ambassador of a member state PERMREP; 19 March 2019 in Brussels, Belgium

CHAPTER 7

DIGITAL DIPLOMACY AND CYBER DEFENCE

LUCAS KELLO

EMERGENCE OF A PROBLEM

AT the turn of the twenty-first century, an organized field of activity in cyber defence and diplomacy did not exist. Governments broadly did not regard cyber issues as relevant to national security or foreign policy. Cybersecurity did not feature prominently (if at all) in national rankings of security threats. No country had published a national cyber strategy paper. None fielded a dedicated command of military cyber forces. The peculiar breed of cyber ambassadors had not yet emerged within the halls of diplomacy. Although the notions of a 'digital society' and the 'e-state' had begun to take shape in some countries at the forefront of the emerging cyber revolution—such as Estonia, which held its first 'e-Cabinet' meeting in 1996 and declared Internet access a human right in 2000 (Laar 2002; Kello, 2012)—they were not closely linked to considerations of national and international security. The concept of cybersecurity, in short, was not part of the lexicon of statecraft.

This situation changed dramatically in the spring of 2007. Between April and June, Estonia suffered three waves of distributed denial of service (DDOS) attacks, which interrupted the country's financial and governmental systems by flooding webservers with torrents of data requests from 'botnets'—networks of hijacked or volunteered computers controlled mainly by private 'hacktivists' inside Russia. The attacks caused serious disruption to Estonia's financial and governmental systems owing to the country's high level of digitization (Ilves, 2009). For example, approximately 99% of banking transactions occurred online. And in March, the month before the attacks began, the country held the world's first online national election (although the DDOS attacks did not affect voting systems). The incident gave rise to an irony that endures to this day: societies that are most adept at harnessing the social and economic benefits of cyberspace are also the most exposed to threats propagating through it.

The Estonia incident was the first international cyber crisis. It marked the beginning of the first generation of cyber statecraft. The period is most notable for the elevation of cyber issues to the top of national and international security agendas. Nations began to realize the enormity of the societal challenge of cybersecurity: how to enjoy the social and economic benefits of the modern information society while limiting its new risks. From a national security perspective, defence planners began to consider complex questions: If the government and financial systems of Estonia could be disrupted by torrents of foreign code, could other technologically advanced nations that also relied heavily on Internet services experience a similar (or worse) cyberattack? What new technological vulnerabilities does the expansion of computers and networks into the financial sector and public institutions create? Who are the main cyber threat actors, what are their driving motives and offensive capacities, where do they reside, what is their relationship to foreign governments, and what defensive measures could thwart their actions? But that is not all. There also arose vexing questions of international law and diplomacy: How do the laws and norms of armed conflict apply (if at all) to the regulation of interstate cyber conduct? Can the proliferation of weaponized code be curtailed by arms control mechanisms and dual-use technology treaties (such as the Wassenaar Agreement)? What is a legitimate and proportionate response to a major international cyberattack? How can regional security organizations such as the North Atlantic Treaty Organization (NATO) and integrative bodies such as the European Union (EU) or the Association of Southeast Asian Nations (ASEAN) adapt their institutions to defeat external cyber threats?

Although the cyberattacks against Estonia did not inflict lasting damage on the country's computer systems, it launched the era of international cyber conflict. Until then, cybersecurity was chiefly the concern of esoteric computer scientists who had been dealing with malware incidents (such as the 'Morris worm' of 1988) (Eichin and Rochlis, 1989) that typically did not rise to the level of national security significance. Immediately in the spring of 2007, however, the issue became a legitimate and pressing matter for national security planners and diplomats. A similar DDOS attack against Georgia's central bank and government communication systems during the country's military invasion by Russia in August 2008 crystallized cybersecurity concerns. The attacks showed that cyberspace could be used as an adjunct of conventional war in ways that confer tactical benefits (for example, the DDOS attacks hindered Georgia's ability to procure essential war materiel) (Bumgarner and Borg, 2009). As NATO's former military commander Admiral James Stavridis put it, the attacks provided a 'glimpse of this future [of conflict]' (Miles, 2012).

The second generation of cyber statecraft was not long in coming. Cybersecurity policy questions gained further traction in the years after the Estonia crisis. In 2010, security researchers uncovered an American-Israeli computer worm—'Stuxnet'— that had infiltrated the industrial control system at the nuclear facility in Natanz, Iran to destroy approximately 1,000 of its uranium enrichment centrifuges (Falliere et al., 2011). The proven scale of harm from cyberattack thereby grew larger; it now encompassed the physical destruction of security and defence infrastructure. The arc of disruption in cyberspace also grew wider. In 2012, an Iranian wiper virus named 'Shamoon' incapacitated about 30,000 workstations at Saudi Aramco, the world's largest company at the time (Cybersecurity and Infrastructure Security Agency, 2012). Two years later, three-quarters of computers and servers at Sony Pictures Entertainment were taken down by the 'Lazarus Group', a North Korean military hacking unit (Sanger and Perlroth, 2014). These and other incidents showed that private industry lay at the frontlines of geopolitical cyber conflict. In 2016, North Korean state hackers struck again by seizing almost one-billion dollars from the Bangladeshi Central Bank (BBC, 2021).

An incident later that year marked the beginning of a third generation of problems: interference in the democratic processes of other states. On 22 July 2016, just three days before the Democratic Party Convention to elect the party's candidate in the US presidential election against Republican Party candidate Donald Trump, Russian military hackers in the GRU leaked stolen emails of the party leadership's communications (Lipton et al., 2016). The revelation via Wikileaks caused an uproar within the party at the height of the presidential election. The emails showed that the party's leadership had secretly favoured Hillary Clinton over her contender for the nomination, the firebrand Bernie Sanders. Plausibly, but improvably, the controversy arising from the leak of the hacked emails cost Clinton the election on November 3 (Kello 2017, chapter 8). Also in 2016, Russian operatives spread misinformation on social media such as Twitter and Facebook to aggravate political divisions in the United Kingdom during the acrimonious 'Brexit' referendum, an intrusion that the head of the country's foreign spy agency MI6 described as 'a fundamental threat to our [nation's] sovereignty' that 'should be a concern to all those who share democratic values...' (MacAskill, 2016).

State institutions and democratic processes thus became a central plane of offensive cyber activity. They remain in the frontlines of cyber conflict as expansionist autocracies such as Russia and China seek to exploit vulnerabilities within the open information systems of democratic nations—such as Ukraine or Taiwan—which they seek to subvert under their control.

The evolution in cyber threats, in sum, is clear. Whereas the first generation of incidents (from 2007 to 2010) involved the use of unsophisticated techniques to disrupt the financial and governmental systems of small nations, thereby elevating cybersecurity to the top of national security concerns, the second generation (from 2010 to 2016) featured more sophisticated incidents targeting vital defence infrastructure and producing systemwide computer malfunction in strategic industries. The third generation (from 2016 to the present) is marked by an expansion of cyber threats beyond traditional concerns of infrastructure protection to new concerns about the integrity of information flows within the democratic polity. Today, the statecraft of cybersecurity involves a combination of all three sets of problems. The evolution among generations of threats and problems has been decidedly negative, especially for democracies that have not traditionally experienced the threat of foreign information intrusions at a scale which can disrupt the foundations of the political system. The view from Beijing or Moscow, however, will be different. For them, the tables have turned. Long accustomed to the challenge of fending off the incursion of ideals that imperilled the autocratic regimes' existence, the governments have found new ways of inserting themselves within foreign democratic societies, whose divisions they can inflame from afar.

The empirical record in all three generations of problems reflects a singular trend: the growing convergence of geopolitics and cyberspace. Larger powers understand that in a world of nuclear plenty and tight globalization, a direct military clash among them could result in enormous economic and human loss. While interstate war still mars aspects of international relations, especially in the periphery of great power contests (think of Russia's invasion of Ukraine in 2014 and 2022), the likelihood of a millenarian war among the nuclear powers remains low. Hence they have sought new opportunities for strategic competition within realms of conflict that lie below the traditional threshold of war, thereby avoiding its potentially existential risks (Kello 2022).

This is the realm of unpeace: harmful actions that are not warlike because they do not destroy property or take human life, but which are also not peaceful because their political, social, and economic costs are too high for victim states to tolerate (Kello, 2017). Therein lies the chief implication of the cyber revolution for international affairs: the dependence of governments, the economy, and society on computer systems and networks has created new opportunities for adversaries to pursue their foreign policy goals short of war. At the same time, intensifying geopolitical competition beyond cyberspace provides growing motives for unpeaceful activity within it. Here, the main goal is not to seize geographic territory (how could intangible zeros and ones do that?) or even to coerce state behaviour. Rather, the primary goal is to weaken the internal political bases of adversaries' foreign and security policy, thereby diminishing its assertiveness and effectiveness. The defining precept of technological unpeace, then, is that nations can seize strategic gains while avoiding the potentially high retaliatory costs of attempts at conquest or coercion. An important theoretical point flows from this observation: the traditional lens of war and conquest through which much of security studies scholarship evaluates cyber issues is not relevant because it misses the essence of the cyber revolution in strategic affairs. In other words, the traditional perspective gives the right answers but poses the wrong questions (Kello 2022, chapter 10).

Consider the war between Russia and Ukraine. The war's tragedies reveal the enormous economic and human costs of military conflict involving large powers such as Russia. Although the risk of an accidental or unwanted war between Russia and NATO is always present, both sides have sought to reduce it. Leaders on both sides have warned about the perils of nuclear destruction should a direct war between them break out—a 'World War 3', in the words of US President Joe Biden (Tsvetkova, 2022; Blake, 2022).

Cyberspace offers attractive options of strategic competition short of an epochal war. Cyber activity has not altered the reality of fighting on the ground in the planes and cities of Ukraine. But that (and other military battlefields) is not the right place to seek out its strategic implications. When missiles are raining down on large urban centres and when rural populations have suffered deprivation and mass atrocities, the salience of non-violent cyber activity—however disruptive—seems comparatively low. Instead, one should search for cyber effects elsewhere, in the plane of contention among the large rivals who are reluctant to lock horns directly on the battlefield and who must therefore seek to affect interests elsewhere. Here, the possibilities begin to appear. Hackers in Moscow could seek to retaliate for Western economic and financial sanctions by disrupting Western cyberspace: for example, by interrupting stock trading at the NASDAQ or the London Stock Exchange (thereby seeking to mirror the sanctions' effects on the Moscow Exchange (MOEX) index, which at one point in the conflict lost almost 50% of its value). Or else they could seek to corrupt the data servers of financial institutions that prohibit the transfer of hard currency into the Russian banking system (thus responding to the ejection of major Russian banks from the SWIFT interbank payment system). For their part, Western operators could seek to punish Russia for its military adventure by disrupting Russian cyberspace—for instance, by taking down the companies and financial institutions that have found ways to evade Western sanctions. Past cyber incidents show that the effects of such operations could quickly cascade beyond the immediate war scenario. In 2017, for example, the wiper virus 'NotPetya' devastated Ukrainian businesses and produced cascading effects across multiple countries—including the disruption of the operations of Maersk, a giant Danish company that handled 20% of global shipping volume (Turner, 2017).

For their part, Western and Western-aligned nations that have punished Russia economically could seek to impose further costs on it via cyberspace—especially if the economic sanctions toolbox has been largely used up (in March 2022, Russia became the world's most heavily sanctioned country) (Wadhams, 2022; Kello and Kaminska, 2022). Targets for disruptive cyber activity would likely exclude military command and control systems because, in the midst of war in Ukraine, such attacks could be construed as acts of war. More likely are cyberattacks against Russian banks and companies (e.g. in the oil and gas industry) that have enabled the Kremlin to circumvent sanctions and acquire hard currency in foreign markets. Or else NATO allies could work together to carry out information operations within Russia seeking to contravene the Kremlin's tightly controlled and mainly false narrative about Russian setbacks in the Ukraine battlefield or about the commission of war crimes and other atrocities by invading Russian troops. Although Russian authorities operate a tight Internet surveillance regime, its censorship apparatus is not yet as strict as China's. And while the country has banned Western social media companies such as Facebook and Twitter, alternative Russian services such as vKontakte and OdnoKlassniki remain accessible to foreign operatives seeking to counter the Kremlin's propaganda efforts (Soldatov and Borogan, 2015).

In sum, Russia's aggressive resurgence in Europe and China's growing assertiveness in Asia-Pacific and beyond have sparked geopolitical flashpoints. Consequently, not just the opportunities but also the political motives for unpeaceful cyber activity are increasing. Cyber conflict will remain a core preoccupation of national security planning and a central phenomenon in the world of diplomacy.

Theoretically and conceptually, the cyber revolution presents international relations specialists and diplomats with vexing questions of strategy and law. Perhaps the foremost challenge, one that this chapter addresses, is how to fit offensive activity whose effects fall short of war but which nevertheless potentially harm national and economic security within the existing legal and normative framework of international affairs.

Much like Western security doctrine, the framework prioritizes the use of force and armed attack—which entail significant destruction of physical property and human death—and sovereignty rights—which emphasize the protection of the nation's geography against foreign incursion. In other words, the legal system prioritizes the physical world over the virtual world; consequently, it offers few clear benchmarks to guide state responses to acts of technological unpeace—hence why they go largely unpunished (more on this problem below) (Kello, 2021 and 2022). Although world leaders routinely warn about the gravity of major hacking incidents such as the DNC email leak or the disruption of energy supplies in the US East Coast by ransomware in 2021, and while leaders commonly promise to punish such activities, they repeatedly fail to do so sternly enough to deter further ordeals. As former US Ambassador to Russia Michael McFaul stated about the 2016 incident: 'The punishment'—which involved the expulsion of Russian diplomats as well as targeted financial sanctions and criminal indictments— 'did not fit the crime. Russia violated our sovereignty, meddling in one of our most sacred acts as a democracy—electing our president. The Kremlin should have paid a much higher price for that attack' (Miller et al., 2017).

In other words, whereas Western security doctrine and the legal system are essentially binary, emphasizing the conditions of war and peace, or the violation and integrity of national territory, much of modern interstate rivalry is in fact *spectral*. It encompasses the widening space of technological unpeace within which large powers can pursue their strategic goals without firing a single gun, thereby avoiding the serious repercussions and tragedies of war. For national security planners wedded to binary notions of war and peace, the growing spectrum of technological unpeace raises unresolved questions about thresholds of response—when and how to retaliate for activity that is harmful to core interests but not recognizably punishable under international law. For diplomats and lawyers seeking international consensus on new rules and norms to restrain unpeaceful state behaviour, the existing rulebook offers few clear guidelines; nations that seek to draw them up based on liberal political values that the challenger states reject will not go far in the enterprise of global norm construction.

CLASHING NATIONAL PERSPECTIVES

Among the greatest obstacles to international agreement on cyber issues is the fundamental divergence that exists between large nations on the very meaning and priorities of cybersecurity. Western and other democratic nations have traditionally prioritized the protection of the functionality of the vital computer systems that run transportation systems, government communications networks, stock trading platforms, and so forth. They have also defended the original model of a global open Internet that operates largely beyond governmental control. By contrast, authoritarian nations such as China and Russia have instead prioritized 'information security', which entails controlling the domestic flow of information via the Internet, especially politically sensitive views such as democratic beliefs that challenge the ruling elite. These regimes operate comprehensive systems of Internet surveillance and censorship (the latter requires the former), which in Russia centres on the 'SORM' system for the interception of online communications and in China is dubbed 'The Great Firewall'.

This disparity of conception and priorities reflects a fundamental divergence in political values between competing Internet governance models. The Western democratic model prioritizes machine functionality and the nearly unfettered access to the Internet. The authoritarian model championed by China and Russia emphasizes the necessity to surveil and control digital information tightly—even at the cost of disrupting machines and networks: for example, the Russian government's DDOS attacks against the web servers of the election monitoring group Golos during the Russian legislative elections in 2011. The open model envisaged by early Internet pioneers such as Vint Cerf and embraced by democratic nations seeks to preserve nearly unlimited information exchange, especially against government interception (domestic or foreign). The closed model, involving the construction of domestic authoritarian 'intranets', imposes stringent information controls, which the regimes sometimes work together to develop (e.g. within the framework of the Shanghai Cooperation Organization, which has produced intergovernmental agreements on information security practice) (People's Daily, 2010) or which Russia and China export to authoritarian regimes abroad (e.g. Zimbabwe) (Weber, 2019). Political activists and scholars have long warned about the 'splintering' of the global Internet as the closed model of information security took hold in nations that had once adopted unfettered networks (Malcomson, 2016). The so-called Splinternet has become a firm reality; it is a reality of domestic and international life that the champions of openness can do little to defend their model within nations whose governments are bent on building walls where information once flowed freely. Politically and technically, splintering the Internet is generally easier than unblocking it.

In sum, when Western nations speak of cybersecurity, they often refer to vital infrastructure protection; when China and Russia discuss it, they ordinarily reference domestic information controls. True, closed regimes also worry about securing their infrastructure against foreign attack. But that is not their main concern; rather, the autocrats have worried far more about their ability to control the space of political and social ideas within their own borders, as reflected in the statements of the Shanghai Cooperation Organization that routinely emphasize information security and propose common measures to achieve it (Shanghai Cooperation Organization, 2009). Although such documents often identify as a central goal of information security the stability of the states system, what they really mean is the preservation of their own centralized political systems within a liberal international order that they increasingly challenge.

Let us return to the question of legal interpretation of interstate cyber conflict. It is important to recognize where there is international consensus and where there is enduring discord. Almost all nations agree that international law—in particular the United Nations Charter principles and the laws of armed conflict—applies to cyberspace. This consensus was formalized in a landmark agreement during the fifth round of the UN Group of Governmental Experts in 2015 (United Nations General Assembly, 2015). But nations disagree on when and how the international legal rulebook applies, with important implications for security relationships and diplomacy.

Western nations have put law and norms at the centre of international efforts to reduce the number and intensity of offensive cyber activity. For example, building a 'global consensus' around norms of interstate conduct is a key 'pillar' of the United States' international strategy for cyberspace (US Office of the Coordinator for Cyber Issues, 2009). The effort was a core responsibility of Christopher Painter, the country's first US Coordinator for Cyber Issues who described his remit as one of creating 'a new area of foreign policy' (Painter, n.d.). The United Kingdom has supported this effort. Its national cyber strategy stresses the objective of assembling a 'global alliance' to advance the application of international laws and norms of restraint in cyberspace (UK Government, 2016). EU officials have toed a similar line. In the eyes of the European Commission, the EU's new Cybersecurity Strategy seeks to 'step up leadership on international norms and standards in cyberspace, and to strengthen cooperation with partners around the world to promote a global, open, stable and secure cyberspace, grounded in the rule of law, human rights, fundamental freedoms and democratic values' (European Commission, 2020). The NATO alliance, for its part, declared: 'We all stand to benefit from a rules-based, predictable, open, free, and secure cyberspace' (NATO, 2020). This stance, too, is not new. Concluding the Warsaw Summit in July 2016, the alliance's heads of state issued a communiqué emphasizing their commitment to build 'international norms of responsible state behaviour and confidence-building measures regarding cyberspace' (NATO, 2016). And it lives strong despite the incessant transgression of norms. Following Iranian agents' intrusion into Albania's governmental systems in the summer of 2022, NATO heads 'called on all states to respect their international commitments to upholding a norms-based approach to cyberspace' (NATO, 2022).

This normative approach is based on an expansive interpretation of the law's applicability. As we saw, the law of armed conflict (LOAC) traditionally privileges the regulation of armed attacks and uses of force—which involve significant destruction of physical property and loss of life—as well as violations of states' physical territory. It does not customarily regulate interstate rivalry below those thresholds. Yet no single cyberattack has cleanly met the criteria established by LOAC. The Stuxnet incident perhaps comes closest, because it featured physical destruction of infrastructure—but even the Iranian authorities publicly played down the significance of the effects (Clayton, 2010).

Regardless, the Western approach of 'cyber legalism' (Kello, 2021) presumes that some forms of cyber activity, such as Russia's disruption of public infrastructure or its information campaigns during foreign elections, violate the boundaries of acceptable state conduct. To illustrate, President Barack Obama decried Russia's hack-and-leak operation during the 2016 presidential election as a breach of 'established international norms of behaviour' (Obama, 2016), an interpretation of law and norms that survived the vicissitudes of Donald Trump's foreign policy and which endures under Joe Biden (Fidler, 2021). Referring to problems of technological connectivity, in March 2021 the White House affirmed the United States' 'leadership role in multilateral organizations' and the importance 'that these institutions continue to reflect the universal values, aspirations, and norms that have underpinned the UN system since its founding 75 years ago, rather than an authoritarian agenda' (The White House, 2021). Similarly, NATO's Secretary General Jens Stoltenberg has condemned Russia's 'blatant attempts to undermine international law and institutions' through its foreign cyber meddling (Stoltenberg, 2018). This expansive interpretation of the law might find a basis in a 1996 ruling of the International Court of Justice stating that the UN Charter principles 'apply to any use of force, regardless of the weapons employed' (Bekker, 1996), although it would imply a relaxation in the conventional understanding of a use of force so that it encompasses actions that harm national security without causing physical destruction or death.

Russia and China agree that the international legal framework applies but for the opposite reason: it does not clearly constrain harmful activity that lies below the threshold of war or which does not directly violate states' physical territory. Whereas Western officials have described unpeaceful behaviour such as Russia's social media operations during the Brexit referendum as threat to sovereignty (MacAskill, 2016), the aadversaries apply a narrower interpretation of sovereignty rights that covers territorial violations of the national soil—that is, material interventions in other nations' domestic affairs. According to some legal scholars, it is not clear that positivist international law supports a more expansive interpretation of the rule of non-intervention (Moynihan, 2019; Goldsmith and Loomis, 2021; Hollis, 2021; Fischerkeller, 2021; Tsagourias and Buchan, 2021).

Taking Stock: Successes and Failures of Cyber Diplomacy

On this backdrop of interstate contention, it is important to distinguish between problems of Internet governance and problems of cyber governance. The two sets of issues are related but also separate. They have experienced different degrees of success and failure in international cooperation.

Internet governance concerns the regulation of the world's sprawling computer networks, in particular flows of information across them. It involves many of the technical aspects of cyberspace itself—the servers, routers, and protocols that govern information exchanges (DeNardis, 2009; DeNardis and Raymond, 2013). It has been a primary concern of states within intergovernmental forums such as the International Telecommunication Union (ITU), which helps to set Internet standards. Despite the deepening clash between open and closed models, important advances in cooperation have occurred in this technical realm. Among them, for instance, is the transition to IPv6. All computers on the Internet must be assigned an identification that locates them within the global network—a kind of virtual address comprising a series of digits. The original addressing system, IPv4, which was established in the early 1980s when the Internet comprised only a few tens of thousands of machines, suffered the in-built limitation that it could issue a maximum of four billion addresses—far less than the demand of rapidly multiplying computer devices. The transition to the new addressing system, IPv6, which could encompass an extremely large number of devices—essentially a brain transplant of the Internet—required extensive technical testing and coordination among the world's authorities. Forums such as the ITU, which ran training programmes on the IP migration, were essential in drumming up support for the new protocol's adoption among governments and in assisting with the technical aspects of the transition, including the challenge of ensuring IPv4 and IPv6 interoperability during the migration (International Telecommunication Union, n.d.). As a result of the broadly seamless migration between protocols, vast amounts of information continue to flow freely even between machines in the open Internet and those in the authoritarian intranets, except where the latter are subject to state checks.

Cyber governance is different and much thornier. It involves the regulation of harmful activity in cyberspace among nations—DDOS attacks (e.g. against Estonian and Georgian computer systems), physical infrastructure destruction (e.g. the Stuxnet operation), foreign information operations and hack-and-leak campaigns (e.g. the 2016 DNC hack), cyber espionage (e.g. China's 'Operation Aurora' targeting Chinese dissidents' Gmail accounts), and so on. While international discussions of Internet governance have often focused on the technical dimensions of cyberspace, issues of cyber governance are more complex because they involve the broader cyber domain—a plane of action that includes not just machines but also the humans and institutions that operate or seek to disrupt them (Kello, 2017). More than just a technical realm, it is a social and political environment.

In the cyber domain, as we saw, vast differences of opinion, interests, and standards of acceptable conduct exist among states. Nations such as the United States and the United Kingdom that advocate for a law and norms oriented approach to conflict prevention seek to curtail unpeaceful activity that international law and custom do not normally prohibit. Nations such as Russia and China that apply a narrower interpretation of the law find in the international rulebook no clear prohibitions against their offensive cyber manoeuvres below the threshold of a use of force and territorial infringements of state sovereignty.

Conceptually, it is important to distinguish three broad realms of activity within the legal and normative framework. At one end of the spectrum is cyberwar: attacks whose destructive and fatal effects meet the traditional criteria of armed attack under international law. Although scholars have debated whether Stuxnet represented a use of force—a vaguer notion than armed attack but which entails physical destruction—no true act of cyberwar has occurred so far. Plausible scenarios are not hard to find and include the disruption of rail networks derailing passenger trains or the corruption of air traffic control data causing aviation accidents. Because such incidents would clearly meet the legal benchmark of war, they would be the easiest to fit within the law of armed conflict—hence why they have not occurred. Cyberwar is an area of activity where the lines of prohibited conduct are drawn the reddest (e.g. in UN Charter Article 51 on 'self-defense' or in NATO's Article 5 on 'collective defense') and where, therefore, the mechanism of deterrence by punishment has worked best.

At the other end of the spectrum is the category of cyber peace. This does not entail the total absence of rivalry; for example, international law and diplomacy says almost nothing about espionage, which continues unabated in operations such as the 'SolarWinds' hack of December 2020 that affected computers and data at dozens of US government agencies and companies. The category of cyber peace also includes low-level crimes (e.g. child pornography or credit card fraud) that are penalized within the domestic legal code but which do not rise to the level of national security significance.

The third and most troublesome governance category is the technological realm of unpeace. Major cyber incidents fall within this box: North Korea's hack in 2014 against Sony Pictures Entertainment that destroyed about three-quarters of the company's computers and servers, North Korea's theft in 2016 of $900m (most of which was recovered) from the Bangladeshi Central Bank, Russian criminals' attack in 2021 on the Colonial pipeline network that disrupted approximately half of fuel supplies to the US East Coast, and so on. While the interpretive task of defining the upper boundary of unpeace and war is typically not difficult, because the benchmark of war is so stark, the lower boundary separating unpeace from peace is harder to define because no violence or death occurs. The key interpretive question is at what point do criminal actions rise to the level of national security significance even if they do not pass the use of force threshold? Among the thorniest conundrum is figuring out how to interpret the law in instances where governments team up with criminal and other private elements to carry out offensive actions abroad, a scenario that complicates the attributional picture and which therefore affords the complicit authorities grounds for plausible deniability. This is a question that governments must answer for themselves and about which, as we saw, they will continue to disagree, although international law provides at least a basis for consensus in the principle of 'state responsibility', which stipulates that governments are responsible for harmful activity emanating from within their borders even if they are not involved in it (Banks, 2021).

Overall, there is little common ground on which to build an international treaty or tighter norms of behaviour regulating interstate cyber conduct. The record of diplomatic achievements reflects this reality. So far, only a single cyber governance treaty exists, the Council of Europe's 2004 Cybercrime Convention (Council of Europe, 2004). As the label implies, the treaty regulates low-intensity activity that states can agree upon— credit card fraud or the dissemination of child pornography, for example. Tellingly, the treaty framework omits strategic level activity whose consequences impinge on national and economic security and about which large states diverge fundamentally. Despite repeated attempts to draw up a wider agreement on norms of responsible state conduct within the UN Group of Governmental Experts (UNGGE) and the Open-Ended Working Group (OEWG)—an intergovernmental forum established by the UN General Assembly in 2019 in which all member states can participate—little progress has been made beyond the by now familiar and vague affirmation that international law applies to cyberspace. Both of these forums have manifested the usual interpretive battle lines among large states. One group of states seeks to advance the principles and values of a free Internet while striving to constrain unpeaceful activity. Another group advocates for the imposition of sovereign controls upon the domestic Internet while refusing to curtail intrusive and disruptive activity abroad. Until the participating nations narrow down the gulf of legal interpretation that separates them, and unless their interests align more closely in the direction of a stabler and more peaceful cyberspace, the prospects of a meaningful treaty in cyber governance will remain dim. Bold attempts at normative breakthrough have also emerged outside conventional diplomatic channels, such as the 'Digital Geneva Convention' championed by Microsoft (Fairbank, 2019). These efforts, too, have not gone far, because they mirror the basic values and borrow the assumptions that underpin cyber legalism. Whereas all nations are bound by the Geneva Convention (which some nations nevertheless infringe), no nation is bound by Microsoft's digital variant of it.

In the absence of a global consensus, the greatest strides in cyber defence diplomacy have occurred within regional settings. The record of NATO stands out. NATO is the most powerful alliance in military history. Yet it, too, suffers the limitations of conventional security thinking that prioritizes the benchmark of war over lesser forms of conflict. Written in 1949 when the spectre of a Soviet invasion of Western Europe loomed large, the alliance treaty's most important clause on collective defence states: 'an armed attack against one or more of [the member states] in Europe or North America shall be considered an attack against them all'. Legally, then, traditional war is the only clear basis upon which allies can invoke the collective defence obligation.

Nevertheless, NATO has achieved notable outcomes in the organization of cyber defence short of the ultimate scenario of a cyberwar. The alliance began to draft its first cyber defence policy in the aftermath of the attacks that hit systems in Estonia, a NATO member state. The ensuing efforts were mostly defensive, as pledged at the Bucharest Summit in 2008, which culminated in the creation of the Cyber Defense Management Authority (CDMA)—which seeks to centralize operational capacities in a crisis—in Brussels and the Cooperative Cyber Defense Centre of Excellence (CCD-COE)—a think tank that seeks to develop new doctrinal understandings—in Tallinn. The alliance reached its most substantial milestone at the Warsaw Summit in 2016, when it formally designated cyberspace as an operational domain. The alliance strengthened the tone of collective defence at the Brussels summit in 2021, where leaders pledged: 'If necessary, we will impose costs on those who harm us. Our response need not be restricted to the cyber domain' (NATO, 2021). Despite the clear allusion to stern punishment, the pledge's credibility was marred by the usual ambiguity about the precise thresholds of response. Risk-taking adversaries would not struggle to conceive scenarios of a major cyberattack that slipped under the bar of Article 5.

These practical and declaratory steps have not appreciably reduced the number or intensity of foreign cyber actions targeting member states—if anything, the scale of threats has increased. But they have gone further than any other international institution in standardizing good practices of cyber defence and coordinating international responses to a crisis than any other intergovernmental forum.

Emerging Challenges

The landscape of cyber defence diplomacy constantly shifts because the underlying technology and its uses in society and government continuously evolve. On the technological front, new threats are appearing in the form of 'deepfakes', which synthetically alter media content to manipulate human perceptions and behaviour, and algorithmically enhanced social bots, which amplify political and social divisions by spreading disinformation within democratic polities (Assenmacher et al., 2020). Perhaps even more vexing are the legal and normative implications of the integration of artificial intelligence into weapons systems. Recall the challenges that already beguile legal minds and norm entrepreneurs—the problem of attributing the identity and origin of an attacker, the conundrum of figuring out how to respond to information threats that do not touch material assets but undermine the democratic process, the question of how to prevent non-violent but harmful activity. Artificial intelligence compounds them and presents new challenges: Can computer code acquire the characteristics of a moral agent in international conflict scenarios? What is the degree of culpability of the humans who design them or the people who activate them? Are states responsible for the unpeaceful (or even warlike) actions of autonomous agents that have adapted beyond the ability of their designers to control or even know?

Perhaps the most fundamental technological change on the horizon concerns quantum computing. Making use of the oddities of quantum physics, a universal quantum computer entails the use of 'qubits', information stored as photons that can be superimposed into more than one state at once—a phenomenon that Albert Einstein famously described as 'spooky action at a distance'. Computationally, this means that digital information would no longer have be stored as either 0's or 1's—it could be both at one and the same time or alternate between them. This development would represent a momentous breakthrough in processing power; it would enable quantum computers to smash even the most advanced 'asymmetric' cryptographic standards that presently secure all aspects of digital life—email exchanges, online banking transactions, online voting, digital identification, etc. A universal quantum computer has not yet been invented. Commercial designations of existing 'quantum' computers such as Google's 'Sycamore' machine mischaracterize their capacity because they cannot be applied beyond specific task sets (thus, they are not universal computers). But the United States, Britain, Russia, China, and the private sector are all locked in a race to be the first to develop one (Zhanna, 2022). The nation or company that wins this race will likely be in a position of 'quantum supremacy', enabling it to deploy enormous hacking and other computational abilities. When it arises in the next decade or more, this situation will only amplify concerns about cyber espionage and aggravate the archaic legal system's gaps in this area.

There is also a growing nexus between cybersecurity and space systems. The phenomenon was demonstrated during the Russia–Ukraine war, when Russian state hackers sought to hack into and jam Elon Musk's 'Starlink' satellite-based Internet service, which the Ukrainian military had been using to locate and attack Russian forces within its territory. Although the Russian hackers did not succeed in disabling Musk's satellite constellation, the incident underscores the growing importance of space as an operational realm for cyber activity. And not just in the area of disruption but also in espionage. Some countries have begun to deploy advanced Earth observation (EO) technology—for example, China's 'Gaofen 12' satellites—that will significantly increase their ability to surveil, in real time and with high precision, populations and military assets on the ground. This development will intensify global debates about the appropriateness of privacy breaches via cyberspace and the risks of cyber espionage. That countries such as China with a history of rampant data intrusions and digital surveillance are at the forefront of EO technology is a cause for concern, especially in democratic societies that will henceforward have to worry about sharper prying eyes from the sky and whose openness foreign actors could exploit to disrupt democratic processes.

But there is more. On the human and institutional plane, nontraditional actors—especially large technology companies such as Facebook, Twitter, and Google—are acquiring greater agency and influence in national security provision and international affairs. The protection of the integrity of political discourse against foreign information campaigns, for example, relies heavily on the monitoring and regulation of social media content in platforms such as Twitter. The private companies that perform these vital functions are not regular participants in intergovernmental forums. Although some of them partake in discussions of the UNGGE and OEWG, for instance, it is the governments that drive the agenda and determine the consensus (or dissensus) over laws and norms. In the end, future advances in cyber diplomacy call forth a new format of diplomatic agency—one that transcends the statist mould of conventional statecraft.

Suggested Readings

DeNardis, Laura, and Mark Raymond. "Thinking Clearly About Multistakeholder Internet Governance." *GigaNet: Global Internet Governance Academic Network, Annual Symposium,* 2013. https://doi.org/10.2139/ssrn.2354377.

Fairbank, Nancy Ayer. "The State of Microsoft?: The Role of Corporations in International Norm Creation." *Journal of Cyber Policy,* Vol. 4, Issue 3 (2019), pp. 380–443.

Hollis, Duncan. "A Brief Primer on International Law and Cyberspace." Carnegie Endowment for International Peace. 14 June 2021. https://carnegieendowment.org/2021/06/14/brief-primer-on-international-law-and-cyberspace-pub-84763

Kello, Lucas. "Cyber Legalism: Why It Fails and What to Do about It." *Journal of Cybersecurity,* Vol. 7, Issue 1 (1 January 2021), pp. 1–15. https://doi.org/10.1093/cybsec/tyab014.

Nye, Joseph S. Jr. "The Regime Complex for Managing Global Cyber Activities." Global Commission on Internet Governance, May 2014.

BIBLIOGRAPHY

Assenmacher, Dennis, Lena Clever, and Lena Frischlich. "Demystifying Social Bots: On the Intelligence of Automated Social Media Actors." *Social Media + Society*, Vol. 6, Issue 3 (2020).

Banks, William. "Cyber Attribution and State Responsibility." *International Law Studies*, Vol. 97 (2021), pp. 1039–1072.

BBC News. "The Lazarus Heist: How North Korea almost Pulled Off a Billion-Dollar Hack." 21 June 2021. https://www.bbc.com/news/stories-57520169.

Bekker, Pieter H. F. "Advisory Opinions of the World Court on the Legality of Nuclear Weapons." *ASIL Insights*, Vol. 1, Issue 5 (1996).

Blake, Aaron. "Why Biden and the White House Keep Talking about World War III." *Washington Post*, 17 March 2022. https://www.washingtonpost.com/politics/2022/03/17/why-biden-white-house-keep-talking-about-world-war-iii/.

Bumgarner, John, and Scott Borg. "Overview by the US-CCU of the Cyber Campaign against Georgia in August 2008." US Cyber Consequences Unit, August 2009.

Clayton, Mark. "Stuxnet: Ahmadinejad Admits Cyberweapon Hit Iran Nuclear Program." *Christian Science Monitor*, 30 November 2010. https://www.csmonitor.com/USA/2010/1130/Stuxnet-Ahmadinejad-admits-cyberweapon-hit-Iran-nuclear-program.

Council of Europe. "Convention on Cybercrime." European Treaty Series - No. 185, 1 July 2004.

Cybersecurity and Infrastructure Security Agency. "ICS Joint Security Awareness Report (JSAR-12-241-01B): Shamoon/DistTrack Malware (Update B)." 16 October 2012.

Eichin, Mark W. and Jon A. Rochlis. "With Microscope and Tweezers: An Analysis of the Internet Virus of November 1988." *1989 IEEE Symposium on Research in Security and Privacy*, 1989, pp. 326–345.

European Commission. "New EU Cybersecurity Strategy and New Rules to Make Physical and Digital Critical Entities More Resilient." 16 December 2020, https://ec.europa.eu/commission/presscorner/detail/en/IP_20_2391.

DeNardis, Laura. *Protocol Politics*. MIT Press, 2009.

DeNardis, Laura, and Mark Raymond. "Thinking Clearly About Multistakeholder Internet Governance." *GigaNet: Global Internet Governance Academic Network, Annual Symposium*, 2013. https://doi.org/10.2139/ssrn.2354377.

Fairbank, Nancy Ayer. "The State of Microsoft?: The Role of Corporations in International Norm Creation." *Journal of Cyber Policy*, Vol. 4, Issue 3 (2019), pp. 380–403.

Falliere, Nicholas, Liam O. Murchu, and Eric Chien. "W32.Stuxnet Dossier," ver. 1.4. Symantec, February 2011.

Fidler, David P. "America's Place in Cyberspace: The Biden Administration's Cyber Strategy Takes Shape," Council on Foreign Relations blog. 11 March 2021. https://www.cfr.org/blog/americas-place-cyberspace-biden-administrations-cyber-strategy-takes-shape.

Fischerkeller, Michael P. "Current International Law Is Not an Adequate Regime for Cyberspace," *Lawfare* blog. 22 April 2021. https://www.lawfaremedia.org/article/current-international-law-not-adequate-regime-cyberspace.

Goldsmith, Jack L., and Alex Loomis. "'Defend Forward' and Sovereignty." *Lawfare* blog. 30 April 2021. https://www.lawfareblog.com/defend-forward-and-sovereignty.

Hollis, Duncan. "A Brief Primer on International Law and Cyberspace." Carnegie Endowment for International Peace. 14 June 2021. https://carnegieendowment.org/2021/06/14/brief-primer-on-international-law-and-cyberspace-pub-84763.

Ilves, Toomas H. "Address Given at the European Union Ministerial Conference on Critical Infrastructure Protection, Tallinn, Estonia." 27 April 2009.

International Telecommunication Union. "Welcome to This IPv6 Website," n.d. https://www.itu.int:443/en/ITU-T/ipv6/Pages/default.aspx.

Kello, Lucas. "The Advantages of Latitude: Estonia's Post-Communist Success Story," in David Bosold, Petr Drulák, and Nik Hynek, eds., *Democratization and Security in Central and Eastern Europe and the Post-Soviet States*. Nomos, 2012, pp. 23–53.

Kello, Lucas. "Cyber Security: Gridlock and Innovation," in Thomas Hale and David Held, eds., *Beyond Gridlock*. Polity, 2017, pp. 205–228.

Kello, Lucas. *The Virtual Weapon and International Order*. Yale University Press, 2017.

Kello, Lucas. "Cyber Legalism: Why It Fails and What to Do about It." *Journal of Cybersecurity*, Vol. 7, Issue 1 (1 January 2021), pp. 1–15. https://doi.org/10.1093/cybsec/tyab014.

Kello, Lucas. *Striking Back: The End of Peace in Cyberspace and How to Restore It*. Yale University Press, 2022.

Kello, Lucas and Monica Kaminska. "Cyberspace and War in Ukraine: Prepare for Worse," *Lawfare* blog. 14 April 2022. https://www.lawfaremedia.org/article/cyberspace-and-war-ukraine-prepare-worse.

Laar, Mart. *Estonia: Little Country That Could*. Centre for Research into Post-Communist Economies, 2002.

Lipton, Eric, David E. Sanger, and Scott Shane. "The Perfect Weapon: How Russian Cyberpower Invaded the U.S." *The New York Times*, 13 December 2016.

MacAskill, Ewen. "Hostile States Pose 'Fundamental Threat' to Europe, Says MI6 Chief." *The Guardian*, 8 December 2016. https://www.theguardian.com/uk-news/2016/dec/08/hostile-states-pose-fundamental-threat-to-europe-says-mi6-chief.

Malcomson, Scott. *Splinternet: How Geopolitics and Commerce Are Fragmenting the World Wide Web*. OR Books, 2016.

Miles, Donna. "U.S. European Command, NATO Boost Cyber Defenses." *American Forces Press Service*, US Department of Defense, 18 May 2012.

Miller, Greg, Ellen Nakashima, and Adam Entous. "Obama's Secret Struggle to Punish Russia for Putin's Election Assault." *Washington Post*, 23 June 2017. https://www.washingtonpost.com/graphics/2017/world/national-security/obama-putin-election-hacking/.

Moynihan, Harriet. "The Application of International Law to Cyberspace: Sovereignty and Non-intervention." *Just Security*. 13 December 2019. https://www.justsecurity.org/67723/the-application-of-international-law-to-cyberspace-sovereignty-and-non-intervention.

NATO. "Warsaw Summit Communiqué Issued by the Heads of State and Government Participating in the Meeting of the North Atlantic Council in Warsaw 8-9 July 2016." 9 July 2016.

NATO. "Statement by the North Atlantic Council Concerning Malicious Cyber Activities." 3 June 2020. http://www.nato.int/cps/en/natohq/official_texts_176136.htm.

NATO. "Brussels Summit Communiqué Issued by the Heads of State and Government Participating in the Meeting of the North Atlantic Council in Brussels 14 June 2021." 14 June 2021.

NATO. "NATO Reaffirms Support for Albania Following Cyber Attacks." 21 September 2022.

Obama, Barack H. "Statement by the President on Actions in Response to Russian Malicious Cyber Activity and Harassment." The White House, 29 December 2016. https://obamawhitehouse.archives.gov/the-press-office/2016/12/29/statement-president-actions-response-russian-malicious-cyber-activity.

Painter, Christopher. "Christopher Painter." Stanford University, n.d. https://cisac.fsi.stanford.edu/people/christopher-painter.

People's Daily Online. "SCO Exercises Show Resolve to Fight Three Evil Forces: Official," 10 September 2010. http://en.people.cn/90001/90777/90851/7136949.html.

Sanger, David E. Sanger and Nicole Perlroth. "U.S. Said to Find North Korea Ordered Cyberattack on Sony." The New York Times, 17 December 2014.

Shanghai Cooperation Organization. "Agreement on Cooperation in Ensuring International Information Security between the Member States of the Shanghai Cooperation Organization (SCO)." 16 June 2009.

Soldatov, Andrei and Irina Borogan. The Red Web: The Struggle Between Russia's Digital Dictators and the New Online Revolutionaries. PublicAffairs, 2015.

Stoltenberg, Jens. "Statement by NATO Secretary General Jens Stoltenberg on Russian Cyber Attacks." NATO, 4 October 2018. http://www.nato.int/cps/en/natohq/news_158911.htm.

Tsagourias, Nicholas and Russel Buchan, eds. Research Handbook on International Law and Cyberspace. Edward Elgar, 2021.

Tsvetkova, Maria. "Putin Puts Nuclear Deterrent on Alert; West Squeezes Russian Economy." Reuters, 28 February 2022. https://www.reuters.com/world/india/war-with-ukraine-putin-puts-nuclear-deterrence-forces-alert-2022-02-27/.

Turner, Giles. "New Cyberattack Goes Global, Hits WPP, Rosneft, Maersk." Bloomberg, 27 June 2017. https://www.bloomberg.com/news/articles/2017-06-27/ukraine-russia-report-ransomware-computer-virus-attacks?utm_source=website&utm_medium=share&utm_campaign=copy&leadSource=uverify%20wall

UK Government. "National Cyber Security Strategy 2016-2021." 2016.

United Nations General Assembly. "Report of the Group of Governmental Experts on Developments in the Field of Information and Telecommunications in the Context of International Security (A/70/174)." 22 July 2015.

US Office of the Coordinator for Cyber Issues. "Pillars of The International Strategy for Cyberspace." 2009. https://2009-2017.state.gov/s/cyberissues/strategy/index.htm.

Wadham, Nick. "Russia Is Now the World's Most-Sanctioned Nation, Surging Past Iran, North Korea." Bloomberg, 7 March 2022. https://www.bloomberg.com/news/articles/2022-03-07/russia-surges-past-iran-to-become-world-s-most-sanctioned-nation.

Weber, Valentin. The Worldwide Web of Chinese and Russian Information Controls. Oxford University Centre for Technology and Global Affairs, 2019.

White House. "International National Security Strategic Guidance." March 2021.

Zhanna, Malekos Smith. "Make Haste Slowly for Quantum." Centre for Strategic and International Studies, 11 February 2022. https://www.csis.org/analysis/make-haste-slowly-quantum.

CHAPTER 8

DIGITAL NUCLEAR DIPLOMACY

RHYS CRILLEY

INTRODUCTION

ON 28 August 2022, six months into Russia's brutal invasion of Ukraine, the Ukrainian Ministry of Defence tweeted their thanks to an unusual supporter. 'We usually express gratitude to our international partners for the security assistance. But today we want to give a shout-out to a unique entity' they said, announcing their thanks to the 'North Atlantic Fellas Organization #NAFO'. The tweet then read 'Thanks for your fierce fight against Kremlin's propaganda & trolls. We salute you, fellas!' This was accompanied by a photoshopped picture of a dog (a Shiba Inu) wearing a Ukrainian military uniform as missiles launched in the background. Whilst Putin was waging an absurdly horrific war on Ukraine, Ukraine was ridiculing his actions with absurdly humorous memes. As Putin was making threats to use nuclear weapons against anyone who opposed his invasion, the internet was responding with pictures of dogs riding missiles and 'bonking' Putin.

The rise of the North Atlantic Fella Organization (NAFO)[1] is just one example that demonstrates the significance of what I refer to as digital nuclear diplomacy—where digital communication technologies have had the effect of changing central aspects of nuclear diplomacy such as the information ecology that provides the contextual back-drop for nuclear diplomacy, thereby enabling new actors, practices, and narratives to become prominent in the field of nuclear diplomacy, where issues such as nuclear

---

[1] NAFO was created in May 2022 by a 27-year-old Polish artist who wanted to support Ukraine by using memes to raise online donations. Since then, what began as a single tweet, has grown into a team of thirty-four people that produce NAFO social media content every day, and their efforts have led to over 5,000 tweets a day linking to NAFO content. NAFO has over 69,000 Twitter followers and has helped to raise between $400,000 and $1 million for military forces in Ukraine, and has been lauded by the Ukrainian government, NATO's head of public diplomacy, the Prime Minister of Estonia, and other officials in NATO member states (Scott, 2022).

signalling and conflict escalation are affected in novel ways. Nowadays, for example, signalling is not just the preserve of government leaders, but is also conducted by online trolls, and memes can affect the relations between nuclear weapon states (Speece, 2022; Hersman, 2020).

In this chapter, amidst the context of the renewed risk of nuclear war, I examine the impact of digital communication technology on nuclear diplomacy. I draw together the burgeoning scholarship on the intersections of digital diplomacy and nuclear politics to outline and examine digital nuclear diplomacy. The chapter then unfolds in four sections. First, I outline a brief history of nuclear diplomacy and the role of communication technologies. I then introduce the concept of digital nuclear diplomacy, before exploring several case studies of digital nuclear diplomacy, ranging from accidentally published nonsensical tweets sent by US Strategic Command in March 2021 to how the International Campaign to Abolish Nuclear Weapons (ICAN) uses Instagram. Ultimately, this section demonstrates that nuclear diplomacy in the digital age involves multiple actors, novel technologies, visual media, and the use of humour that all impact nuclear signalling, crisis stability, conflict escalation, and the communication of nuclear issues in important ways. Because of these developments, in the conclusion I articulate a need for multiple, interdisciplinary, and critical perspectives as we move into an uncertain future where digital nuclear diplomacy may shape the future of life, and death, on planet earth.

A Brief History of Nuclear Diplomacy

In August 1945, American nuclear weapons devastated the Japanese cities of Hiroshima and Nagasaki. Estimates of those killed in the attacks range massively from 110,000 to 210,000 people, largely because 'the two cities were places of anonymous, uncountable death ... there were no bodies left to count near the hypocenter: The heat and energy literally vaporized the closest persons. And many bodies were swept out to sea with the tides, after dying burn victims sought relief in Hiroshima's numerous rivers' (Lindee, 1997: 7). Whilst we are still unsure about the exact death toll caused by nuclear weapons in 1945, their long-lasting effects on global politics are much clearer. As the Soviet Union developed and tested their own nuclear weapons in 1949, the Cold War came to be marked by nuclear proliferation, arms races, strategies of nuclear deterrence, and the ever-present threat of nuclear war. Despite the end of the Cold War and subsequent steps to reduce nuclear arsenals, nuclear weapons persist and the world goes on—for now—under the spectre of 'nuclear eternity' (Pelopidas, 2021a) where it is seemingly impossible to even imagine a future without them.

The development of nuclear weapons gave rise to the practice of nuclear diplomacy, and nuclear diplomacy remains a vital aspect of global politics to this day. The term 'atomic diplomacy' was coined in the early 1960s to refer to President Truman's July 1945 disclosure to Stalin that the US had a new, extremely destructive weapon (Alperovitz,

1965). Here, atomic diplomacy was understood as a state's ability to use their possession of nuclear weapons to gain a diplomatic advantage in negotiations with other states. With the progression of the Cold War and the development of thermonuclear weapons, 'nuclear diplomacy' came to be mainly associated with how states used deterrence and the threat of nuclear use, bilateral negotiations, multilateral negotiations, and cooperative measures such as arms control treaties to survive the Cold War and produce some semblance of a global nuclear order (Ito and Rentetzi, 2021: 7).

Nuclear diplomacy therefore encapsulates a range of issues such as how nuclear weapon states use nuclear weapons for the purposes of deterrence, how these states use signalling to communicate their intentions with others, how they maintain stability through communication with others, how states have negotiated arms control measures, and how states have cooperated with allies to proliferate nuclear weapons, or indeed how they have worked to stop nuclear proliferation through measures such as the implementation of the Non-Proliferation Treaty (NPT). Nuclear diplomacy also concerns the development and maintenance of nuclear alliances and nuclear umbrellas (where the nuclear weapons of one state are used to deter others from attacking their allies), as well as international institutions working on nuclear issues such as the International Atomic Energy Agency (IAEA).

Such an understanding of nuclear diplomacy has, however, been critiqued for being limited for several reasons. First, for failing to account for the humanitarian impact of nuclear weapons development, testing, use, and potential use (Ritchie, 2013; Cohn, 1987). Second, for being too narrowly focused on the role of 'high politics'—states, state leaders, and foreign policy—at the expense of understanding the 'everyday' dimensions of nuclear issues (Eschle, 2018). For example, how the maintenance of nuclear arsenals is underpinned by the exploitation of uranium miners (Hecht, 2014), or how popular culture shapes public opinion about nuclear weapons (Pelopidas, 2021b). Third, conventional accounts of nuclear diplomacy have been challenged for being too optimistic about the control that humanity has over nuclear weapons and the ability to avoid disaster (Pelopidas, 2017), whilst also being too positive about prior steps to achieve nuclear disarmament (Egeland, 2020).

Subsequently we can, and should, understand nuclear diplomacy in a much broader sense than something that simply concerns the high politics of state leaders and militaries. One way of doing so is to understand nuclear diplomacy '*as emergent processes* by which state and non-state actors build and manage relationships on multinational and multidisciplinary levels, shaping themselves and nuclear knowledge at the same time' (Ito and Rentetzi, 2021: 8; emphasis in original). This understanding allows us to account for more actors and practices in our accounts of nuclear diplomacy, whilst also being attuned to how it 'shapes and is shaped by political and economic interests, geostrategic contexts, epistemic claims, technological products and materials and even the nitty-gritty details of knowledge production' (Ito and Rentetzi, 2021: 8). This approach to nuclear diplomacy aligns with more recent influential works in the field of diplomacy that recognize that diplomacy concerns much more than meetings between high-level state officials in traditional halls of power.

An analysis of nuclear diplomacy as processes and practices occurring at a broad range of sites allows us to account for the historical role of communication technologies in shaping our nuclear world, which can then give us an insight into the rise of digital nuclear diplomacy. The nuclear age began with a letter, written by the scientists Leo Szilard and Albert Einstein to President Roosevelt and imploring him to develop a nuclear weapon before the Nazis did. After the American use of nuclear weapons against Japan in 1945, face-to-face diplomacy and international means of communication between state leaders and diplomats became central to nuclear diplomacy as they helped to send signals about each other's intentions, aims, and wishes whilst also helping nuclear weapon state leaders implement arms control measures. Key here was how, prior to the Cuban Missile Crisis in 1962, there was limited communication between state leaders in the USA and USSR, but during the crisis letters exchanged between President Kennedy and his Soviet counterpart Nikita Khrushchev helped to generate trust between the two leaders and helped to avert nuclear war (Wheeler and Holmes, 2021: 737–743). After the Cuban Missile Crisis, a hotline was set up between the White House and the Kremlin, and a year later the two superpowers signed their first nuclear arms control agreement, the Partial Test Ban Treaty (Wheeler and Holmes, 2021: 746), clearly demonstrating that communication matters in nuclear diplomacy.

Beyond state-to-state communication, the media and the press were key to nuclear diplomacy as they shaped public and elite opinion about nuclear issues. John Hershey's reporting of the Hiroshima bombing in the pages of the New Yorker is attributed with uncovering the true devastating cost of the bombing after the American government attempted to control knowledge about it (Blume, 2020). Films such as *Dr Strangelove* also become a key medium by which nuclear weapons were critiqued, and the televised anti-nuclear speeches of Martin Luther King Jr were essential in building up an anti-nuclear mass movement during the Cold War (Intondi, 2015). This brief overview demonstrates the important role that communication technologies have played in shaping nuclear diplomacy over the course of history.

However, despite fundamental changes to diplomacy that have been facilitated by the rise of digital technologies, the internet, and social media, research on digital nuclear diplomacy is only in its ascendancy (Hersman, 2020; Williams and Drew, 2020; Trinkunas et al., 2020a). In the next section of this chapter, I introduce the concept of digital nuclear diplomacy and engage with the burgeoning body of work that helps to understand it.

DIGITAL NUCLEAR DIPLOMACY

The rise of digital communication technologies such as the internet, social media, and smart phones, and their widespread integration into daily life for billions of people has had a profound impact on politics, international relations, and diplomacy. The old broadcast model of media communication as being one-to-many has now been usurped by many-to-many communication where a cacophony of voices can now communicate with each other instantaneously in different ways on many platforms. Because of this, traditional elite media gatekeepers have been bypassed, and whilst they still maintain power in shaping news agendas they are no longer the only source of news and opinion in global politics, nor do they control what can be published online. Anyone with internet access is now no longer simply a consumer of media, but a potential producer of it, with the ability to share their own views, ideas, opinions, and content with the rest of the world. We live in an age where a teenage dancer from Connecticut has fifteen times as many followers on TikTok (Charli D'Amelio—146 million) as the *New York Times* has paid subscribers (9.17 million). In the age of the influencer our attention is focused on new actors, who communicate in novel ways, where visual images—videos, memes, photographs—reverberate around the world instantaneously on ever changing platforms.

The effects of the new information ecology on global politics are wide ranging, and have given rise to digital diplomacy, where digital technology is now an integral part of diplomacy itself. Nuclear diplomacy has also been shaken by the rise of digital communication technologies, so much so that we can now talk of digital nuclear diplomacy. Whilst the term 'digital nuclear diplomacy' has rarely been used in studies to date, it is a helpful way of referring to the study of how digital communication technologies and associated practices are now having an impact on nuclear diplomacy. By reviewing recent studies on the topic of digital communication technologies and nuclear weapons we can outline the contours of the emerging issue of digital nuclear diplomacy.

One of the most comprehensive insights into digital nuclear diplomacy to date is a collection of research articles edited by Harold Trinkunas, Herbert S. Lin, and Benjamin Loehrke titled *Three Tweets to Midnight: Effects of the Global Information Ecosystem on the Risk of Nuclear Conflict* (2020). The volume explores the impact that the contemporary media ecology has on crisis stability and decision making in nuclear states. In the introduction to the collection, Danielle Jablinski and the editors point out that 'the current global information ecosystem' could have exacerbated previous nuclear crises such as the Cuban Missile Crisis and led to these crises 'escalating into all-out nuclear war' (2020: 2). This potentially catastrophic impact arises from how digital communication technologies have led to a radical increase in both the 'volume' and 'velocity' of information and communication that circulates online as well as how digital platforms have led to the 'microsegmentation of audiences and direct targeting' where gatekeepers don't have control over what news circulates, and audiences are susceptible to disinformation from 'inauthentic voices' such as trolls, bots, and adversaries who work to polarize citizens and confuse state leaders (Jablinski et al., 2020: 2–3). This is a worrying development given that mainstream approaches to nuclear diplomacy are underpinned by a belief that deterrence takes place between rational actors making rational decisions based on facts, but in the new media ecology emotion, irrationality, and post-truth representations of the world reign supreme. As such, the new media ecology 'provides unprecedented opportunities for manipulation of leaders' and publics' perceptions about intentions, capabilities, and consequences of conflicts—cheaply, rapidly, and at scale' (Jablinski et al., 2020: 6).

Support for Jablinski et al.'s thesis is then explored in each chapter of the collection. McDermott analyses how narratives and emotions psychologically underpin what people believe to be true (2020). Slovic and Lin draw upon further developments in psychology to point out that the existence of nuclear weapons, and state leaders willingness to use them to potentially cause mass casualties, is shaped by 'psychic numbing, compassion collapse, tribalism, dehumanization of others, blaming of victims, attentional failures, and faulty decision-making processes' (Slovic and Lin, 2020: 58–59). They conclude that if the world is not going to disarm, then the best way forward to avoid a catastrophic nuclear war is to 'improve the circumstances under which nuclear decision making takes place' (Slovic and Lin, 2020: 59).

Kumbleben and Wooley then explore how nuclear decision-making during crises can be affected by nefarious political actors who use bots, trolling, and harassment to confuse and disrupt the flow of information (2020: 73). Kate Starbird also explores computational propaganda and how online discussions of NATO have been shaped not only by mainstream media outlets but also by Russian media outlets and the alt-right. NATO's official social media accounts were found not to have much influence over how it was discussed online, suggesting that discussions of nuclear issues can be shaped by 'loose online communities' who are malignly influenced by others (Starbird, 2020: 100).

Kelly M. Greenhill finds that 'unverified and unverifiable information, such as rumors, propaganda, so-called fake news' (2020: 115) can lead to conflict escalation, either intentionally, accidentally, or inadvertently. Greenhill finds that the 'derogatory, provocative, and inflammatory' (2020: 128) social media posts of states and actors on the topic of nuclear weapons—such as Donald Trump's infamous Twitter threats of 'fire and fury'—can have 'destabilizing, escalatory effects' (Greenhill, 2020: 128–129).

Kristin Ven Bruusgaard and Jaclyn Kerr also demonstrate that the new media ecology threatens crisis stability. Crisis stability is reliant on decision makers being able to effectively and accurately interpret and process information (Ven Bruusgaard and Kerr, 2020: 152). Whilst decision makers never have full certainty or complete information in a crisis, the new media ecology increases the likelihood that leaders will have bad information and be dealing with a confused and panicked public, whilst also being more likely to miscalculate and misperceive the intentions, actions, and goals of others (Ven Bruusgaard and Kerr, 2020: 146).

Jeffrey Lewis also finds that digital communication technologies can affect crisis stability, because elite policy makers often articulate public rhetoric that has a propagandistic formulation but then comes to be believed (Lewis, 2020: 159). By analysing historical crises, Lewis shows that policy elites often believe false ideas and make important decisions based on bad, if not ridiculous ideas about others (Lewis, 2020: 173). Lewis suggests we should not naively assume that 'elites are immune to the bad information on social media, particularly involving issues relating to nuclear weapons and nuclear war' (Lewis, 2020: 160).

Ben O'Loughlin highlights that 'nuclear crises allow the public articulation of narratives about how international order works and that narratives about the identities of the key protagonists often remain central to the reaction of public opinion' (O'Loughlin, 2020: 179). O'Loughlin does, however, argue that digital communication technologies like social media won't immediately shape public opinion during crises, mainly because publics react with uncertainty to complex issues such as nuclear weapons, and often fall back on long-standing feelings of identity during crises (O'Loughlin, 2020: 185).

Finally, Trinkunas et al. conclude the collection by noting that in the new media ecology the accelerated speed of communication, overwhelming volumes of information, and 'intemperate, ill-considered, and impulsive outbursts' have combined to be an important aspect of contemporary crises (Trinkunas et al., 2020b: 193). Because of this, they argue that we need to acknowledge the role that social media platforms themselves now play in the age of digital nuclear diplomacy, whilst also imploring decision makers to be level headed, and to move away from nuclear decision-making authority being vested in the sole authority of a state leader (Trinkunas et al., 2020b: 209).

In another central contribution to the field, Heather Williams and Alexi Drew examine how social media can escalate nuclear crises into nuclear conflicts. They note that earlier understandings of escalation as a linear, predictable ladder have been surpassed by a complex, unpredictable 'escalation web' in the digital age (Williams and Drew, 2020: 10) because of the 'speed, informality, and openness' of social media platforms such as Twitter that can escalate crises in three ways. First, inadvertent escalation can occur through the phenomena of 'collateral messaging' where social media content for a domestic audience impacts foreign audiences, and a digital fog of war causes information overload and background noise in a crisis. Second, deliberate escalation can occur when state leaders and governments use social media to show resolve, and when they spread disinformation. Third, catalytic escalation can occur when a third party prompts another actor to escalate a conflict through social media—this can be through the likes of bots and trolls, but also by the public, or allies (2020: 16). The exact pathways that might turn a crisis into a conflict cannot be precisely predicted, and as Williams and Drew point out, the impact of social media depends on its content and context on a case-by-case basis (2020: 12–16).

The complexity of conflict escalation as a result of digital nuclear diplomacy is also the focus of Rebecca Hersman's work on 'wormhole escalation'. Hersman notes that 'the accessibility of information technology suggests a levelling of the playing field for great powers, non-state actors, states, and non-government entities alike' (2020: 92). In an age of information warfare that is hybrid and occurs in a grey zone between all-out war and peace, conflict escalation may 'follow a wormhole dynamic ... in accelerated and decidedly non-linear ways' (Hersman, 2020: 93). Digital communication technologies are key to this 'wormhole escalation' as they can alter 'public perception, institutional legitimacy, and leadership credibility' (Hersman, 2020: 95). False information and developments in deep-fake technology may not only influence leaders into making hasty designs in a crisis but may also lead to 'a "deception revolution," where elements of the public, deceived by a disinformation campaign, become unwitting soldiers on behalf of an adversary' (2020: 96).

Beyond the focus on the impact of digital information communication technologies on crisis stability and conflict escalation, other scholars have examined how such technologies now play a key role in underpinning communication and the construction of identifies in nuclear diplomacy. Constance Duncombe points out that social media facilitates 'interstate dialogue' (2017: 546) and that this dialogue was integral to the success of nuclear diplomacy initiatives like the Joint Comprehensive Plan of Action (JCPOA/Iran Nuclear Deal). Alister Miskimmon and Ben O'Loughlin agree that the use of social media was key to the successful negotiation of the Iran Deal as social media helped the US and Iranian strategic narratives of shared interests and goals to align, even 'amid uncertainty, sometimes chaotic media dynamics, lack of evidence, and asymmetries of power' (2020: 794).

Others have examined how social media is now an integral part of how NATO communicates with the world. Katherine Wright has found that NATO uses social media to construct an identity of itself as a masculine protector of women (Wright, 2019: 88). Other studies have found that NATO uses digital influencers to represent itself as 'militarily muscular' but also 'caring, democratic, and progressive' (Hedling et al., 2022: 1), whilst also using celebrities like Angelina Jolie to represent itself as a global leader on the issue of sexual violence in conflict (Wright and Rosamond, 2021). The explicit role of social media in how NATO communicates information about nuclear weapons was also examined in a study that found that NATO represents its nuclear weapons as a source of 'safety, security, peace, and pride' (Crilley, 2021: 42), but that online audiences challenge these representations (Crilley, 2021: 43). Subsequently, social media is a site where members of the public now participate in nuclear diplomacy by conferring but also contesting the legitimacy of nuclear weapons, nuclear alliances, and policies of deterrence.

The centrality of social media in maintaining the legitimacy of nuclear weapons has also been recently demonstrated. Kjølv Egeland shows that nuclear weapon states claim legitimacy for their nuclear weapons in print media, on broadcast news, and increasingly with 'outreach through social media' (Egeland, 2022: 603). According to Egeland, significant examples of legitimation in digital nuclear diplomacy include US Strategic Command's maintenance of a Twitter account and the use of social media by arms companies involved in the production of nuclear weapons. Alongside this, there is an emerging area of research in how populism poses a threat to the nuclear order, where scholars have examined how populist actors have used social media in ways that increase the risk that nuclear weapons might be used (Meier and Vieluf, 2021).

Ultimately, the field of digital nuclear diplomacy is one of diverse and burgeoning approaches, insights, and cases. Despite this, the above engagement with the literature suggests that two broad areas of study currently coincide. First, there are the studies that focus specifically on how the use of social media and digital technology can affect crisis stability and conflict escalation. Second, there are studies that explore how social media and digital technology is key to the communication of nuclear issues and central to the construction of the identities, interests, values, norms, and beliefs of the actors at the heart of nuclear diplomacy. In the next section of this chapter, I examine recent examples that reveal important dynamics about contemporary digital nuclear diplomacy.

THE MANY FACETS OF DIGITAL NUCLEAR DIPLOMACY

Recent analysis suggests that we have now entered a dangerous, new nuclear age because of the collapse of nuclear arms control treaties, a shift towards a multipolar world, increased tensions between nuclear weapon states, and the development of new nuclear weapon systems such as hypersonic missiles (Legvold and Chyba, 2020). In this new nuclear age, the risk of nuclear war is as high as it was during the Cold War, yet to date, beyond those studies discussed above, scholars have not examined the role that digital communication technologies play in mediating the very developments, events, and issues that constitute the new nuclear age itself.

Subsequently, in this section I explore several examples of digital nuclear diplomacy that demonstrate its significance in the new nuclear age. I explore first how digital nuclear signalling can affect crisis stability and conflict escalation through the case study of US tweets about arms control with China, and then a nonsensical tweet sent by US Strategic Command. I then turn to examining how a diverse range of actors—from civil society, such as ICAN, international organizations such as the IAEA, and new networked actors such as NAFO—use social media to construct identities and project their interests through visual media. Significantly, digital nuclear diplomacy involves many issues that are often overlooked in traditional accounts of nuclear diplomacy: such as a plurality of actors beyond state leaders and diplomats, novel communication technologies, visual media, and the use of humour.

The Cold War was characterized by bipolar competition between the nuclear armed superpowers of the United States and the Soviet Union. With the recent rise of China as a nuclear-armed, economic, and military international heavyweight, the new nuclear age is characterized by three global superpowers (the US, Russia, and China) maintaining nuclear arsenals, developing new nuclear weapons systems, and potentially causing a nuclear arms race with three or more participants. In the age of digital nuclear diplomacy the dynamics of tri-lateral nuclear arms competitions also play out on social media spaces, further complicating how the contemporary nuclear arms race is developing.

One example of social media's role in complicating efforts towards nuclear arms control occurred during negotiations between the USA and Russia to discuss renewing the New START treaty in the summer of 2020 (Crilley et al., 2020). At the time, New START—a key nuclear arms control treaty that limits the number of nuclear weapons that the USA and Russia can deploy—was set to expire. At one meeting in Vienna, the US delegation arrived early and placed small Chinese flags on the tables around the room next to empty chairs. A picture was taken, and the Trump administration's Envoy for Arms Control tweeted it out with the caption 'Vienna talks about to start. China is a no-show. Beijing still hiding behind #GreatWallofSecrecy on its crash nuclear build-up, and so many other things. We will proceed with #Russia, notwithstanding'. Given that China is a non-signatory to this bilateral treaty between Russia and the US, their attendance in Vienna would have been inappropriate, as the Chinese director of arms control himself said: 'What an odd scene! Displaying Chinese National Flags on a negotiating table without China's consent! Good luck on the extension of the New START! Wonder how LOW you can go?'.

Former American diplomats were also critical of the American tweet, and said 'turning crucial US #Russia discussions into a cheap stunt aimed at humiliating rather than persuading #China is a feature of Trump's @USArmsControl. It's bad diplomacy in any administration'. News commentators referred to the tweet as a 'misleading photo stunt' and the Chinese mission to the UN questioned whether the photograph was 'US performance art?' As S. Mahmud Ali has recently noted, 'serious negotiations over horrifying aspects of the world's grim reality began with farcical drama' (Ali, 2022: 10). This example demonstrates how serious nuclear arms control negotiations are now used by diplomats to conduct stunts designed to be shared on social media, and that these stunts—visually represented and told in 240 characters or less—can impact diplomatic relations. Rather than making China more likely to enter into tri-lateral negations, the US tweet enraged Chinese diplomats and made them double-down on their policy of non-engagement with any tri-lateral nuclear arms control agreements until Washington and Moscow radically reduce their nuclear arsenals.

The rise of nuclear digital diplomacy, and its broader importance in the new nuclear age, can also be seen in how military actors responsible for maintaining nuclear weapons now use social media to communicate with online audiences on a daily basis. For example, the United States Strategic Command has maintained a presence on Twitter and Facebook since 2009, regularly posting about '#StrategicDeterrence' and the nuclear capabilities of the US and its allies. In recent years, Strategic Command's Twitter account has come under scrutiny. In 2018, on New Year's Eve, Strategic Command tweeted '#TimesSquare tradition rings in the #NewYear by dropping the big ball ... if ever needed, we are #ready to drop something much, much bigger', and they had to delete the tweet and apologize for it being in 'poor taste' after complaints that the tweet made light of nuclear weapons being used.

In March 2021, Strategic Command again went viral with the garbled tweet ';l;;gmlxzssaw' (see Figure 8.1). Twitter users speculated that the tweet indicated that those responsible for America's nuclear weapons had been hacked, or that someone had even accidentally tweeted out a nuclear code. In fact, as a Freedom of Information request by a journalist soon found, the cause of the tweet was much more benign: 'The command's Twitter manager', whilst working from home, 'momentarily left the command's Twitter account open and unattended. His very young child took advantage of the situation and started playing with the keys and unfortunately, and

FIGURE 8.1 US Strategic Command tweet
Source: Now deleted, see https://www.bbc.co.uk/news/technology-56578544 (accessed 8 February 2023).

unknowingly, posted the tweet' (Thalen, 2021). By accident, a toddler had inadvertently made a nonsensical nuclear signal to hundreds of thousands of Strategic Command's Twitter followers.

Soon after, in April 2021, Strategic Command were again mocked online, but this time for suggesting that 'We must account for the possibility of conflict leading to conditions which could very rapidly drive an adversary to consider nuclear use as their least bad option' in their preview of their nuclear posture statement. This tweet elicited panicked, and humorous responses where Twitter users asked 'What should we raid first? Alcohol or toilet paper?' Others said the tweet was 'truly frightening, chilling', and an 'ominous statement' that seemed to normalize the potential of nuclear war.

These controversies reveal that militaries themselves are now involved in digital nuclear diplomacy. Despite these examples being somewhat humorous with little serious impact on contributing to crisis escalation, they indicate there is a clear potential to do so; by instigating panic, misinterpretation, or miscalculation in their audiences. In a broader sense, military social media sites also function to normalize the use of force, and Strategic Command's online presence is 'a response to mounting online criticism of nuclear armament and purportedly wasteful defence spending' (Egeland, 2022: 603).

The online normalization of nuclear weapons and deterrence is, however, also challenged and contested on social media. This is another important aspect of digital nuclear diplomacy, as social media platforms have also provided anti-nuclear activists with cheap, accessible tools to reach mass audiences with their messages. Take, for example, ICAN, which not only won the Nobel Peace Prize in 2017 but has also played an integral role in helping the Treaty on the Prohibition of Nuclear Weapons (TPNW) enter into force. Whilst ICAN has proven to be an exceptionally effective organization in facilitating diplomatic organization to ensure that states support an international ban on nuclear weapons (Acheson, 2021), it has also been successful in using social media to build a broader movement in support of #BanningTheBomb. ICAN has a presence on all major social media platforms, and regularly posts content across all of them. In particular, ICAN has success in using visual platforms such as Instagram and TikTok to reach young audiences with engaging content that supports their aims of a nuclear-weapon-free world.

Several significant themes are constructed through ICAN's visual messaging on Instagram (see Figure 8.2). First, ICAN depicts the anti-nuclear movement as one that is highly professional, with widespread support at an international level. This is seen in images of politicians and experts from across the globe expressing their support, photographs of meetings at the UN, and in briefings from ICAN staff that summarize diplomatic summits. Second, ICAN frames the anti-nuclear movement as popular, young, and diverse, and thereby attractive to young social media users with progressive social values. Short videos made and shared by young activists, as well as images of

FIGURE 8.2 ICAN's Instagram

Source: www.instagram.com/nuclearban (accessed 8 February 2023).

groups of activists, depict a sense of widespread support. Third, ICAN uses infographics to provide information about nuclear weapons in an accessible way. These include facts about the harms of nuclear weapons, global spending on nuclear weapons, and short briefings on current affairs such as Putin's threats to use nuclear weapons. Fourth, ICAN provides a platform for survivors of nuclear testing and nuclear weapons use to tell their stories. Images of survivors from the American bombing of Hiroshima and Nagasaki present a human face to the extreme violence of nuclear weapons use that is often abstracted in policies of nuclear deterrence.

Finally, ICAN uses visual media to personalize their work on nuclear abolition. This personalization occurs through the #ICANSAVE campaign, where images of cities that have signed up to support the abolition of nuclear weapons are shared across their platforms. These images function in a way similar to those shared by other political actors that attempt to make far away issues personal to people across the planet by presenting them with images of their hometowns (Manor and Crilley, 2018). Such images function not only to depict global support for disarmament, but also to engage social media users and invite them to imagine why they need to support ICAN in order to prevent nuclear war destroying their hometown. ICAN also encourages social media users to use ICAN templates and to create their own content in support of disarmament. Taken together, ICAN's visual social media output illustrates how non-state actors, civil society organizations, and activists can be effective at countering nuclear weapon state narratives, and how images are a key aspect of driving public engagement with disarmament in the age of digital nuclear diplomacy.

A further novel development in digital nuclear diplomacy concerns the role it has played in global politics following Russia's invasion of Ukraine in February 2022. Whilst social media was a central aspect of Russia's attempts to influence the world via their state-funded international broadcaster RT, directives by states across Europe and elsewhere have banned access to RT and limited how Russia can communicate with global audiences. Whilst Russian attempts to gain support via social media have been blunted, those of others have not. Zelensky has used social media to build up international support by directly communicating with audiences in first-person selfie videos and by highlighting the threat posed by Putin's nuclear sabre rattling. In a similar vein, international institutions such as the IAEA under the directorship of Rafeal Mariano Grossi have also used social media to project an image of strength, authority, and legitimacy in response to Putin's actions. Grossi's tweets stress the need for safety and security around nuclear sites in Ukraine, and whilst most of his tweets show him shaking hands with other diplomats in front of an IAEA sign, others are taken from his visit to the Zaporizhzhya power plant and project an image of a responsible, powerful, authoritative leader who is not afraid to visit a war zone to prevent a nuclear catastrophe (see Figure 8.3).

The state of Ukraine and international institutions like the IAEA have turned to social media as a key aspect of their political communication in response to Vladimir Putin's nuclear threats, and so too have a loose network of anonymous individuals. The aforementioned NAFO is an online collective of social media users with Shiba Inu dog

FIGURE 8.3 Rafael Mariano Grossi and the IAEA head to Ukraine
Source: https://twitter.com/rafaelmgrossi/status/1564096717397659649 (accessed 8 February 2023).

avatars (referred to as fellas) who mock Putin's invasion of Ukraine, post pro-Ukraine memes, and shitpost against other social media users who express support for Putin and Russia. NAFO works to have pro-Russia social media accounts removed from platforms like Twitter whilst coordinating people to respond to and challenge Russian misinformation. They aim to keep Russia's invasion of Ukraine in the mind of foreign audiences by using humour in a way that Russia itself has often attempted to do in the past (Manor, 2021; Crilley and Chatterje-Doody, 2021; Chernobrov, 2022). However, NAFO's impact extends beyond the digital realm and has a direct impact on the conflict as NAFO crowdfunds support for Ukrainian aid and weapons. NAFO have fundraised for 'The superbonker 9000'—a large artillery gun that's been outfitted with memes and symbols (see Figure 8.4). This piece of artillery attached to a Soviet-era tank was funded through signmyrocket.com—a website set up by a Ukrainian student. On this website you can pay to have a message written on an artillery shell, or if you've got $30,000 you can have your message written on the side of a Ukrainian fighter jet.

NAFO indicates a new dynamic of digital nuclear diplomacy, as NAFO can be understood as a network of crowdsourcing 'violence entrepreneurs' who rely on contemporary forms of networked communication to wage combat and challenge traditional notions of sovereignty and power. In a study of the emergence of crowdsourcing in war,

FIGURE 8.4   NAFO and 'the superbonker 9000'
Source: https://twitter.com/Osinttechnical/status/1563188524324573185 (accessed 8 February 2023).

Nicole Sunday Grove suggests that social media and online funding lead to 'a radical deviation from conventional national and corporate organizational structures for waging combat' (Grove, 2019: 87). Through social media, warfare has now become participative, and individuals can circumvent the state to participate in international security and nuclear crises in novel ways facilitated through social media. The implications of this for digital nuclear diplomacy remain to be fully understood, but they indicate that individuals can now play a role in contributing directly to conflicts in ways that circumnavigate states, and can potentially contribute to conflict escalation and crisis instability.

Conclusion

We once again live in an era where the shadow of nuclear war looms over us. As scholars have identified the contours of this dangerous new nuclear age, few have so far indicated how digital information communication technologies might play a significant role in shaping our nuclear future. The nascent literature that does engage with the topic of digital technologies, social media, and nuclear weapons provides an important foundation for studying digital nuclear diplomacy.

In an age of renewed nuclear threats and an increasing likelihood of nuclear weapons being detonated, it is imperative that students and practitioners of digital nuclear diplomacy do all they can to reduce rather than exacerbate the threat of nuclear war. Digital nuclear diplomacy is complex, multifaceted, and involves a range of actors old and new communicating in multiple, novel ways to different audiences. Further research is therefore needed to understand these issues. As the nuclear age has clearly gone digital, we need more studies to understand how, why, when, and where social media and digital technologies shape nuclear politics. What effect is digital media having on how nuclear issues are communicated, understood, and acted upon? Who is communicating about nuclear issues, and to whom are they communicating? How are nuclear weapons and policies of deterrence, disarmament, arms control, and so on framed and represented? What media and platforms are significant? Why are they so? How is the emergence and proliferation of new technologies such as generative Artificial Intelligence impacting these issues? When does digital nuclear diplomacy matter? During crises? During periods of relative stability? Where does digital nuclear diplomacy have an impact on global politics? All of these questions and more should shape an emerging research agenda. In terms of practice, it is of course imperative that states and institutions formulate best practices for digital nuclear diplomacy that ensure that crises don't escalate into nuclear confrontation because of what is said and done online. At the same time, with the increasing risk of nuclear conflict we need advocates of arms control and disarmament to harness the affordances of digital technology to engage audiences and build support and legitimacy for nuclear disarmament alongside meaningful measures to reduce nuclear risks that will avert a global catastrophe. As the horror of a nuclear war once again provokes a sense of atomic anxiety in the wider public, understanding the potential and pitfalls of digital nuclear diplomacy is of the upmost urgency.

SUGGESTED READING

Cohn, Carol (1987) Sex and death in the rational world of defense intellectuals. *Signs: Journal of women in culture and society* 12(4): 687–718.

Crilley, Rhys (2023) *Unparalleled catastrophe: Life and death in the Third Nuclear Age.* Manchester University Press.

Egeland, Kjølv (2022) Sustaining social license: nuclear weapons and the art of legitimation. *International Politics* 60(3): 598–615.

Hersman, Rebecca (2020) Wormhole escalation in the new nuclear age. *Texas National Security Review* 3(3): 90–109.

Ito, Kenji and Rentetzi, Maria (2021) The co-production of nuclear science and diplomacy: towards a transnational understanding of nuclear things. *History and Technology* 37(1): 4–20.

Trinkunas, Harold A, Lin, Herbert S, and Loehrke, Benjamin (2020) *Three Tweets to Midnight: Effects of the Global Information Ecosystem on the Risk of Nuclear Conflict.* Hoover Institution Press.

Williams, Heather and Drew, Alexi (2020) *Escalation by Tweet: Managing the New Nuclear Diplomacy.* Kings College London.

REFERENCES

Acheson, Ray (2021) *Banning the Bomb, Smashing the Patriarchy.* Rowman & Littlefield.

Ali, S Mahmud (2022) *The US–China–Russia Triangle.* Springer.

Alperovitz, Gar (1965) *Atomic Diplomacy: Hiroshima and Potsdam.* New York: Simon and Schuster.

Blume, Lesley (2020) *Fallout: The Hiroshima Cover-Up and the Reporter Who Revealed It to the World*. Scribe.

Chernobrov, Dmitry (2022) Strategic humour: public diplomacy and comic framing of foreign policy issues. *The British Journal of Politics and International Relations* 24(2): 277–296.

Cohn, Carol (1987) Sex and death in the rational world of defense intellectuals. *Signs: Journal of women in culture and society* 12(4): 687–718.

Crilley, Rhys (2021) NATO's nuclear narratives in the digital age. *NATO Defence College Research Paper* Challenges to NATO's nuclear strategy (22): 35–44.

Crilley, Rhys and Chatterje-Doody, Precious N (2021) From Russia with lols: humour, RT, and the legitimation of Russian foreign policy. *Global Society* 35(2): 269–288.

Crilley, Rhys, Manor, Ilan, and Bjola, Corneliu (2020) Visual narratives of global politics in the digital age: an introduction. *Cambridge Review of International Affairs* 33(5): 628–637.

Duncombe, Constance (2017) Twitter and transformative diplomacy: social media and Iran–US relations. *International Affairs* 93(3): 545–562.

Egeland, Kjølv (2020) Who stole disarmament? History and nostalgia in nuclear abolition discourse. *International Affairs* 96(5): 1387–1403.

Egeland, Kjølv (2022) Sustaining social license: nuclear weapons and the art of legitimation. *International Politics* 60(3). 598–615.

Eschle, Catherine (2018) Nuclear (in) security in the everyday: peace campers as everyday security practitioners. *Security Dialogue* 49(4): 289–305.

Greenhill, Kelly M (2020) Of Wars and Rumors of Wars: Extra-factual Information and (In)Advertent Escalation In: Trinkunas HA, Lin HS, and Loehrke B (eds), *Three tweets to midnight: Effects of the global information ecosystem on the risk of nuclear conflict*. Hoover Institution Press, pp.113–136.

Grove, Nicole Sunday (2019) Weapons of mass participation: social media, violence entrepreneurs, and the politics of crowdfunding for war. *European Journal of International Relations* 25(1): 86–107.

Hecht, Gabrielle (2014) *Being nuclear: Africans and the global uranium trade*. MIT press.

Hedling, Elsa, Edenborg, Emil, and Strand, Sanna (2022) Embodying military muscles and a remasculinized west: influencer marketing, fantasy, and "the face of NATO". *Global Studies Quarterly* 2(1): ksac010.

Hersman, Rebecca (2020) Wormhole escalation in the new nuclear age. *Texas National Security Review* 3(3): 90–109.

Intondi, Vincent J (2015) *African Americans against the bomb: nuclear weapons, colonialism, and the black freedom movement*. Stanford University Press.

Ito, Kenji and Rentetzi, Maria (2021) The co-production of nuclear science and diplomacy: towards a transnational understanding of nuclear things. *History and Technology* 37(1): 4–20.

Jablinski, Danielle, Lin Herbert S, and Trinkunas Harold A (2020) Retweets to Midnight: Assessing the Effects of the Information Ecosystem on Crisis Decision Making between Nuclear Weapons States In: Trinkunas HA, Lin HS, and Loehrke B (eds), *Three tweets to midnight: Effects of the global information ecosystem on the risk of nuclear conflict*. Hoover Institution Press, pp.1–16.

Kumbleben, Mark and Wooley, Samuel C (2020) Gaming Communication on the Global Stage: Social Media Disinformation in Crisis Situations In: Trinkunas HA, Lin HS, and Loehrke B (eds), *Three tweets to midnight: Effects of the global information ecosystem on the risk of nuclear conflict*. Hoover Institution Press, pp.63–78.

Legvold, Robert and Chyba, Christopher F (2020) Introduction: the search for strategic stability in a new nuclear era. *Daedalus* 149(2): 6–16.

Lewis, Jeffrey (2020) Bum Dope, Blowback, and the Bomb: The Effect of Bad Information on Policy-Maker Beliefs and Crisis Stability In: Trinkunas HA, Lin HS, and Loehrke B (eds), *Three Tweets to Midnight: Effects of the Global Information Ecosystem on the Risk of Nuclear Conflict*. Hoover Institution Press, pp.159–178.

Lindee, M Susan (1997) *Suffering Made Real: American Science and the Survivors at Hiroshima*. University of Chicago Press.

Manor, Ilan (2021) The Russians are laughing! The Russians are laughing! how Russian diplomats employ humour in online public diplomacy. *Global Society* 35(1): 61–83.

Manor, Ilan and Crilley, Rhys (2018) Visually framing the Gaza War of 2014: The Israel ministry of foreign affairs on Twitter. *Media, War & Conflict* 11(4): 369–391.

McDermott Rose (2020) Psychological Underpinnings of Post-truth in Political Beliefs In: Trinkunas HA, Lin HS, and Loehrke B (eds), *Three Tweets to Midnight: Effects of the Global Information Ecosystem on the Risk of Nuclear Conflict*. Hoover Institution Press, pp.17–38.

Meier, Oliver, and Vieluf, Maren (2021) Upsetting the nuclear order: how the rise of nationalist populism increases nuclear dangers. *The Nonproliferation Review* 28(1–3): 13–35.

O'Loughlin, Ben (2020) The Impact of the Information Ecosystem on Public Opinion during Nuclear Crises: Lifting the Lid on the Role of Identity Narratives In: Trinkunas HA, Lin HS, and Loehrke B (eds), *Three Tweets to Midnight: Effects of the Global Information Ecosystem on the Risk of Nuclear Conflict*. Hoover Institution Press, pp.179–192.

Pelopidas, Benoît (2017) The unbearable lightness of luck: three sources of overconfidence in the manageability of nuclear crises. *European Journal of International Security* 2(2): 240–262.

Pelopidas, Benoît (2021a) The Birth of Nuclear Eternity In: Kemp S, and Andersson J (eds), *Futures*. Oxford University Press, pp.484–500.

Pelopidas, Benoît (2021b) Imaginer la possibilité de la guerre nucléaire pour y faire face. Le role de la culture populaire visuelle de 1950 à nos jours. *Cultures & Conflits* 3–4(123–124): 173–212.

Ritchie, Nick (2013) Valuing and devaluing nuclear weapons. *Contemporary Security Policy* 34(1): 146–173.

Scott, Mark (2022) The shit-posting, Twitter-trolling, dog-deploying social media army taking on Putin one meme at a time. *Politico*. Available at: https://www.politico.eu/article/nafo-doge-shiba-russia-putin-ukraine-twitter-trolling-social-media-meme/ (accessed 22 November 2022).

Slovic, Paul and Lin, Herbert S (2020) The Caveman and the Bomb in the Digital Age In: Trinkunas HA, Lin HS, and Loehrke B (eds), *Three Tweets to Midnight: Effects of the Global Information Ecosystem on the Risk of Nuclear Conflict*. Hoover Institution Press, pp.39–62.

Speece, Steve (2022) On trolls and nuclear signaling: strategic stability in the age of memes. Available at:https://mwi.usma.edu/on-trolls-and-nuclear-signaling-strategic-stability-in-the-age-of-memes/ (accessed 14 November 2022).

Starbird, Kate (2020) Information Operations and Online Activism within NATO Discourse In: Trinkunas HA, Lin HS, and Loehrke B (eds), *Three Tweets to Midnight: Effects of the Global Information Ecosystem on the Risk of Nuclear Conflict*. Hoover Institution Press, pp.79–112.

Thalen, Mikael (2021) The agency that controls U.S. nukes had its Twitter account accessed by a child. Available at: https://www.dailydot.com/debug/gibberish-tweet-u-s-strategic-command-child/ (accessed 14 November 2022).

Trinkunas, Harold A, Lin, Herbert S, and Loehrke, Benjamin (2020a) *Three Tweets to Midnight: Effects of the Global Information Ecosystem on the Risk of Nuclear Conflict*. Hoover Institution Press.

Trinkunas, Harold A, Lin, Herbert S, and Loehrke, Benjamin (2020b) What Can Be Done to Minimize the Effects of the Global Information Ecosystem on the Risk of Nuclear War? In: Trinkunas HA, Lin HS, and Loehrke B (eds), *Three Tweets to Midnight: Effects of the Global Information Ecosystem on the Risk of Nuclear Conflict*. Hoover Institution Press, pp.193–214.

Ven Bruusgaard, Kristin and Kerr, Jacyln A (2020) Crisis Stability and the Impact of the Information Ecosystem In: Trinkunas HA, Lin HS, and Loehrke B (eds), *Three Tweets to Midnight: Effects of the Global Information Ecosystem on the Risk of Nuclear Conflict*. Hoover Institution Press, pp.137–158.

Wheeler, Nicholas J and Holmes, Marcus (2021) The strength of weak bonds: substituting bodily copresence in diplomatic social bonding. *European Journal of International Relations* 27(3): 730–752.

Williams, Heather and Drew, Alexi (2020) *Escalation by Tweet: Managing the New Nuclear Diplomacy*. Kings College London.

Wright, Katharine AM (2019) Telling NATO's story of Afghanistan: gender and the alliance's digital diplomacy. *Media, War & Conflict* 12(1): 87–101.

Wright, Katharine AM, and Rosamond, Annika Bergman (2021) NATO's strategic narratives: Angelina Jolie and the alliance's celebrity and visual turn. *Review of International Studies* 47(4): 443–466.

CHAPTER 9

DIGITAL FEMINIST
FOREIGN POLICY

JENNIFER A. CASSIDY

Introduction

THE ability to get what you want through attraction and cooperation has been the subject of considerable and open debate in the realm of academia, policy making, and foreign affairs. As both a concept and framework, it has become more commonly known by the term: *soft power*. Being coined and launched by Joseph Nye in the early 1990s, soft power is defined as the ability of one actor to influence the behaviour of another. This influence is crafted and exerted in order to obtain a favourable outcome; an outcome which is obtained through attraction and cooperation rather than military and/or economic coercion. If a state engages in a process and acceptance of soft power, we see them reject threats or sanctions and, instead, tempt actors by shaping their preferences and eliciting attraction. In seeking to summarize this process, Nye (2004a) writes:

> If I am persuaded to go along with your purposes without any explicit threat or exchange taking place – in short, if my behaviour is determined by an observable but intangible attraction, soft power is at work. Soft power uses a different type of currency, not force, not money – to engender cooperation – an attraction to shared values and the justness and duty of contributing to the achievement of those values.

The success of this diplomatic strategy can be seen to rely on two factors. First, the state must be able to generate an image that the rest of the world considers desirable and worth emulating. This is achieved through intangible resources such as a nation's: *culture*, defined as a set of practices that create meaning and identity for a society; *political values*, when lived up to home and abroad; and *foreign policy*, when regarded as legitimate and having moral authority. Second, others must be aware that the state possesses these qualities, which places a considerable emphasis on the latter's ability to communicate (Beadle and Hill, 2014), an ability which has now been irrevocably transformed through an evolutionary process towards 'real-time' communication, particularly that conducted on novel digital platforms which are aimed at crafting, projecting, and receiving messages of intention to a wider international audience. Situated within this debate is the examination of how a state constructs and promotes its individual foreign policy, and how this promotion works towards crafting and cementing influence and attraction on behalf of the state. In short, how a state can use its foreign policy, as a tool of attraction.

The objective of this chapter is therefore to theorize and empirically demonstrate the understanding of *feminist* foreign policy as a tool within the digital diplomacy strategies of foreign ministries—a tool that is digitally crafted, enhanced, and shared in order to increase digital nation branding, online image-making to increase the attractiveness of the nation online, and online cultural and political attraction. This demonstration of understanding will be achieved by undertaking a unique analytical analysis of the chosen ministry of foreign affairs (MFA), their digital diplomacy strategies, and digital public diplomacy tools of attraction, as they relate to the active promotion of their states feminist foreign policy. The strategies and tools analysed are those projected and carried out through the MFA's selected and prominent social media tools and applications. The aim of this contribution to the domains of diplomatic studies is threefold: (1) to expose and confront the politics of attraction; (2) to shed light on the overlooked use of digital tools to craft a state's image and brand, with a focus on the critical juncture of a feminist foreign policy adoption; (3) to examine the current state of a feminist foreign policy as a digital diplomacy strategy for states to promote their nation's brand and country's image and to express their state's morals and values.

To achieve these objectives and contributions, this chapter unfolds as follows. First, the chapter outlines its conceptualization of soft power in the digital age and discusses how it applies it to states' adoption and promotion of a feminist foreign policy as an integral part of their public diplomacy. This chapter argues that adoption and promotion of a feminist foreign policy, and consequently the advocacy of gender equality worldwide, provides states with the potential to practise public diplomacy to attract the citizens of other states using the global media. The chapter suggests that these tools and policies of attraction are performative political practice and, as such, are evidence of their increasing global reach, as well as their ability to leverage international credibility and status and project their carefully managed image abroad through the discursive praxis of public diplomacy (Grix and Brannagan, 2016). The subsequent sections then apply these conceptual insights to the cases of Sweden and Mexico, who have adopted a feminist foreign policy and actively seek to promote its adoption and ideals through online means.

These empirical examples highlight strategies of online attraction and influence by states who are using similar, if not identical, tools of attraction online. These cases were chosen for examination as they represent the first state to ever adopt a feminist foreign policy (Sweden) and the last state to do so (Mexico). Furthermore, both states have been shown to frequently enact public and state-sanctioned uses of gender tropes to identify the universal applicability of soft power. However, it must be noted that the possible pitfalls of any soft power strategy are also highlighted before concluding how this ideal type might be used in future research to help further identify, and explain, the mechanisms through which a state can acquire soft power for diplomatic purposes, which align with their aforementioned digital diplomacy ministry strategies.

POLITICS OF ATTRACTION AND DIGITAL DIPLOMACY

Politics of Attraction

One could be forgiven for presuming that with the quantity of commentators making use of Nye's (2004b) soft power concept—a framework to explain how, and why, states engage in the politics of attraction on the international stage would have already been developed. Unfortunately, although the concept has shed some light on *why* states undertake a soft power strategy—for international prestige, increased trade, raised diplomatic presence on the global stage—sparse and varied analysis has emerged relating to the *how*. Indeed, despite its growing significance, soft power, as both a concept and more importantly a strategy, continues to be questioned on four specific levels.

First, many have raised concerns over what soft power actually is and, more specifically, whether it is merely another buzzword for conceptualizing that of nation branding and/or place marketing. Second, many have suggested that those writers taking up the soft power gauntlet fail to deliver a clear description of how one actually acquires soft power, leading to a highly confusing and problematic concept with which to work (Jezierska, 2021). Third, due to the existing literature's reliance on discussions of the West, many equate soft power as being either too structural or Western-centric (Jezierska, 2021). Finally, an increasing amount of scholarship has argued for greater academic attention in identifying and highlighting the potential pitfalls for any state that attempts to acquire soft power forms.

Yet scholars have gone further than simply arguing for greater academic attention, and have actively sought to apply the concept of soft power in their attempt to theorize various state-led pursuits. In commenting on the field of international relations, Jan Melissen (2005), for example, advocates that, 'it is now a cliché to state that soft power is increasingly important in the global information age'. Such an observation finds support from those scholars who have argued that states are currently engaged in a soft power offensive, such as China's promotion of its Confucius Institutes abroad, its involvement in United Nations peacekeeping missions, and various humanitarian efforts, as well as the rise and international reach of its media outlets: Central China Television (CCTV) and Xinhua News Agency (Bandurski, 2007). This chapter places its unique investigation amongst these previous academia endeavours, exploring and investigating new avenues and tools for states; specifically the adoption and promotion of a feminist foreign policy through digital diplomacy strategies. Cumulatively, it investigates the pitfalls and benefits of these states' attempts to acquire soft power forms through this foreign policy framework and means.

In responding to the first criticism, Nye—along with a plethora of other scholars—has been quick to point out that soft power should not merely be considered another term for nation branding. As Nye has been at pains to advocate, soft power is not simply the ability to persuade; it is the ability to entice and attract, which leads to acquiescence and imitation. Leading from this, we posit that in an age of real-time governance, states are increasingly using a range of novel, diverse, and online tools to garner soft power, with one of those tools and strategies being the adoption of a feminist foreign policy, and its public cultivation and promotion as part of a state's digital diplomacy strategy. Arguably, all states that have made the diplomatic and political decision to adopt a feminist foreign policy see it as part of their wider diplomatic armoury; an armoury which can increase a state's international prestige, improve a state's current image, and increase the likelihood of strengthening their diplomatic relations on the world stage.

When discussing, analysing, and obtaining data in the field of soft power investigations, we cannot forget about the notorious elephant in the Microsoft breakout room, recognizing here that soft power is, and always has been, extremely difficult to measure. Jonathan McClory (2019) and colleagues have produced some interesting indices. Key components like image, reputation, and trust are difficult to operationalize even via opinion polls, but in terms of the attitudes of foreign decision makers the task becomes impossible, because the data is simply unavailable. Therefore, we should acknowledge the fact soft power is primarily an instrument and not a policy, and that it may ultimately represent desirable values, in that it stresses cooperative rather than coercive approaches, but otherwise it tells us little about the content of strategies to be followed. It is this philosophy of examination and analysis that stands as the methodological underpinning of this chapter and its investigation.

Digital Diplomacy and Feminist Foreign Policy

Digital diplomacy, as both a strategy and medium, has revealed itself as an increasingly vital tool for the strategies, objectives, and ideals discussed within the previous section, that is, an increasingly vital tool for, inter alia, articulating a state's identity and projecting their chosen strategic narratives (Wright and Guerrina, 2020). This trend thus represents something of a transformation in diplomatic practice, altering not just the methods but the meaning of diplomacy, with the potential to increase transparency and accountability of both outcomes and process (Bjola, 2016: 2). Digital diplomacy has changed the way in which governments and international organizations seek to share and manage messages, with social media enabling the circumnavigation of the traditional routes for information dissemination through the media, and to engage directly with consumers (Bjola, 2016: 55). Digital diplomacy, as both a practice and strategy, therefore represents a pertinent arena in which to investigate how states seek to acquire soft power within the digital age.

Existing literature on digital platforms, and diplomatic strategies, appears on the surface to present a different picture. The platform has shown to provide a space for both communication and relationship building between different actors, for example the resolution of a territorial dispute in 2016 between the foreign ministers of Iran and the United States. This chapter considers case studies of selected foreign ministries' use of digital diplomacy to promote their feminist foreign policies and, through it, to craft an image of a nation state committed to and supportive of gender equality worldwide. At first glance, the selected cases of Sweden and Mexico may seem representative of the more 'day-to-day' use of digital diplomacy as a public diplomacy tool, as opposed to high-stakes politics or attempts to provoke a reaction. However, if projected effectively online, these states have the potential to use their soft power resources to move beyond the scope of 'day-to-day' use of digital diplomacy as public diplomacy. Thus, this chapter's investigation provides a useful point from which to interrogate whether the utility of Twitter as an engagement tool has carried over into other forms of digital diplomacy, in promoting and strategically narrating soft power resources that currently remain unique to states.

CONCEPTUALIZING FRAMEWORK

A central component of this chapter's analysis and empirical investigation arises from the contributions of Jonathan Grix and Paul Michael (2016) in their work titled 'Of Mechanisms and Myths: Conceptualising States' "Soft Power" Strategies through Sports Mega-Events'. This work saw the development of an ideal type, as it relates to soft power. This proposed ideal type forms the foundational basis for this chapter's overarching conceptual framework, and subsequent empirical analysis. While its creators linked the ideal type to offline analysis and evaluation, this chapter adapts and sculpts the framework to analyse how selected states use their adoption of a feminist foreign policy as a soft power resource as an integral component of their digital diplomacy strategy.

Reflecting on the development of this ideal type, we can see that Grix and Michael crafted it through an iterative process between concepts and empirical data, seeking to reflect the soft power strategies of a number of nation states. The development of this ideal type, as it relates to soft power strategies and resources, made two primary propositions. First, an ideal type's purpose was to be parsimonious. Second, the ideal type's purpose is not to advance a 'theory' of soft power or an explanatory framework for predicting outcomes, but rather to produce a tool that researchers can use and adapt by looking at a variety of states and their soft power strategies. This chapter, and its corresponding proposed conceptual framework, will seek to do just that. This will be achieved by adapting this ideal type in a bid to investigate the selected empirical cases of Sweden and Mexico, with the investigation centring on these states' use of soft power strategies and resources online, particularly their adoption and online promotion of a feminist foreign policy.

The ideal types of soft power, and the states within which they are likely to be found, are revealed from the two selected foreign ministries and their feminist foreign policies: Sweden and Mexico. The primary reasons for selecting the adoption and online promotion of a feminist foreign policy for analysis are twofold. First, feminist foreign policies in particular have brought with them the potential to become significant soft power opportunities, acting as major contributions in the process of improving a nation's image, by allowing states to profile and highlight themselves globally whilst attracting others to their values and ideals. We can posit that promoting and engaging with human rights-centred issues, whether through foreign policy strategy or a strong moral leadership, is arguably a strong opportunity for states to attract others with their values and culture and persuade them to 'want what they want' by projecting specific images, principles, achievements, and visions to foreign publics. Second, gender plays a role in all five of the distinct but interlinked proposed resources that appear essential in a state's successful soft power strategy—see Figure 9.1. Furthermore, gender is, and has always been, an intricate part of a nation's cultural make-up. Nevertheless, how a state uses and expresses their political and diplomatic views on this issue will ultimately be the difference on whether or not gender has the potential to be an effective soft power resource online, or indeed off.

The analysis begins with the resource 'Culture', to which a feminist foreign policy and its adoption clearly belongs. Often leveraged to improve global standing, a state's culture

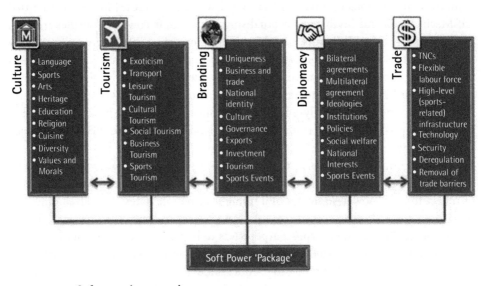

FIGURE 9.1 Soft power 'resources'

Source: Soft power 'package' taken from Johnathan Grix and Paul Michael (2016) 'Of Mechanisms and Myths: Conceptualising States' "Soft Power" Strategies through Sports Mega-Events'.

(in which values and morals are central components) is often central to making a state more attractive to others, one of the reasons Germany and China invest heavily in language institutes abroad; art, heritage, history, and literature fall under this category, too. Nations such as Sweden, even before the adoption of a feminist foreign policy, sought to actively promote the values and ideals of gender equality in all areas of their society, and the corresponding image this produced worldwide.

The second resource, 'Tourism', has close links with both 'Branding' and 'Diplomacy', the third and fourth resources respectively. It serves the purpose of attracting foreigners to a state, be this political or diplomatic tourism, or otherwise. In the case of political or diplomatic tourism, states who promote or sell certain ideals, such as human rights or gender equality, tend to host summits or conferences surrounding such areas; with satisfied diplomatic or political 'tourists' then having the opportunity to act as multipliers, passing on positive messages about the host country on their return home. 'Branding', the third resource, takes aspects such as 'tourism' and 'culture' and attempts to package them to 'sell' a country externally. 'Diplomacy', the fourth resource, is a broad framework that entails formal state-to-state relations, but it also encompasses the multitude of actors now involved in diplomatic relations. Public diplomacy studies differentiate between the old *modus operandi* via hierarchical state-centric structures and the new model of a network environment in which several actors, of which the state is but one, undertake public diplomacy (Melissen, 2005). The arena of foreign policy is one of the most well-known examples of this process and strategy. The final resource 'Trade' is straightforward: states use all of the resources discussed above to increase their global trade and grow their economies; it can entail finding new markets within which to sell both products that they manufacture or their own 'goods' such as financial services. The adoption of a feminist foreign policy often finds use in sending out a 'signal' that a state has certain values and morals attached to their trading agreements, and that they expect the same from their trading partner.

METHODOLOGY: TWITTER AS A DIGITAL DIPLOMACY TOOL

The versatility of online media platforms has opened up space for debates on political participation and citizenship. Twitter has a 'human-centric' approach, which sets it apart from other social media platforms. The platform represents much more than a one-way broadcast medium and is premised on engagement. Indeed, digital diplomacy, with public diplomacy a core component of it, is increasingly important in a world where traditional diplomacy is seen to be less effective and therefore in relative decline (Wright and Guerrina, 2020). Indeed, the link between the digital sphere and soft power (Bjola and Holmes, 2015) makes the use of Twitter in public diplomacy an important site for examination.

The chapter now turns to examine in detail its methodological underpinnings and the tools used to interrogate whether the utility of Twitter as a digital diplomacy tool has enabled state promotion and acquisition of soft power resources, through the adoption and promotion of feminist policies and values. In the context of our proposed questions, this research employs mixed, mutually supportive methods, relying on both quantitative and qualitative approaches for data collection and analysis. This approach results from the objective and subjective strands of foreign policy analysis and soft power resources, and reveals in part the complexity of studying this space. In the case of our research, it may therefore be helpful to think about the study of foreign policy and soft power as dips into a fluid environment and that analytical choices depend on what aspect of the foreign policy we are seeking to explain along the spectrum of persuasion (Miskimmon et al., 2014).

This chapter analysis engaged with distinct methods to accurately capture each aspect and use of the unique resources, and ideals, embedded within a feminist foreign policy. The subjective nature of these soft power resources, namely cultural, branding, and tourism resources (see ideal type), requires the use of qualitative methods for their discovery and analysis. Within the formation of narratives specifically, we used process-tracing, textual analysis, which enabled us to understand the domestic political pressures evident when studying foreign policy narratives, and how national or international foreign policy projected narratives constrained how political actors conceive the realm of the possible. Conversely, other core aspects of this investigation required a vastly different approach in order to accurately obtain pertinent data for analysis. Here social media analytical tools, primarily Twitonomy, Visone, and Netvizz, were used to discover, collate, and categorize these mechanisms within the three selected case studies and their adoption, and online promotion of their respective feminist foreign policies: Sweden and Mexico. Due to their consistent analytical make-up, these tools allowed for a concrete comparison between all actors analysed, a consistency not able to be achieved even by the most rigorous qualitative methods.

The methodological investigation conducted regarding the content analysis of this work can be divided into a number of distinct but interlocking sections. The first stage was the collection and collation of the online data. On Twitter, this was achieved by using the Twitonomy application, which allowed each foreign ministry's Twitter account tweets to be easily collated, viewed, and analysed via an Excel document, a document produced by the application itself. The collection of data for all three states produced a structured and categorized Excel document, revealing the last 3,200 tweets for each selected online foreign ministry account selected. It should also be noted that tweets deleted before our collection date are not included in the data set, and while there are likely to be relatively few deleted tweets (if any), our sample reflects only tweets that the selected foreign ministries were prepared to uphold as an integral part of their digital narrative. Each document created a firm foundation on which to begin the second aspect of our content analysis, that of coding and categorizing of the data gathered. This was undertaken manually, and not through an online methodological tool. In short, the aim of this stage was to code and categorize the data gathered, as although raw data can be interesting to observe, it does not help the reader to understand the social world under scrutiny and the way the participants view it, unless such data has been systematically analysed to illuminate an existent situation.

Once the data was collected (manually or through Twitonomy), we then engaged in content analysis on each tweet generated. Although time consuming, content analysis on every tweet was necessary, if we were to a) understand exactly what the actors were saying or not saying when it came to their state's feminist foreign policy; b) collate and categorize the content into the two distinct content categories, namely the tweets which related directly to a feminist foreign policy, and the tweets which related to key issues of gender equality and equity without explicitly mentioning a feminist foreign policy; and c) categorize the coded tweets into the constructed ideal type for soft power resources.

It is worth briefly clarifying the ontological and epistemological underpinnings of this study, and in part, its limitation. This research is structured around the proposition that how we 'read' and interpret diplomatic communication activities shapes how we interpret it and how we then respond to it. This means that we do not imply a definitive or mono-causal relationship between meanings, interests, behaviours, and outcomes, but contend that we cannot fully explain interests and behaviours, and thus the outcomes of interactions, without being aware of how actors understand the entities and social worlds with which they interact. In short, this research highlights one piece of the complex puzzle that is diplomatic communication in the digital age, and therefore should be read as one approach that complements a range of other approaches that might do better at filling in other gaps of this complex and multi-faceted problem.

Case Study Analysis

Sweden

Foundational Overview

To provide a foundational overview of this empirical case, we first see that in 2014, Sweden declared its intention to pursue a feminist foreign policy, becoming the first state in the world to do so. This intention, and corresponding adoption of this foreign policy, can be read as an intensification of Sweden's long-standing ambition to champion and promote an array of policies, including gender equality, the role of women within decision making processes, and improving the lives of women and girls, not only in Sweden but also worldwide. Indeed, two years after Sweden declared its intention, the Swedish MFA presented long-term objectives for its novel foreign policy, with a focus on six core areas. These areas have explicitly outlined the promotion of women's rights as human rights, women's participation in politics and peace processes, economic rights, freedom

from violence, and sexual and reproductive health and rights (Swedish Foreign Service Action Plan for Feminist Foreign Policy 2015–2018) Being comprehensive, this policy applies a gender lens to diplomacy, trade, aid, and security spheres of action. While the foreign policy rests on existing norms, as expressed in previously adopted international conventions, it constitutes a novel and enhanced normative approach, as 'the feminist foreign policy entails applying a systematic gender equality perspective throughout foreign policy' (Statement of Government Policy on Foreign Affairs
2015, 2015, 2018: 9).

Ultimately Sweden's adoption and promotion of a feminist foreign policy online offers an excellent example of how states are seeking to project certain morals, values, and diplomatic relationships in the digital age, in an active attempt to make itself more attractive, more influential, and more powerful (at least in one arena) on the world stage.

Twitter Account @SweMFA: An Analysis

Sweden's adoption and promotion of a feminist foreign policy offers an excellent example of how a state can actively seek to make itself more attractive and influential on the world stage through cultivating and promoting soft power resources within the digital sphere. Within this case, data was first collected from Sweden's primary and central foreign ministry Twitter account (@SweMFA).[1] From this account, the last 3,200 tweets of the account were collected and coded. The date range of these tweets ran from 14 November 2017 (14:09:23) to 04 December 2021 (14:34:31). Content analysis was then conducted on all 3,200 tweets, with those tweets specifically relating to Sweden's feminist foreign policy, and its direct components being chosen and categorized as per the proposed conceptual framework. The findings revealed 299 tweets which directly related to these subjects, with forty-three of these tweets referring explicitly to the title of Sweden's feminist foreign policy and 256 relating to the promotion of the ideals and norms present within Sweden's feminist foreign policy that reflect Sweden's ambition to champion and promote gender equality, increase the presence, status and role of women within decision making processes, and improve the lives of women and girls. Finally, the coded tweets were categorized into the relevant constructed ideal type for soft power resources, as explained above. It should also be noted that tweets deleted before our collection date are not included in the data set, and while there are likely to be relatively few deleted tweets (if any), our sample reflects only tweets that the selected MFAs were prepared to uphold as an integral part of their digital narrative. The tweets collected, coded, and categorized are illustrated in Figure 9.2 and Figure 9.3.

Twitter Account @SweMFA: Soft Power 'Resources'

The following analysis is succinct, focusing on illustrative examples from the aforementioned soft power resources and their projection online, as highlighted in detail

---

[1] Swedish Ministry of Foreign Affairs Twitter Account (@SweMFA), URL: https://twitter.com/SweMFA, Last Accessed: 07/02/2022.

DIGITAL FEMINIST FOREIGN POLICY   167

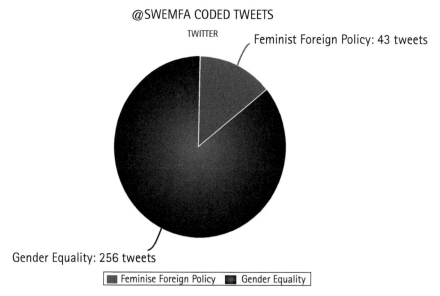

FIGURE 9.2 @SweMFA coded tweets online (2021)
Source: Created by the chapter author, based on the tweets collected and collated by the author. The process is outlined in detail in the section 'Twitter Account @SweMFA: An Analysis'.

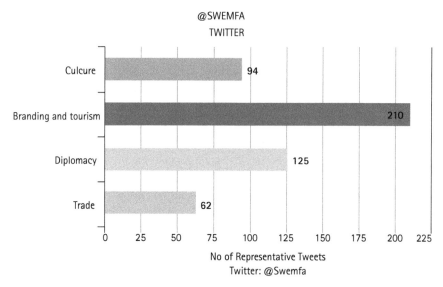

FIGURE 9.3 Sweden's soft power 'resources' online (2021)
Source: Created by the chapter author, based on the tweets collected and collated by the author. The process is outlined in detail in the section 'Twitter Account @SweMFA: An Analysis'.

within the ideal type above. Relating directly to the proposed ideal type categories, the analysis of @SweMFA's account and corresponding tweets reveal that, of the 299 coded tweets, the categorization was as follows: Culture (94), Tourism and Branding (210), Diplomacy (125), and Trade (62). See Figure 9.3. Engaging in a more focused investigation, our findings reveal that for the first soft power resource of *Culture*, Sweden digitally projected ninety-four tweets relating directly to this distinct conceptual lens. With these tweets they actively projected Sweden's values, morals, and advocacy—pertaining to gender equality, human rights, rule of law, and respect for all people—through the crafting of an online narrative, which is illustrated through individual tweets directly relating to Sweden's adoption and promotion of their feminist foreign policy. Situated within these culturally based tweets, we gained a clear insight (albeit not a comprehensive one) into a number of distinct tweets which clearly represent Sweden's projection and crafting of their soft power cultural resource online, as per the ideal type's strategy of culture. However, this time it was done through digital diplomacy means, through the projection of a feminist foreign policy. Tweets were crafted and digitally produced to represent Sweden's projection and crafting of their soft power cultural resource online.

Turning to the blended soft power resources of *Tourism* and *Branding*, we see key tenets such as national identity, uniqueness, culture, and (political or diplomatic) tourism emerge within this ideal type's categorization. Here Sweden sent out 210 tweets which directly related to both conceptual categorizations, crafting a stronger narrative projection than any other categorization. These tweets focused on ideals concerning the state's identity, its unique place in the international arena, and its ability to engage successfully in political and diplomatic tourism through hosting events and leading conferences related to the morals, values, and ideals it holds and projects. Through coding, collating, and engaging in discourse analysis on the 201 Tourism- and Branding-based tweets, we found that the ideal type and its propositions hold true. These tweets promoted online the national identity, uniqueness, culture, and (political or diplomatic) tourism of Sweden, under the digital diplomacy strategy and framework of their unique feminist foreign policy.

Turning to the broad and highly expansive soft power resources of *Diplomacy*, we see key tenets such as bilateral engagement, multilateral agreements, political and diplomatic institutions, and shared state ideologies emerge within this ideal type's categorization. Sweden here sent out 125 tweets which directly related to this conceptual lens, thereby crafting the second strongest narrative projection within this soft power resource categorization. The final examination of these soft power resources turns to the category of *Trade*, where labour force policies, diversification, security, fair trade, deregulation, and removal of trade barriers emerged as key tenets within this ideal type for Sweden, with the Swedish MFA Twitter account digitally producing sixty-two tweets which can be categorized within this individual conceptual category. An in-depth analysis, more specifically a comparative analysis of both Sweden and Mexico's adoption and online promotion of a feminist foreign policy, will be presented after Mexico's soft power resources are categorized.

Mexico

Foundational Overview

To provide a foundational overview of the second empirical case, we turn to the state which has most recently announced its adoption of a feminist foreign policy. Announced in early 2020, Mexico's feminist foreign policy openly sought to include five priority areas (with a feminist approach across all five), including foreign policy processes, making equality visible, gender parity within the foreign ministry, combatting gender-based violence, and an intersectional approach to foreign policy (Government of Mexico Press Release, 2020). Mexico specifically stated its focus would be on working within the Latin American region and regional forums using an intersectional lens. Indeed, that continued focus remains two years on. Within the diplomatic sphere, Mexico also followed Sweden's recent diplomatic route by winning a non-permanent UN Security Council (UNSC) seat in 2020. We suggest that each country's different take on feminist foreign policy can be understood through how it seeks to craft and project its soft power resources, which we have conceptualized previously and analysed below. Overall, Mexico's public adoption and online promotion of a feminist foreign policy is another example, offering us excellent insight into how states use and modify the online sphere, in order to make their nation more attractive and influential on the world stage.

Twitter Account @SRE_mx: An Analysis

The following analysis is a focused insight on how Mexico's feminist foreign policy engages and embodies their soft power resources as highlighted previously, in the ideal type presented. Speaking directly to this case, data was first collected from Mexico's primary and central MFA Twitter account (@SRE_mx).[2] From this account, 3,200 tweets were collected and coded. The date range of these tweets ran from 28 June 2021 (17:14:1) to 05 December 2021 (20:07:43). Content analysis was then conducted on all 3,200 tweets, with those tweets specifically relating to Mexico's feminist foreign policy, and its direct components being chosen and categorized as per the proposed conceptual framework. The findings revealed a mere thirty-one out of 3,200 tweets relating directly to these subjects, which should be noted was significantly less than Sweden's 299 out of 3,200 selected tweets. Both Mexico and Sweden have created public diplomacy strategies that are intertwined with their corresponding digital diplomacy policies, which directly relate to their state promotion of gender equality, the role of women within decision making processes, and improving the lives of women and girls, not only in their states, but also worldwide. As a result, when comparing the quantity of tweets between both nations, such similar conditions and varying outputs should be acknowledged and respected within the analysis.

---

[2] Mexican Ministry of Foreign Affairs Twitter Account (@SRE_mx), URL: https://twitter.com/SRE_mx, Last Accessed: 07/02/2022.

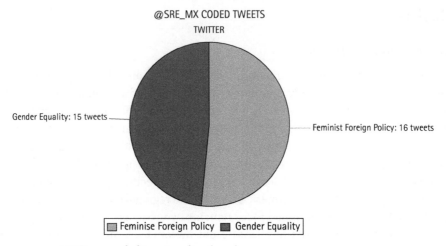

FIGURE 9.4 @SRE_mx coded tweets online (2021)

Source: Created by the chapter author, based on the tweets collected and collated by the author. The process is outlined in detail in the section 'Twitter Account @SRE_mx: An Analysis'.

Situated with these thirty-one tweets, sixteen referred explicitly to the title of Mexico's feminist foreign policy and fifteen referred to the promotion of the ideals and norms present within Mexico's feminist foreign policy. Finally, the coded tweets were then categorized into the relevant constructed ideal type for soft power resources, as explained in detail above. It should also be noted that tweets deleted before our collection date are not included in the data set, and that our sample reflects only tweets that Mexico's MFA was prepared to uphold as an integral part of its digital narrative. The tweets collected, coded, and categorized are illustrated also in Figure 9.4 and Figure 9.5.

Twitter Account: @SRE_mx: Soft Power 'Resources'

As previously noted, Mexico's adoption and promotion of a feminist foreign policy offers an excellent example of how a state seeks to project certain morals, values, and diplomatic relationships, in an active attempt to make itself more attractive, more influential, and more powerful (at least in the online arena) on the world stage. The following analysis is necessarily brief, focusing on illustrative examples from the aforementioned soft power resources and their projection online, as highlighted in detail within the ideal type above.

Relating directly to the proposed ideal type categories, the analysis of @SRE_mx account and corresponding tweets reveal, of the thirty-one coded tweets, the categorization was as follows: Culture (14), Tourism and Branding (16), Diplomacy (29), and Trade (9) (see Figure 9.5). Engaging in a more focused investigation our findings reveal that for the first soft power resource of *Culture*, Mexico digitally projected fourteen tweets relating directly to this distinct conceptual lens. These tweets actively projected Mexico's values, morals, and advocacy—pertaining to gender equality, human rights, rule of law, and respect for all people—through the crafting of an online soft power narrative, which

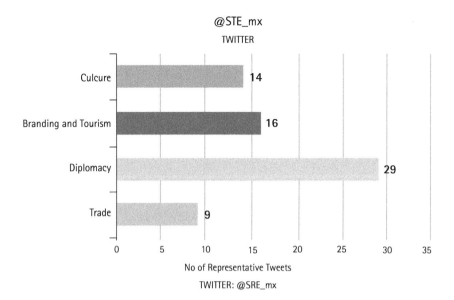

FIGURE 9.5 Mexico's soft power 'resources' online (2021)
Source: Created by the chapter author, based on the tweets collected and collated by the author. The process is outlined in detail in the section 'Twitter Account @SRE_mx: An Analysis'.

is illustrated through individual tweets directly relating to Mexico's adoption and promotion of their feminist foreign policy. Situated within these culturally based tweets, we gained a clear insight (albeit not a comprehensive one) into a number of distinct tweets which clearly represent a similar comparative context to Sweden's analysis, where we note Mexico's projection and crafting of their soft power cultural resource online, as per the ideal type's strategy of culture. However, this time it was done through digital diplomacy means, through the projection of a feminist foreign policy. Tweets were crafted and digitally produced to represent Mexico's projection and crafting of their soft power cultural resource online.

Turning to the blended soft power resources of *Tourism* and *Branding*, we see key tenets such as national identity, uniqueness, culture, and (political or diplomatic) tourism emerge within this ideal type's categorization. Here Mexico sent out sixteen tweets directly relating to these conceptual lenses, crafting a stronger narrative projection than any other categorization. These tweets focused on ideals concerning the state's identity, its unique place in the international arena, and its ability to engage successfully in political and diplomatic tourism through hosting events and leading conferences related to the morals, values, and ideals it holds and projects. Through coding, collating, and engaging in discourse analysis on these Tourism- and Branding-based tweets, we found that the ideal type and its propositions hold true. These tweets promoted online the national identity, uniqueness, culture, and (political or diplomatic) tourism of Mexico (just as was seen with the analysis of Sweden under this conceptual idea type), under the digital diplomacy strategy and framework of their unique feminist foreign policy.

Turning to the broad and highly expansive soft power resources of *Diplomacy*, we see key tenets such as bilateral engagement, multilateral agreements, political and diplomatic institutions, and shared state ideologies emerge within this ideal type's categorization. Here Mexico sent out twenty-nine tweets which directly related to this conceptual lens, thereby crafting the second strongest narrative projection within this soft power resource categorization. The final examination of these soft power resources turns to the category of *Trade*, where labour force policies, diversification, security, fair trade, deregulation, and removal of trade barriers emerged as key tenets within this ideal type for Mexico, with Mexico's MFA Twitter account digitally producing nine tweets which can be categorized within this individual conceptual category. An in-depth analysis, more specifically a comparative analysis, of both Sweden and Mexico's adoption and online promotion of a feminist foreign policy will be presented below.

COMPARATIVE STATE ANALYSIS

When viewed from a comparative analysis context, the soft power resources within both selected case studies overlap, frequently and distinctly. This investigation revealed that they overlap not only within individual state analysis, but also between them. Furthermore, what emerges with clarity as a result of this chapter's analysis, and the insight garnered from it, is that regardless of the numerical diversity of projected tweets between states (see Figure 9.6), it remains distinctly evident that each online foreign ministry account analysed within this investigation has engaged, and continues to engage, with their state's own adoption and promotion of a feminist foreign policy in distinctly different but interlocking ways.

Speaking directly to this point of comparative context between states, Ann Towns (2010: 6), in her work *Women and States: Norms and Hierarchies in International Society*, proposes that '[s]tate behaviour towards women has often provided an opportunity not only to differentiate among states but also to evaluate and rank states in a hierarchical manner'. Some feminist foreign policy countries (Sweden specifically) have a long-standing reputation as ethical powers with an ideological heritage as promoters of human rights, and not least gender equality (Zhukov et al., 2021). Being a pioneer by initiating a feminist policy attracts attention and can consolidate a country's image as a vanguard and frontrunner. This is a narrative which runs remarkably strong within the online sphere and strategic narratives presented by Sweden. In comparison to Mexico, their feminist foreign policy and promotion of it online both supports its ambitions as a regional leader and adds credibility to its domestic fight against femicide. As the year progressed, however, we also witnessed a strong narrative of multilateral cooperation and 'ideal sharing' emerge from the Mexican MFA online, with increasing messages of support and acknowledgement of other states and multilateral actors who shared and supported Mexico's views and policies on gender

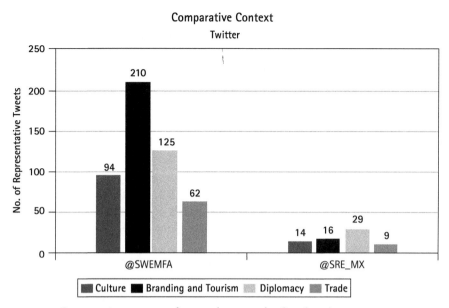

FIGURE 9.6 Comparative context soft power 'resources' online (2021)
Source: Created by the chapter author, based on the tweets collected and collated by the author. The process is outlined in detail in the sections: 'Twitter Account @SweMFA: An Analysis' and 'Twitter Account @SRE_mx: An Analysis'.

equality and equity, in particular retweeting and quoting those states who explicitly promote a feminist foreign policy of their own. This open shared acknowledgement of understanding brings with it possible opportunities of increasingly stronger state-to-state relations between these states, increased trade, and/or multilateral cooperation, even outside the shared arena of a feminist foreign policy. Finally, a feminist foreign policy may also become a catalyst for recognition at a multilateral arena, as evidenced by the Canadian (2018) and French (2019) presidency in the Group of Seven (G7), and the Swedish (2017–18) and Mexican (2021–22) non-permanent seats on the UNSC after their feminist foreign policy launch. How these distinct narratives progress online, and their continued impact in the online and offline sphere, is without question an arena worth watching.

The revealed differences, as highlighted in Figure 9.6, between these states in approaching their respective feminist foreign policies may allow us to conclude that when international norms get translated into online strategic narratives of states, in this case projected through the medium of Twitter, they become part of stories that states tell about themselves and others in solving urgent problems. In these circumstances, the content of individual soft power resources and how it is projected is no longer solely about the ideals, morals, and values within that resource, but about the states themselves and their place in the world. This leads us to suggest that a feminist foreign policy is not simply about localization of international norms surrounding gender equality and equity or about internationalization of local norms surrounding the same conceptual beacons. Nor is it not primarily about national identities, images of Self and Others, and perceptions of roles that different states embrace or reject in solving pressing global issues. The findings of this analysis also demonstrate that feminist foreign policies are not a unified phenomenon. The two states examined throughout this chapter revealed their unique feminist foreign policies to be conceptualized and articulated in different ways related to strategic considerations. To a certain extent, feminist foreign policies states may thus compete by bringing attention to their specific interpretation of feminist foreign policies and to their specific role or niche in promoting feminist policies.

When assessing the instrumentalization of a feminist foreign policy online, it is necessary to address not only the potential *benefits* of it at a state level, but also the possible backlash that the foreign ministry may receive online, from promoting what is still a divisive issue amongst a number of people online, with one possible harm and pitfall being the establishment of state feminism in other parts of the world. Based on this possible harm, and backlash against a state, for not only adopting, but actively digitally projecting its promotion, it is vital for any researcher and policy maker alike, to address the very idea of this policy being 'foreign' reproducing differences in race, ethnicity, religion, culture, and class between those who promote a feminist foreign policy and those who receive it. By being formulated as a coherent state narrative, feminist foreign policies have the distinct possibility to silence internal contradictions—whether between 'progressive' elites and the business community, between state representatives and civil society, or between well-off and marginalized women at home and abroad. Therefore, the acknowledgement of possible harms, and reproduction of a feminist foreign policy both online and off, must be undertaken and respected by all states who seek to adopt and promote it.

This comparative analysis also illustrates the argument that these digital policies of attraction are performative tools of political practice and, as such, are evidence of both states' increasing global reach, as well as their ability to project their carefully managed image abroad through the discursive praxis of public diplomacy. With that said, further research needs to develop the ideal type of soft power put forward in this analysis. However, attempting to fill a substantial gap in the literature offers a start to the debate on grounding soft power in empirical research when it comes to investigating this increasingly powerful tool of attraction on the international stage: feminist foreign policy. Indeed, the significance of the current analysis lies in its ability to spell out soft power resources, which then allow researchers and policy makers to consider the potential gains and drawbacks of strategies designed to win over opinion abroad and make states more attractive to others. Therefore, rather than rendering the ideal type problematic, researchers should better seek to understand such 'outliers' by the way in which they differ from the mainstream. This chapter thus invites further studies and deeper investigations within this pressing area of academic discovery. Investigating and examining states, such as Canada and France, who have also adopted a feminist foreign policy would be a worthy avenue for comparative investigation and future research.

Conclusion

This chapter contributed three distinct but interlocking aims: (1) it exposed and confronted the politics of attraction as constructed and projected online; (2) it shed light on the overlooked use of digital tools to craft a state's image and brand, through the use of critical junctures, with the focus of this chapter being the adoption and online promotion of a feminist foreign policy; (3) it examined the current state of a feminist foreign policy as a digital tool for Sweden and Mexico to promote their nation's brand and country's image and to express their state's moral values. By engaging in and producing these core contributions, this chapter has made substantial progress in theorizing and empirically demonstrating the understanding of a feminist foreign policy, as a state tool for twenty-first century image-making and cultural, political attraction. Through qualitative and quantitative analysis, this chapter presented the findings that adoption and promotion of a feminist foreign policy, and consequently the advocacy of gender equality worldwide, has provided a number of states with limited ability, but a strong and increasing potential to practise digital diplomacy, by constructing strategic narratives to further utilize to advance their soft power online. Further research, be this through comparative analysis or through singular state examination, should be undertaken and encouraged, to garner further insight within this diplomatic arena.

Suggested Readings

Aggestam, Karin, and Annika Bergman-Rosmand. 2019. 'Feminist Foreign Policy 3.0. Advancing Ethics Equality in Global Politics'. SAIS Review of International Affairs 39 (1): pp. 37–48.
Duriesmith, D. 2017. *Engaging Men and Boys in the Women, Peace and Security Agenda*, LSE Centre for Women, Peace and Security.
- hooks, b. 2015. *Feminist Theory: from Margin to Center*. New York: Routledge.
- Zack, N. 2005. *Inclusive Feminism: A Third Wave Theory of Women's Commonality*. Maryland: Rowman & Littlefield Publishers.
- Sjoberg, L. 2013. *Gendering Global Conflict: Toward a Feminist Theory of War*. Columbia University Press.
- Zimmerman, S. 2020. *The Value of a Feminist Foreign Policy*. Women In International Security.

Bibliography

Bandurski, David. 2007. 'Propaganda Head Liu Yunshan Promotes Commercialization of Media to Strengthen China's "Cultural Power". *China Media Project*, 10 April 2007
Bjola, Corneliu. 2016. 'Digital diplomacy – the state of the art'. *Global Affairs* 2 (3): pp. 297–299.
Bjola, Corneliu and Marcus Holmes. 2015. *Digital Diplomacy: Theory and Practice*. London: Routledge.

Grix, Jonathan and Paul Michael Brannagan. 2016. 'Of Mechanisms and Myths: Conceptualising States' "Soft Power" Strategies through Sports Mega-Events'. *Diplomacy and Statecraft* 27 (2): pp. 251–272.

Grix, Jonathan, Paul Michael Brannagan, and Houlihan, Barrie. 2015. 'Interrogating States' Soft Power Strategies: A Case Study of Sports Mega-Events in Brazil and the UK'. *Global Society* 29 (3): pp. 463–79.

Government of Mexico. 2020. 'Mexico Adopts Feminist Foreign Policy' Secretaría de Relaciones Exteriores. 09 January. https://www.gob.mx/sre/prensa/mexico-adopts-feminist-foreign-policy?idiom=en.

Government Offices of Sweden. 2019. '*Swedish Foreign Service action plan for feminist foreign policy 2015-2018*', https://www.peacewomen.org/sites/default/files/action-plan-feminist-foreign-policy-2015-2018.pdf, Last Accessed 6 August 2023.

Government Office of Sweden. 2019. 'Statement of Government Policy on Foreign Affairs, Policy', https://www.government.se/contentassets/da51fffff1e3848b4bc5597190bdd8c4e/Statement-of-Foreign-Policy-2018/. Last Accessed 6 August 2023.

Hill, Christopher and Sarah Beadle. 2014. *The Art of Attraction: Soft Power and the UK's Role in the World*. The British Academy.

Jezierska, Katarzyna. 2021. 'Incredibly Loud and Extremely Silent: Feminist Foreign Policy on Twitter'. *Cooperation and Conflict* 36 (1): p. 177.

Melissen, Jan. 2005. *The New Public Diplomacy: Soft Power in International Relations*. Basingstoke UK: Palgrave Macmillan.

McClory, J. 2019. *The Soft Power 30*. London: Portland.

Nye, Joseph. 2004a. The Benefits of Soft Power. *Harvard Business School* [online] 8 February 2004. hbswk.hbs.edu/archive/4290.html

Nye, Joseph. 2004b.'Soft Power and American Foreign Policy'. *Political Science Quarterly* 119 (2): pp. 255–270.

Roselle, Laura, Alister Miskimmon, and Ben O'Loughlin. 'Strategic Narrative: A New Means to Understand Soft Power'. *Media, War & Conflict* 7 (1) (2014): pp. 70–84.

Towns, Anne E. 2010. *Women and States: Norms and Hierarchies in International Society*. Cambridge, UK: Cambridge University Press.

Wright, Katharine A.M. and Roberta Guerrina. 2020. 'Imagining the European Union: Gender and Digital Diplomacy in European External Relations'. *Political Studies Review* 18 (3): pp.393–409. https://doi.org/10.1177/1478929919893935. Last Accessed 6 August 2023.

Zhukova, E., M. Rosén Sundström, and O. Elgström. 2021. 'Feminist Foreign Policies (FFPs) as Strategic Narratives: Norm Translation in Sweden, Canada, France, and Mexico'. ; *Review of International Studies* 48 (1): pp. 217–217.

CHAPTER 10

HISTORY AND DIGITAL PUBLIC DIPLOMACY: MEDIA DISRUPTION AND GLOBAL PUBLIC ENGAGEMENT ONLINE IN HISTORICAL PERSPECTIVE

NICHOLAS J. CULL

WHEN the word 'history' is linked to the term 'digital diplomacy' it is most often as a blaring fanfare statement of scale and tied to the present: a negative marker of the catastrophic degree of disruption or a monumental challenge encountered in digital space or perhaps a positive indicator of the unprecedented nature of some special opportunity adjudged to flow from the digital sphere. An example of the latter occurred in October 2021 when the US Secretary of State, Antony Blinken, spoke of his hopes for reinvigoration both digital and in-person diplomacy as a window for 'historic, lasting change' (Blinken, 2021). As other chapters in this book make clear, the digital has impacted widely on diplomacy with activities including but not limited to the use of virtual meetings, big data analysis, algorithm coding, crowd sourcing policy, digital analysis of public opinion, open-source intelligence, and even experiments in gaming and virtual worlds. This chapter will focus on one specific dimension of digital diplomacy—digital public diplomacy (those elements of diplomacy which operate through engagement with a foreign public)—and consider the value of history in understanding both the micro-processes at work within foreign ministries and the macro-trends unleashed in wider society, which in turn generate the wider landscape of foreign policy. The focus is apt given that the invocation of history to emphasize a watershed is a particular feature of digital public diplomacy. In recent years, the claim has been predominantly negative. Observers have spoken of history made by the challenge of an adversary's new digital propaganda tactics or history repeating in a return to old habits of mutual demonization but in the new platforms of digital space.

This chapter will acknowledge the scale of the current challenge in the digital realm but will focus on history not in a metaphoric sense but as a source of relevant precedent. As the book of Ecclesiastes (1:9) puts it: 'The thing that hath been, it is that which shall be; and that which is done is that which shall be done: and there is no new thing under the sun.' In so doing the chapter hopes to illuminate the exceptional dangers to the international system inherent in the special forms of instability associated with the coming of a new medium of political communication. There have been paradigm shifts in communication technology before and their impact on diplomatic engagement is instructive. This chapter will both outline an underlying pattern in the acceptance of technology in public diplomacy, which appears to be repeated in the digitization of public diplomacy, and—more worryingly—show the links between innovation in news media technology and extreme instability on the international stage. I will argue that shifts in new media technology are the forgotten dimension in our worst global crises. Yet there is hope. History also suggests a process of rebalancing and adaptation to new media technologies and their integration over time into the processes of building peace and resolving conflict. The research for this piece is in many places a revisiting of periods and processes addressed in the author's own work on the history of propaganda and the role of media in diplomacy over three decades (hence the multiple instances of self-citation) now reconsidered in the light of the scale of the present crisis in both international and media affairs.

Our Moment of Crisis

Our world is in the midst of crisis and digital media are an integral part of it. Digital media provide our collective window on that crisis, are embraced as tools to manage it, and are themselves catalysts of underlying difficulties. The diplomatic sphere has been destabilized by a widespread weaponization of media by hostile actors on the world stage seeking to advance their goals. The hostile intent has been compounded by the problem of the public around the world lacking long-term familiarity with the dominant platforms. The world may have come to terms with digital platforms broadly, but the advent of social media, with its ability to connect many to many, to sidestep traditional sources of editorial authority, and to trade in sensation whereby the most emotionally rewarding story travels furthest, has upended the public sphere. Social media platforms hit the global public like a virus to which they had yet to develop an immunity, displacing media legacy platforms as sources of information even as they simultaneously eroded the advertising base on which the profitability of the legacy media platforms depended. Matters were made worse by the simultaneous crisis in politics in which governments around the world faced problems that were too big for any one country to fix: climate, migration, economic crisis, and so forth. Multiple countries looked to the reassuring but ultimately counterproductive charms of strong man leaders promising quick fixes and identifying clear scapegoats, often amplified by digital platforms. This whole situation lay on top of existing trends towards a more prominent role for the public in foreign policy and an emphasis on reputation-focused concepts like Soft Power. It was a recipe for chaos (Bjola and Pamment, 2019; Seib, 2021).

The crisis found public diplomacy already engaged in managing a transition to a digital world. It is a mark of the significance of the digital revolution that its impact can be detected in all aspects of public diplomacy. Each of the five core areas of public diplomacy activity identified in Cull's classic schema (Cull, 2019)—listening, advocacy, culture, exchange, and international broadcasting/news—all now have digital dimensions. In listening, tracking of online media and trending topics in real time is now commonplace. The first response of both Japan and Saudi Arabia in 2020 following the outbreak of COVID was to inaugurate new real-time listening activity using artificial intelligence to better understand opinion in crucial markets. In advocacy, the embassy and foreign ministry twitter feed is a universal feature of self-presentation. In cultural work, actors have not only developed online methods for delivery of some programmes, such as language instruction, but also have developed cultural collaborations in digital space. In October 2020 the British Council launched a Digital Collaborations Fund for exactly this purpose to link British arts organizations with counterparts in foreign countries eligible for overseas development aid (ODA) funds (British Council, 2020). Exchange providers have experimented with hybrid programmes mixing in-person and digital contact, have substituted all-virtual meetings for physical trips to maintain operations during the pandemic, and have focused on developing links with digital leaders. An excellent example of the latter is the US Department of State's TechWomen and TechGirls programmes, linking the next generation of female innovators in places like the Middle East and Africa with Silicon Valley. In international broadcasting, the world's state-funded media have developed digital platforms. Canada and Netherlands now use these exclusively. News output is conceptualized as packages of material which can be shared through multiple channels. The US government now co-locates efforts to promote connectivity around the world beside its international news media in the US Agency for Global Media. The associated programme, known as the Open Technology Fund (OTF), claims to have supported Internet access for more than two billion people in 200 languages around the world for an annual budget of $20 million (OTF, 2022).

Digital activities have become a key source of Soft Power. Estonia has placed especial emphasis on its digital dimension, offering online citizenship to qualified netizens. The US points to Silicon Valley as an aspect of its Soft Power while Israel plays up its status as a start-up nation with digital businesses strongly represented. More than this, the digital is also a vector for attack on the image of rivals. Analysts in NATO had long since popularized the term hybrid-warfare to refer to the mix of media and physical assault deployed against Ukraine in 2014 (Wither, 2020). It is increasingly common for hostile actors to deploy disinformation online to smear an adversary or simply to undermine the impression that facts are knowable, with the underlying assumption that when audiences are confused or uncertain they will gravitate to the strength of the regime promoting the uncertainty. Bjola and Pamment have written of the 'dark side' of digital diplomacy (Bjola and Pamment, 2019). Struggles over reputation have included a concerted assault by media associated with the regime in Russia on the reputation of the Nordic countries, associating them with the neglect and abuse of children. The association serves to undermine what has historically been one of the strongest reputations on the global stage. It also turns part acts of goodness such as the Nordic countries' interest in adopting children from Russia into more sinister behaviour (Deverell, Wagnsson, and Olsson, 2021).

The convergence of crisis and new technology has encouraged an emphasis on the unprecedented nature of the moment. Even a cursory analysis of the historical record reveals that while the present moment rests on new technologies with unprecedented capacities the underlying strategies are familiar. Propaganda has a well-established role in international relations: making home audiences supportive, foreign friends friendlier, demoralizing enemies, and appealing to neutrals. At its most powerful, propaganda is not communicating facts. It is speaking to underlying and even unspoken prejudices and connecting them to political activity in the present. The tactics visible online come from a familiar playbook even if the technologies are brand new.

There is a distinct three-phase pattern to the introduction of new technology to public diplomacy. Its application to the emergence of digital public diplomacy suggests that we are in the midst of the process and not at the end. The phases are as follows. First comes a period of symbolic use when the communication technology is used as a statement in the hope that its use will be newsworthy in existing media rather than for any communicative freight which the mechanism itself might hope to carry. Second comes the phase of early application when the new technology is used to accomplish a task accomplished by a former technology without integrating the full potential of the new medium. The third comes a phase of mature application when new technology is used in a new way, harnessing the full capabilities of the new medium. By way of illustration consider first the adoption of radio as a mechanism of public diplomacy.

Case One: Radio

The first use of radio in public diplomacy was symbolic. In January 1903 President Theodore Roosevelt of the United States used the new wireless apparatus created by Guglielmo Marconi to send a morse coded message of friendship to King Edward VII and his people. The message read:

> In taking advantage of the wonderful triumph of scientific research and ingenuity which has been achieved in perfecting a system of wireless telegraphy, I extend on behalf of the American people most cordial greetings and good wishes to you and the people of the British Empire.

The King, who received the message at a transmitter in Cornwall, replied:

> I thank you most sincerely for the kind message which I have just received from you through Signor Marconi's transatlantic wireless telegraphy. I sincerely reciprocate, in the name of the people of the British Empire, the cordial greetings and friendly sentiment expressed by you on behalf of the American nation, and I heartily wish you and your country every possible prosperity
>
> (*Times of London*, 1903)

Both messages were crafted to resonate with a wider public but that public would be reached through press reports of the innovative exchange and not through the inherent capacity of Marconi's system. The system itself was used in a limited way as a mechanism for point-to-point contact along the lines of a telegraphic cable system, rather than as a mechanism for one-to-many dissemination or broadcasting, which the medium eventually made possible.

The emergence of radio broadcasting opened new communication possibilities for nation states. It was notable, however, that the first generation of international broadcasters were recreating the capabilities and conventions of the printed word. Specifically, they aimed their broadcasts at their own publics overseas, seeing broadcasting as a mechanism for maintaining a connection with colonies and diasporas rather than a way to win friends. This was the dynamic behind the creation of Radio Netherlands, France's Poste Colonial, and the BBC's Empire Service. The Soviet Union—which sought to use the new medium to export its political philosophy—still did so by clearly labelling the origin of its transmissions as Radio Moscow (Wood, 1992). Content of the new services was news from the point of view of the sponsoring government. It was read over the air essentially as it would have been printed.

The programming materials for their audio value—music, conversation, recorded sound reportage, and even drama—was part of the transition to a third phase of radio diplomacy, but the real innovation was the insight that a station could be distanced from and even conceal its sponsor. The Second World War saw the emergence of new types of international broadcasting, what would now be called surrogate stations—proxy broadcasters funded by one country but whose broadcasters were from another, broadcasting to their home audience: French exiles broadcasting from London to German-occupied France; Danish-exiles broadcasting from London to German-occupied Denmark and so on, all under the auspices of BBC external services (Stenton, 2000). Such an approach was also a mainstay of Cold War broadcasting and the work of stations like the US-government-sponsored Radio Free Europe. Beyond this were the so-called Black Propaganda radio stations whose sponsor was deliberately misattributed, the most famous being the stations which purported to be operated by the anti-Nazi factions within the German military but which were in reality created by the British Political Warfare Executive (Delmer, 1962). The US government followed the same strategy with its own line-up of 'black' and 'grey' clandestine stations in the early Cold War (Cummings, 2021). With this line-up of activity, radio at last had a range of outlets which fitted its capacities. The medium had realized its potential. What followed was a series of radio duels as various kinds of stations competed for the attention of audiences, built or lost reputations for credibility, and intersected with other communication networks. Surrogate broadcasters in Polish, for example, had by the 1980s become an essential component of Poland's media ecology. An estimated 80% of Poles tuned in to Voice of America's broadcasts in Polish at least once a week (Nelson, 1997).

CASE TWO: TERRESTRIAL TELEVISION

The same three phases played out in the adaptation of terrestrial television to diplomatic use. At the start it was a novelty, featured as an exhibit at international expositions. In the early days of scheduled television services there were sometimes attempts to use the medium as a tool of public diplomacy. A good example was the TV spectacular in support of the United Nations which graced the screens of New York City in 1943. The event could not be expected to reach a significant audience but it was plainly hoped that print and radio news reports of the performance would circulate and that the association of the cause with the latest technology would be a positive thing (Cull, 1996).

The second phase of television diplomacy was the attempt to use stations around the world as simple platforms for a dominant country's film programming. The early years of US Cold War public diplomacy focused on distributing documentary films of political value to foreign stations. An associated gambit was technical aid to help allied nations develop television stations with an eye to upgrading their domestic political communication. The medium had immense qualities of its own but was used as an extension of either radio or the educational film circuit. By the 1960s a more complex use of television consistent with the nature of the medium could be seen. The United States Information Agency produced Spanish language talk shows for distribution to Latin America and developed regional production to embed output more closely in target regions. Success stories included the creation of a fabulously successful soap opera for Latin American audiences called *Nuestro Barrio* (Our Neighbourhood) in which storylines were both entertaining (focusing of the adventures of an idealistic young doctor) and included anti-communist and pro-public health messaging. Failures included the televisual assistance provided to South Vietnam, which seems less to have provided an all-powerful ideological weapon for America's client regime in Saigon and rather more revealed nationally the corruption of traditional culture associated with the American presence. The 'cowboy shows' with Vietnamese singing American pop-songs may have charmed urban sophisticates but they appalled viewers in the countryside and bore out the anti-American narratives of Hanoi. Perhaps the Vietnam War really was lost on television but not necessarily on American screens (Cull, 2008; Vukoder and Garabaghi, 2022).

CASE THREE: SATELLITE TELEVISION

The full force of television as a diplomatic medium was apparent only with the advent of satellite broadcasting, which freed the medium from its relatively local footprint and made transnational broadcasting possible. The same three-stage trajectory may be perceived. First there were the symbolic uses: the transmission of signals with leader greetings to inaugurate a service. In November 1963 President Kennedy prepared a message to the Japanese people to inaugurate the Relay 1 satellite. Tragically events overtook the broadcasts and Japan heard coverage of the Kennedy assassination instead (National Air and Space Museum, 2018).

The middle phase of satellite television diplomacy was the technology's use as a mechanism of distribution allowing standard programming to reach international audiences more swiftly. US embassies were equipped with facilities to download programming and pass it on to news organizations around the world. The third phase—a full integration of satellite techniques into public diplomacy—involved more complex interactive broadcasts allowing journalists in foreign countries to interview US officials and experts over a satellite link, which embassies found made it far more likely that material would be broadcast (Cull, 2008; Snyder, 1995). The use of satellite capabilities was not just on the US side. Soviet authorities agreed to participate in direct person-to-person exchanges via satellite links called Space Bridges, connecting civil society groups in the US and Soviet Union, and transmitted the resulting meetings in prime time, by some accounts significantly challenging Cold War assumptions and the status quo in the process (Brainerd, 1989).

THE COMING OF THE INTERNET

What, then, was the path of digital media in public diplomacy? It is possible to see two distinct waves. An experience in the 1990s as public diplomacy embraced the World Wide Web and a second process was based around social media and user-generated content. The initial digital transition began with the symbolic use. Swedish Prime Minister Carl Bildt emailed President Bill Clinton. His message included a rider for an assumed general public, which fell into what later that decade would be termed Nation Branding:

> Sweden is—as you know—one of the leading countries in the world in the field of telecommunications, and it is only appropriate that we should be among the first to use the Internet also for political contacts and communications around the globe.
>
> (Bildt, 1994)

While the White House avoided use of email for presidential communication for some time after that, the United States Information Agency proved to be an early adopter of the Internet. Early uses to simply replicate or accelerate existing capacities included Voice of America issuing copies of its scripts online (using the now forgotten gopher protocol) and at an early state making it possible to access entire services. Innovations which played directly to the strengths of the new medium included initiatives in digital connectivity such as those provided for schoolteachers in the former Soviet Union or refugees in Kosovo. Such work had no immediate analogue in the public diplomacy of the previous decade (Cull, 2012). The Clinton administration's decision to merge the innovative United States Information Agency into the risk averse State Department represented an undoubted step backwards in that country's path to digital diplomacy. The leadership of Colin Powell and communication pressures which followed the terrorist attacks of 11 September 2001 provided the impetus for such innovations as websites at every embassy. By the end of the George W. Bush presidency the incumbent Under Secretary of State for Public Diplomacy and Public Affairs—James K. Glassman—spoke often of the importance of what he termed 'public diplomacy 2.0'—a approach to public diplomacy which integrated the ability of the second wave of Internet platforms to present user-generated content (Cull, 2013).

'PUBLIC DIPLOMACY 2.0'

The transition to a public diplomacy integrating user-generated and social media platforms also began with high profile but essentially symbolic initiatives. In 2007 Sweden opened an embassy on the virtual world Second Life. As Stina Bengtsson has shown, the gambit was of more significance for the coverage that it generated in legacy media than people actually reached on the platform. It was—she argued—'virtual nation branding' (Bengtsson, 2011). In the years that followed there was a distinct pattern of digital diplomacy initiatives being trumpeted to showcase the sponsor's innovative approach. This was a regular feature of the presentation of the Obama administration. Secretary of State Hillary Clinton spoke of Twenty-First Century Statecraft. The emphasis was perhaps less an attempt to convince foreign audiences of the innovative nature of the US than a bid to stress to domestic audiences that the administration was managing the digital revolution (Cull, 2013).

Behind the bluster of grand declarations and symbolic 'firsts' much digital and social media fell into the category of using new technology in old ways. Twitter feeds reproduced the one-way dynamics of press releases or served as flags for reports or statements placed on websites. The potential for social media to enable mass participation in and transmission of ideas was neglected; there seemed to be little attention to the potential virality of messages and, indeed, regulations requiring clearances from superiors for messages argued against the kind of shooting from the hip rewarded on social media. And yet, while the Department of State lingered on the brink, the social media impacted the world.

Scholars of the process of transitions in new technology include Marshall McLuhan, who proposed a tetrad of media effects to help understand its impact. Every new technology—he argued—will enhance something, retrieve something from the past, render another technology obsolete, and reverse an existing trend. The telephone had enhanced direct person to person communication, retrieved the power of speech, rendered messenger boys obsolete, and reversed the trend towards written communication (McLuhan and McLuhan, 1988). Social media maps interestingly into these categories. It has plainly enhanced person to person communication, but it has retrieved the free circulation of memes and rumours as if turning the whole world into the marketplace of old, abuzz with scandal and the latest jokes. It has revived the importance of the visual in outreach. What has been rendered obsolete? The social turn has effectively obsolesced the gate-keepers of media—the editors and authorities who ensured standards albeit by their own lights. What has been reversed? Most observers would concede that the emphasis on writing seen in the era of email has been reversed. Some would go so far as to argue that the social coherence that came from centuries of stable, national media has also been reversed. The world is certainly in a state of disruption.

MEDIA DISRUPTION IN HISTORICAL PERSPECTIVE

New media have been appearing for centuries and while all bring a certain disruption not all are harbingers of doom. It is not uncommon for new media to become visible at a time of crisis simply because the crisis story requires reporting and audiences are open to experimenting with a new platform at such times. Hence the first Gulf War accelerated the transition to rolling news formats and the Desert Fox bombings of Iraq 1998 were associated with early attention to Al Jazeera's news in Arabic. Historically the Anglo-Boer War and Spanish American wars both saw innovations in news reporting on film in response to audience demand. Both conflicts produced staged films falsely claiming to be actual scenes of their respective conflicts. In neither case is the innovation considered to have impacted on the cause or outcome of the war (Barnes, 1992; Chapman, 2008). This is not the case with the three most significant conflicts of the Twentieth Century. World War One, World War Two, and the Cold War are all profoundly connected to the evolution of new technologies. In fact, the disruption caused by new technology should be included as a causal factor in the onset and escalation of these events.

CASE ONE: WORLD WAR ONE

The crisis leading to the outbreak of World War One overlapped with the emergence of mass audience popular press. The international tensions which had been containable in the later nineteenth century now had also to reckon with each grievance on the international stage being presented in a way calculated to maximize the audience in that newspaper's market, which in the context of 1914 meant a Europe-wide emphasis on national perspectives. It suited the commercial and political priorities of editors to demonize neighbours. It was also in no one's immediate interest to pay attention to events in the Balkans in the early summer. As Jack Hamilton and others have noted, it is revealing that in the summer of 1914 the French popular press had little interest in the assassination of Archduke Franz Ferdinand in Sarajevo but was much more interested in the trial of the wife of the Minister of Finance, one Mme Henriette Caillaux, for murdering the editor of *Le Figaro*, an old lover who had damaged her husband's career (Hamilton, 2020).

CASE TWO: WORLD WAR TWO

The crisis leading to the outbreak of World War Two also coincided with new media destabilization. In that case it was the emergence of the powerful national media of radio and newsreel which enabled the leaders of the era to dramatize their politics in new ways and marshal their populations back onto collision courses with their neighbours. Hitler and Goebbels made no secret of the debt that they owed to radio as a mechanism for sealing the inner worldview of Germans along Nazi lines once they had taken power. Mass production and distribution of inexpensive radios became a priority for the regime even as Goebbels tightened control over on-air content. Radio worked in tandem with the use of air travel, which allowed an unprecedented personal visibility for Hitler across the entirety of Germany, ensuring that Germans were exposed to a heady mix of virtual and in-person encounters with the leader. Waxing lyrical on the power of the medium at the opening of a radio exhibition in the summer of 1933, Goebbels called radio the 'eighth great power' and stated:

> It would not have been possible for us to take power or to use it in the ways we have without the radio and the airplane. It is no exaggeration to say that the German revolution, at least in the form it took, would have been impossible without the airplane and the radio.

(Goebbels, 1933/Bytwerk, 1999)

There was no airtime for voices of restraint or international conciliation. The decade of the 1930s unfolded with a cycle of crises precipitated by the dictators who then further enhanced their power by providing solutions.

The democracies were also touched by media disruption in the run up to World War Two. In the United States, President Roosevelt was able to use the intimacy of the new medium to rally his country behind New Deal reforms but did not have everything his way. Dissenting voices like radio priest Charles Coughlin succeeding in complicating the politics of US foreign policy and using the new medium to stoke the fires of US isolationism. As late as 1938 a sizeable slice of the United States radio audience still lacked the media-specific literacy necessary to accurately assess the veracity of information received over the wireless at a moment of crisis: a fact famously exploited by Orson Welles in his mischievous *War of the Worlds* broadcast on Halloween that year. By the end of the war-that-radio-helped-make, the US public seems to have had a clearer grasp on the medium but had to adjust to the new medium of television.

CASE THREE: THE EARLY COLD WAR

The Cold War is less clearly related to a media disruption, but the coincidence of the political crisis which followed the shocks of the Soviet A-bomb and outbreak of the Korean War with the learning-cure associated with the new medium of television made matters worse. Senator Joe McCarthy proved an early innovator in playing to the cameras and staged televised hearings to expound his theory of a vast Communist conspiracy against the United States and build his own career in the process. Edward R. Murrow's famous riposte in his *See It Now* broadcast of March 1954 was part of a process of the country learning to interpret televised events (Doherty, 2003). As noted earlier in this chapter, television was one of the gifts which Cold War superpowers offered to their satellites, helping to create a broadcast system which overlapped with and reinforced political alignments.

This argument as to the toxic nature of media disruption raises the issue of why this isn't a more regularly discussed element of the history of these events. In the first instance it seems that human nature prefers to personalize conflicts and speak in terms of guilty parties—the Kaiser, Hitler, Stalin—or geographical theatres of conflict like the Western Front, Pacific War, or Iron Curtain rather than the war of the popular press, the war of radio, or the crisis that TV made worse. Integrating media disruption into an understanding of these crises is made still less likely by our collective reliance on these selfsame channels for our understanding of the conflict. Propaganda in the Great War is a case in point. The detailed work of scholars on what actually happened in the Great War suggests that the popular press was much freer with rumours and atrocity stories that the government bureaucracies who received blame in the post war years (Badsey, 2019).

Culpability for crisis is only part of the story. It is also clear that the solutions to our most serious crises have involved a systematic reassessment of the media; an honesty about its disruptive qualities and a process to promote or even restore balance. To return to our three cases:

MEDIA DISARMAMENT: GREAT WAR, WORLD WAR TWO, COLD WAR

The aftermath of the Great War spurred a global examination of the causes of the conflict. The media was implicated, with the major culprit being state propaganda rather than the private enterprise of the popular press. The new League of Nations saw the need to work against the tendency of mutual demonization between nations and championed dialogue between thought-leaders. The league established a Committee on Intellectual Cooperation and undertook projects such as textbook studies to identify and remove counterproductive bias and tendentious misinformation. Idealists established organizations for student and faculty exchange like the Institute of International Education (IIE) founded in New York in 1919 or exchanges created as a postwar project of the American Field Service. Individual scholars like Harold Laswell worked to expose the danger of propaganda and launched the discipline of communication studies in the process. Attempts to defang the media and reign in the power of propaganda in general continued into the 1930s. Milestones included the creation in 1937 of an Institute for Propaganda Analysis also based in New York. Such efforts were unequal to the forces sweeping the world back to war.

The years following World War Two saw renewed attempts to address the media causes of war. The occupation of Japan and Germany included a top-down reconstruction of the state media apparatus: founding democratic platforms, purging the ideologues of the old regime, and so forth. At an international level the creation of UNESCO represented a concerted effort to head off media misrepresentation and reconstruct the world in a spirit of transparency and openness. The constitution of the new organization famously began: 'since wars begin in the minds of men, it is in the minds of men that the defences of peace must be constructed.' The spirit of the era was overshadowed by the emergence of the Cold War and UNESCO became a stage on which the global division was acted out.

In time the blocs engaged in the Cold War also looked to address media as a factor in mutual tension. The exploration took multiple forms from a US-Soviet mutual history textbook review process, launched in the wake of détente to an increase in educational exchanges built into the Helsinki accords of 1975. In the era of direct negotiation between Reagan and Gorbachev, media disarmament became a distinct strand of engagement. Media leaders discussed mutual stereotyping and agreed steps to improve access to one another's media space. The Soviets, whose secret elements had come to rely on disinformation as a core tactic, backed away from those methods when threatened with a suspension of cooperation in the field of AIDS research. The claim that AIDS was an American bioweapon was a favourite gambit. Finally, the US and USSR agreed to operate a disinformation hotline so that stories which one or the other considered inaccurate could be speedily corrected. This process was predicated on the perceived symmetry of power between the US and USSR. As the Soviet state collapsed, attention to media issues shifted into a cruder discussion of the opening of former-Soviet space to US media business. A dimension of the process by which the Cold War ended was forgotten in favour of a more simplistic narrative of the victory of one system over another (Cull, 2021).

Taken together these three cases may be seen as examples of media disarmament, a logical response to the role of destabilization flowing from media disruption in exacerbating these conflicts.

Conclusion: An Agenda for Leadership in Digital Public Diplomacy

This chapter argues that the disruption caused by new media has historically been a catalyst in the escalation of international crises that might otherwise have been contained. The precedents should compel action in the face of the convergence of media disruption and crisis in our own time. In the first instance it is essential that the democracies move into the third phase of adoption of this particular new media themselves. In the sub-fields of digital public diplomacy this will require being better in listening: investing in using social media to understand opinion in the field; in advocacy: empowering rapid responses and creative processes which produce material that audiences would be willing and able to share; in cultural diplomacy: building culture on and off line to be resilient to disruption; and in exchange diplomacy: using the relationship-building capacity of social media not just to establish and contribute to new communities of shared interest focused on core values like human rights but also to reinvigorate existing relationships. Key networks in need of attention include the alumni of past exchange programmes. Finally, state-sponsored international broadcasters need to invest in maintaining the circulation of credible news and to assist communities around the world in developing skills of media literacy.

The challenge requires a major readjustment in the priorities of global public engagement. Public diplomacy has long rested on the question 'what can I say to persuade this audience?' Public diplomacy in the era of digital social media requires a different question: 'who can I empower to persuade this audience?' Helping allies to engage with their own people is part of the way forward—assisting in the development and maintenance of free media; promoting media literacy to diminish the disruptive quality of the new platforms; encouraging concepts of citizenship that incorporate discussion not only of what the user has a right to access but what it is wise to share. Finally, the previous history of information disarmament should be remembered. There comes a time in the life-cycle of every unchecked weapon when the international community see greater interest in restraint than the hope of a unilateral advantage. Diplomats should be alert for that moment.

The process of mitigating the disruption associated with social media and its abuse in foreign policy is plainly now well underway. While the Ukraine crisis of 2014 suggested that audiences were astonishingly malleable in the face of disinformation and state media crafted to obscure realities on the ground, the years following saw the introduction of countermeasures such as the creation of and/or investment in fact check websites and tactical remedies. The British government successfully handed hostile and deliberately confusing digital messaging around the Skripal affair in March 2018 during which Russian agents used the novichok nerve agent in an attempted assassination on British soil. The Foreign and Commonwealth Office found that it achieved traction by simply tracking and drawing attention to the absurd range of denials and counter explanations proffered by the Russian embassy in the wake of the attack, undermining any vestige of credibility that the Russian diplomats might have had and successfully rallying European partners behind collective action (Cull, 2020). The run up to Russia's invasion of Ukraine on 24 February 2022 showed the extent to which Western countermeasures had adapted. As evidence mounted of Putin's hostile intentions, Western government messaging not only paid careful attention to reports of Russian propaganda gambits in circulation but began predicting likely media strategies to accompany any invasion. Predictions included false flag operations designed to shift culpability for the invasion onto Kyiv. The strategy reflected a foreign policy application of an approach used to combat disinformation during the Covid-19 pandemic, which was widely dubbed 'prebunking', by which a population could be successfully inoculated against a particular argument or allegation by being warned that it was coming (Vivion et al., 2022). The effect in the context of the Ukraine War seemed undeniable. The prediction of Russian falsehood drew attention to that aspect of Kremlin statecraft and then the boldfaced use of the anticipated tactic confirmed the untrustworthiness of Russian messaging and made Russia even less credible as a voice. The moment for direct negotiation over social media behaviour has yet to arrive.

As the war unfolded it became clear that Ukraine itself had mastered multiple dimensions of digital public diplomacy using the technology to its utmost. The entire experience of the war seemed digitally visible. Ministers tweeted and retweeted. NGOs rebutted Russian disinformation. Citizens engaged global publics directly not merely to share their experience of the conflict or circulate memes but to accomplish specific ends such as recruiting volunteers or crowd funding the purchase of drones. Ukrainian sources shared cellphone messages intercepted from Russian troops themselves variously revealing their low morale, looting, and confusion and undermining Kremlin claims. Video conferencing platforms allowed President Zelensky to speak at a bewildering variety of venues without geographical limitation, engaging parliaments and wider audiences with speeches skilfully crafted to resonate with local political culture. Global audiences responded not merely by passively receiving the messaging but by actively participating in its onward recirculation and generating memes of their own. Ukraine and its cause became part of the lives of a broad swathe of citizens across the West, permitting aid, civil support, and policy initiatives including the promise of a fast-tracked Ukrainian entry into the European Union. The surge in public opinion was such that corporations who had been happy to do business with Russia in the years following 2014 scrambled to abandon the market lest publics elsewhere tar them with a Putinist brush. Thus digital public diplomacy became a force multiplier, a major reason that the easy victory expected by Moscow failed to materialize.

Looking to the future, analysts should expect the cycle of symbolic use, limited use, and innovative use to be repeated as each new technology becomes available. More than this the frequency of major technological changes has plainly increased, arguably to the stage when it is a permanent part of the foreign policy landscape. Diplomats can easily find themselves symbolically using one new technology while making limited use of another and mastering a third all simultaneously and while endeavouring to signal competence to their domestic public and political masters. In such circumstances the inherently conservative culture of diplomatic agencies seems of necessity to have changed. Historical precedent suggests that diplomats should also be deeply concerned by the disruptive potential of media technologies and their associated role in our foreign policy's darkest moments. They should be open to bringing the traditional expertise of diplomacy—face to face negotiation—to bear to reduce threats through mechanisms of media disarmament. Bureaucracies which are actively mindful of the difficulty in seeing new technologies in their own terms are more likely to master them than those who 'linger shivering on the brink' of change and limit use to performing the tasks of the processor technology.

RECOMMENDED READING

Cull, Nicholas J. 2008. *The Cold War and the United States Information Agency: American Propaganda and Public Diplomacy, 1945-1989.* New York: Cambridge University Press.

Cull, Nicholas J. 2012. *The Decline and Fall of the United States Information Agency: American Public Diplomacy, 1989-2001.* New York: Palgrave.

Cull, Nicholas J. 2013. 'The Long Road to Public Diplomacy 2.0: The Internet in US Public Diplomacy.' *International Studies Review*, Vol. 15, No. 1, March, pp. 123–139.

Cull, Nicholas J. 2019. *Public Diplomacy: Foundations for Global Engagement in the Digital Age.* Cambridge: Polity.

McLuhan, Marshall and McLuhan, Eric. 1988. *Laws of Media: The New Science.* Toronto: University of Toronto Press.

REFERENCES

Badsey, Stephen. 2019. *The German Corpse Factory: A Study in First World War Propaganda.* Wolverhampton: University of Wolverhampton Press.

Barnes, John. 1992. *Filming the Boer War.* Tonbridge: Bishopsgate Press.

Bengtsson, Stina. 2011. 'Virtual Nation Branding: The Swedish Embassy in Second Life,' *Journal of Virtual World's Research*, Vol. 4, No. 1, July, pp. 1–28.

Bildt, Carl. 1994. quoted in Clinton, William J. 1997. *Public Papers of the Presidents of the United States: William J. Clinton (1994, Book I).* Washington DC: GPO, p. 273

Bjola, Corneliu and Pamment, James (eds.). 2019. *Countering Online Propaganda and Extremism: The Dark Side of Digital Diplomacy.* Abingdon: Routledge.

Blinken, Antony. 2021. 'Secretary Antony J. Blinken on the Modernization of American Diplomacy,' Speech to the Foreign Service Institute, Arlington, VA, 21 October: https://www.state.gov/secretary-antony-j-blinken-on-the-modernization-of-american-diplomacy/

Brainerd, Michael (ed.). 1989. *Spacebridges: Television and U.S.–Soviet Dialogue.* Lanham, MD: University Press of America.

British Council. 2020. 'British Council announces Digital Collaboration Fund to support virtual international Arts partnerships,' Online announcement, 28 October: https://www.britishcouncil.org/about/press/british-council-announces-digital-collaboration-fund-support-virtual-international-arts#:~:text=The%20British%20Council%20today%20opened,Assistance%20(ODA)%20recipient%20countries.

Chapman, James. 2008. *War and Film*, London: Reaktion Books.

Cull, Nicholas J. 1996. 'Selling Peace: The Origins, Promotion and Fate of the Anglo-American New Order During the Second World War,' *Diplomacy & Statecraft*, Vol. 7, No. 1, pp. 1–28.

Cull, Nicholas J. 2008. *The Cold War and the United States Information Agency: American Propaganda and Public Diplomacy, 1945-1989*. New York: Cambridge University Press.

Cull, Nicholas J. 2012. *The Decline and Fall of the United States Information Agency: American Public Diplomacy, 1989-2001*. New York: Palgrave.

Cull, Nicholas J. 2013. 'The Long Road to Public Diplomacy 2.0: The Internet in US Public Diplomacy.' *International Studies Review*, Vol. 15, No. 1, March, pp. 123–139.

Cull, Nicholas J. 2019. *Public Diplomacy: Foundations for Global Engagement in the Digital Age*. Cambridge: Polity.

Cull, Nicholas J. 2020. '"Rough Winds Do Shake the Darling Buds of May," Theresa May, British Public Diplomacy and Reputational Security in the Era of Brexit' in Surowiec, Pawel and Manor, Ilan (eds.), *Public Diplomacy and the Politics of Uncertainty*. London: Palgrave, pp. 83–107.

Cull, Nicholas J. 2021. 'The Forgotten Process: Information Disarmament in the Soviet/ US Rapprochement of the 1980s,' *Vestnik of St. Petersburg State University, International Relations*, Vol. 14, No. 3, pp. 257–272.

Cummings, Richard H. 2021. *Cold War Frequencies: CIA Clandestine Radio Broadcasting to the Soviet Union and Eastern Europe*. McFarland.

Delmer, Sefton. 1962. *Black Boomerang*. London: Secker & Warburg.

Deverell, Edward, Wagnsson, Charlotte, and Olsson, Eva-Karin. 2021. 'Destruct, Direct and Suppress: Sputnik Narratives on the Nordic Countries,' *The Journal of International Communication*, Vol. 27, No. 1, pp. 15–37.

Doherty, Thomas H. 2003. *Cold War, Cool Medium: Television, McCarthyism, and American Culture*. New York: Columbia.

Goebbels, Josef. 1933. 'Der Rundfunk als achte Großmacht,' Speech at opening of 10th German Radio Exhibition, translated by Bytwerk, Randall, 1999: https://research.calvin.edu/ger man-propaganda-archive/goeb56.htm, quoted with the translator's permission.

Hamilton, John Maxwell. 2020. *Manipulating the Masses: Woodrow Wilson and the Birth of American Propaganda*. Baton Rouge: University of Louisiana Press.

McLuhan, Marshall and McLuhan, Eric. 1988. *Laws of Media: The New Science*. Toronto: University of Toronto Press.

National Air and Space Museum. 2018. 'How Communication Satellites Helped World Mourn JFK,' Editorial, November: https://airandspace.si.edu/stories/editorial/how-communicati ons-satellites-helped-world-mourn-jfk

Nelson, Michael. 1997. *War of the Black Heavens: The Battles of Western Broadcasting in the Cold War*. London: Brasseys.

OTF. 2022. 'Open Technology Fund,' Information page: https://www.usagm.gov/networks/otf/

Seib, Philip. 2021. *Information at War: Journalism, Disinformation, and Modern Warfare*. Cambridge: Polity.

Snyder, Alvin. 1995. *Warriors of Disinformation: American Propaganda, Soviet Lies, and the Winning of the Cold War, an Insider's Account*. New York: Arcade.

Stenton, Michael. 2000. *Radio London and Resistance in Occupied Europe: British Political Warfare 1939-1943*. Oxford: Oxford University Press.

Times of London. 1903. 'The King and President Roosevelt: Messages by Wireless Telegraphy,' 21 January, p. 3.

Vivion, Maryline et al. 2022. 'Prebunking Messaging to Inoculate Against COVID-19 Vaccine Misinformation: An Effective Strategy for Public Health,' *Journal of Communication in Healthcare*, Vol. 15:3, pp. 232–242. DOI: 10.1080/17538068.2022.2044606

Vukoder, Bret and Gharabaghi, Hadi (eds.). 2022. 'Special Issue: Motion Picture Legacies of the USIA,' *Journal of E-Media Studies*, Vol. 6, No. 1, pp. 1–37.

Wither, James K. 2020. 'Defining Hybrid Warfare,' *per Concordiam: Journal of European Security Defense Issues*. Vol. 10, No. 1, pp. 7–9.

Wood, James. 1992. *The History of International Broadcasting Vol. 1*. Stevenage: Institution of Engineering and Technology.

CHAPTER 11

DIGITAL CULTURAL DIPLOMACY: FROM CONTENT PROVIDERS TO OPINION MAKERS

NATALIA GRINCHEVA

INTRODUCTION

CULTURAL diplomacy, understood as a form of cross-cultural communication between countries to improve international relations, has traditionally played a unique role. Its intangible form of power can bring people together for establishing bridges of mutual trust and understanding, which can further improve international economic and political relations among nation states (Schneider, 2003). Though cultural diplomacy remains an important part of international communication, the new century, marked by such processes as economic and cultural globalization, has introduced new diplomatic players. Furthermore, technological developments in the twenty-first century have offered new digital tools to exercise cultural diplomacy. They made cross-cultural communication among governments, peoples, and institutions faster and more transparent, though more unpredictable and less centralized and controlled. Known as digital diplomacy, diplomacy 2.0, or e-diplomacy, diplomatic practices through digital and networked technologies (including the Internet, mobile devices, and social media channels) have become increasingly important and popular among various actors (Melissen, 2006).

The digital environment made possible a much larger set of diplomatic actors than before. State actors and mainstream cultural institutions as key 'cultural ambassadors' share the global communication space with cultural communities and even individuals without parties, including solo performers or influencers. Specifically, the digital environment empowered non-state actors of diplomacy who became more informed, mobile, flexible, and influential in the global arena because they can communicate their ideas and beliefs to international audiences 'often more effective[ly] than the states' (Jora, 2013: 46). As a result, cultural diplomacy in the digital environment is operationalized in a much more heterogenic and saturated space. Civil society, non-partisan cultural institutions, transnational corporations, and even individual artists or cultural leaders can successfully exist and even thrive in digital networks.

While academic scholarship made a clear distinction between state and non-state actors of digital diplomacy (Kelley, 2014), new research indicated that this dichotomy is not necessarily productive to explain diplomatic actorness in a much more complex networked environment (Grincheva and Kelley, 2019). Moreover, some scholars interrogated what exact types of actors tend to become more powerful under digital conditions, questioning how exactly individual and group actors come together online to produce 'longer chains of action' (Couldry, 2015: 615). Finally, new players complicate directions and messages of cultural diplomacy that can no longer be closely aligned with government foreign policy objectives and even create conditions for adversarial diplomacy (Wiseman, 2015).

This chapter proposes a new typology of cultural diplomacy actors, focusing on the roles they play in the global digital space and the power they can accumulate to exert impact. It argues that traditional government actors of cultural diplomacy in the digital realm increasingly become more dependent on cultural institutions and communities who serve as key cultural *content providers*. Furthermore, their activities in the digital domain are shaped by interfaces, digital capabilities, and algorithms of dominant communication platforms, designed by transnational corporations as main digital *infrastructure builders*. Finally, they operate in a very dynamic communication space populated by various *opinion makers*, including individual influencers, who gain in certain cases a significant diplomatic clout to shape global discourses.

The chapter starts with a literature review that identifies and sketches important changes in cultural diplomacy practices under the pressures of increasing digitalization and globalization processes. It proceeds with the section 'Actors' Typology' that provides clear definitions of three actors of digital cultural diplomacy and explains the rationale behind the proposed framework. It also contains three dedicated sections which further investigate and illustrate each of these types of diplomatic actors respectively. They aim to reveal what digital conditions and digital cultural and communication processes enabled three different types of actors and how they share power in the global media space.

TRANSFORMATIONS OF CULTURAL DIPLOMACY IN THE DIGITAL AGE

Content: Digitizing Arts and Cultures

Visual and performing arts shared across borders through cultural diplomacy activities have traditionally been a powerful tool to communicate political messages, ideologies, and world views to shape public perceptions 'on the other side'. For instance, during the time of the strong political tensions between the US and the Soviet Empire, jazz very quickly 'developed into a popular form of music' among Russians (Lucke, 2002: 1). During the Stalinist regime, the attitude toward jazz, a musical style with strong connotations of freedom, moved from state sponsorship to censorship and severe restrictions. However, throughout the entire Stalinist era, even when it was strictly forbidden by the government, jazz remained an important element of cultural life of the Soviet people. Many attempts were made 'to ban music and the mere mention of the word "jazz." This did succeed on the surface, but, through the burgeoning black market as well as in the Baltic republic, it was nevertheless possible to buy, hear and experience live performances in the USSR' (Zubok and Shiraev, 2000).

Before this thirst for jazz consumption reached this level, though, the US government invested almost $2.25 million to send 1,313 Americans jazz musicians (Prevots, 2001) to Eastern Europe to 'showcase the values of a democratic society in juxtaposition to a totalitarian system' (Schneider, 2003: 2). Technological developments in the digital era and the increased use of instant communication platforms have drastically changed and simplified the process of cultural sharing on the global scale. First, digital technologies immaterialized cultural consumption and interactions, and second, they deterritorialized these experiences, increasingly disconnecting place and culture (Beck, 2006). Digital technologies have created an unlimited storage capacity to preserve, share, and exchange human heritage and cultural capital accumulated by present and past generations. They offered new and more efficient means for cultural representation, promotion, and distribution, as well as its re-use and reproduction (Hernandez, 2010).

Encoded in electronic format, culture becomes a resource that is easy to share across borders to 'win hearts and minds' of international audiences. As a result, cultural diplomacy that used to be based on 'here and now' types of human experiences of engaging with other cultures transformed into a more 'on demand' interaction. In the current media landscape, cultural diplomacy shifted from the live performances and broadcasting schedules to a streaming mode, 'where audiences are subjected to a constant stream of information that adapts to them, using tools such as social media sites, search engines and messaging services' (Lutkenhaus, 2019: 2). However, the cultural content cannot exist in vacuum; there should be robust transmission channels that allow this content to travel to and reach target audiences.

Environment: Digitalizing Exchange Infrastructures

In the past, a facilitation of traditional cultural exchanges has been conducted exclusively with the help of national governments who defined the content, form, and main players of cross-cultural programmes and international travelling tours (Krenn, 2005). Nation states remained quite powerful political and economic infrastructure providers of these cross-cultural exchanges, when travelling and communication technologies posed significant barriers. It is worth mentioning, for example, that the first and the only visit of the famous Mona Lisa painting by Leonardo da Vinci from Louvre to the US in 1963 was 'an official matter of the White House', facilitated directly by the president of the USA and his wife (Zollner, 1997: 472). Securely packaged in a temperature-controlled, custom-built container, Mona Lisa arrived in the US under the patronage of fifty soldiers and six permanent bodyguards. Transformed through this highly expensive operation into a symbol of the Cold War, Mona Lisa did more than merely help to improve the frosty relationship between the USA and France. More importantly, the painting demonstrated to the whole world the major geopolitical shift of power from the old world to the US (Zollner, 1997).

However, in the times of increasing digitalization (Peters, 2016), datafication (van Dijck, 2014), and, more recently, platformization (Jin, 2017), cultural diplomacy infrastructure is no longer solely defined by national governments. Digital platforms (including social networks and instant communication providers), run by private transnational corporations, offer powerful infrastructural arrangements which in many cases 'mediate—and to a considerable extent, dictate—economic and political relationships' (Schwarz, 2017: 347). Platforms' algorithms govern the news, opinions, and friends, creating the social world of people. They are powerful enough to accelerate cultural and political fragmentation of society, in many cases exacerbating the differences between cultural communities (Riordan, 2019). Furthermore, platforms increase the 'vulnerability of all political institutions to leaks so that they become more porous, more open to disruption across their boundaries' (Couldry, 2015: 616).

As a result, developing robust digital infrastructures for cultural exchanges and international communications is critical for governments and cultural organizations to remain relevant and visible in the global media space. While digital technologies increasingly benefit powerful actors on the world stage, many arts and cultural organizations in countries with fewer resources and less-developed digital infrastructures drag behind in the global competition of cultural sharing. Moreover, a few global social media platforms dominate the international media space. They leave a small room for developing countries to compete in global informational environments, shaped by algorithmic cultures perpetuating neocolonialism (Jin, 2017). Despite these limitations on the macro level, cultural diplomacy in the digital realm allows more diverse actors to intervene in cross-cultural dialogue and exchanges and become more subjected to influences from solo-players.

Cross-Cultural Dialogue: Digitalizing Communications

From its inception, cultural diplomacy as a practice has always operated through international exchanges and stressed a two-way interactive dialogue that offers an arena for contested ideas and beliefs to be discussed and negotiated (Melissen, 2006). For example, in the context of US cultural diplomacy, 'triumphant success' and the strong power of exchange as a means of establishing a productive dialogue with foreigners is documented in various practices of Cold War diplomacy. Described in many historical works or memoirs written from both sides of the Iron Curtain (the USA and Soviet Russia), cultural exchanges had a strong impact on the participants' perceptions of each other's cultures (Richmond, 2003) and even 'played a great role in undermining the Soviet Union and sowing the seeds for its eventual dissolution' (Schneider, 2006: 147).

However, officially supported cultural exchange programmes could reach only an 'elite population' (Ivey, 2007: 37). National governments traditionally supported institutions of high arts to travel abroad, as opposed to popular culture and mass cultural products. In this regards, cultural diplomacy programmes were quite poorly positioned to embrace a broad audience. Outreach to wider foreign publics has been a real challenge, when international travelling arrangements proved to be an expensive and resource-demanding exercise, requiring a high level of long-term commitment. However, in the twenty-first century, a multitude of players with affordable and easy access to various digital tools—not only for information consumption, but also for its production and distribution—have changed the very nature of diplomatic conduct. Social networks have introduced important changes in the field of political communication.

One of them is the emergence of influencers or digital opinion leaders, who have acquired the ability to publish and, in certain cases, co-produce cultural stories to engage with various communities in a multi-directional way. Drawing on the two-step flow model of communication (Lazarsfeld et al., 1944), digital diplomacy scholarship explains the powerful role of influencers by prescribing them the role of important media transmitters who are capable to target and successfully reach less-active members of the audiences (Choi, 2014).

Employing technologically mediated personal influence, opinion makers attempt to condition the configuration of the public agenda, 'often lending their credibility to these messages' (Pamment, 2014: 57). The power of influencers rests on their ability to personalize messages, which dramatically amplifies the trustworthiness of their communication, appealing to wider publics (Uzunoglu and Kip, 2014). In these conditions, a cross-cultural dialogue is increasingly transforming from a high-level mediated diplomacy among elite stakeholders to many-to-many mobile communications where public perceptions could be shaped by a variety of actors, including independent non-partisan players.

* * *

Three foundational transformations of cultural diplomacy, namely digitization of cultural content, virtualization of exchange infostructures, and a rise in new online participants, enable three types of diplomatic actors. They include (1) actors who provide or produce digital cultural content for global circulation, (2) players who develop platforms for communication and exchange, and (3) cultural leaders, whose opinions matter in shaping global public discourses. The national governments have traditionally assumed and played all these three roles, by curating, commissioning, and enabling cultural exchanges while delivering specific ideological messages to the foreign public. With the increasing digitalization of global communication, though, which to certain degrees democratized, automated, and simplified cultural exchanges, these roles started to be shared among various stakeholders. However, these functions in diplomatic exchanges require further academic attention, especially recognizing that the existing academic scholarship does not necessarily consider them as important variables. The chapter addresses this gap in the academic scholarship and contributes to the current conceptualization of cultural diplomacy actorness by identifying three roles that actors could assume and play in the global media space.

Actors' Typology

Framework and Rationale

This chapter suggests exploring cultural diplomacy actors from the perspective of their involvement in the processes of cross-cultural communication and the role they could play in cultural diplomacy. Surveying the most recent practices of cultural diplomacy reflected in the academic scholarship, this research conceptualizes three key actors of digital cultural diplomacy: (1) content providers, (2) infrastructure builders, and (3) opinion makers.

(1) *Content provider* is a cultural actor who is capable to produce a creative content for sharing in the global media environment. Traditional cultural institutions, like museums, galleries, or performance arts groups, usually supported by state funding, remained main content providers in the historical past. In the digital age, though, many much smaller cultural communities and marginal art groups can create engaging content that can go viral and change public perceptions toward specific political issues. These new players blur the boundaries between state and non-state actors in digital cultural diplomacy as well as complicating the message of such diplomacy that can either be aligned with government foreign policy objectives or create conditions for adversarial diplomacy.

(2) *Infrastructure builder* is a powerful stakeholder in the global media space who develops sustainable channels and platforms for international information transfer, content sharing, and public communications. Actors can exercise these roles only if they acquire enormous economic resources and significant political power to build robust platforms for global many-to-many communications. Despite the muti-stakeholder aspirations of the global Internet governance, which promotes a wide range of actors, the existing situation in fact reinforces existing power dynamics, privileging governments and transnational private corporations, leaving no space to civil society (Carr, 2015). As a result, infrastructure builder roles are shared across most powerful actors on the hierarchy of the global governance, such as states, intergovernmental organizations, and transnational media corporations, predominantly from the USA.

(3) *Opinion Maker* is another important type of cultural diplomacy actor in the digital realm who can mobilize crowds by communicating cultural and political messages with an international resonance. Online opinion makers could become key power points in a highly networked digital environment who project messages of political significance. This mediated influence in many cases builds on the affordances of digital communication that elevates the personal connectivity one can achieve, increases the scope of self-communication, and provides many opportunities for more dynamic interactive forms of dialogue with publics than any bureaucratic institution or government can ever sustain in a technologically mediated field (Casero-Ripollés, 2020).

This typology is designed to account for such variables as functions, dependency, and agency. First, it interrogates and explores key functions different stakeholders choose to serve while communicating in the global media space. Second, it explores how much political clout they are capable to generate and to what extent they become dependent on other actors in a highly networked online environment. The typology does not necessarily draw a clear boundary between state and non-state actors, and neither does it argue that each actor type is self-sufficient and exists within strict boundaries of its own characteristics. By contrast, the actors' categories are not self-exclusionary, but rather they complement and extend each other.

Each of the following respective sections provides provocative illustrations that help describe major functions of each actor, demonstrating their mutual dependencies. Questioning the agency and power of each actor, the following examples highlight how the government actors play or fail to play three respective roles in the global digital media space. While the chapter reveals that some actor types might lack an agency, it also exposes a highly saturated, heterogenous, and complex nature of global cross-cultural communications that requires a more nuanced actors' typology to help its deeper analysis.

Content Providers

Content providers might include a large spectrum of visual and performing arts organizations, communities, and even independent artists, who can acquire critical diplomatic powers if they can grab and retain global audiences' attention through a meaningful content. For example, in the digital realm, museums, as key repositories of national cultural heritage, acquired significant powers to serve as state-sponsored or even unofficial cultural ambassadors. Bringing the wealth of their cultural resources to international audiences to the digital environments, they offer a robust platform for a dynamic cross-cultural sharing and dialogue. The recently published monograph *Museum Diplomacy in the Digital Age* aimed to draw attention to particular cases of unofficial, non-state cultural diplomacy that occur in the global communication space of online environments (Grincheva 2020a). Exploring the digital heritage repatriation diplomacy implemented by the Australian Museum, the digital nation-branding campaign by the British Museum, and a peculiar case of cosmopolitan corporate diplomacy exercised by the Guggenheim Museum in collaboration with Google, the book exposed political implications of museums' digital exhibitions and collections. It revealed the multiplied potentials of digital cultural content in the context of online museums to speak for the nation, construct informational environments of global audiences, and make important contributions to the cultural projection efforts of respective nation states in specific geopolitical contexts (Grincheva 2020a).

While all three analysed cases revealed that state governments were not involved in each of these online diplomatic initiatives, one cannot deny that such digital diplomacy is enabled by the level of national cultural heritage digitization, directly dependent on government support efforts. In the past several decades, national governments heavily subsidized their cultural institutions to digitize their content and provide global access to their cultural resources. For example, in the 2000s the UK government launched a nation-wide digitization programme through the New Opportunities Fund that allocated over $72 million to more than 150 digitization projects (Gill and Miller, 2002). More recently, the government's *Culture White Paper* emphasized the national commitment to making the United Kingdom 'one of the world's leading countries for digitized public collections content' (DCMS, 2018: 39). By 2018 more than 60% of arts and culture organizations in the country had digitized significant portions of their collections (DCMS, 2018: 11–12). Furthermore, in 2020 the UK Arts and Humanities Research Council invested £18.9 million to support digital humanities research projects under the framework of its flagship initiative 'Towards a National Collection'. It invests in world-renowned museums, archives, libraries, and galleries to mobilize their heritage, remove barriers between different collections, expand and diversify virtual access, and enhance the storytelling potentials of cultural heritage to create new interdisciplinary and cross-cultural experiences for global audiences (AHRC, 2020).

Similar state-enabled processes of national cultural digitization are evident in other developed countries, including Australia, Canada, and the European Union (Kremers, 2019). They aim to increase the national cultural competitiveness of heritage institutions as main content providers in the cyberspace to successfully shape and dominate the informational environments of global audiences (Ronfeldt and Arquilla, 2020). However, while governments still play an important role in enabling the digital infrastructures for state funded cultural organizations, they can no longer control new emerging actors who assume content-provider functions in the global digital media space, nor are they able to censor messages and ideologies communicated by traditional and new actors. It is worth mentioning, for example, that while in 2020 the US government made significant efforts in mitigating Back Lives Matters public protests across the country, many museums actively employed social media to take a public stance and incorporate Black collective memory into their activities, significantly amplifying the scope and the importance of the movement (Salahu-Din, 2019). More importantly, as Lynch's (2021) analysis of five case studies indicates, American museums 'utilized the Black Lives Matter Movement's momentum to create new content for the public'. They enriched their collections with new acquisitions, aiming to debunk the 'Eurocentric worldview that diminished the contributions of Black Americans' in the past (Lynch, 2021: 3).

A wide variety of cultural content creators and providers, from major arts institutions to marginalized arts groups, significantly democratize the processes of cultural diplomacy. Specifically, they diversify the cultural content and eventually cultural messages that could be shared across borders to reach different target audiences and can either support or contest nation states' agendas. For example, in the rhizomatic horizontal digital environment different fringe arts groups or smaller sub-cultures' creative media producers can capitalize on the affordances of digital tools and platforms to produce and circulate their content to become new diplomatic actors. Moreover, cultural content acquires many new experimental, ad-hoc forms, which in some cases lead to viral effects. For instance, cultural memes, an audio-visual content of a humorous nature that is usually rapidly shared by Internet users with some variations, have become an important medium through which people call for political changes and instigate activism (Davis et al., 2015).

'Playing with meaning', memes produce new politically active narratives and subjectivities while agitating social groups (Gal et al., 2015). For example, Fraser and Carlson (2017) explored memes produced by Australian Aboriginal activist group Blackfulla Revolution (BFR) who employed meme culture to advocate for anti-colonial politics. Their analysis revealed that in this case memes served as a diplomatic narrative to challenge the wide-spread national myth of 'peaceful' British settlement and gave voice to indigenous peoples. The content of the memes 'intentionally produced a discord with the dominant colonial narrative' and provoked a consolidation of small communities who 'prompted a spontaneous collective policing of racism and, in doing so, intensified the anti-colonial politics' (Fraser and Carlson, 2017: 10).

This example is a good illustration that content producers as key actors of digital cultural diplomacy could include a wide variety of subgroups, smaller communities, and non-partisan organizations. They are capable to reach larger targeted audiences within and across borders, competing not only with traditional 'cultural ambassadors', like major museums or performing arts centres, but also with government actors, in this case engaging in adversarial diplomacy. However, all of them are a subject to norms, regulations, and interfaces of existing digital infrastructures, which is explored in more detail in the next section.

Infrastructure Builders

Infrastructure builders are crucial actors of digital diplomacy who actively shape global informational environments by regulating cultural circulation and setting boundaries, thereby defining important processes of cultural production and consumption. While cross-cultural sharing and arts diplomacy implemented via Facebook and Instagram or Twitter are established practices that are able to enhance international relations (Rashica, 2019), they come with significant limitations. In many cases, mega-popular global social media platforms, like Twitter or Facebook, fail to serve as trusted avenues of cultural diplomacy. Social media algorithms reinforce echo chambers and increase the fragmentation of social and political debates online, making it much harder for cultural practitioners to engage with foreign publics, especially targeted groups (Riordan, 2019). The fact that algorithms ensure that online users receive only content which they already favour minimizes the chances of cross-cultural exposure to new languages, cultural offerings, and activities, only reinforcing prejudices against other cultures. Furthermore, algorithms increasingly intervene in the flow of communications of cultural institutions by censoring the content that they deem to be inappropriate for public spaces, while reinforcing their own cultural biases (Cobbe, 2020).

A good example of a powerful platform that competes in the global media environments with state actors in the race for digital heritage preservation and promotion is Arts and Culture Institute, founded in 2011 by Google, one of the largest transnational media corporations. It is a 'not-for-profit initiative that partners with cultural organizations to bring the world's cultural heritage online' (Google, 2015). This institute has been working closely with museums around the world, providing free tools, expertise, and resources to digitize global cultural heritage and make museums 'more widely accessible to a global audience' (Google, 2015). While promoting universal access to knowledge, culture, and heritage across languages and communities, the Google Arts and Culture platform is argued to propel digital cultural colonialism (Terras et al., 2021). As Van Dijck et al. (2018: 3) stressed, aggregated digital content is a powerful tool 'producing the social structures we live in'. In the case of Google Institute, for instance, the top five countries represented through 93.4% of the published content on the platform are the USA, the UK, the Netherlands, Italy, and South Korea, with the USA alone accounting for 82% of images found on the site (Terras et al., 2021). The digital infrastructure offered by the platform and algorithms which produce more information of similar content (Zuboff, 2019) represent the epistemologies of dominant countries. They shape the informational realities of the world outside European or Western culture, while amplifying existing biases and strengthening cultural prejudices (Terras et al., 2021).

Furthermore, in many cases private corporate platforms instigate a direct response from governmental and intergovernmental actors, convincingly demonstrating significant political implications of platforms' global competition, going beyond the mere economic. For instance, Europeana, the largest digital heritage aggregator in Europe, was developed in response to the Google Books Project that commenced in 2005 (Purday, 2009). The idea to create the European digital heritage repository to bring together hundreds of museums and collections online was a direct response to Google's global cultural digitization activities. Its world leadership in building digital platforms to provide access to the world's heritage, in fact, was seen by European cultural institutions as a threat to appropriate a large volume of cultural resources and transfer them into a private sector (Purday, 2009). Europeana, in its turn, as a digital heritage aggregator platform, serves EU diplomatic goals as a site of supranational identity construction and a political media tool to facilitate regional cohesion. As a strategically designed digital heritage space that brings together diverse collections of thousands of European museums and archives, Europeana is directly supported by the EU Commission to realize the EU's ambitions to establish legitimacy as a supranational actor on the world stage (Valtysson, 2020).

These two cases of Europeana and Google Arts and Culture offer interesting examples of the power dynamics among digital infostructure builders as actors of cultural diplomacy on the global arena. To the complexity of this rivalry dynamics, though, can be added another peculiar case which demonstrates a collaborative effort between a national government and major media corporations in building digital infrastructure for reinforcing efforts in digital cultural diplomacy and national projection. For example, being the world's fourth-largest gaming market, South Korea announced ambitious plans to build the first nation-wide metaverse. First coined by Neal Stephenson (1992) in his highly influential science-fiction novel *Snow Crash*, metaverse is a shared online space that incorporates 3D graphics either on a screen or in VR and allows synchronous virtual social interactions among geographically dispersed participants. In May 2021, South Korea's Ministry of Science and Information Technology created a metaverse board and launched an industry alliance to bolster the development of the national metaverse ecosystem, composed of seventeen major IT companies. 'Throughout 2022, President Moon Jae-in is deploying 30 billion Won, equivalent to US $26 million, as part of the Digital New Deal' (Andreula and Petruzzelli, 2022: 148).

This government initiative has strong implications for national efforts in cultural diplomacy and branding. In the past three decades the governments' investments in wielding its cultural soft power have produced a phenomenal growth and global popularity of Korean culture, known as a Hallyu or Korean Wave (Kim, 2021). Despite the coronavirus restrictions in 2020, the number of global Hallyu fans topped 100 million, while the total number of fan clubs rose to 104,770,000 in 109 countries worldwide (KF, 2020). Furthermore, in the challenging pandemic times, K-pop groups established new metaverse practices. For example, in 2021, Hybe, the company behind popular musical groups like BTS or Tomorrow X Together, launched Weverse, a global fandom platform for VR communication and a market space of cultural products from music to cosmetics (Weverse, 2021). SK Telecom, the largest South Korean wireless telecommunications operator with more than 27 million subscribers, launched its 'K-pop Metaverse Project', which created a social world for global fans to experience Hallyu on a new level (SK T, 2021). The most recent research confirmed that global K-pop fans value continuity, sense of presence, interoperability, and simultaneity as enhanced metaverse experiences, which they find more relevant and enriching in comparison to creative content consumption through social media or streaming channels (Hwang and Lee, 2022).

This case moves forward the analysis of digital cultural diplomacy by revealing the importance of infrastructure builders as vital actors of digital cultural diplomacy. Digital infrastructures, in fact, enable all other actors, including governments, content providers, and even opinion makers, to co-exist in the digital realm and participate in the complex flows and contraflows of digital cultural circulation which shape social and cultural realities of global audiences.

Opinion Makers

Digital tools, social networks, and new media technologies empowered a birth of many digital performers, street artists, animators, or crypto artists, who, in certain cases, achieve a global popularity. Most of them share their art online, including featuring their musical, visual, or mixed media creations through the most popular social networks, from Facebook to Tik Tok. In this context, conventional arts institutions like galleries, museums, or performance arts centres increasingly share their cultural information gate-keeping functions in the digital domain with these emerging actors. Social media have provided a powerful tool for independent artists to communicate their messages across borders, which can contest and challenge government regimes and even incite political activism and social movements.

For example, Bansky, a globally famous anonymous graffiti artist, known for his highly influential ironic and politically urgent graphic arts like 'Balloon Girl', 'Love Rat', and 'There Is Always Hope', currently enjoys Instagram fellowship reaching almost eleven and a half million followers. Banksy is an artist from Bristol in the UK 'whose anonymity, ubiquity and creativity have garnered him an international following among the art establishment and the general public' (DeTurk, 2015: 22). His street art in the Palestinian territories, in Cairo during and after the revolution of 2011, and in Tunisia in the form of the Djerbahood campaign have given rise to a so-called 'Banksy effect'. Banksy street art in the Middle East and North Africa, particularly during and in the wake of the Arab Spring of 2011, has been widely documented through social media, websites, and several published photo essays. His street art images shared in social networks in the context of war and political upheaval played a unique political role 'in liberating the voices of the people of this region during times of revolution and change' (DeTurk, 2015: 24).

The resonance and importance of online influencers become even more significant if their protests overcome the digital limitations and restrictions established by political regimes. For example, no government in the world invests so heavily in patrolling the Internet than China's, constantly censoring online content with a large army of censors and advanced filtering algorithms (Roberts, 2020). Yet despite these restrictions—or precisely because of them—the cyberspace activism of Chinese contemporary political dissident artist Ai Weiwei has become a global phenomenon. Known as 'China's most important creative virtuoso, flagrant public intellectual and intrepid antiestablishment activist' (Thomas, 2014: 184), Weiwei started blogging in 2006, even though he could barely type at that time (Weiwei, 2011). Shortly after Ai's blog was deleted by the Chinese authorities, he started to tweet, reaching 60,000 published posts (over 100,000 words) in the first few months of opening his account (Thomas, 2014). Now enjoying a global followship of hundreds of thousands of users on Twitter and Instagram, Ai Weiwei employs his art to fight for human rights and democratic liberties that are being denied to people both in China and internationally (Lentz and Buffington, 2019).

Ai's digitally publicized criticism of Chinese policies through his 'pithy online Tweets has become an integral part of his antagonistic political posturing', contributing to an 'ongoing battle on behalf of China's collective' (Thomas, 2014: 185). Weiwei's strong declarations about China's woes through social media as a combative device represents a case of digital adversarial diplomacy, empowered and enabled by the Internet as an optimal space to manifest artistic activism. Weiwei himself shared, 'my artwork is an extension of the Internet. If there's no Internet, there's no Ai Weiwei of today. I'm a pure product of the Internet' (Gao, 2014). These, and many other cases of artists or artistic groups employing social media as a tool for voicing political concerns, provide convincing illustrations that digital cultural diplomacy is no longer a domain of state actors and official cultural ambassadors. It operates in a more complex and heterogenic field shared across multiple actors, including ordinary Internet users whose online activity shapes public discourses and perceptions.

In a high competition for attention from global audiences, state actors frequently attempt to capitalize on opinion makers and even build on their abilities to engage digital publics to promote political ideas. For example, many (inter)governmental actors attempted to employ crowdsourcing as a tool to 'address governance issues, strengthen communities, empower marginalized groups, and foster civic participation' in their diplomatic activities (Bott et al., 2011: 1). However, the instrumental approach to, and 'guardianship' of, citizen diplomacy significantly undermines the credibility of the relationship among actors and destroys the positive impact of cross-cultural contacts (Scott-Smith, 2014: 52). Furthermore, the collaborative and dialogic format of digital cultural diplomacy activities does not necessarily guarantee that they will inspire a genuine cross-cultural dialogue that translates into cultural influence.

For example, a New Museum Definition crowdsourcing campaign delivered by the UNESCO International Commission of Museums (ICOM) in 2019 served 'a severe blow to the NGO's global leadership' (Noce, 2019). Despite its inclusiveness, openness, and democratic aspirations to invite museum professionals around the world to share their ideas about what a museum could be in the twenty-first century, the online campaign resulted in a failure to adopt a new proposed definition during the ICOM Extraordinary General Conference in Kyoto. The decision to postpone the vote was taken by more than 70% of participants, who accused ICOM of ignoring public voices and delivering 'a definition, which was not submitted as part of the public campaign' (Hatfield, 2019). A close analysis of the case confirmed that when crowdsourcing is used only as a democratic frame to engage the publics without a real distribution of power across participants, such a campaign is doomed to failure (Grincheva, 2020b). Contemporary audiences are well equipped with multiple digital communication tools that make their voice an important part of the global media discourse and this power is potent to challenge and contest government decisions and policies.

Individual artists, cultural leaders, and solo opinion makers actively participate in the formation of global informational environments and can even create certain dependencies for infrastructure builders, who thrive on individual platform users' triumphs. On the one hand, social media influencers are subject to platforms' communication norms and to regulations of infrastructure builders, and their success in many cases depends on their understanding of algorithmic cultures (Cotter, 2018). On the other hand, the power of platforms to attract new audiences can also grow exponentially if they are able to attract influential opinion makers capable to create online communities by sharing engaging content. For example, launched during the global pandemic crises in 2020, Clubhouse reached 10 million active weekly users within just a year, due to its influencers (TI, 2022). The fact that it was an invite-only platform is evidence that it capitalized on users' already established networks, who also served as gatekeepers to their online communities. This section is evidence that opinion makers who even lack an agency, in comparison to other actor types, can become very powerful players in the global media space.

Conclusion

This research explores key actors of digital cultural diplomacy, approaching this task from a new perspective. It proposes a new typology of diplomatic actorness in the digital realm by analysing different players based on their key functions and the contributions they make in the construction of global media flows. The chapter reveals that those actors who can produce meaningful and engaging cultural content acquire strong powers to reach wider audiences, to 'win hearts and minds', even to mobilize publics, and to instigate social action. Specifically, *cultural content providers* and *opinion makers* are influential actors of digital cultural diplomacy, whose functions could overlap in certain scenarios. For example, cultural organizations and even individuals, like independent artists, bloggers, or experimental creators, can become important opinion makers. By populating the informational space with meaningful cultural content that raises new sets of critical questions, empowers marginalized voices, or resonates with global concerns, they can generate considerable political clout.

However, online behavioural norms and digital consumption demands, expectations, and practices are in many cases defined by the rules and interfaces of digital *infrastructure builders*. Social media platforms, search engines, communication applications, or cultural heritage aggregators, operating on the global level, become important hosting media environments where cultural diplomacy takes place. While the chapter confirms that state actors retain their power in the global communication space as key actors in building digital infrastructures, it also illustrates how they increasingly share the world arena with a multitude of other actors, like transnational media corporations or intergovernmental organizations. These new actors come to stage to push their own agendas and establish new communication norms, which can even create unfavourable conditions and algorithmic barriers for cultural diplomats to reach their targeted audiences and communicate their messages.

These power dynamics evidence a certain level of dependencies among actors, especially in the fulfilment of their functions in the global media space. These dependencies are evident, for instance, between state digital infostructure builders and content providers, like large national cultural organizations, whose level of digitalization in many cases would depend on direct state support for their digital transformations. In return, national cultural projection or digital country branding is no longer in the full control of the state governments who share global communication spaces with a large variety of various content providers. Interesting dependencies could also be observed among actors with agency and those who lack it, such as individual artists as solo non-partisan actors. Intervening in international informational flows, these actors are capable to produce their own cultural imagery and narratives going beyond accepted mainstream ideologies. They can generate large cultural communities of their followers, reaching in certain cases millions of users, competing with governments and traditional cultural ambassadors in public influence. Their abilities to attract and mobilize the masses also work as a legitimizing force for social media platforms to position themselves as vital public communications spaces as well as trendy avenues for global cultural consumption.

The chapter starts an important conversation on the actors of digital cultural diplomacy, profiled from the perspective of their roles and powers in the cyberspace. While this work conceptualized the actors' typology, exploring existing players, future research should pay more attention to the rise of new non-human actors of cultural diplomacy who increasingly participate in international cultural flows of information exchange. Chat bots, AI artists, AI curators, and deep fake-enabled historical figures are becoming important players of cultural diplomacy in the post-human era. Non-human actors who could potentially serve on all three levels of actorness—content providers, infrastructure builders, and opinion makers—should be further explored and critically scrutinized to analyse implications for contemporary cultural diplomacy.

SUGGESTED READING

Bjola, Corneliu and Ruben Zaiotti. 2020. *Digital Diplomacy and International Organisations: Autonomy, Legitimacy and Contestation.* London: Routledge.

Cameron, Fiona. 2021. *The Future of Digital Data, Heritage and Curation in a More-than Human World.* New York: Routledge.

Grincheva, Natalia. 2020. *Museum Diplomacy in the Digital Age.* London: Routledge.

Grincheva, Natalia and Liz Stainforth. 2023. *Geopolitics of Digital Heritage.* Cambridge: Cambridge University Press.

Valtysson, Bjarki. 2020. *Digital Cultural Policy: From Politics to Practice.* Cham, Switzerland: Palgrave Macmillan.

REFERENCES

Andreula, Nicolò and Petruzzelli, Stefania. 2022. "Meta-Soft Power: Flipping the Scales Between Art & Culture." *Raisina Dialogues* 6: 143–150.

Arts and Humanities Research Council (AHRC). 2020. *Towards a national collection – opening UK heritage to the world.* Accessed July 26, 2023. https://www.nationalcollection.org.uk/about

Beck, Ulrich. 2006. *The Cosmopolitan Vision.* Cambridge: Polity Press.

Bott, Maja, Gigler, Bjorn, and Young, Fregor. 2011. *The Role of Crowdsourcing for Better Governance in Fragile State Contexts.* Washington, DC: World Bank Publications.

Carr, Madeline. 2015. "Power Plays in Global Internet Governance." *SSRN Electronic Journal.* https://doi.org/10.2139/ssrn.2809887

Casero-Ripollés, Andreu. 2020. "Political Influencers in the Digital Public Sphere." *Communication and Society* 33(2), 171–173.

Choi, Sujin. 2014. "The Two-Step Flow of Communication in Twitter-Based Public Forums." *Social Science Computer Review* 33(6): 696–711.

Cobbe, Jennifer. 2020. "Algorithmic Censorship by Social Platforms: Power and Resistance." *Philosophy & Technology* 34:739–766.

Cotter, Kelley. 2018. "Playing the Visibility Game: How Digital Influencers and Algorithms Negotiate Influence on Instagram." *New Media & Society* 21(4): 895–913.

Couldry, Nick. 2015. "The Myth of 'Us': Digital Networks, Political Change and the Production of Collectivity." *Information, Communication & Society* 18(6): 608–626.

Davis, Corey B., Glantz, Mark, and Novak, David. 2015. "'You Can't Run Your SUV on Cute. Let's Go!': Internet Memes as Delegitimizing Discourse." *Environmental Communication* 10(1): 62–83.

Department for Digital, Culture, Media and Sports (DCMS). 2018. *Culture is Digital.* https://www.gov.uk/government/publications/culture-is-digital

DeTurk, Sabrina. 2015. "The 'Banksy Effect' and Street Art in the Middle East." *Street Art and Urban Creativity Scientific Journal* 1(2): 22–30.

Fraser, Ryan and Carlson, Brownwyn. 2017. "Indigenous Memes and the Invention of a People." *Social Media + Society* 3 (4): https://doi.org/10.1177/2056305117738993.

Gal, Noam, Shifman, Limor, and Kampf, Zohar. 2015. "It Gets Better: Internet Memes and the Construction of Collective Identity." *New Media & Society* 18(8): 1698–1714.

Gao, Yuan. 2014. "Interview: Ai Weiwei." *Time Out Beijing,* 30 July. https://bit.ly/3w8M398.

Gill, Tony and Paul Miller. 2002. "Re-inventing the Wheel? Standards, Interoperability and Digital Affairs." *D-Lib Magazine* 8(1): 1–5.

Google. 2015. *Google Arts and Culture Institute.* https://www.google.com/culturalinstitute

Grincheva, Natalia. 2020a. *Museum Diplomacy in the Digital Age.* London: Routledge.

Grincheva, Natalia. 2020b. "Is there a Place for a Crowdsourcing in Multilateral Diplomacy? Searching for a New Museum Definition ICOM vs the World of Museum Professionals." In *International Organisations and Digital Diplomacy: Autonomy, Legitimacy and Contestation,* edited by Bjola, Corneliu and Zaiotti, Ruben, 74–98. London: Routledge.

Grincheva, Natalia and Rob Kelley. 2019. "Non-Western Non-state Diplomacy." *The Hague Journal of Diplomacy* 14(3): 199–208.

Hatfield, Boodle. 2019. "The Definition of a Museum Revealed." *Art, Law & More* 20 August. https://artlawandmore.com/2019/08/20/the-definition-of-a-museum-revealed/

Hernandez, Trilce. 2010. *Does Digitization Bring a Productivity Lag in Museum Work?* Media Studies: University of Amsterdam.

Hwang, RakGun and Lee, MinKyung. 2022. "The Influence of Music Content Marketing on User Satisfaction and Intention to Use in the Metaverse: A Focus on the SPICE Model." *Businesses* 2: 141–155.

Ivey, Bill. 2007. *Cultural Diplomacy and The National Interest*. Arts Industry Policy Forum. http://www.interarts.net/descargas/interarts673.pdf

Jin, Dal Yong. 2017. *Digital Platforms, Imperialism and Political Culture*. London: Routledge.

Jora, Lucian. 2013. "New Practices and Trends in Cultural Diplomacy." *Political Science and International Relations* 10(1): 43–52.

Kelley, Rob. 2014. *Agency Change: Diplomatic Action Beyond the State*. Lanham: Rowman & Littlefield.

Kim, Youna. 2021. *The Soft Power of the Korean Wave*. London: Routledge.

Korean Foundation. 2020. *Global Hallyu Trends*. https://bit.ly/3yuRgIb.

Kremers, Horst. 2019. *Digital Cultural Heritage*. Cham Springer.

Krenn, Michael. 2005. *Fall-out Shelters for the Human Spirit*. Chapel Hill: The University of Northern California Press.

Lazarsfeld, Paul, Berelson, Bernard, and Gaudet, Hazel. 1944. *The People's Choice*. Columbia University Press.

Lentz, Alex and Buffington, Melanie L. 2019. "Art + Politics = Activism: The Work of Ai Weiwei." *Art Education* 73(1): 52–58.

Lucke, Martin. 2002. "Vilified, Venerated, Forbidden: Jazz in the Stalinist Era". *Music and Politics* 1(2): 1–9.

Lutkenhaus, Roel, Jansz, Jeroen, and Bouman, Martine P.A. 2019. "Tailoring in the Digital Era: Stimulating Dialogues on Health Topics in Collaboration with Social Media Influencers." *Digital Health* 5(1): 1–11.

Lynch, Jessica. 2021. "'Interrupt the status quo': How Black Lives Matter Changed American Museums." *Student Research Submissions* 397. https://scholar.umw.edu/student_research/397

Melissen, Jan. 2006. *The New Public Diplomacy: Between Theory and Practice*. UK, USA: Palgrave.

Noce, Vincent. 2019. "Vote on ICOM's New Museum Definition Postponed." *The Art Newspaper*, 9 September.

Pamment, James. 2014. "Articulating Influence: Toward a Research Agenda for Interpreting the Evaluation of Soft Power, Public Diplomacy and Nation Brands." *Public Relations Review* 40(1): 50–59.

Peters, Benjamin. 2016. *Digital Keywords: A Vocabulary of Information Society and Culture*. Princeton, NJ, Cambridge & Oxford: Princeton University Press.

Prevots, Naima. 2001. *Dance for Exports. Cultural Diplomacy and the Cold War*. Middletown, CT: Wesleyan Univ. Press.

Purday, Jon. 2009. "Think Culture: Europeana.eu from Concept to Construction." *Bibliothek: Forschung und Praxis* 33(2): 170–180.

Rashica, Viona. 2019. "Digital Diplomacy: Aspects, Approaches and Practical Use." *European Perspectives – International Scientific Journal on European Perspectives* 10(17): 21–39.

Richmond, Yale. 2003. *Cultural Exchange and the Cold War: Raising the Iron Curtain*. University Park, Pa.: Penn State University Press.

Riordan, Shaun. 2019. *Cyberdiplomacy: Managing Security and Governance Online*. Cambridge: Polity.

Roberts, Margaret E. 2020. *CENSORED: Distraction and Diversion inside China's Great Firewall*. Princeton, New Jersey: Princeton University Press.

Ronfeldt, David and Arquilla, John. 2020. *Whose Story Wins?* Santa Monica, Calif: Rand Corporation.

Salahu-Din, Deborah Tulani. 2019. "Documenting the Black Lives Matter Movement in Baltimore through Contemporary Collecting: An Initiative of the National Museum of African American History and Culture." *Collections: A Journal for Museum and Archives Professionals* 15(2–3): 101–112.

Schneider, Cynthia. 2003. *Diplomacy That Works: Best Practices in Cultural Diplomacy*. Center for Arts and Culture.

Schneider, Cynthia. 2006. "Culture Communicates: US Diplomacy that Works." In *The New Public Diplomacy*, edited by Melissen, Jan, Donna, Lee, and Sharp, Paul, 147–168. London: Palgrave Macmillan.

Scott-Smith, Giles. 2014. "Introduction: Private Diplomacy, Making the Citizen Visible." *New Global Studies*. https://doi.org/10.1515/ngs-2014-012.

Schwarz, Jonas. 2017. "Platform Logic: An Interdisciplinary Approach to the Platform-Based Economy." *Policy and Internet* 9(4): 374–394.

SK Telecom (SK T). 2021. *Introduce Metaverse*. https://www.sktelecom.com/en/view/introduce/metaverse.do

Stephenson, Neal. 1992. *Snow Crash*. New York: Random House Publishing Group.

Terras, Melissa, Kizhner, Inna, Rumyantsev, Maxim, Khokhlova, Valentina, Demeshkova, Elisaveta, Rudov, Ivan, and Afanasieva, Julia. 2021. "Digital Cultural Colonialism: Measuring Bias in Aggregated Digitized Content Held in Google Arts and Culture." *Digital Scholarship in the Humanities* 36(3): 607–640.

ThinkImpact (TI). 2022. "2022 Clubhouse User Statistics - Trends & Data." 23 March 2021. https://bit.ly/3w5mNRe

Thomas, Taliesin. 2014. "The 'Post-Human' Internet Dimension: Ai Weiwei and Cao Fei Online." *Journal of Contemporary Chinese Art* 1(2): 177–99.

Uzunoglu, Ebru and Kip, Sema. 2014. "Brand Communication through Digital Influencers: Leveraging Blogger Engagement." *International Journal of Information Management* 34(1): 592–602.

Valtysson, Bjarki. 2020. *Digital Cultural Policy: From Politics to Practice*. Cham, Switzerland: Palgrave Macmillan.

van Dijck, Jose, Poell, Thomas, and de Waal, Martijn. 2018. *The Platform Society*. New York: Oxford University Press.

van Dijck, Jose. 2014. *The Culture of Connectivity: A Critical History of Social Media*. New York, NY: Oxford University Press.

Weverse. 2021. *About*. https://about.weverse.io/en.html

Weiwei, Ai. 2011. *Ai Weiwei's Blog: Writings, Interviews, and Digital Rants, 2006-2009*. MIT Press.

Wiseman, Geoffrey. 2015. *Isolate or Engage: Adversarial States, US Foreign Policy, and Public Diplomacy*. Stanford, Calif.: Stanford University Press.

Zollner, Frank. 1997. "John F. Kennedy and Leonardo's Mona Lisa: Art as the Continuation of Politics." In *Radical Art History. Internationale Anthologie*, edited by Kersten, Wolfgang, 466–479. Zurich: Zurich InterPublishers.

Zuboff, Shoshana. 2019. *The Age of Surveillance Capitalism: The Fight for a Human Future at the New Frontier of Power*. New York: Profile Books.

Zubok, Vladislav and Erick Shiraev. 2000. *Anti-Americanism in Russia: From Stalin to Putin*. New York: Palgrave MacMillan.

CHAPTER 12

DIGITAL PROPAGANDA AND DIPLOMACY

PAWEŁ SUROWIEC-CAPELL

INTRODUCTION

SINCE the publication of *Diplomacy*, a classic volume by Sir Harold Nicolson (1950: 169) recognizing that technological advances proffer 'a vast impetus to propaganda as a method of policy', the emerging types of media are inherent to understanding the relationship between diplomacy and propaganda. Unsurprisingly, digital technologies hold great promise for diplomacy. If diplomacy is 'the conduct of relationships, using peaceful means, by and among international actors, at least one of which is usually governmental' (Cooper et al., 2013: 2), propaganda is paramount to the ways these relationships are mediated, online and offline, and received by the public. With the advancement of digital technologies, propaganda as a form of persuasion has been adapted to hybrid media landscapes. Yet, in the study of diplomacy, these advancements have left an epistemic gap. Therefore, the departure point for the examination of how propaganda affects the public experience of diplomacy is to ask questions about taxonomy at the intersection of the study of both practices. This chapter discusses ways in which propaganda as a practice inherent to diplomacy has been reshaped by digital technologies in order to aid goals of diplomatic actors and actors of diplomacy.

The term 'digital propaganda' has been introduced to the study of diplomacy as a proposition aiming to make sense of '*how*' and '*why*' this form of persuasive communication has been affected by digitalization. Bjola and Papadakis (2020: 641) makes the distinction between the traditional, 'information-oriented aspect of propaganda' and non-traditional 'digital or computational component of the concept'. While this term has an exploratory power, digital propaganda cannot be understood as being solely confined to digital technologies, as the flows of propaganda about diplomatic relations occur across 'old' and 'new' media, the logics of which define hybrid media landscapes (Chadwick, 2013). As digitalization has opened new opportunities for propaganda, marking a shift in the ways in which its messages are disseminated in diplomatic settings, its analysis ought to consider it not as a stand-alone concept, but rather as a multimodal practice co-created with the use of legacy and new media.

As competitive media-rich landscapes are the contemporary settings for diplomacy, they afford the dissemination of propagandistic messages across national borders at accelerated speed and with customized style. Hybrid media landscapes, particularly the proliferation of social media among diplomatic actors and actors of diplomacy, which since 2009 have been *en masse* migrating onto platforms, have created the abundance of digital spaces shaping and re-shaping the relationship between propaganda and diplomacy. Prior to the digitalization and platformization, the study of propaganda in 'old' media landscapes reveals the profusion of its messages referred to as the 'Niagara of spin' (Moloney, 2006: 1). This analogy can be extended to the inquiry of digital propaganda. Hybrid media landscapes reveal that the Niagara of propagandistic messages has spilled over the confines of traditional news media, creating the abundance of opportunities for free-flowing propagandistic messages. This spill-over effect can be best described as 'post-truth culture', a transnational condition foregrounding uncertainty about public claims over truth, legitimacy, and authority, which profoundly affects diplomacy (Surowiec and Manor, 2021). Questions navigating this chapter therefore include: How best to define digital propaganda in hybrid media landscapes? How is propaganda re-modelled in diplomatic settings? Who are the new propagandists?

TERMINOLOGICAL MAPPING: DIFFERENT SHADES OF PROPAGANDA

Since 'post-truth' culture intertwines with the norms and cultures of diplomacy, for the sake of terminological clarity, it is useful to acknowledge the sibling concepts affiliated with the practice of propaganda. As the analysis of disinformation, misinformation, and fake news has gained momentum due to the unprecedented developments of 'post-truth' culture, Freelon and Wells (2020: 145) has brought the definition of disinformation by the High Level Expert Group on Fake News and Online Disinformation of the European Commission to the study of propaganda, which captures it as 'all forms of false, inaccurate, or misleading information designed, presented and promoted to intentionally cause public harm or for profit'. This definition underscores deception, potential for harm, and an intent to harm. It does, however, exclude deception that may cause harm without the disseminators' knowledge and non-deceptive messages intended to harm others. To that end, it differentiates disinformation from misinformation, highlighting that the former are munitions of information warfare, non-lethal weapons intended to subdue adversaries rather than reason with them, whereas the latter is sporadic, and does not rely on a campaigning mode.

As diplomacy has been affected by the emergence of fake news (Nisbet and Kamenchuk, 2019), another by-product of the interplay between digitalization and post-truth culture, it is useful to define this digital genre. Here the studies of media and communication offer substantive insights relevant to the study of diplomacy. In a pioneering analysis, Farkas and Schou (2018) align fake news with critiques of digital capitalism, right-wing politics and media, liberal and mainstream journalism, and mobilizations of this genre in techno-deterministic critiques of digital media. Despite the proximity to other digital *genres*, fake news is defined as 'information that is intentionally false, and are often malicious stories propagating conspiracy theories' (Molina et al., 2021: 189). For the sake of clarity, the auxiliary term 'conspiracy theory' is a *content* category, which, in the settings of diplomacy, can be best described as a 'discursive position, attaching associations of paranoia and irrationality to particular interpretations of diplomatic relations (Aistrope, 2016: 6). To that end, conspiracy theories can be delegitimizing of views that do not fall within an acceptable range, in this case, of diplomatic positions, and productive as spaces where diplomacy can occur as juxtaposed with the irrational views of its propagators.

Disinformation and misinformation may be epistemic sensibilities underpinning propaganda; they are phenomenologically broader as they pertain to other fields of practice. While disinformation and misinformation mark the scope of 'post-truth' culture, the digitalization of propaganda shows a state of flux, namely its adaptability to evolving media landscapes. Until recently, the concept of 'computational propaganda' has been centre stage in the analysis of deceptive campaigning on social media. Wooley and Howard (2019: 4) coined this term with the purpose of opening the strand of research on propaganda that involves 'the use algorithms, automation, and human curation to purposefully manage and distribute misleading information over social media networks', and while the digitalization underpins their definition, they emphasize the role of actants among propaganda tactics, that is 'automated social actors' such as bots, a computational tactic in 'manufacturing consensus'. Other tactics of computational propaganda involve dubious devices such as astroturfing, state-sponsored trolling, and forms of online warfare such as PsyOps and InfoOps, the goal of which is to manipulate information in order to shape opinions, attitudes, and behaviours.

In general terms, digital propaganda has been described as a 'product of the culture of social interactivity as well as hybridisation of political news' (Lilleker and Surowiec, 2020: 171). In the study of diplomacy, it has been positioned vis-à-vis digital diplomacy, an analytical avenue theorized as a middle-range approach to international change management (Holmes, 2015). At early stages of digitalization in the field, digital propaganda was deemed an undesirable side-effect of digital diplomacy, but post-truth culture triggered the further need to counter and contain it. Unlike propaganda messages challenging the truth and relying on media effects in international broadcasting, digital propaganda thrives on 'reality effects' with its main focus being assaulting the truth. The epistemic crisis stemming from 'reality effects' is manifested by the inability of diplomats to bridge the differences in foreign policies as their strategic landscapes are oftentimes distorted to serve ad hoc interests. This digitally constructed reality became a foundation on which undermining trust in democratic institutions, including the apparatus of diplomatic affairs, proceeds to conflict and war (Bjola and Pamment, 2019). Unsurprisingly, then, digital propaganda has been labelled as 'the dark side' of digital diplomacy and its conceptual distorting mirror.

Beyond the study of diplomacy, the analysis of propaganda uncovers a transnational dynamic of its organization, which has been advanced due to the rapid proliferation of social media enabling campaigning on the platforms, and subsequently affecting reception of diplomatic messages. Unlike in the institutional settings of diplomacy, in which the transduction of propaganda into other communicative practices such as public diplomacy is well-documented (Cull, 2008), the relative openness of the Internet, its net-neutral architecture, and the sheer volume of platform users has demonstrated that propaganda on the Web cannot be simply re-invented by changing the name of the practice into something more palatable or re-modelled with normative claims. To that end, propaganda on social media became seemingly more visible but less traceable and—given digital innovations, the roll-out of which entails an element of surprise—it has potential to be disruptive (Boyd-Barrett, 2019). This dynamic was a defining feature of 'RussiaGate', the campaigning behind which has shown that the principles and objectives of propaganda remain constant but the technologies and the repertoire of strategies and tactics evolve and become more sophisticated. This evolving pattern in the practice of propaganda has led Hall-Jamieson (2018: 7) to make a case for the conceptualization of the foreign intervention into the 2016 US election campaign as a 'cyberwar', that is 'actions by a nation-state to penetrate another nation's computers or networks for the purpose of causing damage or disruption' (Clarke and Knake, 2014: 6).

The 2016 US election was a unique site of digital propaganda. Cyberwar typically involves hacking; posting; impersonating; strategic release of misappropriated content; presupposition of ill-intent; expression of the believe that the perpetrators are enemies; labelling hackers and trolls as soldiers or saboteurs; setting an expectation that the attacked state will retaliate; calls for arms; and reliance on a politically charged term— 'meddling'—which leaders as well as journalists tend to use to obscure the enemy and delineate the reaction to cyberattacks, all of which feed into the notion of 'being attacked'. Bjola (2019) makes sense of the Russian-state disruption of the US elections using the long-standing information doctrine of the Soviet intelligence service, reflexive control, which is 'a means of conveying to a partner or an opponent specially prepared information to incline him to voluntarily make the predetermined decisions desired by the initiator of the action' (Thomas, 2004: 237). Using it to qualify digital propaganda, he argues that it aims to exert influence by shaping the decision-making of the adversary, who is covertly persuaded to pursue the course of action advancing the goals of the propagandist or its intermediaries.

In general terms, the contemporary approaches to propaganda describe it as 'the deliberate, systematic attempt to shape perceptions, manipulate cognitions, and direct behavior to achieve a response that furthers the desired intent of the propagandist' (Jowett and O'Donnell, 2019: 6). In particular terms, the study of diplomacy recognizes the networked architecture of media landscapes in which propaganda is practised (Bjola and Pamment, 2019), but it was the 2016 US elections, a watershed event involving a foreign-sourced disruption of the campaign, that inspired the redefinition of propaganda considering the logics of networks. In particular terms, then, as 'network propaganda' it is defined as 'the overall effects on beliefs and attitudes [that] emerges from the interaction among a diverse and often broad set of discrete sources and narrative bits' (Benkler et al., 2018: 29–33). This definition foregrounds the architecture aiding the flow of messages.

Notwithstanding the intentionality of propaganda behind online campaigning, the networked ecosystem of propaganda in hybrid media landscapes gave rise to a breath of tactics such as 'bullshite', that is communicating with no regard to truth or falsehoods about reality. In its archetypal form, fake news pages geared solely toward generating advertising revenue exemplified this tactic. Another digital tactic, 'feedback loop', refers to a dynamic in which political actors, media, and the public form and break connections made on the content of statements, which gradually lowers the cost of telling falsehoods consistent with a shared narrative, while increasing the costs of resisting that narrative in the name of truth. In addition, the analysis of propaganda reveals 'attention backbone' and 'propaganda pipeline' as two techniques associated with the network dynamics of the flow of propaganda. The former tactic describes the flow of messages from peripheral nodes in the network that garner attention for their content in order to push its agenda within a sub-network of users who *amplify* their messages to more visible sites and its users. The latter tactic, propaganda pipeline, concerns the periphery-core dynamic, but describes the content *sameness* rather than the direction of the flow of propagandistic messages (Benkler et al., 2018).

The above definitions position propaganda vis-à-vis other concepts, which have gained prominence in the study of diplomacy—disinformation, misinformation, fake news, and conspiracy theory—recognizing, however, differences between them. Those definitions have neither tackled nor reflected the practice of propaganda in the settings of diplomacy, and predominantly emphasize technological innovations associated with the flow of messages or the political economy underpinning it (Zuboff, 2019) rather than propaganda in diplomacy as such. While it is widely acknowledged that digital innovations drive the evolution of propaganda in the settings of diplomacy, and that social media platforms are the spaces where transnational campaigning or indeed institutionalized discussions on foreign policy issues occur, here, too, conceptual clarity is missing. By introducing new concepts such as 'digital propaganda', scholars seemingly suggest the emergence of a new form of influencing, but critiques of this approach argue that the aggregation of social media, bots, and big data are the latest tactics deployed to shape public opinion, using algorithms to target publics with unprecedented accuracy and speed, creating the potential for extraordinary influence among publics, while indeed not changing what is at the core of propaganda (Hyzen, 2021).

Digital Propaganda and Digital Diplomacy

The aforementioned public diplomacy, that is a public-facing strategic communication on foreign policy issues, has entered the path toward multi-faceted digitalization. The analysis of the adoption of digital tools and social media platforms by diplomatic actors and actors of diplomacy engaging with foreign policy issues makes public diplomacy one of the most vibrant research areas in the field. Given the centrality of media to public diplomacy, as an axiom in the field, the definition of 'mediated public diplomacy' has been recently updated to reflect the changing media landscapes. Golan et al. (2019: 1670) have defined it as 'the organized attempts by governments to influence foreign public opinion via mediated channels including paid, earned, owned and shared media for the purpose of gaining support for its foreign policy objectives'. This conceptualization of mediated public diplomacy encompasses digital diplomacy as it relies on owned and shared media and content, supplanting the use of earned and paid media strategies by governments. In this theorization, the place of digital propaganda vis-à-vis digital diplomacy requires a broader consideration (Table 12.1).

The Cold War became a background for debate on the similarities and differences between propaganda and public diplomacy, central to which was the dominance of international broadcasting. There is a consensus among scholars of diplomacy that public diplomacy was the then US government's measure to counter-balance Soviet propaganda of the totalitarian 'communist' Russia (Cull, 2008), which in itself was an ideologically momentous move. This distinction, however, has left a mark on the trajectories of diplomacy as it has opened a strand of research aiming to understand the public aspects of diplomacy vis-à-vis propaganda. Nowadays, the contested notion of a rival diplomatic game between the US and, this time, authoritarian right-wing Russia, the 'New Cold War', became the stage for attuning digitized public diplomacy *versus* digitized propaganda. The bulk of analysis of the adoption of digital tools for public diplomacy fell on, on the one hand, the US presidency of Barack Obama (Hayden, 2011; Tsvetkova et al., 2020) and, on the other hand, the presidency of Vladimir Putin of Russia. The early signs of the revival of the Russian state-sponsored propaganda to posture and position itself as an 'equal' diplomatic player were aided by an array of propaganda campaigns utilizing digital technologies (Surowiec, 2017). In a study of mutual allegations in the inter-state diplomacy, Chernobrov and Briant (2022) reveal how policy makers and international broadcasters conceive propaganda as a threat, signalling the deteriorating relationship mirrored by public diplomacy of both states.

In addition to digital technology, it is the developments in the conduct of foreign policy and the ensuing escalation-de-escalation dynamic that drives changes to the scale and scope of propaganda. Russia is not the only state or regional power that engages in state-sponsored propaganda but its routinized statecraft and campaigning is politically significant in the study of diplomacy. Russian-state actors and its intermediaries

Table 12.1. Key differentiators between digital propaganda and digital diplomacy

Point of differentiation	Digital propaganda	Digital diplomacy
Foreign policy function	Open rivalry, disruption, and societal discord (Surowiec and Manor, 2021) Evidence shows links to spheres of interests (Szostek, 2018) Evidence shows ties to military strategy and operations (Valeriano, Jensen, and Maness, 2019)	International change management (Bjola and Holmes, 2015) Evidence shows reliance on international advocacy (Bjola and Manor, 2018) It yields potential to overcome prestige deficits (Manor and Pamment, 2019)
Diplomatic intelligence function	Links to intelligence services information doctrines (Bjola and Pamment, 2019; Szostek, 2021)	Links to listening and virtue signalling (Cull, 2008; Eggeling and Adler-Nissen, 2021)
Commitment to facts and truth	Thrives on disinformation and misinformation (Gaber and Fisher, 2021) Assaults the truth by co-creating alternative realities (Bjola and Pamment, 2019)	Commitment to informing and educating (Danziger and Schreiber, 2021) Aims to facilitate mutual understanding (Bjola, 2019)
Projecting ideologies	Disseminates ideological content across national borders (Golovchenko, 2020)	Driven by foreign policy issues (Antwi-Boateng and Al Mazrouei, 2021)
Intent and motivation	Persuasion by manipulation and deception (Bjola, 2019)	Persuasion by open dialogue (Kampf, Manor, and Segev, 2015)
Underpinning logic on the Web	Networked logic and adversarial or antagonistic relationships (Benkler, Faris, and Roberts, 2018; Bjola and Pamment, 2019)	Networked logic and the relationship management (Zaharna, 2013; Park, Chung, and Park, 2019)
Relationship to media landscapes	Thrives in echo chambers, on fake social media accounts, and through bots and astroturfing technologies on open Web (Bjola and Papadakis, 2020)	Relies on transmedia and meanings negotiated in a relatively open media environment (Pamment, 2016)

Mode of delivery	Campaigning mode, either overt or covert (Briant, 2015) Multimodal (Hyunjin, 2014)	Routinized modes of delivery and campaigning modes (Surowiec and Miles, 2021) Multimodal (Hedling and Bremberg, 2021)
Style of delivery	Relies on affect and tends to break diplomatic norms (Surowiec, 2017)	Adheres to publics' sensibilities, but stretches diplomatic norms (Hayden, 2011)
Content and messages	Curated content and mediated messages (Jack, 2019) Self-produced content and messages (O'Shaughnessy, 2012) Micro-targeted messages (Ó Fathaigh, Dobber, Borgesius, and Shires, 2021)	Mediated content and messages (Golan, Manor, and Arceneaux, 2019) Self-mediated content and messages (Bos and Melissen, 2019)
Flow of messages	Fast-spreading between open-web, social media platforms, and news media (Benkler, Faris, and Roberts, 2018)	Content and its flow partially controlled and managed (Bjola, 2016)
Desired effects	Geared toward 'deception effects' (Chadwick and Stayer, 2022) Geared toward 'disruptive effects' (Elswah and Howard, 2020) Geared toward 'coercive effects' (Bjola and Pamment, 2016)	Geared toward 'attraction effects' (Surowiec and Long, 2020)

such as the (in)famous Internet Research Agency invested in digital propaganda are trend-setters in aligning this practice to the strategic landscape, redefined by the rivalry labelled as the 'New Cold War'. This confrontation, convulsing Russia's relations with the US and its allies, recasts again the characteristics of international politics and, like a vortex, sucks other actors into the diplomatic game that entails propaganda campaigning on an unprecedented scale, one in which digital propaganda aids the imagining of regional 'spheres of interests' (Szostek, 2018). If the US–Russia rivalry is a ground to innovate digital propaganda, the post-September 11 theorization of public diplomacy had shown a revival of the debate on conceptual similarities and differences between both forms of persuasion extended to cyberspace. It was particularly the development of 'new' public diplomacy that became a benchmark in the assessment of the links between them. Although public diplomacy and propaganda overlap, not least in their goal to strategically aid foreign policy, public diplomacy as 'persuasion by means of dialogue' is more open to listening to and engaging publics (Melissen, 2005: 18). In an attempt to further challenge unidirectional propaganda, Zaharna et al. (2013: 6) argue that networks as the hubs of persuasion illustrate a differential of how networked communication trumps international broadcasting in co-creating as opposed to wielding influence.

It is beyond the scope of this chapter to offer a comprehensive overview of the similarities and differences between digital diplomacy and digital propaganda, a task no less challenging by virtue of still limited evidence on the effects of digital propaganda. However, a review of literature on diplomacy and propaganda reveals that scholarship on the digitalization of public diplomacy emphasizes the building of, and the management of, relationships between a state and foreign publics, primarily with a view to broadening the public appeal of its foreign policies. The persuasion strategies that this approach has favoured have intrinsically focused on engendering positive public sentiments around a state and its principal diplomatic actors (Surowiec and Miles, 2021). The binary associations of public diplomacy with liberal democracies (soft power of the US) and propaganda with authoritarian rule (sharp power of China or Russia) (Hedling, 2021) requires careful contextual consideration as the evidence suggests that liberal democracies engage in digital propaganda at home and abroad (Wooley and Howard, 2019: 4), although for different reasons and on a scale dissimilar to authoritarian regimes. While the public diplomacy of democracies is more likely to embrace deliberation enshrined in participatory ideals of this practice, an assessment of the features of digital propaganda solely on the basis of the type of regime is a risky analytical avenue. As such, 'attraction effects' is a principle navigating the communicative outcomes of public diplomacy, whereas these are less significant in propaganda, which in relation to the public tends to be geared toward 'deception effects', 'disruptive effects', or 'coercive effects'.

Among other principles differentiating the two forms of persuasion is the approach to facts and truth. While public diplomacy remains committed, however narrated or framed, to facts or even at times debunking misinformation or disinformation disseminated by propagandists, the study of digital propaganda reveals fluid attitudes to them. For example, Archetti (2019) argues that irrespective of propagandists' intentions, neither truth nor facts are self-evident, and highlights that no statement can be verified or falsified without a broader structure of meanings. She considers the network as a source of meaning structure constituting the 'reality' of the network itself and 'truth' as the make-up of core beliefs in the network. In the absence of firm epistemic grounds for falsifying truth-claims within networks, a peripheral route to persuasion takes precedent over the central route, reinforcing the authenticity of false claims, facilitating identity-affirming interactions among publics, which tend to exclude rather than include users who oppose a dominant narrative within the given ecosystem.

In an environment in which a closed system of echo chambers is immune to rebuttal or change, the assessment of the effects of digital propaganda prioritizes the digital construction of 'alternative realities'. Here, the focus on interpretation of loosely linked public frames, utterly unconnected to facts and evidence-based reasoning, tends to undermine the confidence in institutions, including diplomatic actors, the governance of which relies on openness, societal trust, and reputation (Bjola and Pamment, 2019). Consequently, instead of relying on media effects, as in the case of digitized public diplomacy, Manor and Bjola (2021) have identified 'reality-effects', engendered by disinformation-fuelled digital propaganda, and the adjustments to public diplomacy in order to contain its spread by means of the following tactics: debunking, setting the record straight, turning the tables, discrediting, and disrupting.

Moving beyond 'technological fetishism' underpinning the early analysis of digital propaganda and digital diplomacy, Surowiec and Manor (2021) link the impact of digital technologies with particular diplomatic actors and issues. By capturing the relationship between public diplomacy and 'post-truth' culture thriving on disinformation engendered, *inter alia*, by digital propaganda, they define the *zeitgeist* of international politics as 'the politics of uncertainty', that is the 'episteme foregrounding hyperrealities of a heteropolar world order characterised by the simultaneity of the weakening of global leadership, competitive struggles of regional powers, highly particularised interests of political actors and the governance modes focusing on a perpetual crisis' (Surowiec and Manor, 2021: xiii).

The area of foreign policy where public diplomacy overlaps with propaganda most vividly is national security. As the conjunction of the politics of uncertainty and digital propaganda is rendered an ominous prelude to international conflict or war, unsurprisingly analyses of communicative practices in international politics have focused on 'information war'. Here, the differences between public diplomacy and propaganda are, arguably, least conceptually discernible, and overlapping. Snow (2003) has talked about the role of propaganda in the information war enacted by the US government's public diplomacy actors in the aftermath of 9/11. The recent analysis emphasizes the role digital media technologies and propaganda play in information wars. A departure point here is the recognition that public diplomacy tends to be thought about as used to win an argument, whereas the language of information war increases the stakes by aligning 'the communicative battles with an existential threat' (Szostek, 2021: 2737). This argument, inspired by the rivalry between Russia and liberal democracies, has led to the rethinking of the means of influence in international politics. While, arguably, public diplomacy and information war overlap, the former represents a distinct ideal that is worth defending, particularly if the strategic landscape shaping international politics is adversarial. Additionally, the logic of 'information war' rests on the weaponization of information that ensues in an informational 'arms race', the assumption of the vulnerability of audiences, and the assumption that winning the information war means securing belief in facts. On both sides of the antagonistic relationship, 'information war' is inherently a doctrine embedded into a broader grand strategy mapping out landscapes in which diplomacy unfolds—proactive, in the case of Russia, reactive, however, in the case of West. Digital media technologies and propaganda are deemed as the means of delivery of this doctrine.

INTERNATIONAL EVENTS, DIPLOMACY, AND DIGITAL PROPAGANDA

While the rivalry between Russia and the Western liberal democracies has reinvigorated the debate about the relationship between digital propaganda and digital diplomacy, research demonstrates that other international events with diplomatic repercussions provide revealing insights about digital propaganda. Despite the escalation of diplomatic tension between Russia and liberal democracies, the rise of digital media technologies coincided with propaganda accompanying the Global War on Terror launched by the US government. Briant (2015) offers early insights into the ways in the US–UK 'special relationship' became a setting capable of overcoming the limitations in the cultures of propaganda for purposes of counter-terrorism. While her study considers the role of US–UK diplomatic and intelligence collaboration in the process of re-planning the practice of propaganda to the needs of counter-terrorism, notably, her analysis does not explicitly discuss digital propaganda beyond adapting governmental propaganda to media environments, one that includes social media and affords overt and covert 'insertions', 'viral videos', and 'story planting'.

Paralleled to the Global War on Terror, the upward trajectory of China's rise to a global superpower status has inspired a body of research demonstrating how statecraft capabilities of this state are used to accustom foreign publics to its foreign policies and its aspiring status in international politics. Over the past forty years, China has remained on track to become a powerful diplomatic actor on the world geopolitical stage. It has invested in digital media technologies to be a competitive global media player. Yet, the centralized approach to diplomatic communication of the Chinese state obscures the debate about the uniqueness of digital propaganda. Until recently, the Chinese government did not make a distinction between propaganda and public diplomacy, which has made the differentiation between the two practices challenging to interpret (Wang, 2008). The use of *wai xuan* (org. 'external propaganda') was, in 2004, rebranded to 'external publicity' when China embarked on the adoption of digital tools to expand the digital capabilities of diplomacy (Huang and Wang, 2019). The ongoing development of digital capabilities indicates that the ambition of the Chinese diplomatic service to move toward digital public diplomacy might not be in line with the government's goal to pursue 'improvement of online propaganda' with the purpose to 'guide public opinion on the Internet' (Huang and Rang, 2020: 122). Additionally, the Chinese government reduces negative digital content *via* censorship (Roberts, 2018), and its state-owned press, published internationally, has undergone a re-invention of its digital content away from a 'rigid propagandistic writing style to a much more energetic and literary form of expression' (Li, 2015: 19). According to Hartig (2016), the debate on the relationship between propaganda and public diplomacy by the Chinese state duplicates 'non-Chinese' arguments about the benignancy or evilness of some forms of persuasion. As it stands, more long term evidence is required to understand the differences and similarities between China's approach to digital propaganda vis-à-vis digital diplomacy, which, at this point, is hindered by governance habits and an authoritarian approach to public opinion.

The event that captured the imagination of publics across the world was the 2016 referendum on the United Kingdom's membership of the European Union. Embodying the politics of uncertainty, the referendum campaign as a precipitating event for a diplomatic crisis between the UK and the EU was a playground for the re-invention of propaganda. The propagandistic invention that became the trademark of the campaign was 'strategic lying', that is a rhetorical content device representing a unique transformation in 'spin'. Strategic lying is defined by manipulative content and its deployment within political campaigns. The goal of the 'strategic lie' is to set the news agenda and to prime the issue, both of which are achieved, first, by the attention-grabbing lie itself, and, second, by the rebuttal that ensures that the lie is widely disseminated and, as a statement, amplified across hybrid media landscapes. Gaber and Fisher (2022) argue that social media has increased the attractiveness of 'strategic lying' among political actors, and they reveal how it was deployed during the 2016 referendum campaign, the event with wide-ranging strategic diplomatic consequences. It was the Leave campaign's claim that Britain sent £350 million a week to Brussels as part of the contribution to the EU budget, funding which could, allegedly, otherwise be directed toward the National Health Service. Its rebuttals by the Remain campaigners kept reminding the public of the initial claim, which primed the issue, turning it into a shortcut in the argument about the financial costs of EU membership. Dominic Cummings (2017), the chief strategist of the Leave campaign, recalled this claim as a devise to 'to provoke people into argument'. Put simply, it was deployed to keep the news agenda on this issue, irrespective of its veracity.

Propaganda, however, has not only been remastered by global or regional powers. Since 2015, Poland, governed by the conservative Law and Justice party, has been a site of intensified clashes in local, national, and international politics, leading to the escalation of diplomatic tensions with the European Commission. Focused on the wedge issue of gender minorities rights, clerical leaders in the Catholic Church in comradeship with right-wing commentators, think-tanks, and parties have campaigned against what they perceive as a 'gender ideology', which entails promoting same-sex marriages and reproductive rights, allegedly undermining 'traditional family' values (Isaacs et al., 2021). This campaigning in Poland has turned into a multi-faceted international culture war between the right-wing government and the EU. One of the distinct propagandistic inventions which emerged during this culture war was the announcement of the formation of 'LGBT-free zones', a strategic branding deployed in online and offline campaigning to mark out municipalities, cities, and regions in Poland, which have embraced it as a self-affirmation strategy pertaining to the alleged 'LGBT ideology'. The issue escalated: not only did European cities such as Fermoy break twinning agreements, one of the pillars of city diplomacy, but the European Commission (2021) took a position on the issue, arguing that such campaigns would lead to freezing of the development funding for Polish regions. As a consequence, some regions begun easing off their campaigning stance.

On a global stage, the Covid-19 pandemic became a backdrop for the circulation of disinformation and misinformation about the virus. Propaganda played a role in shaping environments in which remedies such as vaccines were introduced. For example, Manfredi-Sánchez (2023) notes that selective exposure, as a derivative of the engagement with digital technologies, affected ways in which legitimacy narratives over Covid-19 policies were secured by diplomats. He argues that propagandistic narratives carried some disinformation and, in the case of China, were coercively pushed by 'wolf warrior' diplomacy. Rising to prominence during the pandemic, this coinage inspired by the 2017 film '*Wolf Warrior 2*' came to signify the coercive diplomatic style aimed at challenging anti-Chinese hostilities in international politics (Huang, 2022). The 'wolf warrior' diplomacy entailed rebutting falsehoods, a dynamic which foregrounds China's defensive stance. In the EU, according to Vértier et al. (2020), the sources of disinformation during the pandemic were foreign actors such as China, the digital propaganda of which used the self-portrayal as a humanitarian partner, while acting as an opportune do-gooder aiming to strengthen its foothold in vulnerable parts of Europe and masking its own handling of the pandemic. Vértier et al. (2020) speak of digital propaganda in metaphorical terms as a 'virus' that infects the 'informational body', and one that needs to be cured by proactive yet defensive policy measures which inhibit its development and by the cognitive resilience of the publics which, in turn, challenge its spread.

CHALLENGES IN THE ANALYSIS OF DIGITAL PROPAGANDA

The intersections of the field of diplomacy and propaganda echo a broader fragmentation of international politics manifested by the practice of digital propaganda by diplomatic actors as well as actors of diplomacy. The former pertains to institutional diplomatic actors, whereas the latter, similarly as in the practice of public diplomacy (Manor and Bjola, 2021), highlights the de-institutionalization of diplomacy displayed by the self-production of propaganda messages by non-diplomatic actors, which, pursuing their interests, engage with diplomatic conversations on social media. O'Shaughnessy (2012) notes that classical propaganda is a practice of well-resourced governments and other political actors. The proliferation of digital technologies has reduced the costs of propaganda and shifted the entry point of participation in diplomacy. The existing research demonstrates that platformization has afforded terrorist groups or rogue states such as ISIS the self-production of propaganda in order to radicalize or recruit supporters across national borders (Farkas et al., 2018), both of which have far-reaching security and diplomatic consequences regarding threat perceptions. Diaspora communities, too, have been long recognized (Orjuela, 2008) either as actors of diplomacy involved in propaganda, advocacy, and fundraising for armed actors or, conversely, for their untapped potential as peacebuilders (Crilley et al., 2020). Keeping in mind the self-production of propaganda, it is worth emphasizing that transnational activism or other counter-publics as sources of digital propaganda affect diplomacy and its outcomes (Bjola and Papadakis, 2020). In a fragmented landscape of international politics, tracing propaganda requires analytical approaches that go beyond the analysis of propagandistic content and that take under consideration relationships between diplomatic actors and actors of diplomacy.

Even less attention has been paid to the reception of propaganda messages in the context of diplomacy. In a recent survey of perceptions of falsehoods among publics in three countries, 36% of the US-based participants reported a belief they were exposed to falsehoods, followed by 29% in France and 19% in the UK. In all three countries, political use of social media is the strongest among all the predictors of belief in the public exposure to falsehoods (Koc-Michalska et al., 2020). While this study does not isolate perceptions of news on diplomatic affairs, it shows that social media is most likely to be associated with the perception of falsehoods. Studies also explore public engagement with the *RT* Twitter. For example, Crilley et al. (2022) reveal that its users tend to follow other broadcasters on Twitter, and that its followers are more likely to be an older male or bots. While existing studies have shown ways in which digital propaganda has evolved in hybrid media landscapes and set the agenda for the study and the practice of diplomacy, the effects of digital propaganda on publics across the world require further comparative evidence.

In the study of diplomacy, digital propaganda has not yet been re-modelled, but its existing models have been adapted to hybrid media landscapes. As propaganda is neither exclusively horizontal nor vertical any more, the networked logic of propaganda (Benkler et al., 2018) is a promising analytical avenue, but it still needs to be applied to the study of diplomacy. The information influence model proposed by Nothhaft et al. (2018) focuses on the formation of opinions as a means of understanding the systemic vulnerabilities of democracies rather than actual propaganda and its effects. In a study of the cross-platform propaganda executed on behalf of the Russian state by the Internet

Research Agency, Golovchenko et al. (2020) draws from classical models of propaganda (Ellul, 1973; Jowett and O'Donnell, 2019), particularly from the deflective source model to explain how, by engaging directly with targeted publics, cross-platform messages are shared covertly by a source that has no explicit connection to the propagandist. This mechanism enabled Russian-state actors dissemination of the ideologically conservative propagandistic content *via* liberal-leaning YouTube and Twitter accounts, which were sources of 'pre-propaganda', that is a mobilizing strategy not immediately related to the message of propagandist. In the light of that, the modelling or re-modelling of propaganda remains to be an ongoing task for the study of diplomacy.

Conclusions

The positioning of digital propaganda vis-à-vis digital diplomacy in scholarship enables the field of diplomacy to embark on the discussion of differences and similarities as pathways to understanding the effect digitalization has had on propaganda and public diplomacy as practices as well as forms of persuasion. The epistemic crisis affects publics on the open Web, those engrossed in echo chambers ringing with fake news and other digitized genres of propaganda, making liberal democracies increasingly ungovernable and posing a diplomatic challenge for the liberal order. Additionally, the epistemic crisis experienced by the publics of diplomacy opens the study of diplomacy, which appears to be playing catch-up with changes driven by the impact of digitalization on the practice, to new avenues in a still fragmented field.

As well as gaining empirical and comparative insights about the style, content, and intentions of a growing portfolio of actors behind digital propaganda, more work is required to systematize taxonomies in the field, in which the contestation of propaganda, the most established form of persuasion, is pursued by de-contextualized descriptors of this practice and the embrace of the latest conceptual containers. For example, Deverell et al. (2020: 19) justify the use of the concept of strategic narrative in the analysis of Sputnik thusly: 'Alongside processes of militarisation and conflict, another phenomenon has developed—broader in scope than disinformation, not as structured, strategic or military dominated as information operations and lacking the negative connotations and simplicity of propaganda'. Along with the review of literature, this quote suggests that the field would benefit from taxonomic systematization of the newer concepts vis-à-vis established practices, all of which are nowadays subjected to digitalization, including the latest interventions to diplomacy in the form of deepfakes and virtual and augmented reality. Finally, as only a few international events in international politics have dominated the analysis of digital propaganda, evidence of the inner-workings and effects of digital propaganda from other parts of the world would help to aid the understanding of the evolving relationship between digital propaganda and diplomacy.

Suggested Reading

Bjola, C. and Pamment, J. (2016) 'Digital containment: revisiting containment strategy in the digital age', *Global Affairs*, 2(2), pp. 131–142.

Lam, V. (2021) 'Information and communications technologies, online activism, and implications for Vietnam's public diplomacy', *Journal of Current Southeast Asia Affairs*, 41(1), pp. 3–33.

Sparkes-Vian, C (2022) 'Digital diplomacy: the tyranny of ignorance', *Critical Sociology*, 45(3), pp. 393–409.

Wooley, S. C. (2022) 'Digital propaganda: the power of influencers', *Journal of Democracy*, 33(3), 115–129.

References

Aistrope, T. (2016) *Conspiracy theory and American foreign policy*. Manchester: Manchester University Press.

Antwi-Boateng, O. and Al Mazrouei, K. A. M. (2021) 'The challenges of digital diplomacy in the era of globalization: the case of the United Arab Emirates', *International Journal of Communication*, 15, pp. 4577–4595.

Archetti, Ch. (2019) 'The unbearable thinness of strategic communication', in Bjola, C. and Pamment, J. (eds.) *Countering online propaganda and extremism: the dark side of digital diplomacy*. London: Routledge, pp. 81–95.

Benkler, Y., Faris, R., and Roberts. H. (2018) *Network propaganda: manipulation, disinformation and radicalization in American politics*. New York: Oxford University Press.

Bjola, C. (2019) 'Propaganda as reflexive control: the digital dimension' in Bjola, C. and Pamment, J. (eds.) *Countering online propaganda and extremism: the dark side of digital diplomacy*. London: Routledge, pp. 13–27.

Bloja, C. and Manor, I. (2018) 'Revisiting Putnam's two-level game theory in the digital age: domestic digital diplomacy and the Iran nuclear deal', *Cambridge Review of International Affairs*, 31(1): 3–32.

Bjola, C. and Pamment, J. (2019) *Countering online propaganda and extremism: the dark side of digital diplomacy*. London: Routledge.

Bjola, C. and Papadakis, K. (2020) 'Digital propaganda, counterpublics and the disruption of the public sphere: the Finnish approach to building digital resilience', *Cambridge Review of International Affairs*, 33(5), pp. 638–666.

Bos, M. and Melissen, J. (2019) 'Rebel diplomacy and digital communication: public diplomacy in the Sahel', *International Affairs*, 95(6), pp. 1331–1348.

Boyd-Barrett, O. (2019) 'Fake news and "RussiaGate" discourses: propaganda in the post-truth', *Journalism*, 20(1), pp. 87–91.

Briant, E. (2015) 'Allies and audiences: evolving strategies in defence and intelligence propaganda', *The International Journal of Press/Politics*, 20(2), pp. 145–165.

Cull, N. (2008) *The Cold War and the United States Information Agency: American propaganda and public diplomacy, 1945-1989*. Cambridge: Cambridge University Press.

Chadwick, A. (2013) *Hybrid media system: power and politics*. Oxford: Oxford University Press.

Chadwick, A. Stanyer, J. (2022) 'Deception as a bridging concept in the study of disinformation, misinformation, and misperceptions: toward a holistic framework', *Communication Theory*, 32(1), pp. 1–24.

Chernobrov, D. and Briant, E. L. (2022) 'Competing propagandas: how the United States and Russia represent mutual propaganda activities', *Politics*, 42(3), pp. 393–409.

Clarke, R. A. and Knale, R. K. (2014) *Cyber war: the next threat to national security and what to do about it?* New York: HarperCollins.

Cooper, A. F., Heine. J., and Thakur, R. (2013) 'Introduction: the challenges of 21st century diplomacy', in Cooper, A., Heine, J., and Thakur, R. (eds.) *The Oxford handbook of modern diplomacy*. Oxford: OUP, pp. 1–31.

Crilley, R., Manor, I., and Corneliu, B. (2020) 'Visual narratives of global politics in the digital age: an introduction', *Cambridge Review of International Affairs*, 33(5), pp. 628–637.

Crilley, R., Gillespie, M., Vidgen, B., and Wills, A. (2022) 'Understanding RT's audiences: exposure not endorsement for Twitter followers of Russian state-sponsored media', *The International Journal of Press/Politics*, 27(1), pp. 220–242.

Cummings, D. (2017) 'On the referendum #21: Branching histories of the 2016 referendum and the frogs before the storm', *Dominic Cummings Blog*. Available at: https://dominiccummings.com/2017/01/09/on-the-referendum-21-branching-histories-of-the- 2016-referendum-and-the-frogs-before-the-storm-2/. (Accessed on: 22 February 2022).

Danziger, R. and Schreiber, M. (2021) 'Digital diplomacy: face management in MFA Twitter accounts', *Policy Internet*, 13, pp. 586–605.

Deverell, E., Wagnsson, Ch., and Olsson E. K., (2020) 'Destruct, direct and suppress: sputnik narratives on the Nordic countries', *The Journal of International Communication*, 27(1), pp. 15–37.

Ellul, J. (1973) *Propaganda: the formation of men's attitudes*. New York: Random House.

Elswah, M. Howard, P. N. (2020) ' "Anything that causes chaos": the organizational behavior of Russia Today (RT)', *Journal of Communication*, 70(5), pp. 623–645.

Farkas, J. and Schou, J. (2018) 'Fake news as a floating signifier: hegemony, antagonism and the politics of falsehood', *Javnost – The Public*, 25(3), pp. 298–314.

Farkas, J., Schou, J., and Neumayer, C. (2018) 'Cloaked Facebook pages: exploring fake Islamist propaganda in social media', *New Media & Society*, 20(5), pp. 1850–1867.

Freelon, D. and Wells, Ch. (2020) 'Disinformation as political communication', *Political communication*, 37(2), pp. 145–156.

Eggeling K. A., and Adler-Nissen, R. (2021) 'The synthetic situation in diplomacy: scopic media and the digital mediation of estrangement', *Global Studies Quarterly*, 1(2), pp. 1–14.

European Commission (2021) 'EU founding values: Commission starts legal action against Hungary and Poland for violating fundamental rights of LBBTIQ people'. Available at: https://ec.europa.eu/commission/presscorner/detail/en/ip_21_3668 (Accessed on: 22 February 2022).

Gaber, I. and Fisher, C. (2022). ' "Strategic lying": the case of Brexit and the 2019 U.K. Election'. *The International Journal of Press/Politics*, 27(2), pp. 460–477.

Golan, G. J., Manor, I., and Arceneaux, P. (2019) 'Mediated public diplomacy redefined: foreign stakeholder engagement via paid, earned, shared, and owned media', *American Behavioral Scientist*, 63(2), pp. 1665–1683.

Golovchenko, Y., Buntain, C., Eady, G., Brown, M. A., and Tucker, J. A. (2020) 'Cross-platform state propaganda: Russian trolls on Twitter and YouTube during the 2016 U.S. Presidential election', *The International Journal of Press/Politics*, 25(3), pp. 357–389.

Hall-Jamieson, K. (2018) Cyber-war: how Russian hackers and trolls helped elect a president. New York: Oxford University Press.

Hartig, F. (2016) 'How China understands public diplomacy: the importance of national image for national interests', *International Studies Review*, 18(4), pp. 655–680.

Hayden, C. (2011) 'Beyond the "Obama Effect": refining the instruments of engagement through U.S. public diplomacy', *American Behavioral Scientist*, 55(6), pp. 781–802.

Hedling, E. (2021) 'Transforming practices of diplomacy: the European External Action Service and digital transformation', *International Affairs*, 97(3), pp. 841–859.

Hedling, E., Bremberg, N. (2021) 'Practice approaches to the digital transformations of diplomacy: toward a new research agenda', *International Studies Review*, 23(4), pp. 1595–1618.

Holmes, M. (2015) 'Digital diplomacy and international change management' in Bjola, C. and Holmes, M. (eds.) *Digital diplomacy: theory and practice*. London: Routledge, pp. 13–32.

Hyzen, A. (2021) 'Revisiting the theoretical foundations of propaganda', *International Journal of Communication*, 15, pp. 3479–3496.

Huang, Z. H. (2022) '"Wolf warrior" and China's digital public diplomacy during the COVID-19 crisis', *Place Branding and Public Diplomacy*, 18, pp. 37–40. doi.org/10.1057/s41254-021-00241-3.

Huang, Z. A. and Wang, R. (2019) 'Building a network to "tell China stories well": Chinese diplomatic communication Strategies on Twitter', *International Journal of Communication*, 13, pp. 2984–3007.

Huang, Z. A. and Wang, R. (2020) '"Panda engagement" in China's digital public diplomacy', *Asian Journal of Communication*, 30(2), pp. 118–140.

Hyunjin, S. (2014) 'Visual propaganda in the age of social media: an empirical analysis of Twitter images during the 2012 Israeli–Hamas Conflict', *Visual Communication Quarterly*, 21(3), pp. 150–161.

Isaacs, R., Wheatley, J., and Whitmore, S. (2021) 'Culture wars in the post-Soviet space', *Europe-Asia Studies*, 73(8), pp. 1407–1417.

Jack, C. (2019) 'Wicked content', *Communication, Culture and Critique*, 12(4), pp. 435–454.

Jowett, G. and O'Donnell, V. (2019) *Propaganda and persuasion*. Sage: London.

Kampf, R., Manor, I., and Segev, E. (2015) 'Digital diplomacy 2.0? A cross-national comparison of public engagement in Facebook and Twitter', *The Hague Journal of Diplomacy*, 10(4), pp. 331–362.

Koc-Michalska, K., Bimber, B., Gomez, D., Jenkins, M., and Boulianne, S. (2020) 'Public beliefs about falsehoods in news', *The International Journal of Press/Politics*, 25(3), pp. 447–468.

Li, A. K. (2015) 'Towards a more proactive method: Regulating public opinion on Chinese microblogs under Xi's new leadership', *China Perspectives*, 4, pp. 15–23.

Lilleker, D. and Surowiec, P. (2020) 'Content analysis and the examination of digital propaganda on social media', in Baines, P. R., O'Shaughnessy, N. J., and Snow, N. (eds.) *The Sage handbook of propaganda*. London: Sage, pp. 171–188.

Manfredi-Sánchez, J. (2022) 'Vaccine (public) diplomacy: legitimacy narratives in the pandemic age', *Place Branding and Public Diplomacy*, 19, pp. 398–410.

Manor, I. and Bjola, C. (2021) 'Public diplomacy in the age of "post-reality"', in Surowiec, P. and Manor, I. (eds.) *Public diplomacy and the politics of uncertainty*. Cham: Palgrave, pp. 111–143.

Manor, I. and Pamment, J. (2019) 'Towards prestige mobility? Diplomatic prestige and digital diplomacy', *Cambridge Review of International Affairs*, 32(2), pp. 93–131.

Molina, M. D., Sundar, S. S., Le, T. and Lee, D. (2021) '"Fake news" is not simply false information: a concept explication and taxonomy of online content', *American Behavioral Scientist*, 2(2), pp. 180–212.

Melissen, J. (2005) *The new public diplomacy: between theory and practice*. Basingstoke: Palgrave.

Moloney, K. (2006) *Rethinking public relations*. London: Routledge.

Nothhaft, H., Pamment, J., Agardh-Twetwan, H., and Fjällhed, A. (2018) 'Information influence in Western democracies: a model of systemic vulnerabilities', in Bjola, C. and Pamment, J. (eds.) *Countering online propaganda and extremism: the dark side of digital diplomacy*. London: Routledge, pp. 28–43.

Nicolson, H. (1950) *Diplomacy*. London: Oxford University Press.

Nisbet, E. C. and Kamenchuk, O. (2018) 'The psychology of state-sponsored disinformation campaigns and implications for public diplomacy', *The Hague Journal of Diplomacy*, 14(1–2), pp. 65–82.

Orjuea, C. (2008) 'Distant warriors, distant peace workers? Multiple diaspora roles in Sri Lanka's violent conflict', *Global Networks*, 8(4), pp. 436–452.

O'Shaughnessy, N. (2012) 'The death and life of propaganda', *Journal of Public Affairs*, 12(1), 29–38.

Ó Fathaigh, R., Dobber, T., Zuiderveen Borgesius, F., and Shires, J. (2021) 'Microtargeted propaganda by foreign actors: an interdisciplinary exploration', *Maastricht Journal of European and Comparative Law*, 28(6), pp. 856–877.

Pamment, J. (2016) 'Digital diplomacy as transmedia engagement: aligning theories of participatory culture with international advocacy campaigns', *New Media & Society*, 18(9), pp. 2046–2062.

Roberts, M. E. (2018) *Censored: distraction and diversion inside China's great firewall*. Princeton, NJ: Princeton University Press.

Snow, N. (2003) *Information war: American propaganda, free speech and opinion control since 9/11*. New York: Seven Stories Press.

Surowiec, P. (2017) 'Post-truth soft power: changing facets of propaganda, kompromat and liberal democracy', *Georgetown Journal of International Affairs*, 18(3), pp. 21–27.

Surowiec, P. and Long, P. (2020) 'Hybridity and soft power statecraft: the 'GREAT' campaign', *Diplomacy & Statecraft*, 31(1), pp. 168–195.

Surowiec, P. and Manor, I. (2021) *Public diplomacy and the politics of uncertainty*. Cham: Palgrave.

Surowiec. P. and Miles. Ch. (2021) 'The populist style and public diplomacy: keyfabe as performative agonism in Trump's Twitter posts', *Public Relations Inquiry*, 10(1), pp. 5–30.

Szostek, J. (2018) 'The mass media and Russia's "spheres of interest": mechanisms of regional hegemony in Belarus and Ukraine', *Geopolitics*, 23(2), pp. 307–329.

Szostek, J. (2021) 'What happens to public diplomacy during information war? Critical reflections on the conceptual framing of international communication', *International Journal of Communication*, 14, pp. 2728–2748.

Thomas, T. (2004) 'Russia's reflexive control theory and the military', *The Journal of Slavic Military Studies*, 17(2), pp. 237–256.

Tsvetkova, N., Rushchin, D., Shiryaev, B., Yarygin, G., and Tsvetkov, I. (2020) 'Sprawling in cyberspace: Barack Obama's legacy in public diplomacy and strategic communication', *Journal of Political Marketing*, pp. 1–13. DOI: 10.1080/15377857.2020.1724425

Valeriano, B., Jensen, B. and Maness, R. C. (2019) *Cyber strategy: the evolving character of power and coercion*. Oxford: Oxford University Press.

Vériter, S. L., Bjola, C., and Coops, J. (2020) 'Tackling Covid-19 disinformation and external challengers for the European Union', *The Hague Journal of Diplomacy*, 15, pp. 569–582.

Wang, Y. (2008) '@public diplomacy and the rise of Chinese soft power', *The Annals of the American Academy of Political and Social Sciences*, 616, pp. 257–273.

Wooley, S. C. and Howard, P. (2019) *Computational propaganda*. Oxford: Oxford University Press.

Zaharna, R. S., Arsenault, A., and Fisher, A. (2013) *Relational, networked and collaborative approaches to public diplomacy*. New York: Routledge.

Zuboff, S. (2019) *The age of surveillance capitalism: the fight for a human nature at the new frontier of power*. |London: Profile Books.

CHAPTER 13

ETHICAL CHALLENGES IN THE DIGITALIZATION OF PUBLIC DIPLOMACY

ZHAO ALEXANDRE HUANG AND PHILLIP ARCENEAUX

FROM certain perspectives, digital diplomacy is oxymoronic. Historically, diplomacy has been exclusive, i.e., lateral negotiation between societal elites. Digital diplomacy, however, involves inclusive, two-way, vertical dialogue between multiple levels of a networked society. *The Digitalization of Public Diplomacy* highlights a key contradiction in diplomatic engagement in a networked world.

> Diplomacy . . . should not be subject to the demands of 'open government'; whenever it works, it is usually because it is done behind closed doors. But this may be increasingly hard to achieve in the age of Twittering bureaucrats.
>
> (Manor, 2019: 1)

This articulates core ethical challenges for diplomats in a digital society: balancing secrecy versus transparency, exclusivity versus inclusivity, and state interests versus public interest.

Brittney Griner's detainment in Russia is an ideal case study. While US and Russian diplomats negotiate for her release, this NBA star's social media fandom has placed pressure on the Biden administration to secure a prisoner exchange. While US diplomats attempt daily to assuage public concern they will bring Griner home, growing public outcry plays into Russian interests. It tips the scales of negotiation into Russia's favour at the expense of US interests. The Department of State has struggled to balance the secrecy of its negotiation strategy with transparent accountability to the US public. A similar case involves the repatriation of Nazanin Zaghari-Ratcliffe to the United Kingdom from Iran during the Theresa May and Boris Johnson administrations.

For diplomats, negotiation and mediation require secrecy. Diplomatic confidentiality resolves conflict and ensures peace in uncertain geopolitical environments. This *closed-door* diplomacy provides a necessary condition to ensure effective implementation of foreign policy strategy. While secret diplomacy is subject to ethical scrutiny in democratic societies, it remains justified, legitimate, and necessary (Bjola, 2014).

Digital diplomacy, however, invites a re-examination of the ethical legitimacy of secret diplomacy. Since Woodrow Wilson advocated 'open diplomacy' (Cull, 2009), democracies have pursued more transparent and democratic mechanisms for international engagement. The principle of openness versus secrecy, inclusivity versus exclusivity, and state versus public interest in diplomatic operations is now a matter of debate and compromise in the digital age.

Digital diplomacy also challenges traditional information systems, creating uncertainty in the public sphere (Surowiec and Manor, 2021). This involves the use of disinformation, computational propaganda, misinformation, and other forms of fake news to deliver more fragmented, one-sided, and emotional messages that disrupt or reshape the international order (Arceneaux and Harman, 2021). Take for example the Trump administration's denial of global warming amid catastrophic climate anomalies, the competing origin theories for Covid-19 promoted by the United States and China, or the justifications by *Russia Today* for the invasion of Ukraine.

This accentuates the necessity, and urgency, for considering the ethics of digital diplomacy. Due to the specificity and political sensibility of their mission, diplomats must find ways to reconcile competing ethical constraints with their professional responsibilities (Bjola, 2016). To explore this nexus, this chapter opens by defining ethics. It then summarizes the professionalization of the public diplomat. From there, the chapter posits three key challenges at the intersection of ethical digital diplomacy: secrecy versus transparency, advancing state versus public interests, and creating trust versus chaos. The chapter does not provide ethical standards or codes for the practice of digital diplomacy. Rather, it explores the ethical puzzles inherent in digital diplomacy.

How to Define Ethics

Ethics can be applied to every aspect of human life. Efforts to conceptualize the term must account for the universality of good and honest belief, diversity of practice, and the professionalization of specific occupations. For Weil-Dubuc, ethics refers to 'a nebula of labeled professional practices' (2019: 23). It represents the duties or responsibilities of a professional field. Ethics, however, are not 'moral rules', though the former 'refers to values that allow one to judge' (Simonnot, 2018: 14). While morality derives from self-discipline, personal will, and individual goodness, the ethical life embraces 'the concept of freedom developed into the existing world and the nature of self-consciousness' (Horowitz, 1966: 13).

Ethics is collectivist, implying the normalization and institutionalization of multiple viewpoints and practices, and the value orientation of a specific group. Ethics take root in various organizational forms, from family to community, civil society to the nation-state. Ethical issues point to the observance and defence of collectivity. Thus, ethical values are more important than individual moral values, and ethical concerns lead to feelings of discomfort that one should not try to extinguish or calm by an appeal to static values or deontological charters. Ethical concerns are 'a reflection on the means adopted to implement this concern for non-harm to another who is our fellow human being' (Ricœur, quoted by Desmoulins, 2017: 130).

People use equivocal descriptions to define ethics due to its ontological vagueness. Intellectuals attribute such ambiguity to the disagreement between philosophical schools on social order, e.g., meta-ethics, materialism, philosophico-political, and metaphysics. For example, monists and pluralists debate whether ethical achievement involves identifying common visions and interests or shared value in diversity (Weil-Dubuc, 2019). The debate revolves around whether ethical rules create consensus, achieve compromise, or justify and legitimize differences among people (Mouffe, 2016).

Scholars regard ethics as a 'teleologically' oriented social tradition (Couldry, 2008: 62). Plato viewed ethical virtue as a complex set of rational, emotional, and social skills. Aristotle called ethical virtue the 'center of a well-lived life' (Kraut, 2018: para. 1), while Kant offered a 'deontological' interpretation of ethics as rules for distinguishing right from wrong (Alexander and Moore, 2021: para. 2).

Given this variety, ethical concepts indicate a developmental regulation applying to an embodied social group. The ambiguity of ethics is derived from the breadth of practice it covers, i.e., the heterogeneity of different professions. This is exemplified between professional diplomatic and communication practice.

Specificity of practice depends on not only the geographic and historical characteristics of an occupation, but also its professionalization. Professionalization is polysemic and covers multiple aspects layered within a dynamic process. This includes not only the creation of new occupations, the socialization of career development, and the institutionalization of professional training programmes, but also legalization and specialization.

The Professionalization of the Public Diplomat

As a modern complement to traditional diplomacy, public diplomacy broadens the channels of negotiation and mediation. Diplomacy is no longer limited to exchanges among elites, closed-door coordination of stakeholders, or administrative communication. Public diplomacy gives rise to open diplomatic communication between governments and their domestic and foreign publics. The development of public diplomacy depends on and responds to mutations in the global environment, various forms of international communication, and normalizing para-diplomacy. The fundamental categories of public diplomacy include five forms: listening, advocacy, cultural diplomacy, exchange diplomacy, and international broadcasting (Cull, 2019).

Digital diplomacy's diffusion, however, enlarges diplomats' professional boundaries, such as the popularization of community management. This expands the professionalization of public diplomacy, adding place branding, national image and reputation management (Ingenhoff et al., 2019), and partnership management (Cull, 2019) into the day-to-day responsibilities of communication staffs.

Such diversity demonstrates the openness and inclusiveness of diplomacy's professionalization. It also prompts scholars to examine diplomatic action from a 'transprofessionalization perspective' (Constantinou, Cornago, and McConnell, 2016: 3). This seeks to understand how multiple actors coordinate cross-cutting strategies to co-participate in the construction of a government's influence and legitimacy.

Public diplomacy actors in the digital age are no longer limited to a single profession. They need an interdisciplinary knowledge base; their skillsets need to be inspired by other fields. They also need to continuously learn new technics and methods to adapt to globalization and technological change. For Constantinous et al. (2016), current diplomats need to be innovative and flexible in coordinating and organizing strategies, tactics, methods, and techniques, and facilitate interactions of multiple actors in deploying foreign policies to obtain advantages in legitimacy and frame competition.

For instance, the gender initiative launched on Twitter by then Swedish Minister of Foreign Affairs Margot Wallström (2014–2019) successfully built an online narrative network with #FeministForeignPolicy, engaging numerous international organizations (i.e., UN, Plan International) to advocate and protect women's rights at the global level (Aggestam, Rosamond, and Hedling, 2021). The campaign also contributed to Sweden's international image- and reputation-building as a progressive country, deploying its foreign policy for supporting 'global gender equality' (Government Offices of Swenden, 2019: 6).

Moreover, the Association of Southeast Asian Nations (ASEAN) engages its youth organization (@ayoasean on Twitter) and think tanks (The Habibie Centre and ASEAN Studies Centre) in its digital diplomacy network (Intentilia, Haes, and Suardana, 2022). This not only extends and dynamizes ASEAN's online communication and audiences, but also demonstrates the dynamism of ASEAN's members, their contributions to global economic development, and the opportunities they provide for other geopolitical players.

This transprofessional diversity also drives the digitalization of public diplomacy toward the nature of a discipline, gaining conceptual strength by scholars. As 'the sunrise of the academic field' (Gregory, 2008: 274), public diplomacy and its digitalization appear frequently in political science, political communication, and public relations textbooks. Political scientists describe public diplomacy's core objective as 'the transfer of values, attitudes, opinions, and information through the interactions of individuals, groups, governments, and technologies' (Mowlana, 1997: 207). Communication scholars understand it as a mixture of the discursive and relational dimensions of influence (Cowan and Arsenault, 2008).

Social media's popularity emphasizes the vital role of discourse and relationship-management in the process of online meaning (co-)construction. Practitioners regard the enhancement of the communication management underpinning diplomatic relationship-building as 'central to the field of soft power statecraft' (Surowiec and Miles, 2021: 6). Scholars therefore increasingly conceptualize digital diplomacy as pre-planned, goal-oriented, network-synergistic, and dynamically coordinated strategic communication (Zaharna, 2018; Nye, 2019). This indicates the vital role of digital diplomacy in mediating foreign policy by mobilizing social media affordances and implies the *transprofessionality*, flexibility, complexity, diversity, and sustainability of its practice.

The professionalization of digital diplomacy also highlights the construction of its values and representation. This includes global communications embedded in foreign policy by various actors: diplomats, politicians, journalists, etc. (Huang, 2021). Its professionalization implies the emergence of a new career category: public diplomats. Like other professions, this requires following a set of established professional identities and missions in daily routines.

The application and rapid change of digital technology provides a wealth of means and channels for governments to build their geopolitical agenda on the international stage. Accordingly, digital diplomacy bid farewell to traditional top-down communication models. As social media continue to expand information transmission methods and channels, this increasingly widens the scope of public diplomacy to include non-state actors, horizontal two-way communication, and interaction (Manor, 2019).

Public diplomacy now also includes multinational corporations, NGOs, and cultural institutions. Even individuals can now engage in low-cost, sustainable, and efficient international communication. Actors can execute short-term and day-to-day political communication campaigns, promote national image, forge national reputations, and manage relationships with foreign audiences (Golan, Manor, and Arceneaux, 2019).

For example, the Louvre Museum operates Twitter, Instagram, and Weibo accounts for audiences from different countries, languages, and cultural backgrounds. It not only increases the reputation and traffic of this French national museum, but also implicitly endorses French values, ideas, and policies through mediating French knowledge, culture, history, and republican values (Huang and Hardy, 2021). Further, unlike China's aggressive wolf warrior diplomacy, Chinese Internet celebrity Li Ziqi presents her peaceful life in rural China to the world on YouTube. By combining a variety of Chinese cultural symbols (food, music, clothing) in her non-verbal visual communication, Li conveys the simple, positive, and traditional Chinese rural values while deliberately displaying the diversity of Chinese culture. This contributes to eliminating the stereotype in international public opinion of China's one-Party-controlled ideology (Fan, 2021).

Digital diplomacy not only allows practitioners 'to share, to co-operate, with one another, and to take collective action, all outside the framework of traditional institutional institutions and organizations' (Fuchs, 2014: 35), but also provides a platform for user-centred community activities (Huang and Wang, 2021; Manor and Huang, 2022). In addition to being information releaser, communicator, and mediator, public diplomats are increasingly becoming managers of online communities and public opinion. They are involved not only in the formulation, development, and implementation of communication strategies and assessment, but also in the management of needs, partnerships, and online relationships (Fitzpatrick, 2007).

Social media provide the means for an interactive communication network that 'promotes connectedness as a social value' (Dijk, 2012: 11) through long-term, durable online engagement led by public diplomats. This is an ethical form of two-way communication (Cowan and Arsenault, 2008; Zaharna, 2018) because the engagement has the potential to achieve symmetry (Grunig, 2001), enhance mutual understanding, build trust, accumulate social capital, and 'promote diversity and help create democracy' (Pisarska, 2016: 24).

Despite established roles and practices, the professionalization of public diplomacy remains rocky. The coordination of state actors has standardized digital diplomacy activities, and the diversity of those activities has created new disciplines. At the same time, the ambiguous boundaries of its professionalization have made peer oversight difficult, allowing monopolies to emerge. While everyday professions such as police officers, doctors, lawyers, and pharmacists have professional codes of conduct to regulate the ethical boundaries of their work, such a framework is still missing for public diplomats (Bessières and Huang, 2021).

Challenge 1. Balancing Secrecy versus Transparency

Diplomacy is international communication by a political entity to negotiate with exogenous counterparts. It is the 'conduct of relations between sovereign states' through diplomats (Berridge and James, 2001: 62). Diplomacy involves the strategic calculation and exercise of power; contemporary diplomacy is 'the institutionalization of bilateral or multilateral discussions' to promote the proper functioning of a world order (Fernandez, 2018: 144).

Diplomacy differs, however, from other types of organizational communication. Diplomats exercise authority on behalf of a political collectivity. This diplomatic agency is 'the result of a conditional transfer' (Bjola, 2016, 124) of plenipotentiary privileges from legitimate authorities to specific actors. While modern diplomats have power, they rarely exercise it directly and autonomously. This is because the conditions for executing diplomatic agency are strictly institutionalized and normalized. Diplomats must ensure the sustainability of negotiations with their counterparts (Fernandez, 2018) to reach consensus or compromise under better political conditions (Constantinou and Sharp, 2016).

One way for ensuring the sustainability of diplomatic negotiations is through secrecy. Secret diplomacy creates favourable conditions for unlocking 'peace negotiations and providing a conducive environment for constructive talks' (Bjola 2014: 87). This allows the mediation process to avoid interference and informational noise from international media. It also helps diplomats defuse contradictions in a closed-door manner and reach consensus. Secret diplomacy can 'prevent dangerous escalations by protecting the reputation of a government from political embarrassment or damage' (Bjola, 2014: 87). This offers the benefit of enhancing the diplomatic standing of small states by legitimatizing their mediation role in geopolitical conflicts.

Diplomats are also 'interpreters' or 'translators' (Ollivier-Yaniv, 2015: para. 14) who occupy the transitive position of foreign policy explicator. This reorganizes and mediates various registers of language coming from different levels of authority to 'articulate multiple and often divergent influences into a coherent discourse' (Ségas, 2012: para. 26). By having diplomats wield power on their behalf, governments perform a kind of ventriloquism (Huang and Wang, 2020), empowering diplomats to speak words aligning with organizational strategies on the global stage. This proxy communication, operating under a set of constraints between actors and their authorities, involves traditional diplomatic ethics: serving, keeping secrets for, and being loyal to, the interests of a government.

The emergence of digital diplomacy represents the rise of an open diplomacy model, extending diplomacy beyond the secret and exclusive interaction of elites to include the public sphere. As a 'ubiquitous and pluralistic social practice' (Petiteville and Placidi-Frot, 2013: 19), public diplomacy in the digital age fosters comprehensive social cooperation openly and democratically (Cowan and Arsenault, 2008). The significant difference between public diplomacy and secret diplomacy is the insistence of the former on deliberative democracy, calling for 'an ethics of discussion' (Habermas, 1987: 26).

In other words, digital diplomacy contributes to 'a communication structure anchored in the lifeworld through the foundations of civil society' (Dacheux, 2000: 132). This democratic ideal emphasizes 'pluralism and communication games among civil society actors' (Pirotte, 2018: 56). Digital diplomacy works to achieve mutual understanding and social consensus. Its actors must not only shape the authority, image, and reputation of their respective governments in the public sphere, but also coordinate various symbolic forms to facilitate the creation of meaning.

The difference between traditional and digital diplomacy is a distinct understanding of ethics in the fields of diplomacy and communication. Realism's influence is evident in political science's analysis of ethical issues: the justice and legality of war (Capizzi, 2015), how ethical principles affect international affairs and negotiations (Rosenthal and Barry, 2009), and the status and role of ethics in geopolitical chess games (Hoffmann, 1981). For diplomacy, ethics is a value lever used to reconcile the dilemma between crystallizing national responsibility and defending national interests (Ellis, 2009). In this framework, two philosophies compete for ethical supremacy: cosmopolitanism and communitarianism (Brown, 2011, 2019).

In communication, however, ethics is the perception of right versus wrong and the definition of truth versus falsehood (Catellani, Zerfass, and Tench, 2015). This relates to the mediatization of information and influence. Plato analysed the role of information dissemination in constructing legitimacy and authority; he noted some people have inherent abilities to communicate ideas and persuade audiences to hold or change certain beliefs (Plato and Lamb, 2007).

Leveraging this influence, however, comes with ethical mandates. Plato used the metaphors of 'evil lover' and 'noble lover' (Weaver, 1985: 6) to judge the ethics of persuasive communicators in influencing beliefs and ideas. While evil lovers create relationships in which they play superior roles, noble lovers help elevate their audiences.

Scholars conceptualize this metaphor as the distinction between two-way asymmetrical and symmetrical communication (Marsh, 2003; Porter, 2010). If two-way asymmetric communication is 'a form that promotes advocacy and selective truth' (Marsh Jr., 2001: 85), the symmetrical paradigm facilitates the search for win-win relationships and permits organizational change to foster meaningful relationships. The latter aligns with Plato's teaching on the ethics of communication: the constant mobilization of communication skills to advance the public good and make others better (Elliott and Spence, 2017).

Ethically examined, the transition from traditional diplomacy to digital diplomacy implies a reconciliation of the tension between diplomatic and communication ethics. Digital diplomacy increasingly involves information exchange and meaning co-creation through dialogue; thus, 'participants are committed to each other and care about each other' (Taylor and Kent, 2014: 389). This forges trust, thereby defending public interests through a long-term accumulation of mutual awareness and understanding (Huang, 2021).

CHALLENGE 2. ADVANCING STATE VERSUS PUBLIC INTEREST

Diplomacy entails the commitment of diplomats to defend the interests of their state. In this framework, loyalty is the willingness to engage with persistent belief and complete dedication (Fletcher, 1995). This loyalty takes precedence over personal emotions and is superior to friendship, gratitude, and respect. The history of diplomatic ethics is the evolution of this concept of loyalty, which includes debates about the interests diplomatic actions serve.

The evolution of diplomatic objectives has moved through three stages: 'loyalty to the Prince; loyalty to the State; loyalty to People' (Bjola, 2016: 125). These phases correspond to the principles of dynastic sovereignty, territorial sovereignty, and international norms. The debate of diplomatic allegiance continues to focus on these principles. Diplomats use the term 'national interest' to construct the rationality and legitimacy of their actions because it is the basis of the strategic formulation of a state's foreign policy. The conceptual boundaries of national interest, however, are unclear, leading to differences in the perception of diplomatic ethics.

For realists, states engage in competition as the need for survival and the desire to dominate overlap (Carlsnaes, Risse-Kappen, and Simmons, 2013). The construction and acquisition of power are at the heart of geopolitics. Countries gain international status by mobilizing coercive power: military, economic, cultural (Nye, 2019). Therefore, the *raison d'État* has an anarchic essence: power deployment and strategic calculation based on self-interest and need. Though neorealists shifted the discussion on *raison d'État* from the pursuit of power to maximizing national security (Waltz, 1979), realism's central ideas remain power and conflict.

This questions national interest at the ethical level. 'The *raison d'État* made the line between diplomatic loyalty and vice more difficult to hold' (Bjola, 2016: 126). Russia, for example, waged war in Ukraine in the name of national survival and security. Regarding the Bucha massacre where Russian troops killed 300 civilians, Russian diplomats denied the allegations and organized a fake fact-check-themed campaign to influence public opinion (Gunter, 2022). This highlights the use of propaganda and mass persuasion techniques inherent in public diplomacy. It encapsulates the deliberate use of lies and half-truths to influence the judgements, values, attitudes, emotions, beliefs, and behaviours of others. It defends Russia's national interests while influencing audiences to approve Kremlin's actions (France 24, 2022).

Public diplomacy's influence is a weapon for peace, and the ammunition is persuasive information (Taylor, 2009). This international communication influence is like 'an instrument for taking power over the other. This weapon does not kill. More exactly, it only kills the contrary opinion to replace it with that of the owner of the weapon' (Revel, 2012: 8). Such thinking derives from ancient military theory; Sun Tzu underlines a 'moral destructuring' strategy (Jullien, 2010: 41) for disseminating information to create insecurity, anxiety, and confusion in the enemy. Diplomatic acts are a defence of national interests, but this threatens the shared norms and rules for maintaining international order.

For liberals (Doyle, 1986; Zacher and Matthew, 1995) and global humanists (Gurtov, 2007; Dodds, 2000), states participate in constructing a better system of international cooperation and globalization. This shift from *raison d'État* to *raison de système* emphasizes the rationality and legitimacy of international norms and conventions (Fernandez, 2018). If liberalism focuses on the value of promoting openness, democracy, and cooperation for the common good, global humanism underlines the interdependence of states and people in the age of internationalization.

Interdependence and *raison de système* change the definition of diplomatic loyalty. When diplomats guard the international community and promote globalization (Bjola, Cassidy, and Manor, 2019), diplomatic ethics reflect a set of norms defending a peaceful and fraternal international order and community. Accordingly, national interests serve civil society and humanity i.e., the public interest.

Discussions on public diplomacy and digitalization focus on the shift to public-centric models to observe how diplomats promote harmony and cooperation through diverse online communication (Cowan and Arsenault, 2008; Zaharna, 2018; Huang, 2022; Huang and Zhang, 2022). Social media allow for 'extensive collaboration and networking' between para-diplomatic stakeholders and participants (Aggestam, Rosamond, and Hedling, 2021: 5). In liberal terms, the ethics of public diplomacy centre on 'the pursuit of peace—a harmony between nations' (Burchill, 2014: 125).

In other words, political entities implement digital diplomacy rather than coercive power in the international public sphere. This encourages institutions, non-state organizations, and citizens to speak publicly about their state's beneficial policies, culture, and attractiveness. Exemplifying greater authenticity, such advocacy is based on the personal experiences of everyday people and organizations. This legitimizes government achievements and policies, advancing reciprocal dialogue and understanding.

To this end, public communications reflect the national interests served by digital diplomacy (L'Etang, 2009). If digital diplomacy aims to promote institutionalized democracy and quell dispute, it has public communication attributes that defend the general interests of civil society for the public good (Fitzpatrick, 2017). This includes the 'exchange and sharing of public utility information' (Zémor, 2008: 5), as well as listening and adopting different opinions (Bessières and Huang, 2021). It contributes to the construction and maintenance of social relations while promoting social progress (Bessières, 2009). The conceptual category of national interest, expanded by public interest and universal social values, includes the needs of specific civil societies (Mitzen, 2005).

Zaharna (2022) embedded global humanism in her discussion of humanity-centred diplomacy. For her, the humanity-centred approach 'reflects and responds to the needs of human societies, centring our capacity to collaborate for collective decision-making and problem-solving' (Zaharna, 2022: 31). In the context of Covid-19, foreign policy and diplomatic actions should not only consider the drive of national interests, but also pay attention to global interests. This expands the ethical boundaries of public diplomacy in the digital era, which now aims to defend universal values and humanity's well-being. Digital public diplomacy provides 'problem-solving and relationship-coordinating communication logics' (Zaharna and Huang, 2022: 12), emphasizing horizontal social interaction and cooperation, abandoning political benefits, and overcoming ideological barriers.

For diplomats, national interests from a liberal and global humanism point of view establish an ethical image of public diplomacy 2.0, but in practice, foreign policy executors are on 'a collision course with the other sources of diplomatic loyalty' (Bjola, 2016: 127). Choosing between upholding universal values, defending international norms and international cooperation, and maintaining the political interests of governments might seem like a confusing, if not impossible, task.

Challenge 3. Building Trust versus Fermenting Chaos

The generalization of social media creates a new 'hybrid media system' (Gilardi et al., 2022: 39) which weakens traditional gatekeeping power and authority while involving new actors in a global agenda-building. Digital diplomacy actors are deliberately and proactively reshaping the global balance of power, weaponizing social media, and engaging in frame competition (Golan, Manor, and Arceneaux, 2019).

In this reshaping, reality and truth become scarce resources, since 'the fundamental form of power is the power to define, allocate, and display this resource' (Carey, 2009: 66). This is significant for analysing the ethical challenges of shifting to digital diplomacy. In an ever-increasing divergence to define the reality of international politics, the digitalization of diplomacy has seen the adoption of sharp power tactics ranging from disinformation to computational propaganda, information operations, and, at its simplest, fake news.

On Speaker Nancy Pelosi's visit to Taiwan, Chinese diplomats used 300 Twitter accounts to weave a narrative network of nationalism and violence. Chinese diplomats cast Pelosi as a 'selfish, opportunistic, hypocritical ugly politician', equating her acts to the US' undermining of China's claimed territorial sovereignty (Xinhua, 2022: para. 1). Such narratives, while ignoring the genesis and complete picture of this sophisticated geopolitical event, allow Beijing to participate in 'international public opinion struggles' (Xi, 2021: para. 7) and gain the dominance over the narratives (Tan, 2016) on the China–Taiwan issues in the uncertain time.

Accordingly, digital diplomacy practitioners also face ethical issues in communication strategy formulation. This is because the construction and competition for influence implies the decisive role of information in legitimacy- and authority-building. Information is 'capable of giving [actors the opportunity] to maintain a decisive competitive advantage' (D'Almeida, 2012: 39). Its content is not simply a linguistic device or a semiotic mechanism. Language elements installed in discourse comprise 'a strategic vision of communication, in which we strive to control, by their preconstruction, the 'good' reception of the discourses by the target audiences' (Krieg-Planque and Oger, no date: para.1). In other words, discourse is at the centre of the social construction of reality. Individual attitudes, behaviours, and perceptions depend on the interactions and discourses in which they engage.

Trust-building, moreover, is the ethical basis for constructing legitimacy and deploying authority in the digital environment (Elliott and Spence, 2017). Though there is no consensus on the term 'trust', it is often described as a reciprocal power game in human communication. Trust is 'the willingness of a party to be vulnerable to the actions of another party based on the expectation that the other will perform a particular action important to the trustor, irrespective of the ability to monitor or control that other party' (Mayer, Davis, and Schoorman, 1995: 712).

Granting trust, however, is not eternal. Much less so in the digital age. Long-term trust-building in digital diplomacy is inherently risky due to the cognitive uncertainty generated by asymmetric information exchange. The advancement of digitalization makes trust-building increasingly difficult as people have difficulty confirming the truth amid a flood of equivocal and complex information (Rathbun, 2007).

By complicating the production and dissemination of information, and given the dual attributes of information producers and receivers, digitalization has fragmented the definition, allocation, and display of reality (Lee, 2020). The rise of cyberbalkanization, social media platformization and deplatformization, and post-truth politics make truth increasingly difficult to grasp, and create for digital diplomacy practitioners public opinion environments filled with competition and volatility. This change lies in the progressively deepening political parallelism brought on by digitalization (van der Pas, van der Brug, and Vliegenthart, 2017), weakening the ability of ethical communicators to establish authority.

In the aftermath of Nazi propaganda following World War II, democracies established a system of checks and balances (Waisbord 2018b). Various institutions, public communicators and expert systems, and professional media acting as gatekeepers gained public trust and helped society confirm truth in public and global affairs. The post-truth era, however, has produced much information deviating from reality. In some cases, even machines manufacture information using algorithms (Bjola, Cassidy, and Manor, 2019), the result is the proliferation of unethical and misleading emotional content causing confusion and devaluing the legitimacy, authority, and reputation of qualified communicators (Waisbord, 2018b, 2018a).

CONCLUSION

By combing literature from political science and communication, we outline various ethical challenges in the practice of digital diplomacy. Though the professionalization of diplomacy principally involves political meanings and actors, it should not exist in an ethical vacuum. This is tantamount as digital diplomacy expands the boundaries of traditional diplomacy, extending to civil society, and touching public interests and the public good. Practitioners need to disentangle diplomatic and communication ethics to better shape the image and reputation of their governments.

Moscow continues to use bots and false information to justify its invasion of Ukraine, while Beijing's wolf warrior diplomats frequently publish hurtful, demeaning, and insulting stories to intimidate Taiwan with allusions to war. Especially since 2022, the generative artificial intelligence (AI) represented by ChatCPT has also allowed its users to leverage its massive data resources and personalized algorithms to fabric narratives mixing the spurious with the genuine. The need for peer oversight to subdue the anarchic character of current digital diplomacy practices is paramount. Future research on digital diplomacy should reflect on the ethical significance of public diplomacy and address the following questions.

First, how do foreign policy executors balance the tension between personal morality, professional ethics, and international norms in practicing digital diplomacy? Second, do cultural differences influence the ethics of digital diplomacy? Third, what is the best way to coordinate the relationship between freedom and order in digital diplomacy? And fourth, in spaces where globalization and digitalization continue to deepen, how will the ethics of responsibility of nations affect others?

SUGGESTED READING

Sebastião, Sónia Pedro. 2021. 'Becoming an Ethical Ambassador: Proposal for a Public Relations and Public Diplomacy Practitioner Course on Ethics'. In *Diplomacy, Organisations and Citizens*, edited by Sónia Pedro Sebastião and Susana de Carvalho Spínola, 275–289. Springer, Cham.

Fitzpatrick, Kathy. 2013. 'Public Diplomacy and Ethics: From Soft Power to Social Conscience'. In *Relational, Networked and Collaborative Approaches to Public Diplomacy*, edited by R. S. Zaharna, Amelia Arsenault, and Ali Fisher, 43–57. New York: Routledge.

Fitzpatrick, Kathy. 2017. 'Public Diplomacy in the Public Interest'. *Journal of Public Interest Communications* 1(1), pp. 1–16. doi: 10.32473/jpic.v1.i1.p78.

Rashica, Viona. 2019. 'Digital diplomacy: Aspects, approaches and practical use'. *European Perspectives – International Scientific Journal on European Perspectives* 10(1), pp. 21–39.

Zhang, Juyan and Brecken Chinn Swartz. 2009. 'Public diplomacy to promote Global Public Goods (GPG): Conceptual expansion, ethical grounds, and rhetoric'. *Public Relations Review* 35(4), pp. 382–387. doi: 10.1016/j.pubrev.2009.08.001.

REFERENCES

Aggestam, K., Rosamond, A.B., and Hedling, E. (2021) 'Feminist digital diplomacy and foreign policy change in Sweden', *Place Branding and Public Diplomacy* 18(4), pp. 314–324. doi: 10.1057/s41254-021-00225-3.

Alexander, L. and Moore, M. (2021) 'Deontological Ethics', in E.N. Zalta (ed.) *The Stanford Encyclopedia of Philosophy*. Winter 2021. Metaphysics Research Lab, Stanford University. https://plato.stanford.edu/archives/win2021/entries/ethics-deontological/.

Arceneaux, P. and Harman, M. (2021) 'Social cybersecurity: A policy framework for addressing computational propaganda', *Journal of Information Warfare*, 20(3), pp. 24–43.

Berridge, G. and James, A. (2001) *A Dictionary of Diplomacy*. New York: Palgrave.

Bessières, D. (2009) 'La définition de la communication publique: des enjeux disciplinaires aux changements de paradigmes organisationnels', *Communication et organisation*, 35, pp. 14–28. doi: 10.4000/communicationorganisation.686.

Bessières, D. and Huang, Z.A. (2021) 'La communication publique et d'intérêt général', in C. Guillot and S. Benmoyal (eds) *Les fondamentaux de la communication: Pratiques et métiers en évolution*. Louvain-la-Neuve: De Boeck, pp. 201–220.

Bjola, C. (2014) 'The ethics of secret diplomacy: A contextual approach', *Journal of Global Ethics*, 10(1), pp. 85–100. doi: 10.1080/17449626.2013.858761.

Bjola, C. (2016) 'Diplomatic Ethics', in C.M. Constantinou (ed.) *The SAGE Handbook of Diplomacy*. Los Angeles: SAGE, pp. 123–132.

Bjola, C., Cassidy, J., and Manor, I. (2019) 'Public diplomacy in the digital age', *The Hague Journal of Diplomacy*, 14(1–2), pp. 83–101. doi: 10.1163/1871191X-14011032.

Brown, C. (2011) 'The only thinkable figure? Ethical and normative approaches to refugees in international relations', in A. Betts and G. Loescher (eds.) *Refugees in International relations*. Oxford: Oxford University Press, pp. 151–168.

Brown, C. (2019) *Understanding International Relations*. Macmillan International Higher Education.

Burchill, S. (2014) *National Interest in International Relations Theory*. New York: Palgrave Macmillan.

Capizzi, J.E. (2015) *Politics, Justice, and War: Christian Governance and the Ethics of Warfare*. Oxford: OUP Oxford.

Carey, J.W. (2009) *Communication as Culture: Essays on Media and Society*. New York: Routledge.

Carlsnaes, W., Risse-Kappen, T., and Simmons, B.A. (eds) (2013) *Handbook of International Relations*. 2nd edition. Los Angeles: SAGE.

Catellani, A., Zerfass, A., and Tench, R. (2015) *Communication Ethics in a Connected World*. Peter Lang. doi: 10.3726/978-3-0352-6555-2.

Constantinou, C.M., Cornago, N., and McConnell, F. (2016) 'Transprofessional diplomacy', *Brill Research Perspectives in Diplomacy and Foreign Policy*, 1(4), pp. 1–66. doi: 10.1163/24056006-12340005.

Constantinou, C.M. and Sharp, P. (2016) 'Theoretical Perspectives in Diplomacy', in C.M. Constantinou (ed.) *The SAGE Handbook of Diplomacy*. Los Angeles: SAGE, pp. 13–27.

Couldry, N. (2008) 'Media Ethics: Towards a Framework for Media Producers and Media Consumers', in S.J.A. Ward and H. Wasserman (eds) *Media Ethics Beyond Borders: A Global Perspective*. Heinemann, pp. 59–72.

Cowan, G. and Arsenault, A. (2008) 'Moving from monologue to dialogue to collaboration: The three layers of public diplomacy', *The ANNALS of the American Academy of Political and Social Science*, 616(1), pp. 10–30. doi: 10.1177/0002716207311863.

Cull, N.J. (ed.) (2009) *Public Diplomacy: Lessons from the Past*. Los Angeles: Figueroa Press.

Cull, N.J. (2019) *Public Diplomacy: Foundations for Global Engagement in the Digital Age*. Cambridge: Polity Press.

Dacheux, E. (2000) *Vaincre l'indifférence. Les Associations dans l'espace public européen*. Paris: CNRS Editions.

D'Almeida, N. (2012) *Les promesses de la communication*. Paris: Presses Universitaires de France.

Desmoulins, L. (2017) 'Pédagogie et dilemmes de l'enseignement de l'éthique du lobbying', *Revue Communication & professionnalisation*, 5, pp. 122–144. doi: 10.14428/rcompro.vi5.913.

Dijk, J. van (2012) *The Network Society*. 3rd edition. London: Sage Publications.

Dodds, K. (2000) *Geopolitics in a Changing World*. New York: Pearson Education.

Doyle, M.W. (1986) 'Liberalism and World Politics', *American Political Science Review*, 80(04), pp. 1151–1169. doi: 10.2307/1960861.

Elliott, D. and Spence, E. (2017) *Ethics for a Digital Era*. Hoboken: Wiley-Blackwell.

Ellis, D.C. (2009) 'On the possibility of "international community"', *International Studies Review*, 11(1), pp. 1–26. https://www.jstor.org/stable/25482041.

Fan, Q. (2021) 'On the role of nonverbal communication in Li Ziqi's videos in intercultural communication', in *Proceedings of the 6th Annual International Conference on Social Science and Contemporary Humanity Development (SSCHD 2020)*. Xi'an: Atlantis Press. doi: 10.2991/assehr.k.210121.031.

Fernandez, J. (2018) *Relations internationales*. Paris: Dalloz.

Fitzpatrick, K. (2017) 'Public diplomacy in the public interest', *The Journal of Public Interest Communications*, 1(1), p. 78. doi: 10.32473/jpic.v1.i1.p78.

Fitzpatrick, K.R. (2007) 'Advancing the new public diplomacy: A public relations perspective', *The Hague Journal of Diplomacy*, 2(3), pp. 187–211. doi: 10.1163/187119007X240497.

Fletcher, G.P. (1995) *Loyalty: An Essay on the Morality of Relationships*. New York: Oxford University Press.

France 24 (2022) 'Truth or fake – pro-Russian accounts share images falsely suggesting Bucha massacre was staged', *France 24*, 6 April. https://www.france24.com/en/tv-shows/truth-or-fake/20220406-pro-russian-accounts-share-images-suggesting-bucha-massacre-was-staged.

Fuchs, C. (2014) *Social Media: A Critical Introduction*. Los Angeles: SAGE.

Gilardi, F. et al. (2022) 'Social media and political agenda setting', *Political Communication*, 39(1), pp. 39–60. doi: 10.1080/10584609.2021.1910390.

Golan, G.J., Manor, I., and Arceneaux, P. (2019) 'Mediated public diplomacy redefined: Foreign stakeholder engagement via paid, earned, shared, and owned media', *American Behavioral Scientist*, 63(12), pp. 1665–1683. doi: 10.1177/0002764219835279.

Government Offices of Sweden (2019) 'The Swedish Foreign Service action plan for feminist foreign policy 2019–2022, including direction and measures for 2020'. https://www.governm ent.se/499195/contentassets/2b694599415943ebb466af0f838da1fc/the-swedish-foreign-serv ice-action-plan-for-feminist-foreign-policy-20192022-including-direction-and-measures-for-2020.pdf.

Gregory, B. (2008) 'Public diplomacy: Sunrise of an academic field', *The ANNALS of the American Academy of Political and Social Science*, 616(1), pp. 274–290.

Grunig, J.E. (2001) 'Two-Way Symmetrical Public Relations: Past, Present, and Future', in R. L. Health (ed.) *Handbook of Public Relations*. Thousand Oaks: SAGE Publications, pp. 11–30. doi: 10.4135/9781452220727.n1.

Gunter, J. (2022) 'Bucha killings: "I wish they had killed me too"', *BBC News*, 5 April. https://www.bbc.com/news/world-europe-61003878.

Gurtov, M. (2007) *Global Politics in the Human Interest*. Boulder: Lynne Rienner Publishers.

Habermas, J. (1987) *Théorie de l'agir communicationnel*. Paris: Fayard.

Hoffmann, S. (1981) *Duties Beyond Borders: On the Limits and Possibilities of Ethical International Politics*. Syracuse: Syracuse University Press.

Horowitz, I.L. (1966) 'The Hegelian concept of political freedom', *The Journal of Politics*, 28(1), pp. 3–28. doi: 10.2307/2127632.

Huang, Z.A. (2022) 'A historical–discursive analytical method for studying the formulation of public diplomacy institutions', *Place Branding and Public Diplomacy*, 18(3), pp. 204–215. doi: 10.1057/s41254-021-00246-y.

Huang, Z.A. (2021) 'The Confucius Institute and Relationship Management: Uncertainty Management of Chinese Public Diplomacy in Africa', in P. Surowiec and I. Manor (eds) *Public Diplomacy and the Politics of Uncertainty*. Cham: Palgrave Macmillan, pp. 197–223. doi: 10.1007/978-3-030-54552-9_8.

Huang, Z.A. and Hardy, M. (2021) 'Vers une diplomatie publique française des musées en Chine?: La sinisation des stratégies communicationnelles du Louvre à l'ère numérique', *Les Enjeux de l'Information et de la Communication*, 21(3A), pp. 71–87. doi: 10.3917/enic. hs10.0071.

Huang, Z.A. and Wang, R. (2020) '"Panda engagement" in China's digital public diplomacy', *Asian Journal of Communication*, 30(2), pp. 118–140. doi: 10.1080/01292986.2020.1725075.

Huang, Z.A. and Wang, R. (2021) 'Exploring China's digitalization of public diplomacy on Weibo and Twitter: A case study of the U.S.-China trade war', *International Journal of Communication*, 15(2021), pp. 1912–1939. https://ijoc.org/index.php/ijoc/article/view/15105.

Huang, Z.A. and Zhang, R. (2022) 'Understanding China's "Intermestic" Online Vaccination-themed Narrative Strategy', in F. Rossette-Crake and E. Buckwalter (eds) *COVID-19, Communication and Culture: Beyond the Global Workplace*. New York: Routledge, pp. 52–75. doi: 10.4324/9781003276517-6.

Ingenhoff, D. et al. (eds) (2019) *Bridging Disciplinary Perspectives of Country Image, Reputation, Brand, and Identity*. New York: Routledge.

Intentilia, A.A.M., Haes, P.E., and Suardana, G. (2022) 'Utilizing Digital Platforms for Diplomacy in ASEAN: A Preliminary Overview', *Journal of Communication Studies and Society*, 1(1), pp. 1–7. doi: 10.38043/commusty.v1i1.3685.

Jullien, F. (2010) *Le détour et l'accès: Stratégies du sens en Chine, en Grèce*. Paris: Points.

Kraut, R. (2018) 'Aristotle's Ethics', in E.N. Zalta (ed.) *The Stanford Encyclopedia of Philosophy*. Summer 2018. Metaphysics Research Lab, Stanford University. https://plato.stanford.edu/archives/sum2018/entries/aristotle-ethics/.

Krieg-Planque, A. and Oger, C. (no date) *Eléments de langage, Publictionnaire*. Nancy, France: Université de Lorraine. http://publictionnaire.huma-num.fr/notice/elements-de-langage/.

Lee, F.L.F. (2020) 'Social movements, media, and information politics in the post-truth era: The experience of Hong Kong's anti-extradition bill movement', *Chinese Journal of Communication Research*, 37, pp. 3–41. doi: 10.3966/172635812020060037001.

L'Etang, J. (2009) 'Public relations and diplomacy in a globalized world: An issue of public communication', *American Behavioral Scientist*, 53(4), pp. 607–626. doi: 10.1177/0002764209347633.

Manor, I. (2019) *The Digitalization of Public Diplomacy*. Cham: Palgrave Macmillan.

Manor, I. and Huang, Z. A. (2022) 'Digitalization of public diplomacy: Concepts, trends, and challenges', *Communication and the Public*, 7(4), pp. 167–175. doi: 10.1177/20570473221138401.

Marsh, C. (2003) 'Antecedents of two-way symmetry in classical Greek rhetoric: The rhetoric of Isocrates', *Public Relations Review*, 29(3), pp. 351–367. doi: 10.1016/S0363-8111(03)00039-0.

Marsh Jr., C.W. (2001) 'Public relations ethics: Contrasting models from the rhetorics of Plato, Aristotle, and Isocrates', *Journal of Mass Media Ethics*, 16(2–3), pp. 78–98. doi: 10.1080/08900523.2001.9679606.

Mayer, R.C., Davis, J.H., and Schoorman, F.D. (1995) 'An integrative model of organizational trust', *Academy of Management Review*, 20(3), pp. 709–734. doi: 10.5465/amr.1995.9508080335.

Mitzen, J. (2005) 'Reading Habermas in anarchy: Multilateral diplomacy and global public spheres', *American Political Science Review*, 99(03), pp. 401–417. doi: 10.1017/S0003055405051749.

Mouffe, C. (2016) *L'illusion du consensus*. Paris: Albin Michel.

Mowlana, H. (1997) *Global Information and World Communication: New Frontiers in International Relations*. Los Angeles: SAGE.

Nye, J.S. (2019) 'Soft power and public diplomacy revisited', *The Hague Journal of Diplomacy*, 14(1–2), pp. 7–20.

Ollivier-Yaniv, C. (2015) '8. Des conditions de production du discours politique: les "écrivants" des prises de parole publiques ministérielles', in S. Bonnafous et al. (eds) *Argumentation et discours politique: Antiquité grecque et latine, Révolution française, monde contemporain*. Rennes: Presses universitaires de Rennes, pp. 89–98.

van der Pas, D.J., van der Brug, W., and Vliegenthart, R. (2017) 'Political parallelism in media and political agenda-setting', *Political Communication*, 34(4), pp. 491–510. doi: 10.1080/10584609.2016.1271374.

Petiteville, F. and Placidi-Frot, D. (2013) 'Introduction', in F. Petiteville and D. Placidi-Frot (eds) *Négociations internationales*. Paris: Presses de Sciences Po, pp. 19–24.

Pirotte, G. (2018) *La notion de société civile*. Paris: La Découverte.

Pisarska, K. (2016) *The Domestic Dimension of Public Diplomacy*. London: Palgrave Macmillan UK.

Plato and Lamb, W.R.M. (2007) *Plato. 3: Lysis. Symposium. Gorgias*. [Repr. der Ausg.] 1925. Cambridge: Harvard Univ. Press.

Porter, L. (2010) 'Communicating for the good of the state: A post-symmetrical polemic on persuasion in ethical public relations', *Public Relations Review*, 36(2), pp. 127–133. doi: 10.1016/j.pubrev.2009.08.014.

Rathbun, B.C. (2007) 'Uncertain about uncertainty: Understanding the multiple meanings of a crucial concept in international relations theory', *International Studies Quarterly*, 51(3), pp. 533–557. doi: 10.1111/j.1468-2478.2007.00463.x.

Revel, C. (2012) *La France: un pays sous influences?* Paris: Vuibert.

Rosenthal, J.H. and Barry, C. (2009) *Ethics & International Affairs: A Reader*. Washington, D.C.: Georgetown University Press.

Ségas, S. (2012) 'La diplomatie en images. Discours politique et mythe technocratique dans la bande dessinée Quai d'Orsay (tome I)', *Mots. Les langages du politique*, 99, pp. 61–78. doi: 10.4000/mots.20692.

Simonnot, B. (2018) 'Conduire des recherches en régime numérique: vers un cadre conceptuel de réflexion éthique', in L. Balicco et al. (eds) *L'éthique en contexte de communication numérique: déontologie, régulation, algorithme, espace public*. Louvain-la-Neuve: De Boeck Supérieur, pp. 13–23.

Surowiec, P. and Manor, I. (2021) *Public Diplomacy and the Politics of Uncertainty*. Cham: Palgrave Macmillan.

Surowiec, P. and Miles, C. (2021) 'The populist style and public diplomacy: Kayfabe as performative agonism in Trump's Twitter posts', *Public Relations Inquiry*, 10(1), pp. 5–30. doi: 10.1177/2046147X20979294.

Tan, Y. (2016) *Construction Strategy for Chinese Public Diplomacy from the Perspective of International Discourse Power*. Beijing: China Social Sciences Press.

Taylor, M. and Kent, M.L. (2014) 'Dialogic engagement: Clarifying foundational concepts', *Journal of Public Relations Research*, 26(5), pp. 384–398. doi: 10.1080/1062726X.2014.956106.

Taylor, P.M. (2009) 'Public Diplomacy and Strategic Communication', in N. Snow and P.M. Taylor (eds) *Routledge Handbook of Public Diplomacy*. New York: Routledge, pp. 12–16.

Waisbord, S. (2018a) 'The elective affinity between post-truth communication and populist politics', *Communication Research and Practice*, 4(1), pp. 17–34. doi: 10.1080/22041451.2018.1428928.

Waisbord, S. (2018b) 'Truth is what happens to news: On journalism, fake news, and post-truth', *Journalism Studies*, 19(13), pp. 1866–1878. doi: 10.1080/1461670X.2018.1492881.

Waltz, K.N. (1979) *Theory of International Politics*. Menlo Park: Waveland Press.

Weaver, R.M. (1985) *The Ethics of Rhetoric*. Davis: Hermagoras Press.

Weil-Dubuc, P.-L. (2019) 'Introduction. Les pratiques de l'éthique: un flou nécessaire?', *Revue française d'éthique appliquée*, 7(1), pp. 22–27. doi: 10.3917/rfeap.007.0022.

Xi, J. (2021) 'Xi Jinping zai zhonggong zhongyang zhengzhiju di sanshici jiti xuexi shi qiangdiao, jiaqiang he gaijin guoji chuanbo gongzuo, zhanshi zhenshi liti quanmian de zhongguo' ['During the 30th collective study session of the Political Bureau of the CPC Central Committee, Xi Jinping emphasized strengthening and improving international communication work, showing a real, three-dimensional and comprehensive China'], Xinhua. 1 June. http://www.xinhuanet.com/politics/leaders/2021-06/01/c_1127517461.htm.

Xinhua (2022) 'Let's look at Pelosi's selfishness and sinister intentions', Xinhua. 5 August. http://www.news.cn/2022-08/05/c_1128893791.htm.

Zacher, M.W. and Matthew, R.A. (1995) 'Liberal International Theory: Common Threads, Divergent Strands', in C.W. Kegley (ed.) *Controversies in International Relations Theory: Realism and the Neo-Liberal Challenge.* Basingstoke: Macmillan, pp. 107–150.

Zaharna, R.S. (2018) 'Global Engagement: Culture and Communication Insights from Public Diplomacy', in K.A. Johnston and M. Taylor (eds) *The Handbook of Communication Engagement.* Medford: Wiley-Blackwell, pp. 313–330.

Zaharna, R.S. (2022) *Boundary Spanners of Humanity: Three Logics of Communications and Public Diplomacy for Global Collaboration.* New York: Oxford University Press.

Zaharna, R.S. and Huang, Z.A. (2022) 'Revisiting public diplomacy in a postpandemic world: The need for a humanity-centered communication logic', *Communication and the Public,* 7(1), pp. 7–14. doi: 10.1177/20570473221078619.

Zémor, P. (2008) *La communication publique.* Paris: Presses Universitaires de France.

CHAPTER 14

TRANSFORMING INTERNATIONAL DEVELOPMENT: NAVIGATING THE SHIFT TOWARDS DIGITAL COOPERATION

LUCIANA ALEXANDRA GHICA

ONCE marginal subjects for both the practice and the study of international affairs, digital technologies and international development for cooperation are nowadays at the core of the latest global strategic framework for managing present and future challenges, and for ensuring social and economic progress worldwide (UN Secretary General, 2021). Emerging from a multistakeholder dialogue under the leadership of the United Nations, this new agenda builds on almost eight decades of conceptual, institutional, and normative advancements on international cooperation. However, its story is not one of linear accumulations but rather of constant changes, under conditions of uncertainty, and full of elements that, although having appeared in different periods and specific contexts, are present simultaneously in a continuous transformation and negotiation of relevance. In other words, like other modern processes, this is also 'liquid' (Bauman, 2000): as new technologies emerge and new social practices develop, it liquefies some of the previously solidified orthodoxies and adds more substance to others, triggering on the way constant redefinitions of power relations and new modes of governance.

Against this background, this chapter first provides an overview of the milestones in the evolution of the global agenda on development cooperation that are relevant to understand the current situation. Then, it shows how digital technologies gradually became a priority for it, especially in institutional terms. Finally, the chapter identifies a series of challenges and trends for diplomatic work in relation to digital cooperation for sustainable development. The chapter presents the argument that, given the complexity, interconnectedness, and shifting nature of issues and actors relevant for the topic, digital diplomacy can be framed for both analytical and practical purposes also as a 'liquid' landscape with quantum features: (1) observing it modifies it (Schultz, 1998) and (2) it is continuously '[shifting] from a negotiation between states to negotiation among cities, municipalities, streets, and other byways of authority and representation […] rapidly and repeatedly [oscillating] from the national and the local, the public and the private' (Der Derian, 2011: 375). Under such circumstance, beyond being a method of change management (Bjola and Holmes, 2015), digital diplomacy can be understood as a means through which international interaction is conducted making use of digital technologies. In this sense, it is a constitutive part and an instrument of governance dynamics, serving 'both traditional and new foreign policy goals of states and non-state actors' (Gilboa, 2016: 541).

THE INVENTION OF DEVELOPMENT

Initially, the developmental success of a country was equated with its economic output—the richer, the better. It was also assumed that social progress would follow automatically once the country reached a certain level of wealth and industrialization (Rostow, 1960). Since within this model some countries were already better-off than others, i.e. more developed, the world started to be represented as divided between the 'developed' and the 'underdeveloped' (later 'developing') states, with the first serving as a model for the latter (Escobar, 1995). Consequently, international cooperation in this field was also gradually framed mostly around the transfer of usually technical and financial resources (i.e. Official Development Aid—ODA) from a developed country to a developing country to support the economic development and welfare of the latter. Established in 1961 by the governments of the most industrialized states, the Organisation for Economic Co-operation and Development (OECD) soon took a leading role in the process of setting global standards and technical definitions for ODA and for compiling a list of countries eligible to receive ODA, based mostly on the degree of economic vulnerability (Hynes and Scott, 2013).

Such definitions and standards were far from being mere technicalities. Particularly within the context of the decolonization process, international cooperation for development served both as a battleground for political influence and as experimentation laboratory for creating viable states, based on often opposing views on how economy and politics can be connected for the public interest (Harris, 2014). Representing mostly newly independent / postcolonial states from Africa, Asia, and Latin America, these started to be collectively known as the 'Third World' but, since they were characterized by complex developmental and governance problems, the term became increasingly pejorative (Tomlison, 2003) and was eventually replaced with others, most frequently the 'Global South', currently still a contested label (Haug et al., 2021). In parallel, the label 'Global North' started to be used to designate countries mostly in the Northern Hemisphere that ranked high on the (economic) development measurements of the time, while the focus of the debates shifted towards explaining the developmental gap between the 'Global North' and the 'Global South'. However, since such rankings were created based on definitions generated from the economic and political development models of the countries from the 'Global North', the relevance of these classifications was increasingly questioned not only for ideological reasons but also for methodological ones. Partly from these processes, other forms of international cooperation for development also emerged, some still in existence, the most notable being 'South-South cooperation' (i.e. among states from the 'Global South') and 'triangular cooperation' (i.e. in which a pivotal partner and a facilitating partner provide expertise and financial resources for the benefit of a developing country).

The Emergence of the Sustainable Development Framing

After the Cold War, addressing many of these challenges and critiques, the mainstream perspectives on development and the international practices associated to them have gradually changed. Most significantly, some of the previous economic orthodoxies have been abandoned, following substantive evidence that the wealth of a country expressed exclusively in economic development terms does not necessarily reflect or positively correlate with social progress (Piketty, 2014) and that traditional economic growth models are inadequate (Yusuf, 2014). Consequently, policy recommendations started to focus also on social measures (Serra and Stiglitz, 2008; Banerjee and Duflo, 2011), while the connections between political institutions and economic performance have started to be re-examined (Acemoglu and Robinson, 2012). International measurements of development started to include more indicators reflecting social dimensions, and, with the advancement of technology, especially ICTs, measures of digital literacy, and access to the benefits created through new technologies have been also increasingly considered (UNDP, 2022). Furthermore, the recommendations that international institutions such as the World Bank and the International Monetary Fund (IMF) have traditionally provided since the mid-twentieth century to states confronted with developmental challenges became more sensitive to the social impact of economic measures (Stiglitz, 2002; Fine et al., 2003; World Bank, 2005; Serra and Stiglitz, 2008), as well as to the local conditions (Rodrik, 2008) and the impact that (access to) new technologies can have on development (UNDP, 2022).

At the same time, the concept of 'development' itself transformed. Already during the last two decades of the Cold War and largely via multilateral forums, there had been an increased international acknowledgement of the complex nexus between economic and social development, as well as of the relevance of the environmental protection in such processes. It was partly within this context that, under the aegis of the UN, the independently established World Commission on Environment and Development (WCED) adopted the so-called Bruntland report (WCED, 1987). This put forward the concept of 'sustainable development', defined as a type of development that 'meets the needs of the present without compromising the ability of future generations to meet their own need'. Although this was not the first time the concept had been proposed (Caradonna,

2022), the report became the standard reference on sustainability for policy purposes and served as basis for the widely used and more operationalizable representation of sustainable development as being produced at the intersection of economic efficiency, social inclusion, and environmental responsibility.

In the next three decades following the 'Bruntland report' sustainability gradually permeated the vocabulary of international dialogue, generating in the process several major initiatives and strategic documents (e.g. *The Rio Declaration, Agenda 21*), as well as an institutional setting for coordination on these matters within the UN system, including most significantly a UN Commission on Sustainable Development (UN CSD), currently known as a High-Level Political Forum (HLPF) on Sustainable Development. However, it was only in 2015, in the form of the *Agenda 2030* and of the ensuing so-called Sustainable Development Goals (SDGs, 2015–2030), that sustainability truly became the focus of an increasingly integrated global agenda in the field. Addressing some of the previous criticism, the SDGs acknowledge the need to create partnerships rather than donor–recipient relations, and in relation to that, to enhance the ownership of actions and policy design so that developing countries can have more decision power in setting their developmental priorities (UN General Assembly, 2015). At the same time, the SDGs signal that sustainable development is currently understood as deeply connected not only to economic, social, and environmental concerns but also with democratic governance and with the protection of human rights. They also convey the message that unsustainable development generates security threats at individual, local, national, and international levels. From this perspective, topics usually on the security agenda could now be framed as matters of improper development and governance, with some governments going even further and starting to join security and development concerns in their foreign policy strategies. In this respect, probably the best-known case is the US, for which the integrated 3D (Defence, Diplomacy, and Development) approach gradually permeated the larger diplomatic circles and parlance, even if the label was initially used exclusively in connection to post-conflict situations (Constantinou and Opondo, 2016).

Coherence, Effectiveness, and Transparency Mechanisms

The degree of this evolving agenda's complexity made *policy coherence* for development an increasingly relevant topic, both at the national level and in multilateral settings (OECD, 2016), as well as in direct connection with the SDGs (UN, 2018; UN General Assembly, 2018a, 2018b). The matter of coordination is further complicated by the fact that governments are not the only providers of development funds and expertise. States and bilateral development projects remain the main sources of development aid flows, and about a third of reported development funding is disbursed through intergovernmental organizations (OECD, 2022). But other stakeholders such as private companies (Kolk, 2016), civil society actors and initiatives (Fowler, 2011; Jordan, 2011), social movements (Della Porta and Tarrow, 2005), media outlets (Scott, 2014; Schwittay, 2015), religious organizations (Tomalin, 2018), and celebrities (Kapoor, 2013) are increasingly visible and instrumental in the field at a global level.

At the same time, given the interaction of so many stakeholders and initiatives, *effectiveness* increasingly became the focus of concern, with the Busan High Level Forum of Aid Effectiveness (2011) establishing the first multistakeholder dialogue on the topic (OECD, 2011). Simply put, aid effectiveness refers to the success or failure of international development aid. Although the concept seems to refer to development aid outputs, in practice a large part of the discussions around this subject are inevitably related to the input aspects, particularly funding for development. In this respect, the debates have traditionally centred on two issues: how much the better-off states should contribute to the global efforts, and how much should be specifically allocated to the most vulnerable states. As early as 1970, the UN members agreed that high-income countries should allocate 0.70% of their Gross National Product (GNP) for ODA (UN General Assembly, 1970). Later, GNP was replaced with an equivalent concept—the Gross National Income (GNI), still in use—but less than a dozen states ever achieved this goal, not all maintained the pace, and for the moment only five states, all European, meet the minimum ODA allocation target (OECD, 2022).

Existing public data remains highly fragmented and biased towards ODA and entities originating from the 'Global North'. Under such circumstances, it is rather difficult to assess the global amount of development aid flows. Although a multistakeholder International Aid Transparency Initiative (IATI, https://iatistandard.org/) has existed since 2008, OECD is still the main global reference for data on such issues, compiling it from the mandatory reporting of its members, from the voluntary reporting of a handful of non-members, and from about a dozen other countries and around forty major private donors that it chose to monitor. Based on its latest evaluation (OECD, 2022), global aid development flows are at the highest level ever in nominal terms (about US$180 billion), double when compared to 2000, while the largest donors are the European Union (US$70 billion through its members and institutions) and the US (US$48 billion). Of the countries that are not OECD members, the People's Republic of China (with estimates varying between US$3 billion and almost US$8 billion), India (US$1 billion), and the Republic of China (Taiwan, US$330 million) are the top providers of funding for development. The private entities that OECD profiles are mainly foundations created around some of the richest companies in the world, are located mostly in the US and Europe, and their contribution to development funding worldwide ranges from a couple of million US dollars to more than US$4.5 billion. The top three private donors are currently initiatives built around (the founders of) companies from the digital technology sector (Bill & Melinda Gates Foundation: US$4.6 billion) and the banking and financial sector (BBVA: US$925 million; Mastercard: US$870 million) (OECD, 2022).

Especially given the increasing weight of the private sector in the field, a fact which 'liquefies' the current institutional and normative settings of public *accountability*, it is highly likely that debates on further regulation, at least on data reporting, for both funding elements and non-financial sustainability / environmental, social, and governance (ESG) issues will continue to develop in the next decade. Within this context, the collection, maintenance, and accessibility of robust digital data that can be adapted to quickly evolving circumstances become not only a matter of monitoring development but also one of building critical governance infrastructures, essential for generating further sustainable development. From a public interest viewpoint, since companies from the digital technology sector may have an upper hand in providing services for managing such data, it will become necessary to build more international cooperation, coordination, and norm-building with a focus on digital technology as part of the larger framework of sustainable development.

BUILDING A DIGITAL COOPERATION AGENDA IN INTERNATIONAL DEVELOPMENT

Discussions on new technologies in the context of development are as old as the concept of development itself, since technological innovations are considered crucial for economic growth in most economic models (Yusuf, 2014). That is why one would expect that the emergence of highly disruptive technologies such as the digital ones would become immediately the focus of international dialogue on development. However, as debates on development were moving away from an exclusively economic approach at the time when digital innovations started to emerge, the issue became more visible on the global agenda rather in connection to social aspects such as the role of these technologies in widening or narrowing developmental gaps and inequality. Following the 'infodemic' that emerged during the Covid-19 pandemic, as well as the fast, non-linear, and unpredictable evolution of newer digital technologies such as artificial intelligence (AI) that make human control and accountability more difficult or even impossible, the matter gained more prominence and became a key dimension for building the next global agenda on development. This prioritization requires both *operational* and *structural* changes, which transform the existing landscape of international cooperation for development and integrate it further with security and governance puzzles.

The Current Framework

At the UN, the dialogue on issues related to science, technology, and innovations (STI) such as those pertaining to digital technologies has been traditionally coordinated within the Economic and Social Council (ECOSOC), especially through its Commission on Science and Technology for Development (CSTD) serviced by the UN Conference on Trade and Development (UNCTAD). This commission is also the focal coordination point for the system created around the World Summit on the Information Society (WSIS), an initiative of the International Telecommunication

Union (ITU), convened since 2003 under the patronage of the UN Secretary General. Currently meeting every year within a mandate renewed until 2025, WSIS produced a series of major framework documents for multistakeholder coordination in the field (i.e. *Geneva Declaration of Principles, Geneva Plan of Action, Tunis Commitment, Tunis Agenda for Information Society*), as well as the Internet Governance Forum (IGF), a multistakeholder policy dialogue structure created in 2006 (UN General Assembly, 2001; UN General Assembly, 2022).

Following the adoption of *Agenda 2030*, the UN also established the Technology Facilitation Mechanism (TFM, https://sdgs.un.org/tfm), which coordinates with the HLPF and aims to support the implementation of the SDGs as a multistakeholder collaboration on STI between member states, UN structures and initiatives, civil society organizations, the private sector, the scientific community, and other stakeholders (UN General Assembly, 2015: para. 70). The TFM has four components: (1) an Interagency Task Team on STI for the SDGs (IATT); (2) a 10-Member Group of High-level Representatives of Scientific Community, Private Sector and Civil Society (all appointed by the UN Secretary General); (3) an annual multistakeholder forum prepared by the 10-Member Group; and (4) an online database (2030 Connect) of various projects, initiatives, and publications in the field. Coordinated within the UN Secretariat, IATT currently has a membership of more than forty UN agencies and works in collaboration with the 10-Member Group on ten thematic 'streams', one of which is dedicated to 'emerging technologies and the SDGs'.

In addition, under the aegis of the UN General Secretary, UN Global Pulse was created in 2009. For the moment, this is an initiative in the form of a network of offices located in Africa, Europe, North America, and South-East Asia which aims to '[bring] together governments, UN entities and partners from academia and the private sector to test, refine and scale methods for using big data and AI to support the achievement of the Sustainable Development Goals' (www.unglobalpulse.org/labs/). Among its most notable results so far one may count a collaboration with several global companies in the sectors of banking, telecommunications, data analytics, and energy to open their databases for the international scientific community especially for work related to SDG 13 (http://dataforclimateaction.org/), as well as an agreement with Twitter for access to its anonymized data for scientific research (UN Academic Impact, 2016). It also co-chairs the UN Data Privacy Policy Group (UN DPPG), which coordinates the UN institutional framework in matters related to data privacy and protection.

Within the original SDGs framework there are only four indicators directly relevant for digital technologies: 4.4.1, 9.c.1, 17.6.1, 17.8.1. As part of the goals related to 'inclusive and equitable quality education and lifelong learning opportunities for all' (4), 'resilient infrastructure, inclusive and sustainable industrialization and innovation' (9) and 'Global Partnership for Sustainable Development' (17), they address just two issues— the ability to use digital technology (*digital literacy*) and the unequal access to digital technology (*digital divide*). With their respective targets referring mostly to developing states, these indicators measure the type and distribution of ICT skills by age, as well as the type, spread, and accessibility of mobile networks and the Internet.

However, both digital literacy and digital divide concerns are connected indirectly to most of the other goals. In this respect, in its latest assessment on the matter (UN General Assembly, 2022), the UN identifies that there are still 'substantial continued digital and broadband divides', with 90% of the population in developed countries using Internet compared to only 57% in developing states. Moreover, the costs of access to ICTs measured as proportion of household income are still much higher in developing countries than in the developed ones. Rural–urban cleavages and age gaps in digital skills and ICTs use are also significant, and there is a persistent gender digital divide both at a global level and in the more vulnerable environments, as illustrated for instance by data on Internet use—62% of men vs. 57% of women worldwide and 31% of men vs. 19% of women in developing countries (UN General Assembly, 2022). At the same time, the UN acknowledges the relevance of rapid technological changes and the impact of ICTs in all sectors, most notably trade, commerce, agriculture, health services, governance, science, and education, and notes that ICTs can accelerate progress across all the SDGs. For such reasons, the UN urges all stakeholders to engage in development cooperation, including via aid flows, aiming to promote digital transformation and bridge the digital divides (UN General Assembly, 2022).

Preparing for the Future

The UN approach to digital technologies and sustainable development is nonetheless more ambitious than what could be read through the SDGs indicators. In fact, a new global agenda is gradually emerging, with ICTs and digital cooperation as one of twelve priorities at the global level (UN General Assembly, 2020b; UN General Secretary, 2021). Already in 2018, following proposals from ITU, the UN Secretary General established the High-level Panel on Digital Cooperation (HLP DC), a group of twenty independent experts representing governments, the business and technical sectors, civil society, and academia co-chaired by Melinda Gates (Bill & Melinda Gates Foundation) and Jack Ma (founder of e-commerce company Alibaba Group). Based on this panel's report and recommendations (UN Secretary General, 2019) and following further consultations with more than one hundred entities and organizations deemed relevant for the topic by the UN, the Secretary General then issued a *Roadmap for Digital Cooperation* (UN General Assembly, 2020a), which defines eight major goals addressing the current global challenges in the field and proposes a set of priorities and measures (Table 14.1). In 2022, a Secretary General's Envoy on Technology was also appointed for the co-ordination of this *Roadmap*, which will serve as basis for international dialogue and negotiations on the topic in the coming years.

These institutional developments on digital cooperation are also part of the larger process outlined in the Secretary General's report *Our Common Agenda* (UN Secretary General, 2021), a document proposing the plan to put in practice all priorities adopted by UN members at the 75th anniversary of the organization (UN General Assembly, 2020b), following a public and stakeholder consultation to which more than 1.4 million

Table 14.1 UN Roadmap for digital cooperation (2020)

HLP DC Recommendation	*Roadmap for digital cooperation* goals	Identified challenges	Proposed priorities and measures
I. Build an inclusive digital economy and society	**1A.** Achieve universal, affordable connectivity by 2030	• Lack of access to Internet for almost half of the world population • Especially in developing countries: costly installation and maintenance of connectivity due to unfavourable market dynamics • Direct risks to individuals and Governments due to lack of connectivity	• Establishing baselines and targets of Internet connection affordability • Financing platforms • National and local connectivity plans • Policies and regulations promoting connectivity, including via smaller-scale providers • Identify and use emerging technologies for ensuring connectivity
	1B. Promote digital public goods to create a more equitable world	• Decreasing percentage of open-source and public resources on the Internet • Increasing costs of access to online information • Uneven distribution of digital public goods (language, content, and infrastructure to access them)	• Using big data and AI tools to create digital public goods that can be used in real time or for foresight • Open-source digital data packages, including open educational resources, for use especially in future health emergencies • Global effort to create digital public goods as a key measure to achieving the SDGs
	1C. Ensure digital inclusion for all, with special attention to the most vulnerable	• Digital divide (affecting particularly women, migrants, refugees and internally displaced persons, rural populations, indigenous populations, older persons, young people and children, persons with disabilities) • Lack of universal definitions and standards for measuring digital inclusion	• Multistakeholder coalition on innovation and technology for gender equality • Inclusive digital infrastructure as part of the post-pandemic recovery effort • Incorporate various forms of accessibility in user experience design • International standards for defining and measuring digital inclusiveness • Public-private cooperation for collecting anonymized and disaggregated data • Improved coordination and information-sharing based on policies and actions capable of mitigating multiple digital gaps

II. Develop human and institutional capacity	2. Strengthen digital capacity-building	• Digital capacity-building has been largely supply-driven, thus not answering properly the existing needs • Specific local and national needs • Insufficient investment	• Improved coherence and coordination • Concerted effort to scale up solutions • Coordinated mapping and needs assessment exercises • Multistakeholder dialogue • Digital help desks • Involving local young people in UN-coordinated country-level support teams
III. Protect human rights and human agency	3A. Ensure the protection of human rights in the digital era	• Abuse and overuse of new technologies for surveillance, repression, censorship, and online harassment • Potential appearance of protection gaps as technology evolves • Data protection and privacy • Digital identity • Surveillance technology, including facial recognition	• Effective due diligence for ensuring compliance with human rights and principles for all digital items, policies, practices, and terms of service • Using new technologies to advocate, defend, and exercise human rights • Within the UN system and with multistakeholder participation, develop improved guidance on how human rights standards apply in digital contexts • Developing legal and additional mechanisms to sanction and prevent abuse against human rights connected to digital technologies, in both digital environments and the physical world • Changes to the financial model of social media platforms that currently encourages the collection of personal data for commercial purposes • Design digital identity tools that consider personal data protection and privacy • Multistakeholder advocacy for transparent and accountable digital content governance that protects freedom of expression and the most vulnerable
	3B. Promote global cooperation on artificial intelligence	• AI can also pose significant risks to the safety and agency of humans worldwide • Lack of representation and inclusiveness in the global dialogue on the matter • Lack of overall coordination • Limited use of AI in the public sector	• Global ban on lethal autonomous weapons systems • Stimulate and facilitate the participation of developing countries to international forums on AI • Common platform of international dialogue on AI • Develop knowledge and tools allowing AI to facilitate the achievement of the SDGs

(*continued*)

Table 14.1 Continued

HLP DC Recommendation	*Roadmap for digital cooperation* goals	Identified challenges	Proposed priorities and measures
IV. Promote digital trust, security, and stability	**4.** Promote digital trust and security	• Increasing numbers and severity of global data breaches • Increase of severe cyberattacks, including those targeting public services and critical infrastructure • Digital disinformation campaigns targeting the foundations of democratic institutions • Lack of organization and technical capacity to respond to cyberattacks for about half of all countries • Limited understanding and development of the potential normative framework on the responsible use of ICTs	• Improve the coordination and geographical coverage of multistakeholder and issue-specific initiatives on trust and security in the cyberspace • Prioritize issues of trust and security for SDGs in digital contexts • Adopt a universal statement on core values and a shared vision on digital cooperation, emphasizing the need to safeguard critical infrastructure
V. Foster global digital cooperation	**5.** Build a more effective architecture for digital cooperation	• Increased complexity and diffusion of the digital cooperation architecture • Lack of inclusiveness in the global dialogue on the matter, partly due to the lack of a unique entry point • Three different potential models for addressing global digital cooperation gaps: (1) Internet Government Forum Plus; (2) distributed co-governance; (3) digital commons	• Ongoing dialogue and negotiation on selecting and refining the most appropriate model, although model (1) appears to gain momentum • Multistakeholder taskforce to pilot model (2) at national and regional levels

Source: Compiled by the author from UN General Secretariat (2019) ©2019 United Nations, and UN General Assembly (2020a), ©2020 United Nations. Reprinted with the permission of the United Nations.

people contributed individually or on behalf of their organizations (UN Secretary General, 2022: 10). Reflecting development, security, and governance concerns, these priorities are grouped into twelve major areas of interest ('commitments'): social and economic inequalities, environmental protection, peace and international security, international law and justice, gender equality and empowerment, trust-building, digital cooperation, UN reform, sustainable financing, international and multistakeholder partnerships, youth, and strategic foresight.

Within the distinct commitment on digital cooperation, the new agenda proposes the adoption of a *Global Digital Compact (CDG)*—an international agreement on the 'shared principles for an open, free and secure digital future for all' (UN Secretary General, 2021: 63). In this respect, it identifies a set of seven goals/areas of concern: Internet connectivity for all, including schools; 'avoid internet fragmentation'; data protection; human rights in digital contexts; 'accountability criteria for discrimination and misleading content'; 'regulation of artificial intelligence'; and 'digital commons as a global public good'. At the same time, it defines digital public goods as including 'open-source software, open data, open AI models, open standards and open content that adhere to international and domestic laws' (UN General Assembly, 2022: para. 45), and it acknowledges that they are essential for accelerating development and for narrowing developmental gaps. In addition, as part of some of the other commitments, it also proposes to define universal access to Internet as a human right, as well as to improve digital inclusivity and the regulation of cyberwarfare. Not least, as part of the commitment on UN reform, it introduces a so-called quintet of change for UN 2.0, which is defined as a set of 'cross cutting agendas [including] data, analytics and communications; innovation and digital transformation; strategic foresight; behavioural science; and performance and results orientation' (UN Secretary General, 2021: 76).

So far, within this new agenda the most significant institutional advancement seems to be in the field of Internet connectivity, where the multistakeholder alliance Partner2Connect Digital Coalition (https://www.itu.int/itu-d/sites/partner2connect/) was created in 2021 aiming to address particularly the needs of the least developed countries (LDCs), landlocked developing countries (LLDCs), and small island developing states (SIDS). Under the aegis of UNESCO, dialogue on global standards related to AI ethics has also reached a first agreement in 2021 (UNESCO, 2022).

DIPLOMATIC WORK IN THE CONTEXT OF THE DIGITAL COOPERATION AGENDA

Web 3.0, and especially AI, is predicted to significantly transform how sustainable development is measured and achieved, raising various practical and ethical concerns in the process (Bjola, 2022) and thus further 'liquefying' the field. With digital cooperation becoming a major commitment in the latest UN agenda, one may expect that debates on the nature, role, opportunities, and limits of digital diplomacy will become increasingly visible in other corners of the practice of and studies on international affairs, such as international development. The framing of the proposals within the UN *Roadmap for Digital Cooperation* seems to indicate that 'blended' (Adler-Nissen and Eggeling, 2022) or 'hybrid' (Bjola and Manor, 2022) forms of diplomacy will be the most likely outcome. However, as illustrated below, it is very likely that the hybrid character of diplomatic work in international development does not remain limited only to multilateral settings.

A striking example in this sense is that of Tuvalu. During the 2022 UN Climate Change Conference (COP27), its foreign affairs minister announced that his country will replicate itself in the metaverse, becoming thus 'the world's first digital nation' (Kofe, 2022). In addition to a full digital mapping of its physical territory, the project (*Future Now*) also includes the digital preservation of material and immaterial heritage (Lesa, 2022). While this might look like a straightforward use of Web 3.0 technologies in a diplomatic context, the case is far from being a mere poster for a potentially upcoming Digital Diplomacy 3.0 or an upgrade of the virtual embassy model. At the current pace of global warming, the territories of low-lying atoll states such as Tuvalu and Kiribati are expected to be almost fully submerged by 2100. Adding to the complex set of developmental challenges that characterize SIDS, the rising sea-level has already generated major environmental, social, and economic costs throughout the entire Pacific region (Campbell and Warrick, 2014), as well as some of the first 'climate refugees', a topic currently barely covered in international law (UNHCR, 2020). A plan to amend the country's constitution so that the state's boundaries are legally defined even when its territory will be fully submerged is already in place. However, since there is no international convention to cover this specific situation, Tuvalu's government is currently using some of the existing international norms, while also seeking international legal advice and engaging in advocacy on the matter.

Currently, roughly half of the world population is estimated to be highly vulnerable due to climate change, while no significant improvement seems to have been achieved in mitigating its negative effects (IPCC, 2022). Therefore, it is very likely that other cases as complex as Tuvalu's may emerge soon, accelerating the need for action often under conditions of increased uncertainty. Furthermore, although it may look like an extreme case, Tuvalu's example raises fundamental questions on statehood, sovereignty, national identity, and governance in the larger context of development relevant for most states, while bringing forward both tested and untested means to answer them. The digital replica of elements existing in the physical reality that it proposes is a means to preserve that reality for both its citizens and the rest of the international community, with the country's diplomatic expertise continuing to remain essential not only for ensuring international recognition but, via its representation function, also for providing the rest of the Tuvaluans a sense of still existing as a collective group. From this perspective, even when they use ICTs to communicate, diplomats epitomize the idea of a physical connection between the virtual and the physical reality, a fact that, although valid for all states, is more visible in this case.

Then again, such connections are continuously challenged by the ever-transforming landscape of competing authorities and stakeholders. Most significantly, as technological development happens largely in cities, which are also where most of the world population currently lives, some of them become hubs of digital innovation and leaders in the use of digital technologies for developmental purposes. This dynamic also generates new forms of interaction, knowledge transfer, and power relations, ranging from 'smart cities' aiming to address local development issues through digital technologies and then sharing their experience with the government, other cities, or countries to international coalitions of local authorities from more technologically developed cities and regions aimed at lobbying and advocacy around certain developmental models and solutions (Acuto, 2013; Kihlgren Grandi, 2020). In turn, such processes also fuel new forms of 'city diplomacy' (Marchetti, 2021), 'municipal foreign policy' (Leffel, 2018) or 'quantum diplomacy' (Der Derian, 2011), which, given the widespread use of ICTs, can increasingly bypass national authorities in matters of international dialogue. All these transform international norms and governance structures, further accelerating the 'liquefication' of the field in unpredictable and non-linear patterns.

Under these circumstances, a key aspect for both foresight and action will be the collection of, maintenance of, and access to robust and extensive databases. Consequently, open-data initiatives will become increasingly valuable for the global sustainable development, governance, and security architecture. However, digital data also generates substantial environmental costs, estimated to be at present 'on par with the aviation industry's emissions' (Jones, 2018). While future technology might solve some of these issues and additionally contribute to further global development, for the moment only some countries have the human and economic resources to look for such solutions. Even fewer countries can compete in the 'quantum race', i.e. the quest for faster computational devices that use quantum physics to achieve the goal. Without addressing such structural inequalities, these dynamics can deepen developmental gaps within the global system and may reignite older debates on colonialism reinvented for the digital era. Some of these concerns are already included in the most recent digital diplomacy strategies of the two largest ODA donors—the EU and the US, both acknowledging and committing to support especially the needs of Africa's digital development (Council of the European Union, 2022; US Government, 2022). However, global level a more consistent commitment on the matter has only recently been the focus of the conversation (UN Secretary General, 2021).

Another related aspect is the reputational one. Like other desirable items, digital technologies are an asset that can contribute to the reputation not only of the companies providing them but also of the countries of origin or hosting such companies. From this perspective, possessing and displaying digital technologies will add to the already existing set of classic diplomatic tools related to signalling both 'hard' and 'soft' power (Kaltofen et al., 2019). Cooperation in the context of sustainable development around such matters will imply negotiation on how much those who are already better-off are willing to share with those who are in more vulnerable situations, as well as public communication around such topics. The two may not always align, while inappropriate actions and/or communication may redraw or invent division lines that can then make international dialogue more difficult and thus hinder the local and global efforts for sustainable development.

Furthermore, as ICTs become a basic tool for diplomatic work and for building networks crucial for communicating, signalling presence, and negotiating, the independence and accountability of digital platforms through which dialogue is conducted will become vital for both diplomats and the larger public. For the moment there is a limited number of such platforms with global reach, and they have become intrinsically linked to various processes relevant for sustainable development, allowing people to reach information faster and to share it with wider audiences, accelerating the non-linear and simultaneous transformations that further enhance the 'liquid' character of this shifting landscape. In the absence of norms that protect the users and the trust invested in these platforms as part of the digital common goods, the processes and institutions that ensure the foundations of sustainable development and good governance in the physical reality can be also eroded. The viral spread of harmful, misleading, or fabricated digital content during recent elections and the Covid-19 infodemic, as well as the chaotic recent evolution of Twitter (currently X), a major social media tool for diplomats, represent illustrations of such vulnerabilities.

Not least, as the level of interconnectedness between different issues and areas increases, so does the likelihood to find relevant expertise and skills in teams rather than in single individuals. Therefore, in addition to its traditional functions, diplomatic work will increasingly require project and team management abilities and infrastructures, elements that become vital in digital environments characterized by high amounts of data and significant levels of complexity. Since relatively similar skills are necessary also for the other stakeholders in the field, the circulation of human resources across the stakeholder ecosystems is also likely to increase, a fact that might contribute to shifting the traditional perception on diplomacy as a lifetime career. To ensure the recruitment and retention of talent, ministries of foreign affairs and intergovernmental organizations will have to find new ways to incentivize and increase trust in the public sector, which is also one of the major goals of the newly emerging agenda.

CONCLUSION

The future is already here. The type of institutional framework in which the digital co-operation agenda has developed so far requires multistakeholder dialogue, but states remain the key actors for advancing the normative and institutional settings in the field, with the UN system serving as main forum for addressing such issues at a global level from a public interest perspective. Consequently, diplomats will likely continue to have a significant role especially in facilitating negotiation on such matters. From a foreign policy perspective, it may be also rational that states wishing to build or consolidate advantages related to digital cooperation identify and develop a multistakeholder dialogue also at national and sub-national levels. However, since stakeholders are increasingly connected internationally and, particularly in the context of digitalization, national borders, identities, and stratifications, might not be as strong as traditionally imagined, additional 'liquefication' is also quite likely. Therefore, and particularly through the global agenda on development, digital diplomacy becomes a nexus of norms, institutions, knowledge, and digital products, including ICTs, through which action can be furthered for diplomatic purposes. In this sense, digital diplomacy is not necessarily what diplomats do but rather the landscape they inhabit and share with other stakeholders in an increasingly digitalized and 'liquefied' environment, in the observation and transformation of which they also continue to actively participate.

SUGGESTED READING

Adler-Nissen, Rebeca, and Kristin Anabel Eggeling. 2022. 'Blended Diplomacy: The Entanglement and Contestation of Digital Technologies in Everyday Diplomatic Practice'. *European Journal of International Relations* 28(3): 240–266. doi: 10.1177/13540661221107837.
Bjola, Corneliu. 2022. 'AI for development: Implications for theory and practice'. *Oxford Development Studies* 50(1): 78–90. doi:10.1080/13600818.2021.1960960.
Bjola, Corneliu, and Ilan Manor. 2022. 'The Rise of Hybrid Diplomacy: From Digital Adaptation to Digital Adoption'. *International Affairs* 98(2): 471–491. doi: 10.1093/ia/iiac005.
Currie-Alder, Bruce, Ravi Kanbur, David Malone, and Rohinton Medhora, eds. 2014. *International Development: Ideas, Experience and Prospects*. Oxford: Oxford University Press.
UN General Assembly. 2020. *Road Map for Digital Cooperation: Implementation of the Recommendations of the High-level Panel on Digital Cooperation*, 24 May 2022 (A/RES/74/821).

REFERENCES

Acemoglu, Daron, and James A. Robinson. 2012. *Why Nations Fail: The Origins of Power, Prosperity, and Poverty*. New York: Crown Business.
Acuto, Michele. 2013. *Global Cities and Diplomacy. The Urban Link*. New York: Routledge.
Adler-Nissen, Rebeca, and Kristin Anabel Eggeling. 2022. 'Blended Diplomacy: The Entanglement and Contestation of Digital Technologies in Everyday Diplomatic Practice'. *European Journal of International Relations* 28(3): 240–266. doi: 10.1177/13540661221107837.
Banerjee, Abjihit V., and Esther Duflo. 2011. *Poor Economics: A Radical Rethinking of the Way to Fight Global Poverty*. New York: PublicAffairs.
Bauman, Zygmunt. 2000. *Liquid Modernity*. Cambridge: Polity Press.
Bjola, Corneliu. 2022. 'AI for Development: Implications for Theory and Practice'. *Oxford Development Studies* 50(1): 78–90. doi:10.1080/13600818.2021.1960960.
Bjola, Corneliu, and Marcus Holmes, eds. 2015. *Digital Diplomacy: Theory and Practice*. London: Routledge.
Bjola, Corneliu, and Ilan Manor. 2022. 'The Rise of Hybrid Diplomacy: From Digital Adaptation to Digital Adoption'. *International Affairs* 98(2): 471–491. doi: 10.1093/ia/iiac005.
Campbell, John, and Olivia Warrick. 2014. *Climate Change and the Migration Issues in the Pacific*. United Nations Economic and Social Commission for Asia and the Pacific (ESCPA)

Pacific Office. Available at: https://www.ilo.org/dyn/migpractice/docs/261/Pacific.pdf (Accessed: 23 December 2022).

Caradonna, Jeremy. 2022. *Sustainability: A History*, revised and updated edition. Oxford: Oxford University Press.

Constantinou, Costas M, and Sam Okoth Opondo. 2016. 'Engaging the "Ungoverned": The Merging of Diplomacy, Defence and Development'. *Cooperation and Conflict* 51(3): 307–324. doi: 10.1177/0010836715612848.

Council of the European Union. 2022. *Council Conclusions on EU Digital Diplomacy*. Brussels, 18 July (11406/22).

Della Porta, Donatella, and Sidney Tarrow. 2005. *Transnational Protest and Global Activism*. Lanham: Rowman & Littlefield.

Der Derian, James. 2011. 'Quantum Diplomacy, German–US Relations and the Psychogeography of Berlin'. *The Hague Journal of Diplomacy* 6(3–4): pp. 373–392. doi: 10.1163/187119111X598152

Escobar, Arturo. 1995. *Encountering Development: The Making and Unmaking of the Third World*. Princeton: Princeton University Press.

Fine, Ben, Constantine Lapavistas, and Jonathan Pincus, eds. 2003. *Development Policy in the Twenty-First Century: Beyond the Post-Washington Consensus*. London: Routledge.

Fowler, Alan. 2011. 'Development NGOs'. In *The Oxford Handbook of Civil Society*, edited by Michael Edwards, pp. 42–54. Oxford: Oxford University Press.

Gilboa, Eytan. 2016. 'Digital Diplomacy'. In *The SAGE Handbook of Diplomacy*, edited by Costas Constantinou, Pauline Kerr, and Paul Sharp, pp. 540–551. Los Angeles [etc.]: SAGE.

Harris, John. 2014. 'Development Theories'. In *International Development: Ideas, Experience, and Prospects*, edited by Bruce Currie-Alder, Ravi Kanbur, David Malone, and Rohinton Medhora, pp. 35–49. Oxford: Oxford University Press.

Haug, Sebastian, Jacqueline Braveboy-Wagner, and Günther Maihold. 2021. 'The "Global South" in the Study of World Politics: Examining a Meta Category'. *Third World Quarterly* 42(9)1923–1944. doi: 10.1080/01436597.2021.1948831.

Hynes, William, and Simon Scott. 2013. *The Evolution of Official Development Assistance: Achievements, Criticisms and a Way Forward*. OECD Development Co-operation Working Papers 12. Paris: OECD. doi: 10.1787/5k3v1dv3fo24-en.

IPCC. 2022. *Climate Change 2022: Impacts, Adaptation and Vulnerability* [Contribution of Working Group II to the Sixth Assessment Report of the Intergovernmental Panel on Climate Change]. Cambridge: Cambridge University Press. doi:10.1017/9781009325844.

Jones, Nicola. 2018. 'How to Stop Data Centres from Gobbling Up the World's Electricity'. *Nature* 561: 163–166. doi: 10.1038/d41586-018-06610-y.

Jordan, Lisa. 2011. 'Global Civil Society'. In *The Oxford Handbook of Civil Society*, edited by Michael Edwards, pp. 93–108. Oxford: Oxford University Press.

Kaltofen, Carolin, Madeline Carr, and Michele Acuto, eds. 2019. *Technologies of International Relations: Continuity and Change*. Cham: Palgrave Macmillan.

Kapoor, Ilan. 2013. *Celebrity Humanitarianism: The Ideology of Global Charity*. London: Routledge.

Kihlgren Grandi, Lorenzo. 2020. *City Diplomacy*. Cham: Palgrave Macmillan.

Kofe, Simon. 2022. 'Rising Sea Levels Force Tuvalu to Move to the Metaverse'. COP27 speech, 15 November 2022. Available at: https://youtu.be/hpPTFGwFExg (Accessed: 27 December 2022).

Kolk, Ans. 2016. 'The Social Responsibility of International Business: From Ethics and the Environment to CSR and Sustainable Development'. *Journal of World Business* 51(1): 23–34. doi: 10.1016/j.jwb.2015.08.010.

Leffel, Benjamin. 2018. 'Animus of the Underling: Theorizing City Diplomacy in a World Society'. *The Hague Journal of Diplomacy* 13(4): 502–522. doi: 10.1163 /1871191X-13040025.

Lesa, Sosikeni. 2022. 'Tuvalu's Innovative Contingency Plan to Address Scientific Predictions of Being Uninhabitable by 2050'. Secretariat of the Pacific Region Environmental Programme, 15 November 2022. Available at:https://www.sprep.org/news/tuvalus-innovative-continge ncy-plan-to-address-scientific-predictions-of-being-uninhabitable-by-2050 (Accessed: 27 December 2022).

OECD. 2022. *Development Co-operation Profiles*. Paris: OECD Publishing. doi: 10.1787/ 2dcf1367-en.

OECD. 2016. *Better Policies for Sustainable Development 2016: A New Framework for Policy Coherence*. Paris: OECD Publishing. doi: 10.1787/9789264256996-en.

OECD. 2011. 'Busan Partnership for Effective Development Co-Operation'. Fourth High Level Forum on Aid Effectiveness, Busan, 29 November–1 December 2011. Available at: https:// www.oecd.org/dac/effectiveness/49650173.pdf (Accessed: 5 January 2023).

Marchetti, Raffaele. 2021. *City Diplomacy: From City-States to Global Cities*. Ann Arbor: Michigan University Press.

Piketty, Thomas. 2014. *Capital in the Twenty-First Century*. Cambridge, MA: Harvard University Press.

Rodrick, Dani. 2008. *One Economics, Many Recipes: Globalization, Institutions and Economic Growth*. Princeton: Princeton University Press.

Rostow, Walt W. 1960. *The Stages of Economic Growth: A Non-Communist Manifesto*. Cambridge: Cambridge University Press.

Schultz, George P. 1998. 'Diplomacy, Wired'. *Hoover Digest*, 30 January 1998. Washington, DC, and Stanford University: Hoover Institution. Available at: https://www.hoover.org/research/ diplomacy-wired (Accessed: 27 December 2022).

Schwittay, Anke. 2015. *New Media and International Development: Representation and Affect in Microfinance*. London and New York: Routledge.

Scott, Martin. 2014. *Media and Development*. London and New York: Zed Books.

Serra, Narcís, and Joseph E. Stiglitz, eds. 2008. *The Washington Consensus Reconsidered: Towards a New Global Governance*. Oxford: Oxford University Press.

Stiglitz, Joseph. 2002. 'Challenging the Washington Consensus, an interview with Lindsey Schoenfelder'. *The Brown Journal of World Affairs* 9(2): 33–40.

Tomalin, Emma, ed. 2018. *The Routledge Handbook of Religions and Global Development*. London: Routledge.

Tomlinson, B. R. 2003. 'What was the Third World?' *Journal of Contemporary History* 38(2): 307–321. doi: 10.1177/0022009403038002135.

UN. 2018. *Global Compact on Refugees*. New York: United Nations. Available at: https://www. unhcr.org/5c658aed4 (Accessed: 3 January 2023).

UN Academic Impact. 2016. 'UN Unveils Data Partnership with Twitter in Support of Global Goals', 23 September 2016. Available at:https://www.un.org/en/academic-impact/un-unve ils-data-partnership-twitter-support-global-goals (Accessed: 4 January 2023).

UN General Assembly. 2022. *Information and communications technologies for sustainable development*, 14 December 2022 (A/RES/77/150).

UN General Assembly. 2020a. *Road Map for Digital Cooperation: Implementation of the Recommendations of the High-level Panel on Digital Cooperation*, 24 May 2022 (A/RES/74/821).

UN General Assembly. 2020b. *Declaration on the Commemoration of the Seventy-Fifth Anniversary of the United Nations*, 21 September 2020 (A/RES/75/1).

UN General Assembly. 2018a. *Intergovernmental Conference to Adopt the Global Compact for Safe, Orderly and Regular Migration: Draft Outcome of the Conference*, 30 July 2018 (A/CONF.231/3).

UN General Assembly. 2018b. *Resolution Adopted by the General Assembly on 17 December 2018 [on the Report of the Third Committee] (A/73/583)*, 5 December 2018 (A/RES/73/51).

UN General Assembly. 2015. *Transforming our World: The 2030 Agenda for Sustainable Development*, 25 September 2015 (A/RES/70/1).

UN General Assembly. 2001. *World Summit on Information Society*, 21 December 2001 (A/RES/56/183).

UN General Assembly. 1970. *International Development Strategy for the Second United Nations Development Decade*, 24 October 1970 (A/RES/2626(XXV)).

UN Secretary General. 2022. *Implementing the Secretary-General's Roadmap for Digital Cooperation: July 2022 Update*. New York: UN Office of the Secretary General's Envoy for Technology.

UN Secretary General. 2021. *Our Common Agenda: Report of the UN Secretary General*. New York: United Nations.

UN Secretary General. 2019. *The Age of Digital Interdependence: Report of the UN Secretary General's High-level Panel on Digital Cooperation*. New York: United Nations.

UNDP. 2022. *Uncertain Times, Unsettled Lives: Shaping Our Future in a Transforming World, Human Development Report 2021-2022*. New York: United Nations Development Programme.

UNESCO. 2022. *Recommendation on the Ethics of Artificial Intelligence Adopted on 23 November 2021*. Paris: UNESCO (SHS/BIO/PI/2021/1).

UNHCR. 2020. *Legal Considerations Regarding Claims for International Protection Made in the Context of the Adverse Effects of Climate Change and Disasters*, 1 October 2020. Available at: https://www.refworld.org/docid/5f75f2734.html (Accessed: 27 December 2022).

US Government. 2022. *U.S. Strategy Towards Sub-Saharan Africa, August 2022*. Washington, DC. Available at: https://www.whitehouse.gov/wp-content/uploads/2022/08/U.S.-Strategy-Toward-Sub-Saharan-Africa-FINAL.pdf (Accessed: 27 December 2022).

WCED. 1987. *Our Common Future: Report of the World Commission on Environment and Development*. Oxford: Oxford University Press.

World Bank. 2005. *Economic Growth in the 1990s: Learning from a Decade of Reform* Washington, D.C.: World Bank Group.

Yusuf, Shahid. 2014. 'Fifty Years of Growth Economics'. In *International Development: Ideas, Experience, and prospects*, edited by Bruce Currie-Alder, Ravi Kanbur, David Malone, and Rohinton Medhora, pp. 50–64. Oxford: Oxford University Press.

CHAPTER 15

NEW TRENDS IN DIGITAL DIPLOMACY: THE RISE OF TIKTOK AND THE GEOPOLITICS OF ALGORITHMIC GOVERNANCE

ALICIA FJÄLLHED, MATTHIAS LÜFKENS, AND ANDREAS SANDRE

INTRODUCTION

WHILE there is a range of diplomatic studies on how actors use digital platforms as mediums for their message, this chapter address how influence works in relation to the infrastructure containing such messages. That is, both through influence over the algorithmic setup of each platform—allowing certain behaviour but not others—as well as opportunities of influence through the access to data.

Platforms' infrastructural influence over our societies has been theorized through various concepts, one of which is *platformization*. When introduced, the concept was used 'to refer to the rise of the platform as the dominant infrastructural and economic model of the social web and the consequences of the expansion of social media platforms into other spaces online' (Helmond, 2015: 5). Scholars have since argued for an emerging *platform society* (Van Dijck, Poell, and De Waal, 2018) as online platforms have 'penetrated the heart of societies' by converging with pre-existing institutions, 'forcing governments and states to adjust their legal and democratic structures' (Van Dijck et al., 2018: 2). Building on these concepts, Kaye, Chen, and Zeng (2021) have argued for *parallel platformization* through the case of TikTok and its twin Douyin, both owned by ByteDance. Formed to fit 'two opposing media systems' (2021: 290)—the first available on a global market, the second only in China—the two 'exist in radically different markets and are governed by radically different forces' and so 'adapts its products to better fit divergent expectations, cultures, and policy frameworks in China and abroad' (2021: 290).

TikTok is also a case where the international geopolitics of *algorithmic governance* has grown salient in the public debate. The concept concerns how one can govern automated decision-making processes through algorithms' design (see the special issue by Gritsenko, Markham, Potzsch, and Wijermars, 2022)—spanning from smart cities using algorithms to regulate traffic lights with the purpose of reducing emissions, using algorithmic solutions to manage stock-exchanges, for the recruitment of new staff, or for decisions concerning loans to name but a few examples. The debate also covers the use of algorithms by social media companies to regulate the flow of communication on their platforms, dictating the rules of social interactions online through 'direct interference with speech, through content moderation practices, and indirect algorithmic control' (Aytac, 2022: 17). This, as the chapter would argue, opens up for a new dimension of influence of relevance for digital diplomacy, in terms of both prospective opportunities and critical risks.

To drive this argument, the chapter focuses on TikTok as a case, later used in this chapter to spark a theoretical discussion within digital diplomacy on how *all* platforms (including Facebook, Twitter, Instagram etc.) are bound to geopolitical systems implicitly influencing the nature of public conversations online. TikTok has been argued to enable discussions on 'the new dynamics in geopolitics and the emerging platform governance' (Yu and Li, 2022: 104) where 'lawmakers have questioned whether ByteDance, the company that owns TikTok, sufficiently protects users' data against access by the Chinese state' (2022: 2). This, the chapter argues, requires a geopolitical analysis in digital diplomacy. It also opens up the possibility of critically not only reviewing TikTok but in the future other platforms and how diplomatic actors may implicitly or explicitly influence their algorithmic structures.

For this chapter, however, the case of TikTok is used as the epicentre of the critical discussion of the twenty-first century on geopolitical concerns connected to digital platforms and explores how the platform was received by diplomatic actors abroad— spanning from early adaptors to critical sceptics. So far, TikTok's implications on digital diplomacy practice and theory has remained unexplored within the field—a literature review of academic articles revealing none yet published that mention both *TikTok* and *diplomacy* in the same piece. Similarly, only a limited number of world leaders, foreign ministries, and embassies' actors have chosen to establish a direct presence on the platform as of this writing. As such, the chapter starts with an introduction to TikTok, with some background to its rise, user base, and technical features, and presents a review of published journal articles beyond diplomacy studies on TikTok. After that, the paper presents a few cases of diplomatic actors' attitudes towards and early adapters' use of TikTok. Finally, the literature review and case studies are used as a stance for a critical concluding discussion that explores the theoretical aspects of algorithmic geopolitics argued by this chapter.

Introducing TikTok

The journey starts with the Chinese company *ByteDance* launching the social media platform *Douyin* in 2016, the next year acquiring *Musical.ly*, and integrating the two in 2018 to produce the platform *TikTok* for a global market (Gray, 2021: 7). Continuously, there has been two versions of the platform—TikTok for a global market and Douyin (or 抖音) for the Chinese market (for a popular introduction to the platform, see Stokel-Walker, 2021).[1] Since then, TikTok has developed into one of the major competitors of previously introduced US platforms from Silicon Valley, confirming 'that users will adopt innovative new platforms ... regardless of their geopolitical orientation' (Gray, 2021: 2). The two have slightly different features (Kaye et al., 2021; Liu and Yang, 2022) but essentially form video communities containing a feed of short videos ranging from 15 seconds to a few minutes,[2] all appearing in an infinite scroll regulated by the platforms' algorithm.

> TikTok applies a powerful recommendation AI algorithm to learn users' interests from their viewing habits ... and to analyse the correlation among video content, user characteristics, and user behaviours. The short video format trains the algorithm very fast [and] once the algorithm has gauged a user's preferences, it feeds them more targeted material. What's next is extremely simple and effective: TikTok bombards the 'known' user with self-repeating clips ..., in an increasingly personalized stream, until users are hooked ... On top of the algorithm, TikTok also puts in human capital to cultivate KOLs [key opinion leaders].
>
> (Ma, 2021: 134–135)

When videos reach large number of users, 'a person on the content moderation team will watch the video and confirm that it does not violate the platform's terms of service or have any copyright issues' (Brennan, 2020). As with other social media platforms, the algorithm is designed to feed the user with content matching their behavioural profile—aiming to retain users for a longer time. The algorithm has also been criticized for skewing the selection of content (expanded presentation in the chapter's concluding discussion) where, as Gray (2021: 8) emphasizes, 'what the TikTok controversy reveals is the extent to which the politics of platforms is immersed in geopolitical tensions'. This expands to accusations of TikTok extracting data from users' phones and tracking them geographically, broadly tied to a wider discussion on platforms' data security, moderation practices, and a critical discussion on regulation of free speech (2021: 7–8).

TikTok has ever since the merging with Musical.ly held a younger user base in comparison to other platforms and is described as an important platform for the collective '*we-sense* of Gen Z' (Zeng and Abidin, 2021: 2461), sparking a moral panic as

---

[1] For scholarly pieces about Douyin, see i.e. Liang (2022), Jia and Ruan (2020), or Kaye et al. (2021).

[2] The maximum length has varied throughout the years, expanding from some three to ten minutes.

an 'adult-free social network' (Savic, 2021: 3173). While described by scholars as 'largely constituted of user-generated content (UGC) as opposed to professionally generated content (PGC)' (Kaye et al., 2021: 230), today the platform—as the empirical sections will show—also hold the presence of activist groups and private, non-profit, and public organizations.

As one of the latest additions to our contemporary global communication platforms, TikTok is not extensively studied in academia and only a few publications can be found within the fields of communication science and international relations.[3] The vast majority of studies are using TikTok content as empirical material—i.e. studies of political debates around climate change (Hautea, Parks, Takahashi, and Zeng, 2021), studies about the influencers on the platforms (Balaban and Szambolics, 2022; Huber, Lepenies, Baena, and Allgaier, 2022), and studies about politicians' use of TikTok (Cervi and Marin-Llado, 2021). Some papers accentuate the *possibilities* with TikTok to e.g. enable public participation and the empowerment of publics (Cervi and Marin-Llado, 2022; Kaur-Gill, 2023; Krutrok and Akerlund, 2023; Vizcaino-Verdu and Aguaded, 2022)—such as to support identify formation (Civila and Jaramillo-Dent, 2022; Darvin, 2022; Gentry; Steele, 2021), to connect with others of the same profession (Hartung, Hendry, Albury, Johnston, and Welch, 2023), to push for a feminist agenda (Sued et al., 2022), or to challenge traditional notions of masculinity (Foster and Baker, 2022), to take but a few examples.

Another cluster of studies accentuates the *risks* with the platform. One piece describes how traditional media initially introduced it as merely a popular platform on the rise, but since the 2020s there has been rather a critical discussion in relation to concerns for national security, increasingly 'embedded in the escalating geo-political tensions' between China, the US, and India (Miao, Huang, and Huang, 2021: 1).[4] The core in such discussion concerns TikTok's ties to the Chinese government. On the one hand, authors such as Gray (2021: 8) argue that 'while the Chinese government has been known to influence the content available on Douyin, the evidence of similar influence on TikTok is limited', and TikTok repeatedly issues statements insisting that the app is independent from the Chinese government. On the other hand, various journalistic investigations have found evidence of questionable unethical practices either planned (Forbes, 2022a) or executed (BuzzFeed, 2022; CNBC, 2021; Forbes, 2022b; Post, 2022) and—as the final discussion will address—several governments have banned the platform for security reasons. To that, papers also accentuate the risks of mis- and disinformation on the platform (Grandinetti and Bruinsma, 2023; Lopez, Sidorenko-Bautista, and Giacomelli, 2021). Others express concerns for the content-moderation practices forming an environment

---

[3] A search for all journal articles registered as of 5 December 2022 on *Web of Science* (previously *Web of Knowledge*) reveal no pieces mentioning both *diplomacy* and *TikTok*. Expanding the search for mentions of *TikTok* revealed 396 English journal articles, 88 within communication studies (six not accessible and thus removed from the review) and one within the field of international relations.

[4] Additional scholarly commentaries within communication studies by Gray (2021), Mishra, Yan, and Schroeder (2022), and Mazumdar (2022).

where 'marginalized communities claim the platform's underlying algorithms and content moderation policies remove and suppress explicitly anti-racist content, as well as content that features fat, queer, and disabled creators' (Peterson-Salahuddin, 2022: 2, in reference to Botella, 2019; McCluskey, 2020).

As studies on the application of TikTok in diplomacy studies remain scarce, the following sections introduce some of the early adaptors of TikTok with stories arising from one-on-one interviews with thirty-four social media managers and policy communications staffers at international organizations and global non-governmental organizations, as well as with researchers, journalists, influencers, and creators already active on TikTok or studying the platform. The interviews were conducted between 2020 and 2021. Just as the literature points to academically observed possibilities and risks with TikTok, so does the following review illustrate how diplomatic actors walk this line—on the one hand drawn to a platform with a global user base while at the same time expressing concerns for security reasons.

DIPLOMATIC INSTITUTIONS ON TIKTOK

Embracing TikTok has not come as an easy process for many social media managers at diplomatic and for-good organizations. Communication teams at several institutions needed to convince higher echelons that the move to TikTok was a strategic one, facing internal resistance due mainly to political and geopolitical reasons, mindful to the Chinese ownership of TikTok. So far, India has taken the harshest measures as the government banned the app in 2020 in the country (Aronczyk, 2021) along with over fifty other Chinese apps. In the US, authorities banned the app on government-issued devices—starting with the White House and the defence, homeland security, and state departments (Gray, 2021), expanded in December 2022 to cover all government-issued cell phones (Bhuiyan, 2022).

As a solution, actors have worked with influencers or *creators* to reach a TikTok-audience without having to create an account. To take one example, in June 2021 the then German Permanent Representative to the United Nations in New York, Ambassador Christoph Heusgen, joined TikTok influencer Nikolas Kappe for a conversation on foreign policy and the role of the UN (German Mission to the UN, 2021). Another case is when in Washington DC, the embassies of both Finland and France participated in videos posted by the popular official TikTok of *The Washington Post*, an experiment that ended up convincing the French embassy in the US to join TikTok shortly after in April 2022 (Embassy of France, 2022). Such examples abound, found in e.g. TikTok's Australia affiliate, partnering with former Australian Prime Minister Julia Gillard and creator Abbey Hansen to talk about women's rights and gender equality in March 2021 (TikTok, 2021), and when the White House partnered with TikTok stars in summer 2020 including the eighteen-year-old pop star Olivia Rodrigo to fight vaccine disinformation and hesitancy (The White House, 2021), and more recently when the White House started to work with non-profit advocacy group *GenZ For Change* to reach out to thirty TikTok young creators to talk about Ukraine and the US's role (Lorenz, 2022).

In this we see a continuous struggle, with a reluctancy from political organizations and individuals to join the platform for political, security, and economic reasons (as establishing a presence on a new platform takes commitment and thus inevitably time and money), while at the same time they find themselves drawn to leverage the platform's large and young user base. To push for a presence of more organizations on TikTok, the company offered some of these organizations to be paired with a representative from TikTok, or to be introduced to the platform in mentoring and training with their CSR-initiative *TikTok For Good*.[5] The latter is specifically aimed at a limited number of international organizations and non-profits, starting in November 2020 with programmes better known as *Elevate* rounds including 6–8 weeks of guidance and mentorship. The first three rounds included the UN Secretariat and other UN agencies, the International Committee of the Red Cross (ICRC), and the International Campaign to Abolish Nuclear Weapons (ICAN)—today all three having amassed a sizeable presence and reached the status of *Key Opinion Leaders* (KOL) on TikTok.

For beyond the political concerns, early users also need to learn the TikTok-specific milieu and by extension what forms of campaigns could run on it. The short videos—also called TikToks—are characterised by platform-specific storytelling, oftentimes with text overlays, visual effects, and filters. The best performing campaigns are TikTok challenges that form around a specific hashtag with videos following a set story-ark. These videos include a call to action, which in turn drives engagement and generates content by additional TikTok users. Thus, simply reposting videos from other platforms will not attract TikTok users. Instead, diplomats have come to prioritize communication on TikTok to target their large user base of younger publics. And so, while TikTok would seem as an easy switch from the pre-existing social media platforms, social media teams were quite aware of the need to adapt to the new creative possibilities enabled and restricted by the platform. TikTok, as some social media managers explain, has a specific 'feel' that one needs to preserve in order to be successful.

Today, one can see three specific objectives diplomats strive for on TikTok; educating young audiences about political issues, countering mis- and disinformation about the same issues, and empowering young people to engage in political discussions. This can also be seen to pair well with the priorities of TikTok's For Good programme. To take one example; one of the early projects the TikTok For Good team worked on was a partnership with UNICEF and the European Union's European External Action Service (EEAS) in 2019, coinciding with the thirtieth anniversary of the UN Convention on

---

[5] Account managers 'will assist with best practices, manage relationships, and offer guidance every step of the way until you've reached your end goal' (TikTok, 2022) and the TikTok For Good programme is described as an opportunity for organizations to support the company's efforts to 'inspire and encourage a new generation to have a positive impact on the planet and those around them.' (TikTok, 2022)

the Rights of the Child. The project was centred around *#TheRealChallenge*, an educational campaign aimed at empowering children around the globe to demand that their human rights be respected (UNICEF, 2019). Another example is how the Geneva-based International Federation of Red Cross and Red Crescent Societies (IFRC) used TikTok to reach a younger, engaged audience and educate them about the IFRC's humanitarian missions and areas of activity. The IFRC started by directly contacting the TikTok team, who, in return, paired them 'with a representative that was actually an ex-IFRC staffer' to facilitate contacts and, eventually, consolidate the collaboration into a partnership. In the process, the IFRC consulted with a number of social media managers in the advocacy sector to share best practices. The result of the IFRC's partnership with TikTok became the *#ForClimate* campaign aimed at educating younger audiences about the humanitarian impact of climate change and invite them to share their knowledge about the environment and to advocate directly for the protection of the planet (IFRC, 2019).

Following these early success stories, social media teams at various organizations, including Amnesty International and various UN agencies, followed suit. These realized that educational content was very popular and created high levels of engagement among young users, eager to express their opinions and show their support for campaigns and causes by becoming active in online conversation. The focus was not about delivering information in amusing ways, but to target TikTok's very engaged audiences to act on content, empowering the ability of the platform to make each user a social amplifier.

One of the things emphasized by social media managers and strategists is the power of boosting one's message through TikTok creators, acting as influencers spreading the message to a large audience. As one marketing expert explain, 'I think there are a lot of opportunities for social impact and digital diplomacy' (Haberman, 2020) where one can find ways to counter false messages in a strong combination of both official sources and powerful influencers with millions of followers on the platform. To take one example, in 2020 the most followed user on the platform[6] Charli D'Amelio with her over 130 million followers and her sister Dixie teamed up with UNICEF for Internet Safety Day to talk 'about how cyberbullying really can affect people', as the TikTok star explained in a March 2020 televised interview with Jimmy Fallon. The TikTok star highlighted the power of the platform in educating young audiences about issues that affect them personally.

But it is not only the mega-influencers that have proven valuable for organizations seeking to reach an audience on TikTok. Similarly, micro-influencers have also been engaging with global entities to educate audiences about specific causes, a trend that surged in 2020 at the height of the Covid-19 pandemic. US singer-songwriter Tiana Kocher, for example, partnered with TikTok, the American Red Cross, and the Philippines Red Cross for her *#DontTripChallenge*, launched alongside her new single *Don't Trip*. In the campaign, users were asked to create TikTok videos and dances to the beat of Kocher's new song and, each day, one entry was selected to win—both a gift

---

[6] Surpassed in 2022 by Khabane 'Khaby' Lame.

card furnished by campaign partners Amazon and Lazada, and a $100 donation to the Red Cross made in their name. The participation of TikTok influencers like Mary Lite Lamayo, Sai Datinguinoo, Marvin Fojas, Lennie Enverga, each with about 10 million followers, enabled the campaign to attract more than 14 million views (Kocher, 2020). In various ways, these influencers become social amplifiers of diplomatic messages.

But the dynamics of messages going viral is not always a good thing, which became particularly clear during the Covid-19 pandemic. On the one hand, organizations such as the World Health Organisation (WHO) identified a need to influence the TikTok conversation to also cover a conversation about their issues, as one social media manager describes:

> The platform was lacking educational content on health, so it was a great opportunity for us to collaborate with TikTok to provide their users with health-related information, and to communicate about health risks to audiences younger than 25.
>
> (Kuzmanovic, 2020)

Their decision to launch a TikTok account in March 2020 is described by the same interviewee as a strategic decision, not just as an educational tool to spread information but also as a way to correct misinformation (Kuzmanovic, 2020). And the WHO was not alone. Similarly, in the summer of 2021 the global movement campaign ONE setting out with the mission to end extreme poverty and preventable disease, UNICEF, and the African Union (AU) co-launched the campaign #MythOrVax to counter false information about Covid-19 vaccines. The goal was to dispel myths and combat inaccurate information about vaccines, address ongoing fears and concerns, and raise awareness about the importance of vaccinations in Africa—or, as the UNICEF Regional Director for Eastern and Southern Africa explains—to 'help to further engage young people in learning about Covid-19 vaccines and to clarify some of the common misconceptions that are circulating' (UNICEF, 2021). Thanks to the contribution of some of the continent's biggest music and entertainment acts—like Yemi Alade from Nigeria, SautiSol from Kenya, Maps from South Africa, and Pearl Thusi—the campaign garnered nearly 75 million views globally. Each element in the challenge featured a live stream on TikTok that paired celebrities with health experts from across the continent and the globe, including Dr John Nkengasong, Director of the Africa Center for Disease Control and Prevention. The TikTok approach of countering misinformation with expert organizations presenting facts to be amplified through celebrity spokespeople and influential TikTok creators, packaged as challenges to engage the audience, is also one supported by TikTok.

As their own Covid-19 community guidelines read 'We believe that one of the best ways to counter misinformation is through engaging, informative content, and we continue to partner with public health experts to create content that resonates with our community' (TikTok, n.d.). At the same time, the power of viral stories could just as well mean that false information gains influence on TikTok. As Singer and Brooking (2018) describe, it is an environment where 'virality is inseparable from reality' and where 'a fake story shared by millions become "real" in its own way', while 'an actual event that fails to catch the eye of attention-tracking algorithms might as well never have happened' (2018: 137). In the same presentation of TikTok's Covid-19 guidelines, they also emphasize the prohibition of content 'that's false or misleading, including misinformation related to Covid-19, vaccines, and anti-vaccine disinformation more broadly' as well as not allowing 'paid advertising that advocates against vaccinations, though public service announcements (PSAs) or calls to action related to vaccines are accepted on a case-by-case basis if they're in the interest of public health and safety'.

Moving from the goal of informing the public and countering false claims, the third goal of empowering vulnerable communities by leveraging the power of young generations using the palatform has also been driven by a series of campaigns. One example is the Malala Fund, the digital communications manager describing how this has been the focus of their presence on TikTok since the start. Their strategy conveys this stance as it describes how 'Young women are passionate, knowledgeable, and really eager to make a change, and Malala [Yousafzai] and the Malala Fund work to amplify their voices by creating content that resonates with young women' (Regmi, 2020). Their TikTok strategy can be summed up in three points:

> We put girls at the forefront of our messaging and celebrate their comradery and activism; we don't impart our values onto girls, instead, we let them speak for themselves and open up our platforms for girls to talk about the issues that matter to them; and we position young women as the experts of their own stories, experts in their communities, and the issues they care about.
>
> (Regmi, 2020)

When launching their TikTok account in October 2020, the Malala Fund's strategy was indeed to empower these groups, in an open call for girls around the world to submit their stories to be features on their new account as they described how 'We want to help amplify girls' voices so we can all learn from each other's stories' (Malala Fund, 2020). And they are not alone; the UNHCR is another example of an organization seeking to use TikTok to empower vulnerable communities online. Their social video lead and social media officer describe how *'We want to make sure we include refugees themselves in the ideas and content production'*, again emphasizing the target being younger audiences.

> We want to reach a young and diverse audience: young people have a lot of compassion and they can really help us change the narrative around refugees. What is really lovely to see on TikTok is a lot of young people commenting on their support for refugees and also defending them against the haters in comments.
>
> (Bitetti, 2021)

This strategy was particularly successful during the Tokyo Olympics in 2021. As their senior communication officer described, 'social media videos detail an incredible journey of refugee athletes to the Olympics and Paralympics, in conversation pieces between the athletes themselves and celebrity supporters, with content and messages shared directly from the refugee athletes' handles and on UNHCR platforms'. In this, the interviewee points out the importance of the collaboration between UNHCR and TikTok, in that 'to reach young audiences where they are, UNHCR worked closely with TikTok For Good and influencers to build awareness and support not only for the refugee teams but about issues that forced displacement' and the help from TikTok enhancing their ability to achieve measurable results, amplifying content and calls to actions.

WORLD LEADERS ON TIKTOK

When it comes to the application of TikTok in diplomatic circles, this covers not only organizations' use, but also early adapters on an individual level—from world leaders to cabinet ministers and other high-level politicians, to mention but a few examples. As of February 2022, seventy-one heads of state and government and foreign ministries had an active presence on TikTok, though only thirty-four verified by TikTok. These accounts had a combined following of over 10 million followers, with more than 5,000 videos posted, 65 million likes, and 755 million video views (DigiTips, 2022). The leaders adopting TikTok tend to become more active during election campaigns, quite a few downloading the app to reach younger voters.

For example, Polish President Andrzej Duda joined TikTok at the end of March 2020, exactly three months before the presidential elections in June 2020. His goal was to encourage teenagers confined at home due to the pandemic to join e-sports and on-line contests on a bespoke website developed by the Polish Ministry of Digital Affairs. President Duda's TikTok adventure, although very successful in terms of engagement, didn't last long, and the account is now set to private (Duda, 2020). Another example is the use of TikTok by Israeli politicians. Ahead of the 2020 elections, all three contenders for the role of Prime Minister joined TikTok. Former Israeli Prime Minister Benjamin Netanyahu launched his TikTok account in December 2020, three months before the March 2021 elections, while Naftali Bennett and Yair Lapid also joined TikTok during the election campaign in January and February 2021 (Bennett, 2021; Lapid, 2021). In the French presidential elections of April 2022, all but one of the eight leading candidates had set up official accounts on TikTok. French President Emmanuel Macron started his TikTok journey in early July 2020 with a video congratulating French high school graduates for a challenging school year amid the pandemic and stringent lockdown. The one-minute video of the president dressed in suit and tie and filmed in the Élysée gardens is still his most viewed video, with over 14 million views, 1.6 million likes, and almost 200,000 comments (Macron, 2020a).

As a review of best-case practices, one can zoom in on the most followed world leaders on TikTok in 2022 (covering foremost presidents and prime ministers)—starting at the top with three leaders all with more than a million followers, first Emmanuel Macron

(France), continuing with Nayib Bukele (El Salvador), and Guillermo Lasso (Ecuador). The French president has become the most followed world leader on TikTok with 2.8 million followers, 18.8 million likes, and 182 million video views. The median average views of each video stands at 3 million. When Macron tested positive for Covid-19 in December 2020, he recorded himself a 3:22 minute-long piece to camera, which was posted on Instagram and a 30-second extract on TikTok (Macron, 2020b). In August 2021, Macron used TikTok and Instagram to answer a series of twelve questions from social media users about Covid-19 health policies, vaccines, and vaccination programmes. The videos were simple statements—video selfies—shot on a hand-held mobile device. The French president was dressed in a T-shirt. He held the phone himself and looked straight into the camera, addressing his viewers in a very personal and direct way, while at his holiday retreat in southern France. This is a far cry from official videos on other platforms that usually include world leaders in suites speaking from behind podiums.

El Salvador's President Nayib Bukele is the second most followed world leader on TikTok with 2.5 million subscribers. His forty-one videos have been viewed 112 million times and the median average views stand at 1.9 million views per video. The forty-year-old president first started using TikTok in September 2020 with a two-scene video of his motorcade passing along a highway and a shot of his daughter Layla happily ensconced in the child seat inside. His account uses the different TikTok editing features for short storytelling including trending hashtags and popular sounds. His nine-second clip showing him in the presidential office through the ages was set to the tune of the song 'Vacation' from the group Dirty Heads. The video with the description 'I'm (never) on vacation' has been viewed more than twenty-five million times (Bukele, 2021). The video clips of his official engagements, visits, speeches, and military parades set to popular soundtracks help the president create a decidedly youthful and rock-infused digital persona.

Guillermo Lasso, the president of Ecuador, is the third most followed world leader on TikTok with 1.3 million followers as of February 2022. The sixty-six-year-old politician is also one of the few leaders who dares TikTok dance moves. In his February 2021 inaugural video, he moves to the sound of Michael Jackson's *Bad,* throwing his left arm backwards and arching his entire body. The eight-second clip, which celebrates his victory in the first round of the presidential elections, has been viewed 5.3 million times and has become a signature move on his TikTok channel (Lasso, 2021). Since becoming president, Lasso has continued to use the platform as a tool to explain his policies and engage with his youth audience. In one of his first videos after coming to power, Lasso vowed to continue the conversations and engage with his communities on social media via Facebook, Instagram, and TikTok live broadcasts. It comes as no surprise that the median average views of each of his eighty videos stands at almost 1 million.

What these world leaders have in common is not merely a large following on TikTok, but arguably similarities in posted content on the platform. And it is a common feature beyond the integration of musical elements. Instead, success factors arguably seems to be an acknowledgement of the type of target audience one addresses in each video—the younger audience—and the format they are used to encountering on the platform—shorter videos with more relaxed content or, as e.g. Sot (2022) emphasizes, a sense of intimacy. While it might be more medium-appropriate to appear dressed in a shirt or even suit on other social media channels, TikTok is a more relaxed medium for if not entertaining then at least less-strict content. This covers not only the dress code but other aspects of the visual impression one makes too, such as the use of hand-held smartphones to record addresses to the audience rather than a professionally recorded video from a stiff press-room. Similarly, it seems to have provided a platform for politicians to 'be themselves'—in the sense of inviting people to learn more about the *person* rather than the *public profile*.

Beyond these world leaders, foreign ministries, too, have embraced TikTok, although few. As of February 2022, only five foreign ministries (Israel, Mexico, Russia, Somalia, and Thailand) had set up TikTok accounts and only four foreign ministers (Belgium, Israel, North Macedonia, and Togo) maintain personal profiles and only a few of these are active on the platform. But there are exceptions to these rules—as in the foreign ministry of Israel. With a total of 400,000 followers and 3.2 million likes as of February 2022, they have established a large presence on TikTok—with three separate channels in Arabic, English, and Spanish—and have a dedicated team of young staffers who produce videos about Israeli culture, customs, and cuisine, promoting Israel to foreign audiences. The @Israel channel made headlines in May 2021 when it documented the life of Israelis under Hamas's rocket attacks. A fifteen-second clip showing Tamar Schwarzbard, the head of digital operations at the Israeli foreign ministry, sitting in a bomb shelter as air raid sirens are wailing asked the question 'Israelis have 15 seconds to run to bomb shelters when rockets hit. Would you make it?' The most poignant video, totalling 6.3 million views, is a clip of an Israeli youth protecting his younger sister from an incoming rocket. On the Spanish channel, the clip showing Israelis running for cover on a beach has been viewed 3.3 million times (Israel in Spanish, 2021). On a more upbeat note, the most watched video on the Arabic language channel is a clip of an Arab-Israeli citizen singing *a cappella* his love for Israel, with 2.4 million views and 41,000 comments. A clip entitled 'The peace train has started', celebrating the six Arab countries with which Israel has established diplomatic relations over the years, poses the question: 'Who is the next?' (Israel Arabic, 2021).

A final interesting example is China's use of TikTok for digital diplomacy, since TikTok is not available within the country. Instead, the ministry of foreign affairs of China has formed a presence on the Chinese equivalent Douyin, with the official account of the spokesperson's office of the ministry joining the platform in July 2019. The move shows an attempt by the foreign ministry to reach out directly to its domestic audience, rather than operate a digital diplomacy channel, and it follows similar moves on other Chinese-only platforms, including Weibo. As Purayil (2019) reflects, 'opening a social media platform is intended to bolster the government's positive image through dialogue and interaction with the public. This can certainly boost its image in the domestic realm, which will have implications at the global level', thus emphasizing how the choice to establish a presence on Douyin may be an attempt to leverage the domestic–foreign dimensions in a strategic way, including strengthening China's relations with its own diaspora overseas that number at about 60 million. For when it comes to TikTok, the foreign ministry does not have a presence, and only a few Chinese embassies have established accounts. Interestingly, on TikTok, the Chinese government and the Ministry of Culture and Tourism, which runs state-affiliate media outlet *China Daily*, have witnessed an increase in the number of Chinese Cultural Centers (CCCs) with a presence on the platform. CCCs now count dozens of accounts on the platform, but only very few have large followings, including in Cairo and Bangkok. Content on those accounts follows the same playbook used initially for Twitter—namely building a large audience with click-bates, memes, and polarizing, confrontational content.

Concluding Discussion

TikTok has grown into a digital platform which the diplomatic realm can no longer disregard. Or—that is—if one chose to not engage with it, this would also send a message. Not only do diplomatic actors need to consider the security dimensions of downloading any app to their phones feared to provide access to contact-lists, photos, message, records of phone-calls, and other information stored on their device—but one also needs to acknowledge that it is a *political* decision to establish a visual presence on such a platform. To be clear, such visible endorsement not only covers whether you start an account in the organizations' name, but also if you campaign on TikTok through influencers—implicitly communicating to your publics on TikTok that *they* should remain in an environment fitted with an app that you yourself are not comfortable with installing. Drawing upon the literature's emphasis on the possibilities and risks of TikTok, the empirical presentation has shown the dilemmas of walking this line for diplomatic actors. But more essential to this paper, the critical discussions around TikTok have opened up a wider discussion on how the algorithmic structure of platforms could be used for geopolitical influence. This leads to a new dimension of concern for digital diplomats, as how political influence could be embedded in the very design of platforms' algorithmic structures—either influencing or influenced by digital diplomatic practices.

The centre lies in a shift from previously journalistic gatekeepers in the old media landscape to an acknowledgement of the algorithmic gatekeepers in the digital landscape. As Gray (2021: 2) phrases it, 'digital platforms are information gatekeepers, with the capacity to influence social conditions by determining the ideas and information that are shared and amplified across vast socio-technical systems'. In this, critics have argued that TikTok silence political discussions through their algorithms (Peterson-Salahuddin; Zeng and Kaye, 2022), supported by documents from internal leaks of content-moderation policies. For example, *The Intercept* (2020) reported how moderators were instructed to supress videos with too ugly, poor, or disabled people, and censor political speech deemed harmful for the Chinese state. Another leak reported by *The Guardian* (2019) argued that obtained content-moderation documents revealed how ByteDance 'is advancing Chinese foreign policy aims abroad through the app'.

> The guidelines divide banned material into two categories: some content is marked as a 'violation', which sees it deleted from the site entirely, and can lead to a user being banned from the service. But lesser infringements are marked as 'visible to self', which leaves content up but limits its distribution through TikTok's algorithmically-curated feed.
>
> (Guardian, 2019)

Learning from these stories, digital diplomacy should not only direct their future focus in studies towards the content of campaigns by digital diplomacy actors, but incorporate a deeper analysis of the mediums and their algorithmic character to gain a deeper understanding of the forces of influence at play. Even more important, this chapter hopes to serve as a first step towards a theoretical conversation in digital diplomacy on the geopolitics of algorithmic governance, and how platforms are used to shape public political debates. Just as China was sceptical about Facebook—eventually banned in most parts of the country—we see the same geopolitical scepticism in reverse in e.g. India's and the US government's attitude towards TikTok. This means that inquiries into the geopolitical dimensions in algorithmic governance can be refocused to studies of all platforms, not just TikTok. Furthermore, on a strategic level one can explore how TikTok's efforts to support certain organizations such as branches of the UN and various governments can be seen as part of their own efforts to establish their reputation as legitimate actors—hopefully paving the way for other sceptical organizations to follow suit in establishing their presence on the platform, and by extension attracting previously sceptical audiences as new users. They are therefore not simply striving to attract *more* organizations to join but, more importantly, focusing strategically on *which* to attract for organizational endorsement. It is these processes influencing the underlying, embedded, structures of influence of each platform that should attract more attention among the future scholarship in digital diplomacy—either incorporated as dimensions in case studies of campaigns or as the sole focus in studies of how geopolitical influence has travelled to the digital domain.

SUGGESTED READING

Gray, J. E. (2021). The geopolitics of 'platforms': The TikTok challenge. *Internet Policy Review, 10*(2), 1–26. doi:10.14763/2021.2.1557

Kaye, D. B. V., Chen, X., and Zeng, J. (2021). The co-evolution of two Chinese mobile short video apps: Parallel platformization of Douyin and TikTok. *Mobile Media & Communication, 9*(2), 229–253. doi:10.1177/2050157920952120

Stokel-Walker, C. (2021). *TikTok Boom: China's Dynamite App and the Superpower Race for Social Media*. Canbury: Canbury Press.

Gritsenko, D., Markham, A., Potzsch, H., and Wijermars, M. (2022). Algorithms, contexts, governance: An introduction to the special issue. *New Media & Society*, 24(4), 835–844. doi:10.1177/14614448221079037

Zeng, J., and Kaye, D. B. V. (2022). From content moderation to visibility moderation: A case study of platform governance on TikTok. *Policy and Internet*, 14(1), 79–95. doi:10.1002/poi3.287

REFERENCES

Aronczyk, A. (2021). A look at the fallout of TikTok ban in India. *NPR*, 15 January. Retrieved from https://www.npr.org/2021/01/15/957371287/a-look-at-the-fallout-of-tiktok-ban-in-india

Aytac, U. (2022). Digital domination: Social media and contestatory democracy. *Political Studies*, 0(0), 1–20. doi:10.1177/00323217221096564

Balaban, D. C., and Szambolics, J. (2022). A proposed model of self-perceived authenticity of social media influencers. *Media and Communication*, 10(1), 235–246. doi:10.17645/mac.v10i1.4765

Bennett, N. (2021). 1 February Available at: https://www.tiktok.com/@naftalibennett_official (Accessed: 19 January 2023).

Bhuiyan, J. (2022). Why did the US just ban TikTok from government-issued cellphones? *The Guardian*, 31 December. Retrieved from https://www.theguardian.com/technology/2022/dec/30/explainer-us-congress-tiktok-ban

Bitetti, D. (2021). 17 December. Available at: https://www.tiktok.com/t/ZTRpUodSy/ (Accessed: 19 January 2023).

Botella, E. (2019). TikTok admits it suppressed videos by disabled, queer, and fat creators. *Slate*, 4 December. Available at: https://slate.com/technology/2019/12/tiktok-disabled-users-vid eos- suppressed.html

Brennan, M. (2020). *Attention factory: The story of TikTok and China's ByteDance*. China Channel.

Bukele, N. (2021). 31 January. Available at: https://www.tiktok.com/@nayibbukele/video/6923 735027192777989 (Accessed: 19 January 2023).

BuzzFeed. (2022). Leaked audio from 80 internal TikTok meetings shows that US user data has been repeatedly accessed from China. 17 June. Retrieved from https://www.buzzfeednews.com/article/emilybakerwhite/tiktok-tapes-us-user-data-china-bytedance-access

Cervi, L., and Marin-Llado, C. (2022). Freepalestine on TikTok: From performative activism to (meaningful) playful activism. *Journal of International and Intercultural Communication*, 15(4), 414–434. doi:10.1080/17513057.2022.2131883

Cervi, L., and Marin-Llado, C. (2021). What are political parties doing on TikTok? The Spanish case. *Profesional De La Informacion*, 30(4), 1–17. doi:10.3145/epi.2021.jul.03

Civila, S., and Jaramillo-Dent, D. (2022). #Mixedcouples on TikTok: Performative hybridization and identity in the face of discrimination. *Social Media + Society*, 8(3), 1–14. doi:10.1177/20563051221122464

CNBC. (2021). TikTok insiders say social media company is tightly controlled by Chinese parent ByteDance. 25 June. Retrieved from https://www.cnbc.com/2021/06/25/tiktok-insid ers-say-chinese-parent-bytedance-in-control.html

Darvin, R. (2022). Design, resistance and the performance of identity on TikTok. *Discourse Context & Media*, *46*, 1–11. doi:10.1016/j.dcm.2022.100591

DigiTips (2022). 4 May. Available at: https://twitter.com/digitips/status/1521775574452166657 (Accessed on 19 January 2023).

Duda, A. (2020). 1 February. Available at: https://www.tiktok.com/@andrzejdudanatiktoku (Accessed: 19 January 2023).

Embassy of France (2022). 1 April. Available at: https://www.tiktok.com/@franceintheus/video/7081644278761524523 (Accessed: 19 January 2023).

Forbes. (2022a). The project, assigned to a Beijing-led team, would have involved accessing location data from some U.S. users' devices without their knowledge or consent. 20 October. Retrieved from https://www.forbes.com/sites/emilybaker-white/2022/10/20/tiktok-bytedance-surveillance-american-user-data/?sh=cde545e6c2db

Forbes. (2022b). TikTok spied on Forbes journalists. 22 December. Retrieved from https://www.forbes.com/sites/emilybaker-white/2022/12/22/tiktok-tracks-forbes-journalists-bytedance/?sh=30c035397da5

Foster, J., and Baker, J. (2022). Muscles, makeup, and femboys: Analyzing TikTok's 'radical' masculinities. *Social Media + Society*, *8*(3), 1–14. doi:10.1177/20563051221126040

Gentry, B. A. (2022). TikTok's 'Republicansona' trend as cross-party cross-dressing: Legible normativity, (in)dividual representation and performing subversive ambiguity. *Convergence-the International Journal of Research into New Media Technologies*, *0*(0), 1–21. doi:10.1177/13548565221113469

German Mission to UN (2021). 9 June. Available at: https://twitter.com/GermanyUN/status/1402622981394911233 (Accessed: 23 February 2022).

Grandinetti, J., and Bruinsma, J. (2023). The affective algorithms of conspiracy TikTok. *Journal of Broadcasting & Electronic Media*, *67*(3), 274–293. doi:10.1080/08838151.2022.2140806

Gray, J. E. (2021). The geopolitics of 'platforms': The TikTok challenge. *Internet Policy Review*, *10*(2), 1–26. doi:10.14763/2021.2.1557

Gritsenko, D., Markham, A., Potzsch, H., and Wijermars, M. (2022). Algorithms, contexts, governance: An introduction to the special issue. *New Media & Society*, *24*(4), 835–844. doi:10.1177/14614448221079037

Guardian, The (2019). Revealed: How TikTok censors videos that do not please Beijing. 25 September. Retrieved from https://www.theguardian.com/technology/2019/sep/25/revealed-how-tiktok-censors-videos-that-do-not-please-beijing

Haberman, L. (2020). 13 July. Available at: https://www.tiktok.com/t/ZTRpU6VEA/ (Accessed: 19 January 2023).

Hartung, C., Hendry, N. A., Albury, K., Johnston, S., and Welch, R. (2023) Teachers of TikTok: Glimpses and gestures in the performance of professional identity. *Media International Australia*, *186*(1), 81–96. doi:10.1177/1329878X211068836

Hautea, S., Parks, P., Takahashi, B., and Zeng, J. (2021). Showing they care (or don't): Affective publics and ambivalent climate activism on TikTok. *Social Media + Society*, *7*(2), 1–14. doi:10.1177/20563051211012344

Helmond, A. (2015). The platformization of the web: Making web data platform ready. *Social media+ society*, *1*(2), 2056305115603080.

Huber, B., Lepenies, R., Baena, L. Q., and Allgaier, J. (2022). Beyond individualized responsibility attributions? How eco influencers communicate sustainability on TikTok. *Environmental Communication-a Journal of Nature and Culture*, *16*(6), 713–722. doi:10.1080/17524032.2022.2131868

Intercept, The (2020). Invisible censorship. 16 March. Retrieved from https://theintercept.com/2020/03/16/tiktok-app-moderators-users-discrimination/

International Federation of Red Cross and Red Crescent Societies (IFRC) (2019). IFRC joins forces with social media giant TikTok to recruit climate volunteers [Press release]. 7 October. Available at: https://www.climatecentre.org/711/ifrc-joins-forces-with-social-media-giant-tiktok-to-recruit-climate-volunteers/ (Accessed: 16 February 2022).

Israel Arabic (2021). 1 February. Available at: https://www.tiktok.com/@israelarabic/video/6924308760324279554 (Accessed: 19 January 2023).

Israel in Spanish (2021). 15 May. Available at: https://www.tiktok.com/@israelinspanish/video/6962486926041435393 (Accessed: 19 January 2023).

Jia, L. R., and Ruan, L. (2020). Going global: Comparing Chinese mobile applications' data and user privacy governance at home and abroad. *Internet Policy Review*, 9(3), 1–22. doi:10.14763/2020.3.1502

Kaur-Gill, S. (2023). The cultural customization of TikTok: Subaltern migrant workers and their digital cultures. *Media International Australia*, 186(1), 29–47. doi:10.1177/1329878X221110279

Kaye, D. B. V., Chen, X., and Zeng, J. (2021). The co-evolution of two Chinese mobile short video apps: Parallel platformization of Douyin and TikTok. *Mobile Media & Communication*, 9(2), 229–253. doi:10.1177/2050157920952120

Kocher, T. (2020). Interview by Andreas Sandre, 12 August.

Krutrok, M. E., and Akerlund, M. (2023) Through a white lens: Black victimhood, visibility, and whiteness in the Black Lives Matter movement on TikTok. *Information Communication & Society*, 26(10), 1996–2014. doi:10.1080/1369118X.2022.2065211

Kuzmanovic, A. (2020). 17 June. Available at: https://www.tiktok.com/t/ZTRpUted4/ (Accessed: 19 January 2023).

Lapid, Y. (2021). 1 February. Available at: https://www.tiktok.com/@yair_lapid (Accessed: 19 January 2023).

Lasso, G. (2021). 26 February. Available at: https://www.tiktok.com/@guillermolasso/video/6933381188698541318 (Accessed: 19 January 2023).

Liang, M. (2022). The end of social media? How data attraction model in the algorithmic media reshapes the attention economy. *Media Culture & Society*, 44(6), 1110–1131. doi:10.1177/01634437221077168

Liu, J. H., and Yang, L. (2022). 'Dual-Track' platform governance on content: A comparative study between China and United States. *Policy and Internet*, 14(2), 304–323. doi:10.1002/poi3.307

Lopez, N. A., Sidorenko-Bautista, P., and Giacomelli, F. (2021). Beyond challenges and viral dance moves: TikTok as a vehicle for disinformation and fact-checking in Spain, Portugal, Brazil, and the USA. *Analisi-Quaderns De Comunicacio I Cultura*, 64, 65–84. doi:10.5565/rev/analisi.3411

Lorenz, T. (2022). 'The White House is briefing TikTok stars about the war in Ukraine'. *The Washington Post*, 11 March. Available at: https://www.washingtonpost.com/technology/2022/03/11/tik-tok-ukraine-white-house/ (Accessed: 14 March 2022).

Ma, W. (2021). *The Digital War: How China's Tech Power Shapes the Future of AI, Blockchain and Cyberspace*. John Wiley & Sons.

Macron, E. (2020a). 7 July. Available at: https://www.tiktok.com/@emmanuelmacron/video/6846719957561052421 (Accessed: 19 January 2023).

Macron, E. (2020b). *Covid*. 18 December. Available at: https://www.tiktok.com/@emmanuelmacron/video/6907655341060738305 (Accessed: 19 January 2023).

Malala Fund (2020). Get featured on Malala Fund's TikTok!. Available at: https://malalafund.typeform.com/to/eFp7lrGw (Accessed: 19 January 2023).

Mazumdar, S. (2022). Loving the enemy app: Resistance versus professionalism in 'post-TikTok' India. *Global Media and China*, 7(3), 340–356. doi:10.1177/20594364221116018

McCluskey, M. (2020). These TikTok creators say they're still being suppressed for posting Black lives matter content. *Time*, 22 July. Available at: https://time.com/5863350/tiktok-black-creators/

Miao, W. S., Huang, D. L., and Huang, Y. (2021). More than business: The de-politicisation and re-politicisation of TikTok in the media discourses of China, America and India (2017-2020). *Media International Australia*, 186(1), 97–114. doi:10.1177/1329878X211013919

Mishra, M., Yan, P., and Schroeder, R. (2022). TikTok politics: Tit for tat on the India-China cyberspace frontier. *International Journal of Communication*, 16, 814–839.

New York Post (2022). Leaked TikTok memo told employees to 'downplay the China association'. 27 July. Retrieved from https://nypost.com/2022/07/27/leaked-tiktok-memo-told-workers-to-downplay-the-china-association/

Peterson-Salahuddin, C. (2022). 'Pose': Examining moments of 'digital' dark sousveillance on TikTok. *New Media & Society*, 0(0), 1–20. doi:10.1177/14614448221080480

Purayil, M. P. (2019). Why did China's foreign ministry make its debut on Weibo? *The Diplomat*, 5 June. Retrieved from https://thediplomat.com/2019/06/why-did-chinas-foreign-minis try-make-its-debut-on-weibo/

Regmi, B. (2020). 8 September. Available at: https://www.tiktok.com/t/ZTRpUTaRN/ (Accessed: 19 January 2023).

Savic, M. (2021). From Musical.ly to TikTok: Social construction of 2020's most downloaded short-video app. *International Journal of Communication*, 15, 3173–3194.

Singer, P. W., and Brooking, E. T. (2018). *Like War: The Weaponization of Social Media*. Eamon Dolan Books.

Sot, I. (2022). Fostering intimacy on TikTok: A platform that 'listens' and 'creates a safe space'. *Media Culture & Society*, 44(8), 1490–1507. doi:10.1177/01634437221104709

Steele, C. K. (2021). Black feminist pleasure on TikTok: An ode to Hurston's 'Characteristics of Negro Expression'. *Womens Studies in Communication*, 44(4), 463–469. doi:10.1080/07491409.2021.1987822

Stokel-Walker, C. (2021). *TikTok Boom: China's Dynamite App and the Superpower Race for Social Media*. Canbury: Canbury Press.

Sued, G. E., Castillo-Gonzalez, M. C., Pedraza, C., Flores-Marquez, D., Alamo, S., Ortiz, M., ... Arroyo, R. E. (2022). Vernacular visibility and algorithmic resistance in the public expression of Latin American feminism. *Media International Australia*, 183(1), 60–76. doi:10.1177/1329878X211067571

The White House (2021). Olivia Rodrigo, President Biden, and Dr. Fauci talk vaccines at the White House. 27 July. Available at: https://www.youtube.com/watch?v=2wHOtsQ44HA (Accessed: 19 January 2023).

TikTok (2022). TikTok for Good. Retrieved from https://www.tiktok.com/forgood

TikTok (2021). The Hon. Julia Gillard AC goes LIVE on TikTok, in conversation with the creator who put her iconic 'misogyny speech' back in the headlines in 2020 [Press release]. 17 March. Available at: https://newsroom.tiktok.com/en-au/the-hon-julia-gillard-ac-goes-live-on-tiktok (Accessed: 23 February 2022).

TikTok (n.d.). Supporting our community through COVID-19. Available at: https://www.tik tok.com/safety/en/covid-19/ (Accessed: 23 February 2022).

United Nations Children's Fund (UNICEF) (2021). ONE, UNICEF and African Union join forces with TikTok to strengthen vaccine confidence in Africa [Press release]. 26 August. Available at: https://www.unicef.org/southafrica/press-releases/one-unicef-and-african-union-join-forces-tiktok-strengthen-vaccine-confidence-africa (Accessed: 16 February 2022).

United Nations Children's Fund (UNICEF) (2019). 18 October. Available at: https://www.tiktok.com/tag/TheRealChallenge (Accessed: 19 January 2023).

Van Dijck, J., Poell, T., and De Waal, M. (2018). *The Platform Society: Public Values in a Connective World*. Oxford University Press.

Vizcaino-Verdu, A., and Aguaded, I. (2022). #ThisIsMeChallenge and music for empowerment of marginalized groups on TikTok. *Media and Communication*, *10*(1), 157–172. doi:10.17645/mac.v10i1.4715

Yu, H. Q., and Li, L. Z. (2022). Chinese digital platforms in Australia: From market and politics to governance. *Media International Australia*, *185*(1), 93–109. doi:10.1177/1329878X221095594

Zeng, J., and Abidin, C. (2021). '#OkBoomer, time to meet the Zoomers': studying the memefication of intergenerational politics on TikTok. *Information Communication & Society*, *24*(16), 2459–2481. doi:10.1080/1369118X.2021.1961007

Zeng, J., and Kaye, D. B. V. (2022). From content moderation to visibility moderation: A case study of platform governance on TikTok. *Policy and Internet*, *14*(1), 79–95. doi:10.1002/poi3.287

PART III

DIPLOMATIC INSTITUTIONS

CHAPTER 16

THE DIGITAL HYBRIDIZATION OF MINISTRIES OF FOREIGN AFFAIRS: THE CASE OF THE NORDIC AND BALTIC STATES

CORNELIU BJOLA AND DIDZIS KĻAVIŅŠ

INTRODUCTION

A full decade has now passed since ministries of foreign affairs (MFAs) and embassies started to actively embrace social media as a tool of policy promotion and public engagement. The enthusiasm of the early adopters (US State Department in 2007, UK FCO and Brazil MFA in 2009, and Swedish and Indian MFAs in 2010) soon turned contagious and within a decade the majority of heads of governments and MFAs around the world had opened social media accounts. The fast rate of digital adoption by MFAs and diplomats has been undoubtedly impressive not least because MFAs are known as rather rigid institutions, with a penchant for cultivating tradition, procedure, and risk-avoidance (Roberts, 2017) and with a track record of incremental adaptation to technological innovations.

MFAs' experimentation with digital tools has mainly focused on developing bridges between the online 'front-stage' and the offline diplomatic 'back-stage', especially in public diplomacy, crisis communication, or diaspora engagement (Bjola and Holmes, 2015; Spry, 2019; Cull, 2019). There is little evidence to suggest, at least at this stage, that the traditional diplomatic functions of representation, communication, and negotiation have been made redundant by the arrival of digital technologies. Rather than revolution, we argue, hybridization is the term that best captures and describes the current process of digital transformation of the diplomatic practice. Fears of traditional diplomacy going extinct in the digital age are therefore misplaced as MFA's efforts focus on adapting diplomacy to the digital age rather than on creating digital alternatives to diplomatic functions. Therefore, the interesting question to ask is *how exactly is diplomacy being hybridized by digital technologies and with what effect?*

Drawing on concepts and insights from the assemblage theory (DeLanda, 2016, 2019; Latour, 2007), this contribution advances an original theoretical account to describe and explain the process of digital hybridization of MFAs' diplomatic activities. It will be thus argued that *hybridization involves a process by which digital technologies and diplomatic agency come together to form new entities, which we call digital assemblages.* Importantly, the purpose of these new entities cannot be reduced to the functions of the constitutive elements, but it is the product of the interaction between them. Diplomatic agency is augmented or diluted through relations with digital technologies, but the latter also apply themselves on diplomatic tasks, objectives, or methods. The internal coherence of the resulting digital assemblages varies depending on the degree of digital–human compatibility and on the type of meaning that is being constructed to explain the purpose and identity of the assemblage. Building on this insight we describe three possible forms of digital hybridization—the compact, the mosaic, and the canvas, and discuss the type of relations that constitutes and empowers them, as well as the influence they exert on the way in which diplomats conduct themselves.

The chapter promises to address three important issues that studies of digital diplomacy have failed to properly examine thus far. The first one relates to the difference that digital technology makes to the practice of diplomacy. We already know that many diplomatic activities, ranging from public diplomacy to crisis communication, are conducted digitally. What we do not know, however, is how deep this integration has infiltrated the surface of MFAs' activities, and how much it has transformed the boundary between diplomacy and digital technology. Second, there is limited understanding of why MFAs vary in their efforts to integrate digital technologies in their work and, equally importantly, of the factors that may account for and explain these differences. Third, by advancing an innovative framework for assessing the scope and depth of the digital transformation, the study aims to steer the debate away from the narrow focus on social media communication and to encourage the exploration of the broader technological processes that contribute to the acceleration of the digital hybridization of diplomacy.

To this end, the study will compare the digital diplomatic efforts undertaken by three Nordic countries (Denmark, Finland, and Sweden), in one group, and three Baltic countries (Estonia, Latvia, and Lithuania), in another group. The case study selection was informed by three considerations. First, we wanted to make sure that countries shared sufficiently similar attributes (diplomatic influence, geopolitical context, and domestic regime) so that processes of digital hybridization could be reliably compared. Second, we were interested to compare MFAs with an active interest in digital technologies, but at different stages on the hybridization path so that we could better trace and understand differences in MFAs' approaches to digital adaptation. Third, we sought to include cases that would allow us to compare different institutional responses to digital integration pressures, a factor that could help explain the level of coherence of the resulting digital diplomatic assemblages.

Methodologically, the paper relies on the qualitative data collected through in-depth interviews with diplomats from the Nordic and Baltic countries, which were conducted in person before the arrival of the Covid-19 pandemic. Interviewees were chosen with a view to provide a broader representativity to the sample in terms of position (embassy vs MFA) and status (low vs high ranking official). The interview data was then processed using the NVivo 12.0 software following the four grounded theory strategies described by Charmaz (2008): coding (extracting common themes from the data), memo writing (capturing ideas in progress), theoretical sampling (developing tentative categories), and theoretical saturation (refining the properties of a theoretical category in light of existing data). The analysis has led to the formulation of four categories (objectives, processes, effects, and challenges), which have provided the theoretical foundation for examining the formation of the three digital assemblages, the compact, the mosaic, and the canvas.

THEORIZING DIGITAL HYBRIDIZATION

Diplomacy in the Digital Age

To begin with, it is important to recall that what is commonly referred to as the 'Digital Age' in the public discourse is actually the product of the fourth generation of digital technology, the algorithmic-driven platform society of social media companies (Karpf, 2020). As explained in first chapter, What distinguishes the latest generation of digital technology from the others are the "grammar rules" that inform and shape digital engagement (visual simplicity, emotional framing, computational personalization, and engagement hybridization.) as well as the underlying mechanisms of data collection, analysis, and circulation that inform how digital technologies operate (Van Dijck et al., 2018: 32). In order to truly understand the impact of digital technologies on diplomacy, we therefore need a theoretical model that can explain, in a more comprehensive fashion, how digital technologies weave themselves through the gathering, analysis, and use of data into the texture of diplomatic practice. This brings us, in turn, to the idea of hybridization.

Assemblage Thinking

To understand digital hybridization, we first need to develop an account of how the materiality of digital technology interacts with the social-institutional component of diplomatic practice. As one of the leading theoretical paradigms to study processes of interaction and entanglement between the social and the material, assemblage theory is an ideal approach for addressing such questions.[1] According to Deleuze and Guattari

---

[1] It should be noted, however, there are actually two schools of thought, Actor-Network Theory or ANT (Bueger, 2013) and assemblage thinking, which share many assumptions on socio-material

(1987), the assemblage is neither a part nor a whole, because the properties of the component parts can never explain the relations which constitute the whole. Nail (2017) insists that assemblages are composed of a basic structure including a condition (external relations that hold the assemblage together), elements (ingredients that make up the assemblage) which can be added, subtracted, and recombined with one another, and agents (operators that connect the elements together according to conditions). Importantly, assemblages are also seen as productive as they generate new territorial organizations, new behaviours, new expressions, new actors, and new realities (Müller 2015: 29). DeLanda, whose reformulation of Deleuze and Guattari's original concept has gone probably the furthest, insists that the assemblage could be best understood as a concept with 'knobs' that can be set to different values (2016: 3), an idea that carries good analytical value for our discussion further below on digital hybridization.

Assemblage thinking has made inroads in International Relations (IR), although at slower pace than the ANT counterpart. In one of the first IR books on the topic, Acuto and Curtis (2014: 9, 11) introduced assemblage thinking as a 'method' or *modus operandi* for social scientists to destabilize reified meaning and anthropocentric rationalities in IR scholarship (state, power, ideology). More substantively, assemblage theory has been invoked, mainly in a heuristic fashion, to describe the global ordering of security (Austin, 2019) or the generation of professional expertise (Leander, 2018). The work of Jason Dittmer stands out in particular for his use of assemblage theory to develop an account of posthuman geopolitics (2014), to rethink foreign policy in terms of assemblages that states enter with each other in order to enact their collective agency (2017), and to trace the formation of diplomatic articulations of the British Foreign Office and Overseas Territories (McConnell and Dittmer, 2018; Dittmer, 2016). It is mainly the work of DeLanda, Dittmer, McConnell, and, to a lesser extent, the collection of articles in Acuto and Curtis' volume (2014) that will allow us in the next section to develop an assemblage-focused framework for theorizing digital hybridization.

Digital Hybridization as Assemblage Formation

Central to understanding how the assemblage takes shape and how it works, there is an important distinction between the enduring states or *properties* of the components that make up the assemblage and the dispositions or *capacities* that arise from the interaction between them. As Hoffman and Novak point out, properties are measurable characteristics that specify *what the entity is*. Capacities are directional, they are the result of how properties interact, and they specify *what the entity does* (2018: 1184). The relevance of this distinction is twofold: on the one hand, it explains how components

---

ordering and effects, but they have different intellectual roots and conceptual aspirations. Unlike ANT, which is more action- and outward-oriented, assemblage thinking prioritizes the internal constitution of relationships between social and material entities, and how different entities (individuals, institutions, or technologies) shape each other and form new wholes.

come together to form an assemblage: wholes emerge in a bottom-up way, depending causally on their components (upward causality), but they also have a top-down influence on them. Once an assemblage takes shape, it starts acting as a source of limitation and opportunity for its components (downward causality) (DeLanda, 2016: 21). On the other hand, the distinction also makes clear that the components' capacities, rather than their properties, are particularly relevant for understanding how the resultant assemblages behave. While the properties of a material are relatively finite, its capacities are infinite because they are the result of the interaction with an infinite set of other components (Dittmer, 2014: 387). What matters is the 'knob' that can be set, through interaction, to different values and thus to yield distinct forms of digitally hybrid assemblages. For some settings, the assemblage will take the form of a service delivery, while with other settings it will evolve into a digital entity with its own logic of action.

DeLanda (2016: 22) argues that two parameters are responsible for how the 'knob' may change these settings. The first one is the degree of *territorialization*, a parameter which describes the ability of an assemblage to homogenize its components either spatially, by delineating the physical boundaries within which the assemblage is expected to operate, and/or by generating stable and self-reproductible connections between the properties of the constitutive components. The second parameter is the degree of *coding*, which describes the meaning that helps consolidate the identity and coherence of the assemblage. When interacting through their capacities, the components of the assemblage may play either a material (technical) or expressive (symbolic) role, the significance of which is emphasized through coding. By tuning the coding knob on the material side (tech performance), agents may induce the assemblage to cement itself around the service delivery mode. By contrast, strong coding on the expressive side (social value), may raise the symbolic visibility of the assemblage, which in turn may steer the process of digital hybridization on a more ambitious and complex trajectory.

Building on these ideas, we *define digital hybridization as the ordering process by which digital technologies and diplomatic tasks come together to form relatively stable configurations (digital assemblages) with a distinct internal logic of action.* The definition combines two key elements which researchers can use to empirically unpack the process of digital hybridization: the first one calls attention to the uneven topography forming through the co-junction and co-evolution of digital and diplomatic properties and the need to understand the ordering mechanisms that hold the assemblage together; the second element highlights the inherently dynamic aspect of the assemblage and its sensitivity to change and mutation, which could be captured by tracing the agential dispositions to arise at the border between the digital and physical world.

The empirical analysis should lead to results that approximate the spectrum of possibilities presented in Figure 16.1. The figure incorporates the tetravalence of assemblages concept put forth by Sesay, Oh, and Ramirez (2016: 6) into the realm of digital hybridization. Weak assemblages (the left-bottom corner) are likely to form when the properties of digital technologies and diplomatic tasks do not match well, and little effort is made through territorialization or coding to homogenize the material functions or expressive meanings of the two components. The agential disposition of

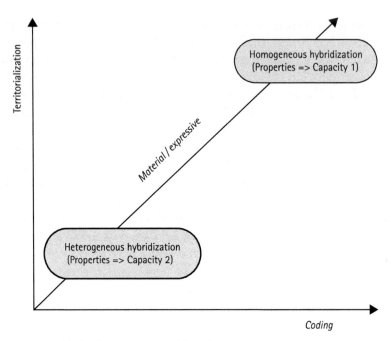

FIGURE 16.1 Digital hybridization as assemblage formation
Source: Author, using data from Sesay, Oh, and Ramirez (2016).

the assemblage to generate new functions remains marginal, while the lack of internal coherence limits the ability of the assemblage to exert downward pressure on digital and diplomatic properties. By contrast, strong forms of assemblages (the top-right corner) are likely to result from situations in which digital and diplomatic functions align well with each other. The agential disposition of the assemblage is strengthened through active efforts of territorialization and coding, which in turn may facilitate the generation of new functions. Enhanced internal coherence may also exert downward pressure on the digital and diplomatic components to fine-tune the mechanisms by which they function together.

The empirical analysis will proceed in two steps. The first part is primarily quantitative and involves the coding, using the NVivo 12.0 software, of the common themes arising in the interviews conducted with Nordic and Baltic diplomats (see Appendix 1). Drawing on grounded theory, these common themes are then developed into analytical categories that reflect properties and capacities of the emergent digitally hybrid assemblages. The second part of the analysis is qualitative and explores how the two 'knob' parameters (territorialization and coding) have contributed to processes of digital hybridization inside the MFAs. To understand the broader context in which the process of hybridization takes place, the analysis will be preceded by a short overview of recent digital efforts undertaken by the Nordic and Baltic MFAs to upgrade their digital capacities and know-how.

Studying Digital Hybridization

Digital Diplomacy 1.0 in the Nordic and Baltic States

Digital diplomacy has followed an uneven trajectory in both the Nordic and the Baltic MFAs. The ministry of foreign affairs of Sweden, one of the early adopters, is perhaps the most visible example of how a digital ecosystem could be quickly established with strong leadership (see Table 16.1). It was Carl Bildt, the former minister of foreign affairs, who urged his fellow diplomats to 'be at the absolute cutting edge in digital diplomacy efforts' (2013), and who insisted that that all embassies and ambassadors must have Twitter and Facebook accounts (Sandre, 2015: 81). Similarly, Latvia gained international attention in the field of digital diplomacy thanks to the efforts of former Foreign Minister Edgars Rinkēvičs, one of the early and leading exponents of Twitter diplomacy.

After Bildt's departure, the Swedish MFA continued to develop its digital capacity and to deploy it effectively in support of his foreign policy priorities, such as the recent feminist agenda (Löfven and Linde, 2019) through a range of digital advocacy campaigns such as #MoreWomenMorePeace, #SheTrades, #SheDecides, and #GenderEqualWorld (Aggestam and Rosamond, 2019: 45). The Latvian MFA, on the other hand, has failed to build on its early start and to leverage the power of digital tools in a similar way as Sweden, mainly due to the absence of a comprehensive digital strategy.

The Danish MFA moved somewhat slowly into the digital realm, but by 2018 it was contributing to thirty-eight initiatives, as part of the new governmental Digital Growth Strategy, aimed at strengthening and improving Denmark's position as an attractive digital hub. It also took over the 'cutting edge' torch from Sweden by creating in 2017 the world's first 'tech ambassador' to Silicon Valley, with the goal to promote Denmark as an IT-friendly place for investment, develop collaboration with technology companies, and forge partnerships on artificial intelligence research. Lithuania also had a slow digital start, with no coherent strategy and limited capacity. However, in recent years, Lithuania has become one of the best digitally connected foreign services, with a comprehensive and innovative digital strategy that turned the MFA into a member of a 'relatively small club of digital diplomatic powerhouses' (Bjola and Paulauskas, 2019). As a key part of its digital strategy, Lithuania has made it a priority to engage not only with foreign target audiences, but also with resident Lithuanian citizens as well as with representatives of the Lithuanian diaspora community (Birka and Kļaviņš, 2020: 120, 126).

Activities carried out by the Finnish foreign service in recent years indicate that its digital diplomacy is mainly focused on developing a distinct nation brand (Eksell and Fjällhed, 2019), which seeks to build on Finland's reputation as the world's happiest country in the world. In 2015, Finland was the first country to launch a set of national emojis, which reached 154 million people and won an international viral campaign award in Berlin. More recently, the MFA launched a new cheerful and award-winning initiative—Capital of Metal—based on Finland's position as the country with the

Table 16.1 The digital presence of Baltic and Nordic MFAs

		Twitter		
Countries	Date	Number of followers	Tweets	Title
Latvia	August 2011	33.5K	14.7K	Latvian MFA
	October 2010	25.8K	18.1K	Ārlietu ministrija (Latvian version)
Lithuania	December 2010	113.2K	25.4K	Lithuanian MFA
Estonia	March 2009	63.7K	12.9K	Estonian MFA
Denmark	April 2013	54K	16.4K	Denmark MFA
Sweden	May 2010	77.4K	13.3K	Swedish Ministry for Foreign Affairs
	May 2010	63.6K	11K	Utrikesdepartementet (Swedish version)
Finland	March 2011	130.8K	28.2K	MFA Finland

		Facebook	
	Date	Number of followers	Title
Latvia	19 August 2011	9.8K	Ministry of Foreign Affairs of the Republic of Latvia
	24 March 2016	12K	Latvijas Republikas Ārlietu ministrija (Latvian version)
Lithuania	10 April 2012	54K	Užsienio reikalų ministerija (Lithuanian)
Estonia	5 March 2009	29K	Estonian Ministry of Foreign Affairs / Välisministeerium
Denmark	22 March 2017	23K	Udenrigsministeriet (Danish)
	14 October 2008	297K	Denmark.dk*
Sweden	10 June 2014	120K	Swedish Ministry for Foreign Affairs
Finland	15 February 2011	35K	Ulkoministeriö – utrikesministeriet

		Instagram		
	Date	Number of followers	Number of posts	Title
Latvia	11 March 2019	3 756	726	arlietuministrija
Lithuania	27 October 2021	1 291	236	urministerija
Estonia	15 May 2020	2 173	187	mfaestonia
Denmark	3 February 2021	6 840	840	udenrigsministeriet
	29 October 2012	126K	1 230	denmarkdotdk*
Sweden	11 October 2018	6 051	626	swedishmfa
Finland	4 November 2015	33.9K	1 340	thisisfinlandofficial**

*Denmark.dk is Denmark's official internet website managed by the Ministry of Foreign Affairs of Denmark.

** ThisisFINLAND is produced by the Ministry for Foreign Affairs of Finland and published by the Finland Promotion Board.

Source: The MFAs' official accounts on Twitter, Facebook, and Instagram (last accessed on 11 August 2023).

highest number of metal bands per capita in the world. The Estonian MFA has also used digital tools to brand itself, especially on Twitter and Facebook (see Table 16.1), but from a different angle. Drawing on its experience in cyber security and digital society, Estonia has launched several initiatives to highlight its digital leadership, including, for instance, the virtual residency project, which offers anyone in the world the opportunity to become an Estonian e-Resident. The Estonian MFA also established a new Department for Cyber Diplomacy in the autumn of 2019, which should enable Estonia to participate more effectively in the global cybersecurity debate.

Digital Hybridization in Practice

The common themes of digital hybridization that we have identified in our interviews can be grouped into four main categories: objectives, processes, effects, and challenges (see Table 16.2). Objectives range, for instance, from general aspirations about increasing the influence of MFAs in the online medium, to specific policy areas in which digital platforms can make tangible contributions, to even the tactics adopted in support of these other objectives (e.g., task management, audience engagement). Processes include the drivers that have prompted the MFAs to embrace digital platforms in their work, the changes the latter have introduced to the way in which MFAs conduct their business such as in public diplomacy or crisis communication, the conditions for the recalibration of the sphere of autonomy that embassies enjoy in their relationship with the MFA, and the training formats that may assist diplomats improve their digital skills. Effects refer to the capacity built by the MFAs for engaging in digital activities, the tools and metrics used for digital analytics, and the lessons learned from successful and less effective cases. Challenges revolve around issues of attracting and maintaining digital talent, coping with strategic disinformation, managing international collaborations, especially in the EU context, and preparing for the next generation of digital technologies such as artificial intelligence (AI) or mixed reality.

As Table 16.3 reveals, processes related to the relationship between embassies and MFAs as well as to training stand out among all hybridization themes in terms of the

Table 16.2 Common themes of digital hybridization across Baltic and Nordic MFAs

Objectives	Processes	Effects	Challenges
Specific	Drivers	Capacity	Recruitment
General	Institutional adaptation	Analytics	Disinformation
Tactics	MFA-embassy relationship	Metrics	EU collaboration
–	Training	Lessons	Tech trends

Source: authors

Table 16.3 Distribution of digital hybridization themes by country (number of references per topic)

MFA	Objectives	Processes	Effects	Challenges
Latvia	4	12	11	8
Lithuania	7	11	5	6
Estonia	2	11	12	6
Denmark	3	16	5	4
Sweden	4	15	8	5
Finland	2	6	9	13

Source: authors

number of references per topic. The Danish MFA has created a special fund of two million Danish crown annually, to which all embassies can apply for organizing public diplomacy events and many of them have a digital focus (Interview 10, see Annex I). Training wise, Sweden has set up a helpdesk to assist diplomats manage digital communication, tailor messages to local audiences, and cope with problems of disinformation (Interview 11). To facilitate coordination with embassies and maximize communication effectiveness, the Lithuanian MFA has developed a 'network of networks' of digital accounts, which it uses for targeting online audiences more precisely through its messaging (Interview 3).

Capacity building dominates concerns about the effects of digital hybridization across all MFAs, especially in Latvia and Estonia due to the unsustainable combination of shortages of skilled personnel, on the one hand, and the growing demand for digital services, on the other hand (Interviews 6 and 9). There is growing preoccupation with questions involving data analytics, algorithmic personalization, and impact metrics, as well as the lessons to be drawn from past experiences. Challenges are acknowledged by all MFAs, especially the recruitment of people with the right mix of skills, combining traditional diplomatic knowledge, communication expertise, and proficiency in data analysis (Interviews 3 and 10). On the question of challenges, it is the Finnish foreign service that appears to be the most forward-thinking institution in our sample, including by taking steps to explore the potential for diplomatic work of new technologies such as AI (Interview 12).

While the four themes discussed above help us make sense of the scope of digital hybridization, the intensity with which MFAs approach these themes can shed light on the depth of the process. Intensity in this context refers to MFAs' level of ambition and commitment to facilitate digital integration throughout their institutions at multiple levels, including by allocating resources, providing leadership, improving coordination, or developing interfaces for new technologies. The distinction between high vs low intensity refers to situations when MFAs set hybridization targets that

Table 16.4 Distribution of the intensity of digital hybridization by country (number of references per category)

MFA	High	Medium	Low
Latvia	1	7	22
Lithuania	8	10	2
Estonia	3	12	8
Denmark	8	5	3
Sweden	9	8	3
Finland	11	11	2

Source: authors

are well above vs under the average. For example, they may seek to develop their data analytics or AI capacity as opposed to merely focusing on updating websites or on providing basic training diplomats on how to use social media. As Table 16.4 indicates, there are significant differences among the six MFAs, with Finland and Sweden being the most digitally enthusiastic MFAs, followed closely by Denmark and Lithuania.

The Finnish MFA has been collecting and sharing best practices of digital practice with its embassies in crisis communication, public diplomacy, and for countering disinformation (Interview 14); Sweden has been expanding its presence in Instagram, WhatsApp, and Weibo (Interview 11); Denmark has been adding new staff with expertise in data analysis (Interview 10); while Lithuania has been upgrading the objectives of its digital diplomacy strategy from communication to achieving behavioural change (Interview 3). Latvia and to a lesser extent Estonia have been lagging behind in their digital efforts as they continue to struggle with bridging the gap between policy execution and communication (Interview 1), and with building up their digital capacity (Interview 9).

As Table 16.5 indicates, the two groups, the Nordic and Baltic MFAs, behave relatively similarly on the four hybridization themes, especially with respect to processes informing the relationship between MFAs and their embassies, as well as to challenges involving, *inter alia*, questions about how to cope with digital disinformation and how to strengthen MFAs' collaboration with the EU counterparts. They differ, however, in a rather significant way, with respect to the intensity with which they approach digital transformation, especially in terms of their determination to develop advanced digital analytical capacities and to facilitate the adoption of new technologies (AI). The Nordic countries clearly lead the way, but interestingly, Lithuania has demonstrated a similar level of intensity in seizing digital opportunities for diplomatic work and even a stronger interest in recalibrating the objectives of their digital diplomatic strategies as the process of hybridization evolves.

Table 16.5 Distribution of digital hybridization themes and intensity by region.

		Nordic MFAs	Baltic MFAs
Themes	Processes	37	34
	Objectives	9	13
	Effects	22	28
	Challenges	22	20
Intensity	Medium	23	28
	Low	8	32
	High	28	11

Source: authors

Digital Hybridization in Theory

The previous analysis has offered us a comprehensive picture of how the two groups of MFAs compare in terms of the scope and intensity of their digital integration efforts. The results suggest that the six MFAs expose an uneven pattern of digital hybridization, with Sweden and Denmark focusing on digitally empowering their embassies, Finland and Lithuania seeking to articulate a more strategically driven vision of the use of digital technologies in diplomacy, and Latvia and Estonia experimenting with different models of capacity building. What we still need to determine is how profoundly the diplomatic practice of the six MFAs has changed as a result of these efforts. This is the point where assemblage theory re-enters our discussion via the two analytical tools, territorialization and coding, which allow us to explore the constitution and impact of the assemblages to emerge inside MFAs as a result of the process of digital hybridization. We argue that our case studies bear evidence of the emergence of three different models of digital assemblages: the compact (Sweden and Denmark), the mosaic (Finland and Lithuania), and the canvas (Latvia and Estonia).

The compact, mosaic, and canvas assemblages reflect responses to different strategic themes that MFAs have decided to pursue with distinct levels of intensity as discussed in the previous section. The formation of these assemblages is influenced, however, by the presence of certain 'attractors' that territorialization and coding help bring to the fore. In the case of Denmark and Sweden, the process of digital hybridization revolves around a dominant 'attractor', digital communication, which favours the integration of digital technology and diplomatic tasks into a *compact* space of communicational activities, tasks, and projects, especially at the embassy level. The Swedish and Danish MFAs see themselves mainly as facilitators rather than champions of digital integration, with a mission to create a conducive environment for diplomats to familiarize themselves with the trends, themes, and ethos of the digital technological culture and to absorb and master the professional skills and cognitive outlook necessary to excel in digital communication.

The Swedish MFA insists, for instance, that embassies should seek to have 'integrated communications from the beginning' and that everyone should be well versed in digital communication including 'first secretaries, deputy head of missions, second secretaries working with trade and promotion' as well as the locally employed staff (Interview 11). In addition to weekly newsletters suggesting themes and policies for digital promotion, the Danish MFA also sends out guidelines to all embassies on digital trends (e.g., on the use of algorithms, digital formats, infographics) and expects those working on public diplomacy to closely follow these guidelines so that they can better tailor their communication to local conditions and contexts. As a way of encouraging digital learning, the Danish MFA also organizes a competition to determine who is the best ambassador on Twitter each year (Interview 10).

In line with assemblage theory, the process of digital hybridization in the case of the Danish and Swedish MFAs occurs at two levels, at the same time. From a territorialization perspective, the emergent assemblage takes shape via facilitative leadership by which internal coherence is built through an incrementally orchestrated process. Efforts are mustered to ensure that the properties of digital tools are properly understood and integrated into diplomatic communication as much as possible via various homogenizing methods, including the sharing of best practices, internal competition, and training. From a coding perspective, the emphasis is firmly placed on task delivery, that is, on how well digital tools are used to reach pre-defined goals. Denmark's digital campaigns are expected, for instance, to align themselves with three branding themes (green, digital, and creative Denmark) (Interview 10), while Sweden's digital efforts aim to support the country's positions on human rights, sustainable development goals (SDG), or feminist foreign policy (Interview 11).

There are, however, important codifying nuances that help solidify the digital communication identity of the compact assemblage. The Swedish MFA insists, for instance, that communication campaigns must follow the 'co.diplomacy method' by tailoring conversations, channels, and connectors to the local context so as to maximize impact. Public diplomacy projects must be also designed with a 'digital first' mindset, which means that the objectives, content, format, and style of the campaign should be tailored for an online audience. This position is also echoed by the Danish MFA, which views social media engagement as a 'natural part' of the ambassadors' work (Interview 10).

The *mosaic* assemblage that characterizes the process of digital hybridization of the Lithuanian and Finnish MFA lacks a dominant attractor and revolves around multiple focal points with an unequal and fluctuating weight distribution, hence the idea of the mosaic. In both cases, the MFA does not limit itself to facilitating digital integration at the embassy level for communication purposes (attractor #1), but it seeks to actively set the overall direction of the process of digital hybridization. For the Lithuanian MFA this includes, for instance, a robust institutional dimension (attractor #2) involving close digital coordination among the four divisions responsible for advancing MFA's strategic objectives (e.g., on public information, strategic communication, information analysis division, and cultural diplomacy) (Interview 3). For the Finnish MFA, experimentation with new concepts (AI) and technological innovations (attractor #3), such as virtual reality formats, travel apps, or chat bots, is seen as a central element of fostering digital adaptation (Interviews 13 and 14). The mosaic profile of this type of digital assemblage is further defined by how components orbiting attractors are included or excluded from the assemblage depending on the type of task that is expected to be delivered.

With more moving parts to connect and coordinate, the mosaic assemblage faces a more serious challenge of managing internal coherence than the compact model discussed above. Territorialization in this case involves a recurring process of compatibility assessment between digital properties and diplomatic tasks based on which various elements are brought in or excluded from the assemblage in line with a specific strategic direction. Leadership makes a significant difference for how such a form of territorialization is pursued. In the case of Sweden and Denmark, the heads of the digital diplomacy units have a professional background in journalism or public relations, hence their sharp focus on communication. However, those in a similar position in Lithuania and Finland are senior and well-connected diplomats, with a broader perspective of the strategic role of digital technology in diplomacy. This allows them to consolidate the internal coherence of the assemblage by drawing on domestic resources (funding and expertise) and external networks (international organizations, think tanks) with relative ease. It also offers them the opportunity to authoritatively codify the assemblage as being more than task delivery, and emphasize its branding value: the ability to project abroad the image of a country increasingly confident in its ability to adapt, innovate, and seize the opportunities offered by the digital age, either by demonstrating they 'are pretty capable in the digital world' (Interview 14) or by striving to make the 'MFA's digital diplomacy go from 1.0 to 2.0, or 3.0' (Interview 3).

The *canvas* assemblage differs from the compact and mosaic models in one crucial aspect: it lacks a clearly defined attractor. Its emergent properties, that is, the properties caused by the interactions between the constitutive elements (digital tools and diplomatic tasks), are yet to form, hence the idea of the canvas. As the process of digital hybridization of the Latvian and Estonian MFAs illustrates, the profile of the digital assemblage in both cases remains work in progress. It may well evolve in the direction of the compact or the mosaic assemblages by developing a preference for a dominant or for multiple points of attraction respectively, or it may even develop a distinct profile that vacillates between the two models. Concerns over capacity building and training currently dominate considerations about the direction of the digital hybridization efforts made by two MFAs. At the same time, the low (Latvia) and medium (Estonia) level of intensity of the hybridization process reveals a minimum level of interaction between the digital and diplomatic components, which explains why they have not yet reached the tipping point to form a more cohesive assemblage. As one the media advisors of the Estonia MFA has acknowledged, 'there's a lot of hunger to actually do more in social media. I think people just sometimes kind of need a little bit more support and guidance from us' (Interview 9).

From a territorialization perspective, there is enough evidence to suggest that the integration of digital technologies into the sphere of diplomatic objectives, tasks, and methods of the two MFAs follows an evolving strategic logic of capacity building— website upgrading, ad hoc advice to embassies, diaspora outreach, distance learning

(Interviews 1 and 9). However, it is the ambiguity over the coding of the digital properties that gives the canvas model its amorphous profile. For Estonia, the coding frame is expected to be primarily material (potential attractor #1). IT technologies should be used in a way that can facilitate better decision-making by reducing, *inter alia*, the time to process information (Interview 8). For Latvia, the coding frame is more ambitious and touches on more subtle matters of policy making (potential attractor #2): digital communication should be seen not merely as something that stems from policy execution but rather an important part of it (Interview 6). As potential building blocks of an emerging digital assemblage, these coding principles (technology as decision- and policy-making aid) can ensure that digital technologies and diplomatic tasks do not just co-exist, but they interact with each other and create specific properties for the resulting assemblage. The problem with these coding formulations is that the internal debate inside the two MFAs about the validity of these principles is still wide open and therefore their operational capacity to promote internal coherence has had only peripheral effects thus far.

As summarized in Table 16.6, the way in which digital artefacts and diplomatic tasks have interacted in the case of the six MFAs has led to the formation of three different types of digital assemblages. Facilitative leadership and materially oriented coding are the key ingredients of the compact model adopted by the Danish and Swedish MFAs, while pro-active leadership and a combination of material and expressive coding inform the mosaic model of the Lithuanian and Finnish MFAs. The canvas model characterizing the process of digital hybridization of the Estonian and Latvian MFAs is the least developed thus far due to a combination of weak territorialization and ambiguous coding. It is important to note that the transition from strategic intention to assemblage formation has been mediated by the way in which territorialization and coding have enabled digital and diplomatic properties to congeal around certain attractors: a dominant one in the case of the compact model, multiple focal points in the case of the mosaic assemblage, and none thus far in the case of the canvas model.

Table 16.6 Key features of the three models of digital assemblages

	Compact	Mosaic	Canvas
Territorialization	Via facilitative leadership	Via pro-active leadership	Work in progress
Coding	Material (task delivery)	Material (task delivery) and expressive (innovation branding)	Possibly material, but the internal debate remains open
Attractor	Communication with a focus on public diplomacy	Communication, cross-institutional integration, and technological innovation	Not yet defined
Digital Hybridization	Homogenous	Semi-homogenous	Heterogenous

Source: authors

Digital Hybridization in Action

Aside from helping us explain how the process of digital hybridization occurs across the six MFAs, which is the primary focus of this paper, assemblage theory also gives us the analytical tools to understand what happens as a result. More specifically, the three models of digital assemblages tend to behave differently as they develop distinct configurations of agential properties. In the compact model, the communication attractor plays a dominant role in shaping these properties. Human agency becomes liquified in digitally saturated spaces of communication giving way to a 'digital first' mindset, by which the materiality of digital technologies becomes the privileged site of translation, modulation, and enactment of diplomatic tasks. The compact model that the Danish and Swedish MFAs have developed is thus geared towards assisting embassies excel in digital communication with a focus on public diplomacy. It does not mean that embassies cannot use their digital capacity for other objectives, but the agential properties of the assemblage have evolved to maximize this form of action, as illustrated by the novelty of the 'co.diplomacy' method created by the Swedish MFA to increase the effectiveness of digital campaigns.

In the mosaic model, the presence of multiple focal points favours the emergence of a distributed form of assemblage agency. Attractors' competition for primacy via processes of territorialization and coding creates a dynamic space of symbiotic connections in which agency 'bounces' between different virtual ordering processes that are yet to be actualized (communication, cross-institutional integration, technological innovation). As illustrated by the case of Lithuania and Finland, the distributed agency of the mosaic model allows the two MFAs to engage in a broader set of activities (including public diplomacy, consular affairs, and crisis management), but with less efficiency than the compact model, unless additional resources are provided. Lastly, the canvas model informing the digital hybridization efforts of the Estonian and Latvian MFAs exposes no clearly defined agential properties on its own. The assemblage is loosely structured in both cases, with modest levels of internal homogeneity and distinctness of identity. Human agency remains largely in control, but this could change if the two potential attractors are activated thus pushing the assemblage to embrace agential properties associated with the compact or mosaic model.

More broadly speaking, the focus on the constitution of digital assemblages also promises to expand the discussion about the centrality of spatiality to the practice of diplomacy into an exciting new direction, the digital context. As McConnell (2019: 47) points out, diplomacy can be imagined not only as a network of bilateral and multilateral relations, but also as a series of material nodes that serve to produce relational spaces and affective atmospheres. In this vein, the digital hybridization models discussed in the paper make it possible to conceptually visualize the transformation patterns of the conventional boundaries between diplomacy and digital technology. Assemblages form, after all, through the interaction of heterogenous elements, so their boundaries are inevitably unstable and mouldable. In contrast to the canvas assemblage, which has limited insight to offer on this issue because of its inchoate status, the compact and mosaic models come with different prescriptions about the patterns of evolution of the boundary between diplomacy and digital technology.

The compact model suggests, for instance, that the said boundary has become increasingly porous, as diplomatic communication has moved away from a text-based, thoughtful, sober, and personal format to a visually oriented, faster, emotionally engaging, and data-driven approach. One direct implication of this entanglement is that datafication processes (Lycett 2013, Mayer-Schönberger and Cukier, 2013) are bound to firmly embed themselves in the MFA's communication approach. The hiring of data analysts by the Swedish MFA to support its strategic communication efforts provides an early illustration of this trend (Interview 11). Data analytics can assist MFAs to better tailor their message to the profile of the target audience (thematic data analysis), reduce the perception gap between the MFAs' self-image and that of the online public (sentiment data analysis), and assess the impact value of alternative communication strategies (prescriptive data analysis). Increased datafication will further blur the boundary between diplomacy and digital technologies by incentivizing the former to adopt the ethos of the latter. Diplomats are thus increasingly expected to embrace a more pro-active profile and to seek to harness the power of Big Data to anticipate and shape events rather than to react to them.

While the compact model is liable to blur the boundary between diplomacy and digital technology, the mosaic model seeks to redraw it in a non-linear fashion. This trajectory is informed by the fact that the mosaic assemblage displays multiple states of 'digital being', revolving around attractors with different 'digital loads' and activated by competing 'digital thresholds'. The technological innovation attractor serves, for instance, as a powerful catalyst for digital hybridization in the case of the Lithuanian and Finnish MFAs, but its thrust is reinforced by its proximity to the other attractors. The digital/diplomatic boundary therefore follows a non-linear path of entanglement with expectations of increased digital disruption when innovation-type attractors move to the centre of the assemblage. The establishment of the Finnish Ambassador for Cyber Diplomacy is a case in point (Interview 13). Diverging attractors, by contrast, may stretch out the digital space that the mosaic assemblage inhabits, thus diluting the connections that sustain the agential properties of the assemblage. 'Digital stretching' may even reach a 'tipping point' which can cause the entire assemblage to reorder itself, should enough attractors fall on the far side of it (Dittmer, 2014: 393).

Conclusion

More than a decade since MFAs started to actively embrace social media in their work and to develop digital capabilities for their embassies, the scope and effect of the process of digital transformation on diplomatic activities remain little understood. Drawing on assemblage theory, this study has argued that this gap could be bridged by using the concept of digital hybridization as a theoretical anchor for unpacking the interplay between the online and the offline dimensions of diplomatic work. We have defined digital hybridization as the ordering process by which new structures with a distinct internal logic (digital assemblages) are formed through the co-junction and co-evolution of digital and diplomatic components. After comparing the digital experience of six Nordic and Baltic MFAs, we have found evidence to distinguish between three different models of digital assemblages: the compact (Sweden and Denmark), the mosaic (Finland and Lithuania), and the canvas (Latvia and Estonia).

The three models of digital assemblages discussed in the paper (the compact, mosaic, and canvas) not only describe a spectrum of entities that help re-organize the structure of relations inside the MFAs; they also offer a conceptual lens for unpacking the agential configurations to arise within the hybrid spaces (online and offline) in which diplomats now work, in either bilateral or multilateral settings. They also tell us that in the digital age, McLuhan's famous remark 'the medium is the message' is hardly obsolete. Today, the 'digital medium is alive', as it contributes in its own way to how diplomats develop connections, project power, and mediate differences. These research directions will thus allow diplomatic scholars to offer more precise answers to the question about whether and how the 'DNA code' of the diplomatic profession is being reset by digital technologies.

SUGGESTED READING

Adler-Nissen, Rebecca, and Kristin Anabel Eggeling. 2022. 'Blended Diplomacy: The Entanglement and Contestation of Digital Technologies in Everyday Diplomatic Practice'. *European Journal of International Relations.* 28(3): pp 640–666.

Bjola, Corneliu, and Ilan Manor. 2022. 'The Rise of Hybrid Diplomacy: from Digital Adaptation to Digital Adoption'. *International Affairs* 98 (2): pp. 471–491.

Bjola, Corneliu, and Ruben Zaiotti. eds. 2020. *Digital Diplomacy and International Organisations: Autonomy, Legitimacy and Contestation.* Abingdon and New York: Routledge.

Buchanan, Ian. 2020. *Assemblage Theory and Method.* London: Bloomsbury Academic.

Constantinou, Costas M. et al. 2021. 'Thinking with Diplomacy: within and Beyond Practice Theory'. *International Political Sociology* 15 (4): pp. 559–587.

REFERENCES

Acuto, Michele, and Simon Curtis. eds. 2014. *Reassembling International Theory: Assemblage Thinking and International Relations.* London: Palgrave Macmillan.

Aggestam, Karin, and Annika Bergman Rosamond. 2019. 'Feminist Foreign Policy 3.0: Advancing Ethics and Gender Equality in Global Politics'. *SAIS Review of International Affairs* 39 (1): pp. 37–48.

Austin, Jonathan Luke. 2019. 'Security Compositions'. *European Journal of International Security* 4 (3): pp. 249–273.

Bildt, Carl. 2013. *Statement of Government Policy in the Parliamentary Debate on Foreign Affairs,* 13 February. Government Offices of Sweden.

Birka, Ieva, and Didzis Kļaviņš. 2020. 'Diaspora Diplomacy: Nordic and Baltic Perspective'. *Diaspora Studies* 13 (2): pp. 115–132.

Bjola, Corneliu, and Marcus Holmes. eds. 2015. *Digital Diplomacy: Theory and Practice.* New York: Routledge.

Bjola, Corneliu, and Rytis Paulauskas. 2019. 'Lithuanian Diplomacy in the Digital Age: Closing the Foreign Policy Gap'. *Lithuanian Foreign Policy Review* 38: pp. 35–37.

Bueger, Christian. 2013. 'Actor-Network Theory, Methodology, and International Organization'. *International Political Sociology* 7 (3): pp. 338–342.

Charmaz, Kathy. 2008. 'Grounded Theory as an Emergent Method', In *Handbook of Emergent Methods,* edited by Sharlene Nagy Hesse-Biber, and Patricia Leavy, pp. 155–172. New York: Guilford Press.

Cull, Nicholas J. 2019. *Public Diplomacy: Foundations for Global Engagement in the Digital Age.* Cambridge: Polity.

DeLanda, Manuel. 2016. *Assemblage Theory.* Edinburgh: Edinburgh University Press.

DeLanda, Manuel. 2019. *A New Philosophy of Society Assemblage Theory and Social Complexity.* London: Bloomsbury Academic.

Deleuze, Gilles, and Felix Guattari. 1987. *A Thousand Plateaus: Capitalism and Schizophrenia.* Minneapolis: University of Minnesota Press.

Dittmer, Jason. 2014. 'Geopolitical Assemblages and Complexity'. *Progress in Human Geography* 38 (3): pp. 385–401.

Dittmer, Jason. 2016. 'Theorizing a More-than-Human Diplomacy: Assembling the British Foreign Office, 1839-1874'. *The Hague Journal of Diplomacy* 11 (1): pp. 78–104.

Dittmer, Jason. 2017. *Diplomatic Material: Affect, Assemblage, and Foreign Policy, Diplomatic Material.* Durham: Duke University Press.

Eksell, Jörgen, and Alicia Fjällhed. 2019. 'A Nordic perspective on Supranational Place Branding', In *The Nordic Wave in Place Branding: Poetics, Practices, Politics,* edited by Cecilia Cassinger et al., pp. 25–38. Cheltenham: Edward Elgar Publishing.

Hoffman, Donns L., and Thomas P. Novak. 2018. 'Consumer and Object Experience in the Internet of Things: an Assemblage Theory Approach'. *Journal of Consumer Research* 44 (6): pp. 1178–1204.

Karpf, David. 2020. 'Two Provocations for the Study of Digital Politics in Time'. *Journal of Information Technology and Politics* 17 (2): pp. 87–96.

Latour, Bruno. 2007. *Reassembling the Social: An Introduction to Actor-Network-Theory.* Oxford: Oxford University Press.

Leander, Anna. 2018. 'International Relations Expertise at the Interstices of Fields and Assemblages', In *The SAGE Handbook of the History, Philosophy and Sociology of International Relations,* edited by Andreas Gofas et al., pp. 386–398. London: SAGE Publications.

Löfven, Stefan, and Ann Linde. 2019. *Sweden's Feminist Foreign Policy.* Government Communication. Stockholm: Ministry for Foreign Affairs.

Lycett, Mark. 2013. '"Datafication": Making Sense of (Big) Data in a Complex World'. *European Journal of Information Systems* 22 (4): pp. 381–386.

Mayer-Schönberger, Viktor, and Kenneth Cukier. 2013. *Big Data: A Revolution That Will Transform How We Live, Work, and Think.* An Eamon Dolan Book. New York: Houghton Mifflin Harcourt.

McConnell, Fiona, and Jason Dittmer. 2018. 'Liminality and the Diplomacy of the British Overseas Territories: An Assemblage Approach'. *Environment and Planning D: Society and Space* 36 (1): pp. 139–158.

McConnell, Fiona. 2019. Rethinking the Geographies of Diplomacy. *Diplomatica* 1 (1): pp. 46–55.

Müller, Martin. 2015. 'Assemblages and Actor-networks: Rethinking Socio-material Power, Politics and Space'. *Geography Compass* 9 (1): pp. 27–41.

Nail, Thomas. 2017. 'What is an Assemblage?'. *SubStance* 46 (1): pp. 21–37.

Roberts, Ivor, ed. 2017. *Satow's Diplomatic Practice*. Oxford: Oxford University Press.

Sandre, Andreas. 2015. *Digital Diplomacy: Conversations on Innovation in Foreign Policy*. Lanham: Rowman & Littlefield.

Sesay, Abdul, Oh, Onook, and Ramirez, Ronald. 2016. 'Understanding Sociomateriality through the Lens of Assemblage Theory: Examples from Police Body-Worn Cameras'. ICIS 2016 Proceedings. 11. https://aisel.aisnet.org/icis2016/Methodological/Presentations/11

Spry, Damien. 2019. 'From Delhi to Dili: Facebook Diplomacy by Ministries of Foreign Affairs in the Asia-Pacific'. *The Hague Journal of Diplomacy* 15 (1–2): pp. 93–125.

Van Dijck, José et al. 2018. *Platform Mechanisms. The Platform Society*. New York: Oxford University Press.

APPENDIX 1

INTERVIEWS

1. Interview with Latvian diplomat, Riga, 3 October 2018.

2. Interview with Lithuanian diplomat, Vilnius, 12 October 2018.

3. Interview with Lithuanian diplomat, Vilnius, 12 October 2018.

4. Interview with Estonian diplomat, Tallinn, 19 October 2018.

5. Interview with Latvian diplomat, Riga, 25 October 2018.

6. Interview with Latvian diplomat, Riga, 2 November 2018.

7. Interview with Lithuanian diplomats, Vilnius, 9 November 2018.

8. Interview with Estonian diplomat, Tallinn, 11 January 2019.

9. Interview with Estonian diplomat, Tallinn, 11 January 2019.

10. Interview with two Danish diplomats, Copenhagen, 25 January 2019.

11. Interview with two Swedish diplomats, Stockholm, 14 February 2019.

12. Interview with Finnish diplomat, conference call, Riga, 18 February 2019.

13. Interview with Finnish diplomat, Helsinki, 21 February 2019.

14. Interview with Finnish diplomat, Helsinki, 21 February 2019.

CHAPTER 17

DIGITAL DIPLOMATIC CULTURES

GEOFFREY WISEMAN

INTRODUCTION

THIS chapter explores the novel idea of 'digital diplomatic cultures'.[1] The chapter suggests that the overall impact of digital technologies on diplomatic practices has been over-generalized and that current debates do not make a clear enough distinction between digital technology's impact on different forms of diplomacy. The reasons for this over-generalization include hasty extrapolations from the heady dominance of scholarly work on digital technologies, public diplomacy, multilateral diplomacy, certain high-tech states, and the European Union; all research areas that are more accessible and quantifiable than others. To better understand digitalization's varied impact on diplomatic practices, the chapter first raises key definitional problems and identifies several research challenges. The chapter then considers how digital technologies are likely to impact four main types, or dimensions, of diplomacy: bilateral (state-to-state relations), multilateral (multi-state relations), polylateral (state–non-state relations), and omnilateral (non-state–non-state relations). Each type is developing its own distinctive amalgam of analogue-digital practices suggestive of emergent, if variable, digital diplomatic cultures.

Defining Digital Diplomatic Cultures

The chapter invites a cautious view of the term 'digital diplomacy' (cf. Bjola and Holmes, 2015). The term does not convey an actual form of diplomacy such as cultural diplomacy, sports diplomacy, celebrity diplomacy, or public diplomacy. Thus, it may be more

---

[1] I am grateful to Corneliu Bjola, Pauline Kerr, Paul Sharp, and David Wellman for comments on a draft and to Allison Scott for research assistance.

accurate to use slightly longer terminology, such as 'diplomacy by digital means' or 'the digitalization of diplomacy' (Cornut and Dale, 2019). Another problem with the shorthand term 'digital diplomacy' is that it implies that diplomacy is conducted only via digital means, whereas many diplomatic acts or interactions have varying degrees of analogue and digital, as several authors have noted. Important conceptual correctives that give due weight to the qualitative difference that digital technologies make in the practice of diplomacy are *hybrid diplomacy* and *blended diplomacy*. In this chapter, I use the metaphor of a spectrum, or continuum, of practices ranging from the *analogue*, at one end, to the *digital*, at the other.

The idea of 'digital diplomatic cultures' consists of three terms, each of which is hotly contested. Here, *digital* refers to 'digital technology and platforms, including social media, mobile devices and teleconference systems' (Adler-Nissen and Eggeling, 2022: 660). From the many definitions of *diplomatic*, I start with the term as an adjective for the noun 'diplomacy', which generally means relations between sovereign states. Contemporaneously, the singular idea of diplomacy is being challenged by scholars referring to plural diplomacy, or diplomacies.

Culture is even more definitionally challenging. As a concept, it can be either inconsequential or momentous. Hofstede's (1991: 5) well-known definition of culture as 'the collective programming of the mind which distinguishes the members of one group or category of people from another' implies that a culture is not innate but is social and constituted in complex ways over time. Thus, it allows that social entities and collectivities of almost any kind might have a distinctive culture. Wells (2021: 822) defines culture as 'patterns of behaviour arising from social learning ... within specific social groups'. Some conceptions see cultures as historically derived and so highly resistant to change, others see them as more pliable. Some give weight not only to *people* and *practices*, but also to *places* (Causadias, 2020). However, concepts such as historical and inter-generational learning will acquire substantially new meaning as time and space become compressed in the digital age. My interpretation of culture here is that it is a social construct, albeit one that hews more towards discernible practices than to readings that see it as 'the inferred ideational codes lying beneath the realm of observable events' (Keesing, 1974: 77). Digitalization accelerates the construction of new mindsets and practices. It does so *inter alia* by speeding up and widening the range of communications between political leaders and diplomats, between officials in home capitals and diplomats in the field, between diplomats in the field and elite contacts and public audiences in host societies, and between consular officers and citizens.

Hedley Bull combined the terms 'diplomatic' and 'culture' to describe 'diplomatic culture', by which he meant 'the common stock of ideas and values possessed by the official representatives of states' (Bull, 2002: 304). Diplomatic culture was not created at any given moment but, rather, developed over centuries from the social, or cultural, practices of official representatives of states (Bull, 2002: 160). For Bull, the diplomatic corps (discussed further below) is the most tangible expression of international society's diplomatic culture.

By diplomatic culture, I mean *the accumulated communicative and representational institutions, rules, norms, and practices devised to improve relations and avoid war between interacting and mutually recognizing political entities* (Wiseman, 2005). Building on the notion of plural diplomatic cultures (Dittmer and McConnell, 2016), the chapter identifies four such cultures—bilateral, multilateral, polylateral, and omnilateral. In each case, I describe key practices of that diplomatic culture. Then, I consider how emergent digitalization practices appear to be changing that culture. These practices include extensive reliance on the Internet for information and a general preference for 'digital' platforms such as social media, smart phones, and online meetings rather than in-person, or 'analogue', methods, including traditional media, such as radio, television, and newspapers, and especially in-person interactions. In all four types of diplomacy, I conclude with a judgement about the direction that culture is taking on a spectrum that is bounded at one end by in-person (analogue) norms and practices and at the other by online (digital) norms and practices. Accordingly, the chapter suggests that we are seeing the emergence of (at least) four digital diplomatic cultures, each one manifesting varying, blended degrees of analogue and digital characteristics.

Some Research Problems

Researching digital diplomatic cultures poses several research challenges which influence the direction of scholarship and risk overstating digitalization's overall impact on diplomacy and understating the variations. First, much scholarly literature has approached the subject from the perspective of the ministry of foreign affairs (MFA). This is a research challenge because the main government department generally responsible for managing a state's bilateral relations, the MFA, is also responsible for managing a state's multilateral and 'functional' affairs. This can leave an impression that bilateral diplomacy is conducted from the 'centre' (the home capital) rather than from the 'periphery' (embassies and consulates abroad), although there is much interaction between headquarters and field (Manor, 2016: 35). Moreover, other writings on MFAs devote far less attention to the digital revolution and foreground factors such as ethnic and gender diversity, politicization, and populism (Aggestam et al., 2021; Lequesne, 2022; Huju, 2022). A second research challenge is that the scholarly focus on social media in technologically advanced societies such as the Nordics and Israel (Manor and Crilley, 2020) can understate the ongoing importance of traditional media in other countries. Third, studies of the diplomacy-digital nexus have been dominated by the digitalization of public diplomacy (Bjola et al., 2019; Cull, 2019; Manor, 2019; Hedling and Bremberg, 2021: 1597; Fletcher, 2023), imparting a sense that all diplomatic practices are going digital. A fourth problem is the difficulty of determining the short-term versus long-term impact of a once-in-a-century event, the Covid-19 pandemic (Bjola, 2021; Eggeling and Adler-Nissen, 2021; Manfredi-Sánchez, 2022). A fifth problem is that digital diplomatic practices tend to be more quantifiable than analogue practices, underscoring the perils of theorizing what is observable (Danziger and Schreiber, 2021). Finally, some forms of diplomacy, such as multilateral relations, are more accessible to researchers than others, such as bilateral relations. How these research challenges affect the discourse on digital technologies becomes more apparent as the chapter considers four diplomatic cultures—bilateral, multilateral, polylateral, and omnilateral.

Bilateral Diplomacy's Digital Culture

The persistence of traditional centuries-long bilateral diplomacy—relations between two sovereign states—in contemporary international relations is often underestimated in scholarly work. However, bilateral diplomacy continues to matter greatly, such as US–Russian and US–Chinese relations. It has not been superseded by institutionalized multilateral diplomacy. Moreover, bilateral diplomacy persists because of an underlying culture that prioritizes the need for continuous dialogue with both friend and foe, manifested tangibly in resident embassies and in the collective diplomatic corps, mentioned above and elaborated below. What, then, has been the impact of digitalization on bilateral diplomacy's culture and is it possible to identify an emerging bilateral diplomacy digital culture?

Bilateral diplomacy today reflects increasingly greater use of digital technologies, notably in two areas that involve close connections with citizens: public diplomacy and consular services. Public diplomacy is increasingly performed online by bilateral missions, sometimes led by digitally aware ambassadors utilizing social media platforms such as Facebook and Twitter. There are also many examples of diplomats in major bilateral posts using social media to respond to host government disinformation (McFaul, 2018: 302–309; Cooper and Cornut, 2019: 15–16). However, the impact of such efforts in 'minor' capitals is unclear. Moreover, many embassies maintain designated public diplomacy/media staff who, under the ambassador, curate both online activity and traditional media outreach, much as embassy public-diplomacy officers have done in the pre-digital past.

Consular services provided for citizens at diplomatic posts abroad show the direct impact of digital technologies. Writing before the Covid-19 pandemic, one observer noted:

> The exercise of the consular function has been deeply transformed over the last two decades by the extraordinary upsurge of IT solutions applied to consular services. This swift adaptation of consular administrations to new technologies can be explained by a need for enhanced security, especially after 9/11, and greater efficiency in the face of growing citizens' expectations and media scrutiny.
>
> (Fernández Pasarin, 2016: 168)

While detecting evidence of a slower adoption of new digital tools in consular work, Melissen (2022: 256) also notes variation regarding states' capacity to coordinate online and offline services (see also Manor, 2016: 15). In short, parts of the world are persistently analogue even as some societies embrace smart phones to offset poor communications infrastructure. Moreover, we should not neglect the importance of the physical presence of consular officers in-country. For citizens incarcerated abroad, such as American basketball star Brittany Griner in Russia in 2022, on-the-ground consular support is essential. Thus, while online advisories and other services for citizens travelling, studying, and working abroad are likely to grow, in-person consular protection from consular staff operating under the Vienna Conventions on Consular Relations will remain crucial.

Beyond digitalization's impact on public diplomacy and consular affairs, three considerations help explain why bilateral diplomacy worldwide—whether characterized as hybrid or blended—will likely tilt towards the analogue rather than towards the digital end of the analogue–digital spectrum.

First, diplomacy's long-standing, professional preference for in-person, field contact remains highly valued at bilateral posts worldwide (Manor, 2016: 25–26; Berridge, 2022: 101–124). Almost universally, diplomats prefer to work in the field rather than at home in the ministry (Neumann, 2012: 35; Wiseman, 2019: 793). And diplomatic memoirs suggest that most prefer bilateral over multilateral postings. Competent bilateral diplomats thrive in physical settings, reaching out beyond the embassy walls to the broader host society. The bilateral diplomat's work typically requires extensive in-country travel and often to other countries when the ambassador is multi-accredited.

This in-person preference is likely to continue in bilateral negotiations at the political-leader level (Holmes, 2018). Wheeler and Holmes (2021) show how 'social bonding' between US President Reagan and Soviet leader Gorbachev in their highly personal bilateral meetings in the 1980s contributed to the Cold War's end. While some authors usefully note the potential of virtual reality apps and 3D holograms (Bjola and Manor, 2022: 486), it is difficult to imagine many Reykjavik-like breakthroughs occurring online. While bilateral online 'summit' meetings will likely increase, physical visits by heads of government and ministers will retain their traditional clout in relationships, which also leave an ongoing diplomatic afterglow for diplomats remaining at the post after the high-level visit. Even in an increasingly high-tech world, land, territory, and material resources still matter a great deal in terms of what causes war to break out, for example, Russia's 2022 invasion of Ukraine. In the war's conduct, however, new media have been important factors in Russian propaganda and in Ukraine's adroit efforts to win ideational and material support from Western governments and to pressure Big Tech companies to curtail their activities in Russia (Cull, 2022: 3; Manor, 2022: 2). Still, traditional media outlets have also been prominent in coverage of bombings, mass graves, and war crimes. Moreover, in crises the in-person diplomatic protest—such as withdrawing ambassadors for 'consultations' and calling in an ambassador to the Foreign Ministry for a 'dressing down' (Bang, 2019)—will preserve their currency as in the analogue era.

A second reason why bilateral diplomacy's hybrid mix will lean towards the face-to-face/analogue end of the spectrum is the ongoing importance of the diplomatic corps—the formal assemblage of diplomats of different sovereign states resident in embassies in the capital of another sovereign state and in permanent missions at the headquarters of major regional and international organizations—which continues to exist in the same physical form as it has for centuries (Sharp and Wiseman, 2016). In the diplomatic corps in some bilateral capitals, there have been innovative physical adaptations such as like-minded countries—e.g. Norway and Denmark—sharing embassy locations and buildings. However, their physical presence is key, conveying status and respect in ways that online representations cannot even as more routine business is conducted online. The physical presence (including the size and architecture) and even location of an embassy in a host-country's capital still matters in most bilateral relationships. Related, closing a diplomatic mission will normally be resisted by the host government. Actual embassies are still needed, as evidenced by Covid-era announcements by governments such as China, Australia, and Canada establishing new missions. And, in wartime, the ongoing presence of a diplomatic corps is even more significant symbolically. For example, after Russia's 2022 invasion of Ukraine, most embassies relocated temporarily from Ukraine's capital to Lviv in western Ukraine or to neighbouring countries, with many of them returning to Kyiv within months to signal support for Ukraine and with some organizing highly publicized in-person visits by their heads of government.

A third reason why digitalization will likely take less hold in bilateral diplomacy lies in the differences between two-party and multilateral diplomacy. As discussed below, much scholarly attention on the diplomacy–digitalization nexus has focused on the impact on diplomatic practices at the multilateral level. However, multilateral institutions tend to be more open to outside access for researchers, journalists, and others than are MFAs and embassies in bilateral capitals. Thus, research on EU diplomacy skews towards Brussels with far less research on the EU's diplomatic missions in world capitals (*pace* Rasmussen, 2018: 81–99; Bicchi and Schade, 2022). Related is the emphasis in the literature to how digitalization impacts diplomatic negotiation. Bjola and Coplen (2023) conclude from their empirical research that 'virtual venues are no longer seen as exotic places, located outside the realm of diplomatic activity. In fact, they are increasingly perceived as a credible alternative to face-to-face negotiation arenas' (2023: 85. See also Fletcher, 2023: 374; cf. Kuus, 2023). While this observation may hold in *multilateral* posts such as Brussels, where negotiations are constant (Maurer and Wright, 2020: 558), the generalization is less likely to hold in many *bilateral* settings outside Europe—say, Abuja, Baghdad, Hanoi, Kampala, or Lima—where ongoing negotiations are less frequent. Accordingly, many of the negotiation adaptations and tactics enabled by digital platforms will be less important in bilateral capitals because fewer negotiations take place there.

Consistent with both the hybrid and blended concepts, resident diplomats in bilateral capitals and consular cities will indeed rely on smart phones and seek to have a social media presence and active embassy websites, although Robertson suggests that even some powerful countries neglect their embassy's websites (2017). And while one study cites a figure of 189 countries of the 193 members of the United Nations (UN) as having some form of official Twitter presence (Danziger and Schreiber, 2021: 4), Sevin and Manor note significant variation between countries in 'levels of adoption of digital technologies' (2019: 338). Another issue is whether technologies such as Twitter contribute to the building of diplomatic cultures or, as Cornut et al. (2022) argue, provide a platform for *un*diplomatic cultures, as with impulsive political leaders such as Donald Trump and Jair Bolsonaro, and China's wolf warrior diplomats (Martin, 2021).

While bilateral diplomatic culture and practices now involve more digital activity than in the past, especially in public diplomacy and consular activities, bilateral diplomacy does not yet display a near-universal, distinctive digitally oriented culture. Professional diplomats in bilateral settings will largely prefer the offline side of the spectrum, while recognizing that they are now operating in a world that is a hybrid of analogue and digital. What matters for bilateral diplomats is knowledge of the host-country language, inter-cultural sensibility, sociability, a sense of place, and mental and physical resilience. The traditional culture of bilateral diplomacy remains strong even if it now has a digital patina. In sum, bilateral diplomacy has thus far been changed in degree but not in kind by digital practices. As for the future, indicators of movement toward a stronger bilateral digital culture include more embassy personnel––not just the ambassador and designated public-diplomacy/media staff––using digital outreach to host-country publics; more online consular services in many more countries across regions; and more online meetings of regional groups in the diplomatic corps of bilateral capitals. However, for now, bilateral diplomacy retains a mixed, sometimes reluctant digital culture, especially when compared to multilateral diplomacy.

Multilateral Diplomacy's Digital Culture

This section considers whether multilateral diplomacy is tilting more towards the digital or analogue end of the digital–analogue spectrum and if there are signs of an emergent multilateral digital culture. A multilateral diplomatic culture has been in the making for centuries, symbolized by landmark conferences and settlements including the 1648 Peace of Westphalia, the 1815 Congress of Vienna, the 1919 Paris Peace Conference, and—its most institutionalized form—the UN system established in 1945. In essence, a multilateral diplomatic culture has emerged from the core normative idea that war is less likely, and international cooperation more achievable, when three or more sovereign entities meet willingly at ad hoc or permanent conferences. Building on Bjola and Zaiotti's (2021) agenda-setting edited volume *Digital Diplomacy and International Organisations*, the section discusses select examples from the UN, the European Union (EU), and the Association of Southeast Asian Nations (ASEAN).

The United Nations

The foundations of the UN's diplomatic culture were laid in the 1945 Charter and evolved from the basic idea of multilateral cooperation, institutionalizing it in a myriad of agencies, funds, and programmes and universalizing it to a current membership of 193 member states. While the organization's culture was originally driven by a post-war concern with international peace and security, it has since shifted, often informally, towards a broader understanding of security via such concepts as peacebuilding and sustainable development. To what extent, then, has digital technology impacted that culture and what might we expect in the future? A plausibility probe of different parts of the UN system—the Security Council, the General Assembly, and the Goodwill Ambassadors programme—points to a complex, varied picture.

The almost continuous in-person meetings of the UN Security Council—the organization's most consequential body—were seriously disrupted by Covid-19's rapid spread in New York City in early 2020. Meetings and consultations shifted online, with permanent representatives generally expressing a wish to return to in-person meetings. As pressures from the pandemic eased, the Council returned to face-to-face meetings with few signs that future Council meetings would move online by choice. The most likely explanation for this preference is the need for confidentiality associated with the traditional high-politics, peace-and-security Council mandate under Chapter VII of the Charter. High-politics issues are less likely to go virtual than low-politics issues. Moreover, since much of the Security Council's work is conducted in the 'grey area' of informal, more discreet, in-person interactions (Pouliot, 2021), the security factor will typically inhibit a move to more 'open' virtual platforms (Bjola and Coplen, 2023: 89). However, a qualification here is whether the Security Council will continue to adapt its high-politics mandate to tackle low-politics thematic issues beyond the informal Arria-formula consultative process. Notable examples in this regard are UNSC Resolution 1325 (2000) and its subsequent iterations on Women, Peace, and Security; UNSC Resolution 2250 on Youth, Peace, and Security; and multiple climate resolutions and statements. This increasing attention to thematic issues implies for some that the Security Council is 'slowly but relentlessly moving from protecting State sovereignty only to protecting humanity' (Deplano, 2022: 168). By implication, a low-politics, human-security countenance of the Council, involving more non-state actors, will likely be both in-person and virtual.

During the pandemic, the parliamentary-style General Assembly adopted a 'hybrid format' of in-person and video speeches (Bjola and Coplen, 2023: 70). Nonetheless, with Covid-19 rampant, some 100 heads of state and government attended the opening of 76th session the 2021 General Assembly in person. Tellingly, in 2022 the General Assembly session mandated that all speeches at the opening of the 77th session be delivered in person (conspicuously granting Ukraine's Zelensky an exception—against Russia's objections). Moreover, many UN Member States have resisted the adoption of digital technologies *inter alia* urging that resources be devoted to traditional media (Bouchard, 2021: 118. Cf. Cornut, 2022).

As with bilateral diplomacy, research on digitalization throughout the sprawling UN system is led by public-diplomacy studies, which have generally drawn attention to the UN's public outreach emanating from the UN Secretariat's Department of Global Communications and the Goodwill Ambassadors and Messenger of Peace programmes.

Regarding the latter programmes, Postema and Melissen argue that they have 'largely moved online' in the past decade (2021: 673), although not always with positive results. They found that Chinese goodwill ambassadors, many of whom have a large Weibo following, opt for 'symbolic activism and sloganization' (683) that reinforces Chinese nationalism rather than promoting the UN's universalist goals.

While digital practices are now evident across the complex UN system, as seen in the public-diplomacy oriented Goodwill Ambassadors programmes, resistance to online meetings is evident in the General Assembly and Security Council. Overall, it seems premature to conclude that multilateral diplomacy at the UN has 'gone digital' (Bouchard, 2021: 104) in the sense of system-wide acceptance of digital multilateral meetings and plenaries, especially when measured against the most successful case of regional integration, the European Union.

The European Union

Diplomatic culture in the EU context has come to mean 'pooling resources toward the creation of a regional diplomatic system, including a set of dedicated institutional structures for performing diplomacy' (Batora, 2018: 308). The EU's unique diplomatic culture combines a dense network of both traditional *intergovernmental* cooperation and evolving *supranational* institutions, the latter involving practices that transcend the sovereign state. The high point of the EU's multilateral diplomatic culture was the creation of the European External Action Service (EEAS) in 2009—the EU's diplomatic service—and the expansion of the EU's 'Delegations' abroad (Bicchi and Schade, 2022).

In recent decades, the EU has embraced new technologies, building on its position as the most advanced example of regional integration with a complex regional diplomatic culture. The EU's generally tech-friendly culture is reflected in aspects of the EU's expanding diplomatic role, Brexit notwithstanding, and can be tracked in the growing literature on the impact of digitalization on the EU's diplomatic practices (e.g. Bicchi and Lovato, 2024).

The Covid-19 pandemic fuelled this literature. Bjola and Manor argued that 'diplomacy is about to enter a new phase of digital transformation' (2022: 471). Bicchi and Schade discussed how the EU's expanding diplomatic footprint was made possible partly by 'contemporary technological developments' (2022: 3). Hedling described how digital disinformation such as Russia's deceptions in the Brexit vote and the 2016 US election 'sparked a transformation of diplomacy' in the EEAS (2021: 859). Bjola and Coplen found that during the pandemic 'virtual venues not only affect the format, but also the substance of negotiations' (2023: 69), concluding that 'coercive approaches (including novel tactics) are more common than persuasive approaches' (69–70). And Eggeling and Adler-Nissen noted how the pandemic 'accelerated the ongoing transformation of diplomacy from "naked" face-to-face interactions to digitally mediated "synthetic situations", producing new interpretations of who is "essential" in diplomacy' (2021: 1). Some of this work reflected the unanticipated scale and social disruption of the Covid-19 pandemic. Some of it produced helpful conceptual advances regarding the diplomacy-digitalization nexus.

Two synthesizing conceptual advances, mentioned above, were *hybrid diplomacy* and *blended diplomacy*. Bjola and Manor predicted diplomats post-Covid-19 'adapting' to and 'adopting' *hybrid diplomacy* 'in which physical and virtual engagements are expected to integrate, complement and empower each other' (2022: 472; see also Hocking and Melissen, 2015). In their model, diplomatic practices merge 'virtual meetings with off-line, face-to-face diplomacy' (487). In short, 'diplomats' imaginary now includes virtual alongside physical meetings' (489). Based on pre-Covid ethnographic observations of EU diplomats in Brussels, Adler-Nissen and Eggeling developed the concept of *blended diplomacy*. Sceptical of the term 'digital diplomacy' for its assumptions about intentionality and its techno-optimism, they also cast doubt on accounts that assume a hard distinction between *traditional* (offline) diplomacy and *digital* (online) diplomacy, because it has become 'impossible to experience a workday without digital technologies' (2022: 661; see also Eggeling and Adler-Nissen, 2021: 12).

These empirical assessments and conceptual overlays of evolving EU diplomatic practices are valuable. However, it is not yet clear whether the digitalization of diplomatic practices is having a generalized impact across all member states. Theories of 'differentiated integration' suggest that there will be variances and, even in a more digital EU culture, that such differentiation might be uncovered as more attention is paid to informal and social diplomatic interactions (Haugevik, 2022: 15). Thus, we need to be mindful of the risk of over-generalization about the diplomacy–digitalization nexus from the EU context. Moreover, the EU is a '*sui generis* post-modern' entity (Rasmussen, 2018: 5). A considerable gap remains between the 'thick' layers of EU diplomatic practices and the 'thin' layers identifiable in other regional organizations such as ASEAN.

The Association of Southeast Asian Nations

Despite its relatively thin institutions, ASEAN is nonetheless thought to have an 'emergent regional diplomatic culture' (Batora, 2018: 317). This culture has long been described as the 'ASEAN Way'. Its key norms are non-interference in the affairs of other members, decision-making based on consultation and consensus, a preference for informal practices, and an aversion to legally binding commitments on the European model. Research on digitalization's impact on ASEAN diplomatic practices is insubstantial compared with the EU, focusing instead on the socio-political underpinnings of the ASEAN Way, such as informal socializing around meetings and face-saving practices that minimize criticism of member states' foreign policies and provide camouflage for domestic authoritarianism (Nair, 2019). ASEAN's putative 'high-context', informal diplomatic culture is more amenable to personal contact, unlike the EU's reputed more technocratic, 'low-context' culture, which is arguably more open to a digital mindset. That ASEAN is so different from the EU, in terms of democratization and formal institutional development, underlines the gap between the EU and other regional diplomacies and highlights the risk of generalizing digitalization's impact. Similarly, many diplomatic capitals that host international or regional organizations— e.g. Nairobi, Addis Ababa, Montevideo, Kathmandu—will likely see everyday diplomatic activities leaning more towards the in-person and less towards the virtual end of the spectrum. More comparative research could show whether the highest levels of digitalization occur in the most 'developed' regional diplomatic cultures (for the foreseeable future, the EU) and the lowest levels in regional diplomatic cultures with lower densities of institutional interaction and where personal, high-context relationships are traditionally seen to be prized, as in parts of the Global South.

Overall, even with significant variations at the UN and regional organizations such as ASEAN, trends in the EU suggest that multilateralism is developing a stronger digitally oriented culture than is the case in bilateral diplomacy. However, as already indicated, diplomacy is by no means limited to its bilateral and multilateral forms. And so, we need to examine these other diplomatic cultures for changes in practices that can be traced to digital developments.

POLYLATERAL DIPLOMACY'S DIGITAL CULTURE

Conceptually different from bilateral and multilateral diplomacy, I see *polylateral diplomacy* as diplomacy's third dimension—a term that characterizes peaceful relations between state and non-state actors (Wiseman, 2010). Well-documented cases of polylateralism are the Ottawa landmines process, the anti-apartheid movement, and the Mozambique peace process brokered by the Catholic NGO Community of Sant'Egidio. Polylateralism is also commonplace at the UN, notably, the long-standing system of NGO accreditation to the Economic and Social Council (Constantinou and McConnell, 2022: 66, 68).

A sovereign state's willingness to engage polylaterally with legitimate non-state actors depends on the state's adaptive capacity, state size, state type, the issue area, the decision phase, and non-state actors' mode of persuasion. The focus here is on the latter criterion: how global civil society actors' persuasive methods reflect digital advances and portend a distinctive polylateral digital culture. A research problem here is that the literature on transnational advocacy involving NGOs and social movements tends to emphasize strategies and tactics rather than organizational culture. Evaluating organizational culture in physical institutions is hard enough but evaluating culture in largely digital networks is even more challenging. Here, we look for a shared mindset manifested in routine practices shared by members of a category of people.

Two distinctions help minimize over-generalizing about what digital cultures are emerging in polylateralism. One is that between service and advocacy NGOs, which have different organizational cultures. *Service* NGOs such as CARE International focus on delivery of humanitarian relief and development assistance. Consequently, their political-influence strategies typically concentrate on elite lobbying of governments and philanthropic sources for funding. *Advocacy* NGOs seek to change national and international policy on politically charged issues such as human rights, development, health, and climate change. Their political-influence strategies concentrate on mobilizing their membership designed to take visible action to influence policy makers. Since Keck and Sikkink's landmark *Activists Beyond Borders* (1998), much scholarship has focused on 'transnational advocacy networks'. However, the service/advocacy distinction is not always easy to discern, as many humanitarian NGOs such as OXFAM have adopted a stronger advocacy profile.

A second distinction is that between well-established advocacy NGOs and more fluid, grassroots organizations and social movements. Here too we see different organizational cultures. As for NGOs, Hall and colleagues (2020) observe a general shift away from centralized, professionalized, brand-name advocacy models to digital-era activist types in which 'supporters make key decisions, including what campaign topics to pursue and how to do so' (160–161). They suggest that the culture of these new-age NGOs is 'less professional in nature' and that it generates more support and legitimacy (161). For these NGOs, digital tools imply a culture of fast feedback from supporters, rapid surges in mobilization, and more decentralized campaigns.

As for broadly based grassroots organizations and social movements, Hall and colleagues concur with others that online practices 'have been widely adopted in social movements' (160) and that the organized NGO sector 'remains far behind … social movements in mobilizing digital technologies' (161). The trend also represents a shift from large, physical, well-organized NGOs towards more spirited, subversive campaigns such as Extinction Rebellion (Gunningham, 2019) and high-profile social movements such as the 'Colour Revolutions' in eastern Europe, the 'Arab Spring' uprising, Black Lives Matter, #Me Too, and School Strike for Climate.

The evidence hints at a polylateral digital culture that is increasingly more participatory and simultaneously more assertive. Cooperation-inclined organizations lean towards the analogue end of the analogue–digital spectrum (aiming to reassure and thus secure face-to-face meetings with decision makers) while conflict-inclined groups lean more to the digital end (aiming to disrupt and thus secure mass involvement, in the streets and online, to pressure decision makers). Strong democracies will cope with both 'cooperative' insider models (e.g. Amnesty International, Transparency International) and even with 'combative' outsider models (e.g. Extinction Rebellion and Greenpeace). Weaker democracies will likely see both types as existentially threatening. Typically, the more contentious the advocacy that tests the limits of state-based notions of civility and decorum, the more likely governments and international organizations will close ranks (McConnell, 2018; Lemke and Habegger, 2021: 231).

Current trends, then, suggest that significant variations of digital adoption will continue within the polylateral, state–non-state diplomatic dimension. Nonetheless, we see the outlines of a polylateral diplomatic culture that is increasingly determined by the analogue vs. digital preferences of non-state groups. As noted above, this culture is likely to reveal tensions—about technology's role in pursuing best influence-practices—between service and advocacy NGOs and between 'professionalized' NGOs and 'grassroots' campaigns and movements. Significantly, there is evidence that digitalization has prompted some states to embrace polylateral relationships. For example, several countries have appointed digital or cyber ambassadors and some, notably Denmark, have established new forms of diplomatic representations to multinational tech companies in Silicon Valley (Klynge et al., 2022: 266, 268).

Overall, a stronger digital-driven polylateral culture is emerging from small to medium-sized tech-smart countries while non-state-driven polylateralism is likely to be both more participatory with supporters and more assertive with decision makers.

Omnilateral Digital Culture

To the three dimensions of diplomacy considered so far—bilateral, multilateral, and polylateral—a fourth is now emergent, *omnilateral diplomacy*, which I have defined as:

> the conduct of relations between at least two non-state entities—with a modicum of standing—in which there is a reasonable expectation of systematic relationships, involving some form of reporting, communication, negotiation, and representation, but not involving mutual recognition as sovereign, equivalent entities.
>
> (Wiseman, 2019: 151)

This fourth dimension becomes more salient given how 'the exponential growth in global interaction capacity between non-state actors' is explained by digital communication (Lemke and Habegger, 2021: 238). Omnilateral diplomacy pushes the boundaries of the debate about who can be called a diplomat. The term omnilateralism derives from the Latin 'omnibus' meaning 'for all and by all'. Immanuel Kant ([1796] 1974: 84) used omnilateral to depict 'the act of all the wills of a community together'. Modern-day authors have offered different perspectives on omnilateralism (Watson, [1982] 2004: 151; Kingsbury, 2005).

My application of omnilateralism to contemporary conditions provides a fourth framework to test digitalization's impact on diplomacy. It suggests peaceful relations between non-state entities, entities that traditionally would not be regarded as diplomatic actors but have social 'standing' of some kind. My conception precludes 'bad' non-state actors such as terrorists, opposed to all negotiations, and malefactors from the 'dark side of digital diplomacy' engaging in 'fake news, disinformation and the deliberate weaponization of information' (Bjola and Pamment, 2019: 1). On a narrow interpretation, when two or more NGOs or activist campaigns collaborate to influence policy, they are engaging in omnilateral diplomacy. Digitalization increases the speed and technical capacity of NGOs, activist groups, and social movement campaigns to communicate with each other, share policy statements, and discuss strategies that include negotiating and proposing compromise positions—all common diplomatic practices.

On a broader interpretation—one that is closer to Kant's idea of 'the will of all individuals'—is the capacious idea of everyday diplomacy (Sennett, 2012). In this everyday/everywhere view of diplomacy, individuals think, act, communicate, and represent themselves to others diplomatically. For Constantinou, everyday diplomacy occurs 'whenever someone successfully claims to represent and negotiate for a territory or a group of people or a cause, or successfully claims to mediate between others engaging in such representations and negotiations' (2016: 23). Related concepts are 'people-to-people' diplomacy, 'humanity-centric' public diplomacy (Zaharna, 2021), 'citizen diplomacy', and 'social diplomacy' (Faizuleyev, 2022).

All these concepts indicate a mindset manifested in patterned practices that point towards a universal digital diplomatic culture. These indications include an easy disposition to connect with others online, including outside national borders, as evidenced by the prodigious numbers of global followers on such platforms as Twitter, Facebook, and Instagram who engage comfortably with such practices as 'liking' and 're-tweeting'. These practices also involve new forms of digital etiquette, or codes of polite behaviour. They also involve digital practices of informality, such as ideographic emoticons and emojis, transcending cultural divides (hence their potential 'universality') and suggesting a shared mindset (hence their belonging to a 'culture'). These evolving informal practices, evident in multilateral diplomacy, are even more likely to proliferate in diplomacy's omnilateral dimension.

Unlike traditional bilateral and multilateral diplomacy, which begins with the sovereign state, omnilateral diplomacy begins with the individual. Concerns about such constructs overtaxing the diplomacy concept notwithstanding, there is growing interest in applying diplomatic language to both inter-state relations and inter-human relations. Digitalization expands the likelihood that omnilateralism, in the narrow and broad senses, will involve more people in digital interaction with others. The question is whether these relations produce cooperative, trust-based solutions to global problems. Lemke and Habegger are pessimistic, concluding that 'while [traditional] diplomacy seeks to ameliorate conflict through convergence and compromise, the communicative logic of digital communication amplifies contentions by pushing users to diverge and radicalize' (2021: 259). Constantinou, Cornago, and McConnell are more optimistic. They argue that the pluralization of diplomatic actors beyond officially accredited, professional state representatives is producing the *trans*professionalization of diplomatic practices, which recognizes 'the "new" skills and knowledges that non-state actors bring to the diplomatic realm, from expertise and specialized knowledge pertinent to the increasing prevalence of issue-based diplomacy to innovations in digital technology and advocacy strategies' (2016: 36).

Thus, an evolving transprofessional diplomatic culture potentially bridges the gap between the narrow and broad variants of omnilateralism and between the generally risk-taking, open communicative disposition of the non-state world and the generally risk-averse, measured communicative disposition of the traditional state-based diplomatic world. This fourth type of diplomacy, which I am casting as omnilateral, is far from a fully conceptualized framework but we perhaps need to leave open the theoretical possibility that a neo-Kantian will of all the world's individuals representing themselves to others, albeit in digital form, is imaginable.

Conclusion

The Covid-19 pandemic prompted a huge surge in digital diplomatic practices, eventually slowing with some return to analogue, in-person pre-pandemic practices. However, in diplomacy's four dimensions—as with other sectors such as business and education—there will be no return to the *status quo ante*. The pandemic shifted the centre of gravity on the analogue–digital continuum in the digital direction. However, this chapter concludes that general claims about how digital technologies have impacted diplomacy need to be heavily qualified in terms of the type of diplomacy under consideration—bilateral, multilateral, polylateral, or omnilateral. All four dimensions of diplomacy continue to evolve, and each has its own emerging digital values that, when seen alongside analogue values, can be roughly said to constitute emergent, identifiable digital cultures.

Contemporary digital advances are likely to have a more enduring impact on multilateral diplomatic practices than on bilateral practices, although with significant variance depending on the multilateral institution, issues, and actors concerned. At the UN, the digital impact will vary considerably from the General Assembly to the Security Council, from agency to agency, and from hard-power to soft-power issues. Digital multilateral practices are most likely to take hold within the EU. Its thick, blended, tech-oriented diplomatic culture will incline towards the digital on the analogue–digital spectrum, depending on such determinants as the issue area at stake. However, there will likely be variance within the EU and considerable variance between the EU and other regional diplomacies such as ASEAN, where diplomatic practices will lean towards the analogue end of the spectrum.

Thus, digital cultures vary widely not only *between* but also *within* the four types of diplomacy, as shown by the differences between the digital practices of highly 'connected' and less 'connected' capital cities that host bilateral diplomatic missions, between 'dense' multilateral cities such as Brussels and 'thin' ones such as Nairobi and Kathmandu, between centralized NGOs and decentralized social movements and grassroots campaigns conducting polylateral diplomacy, and between individuals engaging in narrow or broad variants of omnilateral diplomacy. We can expect the 'in-person, analogue, offline' versus 'virtual, digital, online' dichotomy to be guiding debates for some time to come.

Suggested Reading

Constantinou, Costas M., Noé Cornago, and Fiona McConnell (eds.). 2016. 'Transprofessional Diplomacy'. *Diplomacy and Foreign Policy* 1 (4): pp. 1–66.

Cull, Nicholas J. 2019. *Public Diplomacy: Foundations for Global Engagement in the Digital Age*. Cambridge: Polity Press.

Zaharna, R.S. 2022. *Boundary Spanners of Humanity*. Oxford: Oxford University Press.

References

Adler-Nissen, Rebecca, and Kristin Anabel Eggeling. 2022. 'Blended Diplomacy: The Entanglement and Contestation of Digital Technologies in Everyday Diplomatic Practice'. *European Journal of International Relations* 28 (3): pp. 640–666.

Aggestam, Karin, Annika Bergman Rosamond, and Elsa Hedling. 2022. 'Feminist Digital Diplomacy and Foreign Policy Change in Sweden'. *Place Branding and Public Diplomacy* doi. org/10.1057/s41254-021-00225-3, 18 (4): pp. 314–324.

Bjola, Corneliu, and Ruben Zaiotti (eds.). 2021. *Digital Diplomacy and International Organisations: Autonomy, Legitimacy and Contestation*. London: Routledge.

Bang, Jiun. 2019. 'Addressing the "Dressing Down": Introducing Summonses as Source Material in North-East Asia'. *The Hague Journal of Diplomacy* 14 (4): pp. 357–378.

Batora, Jozef. 2018. 'Regional Institutional Diplomacies'. In *Diplomacy in a Globalizing World. Theories and Practices*, edited by Pauline Kerr and Geoffrey Wiseman, pp. 300–318. Oxford: Oxford University Press.

Berridge, G. R. 2022. *Diplomacy: Theory and Practice*. 6th edition. Cham, Switzerland: Palgrave Macmillan.

Bicchi, Federica, and Marianna Lovato. 2024. 'Diplomats as Skilful Bricoleurs of the Digital Age: EU Foreign Policy Communications from COREU to WhatsApp'. *The Hague Journal of Diplomacy* 9: pp. 1–40. doi:10.1163/1871191x-bja10174.'

Bicchi, Federica, and Daniel Schade. 2022. 'Whither European Diplomacy?'. *Cooperation and Conflict* 57 (1): pp. 3–24.

Bjola, Corneliu. 2021. 'Digital Diplomacy as World Disclosure: the Case of the COVID-19 Pandemic'. *Place Branding and Public Diplomacy* 18 (1): pp. 22–25.

Bjola, Corneliu, and Ilan Manor. 2022. 'The Rise of Hybrid Diplomacy: from Digital Adaptation to Digital Adoption'. *International Affairs* 98 (2): pp. 471–491.

Bjola, Corneliu, and Michaela Coplen. 2023. 'Virtual Venues and International Negotiations: Lessons from the COVID-19 Pandemic'. *International Negotiation*, 28 (1): pp. 69–93. doi.org/10.1163/15718069-bja10060.

Bjola, Corneliu, and Ruben Zaiotti (eds.). 2021. *Digital Diplomacy and International Organisations: Autonomy, Legitimacy and Contestation*. London: Routledge.

Bjola, Corneliu, Jennifer Cassidy, and Ilan Manor. 2019. 'Public Diplomacy in the Digital Age'. *The Hague Journal of Diplomacy* 14 (1–2): pp. 83–101.

Bjola, Corneliu, and Marcus Holmes (eds.). 2015. *Digital diplomacy: Theory and practice*. London: Routledge.

Bjola, Corneliu, and James Pamment (eds.). 2019. *Countering Online Propaganda and Extremism: The Dark Side of Digital Diplomacy*. London: Routledge.

Bouchard, Caroline. 2021. 'The United Nations in the Digital Age: Harnessing the Power of New Digital Information and Communication Technologies'. In *Digital Diplomacy and*

International Organisations: Autonomy, Legitimacy and Contestation, edited by Corneliu Bjola and Ruben Zaiotti, pp. 101–126. London: Routledge.

Bull, Hedley. 2002. *The Anarchical Society: A Study of Order in World Politics*. 3rd edition. New York: Columbia University Press.

Causadias, José M. 2020. 'What is Culture? Systems of People, Places, and Practices'. *Applied Developmental Science* 24 (4): pp. 310–322.

Constantinou, Costas M., Noé Cornago, and Fiona McConnell (eds.). 2016 'Transprofessional Diplomacy'. *Diplomacy and Foreign Policy* 1 (4): pp. 1–66.

Constantinou, Costas M. and Fiona McConnell. 2022. 'On the Right to Diplomacy: Historicizing and Theorizing Delegation and Exclusion at the United Nations'. *International Theory* 15 (1): pp. 53–78. doi.org/10.1017/S1752971922000045.

Constantinou, Costas M. 2016. 'Everyday Diplomacy: Mission, Spectacle and the Remaking of Diplomatic Culture'. In *Diplomatic Cultures and International Politics*, edited by Jason Dittmer and Fiona McConnell, pp. 23–40. Abingdon: Routledge.

Cooper, Andrew, and Jérémie Cornut. 2019. 'The Changing Practices of Frontline Diplomacy: New Directions for Inquiry'. *Review of International Studies* 45 (2): pp. 300–319.

Cornut, Jérémie. 2022. 'Emotional Practices and How We Can Trace Them: Diplomats, Emojis, and Multilateral Negotiations at the UNHRC'. *International Studies Quarterly* 66 (3): pp. 1–12. doi.org/10.1093/isq/sqac048.

Cornut, Jérémie, and Nadia Dale. 2019. 'Historical, Practical, and Theoretical perspectives on the Digitalisation of Diplomacy: An exploratory analysis'. *Diplomacy & Statecraft* 30 (4): pp. 829–836.

Cornut, Jérémie, Susan Gail Harris Rimmer, and Ivy Choi. 2022. 'The Liquidification of International Politics and Trump's (Un)Diplomacy on Twitter', *International Politics* 59 (2): 367–382.

Cull, Nicholas J. 2023. 'The War for Ukraine: Reputational Security and Media Disruption', *Place Branding and Public Diplomacy* 19 (2): pp. 195–199. doi.org/10.1057/s41254-022-00281-3.

Danziger, Roni, and Mia Schreiber. 2021. 'Digital Diplomacy: Face management in MFA Twitter accounts'. *Policy Internet* 13 (4): pp. 586–605.

Deplano, Rossana. 2022. 'The UN Security Council: From Preserving State Sovereignty to Protecting Humanity'. In *International Conflict and Security Law: A Research Handbook*, edited by Sergey Sayapin et al., pp. 149–170. The Hague: Asser Press.

Dittmer, Jason, and Fiona McConnell (eds.). 2016. *Diplomatic Cultures and International Politics*. Abingdon: Routledge.

Eggeling, Kristin Anabel, and Rebecca Adler-Nissen. 2021. 'The Synthetic Situation in Diplomacy: Scopic Media and the Digital Mediation of Estrangement'. *Global Studies Quarterly* 1 (2): pp. 1–14.

Faizullaev, Alisher. 2022. *Diplomacy for Professionals and Everyone*. Leiden: Brill.

Fernández Pasarín, Ana Mar. 2016. 'Consulates and Consular Diplomacy'. In *The SAGE Handbook of Diplomacy*, edited by Costas M. Constantinou, Pauline Kerr, and Paul Sharp, pp. 161–170. Los Angeles: SAGE.

Fletcher, Tom. 'Beyond Meeting and Tweeting: The Next Challenges for Innovation in Diplomacy'. In *The Palgrave Handbook of Diplomatic Reform and Innovation*, edited by Paul Webster Hare, Juan-Luis Manfredi-Sánchez, and Kenneth Weisbrode, pp. 367–374. Cham, Switzerland: Palgrave Macmillan.

Gunningham, Neil. 2019. 'Averting Climate Catastrophe: Environmental Activism, Extinction Rebellion and Coalitions of Influence'. *Kings Law Journal* 30 (2): pp. 194–202.

Hall, Nina, Hans Peter Schmitz, and J. Michael Dedmon. 2020. 'Transnational Advocacy and NGOs in the Digital Era: New Forms of Networked Power'. *International Studies Quarterly* 64 (1): pp. 159–167.

Haugevik, Kristen. 2022. 'United Clubs of Europe: Informal Differentiation and the Social Ordering of Intra-EU Diplomacy', *Cooperation and Conflict*: pp. 1–19. 10.1177/00108367221103494.

Hedling, Elsa. 2021. 'Transforming Practices of Diplomacy: the European External Action Service and Digital Disinformation'. *International Affairs* 97 (3): pp. 841–859.

Hedling, Elsa, and Niklas Bremberg. 2021. 'Practice Approaches to the Digital Transformations of Diplomacy: Toward a New Research Agenda'. *International Studies Review* 23 (4): pp. 1595–1618.

Hocking, Brian, and Jan Melissen. 2015. *Diplomacy in the Digital Age*. The Hague: Clingendael Netherlands Institute of International Relations.

Hofstede, Geert. 1991. *Cultures and Organizations: Software of the Mind*. London: McGraw-Hill.

Holmes, Marcus. 2018. *Face-to-Face Diplomacy: Social Neuroscience and International Relations*. Cambridge: Cambridge University Press.

Huju, Kira. 2022. 'Saffronizing Diplomacy: The Indian Foreign Service Under Hindu Nationalist Rule'. *International Affairs* 98 (2): pp. 423–441.

Keck, Margaret E., and Kathryn Sikkink. 1998. *Activists Beyond Borders: Advocacy Networks in International Politics*. Ithaca, NY: Cornell University Press.

Kant, Immanuel. [1796] 1974. *The Philosophy of Law: An Exposition on the Fundamental Principles of Jurisprudence as the Science of Right*. Translated by W. Hastie. Clifton: Kelley Publishers.

Keesing, Roger M. 1974. 'Theories of Culture'. *Annual Review of Anthropology* 3: pp. 73–97.

Kingsbury, Benedict. 2005. 'Omnilateralism and Partial International Communities'. *Journal of International Law* 98: pp. 98–124.

Klynge, Casper, Mikael Ekman, and Nikolaj Juncher Waedegaard. 2022. 'Diplomacy in the Digital Age: Lessons from Denmark's TechPlomacy Initiative'. In *Ministries of Foreign Affairs in the World: Actors of State Diplomacy*, edited by Christian Lequesne, pp. 263–272. Leiden: Brill.

Kuus, Merje. 2023. 'Bureaucratic Sociability, or the Missing Eighty Percent of Effectiveness: The Case of Diplomacy'. Geopolitics 28(1): pp. 174–195.

Lemke, Tobias, and Michael Habegger. 2021. 'Diplomat or Troll? The Case Against Digital Diplomacy'. In *Digital Diplomacy and International Organisations: Autonomy, Legitimacy and Contestation,* edited by Corneliu Bjola and Ruben Zaiotti, pp. 229–266. London: Routledge.

Lequesne, Christian (ed.). 2022. *Ministries of Foreign Affairs in the World: Actors of State Diplomacy*. Leiden: Brill.

Manfredi-Sanchez. 2023. 'Vaccine (Public) Diplomacy: Legitimacy Narratives in the Pandemic Age'. *Place Branding and Public Diplomacy* doi.org/10.1057/s41254-022-00258-2, 19 (3): pp. 398–410.

Manor, Ilan. 2023. 'The Road not Taken: Why Digital Diplomacy Must Broaden Its Horizons'. *Place Branding and Public Diplomacy* 19 (2): pp. 206–210. doi.org/10.1057/s41254-022-00280-4.

Manor, Ilan. 2019. *The Digitalization of Public Diplomacy*. Cham, Switzerland: Palgrave Macmillan.

Manor, Ilan. 2016. 'Are We There Yet: Have MFAs Realized the Potential of Digital Diplomacy? Results from a Cross-National Comparison'. *Diplomacy and Foreign Policy* 1 (2): pp. 1–110.

Manor, Ilan, and Rhys Crilley. 2020. 'The Mediatisation of MFAs: Diplomacy in the New Media Ecology'. *The Hague Journal of Diplomacy* 15 (1–2): pp. 66–92.

McConnell, Fiona (2018) 'Performing Diplomatic Decorum: Repertoires of "Appropriate" Behavior in the Margins of International Diplomacy'. *International Political Sociology*, 12 (4): 362–381.

McFaul, Michael. 2018. *From Cold War to Hot Peace*. UK: Penguin.

Melissen, Jan. 2022. 'Consular Diplomacy in the Era of Growing Mobility'. In *Ministries of Foreign Affairs in the World: Actors of State Diplomacy*, edited by Christian Lequesne, pp. 251–262. Leiden: Brill.

Martin, Peter. 2021. *China's Civilian Army: The Making of Wolf Warrior Diplomacy*. Oxford: Oxford University Press.

Maurer, Heidi, and Nicholas Wright. 2020. 'A New Paradigm for EU Diplomacy? EU Council Negotiations in a Time of Physical Restrictions'. *The Hague Journal of Diplomacy* 15 (4): pp. 556–568.

Nair, Deepak. 2019. 'Saving face in diplomacy: A political sociology of face-to-face interactions in the Association of Southeast Asian Nations'. *European Journal of International Relations* 25 (3): pp. 672–697.

Neumann, Iver B. 2012. *At Home with the Diplomats: Inside a European Ministry of Foreign Affairs*. Ithaca NY: Cornell University Press.

Postema, Saskia, and Jan Melissen. 2021. 'UN Celebrity Diplomacy in China: Activism, Symbolism and National Ambition Online'. *International Affairs* 97 (3): pp. 667–684.

Pouliot, Vincent. 2021. 'The Gray Area of Institutional Change: How the Security Council Transforms Its Practices on the Fly'. *Journal of Global Security Studies* 6 (3): pp. 1–18.

Rasmussen, Steffen Bay. 2018. *The Ideas and Practices of the European Union's Structural Antidiplomacy: An Unstable Equilibrium*. Leiden: Brill.

Robertson, Jeffrey. 2017. 'Embassy Websites: First Impressions Count'. USC Center on Public Diplomacy blog. 11 August. https://uscpublicdiplomacy.org/blog/embassy-websites-first-impressions-count.

Sevin, Efe, and Ilan Manor. 2019. 'From Embassy Ties to Twitter Links: Comparing Offline and Online Diplomatic Networks'. *Policy and Internet* 11 (3): pp. 324–343.

Sennett, Richard. 2012. *Together: The Rituals, Pleasures and Politics of Cooperation*. New Haven: Yale University Press.

Sharp, Paul, and Geoffrey Wiseman. 2016. 'The Diplomatic Corps'. In *The SAGE Handbook of Diplomacy*, edited by Costas M. Constantinou, Pauline Kerr, and Paul Sharp, pp. 171–184. Los Angeles: SAGE.

Watson, Adam. 2004. *Diplomacy: The Dialogue Between States*. London: Routledge.

Wells, David A. 2021. 'Plasticity-Led Evolution and Human Culture'. *Integrative Psychological and Behavioral Science* 55: pp. 821–849.

Wheeler, Nicholas J., and Marcus Holmes. 2q21. 'The Strength of Weak Bonds: Substituting Bodily Copresence in Diplomatic Social Bonding'. *European Journal of International Relations* 27 (3): pp. 730–752.

Wiseman, Geoffrey. 2019. 'Public Diplomacy and Hostile Nations'. *The Hague Journal of Diplomacy* 14 (1–2): pp. 134–153.

Wiseman, Geoffrey. 2010. ' "Polylateralism": Diplomacy's Third Dimension'. *PD Magazine*, Summer, pp. 24–39.

Wiseman, Geoffrey. 2005. 'Pax Americana: Bumping into Diplomatic Culture'. *International Studies Perspectives* 6 (4): pp. 409–430.

Zaharna, R.S. 2022. *Boundary Spanners of Humanity*. Oxford: Oxford University Press.

CHAPTER 18

THE DIGITALIZATION OF PERMANENT MISSIONS TO INTERNATIONAL ORGANIZATIONS

CAROLINE BOUCHARD

INTRODUCTION

INTERNATIONAL organizations (IOs) have 'gone digital' (see Bjola and Zaiotti, 2020). Created by states with shared interests to foster cooperation and harmonize relations in the attainment of common objectives, these intergovernmental bodies have been significantly impacted by the emergence of new digital information and communication technologies (ICTs) such as social media, video-conferencing platforms, and instant messaging applications. As various chapters in this handbook show, these new technological tools have affected all areas of work of IOs and shaped multilateral diplomatic activities. While other contributions in this handbook examine the digitalization of IOs and their secretariat/bureaucracy (see chs.19, 25 and 26), this chapter aims to explore how the offices established by member states at the headquarters of international organizations, often called missions or permanent missions, have experienced this process.

A permanent mission to an IO can be defined as a 'mission of permanent character, representing the State [and] sent by a State member of an international organization to the Organization.'[1] Missions are 'indispensable tools for members that desire to play any type of serious role in an [international organization]' (Smith, 2006: 34), and hold

[1] See Article 1 (7) of the Vienna Convention on the Representation of States in their Relations with International Organizations of a Universal Character.

both 'shareholders as well as stakeholders' roles (Malone, 2015: 132). Missions work closely with the international secretariat of IOs to ensure negotiations and activities run continuously and the decision-making process 'never stops' (Reinalda and Verbeek, 2004: 14). They are also important interlocutors with other actors involved in multi-lateral diplomacy, including civil society (Rana, 2016). To explore the digitalization of missions to IOs, we focus on the case of the permanent missions to the United Nations (UN) in New York. These entities resemble traditional embassies in their organiza-tional design, but function in a particular setting: the UN system, a complex 'micro-cosm' (Malone, 2015) composed of multiple entities and governed by specific rules of procedures. Most UN member states have missions in other cities hosting UN head-quarters (such as Geneva and Vienna), but New York is considered 'a global listening post' (Rana, 2016: 161) and 'the heart of the UN's political processes' (Smith, 2006: 35). Missions to the UN in this city have usually more staff and resources. Furthermore, in terms of digital diplomacy, studies show that permanent missions located in New York have had a greater online presence than their counterparts in other cities (see Manor and Pamment, 2019).

From the outset, it is important to stress that the digitalization of permanent missions to the UN in New York has not been a homogeneous experience. The digital divide has significantly shaped this process and remains a pressing issue. It is even considered 'the new face of inequality in the COVID-19 era' (UN General Assembly, 2021). Limited access to resources and technical skills as well as high costs of infrastructures remain important challenges, especially for certain countries in the Global South. Conversely, some UN member states have been able and willing to in-vest significant resources to fund their digital diplomacy in New York. This chapter does not presume to provide a complete picture of how all permanent missions from the 193 current UN member states have integrated digital tools into their work. We ra-ther wish to explore factors that have shaped the digitalization (see ch.1) of missions to the UN in New York. We also aim to examine how digital technologies have influenced behaviours, patterns of use, procedures, and norms (Manor, 2017) in the diplomatic activities of permanent missions, as well as consider 'the appropriation of techno-logical tools' (Archetti, 2012: 185–186) by both the missions and their staff.

The chapter begins by examining some of the characteristics of permanent missions to the UN in New York. It then suggests adopting a multilevel approach to study the digitalization of permanent missions. This perspective allows us to pay attention to factors at various levels of decision making (international, domestic, regional) which help explain why and how missions to the UN in New York have incorporated digital ICTs. The chapter then examines how digital tools have been integrated into specific tasks performed by permanent missions and their staff including campaigning, formal and informal negotiations, networking activities, and public diplomacy. It concludes by discussing challenges and impacts linked to the digitalization process of permanent missions. The chapter focuses on first-hand accounts from practitioners working at the UN headquarters in New York as well as official documentary sources published by the UN and UN member states.

Permanent Missions to the UN: Characteristics, Roles, and Responsibilities

Permanent missions in New York represent the interests of member states in the UN system. Like for other embassies, missions to the UN are guided by directives received from the ministry in charge of foreign affairs (MFA). One of their main mandates is to support delegations officially representing their state in UN negotiations and meetings. In a negotiation context, they are responsible for examining draft versions of the negotiating text, communicating questions and progress made to their government, and identifying strategic partners or potential adversaries (Smith, 2006). Missions to the UN also now regularly perform public diplomacy activities (Rana, 2016). Most diplomats working in permanent missions are political officers, but some are experts on specific UN issues (for example, disarmament or climate change) (Malone, 2015).

In the UN system, the role of permanent missions is defined as 'to assist in the realization of the purposes and principles of the United Nations and, in particular, to keep the necessary liaison between the Member States and the Secretariat in periods between sessions of the different organs of the United Nations' (see UNGA Resolution 257 (III)). Permanent missions are crucial players in UN decision making, which can be defined as 'the entire policy process as defined by the international legal framework of [the UN] in which member states, the international secretariat and various other actors participate' (Reinalda and Verbeek, 2004: 14) and includes activities such as agenda setting, informal and formal negotiations, and voting. While performing these tasks, missions and their staff interact with other UN actors. Weiss and colleagues (2009, 2016) have identified three categories of actors who are involved in UN decision making. Diplomats representing the current 193 member states are the 'first UN'. They lead all intergovernmental work done in the organization. The 'second UN' consists of international civil servants working in the UN Secretariat as well as in the various UN agencies, entities, agencies, and programmes. This 'second UN' works closely with diplomats from permanent missions as 'UN officials present ideas to tackle problems, debate them formally and informally with governments' (Weiss, 2016). The 'third UN' is composed of members of non-governmental organizations and other groups representing civil society as well as academics, experts, consultants, and groups of individuals with shared interests. This 'insider-outsider' group (Weiss et al., 2009: 123) has become, over time, extremely active in the UN system (Weiss et al., 2009; Cooper, 2002). Whether as allies or critics, members of this group frequently interact with diplomats from permanent missions at the UN.

Diplomats in permanent missions to IOs are likely to experience more freedom of action, as governments and their MFA often lack the capacities and resources to overview all the issues being discussed in multilateral forums. However, in the UN context, a specific member state's attitude towards the organization, the size of the mission, and the resources available can significantly affect this degree of autonomy (see Smith, 2006). All five of the permanent members of the UN's Security Council (China, France, Russia, the United Kingdom, and the United States) have sizeable permanent representations in New York. The United States mission to the United Nations is the largest mission, with more than 100 diplomatic staff (United Nations Blue Book, 2021). This high number can be explained by the significant role it plays in the UN system, and the fact that the UN's headquarters are located on American soil (Smith, 2006). Conversely, the smallest UN member states, like Nauru or Liechtenstein, only have a handful of diplomatic staff in New York (United Nations, 2021). This variation reveals a stark reality: maintaining a permanent mission to an IO involves significant costs for states, especially if it is located in New York.

Personnel from permanent missions are trained to conduct diplomacy activities in a multilateral setting (Rana, 2016). They must also learn a specific set of skills that will allow them to efficiently perform certain tasks specific to the UN system, which can include chairing a multilateral meeting, acting as a 'rapporteur', and drafting resolutions. Like other diplomatic agents, staff in missions to the UN have been continuously using more digital ICTs to carry out their daily activities. In the next sections, we suggest that a multilevel approach is useful to explore the digitalization of permanent missions to the UN as this process is influenced by the interplay of factors from different levels of decision making (international, domestic, and, in some cases, regional).

Exploring the Digitalization of Permanent Missions: A Multilevel Approach

As other digital diplomacy scholars have done (see, for example, Bjola and Manor, 2018), we consider international negotiations as the product of a multilevel process of decision making that flows through a complex web of actors and institutions. In our view, diplomats of permanent missions to the UN are involved in a multilevel game (Putnam, 1988), that is 'strategic interactions in which [diplomats] simultaneously try to take into account of and, if possible, influence the expected reactions of other actors, both at home and [at the UN]' (Moravcsik, 1993: 15). To be successful in a multilevel game, diplomats must reach an agreement at the international (UN) level that will be accepted, or ratified, at the domestic/regional level. In this perspective, decisions and strategies adopted at different levels of decision making can influence outcomes. We suggest that this multilevel game has influenced the digitalization of permanent missions: the decisions and strategies adopted by diplomats of missions regarding the integration of digital tools into their work have been shaped by interactions at different levels of decision making.

Various first-hand accounts given by diplomats suggest that decisions taken by MFAs (at home/domestic level) pertaining to the integration of digital tools have heavily weighted on the digital diplomacy of permanent missions to the UN. For instance, most of the missions that were early adopters of social media had a minister in charge of foreign affairs at home who was actively using these platforms (see United Nations, 2015b). As stressed above, permanent missions follow guidelines elaborated by their MFA. In the case of their digitalization, the guidance received by missions from their capital has varied greatly. The United States is often cited as one UN member state that early on recognized the need to develop strategies to guide the digitalization of its diplomacy (see Ross, 2011). Another early champion of digital diplomacy is the United Kingdom. In 2012, the UK's Foreign and Commonwealth Office published a *Digital Strategy* to make sure UK diplomacy would take full 'advantage of the opportunities offered by the digital to enhance every element of [its] work' (UK FCO, 2012: 3). In contrast, other UN member states have lagged behind their colleagues and failed to provide clear directions to their missions on how to integrate digital technologies into their activities (United Nations, 2015b). This should not be interpreted as a lack of interest on their part. As discussed above, it is important to recognize that limited resources and skills, and high infrastructure costs have shaped decisions taken by governments and their MFA, particularly in some parts of the Global South, regarding the digitalization of their diplomatic activities (Turianskyi and Wekesa, 2021; Wekesa et al., 2021).

Interactions at the international (UN) level also appear to have influenced the digitalization of missions to the UN in New York. Diplomats of missions work together daily with their peers as well as the 'second' and the 'third' UN. Recent research has shown that the growing use of digital ICTs, particularly social media platforms, in the UN system has led to changes in the ways these three categories of actors interact (see Bouchard, 2020; Ecker-Ehrhardt, 2020; Hofferberth, 2020). We would suggest that the UN system's own digitalization process has affected how diplomats of permanent missions have integrated digital ICTs into their activities. The United Nations, like other international organizations, embodies a 'tightly knit community' or a 'group diplomacy' (Pouliot, 2011) where socializing is not only encouraged but also important to teach actors the 'right' way of doing things within the organization (Smith, 2006; Pouliot, 2011). We contend that this socialization process should be considered an important factor in the diffusion (Rogers, 2003) (introduction, adoption, and spread) of digital ICTs in permanent missions and the UN system in general. Through interactions with other diplomats, as well as actors from the 'second' and 'third' UN, diplomats of missions can be in contact with early adopters of new digital technologies who can 'provide information and advice about [digital] innovations' (Rogers, 2003: 26).

Early evidence of this came at the first (and, so far, only) *UN Social Media Day* organized in New York in January 2015 (United Nations, 2015a). The event had been specifically planned 'to bring the experiences of missions and diplomats that are actively active [on social media] and encourage others to do' (United Nations, 2015b). Throughout the event, diplomats of missions to the UN that were present were encouraged to share their experiences and best practices including during a panel with three high-ranking diplomats from three permanent missions (Canada, Fiji, and Pakistan). The event also included a 'Social Media Medics', managed by staff from the UN Secretariat, to help cure 'the growing pains that we all encounter in our digital identities' (United Nations, 2015a). Two other panels with actors from the 'third UN', including experts from the digital platforms LinkedIn, Twitter, and Tumblr, specialists in the areas of journalism, marketing, and advertising, and speakers from civil society, were also organized. One recurring piece of advice given during the day by multiple participants was that diplomats should identify colleagues in the UN system who were effective communicators on social media platforms and follow their lead (United Nations, 2015b). To better understand the digitalization of permanent missions, attention should be paid to how interactions at the UN level influence the behaviours and patterns of diplomats surrounding the use of digital tools. As the next sections will show, this socialization process is ever-present in the daily work of permanent missions in the digital age.

The Integration of Digital ICTs in Permanent Missions' Activities

As discussed above, permanent missions and their staff are crucial players in various phases of UN decision making such as agenda setting, informal and formal negotiations, and voting. Another important aspect of their work is to gain support and 'sell' their policies to various audiences. The next sections explore how new digital tools have been adopted by diplomats to perform these activities (on some of these issues, see also ch.6 and ch.20 in this handbook), more specifically for sharing information and communicating with various actors and publics. Evidence suggests that digital ICTs such as instant messaging applications, video-conferencing platforms, and social media have progressively been perceived by diplomats as useful, if not essential, tools to perform these tasks.

Permanent Missions, UN Decision Making, and Digital Tools

Diplomats of permanent missions are responsible for presiding over most UN meetings and setting the agenda for issues to be discussed with their UN colleagues. In this context, diplomats must often perform campaigning activities as most top leadership positions in the UN system are elected. For example, the president and vice presidents of the General Assembly are voted by all UN member states. The chairpersons of UN committees and limited-membership UN entities such as the Human Rights Council as well as the non-permanent members of the Security Council are also elected (Smith, 2006). Traditional campaigning tactics usually involved organizing in-person bilateral meetings with significant partners and staging social events for diplomats (Smith,

2006). In recent years, however, campaigning in the UN has now taken a digital turn. Diplomats now increasingly contact their UN colleagues using instant messaging apps to send information about their candidacy, videos, and invitations to events. The number of virtual campaigning events organized has also exponentially grown (Ashley, 2021).

In UN decision making, diplomats are at the centre of formal and informal negotiation sessions. Just like in campaigning activities, instant messaging applications have become a ubiquitous tool to communicate during UN negotiations. One of these messaging applications, WhatsApp, became particularly popular among the UN diplomatic community (see Manor, 2017; Sandre, 2018) leading some observers to brand this new form of communication as WhatsApp diplomacy (Borger et al., 2016). According to diplomats, this application as well as other similar messaging apps are convenient and easy to use in negotiation context at the UN. Not only do they resemble texting (which diplomats are already familiar with), but they also allow diplomats to be in contact with one another during discussions without leaving the room. These apps also have an advantage over texting: they can use Wi-Fi networks instead of phone data. They thus help circumvent connectivity issues experienced by diplomats from some missions and can be employed in rooms with limited or no phone connectivity (Ashley, 2021).

The group chat options available on messaging apps like WhatsApp have also contributed to their success among diplomats and other UN actors. Smith points out that nearly all discussions in the UN involve 'collectivities of Member States working together as groups or voting blocs' (2006: 53). For instance, formal regional groupings play an important role in the decision-making process of the UN General Assembly.[2] UN member states can be part of different groupings. They can be involved in groups representing intergovernmental organizations like the European Union and the Group of 77.[3] They can be members of smaller coalitions such as The Nordics (Denmark, Finland, Iceland, Norway, and Sweden) or CANZ (Canada, Australia, and New Zealand). They may also join other states in temporary interest groups formed in response to a specific issue such as climate change or human rights issues. In some circumstances, diplomats with diverging views may even work together in a group to tackle contentious issues and find consensus (Smith, 2006). Group or 'bloc-diplomacy' (Pouliot, 2011) allows a certain degree of 'informality' as discussions within a group do not usually follow stringent procedures or necessitate simultaneous translation (Smith, 2006). This may also help explain why messaging apps and their chat have been popular in group discussions in the UN.

---

[2] There are five main regional groups of member states in the UNGA: African states; Asia-Pacific states; Eastern European states; Latin American and Caribbean states; and Western European and other states. While not a member of any regional group, the United States attends meetings of the group of Western European and other states as an observer and is considered a member of that group for electoral purposes. Kiribati (located in Oceania) is the only other UN member that is not part of any regional group in the UNGA. https://www.un.org/dgacm/en/content/regional-groups#

[3] The Group of 77 includes 134 UN member states and 'promote[s] South-South cooperation for development'. See https://www.g77.org/doc/

Mirroring the reality of the UN's group negotiations, diplomats are often members of several groups on messaging apps. Experts sent by the capitals, notably for special sessions of negotiations or conferences, are also often provisionally included in these groups. Membership of each group on the app can thus vary over time. In formal UN negotiation sessions, instant messaging apps have been employed by diplomats of missions to communicate with other members of their group(s) in a view to coordinate their position, circulate annotated documents, devise negotiation tactics, gather support for specific policy positions or amendments, and organize their strategy meetings. Instant messaging apps have also become a popular tool used by UN groups to communicate outside formal meetings. Informal discussions and negotiations constitute a significant part of the work done by diplomats (Pouliot, 2011). This is especially true in the context of the UN's internal processes as 'the public and private side of UN diplomacy are two interwoven processes; you cannot assess the impact of one of these without considering both' (Smith, 2002: 130). Diplomats report using messaging applications to contact their colleagues outside formal meetings to update other members of the group about their government's positions, coordinate policy positions, and share and comment on draft documents. Instant messaging apps are also tools employed to informally lobby other diplomats to join coalitions (whether by directly using the app to discuss positions and possible compromises or schedule in-person meetings). These informal digital contacts between group members play an important role in UN decision making as they provide opportunities to strategize, exchange ideas, or clarify their positions (Smith, 2002).

Video-conferencing platforms, another type of digital ICT, have been progressively employed to conduct both formal and informal meetings at the UN. In the 2010s, missions were already using platforms such as Skype, Webex, or Zoom to conduct bilateral or small meetings with other UN member states and UN civil servants (Bouchard, 2020). However, with the COVID -19 pandemic, video conferencing became an essential part of the work done by staff in permanent missions to the UN. As with the rest of society, the pandemic led diplomats to conduct most of their meetings on video-conferencing platforms for long periods (Höne, 2020; Bramsen and Hagemann, 2021; Bjola and Manor, 2022). For permanent missions to the UN, these digital platforms were considered especially helpful to ensure that crucial UN decision making would still happen during the pandemic.

Gaining Internal and External Support in the Digital Sphere

An important part of a diplomat's job at the UN is gaining support and convincing other actors, both inside and outside the UN, to champion their government's preferred policies and positions (see Smith, 2006; Weiss, 2016). Member states and their MFAs have decided to adopt digital ICTs for various reasons including sharing information and ideas and building relationships with potential allies, managing established networks, tailoring their public image, and engaging with outside audiences (Bjola and

Holmes, 2015; Hocking and Melissen, 2015; Bjola et al., 2019). Permanent missions have also progressively turned to the most popular or newest digital tools to help them perform these tasks.

While diplomats have employed instant messaging apps to lobby their colleagues (Ashley, 2001), the emergence of social media platforms, especially the arrival of Twitter, now known as X, in the early 2000s, has significantly transformed how permanent missions approach this aspect of their work.

Recent studies show that permanent missions view social media platforms as networking sites. Permanent missions not only use these platforms to manage existing networks, but also develop relationships with new actors through interactions on social media (see Manor and Pamment, 2019; Manor, 2020). Twitter, especially, was long considered a very useful tool for diplomats to gather information on the work being done by colleagues as well as the 'second' and 'third' UN. Digital platforms are employed by missions to promote joint initiatives with other diplomats as well as partnerships established with UN departments and agencies, and civil society (Bouchard, 2020). By publicly recognizing the initiatives of other diplomats or other actors who support their policies, missions can foster existing working relationships and develop new partnerships. Building these relationships is an integral part of the work of permanent missions.

Furthermore, as other contributions in this book have explored, social media platforms are used by international actors to explain their positions and proposals during international negotiations. Most permanent missions to the UN have followed suit and now prefer using social media to disseminate their messages during negotiations than organizing press conferences at UN headquarters. Social media platforms have appeared especially attractive communication tools to smaller UN member states, which often have problems attracting the interests of international news media (Bouchard, 2020).

Like other international actors, permanent missions have also turned to popular social media sites including Twitter (now X), Facebook, Instagram and, more recently, TikTok to help them conduct their public diplomacy activities (Metzgar 2012; Manor 2019; Bjola et al., 2019; chs.10, 13, and 15 in this handbook). Public diplomacy initiatives are put in place to influence the management of the international environment and achieve specific objectives and have traditionally functioned through engagement with foreign audiences. Nowadays, public diplomacy can entail the promotion of an actor's values and work to both foreign and domestic audiences and aims at shaping public opinion in the actor's favour (Melissen and Wang, 2019). In the digital age, public diplomacy has gone through several transformations. It has become more interactive and interconnected (Bjola et al., 2019). As Manor (2019) argues, 'the digitalization of public diplomacy' has led states and their missions to redefine how they engage with and how they 'listen' to various publics.

It is becoming increasingly evident that diplomats of permanent missions have embraced social media platforms to target specific audiences. They have also adapted their communication strategies to try to engage with the right audience (Ashley, 2021). Some permanent missions to the UN have mobilized social media platforms to specifically engage with foreign audiences. China's permanent mission to the UN is a telling case in point. The Chinese mission has actively used Twitter, a platform inaccessible to the general public in mainland China since 2015, to promote positive narratives about China's contribution to the UN. Publications on the Chinese mission's account (@Chinamission2un) and the account of the Chinese ambassador to the UN (@ ChinaAmbUN) on Twitter (now X) are mostly published in English and openly target a global audience. Research shows that the Chinese government considers engagement on social media has an important component of its growing public diplomacy network (Huang and Wang, 2019; see also ch.28 in this handbook) including in the UN context.

Other permanent missions have opted to use digital platforms to target and engage with domestic audiences. For example, some missions representing the member states from the Global South view social media as an effective tool to explain to their country's citizens how their work at the UN impacts real-life issues (United Nations, 2015b). Permanent missions have also turned to their social media accounts to contribute to the promotion of a specific national image. For instance, in recent years, Sweden has deployed a 'distinctively feminist digital diplomacy strategy'. Sweden's MFA and its mission to the UN have used their social media accounts to champion the adoption of UN norms and resolutions related to gender equality. By doing so, Sweden wished to promote its feminist foreign policy approach as well as its 'self-image as an innovative, progressive and gender aware state' (Aggestam et al., 2021). All these studies demonstrate that social media platforms have been integrated into the work of permanent missions to engage with audiences outside the UN system and broaden support for their work and policies.

THE DIGITALIZATION OF MISSIONS TO THE UN: CHALLENGES AND IMPACTS

The integration of digital ICTs has created unprecedented opportunities for permanent missions to achieve their objectives. However, as we have already alluded to, the growing use of digital platforms in diplomatic activities has had significant impacts on permanent missions, their staff, and the UN system as a whole. In the next sections, we wish to discuss some of the challenges experienced by diplomats from permanent missions to the UN and show how they are often linked to different domestic and regional realities. We also wish to discuss how the digitalization process has produced all sorts of consequences, including some dysfunctional (undesirable) ones (Roger, 2003), both for UN diplomacy and for individuals within the UN system.

Challenges Experienced by Diplomats of Permanent Missions

The UN system is renowned for having specific institutional rules that manage how formal activities (such as negotiating and voting) are performed (see Smith, 2006). However, at least pre-pandemic, no rules existed to organize interactions on video-conferencing platforms during formal UN meetings or to determine who should be part of a UN WhatsApp group. This absence of rules guiding digital interactions between UN actors appears to have created challenges for diplomats. Some diplomats have reported struggling to effectively do their work in virtual meetings with no clear rules of procedures or definitions of hierarchical rankings among the diplomats (Höne, 2020). In this sense, diplomats have also had to consider how diplomatic signalling—that is how other actors perceive and interpret the behaviour of a diplomat, 'whether or not it is spoken or intended or even within the actor's conscious awareness' (Jönsson and Hall, 2003: 199)—has been affected by the digitalization of UN interactions. Signalling can differ online than when meeting in person and diplomats have had to learn to adjust their behaviour accordingly.

Digitalization has also impacted the 'behind the scenes' aspect of UN diplomacy. As mentioned, at the UN, informal discussions are as important as formal interactions. Video-conferencing platforms like Zoom and Teams do offer breakout rooms to conduct smaller, informal discussions. Diplomats of permanent missions have also described using WhatsApp to conduct informal discussions with other UN actors. While digital platforms have been identified as effective tools to foster already existing working relationships, evidence shows that many diplomats still consider in-person meetings crucial for establishing trusting relationships (Höne, 2020; Bjola and Manor, 2022). No existing digital platform has yet been able to replace networking physical spaces like a coffee shop in New York or a lounge at the UN headquarters.

While some UN member states and their MFAs have been willing and able to invest significant resources to develop their digital communications, other countries have faced significant hurdles to follow their colleagues down the digital diplomacy path. This is particularly true for states with smaller permanent missions in New York. Diplomats from smaller missions usually cover several UN issue areas, which means that they are likely to be members of multiple group chats on digital platforms like WhatsApp and thus must follow numerous discussions often taking place simultaneously. This has created a situation where diplomats from smaller missions have often felt overworked, exhausted, and ineffective. It can also affect their visibility and perceived influence among their colleagues (Ashley, 2021). While online meetings were perceived by many diplomats as being more efficient and more inclusive as they allow a higher number of participants and can facilitate contact with members of the 'third' UN (Bjola and Manor, 2022), permanent missions with limited staff can struggle to take part in all the UN virtual meetings that are organized (Höne, 2020).

Some permanent missions from the Global South have also struggled to keep up with their colleagues. For example, Wekesa and colleagues (2021) argue that the COVID-19 pandemic has pushed African diplomats to engage more fully with digital tools. Yet, as Turianskyia and Wekesa explain, most African countries in the digitalization of their diplomacy 'la[g] behind not only the Global North but also other areas of the Global South'. A key explanation for these 'African digital diplomacy deficits is infrastructural' (2021: 347). Infrastructure issues such as low bandwidth and lack of technical resources have significantly affected the capacity of some UN member states from the Global South to effectively mobilize digital tools in their diplomatic activities. It is interesting to note that some countries from the Global North, although they have access to more resources to invest in their digital diplomacy than most other UN member states, have also had issues with their systems and digital capacities. For example, in 2017, widely used digital tools like WhatsApp and Skype were still not supported by the communication system of the Canadian ministry in charge of foreign affairs. This, it was stressed, contributed to slowing down the digitalization process in the ministry and its dependent missions (Global Affairs Canada, 2017).

Maintaining and securing confidentiality in the digital age have become important concerns for permanent missions during their digitalization process. For instance, security concerns over WhatsApp have led some governments and organizations such as the European Commission to recommend to their staff the use of other instant messaging apps such as Signal and Telegram (see Cerulus, 2020). Since July 2019, UN civil servants have also been advised to stop using WhatsApp over privacy and security issues (Reuters, 2020). Several organizations are even now in the process of developing their own instant messaging system. More recently, security concerns have been raised over the use of the platform TikTok. Like for other embassies and MFAs, security questions have been a significant challenge for permanent missions to the UN in New York during their digitalization process. The lack of international cyber security regulations and norms (Pauletto, 2020) has especially put additional pressure on permanent missions that do not have access to in-house cybersecurity expertise and lack the personnel to effectively train their staff on data security.

Consequences Linked to Digitalization

The introduction and adoption of new digital ICTs by permanent missions have had several consequences both on the role played by UN missions in the UN system and its dynamics, and on the communication behaviours and patterns of individuals who are active within these missions. Scholars have pointed out how unintended and problematic outcomes stemming from the use of digital ICTs by diplomats can affect the work being done in multilateral settings (Lemke and Habegger, 2020). There appears to be evidence of this in the case of the digitalization of permanent missions to the UN, which seems to have created a number dysfunctional effects or undesirable consequences (Rogers, 2003).

The increasing use of instant messaging apps like WhatsApp for group diplomacy in the UN, for example, has created a situation where some diplomats (particularly those from smaller missions) have often felt overworked, exhausted, and ineffective as they must follow numerous discussions often taking place simultaneously. For some observers, the level of engagement of missions on messaging apps can have a direct impact on their visibility and influence in UN discussions (Ashley, 2021). Missions with limited personnel have also found that video conferencing can significantly affect their capacities to ensure effective representation (Höne, 2020; Bjola and Manor, 2022). This is especially challenging in a context where UN virtual meetings are often overlapping. The extensive use of digital ICTs can thus lead to the (unintended) exclusion of some permanent missions from crucial UN discussions.

The choice to use some digital ICTs over others has also led to the marginalization of some permanent missions. Twitter, Facebook, and WhatsApp, all American-owned digital platforms, are blocked in some UN member states. All products from American companies like Microsoft and Cisco (Webex) are unavailable in states with US sanctions like Cuba and Iran. Russia and China have limited access to Cisco (Webex) platforms. Access to the popular platform Zoom is also restricted. Fewer than thirty countries, the majority from the Global North, can host free and paid Zoom events. Some states are only allowed to attend (but not host) free meetings. Four UN member states (Cuba, Iran, North Korea, and Syria) have no access to the platform (see Zoom, 2023). These restrictions can limit the role played by certain permanent missions in UN meetings. Furthermore, these choices can also have an important impact on diplomatic relations. As Höne notes, 'some conflicts over video platforms become instrumentalised in the sense that a perceived lack of technical capability could be used to stall the process of deciding on a particular platform and therefore stall an organisation's decision-making capabilities' (2020: 28).

Moreover, the digitalization of permanent missions and the UN system has led actors to reassess how to exert influence and power in the UN. In 2016, an article in the British newspaper *The Guardian* stated that '[i]nfluence [in diplomacy] is no longer defined only by special relationships and old alliances, but which WhatsApp group you are invited into'. Some UN practitioners seem to share this perception. Ashley (2021) notes that an invitation to join a group on an instant messaging app can be understood by certain diplomats as a sign of gaining influence among their peers. Being followed by all the permanent members of the UN Security Council on social media platforms could also be considered by some an indicator of one's importance in the UN system (Manor and Pamment, 2019). Other factors unquestionably shape power politics at the UN (see Acharya and Plesch, 2020). Influence can be linked to the relative position held by the actor in the organization and the international system, as well as the salience of the issue discussed (Smith, 2006). It is important to recognize that, for some UN actors, digital ICTs have become new spaces where UN member states are competing to influence UN politics, but also acknowledge that issues like the digital divide can greatly affect this competition.

Conclusion: Permanent Missions to the United Nations in the Digital Age

Interactions among diplomats of permanent missions to the UN in New York have been transformed by the emergence of instant messaging applications and video-conferencing platforms. Social media sites have changed the ways permanent missions communicate with actors outside the UN system. The integration of artificial intelligence (AI) tools in UN activities is also now being widely debated by the diplomatic community in New York. All missions to the UN have, to a certain extent, gone through some form of digitalization. All diplomats have seen their work impacted by the digitalization of UN diplomacy, especially during the pandemic. Several aspects of the 'hybrid diplomacy' (Bjola and Manor, 2022; Höne, 2020) that have become prevalent during the pandemic are likely to remain. But the pandemic has also been eye-opening regarding the varied experiences of states regarding digital diplomacy: '[i]n some cases, the response to the pandemic has accelerated ongoing digitalisation efforts in ministries of foreign affairs (MFAs). In other cases, missed opportunities regarding digitalisation are creating additional pressures on MFAs' (Höne, 2020: 15). This is also true in the case of permanent missions to the UN in New York.

The digital age and its tools have led many permanent missions to the UN and their diplomats to rethink how they can exert power and influence among their peers. Interestingly, the digitalization of UN permanent missions has reinforced another characteristic of UN dynamics: the United Nations, especially in New York, is a personality-driven environment. Indeed, several studies (Weiss, 2016; Pouliot, 2011; Smith, 2006; Reinalda and Verbeek, 2004) have stressed that the personal attributes of actors (personality, leadership and negotiating skills, knowledge competencies, etc.) can directly influence negotiations at the UN. In the context of the new digital environment, the appropriation and usage of digital media tools (by individual actors in the UN system) can also have a significant effect. Interviews with practitioners suggest that the most efficient communicators in the new digital environment were those who knew how to use the platforms well and whose online communications reflected their personalities. One diplomat even stated that, in his opinion, individual diplomats were doing much better on social media platforms than their member states and their permanent mission (United Nations, 2015b). This is an important finding as diplomats who perform well in the digital environment are perceived as directly contributing to their country's visibility and power in the UN system. Conversely, diplomats of the UN member states who have not invested in or have been unable to invest enough resources in digital communications, as well as diplomats who have not acquired enough 'digital skills', are in danger of being left out of key UN discussions. Individual digital skills and digital personality matter in the UN context. This also underscores the limitations of using a multilevel approach to explore the digitalization of permanent missions.

In many ways, the overarching message that is being sent to diplomats and permanent missions who represent member states is that they must be comfortable using digital tools if they wish to be full participants in the UN system. It tells permanent missions wishing to remain influential in the UN system, or in any international organization for that matter, that they must devote resources to their digital diplomacy. This message highlights that digital ICTs offer unprecedented opportunities for communication and representation in IOs. However, it fails to acknowledge that digitalization has not been a uniform experience for permanent missions. The process has been shaped by domestic, regional, and international factors. The international community must recognize that issues like the digital divide continue to significantly affect the activities of missions to IOs. They must also consider solutions to ensure that all member states are included and can fully participate in multilateral diplomacy in the digital age.

SUGGESTED READING

Bjola, Corneliu, and Ilan Manor. 2022. "The rise of hybrid diplomacy: from digital adaptation to digital adoption." *International Affairs* 98 (2): pp. 471–491. DOI: https://doi.org/10.1093/ia/iiac005

Höne, Katharina E. 2020. *The Future of (Multilateral) Diplomacy? Changes in Response to COVID-19 and Beyond*. Malta: DiploFoundation.

Malone, David M. 2015. "The Modern Diplomatic Mission." In *The Oxford Handbook of Modern Diplomacy*, edited by Andrew F. Cooper, Jorge Heine, and Ramesh Thakur, pp. 122–141. Oxford: Oxford University Press.

Rana, Kishan S. 2016. "Embassies, Permanent Missions and Special Missions." In *The SAGE Handbook of Diplomacy*, edited by Costas M. Constantinou, Pauline Kerr, and Paul Sharp, pp. 149–160. London: SAGE Publications Ltd.

REFERENCES

Acharya, Amitav, and Dan Plesch. 2020. "The United Nations." *Global Governance: A Review of Multilateralism and International Organizations* 26 (2): pp. 221–235. DOI: https://doi.org/10.1163/19426720-02602001

Aggestam, Karin, Annika Bergman Rosamond, and Elsa Hedling. 2021. "Feminist digital diplomacy and foreign policy change in Sweden." *Place Brand Public Diplomacy* 18: pp. 314–324. DOI: https://doi.org/10.1057/s41254-021-00225-3.

Archetti, Cristina. 2012. "The impact of new media on diplomatic practice: an evolutionary model of change." *The Hague Journal of Diplomacy* 7 (2): pp. 181–206.

Ashley, Kavoy Anthony. 2021. "'WhatsApp Diplomacy': The future of multilateralism in a post-COVID 19 world?" Paper prepared for United Nations Institute for Training and Research Workshop for Elections Officers 7–8 April 2021. https://unitar.org/sites/default/files/media/file/Whatsapp%20Diplomacy%20FINAL.PDF—Accessed on 5 November 2021.

Bjola, Corneliu, Jennifer Cassidy, and Ilan Manor. 2019. "Public Diplomacy in the Digital Age." In *Debating Public Diplomacy*, edited by Jan Melissen and Jian Wang, pp. 83–101. Leiden, Nederland: Brill.

Bjola, Corneliu, and Marcus Holmes (eds.). 2015. *Digital Diplomacy—Theory and Practice.* London and New York: Routledge.

Bjola, Corneliu, and Ilan Manor. 2018. "Revisiting Putnam's two-level game theory in the digital age: domestic digital diplomacy and the Iran nuclear deal." *Cambridge Review of International Affairs* 31 (1): pp. 3–32. DOI: https://doi.org/10.1080/09557571.2018.1476836

Bjola, Corneliu, and Ilan Manor. 2022. "The rise of hybrid diplomacy: from digital adaptation to digital adoption." *International Affairs* 98 (2): pp. 471–491. DOI: https://doi.org/10.1093/ia/iiac005

Bjola, Corneliu, and Ruben Zaiotti (eds.). 2020. *Digital Diplomacy and International Organisations Autonomy, Legitimacy and Contestation,* London and New York: Routledge.

Borger, Julian, Jennifer Rankin, and Kate Lyons. 2016. "The rise and rise of international diplomacy by WhatsApp" *The Guardian,* 4 November 2016, https://www.theguardian.com/technology/2016/nov/04/why-do-diplomats-use-this-alien-whatsapp-emoji-for-vladimir-putin—accessed on 20 October 2021.

Bouchard, Caroline. 2020. "The United Nations in the Digital Age: Harnessing the Power of New Digital Information and Communication Technologies." In *Digital Diplomacy And International Organisations—Autonomy, Legitimacy and Contestation*, edited by Corneliu Bjola and Ruben Zaiotti, pp. 101–126. London and New York: Routledge.

Bramsen, Isabel, and Anine Hagemann. 2021. "The missing sense of peace: diplomatic approachment and virtualization during the COVID-19 lockdown." *International Affairs* 97(2): pp. 539–60.

Cerulus, Laurens. 2020. "EU Commission to staff: Switch to Signal messaging app" *Politico,* 20 February 2020. https://www.politico.eu/article/eu-commission-to-staff-switch-to-signal-messaging-app/, accessed 25 November 2021.

Ecker-Ehrhardt, Matthias. 2020. "IO Public Communication Going Digital. Understanding Social Media Adoption and Use in Times of Politicization." In *Digital Diplomacy And International Organisations—Autonomy, Legitimacy and Contestation*, edited by Corneliu Bjola and Ruben Zaiotti, pp. 21–51. London and New York: Routledge.

Hocking, Brian, and Jan Melissen. 2015. *Diplomacy in the Digital Age.* Clingendael Report. The Hague: Clingendael Institute.

Hofferberth, Matthias. 2020. "Tweeting to Save Succeeding Generations from the Scourge of War? UN, Twitter and Communicative Action", In *Digital Diplomacy And International Organisations —Autonomy, Legitimacy and Contestation*, edited by Corneliu Bjola and Ruben Zaiotti, pp. 155–183. London and New York: Routledge.

Höne, Katharina E. 2020. *The Future of (Multilateral) Diplomacy? Changes in Response to COVID-19 and Beyond.* Malta: DiploFoundation.

Global Affairs Canada. 2017. *Evaluation of the Consular Affairs Program. Final Report.* October 2017. Diplomacy, Trade and Corporate Evaluation Division (PRE).

Huang, Zhao Alexandre, and Rui Wang. 2019. "Building a network to 'tell China stories well': Chinese diplomatic communication strategies on Twitter." *International Journal of Communication* 13: pp. 2984–3007.

Jönsson, Christer, and Martin Hall. 2003. "Communication: an essential aspect of diplomacy." *International Studies Perspectives* 4 (4): pp. 195–210.

Lemke, Tobias and Michael Habegger. 2020. "Diplomat or Troll? The Case Against Digital Diplomacy." In *Digital Diplomacy And International Organisations—Autonomy, Legitimacy and Contestation*, edited by Corneliu Bjola, and Ruben Zaiotti, pp. 229–264. London and New York: Routledge.

Malone, David M. 2015. "The Modern Diplomatic Mission." In *The Oxford Handbook of Modern Diplomacy*, edited by Andrew F. Cooper, Jorge Heine, and Ramesh Thakur, pp. 122–141. Oxford: Oxford University Press.

Manor, Ilan. 2017. "The digitalization of diplomacy: toward clarification of a fractured terminology". Working Paper. Exploring Digital Diplomacy. August 2017 available at: https://digdipblog.files.wordpress.com/2017/08/the-digitalization-of-diplomacy-working-paper-number-1.pdf—accessed 27 October 2021.

Manor, Ilan. 2019. *The Digitalization of Public Diplomacy*. Cham: Palgrave Macmillan.

Manor, Ilan. 2020. "Reconceptualising and Measuring Online Prestige in Ios: Towards a Theory of Prestige Mobility." In *Digital Diplomacy And International Organisations—Autonomy, Legitimacy and Contestation*, edited by Corneliu Bjola, and Ruben Zaiotti, pp. 184–206. London and New York: Routledge.

Manor, Ilan, and James Pamment. 2019. "Towards prestige mobility? Diplomatic prestige and digital diplomacy." *Cambridge Review of International Affairs* 32(2): pp. 93–131, DOI: 10.1080/09557571.2019.1577801

Melissen, Jan, and Jian Wang (eds.). 2019. *Debating Public Diplomacy. Now and Next*. Boston, Leiden: Brill Nijhoff.

Metzgar, Emily T. 2012. "Is it the medium or the message? Social media, American public diplomacy & Iran." *Global Media Journal* 12: pp. 1–16.

Moravcsik, Andrew. 1993. "Introduction: International Bargaining and Domestic Theories of International Bargaining." In *Double-Edged Diplomacy. International Bargaining and Domestic Politics*, edited by Peter Evans, Harold K. Jacobson, and Robert D. Putnam, pp. 3–42. Berkeley: University of California Press.

Pauletto, Christian. 2020. "Information and telecommunications diplomacy in the context of international security at the United Nations." *Transforming Government: People, Process and Policy* 14 (3): pp. 351–380. https://doi.org/10.1108/TG-01-2020-0007

Pouliot, Vincent. 2011. "Diplomats as permanent representatives: the practical logics of the multilateral pecking order." *International Journal* 66 (3): pp. 543–561.

Putnam, Robert D. 1988. "Diplomacy and domestic politics: the logic of two-level games." *International Organization* 42 (3): pp. 427–460.

Rana, Kishan S. 2016. "Embassies, Permanent Missions and Special Missions." In *The SAGE Handbook of Diplomacy*, edited by Costas M. Constantinou, Pauline Kerr, and Paul Sharp, pp. 149–160. London: SAGE Publications Ltd.

Reinalda, Bob, and Bertjan Verbeek. 2004. "The Issue of Decision Making within International Organizations." In *Decision Making within International Organizations*, edited by Bob Reinalda and Bertjan Verbeek, pp.25–58. London: Routledge.

Reuters. 2020. "U.N. says officials barred from using WhatsApp since June 2019 over security." 23 January.

Rogers, Everett M. 2003. *Diffusion of Innovations*. 5th ed. New York: Free Press.

Ross, Alec. 2011. "Digital diplomacy and US foreign policy." *The Hague Journal of Diplomacy* 6 (3–4): pp. 451–455. DOI: https://doi.org/10.1163/187119111X590556

Sandre, Andreas. 2018. "WhatsApp for diplomats." *Medium - Digital Diplomacy*. https://medium.com/digital-diplomacy/whatsapp-for-diplomats-c594028042f1

Smith, Courtney B. 2002. "Three perspectives on global consensus building: a framework for analysis." *International Journal of Organizational Theory & Behavior* 5 (1&2): pp. 115–144.

Smith, Courtney B. 2006. *Politics and Process at the United Nations*. Boulder, CO: Lynne Rienner.

Turianskyi, Yarik, and Bob Wekesa. 2021. "African digital diplomacy: emergence, evolution, and the future." *South African Journal of International Affairs* 28 (3): pp. 341–359.

United Kingdom Foreign and Commonwealth Office. 2012. *The Foreign and Commonwealth Office Digital Strategy* (December 2012), https://www.gov.uk/government/publications/the-fco-digital-strategy, accessed on 15 May 2022.

United Nations. 2015a. "UN social media day: schedule and more." *United Nations Blog*, 26 January. New York: United Nations. http://blogs.un.org/blog/2015/01/26/social-media-day-schedule-and-more—accessed on 12 October 2020.

United Nations. 2015b. "UN social media day." https://www.youtube.com/watch?v=I6lobQSH Pg8—accessed on 12 October 2021.

United Nations. 2021. *The Blue Book*, Protocol and Liaison Service for information. New York: United Nations.

UN General Assembly. 2021. *High-Level Thematic Debate on Digital Cooperation and Connectivity: Whole-of-Society Responses to End the Digital Divide*, Summary of the President of the General Assembly, 27 April 2021. New York: United Nations.

Weiss, Thomas G. 2016. *What's Wrong with the United Nations and How to Fix It*. 2nd ed. Cambridge: Polity Press.

Weiss, Thomas G., Tatiana Carayannis, and Richard Jolly. 2009. "The 'third' United Nations." *Global Governance* 15(1): pp. 123–42.

Wekesa, Bob, Yarik Turianskyi, and Odilile Ayodele. 2021. "Introduction to the special issue: digital diplomacy in Africa." *South African Journal of International Affairs* 28(3): pp. 335–339. DOI: 10.1080/10220461.2021.1961606

Zoom. 2023. "Geographic availability for Zoom events." https://support.zoom.us/hc/en-us/articles/4403179347341-Geographic-availability-for-Zoom-Events—accessed on 3 October 2023.

CHAPTER 19

THE DIGITAL ADAPTATION OF INTERNATIONAL BUREAUCRACIES

MATTHIAS ECKER-EHRHARDT

INTRODUCTION

GOVERNMENTS across the globe have delegated substantial political competences to international organizations (IOs) to facilitate cooperation in central policy areas from security, economic development, public health, human rights, or climate change to the management of migration, technical standards, or financial markets. By standard scientific definition, IOs are formal entities of international law established by international treaties among three or more sovereign states (Pevehouse et al., 2004). What is more, IOs not only possess intergovernmental councils, committees, or assemblies inhabited by state diplomats, but also permanent bureaucratic capacities—often named 'secretariats'—tasked to facilitate cooperation among states on a regular basis. These international bureaucracies play an eminent role in contemporary global governance. Competences delegated to IOs by its member states have become increasingly broad and demanding, going beyond the mere facilitation of intergovernmental negotiations— for example by organizing delegates' meetings and gathering knowledge shared with delegates beforehand—to monitoring states' compliance with negotiated agreements, arbitrating conflicts by quasi-judicial processes, and providing operational capacities for implementing ambitious policy programmes such as vaccination campaigns or humanitarian relief (Hooghe et al., 2019). None of this can be done by state delegates alone but has led in most cases to the expansion of international bureaucracies into increasingly complex apparatuses of administrative roles, bodies, and processes (Bauer et al., 2016).

While international bureaucracies have been key for understanding intergovernmental diplomacy for recent decades, their use of digital means of communication is arguably of great importance for understanding the future trajectory of global governance in the digital age. Central issues of this governance—from climate change and migration flows to the spread of contagious diseases across borders—as well as their proper political management are now vehemently commented on and contested in digital spheres of networked communication, such as Facebook, Weibo, Instagram, or X, formerly known as Twitter. In these spheres, the decisions and policies of IOs themselves regularly become the subject of controversy. Like other actors in global governance discussed in this handbook—such as state diplomats (ch.6), civil society organizations (ch.21), or cities (ch.22)—the communication departments of international bureaucracies have consequently begun to use digital means of communication themselves as promising tools of 'digital diplomacy' over the last decade.

International bureaucracies' digital diplomacy is associated with far-reaching hopes, ranging from increased institutional transparency and more effective advocacy for cosmopolitan ideas to a more effective (self-)legitimization to garner support for international cooperation. However, prominent tools of digital diplomacy such as social media seem rather ill-equipped for purposes of communicating the governance of 'complex interdependence' (Keohane and Nye, 1977), characterized by a plurality of issues, actors, and mechanisms (Rosenau, 1995). While the use of social media is not as strongly related to global economic development or levels of education as one might expect, it still reaches younger people much more than the older population, thus remains highly selective as a tool of public communication (Auxier and Anderson, 2021). What is more, technical possibilities often limit the amount of information communicated in remarkable ways—think, for example, of X's maximum length of tweets to 280 characters or Instagram's focus on short video clips of up to 15 seconds. Despite a remarkable abundance of content, public attention in the digital age is nevertheless a surprisingly scarce commodity, especially for institutional communication. On social media, content is vehemently and powerfully curated by other users through selective forwarding, quoting, and commenting. The virality of content therefore follows the logic of social network communication: only what mobilizes users to immediately share content in their private network successfully diffuses through the overall digital sphere and becomes public in this sense (Klinger and Svensson, 2015). Those who aim for a wider reach are accordingly tempted to focus on concise personal or emotional content—without, however, guaranteeing virality (Papacharissi, 2016).

How do international bureaucracies deal with such opportunities and challenges of digital diplomacy? What are the consequences of digital diplomacy regarding the content communicated by international bureaucracies and beyond? While there has been a welcome increase in the number of relevant studies recently, a systematic discussion of the phenomenology, conditions, and impact of digital communication by international bureaucracies has only just begun (Bjola and Zaiotti, 2020). Accordingly, this chapter of the handbook attempts to demonstrate the significance of recent research as well as to demonstrate the need for further exploration. The chapter is divided into three steps: The first part illustrates the current practices of international bureaucracies' 'digital diplomacy' by focusing on social media such as X/Twitter and Facebook in a quantitative perspective, illustrated with recent examples of their use. In the second part, I briefly turn to the 'why' question and discuss motivational factors and conducive conditions that might help to explain why IOs have turned to, and increasingly employ, means of digital diplomacy such as social media. While the first and second parts focus arguably on the opportunities of digital diplomacy, the third part goes full circle by turning to a couple of its challenges—organized hypocrisy, pluralization, acceleration, selectivity, personalization, and polarization—of which little is yet known, but that deserves more attention by scholars, practitioners, and stakeholders of global governance alike.

How Do International Bureaucracies 'Go Digital'?

When writing about the role of international bureaucracy regarding global governance, it is always tempting to start with the most eminent exemplar of this species, the United Nations (UN) Secretariat. It not only facilitates the negotiations of 193 member states across issue areas from international security and economic development to environmental protection, human rights, and humanitarian aid; it monitors global problems as well as governments' compliance with international obligations and also has a tremendous impact by implementing policies on the ground, for example by managing a dozen peacekeeping operation with about 88,686 personnel (as of March 2023).[1] Consequently, its Global Communications Department is arguably one if not the most important actor in global public diplomacy, responsible for 'communicating to the world the ideals and work of the United Nations; interacting and partnering with diverse audiences; and building support for the purposes and principles enshrined in the Charter of the United Nations' (United Nations, 2023: 4). With a total annual budget of about US$102 million in 2023 and 686 staff (United Nations, 2023: 21f) it is also a key branch of the Secretariat that must report annually to member states via the Committee on Information of the UN General Assembly, while the Under-Secretary-General for Global Communications at its helm directly reports to the Secretary-General on a regular basis.

In early 2022, its Social Media Team based in New York has about twenty-five posts and is responsible for 166 accounts on fourteen different social media platforms (in order of relevance: X, Facebook, YouTube, Instagram, LinkedIn, Flickr, Medium, Youku, Weibo, Tumblr, TikTok, WeChat, Snapchat, and Pinterest). Content is provided in the six official languages of the organization—Arabic, Chinese, English, French, Russian, and Spanish—as well as Hindi, Kiswahili, and Portuguese. To make this possible, staff from all over the UN contribute content that is coordinated, streamlined, and published by the Social Media Team. The Social Media Team also advises others across the entire organization on how to provide useful content for the team and to properly employ social media strategies themselves. The last point is important: 'Social media managers' outside of Global Communications are often tasked to run additional social media accounts by the UN's various branches. In the case of Twitter (now X), fifty-four handles

---

[1] <https://peacekeeping.un.org/en/data> (last access on 8 August 2023).

of the UN are officially under direct control of its central Social Media Team, but another 365 credibly claim to belong to UN officials or bodies and thus tweet on behalf of the organization. Additional training for those running these accounts is provided, for example, by courses at the UN System Staff College that include modules on how to effectively implement and evaluate social media campaigns.[2]

The UN Department of Global Communications has an impressive outreach into its social media environment. For 2022, it reports about sixty-six million page views across the multilingual UN News websites to the General Assembly (United Nations, 2023: 15). In August 2023, its main English X handle @UN has about 16.3 million followers, the respective account on Facebook @unitednations about 7.5 million. These numbers add up to an immense amount of total online engagement, because content is promoted across digital platforms: for example, fighting against misinformation on Covid-19, the UN's Verified campaign generated about 660 million video views in 2020 and serves those responsible as a 'flagship example of delivering on the objectives of the UN global communications strategy of leading the narrative, inspiring people to care and mobilizing action' (United Nations, 2021: 9).

Such success according to common engagement metrics is arguably based on various tools of digital diplomacy. For example, the UN has effectively employed its own hashtags as important 'soft structures' of storytelling (Papacharissi, 2016) for a long time (Pamment, 2016). In 2020, the UN-promoted hashtag #ClimateAction successfully generated about thirty-five million engagements (likes, shares, and comments) (United Nations, 2021: 12). What is more, tools of digital diplomacy also include celebrities and influencers as important 'force multipliers' on social media. To illustrate, the K-pop group BTS repeatedly spurred massive user engagement online and journalistic coverage offline—such as in their speech calling for the younger generation to care for sustainable development at the 75th UN General Assembly, which drew about 485,000 likes on Twitter[3] and more than eight million views on YouTube.[4] In the same context, the UN has successfully promoted a mobile phone app *AWorld*, which suggests ways to 'act for the planet', tracks users' habits in order to 'help live a sustainable lifestyle', and also keeps users aware of the overall issue.[5]

What does the picture look like beyond the UN? Communication departments of many IOs have been remarkably active in digital spheres of communication for years now. Virtually all have created their own websites early on, and a recent study on the institutional development of IOs in a global perspective even declared an active webpage to be an operational criterion for the respective IO to be relevant for a systematic investigation of this organizational field (Hooghe et al., 2019). There is more notable

---

[2] for example see <https://www.unssc.org/courses/communications-2030-agenda-and-sdgs-0> (last access on 8 August 2023). On the UN System Staff College itself see https://www.unssc.org/about/what-we-do (last access on 8 August 2023).

[3] <https://twitter.com/bts_bighit/status/1308767112341585921> (last access on 8 August 2023).

[4] <https://www.youtube.com/watch?v=5aPe9Uy1on4> (last access on 8 August 2023).

[5] <https://play.google.com/store/apps/details?id=app.aworld> (last access on 8 August 2023).

variation in the regular use of social media platforms such as Facebook, X, Flickr, or Instagram—platforms that can be categorized as social media to the extent they allow users to connect with others by setting up unique profiles and sharing user-generated content (Ellison and boyd, 2013). To illustrate this variation, I draw on a systematic survey of Facebook and Twitter (now X) profiles of a selection of fifty IOs. Notably, this selection stems from a stratified random sample of the overall population of IOs to provide a representative picture. Consequently, the sample includes organizations across all issue areas of global governance (such as security, environment, development, or trade), global and regional organizations from all over the world (such as the African Union or ASEAN, the Association of Southeast Asian Nations), and major ones such as the UN as well as tiny exemplars most readers might have never heard of such as the Northwest Atlantic Fisheries Organization (Ecker-Ehrhardt, 2020a).[6] At the end of 2021, a total of 486 Facebook pages and 946 Twitter handles can be attributed to these fifty organizations. However, ten of these (20%) are still not actively using Facebook, and seven (or 16%) don't run any official handle on Twitter. While of eminent importance for global governance in their respective policy area(s), many small and specialized organizations—such as the International Telecommunications Satellite Organization or the North East Atlantic Fisheries Commission—neither tweet nor post.

Numbers already suggest another important part of the picture: most organizations beyond the UN are now present with multiple accounts on the same platform, significantly diversifying their presence on social media. On Facebook, the Council of Europe alone runs forty-eight accounts, and the two leading development banks—the World Bank and the Asian Development Bank—are each responsible for thirty-eight. Much smaller ones are also represented by several accounts. For example, the Collective Security Treaty Organization (recently sending 'peacekeeping forces'[7] to Kazakhstan) has three. Figure 19.1 illustrates the relative frequency of social media profiles that can be attributed to the sampled IOs. There had been a steady increase until 2018, with a slight downward trend recently, which indicates a saturation and consolidation process to facilitate coordination and increase resonance. Particularly in the early years, main organizational pages, or handles (such as @UN, @WTO, or @ASEAN) explicitly set up to represent the whole organization, dominated. Since then, official profiles on more specific themes or branches of the respective organization have been added. Most of them reflect the work

---

[6] The sample was originally drawn by Tallberg and colleagues (2013)—a full list of organizations is also provided by the author elsewhere (Ecker-Ehrhardt, 2018, 2020a). This sample included the West European Union that ceased to exist in 2008, that is before social media took off. It has been replaced by another security organization, the Collective Security Treaty Organization, for this article. For the survey of social media activities, search functions of Facebook and Twitter were used to identify accounts related to selected organizations based on acronyms as well as full names. Pages generated independently by Facebook (social community pages) were not taken into account and the profiles of individuals only if explicitly acting in an official capacity. Essential research assistance by Ann-Kristin Kuhnert, Lucas Wotzka, and Philip Kreißel is gratefully acknowledged.

[7] <https://en.odkb-csto.org/news/news_odkb/zayavlenie-predsedatelya-soveta-kollektivnoy-bezop asnosti-odkb-premer-ministra-respubliki-armeniya-n> (last access on 8 August 2023).

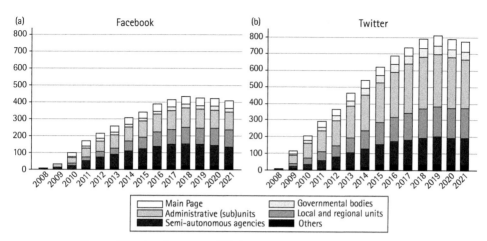

FIGURE 19.1 Types of Facebook pages and Twitter accounts across time
Source: Own calculations, based on the sample of N = 50 IOs discussed in the text.

of specialized sub-units of the respective secretariat and are dedicated to specific policy areas (e.g., human rights, development, energy policy), or administrative functions (e.g., by representing the Human Resources Unit). Larger IOs constitute complex institutional systems including semi-autonomous agencies and local or regional units who increasingly task their staff with running social media profiles. Where existing, special bodies such as parliamentary assemblies and international courts also show a remarkable interest in using social media. For example, all the parliamentary assemblies covered (N = 12) have their own Twitter accounts, and eight are on Facebook. Of the twenty courts or quasi-judicial bodies surveyed, six have Facebook pages, and eight have accounts on Twitter. By comparison, intergovernmental bodies—such as, for example, the UN Human Rights Council or NATO's highest military authority, the Military Committee—only rarely call on staff or those at the respective central communication department to run social media accounts on their behalf. This is remarkable not only because of the enormous decision-making power of intergovernmental bodies—which still have a final say of most what is going on in IOs—but also because nowadays virtually all governments employ some sort of 'digital diplomacy' to address foreign as well as domestic publics (Manor, 2019). Nevertheless, governments leave the presentation of intergovernmental bodies' work (or the decisions taken there) to the main communications departments.

Why Do International Bureaucracies Turn to Digital Means?

The increased use of digital tools such as websites or social media is part of a broader tendency of IOs to proactively address general publics that deserves explanation

(Ecker-Ehrhardt, 2018). Over the past few decades, most have defined public communication as a central task of their bureaucratic apparatus, centralized respective competences in increasingly well-staffed communication departments and intensified efforts toward strategic planning and evaluation. Such endowment with powerful public communication units has significantly favoured the adoption of digital technologies (Ecker-Ehrhardt, 2020a). A number of investigations have also pointed to the central role that innovative leaders—such as Ban Ki-moon and António Guterres at the UN (Bouchard, 2020), Anders Fogh Rasmussen and Jens Stoltenberg at the North Atlantic Treaty Organization (NATO) (Risso, 2014; Olsson et al., 2018), Patricia Scotland at the Commonwealth Secretariat (Goheer, 2020), or Pablo Saavedra at the Inter-American Human Rights Court (IACtHR)—had in making digital communication an organizational priority. Thus, both organizational resources and leadership were crucial for the systematic introduction of social media as a means of digital diplomacy.

Public Information for an Increasingly Diverse Audience

But how else to explain variation across the organizational field beyond such conducive conditions? To start with, practitioners of public communication are tasked with targeting an increasingly broad range of specific audiences in the environment of IOs. Over recent decades, most have opened up towards a plurality of nonstate actors—including experts, activists, and lobbyists—as sources of knowledge and legitimacy (Tallberg et al., 2013). Along the road, public communication has raised its profile as an important intermediary practice between the inside of IOs and the outside of social or transnational publics. It makes the respective communication departments powerful brokers of information in both directions: in terms of channelling information from the inside to the outside, communication departments can have an enormous impact on how the public understands the mandates, procedures, and processes of IOs. Consequently, communication departments have sought to diversify their portfolio of communication channels—including social media—to reach a more diverse organizational environment. In terms of overcoming organizational boundaries outside-in, however, today's communication departments can also help to fulfil organizational mandates. For example, many of them now systematically monitor public discourse to plan and evaluate the effectiveness of communication activities.

Bridging the inside and outside of IOs, communication departments are of normative as well as empirical importance. As transmission belts of information about internal processes and decisions, they can effectively level out corresponding information asymmetries and thus make IOs more accountable to a wider global public, including, for example, journalists, activists, parliamentarians, or interested citizens trying to keep up with international issues. Political accountability presupposes information that is as current and comprehensive as possible, which of course also applies to international governance. Member states and civil society have put increasing pressure on international bureaucracies to provide comprehensive public information as much as possible over recent decades (Grigorescu, 2007). Large-N studies have also provided conclusive evidence that the trend to enhance public communication capacities can, to some extent, be attributed to changing norms of institutional transparency and accountability (Ecker-Ehrhardt, 2018). In this regard, it is instructive to see that communication strategies of large organizations committed their communication departments to use digital channels to provide public information and thereby refer explicitly to corresponding normative expectations of transparency or accountability. For example, in its Public Communications Policy from 2011, Asian Development Bank (2011) already cheered digital media's capability to provide 'more information … to more people in more ways', directly pointing to risen '[p]ublic expectations about the range, type, and delivery of information' (Ecker-Ehrhardt, 2018: 9). Similar references to social media as primary tools to enhance public 'information' have been ubiquitous in similar documents from other organizations, such as the European Bank of Reconstruction and Development (EBRD, 2014).

Self-Legitimation

Second, much of international bureaucracies' communication aims at the *self-legitimation* of their own policies, procedures, and operations because of massive domestic politicization—in the sense of increasing social salience and controversiality of what they are and do (Zürn et al., 2012; Dingwerth et al., 2019). Populist leaders—predominantly from the political right—have successfully used social media to mobilize against specific IOs (such as the UN, the World Health Organization, or the World Trade Organization), often addressing specific organizations as linchpins of a 'liberal international order' (Adler and Drieschova, 2021). Social media have even been experienced by some IOs—such as NATO and the EU—as realms of systematic disinformation campaigns by specific countries (notably Russia and North Korea, Olsson et al., 2018). Lastly, digital means have also empowered citizens and communities at the receiving end of policies and operations of IOs, with very legitimate concerns and allegations—such as sexual exploitation and abuse by UN peacekeepers (Daugirdas, 2019). In these and similar cases, social media have arguably helped to 'elevate marginalized voices and … democratize the ways in which allegations are exposed and documented' (McGregor, 2019: 239). Consequently, the demand for well-managed public communication by the respective organization increases considerably the more it is confronted with public delegitimation—very much explaining how IO communication capacities have been enhanced and channels diversified in the past (Meyer, 2009; Risso, 2014; Ecker-Ehrhardt, 2018), including the timing and intensity of their use of social media (Olsson et al., 2018; Ecker-Ehrhardt, 2020a).

Advocacy

Finally, a decisive part of international bureaucracies' communication is increasingly concerned with campaigns advocating for social change and mobilization. After all, many organizations are not only central arenas of—increasingly contested—multilateral negotiations but are also entrusted with the implementation of ambitious policy programmes that result from these negotiations. In this context, digital campaigns increasingly play a key role as they are perceived as the most efficient means to influence public discourse—for example, in order to improve awareness of human rights or mobilize citizens for a more sustainable lifestyle. Notably, social media afford the immediate and direct communication of visual content, which permits more credible claims of authenticity by providing, for example, timely visual evidence of human suffering or melting ice in the Arctic (Geis and Schlag, 2017). This motivation for 'going digital' also applies to the UN, where the Under-Secretary-General for Global Communications has recently called social media 'a key' for a strategy shift towards 'cause communications' whereby the aim is 'not just to inform, but also to inspire people to care and to mobilize them for action' (United Nations, 2021: 33). Consequently, the Social Media Team has moved from the subprogramme 'News Services' to the 'Communications Campaigns Service' in order to 'strengthen the full integration and the effective use of flagship social media platforms in various UN campaigns on priority themes' (United Nations, 2021: 33). Beyond the UN, quantitative analysis shows that IOs active in thematic areas that are prone to call for public advocacy in terms of 'cause communication'—such as human rights or sustainable development—show a higher probability for enhancing their organizational capacities for public communication (Ecker-Ehrhardt, 2018) and to use social media more extensively (Ecker-Ehrhardt, 2020a). An exemplary comparison of offline and online communication also shows that the possibility of direct online communication—i.e. without journalistic gatekeepers—can also be used to strategically 'orchestrate' advocacy campaigns by disproportionately taking into account the opinions of like-minded states, experts, and NGOs in the public relations work of IOs (Ecker-Ehrhardt, 2020c). Such opportunities for pro-active advocacy may additionally motivate the adoption of social media to some extent.

The expanded use of social media by international bureaucracies can accordingly be attributed to a broad portfolio of goals and motivations, the interaction of which has so far been the subject of too little systematic comparative research. With regard to public information, social media are apparently often used with the expectation of enabling more public information, thus accommodating normative demands for institutional transparency and accountability. At the same time, however, the use of social media also seems to be regularly aimed at improving public support or influencing social discourses by more effective advocacy campaigns.

Challenges of International Bureaucracies' Digital Communication

Maintaining a focus on motivational factors and conducive conditions of digital communication is tempting because it allows us to highlight its opportunities. These are what advocates of change inside and outside international bureaucracies are accustomed to pointing out, and what communication departments prefer to reference when reporting successes to member states. However, there are also important challenges of digital communication, of which six are briefly outlined below: organized hypocrisy, pluralization, acceleration, selectivity, personalization, and polarization. These challenges still define major research desiderata at the intersection of international relations, communication studies, and organizational sociology. At the same time, they should concern practitioners as well as stakeholders of global governance, as they all in some way stress the transformative impact digital technologies arguably have on how global governance involves those at the recipient end of its decisions and operation.

Organized Hypocrisy

Digital means of communication hold the potential to improve global public deliberation on global governance in several ways. As mentioned above, by levelling information asymmetries, they can first of all improve chances to effectively contest decisions and operations, and thus contribute to public accountability. However, beyond the mere dissemination of information, they may also open avenues for a more inclusive dialogue with a wider public in terms of a truly open-minded exchange of reason and arguments (Hofferberth, 2020), thus spurring hopes of a new quality of global governance as a deliberative system (Parkinson and Mansbridge, 2012) if not a 'user-generated democracy' (Loader and Mercea, 2011). Communication strategies in the organizational field indeed regularly allude to such opportunities, for example by stressing social media's 'emphasis on two-way, informal conversation and information sharing, rather than traditional top-down communications' (International Council for the Exploration of the Sea, ICES, 2010: 3). However, communication as practiced by international bureaucracies does not live up to such far-reaching expectations, for at least two reasons. The first one is feasibility in a practical sense. Most organizations use digital tools such as websites and social media predominantly in a top-down mode of broadcasting preferred messages (Hofferberth, 2020; Bjola and Jiang, 2015). Practitioners have noted how they are overwhelmed by the amount of users' questions and replies to their social media content (Groves, 2018), which suggests that they could more actively engage if resources permitted. The use of quantitative engagement metrics that focus on the quantifiable success of one-way information dissemination allows for the circumvention of tricky questions about how much dialogue there really is (Rogers, 2018). Instructively, recent examples of interactive chat bots and mobile phone apps (see above) suggest an easy solution (Bouchard, 2020), even more so if blended with increasingly capable algorithms to emulate human behaviour. However, they arguably do not help because of the second reason for why dialogue is a problematic claim: political feasibility. While theories of 'excellence' in public relations have successfully called for making communication a top priority of strategic management in many organizations of global governance (Grunig,

2009), the everyday experience of many practitioners—especially those in larger organizations—is structurally very much decoupled from the upper echelon of organizational leadership. This is all the more true for international organizations, where intergovernmental bodies ultimately remain the main power houses. In this regard, communication practitioners do not have the authority to engage in a politically significant dialogue that could have an impact on decisions or operations, even if increasingly given time to listen, answer, and even justify what the organization does or does not do. Thus, any simulacrum of such a dialogue by digital means arguably aggravates what organization scholars have long discussed as 'organized hypocrisy' (Lipson, 2007): an over-supply of largely symbolic talk and practices that allude to organizational values but cannot inherently help to materialize them.

Pluralization

Social media not only facilitate control over public legitimation processes but arguably constitute one of its greatest challenges—not only because they facilitate contestations by the many constituents IOs nowadays have (see above). As mentioned earlier, the recent trend of international bureaucracies to 'go digital' reflects an expansion into the breadth of the organization—a proliferation of online presences of individual committees, offices, and units. This is not least due to the comparatively low effort that enables even individual office holders to present themselves on social media and to increase their own visibility within and outside the organization. However, this proliferation of online presences comes at the expense of a coordinated and coherent external presentation as a unified actor in international politics (Olsson et al., 2018: 68). Not surprisingly, it is observed with suspicion by those communication departments increasingly tasked with handling the many voices on behalf of the organization (Groves, 2018). Not least in moments of public scandalization, a pluralization of institutional voices can make effective crisis management—from the perspective of the organization concerned—considerably more difficult (Meyer, 2009). Thus, the recent decline in aggregate numbers can be attributed not to a decreasing need for self-legitimation, but increased efforts to streamline and strengthen it to more effectively speak with 'one voice' in order to facilitate self-legitimation (as well as to increase the impact of advocacy campaigns).

Selectivity

New tools for direct communication with non-expert audiences highlight the demand for the better translation of complex issues. Notably, communication practitioners of international bureaucracies indeed embrace social media's capabilities to use images in order 'to "show" not just "tell" ' (ASEAN, 2019: 49). Similarly, the UN Social Media Team was recently tasked to 'redesign legacy evergreen content from the old platform to suit the new, more visual and mobile-friendly platform ... (for enhancing) reach and deeper engagement' (United Nations, 2021: 16) among audiences. Mostly focused on limited text and attention-grabbing visuals, however, social media seems neither technically nor socially particularly suitable for making people understand and jointly discuss what IOs are and do. Empirical research has shown that the maximum number of characters allowed in tweets, for example, effectively hinders the exchange of detailed arguments and evidence (Jaidka et al., 2019). Like many users, IOs compensate for the lack of information capacity of social media by linking to external content. Even then, however, they face the difficult decision of what information to highlight in the respective tweet or post itself, for example to draw public attention to what is being linked. This favours the questionable reduction of complex issues to colourfully illustrated slogans whose information value is necessarily limited for what global governance is about. It also favours the privileged consideration of certain contents by communication practitioners according to strategic considerations (such as self-legitimization) at the expense of a comprehensive public information desperately needed for spurring the public accountability of IOs (Ecker-Ehrhardt, 2020c). Existing evidence suggests that such selectivity may become a problem in particular when the organization is under considerable pressure to justify itself and soften institutional failures through one-sided success stories (cf., for example, Ecker-Ehrhardt, 2020b). However, much more research is needed to shed light on this possibility.

Acceleration

Acceleration arguably belongs to the most widely acknowledged transformations digital technologies bring to international relations and diplomatic practices (Drezner, 2019). As one practitioner recently pointedly observed, on Twitter, 'when all messaging is shouted and frenetic, discrete diplomacy and slow-paced communication risk to become invisible, and therefore irrelevant' (Summa, 2020: 51). Thus, new digital means of communication foster 'a new sense of urgency and immediacy' also for those who are tasked with informing external audiences with internal developments (Risso, 2014: 259). This problem is enhanced by two affordances of digital tools such as social media. On the one hand, while enabling users to link external content (for example to overcome space constraints as mentioned before), they not only put pressure on a timely tweet or post, but such messaging also presupposes that more detailed statements must also have already been produced at the time the respective tweet or post is sent off—a pressure to speed up that is problematic for internal production and coordination processes of content (Dimitrov, 2014: 304). On the other hand, while enabling timely messaging, digital means also increase the susceptibility of communication to errors that are tricky to correct if content has been shared widely in private networks. To illustrate, the UN's social media unit sent a tweet on 29 November 2012, in which it announced that the Secretary-General was pushing for a one (instead of two) state solution—and this only hours before an important vote in the UN General Assembly on the recognition of the

Palestinian Authority as an observer (Mandel, 2012). Two hours were enough to evoke a flood of both angry and derisive comments online before those responsible went back online and posted a correction—which, however, was not as widely shared as the 'wrong' tweet in the beginning. Thus, 'mistakes can occur more easily ... (those) engaging in social media conversations thus need to be aware of both social media's power and pitfalls' (Asia-Pacific Economic Cooperation, APEC, 2013: 1).

Personalization

Social media have spurred a digital communication that is more focused on the 'people doing global governance' instead of its institutions. Many official accounts of international bureaucracies now belong to representational roles and offices—such as in the case of the United Nations: @UN_PGA regularly tweets for the president of the UN General Assembly, and @antonioguterres tweets for the current UN Secretary-General. What is more, social media allow communication practitioners—including those feeding institutional accounts—to directly target citizens with content that stylizes officials across ranks as the 'personal face' of institutional processes. Both contribute to a new emphasis on the personal, which has its benefits. Ex officio, leading officials of international bureaucracies are important norm entrepreneurs, who are expected to show leadership—internally as well as externally—by credibly representing and promoting community norms and values with a necessary degree of personal authenticity and integrity (Fröhlich, 2014). Social media arguably better allow officials to display emotional states and to stylize as 'sentient beings' vis-à-vis a broader audience of citizens directly. This includes—but is not confined to—an imagery certifying the attentive listening of officials vis-à-vis civil society representatives affirming responsiveness and engagement (Di Martino, 2020). On other occasions, officials have been pictured showing deep regret while apologizing for past failures and firmly committing to comply with highest institutional standards in the future (Daugirdas, 2019). In these and similar situations, the intuitive truth of images blends with a more credible expression of emotional states—such as enthusiasm, affection, anger, or shame—by individual officials and as part of their 'emotional labor' (Hochschild, 2012; Tompea, 2021, Ecker-Ehrhardt, 2023b). Thus, the increased presence of bureaucratic leaders of IOs online might substantially facilitate the public legitimation of IOs as 'community organizations' (Abbott and Snidal, 1998) more credibly representing as well as advocating the norms and values of their constituents. At the same time, however, such benefits seem to come with notable costs. First, some observers have noted a problematic 'trivialization' of public communication that zooms in on officials' personality at the expense of 'hard facts' about decisions and actions themselves (Krzyżanowski, 2018). Second, intuition suggests that the new emphasis on the personal might aggravate existing problems of decoupling action in global governance from its political symbolism. By running personal accounts of officials, organizations suggest to other users that they acknowledge the more horizontal mode of networked communication among peers, but without using it much for engaging other users in terms of an inter-personal dialogue (see above). Third—and most importantly—, there is a sublime but notable tension between foregrounding the personality of individual office holders online and the claim to depersonalized 'rational-legal' authority that international bureaucracies are used to presenting and to which international civil servants are said to adhere (Barnett and Finnemore, 2005: 164ff). While an emphasis on office holders' personal aspects can in some way be read as a strategic response to recent populism's disdain of IOs as 'bureaucratic machineries' (Destradi and Plagemann, 2019), the personalization of its digital diplomacy might be problematic to the degree it reaffirms that 'bureaucratic machinery' is a problem in the first place.

Polarization

In the digital world, competition for attention 'invites affective attunement, supports affective investment, and propagates affectively charged expression' (Papacharissi, 2016: 308). Consequently, current usage of digital communication by larger IOs such as the UN suggests a privileged targeting of audiences that would hopefully empathically connect with moral causes such as humanitarian aid, human rights, or sustainable development (Bouchard, 2020). However, online audiences tend to pick and choose from the abundance of circulating content that confirms their pre-existing attitudes, while avoiding dissonant information (Garrett, 2009). Platforms also rely on algorithms that suggest content, followers, or trending hashtags, notoriously reinforcing the consumption of like-minded content (Flaxman et al., 2016). This favours fragmentation in the form of self-referential echo chambers (Williams et al., 2015), which already structurally impede dialogue across ideological lines of conflict and thus favour polarization of ideological extremes. Network analyses have shown that major organizations such as the UN can achieve a remarkable centrality in debates on climate change (Goritz et al., 2020) or migration (Ecker-Ehrhardt, forthcoming), because their posts or tweets achieve enormous followership and are widely shared. However, such centrality seems to apply mainly to the networks of like-minded users—those that already support the UN's vehement advocacy of more ambitious climate goals or legal and safe migration routes. Online advocacy offers such users considerable opportunities for expressive online activism—they can become publicly visible advocates themselves by liking or sharing relevant content and thus confirm their own identity as activists to themselves and others (Milan, 2015). However, such advocacy only reaches critics to a very limited extent. In particular, the deepening rift between cosmopolitans and anti-cosmopolitans (Strijbis et al., 2018) seems to cause much advocacy to fail bitterly, insofar as it moves the latter to further decouple themselves communicatively and mentally from corresponding communication flows. In the long term, digital advocacy by cosmopolitan IOs could thus involuntarily contribute to their delegitimation and that of the 'liberal international order' (Ikenberry, 2010) they reflect. It could systematically undermine their credibility as a source of trustworthy information—a worrying trade-off in times of post-truth (Adler and Drieschova, 2021), in which shared knowledge across camps has become a scarce commodity not only in digital spheres. At the same time, it could further fragment political debates on international governance along ideological lines—and thus reduce the chances of a transnational consensus in favour of global governance even more.

CONCLUSION

International bureaucracies are important facilitators and authorities of global governance that increasingly use digital means of communication—such as websites, email, social media, or mobile apps—to address their audiences directly in terms of 'digital diplomacy'. Reaching citizens does not get any easier online, given the abundance of competing content and the tendency towards ideological fragmentation. Both pose difficult strategic choices for IO communication departments, especially against the backdrop of complex mandates for neutral information policy, self-legitimation, and advocacy for often liberal or cosmopolitan ideas. More research that addresses such questions is essential for understanding the processes of politicization and (de)legitimation of global governance that are increasingly shifting in digital spheres such as social media. However, such research will only be able to produce illuminating results if it ventures a deeper examination of the specific affordances and mechanisms of networked communication. In this sense, there is a lack of a media-ecological perspective on the communication or legitimation of international governance. Such a perspective would have to consider the techno-social peculiarities of corresponding communication processes—the low-threshold (over)production of content, its network-supported distribution or virality, and the conspicuous tendency towards self-referential fragmentation (echo chambers). It will also have to systematically bring together existing research approaches that have so far been defined by increasingly outdated distinctions between actors and audiences or between the public (communication) and the private (attitudes) in the digital age. These bridges are urgently needed in order to adequately understand virulent struggles about meaning and legitimacy of international governance in spaces of networked communication, in which corresponding distinctions between the private and the public are dissolving and which, perhaps precisely for this reason, are increasingly becoming focal points of political delegitimation of global order.

SUGGESTED READING

Bjola, Corneliu and Ruben Zaiotti, eds. (2020) *Digital Diplomacy and International Organisations: Autonomy, Legitimacy and Contestation*, Routledge.

Dingwerth, Klaus, Antonia Witt, Ina Lehmann, Ellen Reichel, and Tobias Weise (2019) *International Organizations under Pressure: Legitimating Global Governance in Changing Times*, Oxford University Press.

Ecker-Ehrhardt, Matthias (2018) 'International Organizations "Going Public"? An Event History Analysis of Public Communication Reforms 1950–2015', *International Studies Quarterly* 62(4): 723–736.

Groves, Nancy K. (2018) 'Strengthening the United Nations Secretariat's Use of Social Media: The View of One Practitioner', *Revista mexicana de política exterior* 113(marzo): 209–226.

Olsson, Eva-Karin, Charlotte Wagnsson, and Kajsa Hammargård (2018) 'The Use of Political Communication by International Organizations: The Case of EU and NATO', in Corneliu Bjola and James Pamment, eds., *Countering Online Propaganda and Extremism*, 66–80, Routledge.

Zürn, Michael, Martin Binder, and Matthias Ecker-Ehrhardt (2012) 'International Authority and Its Politicization', *International Theory* 4(1): 69–106.

REFERENCES

Abbott, Kenneth W. and Duncan Snidal (1998) 'Why States Act Through Formal International Organizations', *Journal of Conflict Resolution* 42(1): 3–32.

Adler, Emanuel and Alena Drieschova (2021) 'The Epistemological Challenge of Truth Subversion to the Liberal International Order', *International Organization* 75(2): 359–386.

APEC (2013) *APEC Social Media Guidelines*, Singapur.

ASEAN (2019) *The ASEAN Secretariat, ASEAN Communication Master Plan 2018-2025*, Jakarta.

Asian Development Bank (2011) *Public Communications Policy 2011: Disclosure and Exchange of Information*, Mandaluyong City, Philippines.

Auxier, Brooke and Monica Anderson (2021) *Social Media Use in 2021*, Washington D.C.: Pew Research Center.

Barnett, Michael N. and Martha Finnemore (2005) 'The Power of Liberal International Organizations', in Michael N. Barnett and Raymond Duvall, eds., *Power in Global Governance*, 161–184, Cambridge: Cambridge University Press.

Bauer, Michael W., Christoph Knill, and Steffen Eckhard (2016) *International Bureaucracy: Challenges and Lessons for Public Administration Research*, Springer.

Bjola, Corneliu and Lu Jiang (2015) 'Social Media and Public Diplomacy', in Corneliu Bjola and Marcus Holmes, eds., *Digital Diplomacy: Theory and Practice*, 71–88, Routledge.

Bjola, Corneliu and Ruben Zaiotti, eds. (2020) *Digital Diplomacy and International Organisations: Autonomy, Legitimacy and Contestation*, Routledge.

Bouchard, Caroline (2020) 'The United Nations in the Digital Age', in Corneliu Bjola and Ruben Zaiotti, eds., *Digital Diplomacy and International Organisations: Autonomy, Legitimacy and Contestation*, 101–125, Routledge.

Daugirdas, Kristina (2019) 'Reputation as a Disciplinarian of International Organizations', *American Journal of International Law* 113(2): 221–271.

Destradi, Sandra and Johannes Plagemann (2019) 'Populism and International Relations: (Un) predictability, Personalisation, and the Reinforcement of Existing Trends in World Politics', *Review of International Studies* 45(5): 711–730.

Di Martino, Luigi (2020) 'Conceptualising Public Diplomacy Listening on Social Media', *Place Branding and Public Diplomacy* 16(2): 131–142.

Dimitrov, Roumen (2014) 'Bringing Communication up to Agency: UNESCO Reforms Its Visibility', *Public Relations Inquiry* 3(3): 293–318.

Dingwerth, Klaus, Antonia Witt, Ina Lehmann, Ellen Reichel, and Tobias Weise (2019) *International Organizations under Pressure: Legitimating Global Governance in Changing Times*, Oxford: Oxford University Press.

Drezner, Daniel W. (2019) 'Technological Change and International Relations', *International Relations* 33(2): 286–303.

EBRD (2014) 'Public Information Policy. As approved by the Board of Directors at its Meeting on 7 May 2014', London.

Ecker-Ehrhardt, Matthias (2018) 'International Organizations "Going Public"? An Event History Analysis of Public Communication Reforms 1950–2015', *International Studies Quarterly* 62(4): 723–736.

Ecker-Ehrhardt, Matthias (2020a) 'IO Public Communication Going Digital? Understanding Social Media Adoption and Use in Times of Politicization', in Ruben Zaiotti and Corneliu Bjola, eds., *The Digital Diplomacy of International Organizations: Autonomy, Legitimacy and Contestation in the Global Digital Age*, 21–50, Routledge.

Ecker-Ehrhardt, Matthias (2020b) 'Wie und warum kommunizieren internationale Organisationen? Zum problematischen Verhältnis von Politisierung und Öffentlichkeitsarbeit', *ZIB Zeitschrift für Internationale Beziehungen* 27(1): 37–68.

Ecker-Ehrhardt, Matthias (2020c) 'IO Public Communication and Discursive Inclusion: How the UN Reported the Arms Trade Treaty Process to a Global Audience', *Journal of International Relations and Development* 23(2): 385–413.

Ecker-Ehrhardt, Matthias (forthcoming) *Building Bridges or Digging the Trench? International Organizations, Social Media, and Polarized Fragmentation*. Review of International Organizations.

Ecker-Ehrhardt, Matthias (2023b) 'Public Legitimation by "Going Personal"? The Ambiguous Role of International Organization Officials on Social Media', *Politics and Governance* 11(3): 213-225 (https://doi.org/10.17645/pag.v11i3.6767).

Ellison, Nicole B. and danah boyd (2013) 'Sociality through Social Network Sites', in William H. Dutton, ed., *The Oxford Handbook of Internet Studies*, 151–172, Oxford: Oxford University Press.

Flaxman, Seth, Sharad Goel, and Justin M. Rao (2016) 'Filter Bubbles, Echo Chambers, and Online News Consumption', *Public Opinion Quarterly* 80(S1): 298–320.

Fröhlich, Manuel (2014) 'The John Holmes Memorial Lecture: Representing the United Nations—Individual Actors, International Agency, and Leadership', *Global Governance* 20(2): 169–193.

Garrett, R. Kelly (2009) 'Echo Chambers Online?: Politically Motivated Selective Exposure Among Internet News Users', *Journal of Computer-Mediated Communication* 14(2): 265–285.

Geis, Anna and Gabi Schlag (2017) ' "The Facts Cannot be Denied": Legitimacy, War and the Use of Chemical Weapons in Syria', *Global Discourse* 7(2–3): 285–303.

Goheer, Nabeel (2020) 'Clock, Cloud, and Contestation: The Digital Journey of the Commonwealth Secretariat', in Corneliu Bjola and Ruben Zaiotti, eds., *Digital Diplomacy and International Organisations*, 127–152, Routledge.

Goritz, Alexandra, Johannes Schuster, Helge Jörgens, and Nina Kolleck (2022) 'International Public Administrations on Twitter: A Comparison of Digital Authority in Global Climate Policy', *Journal of Comparative Policy Analysis: Research and Practice* 24(3): 1–25.

Grigorescu, Alexandru (2007) 'Transparency of Intergovernmental Organizations: The Roles of Member States, International Bureaucracies and Nongovernmental Organizations', *International Studies Quarterly* 51(3): 625–648.

Groves, Nancy K. (2018) 'Strengthening the United Nations Secretariat's Use of Social Media: The View of One Practitioner', *Revista mexicana de política exterior* 113(marzo): 209–226.

Grunig, James E. (2009) 'Paradigms of Global Public Relations in an Age of Digitalisation', *PRism* 6(2): 1–19.

Hochschild, Arlie Russell (2012) *The Managed Heart: Commercialization of Human Feeling*, University of California Press.

Hofferberth, Matthias (2020) 'Tweeting to Save Succeeding Generations from the Scourge of War? The UN, Twitter, and Communicative Action', in Corneliu Bjola and Ruben Zaiotti, eds., *Digital Diplomacy and International Organisations: Autonomy, Legitimacy and Contestation*, 155–183, Routledge.

Hooghe, Liesbet, Tobias Lenz, and Gary Marks (2019) *A Theory of International Organization*, Oxford University Press.

Ikenberry, G. John (2010) 'The Liberal International Order and its Discontents', *Millennium* 38(3): 509–521.

International Council for the Exploration of the Sea (2010) 'ICES Communications Strategy, CM 2010 Del- 6', Kopenhagen.

Jaidka, Kokil, Alvin Zhou, and Yphtach Lelkes (2019) 'Brevity is the Soul of Twitter: The Constraint Affordance and Political Discussion', *Journal of Communication* 69(4): 345–372.

Keohane, Robert O. and Joseph S. Nye (1977) *Power and Interdependence: World Politics in Transition*, Boston: Little, Brown.

Klinger, Ulrike and Jakob Svensson (2015) 'The Emergence of Network Media Logic in Political Communication: A Theoretical Approach', *New Media & Society* 17(8): 1241–1257.

Krzyżanowski, Michał (2018) 'Social Media in/and the Politics of the European Union: Politico-Organizational Communication, Institutional Cultures and Self-Inflicted Elitism', *Journal of Language and Politics* 17(2): 281–304.

Lipson, Michael (2007) 'Peacekeeping: Organized Hypocrisy?', *European Journal of International Relations* 13(1): 5–34.

Loader, Brian D. and Dan Mercea (2011) 'Networking Democracy? Social Media Innovations and Participatory Politics', *Information, Communication & Society* 14(6): 757–769.

Mandel, Bethany (2012) 'The UN's Freudian Tweet'. *The Commentary*, November 29. Available at: "https://www.commentary.org/bethany-mandel/the-uns-freudian-tweet/"

Manor, Ilan (2019) *The Digitalization of Public Diplomacy*, London: Palgrave Macmillan.

McGregor, Lorna (2019) 'Are New Technologies an Aid to Reputation as a Disciplinarian?', *American Journal of International Law* 113: 238–241.

Meyer, Christoph O. (2009) 'Does European Union Politics Become Mediatized? The Case of the European Commission', *Journal of European Public Policy* 16(7): 1047–1064.

Milan, Stefania (2015) 'From Social Movements to Cloud Protesting: the Evolution of Collective Identity', *Information, Communication & Society* 18(8): 887–900.

Olsson, Eva-Karin, Charlotte Wagnsson, and Kajsa Hammargård (2018) 'The Use of Political Communication by International Organizations: the Case of EU and NATO', in Corneliu Bjola and James Pamment, eds., *Countering Online Propaganda and Extremism*, 66–80, Routledge.

Pamment, James (2016) 'Digital Diplomacy as Transmedia Engagement: Aligning Theories of Participatory Culture with International Advocacy Campaigns', *New Media & Society* 18(9): 2046–2086.

Papacharissi, Zizi (2016) 'Affective Publics and Structures of Storytelling: Sentiment, Events and Mediality', *Information, Communication & Society* 19(3): 307–324.

Parkinson, John and Jane Mansbridge (2012) *Deliberative Systems: Deliberative Democracy at the Large Scale*, Cambridge University Press.

Pevehouse, Jon, Timothy Nordstrom, and Kevin Warnke (2004) 'The Correlates of War 2 International Governmental Organizations Data Version 2.0', *Conflict Management and Peace Science* 21(2): 101–119.

Risso, Linda (2014) *Propaganda and Intelligence in the Cold War: The NATO Information Service*, Milton Park, Abingdon, Oxon; New York: Routledge.

Rogers, Richard (2018) 'Otherwise Engaged: Social Media from Vanity Metrics to Critical Analytics', *International Journal of Communication* 12: 450–472.

Rosenau, James N. (1995) 'Governance in the Twenty-First Century', *Global Governance* 1(1): 13–43.

Strijbis, Oliver, Joschua Helmer, and Pieter De Wilde (2018) 'A Cosmopolitan–Communitarian Cleavage Around the World? Evidence from Ideological Polarization and Party–Voter Linkages', *Acta Politica* 55(3): 1–24.

Summa, Giancarlo (2020) *"We the People" in the Twitter Age: Digital Diplomacy and the Social Legitimacy of the United Nations*, Media@ LSE Working Paper Series, London: London School of Economics and Political Science.

Tallberg, Jonas, Thomas Sommerer, Theresa Squatrito, and Christer Jönsson (2013) *The Opening up of International Organizations: Transnational Access in Global Governance*, Cambridge: Cambridge University Press.

Tompea, Roxana Claudia (2021) 'Truth or Tale? the Implications of Emotional Commodification in Shaping Public Diplomacy', Paper presented at European Workshops in International Studies, 30 June to 2 July 2021, virtual, European International Studies Association.

United Nations (2021) 'General Assembly, Proposed Programme Budget for 2022, Part VII Global Communications, Section 28 Global Communications, A/76/6 (14 April 2021)', New York.

United Nations (2023) 'General Assembly, Proposed Programme Budget for 2024, Part VII Global Communications, Section 28 Global Communications, A/78/6 (4 April 2023)', New York.

Williams, Hywel TP, James R. McMurray, Tim Kurz, and F. Hugo Lambert (2015) 'Network Analysis Reveals Open Forums and Echo Chambers in Social Media Discussions of Climate Change', *Global Environmental Change* 32: 126–138.

Zürn, Michael, Martin Binder, and Matthias Ecker-Ehrhardt (2012) 'International Authority and Its Politicization', *International Theory* 4(1): 69–106.

CHAPTER 20

VIRTUAL DIPLOMATIC SUMMITRY

ELSA HEDLING

INTRODUCTION

DIPLOMATIC summitry, high-level diplomacy conducted by heads of state or government, is a beacon of multilateralism. The term was supposedly given its diplomatic and political meaning by Winston Churchill in the 1950s with reference to the increased frequency and significance of regular meetings between world leaders during the Cold War (Melissen, 2003). Since then, summitry has been established as a core practice of 'diplomacy at the highest level', necessary because of global interdependence and perpetual threats of weapons of mass destruction and possible because of the convenience of modern travel (Dunn, 1996). Summits between two heads of state, which were previously the norm, still occur but the rapid increase in summitry is a result of the upsurge in international and regional constellations such as the North Atlantic Treaty Organization (NATO), the Group of Seven (G7), the Group of Twenty (G20), the Association of Southeast Asian Nations (ASEAN), and the African Union (AU), which have become key sites for political leadership in global politics. Diplomatic summitry, however, remains a controversial practice as the leaders' roles and skills in diplomacy rest on contested grounds (Berridge, 2010: 164). At the centre of this controversy is the difficulty in assessing the relative success of summits and the influence of face-to-face interaction between leaders in times of crises, which have also been affected by increased digitalization (Duncombe, 2017). The resort to *virtual diplomatic summitry* during and after the Covid-19 pandemic has therefore further stressed the need to rethink the role of summitry and the implications of digitalization in diplomacy.

Summits serve to offer a common ground for world leaders to meet and settle politics in person, they provide opportunities to generate trust through social bonding, and they become a stage from which leaders can signal reassurance to their domestic publics in turbulent times (Dunn, 1996; Melissen, 2003). Summit diplomacy therefore blurs the lines between substantive and symbolic politics (Day and Wedderburn, 2022).

Indeed, it is precisely this illusive nature of summit meetings as multifaceted diplomatic sites that has meant that this form of diplomatic interaction has been unlikely to embrace virtualization. The rise of technology that enables face-to-face interaction through video calls since the late 1990s was anticipated as 'a mouth-watering prospect to the prophets of virtual diplomacy' (Berridge, 2010: 199). Still, despite arguments in favour of cost-efficiency, increasing environmental concerns, and constant security risks, ideas of replacing physical summit venues in high diplomacy never took off before the Covid-19 pandemic (Danielson and Hedling, 2022). Adaptations to travel restrictions therefore greatly accelerated the digitalization of diplomacy in this field by introducing new routines of *virtual diplomatic summitry*. While restrictions on physical meetings and international travel were enforced, summit meetings were postponed or replaced by virtual or hybrid meetings to the extent that virtual diplomatic meetings became established in the diplomatic toolbox (Bjola and Coplen, 2022). The interrogation of virtual diplomatic summitry in this chapter seeks to contribute to advance our understanding of this phenomenon by addressing two broad questions: what happens when diplomatic summits are conducted in a virtual format, and how can we conceptualize virtual diplomatic summitry?

Virtual diplomatic summitry in this chapter refers to the diplomatic summit meetings that are conducted through technologies for virtual interaction, such as video-conferencing tools, and that take place partly or completely in virtual venues. While the phenomenon of virtual summitry originally was associated with adaptation in the light of pandemic restrictions, this chapter argues that it also serves as a focal point for the assessment of the role of digitalization in diplomacy. Diplomatic summitry is the ultimate symbol of the pre-digital institutionalization of diplomacy that took place after the end of the Second World War (Feinberg, 2013). The rapid increase in diplomatic summitry was testament to the force of globalization and the liberal world order. In a rapidly changing world, the future of diplomatic summits must therefore also be seen in light of contestations of the multilateral diplomatic system (Schuette, 2021). Virtual diplomatic summitry is then to be viewed partly as a method for preserving the continuity of multilateral diplomacy but, alas, also as a balancing act that may risk disruption and unforeseen change in diplomatic practice.

Guided by the open questions about the role of virtual diplomatic summitry the chapter adopts a theoretical framework that draws on practice theory and relationalism. Practice theory focuses the attention on context-dependent practical enactments and relationalism situates political phenomena in ongoing social processes (Jackson and Nexon, 1999; McCourt, 2016). With the aim of advancing scholarship on the digitalization of diplomacy, the chapter therefore proposes an analytical focus on key situational factors: time and space, and how they condition and co-produce practices and relations in virtual diplomatic summitry. Informed by this framework, a brief analytical reflection of the lessons learned from virtual summits during 2020–2021 is offered. It suggests that assessments of virtual summitry will depend on relations to non-virtual practices, relationships, and processes. Virtual diplomatic summitry therefore cannot be analysed as an isolated diplomatic occasion, nor simply as a replacement or complementary practice—it should be approached as a relational site, mode, and practice within diplomacy with transaction costs that depend on locations in time and space.

The chapter unfolds as follows. First virtual diplomatic summitry is situated in the broader institutionalization of diplomatic summits. It then outlines theoretical considerations in the study of summitry and advances a relational and practice-oriented perspective. The chapter then turns to offer a brief illustration of diplomatic entanglements and virtual practices by drawing on initial experiences of virtualization since 2020. Finally, the conclusion revisits the research questions and discusses the role of virtual diplomatic summitry in future studies of the digitalization of diplomacy.

DIPLOMATIC SUMMITRY: FROM INSTITUTIONALIZATION TO DIGITALIZATION

The rapid increase and frequency of diplomatic summit meetings since the 1970s mark a stark contrast to previous times, when meetings at the highest level of political authority were few and rare (Melissen, 2003). Summitry has historical roots; sovereigns did meet to engage in diplomatic activities in medieval and early modern times but it was a risky and rather uncommon practice (Goldstein, 1996). Maintaining international relations was not an urgent concern—trade and security arrangements were of course highly valued and dealt with through diplomatic means of correspondence and representation, but there was less systemic interdependence between nations and geographical distance guaranteed warnings of invasion (Dunn and Lock-Pullan, 2016). The dawn of the nuclear age reflected a new level of global interdependence among nations and markets that resulted in the necessity to deal with complexities and threats collectively (Feinberg, 2013). Attempts to preserve peaceful relations and to avoid the Cold War escalating between the superpowers called for a move beyond bilateralism to multi-stakeholder relationships in multilateral form. Diplomatic summits of this nature have been held since 1955, but it was not until the 1970s that they significantly increased in form and frequency (Dunn and Lock-Pullan, 2016: 233).

The increase in diplomatic summitry reflects the rapid growth of multilateral diplomacy, but rather than replacing bilateral diplomacy, multilateralism has complemented and increased the venues for diplomatic relations (Mahbubani, 2013). There are hence many different forms of summit meetings and they are institutionalized to different degrees, which makes generalizations of its diplomatic genre difficult. The common denominator of summits is that they, unlike high-level meetings between ministers or diplomats, refer to meetings between the highest representative of states or organizations (most commonly heads of state or government) (Melissen, 2003). There is, however, a vast difference between summits held between two heads of states or government (bilateral summits), summits held between the members of international or non-governmental organizations (multilateral summits), and summits held between members of such organizations and external partners (e.g., European Union (EU)—AU summits or the ASEAN + 3 meetings).

While leaders are the front figures of summits, diplomats are very much involved (and in growing numbers) in the preparations and negotiations of before, during, and after summits. Pre-summit meetings and base camp meetings gather the staff of diplomats, sometimes called 'Sherpas', in preparatory bargaining sessions and pre-negotiations (Dunn, 1996). The precise role of Sherpas (and sub-Sherpas) differs in summit contexts. In the G20 process, Sherpas are designated as the personal representative of the leader and maintain a close relationship to the leader before and during the summit itself (Feinberg, 2013). While multilateral diplomacy in practice thus depends foremost on the cooperation of diplomats and bureaucrats, summits have important functions in multilateral agenda-setting. In addition to shared security needs, new global concerns such as the environment, the economy, and terrorism are often addressed by international summits or by hosted summits (such as President Obama's 2015 'Summit on Countering Violent Extremism') (Dunn and Lock-Pullan, 2016: 234). The rise and enlargements of regional and international organizations (in many of which summits are embedded in founding charters or treaties) has also contributed to the growth of summitry. For instance, the leaders of the EU member states are bound by the treaties to convene in the European Council at minimum twice every six months in so-called 'EU summits' (European Union, 2007). Other organizations hold summit meetings annually, bi-annually, or with other regularities but allowances are typically made for emergency sessions.

Diplomatic summitry has indeed evolved alongside and as an effect of technological advancements (Berridge, 2010: 162). The machinery of summits, the organization by hosts, and the participation by leaders and their delegations have been facilitated by modern technology, most notably by air travel and telecommunications. Feinberg suggests that air travel and telecommunications have facilitated three ancillary components of modern summitry: 1) the active participation of civil society and the private sector, 2) the massive presence of media representatives, and 3) the visible petitions of celebrities and contestation of protesters and counter-summits (Feinberg, 2013). The ability to travel to participate and to be seen and heard as a participant of summits has thus also broadened the set of actors involved in summitry. Telecommunications have foremost been essential in the preparations and pre-negotiations but also as a way for leaders to stay in contact between summit meetings.

In addition to overcoming practical hurdles for participation and communication, technological advancements in a mediatized world have also contributed to the global visibility of summits and therefore increased its symbolic role (Constantinou, 2018). In the post-war era, summits were seen to serve propaganda purposes as spectacular events that, unlike meetings between foreign ministers or diplomats, would generate media attention preferably on television (Melissen, 2003: 13). In a crowded media environment, leaders still participate in summits to be seen—both by their domestic publics and by their international peers. Sharing the spotlight with influential world leaders is a source of status and prestige. Summits are therefore important demonstrations of hierarchy and 'rites of passage' for newly elected leaders (Danielson and Hedling, 2022). Digital communication and social media have further amplified the opportunities for leaders to be seen during summit meetings—both through the lenses of news media actors that report from summits in real time and through social media where leaders can self-narrate their participation. At the dawn of 'digital diplomacy', it was for a time popular among leaders to post 'selfies' of themselves with other leaders during summits (Manor and Segev, 2015). When video became favoured on social media, short video clips from summits often 'went viral', offering a rare glimpse of the interaction between leaders when not performing before the cameras (Hedling and Bremberg, 2021). The undiplomatic ways of US President Donald J. Trump, pushing himself to the front during photo-ops and leaving summits early, produced such glimpses of back-stage interactions and peer reactions to major faux pas (Day and Wedderburn, 2022).

These opportunities for visibility and self-reporting also extend to civil society actors, celebrities, and protesters—all part of the gradual inclusion of untraditional actors in diplomacy. For example, Swedish environmental activist Greta Thunberg, who has gained celebrity status through her digitally mediated protest movement 'Fridays for Future', has on several occasions spoken both during and outside summits (Murphy, 2021). In 2019, while still a teenager, she gave an emotional speech during the United Nations Climate Actions Summit that became widely circulated in news media and on social media, illustrating the power of digital platforms to make and mediate celebrity and broaden the scope of actors involved at the highest level of global governance.

Despite a gradual digitalization of diplomacy including practices relevant to diplomatic summitry, such as inter-state communication (Duncombe, 2017) and pre-negotiations (Adler-Nissen and Drieschova, 2019), virtualization was largely resisted before the Covid-19 pandemic. 'Virtual diplomacy' was discarded as risky and un-necessary. This was in part related to the high costs and technical demands involved. It was not until Instant Unified Communications (IUC) technology drastically reduced the costs of video conferencing, and allowed remote participation with far greater ease than before, that virtual meetings were considered as having the potential to add value (Pilegaard, 2016). Still, arguments in favour of maintaining costly and travel-intensive summitry have continuously emphasized the value of social rituals and ceremonies as well as interpersonal practices in building international trust—all believed to require physicality and face-to-face interaction (Holmes and Wheeler, 2020; Bjola and Coplen, 2022).

The Covid-19 pandemic disrupted institutionalized diplomatic summitry in unprecedented ways. In 2020 and 2021, the G7, the G20, the EU, NATO, the Organisation of Petroleum Exporting Countries (OPEC), the World Bank, the International Monetary Fund (IMF), ASEAN, and the AU, among many other configurations of multilateral diplomacy, held virtual diplomatic summits. When in February 2020 it became known that the world was facing a global pandemic, summits were postponed and gradually replaced by the first truly virtual summits. When travel restrictions were removed and vaccination rates gradually increased in 2022, virtual meetings and hybrid participation remained new elements of diplomatic meetings (Bjola and Manor, 2022). Virtual or hybrid summits have thus become adopted as a fallback option and norm for overcoming the constraints of time and co-location, marking a new phase in the institutionalization and digitalization of summitry.

Debating the Role of (Virtual) Diplomatic Summits

Historically, diplomatic summitry was foremost of interest to realist scholars that viewed meetings between leaders as key opportunities to advance state interests in power politics (Dunn, 1996). The rapid growth of summitry after the end of the Cold War, its role in upholding the multilateral system, and its potential for transforming conflictual relationships have attracted the interest of other perspectives that have reinvigorated the debate (Wheeler, 2013). At the centre of this debate is the role played by political leaders, their personalities and the impact that their interaction with other leaders may have in international politics (Melissen, 2003). As stated in the introduction, the success of summits is inherently difficult to assess—scholarly interventions are instead guided by theorizations and case studies that seek to pinpoint the influence of social and political dynamics of leadership interaction (Wong, 2021; Day and Wedderburn, 2022). Before turning to advance a relational perspective, it is therefore relevant to briefly consider how previous interventions would produce different approaches to virtual diplomatic summitry.

From a strictly systemic perspective on international relations, where the structure of the international system is considered to explain state behaviour, diplomatic summits serve to sustain the system (Alexandroff and Brean, 2015). In this view, the continuity of state relations and diplomacy (in its thinnest form as maintained communication between state parties) can be upheld as long as leaders and diplomats can act as guardians of the international system. A key argument in favour of summitry is then the preservation of the system. For neoclassical realists, keeping the system intact also sustains the 'game' of diplomacy and summits become arenas for the competition over material resources.

Realist approaches, however, tend to downplay the 'cheap talk' that leaders engage in during summits where the 'politics' have already been meticulously prepared by lower-ranking diplomats and officials (Trager, 2017). Systemic or realist approaches to virtual diplomatic summitry would thus focus on the ability for 'regimes' to be upheld and performed through virtual interaction.

With a more nuanced understanding of communication and opportunities to send 'costly signals' during the summit situation, emphasis on opportunities for diplomatic signalling could support a restored opportunity structure—the attention of other states and a public display of participation. In this tradition, to credibly communicate its resolve to other states, a state may choose to incur costs (political, financial, etc.) and leaders will therefore assess the sincerity of signals according to the criteria of cost (Jervis, 1970). Costly signals therefore do not depend on generation of interpersonal trust, and cheap talk (without cost) is not given credibility. The role of summits as arenas for costly signals would in theory, therefore, not be restrained by the virtual format. The opportunities and constraints of virtual summitry may then vary depending on the individual leaders' ability to leverage the situation to the advantage of their own state (Wivel, 2017).

In approaches that focus more on the diplomatic (rather than political) agency of political leaders, summits are often argued as problematic because of politicians' alleged poor abilities to practise diplomacy. Unlike diplomats, leaders are not trained to 'think diplomatically' and they are held to be poor negotiators because of inattention to details, their assumed vanity and addiction to publicity, and the tendency for an uneven performance of statesmanship because of the demands that comes with the job (Berridge, 2010: 162). In this view, the ways in which the more controlled virtual format limits the room for manoeuvre that leaders normally have during a summit may be seen as an opportunity to regain 'technocratic control' in high diplomacy. For instance, there are fewer, if any, opportunities for leaders to ignore or challenge the prenegotiated agenda in the shorter and more structured virtual format. In this sense, leaders may become more like 'puppets' during virtual summits, which seen from a rationalist perspective may have positive effects.

The interactions that take place between leaders are seen both as symbolic performances of the relationship between states embodied by their leaders and, from a micro-sociological perspective, as interaction rituals between individuals in positions of power (Wong, 2021). The summit situation is hence both important as a moment of interaction because they bring leaders together, and as a performative act when leaders are on a joint 'front-stage'.

Diplomatic summits are seen as formative of the relationship between leaders and important social situations for the generation of trust. In this view, leaders may, despite their diplomatic shortcomings, fill an important role by being able to retore trust by 'hitting it off' in person when other attempts of generating trust have failed (Holmes and Wheeler, 2020). The limited opportunities to fill this important function in diplomacy may therefore have disastrous effects (Naylor, 2020). From an interactionist perspective, not only do virtual interactions constrain social bonds but they may also risk an already sensitive relationship between leaders by limiting opportunities to read cues and engage in direct feedback.

While the debates of the role of diplomatic summitry contribute to assess the potential and pitfalls of virtualization, the substantialist view of virtual diplomatic summitry as an analytical category is limiting since it fails to assist conceptualizations of the entangled role of virtualization and digitalization in diplomacy. A relational perspective is therefore relevant to advance nuanced (and hopefully eventually more sophisticated) analyses of virtual summitry in diplomacy.

A RELATIONAL PERSPECTIVE ON VIRTUAL SUMMITRY

From a relational perspective all political processes result from ongoing relations—where events become political through their timing and location within ongoing relations (Jackson and Nexon, 1999). As such, it is the meeting of leaders in a specific time and place that renders a summit its relational diplomatic purpose and meaning (Neumann, 2020). Summits are thus contextually situated and embedded in time and in space.[1] To accept the status of virtual diplomatic summitry in diplomacy therefore demands attention to how virtual summits become contextually embedded and recognized as diplomatic sites and how this relational positionality contributes with meaning (Emirbayer, 1997). Since we can never analytically isolate the virtual standing of a virtual summit (this would demand the exact same summit to take place in both virtual and non-virtual forms at the same time, which is impossible), our focus should instead be directed towards the entanglement with virtualization and with the broader digitalization of our time (see, Adler-Nissen and Eggeling, 2022).

Virtualization of summitry represents entanglement at the practical level of planning and participation through tools that seemingly offer opportunities to reproduce time and space. Using video conferencing in diplomacy was adopted as a practice to mimic 'real' summits by creating a 'synthetic situation' (Eggeling and Adler-Nissen, 2021). In practical terms, virtual diplomatic summitry is a set of practices for virtual diplomatic interaction that are meaningful because they enable the repetition and timing of routines and rituals that otherwise risk disruption when physical meetings cannot be held. In this view, virtual summitry is contrasted with traditional summitry through its (in)ability to recreate the social situation (Naylor, 2020). While not accepted as 'real' in its own right, virtual summits are recognized because of their promises to uphold interaction routines and regularity in the institutionalized role of summits. When a virtual summit replaces a physical summit, it is therefore the replaced social situation that grants it its role as a 'site' in diplomacy (Neumann, 2016). However, more attention to 'sited diplomacy', which Neumann defines as a planned setting for something socially significant, also allows us to take into account the circumstances that cause a summit to take place in virtual form and how those circumstances may also influence relations and practices between and among the participating state leaders (Neumann, 2015: 73). A relational perspective must thus seek to disentangle the practical change that results from disruption in path-dependent routines of institutionalized summitry from the situational cues that arise from the virtual situation.

---

[1] This is indicative in how they often receive their name (in popular language), through reference to the city and the year in which they took place.

Leaving aside the extraordinary situation of a global pandemic, virtual meetings have increasingly been accepted in diplomacy (like in other professional institutions) (Bjola and Manor, 2022). As a set of tools and practices, virtual diplomatic meetings can intervene with time by allowing faster processes of pre-negotiations and planning of summits and potentially even by speeding up decision-making processes (Pilegaard, 2016). Virtual tools to overcome constraints of time therefore also challenge key notions of temporality in diplomacy. When diplomatic processes become faster some nuances may, however, be lost (Adler-Nissen and Drieschova, 2019). In addition, lessons from the Covid-19 pandemic indicate that virtual negotiations are not necessarily faster; they may also prolong diplomatic processes by offering new opportunities for 'stalling and stone-walling' (Bjola and Coplen, 2022: 23). Important here is not whether or not virtual interaction increases efficiency, but the signs of substantial change beyond forms of communication, in diplomacy. Speeding up or slowing down the ways diplomacy is practised may have lasting effects on relationships between actors; entanglement with virtual and digital tools may thus gradually shift diplomatic processes. These claims extend to the role of intervals and repetition, since diplomatic summitry depends on long-term processes—it often takes a series of many summits for real policy action to be developed in multilateral contexts (Melissen, 2003). Getting many states on the same rhetorical page often depends on repeated attempts of negotiation and bargains between engaged parties. Time may also shape the situation in the context of crises. An immediate crisis might call for an emergency summit meeting that charges the situation with variables like uncertainty and stress. A summit focused on an ongoing (shared) crisis is more likely to lead to policy commitments (well-illustrated by the G20 leaders' summits that were first summoned in response to the financial crisis in 2008) (Feinberg, 2013). Creeping crises, most notably the climate threat, may instead produce a social situation less receptive to immediate action that is constrained by long-term analyses in tension with current events. At the same time, recurring summits have become important venues for networking, building interpersonal relationships, learning, and fostering a 'sense of community across scales of difference' in an increasingly complex governance regime (Lövbrand et al., 2017). Diplomatic summits are therefore inevitably conditioned by both timing and repetition. Hence, while summits are sometimes conceived of as one-off events, diplomatic summitry is in fact a process of managing international relationships over time and virtual summitry is situated in multiple temporal processes of timing and repetition.

In addition to the relationship between virtual summits and 'real summits', the social situation in virtual summitry also depends on inter-virtual relationships. During the Covid-19 pandemic, virtual summitry was gradually professionalized and diplomats became socialized into shared digital habits (Bjola and Manor, 2022). A virtual summit that follows several virtual summits may therefore be assessed as qualitatively 'better' in terms of less technical disturbances and sensitivity to virtual protocol. At the same time, a virtual summit that follows a series of physical summits may draw more on the past offline interactions and the relatively short time since a last physical meeting and for those reasons carry more 'offline social capital' (Julien, 2015). Hence time works in multiple directions and may contextually contribute to situate the virtual summit in proximity to physical summits or processes of institutionalizing virtual summits.

Moreover, virtual diplomatic summitry is defined by the replacement of a common physical place with a virtual place, but there are still spatial dimensions at play. Rather than replacing a physical place in a true sense, virtual meetings take place in multiple places at same time. This leads to a multidimensional role of space where the missing sense of place co-exists with multiple places. The virtual situation has spatial qualities in its own right—a perfect connection where video and audio are working seamlessly enhances the spatial experience of a virtual meeting (Bjola and Manor, 2022). Attention to a shared repertoire of visual staging, backdrop, dress attire, and lighting also contributes to the experience of virtual meetings as a spatial situation (Danielson and Hedling, 2022). The virtual situation can thus produce qualitatively different senses of common space. Still, difficulties in 'reading the room' reported by diplomats during the pandemic testify to the importance of spatial qualities that can only be 'felt' in co-presence with others. The virtual space is therefore also defined by its missing qualities (Bramsen and Hageman, 2021).

The multiple places where leaders and their delegations are seen to be participating from also contribute to give the virtual summit its contextual location. Space becomes a situational factor when a leader is displaced from the expected scene of participation, a government building or even an expected room (e.g., in the US context, the situation room in times of crises). The place from where a leader participates in a summit may challenge positions in the international hierarchy, for instance by participating while on a state visit in a more powerful state or on site in a war zone. In the aftermaths of the Russian invasion of Ukraine in the early spring of 2022, Ukrainian president Volodymyr Zelensky refused to leave Ukraine and instead engaged in repeated pleas for help through virtual participation during NATO and EU summits (Herszenhorn, 2022). While an extraordinary situation, such performance of staying in the field while still appearing on the 'front-stage' demonstrates how virtual summitry or virtual participation in summitry has spatial qualities. Virtual summitry therefore provides opportunities to disrupt the spaces of highly ritualized behaviour (McConnell, 2019). From a relational or interactionist view, space shapes the social situation but diplomacy has never been restricted to formal or even expected places. Rather, it is often in the marginal spaces that sociability is cultivated in diplomacy (Nair, 2020). This is true also in the summit context, where informal practices on the margins of the formal event take place in spaces in-between—a walk in the garden before dinner or small-talk during a photo session. While participation in virtual summits does not allow for the same informal practices, informal virtual interactions may still alter how a space is 'felt' and 'read' by other participants. Hence, the multiple spaces that virtual participation affords to leaders and their delegations contribute to the specific aesthetics and emotional registers that shape the virtual summit in ways that may differ from traditional rituals.

Virtual diplomatic summits also have spatial implications for the broader summit situation by blurring the lines of transparency and by displacing scenes for protest. While, in theory, limiting interaction to virtual spaces might suggest more transparency for actors invited to observe summits, the controlled protocol may also change moments of informal interaction from 'silent' to 'invisible'. News media actors may not have had access to what is said in a brush-by between world leaders, but interactions could still be seen and deemed politically relevant (Crespo, 2017). An effect of virtual diplomatic summits might therefore be the production of more invisible spaces outside the public gaze. Protest movements are also displaced from summit locations and instead placed in alternative virtual locations (during the pandemic) or in multiple locations likely to further amplify the digitalization of international protest and phenomenon such as 'virtual mobs' (Heinze, 2017). When protesters lose their sense of shared space, social media and technologies for virtual manifestations are likely to shape counter-events giving the counter-summits new spatial qualities entangled with the media environments in which they take place.

DIPLOMATIC ENTANGLEMENTS AND VIRTUAL PRACTICES: BRIEF ILLUSTRATIONS FROM THE RISE OF VIRTUAL SUMMITRY

On 16 March 2020, US President Donald Trump presided over the first virtual G7 summit that was held using video-conferencing tools in replacement of the meeting as planned and it was the first time that the leaders had not met in person since 1975 (G7 Research Group, 2020). Only ten days later, the leaders of the G20 convened in a virtual emergency summit. In the following months of 2020–2021, virtual diplomatic summitry became a default replacement practice. Just like in other professions, heads of state and government shifted from in-person to remote meetings and their participation was showcased through images of the gallery view of video-conference tools to publics around the world (Danielson and Hedling, 2022). The rise of virtual diplomatic summitry was thus not the result of a gradual development; it was an institutional response to an extraordinary situation made possible by available technology and the extent of global digitalization. This context mattered to the ways in which summits were moved online and the way in which we may conceptualize what became recognized as virtual diplomatic summitry. The scope of this chapter does not allow for an in-depth analysis but, in order to illustrate the merits of the relational perspective previously advanced, three main arguments will be made.

First, the relationship between traditional and 'real' summits and summits carried out in virtual format during this time were of a mimicking kind. Rather than drawing on the added value of virtual interaction, the first virtual summits were conducted in lieu of planned physical summits and aimed to deliver a similar situation. The situation, however, was not similar, not just because of the virtual format but also because of the pandemic, a situation of common nature but without a common response. In fact, the first months of the pandemic were charged with a 'great power blame game' (Tyler and Liu, 2020). A first illustration of entanglement was hence that the virtual format was introduced in a time of diplomatic crisis when tensions were high. As such these summits were qualitatively different from the planned summits they replaced both because they dealt with new multilateral circumstances and because the social situation was different regardless of the virtual format. As a practice, virtual summitry did, however, produce new diplomatic routines and habits that gradually altered the relationship between 'real' and 'virtual'. When travel restrictions were abandoned in 2022, virtual summits or virtual participation by some in summits became a continued complementary practice in a new phase of 'hybrid' or 'blended' diplomacy (Bjola and Manor, 2022; Adler-Nissen and Eggeling, 2022; NATO 2022). At a practical level, virtualization gained a life of its own beyond the diplomatic entanglements that charged the inception of virtual summitry.

Second, the Covid-19 pandemic demonstrated that virtual summits can replace in-person summits between leaders in diplomacy but that the qualitative difference from face-to-face interactions extends beyond the format. The difference between face-to-face interaction and virtual interaction is however not clear cut. Virtual interactions are not a static form of communication. Like any social situation, the virtual situation enables learning, which can in itself be a social practice (Wenger, 1998). Learning becomes practice when members of a community negotiate meaning as a collective practice or continue to learn in their interactions within the community and with other communities. Virtualization during the pandemic was a process of collective learning across and between diplomatic and political communities as they learned how to adapt to new ways of planning and participating in summits. In addition to solving the ability for leaders to virtually meet, virtual summits had to be adapted to solve other more technical issues. For instance, organizations that conduct voting were challenged to figure out how to conduct virtual voting for decision-making bodies such as in the EU (Maurer and Wright, 2020). Aside from innovating new habits of voting, other important diplomatic norms, such as not interrupting during others' statements, were initially challenged by the virtual format through mishaps like forgetting to mute one's microphone or uncertainty of how to act in moments of technical disturbances. Such disruptions of diplomatic protocol illustrate the limits of virtual summits as mimicking practices; at a certain point virtual summits instead became sites for innovation and improvisation by learning how to cope with the new situation. By the autumn of 2021, leaders and diplomats were reported to largely have grown accustomed to the ways of virtual interaction (Bjola and Manor, 2022). The pandemic experience was, however, characterized by restricted in-person interaction. The ways of virtual interaction under other circumstances differ from a context of forced adaptation. Furthermore, adoption and shared habits of using virtual meetings do not necessarily reflect a fixed status for virtual interaction in diplomacy. Diplomatic summitry, like other domains in diplomacy, have become a new site for experimentation with virtual practices in which its participating communities continue to learn their possibilities and limits.

Third, digitalization, and in this case virtualization, is not deterministic. Summitry, although highly institutionalized, depends on the agency of its actors (whether individuals or communities). Virtual summitry was not embraced by all during the pandemic; some organizations actively resisted virtualization and instead opted to keep postponing or use hybrid solutions. The COP26 UN climate change conference planned to take place in Bonn in April 2020 was eventually held in Glasgow in November 2021. The decision to avoid a virtual summit was in this case taken with the risks of challenging the sensitive configuration of climate talks in mind and with consideration for the digital divide between developed and developing countries that could result in an additional source of power asymmetry (Calliari et al., 2020). In this particular case, the pandemic situation intersected with climate diplomacy in ways that challenged what was becoming a default mode of adaptation. The COP26 summit was, however, in part a hybrid solution, and the preparations and negotiations leading up to the summit were foremost conducted through virtual meetings. In the summer of 2021, the participating governments held a three-week-long virtual meeting to begin negotiations and hammer out agreements on key aspects of the talks. As such, the pandemic also offered opportunities to rethink alternatives for summitry in ways that can both reduce the carbon footprint and sustain interpersonal contact and negotiations in the face of new waves of pandemic outbreaks, without risking the loss of interpersonal contact and commitment between states. The COP26 summit illustrates how situational factors of time (timing and postponement) and space (social configurations and the digital divide) produced a situation where the diplomatic risks of digitalization were deemed too high.

CONCLUSIONS

This chapter has critically examined the nature and role of virtual diplomatic summitry and the implications for how this phenomenon is conceptualized in the digitalization of diplomacy. When diplomatic summits are conducted in virtual format, they become relational sites in diplomacy that depend both on their positions in ongoing diplomatic processes and on the ways in which the virtual interactions replace or change the practical enactments of diplomacy. The status as a relational site has implications for conceptualizations of virtual summitry. Just like some diplomatic summits are deemed successful and others not, virtual summits are not on equal grounds across all contexts. If the institutionalization of summitry has taught us anything, it is that diplomatic summitry is a multifaceted practice that must be assessed across time and space. Some virtual summits are qualitatively closer to physical summits than others, sometimes because of proximity in time to a physical meeting and sometimes because the virtual situation has spatial qualities that provide a sense of shared place. By contrast, virtual diplomatic summits can also add value through the qualitative distance to physical summits, by offering temporal or spatial advantages otherwise impossible because of the requirement of a shared place. In such cases, it is not the sense of place as a replacement of physical space, but instead the virtual situation as a temporal site that grants virtual summits its own role in diplomacy. The virtual situation then qualifies as its own category of analysis, linked and related to but not dependent on its ability to mimic 'real' diplomatic summitry.

The digitalization of diplomacy is a burgeoning field in both theory and practice. The implications of this account of virtual diplomatic summitry for researchers and students, as well as practitioners and policy makers in diplomacy and global governance, requires more research to articulate fully. Broadly, the findings suggest that more attention should be paid to the complementary role of digital tools and the entangled nature of virtual practices; the specific challenges facing multilateral diplomacy; and fostering a relational awareness in the digitalization of diplomacy. In this task, diplomatic summitry offers a valuable focal point to the ways in which digitalization sustains, disrupts, and alters diplomacy. As such, digitalization is also a process increasingly entangled in the future configurations of multilateral diplomacy where virtual interactions will continue to challenge traditional conceptions of diplomatic practice.

SUGGESTED READING

Bjola, C., and M. Coplen. 2022. 'Virtual Venues and International Negotiations: Lessons from the COVID-19 Pandemic.' *International Negotiation* 8 (1): 69–93

Dunn, D.H., and R. Lock-Pullan. 2016. 'Diplomatic Summitry' In *The SAGE Handbook of Diplomacy*, edited by C. M. Constantinou, P. Kerr, and P. Sharp, pp. 231–241. London: SAGE.

Eggeling, K. A., and R. Adler-Nissen. 2021. 'The Synthetic Situation in Diplomacy: Scopic Media and the Digital Mediation of Estrangement.' *Global Studies Quarterly* 1 (2): 1–14.

Feinberg, R. 2013. 'Institutionalized Summitry' In *The Oxford Handbook of Modern Diplomacy*, edited by A. Cooper, J. Heine, and R. Thakur, pp. 303–318. Oxford: Oxford University Press.

Hedling, E., and N. Bremberg. 2021. 'Practice Approaches to the Digital Transformations of Diplomacy: Toward a New Research Agenda.' *International Studies Review* 23 (4): 1595–1618.

Naylor, T. 2020. 'All That's Lost: The Hollowing of Summit Diplomacy in a Socially Distanced World.' *The Hague Journal of Diplomacy* 15 (4): 583–598.

REFERENCES

Adler-Nissen, R., and K. A. Eggeling. 2022. 'Blended Diplomacy: The Entanglement and Contestation of Digital Technologies in Everyday Diplomatic Practice.' *European Journal of International Relations* 28 (3): 640–666

Adler-Nissen, R., and A. Drieschova. 2019. 'Track-Change Diplomacy: Technology, Affordances, and the Practice of International Negotiations.' *International Studies Quarterly* 63 (3): 531–545.

Alexandroff, A. S., and D. Brean. 2015. 'Global Summitry: Its Meaning and Scope Part One.' *Global Summitry* 1 (1): 1–26.

Berridge, G. 2010. *Diplomacy: Theory and Practice*. 4th ed. Basingstoke and New York: Palgrave Macmillan.

Bjola, C., and M. Coplen. 2022. 'Virtual Venues and International Negotiations: Lessons from the COVID-19 Pandemic.' *International Negotiation* 8 (1): 69–93.

Bjola, C., and I. Manor. 2022. 'The Rise of Hybrid Diplomacy: From Digital Adaptation to Digital Adoption.' *International Affairs* 98 (2): 471–491.

Bramsen, I., and A. Hagemann. 2021. 'The Missing Sense of Peace: Diplomatic Approachment and Virtualization During the COVID-19 Lockdown.' *International Affairs* 97 (2): 539–560.

Calliari, E., J. Mysiak, and L. A. Vanhala. 2020. 'A Digital Climate Summit to Maintain Paris Agreement Ambition.' *Nature Climate Change* 10: 480.

Crespo, G. 2017. 'New Political Bromance Flourishes at G7 Summit.' *CNN*, 29 May. Available from: https://edition.cnn.com/2017/05/28/world/trudeau-macron-bromance-trnd/index.html

Constantinou, C. 2018. 'Visual Diplomacy: Reflections on Diplomatic Spectacle and Cinematic Thinking.' *The Hague Journal of Diplomacy* 13 (4): 1–23.

Danielson, A., and E. Hedling. 2022. 'Visual Diplomacy in Virtual Summitry: Status Signalling During the Coronavirus Crisis.' *Review of International Studies* 48 (2): 243–261.

Day, B. S., and A. Wedderburn. 2022. 'Wrestlemania! Summit Diplomacy and Foreign Policy Performance after Trump.' *International Studies Quarterly* 66 (2): 1–13

Duncombe, C. 2017. 'Twitter and Transformative Diplomacy: Social Media and Iran-US Relations.' *International Affairs* 3 (3): 545–562.

Dunn, D. H. 1996. 'What is Summitry.' In *Diplomacy at the Highest Level: The Evolution of International Summitry*, edited by D. H. Dunn, pp. 3–22. Basingstoke: Macmillan Press Ltd.

Dunn, D.H., and R. Lock-Pullan. 2016. 'Diplomatic Summitry.' In *The SAGE handbook of diplomacy*, edited by C. M. Constantinou, P. Kerr, and P. Sharp, pp. 231–241. London: SAGE.

Eggeling, K. A., and R. Adler-Nissen. 2021. 'The Synthetic Situation in Diplomacy: Scopic Media and the Digital Mediation of Estrangement.' *Global Studies Quarterly* 1 (2): 1–14.

Emirbayer, M. 1997. 'Manifesto for a Relational Sociology.' *The American Journal of Sociology* 103 (2): 281–317.

European Union. 2007. Consolidated version of the Treaty on the European Union. 13th of December. 2008/C 115/01.

Feinberg, R. 2013. 'Institutionalized Summitry.' In *The Oxford Handbook of Modern Diplomacy*, edited by A. Cooper, J. Heine, and R. Thakur, pp. 303–318. Oxford: Oxford University Press.

Goldstein, E. 1996. 'The Origins of Summit Diplomacy.' In *Diplomacy at the Highest Level: The Evolution of International Summitry*, edited by D. H. Dunn, pp. 23–37. Basingstoke: Macmillan.

G7 Research Group. 2020. *2020 G7 Virtual Summit Final Compliance Report*. University of Toronto

Hedling, E., and N. Bremberg. 2021. 'Practice Approaches to the Digital Transformations of Diplomacy: Toward a New Research Agenda.' *International Studies Review* 23 (4): 1595–1618.

Herszenhorn, D. M. 2022. 'Leaders Rebuff Zelensky's Latest Pitch to Join EU.' *Politico*, 25 March. Available from: https://www.politico.eu/article/eu-leaders-zelenskyy-ukraine-euco-summit/

Heinze, A. 2017. 'The G20 Summit's Virtual Mob: Are Courts Prepared for a New Age of Protests?' *E-International Relations*, 17 August. Available from: https://www.e-ir.info/2017/08/17/the-g20-summits-virtual-mob-are-courts-prepared-for-a-new-age-of-protests/

Holmes, M., and N. J. Wheeler. 2020. 'Social Bonding in Diplomacy.' *International Theory* 12 (1): 133–161.

Jervis, R. 1970. *The Logic of Images in International Relations*. New York, NY: Columbia University Press.

Jackson, P. T., and D. H. Nexon. 1999. 'Relations before states: Substance, process and the study of world politics.' *European Journal of International Relations* 5 (3): 291–332. Julien, C. 2015. 'Bourdieu, Social Capital and Online Interaction.' *Sociology* 49 (2): 356–373.

Lövbrand, E., M. Hjerpe, and B-O Linnér. 2017. 'Making Climate Governance Global: How UN Climate Summitry Comes to Matter in a Complex Climate Regime.' *Environmental Politics* 26 (4): 580–599.

Manor, I., and E. Segev. 2015. 'America's Selfie: How the US Portrays Itself on Its Social Media Accounts.' In *Digital Diplomacy Theory and Practice*, edited by C. Bjola and M. Holmes, pp. 88–108. London: Routledge.

Mahbubani, K. 2013. 'Multilateral Diplomacy.' In *The Oxford Handbook of Modern Diplomacy*, edited by A. F. Cooper, J. Heine, and R. Thakur, pp. 249–262. Oxford: Oxford University Press.

McConnell, F. 2019. 'Rethinking the Geographies of Diplomacy.' *Diplomatica* 1 (1): 46–55.

Maurer, H. and N. Wright. 2020. 'A New Paradigm for EU Diplomacy? EU Council Negotiations in a Time of Physical Restrictions.' *The Hague Journal of Diplomacy* 15 (4): 556–568.

McCourt, D. M. 2016. 'Practice Theory and Relationalism as the New Constructivism.' *International Studies Quarterly* 60 (3): 475–485.

Melissen, J. 2003. *Summit Diplomacy Coming of Age*. The Hague: Netherlands Institute of International Relations.

Murphy, P. D. 2021. 'Speaking for the Youth, Speaking for the Planet: Greta Thunberg and the Representational Politics of Eco-Celebrity.' *Popular Communication* 19 (3): 193–206.

NATO. 2022. *Extraordinary Virtual Summit of NATO Heads of State and Government*. Press Release. Brussels.

Nair, D. 2020. 'Emotional Labor and the Power of International Bureaucrats.' *International Studies Quarterly* 64 (3): 573–587.

Naylor, T. 2020. 'All That's Lost: The Hollowing of Summit Diplomacy in a Socially Distanced World.' *The Hague Journal of Diplomacy* 15 (4): 583–598.

Neumann, I. B. 2016. 'Sited Diplomacy.' In *Diplomatic Cultures and International Politics: Translations, Spaces and Alternatives*, edited by Jason Dittmer and Fiona McConnell. pp. 79–92. Routledge: London,

Neumann, I. B. 2020. *Diplomatic Tenses. A Social Evolutionary Perspective on Diplomacy*. Manchester, UK: Manchester University Press.

Pilegaard, J. 2016. 'Virtually Virtual? The New Frontiers of Diplomacy.' *The Hague Journal of Diplomacy* 12 (4): 316–336.

Schuette, L. A. 2021. 'Why NATO Survived Trump: The Neglected Role of Secretary-General Stoltenberg.' *International Affairs* 97 (6): 1863–1881.

Trager, R. F. 2017. *Diplomacy: Communication and the Origins of International Order*. Cambridge: Cambridge University Press.

Tyler, M.C., and T. Liu. 2020. 'Great Power Blame Game: The Ongoing War of Words Over COVID-19.' In *The Viral World*, edited by M. Mirchandani, S. Suri, and L. B. Warjri, pp. 62–71. Asia Institute: University of Melbourne.

Wenger, E. 1998. *Communities of Practice: Learning, Meaning and Identity*. Cambridge: Cambridge University Press.

Wheeler, N. J. 2013. 'Investigating Diplomatic Transformations.' *International Affairs* 89 (2): 477–496.

Wivel, A. 2017. 'Realism in Foreign Policy Analysis.' In *Oxford Research Encyclopedia of Politics*, edited by R. A. Denemark and R. Marlin-Bennett, pp. 1–22. Oxford: Oxford University Press.

Wong, S. 2021. 'One-upmanship and Putdowns: The Aggressive Use of Interaction Rituals in Face-to-face Diplomacy.' *International Theory* 13(2): 341–371.

CHAPTER 21

DIGITAL DIPLOMACY AND NON-GOVERNMENTAL AND TRANSNATIONAL ORGANIZATIONS

FIONA MCCONNELL AND ALEX MANBY

INTRODUCTION

WITH their globe-spanning networks and long-standing use of digital technology in their communication practices and advocacy strategies, non-governmental and transnational organizations have significant experience of using digital tools when practicing diplomacy. Yet, despite such centrality of the digital to the diplomatic engagement of non-governmental organizations (NGOs), diaspora organizations, and transnational advocacy networks (TANs), this has failed to be the subject of sustained academic attention. Existing literature on digital diplomacy has largely overlooked such actors, instead focusing primarily on state-based diplomats, while scholarship on transnational political actors rarely frames their practices as diplomacy. This chapter seeks to address both of these oversights by placing non-governmental and transnational organizations centre stage as digital diplomatic actors that are actively shaping agendas and driving innovation in the 'digitalisation of diplomacy' (Manor, 2019).

The following section sets the context for non-governmental and transnational organizations as diplomatic actors, discussing their position within 'new diplomacy' and tracing synergies between the pluralization and the digitalization of diplomacy. We then chart the evolution of digital diplomacy amongst these non-state actors, identifying the activities and roles they engage with in the digital diplomatic realm and the relationships they forge with other digital diplomatic actors. We argue that without the same codes of conduct to adhere to as state diplomats, these actors are often more flexible, creative, and innovative in their use of digital technologies and strategies than many states. However, in cautioning against an uncritically optimistic perspective on the potential of digitalization, we also outline the challenges and risks that non-state actors face in engaging in the digital diplomatic realm. In the penultimate section we discuss how focusing on non-state actors requires different conceptual lenses to those currently employed in scholarship on digital diplomacy. We make the case for the application of a spatial lens through engagement with literature on digital geographies, and for drawing on theoretical approaches that are attentive to everyday performances and encounters that are recast by digital diplomacy. We conclude the chapter by discussing emerging trends in non-state digital diplomacy, and outlining what a focus on these actors adds to understandings of digital diplomacy more generally.

'New Diplomacy' and the Pluralising Potential of Digital Diplomacy

As Hamilton and Langhorne note, '"non-state actor" is a new name for a not so very new phenomenon in international politics' (1995: 242), with a wide range of political entities, from city states to religious organizations, indigenous communities to think tanks having long sought to cultivate foreign relations through engaging in formal diplomatic practices. The post-Cold War acceleration of processes of globalization, and resultant increasing interconnectedness of humanitarian, environmental, trade, and military issues, has further expanded the range of diplomatic actors (Kerr and Wiseman, 2013). Such diplomatic pluralism has catalysed debates as to where the boundaries of diplomacy lie. Positions range from those who insist that diplomacy is the exclusive preserve of accredited representatives of sovereign states (e.g. Cooper et al., 2013), to those who delineate transnational diplomacy as that 'exclusively conducted by transnational actors—that is, as sovereignty-free actors, such as religious players, economic players, or NGOs' (Badie, 2013: 89) and those who embrace an expansive and open definition of diplomacy as the mediation of estrangement (e.g. Der Derian, 1987; Constantinou, 1996). For the purpose of this chapter, we deem the organizations being discussed here to have a degree of autonomy as diplomatic actors. In doing so we take as a starting point the characteristics of what has been termed 'new diplomacy' (Riordan, 2003). These characteristics include: an expansion of the definition of diplomacy beyond the peaceful conduct of relations between states; an increase in the volume, speed and mode of diplomatic communication; engagement of actors at a range of supra and sub-state scales in public diplomacy; and networked relationships between actors of different statuses (Scholte, 2008). Notably each of these trends has been impacted by the digitalization of diplomacy.

As documented in literature on digital diplomacy, digital technologies have catalysed normative and procedural shifts in the practice of diplomacy through increasing openness and transparency, and expanding the presence and augmenting the agency of non-state actors (Manor, 2017a, 2019; Bjola and Holmes, 2015). (State) diplomats are now routinely tasked with forging alliances and networks with online publics,

NGOs, civil society organizations (CSOs), and transnational activists in order to further their goals (Manor, 2016; Hayden, 2012). Yet, to date, this trend has almost solely been analysed from the perspective of states, their ministries of foreign affairs, and their diplomats.[1] This is particularly the case for the link between digital diplomacy and diaspora diplomacy wherein attention has overwhelmingly been paid to how digital technologies are transforming how states communicate and seek to alter their relationship with their diaspora communities (e.g. Rana, 2013; Brinkerhoff, 2009; Manor, 2017b). In flipping the perspective this chapter asks what digital diplomacy looks like, and how it is being reworked, from the point of view of three particular sets of 'new' diplomatic actors: NGOs, TANs, and diaspora organizations. Before doing so, however, it is necessary to briefly sketch out the nature of these diplomatic actors. We do so in broad brushstrokes, acknowledging that these are far from hermetically sealed categories, with organizations potentially falling between or spanning several of these groupings.[2]

NGOs are, by definition, separate from state apparatuses, and are a key component of civil society. They vary considerably by size, political clout, organizational structure, funding, and the range of issues that they are committed to. In the diplomatic sphere NGOs engage in what has been termed 'parallel diplomacy' (Aviel, 2009), characterized by 'communication and fact-finding; pressure activities; and advocacy' (Badie, 2013: 95). Of these, fact finding—information gathering, generation, and distribution—is a core function. The laser-like focus of NGOs on a single issue or set of cognate issues means that they have 'acquired an expertise on the history and substance of many issues that is often greater than that of government agencies or international organizations' (Aviel, 2009: 161). As a result NGOs have, over the past few decades, played an increasingly important role in epistemic communities, networks of knowledge-based experts who have 'an authoritative claim to policy-relevant knowledge' (Haas, 1992: 3; Cooper and Hocking, 2000). This has led to NGOs being granted consultative status at the UN in increasing numbers: from forty-five in 1948 to 4,045 in 2019. Consultative status also affords NGOs a degree of standing at the UN, and the distinction between NGOs as advice-givers but not decision makers is often blurred in practice, with 'an expanding role of NGOs as agents, implementers, and supervisors of treaty-based norms' (Bhuta, 2012: 67). Relatedly, a key characteristic of NGOs as diplomatic actors is their participation in and use of networks, involving both other NGOs and governmental and international organization (IO) representatives in order to 'combine their expertise and resources' and 'increase their influence at multilateral conferences' (Aviel, 2009: 162). This trend has been enhanced with the shift to digital diplomacy.

Some networks including NGOs come under the label of 'transnational advocacy networks' (TANs), loose groupings of political actors which can include, *inter alia*, social movements, CSOs, journalists, experts, and individual activists. These

---

[1] Some attention has been paid to the digital diplomacy of international organizations, e.g. Corrie (2015) on the International Criminal Court's use of digital technology.

[2] For example, American-Jewish and Vietnamese diasporas that mobilized for the release of political prisoners in their homelands through TANs during the Cold War (Goodwin, 2021).

networks are characterized by 'the centrality of values or principled ideas, the belief that individuals can make a difference, the creative use of information, and the employment by nongovernmental actors of sophisticated political strategies in targeting their campaigns' (Keck and Sikkink, 1998: 2) and have been key players in international diplomacy related to human rights, women's rights, and the environment. Theorized by social constructivists as 'norm entrepreneurs' (Keck and Sikkink, 1998: 2), the primary influence these actors have in the diplomatic realm is in persuading states and IOs about their values and causes. Like NGOs, this is achieved through the quality and quantity of their information generation in the form of both researched data and witness testimony. Notably, despite discussing strategies of communication, representation, and negotiation at an international scale, it is rare for scholarship in this field to frame the practices of TANs as diplomacy per se (for an exception see Wajner, 2017).

In contrast, there is growing recognition of 'diaspora diplomacy'. Building on Ho and McConnell's delineation of diplomacy *by* diasporas and diplomacy *through* diasporas, Brinkerhoff outlines three roles that diasporas play vis-à-vis diplomacy as 'agents; instruments of others' diplomatic agendas; and intentional or accidental partners with other actors through uncoordinated efforts in pursuit of common interests' (2019: 56). As diplomatic actors, diaspora organizations range from being parties to peace negotiations (e.g. the role of the Tamil diaspora in peace-building in Sri Lanka, Cochrane et al., 2009), advocating for regime change in the homeland (e.g. Turkish diaspora organizations in the aftermath of the 2016 coup attempt, Uysal, 2019) and seeking to influence global public opinion in support of their cause (e.g. the role of the Chinese digital diaspora in national image building, Ding, 2007/8).

Commonalities across these three groups of actors include dense exchanges of information, sustained use of 'network diplomacy' (Slaughter, 2009), effective transnational communication to link up diverse constituencies, and creative use of tools of persuasion that challenge 'dominant Western conceptions of static state-centred, state-initiated public diplomacy' (Uysal, 2019: 272). What distinguishes these non-governmental and transnational organizations as diplomats from their state counterparts is that they have a narrower set of defined objectives and, in general, they do not seek to govern, but seek to influence those who do. They leverage this influence from the position of 'outsiders acting upon a world of insiders, that of the system or society of sovereign states' (Constantino, Kerr, and Sharp, 2016: 6).

As 'outsiders' to 'traditional diplomacy' these non-state actors are key beneficiaries of the opening up of diplomacy enabled by digital technologies. Remote participation in diplomacy facilitated through digital tools such as video submissions to international meetings, livestreaming of diplomatic events, and instant communication goes a considerable way to circumventing spatial exclusions inherent in the practice of diplomacy, including the difficulties NGOs, TANs, and diaspora organizations often face in physically attending meetings due to limited human resources and finances, and visa restrictions. The result is diplomacy that is more inclusive and plural, with a wider range and diversity of voices being heard. Three particular dynamics of the digitalization of diplomacy have benefited non-governmental and transnational organizations.

First, digital technologies have allowed the expansion of the number of non-governmental and transnational organizations operating at the global level by levelling the diplomatic playing field and thus broadening access (Bramsen and Hagemann, 2021). This has occurred both in the realm of public diplomacy and formal diplomacy. In the former the amplification generated by social media has meant that NGOs and TANs are increasingly visible as public diplomacy actors (Duncombe, 2019). In formal diplomacy such as peace negotiations digital tools that facilitate large scale synchronous dialogues—digital focus groups which operate at the scale of an opinion poll—have enabled a wider range of participants, and previously underrepresented voices such as women and youth, to engage in conflict resolution negotiations such as those in Libya (*The Economist*, 1 May 2021: 55).

Second, the high intensity communication that digital technologies enable leads to more contacts and greater interdependence between diplomatic actors (Kurbalija, 2013: 146; Slaughter, 2009), thereby fostering a more polylateral mode of diplomacy (Wiseman, 2010). This is apparent both in terms of increased connections between non-state actors as they forge solidarities and exchange knowledge (McConnell, 2017), and between non-state actors and state and IO diplomats. As a result, non-state actors are able to build relationships with wider and more varied audiences (e.g. Manor, 2019). This is a rapidly shifting landscape, and questions remain regarding the extent to which NGOs make use of changes in algorithms used by social media platforms to sort and curate content based on perceived relevancy and prioritizing emotionally charged content, and are investing in social media advertising. However, the extent to which the digitalization of diplomacy has led to a fundamental shift in power relations between diplomatic actors of different statuses remains unclear. Some early work on digital diplomacy lauded its potential to transfer power from institutions (including states) to individuals (Gilboa, 2016), and celebrated the perceived ability of digital communication to enable individuals across the globe to interact without state interference (e.g. Brinkerhoff, 2009; Badie, 2013). In an era of increasing state policing of the Internet these claims now seem somewhat misplaced. Indeed, Amnesty International has recently documented the widespread 'geo-blocking' and content moderation of user-generated posts on Facebook, Google, and YouTube deemed 'anti-state' by the Vietnamese authorities. This is occurring as part of a wider pattern of censorship, harassment, and prosecution of human rights defenders and digital activists operating within the country (Amnesty International, 2020). Yet there is also evidence of digital technologies having a levelling effect in terms of relations between diplomatic actors of different statuses by creating new opportunities for state and non-state actors to collaborate in more equal and inclusive ways, albeit the influence of each over the other varies. In some cases, NGOs and TANs exert influence on state and IO diplomats, for example Amnesty International and Access Now's work in placing digital surveillance on the international agenda.[3] In other cases, social media campaigns initiated by NGOs

---

[3] Side event organized by NGOs at the 76th session of the UNGA in October 2021 https://www.youtube.com/watch?v=8qCbECZWyJs

and TANs are appropriated by states for their own goals, for example the British FCO's campaign to #EndSexualViolence in conflicts (Pamment, 2016; Manor, 2017b).

Finally, digital technologies have facilitated more effective engagement of non-governmental and transnational organizations in multilateral diplomacy. This has been realized through two sets of seemingly divergent trends. First, the digitalization of diplomacy has made some diplomacy more transparent while causing other diplomatic interactions to become more opaque. Enhanced transparency, for example through the webcasting of international meetings, 'enables more continuous and systematic interaction' (Bramsen and Hagemann, 2021: 545) and thus a wider audience of non-state actors to observe and participate in diplomacy. Simultaneously, other diplomatic exchanges have been able to happen more easily outside of public view and media scrutiny. State diplomats can meet with non-state diplomats online in ways that they cannot (be seen to) in person: a phenomenon which is particularly important when it comes to discussion of politically sensitive human right issues. Second, digital technologies have enabled diplomatic interactions to become both more flexible and more formal. Again each of these trends can potentially be advantageous to non-state actors. Flexibility in terms of cyberspace creating 'new possibilities of connection and disjuncture [that are] affective, social, and political' (Bernal, 2018: 3) means that non-state actors are not constrained by conventional diplomatic protocols. Counterintuitively, the shift to online diplomatic interactions can also lead to an increased formality of diplomatic exchanges where side discussions and free-flowing conversations are no longer possible. As we discuss below, this loss of sociality can be a drawback, particularly for non-state actors who have limited exposure to key diplomatic sites. However, the enhanced structure and formality of online meetings and negotiations—with agendas set in advance, schedules more strictly adhered to, and formal order maintained—can move negotiations forward more efficiently and equalize interactions, particularly for marginalized groups (Bramsen and Hagemann, 2021).

NON-GOVERNMENTAL AND TRANSNATIONAL ORGANIZATIONS AS DIGITAL DIPLOMACY PIONEERS AND INNOVATORS

The increasing inclusivity afforded by the digitalization of diplomacy goes hand in hand with non-governmental and transnational organizations being pioneers and innovators within digital diplomacy. This section first traces how NGOs, TANs, and diaspora organizations have evolved as digital diplomacy actors: their role in spearheading the effective use of ICT in multilateral diplomatic settings; professionalization of these actors as diplomats; and a shift from online observation of diplomacy to online participation. Attention then turns to the new skills and knowledge that these actors bring to digital diplomacy, and how their position outside of the state system enables a degree of flexibility and creativity around digital communication and information management that often eludes state actors.

The evolution of non-governmental and transnational organizations as digital diplomacy actors is arguably harder to trace than the evolution of state-based digital diplomacy. The latter has been done through charting the development of MFA initiatives and institutions focused on digital diplomacy, particularly in the US (e.g. Gilboa, 2016). The challenge for undertaking a similar exercise vis-à-vis non-state actors lies precisely in the lack of clarity and consensus around these being diplomatic actors. As noted above, they rarely feature as agents in digital diplomacy scholarship. This oversight is paradoxical given that non-governmental and transnational organizations have been pioneers in digital diplomacy. Indeed, the first major use of computers and ICT at an international diplomatic meeting—the 1992 Earth Summit in Rio de Janeiro—was controversial precisely because it provided the ability for CSOs across the globe to monitor, challenge, and participate in the proceedings. As Kurbalija notes, through online mailing lists, ICT empowered civil society groupings were directly engaged with the negotiations and as a result 'the monopoly that diplomats had over information from this and other later global meetings was greatly diminished' (2013: 151).

Building on this experience, NGOs and TANs capitalized on the expansion and evolution of digital technology in the 1990s. Indeed one of the earliest and most influential uses of the Internet in international diplomacy was initiated by non-governmental and transnational organizations. From 1992 to 1997, the International Campaign to Ban Landmines—a consortium of more than 1,000 NGOs—used the Internet to both mobilize global public opinion and persuade governments to negotiate a new treaty on landmine use (Price, 1998). The successful adoption of the Convention on the Prohibition of the Use, Stockpiling, Production and Transfer of Anti-Personnel Mines and on Their Destruction in 1997 resulted in the Campaign being awarded the Nobel Peace Prize. Internet-facilitated communication and negotiation was also central to the success of the East Timorese freedom movement, which not only brought human rights abuses in East Timor to international attention, for example through the East Timor Action Network's collation and dissemination of online resources (Hill, 2002), but also coordinated global solidarity activities to enhance East Timor's international visibility and exert international political leverage for Timorese independence. These included the declaration of virtual East Timorese sovereignty through the registering of a '.tp' code domain through an offshore Internet Service Provider (Scharfe, 2000) and forging solidarities with international human rights NGOs (Simpson, 2004), which ultimately led to the successful pressuring of Indonesia to allow a referendum on the territory's independence in 1999.

Since the 1990s non-governmental and transnational organizations have become increasingly professionalized as diplomatic actors. Through both formal training organized by NGOs and IOs and 'on the job' experience, individuals and groups from civil society have honed their negotiation skills and developed their communication and representation capacities (Kurbalija, 2013). There has thus been a resultant shift within these organizations from 'a reliance on untrained volunteers to a growing cadre of experienced NGO negotiators, indigenous expert elites and private diplomats' (Constantinou et al., 2017: 39). A related trend has been a shift from these actors primarily following diplomatic deliberations passively through web broadcasting, to actively participating in diplomacy online.

Alongside the professionalization of non-state diplomatic actors has been the cultivation of new skills and capabilities that they have brought to the digital diplomatic realm. In many ways, diasporas, NGOs, and TANs have been leading the way in digital diplomacy. As Constantinou and colleagues note, 'with their reliance on close coordination and their significantly lower operating costs, new digital technologies favour organisations based on decentralised networks, unlike the traditional hierarchies of foreign ministries' (2016: 40). Non-governmental and transnational organizations have capitalized on this advantage, using their flexible and agile structures to adapt quickly to new communication and information management technologies (Cooper and Hocking, 2000), and have thus been innovators in the field. NGOs in particular have taken advantage of the affordances offered by social media, including the ability to easily reach both geographically widespread and locally targeted audiences through hashtag activism campaigns and micro-targeting technologies respectively, as well as an increasing turn towards search-based information seeking and open-source-intelligence networks as a means of uncovering and verifying human rights abuses. These new opportunities have been balanced by anxieties regarding the lack of transparency surrounding the actors and networks involved in many digital campaigns, including concern amongst human rights activists around social media 'astroturfing', in which the sources of putatively grassroots or naturally occurring social media campaigns are deliberately obscured in order to circulate misinformation.

Non-state actors' early embrace of social media stands in contrast to the rather slow and wary adaptation of some state actors to the digital world (Manor, 2016). Underpinning these divergent approaches to and engagements with digital technologies is the fact that non-state actors operate without the constraints of adhering to particular national agendas or the strictures of subscribing to formal diplomatic protocols. Having resonances with paradiplomacy, which is 'more functionally specific and targeted, often opportunistic experimental' (Keating, 1999: 11), this fleet-footedness means that non-state actors are able to direct their (generally limited) resources towards maximizing their direct interests (Dickson, 2014). This includes the use of the digital to engage in capacity building, with the availability of live-streamed diplomatic meetings (e.g. via UN Web TV) and the use of online training facilitating knowledge sharing about best practices that, ultimately, fosters diplomatic agency.

The innovation of non-state actors in digital advocacy strategies, modes of communication, and transnational networking brings to the fore possibilities for generating spaces for creative thinking within diplomacy more generally. Creativity has long been promoted as a key diplomatic skill, but it has conventionally been understood in the context of well-connected elites having the requisite personal 'qualities' of charisma, ingenuity, and initiative-taking (e.g. Moravcsik, 1999). However, a more inclusive examination of creativity in the diplomatic realm reveals inventive practices beyond elite actors.

For example, in their examination of citizen statecraft and digital diplomacy in the Falklands/Malvinas dispute, Pinkerton and Benwell (2014) document how citizenries on both sides use social media as a 'weapon of the weak' to challenge and subvert existing representations of the dispute and thereby creatively engage with international audiences. In the context of UN diplomacy—a bastion of diplomatic status quo—it was CSOs that lobbied for remote participation at the Human Rights Council (HRC) when the Covid-19 pandemic forced the termination of most in-person diplomacy (ISHR, 2020). Not only was the HRC one of the first UN bodies to run hybrid online and in-person sessions in 2020, but non-state actors drew on their repertoire of digital skills and experience to creatively respond to the shifting modalities of participation. This included producing high quality video interventions, including those featuring indigenous adolescents and speakers who would usually be unable to attend the HRC, and hosting unofficial online side events, which often reached tens of thousands of online viewers (UNPO, 2020).

CHALLENGES AND RISKS OF DIGITAL DIPLOMACY FOR NON-GOVERNMENTAL AND TRANSNATIONAL ORGANIZATIONS

While the potential for non-governmental and transnational organizations to innovate in digital diplomacy is clear, the shift to online modes of diplomacy should not be celebrated uncritically. Digitalization does not inevitably open up and democratize diplomacy. Rather, it can also reproduce and, in some cases enhance, existing socio-spatial inequalities. In this section we discuss two sets of challenges and risks that non-governmental and transnational organizations face when seeking to, or having no choice but to, engage with digital diplomacy: inequalities in access to reliable Internet connections and technical support; and cybersecurity risks.

The first and most systemic challenge is ongoing inequalities in access to digital connectivity, technology, and support. Reflecting wider 'digital divides' (Norris, 2001; van Dijik, 2020) in access to and use of the Internet, in the diplomatic sphere this is manifest in stark differences in the ability to participate in remote diplomacy 'between states and civil society, and between NGOs located in different geographic areas and with different financial and human resource capacities' (UNPO, 2020: 27). As documented in relation to online sessions of the UN's HRC in 2020, the ability of CSOs to participate 'live' was dependent on their access to reliable Internet connection and to technical support, both of which were often lacking (UNPO, 2020: 27). This resulted in speakers being unable to join meetings, often cutting out mid-speech, being inaudible, or the video being of insufficient quality to support interpretation. This raises important questions about the nature and extent of digital empowerment and it challenges the assumed correlation between digitalization and diplomatic inclusion. Indeed, there have been cases whereby the digitalization of diplomacy has been used to curtail or even prevent participation by CSOs. An extreme example is state Internet shutdowns which target the international activities of civil society, for instance, the governments of India, Myanmar, Pakistan, and Bangladesh have all faced criticism for intentionally disrupting Internet access to curtail freedom of expression and the two-way flow of health information during the Covid-19 pandemic (HRW, 2020). More mundanely, the digitalization of diplomacy has in some cases reinforced hierarchies between diplomatic actors. This was evident at the UN during the Covid-19 pandemic wherein the cancellation, postponement, or curtailment of particular UN forums disproportionately affected the participation of NGOs and CSOs. This included the cancellation of the 19th Session of the UN Permanent Forum on Indigenous Issues in 2020, and the cancellation of side events at the 43rd, 44th, and 45th sessions of the HRC, despite the presence of state diplomats at the Palais des Nations being permitted. As a result the existing 'pecking order' (Pouliot, 2019) of diplomatic actors was reinforced.

Second, the digitalization of diplomacy brings with it significant cybersecurity risks for some non-governmental and transnational organizations, including the risk of state reprisals against those critical of particular states. This is especially the case in relation to organizations constituted of or seeking to represent human rights defenders, minority groups, and indigenous communities who have reported states using the tools of digital diplomacy to repress dissent (UNPO, 2020). This is a phenomenon that Moss (2018), focusing on the case of the Syrian government's online policing of pro-revolution diaspora activists, terms 'digitally enabled transnational repression'. In the context of diplomacy at the UN this has been manifest in concerns around the UN's use of video-conferencing platforms such as Zoom for official HRC meetings, which have been vulnerable to state surveillance and shutdown, and suspected phishing emails masquerading as communications from UN bodies (Glowacka et al., 2021). In order to analyse how non-governmental and transnational organizations navigate such challenges of digital diplomacy, and how they also capitalize on the opportunities it presents, it is necessary to step back and assess the conceptual framings that we might employ.

THEORIZING THE DIGITAL DIPLOMACY OF NON-STATE ACTORS: THE SPATIAL AND THE EMBODIED PERFORMANCES

Just as non-state actors have been on the fringes of diplomacy studies, so there is a need to widen the conceptual lenses that are used to study their digital practices beyond those conventionally employed in the study of digital diplomacy. Our interrogation of the digital diplomacy of these actors is underpinned by two approaches. First is the application of a spatial lens through engagement with literature on digital geographies.

This facilitates an examination of how the digital practices of these actors reconfigure the relationship between diplomacy and space, for example by unsettling the distinction between online and offline worlds through the fostering of mediated spaces, and by reshaping the digital as a site of socio-spatial exclusion. Second, and relatedly, we engage with theoretical approaches that are attentive to the everyday performances, encounters, and registers of sociability that are recast in the digital realm. Though these framings can also be productively applied to the activities of state diplomats, the transnational character of non-state actors and the creativity with which they have embraced opportunities for remote participation mean that these approaches are of particular utility in understanding this group's digital diplomatic practices.

Turning first to the application of a spatial lens, diplomacy scholars have illustrated how diplomacy is a fundamentally spatial practice, which occurs *in* and is shaped *by* particular sites, and is underpinned by the management of relations at both close proximity and across distance (McConnell, 2019). Digital geographies scholarship, meanwhile, has explored the increasingly important role of digital technologies in shaping the production of such relational space(s), as well as the associated shifts in the speed and nature of digital communications (Ash et al, 2018). Such is the penetration of the digital technologies into nearly all aspects of life, that geographers have rejected binary accounts of 'real' and 'virtual' space to suggest that all space is now digitally mediated, comprised of the coming-together of people, places, and technology, and, crucially, the connections between multiple places that these technologies facilitate (Leszczynski, 2015). Through this spatial lens, we can see how digitalization has expanded and altered the sites of diplomacy for non-state actors. No longer confined to the conference halls that comprise the front-stage of diplomacy, nor to the corridors and back-rooms of the back-stage, digital technologies have extended the spaces of diplomacy to include offices, living rooms, and even bedrooms of diplomatic actors located around the world, as well as the online platforms via which they interact (Bramsen and Hagemann, 2021).

Widening the empirical lens of diplomacy to incorporate these sites not only brings into view a host of alternative digital diplomatic actors, but also exposes the way in which the digital remains a site of socio-spatial exclusion for non-state actors. As McConnell (2020: 2) has illustrated, '(non)membership and (non)belonging in diplomatic space is articulated through spatial practices', including the establishment of norms and protocols which work to effectively exclude representatives of minority groups. Eschewing understandings of 'online' and 'off-line' as distinct spatial realms thus draws attention to the ways in which in-person diplomatic norms continue to pervade digitally mediated space, for example through exacting technical requirements, practices of intimidation such as 'Zoom bombing', and difficulties accessing meeting links. Attending to the 'where' of diplomacy (Kuus, 2015) also highlights how digital technologies are reconfiguring non-state diplomacy's place-based dynamics. Through participating remotely, diaspora organizations in particular are able to collapse the boundaries between formal diplomatic sites and the spaces 'back home', providing new opportunities to both leverage and disrupt geographical imaginaries of distant places. For example, non-state actors are increasingly taking advantage of the livestreaming of diplomatic meetings to produce video content showcasing their choreographed interventions (UNPO, 2020). These videos can take on a 'life of their own' once circulated on social media, reaching global audiences well outside of formal diplomatic networks (Constantinou et al., 2021: 14).

Attending to these circulations also foregrounds the importance of understanding digital diplomatic interventions as embodied performances. Geographers have analysed engagement with the digital as an embodied performance in which subjectivities are both reproduced and subverted online (Cockayne and Richardson, 2017). Digital media is also understood as having the capacity to induce specific emotional responses in viewers, which vary according to platform and across time and space (Longhurst, 2016). In the realm of diplomacy, the shift to the digital has again presented both challenges and opportunities for non-state actors seeking to employ emotional registers to engage both in-person audiences and those following on social media. With regards to challenges, in order for information to gain attention and be deemed to be credible, it must be communicated persuasively and dramatically—often through the use of witness testimony (Keck and Sikkink, 1998)—and it is here that limitations of digital tools are apparent. In both online diplomatic meetings and in video recorded interventions at diplomatic summits the loss of eye contact and body language means that the emotional connection to audiences is more challenging and overall the impact of such interventions are arguably less than in-person advocacy. Likewise informal diplomatic encounters are significantly curtailed when diplomacy is conducted online. This poses particular problems for non-state actors who, excluded from the diplomatic corps and thus lacking access to formal diplomatic networks, rely on these chance interactions between meetings and outside of official diplomatic spaces for the building of trust and rapport with interlocutors. Indeed, the loss of the physicality of everyday interactions when diplomacy moves online has been documented in recent work on 'sociability' (Kuus, 2023) and 'inter-moments' (Naylor, 2020). Yet, in their preoccupation with what is *lost* when diplomacy is digitalized, these accounts neglect the 'creative attempts' that diplomats use to 'perform diplomacy's intimacies' online and to establish bonds of trust (Eggeling and Adler-Nissen, 2021: 3). Specifically, non-state actors have been creative in their use of Zoom backgrounds, lighting, and sound to cultivate an 'affective [diplomatic] atmosphere' in online diplomatic interventions (Constantinou et al., 2021), and have experimented with web-conferencing tools to enable direct audience participation and dialogic interaction at online side events. As such, we suggest that geographical scholarship on the digitally mediated spaces of intimate encounter, with its attention to the circumstances in which intimacies *can* develop without physical contact through the establishment of an 'experiential *sense* of proximity' (Cockayne et al., 2017: 1124) may go some of the way in elucidating the contradictory ways in which non-state actors can continue to engage in the 'mediation of estrangement' (Der Derian, 1987) online.

Finally, the application of these analytical frames also requires a concomitant broadening of researchers' methodological gaze to consider the increasing range of spaces in which digital diplomatic content is produced and consumed. In these circumstances, when the field-site is extended to include the phones, laptops, and tablets which now comprise the core of diplomatic practice, research needs to be both 'sited', in terms of detailed ethnographic observations into the embodied engagement with digital technologies in physical sites of diplomacy, and 'remote', in terms of following diplomatic meetings online, attending virtual side events, and 'lurking' in the inboxes, virtual chat feeds, and social media timelines of non-state diplomatic actors. As Eggeling and Addler-Nissen (2021: 6) argue, these contexts not only offer new opportunities to get closer to 'participants' experiences', but through conducting such virtual ethnography, the researcher is forced to engage directly with the object of study.

CONCLUSION: EMERGING TRENDS IN NON-STATE DIGITAL DIPLOMACY

In concluding this overview of the digital diplomacy of non-governmental and transnational organizations we identify three ongoing and emerging trends, and note how focusing on the digital practices of these non-state diplomatic actors can offer valuable insights into the nature, scope, and potential of digital diplomacy more generally.

First is the increasing pluralization of actors engaging in digital diplomacy. In many ways the digitalization of diplomacy and the multiplication of diplomatic actors form a virtuous circle, and so it follows that to study digital diplomacy we must take the roles and practices of a wide range of actors seriously. This entails expanding our gaze from bilateral and multilateral digital diplomacy to also interrogate the polylateral diplomatic relations (Wiseman, 2010) that are mediated in the digital sphere. As the range of and use of digital diplomatic tools proliferates, it is likely that the trends regarding polylateral relationships that we have set out here will continue and extend in new ways. We are likely to see increasing partnerships between state and non-state diplomatic actors, facilitated by digital tools, and more knowledge exchange between diplomatic actors of different statuses regarding digital strategies. Indeed, just as there is recognition that the multiplication and diversification of diplomatic actors is changing the nature and quality of diplomacy (e.g. Cooper and Hocking, 2000), so there needs to be focused attention on how the digital diplomacy practices of non-governmental and transnational organizations are altering the nature, scope, and potential of digital diplomacy more generally. These non-state actors have the potential to reshape digital diplomatic culture, making it more flexible, inclusive, and transparent, and, in the process, digitalization can facilitate the emergence of new diplomatic subjectivities.

Second is the potential for non-governmental and transnational organizations to lead the way in digital diplomacy innovation. As pioneers in the successful deployment of digital diplomacy strategies, it is surprising that NGOs, TANs, and diaspora organizations have not garnered more attention from scholars working on digital diplomacy. Again, the trends identified in this chapter look likely to continue in terms of nonstate actors that are institutionally adapted to the digital landscape being innovators in the field, experimenting with digital tools, and thereby opening up new modes of doing diplomacy. A case in point is the use of open source intelligence (OSINT) in diplomacy, an emerging trend that NGOs, TANs, and diaspora organizations are spearheading, in some cases in ways that make states wary and confrontational. More generally, this experimentation in diplomatic practices inspires the development of new types of diplomatic methods and has the potential effect of making diplomacy itself more collaborative, open, and 'transprofessional' (Constantinou et al., 2017). As such, a sustained analysis of how non-governmental and transnational organizations engage with digital diplomacy has the potential to widen the definition of digital diplomacy, not only beyond the actions of states, but also in terms of digital cooperation and issues around governance of the Internet.

Related to Internet governance and security is the third trend: that the digital diplomacy sphere is one that is increasingly riven with hierarchies and inequalities. As we have cautioned in this chapter, the digitalization of diplomacy is not a universally positive development for non-governmental and transnational organizations. By focusing on the challenges and risks that these actors face in seeking to do diplomacy in the digital world, generalized claims about the emancipatory potential of digital diplomacy can and should be refuted. For, at the same time as digital technologies facilitate transnational networking for TANs and diaspora organizations, including in advocating against home country regimes in diplomatic forums, ICTs are also being used by authoritarian states to control and repress dissenting voices. More generally, a focus on the digital diplomacy of these non-state actors exposes the power relations that underpin diplomatic exchanges, including the construction and maintenance of hierarchies of actors and the policing of diplomatic spaces.

Suggested Reading

Aviel, J. F. (2009) 'NGOs and International Affairs'. In *Multilateral Diplomacy and the United Nations Today*, edited by J. P. Muldoon, J. F. Aviel, R Reitano, and E. Sullivan, 159–172. Boulder: Westview Press.

Badie, B. (2013) 'Transnationalizing Diplomacy and Global Governance'. In *Diplomacy in a Globalizing World*, edited by P. Kerr and G. Wiseman, 85–102. Oxford: Oxford University Press.

Brinkerhoff, J. M. (2019) 'Diasporas and Public Diplomacy: Distinctions and Future Prospects'. *The Hague Journal of Diplomacy* 14: 51–64.

Cooper, A. F., and B. Hocking. (2000) 'Governments, Non-Governmental Organizations and the Re-Calibration of Diplomacy'. *Global Society* 14(3): 361–376.

Moss, D. (2018) 'The ties that bind: Internet communication technologies, networked authoritarianism, and 'voice' in the Syrian diaspora', *Globalizations*, 15(2): 265–282.

Simpson, B. (2004) 'Solidarity in an Age of Globalization: The Transnational Movement for East Timor and U.S. Foreign Policy'. *Peace & Change*, 29(3–4): 453–482.

UNPO. (2020) 'Compromised Space and Undiplomatic Immunity' *UNPO* https://unpo.org/downloads/2690.pdf

References

Amnesty International. (2020) ' "Let us Breathe!": Censorship and Criminalization of Online Expression in Viet Nam', 30 November 2020 [Online]. https://www.amnesty.org/en/docume nts/asa41/3243/2020/en/ Accessed 12 May 2022.

Ash, J., R. Kitchen, and A. Leszcynski. (eds) (2018) *Digital Geographies*. London: Sage.

Aviel, J. F. (2009) 'NGOs and International Affairs'. In *Multilateral Diplomacy and the United Nations Today*, edited by J. P. Muldoon, J. F. Aviel, R Reitano, and E. Sullivan, 159–172. Boulder: Westview Press.

Badie, B. (2013) 'Transnationalizing Diplomacy and Global Governance'. In *Diplomacy in a Globalizing World*, edited by P. Kerr and G. Wiseman, 85–102. Oxford: Oxford University Press.

Bernal, V. (2018) 'Digital Media, Territory, and Diaspora: The Shape-Shifting Spaces of Eritrean Politics'. *Journal of African Cultural Studies* 21(1): 1–15.

Bhuta, N. (2012) 'The Role International Actors Other than States Can Play in the New World Order'. In *Realizing Utopia: The Future of International Law*, edited by A. Cassese, 61–75. Oxford: Oxford University Press.

Bjola, C. and M. Holmes. (2015) *Digital Diplomacy: Theory and Practice*. London: Routledge.

Bramsen, I. and A. Hagemann. (2021) 'The Missing Sense of Peace: Diplomatic Approachment and Virtualization during the COVID-19 Lockdown'. *International Affairs* 97(2): 539–560.

Brinkerhoff, J. M. (2009) *Digital Diasporas: Identity and Transnational Engagement*. Cambridge: Cambridge University Press.

Brinkerhoff, J. M. (2019) 'Diasporas and Public Diplomacy: Distinctions and Future Prospects'. *The Hague Journal of Diplomacy* 14: 51–64.

Cochrane, F., B. Baser, and A. Swain. (2009) 'Home Thoughts from Abroad: Diasporas and Peace-Building in Northern Ireland and Sri Lanka'. *Studies in Conflict & Terrorism* 32(8): 681–704.

Cockayne, D., Leszczynski, A., and Zook, M., (2017) '#HotForBots: Sex, the Non-Human and Digitally Mediated Spaces of Intimate Encounter'. *Environment and Planning D* 35: 1115–1133.

Cockayne, D.G. and Richardson, L. (2017) 'Queering Code/Space: the Co-Production of Socio-Sexual Codes and Digital Technologies'. *Gender, Place & Culture* 24: 1642–1658.

Constantinou, C. M. (1996) *On the Way to Diplomacy*. Minneapolis: University of Minnesota Press.

Constantinou, C., N. Cornago, and F. McConnell. (2017) 'Transprofessional Diplomacy'. *Brill Research Perspectives in Diplomacy and Foreign Policy* 1(4): 1–66.

Constantinou, C., P. Kerr, and P. Sharp. (2016) 'Introduction: Understanding Diplomatic Practice'. In *SAGE Handbook of Diplomacy*, edited by C. Constantinou, P. Kerr, and P. Sharp, 1–10. London: SAGE.

Constantinou, C. M., J. Dittmer, M. Kuus, F. McConnell, S. O. Opondo, and V. Pouliot. (2021) 'Thinking with Diplomacy: Within and Beyond Practice Theory'. *International Political Sociology* 15(4): 559–587.

Cooper, A. F., J. Heine, and R. Thakur. (2013) *The Oxford Handbook of Modern Diplomacy*. Oxford: Oxford University Press.

Cooper, A. F., and B. Hocking. (2000) 'Governments, Non-Governmental Organizations and the Re-Calibration of Diplomacy'. *Global Society* 14(3): 361–376.

Corrie, K. L. (2015) 'The International Criminal Court: Using Technology in Network Diplomacy'. In *Digital Diplomacy: Theory and Practice*, edited by C. Bjola and M. Holmes, 145–163. London: Routledge.

Der Derian, J. (1987) *On Diplomacy: A Genealogy of Western Estrangement*. Oxford: Blackwell.

Dickson, F. (2014) 'The Internationalisation of Regions: Paradiplomacy or Multi-Level Governance?' *Geography Compass* 8(10): 689–700.

Ding, S. (2007/8) 'Digital Diaspora and National Image Building: A New Perspective on Chinese Diaspora Study in the Age of China's Rise'. Pacific Affairs. 80(4): 627–648.

Duncombe, C. (2019) 'Digital Diplomacy: Emotion and Identity in the Public Realm'. *The Hague Journal of Diplomacy* 14: 102–116.

Eggeling, K.A. and R. Adler-Nissen. (2021) 'The Synthetic Situation in Diplomacy: Scopic Media and the Digital Mediation of Estrangement'. *Global Studies Quarterly*, 2: 1–14.

Gilboa, E. (2016) 'Digital Diplomacy'. In *The SAGE Handbook of Diplomacy*, edited by C. M. Constantinou, P. Kerr, and P. Sharp, 540–551. London: SAGE.

Glowacka, D., R. Youngs, A. Pintea, and E. Wolosik. (2021) *Study: Digital Technologies as a Means of Repression and Social Control*. Brussels: European Union.

Goodwin, M. (2021) '"Let my People Go": Diaspora Mobilization for the Human Rights of Political Prisoners'. *Globalizations* 19(2):1–15.

Haas, P. (1992) 'Epistemic Communities and International Policy Coordination: Introduction'. *International Organization* 46(1): 1–35.

Hamilton, K. and R. Langhorne. (1995) *The Practice of Diplomacy: Its Evolution, Theory and Administration*. London: Routledge.

Hayden, C. (2012) 'Social Media at State: Power, Practice, and Conceptual Limits for US Public Diplomacy'. *Global Media Journal* 21(1) (RP1):1–15.

Hill, D. (2002) 'East Timor and the Internet: Global Political Leverage in/on Indonesia'. *Indonesia* 73: 25–51.

Ho, E. L. E. and F. McConnell. (2019) 'Conceptualising "Diaspora Diplomacy": Territory and Populations Betwixt the Domestic and Foreign'. *Progress in Human Geography* 43(2): 235–255.

HRW. (2020) 'End Internet Shutdowns to Manage Covid-19: Blocking Access Could Cost Lives', 31 March 2020. [Online] https://www.hrw.org/news/2020/03/31/end-internet-shutdowns-manage-covid-19. Accessed 9 November 2020.

ISHR. (2020) 'COVID-19: Principles and Recommendations on Ensuring Civil Society Inclusion in UN Discussions', 24 April 2020 [Online]. https://ishr.ch/latest-updates/covid-19-principles-and-recommendations-ensuring-civil-society-inclusion-un-discussions/ Accessed 9 November 2021.

Keating, M. (1999) 'Regions and International Affairs: Motives, Opportunities and Strategies'. In *Paradiplomacy in Action: The Foreign Relations of Subnational Governments*, edited by F. Aldecoa and M. Keating, 1–16. Portland: Frank Cass.

Keck, M. and K. Sikkink. (1998) *Activists beyond Borders*. Ithaca: Cornell University Press.

Kerr, P. and G. Wiseman. (2013) *Diplomacy in a Globalizing World: Theories and Practices*. Oxford: Oxford University Press.

Kurbalija, J. (2013) 'The Impact of the Internet and ICT on Contemporary Diplomacy'. In *Diplomacy in a Globalizing World*, edited by P. Kerr and G. Wiseman, 141–150. Oxford: Oxford University Press.

Kuus, M., (2015) 'Symbolic Power in Diplomatic Practice: Matters of Style in Brussels', *Cooperation and Conflict* 50: 368–384.

Kuus, M. (2023) 'Bureaucratic Sociability, or the Missing Eighty Percent of Effectiveness: The Case of Diplomacy'. *Geopolitics*, 28: 174–195.

Leszczynski, A. (2015) 'Spatial Media/tion'. *Progress in Human Geography* 39: 729–751.

Longhurst, R. (2016) 'Mothering, Digital Media and Emotional Geographies in Hamilton, Aotearoa New Zealand'. *Social & Cultural Geography* 17: 120–139.

Manor, I. (2016) 'Are We There Yet: Have MFAs Realized the Potential of Digital Diplomacy? Results from a Cross-National Comparison'. *Diplomacy and Foreign Policy* 1(2): 1–110.

Manor, I. (2019) *The Digitalization of Public Diplomacy*. Palgrave.

Manor, I. (2017a) 'The Digitalization of Diplomacy: Toward Clarification of a Fractured Terminology. Working Paper'. *Exploring Digital Diplomacy*.

Manor, I. (2017b) 'The Contradictory Trends of Digital Diaspora Diplomacy. Working Paper #2'. *Exploring Digital Diplomacy*.

McConnell, F. (2017) 'Liminal Geopolitics: The Subjectivity and Spatiality of Diplomacy at the Margins'. *Transactions of the Institute of British Geographers* 42(1): 139–152.

McConnell, F. (2019) 'Rethinking the Geographies of Diplomacy'. *Diplomatica* 1: 46–55.

McConnell, F. (2020) 'Tracing Modes of Politics at the United Nations: Spatial Scripting, Intimidation and Subversion at the Forum on Minority Issues'. *Environment and Planning C* 38: 1017–1035.

Moravcsik, A. (1999) 'A New Statecraft? Supranational Entrepreneurs and International Cooperation'. *International Organization* 53: 267–306.

Moss, D. (2018) 'The Ties That Bind: Internet Communication Technologies, Networked Authoritarianism, and 'Voice' in the Syrian Diaspora'. *Globalizations* 15(2): 265–282.

Naylor, T. (2020) 'All That's Lost: The Hollowing of Summit Diplomacy in a Socially Distanced World'. *The Hague Journal of Diplomacy* 15: 583–598.

Norris, P. (2001) *Digital Divide: Civic Engagement, Information Poverty, and the Internet Worldwide*. Cambridge: Cambridge University Press.

Pamment, J. (2016) Digital Diplomacy as Transmedia Engagement: Aligning Theories of Participatory Culture with International Advocacy Campaigns. *New Media & Society* 18(9): 2046–2062.

Pinkerton, A. and M. Benwell. (2014) 'Rethinking Popular Geopolitics in the Falklands/Malvinas Sovereignty Dispute: Creative Diplomacy and Citizen Statecraft'. *Political Geography* 38: 12–22.

Pouliot, V. (2016) *International Pecking Orders: The Politics and Practice of Multilateral Diplomacy*. Cambridge: Cambridge University Press.

Price, R. (1998) 'Reversing the Gun Sights: Transnational Civil Society Targets Land Mines'. *International Organization* 52(3): 613–644.

Rana, K. S. (2013) 'Diaspora Diplomacy and Public Diplomacy'. In *Relational, Networked and Collaborative Approaches to Public Diplomacy: The Connective Mindshift*, edited by R. S. Zaharna, A. Arsenault and A. Fisher, pp. 70–85. New York: Routledge.

Riordan, S. (2003) *The New Diplomacy*. Cambridge: Polity Press.

Scharfe S. (2000) 'Human Rights and the Internet in Asia: Promoting the Case of East Timor'. In *Human Rights and the Internet*, edited by S. Hick, E.F. Halpin, and E. Hoskins, 129–137. London: Palgrave Macmillan.

Scholte, J.A. (2008) 'From Government to Governance: Transition to a New Diplomacy'. In *Global Governance and Diplomacy*, edited by A. F. Cooper, B. Hocking, and W. Maley, 39–60. Basingstoke: Palgrave Macmillan.

Simpson, B. (2004) 'Solidarity in an Age of Globalization: The Transnational Movement for East Timor and U.S. Foreign Policy'. *Peace & Change* 29(3–4): 453–482.

Slaughter, A. M. (2009) 'America's Edge: Power in the Networked Century'. *Foreign Affairs* 88(1): 94–113.

The Economist. (2021) 'Diplomacy disrupted: The Zoom where it happens'. *The Economist* May 1st 2021: 51–55.

UNPO. (2020) 'Compromised Space and Undiplomatic Immunity' https://unpo.org/downlo ads/2690.pdf

Uysal, N. (2019) 'The Rise of Diasporas as Adversarial Non-State Actors in Public Diplomacy: The Turkish Case'. *The Hague Journal of Diplomacy* 14: 272–292.

van Dijik, J. (2020) *The Digital Divide*. London: Wiley.

Wajner, D. (2017) 'Grassroots Diplomacy in Battles for Legitimacy: The Transnational Advocacy Network for the Brazilian Recognition of the Palestinian State'. *Diplomacy & Statecraft* 28(1): 128–151.

Wiseman, G. (2010) '"Polylateralism": Diplomacy's Third Dimension'. *Public Diplomacy Magazine* 1: 24–39.

CHAPTER 22

DIGITALIZATION OF DIPLOMACY: IMPLICATIONS FOR CITIES

EFE SEVIN

INTRODUCTION

CITIES have been, as compellingly stated by Michele Acuto (2013: 2), the invisible gorillas of international studies. He draws his analogy from a well-known experiment on selective attention during which subjects were asked to watch a video of individuals passing a basketball around and count their passes (Simons and Chabris, 1999). In one of the experiment scenarios, an individual wearing a gorilla costume passed through the players[1] after which 44% of the participants reported not seeing it (Simons and Chabris, 1999: 1069). Our selective analytical attention in international relations is similar, in the sense that we tend to disregard the role of cities within global politics as we focus on what nation-states are doing.

This neglect does not mean we are not studying cities at all. Indeed, there is a growing body of literature working on city diplomacy—an analytical term that acknowledges cities as expected actors (Klaus, 2020) with their own foreign policy agendas, mechanisms, and procedures. The term hints at long-lasting international activities and presences akin to nation-states as opposed to temporary boosts or one-time appearances. It is even possible to argue that recent interest in city diplomacy is solely a revival as the practice is as old as diplomacy with examples found, for instance, in city-states engaging with each other in Ancient Greece (Surmacz, 2018). While our analytical

---

[1] The video for this specific scenario can be found here: https://www.youtube.com/watch?v=vJG6 98U2Mvo Last accessed, 12 February 2022.

interest might make it seem like cities have just entered the global arena, cities in fact have been—and likely will be—operating beyond the borders of their nation-states.

A myriad of drivers revived the interest in cities and their work in the international arena. There is virtually a universal agreement that the increasing share of population living in urban areas is one of the leading causes. It is not extraordinary that these local governments feel the pressure to respond to the needs of their residents. Existing studies highlight various collaborations among cities to tackle common problems faced such as climate change (Acuto, 2013) or terrorism (Marchetti, 2021). Another important push for cities to be more active in the international arena is their status as 'in-between powers' (Amiri, 2020: 236) as they enjoy both the community links that usually belong to non-state actors (e.g. grassroot organizations) and the organizational resources to conduct diplomacy that usually belong to nation-states. This combination of characteristics gives them a unique role to respond to the needs of their residents since they are aware of the demands and have the capacity to propose solutions by working together with other actors.

These collaboration activities, albeit important, fall short of encompassing the presence of cities in the international arena; thus there is a need to go beyond diplomacy (Sevin, 2021) since the term limits this presence to negotiations, treaties, and collaborations while cities also want to attract new foreign investments and to invite new tourists, or even residents, from other countries. Another relatively young field of study, city branding, surveys what other activities are carried out to manage the international reputations of these actors. Merging these two fields present a more inclusive picture of international outreach efforts.

This chapter focuses on what cities do in the international arena, and how cities communicate on digital platforms relevant to these activities, through an illustrative study of four select cities: New York (USA), Izmir (Turkey), Victoria (Canada), and Akureyri (Iceland). The objective is to observe how the digitization of communication methods changes how cities engage with international audiences. The rest of the chapter is composed of five sections. First, an analytical framework combining diplomacy and branding is presented. Second, mediatization and digitization are introduced as theoretical backgrounds to analyse such activities. The following two sections discuss the methodology and share the findings of the empirical part of this chapter. The chapter is concluded by summarizing the chapter's theoretical and practical implications.

Cities in the Global Arena: City Diplomacy and City Branding

City branding and city diplomacy are two distinct but almost complementary concepts. Acknowledging the difference is indeed necessary since doing so enables the researchers to more inclusively explain what activities cities are engaging in. Disregarding the distinctions is also problematic since they include different processes, address different audiences, and seek to achieve different objectives. In brief terms, the former includes bilateral and multilateral cooperation attempts (Klaus, 2020) while the latter discusses outreach to potential investors, residents, and tourists (Anttiroiko, 2015). This separation also has disciplinary and conceptual advantages. Political scientists and international relations scholars study diplomacy (Klaus, 2020), whereas public relations and marketing scholars study branding (Lucarelli and Brorström, 2013). This is to say the conceptual vocabulary used to describe the activities are different. Finally, organizational structures in the practice also reflect a similar split. Branding is predominantly within the purview of destination management organizations (Gómez et al., 2018). Diplomacy tends to be closer to the offices of mayors (Amiri and Dossani, 2019). This section initially explains both terms on their own, then presents a combined framework to analyse city activities in the international arena.

By the early twenty-first century, it became clear that cities—and mayors—were going to be on the forefront of presenting solutions to global problems (Klaus, 2020: 2). As diplomatic actors, they represent a fresh and promising alternative to nation-states, which are deemed 'too large to engage local civic participation [and], too small to address global power' (Barber, 2014: 357). Cities were beacons of hope with their inclination to collaboration (Barber, 2014: 357). Barber's argument is noteworthy in explaining the modus operandi of city diplomacy: identifying common policy issues and establishing mechanisms for cooperation. One of the more oft-used and studied tools has been 'networking' (Pluijm and Melissen, 2007). Categorically, city networks refer to 'formalized organizations with cities as their main members and characterized by reciprocal and established patterns of communication, policy-making, and exchange' (Acuto and Rayner, 2016: 1148–1149). There are over 200 such networks that address a variety of issues (Kosovac et al., 2020). The C40 Cities Climate Leadership Group is one of the more active networks that brings ninety-six countries together to decrease their emissions by 50% through knowledge-sharing and international advocacy (Chan, 2016). United Cities and Local Governments (UCLG) is another similarly active network that brings together over 1,000 municipalities helping them work together on various issues including economic growth and democratic governance (Acuto and Rayner, 2016), as well as taking the voices of its members to the international arena (UCLG, 2017a). Besides networking, there are also more ad hoc or limited bilateral and multilateral cooperations where cities come together to complete certain projects. Unlike the more formal networks, these partnerships rely on individuals in leadership roles (Kosovac et al., 2020: 15). Istanbul Water Consensus was such an initiative spearheaded by former mayor Kadir Topbas in 2009 (World Water Council, 2014). Topbas's leadership pushed the consensus and grew it to over 1,000 signatories. Since Topbas left office, there has not been any activity reported. In brief, cities come together and establish temporary or permanent partnership mechanisms to learn from each other, to carry local issues to the global arena, and to band together to provide solutions to the challenges their residents are facing in city diplomacy.

Cities are not always seeking cooperation or allies in the international arena. There are indeed activities which pit them against each other as they seek to acquire the same resources. Simon Anholt (1998), a practitioner credited with coining the term 'nation brand', lists direct investments, tourism, and sometimes even the attention of target audiences as such resources. Through competition, Anholt builds a link between cities and nation brands. Nation branding posits that countries have brand images of their own (Anholt, 1998). Cities, not unlike countries, have their own brand images. With city branding (Anholt, 2006), each city is known for a handful of qualities and this brand narrative influences people's and organizations' behaviours such as visiting a city or starting a business. These qualities are categorized under six headings (GFK America, 2013):

- Presence: A city's global contribution in science, culture, and governance
- Place: A city's physical aspects
- Pre-requisite: A city's basic qualities
- People: Perception of a city's residents
- Pulse: How exciting a city is perceived
- Potential: Economic and educational opportunities of a city

While these categories fall beyond the scope of diplomacy, they still push cities to the international arena. Since city branding also includes brand narratives, the concept requires cities to communicate and advocate on behalf of their residents to audiences beyond their own and their countries' borders. Thus city branding has an active policy and action aspect (Braun, 2012).

Consequently, there is a need to move beyond diplomatic engagement and focus on the *international dimension* of city activities. This phrase is based on Bruce Gregory's (2016) public dimension of diplomacy concept in which he argues that singling out public diplomacy as a subfield of diplomacy decreases its importance and is detrimental to capturing all relevant activities as we carve out limited definitions for public diplomacy. The public dimension of diplomacy removes these restrictions and makes it possible to study all relevant activities. The international dimension of city activities similarly attempts to combine all communicative activities.

Above explanations and examples have two common points that this chapter attempts to move beyond. Most studies focus on cities and their activities. While cities have a certain level of autonomy, they are 'sub-state' units. Perceptionally—if not bureaucratically and institutionally as well—they are linked to their countries. Their activities affect and are affected by nation-states (Sevin, 2022). Moreover, these two levels do not need to agree. Cities might or might not have the same diplomatic agendas as their countries. The first common point is disregarding this particular complex city–country relationship. Moreover, most networking and formal city diplomacy studies include larger cities that can engage in sustained international relationships (see Marchetti, 2021 for a longer discussion). Once again, such an approach is not surprising. Engaging in city diplomacy assumes the existence of political, institutional, and financial capital to do so. In the United States, only a handful of cities have dedicated international offices such as Washington, DC, New York City, and Atlanta. C40, a climate change city-network often discussed in city diplomacy, started out with eighteen mega cities as members (C40 Cities, 2022) and currently has ninety-six cities with a total population of over 600 million (Sancino et al., 2021). Yet in reality many smaller cities with limited resources are also active in the international arena. Sister Cities International, a non-profit organization matching American cities with foreign cities for grassroots diplomacy projects, has West Springfield, Massachusetts as one of its newest members where fewer than 30,000 people live. The second point is to exclude smaller cities in the discussion. UCLG (2017b) estimates that there are nearly 9,000 intermediary cities, with populations between 50,000 and one million, making up over 20% of the world population and one-third of people living in urban settings.

This section provided a concise overview of the international dimension of city activities through comparing and combining diplomacy and branding. Furthermore, two additional points were made to move beyond existing studies: the link with countries and with size. The next section introduces a digitization concept to these activities. As will be further explained in the methodology section, the arguments in these two sections help shape the chapter's empirical part.

DIGITIZATION OF INTERNATIONALIZATION

'The medium is the message', arguably one of the most famous phrases in communication studies, set the stage for our contemporary discussions on the impact of digital diplomacy as the accessibility and use of these platforms themselves communicate messages about practices (Comor and Bean, 2012) . When Marshall McLuhan (1964) proposed studying the medium as the primary element in communication as opposed to message content, he paved the way for a new wave of studies. Postman (2000: 10–11) summarizes the objectives of this new wave of studies, referred to as media ecology, as such:

> We put the word 'media' in the front of the word 'ecology' to suggest that we were not simply interested in media, but in the ways in which the interaction between media and human beings give a culture its character and, one might say, help a culture to maintain symbolic balance.

Therefore an inclusive analysis requires more than solely an acknowledgement of the platforms. Rather, these platforms should be seen as an 'environment where people act and live their lives, and through which reality is perceived' (Ruotsalainen and Heinonen, 2015: 9).

Pamment (2014) uses the concept of mediatization while bringing similar arguments to the study of diplomacy. Defining mediatization as the integration of communication technologies to our lives to such an extent that their impacts are taken for granted, he argues that mediatization in diplomacy pushes actors to reconsider issues, identities, codes, and norms that existed within different mediated environments (Pamment, 2014: 253). This is to say actors are expected to know how to select appropriate channels, as well as strategies on those particular channels, to engage with target audiences (Pamment, 2014: 268). Similarly Manor and Crilley (2019) posit that mediatization means that social, political, and cultural realities are influenced by changes in platforms.

Put another way, looking at digital diplomacy as a mediatization process shifts the focus to the impact of these new digital tools (Manor, 2019). We are not looking at replication of offline or other mediated diplomacy practices. Rather, the expectation is to observe the peculiarities of digital media platforms changing such practices. For instance, when Manor and Crilley (2018) looked at the framing of the Gaza War of 2014, they remarked on characteristics of social media as a visual platform, pace of conversation, and opportunity to circumvent traditional media for framing. Pamment (2015) argues for the participatory storytelling element made possible by social media. Stories are no longer told solely by the message senders. Rather, audiences can contribute their own takes. Duncombe (2019: 111) concludes digital diplomacy inherently has a shift from monologic broadcast mechanisms to dialogic communication.

Cities are no exception to the changes argued by media ecology and mediatization. Digitization of their international presence assumes an interdependence between social media tools and their activities. There is almost an expectation that these activities, for instance, show awareness of 'the media's attention rules, [and] production routines' (Mazzoleni, 2008: 1). One important addition this chapter proposes to existing studies is a practice angle. Such a linkage between mediatization and practice theory both moves media from a static object to a phenomenon capable of changing and effecting change (Huxley, 2014: 10) and connects produced content to diplomacy as websites, social media posts, and policy documents as the articulations of how actors have adapted to the changes and improvised their practices (Bourdieu, 1990).

While an inclusive debate on definitions of digital diplomacy—as well as city diplomacy and branding—is beyond the scope of this chapter, the succinct discussion provided here underlines the reasons for two conceptual wagers at stake. First, a focus on diplomacy disregards other activities that get cities to engage with audiences beyond the borders of their countries. The international dimension of city activities provides a more inclusive explanation of how cities engage with each other, represent themselves, or simply exist in the international arena. Second, digital diplomacy is situated within mediatization and practice perspectives. Consequently, the digitization of international activities for cities is expected to firstly reflect new norms and structures rather than solely reproducing existing ones on a different platform and secondly be seen as articulation of how practitioners see their professions. The next section discusses how these two wagers inform the research methodology.

METHODOLOGY

This research studies four cities following an illustrative case selection (Gerring, 2004). The cases were selected because a preliminary review deemed them to be most likely to yield content. Therefore, Sister Cities International's membership directory was used (Sister Cities International (SCI), 2019) to ensure at least some activity. Second, since size and relationship with the home country were named as two noteworthy variables to expand existing studies, a 2x2 matrix was created with rows looking at whether city and country are perceptionally linked or not; and with columns looking at the size of the city. Third, only cities that had a website, a social media account, and a policy document regarding their international activities were included.

Four cities, shown in Table 22.1, were selected: New York (USA), Izmir (Turkey), Victoria (Canada), and Akureyri (Iceland). Given their populations, New York and Izmir were categorized as large cities, with respectively over eight and four million residents. Victoria has fewer than 100,000 habitants and Akureyri fewer than 20,000. The relationship between cities and countries was more challenging to pinpoint as the concept itself is complicated. For this particular case selection, an actual and explicit deviance or difference from home country was sought. In the case of Izmir, it is ideologically and politically different from most of the country (Kaefer, 2021). Akureyri has a different climate and landscape than the rest of Iceland since it is located in a deep fjord (Filippusdottir, 2009). In New York and Victoria, there are no such deviations from home countries.

Table 22.2 shows three categories of resources that were identified to gather data on international activities as well as their digitization. First, institutional websites that might have information regarding international activities—mayor's offices and destination management organizations (DMO)—were identified and used as a starting point. From these websites, official social media accounts were added. Data was gathered primarily from Twitter because of its established status as a diplomatic platform (see Jia and Li, 2020 for a discussion) with the exception of Akureyri whose DMO only had a Facebook page. A total of 19,901 was collected. Lastly, strategy documents and annual reports were added to the analysis where possible. New York had *Leading Locally*, a report by the Mayor's Office of International Affairs (MOIA) as a strategy document, and DMO's annual report. Izmir had a municipality strategic plan and tourism plan.

Table 22.1 Case selection

	Large Cities	Small Cities
Concur	New York	Victoria
Not Concur	Izmir	Akureyri

Table 22.2 Data gathered per case

	Website	Social Media	Policy Document
NY	• https://www1.nyc.gov/site/international/index.page • https://www.nycgo.com	@globalnyc	Two documents
Izmir	• https://www.izmir.bel.tr/en/Izmir/14 • https://www.visitizmir.org/en	@Izmirbld @soyertunc_en	Two documents
Victoria	• https://www.victoria.ca/EN/index.html • https://www.tourismvictoria.com/	@victoriavisitor	Two documents
Akureyri	• https://www.akureyri.is/en • https://www.visitakureyri.is/en	Facebook / VisitAkureyri @akureyrarb	Two documents

Table 22.3 Logic of practice

	Diplomacy	Branding	Digitization
References to	- Networks - Bilateral/Multilateral relations - Leaders - Assets for digitization - Other repeated patterns	- Anholt's six categories - Assets for digitization - Other repeated patterns	- Multimedia - Speed - Engagement - Moving beyond traditional media - Impacts on activities - Other repeated patterns

Victoria had the city's annual report and DMO's business plan. Akureyri had the city's annual report and tourism strategy.

In order to understand digital city diplomacy through international activities and digitization frameworks, a logic of practice approach is adopted (Bourdieu, 1990). Table 22.3 shows overall parameters of patterns sought after, based on the literature review. The first two columns are of activities and the third is of messaging surrounding these activities. Through computer-assisted textual analyses of social media content and close readings of policy documents and websites, the objective is to observe 'patterns of meaningful action that are gradually being naturalized into contemporary diplomacy' (Hedling and Bremberg, 2021: 1600). For diplomacy, these patterns include references to participation in city networks, establishing bilateral or multilateral relations, and the presence of mayor or other city leaders as diplomats. For branding, Anholt's six categories are used to categorize references. For digitization, the key question is whether messaging is in line with the expectation of digital media platforms. In this study, four such items are included as important to messaging: use of multimedia content, pace of communication, engagement with audiences, and ability to circumvent traditional media. While it is difficult to argue these criteria cover all the characteristics of digital messaging given the ever-changing complex nature of platforms, they are in line with previous studies on best practices of digital diplomacy (Pamment, 2015; Manor, 2016; Collins and Bekenova, 2019) Across the board, analysis is open to including additional repeated patterns if observed. The analysis, through digitization, technically, looks for an interdependence between projects and communication. These patterns of actions identified can map and explain how encounters with digitization is changing what cities are doing (Hedling and Bremberg, 2021). This is why activities list 'assets for digitization' and digitization lists 'impacts on activities' to highlight how they both impact each other. The next section shares the empirical findings of this chapter.

FINDINGS

In order to observe how digitization is seen in international activities of cities, the practices of four cities are introduced. Given the differences in their sizes, their experiences in international affairs, and even the focus of the documents included here, this study is not necessarily a comparison of city diplomacy performances. Rather, looking at these four cases should be seen as four parts of a larger digitization story.

Diplomatic Activities of Cities

New York City is one of the few cities with a dedicated diplomatic corps (Amiri, 2020), the MOIA. Also, as the home of the United Nations, it is no stranger to a diplomatic presence on its streets. The *Leading Locally* report is not a traditional strategy document for a city office. It is a closer look at the 'Voluntary Local Review' (VLR) process in which cities open their own practices for a closer examination in terms of sustainability (Global Vision, Urban Action, Mayor's Office for International Affairs, NYC, and UN Habitat, 2021). The report has a section dedicated to the evolution of city networks. The VLR movement is portrayed as both an outcome of existing city networks and a candidate to become a new network. The report further highlights the role of New York in developing this particular movement. It also includes various short pieces from multiple mayors, including Bill de Blasio who was the mayor of New York when the report was published. It should be noted that the online version of the report includes hyperlinks and e-mail addresses, and it is published under a creative commons licence. MOIA's website portrayed a compilation of events and news that had a global-local connection, such as news coming from NYC Junior Ambassadors initiatives (nyc.gov, 2022). In addition to various projects and programmes the office runs, the website has a dedicated page for diplomatic immunities and parking. MOIA's Twitter feed is embeded on the front page. Each page also has social media share buttons.

Izmir has a Department of Foreign Relations and Tourism, and a dedicated directorate for foreign relations (ÜNİBEL A.Ş, 2022). The overview of city offices also has sections for European Union-funded projects, and sister cities. The city's strategic plan for 2020–24 lists seven objectives, none of which is directly related to diplomatic activities (İzmir Büyükşehir Belediyesi, 2019). There are no references to networks, or foreign relations. The website includes photos that can be shared on social media platforms.

The city of Victoria does not have an identifiable department dedicated to diplomatic functions. Its strategic plan lists eight objectives and seven operational priorities (City of Victoria, 2021). There are no references to foreign relations. The only time there is a reference to non-domestic issues is through business deals, renovation of the city's convention centre, and international students (City of Victoria, 2021). Apart from links to the city's own social media platforms, there are no assets for digitization.

Akureyri is the smallest city included in this study. There are no specific departments designated for foreign relations (Akureyrarkaupstaður, 2022). However, there is a local business charged with promoting the city named Akureyrarstofa (Akureyrarbær, 2021: 44). The city also operates a condensed version of its website in English. The 2020 annual report makes limited references to international activities. For instance, it has received a 'child-friendly municipality' designation from UNICEF and the mayor acknowledged the achievement in her notes (Akureyrarbær, 2021: 5). Foreign visitors and promotion are also acknowledged (Akureyrarbær, 2021: 44). There are no references to networks or bilateral/multilateral relations. There are no assets for digitization.

Unsurprisingly, the four cities have different capacities and approaches to diplomatic processes as summarized in Table 22.4. Size or relationship with home country do not seem to be strong indicators. Rather, size seems to be a requirement but is not, by itself, enough to increase participation in global processes. The next section explains how cities engage with foreign audiences to manage their reputation.

Table 22.4 Summary of diplomatic activities

	Networks	Bilateral/ Multilateral	Leaders	Assets	Other
New York	Strong	Limited	Strong	Limited (design and share)	UN Host
Izmir	None	Limited	None	Limited (share)	Funding
Victoria	None	Limited	None	None	Business deals
Akureyri	None	None	None	None	Recognition

Branding Activities of Cities

Before moving into the details of what each city has done beyond their diplomatic attempts, the study period should be acknowledged. The Covid-19 pandemic started curtailing travel—especially international travel—in March 2020 and its impacts are still felt as of this writing in 2022. The documents included here all acknowledge the reality of the pandemic and its effects on the travel industry.

New York is a major tourist destination. In its tourism annual report, there is a strong emphasis on the city's unique presence aspects that draws these visitors such as Broadway musicals (NYC & Company, 2022). There are dedicated weeks promoting these aspects such as Broadway Week, Off-Broadway Week, and Must-See Week. Another repeated pattern is the diversity of its people, which is shown both as an organizational priority for DMO and as a strong point to attract visitors. The pulse of the city is observed as the annual report lists various activities that are promoted for the city, such as Broadway Week, Winter Outing, and Restaurant Week. There is only limited reference to pre-requisites and to students and schools. There are no references to the city's physical aspects (place) or its economic opportunities (potential). The website includes various visuals coming from the city, as well as integrated links for third-party vendors, such as hotels and theatre tickets.

Izmir's document presents seven types of tourism opportunities the city has to offer: heritage, religious, 3S (sea, sun, sand), fairs and conventions, health, gastronomy, and ecological (İzmir Büyükşehir Belediyesi, 2018). There is an emphasis on the city's history of nearly 8,000 years, which, more or less, builds upon the foundation for promotional ideas across different types of tourism opportunities. Heritage and religious tourism elements highlight the city's presence in historical terms. 3S tourism showcases natural landscape (place). Health tourism highlights both natural thermal resources (place) and medical infrastructure (pre-requisite). Gastronomy and eco-tourism are built around more modern, and rather exciting, changes happening in Izmir (pulse). Fairs and convention tourism touches upon economic opportunities in the city. There are no references to the city's residents. The visit Izmir website is practically a more dynamic version of the report with similar tourism categories. Posts seem to be designed with engagement in mind as users can share, bookmark, like, or comment on them.

Destination Greater Victoria's (2022) business report is aptly titled 'Wide and Deep Recovery'. The overall objective is to 'get all segments of the visitor economy moving again'. These segments are rather time-based, i.e. short, medium, and long term. The report situates the residents of Victoria as important stakeholders (people). The rest of the plan is geared primarily towards domestic visitors and is sales-oriented. Tourism Victoria's website presents a more vibrant and inclusive picture of the city. A unique aspect is Victoria's relationship with the British Royal Family. Visitors are invited to follow the stops in Royal Family visits during their stays. The rest of the activities geared towards visitors are based on either natural attractions such as beaches, lakes,

Table 22.5 Summary of branding activities

	New York	Izmir	Victoria	Akureyri
Presence	Strong	Strong (History)	Limited (Royal)	Limited (Museums)
Place	No mention	Strong (Landscape)	Strong	Strong (Nature)
Pre-requisite	Limited (Education)	Strong (Hospital)	No mention	No mention
People	Strong (Diversity)	No mention	Strong (Stakeholder)	Strong (Stakeholder)
Pulse	Strong	Limited (Gastro/ Eco)	Limited (Dining)	Limited (Dining)
Potential	No mention	Limited (Fairs)	No mention	No mention
Assets	Visuals / Share	Interactivity	Native documents	Webcams
Other	Event-based sales	History across the board	Domestic focus	Municipality

and parks (place) or local dining options (pulse). There are no references to the city's services (pre-requisites). Overall, the business report highlighted the importance of domestic travel, especially for short-term gains. The website features a few tools that can only be accessed via digital platforms, such as a smart-phone application and an interactive map.

Akureyri's (Akureyrarbær, 2016) tourism policy is based on two objectives: making the city a desirable destination for tourists and becoming a model municipality for residents and companies (people). Virtually everything in the policy is connected to or affected by nature (place) ranging from decreased visitor numbers during winter months to hiking activities. While it might be an oversimplification of its history and offerings, Akureyri's most unique aspect is its mild climate despite its proximity to the Arctic Circle. The circle has technically passed through Akureyri since 2009 when residents of the small island of Grimsey off the coast voted to join the city. In addition to the outdoor recreational activities, there are also museums and cultural centres promoted (presence), and dining options (pulse). Pre-requisites and potential are not observed on the website or in the tourism policy document. One unique aspect of Akureyri was the role of municipality. The policy assigned considerable tasks to develop infrastructure, train individuals, and maintain the tourism industry. Apart from live-streaming webcams on the website, there are no digital assets.

As summarized in Table 22.5, both size and relationship with home country seem to have an impact on branding. Size translates both into marketing budgets as well as experiences a city has to offer. As seen in Akureyri, a deviation from home country repu-tation makes the city a valuable domestic destination but complicates the story it needs to tell foreign audiences. The next section looks at how these activities are observed on digital platforms.

Table 22.6 Descriptive information on tweets

	Visuals		Traditional		Engagement	
	No Media	Media	No Link	Link	No Mention	Mention
New York	78.57%	21.43%	52.68%	47.32%	14.12%	85.88%
Izmir	31.57%	68.43%	22.78%	77.22%	71.12%	28.88%
Victoria	39.69%	60.31%	30.48%	69.52%	23.96%	76.04%
Akureyri	75.01%	24.99%	49.71%	50.29%	95.54%	4.46%

Digitization of International Activities

The study includes a total of 19,901 tweets. Yet, the individual performance of cities varies. Akureyri has the lowest number with 224, followed by Izmir[2] with 4,890. Both Victoria and New York had over 7,000 tweets. Table 22.6 reports descriptive statistics as percentages rather than absolute values. Multimedia is operationalized as having images or videos in tweets. Izmir and Victoria use these elements more often than New York and Akureyri. The inclusion of links is used as an additional step to circumvent traditional media as cities use social media to direct the attention of users to an outside source. Across the board, there is a high percentage of link usage. Engagement looks at whether tweets mentioned other users or not since an engagement on Twitter requires explicitly tagging another user in the text. New York and Victoria mentioned other users in their tweets.

New York's social media presence is strong across the board. One important aspect that should be noted to expand on the descriptive information is that the *globalnyc* account re-tweets its own content regularly. There were over 600 instances of such re-tweets. The next account that received multiple mentions from *globalnyc* belonged to Penny Abeywardena, former commissioner for international affairs. The links and media also share further information about these projects and events. Overall, tweets resemble shorter press releases. On the other hand, there are important signs that New York's branding is investing in digitization and incorporating various projects to their outreach such as the city's influencer marketing programme geared towards Instagram and TikTok influencers (NYC & Company, 2022).

Izmir uses the municipality's Twitter account as an information outlet. Engagement numbers mostly reflect re-tweeted content from other city accounts. Visuals include digital posters. It should be noted that this particular account was in Turkish, and therefore by design does not address foreign audiences. Yet, there have been calls for domestic visitors to experience the city. The Mayor's English language account includes

---

[2] Two accounts were included from Izmir: the municipality (izmirbld) and the mayor's English language account (soyertunc_en). Since the latter is relatively inactive (120 tweets to the municipality's 4,770), the municipality account is used for comparisons.

Table 22.7 Summary of digitization

	Visuals	Pace	Traditional	Engagement	Impact	Other
New York	Limited	Frequent	Yes	Yes	Changing marketing	Various topics Influencer
Izmir	Yes	Frequent	Yes	No	Tour-guide ideas	Various topics Audience Suggest
Victoria	Yes	Frequent	Yes	Yes	Virtual experience	Influencer Virtual
Akureyri	Limited	Infrequent	Yes	No	None	Audience

news about his participation in international representation activities. However, the account has been dormant since late 2021. A novel employment of digital technologies was observed on Visit Izmir's website. There is a suggestion engine which recommends neighbourhoods and places in the city based on the visitors' interests.

Victoria operates the most cooperative Twitter accounts among these four cities, with its frequent mentions of nearby DMOs such as *explorecanada* and *HelloBC*. Overall, *victoriavisitor* is devoted to promoting touristic attractions the city has to offer. Beyond social media, the city is also supporting influencers through its media influencers programme. Last, the DMO's website has a 'virtual experiences' section that compiles various virtual activities, including tea tastings and museum exhibits. Though this might sound counter intuitive as a strategy to attract visitors, it probably put Victoria in the minds of travellers making their post-pandemic destination lists.

Akureyri's social media presence is limited. Its Twitter account, which is in Icelandic, includes information primarily for residents, such as parking regulations or road closures. There are also announcements for local events. Visit Akureyri's Facebook presents a more visual-heavy story on the unique nature and offerings of the city.

Table 22.7 summarizes the digitization processes of cities. Neither size nor home country relationship can completely account for the variation among these cities. Size has a limited impact as it is translated into financial resources as well as content on which cities can report. Home country relationship seems to work in Victoria's favour as the city cooperates with national and local governments. The next section concludes the chapter by summarizing what we can infer from these four cases about digital city diplomacy.

CONCLUSIONS AND IMPLICATIONS

This chapter started out with a few attempts of conceptual tiptoeing. While the focus is on digital city diplomacy, studying a practice with double qualifiers required—for the lack of a better phrase—conceptual wagers in this study. Eventually, the study attempted to avoid using both 'digital diplomacy' and 'city diplomacy'. The former is replaced with digitization to better account for the interdependent relationship as well as the cultural change. What is observed should not be framed as suggesting business-as-usual on different communication platforms but rather a shift in mentality. In order to unpack this change aspect, practice logic was also introduced as a theoretical framework. The theoretical background—using digitization (or mediatization) with practice logic—is not unprecedented. Yet, using it to discuss international activities of cities is likely to pave the way for future studies in both city branding and city diplomacy since the interdependent nature of technology and practice is relatively understudied.

The latter part, city diplomacy, is replaced with international activities of cities since the concept is constraining. It limits the scholarly attention to networks, or other types of formal relationships, primarily carried out by larger cities that can spare resources for diplomatic engagement. However, it is more important to take a step back and look at what cities are doing in the international arena, how they are engaging with foreign audiences without confining the types or subjects of activities. The illustrative cases presented here present evidence for such an approach. Small cities do not engage in networks—even Izmir, a relatively large city, did not acknowledge any formal diplomatic relations. However, all four cities have varying levels of international engagement and seek international recognition. Akureyri boasts about its UNICEF designation, Victoria wants to be internationally recognized as a sustainable tourism spot. All four cities want to attract more tourists.

The empirical part looks at both what cities are doing internationally and communicating digitally, as well as how these two processes change each other. Websites are used as the starting point to gather data. Activities are mainly drawn from policy documents. Messaging is observed on social media posts. The research is not without its limitations. A purposive sampling strategy makes it difficult to generalize the observations. Second, two cities use English as their native language, which blurred the lines between foreign and domestic audiences. Third, capturing a city's entire digital footprint—let alone four cities' footprints—requires a longer study. My selection of data sources might present a more biased (e.g. DMOs talking about visitors only) view of digital rhetoric. With these limitations in mind, there are two points that the study makes in explaining what digitization of diplomacy means for cities.

First, digitization expects a change in logic of practice. Given the variation in activities as well as in cities, this change is more gradual than binary. Not unlike their nation-state counterparts, cities experience different levels of digitization. The starting variables (size and home country) are influential in deciding activity levels but are not the only ones. Size functions as a necessary but not sufficient condition for most international activities. Country relationship complicates, directs, or sometimes facilitates storytelling. But historical background or current business priorities are also important variables. Similarly even within the same city, digitization of activities are not at the same level. Across the four cities studied, for instance, DMOs and tourism-related activities seem to have embraced digitization better than mayor's offices and diplomatic activities. Ranging from interactive maps to influencer marketing projects, activities change digital messages and digital platforms change activities.

Second, digitization brings its own challenges. For instance, targeting audiences becomes a problem. As digital messages can be accessed by everyone, it is not possible to create messages solely for domestic or solely for foreign audiences. In the case of cities, the segmentation is more complex since there are residents, domestic visitors, and foreign audiences. As local governance units, cities introduce a new level while digitization makes it difficult to move from one to another. Institutional and organizational culture make it difficult to capture all the activities and messaging. Who speaks for the city? Who represents the international activities of cities on digital platforms? While it might be easier for trained professionals to navigate through DMOs, MOIAs, municipalities, and other organizations, ordinary audiences might not be able—or might not bother— to do so.

Cities are once again receiving the attention they deserve in the international arena. Digital platforms have shown a limited and varying impact on their activities—which, in return, have started to influence digital messaging. Both digitization and international activities frameworks are instrumental in presenting a more inclusive picture of what cities can do as well as in demonstrating the changes in the ways they approach these activities. Future research can provide further case studies to examine the interdependence between digital platforms and city activities.

Suggested Reading

Anholt, S. (2007) *Competitive Identity: The New Brand Management for Nations, Cities and Regions*. Basingstoke: Palgrave Macmillan.

Anttiroiko, A.-V. (2015) 'City Branding as a Response to Global Intercity Competition: Global Intercity Competition', *Growth and Change*, 46(2), pp. 233–252.

Klaus, I. (2020) 'The State of City Diplomacy', *Urbanisation*, 7(1), pp. 1–6.

Kosovac, A. et al. (2021) 'City Leaders Go Abroad: A Survey of City Diplomacy in 47 Cities', *Urban Policy and Research*, 39(2), pp. 127–142. Available at: https://doi.org/10.1080/08111146.2021.1886071.

Manfredi-Sánchez, J.L. (2022) 'The Political Economy of City Diplomacy', *Economic and Political Studies*, 10(2), pp. 228–249. Available at: https://doi.org/10.1080/20954816.2021.1899622.

References

Acuto, M. (2013) *Global Cities, Governance and Diplomacy: the Urban Link*. Abingdon, Oxon; New York, NY: Routledge.

Acuto, M. and Rayner, S. (2016) 'City Networks: Breaking Gridlocks or Forging (New) Lock-Ins?', *International Affairs*, 92(5), pp. 1147–1166. Available at: https://doi.org/10.1111/1468-2346.12700.

Akureyrarbær (2016) *Ferðamálastefna Akureyrar 2016-2026*. Akureyrarbær. Available at: https://www.ferdamalastofa.is/is/tolur-og-utgafur/utgefid-efni/stefnumotun-og-skipulag/ferdamalastefna-akureyrar-2016-2026.

Akureyrarbær (2021) *Ársskýrsla Akureyrarbæjar 2020*. Akureyrarbær. Available at: https://www.akureyri.is/is/stjornkerfi/stjornsysla/utgefid-efni/index/arsskyrslur.

Akureyrarkaupstaður (2022) *Divisions and Office Hours*. Akureyri. Available at: https://www.akureyri.is/en/administration/about-akureyri/divisions-and-office-hours (Accessed: 26 April 2022).

Amiri, S. (2020) 'Making US MOIA Sustainable Institutions for Conducting City Diplomacy by Protecting Their Precarious Values', in Amiri, S. and Sevin, E., *City Diplomacy: Current Trends and Future Prospects*. Cham: Palgrave MacMillan, pp. 235–252.

Amiri, S. and Dossani, R. (2019) *City Diplomacy Has Been on the Rise. Policies Are Finally Catching Up*. Available at: https://www.rand.org/blog/2019/11/city-diplomacy-has-been-on-the-rise-policies-are-finally.html.

Anholt, S. (1998) 'Nation-brands of the Twenty-First Century', *Brand Management*, 5(6), pp. 395–417.

Anholt, S. (2006) 'The Anholt-GMI City Brands Index: How the World Sees the World's Cities', *Place Branding*, 2(1), pp. 18–31.

Anttiroiko, A.-V. (2015) 'City Branding as a Response to Global Intercity Competition: Global Intercity Competition', *Growth and Change*, 46(2), pp. 233–252.

Barber, B.R. (2014) *If Mayors Ruled the World: Dysfunctional Nations, Rising Cities*. New Haven: Yale University Press.

Bourdieu, P. (1990) *The Logic of Practice*. Stanford, CA: Stanford University Press.

Braun, E. (2012) 'Putting City Branding Into Practice', *Journal of Brand Management*, 19(4), pp. 257–267.

C40 Cities (2022) *About C40, C40 Cities*. Available at: https://www.c40.org/about-c40/ (Accessed: 25 April 2022).

Chan, D.K. (2016) 'City diplomacy and "glocal" governance: revitalizing cosmopolitan democracy', *Innovation: The European Journal of Social Science Research*, 29(2), pp. 134–160.

City of Victoria (2021) *Strategic Plan, City of Victoria, 2019-2022*. Victoria, BC. Available at: https://www.victoria.ca/EN/main/city/strategic-plan.html.

Collins, N. and Bekenova, K. (2019) 'Digital Diplomacy: Success at Your Fingertips', *Place Branding and Public Diplomacy*, 15(1), pp. 1–11.

Comor, E. and Bean, H. (2012) 'America's "Engagement" Delusion: Critiquing a Public Diplomacy Consensus', *International Communication Gazette*, 74(3), pp. 203–220.

Destination Greater Victoria (2022) *Destination Greater Victoria 2022 Business Plan: Wide and Deep Recovery*. Victoria. Available at: https://www.tourismvictoria.com/sites/default/files/dgv_2022_business_plan_final.pdf.

Duncombe, C. (2019) 'Digital Diplomacy: Emotion and Identity in the Public Realm', *The Hague Journal of Diplomacy*, 14(1–2), pp. 102–116.

Filippusdottir, L. (2009) *Connection to Nature - Exploring Opportunities by the Riverside Glerá in Akureyri, Iceland*. Second cycle, A2E. Swedish University of Agricultural Sciences. Available at: https://stud.epsilon.slu.se/301/ (Accessed: 25 April 2022).

Gerring, J. (2004) 'What Is a Case Study and What Is It Good for?', *American Political Science Review*, 98(2), pp. 341–354

GFK America (2013) 'The Anholt-GfK Roper City Brands Index'. Available at: http://marketing.gfkamerica.com/093013-1694/093013-1694.html (Accessed: 21 March 2013).

Global Vision, Urban Action, Mayor's Office for International Affairs, NYC, and UN Habitat (2021) *Leading Locally: The Origins and Impact of the Voluntary Local Review.* New York, NYC: Mayor's Office for International Affairs, NYC. Available at: https://www1.nyc.gov/assets/international/downloads/pdf/Leading-Locally-The-Origins-and-Impact-of-the-Voluntary-Local-Review.pdf.

Gregory, B. (2016) 'Mapping Boundaries in Diplomacy's Public Dimension', *The Hague Journal of Diplomacy*, 11(1), pp. 1–25. https://doi.org/10.1163/1871191X-12341317

Gómez, M. et al. (2018) 'City Branding in European Capitals: An Analysis from the Visitor Perspective', *Journal of Destination Marketing & Management*, 7, pp. 190–201. Available at: https://doi.org/10.1016/j.jdmm.2016.11.001.

Hedling, E. and Bremberg, N. (2021) 'Practice Approaches to the Digital Transformations of Diplomacy: Toward a New Research Agenda', *International Studies Review*, 23(4), pp. 1595–1618. Available at: https://doi.org/10.1093/isr/viab027.

Huxley, A. (2014) *Discovering Digital Diplomacy: The Case of Mediatization in the Ministry for Foreign Affairs of Finland.* Available at: http://urn.kb.se/resolve?urn=urn:nbn:se:uu:diva-232372 (Accessed: 5 August 2022).

İzmir Büyükşehir Belediyesi (2018) *Tourism in Izmir.* Izmir. Available at: https://www.izmir.bel.tr/tr/Yayinlar/22.

İzmir Büyükşehir Belediyesi (2019) *İzmir Büyükşehir Belediyesi Stratejk Planı, 2020-2024.* Izmir. Available at: https://www.izmir.bel.tr/CKYuklenen/Dokumanlar_2020/Stratejik%20Plan2024.pdf.

Jia, R. and Li, W. (2020) 'Public Diplomacy Networks: China's Public Diplomacy Communication Practices in Twitter During Two Sessions', *Public Relations Review*, 46(1), p. 101818.

Kaefer, F. (2021) 'Günter Soydanbay on City Branding, Turkey and Psychology', in Kaefer, F., *An Insider's Guide to Place Branding.* Cham: Springer International Publishing (Management for Professionals), pp. 133–137.

Klaus, I. (2020) 'The State of City Diplomacy', *Urbanisation*, 7(1), pp. 1–6.

Kosovac, A. et al. (2020) *Conducting City Diplomacy: A Survey of International Engagement in 47 Cities.* Research. Chicago, IL: The Chicago Council on Global Affairs. Available at: https://www.thechicagocouncil.org/research/report/conducting-city-diplomacy-survey-international-engagement-47-cities (Accessed: 23 April 2022).

Lucarelli, A. and Brorström, S. (2013) 'Problematising Place Branding Research: a Meta-Theoretical Analysis of the Literature', *The Marketing Review*, 13(1), pp. 65–81.

Manor, I. (2016) *Are We There Yet: Have MFAs Realized the Potential of Digital Diplomacy?* Leiden: Brill (Brill Research Perspectives).

Manor, I. (2019) *The Digitalization of Public Diplomacy.* Cham, Switzerland: Palgrave MacMillan.

Manor, I. and Crilley, R. (2018) 'Visually Framing the Gaza War of 2014: The Israel Ministry of Foreign Affairs on Twitter', *Media, War & Conflict*, 11(4), pp. 369–391.

Manor, I. and Crilley, R. (2019) 'The Mediatisation of MFAs: Diplomacy in the New Media Ecology', *The Hague Journal of Diplomacy*, 15(1–2), pp. 66–92.

Marchetti, R. (2021) *City Diplomacy: From City-States to Global Cities.* Ann Arbor: University of Michigan Press.

Mazzoleni, G. (2008) 'Mediatization of Politics', in Donsbach, W., *The International Encyclopedia of Communication.* Chichester, UK: John Wiley & Sons, Ltd, p. wbiecm062.

McLuhan, M. (1964) *Understanding Media: The Extensions of Man.* New York: McGraw-Hill.

NYC & Company (2022) *Annual Report, NYC & Company, 2021-22.* New York. Available at: https://business.nycgo.com/about-us/who-we-are/.

nyc.gov (2022) *Apply - NYC Junior Ambassadors.* Available at: https://www1.nyc.gov/site/juniorambassadors/apply/apply.page (Accessed: 26 April 2022).

Pamment, J. (2014) 'The Mediatization of Diplomacy', *The Hague Journal of Diplomacy*, 9(3), pp. 253–280.

Pamment, J. (2015) 'Digital Diplomacy as Transmedia Engagement: Aligning Theories of Participatory Culture with International Advocacy Campaigns', *New Media & Society*, 18(9), pp. 2046–2062.

Pluijm, R. van der and Melissen, J. (2007) *City Diplomacy: The Expanding Role of Cities in International Politics.* The Hague: Netherlands Institute of International Relations 'Clingendael' (Clingendael diplomacy papers, no. 10).

Postman, N. (2000) 'The Humanism of Media Ecology'. New York, NY. Available at: https://www.media-ecology.org/resources/Documents/Proceedings/v1/v1-02-Postman.pdf.

Ruotsalainen, J. and Heinonen, S. (2015) 'Media Ecology and the Future Ecosystemic Society', *European Journal of Futures Research*, 3(1), pp. 8–17.

Sancino, A. et al. (2021) 'What Can City Leaders Do for Climate Change? Insights from the C40 Cities Climate Leadership Group network', *Regional Studies*, 56(7), pp. 1224–1233.

Sevin, E. (2021) 'The Missing Link: Cities and Soft Power of Nations', *International Journal of Diplomacy and Economy*, 7(1), p. 19.

Sevin, E. (2022) 'Academic Perspective: Can the "C" in COO Stand for Studies?', in Dinnie, K., *Nation Branding: Concepts, Issues, Practice.* 3rd Edition. New York, NY: Routledge, pp. 93–95.

Simons, D.J. and Chabris, C.F. (1999) 'Gorillas in Our Midst: Sustained Inattentional Blindness for Dynamic Events', *Perception*, 28(9), pp. 1059–1074.

Sister Cities International (SCI) (2019) *Membership Directory.* Available at: http://sistercities.org/membership-directory/ (Accessed: 25 April 2022).

Surmacz, B. (2018) 'City Diplomacy', *Barometr Regionalny. Analizy i Prognozy*, 16(1), pp. 7–18.

UCLG (2017a) *About US, The Global Network of United Cities, Local, and Regional Governments.* Available at: https://www.uclg.org/en/organisation/about (Accessed: 11 August 2017).

UCLG (2017b) *Intermediary Cities, UCLG - United Cities and Local Governments.* Available at: https://www.uclg.org/en/resources/infographics/intermediary-cities-cuclg (Accessed: 3 August 2022).

ÜNİBEL A.Ş (2022) *Departments | Izmir Metropolitan Municipality, İzmir Büyükşehir Belediyesi.* Available at: http://www.izmir.bel.tr/en/Departments/289/ (Accessed: 12 February 2022).

World Water Council (2014) *Moving Forward with the Istanbul Water Consensus | World Water Council.* Available at: https://www.worldwatercouncil.org (Accessed: 28 April 2022).

CHAPTER 23

DIGITAL DIPLOMATIC REPRESENTATION: THE RISE OF TECH AMBASSADORS

ANNE MARIE ENGTOFT MELDGAARD AND TOM FLETCHER

FROM GUTENBERG TO FACEBOOK: HOW TECHNOLOGY SHAPES SOCIETIES

NEW technologies have historically transformed the world. Gutenberg's printing press not only led to a speedier distribution of books in the fifteenth century but diffused revolutionary religious ideas at a time when the Catholic Church was dominating and ultimately drove institutional change during the Protestant Reformation. During the height of the second industrial revolution and the application of scientific principles, a suite of new technologies was introduced, forever altering the environment around us and how we navigate the human experience. In 1885, for instance, Carl Benz built the world's first car. When Karl's wife Bertha demonstrated its feasibility by going on a trip from Mannheim to Pforzheim in Germany in August 1888, the 192 km she and her two sons travelled seemed revolutionary, but it was nothing in comparison with the impact the internal combustion engine would later have on modern society. It has changed how we perceive distance and our notion of mobility, it's come to represent individual freedom, and more recently it has been associated with climate change through the increase in carbon emissions as the world reached 1.4 billion cars in use worldwide.

In recent years, the internet and the rapid digitization of almost all aspects of society have brought new opportunities and challenges to traditional ways of governing our societies (Lupton, 2015). In 2018 a former employee turned whistleblower from the British consulting firm Cambridge Analytica revealed how personal data belonging to millions of Facebook users had been collected without their consent and used predominantly for political advertisement (Issak and Hanna, 2018). The result was much more wide ranging than petty social media campaigns. Research has later shown that the use of personal data for political advertisement potentially influenced the outcome of high profile elections including the US 2016 election, Brexit, and the 2017 election in Kenya (Manor, 2019). The scandal promoted a global interest in privacy and social media's influence on politics and ultimately our democracies.

As technologies mature, commercialize, and have widespread adaptation and use, they not only change the immediate task for which they are used, but drive change in political systems, social institutions, and systems of governance. The same is true for the world of diplomacy and geopolitics. Indeed, digital technologies have consistently impacted both the institutions of diplomacy and its practitioners. Fifteenth-century ambassadors already bore the title of 'Extraordinary and Plenipotentiary', meaning that they were authorized to negotiate and sign treaties on behalf of their monarchs. This was a result of the communication technologies of the day—letters sent by horseback which would take weeks to reach their destination (Roberts, 2007). The telegraph had an immense impact on diplomacy as information could circle the globe within minutes. Slowly, the agency of ambassadors declined as headquarters could now manage negotiations given the new speed of communications (Dizard, 2001). Time and space were further condensed by the fax machine, which could send entire documents between continents (Adesina, 2017). The Internet ushered a new era in diplomacy as diplomats could use websites and blogs to offer the public insight into world affairs. Moreover, the email, and later smartphones, enabled heads of state to directly communicate with one another, diminishing the role of embassies as intermediaries between capitals (Manor, 2019).

The same has been true of social media. The emergence of platforms such as Twitter, Facebook, and LinkedIn brought about a new practice of 'real-time diplomacy' as diplomats narrate and comment on world events in near-real time (Seib, 2012). Yet more profoundly, social media altered yet again the relationship between headquarters and embassies as it is the latter who are tasked with marketing foreign policies to local audiences (Metzgar, 2012), managing a state's image and reputation (Archetti, 2012; Seo, 2013; Manor, 2019) and creating digital relationships with local audiences and stakeholders (Mazumdar, 2021). Manuel Castells (2013) has argued that digital technologies are used primarily to annihilate time and space. This has been true for diplomacy's past and its present. The Covid-19 pandemic saw a new kind of diplomacy practiced by diplomats who met on Zoom given national lockdowns and quarantines. In such meetings, diplomats from across the world could convene and negotiate agreements regardless of the distance between them (Hedling and Bermberg, 2021; Bjola and Manor, 2022). Similarly, world leaders and NATO leaders have routinely met virtually to rapidly respond to the war in Ukraine.

Digital technologies therefore have a profound impact on the practice of diplomacy and on diplomats. Much like society, diplomacy is now increasingly digital. This chapter seeks to offer an in-depth examination of how diplomacy has changed through the eyes of two practitioners who had to adapt to the digital age. The chapter also discusses the relationship between online and offline diplomacy as diplomats are now tasked with creating offline normative frameworks for the use of advanced technologies such as artificial intelligence (AI). Finally, the chapter reflects on the new diplomatic role of tech companies who design and own the platforms through which diplomacy is practiced.

TECHNOLOGY AS FOREIGN AND SECURITY POLICY

Today technology is with us from the moment we wake up to the moment we go to bed. New technologies have changed the way we communicate, work, socialize, interact, but moreover it has changed how societies are governed, how markets function, how democracy is exercised, and even the geopolitical waters each nation-state navigates according to its interests and values (Lupton, 2015). This has caused new avenues for foreign policy to open up and issues of technology now take centre stage in international relations. Artificial intelligence, quantum computing, and 6G become more than simply hardware and software; they are increasingly indicators and arenas of great power politics while cyberattacks and disinformation campaigns call for states to show resolve in the digital arena (Bjola, 2018; Bjola and Pamment, 2019).

Many countries have begun using digital tools to advance foreign policy objectives in the grey area between war and peace. Methods include cyberattacks on critical infrastructure and influence campaigns conducted through social media to undermine democracies and our alliances (Riordan, 2019). New technologies also provide authoritarian regimes with new opportunities for digital surveillance, behaviour control, oppression, and censorship (Bauman and Lyon, 2013). Furthermore, non-state actors are utilizing digitization to cause harm. Advanced hacking tools are readily available to cyber-criminals, and terrorists have gained new means of radicalizing, recruiting, and planning attacks on the Internet (Farwell, 2014; Awab, 2017; Manor and Crilley, 2019).

At a country-level, technology has become a central component of the strategic competition between the United States and China. Investments in research and development of new technologies are a key competitive parameter that is shifting the geopolitical balance of power. Meanwhile, cyberattacks against public authorities, companies, and citizens are an ever present threat. Yet it is important to note the dual nature of digital technology, as the same technology used by terrorist groups and criminals may be used by states and their supporters. For instance, soon after the eruption of the 2022 War in Ukraine, the Ukrainian government launched an IT hacker army which coordinated cyberattacks against infrastructure in Russia (Pearson, 2022). The government also used social media to crowdfund the purchasing of drones while activists created programmes enabling Internet users to call Russian families and sway them against the war in Ukraine (Burgess, 2022).

Similarly, new technologies are giving democracy and human rights activists a new tool for unprecedented mobilization, advocacy, and influence. Social media has given voice to the powerless and advanced freedom of speech far beyond the opinion pages of established newspapers (Postema and Melissen, 2021). New technologies are advancing transparency, data privacy, and accountability whether in the digitization of public services and infrastructure or allowing citizens to understand the digital realm around them with greater ease.

Technology Companies as Foreign and Security Policy Actors

In the twenty-first century, new players have stepped onto the global stage. In just a few years, tech companies such as Google, Meta, Amazon, Tencent, and ByteDance have amassed a size and influence that surpasses that of many countries. They have un-precedented influence on the development of society and the daily lives of ordinary people, and—through corporate decisions dictating what and when digital tools are available to countries and citizens—they often play the role of de facto foreign policy actors. The casting as foreign policy protagonists became evident during Russia's inva-sion of Ukraine in early 2022 where major American tech companies found themselves squeezed between freedom of speech principles and European political pressure for censoring Russian propaganda and protecting Western democracies. The outcome was that the large tech companies took down Russian state media from their platforms and as such went from neutral platforms to taking sides in a high stakes geopolitical conflict (*The New York Times*, 2022).

The war in Ukraine may prove a watershed event as for the first time in history Silicon Valley has chosen a side in a conflict. Since the advent of the war, Ukraine's Minister of Digital Transformation has used Twitter to communicate directly with tech CEOs urging them to exit the Russian market. To date, dozens of tech companies have either exited Russia or suspended their activities including Amazon, PayPal, Meta, Apple, and Netflix (*The New York Times*, 2022). In essence, Silicon Valley has digitally sanctioned Russia much like nation-states who implemented financial sanctions. Lastly, some tech moguls have offered Ukraine much needed aid, as is the case with Elon Musk that supplied Ukraine with thousands of Starlink units maintaining Internet connectivity throughout the country. These are all a testament to Big Tech's new diplomatic role. It is likely that in future wars, diplomats will be tasked with managing relations with Big Tech so as to avoid being digitally sanctioned while winning wars will be achieved by winning the hearts and minds of tech CEOs.

Tech companies' role as foreign political actors will only increase. Private tech companies are operating overwhelming parts of our critical digital infrastructure and are responsible for an increasing share of the research into new technologies. These rapid and wide-ranging developments threw into question many tenets of the existing international order, and thus beckoned nation-states to come up with answers. Part of the answer was to equip their diplomats with the skills necessary to navigate the changed geopolitical waters (Bjola and Manor, 2022), and part of the answer was to redefine and redirect where to send diplomats. Indeed, in recent years, ministries of foreign affairs (MFAs) throughout the world have institutionalized the use of digital technologies by authoring guidebooks, creating new working routines, and offering their diplomats digital training (Manor and Kampf, 2022). This institutionalization has also included the appointment of tech ambassadors, as elaborated next.

THE FOUR WAVES OF
DIPLOMATIC REPRESENTATION

Diplomats have always been sent to the places where power resided, and where matters of importance for their countries were being decided. Does your country have a hostile nation as a neighbour? Dispatch your finest diplomats to smooth things out and try to prevent an invasion. Does your country's prosperity depend on trade? Send diplomats skilled in the local language and customs to your key trading partners, and so on.

Historically, in the first wave of diplomacy, this could mean sending diplomats out to other tribes, kingdoms, or city-states. After the peace of Westphalia in 1648 the second wave of diplomacy began. With the codification of the nation-state as the nexus of power, this predominantly meant sending diplomats to other nations. After the Second World War, the international system began being characterized by international and intergovernmental organizations, and states responded with the third wave of diplomacy, stationing greater and greater numbers of diplomats in cities such as New York, Geneva, Brussels, and Addis Ababa (Bjola and Kornprobst, 2018). Now, as states navigate a new technological era, a fourth wave of diplomacy is taking shape. Diplomats are being asked to represent their governments digitally. Scholars suggest that this new form of representation has altered the relationship between individuals and states as social media users can now interact and converse with nation-states through social media pages (Pamment, 2014; Manor, 2019).

The once opaque entity of the nation-state now has a profile page, a profile picture, and likes and dislikes. The nation-state has come to life and users interact with it daily. In addition, diplomats have been asked to create relationships with the private companies driving so much of the head-spinning societal and geopolitical change. Though nominally very young, this fourth wave of diplomacy is unmistakably here. And it is this fourth wave that demonstrates yet again the impact of digital technologies on diplomacy as a new form of ambassadors have arisen—tech ambassadors tasked with managing relations of friendship and enmity with tech companies, to paraphrase Bjola (2013).

DIPLOMATS WITH DIGITAL TOOLS

Like every industry or craft, diplomacy—a world once dominated by protocol and platitudes, maps and chaps—has already been disrupted by digital technology (Drezner, 2019). Digital technologies have disrupted diplomacy in diverse ways. Using digital technologies, the borders of nation-states can expand digitally so that they include globally dispersed diasporas (Bernal, 2014). Digital technologies have transformed diplomacy into a visual artform as MFAs and embassies now author and disseminate a host of images and videos daily (Manor and Crilley, 2018; Manor, 2022). Even diplomatic procedures have been disrupted as ambassadors to the UN in Geneva now use WhatsApp to coordinate votes in the Human Rights Council or quickly draft new resolutions (Cornut, Manor, and Blumenthal, 2022).

Also, like many professions, the first and immediately visible impact has been on the tools: better communications and faster pace. However, the real impact has been about culture and changed power dynamics: the humility that comes from understanding how power has shifted, the agility that the new tools allow, the effectiveness that comes from being more inclusive, and the transparency that comes from increased public understanding of what was once a closed world. Diplomats' new commitment to transparency was perhaps best exemplified in 2015 when the US State Department published the Iran Nuclear Agreement in full (Bjola and Manor, 2018). This is also true of UN Security Council sessions that are live-streamed on YouTube while diplomats that attend climate summits live-tweet deliberations taking place in closed rooms. Digital diplomacy, the current and fourth wave of diplomacy, has already moved through three phases. Much has been achieved. But if it is to succeed in responding to the geopolitical moment we find ourselves in, we must consider what we did right and wrong.

FIRST PHASE—BABY STEPS

The first phase impacted the tools of diplomacy, and had a distinct 'Brave New World' quality in its enthusiasm for the world that would supposedly be built by digital technologies. Traditionally, the main means of communication between diplomats and capitals had been the telegram. That was swiftly upended with the advent of email, however. The first email between heads of government was sent on 4 February 1994, from Swedish Prime Minister Carl Bildt to US President Bill Clinton. Bildt congratulated Clinton on the lifting of the Vietnam embargo, and added that 'Sweden is one of the leading countries in technology, and it is only appropriate that we should be among the first to use the Internet for political contacts and communications around the globe'. Clinton replied the following day, in hindsight perhaps with less panache than the moment required: 'I appreciate your enthusiasm for the potential of emerging technologies. This demonstration of electronic communication is an important step toward building the global information highway.' The language was as clunky as the software, but e-diplomacy was underway (Clinton, 2001).

With its twenty-first-century statecraft programme under Secretary of State Hillary Clinton, the US State Department led a period of excitement and optimism about the way that diplomats could use the new tools of communication and connection. For the ambassadors of that era who genuinely adopted and adapted, these were heady times. This was a period when we could surprise people with a desire to connect, engage, and show some humility. It seemed possible to imagine that social media would open up societies and promote real agency and freedom. Several foreign ministries adjusted to social media far more quickly than to any previous technology. For a profession without many ways to assess impact, there was real willingness to experiment with social media. Yes, there were risks. But the biggest risks were not to be part of online conversations.

Notably, this stage was marked by great variance between MFAs as some were more eager to venture online than others. Many factors impacted diplomats' willingness to migrate online ranging from MFAs' communicative cultures (Golberg and Kaduck, 2014) to diplomats' risk averse mentality and proclivity for information keeping as opposed to information sharing (Copeland, 2013; McNutt, 2014; Wichowski, 2015). Even the cyber optimism of senior policy makers impacted diplomats' adoption of digital technologies. Digital mavericks such as the State Departments' Alec Ross and Swedish Foreign Minister Carl Bildt pushed an innovative digital agenda and encouraged diplomats to embrace the risks associated with digitization (Hayden, 2012). Moreover, different MFAs adopted different technologies, with Sweden creating virtual embassies, the UK creating a blogosphere, and Kenya opting for diaspora forums (Pamment, 2014; Manor, 2019). MFAs even differed in the terms they employed, with some practicing digital diplomacy and others practicing public diplomacy 2.0 or diplomacy in the digital age.

SECOND PHASE—RUNNING WILD

The second phase was the institutionalization of digital diplomacy, where the impacts moved beyond the tools to include the power dynamics that diplomats found themselves operating within. As the use of digital communication grew exponentially, foreign ministries started facing new trade-offs over agility versus confidentiality of their communication. They became more reliant on that ability to communicate at speed. Traditionally, diplomats have always tried to minimize and manage the amount of direct contact between leaders. They encased their exchanges in protocol, prepared lines, and statements. New ways of communicating broke down the restrictions that officials put up. Leaders started to text, email, and tweet each other directtly. During negotiations, the text or WhatsApp messages between them (and between their advisers) became more important than the conversation at the table. Neither Bildt nor Clinton could have anticipated the speed at which the 'global information highway' was being built around them. Bildt was the first minister to make it compulsory for ambassadors to have social media accounts.

In terms of diplomacy, it was Twitter and Facebook that built it. @jack (aka Jack Dorsey, Twitter's founder) sent the first tweet at teatime on 21 March 2006. Within three years, a billion tweets had been sent. Within another three years, Twitter was the unavoidable global platform for politicians, journalists, and power players, and come 2011 Twitter was widely credited with being an essential component of the uprisings of the Arab Spring. The Arab Spring demonstrated to diplomats that social media were an important arena in which revolution takes shape and people learn about world events (Hayden, 2012). Between 2011 and 2015, MFAs and diplomats adopted social media while creating social media empires spanning hundreds of accounts across many platforms (Hayden, 2012). Some hoped to converse with foreign populations and create digital relationships (Metzgar, 2012). Others hoped to monitor online conversations and anticipate future shocks to the international system brought about by digital publics that were asserting themselves in unpredictable ways (Haynal, 2011). Leaders also began to wrestle control of their own social media accounts from their staff. They recognized that if you were not tweeting yourself, you were not really on Twitter. In early 2014, John Kerry tweeted 'It only took a year but @StateDept finally let me have my own @Twitter account', and used the hashtag #JKTweetsAgain. Increasingly, such accounts replaced carefully scripted formal statements.

Digital media were also increasingly important resources for those responding to humanitarian crises. Humanitarian agencies got social media channels and devices to those hit by disasters, and used Google Earth to locate survivors. In Lebanon, diplomats used smart cards to deliver cash to the neediest refugees, and sophisticated social media mapping tools to locate them. Throughout the past decade diplomats have employed increasingly sophisticated digital technologies to offer humanitarian and consular aid ranging from network analysis to data analysis, dedicated social media pages, and smartphone applications (Melissen and Caesar-Gordon, 2016).

Some of the most innovative digital diplomats were from smaller countries (Manor and Segev, 2020). Their smaller size made it easier to embrace a nimbler, start-up inspired approach. Estonia led the diplomatic market on use of blockchain technology (a way of distributing digital data globally across thousands of computers), and online citizenship. Since its independence in 2008, Kosovo had been recognized by only half the world. Its deputy foreign minister, Petrit Selimi, persuaded Facebook to allow users to place their location in Kosovo, and not in neighbouring Serbia. The success of this effort meant that Kosovo's existence is more widely recognized online than offline. Importantly, digital diplomacy studies suggest that digital platforms enable states to 'punch above their weight'. Studies examining networks of diplomats have found that states with limited resources, and small economies, can become central players in online networks of diplomacy. Kosovo's MFA is one of the most central ministries on Twitter, attracting diplomatic peers from across the globe, as do Iceland and Albania (Manor and Pamment, 2019).

What Kosovo was quick to see, Denmark was the first to codify. Kosovo rightly diagnosed that tucked away in a valley on the west coast of the USA, an incredible power to shape international development and to change minds across the globe had been growing. Denmark was the first country to draw the logical conclusion from this situation. In 2017, Denmark fired the starting gun for the fourth wave of diplomacy when it became the first country in the world to appoint a Tech Ambassador. Naturally, the ambassador was stationed in Silicon Valley. The sun-bathed valley, nestled between the Santa Cruz Mountains and the San Francisco Bay, had joined the likes of Washington, D.C. and New York as the place to send your diplomats. More than just appointing an ambassador, however, Denmark's self-described 'Techplomacy' initiative represented elevating technology as a cross-cutting foreign and security policy issue (Klynge, Ekman, and Waedegaard, 2020).

The Danish government was mindful that digital technology had become a hype-object, its simultaneous effects too many and too varied to comprehend, with the multiple layers of impact reshaping both Danish society and the international context Denmark operated within. As such, the new ambassador had a global mandate to represent the Danish government on matters of technology, both in direct relations with the industry and in relevant bilateral and international conversations about tech and its increasing influence and relevance. Since 2017, more than twenty-five countries have drawn the same conclusions Denmark did, and followed suit in establishing formal diplomatic structures for dealing with the digital technologies and developments that are reshaping the international order. The titles vary, and so do their mandates, and more of them are stationed in their national capitals than in California. The overarching trend is, however, unmistakable.

One of the key examples of how transnational digital diplomacy has evolved in recent years is the Cyber and Tech Retreat (CTR) co-chaired by Denmark and Australia (Office of Denmark's Tech Ambassador, 2020). Through this initiative, Denmark and Australia convene cyber and tech ambassadors from more than twenty-five like-minded countries each year for a series of high-level, closed-doors meetings about the impacts of emerging technologies on our societies, livelihoods, and national and security politics. Aiming to elevate technology to high-level politics and a strategic priority, the CTR brings together governments, tech companies, and industry leaders to discuss the technologies of tomorrow among like-minded peers. In the years since 2019, the group has come together annually to discuss all things cyber—from cyberattacks, critical digital infrastructure, and new cyber threats to quantum technologies, AI, and disinformation online. Through these dialogues, the participating countries are seeking to advance the multilateral, transnational coordination on tech, both at a governmental and corporate level, and to increase information sharing between industry and governments.

The group ventured into new territory in the begining of 2022. During the March 2022 annual meeting, Denmark and Australia co-launched a formalization of the group into the new Global Network of Cyber and Tech Ambassadors. With the formal establishment of this new group, the group of like-minded cyber and tech ambassadors signalled a clear and long-lasting commitment to engage with other governmental entities and with tech companies in an effort to reap the collective benefits of technology—and to work together to avoid the pitfalls presented by new cyber threats and risks facing states today. In the second phase, CTR also started to create structures around the wider dialogue between the old emperors and the new. Both the UN's High Level Panel and the Global Tech Panel were genuine and effective attempts to translate between those disrupting global politics, economics, and society and those nominally still in charge, an alternative to trying to summon the Zuckerbergs before parliamentary or congressional committees.

THIRD PHASE—SOBERING UP

The third phase of digital diplomacy overlapped with the second: the empire struck back, and the shadow sides of the digital technologies that had proliferated across the globe started to make themselves seen. Authoritarian governments found new ways to use digital technology to suppress freedom. Former US President Trump exploited Twitter to fire up xenophobia, prejudice, and insurrection. More creatively he also used it—as at home—to court potential diplomatic allies and to pressurize diplomatic opponents (Cornut, Harris, and Rimmer, 2022). Meanwhile, Russia's Vladimir Putin weaponized the Internet against democracy and built troll factories (Bjola and Pamment, 2019). Twitter mobs made it harder to share the nuance of complex diplomatic positions, let alone use social media to reach compromise and common ground (Bjola, 2020b). Polarization was packaged as clickbait, and the centre did not hold. Governments realized that cyber was the new battleground, and started to think in terms of defence (Bjola and Pamment, 2019).

It should be noted that digital diplomacy has always been shaped by crises, wars, and conflicts. The Arab Spring saw the shift from virtual diplomacy to social media-based diplomacy (Hayden, 2012). The Russian digital interventions in Crimea and the Brexit referendum led MFAs to adopt big data analysis tools and focus on disabling fake social media accounts (Manor, 2019). The Covid-19 pandemic saw a shift towards hybrid diplomacy, a mix of physical and virtual diplomacy (Bjola and Manor, 2022). Meanwhile, Big Tech grew, morphing in some cases into entities more powerful in certain respects than governments. It became clear that a small handful of private companies had become the de facto arbiters of free speech online, and that the guardrails for the global conversation were being constructed through content moderation policies written predominantly by white American men in California. Perhaps even more troubling, some business models of Silicon Valley went extremely far in the pursuit of citizen data that could be sold to advertisers.

To many, this conduct was a fundamental breach of trust. Through the deployment of ethically questionable algorithms and a general disregard for privacy, tech companies had breached an unwritten societal contract that had allowed digital platforms to operate virtually unchallenged by offline norms and conventions. The boundaries of privacy in the digital space were being tested. Demands for change and calls for regulatory oversight followed. In the EU, 'the right to be forgotten' would come to serve as the mantra that guided early regulatory efforts to protect citizen's data in cyberspace. It was clear to all that a fire had been lit under the feet of regulators and tech companies alike. Change was needed. While Big Tech grew and flexed its muscles, it quietly recruited the talent, depriving governments of human capital as well as taxes. As the legal arms race intensified, the EU's titanic clashes with Big Tech over data or incitement were a long way from the idealism of the Brave New World phase, when we genuinely believed that digital technology would enable us to solve more problems together.

What Lies Ahead for Digital Diplomacy?

Where does this leave us today? We can still crack challenges together, but to do so, governments must be more honest about what they can't do alone. Tech needs more patience to stick with slower moving and often clumsy states, and more honesty about where it has become part of the problem. The next phase of digital diplomacy should forge a new social contract with both new technologies and Big Tech, as well as seeing diplomats returning to the basics of the craft. We'll need an old school pen and paper effort, albeit digital pens and paper, to rewrite the global rules for protection of our freedoms in an online world. We'll need embassies to escape from the confines of buildings and return to their original mission as groups of people sent to connect. We'll need diplomats who can still do what Edward Murrow called the 'last three feet' (Seo, 2013), that crucial human connection that will be the last diplomatic skill to be automated.

For a trade that relies on communication, diplomacy has obviously had to adapt to successive waves of dramatic technological disruption. The most important innovations to shape statecraft throughout history were language, writing, ships, rules, the printing press, trains, telephones, and now the Internet (Dizard, 2001). The tools of diplomacy are constantly evolving. Diplomats now compete over who has the most Twitter followers rather than where they are placed at a diplomatic dinner. Talleyrand would have been out of his depth in a twentieth-century summit, just as John Kerry would be in a twenty-second-century summit. Diplomacy had surrounded itself by the late twentieth century with immense paraphernalia—titles, conferences, summits, rules, and codes. But strip these away, and we can identify the diplomatic skills that made our ancestors more likely to survive 200,000 years of hunter-gathering, the eight millennia of the Agricultural Age, and the two centuries of the Industrial Age (Fletcher, 2016). Maybe these can get us through the new uncertainties of the Digital Age.

The history of diplomacy suggests that diplomats have always been most effective when they have understood, channelled, and represented real power. When emperors held power, diplomats were flunkies in their citadels. When monarchs held power, diplomats were courtiers in their palaces. When military leaders held power, diplomats hung around outside their tents. When states became the dominant power brokers, diplomats started ministries and tried to get as close as possible to their elected (or unelected) leaders. As democracy took hold in the West, diplomats reinvented themselves as its most ardent supporters, while trying to ensure that their trade stayed out of its sight. Diplomacy is now in an age when power is once again shifting and diffusing. If diplomats are not where the power is, they are simply slow journalists with smaller audiences.

The history of diplomacy also shows us that, at key points in our collective story, and normally following shocks such as war, shifts in power required diplomats and politicians to work together strenuously to recalibrate systems and establish new rules of coexistence. Third wave diplomats are standing on the shoulders of the curious, canny, and sometimes courageous individuals behind Westphalia, Vienna, the League of Nations, and Bretton Woods. Two centuries after the Congress of Vienna, it can be argued that we again are at such a moment of flux and uncertainty. Diplomats can only gain the legitimacy and credibility to help manage the next global reset by reorganizing for the digital age and starting to deliver solutions and positive outcomes for the publics and governments they represent.

Digital Diplomacy: Fighting with Values in Winning the Global Technological Race

The fight for liberal values and democracy in the twentieth century has been closely linked to technological dominance. The arms race in the First and Second World Wars was a matter of technologically dominating the battlefield. The race to put the first man on the moon was a contest in technological superiority and the ability to conquer space itself. From a geopolitical viewpoint, among the most significant geostrategic technological races was the development of nuclear weapons under the leadership of Robert Oppenheimer in the Manhattan project during World War II. Its mission was not only to break scientific ground as uranium was transformed into plutonium but to defend world peace in a time of war. The result was that the technology that emerged from the Manhattan project became posterity defining for geopolitical dynamics, shaping our multilateral organizations and even impacting how we perceive security and peace today. The Hungarian-American engineer and mathematician John von Neumann joined the Manhattan project and, in addition to his research on explosives, he contributed as the founding father of game theory to the fundamental political understanding of the Manhattan project: the nuclear bomb is not an end but a means in a much more complex geopolitical game.

From Nuclear to Neural: A New Von Neumann Moment

If nuclear was the defining factor of the twentieth century, so is the development and application of AI today. One where a new complex geopolitical game is underway and the means are defined and developed as we try to set the rules (Bjola, 2020a). AI, as a broad technological term, is used in many everyday tasks like search engines, understanding of human language, facial recognition, spam filters, and self-driving vehicles. AI is widely applied across industries including healthcare, production, supply chain management, logistics, and environmental management. But AI is much more than facial recognition to open your phone with, or the ability to give you the fastest route from your home to your office during rush hour. AI is the epitome of dual-use technology. A machine's ability to perceive, evaluate, and act faster and more precisely than any human being will be a comparative advantage in all regards—civilian and military alike. Just as AI is a great advantage for industries that manage to adapt and transition, so too will it be for countries that manage to embrace the technology to their advantage. To that end, AI is taking the role as protagonist in the increasing rivalry between East and West. As AI takes centre stage, it becomes an advantage, a weapon, and a possible hostage amidst global geopolitical tensions (Riordan, 2019).

AI is not necessarily the beginning of a new cold war, but we are faced with a Von Neumann moment: one where it is not enough to try and play the game, but one where we must define the game. What does 'winning' the race for AI development and deployment look like? And how can liberally minded nations ensure that there are multiple winners and that the gains are broad based? Traditional diplomacy won't be sufficient in answering this quest, as it is currently too mired in twentieth-century procedures and assumptions. Tech diplomacy in the twenty-first century is about defining the global game of AI and what winning looks like. If the game is only a race to most quickly develop superior AI to dominate militarily it becomes a zero-sum game. One in which no one wins. Instead this is a values-based game. Not with sophisticated algorithms but what values future advanced computer systems and AI must rely on. In this game tech diplomats can set the rules, and insist that traditional measures of military superiority are inadequate and instead that strategic as well as military and commercial superiority is obtained not at the expense of, but guaranteed by, high demands to privacy, transparency, responsibility, and applicability for solving societal challenges. This is a Von Neumann moment—one where digital diplomats not only learn to play the game, but define and set the very board on which the game of geopolitics of emerging technologies is played.

The Future for Diplomats in a Digital Age

Diplomacy during the Covid-19 pandemic would have been unimaginable without digital communication platforms like Zoom and WhatsApp (Hedling and Bremberg, 2021). For a profession that used to do everything to minimize direct contacts between leaders, diplomats were quick to embrace videoconferencing once the tech made it a serious option. The pandemic drove summits and conferences online, saving enormous amounts of time and carbon with little obvious negative impact on the outcomes. Perhaps we may even look back on an era of social and national distancing and discern ways in which the pandemic *improved* diplomacy. It has reminded the world—and diplomats—why the craft matters. But much as the pandemic gave a much needed technological jolt to diplomacy (Bjola and Coplen, 2022), it also served as a lesson in just how much we have come to rely on the tech sector for the functioning of society. People were already spending increasing amounts of time online, but the pandemic supercharged this trend. Diplomats had to see more clearly than ever before that basic functioning of society had become digital, and the power entailed therein resided with the tech titans found in Silicon Valley, Seattle, and Beijing. Moreover, the pandemic period exposed the fundamental dividing lines between nationalism and internationalism. The inadequacy of the global infrastructure was not created by Covid, the retreat from Kabul, and the invasion of Ukraine: it was exposed by those moments. If passing the pandemic marks the end of the unnecessary summit, of diplomacy measured in air miles rather than outcomes, and a resistance to automating the parts of diplomacy that are better done by technology, that will be a bonus. The updating of diplomacy for the digital age is an exciting and urgent agenda. If diplomacy did not exist, we would need to invent it. Because finding the right societal balance between the digital and physical realms, between Big Tech and states, and between peoples in the digital era, requires patience, insight, and compromise. It requires, in other words, diplomacy.

Suggested Reading

Bjola, Corneliu, and Marcus Holmes. 2015. *Digital Diplomacy: Theory and Practice*. Routledge.

Bjola, Corneliu, and Ruben Zaiotti. 2021. *Digital Diplomacy and International Organisations: Autonomy, Legitimacy and Contestation*, edited by Corneliu Bjola. Routledge.

Drezner, Daniel W. 2019. 'Technological Change and International Relations'. *International Relations* 33(2), 286–303. https://doi.org/10.1177/0047117819834629.

Drum, Kevin. 2018. 'Tech World: Welcome to the Digital Revolution'. *Foreign Affairs* 97: pp. 43–49. https://www.foreignaffairs.com/articles/world/2018-06-14/tech-world.

Fletcher, Tom. 2016. *Naked Diplomacy: Power and Statecraft in the Digital Age*. UK ed. William Collins.

References

Adesina, Olubukola S. 2017. 'Foreign Policy in an Era of Digital Diplomacy'. *Cogent Social Sciences* 3(1): pp. 13. doi:10.1080/23311886.2017.1297175

Archetti, Cristina. 2012. 'The Impact of New Media on Diplomatic Practice: an Evolutionary Model of Change'. *The Hague Journal of Diplomacy* 7(2): pp. 181–206. doi: 10.1163/187119112X625538

Awan, Imran. 2017. 'Cyber-extremism: Isis and the Power of Social Media'. *Society* 54(2): pp. 138–149. doi: 10.1007/s12115-017-0114-0

Bauman, Zygmunt, and David Lyon. 2013. *Liquid Surveillance*. Cambridge: Polity Press.

Bernal, Victoria. 2014. *Nation as Network: Diaspora, Cyberspace & Citizenship*. Chicago: The University of Chicago Press.

Bjola, Corneliu. 2018. 'Understanding Enmity and Friendship in World Politics: the Case for a Diplomatic Approach'. *The Hague Journal of Diplomacy* 8(1): pp. 1–20. doi:10.1163/1871191X-12341242

Bjola, Corneliu. 2018. 'The Ethics of Countering Digital Propaganda'. *Ethics & International Affairs* 32(3): pp. 305–315. https://doi.org/10.1017/S0892679418000436.

Bjola, Corneliu. 2020a. *Diplomacy in the Age of Artificial Intelligence*. Abu Dhabi, UAE: Emirates Diplomatic Academy. http://eda.ac.ae/.

Bjola, Corneliu. 2020b. 'Coping with Digital Disinformation in Multilateral Contexts: The Case of the UN Global Compact for Migration'. In *Digital Diplomacy and International Organisations*, edited by Corneliu Bjola and Zaiotti Ruben, 267–286. Abingdon, Oxon; New York, NY: Routledge, 2021 https://doi.org/10.4324/9781003032724-15.

Bjola, Corneliu, and Ilan Manor. 2018. 'Revisiting Putnam's Two-Level Game Theory in the Digital Age: Domestic Digital Diplomacy and the Iran Nuclear Deal'. *Cambridge Review of International Affairs* 31(1): pp. 3–32. doi: 10.1080/09557571.2018.1476836.

Bjola, Corneliu, and Markus Kornprobst. 2018. *Understanding International Diplomacy: Theory, Practice and Ethics*. 2nd ed. London and New York: Routledge.

Bjola, Corneliu, and James Pamment. 2019. *Countering Online Propaganda and Extremism: The Dark Side of Digital Diplomacy*. Oxon: Routledge.

Bjola, Corneliu, and Michaela Coplen. 2022. 'Virtual Venues and International Negotiations: Lessons from the COVID-19 Pandemic'. *International Negotiation*. pp. 1–25. 0.1163/15718069-bja10060.

Bjola, Corneliu, and Ilan Manor. 2022. 'The Rise of Hybrid Diplomacy: from Digital Adaptation to Digital Adoption'. *International Affairs* 98(2): pp. 471–491. doi: 10.1093/ia/iiac005.

Burgess, Matt. 2022. Hacktivism Is Back and Messier Than Ever. https://www.wired.co.uk/article/hacktivism-russia-ukraine-ddos

Castells, Manuel. 2013. *Communication Power*. Oxford: Oxford University Press.

Clinton, William J. 2001. Electronic Mail Message to Prime Minister Carl Bildt of Sweden. The American Presidency Project. https://www.presidency.ucsb.edu/documents/electronic-mail-message-prime-minister-carl-bildt-sweden

'Companies Are Getting Out of Russia, Sometimes at a Cost'. October 2022. https://www.nytimes.com/article/russia-invasion-companies.html

Copeland, Daryl. 2013. 'Taking Diplomacy Public: Science, Technology and Foreign Ministries in a Heteropolar World'. In *Relational, Networked and Collaborative Approaches to Public Diplomacy*, edited by R.S. Zaharna, Amelia Arsenault, and Ali Fisher, 56–69. New York: Routledge.

Cornut, Jérémie, Susan Gail Harris Rimmer, and Ivy Choi. 2022. 'The Liquidification of International Politics and Trump's (Un) Diplomacy on Twitter'. *International Politics* 59(2): pp. 367–382. doi: 10.1057/s41311-021-00309-0.

Cornut, Jérémie., Ilan Manor, and Corinne Blumenthal. 2022. 'WhatsApp with Diplomatic Practices in Geneva? Diplomats, Digital Technologies, and Adaptation in Practice'. *International Studies Review* 24(4). doi: 10.1093/isr/viac047

Dizard, Wilson Jr. 2001. *Digital Diplomacy: U.S. foreign Policy in the Information Age.* London: Prarger.

Drezner, Daniel W. 2019. 'Technological Change and International Relations'. *International Relations* 33(2): pp. 286–303. doi: 10.1177/0047117819834629.

Farwell, James. P. 2014. 'The Media Strategy of ISIS'. *Survival* 56(6): pp. 49–55. doi: 10.1080/00396338.2014.985436

Fletcher, Tom. 2016. *Naked Diplomacy: Power and Statecraft in the Digital Age.* UK ed. William Collins.

Golberg, Elissa, and Michael Kaduck. 2014. 'Where is Headquarters: Diplomacy, Development and Defence'. In *Diplomacy in the Digital Age*, edited by Janice Gross Stein, 125–140. New York: McClelland & Stewart Ltd.

Hayden, Craig. 2012. 'Social Media at State: Power, Practice, and Conceptual Limits for US Public Diplomacy'. *Global Media Journal-American Edition* 11(21): pp. 1–21.

Haynal, George.2011. 'Corporate Diplomacy in the Information Age: Catching Up to the Dispersal of Power'. In *Diplomacy in the Digital Age*, edited by Janice Gross Stein, 209–224. New York: McClelland & Stewart Ltd.

Hedling, Elsa, and Niklas Bremberg. 2021. 'Practice Approaches to the Digital Transformations of Diplomacy: Toward a New Research Agenda'. *International Studies Review* 23(4): pp. 1595–1618. doi: 10.1093/isr/viab027.

Isaak, Jim, and Mina J. Hanna. 2018. 'User Data Privacy: Facebook, Cambridge Analytica, and Privacy Protection'. *Computer* 51(8): pp. 56–59.

Klynge, Casper, Mikael Ekman, and Nikolaj Juncher Waedegaard. 2020. 'Diplomacy in the Digital Age: Lessons from Denmark's TechPlomacy Initiative'. *The Hague Journal of Diplomacy* 15(1–2): 185–195. https://doi.org/10.1163/1871191X-15101094Lupton, Deborah. 2015. *Digital Sociology*. New York: Routledge.

Manor, Ilan, and Rhys Crilley. 2018. 'Visually Framing the Gaza War of 2014: the Israel Ministry of Foreign Affairs on Twitter'. *Media, War & Conflict* 11(4): pp. 369–391. doi: 10.1177/1750635218780564.

Manor, Ilan. 2019. *The Digitalization of Public Diplomacy.* Cham: Springer.

Manor, Ilan, and Rhys Crilley. 2019. 'The Aesthetics of Violent Extremist and Counter-Violent Extremist Communication'. In *Countering Online Propaganda and Extremism: The Dark Side of Digital Diplomacy*, edited by Corneliu Bjola and James Pamment, pp. 121–139. Oxon: Routledge.

Manor, Ilan, and James Pamment. 2019. 'Towards Prestige Mobility? Diplomatic Prestige and Digital Diplomacy'. *Cambridge Review of International Affairs* 32(2): pp. 93–131. doi: 10.1080/09557571.2019.1577801.

Manor, Ilan, and Elad Segev. 2020. 'Social Media Mobility: Leveraging Twitter Networks in Online Diplomacy'. *Global Policy* 11(2): pp: 233–244. doi: 10.1111/1758-5899.12799

Manor, Ilan, and Ronit Kampf. 2022. 'Digital Nativity and Digital Diplomacy: Exploring Conceptual Differences Between Digital Natives and Digital Immigrants'. *Global Policy* 13: pp. 442–457. doi: 10.1111/1758-5899.13095

Manor, Ilan. 2022. 'Exploring the Semiotics of Public Diplomacy'. *CPD Perspective on Public Diplomacy* 2: pp. 1–69.

Mazumdar, B. Theo. 2021. 'Digital Diplomacy: Internet-Based Public Diplomacy Activities or Novel Forms of Public Engagement?'. *Place Branding and Public Diplomacy*. pp. 1–20. doi: doi.org/10.1057/s41254-021-00208-4.

McNutt, Kathleen. 2014. 'Public Engagement in the Web 2.0 Era: Social Collaborative Technologies in a Public Sector Context'. *Canadian Public Administration* 57(1): pp. 49–70. doi: 10.1111/capa.12058.

Melissen, Jan, and Matthew Caesar-Gordon. 2016. '"Digital Diplomacy" and the Securing of Nationals in a Citizen-Centric World'. *Global Affairs* 2(93): pp. 321–330. doi: 10.1080/23340460.2016.1239381.

Metzgar, Emily T. 2012. 'Is It the Medium or the Message? Social Media, American Public Diplomacy and Iran'. *Global Media Journal*: pp. 1–16.

Office of Denmark's Tech Ambassador. 2020. 'Cyber and Tech Retreat'. https://techamb.um.dk/impact/cyber-and-tech-summit.

Pamment, James. 2014. 'The Mediatization of Diplomacy'. *The Hague Journal of Diplomacy* 9(3): pp. 253–280.

Pearson, James. 2022. Ukraine Launches 'IT Aarmy,' Takes Aim at Russian Cyberspace. https://www.reuters.com/world/europe/ukraine-launches-it-army-takes-aim-russian-cyberspace-2022-02-26/ (Accessed: 3 March 2022).

Postema, Saskia, and Jan Melissen. 2021. 'UN Celebrity Diplomacy in China: Activism, Symbolism and National Ambition Online'. *International Affairs* 97(3): pp. 667–684. doi: 10.1093/ia/iiab042Riordan, Shaun. 2019. *Cyberdiplomacy: Managing Security and Governance Online*. Cambridge: Polity.

Roberts, Walter R. 2007. 'What is Public Diplomacy? Past Practices, Present Conduct, Possible Future'. *Mediterranean Quarterly* 18(4): pp. 36–52.

Seib, Philip. 2012. *Real Time Diplomacy: Politics and Power in the Social Media Era*. Cambridge: Polity Press.

Seo, Hyunjin. 2013. 'The Virtual "Last Three Feet": Understanding Relationship Perspectives in Network-Based Public Diplomacy'. In *Relational, Networked and Collaborative Approaches to Public Diplomacy*, edited by R.S. Zaharna, Amelia Arsenault, and Ali Fisher, 157–172. New York: Routledge.

Wichowski, Alexis. 2015. ' "Secrecy is for Losers": Why Diplomats Should Embrace Openness to Protect National Security'. In *Digital Diplomacy: Theory and Practice*, edited by Corneliu Bjola and Marcus Holmes, 52–70. Oxon: Routledge.

CHAPTER 24

INTERNATIONAL LAW, BIG TECH REGULATION, AND DIGITAL DIPLOMATIC PRACTICE

VICTORIA BAINES

THE infancy of cyberspace and digital communications technology have borne witness to a multiplicity of attempts to regulate them. A plethora of state and non-state actors, including legal specialists and researchers, have sought to disprove John Perry Barlow's (1996) now famous challenge to governments, 'You have no sovereignty where we gather ... Cyberspace does not lie within your borders. Do not think that you can build it, as though it were a public construction project. You cannot.'

Twenty-five years on, sovereignty in cyberspace remains a hot issue. As Barlow predicted, problems of jurisdiction and attribution continue to dominate negotiations for hard and soft international law. As demonstrated in the current United Nations process for the elaboration of a comprehensive international Convention on countering the use of information and communications technologies for criminal purposes, stakeholders' regulatory priorities are diverse and often diverging: states exhibit varying degrees of preoccupation with controlling the information available to their citizens. Meanwhile, cyber-attacks conducted by criminal groups allegedly sponsored by nation states have prompted close consideration of international provisions for non-intervention and state responsibility. While the expert group of contributors to the Tallinn Manuals succeeded in establishing that existing international law applies both to cyber conflict (Schmitt, 2013) and cyber operations (Schmitt, 2017), concern has grown among states and non-state actors alike that it may not be sufficient to prevent and counter some of the most prevalent and high impact cyber threats, including ransomware affecting critical infrastructure, supply chain attacks, and influence operations (Ohlin, 2017; Tsagourias, 2019).

Multilateral Deliberations, Multistakeholder Norm Shaping

At the time of writing (summer 2022), the Council of Europe Convention on Cybercrime (CETS No.185) is the only binding multilateral treaty in the field of cyberspace governance. While largely focused on criminal investigation, an additional protocol criminalizing racist and xenophobic propaganda (ETS 189), and guidance notes on critical infrastructure attacks, election interference, and terrorism, demonstrate a broader scope in practice (Council of Europe, 2013, 2016, 2019). Ratified by sixty-six states parties since its entry into force in 2004—among them eighteen non-members of the Council of Europe including the United States, Australia, Canada, Israel, Japan, and a number of Latin American, African, South Asian, and Pacific nations—and with a number of observer states and international organizations, the Convention is the first point of reference for agreed definitions of cybercrime offences in substantive criminal law, and provisions for international cooperation in investigations and electronic evidence gathering. Before its suspension from the Council of Europe in February 2022, the Russian Federation was the only member state to have neither signed nor ratified the Convention. Reasons adduced for refusal include an assessment that its provision for cross-border data access (Article 32b) constitutes a violation of national sovereignty (Gady and Austin, 2010; Hakmeh and Peters, 2020).

Rejecting the Tallinn Manuals on the basis of their initial sponsorship by NATO and a focus broadly aligned with the United States' position on the applicability of the law of armed conflict to cyber operations (Huang and Mačák, 2017; Mueller, 2019), Russia and China have for a number of years pushed for a comprehensive *lex specialis*. Parallel processes hosted by the United Nations, the First Committee's Group of Governmental Experts on Developments in the Field of Information and Telecommunications in the Context of International Security among them, have at times achieved a certain level of consensus on norms and responsible behaviour in cyberspace (Georgieva, 2020; Austin, McConnell and Neutze, 2015), and at others failed to agree on key concepts of cyberspace governance, not least its militarization (Henriksen, 2019; Tikk and Kerttunen, 2017).

Chairing the Group of Governmental Experts in 2009–2010, the Russian Federation called for a non-binding international code of conduct 'to identify the rights and responsibilities of States in the information space, promote constructive and responsible behaviour on their part and enhance their cooperation in addressing common threats and challenges in the information space' (A/66/359). By 2019—and with the support of China, the Central Asian Republics, and states including Angola, Iran, Myanmar, North Korea, the Syrian Arab Republic, and Venezuela—the Russian Federation was chief sponsor of a resolution 'to establish an open-ended ad hoc intergovernmental committee of experts, representative of all regions, to elaborate a comprehensive international Convention on countering the use of information and communications technologies for criminal purposes' (A/C.3/74/L.11/Rev.1). Despite opposition by Australia, Canada, Israel, Japan, New Zealand, the United States, the United Kingdom, and the European Union's twenty-seven member states, the resolution was adopted by vote on 18th November.

In the course of a decade, then, and with the guidance of the Russian Federation and like-minded states, the multilateral focus appears to have shifted. Hard law in the ostensibly more limited sphere of cybercriminal activity has gained precedence over the establishment of soft law/norms for responsible behaviour. Cyber norms and other measures aimed at confidence and capacity building have not, however, disappeared entirely. Close reading of state contributions to the Ad Hoc Committee for the elaboration of the Convention reveals that they remain matters for contention, disputed inclusion, or conscious exclusion. Moreover, they live on in alternative, often more multistakeholder, initiatives.

Much of the world's information and communications infrastructure is not within direct domestic control. While by no means impervious to politicization (Walden, 2013; Weinberg, 2000), technical Internet and web standards are predominantly maintained and updated by multistakeholder groupings such as the Internet Corporation for Assigned Names and Numbers (ICANN) and Internet Engineering Task Force. Open to governments, the private sector, civil society organizations, academic institutions, and individuals, representation in these fora reflects the multiple constituencies and operational reality of Internet governance: namely, that there is no single owner or group of owners, but common ownership and community operation.

Aligned with this paradigm, a multistakeholder model of cyberspace governance has proliferated in a number of venues, among them the UN's Internet Governance Forum, the Paris Call for Trust and Security in Cyberspace, and thematic initiatives, such as the Global Internet Forum to Counter Terrorism. In the area of cyber norms elaboration, initiatives such as the Global Commission on the Stability of Cyberspace (GCSC), established at The Hague Centre for Strategic Studies and the East West Institute in 2017, not only invite non-state participation but also enjoy promotion by and financial support from the private sector. The GCSC's (2019) report promoted the principles of responsibility, restraint, requirement to act, and respect for human rights and the rule of law. Of note, the concept of responsibility is consciously expanded beyond that in the International Law Commission's Draft Articles on Responsibility of States for International Wrongful Acts (2001). According to the GCSC, 'Everyone is responsible for ensuring the stability of cyberspace'. Similarly, restraint and the requirement to act apply equally to state and non-state actors.

Among the latter, Microsoft has sought a particularly active role in shaping cyber and digital governance in recent years. Opening a United Nations representation office in September 2020, the company set out its priorities for the 75th session in a series of blogs authored by its Vice President, John Frank, and white papers on its work towards the Sustainable Development Goals and Digital Peace in Cyberspace (Art and Emejulu, 2020a, 2020b). Describing an interconnected world requiring collective action, and stressing the need 'to think more broadly and imagine what inclusive global governance can do for society, and to strengthen the systems and institutions that are tasked with this work' (Microsoft, 2020a), the company nevertheless conceded, 'We're not a government; we don't pretend to be. There are some things that we don't get invited to, but there are things that we can help with' (Microsoft, 2020b). With a large number of states, inter-governmental organizations, non-governmental organizations, and Russian cybersecurity firm Kaspersky, Microsoft submitted comments on draft reports of the UN's Open-Ended Working Group on developments in the field of information and telecommunications in the context of international security. This group had the objectives of 'making the United Nations negotiation process on security in the use of information and communications technologies more democratic, inclusive and transparent', and 'to further develop the rules, norms and principles of responsible behaviour of States ... and the ways for their implementation' (A/RES/73/27).

The corporation's increasingly active participation in the cyberspace governance debate has not gone unnoticed. Identifying Microsoft as falling into Finnemore and Hollis' (2016) category of 'norm entrepreneur', an actor who may 'frame the issue, articulate the norm, and organize support', Hurel and Lobato (2018) conclude that 'Not only does the company focus on changing the behaviour of states regarding global cybersecurity norms, but also seeks to stretch its own legitimacy beyond technical and economic services to influence international diplomatic efforts at the forefront of global cybersecurity debates'.

Along with academic institutions and civil society organizations, Microsoft, Meta/Facebook, and Amazon Web Services were among fifty non-state actors who applied to participate in the Ad Hoc Committee to elaborate a comprehensive international Convention on countering the use of information and communications technologies for criminal purposes, as per General Assembly resolution 75/282. States' written contributions indicate diverse sentiment on both the degree and purpose of private sector participation. Some, such as Australia, Indonesia, Mexico, Norway, and Switzerland, have stressed the importance of ensuring that the process of legislative development is itself multistakeholder, receiving expert inputs from the private sector. For others such as Nigeria, the input of non-state actors is envisaged chiefly with regard to information sharing on emerging threats. For Canada, multistakeholder involvement is envisaged in technical assistance and capacity building. Russia, meanwhile, sees a more subordinate role for the private sector, Articles 42 and 43 of its proposed draft text seeking respectively 'to prevent offences and other unlawful acts relating to ICT use in the private sector' and to require 'each private provider (or grouping of such providers) of information and telecommunications services located in the territory of a State party' to 'take appropriate measures, within its power and in accordance with the law of the State where it is located, to support the establishment and implementation of principles and standards for the use of international cyberspace'. The latter provision nevertheless accords at least a supporting role to digital service providers in ensuring responsible behaviour in cyberspace. As it transpires, this is not the only issue on which states diverge.

Sovereign Preoccupations: The Process to Elaborate a UN Cybercrime Convention

Unsurprisingly, digital sovereignty looms large in state submissions to the Ad Hoc Committee, with states including China, Cuba, Indonesia, Mexico, and Jamaica making explicit reference to the need for due regard for national sovereignty. Indeed, Mexico's proposal for the elaboration of a dialogue on 'crimes against national sovereignty' speaks both to the centrality of non-intervention in debates on responsible behaviour in cyberspace, and the extent to which regulation concerning cybercriminal activity inevitably touches on broader issues of multilateral cyberspace governance.

Considerable divergence in the suggested scope of the Convention reflects the fact that there is still so much in cyberspace that *could* be regulated. Something of a spectrum emerges. At one end is the European Union's position that substantive criminal law provisions 'must be clearly and narrowly defined', and 'should in general relate only to high-tech crimes and cyber-dependent crimes, such as illegally gaining access to, intercepting or interfering with computer data and systems'. Moreover, 'matters related to or regulating national security or state behaviour' and 'matters related to or regulating rules on Internet governance, which are already being addressed in the context of dedicated multistakeholder policies and forums' must be considered out of scope of a UN Convention. A further group of countries, Australia, Canada, Japan, Norway, Nigeria, New Zealand, the United Kingdom and the United States among them, propose a 'cyber-dependent plus' model incorporating crimes of unauthorized access, interception, or interference, and crimes such as child sexual exploitation and abuse and certain frauds, whose scale and distribution are significantly enabled by digital communications technology.

Once one leaves the confines of cyber-dependent crimes, national priorities and imperatives of information control become more apparent. Taking the opportunity to propose a full draft text of the Convention, Russia's suggested content crimes include encouragement of or coercion to suicide, the creation and use of digital data to mislead the user, offences related to the involvement of minors in the commission of unlawful acts that endanger their life or health, incitement to subversive or armed activities, and rehabilitation of Nazism, justification of genocide, or crimes against peace and humanity. The first two of these would appear to reflect local preoccupations with social media-based 'suicide games' such as the Blue Whale Challenge, which have been the subject of moral panic and criminal legislation. Establishing an evidence base for the existence of this phenomenon prior to sensational media coverage has been difficult, and it is perhaps telling that similar substantive criminal provisions have not been proposed by any other state. While Indonesia's suggested designation of distribution of adult pornography as a 'core cybercrime offence' is unlikely to achieve consensus, its proposal for the inclusion of 'disinformation, conspiracy, hoax', and 'material that contains racial, nationality, religion or political based hostility' speaks to common societal challenges of digitally mediated falsehoods and hate speech. At the same time, specific reference to 'disinformation' again takes us into the sphere of responsible state behaviour and non-intervention. Even in the process of defining cybercrime, it can prove difficult to avoid entirely wider concerns of cyberspace governance.

So, too, states appear to disagree on the purpose of the Convention. While most contributing states give at least some consideration to substantive criminal law, Brazil's contribution focuses solely on international evidence exchange in relation to 'i) crimes against computer systems; and ii) any crimes that are committed through electronic means'. India's late submission is the most expansive. Noting that the UN process is an 'unprecedented opportunity to arrive at consensus', its recommended scope for the Convention is as follows:

1. Existing and emerging cyber threats and crimes
2. Norms, rules, and principles for the responsible behaviour of states
3. International law on cybercrime
4. Confidence-building measures
5. Capacity building
6. International cooperation measures in the field of cybercrime

The conscious inclusion of norms, rules, and principles for the responsible behaviour of states—explicitly excluded from the mandate by other countries such as New Zealand and the EU27—along with confidence-building measures and capacity building, not only breaks the Convention out of its more limited cybercrime confines to matters that in the words of Nigeria are 'politically volatile'. It also seeks to enshrine in hard international law soft law measures that require the efforts of a host of non-state actors, including digital service providers. That these measures are necessary is beyond doubt: however, their inclusion, and India's additional suggestion that the Convention might simplify issues of jurisdiction in cyberspace, may risk making this particular multilateral instrument unachievable or unenforceable.

The need for any UN Convention to be technology-neutral and as 'future proof' as possible is a key concern in state contributions to the Ad Hoc Committee, perhaps reflecting sovereign preoccupations with the disruptive pace of technological development, especially in those countries in which it is not state-controlled. Current signals are that the importance of the private sector in global technology development and governance will increase. China's recent complaint to the United Nations concerning two near-collisions between the China Space Station and Space X's Starlink satellites (A/AC.105/1262) illustrates the extent to which private sector organizations involved in the provision of digital communications infrastructure already have the potential to contravene international law, in this case actions pertaining to Article 5 of the Outer Space Treaty 'which could constitute a danger to the life or health of astronauts'. The complaint attributed the near misses to 'Space Exploration Technologies Corporation

(SpaceX) of the United States of America', and a statement by China's Foreign Ministry broadcast on Twitter sought to lay SpaceX's alleged errors at the US government's door. Nevertheless, reports that the company controls more than a third of all active satellites in orbit, comments by the Director General of the European Space Agency to the effect that governments are allowing SpaceX CEO Elon Musk to 'make the rules' in space (Hollinger and Cookson, 2021), and extensive media coverage of Musk's response in the absence of an official statement by the US government, have cast SpaceX/Musk in something of a supra-national role for the future of digital connectivity.

Of note, the EU27's contribution to the Ad Hoc Committee advises that 'as an intergovernmental instrument, a future UN Convention should refrain from directly imposing obligations upon non-governmental organisations, including the private sector, such as internet service providers'. A traditional appreciation of international law holds that it can regulate interactions only between sovereign states. Any attempt to regulate digital service providers directly would mark a significant departure from this model. That it is subject to an explicit exclusion by the bloc is perhaps an indicator of the muddiness of current dialogues on, and real-world operations in, cyber governance. Digital service providers' operations against state-sponsored disinformation campaigns (Weedon, Nuland, and Stamos, 2017), legal actions against developers of intrusive surveillance software used by governments, and boycotts of the investment arms of said governments demonstrate the degree to which these companies are already key actors in countering cyber-espionage and forging responsible behaviour.

Digital Regulation as an Expression of National and Regional Sovereignty

Concurrently, national governments have sought to regulate Big Tech, comprising the largest, mostly US-based, digital service providers. Exercise of national sovereignty in the development of new legislation (as opposed to enforcement of existing legislation on taxation, acquisitions, and so forth) has to date concentrated on information control, network security, and data governance as concerns consumer rights, innovation, and government access.

Attention is naturally drawn to legislation introduced by authoritarian regimes such as those in Russia and China. Applying domestic jurisdiction to all users, hardware, and software operated within their territories, national instruments seek to ensure access by government authorities to content and metadata stored by foreign digital service providers. Russia's 2014 Information Act or 'Bloggers' Law' requires all web services to store Russian citizens' user data on Russian soil. Article 49 of China's Cybersecurity Law requires network operators to 'cooperate with cybersecurity and informatization departments and relevant departments in conducting implementation of supervision and inspections in accordance with the law'.

In as much as both countries' conceptions of national security are sufficiently expansive as to facilitate the restriction of political speech and support for political dissidence, data governance measures that enable the investigation of criminal, qua anti-government, activity are closely linked to the objective of information control. Accordingly, both Russian and Chinese authorities have demanded the removal of apps from US-operated app stores—Russia reportedly of opposition leader Alexei Navalny's app providing advice on tactical voting, China of a tool that enabled protestors in Hong Kong to track the movements of police. Although China's restriction of information and access, colloquially known as the Great Firewall, is more systematic than that experienced by Russian citizens, the techniques deployed by the two governments are broadly similar. Both Russia and China block access to undesirable websites, apply financial and political pressure for the removal of undesirable content, and reportedly engage in online influence operations that target their own populations (Kreps, 2021).

Restriction of access to services and content is by no means the preserve of these two countries, however, or even of repressive regimes. It has become a default exercise of national digital sovereignty, particularly as regards the operations of the largest US-based digital service providers. Increasingly, national governments seek to hold Big Tech liable for non-removal of content that is locally illegal, as in the case of Germany's 2017 Network Enforcement Act. For some governments, perhaps most notably that of the United Kingdom, Big Tech's expected obligations extend to user-generated content that is 'legal but harmful', as stated in the draft Online Safety Bill, which seeks to exert an extraterritorial 'duty of care' over digital platforms' global terms of service. Identified by some as prioritizing rhetoric over evidence (Phippen and Bond, 2019), and failing to engage with user responsibility for crimes committed online (Nash, 2019), the Bill has persistently been trumpeted as 'world-leading' legislation that will hold Big Tech to account for its perceived moral and societal transgressions. Policy rhetoric has drawn on well-worn frontier imagery, the Chair of the Bill's joint parliamentary committee stating that 'we need to call time on the Wild West online', and, 'For too long, big tech has gotten away with being the land of the lawless … the era of self-regulation for big tech has come to an end'. The depiction of technology and its providers as outlaws from justice conforms to earlier government constructions of Big Tech as pro-criminal and ideologically opposed to democratic values (Baines, 2021a). Curiously, it is a phenomenon also observed in the United States, Big Tech's legal and spiritual home. In particular, recent prophecies by US law makers of an imminent 'Big Tobacco moment' for Big Tech in the wake of whistle-blower revelations on Facebook's safety and civic integrity operations consciously align legal action with reckoning and the re-establishment of government authority and control over technology.

Assertion of national sovereignty over Big Tech is nevertheless largely dependent on a government's security imperative and jurisdiction. US-based digital service providers have until now been afforded some protection from over-restriction of content by the Communications Decency Act 1996, also known as Section 230, which states that 'No provider or user of an interactive computer service shall be treated as the publisher or speaker of any information provided by another information content provider'

(47 U.S.C. §230(c)1). The Act also provides 'Good Samaritan' protection for 'any action voluntarily taken in good faith to restrict access to or availability of material that the provider or user considers to be obscene, lewd, lascivious, filthy, excessively violent, harassing, or otherwise objectionable, whether or not such material is constitutionally protected' (47 U.S.C. §230(c)2(A)). For governments outside the US, these provisions are problematic privileges that simultaneously exempt large US companies from liability for content and give them freedom to set and enforce their own terms of service without the interference of local notions of legality and morality.

For the technological hegemon itself, China presents the technological security threat. While considerably more discriminate than the Trump administration's designation of 'information and communications technology or services designed, developed, manufactured, or supplied, by persons owned by, controlled by, or subject to the jurisdiction or direction of a foreign adversary' as an 'extraordinary threat to the national security' (The White House, 2019), the Biden administration has nevertheless pressed ahead with signing into law the Secure Equipment Act 2021, which effectively prohibits Chinese companies Huawei and ZTE from selling communications infrastructure components to the US market. Big Tech conceived as external threat appears to be something of a constant, with only the company names subject to change.

Perhaps somewhat paradoxically, draft regional instruments seek to streamline national content restriction processes while also prescribing greater openness in the respects of consumer control of personal data, portability, and sovereign technological innovation. The largest US-based digital service providers are the primary targets of both the EU Digital Services Act and Digital Markets Act, identified respectively as 'very large online platforms' and 'gatekeepers'. In the former framing, providers are in scope by virtue of their size alone; in the latter, market dominance is problematized and given legal remedy. The Digital Services Act's proposed obligation for platforms to provide detailed information on reasons for content restriction (Articles 15.2.(b) and (c)) reflects an admirable drive towards greater transparency, but also presents the risk of disclosing information that 'tips off' bad actors and enables security and safety measures to be circumvented or 'gamed' (Baines, 2021b). Given that the Act mandates public disclosure of additional information on risk assessments pertaining to influence operations aimed at electoral interference (Articles 26 and 33), the possibility that these provisions will be exploited by state authorities and state-sponsored criminal groups cannot be ruled out.

Likewise, the draft Digital Markets Act's obligation on digital service providers designated as gatekeepers to 'refrain from combining personal data sourced from these core platform services with personal data from any other services offered by the gatekeeper or with personal data from third-party services' (Article 5(a)) effectively prohibits one of the predominant techniques of digital security operations at scale, namely attribution via cross-platform forensic investigation. Additional obligations on gatekeepers to allow installation of and ensure interoperability with third party software applications (Articles 6(c)) and (6(f)) raise questions over Big Tech's continued ability to combat cyber-attacks via malicious apps or misuse of their application programming interfaces (APIs). Legislation drafted with consumer choice and market contestability in mind may therefore have unintended consequences for user safety and network security. Moreover, drafting of legislation with the US tech hegemon foremost in mind, even if not explicitly named, risks regulation that may not be sufficiently applicable to e.g. Chinese digital service providers, and without clearly articulated exemptions for security at scale may even make globally popular services more vulnerable to hostile state and state-sponsored actors. Legislation intended to make the market fairer for EU consumers and businesses may in fact simply displace market dominance to and increase the threat from other non-EU states.

In their attempts to resist US technological hegemony, national and regional instruments for regulating Big Tech are more similar to the approaches of Russia and China than might be imagined or politically expedient. At the same time, even when digital service providers are themselves the object/target of regulation, there are evident touchpoints with ongoing multilateral debates over digital sovereignty and responsible behaviour in cyberspace. Platforms are misused by foreign states for influence operations with potential to interfere in democratic processes, and it has been suggested that states with tighter Internet and information controls have a strategic advantage in this field of information operations over those in which a freer Internet accords with democratic ideals (Kreps, 2021). Meanwhile, states seek to exercise or (re)gain jurisdiction over their citizens' communications on foreign digital services. Current debates over the deployment of end-to-end encryption on services such as Facebook Messenger are in one respect the latest manifestation of states' attempts to exert their data sovereignty. Tellingly, some countries such as Australia, with its Assistance and Access Act 2018, have sought a solution in regulation.

Digital Diplomatic Practice: Enabling or Complicating Factor?

As the Chinese government's broadcast via Twitter demonstrates, social media is increasingly the preferred medium for public statements about cyberspace governance and regulation of digital communications technology. Cyberspace has become the subject and the means of debate, platforms objects of regulation and vectors for discourse on that very regulation. In the process, digital diplomatic process has been coloured both by the constraints of short-form rhetoric and platform conventions that require policy makers, law makers, and diplomats to conform to rules and tools developed by mostly US and China-based companies.

As regards Big Tech regulation, the proposed UK Online Safety Bill provides a rich seam of social media content. With a dedicated Twitter account (@OnlineSafetyCom), in late 2021 the Joint Committee on the Draft Online Safety Bill displayed a cover photo of Facebook whistle-blower Frances Haugen giving evidence to a hearing of the committee, the visual rhetoric thereby celebrating the committee's aforementioned aspiration to hold Big Tech accountable. In addition to sharing highlights from its reports on these hearings, the account made statements such as 'Platforms should be made to apply laws written in the @HouseofCommons and @UKHouseofLords, not just terms and conditions written in Silicon Valley', clearly expressing the desire to assert UK sovereignty over US digital service providers. Statements made by committee members in Parliament, heart-warming content produced by children, and articles produced by mainstream media outlets were also re-tweeted.

Politicians and law makers working on tech policy issues therefore put themselves in the somewhat peculiar position of using digital communications technology to grandstand about regulating that same technology. The companies they seek to regulate enable them to draw attention to their actions and derive social capital from demonstrations of power and sovereignty. Moreover, by re-sharing content and posting video clips to increase reach and reaction, including authentic messages from children, the committee plays by the rules of social media engagement—rules that were developed by the objects of their scrutiny. Even efforts to hold Big Tech to account may be forced to dance to Big Tech's tune to some degree.

Use of digital platforms has also impacted the elaboration of international law. Where content is unmediated and not subject to official approval, short statements made by diplomats on social media can at times read as somewhat less than ideally diplomatic, as in this exchange between the Russian and UK ambassadors to the UN in Vienna concerning a postponed meeting on the proposed UN Cybercrime Convention [uncorrected text]:

> Mikhail Ulyanov @Amb_Ulyanov Jan 13, 2021 4:36 PM
>
> 1/2 Leaned with surprise that some states aren't happy with holding the 1st session of Committee on #cybercrime in January and propose to postpone it further. Is it justifiable? No. The conditions in NY are now quite permissible. No objections from the U.N. medical service.
>
> Corinne Kitsell @corinnekitsell Jan 13, 2021 4:55 PM
>
> And we learned with surprise that some states are happy to risk the health of delegates by going ahead with the meeting that cannot be described as urgent. It's certainly a shame that so many multilateral meetings have had to be postponed over the past year due to COVID.
>
> Mikhail Ulyanov @Amb_Ulyanov Jan 13, 2021 11:04 PM
>
> Valuable confession. So many meetings are taking place in the U.N. Headquaters w/o and problem, incl. for example the recent Fifth Committee in- person meetings. But in view of our Western partners it doesn't relate to the cybercrime session . Double standards as usual...

With regard to the UK's request to postpone the meeting due to travel restrictions during the Covid pandemic, Ulyanov responds, 'It seems to be a joke. What kind of expertise do we need to elect Committee's officials or adopt the draft agenda agreed in Vienna last July? Just vote.' That sovereign states' representatives to the UN get frustrated by one another's behaviour is no surprise. Less expected, perhaps, is the extent to which some of these representatives are now prepared to engage in what appears to be short-lived point scoring in front of millions of social media users worldwide. In this respect, digital diplomacy even in the context of the elaboration of international law on the misuse of digital technology—whose Russian-penned draft has proposed criminalization of misleading information—appears to assume the chief characteristics of unguarded debate on Twitter, including unmediated comments with an air of spontaneity as evidenced by spelling errors, and a less than respectful tone. At the same time, the overarching message is consistent with Ulyanov's other statements on the Convention, which celebrate Russia's authorship of the draft, claim a leading role in international cybersecurity, and demonstrate unwillingness to brook any further delay. This new, certainly less formal, short-form rhetoric makes full use of US platforms, which in turn would suggest that they are not viewed merely—or at least not entirely—as extensions of the US government, even if they do represent its technological dominance.

Theoretical Approaches to Understanding International Law on Cyberspace

International Relations theory provides several useful lenses through which to view key challenges and emergent processes of cyberspace governance. Specifically, theoretical perspectives help us to appreciate the different world views of relevant stakeholders, the space in contest, and the highly transitionary status of regulatory development.

State preoccupations with sovereignty, jurisdiction, responsibility, and othering, most visible currently in the construction of the open Internet and foreign technology as a security threat per se (Baines, 2021a), map to a realist world view that prioritizes the accumulation and exercise of power. Westphalian/Hobbesian imperatives to exercise power over citizens and territory are manifest in the plethora of initiatives at a domestic level to regulate the operations of foreign technology companies; also in the deployment of national firewalls, 'sovereign internets', and the promotion of national content standards in contributions to the Ad Hoc Committee to elaborate the UN Convention (Tikk-Ringas, 2016). China's public move on social media to hold the US government to account for the alleged errors of a commercial satellite provider aligns closely with realist conceptions of the state as primary referent and multinational corporations as subordinate.

We may also be inclined to see Morgenthau's (1985) 'drive to dominate' in the actions and reactions of states, especially the role of the United States in discounting a comprehensive Convention as unnecessary, Russia's assumption and celebration of a leading role in the drafting of a Convention text, and huge investments in 'sovereign innovation', particularly in China. Technological hegemony is a key concept in this context. While the US may be deemed to be in 'hegemonic decline' in other areas, it continues to enjoy a dominant position globally with regard to communications technology. Against this backdrop, US-backed multistakeholder initiatives for cyber norm development may be interpreted not so much as pluralist expressions of idealistic liberalism as expressions of hegemonic privilege: one can afford to be inclusive when the majority of the relevant companies are within one's jurisdiction. According to this framing, we may also see in current US/China diplomacy consciousness of imminent hegemonic decline.

At the same time, it is possible to discern evidence of Waltz's (1979) neorealist focus on systemic impact beyond national units. Targeted US anti-trust legislation or reform of the Communication Decency Act's exemption of platforms from liability for user-generated content would have consequences outside the intended domestic jurisdiction. The proposed EU Digital Markets Act and Digital Services Act may in its current form have unintended consequences for information security worldwide (Baines, 2021b). Russian and Chinese data governance legislation is assessed as posing a threat to the security of other states' commercial and personal data (Wallace, 2020).

Multistakeholder initiatives aimed at fostering responsible cyber behaviour and protecting communications infrastructure naturally align with liberal attitudes that favour a free market economy and emphasize both interdependency and pluralist ordering. This conception arguably finds legislative counterparts in suggestions that cyberspace be regulated as a global common or common heritage of mankind (Hollis, 2012; Segura-Serrano, 2006) and a range of proposals for 'international internet law', among them a common customary *ius Internet* on the model of the Roman Empire's *ius gentium* (Balleste and Kulesza, 2013) and the introduction of cyber torts (Crootof, 2018). With respect to the lenses through which stakeholders engage in deliberations on international law and cyber governance, we need only look to the terms of service and press releases of the largest US tech companies for evidence of a universalist—and arguably at times idealistic—perspective on connectivity and access to information, and the rights to and unalloyed benefits of both. The promotion of 'international standards' for online content and behaviour likewise speaks to global standardization that overlooks their interpretation by sovereign governments as primarily US speech standards imposed on the rest of the world.

That the subjects of regulation would also advocate for their involvement in shaping it is to be expected. Moreover, some of the largest technology companies, including but not exclusively those based in the US, have publicly declared their faith in a neoliberal institutionalist approach to cyber governance embodied by the ongoing UN Open-Ended Working Group and Ad Hoc Committee. More striking, perhaps, is the extent to which Big Tech has been depicted as liberal outlaw. The words of a former UK Home Secretary in a 2014 parliamentary debate on access to terrorist communications serves to illustrate:

> Lastly, may I press the Prime Minister again on the issue of the United States based internet companies and ask him to take it up with the US at the highest level? Is there

not a cultural problem among the leadership of some of these companies, which have a distorted 'libertarian' ideology and believe that somehow that allows them to be wholly detached from responsibility to Governments and to the peoples whom we democratically represent in this country and abroad?

(Hansard, Vol. 588, column 754)

Here contrast of the liberal/libertarian ideals of Big Tech on the one hand with democratic governments and their citizens on the other enables a rhetorical re-establishment of control over British cyberspace that aligns closely with regulatory development in the form of the Online Safety Bill. This and the presentation of the issue as a matter for bilateral engagement with the US government may also be seen as something of a re-assertion of realist over liberalist thinking concerning digital technology.

How, then, are we to make sense of regional regulatory developments such as those elaborated by the European Union? On the one hand, they are expressions of digital sovereignty by and on behalf of the twenty-seven Member States. On the other, greater integration in a digital single market with a holistic regional approach to data governance resembles rather liberal functionalist appreciations of complex interdependence and cooperation and Keohane's (1984) insistence that hegemons are inessential for international cooperation.

It is tempting to see in the current legal landscape something of a clash between realist and liberal ideologies. But perhaps the most important theoretical insight concerns the process itself of elaborating international law. Multiple fora and digital diplomatic practice declare cyber governance and technology regulation to be objects of continuous discourse and dialogue. In the UN processes, through multistakeholder initiatives, and on Twitter, responsible behaviour is gradually defined, norms shaped, confidence built or shaken, and capacity built. The centrality of language, negotiation, and communal creation to both soft and hard international law finds a natural paradigm in Habermas' (1984, 1987) conceptions of dialogic politics, communicative action, and discourse ethics, and their application to international relations (Linklater, 1988, 2005). The emergence and definition of cybercrimes as national security threats likewise align with social constructivist readings of the establishment of threats as 'social fact'. Existing international law may assist to some extent, but in fields as young as cyberspace and Internet governance, there has understandably been considerable focus in recent years on defining (qua constructing) responsible/acceptable behaviour by a range of stakeholders, not exclusively states.

Consideration of international law elaboration through this lens encourages us to ask further questions about the persistence of dialogic politics and discursive ethics once the terms of threats and their remedies have been 'settled'. In debate on rules, norms, and principles in the December 2021 meeting of the second Open-Ended Working Group on security of and in the use of information and communications technologies, a number of participating states and the European Union urged their counterparts to focus on implementation of the eleven norms agreed by the Group of Governmental Experts in 2015. Notwithstanding calls for additional norms from states such as Cuba and Iran, with customarily realist emphasis on sovereign equality and territorial integrity, this suggests that a tipping point may be approaching, whereby discourse on creation will give way to iterative discourse on action.

Concluding Remarks—
Future Prospects

Despite the best efforts of multiple stakeholders, it may yet prove impossible to disentangle Big Tech regulation from the elaboration of international law in and on cyberspace, and from digital diplomacy in practice. The world's largest digital service providers are targets of the first, active norms shapers and key delivery partners of the second, and media of the third. Sovereignty is a central concern in all three processes: by this very fact, non-state actors are the subjects of contention while actively seeking participation.

Regulation of digital communications technology is necessarily a foreign policy issue, as acknowledged by the EU and US in their establishment of a new ministerial level Trade and Technology Council with multiple interdependent workstreams, and as evidenced by both Russia's and the UK's attempts to demonstrate extraterritorial force over digital content: one via proposed inclusions in international law, the other by means of a planned global 'duty of care'. Conception of Big Tech regulation as a 'Big Tobacco moment' risks neglecting this complexity, not least in light of emerging technological developments. Big Tech already provides the online spaces in which everyone, diplomat and policy/law maker included, interacts. Progress towards embodied interactions in Metaverses enabled by advances in Virtual and Augmented Reality will further blur the distinction between online and offline, cyberspace and meatspace. Big Tech are already the architects of the hybrid cyber-physical 'Zoom Plus' environments in which personal, business, and political contact will occur.

Equally, national critical infrastructure's increasing reliance on foreign digital service providers is likely to accelerate in many states as advanced processing technologies such as quantum computing become accessible. A cursory review of the locations of organizations engaged in the development of quantum computing or quantum communication reveals a distribution that is dominated by European and US entities, Microsoft and Google among them. As demand increases for ever faster processing of ever larger data sets and new applications of computing, greater political power will inevitably accrue to those companies and countries who control access to enhanced processing power. Whether states will give ground to enable a more inclusive cyber governance process that accommodates non-state actors in all relevant aspects, or whether they will rein in Big Tech power, of course remains to be seen.

Nonetheless, the current fixation with regulating predominantly US Big Tech risks neglecting changes in the global technology market. The 'gatekeepers' of the future may well be based in Shenzhen or Lagos, requiring new modalities for digital diplomacy and sufficient openness and foresight in norm shaping and public international law to accommodate the possibility that technological hegemony may not last forever.

Suggested Reading

Clapham, A. 2012. *Brierly's Law of Nations: An Introduction to the Role of International Law in International Relations. Seventh Edition.* Oxford: Oxford University Press.

Efrony, D. and Shany, Y. 2018. 'A Rule Book on the Shelf? Tallinn Manual 2.0 on Cyberoperations and Subsequent State Practice'. *American Journal of International Law* 112(4): 583–657.

Kreps, S. 2021. *Social Media and International Relations.* Cambridge: Cambridge University Press.

Lowe, V. 2007. *International Law.* Clarendon Law Series. Oxford: Oxford University Press.

Moynihan, H. 2019. *The Application of International Law to State Cyberattacks: Sovereignty and Non-intervention.* London: Chatham House.

Tsagourias, N. and Buchan, R. eds. 2015. *Research Handbook on International Law and Cyberspace.* Cheltenham: Edward Elgar.

Schmitt, M. 2017. *Tallinn Manual on the International Law Applicable to Cyber Operations.* Tallinn: NATO Cooperative Cyber Defence Centre of Excellence.

References

Art, J-Y. and Emejulu, D. 2020a. *Microsoft and the United Nations Sustainable Development Goals.*https://query.prod.cms.rt.microsoft.com/cms/api/am/binary/RE4GSkV

Art, J-Y. and Emejulu, D. 2020b. *Digital Peace in Cyberspace: An Invisible Pillar for the United Nations Sustainable Development Goals.* https://query.prod.cms.rt.microsoft.com/cms/api/am/binary/RWLAhm

Austin, G., McConnell, B., and Neutze, J. 2015. *Promoting International Cyber Norms: A New Advocacy Forum.* New York: EastWest Institute.

Baines, V. 2021a. *Rhetoric of Insecurity: the Language of Danger, Fear and Safety in National and International Contexts.* London: Routledge.

Baines, V. 2021b. 'On Joined Up Law-Making: the Privacy/Safety/Security Dynamic, and What this Means for Data Governance'. *SSRN* 28 Nov 2021. https://dx.doi.org/10.2139/ssrn.3958982

Balleste, R. and Kulesza, J. 2013. 'Signs and Portents in Cyberspace: The Rise of Jus Internet as New Order in International Law'. *Fordham Intell. Prop. Media & Ent. L.J.* 23: 1311–1349.

Barlow, J. P. 1996. *A Declaration of the Independence of Cyberspace.* https://www.eff.org/cyberspace-independence.

Council of Europe. 2013. *Cybercrime Convention Committee (T-CY) Guidance Note #6: Critical Information Infrastructure Attacks (T-CY (2013)11E Rev).* Strasbourg.

Council of Europe. 2016. *Cybercrime Convention Committee (T-CY) Guidance Note #11: Aspects of Terrorism Covered by the Budapest Convention (T-CY (2016)11).* Strasbourg.

Council of Europe. 2019. *Cybercrime Convention Committee (T-CY) Guidance Note #9: Aspects of Election Interference by Means of Computer Systems Covered by the Budapest Convention (T-CY (2019)4).* Strasbourg.

Crootof, R. 2018. 'International Cybertorts: Expanding State Accountability in Cyberspace'. *Cornell L.Rev.* 103: 565–644.

Finnemore, M. and Hollis, D. B. 2016. 'Constructing Norms for Global Cybersecurity'. *American Journal of International Law* 110.3: 425–479.

Gady, F-S. and Austin, G. 2010. *Russia, The United States, and Cyber Diplomacy: Opening the Doors*. New York: EastWest Institute.

Georgieva, I. 2020. 'The Unexpected Norm-Setters: Intelligence Agencies in Cyberspace'. *Contemporary Security Policy* 41.1: 33–54.

Global Commission on the Stability of Cyberspace. 2019. *Advancing Cyberstability: Final Report November 2019*. The Hague.

Habermas, J. 1984. *The Theory of Communicative Action. Vol. I: Reason and the Rationalization of Society*. T. McCarthy (trans.). Boston: Beacon.

Habermas, J. 1987. *The Theory of Communicative Action. Vol. II: Lifeworld and System*. T. McCarthy (trans.). Boston: Beacon.

Hakmeh, J. and Peters, A. 2020. 'A New UN Cybercrime Treaty? The Way Forward for Supporters of an Open, Free, and Secure Internet'. *Council on Foreign Relations* 13 January 2020. https://www.cfr.org/blog/new-un-cybercrime-treaty-way-forward-supporters-open-free-and-secure-internet.

Henriksen, A. 2019. 'The End of the Road for the UN GGE Process: the Future Regulation of Cyberspace'. *Journal of Cybersecurity* 5.1: 1–9.

Hollinger, P. and Cookson, C. 2021. 'Musk is Being Left to Make Up Rules for Space Economy, Says European Agency', *Financial Times* 06 December 2021.

Hollis, D. B. 2012. *Stewardship versus Sovereignty? International Law and the Apportionment of Cyberspace*. Temple University Legal Studies Research Paper No. 2012–25.

Huang, Z. and Mačák, K. 2017. 'Towards the International Rule of Law in Cyberspace: Contrasting Chinese and Western Approaches'. *Chinese Journal of International Law* 16.2: 271–310.

Hurel, L. and Lobato, L. 2018. 'Unpacking Cybernorms: Private Companies as Norm Entrepreneurs'. *Journal of Cyber Policy* 3:1: 61–76.

International Law Commission. 2001. *Draft Articles on Responsibility of States for Internationally Wrongful Acts, with Commentaries*. Geneva.

Keohane, R. 1984. *After Hegemony: Cooperation and Discord in the World Political Economy*. Princeton: Princeton University Press.

Kreps, S. 2021. *Social Media and International Relations*. Cambridge: Cambridge University Press.

Linklater, A. 1988. *The Transformation of Political Community*. Oxford: Polity Press.

Linklater, A. 2005. 'Dialogic Politics and the Civilising Process'. *Review of International Studies* 31.1: 141–154.

Microsoft. 2020a. 'Our Interconnected World Requires Collective Action'. *Microsoft on the Issues* 17 September 2020. https://blogs.microsoft.com/on-the-issues/2020/09/17/micros oft-un-affairs-team-unga/.

Microsoft. 2020b. 'Why Does Microsoft Have an Office at the UN? a Q&A with the Company's UN Lead'. *Microsoft On the Issues* 05 October 2020. https://news.microsoft.com/on-the-iss ues/2020/10/05/un-affairs-lead-john-frank-unga/.

Morgenthau, H. J. 1985. *Politics among Nations*. New York: McGraw Hill.

Mueller, M. L. 2020. 'Against Sovereignty in Cyberspace'. *International Studies Review* 22.4: 779–801.

Nash, V. 2019. 'Revise and Resubmit? Reviewing the 2019 Online Harms White Paper'. *Journal of Media Law* 11.1: 18–27.

Ohlin, J. 2017. 'Did Russian Cyber Interference in the 2016 Election Violate International Law?'. *Texas Law Review* 95: 1579–1598.

Phippen, A. and Bond, E. 2019. 'The Online Harms Spearmint Paper – Just More Doing More?'. *Entertainment Law Review* 30.6: 169–173.

Schmitt, M. N. 2013. *Tallinn Manual on the International Law Applicable to Cyber Warfare*. Tallinn: NATO Cooperative Cyber Defence Centre of Excellence.

Schmitt, M. 2017. *Tallinn Manual on the International Law Applicable to Cyber Operations*. Tallinn: NATO Cooperative Cyber Defence Centre of Excellence.

Segura-Serrano, A. 2006. 'Internet Regulation and the Role of International Law'. *Max Planck Yearbook of United Nations Law Online* 10.1: 191–272.

Tikk, E. and Kerttunen, M. 2017. *The Alleged Demise of the UN GGE: An Autopsy and Eulogy*. Cyber Policy Institute: New York.

Tikk-Ringas, E. 2016. 'International Cyber Norms Dialogue as an Exercise of Normative Power'. *Georgetown Journal of International Affairs* 22.3: 47–59.

Tsagourias, N. 2019. 'Electoral Cyber Interference, Self-Determination and the Principle of Non-Intervention in Cyberspace', *EJIL Talk* 26 June 2019. https://www.ejiltalk.org/electoral-cyber-interference-self-determination-and-the-principle-of-non-intervention-in-cyberspace/.

Walden, I. 2013. 'International Telecommunications Law, the Internet and the Regulation of Cyberspace', in *Peacetime Regime for State Activities in Cyberspace: International Law, International Relations and Diplomacy*. ed. K. Ziolkowski, pp. 261–289. Tallinn: NATO Cooperative Cyber Defence Centre of Excellence.

Wallace, C. 2020. 'Dangerous Partners: Big Tech and Beijing'. *Statement Before the Senate Judiciary Committee, Subcommittee on Crime and Terrorism*. 4 March 2020. Washington, D.C.

Waltz, K. 1979. *Theory of International Politics*. New York: Random House.

Weedon, J., Nuland, W., and Stamos, A. 2017. 'Information Operations and Facebook'. 4 April 2017. https://about.fb.com/wp-content/uploads/2017/04/facebook-and-information-operations-v1.pdf.

Weinberg, J. 2000. 'ICANN and the Problem of Legitimacy'. *Duke Law Journal* 50.1: 187–260.

White House, The. 2019. *Securing the Information and Communications Technology and Services Supply Chain*, Executive Order 13873.

PART IV

DIPLOMATIC RELATIONS

CHAPTER 25

....

THE EUROPEAN UNION AND DIGITAL DIPLOMACY: PROJECTING GLOBAL EUROPE IN THE SOCIAL MEDIA ERA

....

RUBEN ZAIOTTI

INTRODUCTION

UPON taking office as the European Union's (EU) High Representative for Foreign and Defense Policy, Federica Mogherini claimed that the social media platform Twitter represented 'an extraordinary channel of diplomacy and of communication' and committed to using it as 'one of the fundamental tools of our diplomacy' (Mogherini, quoted in Mann, 2015). As a regional organization with an active presence on the world stage, the European Union has indeed embraced social media and other digital technologies as communication tools deployed to engage with foreign audiences and to project its image globally. The use of digital technology to achieve foreign policy objectives, or what is known as 'digital diplomacy' (Bjola and Holmes, 2015), has acquired a central role in EU communication strategy, and more resources and personnel have been dedicated to this policy area. This trend has accelerated during the Covid-19 pandemic, as the EU turned to 'virtual diplomacy' to manage relations among its members and the rest of the world (Maurer and Wright, 2020).

By turning to online platforms to conduct foreign policy, the European Union has followed the lead of public organizations (both national and international) that have been early adopters of digital technologies in their communicating practices (Bjola and Zaiotti, 2020). However, the Union's foray into digital diplomacy differs from other organizations' because of its hybrid institutional arrangement mixing intergovernmental and supranational characteristics and its foreign policy's decentralized structure, with EU-level actors and member states sharing responsibilities in this domain (Soetendorp, 2014). These unique features have shaped the approach and practices that constitute the field of EU digital diplomacy, from its governance (centred on the EU diplomatic unit, the European External Action Service (EEAS), but complemented with other EU units and EU member states) to the narrative it has constructed to engage with foreign audiences. In this context, digital channels of communication (websites, blogs, and social media) represent a compelling tool available to the EU to promote its 'soft power' (Nye, 1990; Cross and Melissen, 2013) in world affairs. Digital diplomacy also offers a unique opportunity for the EU to boost its external reputation (Zaiotti, 2020). Like other international organizations, the EU has limited direct sources of legitimacy, and therefore it has to rely on its performance to justify its existence (Maurer and Morgenstern-Pomorski, 2018). The latter requires a concerted effort to showcase one's achievements, a feature that digital communication platforms can provide.

Despite its newly acquired prominence, EU digital diplomacy faces various challenges in its quest for improving the regional organization' relevance and visibility on the global stage. As the latest addition to its communication and public diplomacy toolkit, the EU digital efforts suffer from a legacy of neglect and self-centredness regarding external communication, which, despite recent improvements, still negatively affects this policy domain (Spanier, 2010; Meyer, 1999; Krzyżanowski, 2012). The EU digital diplomacy is also constrained by the complexity and weakness of the Union's foreign policy. The lack of a unified voice and the limited coordination among the various actors who speak on behalf of the EU (especially member states, which maintain a degree of autonomy with regards to foreign policy) limits the ability of the organization to provide a coherent narrative about what the EU stands for. Another challenge, one that is related to the social nature of the communicative platforms used for digital diplomacy, is the still widespread lack of genuine engagement with the targeted audience, a problem that, in fairness, the EU shares with other international organizations. The EU's digital diplomacy also has to counter the growing number of online activities that openly contest the organization. Some of the forces behind these activities have a malign intent (e.g. cybercrime, trolling, misinformation; Bjola and Pamment, 2016). Others reflect the shortcomings of the EU in tackling the various internal and external crises the organization had to face in the last decade (the 'Euro crisis', the 'refugee crisis', and, more recently, the Covid-19 pandemic).

The present chapter presents an overview of the key features of the EU's digital diplomacy and the challenges it faces. The first section traces the origins and evolution of EU digital diplomacy, highlighting its connections with the organization's efforts in the realms of external communication and public diplomacy. This section introduces the main actors responsible for the planning and the implementation of the EU's digital diplomacy, namely the EEAS, EU delegations around the world, and the European Commission's departments (Directorates General) with an explicit foreign policy mandate. The second section examines the content of the EU-as-'principled and pragmatic global power' narrative that is at the core of the organization's digital diplomacy. The section also provides examples of how EU foreign policy actors have deployed this narrative through social media and other digital channels. The third section considers the challenges that EU digital diplomacy faces and the efforts made by the organization to overcome them. In concluding, the chapter looks at some directions where EU digital diplomacy is headed.

From 'Public' to 'Digital' Diplomacy: The Evolution of the European Union's External Communication

The European Union's digital communication activities aimed at engaging external stakeholders (i.e. citizens and public officials in non-EU countries) are a key component of the EU's public diplomacy (Cross and Melissen, 2013). Winning the 'hearts and minds' of foreign audiences has been recognized as a priority since foreign policy officially became an area of EU competence in the 1990s (White, 2017). In the early years of the Union's involvement in foreign affairs, however, the term *public diplomacy* was not explicitly used to describe its public relations and communication practices, as the EU was concerned about being perceived as distributing overtly political content or straightforward propaganda (Duke, 2013). Its primary efforts were put into disseminating information to foreign publics, or what Lynch calls 'a glossy "facts and figures" approach to public diplomacy' (Lynch, 2005: 24). Most of these endeavours were delivered in traditional 'analogue' formats (press releases, bulletins, publications). The digital presence of the EU was limited to websites providing information and resources on EU activities abroad.[1] The impact of this messaging was also hampered by the fragmented nature of EU external communication policy, and especially the lack of a coordinating structure and common strategy among the various actors speaking on behalf of the EU. The neglect of this policy area meant that public diplomacy remained the 'Cinderella of the EU's global engagement' (Whitman, 2005: 32).

The turning point with regards to EU public diplomacy and its digital dimension occurred with the creation of a dedicated diplomatic corps, the EEAS (Cross, 2015; Hedling, 2020). EEAS, which became operative in January 2011, was tasked with running EU delegations and offices around the world. Leaderships of EEAS was bestowed to the office of the High Representative of the EU for Foreign Affairs and Security Policy, whose profile was upgraded to include the role of European Commission's Vice President. The new unit took over some of the responsibilities with regards to

---

[1] The.*eu* internet domain was established in 2005. EU institutions adopted the *europe.eu* domain on Europe day (9 of May) in 2006 (previously they used *eu.int*).

communication and engagement with foreign publics previously held by the Secretariat of the Council of the European Union (the institution representing EU member states' interests) and the European Commission (the EU's executive agency). The EEAS was tasked to increase the visibility of the EU foreign policy 'footprint' around the world. The High Representative plays a key role in these efforts, as this office's mandate is to articulate 'clear, convincing, coherent, and mutually reinforcing messages' about EU foreign policy (quoted in Duke, 2013: 132).

The importance of public diplomacy, and external communication more generally, was recognized by the creation of a dedicated unit within EEAS, the Strategic Communication and Foresight unit. The unit is composed of three branches ('divisions'): Communications Policy and Public Diplomacy (CPPD); Strategic Communications, Tasks Forces and Information Analysis (StratCom); and Policy Planning and Strategic Foresight. The CPPD division supports the activities of the EU High Representative and communicates about EU external relations (foreign affairs, security, and defence policy). CPPD includes a 'Digital Communication' section, which is responsible for content and delivery of information through digital media.[2] StratCom and its task forces are mandated to manage communication and counter misinformation in selected regions around the world. One of this unit's primary responsibilities is coordinating the message so that all EU foreign policy actors follow the line established in Brussels. In its first configuration, StratCom consisted of a small team managing social media (two people) and the spokesperson's service (5–6 persons). It also included a dedicated task force on digital diplomacy. Over time, staff in this unit has grown substantially and currently employs fifty officers, with ten working on issues related to digital communication.

The push to digitalize EU foreign policy has been a core component of EEAS' communication strategy since the unit was created (Mann, 2015). Despite being one of the more recent additions to the EU institutional scene, EEAS was not far behind other EU units in terms of establishing a presence on social media.[3] The unit established accounts on all major social networking platforms (Twitter, Facebook, Instagram, Flickr, YouTube, Vimeo, and the VK in Russian, plus Sina Weibo and Tencent Weibo in Chinese). On Twitter, the most popular platform in EU foreign affairs, EEAS maintains an institutional account (@eu_eeas) and individual handles for the High Representatives and the spokespersons for foreign and security policy.[4] With the Mogherini tenure, the EEAS

---

[2] https://op.europa.eu/en/web/who-is-who/organization/-/organization/EEAS/EEAS_CRF_249116

[3] The European Parliament was the first EU institution with a social media presence with a Twitter account (April 2009) and a Facebook page (May 2009). The EEAS Twitter account was created in October 2009, while a Facebook page was established in May 2011. It should be noted that the creation of EAAS coincided with the popularization of social media platforms and their adoption as communication tools by public and private organizations.

[4] Followers on the official EEAS's Twitter account have grown from 94,000 in 2015 to 192,000 in 2017 and 372.000 in 2021. The High Representative's followers during the Mogherini tenure grew from 123,000 in 2015 to 347,000 in 2017. As of 2021, Mogherini's successor, Josef Borrel (who took over in 20019) has just over 200,000 followers.

introduced a Digital Diplomacy Task Force, with the specific mandate of curating the unit's social media accounts and content for the senior management (Mann, 2015).

While the EEAS is the central cog in the EU external relations' digital diplomacy machine, an essential role in this domain is played by EU delegations, as they represent EU global interest on the ground. The Lisbon Treaty gave delegations legal personality; it also expanded the scope of their activities, now covering all aspects of EU foreign policy. Besides performing 'classic' diplomatic tasks (maintaining relations with local institutions in areas such as trade, development, and scientific and technical cooperation), the delegations play a frontline role in promoting the EU image, interests, and values abroad. Public communication has therefore become a core feature of their activities. Some of the external messaging is deployed through in-person events (press conferences, talks, workshops, cultural events). More and more, however, the core of the EU delegations' communication activities occurs digitally, whether as sole medium or as complementary to the in-real-life events. To fulfil these communication tasks and reach the targeted audience (mainly within the host state), the majority of EU delegations (ninety-six out of 140 at the time of writing) have established a social media presence on the leading social networking platforms (YouTube, Twitter, FB, Fickr, Instagram). Some EU ambassadors posted outside Europe maintain personal social media accounts, mainly in countries with large populations or strategic relevance to the EU.[5] The amount of financial and human resources dedicated to digital diplomacy varies dramatically. Delegations have a press and information officer, who is typically responsible for managing the social media handles. Some of the largest delegations (i.e. Washington, Moscow, Tokyo, and Beijing[6]) have a dedicated unit for communication and are able to deliver a sleek and professional digital communication operation. In some cases, these units' mandate explicitly includes public diplomacy. The US delegation in Washington, for instance, has a Press and Public Diplomacy Section, which was established in 2006. Most of the other delegations rely on the entrepreneurial spirit of their staff (often hired locally and not part of the EU diplomatic corps) working on a small budget. Not surprisingly, the level of digital activity of EU delegations and their ambassadors and their impact around the world fluctuates dramatically.[7]

---

[5] At the time of writing, the EU ambassadors on social media are 33; see https://eeas.europa.eu/headquarters/headquarters-homepage/9005/. Special Representatives (EUSRs) constitute a sui generis category of EU emissary (Tolksdorf, 2015). The EUSRs' mandate is to collaborate with local and international partners to promote peace and stability in troubled parts of the world or support specific issues (e.g. human rights). In performing their duties, these offices promote EU interests and policies. The number of Special Representatives has fluctuated over time—the first one established in 1996—and at the time of writing they are nine, of whom some are based in the region or country they represent, and the rest in Brussels.

[6] The delegation in Moscow has a Press and Information Department; Tokyo has a Press, Public and Cultural Affairs section, while Beijing has a Press and Information Section.

[7] Other actors within the EU foreign policy family that contribute to organization's digital diplomacy are the civilian and military missions that the EU maintains around the world. These missions all have a digital presence on various social media platforms (e.g. Facebook, Twitter), and their main purpose is to

Despite their prominent role in representing the EU abroad, EEAS and EU delegations are not the only entities populating the Union's digital diplomacy universe. This is the case of the European Commission's departments (Directorates General, or DGs) with a foreign policy mandate, namely the DG for International Partnerships (INTPA)—previously DG for International Cooperation and Development (DG DEVCO)—and the DG for Trade (TRADE). The two departments are responsible for managing EU policies in their areas of competence. Part of their mandate is to communicate with the external world about what the EU does and the impact of its policies. The Directorate General for International Partnerships mission is 'to contribute to sustainable development, the eradication of poverty, peace, and the protection of human rights, through international partnerships that uphold and promote European values and interests' (INFPA, n.d.: 4). DEVCO/INTPA's social media messaging focuses on showcasing the EU action on issues related to cooperation and development, and, in particular, the value of its aid work (European Union External Action Service, 2012: 5). Its core message is geared towards promoting EU actions related to the organization's global commitments, such as the Paris Agreement on Climate Change and the United Nations 2030 Agenda and Sustainable Development Goals. The public relations work of DG TRADE builds on the reality that international trade is one of the most powerful tools in EU foreign policy, given the EU's authority in this domain, and the economic clout that the Union possesses. Traditionally, DG TRADE has emphasized macroeconomic indicators to showcase its successes in its communication practices. With the advent of social media, DG TRADE has tried to boost the appeal of international trade by emphasizing its impact on the everyday life of firms and consumers.

Projecting European Values and Principles: EU Digital Diplomacy and the Quest for International Reputation and Legitimacy

Digital media provide a valuable resource available to EU foreign policy actors to project and, in some cases, expand the European Union's power on the global stage. The EU's ability to exert such power is premised on the existence of a unique and coherent corporate identity vis-à-vis relevant stakeholders. Organizations develop a corporate identity by building a narrative about who they are and what they represent, a narrative that is typically outlined in internal strategic documents, and it is articulated publicly by their

---

inform about their activities. In their digital activities, the missions adopt a communication approach and set of guidelines similar to the ones of EU delegations.

official representatives (Mumby and Kuhn 2018[8]). Since it acquired greater autonomy with regard to foreign policy, the EU has tried to present itself as a 'normative power' in world affairs (Manners, 2002). In this perspective, the EU's global role involves a commitment to deliver peace, security, and prosperity through the promotion of justice, democracy, and human rights. These values are contrasted to traditional realpolitik in international affairs, an approach that relies on 'hard' power (i.e. military capabilities) and national interest. Key pillars of the EU alternative 'soft power' approach that emphasizes persuasion and the support for global progressive causes (e.g., peaceful resolution to disputes, green economic policies, gender equality) are presented as a reflection of the EU's core values. While states (in Europe and beyond) have advanced this normative dimension of their foreign policy, the EU has posited it at the core of its global strategy (EU, 2003). One of the appeals of this narrative is that the EU carries less baggage than its member states, especially the most powerful ones or those with colonial history (Lynch, 2005). The deterioration of the global order (i.e. the growing tensions with Russia and China) and the economic and political crises that hit the continent in the 2010s pushed the EU to reconsider its overemphasis on soft power in the conduct of its foreign policy (Riddervold et al., 2021; Michalski and Nilsson, 2019). Similarly, the growing backlash against the paternalistic approach that the EU had adopted vis-à-vis its international partners, especially those located in Europe's 'neighbourhood', persuaded EU officials to revisit the principles guiding its norm-driven foreign policy (Staeger, 2016). One of the defining elements of this new approach has been a pivot toward the concept of 'resilience' (Juncos, 2017; Tocci, 2020: 177). When applied to the realm of international relations, resilience entails 'the ability of states and societies, communities and individuals to manage, withstand, adapt, and recover from shocks and crises' (European Commission, 2012; quoted in Tocci, 2020: 177). This approach to foreign policy is meant to be more pragmatic, less prescriptive, and more engaged and transformative than earlier iterations of EU foreign policy (Tocci, 2020: 179). Indeed, in *EU Global Strategy for the foreign and security policy of the European Union*, the 2016 policy document outlining the EU's strategic vision, 'engagement' and 'partnership' are mentioned as two principles guiding EU external affairs (EEAS, 2016). This move does not involve the loss of normative principles in EU foreign policy; instead, it encourages the application of a 'realpolitik with European characteristics' (Biscop, 2016) based on 'principled pragmatism' (Tocci, 2020: 180).

EU officials have also recognized that a more sophisticated communication strategy is needed to ensure that this new foreign policy orientation is embedded in the EU's relations with its international partners. The 2016 *Global Strategy*, for instance, lists 'Strategic Communications' as a priority side by side with other more traditional tools of foreign policy. This commitment involves 'joining up public diplomacy across different fields, in order to connect EU foreign policy with citizens and better communicate it to

---

[8] As an organization's projected image, a corporate image is created for the purpose of increasing the organization's reputation (i.e. collective beliefs about organization held by external stakeholders; Orlitzky et al., 2003). In this sense, the creation of a corporate identity is consistent with what in marketing is called 'branding'.

our partners' (EEAS, 2016). Digital tools, including social media, are central to this communication strategy. Since the early 2010s, EU foreign policy officials posted around the world have been urged to deliver online content that reflects the EU's credentials as a pragmatic and principled foreign policy actor (Manners and Whitman, 2013: 189). According to the 'Information and Communication Handbook for EU Delegations', the internal document drafted in December 2012 by EEAS' Strategic Communication division in collaboration with DG DEVCO, the delegations are asked to relay information that is 'inspired by the promotion of EU values and based on the delivery of peace, security and prosperity' (EEAS, 2012). The emphasis should, in turn, be that of promoting the EU as 'a major partner in democratic transition', 'the world's biggest co-operation and development donor', a 'global economic power', a promoter of human rights, and 'a security provider responding to global security threats' (2012). These tenets have underpinned social media campaigns elaborated by the communication units in concomitance to special events or EU-led initiatives. The issuing *Global Strategy* was accompanied by a dedicated digital campaign on the various EEAS-run social media accounts. The 'European Way' campaign, which was launched in March 2017, used hashtags such as *#EuropeanWay*, *#EUGS*, or *#EUGlobalStrategy* to raise awareness about the EU foreign policy priorities and the implications for stakeholders (Hedling, 2020: 149). Another example of the attempts to diffuse the EU foreign policy narrative can be seen in social media communicative practices related to the theme of gender (Wright and Guerrina, 2020). This theme is a flagship in the Union's normative-driven foreign policy, one in which Europe presents itself not only as an example to follow but also as a supporter of gender causes abroad (MacRae, 2010: 157). Posts related to gender matters are a recurring feature in EEAS social media accounts, especially around special events (e.g., International Women's Day; the EU at sixty celebrations; Wright and Guerrina, 2020).

Digital diplomacy does not only help diffuse the EU's identity as global actor; it also allows the organization to defend, and possibly boost, its global reputation (Zaiotti, 2020). By facilitating direct communication with a global audience, digital platforms allow the EU to project a positive narrative about the organization and showcase its accomplishments. At the same time, social media offer a channel for audiences to engage directly with the EU and express their opinions, thus providing useful feedback on the organization's performance. Besides boosting its reputation, digital communicative tools provide a source of legitimacy for the European Union. The narrative that EU foreign policy actors reproduce becomes a legitimating process since it reminds the public of the positive contribution that the EU's foreign policy provides (Cooper, 2019; Hedling, 2020: 149). This is particularly relevant since the EU suffers similar structural problems affecting other international organizations, namely the lack of direct, bottom-up sources of legitimization. The EU, as a result, has to rely on the assessment of its 'output', namely what it does, and how, to determine its legitimacy (Steffek, 2015). The emphasis on outputs as a source of legitimization is apparent in the EU's digital communication related to its activities in the economic realm. In its social media strategy, DG TRADE has tried to boost the appeal of international trade by emphasizing its impact on the everyday life of firms and consumers. It has therefore embraced what commentators have called 'Trade Policy 2.0'. An example of these efforts was the social media campaign during the Canada–EU Comprehensive Economic Trade Agreement (CETA) ratification process. The DG TRADE communication team created a Twitter hashtag #CETAcomes2town (Cernat, 2018). It complemented this campaign by posting infographics and entries with references to examples of European-made products that could be appealing for a North American market. The department has employed a similar approach for other trade agreements, using the hashtag #FTAcomes2town. These types of campaigns are occurring in a global climate that has become more hostile to international trade, and therefore more needed to boost EU economic interests.

The EU has historically been shielded from popular scrutiny, and, as a result, the issue of legitimacy has been relatively invisible as a subject in public and academic debates. Of late, however, attention to its actions has increased due to the various 'crises' it has faced. As a result, the EU has become more active in seeking popular support. As a popular means of communication, social media represent a novel source for the discursive practices of legitimation (Denskus and Esser, 2013). These practices, which can take the form of anything from individual social media posts of influential foreign policy actors to full-fledged social media campaigns, have become a central component of EU digital diplomacy. Indeed, the quest for greater legitimacy was at the core of one of the most compelling examples of EU digital diplomacy to date, namely the Union's involvement in the negotiations over the Iran nuclear deal (Blockmans and Viaud, 2017). In these negotiations, which started in 2013 and were concluded in 2015, the EU's High Representative, together with other international partners (known as the P5 + 1, i.e., the five permanent members of the United Nations Security Council plus Germany) engaged with the Iranian authorities to achieve an agreement on how to manage Iran's efforts to acquire nuclear capabilities. Although these talks were held behind closed doors, the EU maintained a direct channel of communication via social media (mostly Twitter) throughout this time. With the hashtag #IranTalks, the High Representative (HR) regularly updated journalists and the public on the state of the negotiations through tweets and the insertion of 'behind the scenes' images of key players at work. The content of tweets was mostly generic rather than including details about the content of the discussions. The stated objective of these digital communication practices was to control the message and avoid misinformation. Yet, this communication also provided a (not so subtle) means to boost the legitimacy and reputation of the EU, and the HR (Federica Mogherini) more specifically. As the EEAS official running the account explicitly admits, this communication was aimed at 'carefully reflecting the HR/VP's role as facilitator of the talks'.[9] This role, combined with a proactive presence on social media, meant that the HR could grow her social media profile. She was able to grab the attention of a larger audience. The news of the Iran deal was announced on HR's Twitter account, and the tweet became the most popular item issued on the platform.

---

[9] https://twiplomacy.com/blog/the-european-external-action-service-and-digital-diplomacy/

Challenges in EU Digital Diplomacy: The Quest for Coordination and Coherence

The Lisbon Treaty and the creation of EEAS raised the prospect for greater institutional coherence and consistency in EU external communication. It also provided a framework for the emergence of a common 'communication culture' spanning all the EU foreign policy institutions (Duke, 2013: 10). Indeed, the number of voices speaking for the EU was reduced (e.g., the elimination of a rotating presidency). Practical steps were taken to coordinate communication and public diplomacy within the foreign policy establishment. These efforts included strengthening the collaboration with the EU 'internal' communication units, and in particular with the European Commission's DG Communication. After the Lisbon Treaty, this task fell to the newly established External Relations Information Committee (ERIC), which brought together the Commission's communications units and, unlike its predecessor (RIC), is now responding to the Strategic Communications Division in the EEAS.

Related to the issue of coordination, another task the EU has taken up is that of improving the coherence of its external communication. This topic is explicitly mentioned in the 2016 EU Global Strategy. The document called for action to 'improve the consistency and speed of messaging on our principles and actions', both in terms of factual rebuttals of disinformation and 'fostering an open and inquiring media environment within and beyond the EU' (EEAS, 2016: 23). This 'retooling' of external communication is apparent in the approach the EU has taken regarding content delivery on digital platforms. In 2020, the DG for International Partnerships issued 'Digital Content Guidelines', a manual directed at EU delegations and external service providers.[10] These actors are encouraged to promote the EU through 'positive, inspiring and challenging communication, which is values-driven and impact-focused'. The 'European values' it envisions are sustainability, equality, democracy, human rights, and partnership (INTPA, 2020: 5). The principles that this messaging should follow are 'professional yet human (...) complete yet concise (...) sincere yet positive'.

Despite these efforts at achieving greater coherence, the EU's digital diplomacy is still riddled with obstacles that limit its effectiveness. The first has to do with the continued existence of a plethora of actors speaking on behalf of the EU on the world stage. Some of these actors fall under the EU common foreign and security policy mandate (the President of the European Council, the High Representative, the EEAS, and the member states), others under the Commission (the President of the Commission and Directorates General with an external mandate). Even within the External Action Service, multiple hands are on the communication file. In the original plans leading to

---

[10] DG INTPA, Digital Style Guide, December 2020.

the creation of EEAS, the High Representative was assigned a department for information and public diplomacy. This department did not materialize, and the public diplomacy file was instead scattered within EEAS (Duke, 2013). Member states also continue to have an active voice in matters of EU external communication. Their influence is exerted through the Political and Security Committee (PSC), a unit within the European Union dealing with common foreign and security policy issues.[11] In its remit, the PSC negotiates 'master messages' for civilian missions, and 'communication strategies' for military missions, all of which need to be approved by member states.

Since the creation of EEAS and the move to digital communication, the EU has pledged to streamline how the organization engages with the rest of the world. Rather than relying on a traditional approach based on strategic communication, the emphasis is now on a more nuanced and engaged method. As a communication expert at EEAS put it:

> It is about different things, using different channels, different events, communication strategies and public affairs but the central thing is that this is no longer about informing it is about explaining, engaging and listening.
>
> (Quoted in Hedling, 2020: 148).

The digitalization of EU external communication, however, has not eliminated the organization's old habits. Indeed, this shift might have actually reinforced the deep-seated dispositions in EU communicative practices (Krzyżanowski, 2020). One of these dispositions is that of tightly controlling the messages that EU delegations and other EU foreign policy actors sent to the outside world. Social media content must be approved by the External Action Services' headquarters in Brussels ahead of time. The broadcasting of pre-approved messages is acceptable, but not public interactions that could derail delicate negotiations. While this control is common to other foreign policy actors, especially foreign affairs ministries, the EU must tread a finer line, as it must ensure it does not breach the delicate balance of consensus among the twenty-seven members.

Other problems persist regarding how the EU engages its global audience in the digital realm. Looking at the EEAS' 'footprint' on social media (Facebook, Flickr, Twitter), we notice a degree of interactivity ('likes', re-tweets, and comments). Yet, these efforts fall short of continued engagement. Only a few comments posted on the EEAS handles contain a reply from the administrators. The attempts to project a normative foreign policy through digital channels are also underwhelming. In their study covering social media activity during International Women's Day and the EU's sixtieth anniversary in 2017, Wright and Guerrina (2020) found that the EU did not effectively integrate gender equality in its digital diplomacy, keeping it on the margins of

---

[11] PSC, which is based in Brussels, consists of ambassadorial-level representatives from all the EU member states and is chaired by the EEAS.

EU external communication practices. Another challenge the EU digital diplomacy faces is the growing level of scrutiny and contestation that social media platforms have brought. Like other international organizations active on the world stage, the EU has been historically shielded from popular scrutiny. As a result, the EU has rarely been an object of contention in global public discourse (Ecker-Ehrhardt, 2017). However, the growth of the EU's role in world affairs, and the visibility that it has brought, have led to greater politicization of the organization, and with it, the potential for criticism (Zürn et al., 2012: 71). More and more, this criticism has been delivered through digital channels. As a popular means of expressing opinions, social media have become a powerful tool of political contestation, especially when coming from civil society (Zaiotti, 2020). Social media have also been used to spread misinformation about the EU (Bentzen, 2019; Scheidt, 2019; Vériter et al., 2020). When faced with open contestation, the EU, like other organizations in similar situations, have felt compelled to respond to avoid further negative backlash, with a view to rebuilding the trust of their audience (Bentzen, 2019). Fighting misinformation online is a central component of the EU cybersecurity strategy.[12] The EU has set up a dedicated agency whose task is to contain or prevent malicious efforts carried out on social media and other digital platforms. The *European Network and Information Security Agency* (ENISA), originally established in 2004, has seen its mandate and resources boosted in recent times. Responding to critical situations is particularly needed for organizations such as the EU since it relies heavily on output legitimacy. Yet, the core component for a successful response to a crisis is to focus on its communication strategy, which involves being open to external feedback and adjustments of actions to reflect the public mood (Steffek, 2015: 275). To date, however, most of the focus of EU action has been internal (i.e., on misinformation within the EU), and limited resources have been allocated to the external dimension.

The EU management of its global reputation through digital channels has also been underwhelming and overtly passive in the face of the series of economic and political crises the EU faced in recent times (Zaiotti, 2020). These crises—from the one involving the Euro in the early 2010s ('Eurozone crisis'), to the surge in migration flows around Europe's south-eastern borders in the summer of 2015 ('refugee crisis'), to the Covid-19 pandemic in 2020—were 'internal' matters, as they affected the stability of the European integration project; they nonetheless had important 'external' implications, because they threatened to tarnish the global image of the EU as a successful political project and a model to follow elsewhere (Nedergaard, 2018; Georgiou and Zaborowski, 2017). EU officials acknowledged that these events negatively affected the EU brand. At the height of the refugee crisis, for instance, then High Representative for Foreign Affairs and Security policy of the EU, Federica Mogherini, stated that EU action on the issue

---

[12] European Commission 2020, 'Joint Communication to the European Parliament and the Council: The EU's Cybersecurity Strategy for the Digital Decade', JOIN (2020) 18 final. Available at: https://eur-lex.europa.eu/legal-content/EN/TXT/PDF/?uri=CELEX:52020JC0018&from=ga

of the refugee crisis 'greatly weakens our credibility abroad'.[13] The EU public diplomacy machine, however, did not effectively mount a consistent effort to address this challenge by engaging the public on the meaning of these crises and the responses by the EU. As a result, these issues were mostly ignored in the digital communication conducted by EEAS officials in Brussels and delegations around the world (Zaiotti, 2020).

CONCLUSIONS: OVERCOMING THE CAPABILITY-EXPECTATIONS DIGITAL GAP

The EU as an organization has been slow in realizing that actively engaging with foreign audiences was a crucial component in its efforts to become a prominent actor in foreign affairs. Because of its recent emergence and difficult gestation, EU foreign policy has been conservative and inward-looking. The creation of a dedicated foreign policy service changed this stance. The concomitant emergence of social media and their embracing by foreign policy actors meant that the EU had to become more proactive in the digital domain. The EU has recognized that digital platforms are an essential tool in contemporary world affairs for the purpose of communicating and engaging with the outside world, particularly foreign audiences. Arguably, the EU needs to rely on these platforms more than other policy actors, given its still-limited visibility and ability to influence world affairs through traditional diplomatic means. The EU has made important strides in upgrading its digital presence, as witnessed by its active involvement in various social media platforms. The EU has also made efforts to provide a more coherent message to be conveyed on these platforms and to rationalize the management of its external communication.

The EU's efforts in digital diplomacy, however, still face serious hurdles. The main challenges have to do with the enduring cacophony of voices speaking for the EU, the tension with its 'internal' public diplomacy (i.e. engaging with EU stakeholders within Europe), and the still underwhelming level of coordination among all these actors. These lingering problems raise the question of whether the solutions the EU has pursued (striving for greater centralization, common message) might not actually be wrongly conceived or even deleterious. In the absence of a well-defined strategic view, a path to follow might be greater decentralization, with more direct involvement of EU delegations in shaping the EU's message, core themes, and engagement strategies (Duke, 2013: 33). The rivalry between member states and the EU foreign policy apparatus might be managed more effectively if the emphasis is put on the complementarity

---

[13] 'Mogherini: EU will lose its reputation because of refugee crisis', Meta MK, 25 September 2015, Available at http://meta.mk/en/mogerini-eu-go-gubi-ugledot-poradi-begalskata-kriza/

of their actions. It should be noted that EU member states' public diplomacy strategies typically include a reference to boosting the Union's global profile, and it would not be unreasonable to expect that this could also be done for its digital counterpart.

Complementarity could also be the way ahead to overcome the tensions between efforts to engage stakeholders in Europe and beyond. The internal and external dimensions of EU digital diplomacy are not incompatible. Indeed, in both cases the purpose is, as the European Commission puts it, that of 'promot(ing) EU interests by understanding, informing and influencing. It means clearly explaining the EU's goals, policies and activities and fostering understanding of these goals through dialogue with individual citizens, groups, institutions and the media' (European Commission, 2007: 12). Establishing a cogent narrative about what the EU represents aimed at individuals residing within Europe can also provide a model and a boost for efforts to project this identity to the rest of the world. In this reading, digital diplomacy should be considered as a type of 'intermestic' domain, one that merges domestic and international dimensions.

The case for greater digitalization of EU foreign policy should not be overstated, however. Social media have been hailed as having a positive impact on private and public organizations in terms of meeting their mandates and performing their functions (Collins and Bekenova, 2019; Sandre, 2015); yet it is not clear this assessment applies to foreign policy, and particularly for the EU, given its sui generis status. For all this talk about digitalization as the future of EU foreign policy, digital tools might not be the solution to EU foreign policy problems after all; on the contrary, there are inherent tensions with these tools that might be detrimental to the success of the EU on the world stage (Hedling, 2018). Some of these issues have to do with the very characteristics of social media. While social media platforms promote a more visible digital presence, their decentralized, informal, and personal nature, combined with their capacity to multiply the number of voices who speak on behalf of an organization, means that the message they convey can come across as inconsistent and confusing, and, as a result, it weakens their efforts at projecting a coherent identity (Bjola and Zaiotti, 2020). In this way, social media can exacerbate an inherent tension that characterizes the EU's identity, namely the one between the EU's quest for a collective sense of community and member states' emphasis on their unique features and histories. There are also questions about the compatibility of digital channels and EU foreign policy. Part of the reason is that, unlike domestic politics, foreign policy in general is resistant to what Brommesson and Ekengren (2020) call the 'media logic'. As the authors put it:

> Foreign policy is traditionally seen as a conservative policy area characterized by caution and prudence. Because foreign policy decisions are frequently made in small, closed groups, it is not publicly debated as frequently as other policy areas. Foreign policy issues are therefore less public and debate in the media is more limited. These characteristics stand in sharp contrast to the media logic, with its short-sightedness and focus on individual cases along with its sensationalism rather than long-term perspective.
>
> (Brommesson and Ekengren, 2020: 3–18)

This characterization does not imply that mediatization of foreign policy never occurs, but only under certain circumstances, which depend on contexts, time periods, and types of questions (Brommesson and Ekengren, 2020).

The EU is not unique in its struggles to use digital diplomacy effectively. Indeed, other organizations (including international organizations) are in a similar predicament. For digital diplomacy, however, as it is the case for other aspects of its foreign policy, the EU suffers an additional handicap, namely the digital version of what is known in the EU foreign policy literature as the 'capability-expectations gap' (Hill, 1993). This term refers to the belief that the EU should be able to perform its duties as a major foreign policy power, given its size and its constituent parts' political and economic prowess. Since the EU presents itself as a progressive, future-oriented entity at the forefront of innovation, it has raised the expectation that it should be a leader in digital diplomacy as well. In reality, the resources allocated to support these efforts, and still-limited autonomy of the EU in foreign affairs, means that these expectations have not been met. Until this gap is bridged, the EU digital tools might not turn out to be such 'an extraordinary channel of diplomacy' for the EU as Mogherini envisioned them.

Suggested Reading

Bjola, C., and Zaiotti, R. (eds.). (2020). *Digital Diplomacy and International Organisations: Autonomy, Legitimacy and Contestation*. London: Routledge.

Brommesson, D., and Ekengren, A. M. (2020). EU Foreign and Security Policy in a Mediatized Age. In: Bakardjieva Engelbrekt, A., Bremberg, N., Michalski, A., and Oxelheim, L. (eds.) *The European Union in a Changing World Order* (pp. 193–215). Cham: Palgrave Macmillan.

Cross, M. K. (2015). The Public Diplomacy Role of the EEAS: Crafting a Resilient Image for Europe. In: Spence, D.id and Bátora, J.F. (eds.) *The European External Action Service* (pp. 341–355). London: Palgrave Macmillan.

EEAS. (2016). *Shared Vision, Common Action: A Stronger Europe. A Global Strategy for the European Union's Foreign and Security Policy*. Available at http://europ a.eu/globalstra tegy/ en/global-strategy-foreign-and-security-policy-european-union

Hedling, E. (2021). Transforming practices of diplomacy: the European External Action Service and digital disinformation. *International Affairs*, 97(3), 841–859.

Valentini, C. (2020). The European Union and Its Public Relations: Context, Actions, and Challenges of a Supranational Polity. In: Sriramesh, K., and Verčič, D. (eds.) *The Global Public Relations Handbook: Theory, Research, and Practice* (3rd Edition, pp. 120–130).

References

Bentzen, N. (2019). *Online Disinformation and the EU's Response*. European Parliamentary Research Service.

Biscop, S. (2016). The EU Global Strategy: Realpolitik with European Characteristics. *Egmont Security Policy Brief No.75*. Brussels: Egmont Institute.

Bjola, C., & Pamment, J. (2016). Digital containment: Revisiting containment strategy in the digital age. *Global Affairs*, 2(2), 131–142.

Bjola, C., and Holmes, M. (2015). *Digital Diplomacy: Theory and Practice*. London: Routledge.

Bjola, C., and Zaiotti, R. (eds.). (2020). *Digital Diplomacy and International Organisations: Autonomy, Legitimacy and Contestation*. London: Routledge.

Blockmans, S., and Viaud, A. (2017). EU Diplomacy and the Iran Nuclear Deal: Staying power? *CEPS Policy Insights No 2017-28/14 July 2017*.

Brommesson, D., and Ekengren, A. M. (2020). EU Foreign and Security Policy in a Mediatized Age. In: Bakardjieva Engelbrekt, A., Bremberg, N., Michalski, A., and Oxelheim, L. (eds.) *The European Union in a Changing World Order* (pp. 193–215). Cham: Palgrave Macmillan.

Cernat, L. (2018). How to make trade policy cool (again) on social media? European Centre for International Political Economy (ECIPE) Blog, May 2018. Available at https://ecipe.org/blog/how-to-make-trade-policy-cool-again-on-social-media/

Collins, N., and Bekenova, K. (2019). Digital diplomacy: Success at your fingertips. *Place Branding and Public Diplomacy*, 15(1), 1–11.

Cooper, I. (2019). The Inter-Parliamentary Conferences of the European Union: discussion forums or oversight bodies? In: Kolja Raube, K., Müftüler-Baç, M. and Wou, J. (eds.) *Parliamentary Cooperation and Diplomacy in EU External Relations* (pp. 139–157).

Cross, M. K. (2015). The Public Diplomacy Role of the EEAS: Crafting a Resilient Image for Europe. In: Spence, D., and Bátora, J. (eds.) *The European External Action Service* (pp. 341–355). London: Palgrave Macmillan.

Cross, M. K. D., and Melissen, J. (2013). *European Public Diplomacy* (pp. 111–112). New York: Soft Power at Werk.

Denskus, T., and Esser, D. E. (2013). Social media and global development rituals: a content analysis of blogs and tweets on the 2010 MDG Summit. *Third World Quarterly*, 34(3), 405–422.

Duke, S. (2013). The European External Action Service and Public Diplomacy. In: *European Public Diplomacy* (pp. 113–136). New York: Palgrave Macmillan.

Ecker-Ehrhardt, M. (2018). Self-legitimation in the face of politicization: Why international organizations centralized public communication. *The Review of International Organizations*, 13(4), 519–546.

EEAS. (2016). *Shared Vision, Common Action: A Stronger Europe. A Global Strategy for the European Union's Foreign and Security Policy*. Available at http://europ a.eu/globalstra tegy/en/global-strategy-foreign-and-security-policy-european-union

EEAS. (2017). *The European Way*. Available at https://eeas.europa.eu/headquarters/headquart ers-homepage/search/site_en?f%5B0%5D=im_field_tags%3A899

European External Action Service (2016). Shared Vision, Common Action: A Stronger Europe - A Global Strategy for the European Union's Foreign and Security Policy.

European Commission. (2007). *A Glance at EU Public Diplomacy at Work: The EU's 50th Anniversary Celebrations around the World*. Luxembourg: Office for Official Publications of the European Communities.

European Commission. (2020). Joint communication to the European parliament and the council–the EU's cybersecurity strategy for the digital decade. JOIN (2020) 18 Final.

European Union (2003). *A Secure Europe in a Better World - European Security Strategy*. Brussels, 12 December 2003.

European Union External Action Service (2012). *Information and Communication: Handbook for EU Delegations in Third Countries and to International Organisations*.

European Union. (2017, November 27). Public Diplomacy (working definition). Retrieved from https://europa.eu/capacity4dev/pd-cd/wiki/public-diplomacy-working-definition

Georgiou, M., and Zaborowski, R. (2017). *Media Coverage of the "Refugee Crisis": A Cross-European Perspective*. Council of Europe.

Hedling, E. (2018). *Blending Politics and New Media: Mediatized Practices of EU Digital Diplomacy* (No. 193). Lund University.

Hedling, E. (2020). Storytelling in EU public diplomacy: Reputation management and recognition of success. *Place Branding and Public Diplomacy, 16*(2), 143–152.

Hill, C. (1993). The capability-expectations gap, or conceptualizing Europe's international role. *Journal of Common Market Studies, 31,* 305–328(3)

INFPA – Directorate General International Partnership (n.d.). "Our Mission".https://international-partnerships.ec.europa.eu/our-mission_en

Juncos, A. (2017). Resilience as the new EU foreign policy paradigm: A pragmatist turn? *European Security, 26,* 1–18. doi:10.1080/09662839.2016.1247809

Krzyzanowski, M. (2012). (Mis) Communicating Europe?: On Deficiencies and Challenges in Political and Institutional Communication in the European Union. In *Intercultural Miscommunication Past and Present* (pp. 185–213). Peter Lang Pub.

Krzyżanowski, M. (2020). Digital Diplomacy or Political Communication? Exploring Social Media in The EU Institutions from a Critical Discourse Perspective 1. In: Bjola, C., and Zaiotti, R. (eds.) *Digital Diplomacy and International Organisations* (pp. 52–73). Routledge.

Lynch, D. (2005). Communicating Europe to the world: what public diplomacy for the EU?', EPC Working Paper No. 21, November 2005, pp. 40–62.

MacRae, H. (2010). The EU as a gender equal polity: Myths and realities. JCMS: Journal of Common Market Studies, 48(1), 155–174.

Mann, M. (2015). The European External Action Service and digital diplomacy. Twiplomacy Blog Post, 28 April 2015. Available at http://twiplomacy.com/blog/the-european-external-action-service-and-digital-diplomacy/

Manners, I. (2002). Normative power Europe: A contradiction in terms? *Journal of Common Market Studies, 40*(2), 235–258.

Manners, I., and Whitman, R. (2013). Normative Power and the Future of EU Public Diplomacy. In: Cross, M.K.D., and Melissen, J. (eds.) *European Public Diplomacy: Soft Power at Work* (pp. 183–203). Basingstoke: Palgrave Macmillan.

Maurer, H., and Wright, N. (2020). A new paradigm for EU diplomacy? EU Council negotiations in a time of physical restrictions. *The Hague Journal of Diplomacy, 15*(4), 556–568.

Maurer, H., and Morgenstern-Pomorski, J.-H. (2018). The quest for internal legitimacy: The EEAS, EU delegations and the contested structures of European diplomacy. *Global Affairs, 4*(2–3), 305–316.

Meyer, C. (1999). Political legitimacy and the invisibility of politics: Exploring the European Union's communication deficit. *JCMS: Journal of Common Market Studies, 37*(4), 617–639.

Michalski, A., and Nilsson, N. (2019). Resistant to change? The EU as a normative power and its troubled relations with Russia and China. *Foreign Policy Analysis, 15*(3), 432–449.

Mumby, D. K., and Kuhn, T. R. (2018). *Organizational Communication: A Critical Introduction*. Sage Publications.

Nedergaard, P. (2019). Borders and the EU legitimacy problem: the 2015–16 European Refugee Crisis. *Policy Studies, 40*(1), 80–91.

Nye, J. S. (1990). Soft power. *Foreign Policy, 80,* 153–171.

Orlitzky, M., Schmidt, F. L., & Rynes, S. L. (2003). Corporate social and financial performance: A meta-analysis. *Organization Studies*, 24(3), 403–441.

Riddervold, M., Trondal, J., and Newsome, A. (2021). Crisis and EU Foreign and Security Policy: An Introduction. In: Riddervold, M., Trondal, J., and Newsome, A. (eds.) *The Palgrave Handbook of EU Crises* (pp. 545–552). Cham: Palgrave Macmillan.

Sandre, A. (2015). *Digital Diplomacy: Conversations on Innovation in Foreign Policy*. Rowman & Littlefield

Scheidt, Melanie (2019). The European Union versus external disinformation campaigns in the midst of information warfare: Ready for the battle? *College of Europe EU Diplomacy Paper 01/2019*, pp. 1–33.

Soetendorp, B. (2014). *Foreign Policy in the European Union: Theory, History and Practice*. London: Routledge.

Spanier, B. (2010). *The 'Communication Deficit' of the European Union Revisited. Structures, Key Players and the New Communication Policy* (Doctoral dissertation, University of Zurich).

Staeger, U. (2016). Africa–EU relations and normative power Europe: A decolonial pan-African critique. *JCMS: Journal of Common Market Studies*, 54(4), 981–998.

Steffek, J. (2015). The output legitimacy of international organizations and the global public interest. *International Theory*, 7(2), 263–293.

Tocci, N. (2020). Resilience and the role of the European Union in the world. *Contemporary Security Policy*, 41(2), 176–194.

Tolksdorf, D. (2015). Diplomacy at the Individual Level: The Role of EU Special Representatives in European Foreign Policy. In: Koops J.A., and Macaj G. (eds.) *The European Union as a Diplomatic Actor* (pp. 69–87). The European Union in International Affairs Series. London: Palgrave Macmillan.

Vériter, S. L., Bjola, C., and Koops, J. A. (2020). Tackling COVID-19 disinformation: Internal and external challenges for the European Union. *The Hague Journal of Diplomacy*, 15(4), 569–582.

White, B. (2017). *Understanding European Foreign Policy*. Macmillan International Higher Education.

Whitman, R. (2005). Winning Hearts and Minds for Europe. In: Youngs, R. (ed.) *GLOBAL EUROPE Report 2: New Terms of Engagement* (pp. 30–37) London: Foreign Policy Centre/British Council/European Commission.

Wright, K. A., and Guerrina, R. (2020). Imagining the European Union: Gender and digital diplomacy in European external relations. *Political Studies Review*, 18(3), 393–409.

Zaiotti, R. (2020). The (UN) making of international organisations' digital reputation: The European Union, the "refugee crisis," and social media. In *Digital Diplomacy and International Organisations* (pp. 207–226). Routledge.

Zürn, M., Binder, M., & Ecker-Ehrhardt, M. (2012). International authority and its politicization. *International Theory*, 4(1), 69–106.

CHAPTER 26

NATO's DIGITAL DIPLOMACY

KATHARINE A. M. WRIGHT

INTRODUCTION

THE focus of this chapter is on NATO's digital diplomacy and its move from the 'stone age' towards a sophisticated engagement through the employment of strategic narratives to shape specifically the alliance's own identity narrative, issue narratives (from Women, Peace, and Security (WPS) to the Russia–Ukraine War), and system-level narratives (what is NATO's role and relevance in the world). The way in which war is mediated through television and media (and now social media) means that this is where the battles over 'legitimacy, effectiveness, and consequences are fought' (Behnke, 2002), bringing to the fore the importance of digital diplomacy. To understand the role of digital diplomacy, we also need to understand the wider environment and context in which it operates and how NATO has evolved from a Cold War defensive alliance to the globally engaged actor we see today.

NATO: Between 'Values' and 'Realpolitik'

NATO has moved significantly beyond its Cold War origins, to expand into crisis management and cooperative security, for example, with involvement in Afghanistan, Libya, and Kosovo. NATO's remit has therefore expanded from a regional one to a global one. However, more recently, and in the face of Russian aggression and their full-scale invasion of Ukraine, the alliance's founding purpose has come to the fore again, with a promise to provide collective defence to its members under Article 5 of the Washington Treaty with: 'an armed attack against one . . . considered an attack against them all'. It has also expanded from an alliance of fifteen to one of thirty one, soon to be thirty-two with Sweden's accession. NATO is a political-military alliance built on consensus, with the 'pecking order' and hierarchy underpinning NATO decision making, making it particularly successful in terms of producing outcomes, with relations among allies remaining harmonious despite its large membership. Its status as a multilateral institution means it is limited by its members' priorities and therefore sensitive not to implicate NATO or NATO member states in wrong doing.

Since Russia's full-scale invasion of Ukraine in 2022, NATO has moved from the margins to the centre of global politics. As a result, questions over the relevance of NATO to the contemporary security environment are perceived by many as now null and void; NATO is at front and centre of the news and in debates on the West's response to the full-scale Russian invasion of Ukraine. In this sense it could be argued that we are seeing a move away from the alliance framed 'in terms of democracy, freedom, and "European values"', which characterized the accession processes in Central and Eastern Europe, in a dichotomy embodying the banal/common-sense/boring and the existential/essential above debate (Kuus, 2007: 269), and a return to a projection of NATO as a military power. NATO no longer needs to project its relevance in the same way, with a military response accepted by many as the default means to provide security in the current situation and in response to Russian aggression. Yet digital diplomacy remains important for the alliance as a communication tool whether it is responding to a situation in a collective defence or crisis response mode.

Digital Diplomacy

Digital diplomacy remains a contested concept, as does its impact on global politics. On the one hand there are those who argue that digital diplomacy remains a new tool to achieve the traditional goals of diplomacy; on the other are those who contend 'it has caused a paradigmatic shift, completely changing the environment and conduct of diplomacy and the role of diplomats' (Bjola and Holmes, 2015: 542). It has provided an important platform through which international organizations can articulate their identity narrative, reaching publics but also through engaging in building diplomatic relations with other global actors. The digitization of diplomacy has also enabled the circumnavigation of traditional routes of information dissemination through the media, allowing actors to engage directly with consumers, even if the traditional media also remains a key receptor of digital narratives (Wright and Bergman Rosamond, 2021). It has also transformed the practice of public diplomacy, providing instantaneous access to domestic and foreign publics without the media as a mediator. Yet as Elsa Hedling and Niklas Bremberg (2021: 1613) argue, digital diplomacy is far more than the use of Twitter by state leaders, it has become a 'fundamental dimension of contemporary international politics'. In this sense, it is necessary to resist conceptualizing it just as a subfield of diplomacy, but rather to integrate it into broader IR theories (Hedling and Bremberg, 2021: 1613). This chapter takes up that call, asking what strategic narratives can tell us about NATO's approach to digital diplomacy through its practice of public diplomacy in the digital sphere, including on social media.

In addition, in times of crisis, digital diplomacy plays a crucial role; social media posts, for example, can incite strong reactions online and off, further enflaming situations and making them a necessary site of analysis if we are to understand the 'global political consequences' (Duncombe, 2019: 92). It is also necessary to account for the role of other global actors' digital diplomacy, including international organizations such as NATO, who are on an equal footing with states in their use of social media. NATO's digital diplomacy matters both in respect to the-day-to-day way in which it contributes to shaping global politics and the meanings within it, and at times of crisis when the alliance's public diplomatic response is just as crucial as its material one. For example, in response to Russia's full-scale invasion of Ukraine, NATO has trodden a difficult line between defending NATO values, including democracy, the rule of law, and individual liberty, and seeking to avoid escalating tensions with Russia.

This chapter proceeds as follows. First, I introduce NATO's digital diplomacy, where it has come from, and NATO's current approach. I then turn to examine a case study of how gender, celebrity, and star power are invoked in the alliance's digital footprint to engage 'new' audiences. Finally, I turn to examine the digital diplomatic response by NATO to Russia's full-scale invasion of Ukraine, arguing that this represents a missed opportunity for NATO to reaffirm its values and seek to shape the system-level narrative concerning the war and Putin's actions.

EMERGING FROM THE 'STONE AGE'

In 2007, former NATO Secretary General Jaap de Hoop described the alliance as being in the 'stone age' when it came to engaging online and through multimedia (de Hoop Scheffer, 2007). The 2009 Strasbourg-Kehl Summit was a pivotal moment; here NATO recognized the importance of strategic communications as 'an integral part of our efforts to achieve the alliance's political and military objectives' (NATO, 2009b). Since this point, NATO's approach to digital diplomacy has evolved significantly beyond a focus on the main NATO accounts with its press releases and officials statements, to provide space for a number of different official NATO personal accounts to amplify the alliance's message to key audiences in more personalized ways (Ildem, 2017). NATO engages with digital diplomacy across a range of social media platforms, including YouTube (created 2008), Twitter (created 2009), Facebook (created 2010), Instagram (date of creation unknown), LinkedIn (date of creation unknown), and now Telegram (created 2022).

NATO's digital diplomacy falls between strategic communications (StratComm) and public diplomacy, with StratComm defined as 'the coordinated and appropriate use of NATO communications activities and capabilities ... in support of alliance policies, operations and activities, and in order to advance NATO's aims' (NATO, 2009a). While public diplomacy is defined as 'NATO civilian communications and outreach efforts responsible for promoting awareness of and building understanding and support for NATO's policies, operations and activities, in complement to the national efforts of Allies' (NATO, 2009a). Importantly, the digital aspect, particularly in relation to social media, enables NATO to engage in a two-way process of both projecting and listening.

For example, former NATO Assistant Secretary General for Public Diplomacy Tacam Ilden has stated that social media 'can also be used to listen to what the public is saying about NATO, to understand which topics they are interested in and to gauge their knowledge and understanding of the alliance, thus helping us to define our future communication topics' (Ildem, 2017).

NATO's involvement in Afghanistan, specifically the Taliban's ability to capture international media attention, also contributed to the shift in NATO's public diplomacy towards engagement with digital platforms. As a result, NATO has invested significantly in its digital diplomacy in recent years. During the NATO-led International Security Assistance Force (ISAF), for example, NATO created a specific media centre hosted in Afghanistan, the web-based NATO TV platform, to reach consumers. At this time NATO also appointed Michael Stopford, credited with bolstering Coca-Cola's reputation in his previous role as an executive for the company, as Deputy Assistant Secretary General for Strategic Communication (Wright, 2019: 90). NATO has also had to adapt in the face of the Russian annexation of Crimea and to counter Russian disinformation, establishing a Strategic Communications Center of Excellence in Riga, Latvia, in 2014. Russia's engagement in hybrid warfare and the influence of Islamic State in NATO member states led to the creation of an Assistant Secretary General for Intelligence and Security in 2017, effectively merging the political and military elements of NATO's communication strategy and demonstrating the overlap between information warfare and public diplomacy (Olsson, Wagnsson, and Hammargård, 2019: 77).

NATO's historic approach to public diplomacy messaging has set the alliance up well for the digital transition, particularly its experience in proliferating messages through civil society, which has collaborated (although not officially affiliated) with NATO to produce and project the alliance's strategic narratives. In so doing, civil society, including the Atlantic Treaty Organisations, have become crucial to fostering public understanding of NATO (Risso, 2011: 348). Yet a key challenge for NATO remains the contradiction between a projection of itself as a military force and, at the same time, seeking to align with an image of a 'nonthreatening cosmopolitan force for good' (including through civil society engagement) (Olsson, Wagnsson, and Hammargård, 2019: 79). It therefore makes sense to examine NATO's role in constructing strategic narratives in order to shed further light on such challenges.

SHAPING STRATEGIC NARRATIVES IN NATO's DIGITAL DIPLOMACY

Strategic narratives is an approach introduced by Alister Miskimmon, Ben O'Loughlin, and Laura Roselle (2013) and provides a useful framework for understanding the role of digital diplomacy given the complexity they can account for. Narratives are distinct from discourse and frames in the sense that they have a temporal dimension and can 'orient audiences to a future', while discourse provides the raw material from which actors can craft their narrative based on what is available to them in a particular historical moment (Miskimmon et al., 2013). Frames lack the temporal and causal features narratives possess, so understanding narratives 'helps us understand why and how framing works'. At the same time, parts of a narrative must be framed in a particular way, so framing also aids our understanding of narratives (Miskimmon et al., 2013). As Hanska (2015: 323) notes, the military concept of strategic communications (StratComm) can 'be viewed as the praxis of drafting and distributing narratives'; therefore applying the framework of strategic narratives is all the more relevant to understanding an actor such as NATO.

The reach of strategic narratives is also important to account for since they speak to a potentially global audience even if a message is targeted at a particular demographic. The audience for NATO's digital diplomacy is vast and varied. They need to address audiences in member, partner, and other states globally, from the public to elites. For example, NATO's strategic narratives also influence views of the alliance further away in places such as New Zealand and Australia, which proved important partners to NATO in Afghanistan (Wellings et al., 2018) and have gained reception in popular culture in particularly gendered ways (Wright and Bergman Rosamond, 2021). This means that for NATO, 'every word, image and deed can be a StratCom product if they are well-planned in advance to play their part in furthering the intentions of the metanarratives' (Hanska, 2015: 324). As well as engaging directly with consumers, the use of digital diplomacy can also be an attempt to engage the media, and at its most successful such use of strategic narratives turns the media into a 'conveyor belt transmitting elite cues to the public' (Jakobsen and Ringsmose, 2015: 217). It is therefore an essential part of NATO's toolbox as it responds to crisis, which in itself shapes NATO's digital diplomacy; the effective use of strategic narratives can justify a course of action, whether it be in response to ISIS, Afghanistan, or the full-scale Russian invasion of Ukraine.

System narratives concern the nature of the international system, specifically how this structure emerges and is shaped, sustained, and transformed through time (Miskimmon, O'Loughlin, and Roselle, 2013: 7). Identity narratives concern the identities of international actors, including states and international organizations and are 'in a process of constant negotiation and contestation' (Miskimmon, O'Loughlin, and Roselle, 2013: 7). For example, Trine Flockhart has argued that NATO suffered an identity crisis ten years after the intervention in Afghanistan when the alliance was more active than ever, caused by a failure to invoke an effective (identity) narrative to maintain ontological security (Flockhart, 2012). Issue narratives relate to a particular subject/topic and are strategic because 'they seek to shape the terrain on which policy discussions take place' (Miskimmon et al., 2013: 7). For example, this can involve making the case for (continued) war by building a strategic narrative which appeals 'to pre-existing broadly shared national interests, values and role conceptions as well as international support and a promise of success' (Jakobsen and Ringsmose, 2015: 216).

As the growing scholarship on visual IR attests to, it is increasingly difficult to ignore the role of the visual in shaping global politics (Bleiker, 2018), including in NATO's public diplomacy (Jude, 2023). Digital diplomacy is no exception; there is a significant role for the visual in digital diplomacy given the traction of images and video and that they are the sole focus of a number of social media platforms (e.g. TikTok and YouTube). The visual also plays an important role in the reception of strategic narratives, particularly amongst publics not usually predisposed to an interest in such matters (Wright and Bergman Rosamond, 2021). Narratives become visual when actors use images to communicate their strategic narratives to audiences, while it is the representation of the broader narrative reflected in the images which matters over the image itself (Miskimmon et al., 2013: 125). The use of the visual is always contextual against the wider historical narrative against which an image is situated (Pears, 2016).

A strategic narrative approach enables us to ask questions about how states and other actors in the international system communicate their role, and seek to shape the nature of the international system and issues which impact it through digital diplomacy. It enables us to interrogate the interplay between the domestic and international, power and ideas, and state and non-state actors (Miskimmon, O'Loughlin, and Roselle, 2013). Ultimately, strategic narratives matter because they '(re)produce and shape the socio-political environment, helping to determine priorities and policies that at the most basic level determine who live and who dies' (Wilkinson, 2015: 339). In the context of Russia's invasion of Ukraine and the ongoing war this has never felt so relevant. While NATO may not be a participant, its response and contribution to the issue narrative through the deployment of digital diplomacy has real life consequences. This framework enables us to interrogate NATO's digital diplomatic footprint and the role of gender and the visual in shaping strategic narratives from the 'everyday' to crisis. It also aids us in identifying silences in the projection of strategic narratives which both undermine them and can limit their efficacy.

Method and Approach

Drawing on a strategic narrative approach I first examine the gendering and 'celebrification' of NATO's digital diplomacy, drawing on the case studies of *Return to Hope*, a digital diplomacy initiative to 'tell NATO's story of Afghanistan', Angelina Jolie's partnership with NATO, and the use of Instagram influencer and Norwegian Naval Lieutenant Lasse Matberg as the 'face of NATO'. I then go on to interrogate the narratives underpinning NATO's response to Russia's invasion of Ukraine in respect to digital diplomacy, focusing on the first two weeks of tweets from the official @NATO account, drawing on content analysis. This account was chosen because it is the main NATO account and acts as a filter for the identity narrative NATO wishes to project, through the production of original tweets but also the re-tweeting of other NATO and external Twitter accounts. It is this collection of voices which forms part of NATO's identity projection and attempts to shape the issue narrative concerning the Russia–Ukraine war.

Public Digital Diplomacy: Gender, Celebrity, and Star Power

Over the last decade NATO's digital diplomacy efforts have begun to construct an identity for the alliance as a cosmopolitan defender of gender justice and human rights to legitimize its actions and existence. This has been used to contribute to particular issue narratives. A primary, though not the only, focus of this messaging has been in relation to NATO's involvement in Afghanistan. Celebrity has also been used to send this message, through the elevation of Angelina Jolie as a partner of NATO in efforts to address conflict-related sexual and gender-based violence (CRSGBV). Perhaps the most notable example though is NATO's use of Lasse Matberg, 'an Instagram influencer, model, and lieutenant in the Royal Norwegian Navy, with an impressive physique and Viking looks' (Hedling et al., 2022: 1), projected as 'the face of NATO' as part of shaping the alliance's identity narrative in its digital diplomacy surrounding its largest military exercise since the end of the Cold War, Trident Juncture. These are not the only examples, but they are some of the most striking and add to our understanding of how identity, issue, and system narratives are shaped. Together, all three of them contribute to an understanding of how using the framework of strategic narratives can help us understand the efficacy of NATO's digital diplomacy, both in its projection and reception, and the importance of gender and the visual within it.

NATO's approach to the implementation of the WPS agenda includes a core focus on public (and by extension digital) diplomacy since the adoption of the first policy in 2007. Initially, this was limited to a focus on increasing the visibility of NATO's WPS work, rather than seeking to mainstream a gender perspective into public diplomacy (Wright, 2019: 88). The 2016 revision of the NATO/EAPC policy on WPS marked a departure in NATO's approach, with the latest iteration of the associated action plan adding to this that 'The principles of NATO's WPS agenda are consistently and appropriately reflected in its communications products and activities' (NATO, 2021). This has included an enhanced digital presence for NATO's WPS work, perhaps also reflective of the global Covid-19 pandemic, which necessitated a move of many activities online. For example, in 2020 to mark the twentieth anniversary of UNSCR 1325, NATO hosted a high-level Digital Dialogue on the Future of WPS broadcast live on the NATO website, with an introduction from the Secretary General and discussion between government officials, academics, and civil society chaired by the NATO Secretary General's Special Representative (SGSR) on WPS. The event was promoted on Twitter, primarily through @NATOWPS (the official SGSR WPS account), and 450 participants attended the dialogue, with over 740 subsequently watching it back on YouTube (NATO News, 2020). It was one of a series of such digital dialogues, including 'Conflict-Related Sexual Violence', 'Human Security', and '#Gender Infodemic: Data, Disinformation & a Digital Future'.

NATO's digital turn and in particular its projection of an identity narrative of itself as a gender-just actor has its roots much earlier than this. To coincide with the end of the NATO-led International Security Assistance Force (ISAF) and expected draw down of NATO forces in 2014, NATO launched a showcase digital diplomacy initative to tell 'NATO's story of Afghanistan'. The award winning *Return to Hope* utilized a dedicated interactive website and wider social media footprint across Twitter and YouTube to highlight the stories and narratives of individuals involved with or on the receiving end of ISAF (Wright, 2019). It was an attempt by NATO to shape both the issue narrative (concerning Afghanistan) and simultaneously contribute to NATO's identity or self-narrative, though the two here are co-constitutive. It built on a longer history of Western involvement in Afghanistan, where Afghan women have been presented instrumentally (but also selectively) as victims by the West to justify interventions and invasions, denying their agency, with a specific focus on telling stories related to [Afghan] 'women's struggle'. As Annick T. R. Wibben argues, by placing narratives (including in this case strategic narratives) in a broader historical perspective it is possible to expose and understand their political underpinnings (Wibben, 2010: 45). More broadly, *Return to Hope* articulated the masculinist protection logic, whereby the feminized (in this case Afghanistan) is framed as helpless and in adoration of her protector (NATO) in return for the promise of security they can provide and so contributed to shaping the system narrative. Thereby NATO was conferred with moral legitimacy to act in Afghanistan, in opposition to the 'evil' Taliban (Wright, 2019). *Return to Hope* was a significant digital diplomacy investment by NATO, which utilized individual's stories (from NATO soldier to Afghan woman) and served both to shape NATO's identity narrative concerning the alliance's role in Afghanistan and to depoliticize the issue narrative of women's rights (Wright, 2019). This case shows us that the projection of NATO's strategic narrative across identity, issue, and system level narratives is gendered.

Celebrity has also come to play a part in NATO's more recent forays into digital diplomacy, providing a crucial tool for the alliance to use to shape strategic narratives. In January 2018, celebrity film star and Special Envoy for the UN High Commissioner for Refugees, Angelina Jolie made a high-profile visit to NATO headquarters in Brussels to meet with Secretary General Jens Stoltenberg to discuss NATO's role in addressing CRSGBV (Wright and Bergman Rosamond, 2021). This was not the first time Jolie had partnered internationally on the issue; she previously worked with then UK Foreign Secretary William Hague culminating in the Global Summit to End Sexual Violence hosted in London in 2014. Her visit to NATO was preceded by a joint op-ed published in *The Guardian*, and ended with a press conference which caught the imaginary of the world's media, specifically publications not usually concerned with the Alliance's activities, for example, in *PopSugar* and *People*, publications more usually read by women (Wright and Bergman Rosamond, 2021). NATO's digital diplomacy is therefore gendered both in the way it is projected and in the way it is received in NATO publics and by nations. The visit was highly digitized, relying on social media for the promotion and articulation of NATO's self-narrative. Jolie's promised partnership with NATO transpired to be short lived (she never returned as promised) but it was instrumental in the reception of NATO as a 'gender just' global actor in popular culture and in shaping NATO's identity narrative at this juncture (Wright and Bergman Rosamond, 2021). At the issue level, the projection of Jolie's visit digitally sought to shape the scope of discussion around CRSGBV and policy responses to it, to convince publics that it is possible to 'end' CRSGBV, a simplistic framing which captures headlines. Despite this problematic framing, and while the partnership was short lived, as Wright and Bergman Rosamond note, the NATO–Jolie partnership was a success in terms of digital diplomacy, evidenced by the continued circulation of images of Jolie at NATO on social media (Wright and Bergman Rosamond, 2021: 455). This example adds to our understanding of NATO's digital diplomacy by focusing on the reception of strategic narratives through the visual; building on *Return to Hope* we again see how the projection of strategic narratives is a gendered process.

Jolie represented an engagement with a globally recognized celebrity superstar, yet NATO has engaged with celebrity and glamour on a more 'everyday' level too. A case in point is the role of Instagram influencer and lieutenant in the Norwegian Navy, Lasse Matberg, as the 'face of NATO', promoting NATO's largest ever military exercise, Trident Juncture in autumn 2018 (Hedling, Edenborg, and Strand, 2022). The approach to digital diplomacy here represents an innovation for NATO, with Matberg's own account playing a central role shaping the strategic narratives concerning primarily NATO's identity narrative in a joined-up approach with NATO's central channels. NATO identified the value of influencers for filtering out the 'noise' of social media to reach audiences directly, given some attract followings far exceeding many official institutional accounts (Hedling, Edenborg, and Strand, 2022: 4). In line with Jolie's partnership with NATO, Matberg's role in digital diplomacy draws heavily on the visual to support the narrative projection (Wright and Bergman Rosamond, 2021; Hedling, Edenborg, and Strand, 2022). For example, Matberg has shared images of himself working out with the NATO Secretary General in an exercise class and revealing the content of his backpack (a popular format among women Instagram influencers). These build on but also contrast with the first video NATO released of Matberg, arriving at NATO HQ as a muscular figure in front of member state flags to shake hands with the Secretary General (Hedling, Edenborg, and Strand, 2022).

In their work on Matberg, Elsa Hedling, Emil Edenborg, and Sanna Strand (2022) draw on the concept of 'fantasmatic logics' to illustrate how narratives and images 'hook' audiences in through 'desire and appeal and turns attention away from conflict and antagonism' (Hedling, Edenborg, and Strand, 2022). In such a way military exercises and build-up are produced through a NATO soldier so as to appear normal, depoliticized, and even desirable: 'allowing an ambivalent gendered geopolitical imaginary to emerge' (Hedling, Edenborg, and Strand, 2022). This approach echoes that of *Return to Hope* with individual stories, including those of NATO soldiers, contributing to broader strategic narratives (Wright, 2019), in this case NATO's military build-up. Likewise, it is also a highly gendered process through which 'the figure of Lasse Matberg is co-constructed as a desirable, masculine military protector of the feminized home and nation', with Matberg cautious that images of him posing with women can lose him women followers and so his becomes about renegotiating military masculinities. As in the case of Jolie,

NATO's use of Matberg was successful in drawing the attention of a wide range of media, including the Russian state media agency Rossiya Segodnya (Hedling, Edenborg, and Strand, 2022: 4). This example builds on *Return to Hope* and Jolie to again emphasize the importance of the visual and the gendered individual to the projection of effective strategic narratives. More specifically it demonstrates how the effective use of a 'fantasmatic logic' of unity, in the face of disagreement among allies about relations with Russia and involvement in Syria (Hedling, Edenborg, and Strand, 2022: 8), contributes to shaping system-level narratives.

The examples of *Return to Hope,* Jolie's partnership with NATO, and Matberg as the 'face of NATO' show NATO's more sophisticated approach to digital diplomacy through using individuals and their stories to shape wider strategic narratives, primarily identity and issue narratives but also system-level narratives, for example, in relation to NATO's role vis-à-vis Afghanistan and Russia. These show us the significant investment NATO makes in shaping its own identity narrative and that this in turn influences the issue narrative (WPS); demonstrating that different types of strategic narrative can be co-constitutive. These three cases also focus on personifying NATO. This 'human' element has also been replicated in other digital diplomacy campaigns, including #WeAreNATO (Bjola and Manor, 2020). The #WeAreNATO tag was also used to project Angelina Jolie's visit to NATO in 2018 (Wright and Bergman Rosamond, 2021) and Lasse Matberg's engagement with the alliance (Hedling, Edenborg, and Strand, 2022). Yet during the global Covid-19 pandemic, a study by Corneliu Bjola and Ilan Manor suggests NATO's response, which emphasized the unity behind #WeAreNATO through the projection of 'a reassuring emotional tone' in itself well received by publics, was 'less successful in creatively leveraging digital technologies toward public engagement' (Bjola and Manor, 2020: 77). Given NATO's track record in engaging in a myriad of different ways in the digital diplomatic sphere, this could be seen as something of a surprise. Yet the success NATO has enjoyed in digital diplomatic innovation has come as a result of future facing projects, not in response to crisis, suggesting NATO is less prepared to react effectively digitally. Interrogating NATO's response to the Russia–Ukraine war is the next step in understanding NATO's digital diplomacy; building on the gendered and visual aspects which have shaped it to date, this case also emphasizes the role of silences in undermining the efficacy of strategic narrative projection.

Digital Diplomacy as a Battlefront: The Fight for Values in the Russia–Ukraine War

Russia's full-scale invasion of Ukraine in February 2022 has been a challenge for NATO to respond to without escalating the war. The alliance has had to tread a tightrope between being seen to support Ukraine and allies on NATO's 'eastern flank', for example through the deployment of the NATO Response Force for the first time under a collective defence remit, and avoiding an escalation of the conflict, with the ever-present threat of a nuclear response to NATO actions. Beyond the territorial threat, Russia's actions have provided a significant threat to the existing international order and Putin's actions here and more broadly represent a challenge to the values underpinning NATO, namely; individual liberty, democracy, human rights, and the rule of law. We might expect then for strategic communications, including digital diplomacy, to be at the forefront of NATO's response, particularly in projecting NATO's identity narrative. In actuality, as I examine here, NATO has been muted in reaffirming such values. An examination of such silences matters because as Cai Wilkinson (2015: 338) argues:

> ignoring silences and invisibilities in the analysis of strategic narratives is akin to viewing a painting and paying attention only to the figures in the foreground and their immediate surroundings, rather than seeing the whole picture.

The silences tell us that NATO is not engaging strategically through its digital diplomatic response to Russia's invasion and has missed an opportunity to uphold, reaffirm, and defend the values the alliance stands for, as we might expect in response to a hybrid war.

The focus here is on content analysis of the output of the official @NATO Twitter account in the two weeks immediately preceding the invasion (24 February to 10 March), which included 287 tweets or re-tweets. This provides a snapshot of NATO's digital diplomacy deployed in response to an immediate crisis, something we would expect NATO to have prepared for. The @NATO account is also the main filter point for NATO's projection of itself digitally; it produces original content but also re-tweets other NATO entities, member states, partners, other IOs, NATO staff. It also provides a chance to see what NATO did not re-tweet (from other NATO entities and staff); interrogating these silences gives us another insight into the strategic narratives NATO is seeking to influence in relation to the issue of the Russia–Ukraine War. The audience for NATO's Twitter diplomacy is publics within NATO nations. Twitter does not work in Russia, so this is therefore primarily about public diplomacy, rather than strategic communications even if it becomes increasingly difficult to separate the two. That being said, NATO's Twitter account also maintains an important role in responding to the threat of digital disinformation, in this case from Russia (Duncombe, 2019). It is important to note that we cannot know the intent of those managing the account, but we can see how such tweeting provides a particular representation of NATO and begin to evaluate just *what* NATO is projecting about itself, and its role, in the context of the full-scale Russian invasion of Ukraine in early 2022 and how that is likely to be received by NATO publics.

The significant public support for Ukraine and Ukrainians amongst Western publics and outrage at Russia's horrific actions is another contextual element to consider in understanding how NATO sought to contribute to both its identity and issue narrative through its digital diplomacy (Ipsos, 2022). At this juncture there was public appetite for

NATO's response, notably in the Netherlands, the UK, Canada, France, and Belgium, where there was majority support for sending troops to NATO countries neighbouring Ukraine (Ipsos, 2022), although there was less of a consensus on support for Ukraine militarily. For example, an Ipsos poll conducted between 25 March and 3 April 2022 found global support for going to the aid of states when they were attacked (70%), at the same time as a view that their state should avoid getting involved militarily (72%) with a perception that military involvement in Ukraine would encourage attacks on other states (68%). Among NATO member states opinion was also split; while more than three out of four people in the UK, the US, and Poland believed that inaction in Ukraine would encourage Russia to attack other countries, less than half in Hungary believed the same (Ipsos, 2022). Given this support, NATO does not need to sell its response in the same way it did in Afghanistan, where the reason for NATO's involvement was not immediately obvious and the case had to be made (Wright, 2019). The public supported a response to Ukraine, and arguably wanted NATO to go further. NATO is therefore projecting a very particular form of militarized masculinity through images of war paraphernalia to support an issue narrative that it is responding, and responding to in a 'strong way', but is wary of being seen to cross any 'red lines' to avoid escalating the conflict further, highlighting the blurred line between public diplomacy and strategic communication.

NATO's digital diplomatic response to the full-scale Russian invasion of Ukraine is a significant departure from this previous approach of projecting the alliance as a progressive gender-just actor through invoking a softer, more feminized side of the alliance in its strategic narratives. In the first two weeks of the war, we see a return to 'realpolitik' in the narrative NATO projects about itself. Even on International Women's Day in March 2022, a date NATO usually used to promote its work on WPS, we find NATO muted on the topic—it re-tweets others' approaches/responses to International Women's Day but is limited in how it articulates its own understanding. Most notable is an original content tweet of the Secretary General greeting a NATO woman soldier, in which nothing is mentioned of the alliance's values and their relevance to the date, representing an opportunity missed. This is not to say that there was no content making the link between the WPS agenda and the situation in Ukraine; the NATO Special Representative on WPS tweeted a poster of herself, making the link between gender equality and an effective response to the Russian invasion. The US mission to NATO also tweeted about women and Ukraine to mark International Women's Day (US Mission to NATO, 2022). Yet these were not re-tweeted and showcased as part of NATO's central story, they remained on the margins of the narrative NATO sought to project.

The initial digital diplomatic response by NATO was reactionary. NATO sought to project its identity/self-image as one of a muscular military power with allies united in the face of Russian aggression drawing heavily on the use of imagery, contrasting with its previous softer articulation of NATO military build-up (Hedling, Edenborg, and Strand, 2022). During the first two weeks following the Russian invasion of Ukraine, almost a quarter of tweets and re-tweets included a military image; either of tanks, equipment, or military personnel. NATO invested in developing its identity narrative through emphasizing its role as an alliance, through projecting the strength of relationships among member states, and their attention to the war, for example, 12% of tweets included images of leaders shaking hands, at their desks working, or on visits to Estonia, Poland, or Romania. There is also an emphasis on flags, with 6% of tweets containing images of either the NATO flag, members' flags, Ukraine's flags, or a combination.

NATO retweeted delegations to NATO, member states, and partners including Japan, and there are also a significant number of re-tweets of the UN and the UN Secretary General. The latter could be seen as an attempt to align NATO with global outrage at Russia's actions, while re-tweeting more distant partners reflects the reality that NATO's strategic narratives find an audience here (Wellings et al., 2018). Beyond flags and imagery, what we do not see is the voice of Ukrainians or Ukraine in NATO's digital diplomacy. On the one hand this could be viewed as unsurprising given this is the pro-jection of NATO's response, not Ukraine's experience, contributing to NATO's identity narrative. However, it is a significant silence in the issue narrative NATO is contributing to; in contrast in shaping its issue narrative on Afghanistan, NATO drew on the voices and stories of Afghans, and Afghan women in particular (Wright, 2019). This is more difficult for NATO to navigate here, particularly at the outset of the war in Ukraine; while NATO wants to be seen to support Ukraine in the face of Russian aggression the allies are not willing to go as far as Ukrainians want them to in closing Ukrainian skies.

There has also been a significant emphasis on seeking to shape the issue narrative of the Russia–Ukraine war using images containing slogans. In addition, there has been an emphasis on infographics or short video explainers, for example on what the NATO Response Force or Article 4 is, so 'educational tweets'. This reflects the reality that know-ledge of NATO—what it is and does—remains very low amongst the public (Kuus, 2007), but ultimately NATO wants to be seen to be doing *something* even if that is a diffi-cult line to tread. The tweets analysed here demonstrate NATO is in a reactionary phase. They therefore lack the innovation in terms of digital outreach showcased in NATO's earlier digital diplomatic initiatives, potentially limiting their reach and ability to shape strategic narratives, in line with NATO's more muted digital diplomatic response to the Covid-19 pandemic (Bjola and Manor, 2020). This suggests NATO could do more to invest in embedding the innovative aspects of its digital diplomacy strategy in future planning for emerging crises going forward, to ensure it is not tweeting in reactionary mode but tweeting with the intention of shaping narratives strategically, specifically through invoking NATO values, which has proved successful in the past.

Conclusion: Future Directions

This chapter has highlighted the value of strategic narratives as an approach to under-stand NATO's engagement with digital diplomacy. Undoubtedly, this framework would have useful application for interrogating another actor's digital diplomatic footprint. In the case of NATO it is particularly useful given NATO's purpose as a political-military alliance and the role of strategic communications, which forms an integral part of the military, and NATO's, approach to digital diplomacy. This approach as applied here specifically concerns the deployment of narratives to shape meaning within a particular situation, focusing on the role of gender, the visual, and silences.

NATO has demonstrated significant innovation in its use of digital diplomacy to shape strategic narratives, specifically in relation to Afghanistan, the issue of CRSGBV, and in justifying NATO exercises and military build-up. These three examples also draw attention to the role of celebrity (on different scales) and star power, and to the effective reception of such narratives in popular culture, co-constituted in their reception through both consumers and the media. The use of digital diplomacy has also been gendered both in the ways it is projected, invoking masculinities and femininities to different affect, and in how it is received. Yet, in NATO's digital diplomatic response to crisis, be it Covid-19 or more relevantly Russia's full-scale invasion of Ukraine in 2022, we find NATO's digital intervention less effective at actively shaping strategic narratives containing significant silences and undermining the alliance's response to the broader hybrid war conducted by Russia.

This chapter provided a short snapshot of NATO's current engagement with digital diplomacy following the full-scale Russian invasion of Ukraine. More attention is needed on NATO's digital diplomatic footprint here to understand the place of NATO values versus the projection of military power in shaping the alliance's identity narrative. It is beyond the scope of this chapter, but future research looking at the strategic narratives NATO deploys in its Russian language Telegram account would add an important dimension to understanding how the Alliance is seeking to shape its own identity narrative, the system narrative, and the wider issue narrative concerning the Russian invasion beyond the West and in publics in Russia specifically.

Suggested Reading

Bjola, C. and Manor, I. (2020) 'NATO's digital public diplomacy during the Covid-19 pandemic', *Turkish Policy Quarterly*, 19(2), pp. 77–87.

Hedling, E., Edenborg, E., and Strand, S. (2022) 'Embodying military muscles and a remasculinized West: Influencer marketing, fantasy, and "the face of NATO"', *Global Studies Quarterly*, 2(1), pp. 1–12.

Jude, S. (2023) 'Geopolitical imaginations of war preparations: Visual representations of the Romanian armed forces' military exercises', *Critical Military Studies*, 9(3), pp. 404–424.

Olsson, E.-K., Wagnsson, C. and Hammargård, K. (2019) 'The use of political communication by international organizations: The case of EU and NATO', in J. Pamment and C. Bjola (eds) *Countering Online Propaganda and Extremism: the Dark Side of Digital Diplomacy*. Abingdon: Routledge, pp. 66–80.

Wright, K.A.M. (2019) 'Telling NATO's story of Afghanistan: Gender and the alliance's digital diplomacy', *Media, War & Conflict*, 12(1), pp. 87–101.

Wright, K.A.M. and Bergman Rosamond, A. (2021) 'NATO, Angelina Jolie and the alliance's celebrity and visual turn', *Review of International Studies*. 47(4), pp. 443–466.

References

Behnke, A. (2002) "'vvv.nato.int.": Virtuousness, virtuality and virtuosity in NATO's representation of the Kosovo campaign', in P. van Ham and S. Medvedev (eds) *Mapping European Security After Kosovo*. Manchester University Press, pp. 126–141.

Bjola, C. and Holmes, M. (2015) 'Digital diplomacy', in C. M. Constantinou, P. Kerr and P. Sharp (eds) *The SAGE Handbook of Diplomacy*, pp. 123–133.

Bjola, C. and Manor, I. (2020) 'NATO's digital public diplomacy during the Covid-19 pandemic', *Turkish Policy Quarterly*. 19(2). Pp. 77-87.

Bleiker, R. (2018) *Visual Global Politics*. Abingdon: Routledge.

Duncombe, C. (2019) 'Twitter and the challenges of digital diplomacy', *SAIS Review of International Affairs*, 38(2), pp. 91–100.

Flockhart, T. (2012) 'Towards a strong NATO narrative: From a "practice of talking" to a "practice of doing"', *International Politics*, 49, pp. 78–97.

Hanska, J. (2015) 'From narrated strategy to strategic narratives', *Critical Studies on Security*, 3(3), pp. 323–325.

Hedling, E. and Bremberg, N. (2021) 'Practice approaches to the digital transformations of diplomacy: Toward a new research agenda', *International Studies Review*, 23(4), pp. 1595–1618.

Hedling, E., Edenborg, E., and Strand, S. (2022) 'Embodying military muscles and a remasculinized West: Influencer marketing, fantasy, and "the face of NATO"', *Global Studies Quarterly*, 2(1), pp. 1–12.

de Hoop Scheffer, J. (2007) 'Speech by NATO Secretary General, Jaap de Hoop Scheffer at the Seminar on "Public Diplomacy in NATO-led Operations"'. Available at: http://www.nato.int/docu/speech/2007/s071008a.html (Accessed: 20 July 2015).

Ildem, T. (2017) 'NATO and digital diplomacy in 2017 / Tacan İ ldem', *The State of Digital Diplomacy 2016*. Available at: http://www.sodd16.com/nato-and-digital-diplomacy-in-2017-tacan-ildem/ (Accessed: 5 May 2017).

Ipsos (2022) 'Global public opinion about the war in Ukraine'. Available at: https://www.ipsos.com/en-us/news-polls/war-in-ukraine-april-2022 (Accessed: 28 April 2022).

Jakobsen, P.V. and Ringsmose, J. (2015) 'In Denmark, Afghanistan is worth dying for: How public support for the war was maintained in the face of mounting casualties and elusive success', *Cooperation and Conflict*, 50(2), pp. 211–227.

Jude, S. (2023) 'Geopolitical imaginations of war preparations: Visual representations of the Romanian armed forces' military exercises', Critical Military Studies, 9(3), pp. 404–424.

Kuus, M. (2007) "'Love, peace and NATO": Imperial subject-making in Central Europe', *Antipode*, 39(2), pp. 269–290.

Miskimmon, A., O'Loughlin, B., and Roselle, L. (2013) *Strategic Narratives: Communication Power and the New World Order*. Abingdon: Routledge.

NATO (2009a) *NATO Strategic Communications Policy*. Available at: https://info.publicintelligence.net/NATO-STRATCOM-Policy.pdf (Accessed: 21 April 2022).

NATO (2009b) 'Strasbourg-Kehl Summit Declaration'. Available at: http://www.nato.int/cps/en/natohq/news_52837.htm?mode=pressrelease (Accessed: 31 August 2017).

NATO (2021) *Action Plan for the Implementation of the NATO/EAPC Policy on Women, Peace and Security 2021-2025*. Available at: https://www.nato.int/cps/en/natohq/official_texts_187485.htm (Accessed: 25 April 2022).

NATO News (2020) 'NATO Secretary General at "Digital Dialogue on the Future of Women, Peace and Security"', 15 October 2020. YouTube. Available at: https://www.youtube.com/watch?v=3HuHZQBCmM8 (Accessed: 15 February 2022).

Olsson, E.-K., Wagnsson, C., and Hammargård, K. (2019) 'The use of political communication by international organizations: The case of EU and NATO', in J. Pamment and C. Bjola (eds) *Countering Online Propaganda and Extremism: the Dark Side of Digital Diplomacy.* Abingdon: Routledge, pp. 66–80.

Pears, L. (2016) 'Ask the audience: Television, security and homeland', *Critical Studies on Terrorism*, 9(1), pp. 76–96.

Risso, L. (2011) 'Propaganda on wheels: The NATO travelling exhibitions in the 1950s and 1960s', *Cold War History*, 11(1), pp. 9–25.

US Mission to NATO (2022) 'On #InternationalWomensDay #IWD2022 we stand with the brave women of Ukraine against Russian aggression. #UnitedWithUkraine #WeAreNATO' [Twitter post]. Available at: https://twitter.com/USNATO/status/1501231977374044166.

Wellings, B. et al. (2018) 'Narrative alignment and misalignment: NATO as a global actor as seen from Australia and New Zealand', *Asian Security*, 14(1), pp. 24–37.

Wibben, A.T.R. (2010) *Feminist Security Studies A Narrative Approach.* Abingdon: Routledge.

Wilkinson, C. (2015) 'The unsaid and unseen: On hearing silences and seeing invisibilities in strategic narratives', *Critical Studies on Security*, 3(3), pp. 338–340.

Wright, K.A.M. (2019) 'Telling NATO's story of Afghanistan: Gender and the alliance's digital diplomacy', *Media, War & Conflict*, 12(1), pp. 87–101.

Wright, K.A.M. and Bergman Rosamond, A. (2021) 'NATO, Angelina Jolie and the alliance's celebrity and visual turn', *Review of International Studies*, 47(4), pp. 443–466.

CHAPTER 27

··

DIGITAL DIPLOMACY OF THE CENTRAL ASIAN COUNTRIES

··

ALISHER FAIZULLAEV

THIS chapter aims to analyse the features, trends, and challenges of digital diplomacy (DD) in the Central Asian countries (CAC)—the Republic of Kazakhstan, the Republic of Kyrgyzstan, the Republic of Tajikistan, Turkmenistan, and the Republic of Uzbekistan. I focus on *social media DD* or *social media diplomacy* (SMD),[1] which usually appears as a part of public diplomacy and uses the construction and presentation of the diplomatic actor's political, social, economic, cultural, and other narratives, particularly visual ones, through social media. The chapter argues that CAC have begun to develop their SMD and at this stage it takes place mostly through the dissemination of information about ongoing meetings and events, rather than by way of the engagement with other state and non-state actors regarding their long-term fundamental objectives and critical international problems. Now CAC are faced with a choice—to continue to use Social Media Diplomacy (SMD) mainly at the level of dissemination of everyday information, or to raise it to a more strategic level, which implies the development of a comprehensive strategy in this area with the consideration of long-term objectives, intensive training of diplomats, and specialists with competence in big data and social data analysis. The second option is more promising and effective but also more challenging and will require CAC to raise diplomatic work in general to a new level.

SMD may have different objectives, including impression management, image-making, reputation-building, managing relationships, value-promotion, defending a cause, and developing social networking but, by and large, it serves as a digital

---

[1] Apart from SMD, we can distinguish such areas or types of DD as the application of digital technologies to perform basic diplomatic functions, which can be called *functional* or *operational DD* (FDD), and the analysis of digital data by diplomatic actors or for the purposes of diplomacy, which can be identified *analytical DD* (ADD).

instrument of influencing other stakeholders, including foreign and domestic audiences. From this perspective, the diplomatic actor involved in the SMD can be compared to a social media influencer.

SMD can serve the fundamental and long-term goals of the state, and we can analyse it from the strategic interactions point of view. In this respect, game theory can be useful in discussing SMD, and the chapter explores diplomatic social media activities as elements of the strategic interaction in diplomacy.

THE CENTRAL ASIAN
COUNTRIES: AN OVERVIEW

Kazakhstan, Kyrgyzstan, Tajikistan, Turkmenistan, and Uzbekistan became independent states in 1991, and for the last three decades they have been actively involved in statecraft, including the development of their foreign policy, international politics, and diplomacy. After the collapse of the former Soviet Union, these newly established states had to face many similar problems: to become not only *de jure* but also *de facto* independent countries, build state institutions, develop domestic and international policies, strengthen the economy and security, create a financial system, deal with many challenges in the social, environmental, and educational spheres and human rights issues, and negotiate with neighbours on the delimitation and demarcation of borders. Among the problems that have affected CAC are the situation in Afghanistan, the environmental disaster on the Aral Sea, some ethnic conflicts, terrorist acts, and unrest. Despite many difficulties, CAC became members of the international community and are developing as independent states.

After thirty years of such a development, the countries of the region have both common and specific features in their foreign and domestic policies. In general, for all CAC, the priority areas of diplomatic activities are the further strengthening of independence, attracting and supporting foreign investment, trade, and tourists, and overcoming security threats and ecological challenges, as well as the development of political and economic relations with significant international actors.

As noted earlier, DD of the state may include FDD, ADD, and SMD. As examples of FDD we can refer to carrying out such traditional diplomatic functions as sending and receiving messages and conducting meetings, conferences, and negotiations with the help of digital technologies. Because of Covid-19, CAC, like many other countries in the world, have significantly increased the use of information and communication technologies (ICT) in everyday (or operational) diplomatic activities. Diplomats of CAC have begun to widely use video conferences in their diplomatic practice, and apply digital technologies to communicate with other diplomats and compatriots, especially with those who are in emergency situations abroad. As a tool of communication with home-based citizens and compatriots abroad, the Telegram messenger has become

Table 27.1 Population, spread of the Internet, social media, and mobile connection in CAC as of early 2022

CAC	1	2	3	4	5	6	7	8	9	10
KAZ	19.10M	85.9%	+1.1%	127.9%	+0.5%	72.3%	+15%	2.3M	11.75m	202.9K
KGZ	6.68M	51.1%	+3.4%	158.8%	+3.6%	53.9%	+12.5%	786.7K	2.95M	65.5K
TJK	9.85M	40.1%	+18.1%	105.9%	+2.0%	14.5%	+42.6%	443.4K	1.04M	17.4K
TKM	6.16M	38.1%	+16.4%	79.9%	+0.7%	5.5%	+125%	20.5K	308.4K	2.650K
UZB	34.16M	70.4%	+1.4%	86.8%	+7.2%	18.3%	+35.9%	1.55M	4.80M	29.0K

About the columns: 1) Population. 2) The Internet penetration. 3) The increase of the number of the Internet users between 2021 and 2022. 4) Mobile connections in January 2022 equivalent to the % of the total population. 5) The increase in the number of mobile connections between 2021 and 2022. 6) Percentage of the population using social media. 7) The increase in the number of social media users between 2021 and 2022. 8) Facebook users. 9) Instagram users. 10) Twitter users.

Source: DataReportal.

particularly widespread in many ministries of foreign affairs (MFAs) and diplomatic missions of CAC.[2]

DD is part of a country's diplomacy, and it is also affected by the digital environment in it. The diplomacy of CAC has not yet used to a noticeable extent the possibilities of analysing digital data, especially big data and social data analytics. ADD requires relevant specialists and skills, the collaboration of foreign ministries and diplomatic missions abroad with high-tech companies, and the availability of mobile applications and other appropriate software instruments. It can be assumed that in the future, the countries of the region will take up this matter because diplomatic digital analytics is a natural way of the symbiosis of modern diplomacy with digital technologies.

In 2022, on average, 60% of the world's population uses the Internet (The World Bank). Table 27.1 provides the DataReportal website's information on the population, spread of the Internet, social media, and mobile connection in CAC as of early 2022.[3]

The use of the Internet, social media, and mobile communications in CAC is rising quite dynamically. However, in Freedom House's assessment of the level of Internet freedom in seventy countries, Kazakhstan and Uzbekistan have a status of 'not free', and Kyrgyzstan is specified as 'partly free'. The countries have the following scores for Internet freedom, which 'are based on a scale of 0 (least free) to 100 (most free)': thirty-three for Kazakhstan, fifty-three for Kyrgyzstan, and twenty-eight for Uzbekistan

---

[2] Many diplomats of CAC also use WhatsApp messenger, and practice communication with their home and foreign colleagues through Telegram and WhatsApp.

[3] For brevity and convenience, this chapter uses the following international country codes in tables: KAZ for Kazakhstan, KGZ for Kyrgyzstan, TJK for Tajikistan, TKM for Turkmenistan, and UZB for Uzbekistan.

(Freedom House). The assessments of two countries—Tajikistan and Turkmenistan were not reflected in this report.

The countries of the region provided their diplomats with professional training, including some workshops in DD. Thus, Kyrgyzstan's MFA and Facebook organized a webinar on DD for the country's diplomats (MFA of Kyrgyzstan). USAID provided courses on DD to diplomats from Turkmenistan (USAID, 2021). In Uzbekistan, the United Nations Development Program (UNDP) provided assistance to the MFA with the project 'Enhancing Capacities for Digital Economic Diplomacy in Uzbekistan' (UNDP Uzbekistan); a webinar on digital diplomacy was held for diplomats with the participation of Meta (MFA of Uzbekistan). DD was among the issues discussed in the Organization for Security and Co-operation in Europe's (OSCE's) international summer school for junior diplomats from CAC, Afghanistan, and Mongolia (OSCE, 2019).

CAC adopted various programmes and strategies for the development of digital technologies and the digital economy. Thus, in 2017, the state programme 'Digital Kazakhstan' was approved by Decree of the Government of Kazakhstan (Ministry of Justice of the Republic of Kazakhstan, 2017). In 2018, by the decision of the Security Council of Kyrgyzstan dated 14 December 2018, the Concept of Digital Transformation 'Digital Kyrgyzstan 2019-2023' was approved; in 2019, the Roadmap for the implementation of this concept was approved by the Government of Kyrgyzstan (Ministry of Justice of the Kyrgyz Republic, 2019). In 2019, the Government of Tajikistan approved the Concept of the Digital Economy of this country (Adlia, 2019). In 2018, the Concept of Development of the Digital Economy in Turkmenistan in 2019–2025 was approved by the decree of the President of Turkmenistan (The State Bank for Foreign Economic Affairs of Turkmenistan). In 2020, the Digital Uzbekistan 2030 Strategy was approved by the presidential decree (LexUz online, 2020).

Some government and MFA documents of CAC indicate the need for the development of DD. DD is mentioned in the Concept of the Foreign Policy of Tajikistan (MFA of Tajikistan) and Kazakhstan (Legal Information System of Regulatory Legal Acts of the Republic of Kazakhstan). In Kazakhstan, the presidential decree titled 'On the Foreign Policy Concept of the Republic of Kazakhstan for 2020-2030', from 6 March 2020, points to 'expanding the use of "digital diplomacy"' 'to achieve foreign policy goals, promote international initiatives, and develop cooperation with foreign countries' as one of the priorities of the country's diplomacy (Legal Information System of Regulatory Legal Acts of the Republic of Kazakhstan). The Resolution of the President of Uzbekistan regarding MFA from 4 April 2018 refers to 'expanding the use of digital diplomacy, which implies extensive use of the Internet, including social platforms' (LexUz online, 2018).

So, CAC have made certain important steps in to develop DD, and this became a topic of some studies (Tassilova et al., 2018; Hudaykulov, 2021). In the foreign ministries, various departments deal with DD.[4] However, so far none of these states has developed

---

[4] According to their official websites, Kazakhstan MFA has 'Department of Digitalization'; Tajikistan MFA has 'Information and Communication Technologies Unit'; and Uzbekistan MFA has 'Department for Information Technologies and Communications'.

a detailed and comprehensive strategy for the development of their DD or the system for evaluating the effectiveness of using SMD by diplomats and diplomatic missions abroad.

Digital Diplomacy of the State as an Instrument of Strategic Interaction with Other Actors

Corneliu Bjola, by differentiating strategic and tactical use of DD, remarked 'The strategic use of digital platforms imposes order on digital activities through the definition of measurable goals, target audiences, and parameters for evaluation. The goals determine the target audience, which in turn determines the platforms, methods, and metrics to be used' (2018). Along with such an approach, we can consider SMD itself as a game of strategy that is played by the diplomatic actor through postings, re-postings, likes, comments and other 'moves' on digital platforms. Thomas Schelling, who distinguished the game of chance, the game of skill, and the game of strategy, pointed out that in the last one 'the best course of action for each player depends on what the other players do. The term is intended to focus on the interdependence of the adversaries' decisions and on their expectations about each other's behavior' (1980: 3). It can be assumed that diplomatic actors make their moves on social media by considering the possible responses of their counterparts, and this kind of strategic interaction through social media provides the opportunities to apply some provisions of game theory for the analysis of SMD.

From the game theory perspective, any use of SMD can also be considered as an element of a broader strategic interaction of a diplomatic actor with other entities although such a game can be connected to the strategic goals and objectives of the actor to varying degrees and with different levels of conceptualization. So, the degree of strategic use of SMD may vary within the framework of the actor's diplomatic strategy. In other words, although SMD itself is a strategic interaction with other entities, some countries can use it in strong connection to their main and conceptualized strategic objectives of foreign policy and diplomacy, while others may engage in social media activities more sporadically and with less of a link to the actor's major diplomatic objectives.

The application of game theory to the analysis of SMD can assume the identification of (1) players, or the actor, and its strategic counterparts, (2) the game setting, or major conditions affecting the strategic interaction through social media, (3) the strategic goal and objectives of the actor and its counterparts, (4) a dominant strategy of the actor supported by prevailing actions and interactions, (5) the payoff, or outcome from strategic interactions on digital platforms. Therefore, in the analysis of SMD of CAC, the focus of our attention will be on a country as a diplomatic actor and its strategic counterparts, the social media game setting, the actor's goals/objectives, moves, and payoff.

1. *Actors.* This chapter considers CAC as diplomatic actors involved in the strategic game of SMD, and their foreign ministries and diplomatic representatives

abroad as well as presidential administrations and the presidents' press services as organization-agencies of the actors, and individuals such as presidents, foreign ministers, and ambassadors as individual-agents of the actor, or the DD field players. Counterplayers, in this respect, are international actors, such as other states and intergovernmental, non-governmental, and media organizations, as well as domestic entities—social, political, broadcasting, and professional groups, organizations, companies, journalists, analysts, activists, and individuals.

2. *Game setting.* The availability of technological means (computers, smartphones, the Internet, software, mobile applications, and access to social media) and people with the ability to use social media skilfully, as well as the digital environment in a home and host country, affect the SMD activities.

3. *Strategic goal and objectives.* The game of SMD is about influencing through constructing and presenting narratives on social media in the context of public diplomacy and strategic objectives. This can be seen as a form of narrative practice in diplomacy (Faizullaev and Cornut, 2017), or digital storytelling. Here we should distinguish strategic narratives of diplomatic actors, which 'are a vital component of how states seek to establish and maintain influence in the world' (Miskimmon et al., 2018). As Ilan Manor pointed out, 'Strategic narratives are used by diplomats to make sense of world events' (2019: 117). Strategic narratives of diplomatic actors may have different degrees of conceptualization and formalization.

4. *Dominant strategy.* Generally, the strategy of public diplomacy is a communication and interaction strategy for building influence, reputation, image, and relationship. These general strategies can be supported by such SMD game strategies as *notification,*[5] *engagement,*[6] *advocacy,*[7] *confrontation,*[8] *cooperation,*[9] *bargaining,*[10] *troubleshooting,*[11] and *networking*[12] or a combination of them.

For the diplomatic actor, each of these SMD strategies can be dominant in its interactions with other actors through social media. A combination of different strategies can also appear as a mainstream strategy. Among all these strategies, the most dialogical and corresponding to the spirit of diplomacy is the strategy of engagement. Apart from the strategy of confrontation, all other strategies can serve relationship-building between the involved actors.

Of course, the number of followers, likes, and re-posts, and users reading/watching and commenting on posts on social media accounts, can be considered

---

[5] Mainly publishing notifying posts and re-posts, that is, to report news, inform about happenings, and cover some events, primarily with the actor's own participation.

[6] Engaging in conversation, discussion, and exchange of opinion with other actors.

[7] Defending or promoting some values or causes.

[8] Disagreeing or debating with some other actors—international or domestic adversaries or critics.

[9] Supporting someone by expressing solidarity and sympathy.

[10] Bargaining—tacitly—with some other actors on issues of mutual importance. The concept of tacit bargaining was developed by Thomas Schelling in his seminal book, *The Strategy of Conflict.*

[11] Addressing a crisis that could be a part of crisis management.

[12] Developing a network of contacts with the utility potential.

as some indicators of engagement. However, the most important and effective engagement is a strategic one that is based on the dialogical interaction or conversation of the user with the followers.

5. *Payoff.* For diplomatic actors, as social media influencers who strive to be noticeable, make an impact on other players, and achieve their strategic goals, the payoff in the game of SMD cannot always be clearly recognized, but in general, the number of followers of the social media accounts, as well as the number of interactions such as reading/watching, reactions/comments, and likes/re-posts of the actor's posts/comments, can be considered as observable indicators of it. Sometimes just one tweet can become well known and viral and be an important act in the whole and multifaceted game of diplomacy. One of the payoffs of the social media activity or campaign could be drawing the attention of significant and powerful players, including other diplomatic social media influencers. So, comments or re-posts from such players can also be considered as an important payoff in SMD.

SOCIAL MEDIA DIPLOMACY ACTIVITIES OF THE CENTRAL ASIAN COUNTRIES

This chapter mainly focuses on using such social media as Twitter, Facebook, Instagram, and YouTube by diplomatic actors, because they are commonly recognized as principal instruments of SMD. Diplomatic players of the region also widely use Telegram messenger as an instrument of communication with people, including other diplomats, and as a digital platform for providing information.

To understand the basic features of CAC's SMD, we can look at some of the important social media and messenger accounts of these diplomatic actors. Considering the key role of CAC presidents in the foreign policy and diplomacy of their countries, we start with an overview of their main social media accounts. Table 27.2 shows some features of the social media accounts of CAC presidents as of 01August 2023 (the percentage of the followers' growth compared to 01 January 2022 is indicated in parentheses).

On 1 August 2023, the Kazakhstan, Tajikistan, and Uzbekistan presidents' press services had Telegram channels with the following number of users: 37,883 (KAZ); 1,040 (TAJ); and 171,595 (UZB). In their Facebook, Instagram, YouTube, and Telegram accounts, the presidents and, as we will see later, MFAs and diplomatic missions abroad of CAC mainly use the national languages of their countries and Russian, and their Twitter accounts also often employ English. This fact and existing comments on their posts indicate that they use Facebook, Instagram, YouTube, and Telegram accounts to communicate primarily with a home audience, while Twitter accounts are intended for both domestic and foreign audiences. This also follows from the very nature of

Table 27.2 Social media accounts of CAC presidents as of 01 August 2023.

Presidents	Twitter	Facebook	Instagram	YouTube
KAZ: Kassym-Jomart Tokayev	352.8K (+76,4%)	81K (+55,76%)	2.6M (+597,05%)	
The President's Press Office	523.8K (+135,83%)		444K (+19,04%)	9.23K (+47,68%)
KGZ: Sadyr Japarov	7,365 (+13,56%)	87,837 (+46,13%)	495K (+32%)	
The President's Administration		25K (+594,44%)	92.4K (+111,92%)	
TJK: Emomali Rahmon				
The President's Press Service	2,300 (+54,25%)	230K (+27,07%)	54K (+116,86%)	7,620 (+27,85%)
TKM: Serdar Berdimuhamedow[1]				
UZB: Shavkat Mirziyoyev				
The President's Press Service	137.8K (+142,17%)	383,045 (+14,67)	4.7M (+23,68)[2]	201K (+91,42%)

[1] The President of Turkmenistan—Gurbanguly Berdimuhamedow and then Serdar Berdimuhamedow since 19 March 2022—has no official social media accounts. There exists an Instagram account for Gurbanguly Berdimuhamedow with 13.9K followers (01 August 2023), and an Instagram account for Serdar Berdimuhamedow with 7,111 followers (01 August 2023), but it is not known who manages these accounts.

[2] There is an Instagram account of the President's Press Service in English with 858K followers (01 August 2023). In its 2018 research, Twiplomacy website noted the Instagram account of President Shavkat Mirziyoyev's Press Service: it ranked twenty-three among the fifty world leaders with the most interactions, fifteen among the fifty most followed world leaders, and thirty-nine among the fifty most effective world leaders (Twiplomacy).

these social media platforms: Twitter, unlike the others, is more instrumental for informational interaction within international political, diplomatic, and media circles. Obviously, social media accounts of the head of state cover not only foreign policy, international politics, and diplomacy but a wider range of issues.

Dissimilar to many of the world leaders who are most followed on social media, most social media accounts of the presidents of CAC are conducted not on behalf of the first person but by their press services or administrations. So, in most cases, CAC presidential social media accounts use third-person narration. Usually, the first-person narration in social media may help in decreasing the power distance between the parties of SMD, and increasing the attractiveness of the social media posts.

Social media accounts of the CAC presidents mainly inform about the activities of the heads of state and their positions on a variety of issues, that is, they are primarily of a notification nature. We can see many comments on them; this is especially true for the Instagram accounts. But we can also notice that those who manage these accounts are not particularly involved in dialogue or conversation with the followers and those who

Table 27.3 Social media accounts and Telegram channels of CAC foreign ministries as of 01 August 2023 (with percentage of followers' growth compared to 01 January 2022)

MFA	Twitter	Facebook	YouTube	Instagram	Telegram
KAZ	46.4 (+31,81%)	21K (+10,51%)	4.81K (+5,02%)	11.6K (+50,1%)	4,158 (+33,18%)
KGZ	8,513 (+58,46%)	13K (+8,33%)	636 (+46,88%)	11.9K (+42,25%)	1,134 (+382,55%)
TJK					
– in Russian	3,720 (+27,57%)	22K (+10%)		1,208 (+130,97%)	
– in English	4,235 (+54,9%)			823 (N/A)	
TKM					
UZB	5,912 (+204,74%)[1]	26K (+3,27)		2,751 (First posted on 13 June 2023)[2]	5,224 – The name of the channel is in Uzbek (N/A) 3,239 – The name of the channel is in Russian (+15,02%)

[1] In Uzbekistan, Twitter was blocked from 2 June 2021 to 1 August 2022. From 2 August 2022, MFA has again started using it.

[2] Before that, the ministry indicated other accounts.

left comments. Informing about meetings, events and other activities, on the one hand, and the perception of such information by the public, on the other, is an important part of political and social affairs. But a more engaging strategy of SMD that contains a dialogue with social media followers requires more human and technological resources, including digital analytical ones.

Now, we look at the MFAs' social media accounts. Table 27.3 presents the information about social media accounts and Telegram channels of CAC foreign ministries as of 01 August 2023 (the percentage of the followers' growth compared to 01 January 2022 is indicated in parentheses).

As we can see by the number of followers, Twitter ranks first among social media accounts of Kazakhstan's MFA, and Facebook occupies a leading position in this respect for the foreign ministries of Kyrgyzstan, Tajikistan, and Uzbekistan. Table 27.4 shows some features of the Twitter accounts of the foreign ministries of CAC as of 01 January 2022 and 01 June 2022.[13]

[13] By the beginning of October 2022 and August 2023, of the current foreign ministers of CAC, only Minister of Foreign Affairs of Uzbekistan used Twitter.

Table 27.4 The Twitter accounts of the foreign ministries of CAC as of 01 January 2022 and 01 June 2022.

MFA	1	2	3	4	5	6	7
KAZ	12.2011	12.9K	374[1]	252	101	104	66
KGZ	08.2012	3,597	160[2]	58	20	1	7
TJK							
– in Russian	01.2014	1,413	70	17	7		2
– in English[3]	12.2017	1,163	164	14	8		58
TKM							
UZB	05.2020	180					

About the columns: 1) The date of joining Twitter. 2) The total number of tweets (01 June 2022. 3) The number of tweets from 01 January 2022 to 01 June 2022. 4) The highest number of likes of one of their tweets for this period. 5) The highest number of re-twits of their single post for this period. 6) The number of their re-twits of others' posts for this period. 7) The highest number of comments on one of their tweets.

[1] Tweets are mostly in English as well as in Russian and Kazakh languages. One tweet was in French, and one in Spanish.

[2] Tweets were in Russian.

[3] In 2015–2016, MFA of Tajikistan had another Twitter account in English with 415 tweets.

Most of the tweets of the marked accounts have a visual component, such as photos of various meetings of politicians and diplomats. Such visualization helps in attracting attention. There are very few videos on these Twitter accounts (which usually requires more skills and labour). Most photos represent visual accounts of diplomatic meetings, and they are quite formal in the setting. Foreign ministries of CAC have very little recourse to unofficial photographs, such as pictures of ordinary people in everyday situations. The MFA of Kazakhstan re-tweeted most of all from their President's Twitter account and posted photos of the head of state on its Twitter account.

Table 27.5 provides information about posts on the Facebook accounts of the MFAs of CAC for the period from 01 October 2021 to 25 December 2021.

We can say that the Facebook accounts of the foreign ministries of CAC are intended mainly for the home audience. Basically, all posts in this period inform about the activities of the MFAs, many of them containing photos of various meetings and events. No posts were found about the goals, principles, and missions of the ministries, foreign policy objectives, discussing international problems, and global challenges. In general, there are very few comments on the Facebook posts of the ministries.

The Facebook account of the Kazakhstan MFA used two languages—Kazakh and Russian—and it had no videos for the specified period. Kyrgyzstan's foreign ministry used in its Facebook account also two languages—Kyrgyz and Russian—but most posts were in Russian. It had weekly photo digests designed as slide shows as well as videos.

Table 27.5 Posts on the Facebook accounts of the MFAs of CAC for the period from 01 October 2021 to 25 December 2021

MFA	1	2	3	4
KAZ	56	319	103	8
KGZ	206	126	35	11
TJK	276	183	9	76
TKM				
UZM	98	117	11	38

About the columns: 1) The number of posts. 2) The highest number of likes of a single post. 3) The highest number of comments on a single post. 4) The highest number of re-posts of their single post.

The Facebook account of the Tajikistan MFA is conducted mainly in the Tajik language, but there are a few posts in English and Russian. It covers not only the activity of the ministry but also the President's activities. The account has no videos for the specified time.

The MFA of Uzbekistan used the Uzbek and Russian languages in its Facebook account. Some posts are duplicated in these two languages. For the specified time, there was only one post in English. No videos were posted during this period.

Now let's look at the SMD activities of the diplomatic missions of CAC in some key places. Table 27.6 is about social media accounts of the permanent missions of CAC to the UN as of 01 August 2023 (in parenthesis, the percentage of growth in the number of followers since 01 October 2021).

As we can see, both Kazakhstan's MFA and the mission to the UN have the largest number of social media followers on Twitter, and, given the intensity of its use by these diplomatic agencies, Twitter can be considered the main one for them. The foreign ministries of Kyrgyzstan and Uzbekistan have the largest number of followers on Facebook, but the representations of these countries to the UN have the biggest number of followers on Twitter. Perhaps this kind of 'shift' is due to the geographical alteration of the social media account: while an MFA in the capital communicates with both local and foreign followers, the diplomatic mission in New York should interact more with the international audience. However, for both the Tajik MFA and the mission to the UN, Facebook remains the main social media with the largest number of followers. We can assume that with the further development of Tajikistan's SMD, its diplomatic missions abroad will use Twitter more actively.

Tweets of the permanent missions of CAC to the UN, as in the case of their foreign ministries' tweets, are mostly informational posts about meetings and other activities of their diplomats. However, the Twitter account of Kazakhstan's mission has reacted, mostly by re-tweets, to a number of significant events and issues such as world animal day, pink flamingos, human rights, carbon neutrality, climate change, leopards, and

Table 27.6 Social media accounts of the permanent missions of CAC to the UN as of 01 August 2023 (with the percentage of growth in the number of followers since 01 October 2021).

Permanent Mission	Twitter	Facebook	Instagram	YouTube
KAZ	8,162 (+14,86%)	2.7K (+3.84%)	2,492 (+3,53%)	
KGZ	3,178 (+32,03%)	1.6K (+8,91%)	69 (+43,75%)	
TJK	717 (+100,84%)	2.6K (+11,01%)		
TKM	51 (The account functions since 4 May 2023)	7 (The account functions since 5 May 2023)	409 (The account functions since 4 May 2023)	
UZB	2,245 (+47,79%)	311 (+2,98%)	330 (starting from 23 May 2022)	

Table 27.7 The Twitter activity of the permanent missions of CAC to the UN from 01 October 2021 to 01 June 2022 (data from 06 June 2022)

Permanent Mission	1	2	3	4	5	6	7
KAZ	04.2015	4,491	47	357	287	52	9
KGZ	03.2017	1,270	43	54	130	214	181
TJK	04.2016	989	27	26	36	5	3
TKM							
UZB	12.2017	655	6	28	1	3	3

About the columns: 1) The date of joining Twitter. 2) The number of tweets from the date of joining to 01 June 2022. 3) The number of their tweets from 01 October 2021 to 01 June 2022. 4) The number of their re-tweets of others' tweets from 01 October 2021 to 01 June 2022. 5) The number of re-tweets of their own tweets from 01 October 2021 to 01 June 2022. 6) The number of comments on their tweets from 01 October 2021 to 01 June 2022. 7) The highest number of comments on a single tweet from 01 October 2021 to 01 June 2022.

biodiversity. The same can be noted regarding Kyrgyzstan and Tajikistan missions' reactions to some significant matters and dates related to mountains and water, and Uzbekistan's noting certain sporting, cultural, and gender-related occasions. The missions re-tweet others' tweets quite a lot. Certainly, the creation of the actor's own content enhances the uniqueness and attractiveness of its social media account.

DIGITAL DIPLOMACY OF CENTRAL ASIAN COUNTRIES 503

Table 27.8 The use of Twitter by Permanent Representatives of CAC to the UN as of 01 October 2022

Permanent Representative	1	2	3	4	5	6
KAZ: Magzham Ilyassov	26.10.2020	December 2020	1,099 (+15.6%)	71	29	7
KGZ: Aida Kasymalieva	15.02.2022	February 2022	283 (+45.9%)	192	11	9
TJK: Jonibek Hikmat	04.06.2021	February 2011	733 (+16%)	583[1]	151	13
TKM: Aksoltan Ataýewa	23.02.1995					
UZB: Bakhtiyor Ibragimov	23.05.2017	May 2017	2,211 (+15%)	220	13	6

About the columns: 1) Presentation of credentials. 2) Joining Twitter. 3) The number of followers (in parenthesis, the percentage increase compared to 01 June 2022). 4) The highest number of likes of a single tweet from 01 January 2022 to 01 October 2022. 5) The highest number of re-tweets of a single tweet from 01 January 2022 to 01 October 2022. 6) The highest number of comments on a single tweet.

[1] Tajikistan's Permanent Representative's Tweet from 18 July 2022, which received 583 likes and 151 re-tweets (that is significantly more than tweets with many interactions of his Central Asian colleagues at the UN), deserves attention. It is dedicated to the Nelson Mandela International Day and contains four photos of Nelson Mandela, Prince Harry, New York City Mayor Eric Adams, Deputy Secretary-General of the UN Amina J. Mohammed, and the President of the 76th session of the UN General Assembly Abdulla Shahid—all at the UNGA—as well as hashtags #MandelaDay and #PrinceHarryAtTheUN, and links to the Twitter accounts of Csaba Kőrösi, President of the 77th session of the UNGA with 241.9K followers, of Amina J. Muhammed's with 399.9K followers, of Mayor Eric Adams with 1.6M followers. It can be assumed that such a combination of an important and attractive topic with interesting photos and links to well-known people and their influential Twitter accounts played a role in the success of the tweet of the Tajikistan's UN Ambassador.

Twitter activity is becoming an important part of the work of senior diplomats in international diplomatic centres such as New York, and the UN Ambassadors of CAC (except Turkmenistan) use this social media quite actively. Three of the Permanent Representatives of CAC to the UN joined Twitter after being appointed to this post or presenting credentials. Table 27.8 provides some information about the use of Twitter by Permanent Representatives of CAC to the UN as of 01 October 2022.

A significant percentage of the CAC Permanent Representatives' Twitter activity is their re-tweets. Representing the country at the UN, re-tweeting about important international and domestic events is usual and expected. But when the number of re-tweets almost equals or even exceeds the number of one's own tweets, it indicates a lack of content for posts on Twitter.

Table 27.9 Social media accounts of the embassies of CAC in Washington, DC, as of 01 August 2023 (with percentage of growth in the number of followers since 01 January 2022)

Embassy	Twitter	Facebook	YouTube	Instagram
KAZ	7,520 (+4,91%)	4.5K (+2,11%)		2,516 (+26,81%)
KGZ	2,516 (+26,81%)	5K (+10,27%)		4,451 (+60,51)
TJK	148 (+49,49%)	2K (+25%)		
TKM	184 (+300% since 01 June 2022)	43 (+138,88% since 01 June 2022)		627 (+96,55% since 01 October 2022)
UZB	2,864 (+96,7%)	4.7K (+42,42%)	121 (+42,35%)	1,812 (+188,53%)

Table 27.10 Social media accounts of the embassies of CAC in Moscow, Russia as of 01 August 2023 (with percentage of growth or decline in the number of followers since 01 October 2021)

Embassy	Twitter	Facebook	YouTube	Instagram	Telegram channel
KAZ	821 (+10,49%)	10K (-8%)	7.92K (+12,02%)	15.9K (0%)	3,119 (+24,95%)
KGZ	155 (N/A)	4,7K (N/A)	624 (+212%)	17.6K (+2.32%)	901 (N/A)
TJK	297 (N/A)	8.1K (+7,25%)			492 (N/A)
TKM				797 (+15,840%)	
UZB		9.3K (+10,5%)	53 (+130,43% since 01 October 2022)	2,706 (+1,12% since 01 October 2022)	322 (+51,88% since 01 October 2022)

Table 27.9 displays some characteristics of the social media accounts of the embassies of CAC in Washington, DC, as of 01 August 2023 (in parenthesis, the percentage of growth in the number of followers since 01 January 2022).

Table 27.10 is about the social media accounts of the embassies of CAC in Moscow, Russia as of 01 August 2023 (in parenthesis, the percentage of growth or decline in the number of followers since 01 October 2021).

Some embassies of CAC in Moscow also use the Russian social media Vkontacte (VK). In this regard, the embassies of Kazakhstan and Uzbekistan are noticeable: on 01 August 2023, the former had 25K followers (-3,88% compared to 01 October 2022), and the number of followers of the latter were 797 (+230% compared to 01 October 2022).

Analysis

CAC are expanding the use of social media in their diplomatic practice and this is reflected in the growth of the number of accounts and followers. However, they haven't developed a sustainable strategy for their SMD yet. Not all MFAs, foreign ministers, diplomatic missions, and ambassadors are active in social media. Some embassies use many social media platforms, but others just a few or none. The same applies to individual diplomats. Apparently, a certain unsystematic nature in the development of SMD is explained by the lack of a comprehensive strategy in this area.

A game theory-based analysis shows the following features of the players (actors), game setting, strategic goals and objectives, dominant strategy, and payoffs of CAC's SMD.

Actors. In CAC, the state actors are the main players in SMD. Although they communicate with ordinary people and organizations on their social media platforms, in their SMD activities, these players interact and coordinate little with NGOs and civil society. In the social media accounts, there are very few links to the domestic and international NGOs as well as mutual re-posts. NGOs and civil society can be the main strategic partners in state actors' SMD, but to achieve this the state actors need to develop related objectives and strategy.

In their SMD, the countries of the region are not involved in confrontation with other actors. People reading or watching their narratives on social media mainly appear as networkers, or rather consumers than active partners or opponents.

Game setting. Analysing SMD of CAC, it is worth emphasizing the importance of the domestic digital environment because the game strategy of the state actors, including their representatives abroad, considerably depends on the instructions and feedback of principals operating at home. For example, because of the domestic restrictions, until recently, Twitter was relatively little used in the SMD of Uzbekistan. But the lifting of these restrictions has led to a significant intensification of the use of this social media by diplomats and diplomatic representatives of Uzbekistan both domestically and internationally. In Kazakhstan, during the unrest in early January 2022, the Internet was turned off, and the social media of the MFA and other government agencies did not work, and this has affected the ability of diplomatic missions abroad to repost the government messages.

Another important factor influencing the game setting of SMD is the choice of languages used in social media. On many social media platforms, CAC mainly use three languages: national, Russian, and English. While all these three languages are often used on Twitter, the national and Russian languages are employed more on Facebook, Instagram, and Telegram. This means, while Twitter often works for both domestic and foreign audiences, other social media and Telegram are mainly directed to the home audience.

Strategic goal and objectives. So far CAC mainly conduct their SMD in the framework of the following diplomatic objectives: strengthening political independence and enhancing security; making the country more attractive for foreign investment, tourists, trade, and joint projects in various areas including the economy, energy, transportation, education, and technology; and achieving good and sustainable relations with other actors of importance to them. Accordingly, they construct and present various interrelated narratives in their public diplomacy activities, particularly on social media. At this stage of their statecraft, the major strategic narrative in SMD of CAC is portraying the effective development of statehood through managing political, social, and economic problems as well as showing wide opportunities in these states. In other words, currently, SMD of CAC, along with informing about current affairs and events, mainly takes place within reputation-building public diplomacy with the elements of impression management and image-making. Such a meta-narrative is rather an implicit model of making sense of self, others, and the world, and it is mostly designed to help these still newly independent states become more significant players in the international arena and strengthen their global, regional, and domestic authority.

Dominant strategy. Presently, the dominant strategy of CAC's SMD is the *notification* one. Focusing on providing information about events and news related to them, CAC intend to build their reputation, manage impressions, and advance their images for becoming more influential and attractive actors. Although they promote their cultural traditions and values to a certain extent, the countries of the region are little involved in discussing on social media many global and regional challenges and acute problems of world affairs. They are careful to show their sympathies and antipathies with the major international players, avoiding involvement in any sort of disputes and confrontations. Little use of the engagement strategy by them can be explained by the lack of resources, skills, and clear SMD strategies.

Payoff. The number and geography of followers of the diplomatic social media accounts of CAC are growing, and the region's diplomats are becoming more skilful in notification, image-making, and impression management. This helps CAC to be more influential in SMD. However, because of the weakness of the engagement strategy, dialogical interaction between diplomatic players and their social media followers lags behind such growth.

CONCLUSION

The development of DD in CAC should be considered in the context of the evolution of their statecraft, foreign and domestic policy, and diplomacy in general, as well as the spread of digital technologies and ideas in these countries and internationally. In other words, it appears as a part of political, social, economic, and technological development in the CAC and world.

Currently, CAC are experiencing a dynamic development of the Internet and mobile technologies. However, they are still relatively new actors in SMD, and if we take the diplomatic agencies of CAC, Kazakhstan is arguably the most advanced player in the region, and Turkmenistan is a clear outsider.[14]

The coronavirus pandemic has significantly affected the penetration of ICT into the diplomatic activities of CAC, including their consular work. But despite certain development of DD in the countries of the region, SMD has not yet become one of the main and proactive instruments of international diplomacy of these states. Not all social media accounts indicated on the websites of some MFAs and embassies of these countries were available, and that shows some carelessness in managing and presenting the existing accounts on digital platforms.

The analysis shows that so far CAC make little use of the opportunities of SMD to engage with the audience, i.e. dialogically. For most diplomats from CAC, SMD mainly remains an instrument for informing foreigners and their own citizens about ongoing meetings and events, the current affairs of their governments, foreign ministries, embassies, and diplomats. Diplomatic actors of CAC are especially active in informing the home audience about their activities in the national and Russian languages, and their domestically oriented social media accounts have quite large numbers of followers. This is partly linked to the relative easiness of using these languages for many diplomats from CAC. To become more influential diplomatic players internationally, diplomats of these countries need to use English and other major world languages more effectively on social platforms.

The state-based diplomacy requires hierarchy and coordination within the state system. However, even in such a system diplomats need a sufficiently high level of independence and flexibility to practice the engagement strategy of SMD. As Shaun Riordan pointed out, 'Social media are not about getting messages across but participating in conversations. This means responding to comments, questions or messages' (2017). He also noted that social media campaigns and engagement are resource intensive, and digital diplomacy requires monitoring the social media as well as the flexibility to respond in real time. However, Riordan remarked, this is not always possible within hierarchically structured diplomatic services and foreign ministries: the new ICTs have been used by most MFAs to micromanage their diplomats abroad so that they stay within the government-approved messaging, and this prevents diplomats from responding on social media with the necessary speed and flexibility, especially in foreign languages and in other cultures (2017).

---

[14] Recently, there have been some developments of Turkmenistan's activities in SMD: several diplomatic missions of this country abroad created social media accounts, and the website of Turkmenistan's MFA contains a section about these accounts (MFA of Turkmenistan). Although the accomplishments of this country in SMD are very modest, considering the noted trend, we can expect that Turkmenistan will develop its DD more actively.

The small number of diplomatic personnel in foreign missions of CAC does not contribute to the greater involvement of these diplomats in SMD. The existing strong centralized information management system helps diplomats from these states to focus more on other areas of work without spending much time on social media. But at the same time, this prevents them from being more independent, prompt, and flexible in their SMD activities.

Currently, SMD of CAC is largely based on reputation-building public diplomacy, which includes impression management, image-making, and spreading their own narratives—their sense of achievements, opportunities, and successful statecraft. The development of the engagement strategy in SMD will require from diplomats more independence and quick reactions to the acute problems of the modern world as well as patient and attentive conversation with the audience, reaction and response to people's concerns and questions, and a more proactive approach to the social media activities related to the strategic objectives of their foreign policy and diplomacy. Such a strategy can be supported not only by the digital technologies and DD professionals but also by the conceptual vision and the coordination of efforts with non-state actors and civil society.

In their mostly informing strategy of SMD, CAC diplomatic actors widely use visual images like photographs of officials during meetings and other formal events. The quality of their visual images has improved recently. The attraction of more informal and creative images and short videos can help them to develop their SMD engagement strategies.

So far CAC are little involved in conducting effective and coordinated social media campaigns to support some globally important causes and values. Apparently, to play a more prominent role in international relations and diplomacy, they need to be more engaged with global problems and challenges and to develop and propose their own approaches to solving them. Currently, the countries of the region are more active in mostly home-oriented social media activities and covering some regional issues and problems. For being more effective in the international arena and diplomacy, they need to constantly create their own SMD content that would be attractive and important from the global and regional perspectives.

For SMD to be used at a more strategic level, that is, as a pivotal instrument of foreign policy and diplomacy, CAC need to develop some comprehensive strategies of engagement with other state and non-state stakeholders around their long-term fundamental objectives and critical international problems. To raise the effectiveness of SMD, CAC need to have a more conceptualized SMD with clearly defined strategic goals and measurable objectives. Strategic narratives developed and used on social media platforms should have significance not only for the narrator but also for other actors and targeted audiences. That requires knowledge, skills, resources, and strategic thinking. The widespread use of modern digital analytics tools acquires special importance.

In CAC, certain training in the field of DD has been conducted, but not systematically and regularly. To develop their effectiveness in this area, CAC need to enhance their training for diplomats in various forms of DD, digital storytelling, social data analytics, and artificial intelligence as well as to strengthen their SMD teams. It is also important for them to create a clear strategy and assessment of using social media by diplomats and diplomatic agencies by taking into consideration other countries' experiences. The field of SMD is rapidly developing, and such a policy can help the countries of the region to become effective players in this game of strategic interaction sooner rather than later.

SUGGESTED READING

Bjola, Corneliu and Holmes, Markus, eds., *Digital Diplomacy: Theory and Practice* (London and New York: Routledge, 2015).

Bjola, Corneliu and Pamment, James, eds., *Countering Online Propaganda and Extremism: The Dark Side of Digital Diplomacy* (London and New York: Routledge, 2019).

Cull, Nicholas J. *Public Diplomacy: Foundations for Global Engagement in the Digital Age* (Cambridge, UK: Polity, 2019).

Fletcher, Tom, *Naked Diplomacy: Power and Statecraft in the Digital Age* (London: William Collins, 2016).

Manor, Ilan, *The Digitalization of Public Diplomacy* (Cham, Switzerland: Palgrave Macmillan, 2019).

REFERENCES

Adlia (Centralized Legal Information Bank of the Republic of Tajikistan) 'Decree of the Government of Tajikistan No.642' (30 December 2019). http://www.adlia.tj/show_doc.fwx?rgn=135392 (Accessed 3 October 2022).

Bjola, Corneliu, 'Digital Diplomacy: From Tactics To Strategy', *The American Academy in Berlin*, 2018. https://www.americanacademy.de/digital-diplomacy-tactics-strategy/ (Accessed 3 October 2022).

DataReportal. https://datareportal.com/ (Accessed 3 October 2022).

Hudaykulov, Azam, 'Prospects for digital diplomacy in Central Asia: the experience of Uzbekistan', *Oriental Renaissance: Innovative, Educational. Natural and Social Sciences*, no. 1, (Issue 8, 2021): pp. 540–546.

Faizullaev, Alisher and Cornut, Jérémie, 'Narrative practice in international politics and diplomacy: the case of the Crimean crisis', *Journal of International Relations and Development*, no. 20 (Issue 3, 2017): pp. 587–604.

Freedom House. https://freedomhouse.org/countries/freedom-net/scores (Accessed 3 October 2022).

Legal Information System of Regulatory Legal Acts of the Republic of Kazakhstan. https://adilet.zan.kz/eng/docs/U2000000280 (Accessed 3 October 2022).

LexUz online, 'On the Approval of the Strategy "Digital Uzbekistan-2030" and Measures for its Effective Implementation', *Decree of the President of the Republic of Uzbekistan*, 5 October 2020 (in Russian). https://lex.uz/ru/docs/5031048 (Accessed 3 October 2022).

LexUz online, 'Resolution of the President of the Republic of Uzbekistan on organizational measures to further improve the activities of the Ministry of Foreign Affairs of the Republic of Uzbekistan', 4 April 2018. https://lex.uz/docs/3611280 (Accessed 3 October 2022).

Manor, Ilan, *The Digitalization of Public Diplomacy* (Cham, Switzerland: Palgrave Macmillan, 2019).

MFA of Kyrgyzstan. https://mfa.gov.kg/en/Main-menu/Press-service/novosti/-613b427fe3069 (Accessed 3 October 2022).

MFA of Tajikistan. https://mfa.tj/en/main/view/4255/concept-of-the-foreign-policy-of-the-republic-of-tajikistan (Accessed 3 October 2022).

MFA of Turkmenistan. https://www.mfa.gov.tm/en/social-media (Accessed 3 October 2022).

MFA of Uzbekistan. https://mfa.uz/31351 (Accessed 3 October 2022).

Ministry of Justice of the Kyrgyz Republic, 'Order of the Government of the Kyrgyz Republic', 15 February 2019 (in Russian). http://cbd.minjust.gov.kg/act/view/ru-ru/216896?cl=ru-ru (Accessed 3 October 2022).

Ministry of Justice of the Republic of Kazakhstan, Informational-legal System of Regulatory Legal Acts, 'On the Approval of the State Program "Digital Kazakhstan"', Resolution of the Government of the Republic of Kazakhstan, 12 December 2017 (in Russian). https://adilet.zan.kz/rus/docs/P1700000827 (Accessed 3 October 2022).

Miskimmon, Alister, O'Loughlin, Ben, and Roselle, Laura, 'Strategic narrative: 21st century diplomatic statecraft', *Revista Mexicana de Política Exterior*, no. 113 (2018). https://revistadigital.sre.gob.mx/images/stories/numeros/n113/miskimmonoloughlinrosellei.pdf (Accessed 1 June 2022).

OSCE, 'OSCE promotes dialogue and cooperation between junior diplomats from Central Asia, Afghanistan and Mongolia', 24 June 2019. https://www.osce.org/programme-office-in-bishkek/423932 (Accessed 3 October 2022).

Riordan, Shaun, 'Digital diplomacy in 2016: The need for strategy', *University of Southern California Center for Public Diplomacy Blog*, 27 March 2017. https://uscpublicdiplomacy.org/blog/digital-diplomacy-2016-need-strategy (Accessed 1 June 2022).

Schelling, Thomas, *The Strategy of Conflict* (Cambridge, MA: Harvard University Press, 1980).

Tassilova, Aigerim, Zhappasov, Zharilkasyn, Shyngyssova, Nazgul, Sarybayev, Meiram, Sadenova, Aigul, Tasylova, Nazyia, and Kozgambayeva, Gulnar, 'Comparative analysis on digital diplomacy in Kazakhstan, Uzbekistan and Kyrgyzstan', *Astra Salvensis*, no. 11 (Volume VI, 2018): pp. 321–332.

The State Bank for Foreign Economic Affairs of Turkmenistan, 'The Concept of Development of Digital Economy in 2019-2025 has been approved', 30 November 2018 (in Russian). https://www.tfeb.gov.tm/index.php/ru/2013-09-20-04-46-10/802-2018-11-30-10-53-29 (Accessed 3 October 2022).

The World Bank. Data. https://data.worldbank.org/indicator/IT.NET.USER.ZS (Accessed 3 October 2022).

Twiplomacy, 'Uzbekistan, Shavkat Mirziyoyev's Press-service, President Shavkat Mirziyoyev'. https://twiplomacy.com/info/asia/uzbekistan/president_uz/ (Accessed 23 December 2021).

UNDP Uzbekistan, 'Enhancing Capacities for Digital Economic Diplomacy in Uzbekistan'. https://www.uz.undp.org/content/uzbekistan/en/home/projects/enhancing-capacities-for-digital-economic-diplomacy-in-uzbekista.html (Accessed 3 October 2022).

USAID, 'USAID Advances Digital Diplomacy in Turkmenistan', 15 April 2021. https://www.usaid.gov/turkmenistan/press-releases/apr-15-2021-usaid-advances-digital-diplomacy (Accessed 3 October 2022).

CHAPTER 28

CHINESE WOLF-WARRIOR DIPLOMACY: MOTIVATIONS, MODALITIES, AND SITES OF PRACTICE

ANDREW F. COOPER AND JEFF HAI-CHI LOO

INTRODUCTION

PROMPTED by the US–China trade war in 2018, and outbreak of Covid-19 in 2019, the People's Republic of China (PRC) developed a distinctive diplomatic practice with an assertive even provocative approach towards the Western powers (Zhu, 2020).

This constituted a very different repertoire from the one used by the PRC over the past two decades, especially with special reference to the use of mass media and open conferences to project the PRC's diplomatic strategy. Most significantly, the new diplomatic approach emphasizes new technology, especially social media, to amplify the PRC's position on specific issues in the international system. To a considerable extent, the utilization of new digital technology as a platform is connected to traditional statecraft: with the privileging of 'national interest' and 'territorial integrity' as the core ingredient in the PRC's foreign policy (Hackenesch and Bader, 2020; Verma, 2020; and Weiss and Dafoe, 2019). But in style, the application of digital diplomacy with wolf-warrior characteristics taps into a deep reservoir of emotions, including resentment, frustrations, anger, pride, and status deprivation. Indeed, it is this emotional component that gives wolf-warrior diplomacy its name. Only through an awareness of this combination of animating factors can a fuller understanding of the nature of wolf-warrior diplomacy be deduced.

A more constricted argument is that wolf-warrior diplomacy is consistent with realist traditions, especially since the major focus on motivations is on the fundamental tenets of the defence of 'national sovereignty' reflected in the deep priorities of PRC's national security attached to the survival of the PRC as a Communist Party of China (CPC) party-state. However, distinct from the logic of rationality and strategic calculus of classical realism, wolf-warrior diplomacy also taps into a deep reservoir of populist-oriented calculations which demonstrate the CPC's close attention to public demands facilitated by the use of new technology and social media. Where this chapter extends the debate is in its detailed analysis of how PRC diplomats as specific practitioners operate to impact the shift in diplomatic practice. The most robust promoters were several young diplomats, notably Geng Shuang, Hua Chunying, and Ziao Lijian (Shepherd, 2020). By contrast, many of the old generation refrained from adopting this approach (Weichieh Wang, 2022). This generational gap was especially prominent in relation to sites of practice. As the main game of PRC diplomacy—the US, Japan, Australia, and the UK—became managed over time by new hands instead of old hands, wolf-warrior practice gained traction. With a very different set of motivations and technical skill sets, this new cluster of diplomats embraced new technology as a tool of comparative advantage. Equally, wolf-warrior diplomacy also serves as a key tool to respond to populist sentiment from ordinary citizens. By looking into three major cases, including 1) the responses over the outbreak of the Covid-19 pandemic; 2) the critiques over US democracy; and 3) the attack on external actors on their involvement in Hong Kong, Tibet, Xinjiang, and Taiwan matters, the chapter will demonstrate how wolf-warrior diplomats strengthen the PRC's state responsiveness through stimulating nationalistic and populist sentiment to ultimately consolidate the CCP's legitimacy and regime security. As the PRC regime has ample control in the domain of cyberspace, the PRC party-state was able to develop strategic narratives through social media to consolidate support from the masses.

THEORETICAL PERSPECTIVES IN TERMS OF THE DEBATE OVER DIGITAL DIPLOMACY

This section of the chapter aims to review relevant theoretical debate about digital diplomacy under realist, nationalistic, and populist considerations. On this basis, we extend the discussion in an effort to merge different currents together and develop a comprehensive framework to explain the emergence of Chinese wolf-warrior diplomacy and its motivations, modalities, and sites of practice.

Scholars have studied digital diplomacy in an increasingly detailed fashion for the past decade. These studies concentrate on how the development of new technology, especially the Internet, has influenced international relations. Some of the literature focuses on how digital diplomacy has the ability to set the agenda in shaping world politics through persuading, enticing, and attracting others through the force of a country's beliefs, values, and ideas instead of through coercion militarily and economically. This approach also takes into account how digital diplomacy acts as an important supplement to traditional diplomacy that can assist a country to achieve diplomatic goals, extend its external ties, and influence people who will never interact with any of the world's embassies (Adesina, 2017). Also, some of the literature asserts that digital diplomacy is an alternative form of international practice that is not merely a strategy of public diplomacy but also a mechanism for states to manage the dynamic change in the international arena (Holmes, 2015; and Bjola and Jiang, 2015).

Digital diplomacy serves as a key tool for states to resolve the challenges of the competent political performances of different types of actors in the international system. This alternative dimension argues that social media is a crucial tool to perform three key aspects of public diplomatic engagement, namely digital agenda setting, digital presence expansion, and digital conversation generation (Bjola and Jian, 2015). Such a form of public diplomatic management speaks to an essential aspect of exerting influence to change another country's behaviour through the informal diplomatic channel, including message content, informational reach, and mode of engagement with the audience (Bjola and Jian, 2015: 77). From this perspective, the debate follows a suggestive line that highlights the capability of digital diplomacy to develop an instrumental platform in attracting public engagement.

Finally, it must be added, some of the literature treats digital diplomacy as a crucial means for states to expand the reach to connect and inform others (Abbasov, 2007; Lowy Interpreter, 2015; and Lewis, 2014). This more speculative perspective views digital diplomacy as essential for the state to widen its diplomatic space and as a possible way to compete with the influence and power of non-state entities in cyberspace. As the advancement of information technology boosts the connection between citizens and diplomats, it has become a prominent diplomatic communication that changes the sites of practice for most diplomats (Lowy Interpreter, 2015). In specific terms, the government can utilize social media to connect with ordinary citizens from other countries in real time (Lewis, 2014).

Consistent with this perspective, China believes external propaganda is a crucial strategy to express the 'China Story' globally, and the use of new digital technology and social media remains significant in facilitating China to develop its new sentiment to respond to different global issues. More specifically, President Xi Jinping stresses the significance of diplomats struggling with possible enemies in the international arena (Shi, 2020). As such, digital diplomacy is considered as the most useful tool and one of the important strategies for China to express its real-time influence in the international arena to counterbalance the influence of Western powers by intensifying the connection between ordinary citizens and diplomats.

Building in the Debate over Assertive Nationalism and Populist Authoritarianism

The theoretical discussion on assertive nationalism is one of the most integral in developing PRC's diplomatic strategies. As Allen S. Whiting (1993) argues, assertive nationalism has the following characteristics: 1) advocating how Western Imperialism humiliated China in the pre-1949 period, 2) embracing how CCP developed its independence and self-reliance path to tackle international isolation in the post-1949 era, and 3) stressing the notion that another external force could not humiliate the PRC and undermine its national security and developmental interests. The idea of assertive nationalism demonstrated the PRC's convoluted path in developing its diplomatic space and international recognition.

In operational terms, assertive nationalism serves as a guide to diplomats in foreign relations and cultivates an environment that public opinion favours the PRC government. More specifically, the PRC utilized mouthpieces in propaganda efforts with respect to ordinary citizens and bureaucrats to develop a series of nationalistic sentiments (Whiting, 1993: 929). In other words, the PRC developed assertive nationalism as a means for ideological indoctrination of both government officials and ordinary citizens to intensify the national unity and justify the state's response and position on different issues.

The aforesaid theoretical discussions on assertive nationalism helps to explain the evolution of PRC diplomacy from conservative and inactive to wolf-warrior-style diplomacy. In particular, the PRC under Xi Jinping's administration had been drifting incrementally from hard authoritarianism to neo-totalitarianism (Beja, 2019). The neo-totalitarian leader overwhelmingly stressed how the hegemonic forces, notably the US and the UK, challenge some critical internal issues, such as Hong Kong, Xinjiang, and Tibet. In addition, the neo-totalitarian leader stresses the need to emphasize the significance of the 'Four Self-Confidences', namely confidence in the chosen path, confidence in the political system, confidence in the guiding principles, and confidence in Chinese culture (Hui, 2020).

From Xi Jinping's point of view, these self-confidences not only facilitate the bureaucrats to overcome any challenges, particularly external matters, but could also maintain national unity (Hui, 2020). Also, many of the PRC's leaders and former leaders stress the need to ensure national interests as the bottom line of foreign policy (Zhang, 2018). There is no doubt that the PRC developed an assertive nationalistic sentiment in external affairs to show its confidence in internal development and visions. More crucially, these nationalistic sentiments can allow the PRC's leadership to develop a strategic narrative for their citizens to show their confidence to deny any negotiation with an external threat, especially those related to national sovereignty and territorial integrity (Swine, 2010). To summarize, assertive nationalism can reflect how the PRC's officials utilized strategic nationalistic narratives to show their confidence and commitment to the ordinary citizens in tackling external challenges.

The concept of populist authoritarianism is another integral concept by which to understand how the PRC formulates its diplomatic strategies. According to Tang, the PRC had developed a political culture that can be defined as populist authoritarianism (PA model). It consists of multiple factors, including the majority acceptance of mass-line ideology foundation, relatively dense social capital and interpersonal trust, a high degree of political trust and regime support, strong national identity determination, underdevelopment of civil society, and direct public political involvement (Tang, 2016: 54). The PA model specifically highlights how populist orientation could exert influence on the ruling style of the CCP. In other words, it concentrates on how the CCP's leadership utilized mass political campaigns as a key institutional measure and practice to garner sufficient public support. Furthermore, the PA model also serves as a framework to show how the CCP considers regime survival as an issue of ultimate importance. Specifically, the populist authoritarian state is insecure with public opinion and considers it a root of instability (Tang, 2019: 159).

By set of practice, the CCP party-state is able to create an environment that illustrates its hyper-responsiveness to public opinion. By censoring certain critical opinions from the public and the use of security apparatus to maintain stability, the CCP regime was able to maintain its regime legitimacy without concerning most of the public opinion (Tang, 2016: 159). Objectively speaking, the formulation of PRC's diplomacy can be explained by the PA model in which the state overwhelmingly utilizes populist sentiment to maintain internal support and safeguard regime survival. These populist sentiments can be seen from the antiforeign protests where the CCP regime mobilized popular expression when facing severe diplomatic challenges (Zhao, 2017). The CCP state apparatus was normally quick to respond and to curb even very small-scale demonstrations but tolerated and even encouraged these protests until protestors not only became violent but also turned to criticize the PRC government for its relative soft line position towards their 'enemies', including the US and Japan (Weiss, 2013 and Zhao, 2017). As such, the PA model can demonstrate the PRC regime's hyper-responsiveness to achieve external challenges and maintain its regime legitimacy and status quo.

The Internal and External Goals of Wolf-Warrior Diplomacy

Figure 28.1 develops an analytical framework to explore PRC's wolf-warrior diplomacy. In essence, PRC's wolf-warrior diplomacy can be considered as a new diplomatic strategy, with both internal and external goals. Internally, the wolf-warrior diplomacy serves as a tool to consolidate the CCP's legitimacy and regime survival; in other words, to ensure CCP's leadership as the utmost objective for diplomats to achieve. As the PRC's foreign policy strategies tend to be in a populist orientation, a provocative and assertive position on some critical issues could enhance national unity. Therefore, the CCP could maintain its legitimacy and dominant position in the PRC. Also, the PRC utilized social media to spread assertive nationalistic sentiments to influence the masses' opinions. By manipulating new technology, social media, and artificial intelligence, the PRC's state is able to create an environment and develop strategic narratives

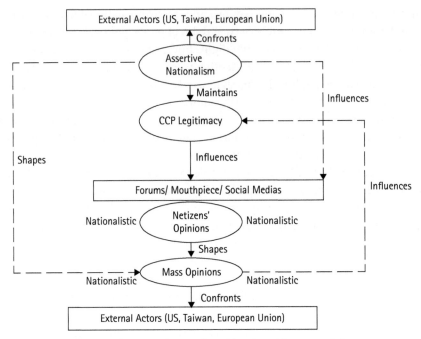

FIGURE 28.1 An analytical framework to explain China's wolf-warrior diplomacy

that show its commitment and confidence in a struggle with external challenges. As the state is able to censor and filter netizens' opinions, it can eliminate some critical arguments against the CPC. More essentially, the PRC is able to develop sufficient public support to legitimate its aggressive struggle with foreign countries. More crucially, the PRC official can enhance the diplomatic communication between ordinary citizens and diplomats through the spread of nationalistic sentiments virtually. As such, the PRC could maintain a stable environment to demonstrate its strong public support in struggling with foreign forces.

Externally, the wolf-warrior diplomacy serves as propaganda to oppose any external threats and criticisms which are considered key challenges to PRC's national security and developmental interests. More specifically, the PRC leaders overwhelmingly emphasize the Marxian approach to counteract the influence of hegemony. Xi Jinping stressed the need to use a 'fighting spirit' to overcome diplomatic challenges. As President Xi Jinping remarks, 'CCP had braced for a continuous struggle against a variety of threats, including the external forces that are challenging 'China' (Shi, 2020). Struggling with external actors has become a crucial strategy for the diplomats to overcome the hegemonic challenge and defend the PRC's core interest. More importantly, the PRC could grasp this golden opportunity to show the superiority of the China model with the use of social media and new technology. In particular, it can unify the support from different parts of the world, especially consolidating the support from overseas Chinese. With the use of new digital technology to achieve diplomatic goals, the PRC diplomats are able to create a new image in international society, which demonstrates the PRC's ability to confront possible enemies in the internal arena.

CASE STUDY 1: THE RESPONSE TO THE OUTBREAK OF COVID-19 PANDEMIC

Unlike the outbreak of Severe Acute Respiratory Syndrome (SARS) in 2003, when the PRC party-state acted conservatively to external criticisms, the PRC's wolf-warrior diplomats rather adopted a far more assertive, aggressive, and provocative position to criticize and struggle with all the external criticisms about the origin of the outbreak of Covid-19.

Firstly, the PRC government attempted to shift the external criticisms over the PRC's role in mishandling the outbreak of the virus in Wuhan to garner public support with the use of social media. From the PRC's perspective, the external criticisms over the Covid-19 mismanagement had derived tremendous impact to regime legitimacy and security. In reality, the PRC's wolf-warrior diplomats tried to show how China acts as 'prompt and decisive' in combating the outbreak of the Covid-19 pandemic (Aljazeera, 2021). According to a tweet from Chinese foreign ministry spokeswoman Hua Chunying, China was the first country that alerted the outside world to a struggle with the pandemic. Hua even argued that Beijing had imposed sufficient measures to avoid infection (Aljazeera, 2021). From Hua's remarks, it is crystal clear that the PRC intends to show its responsiveness in handling the virus to external actors. More importantly, Hua intended to develop narratives virtually by showing how China's success in combating the spread of Covid-19, which is distinct from other countries, such as the UK and the US, shows the hyper-responsiveness of the PRC. As such, the PRC can develop a discourse that demonstrates how it successfully combats diseases to consolidate public support.

Secondly, the PRC diplomats overwhelmingly stressed the stigmatization of external actors, notably the US, in cyberspace. One of the major criticisms that stimulated the PRC's nerve is whether the outbreak of Covid-19 originated in Wuhan. The US State Department claimed Covid-19 emerged from the Wuhan Institute of Virology (WIV), in particular arguing that the Covid-19 pandemic outbreak related to the secret military activity conducted at the WIV's laboratory (US Embassy, Beijing, 2021). The US State Department even urged for an independent investigation with access to WIV to explore some critical information about the origins of Covid-19.

To respond to such provocative criticisms made by the US, the PRC diplomats express their anger by calling former US Secretary of State Mike Pompeo 'Mr. Liar' in different social media, like Weibo, Twitter, and Forum (*The Week*, 2021). The Chinese diplomats also contended that Pompeo had spread out 'conspiracies and lies' by connecting the WIV to the Chinese Military. Furthermore, the Chinese foreign ministry spokeswoman,

Hua Chunying, even asserted that the US intended to blame China to avoid any internal criticisms about the passive way it dealt with the pandemic. Another Chinese foreign ministry spokesman, Zhao Lijian, rather echoes a conspiracy theory that suggested the outbreak of Covid-19 was a matter imported from the US army (*Hong Kong Free Press*, 2020). By attacking the US, the PRC stressed how the Western powers, notably the US, politicized the pandemic narrative. More importantly, the PRC intended to show the US's information was misleading and unauthoritative to stimulate the assertive nationalistic sentiment to indoctrinate mass opinion in cyberspace. As such, the PRC is able to show its confidence to demonstrate its ability to struggle with any further stigmatization by the outside world.

Finally, the PRC utilized cyberspace to manipulate netizens' opinions to openly criticize foreign countries' efforts to contain the outbreak of Covid-19. In particular, the PRC manipulated formal and informal channels to stress the superiority of authoritarian measures in combatting the outbreak of Covid-19. In particular, Beijing's online mouthpiece *Global Times* stressed the Covid-19 epidemic in the US had evolved into a humanitarian disaster (*Global Times*, 2020c). Also, the *Global Times* describes the US as a 'living hell' that illustrates the Western-model failure in handling the health crisis (*Global Times*, 2020a). More significantly, the *Global Times* openly criticized the US's human rights accusation against China. By describing the US's situation as a 'massacre' and 'a shame for humanity', the *Global Times* stressed how the US failed to protect human rights during the Covid-19 pandemic (*Global Times*, 2020a, 2020b). As a matter of interest, these accusations appear from netizens' opinions towards the US. Many Chinese netizens overwhelmingly focus on how the US and its mainstream media utilized the misinformation to attack China while neglecting its human rights situation (*Global Times*, 2020c). These netizens even blamed the existence of racism towards the overseas Chinese for showing how the US violates human rights. By manipulating the mouthpiece, the PRC was able to censor all politically incorrect comments toward the CCP. In reality, it can also lead to netizens' opinions being more nationalistic. More importantly, the PRC authorities are able to manipulate these netizens' opinions to consolidate national unity. Therefore, the CCP was able to maintain its dominant position without any internal criticisms.

The way that the PRC authority responded to the Covid-19 crisis shows the PRC's wolf-warrior diplomacy as an aggressive response to the severe external challenge with a strong concentration on the use of cyberspace. In particular, the PRC authorities see that such an aggressive and assertive approach can enhance their confidence to struggle with external criticisms. Furthermore, the wolf-warrior diplomacy can also illustrate the CCP's commitment to struggle with any external threats that narrow the gap between ordinary citizens and diplomats. By utilizing the mouthpieces and netizens' opinions, the PRC was able to develop an assertive and nationalistic sentiment to legitimate its accusation of the external threats. Unlike the previous diplomatic approach, which passively responded to Western power, the wolf-warrior diplomacy has its flexibility with the massive use of cyberspace, which is able to consolidate national unity and enhance CPC's legitimacy.

Case 2: The Critiques Over Confrontations in Washington on 6 January 2021

The frequent remarks from the PRC's diplomats on the clashes in Washington on 6 January 2021 demonstrates how the PRC wolf warrior was a dominant feature. The PRC utilized cyberspace to project an image that the US shows a double standard in condemning the clashes in Washington but not on other issues. In particular, the Chinese Officials draw a comparison between Washington on 6 January 2021, and the Occupation of the Legislative Council (LegCo) in Hong Kong on 1 July 2019. According to Chinese foreign ministry spokesperson Hua Chunying, the scenes in Washington were similar to Hong Kong and the US government should not condemn such a 'violent incident'. Hua also asserted that the response from the US and officials to the confrontation in Washington was different from those that happened in Hong Kong. Hua even argues the American people should stand with those 'rioters' and 'extremists' (Tiezzi, 2021). From Hua's comment, it is clear that such comparisons are used to attack the US's moral authority in the support democracy movement. Furthermore, the PRC officials even utilized such a scene to show the failure of the US in handling internal affairs. By projecting a negative image of the US, the PRC authorities could legitimize the assertive position on some critical issues, such as Hong Kong and Taiwan matters. As such, the PRC was able to defend its human rights situation by discrediting the US's response to the confrontation in Washington (Global Times 2021a).

Also, the PRC authorities use their formal and informal channels to accuse US politicians in order to consolidate internal support. In particular, the PRC diplomats targeted those US politicians who have a strong anti-China sentiment to show that the US has to bear all the responsibility for such conflict-ridden US–China relations. As Chinese foreign ministry spokesperson Zhao Lijin mentioned, the former Secretary of State Mike Pompeo's biggest legacy in his administration is 'lying diplomacy' (*Global Times*, 2021b): arguing that Pompeo had undermined the US's reputation and its intention to spread the political virus. He even argued that Pompeo's accusation of the CCP was also an attack on all Chinese people in the territory (*Global Times*, 2021b). Similarly, Chinese foreign ministry spokesperson Hua Chunying asserted that those anti-China US politicians 'have been staging a final show of madness'. She also argues such anti-China sentiments reflect those US politicians who intend to grasp this opportunity to earn votes. She believed such clashes in Washington had delegitimized Trump's policy towards China (Tiezzi, 2021). The editor of PRC's mouthpiece, *Global Times*, Hu Xijin, argues that former US President Donald Trump excessively uses China as a scapegoat to promote US democracy. Hu further argues Trump's legacy has become a major threat to democracy (Hu Xijin, 2021). From the above critiques over US politicians made by Chinese diplomats, there is no doubt that the PRC authorities intend to blame these US politicians' actions for undermining US–China relations. By linking the violence in Washington to these politicians' anti-China sentiment, the PRC authorities intend to show how China intends to avoid conflicts with the US. In addition, these attacks on anti-China US politicians can strengthen the spread of nationalistic sentiments. More importantly, the PRC is able to stress the superiority of the China model and its institutional uniqueness in responding to people's demand. Therefore, the PRC was able to consolidate its internal support and maintain its regime legitimacy.

The critiques over the clashes in Washington on 6 January 2021 show the PRC authorities intend to blame the failure of US democracy. By projecting a negative image toward the US virtually, the PRC authorities were able to discredit the US's moral authority in supporting the democracy movement. The PRC even grasped this opportunity to justify their hardline position in handling some critical issues. Finally, the wolf-warrior criticisms over the anti-China US politicians also facilitate the spread of nationalistic sentiments in cyberspace that result in a consolidation of netizens' support and gaining internal recognition of the superiority of China model.

CASE 3: THE ATTACK ON EXTERNAL ACTORS FOR THEIR INVOLVEMENT IN HONG KONG, TIBET, XINJIANG, AND TAIWAN MATTERS

The continued attack on external actors, notably the US, UK, Australia, and Canada about their involvement in Hong Kong, Tibet, Xinjiang, and Taiwan matters shows that wolf-warrior diplomacy serves as a tool to show its confidence to struggle with external threats.

Internally, the PRC authorities targeted various external actors in critical issues and openly accused them of stimulating nationalistic sentiments. By exaggerating external actors' involvement in those critical issues, the PRC intends to show the ordinary citizens how the foreign force intends to subvert the PRC's political system. For example, the PRC's Foreign Ministry Spokesman Zhao Lijian openly criticized the Western countries with the use of Twitter, stating that especially the US, the UK, Australia, and Canada did not respect China's sovereignty and were continuously interfering in Hong Kong matters, which was considered an intervention in China's internal affairs (Ministry of Foreign Affairs of the People's Republic of China, 2021). Zhao's remark is obvious to demonstrate the PRC's intention to express how foreign countries threaten their core interests. More importantly, Zhao's remark further exaggerates these foreign countries as a challenge to China's national sovereignty rights and territorial integrity. To stimulate the nationalistic sentiments on foreign countries' involvement in Hong Kong, Tibet, Xinjiang, and Taiwan Mainland matters, the PRC authorities also manipulated the netizen's opinions to exert influence on mass opinions. Many Chinese netizens continue to attack the pages on social media that are managed by the pro-Taiwan independence groups, the Taiwanese government, pro-Uyghur groups, pro-Tibet groups, and pro-Hong Kong groups to show their ability to curb any opinions that cross PRC's political red line. Some Chinese netizens even proposed a boycott campaign on those companies who offended China by supporting the politically incorrect movement (Griffiths, 2020). The most typical example was Thai actor Vachirawait. He was boycotted by the Chinese netizens as he wrongly listed Hong Kong as a 'country' on Twitter. He was criticized by millions of Chinese netizens as advocating 'Hong Kong independent'. He soon posted an apology, but the Chinese netizens are not satisfied with his action. The case of Vachirawait demonstrates how the PRC authorities utilized the netizen's opinions to attack any politically inappropriate claims to enhance national unity. By using these formal and informal channels, the PRC authority can guide the mass opinions on critical issues. As such, it can consolidate internal support by showing their confidence to struggle with the hegemonic force.

Externally, the PRC authorities continue to showcase Western prejudice towards China as a means of winning the hearts and minds of the countries who offend by the Western hegemonic power. In particular, the PRC stressed their commitment to human rights affairs. For example, the PRC official condemned the external criticisms about Xinjiang's 're-education centers'. Most Western countries have accused the PRC authority of detaining millions of Uighur Muslims in concentration camps. More than thirty-nine democratic countries expressed the view that such political re-education programmes restrict freedom of speech, assembly, religion, and belief (US Mission to the United Nations, 2020). The US even sees such a 'political re-education camp' as a repression campaign and even genocide on ethnic minorities (Ramzy, 2021). In responding to these external criticisms, the PRC authorities called these Uighur Muslims 'students' influenced by extremist ideology (ABC News, 2019). The PRC authorities even claimed such a 're-education camp' is a vocational training programme to increase their competitiveness (CGTN News, 2019). The PRC authorities in response organized a tour of these re-education centres for some media and diplomats to better understand the objectives of setting up these vocational training programmes for ethnic minorities. The PRC authorities also utilized the mouthpiece and social media to interview these students to demonstrate China's intention to resolve deep-rooted problems in ethnic minority regions. Some of the PRC diplomats even used 'Black Lives Matter' to compare the human rights situation to show the superiority of the China model. The PRC authority also uses similar tactics and practices to tell the 'truth' about Hong Kong, Taiwan, and Tibet matters to show the significance of specific implementation measures to assure regime security (MERICS, 2020; US Consulate, Hong Kong, 2020). More importantly, these propaganda campaigns allow the PRC to show its confidence to resist any external criticisms. As such, the PRC was able to develop an alliance to confront the dominance of Western hegemony.

To summarize, the enduring attack on external actors for their involvement in some critical issues demonstrates how the PRC attempts to utilize both formal and informal networks not only to consolidate internal support but also to struggle with any external criticisms. More significantly, wolf-warrior diplomacy serves as a tool to formulate alliances with developing states to confront Western power.

DISCUSSIONS AND LIMITATIONS

The analysis of wolf-warrior diplomacy has become overwhelmingly politized: an approach which neglects conceptual clarity. These discussions concentrate on specific actors and their behaviour at the expense of analytical utility and the ability to capture the special features of the China case.

The case of the PRC authority responding to the Covid-19 crisis specifically demonstrated wolf diplomacy as an assertive even aggressive response of the PRC's diplomats with the use of cyberspace. This approach can enhance and earn the confidence of the general public, narrowing the gap between ordinary citizens and diplomats. With the use of mouthpieces and netizens' opinions, the PRC was able to cultivate an assertive and nationalistic sentiment to legitimize any decision to accuse external threats. This case also demonstrates the PRC diplomat's flexibility in the use of cyberspace to enhance national unity and remain the CPC's legitimacy ultimately. The case of critiques over the clashes in Washington on 6 January 2021, demonstrates the PRC diplomats intend to blame the failure of US democracy and demonstrate its institutional supremacy. With the use of cyberspace and social media, the PRC's authorities were able to project a negative image towards the US and discredit the US's moral authority in supporting the democratic movement. At the same time the PRC enhanced netizens' support and gaining not only internal but also external recognition of the superiority of the China model. The case of enduring attacks on external actors for their involvement in some critical issues especially shows how the PRC attempted to utilize both formal and informal digital networks not only to consolidate internal support but also to struggle with any external criticisms. More significantly, the use of cyberspace serves not merely as a tool to resolve internal challenges but also an alternative to formulate alliances with developing states to resist the dominance of Western powers in the international system.

This chapter aims to provide embellished explanations of how the populist nature of China's society could shape its diplomacy, especially demonstrating how such a 'fighting spirit' represents China's top leadership perception of a possible solution to stand up for China's national interests to resist external criticism and interference. Furthermore, this chapter reveals how the PRC utilizes patriotism and heroism sentiments to justify the PRC as a powerful nation that stands for the people who are from developed countries. With a specification of using 'populist authoritarianism' as a key concept to operationalize wolf-warrior diplomacy, we provide a nuanced analytical lens to understand the PRC's foreign policy.

This framework also helps explain how the emergence of grassroots cyber nationalism can be the key root of wolf-warrior diplomacy, which demonstrated the significance of assertive nationalism as a key component of wolf-warrior diplomacy. The framework is also consistent with the recent trend in the PRC's presentations, propaganda, and purpose under Xi, which is to show to the outside world China's capability to confront external enemies, especially the US (Brazys and Dukalskis, 2020). As a matter of fact, this framework also raised the question of whether wolf-warrior diplomacy garners support through the use of new technology and whether such an assertive and nationalistic approach not only consolidates internal support but also intensifies external support, especially the support from overseas Chinese.

However, the recent cross-national survey data illustrates a significant decline in favourable opinions towards China among the public from Western countries, Japan, and South Korea and with a relatively high negative perception of the rise of the PRC in global affairs (Xie and Jin, 2021). This set of data demonstrates the alternative form of impact of wolf-warrior diplomacy, which facilitates the Western powers to spread the sentiment that China is a threat to global governance architecture instead of a responsible actor in global affairs. Departing from the traditional diplomatic approach, this approach rather demonstrates the generational change of the PRC's diplomats. Unlike the methods used by the old generation, thousands of Chinese diplomatic voices were made in cyberspace, especially Twitter, as to be more assertively pushing back against external criticism (Miller, 2022). As such, digital diplomacy becomes crucial in the making of the PRC's foreign policy. It also highlights digital diplomacy as a means to boost the generational change of diplomats from passive to more assertive in facing external criticism. Overall, this framework demonstrates the significance of new technology and digital diplomacy not merely manifesting a robust foreign policy posture but also salving the preferences of popular nationalism in both China and the Western powers (Sullivan and Wang, 2022: 17; Repnikova and Fang, 2018). It especially illustrates the salience of digital diplomacy, particularly in the context of the use of cyberspace in contributing to the rise of populism and nationalism locally and globally.

CONCLUSION

This chapter argues the PRC's wolf-warrior diplomacy can be considered as a new diplomatic strategy, split between achieving internal and external goals with the massive use of digital technologies. Internally, digital technology is used to communicate with ordinary citizens through the development of nationalistic and populist sentiments towards the outside world. More crucially, it is considered a major tool to consolidate the CPC's regime legitimacy to assure the dominant position of the CPC in ruling the PRC. Externally, wolf-warrior diplomacy considers online propaganda a central means to confront external actors and criticisms and overcome the challenges of hegemonic power. The above cases illustrate that wolf-warrior diplomacy is deemed to enhance national unity and strengthen the diplomats' confidence to resist external threats. As Chinese diplomats have realistic considerations, such strong and aggressive criticisms of the external actors and their criticisms can create a new image in international society which demonstrates PRC's ability to confront possible enemies in the international arena. More crucially, it can promote the 'China model' in developing countries by demonstrating the PRC's institutional superiority and uniqueness to counteract Western hegemonic influence in the international system.

SUGGESTED READING

Brazys, Samuel, and Alexander Dukalskis (2020) 'China's message machine', *Journal of Democracy* 31:4, 59–73.

Hackenesch, Christine, and Julia Bader (2020) 'The struggle for minds and influence: The Chinese Communist Party's global outreach', *International Studies Quarterly* 64:3, 723–733.

Sullivan, Jonathan, and Weixiang Wang (2022) 'China's "wolf warrior diplomacy": The interaction of formal diplomacy and cyber nationalism', *Journal of Current Chinese Affairs* 52, 1–21.

Verma, Raj (2020) 'China's diplomacy and changing the COVID-19 narrative', *International Journal* 75:2, 248–258.

Weichieh Wang, Ray (2022) 'China's wolf warrior diplomacy is fading', *The Diplomat*, 27 July https://thediplomat.com/2022/07/chinas-wolf-warrior-diplomacy-is-fading/.

Weiss, Jessica Chen (2013) 'Authoritarian signaling, mass audiences, and nationalist protest in China', *International Organization* 67:1, 1–35.

REFERENCES

Abbasov, A. (2007) 'Digital diplomacy: Embedding information and communication technologies in the department of foreign affairs and trade'. Retrieved from http://www.academia.edu/1058526/Digital_Diplomacy_Embedding_Information_and_Communication_Technologies_in_the_Department_of_oreign_Affairs_and_Trade (access date: 2 February 2022).

ABC News (2019) ' "Nightline" granted a rare tour of Chinese "vocational" centers where Muslim citizens are allegedly held as prisoners', 29 August, available at https://abcnews.go.com/International/nightline-granted-rare-tour-chinese-vocational-centers-muslim/story?id=65248173 (access date: 20 February 2021).

Adesina, O.S. (2017) "Foreign policy in an era of digital diplomacy", *Cogent Social Sciences*, 3:1, DOI: 10.1080/23311886.2017.1297175

Aljazeera (2021) 'China defends Covid responsive action after criticism by experts', 19 January, available at https://www.aljazeera.com/news/2021/1/19/china-defends-covid-responsive-action-after-criticism-by-experts (access date: 19 February 2021).

Aljazeera (2021) 'China Covid-19: How state media and censorship took on coronavirus', 19 January, available at https://www.bbc.com/news/world-asia-china-55355401 (access date: 19 February 2021).

Beja, Jean-Phillippe (2019) 'Xi Jinping's China: on the road to neo-totalitarianism', *Social Research: An International Quarterly* 86, 203–230.

Bjola, Corneliu, and Lu Jiang (2015) 'Social Media and Public Diplomacy: A Comparative Analysis of the Diplomatic Strategies of the EU, US, and Japan in China', In Corneliu Bjola and Marcus Holmes (eds), *Digital Diplomacy: Theory and Practice*, Routledge: New York, 71–88.

Brazys, Samuel, and Alexander Dukalskis (2020) 'China's message machine', *Journal of Democracy* 31:4, 59–73.

CGTN News, 'President Xi calls for confidence, resolve in reform, opening up', available at https://news.cgtn.com/news/3d3d674d3259544e30457a6333566d54/share_p.html (access date: 16 February 2021).

CGTN News (2019) 'CGTN Exclusive: A tour of a closed "re-education camp" in Xinjiang', available at https://news.cgtn.com/news/2019-12-30/CGTN-Exclusive-A-tour-of-a-former-re-education-center-in-Xinjiang-MQ7rursV3i/index.html (access date: 20 February 2021).

Global Times (2020a) 'Patriotic Chinese Internet users refute US media's nationalist label', 22 April, available at https://www.globaltimes.cn/content/1186383.shtml (access date: 19 February 2021).

Global Times (2020b) 'With epidemic raging, US is becoming a living hell: Global Times editorial', 6 December, available at https://www.globaltimes.cn/content/1209123.shtml (access date: 19 February 2021).

Global Times (2020c) 'The US unrecognizable to the world in 2020: Global Times editorial', 28 December, available at https://www.globaltimes.cn/content/1211273.shtml (access date: 19 February 2021).

Global Times (2021a) 'The US is its enemy on democracy: Global Times editorial', 8 January, available at https://www.globaltimes.cn/page/202101/1212254.shtml (access date: 20 February 2021).

Global Times (2021b) 'Pompeo's attacks on CPC are an evil legacy: FM', 11 January, available at https://www.globaltimes.cn/page/202101/1212458.shtml (access date: 20 February 2021).

Griffiths, James (2020) 'Nnevvy: Chinese troll campaign on Twitter exposes a potentially dangerous disconnect with the wider world', *CNN*, 15 April, available at https://edition.cnn.com/2020/04/14/asia/nnevvy-china-taiwan-twitter-intl-hnk/index.html (access date: 20 February 2021).

Hackenesch, Christine, and Julia Bader (2020) 'The Struggle for Minds and Influence: The Chinese Communist Party's Global Outreach', *International Studies Quarterly* 64:3, 723–733.

Holmes, Marcus (2015) 'Digital Diplomacy and International Change Management', In Corneliu Bjola and Marcus Holmes (eds), *Digital Diplomacy: Theory and Practice*, Routledge: New York, 13–32.

Hong Kong Free Press (2020) 'Chinese official Zhao Lijian echoes a conspiracy theory that the US is to blame for coronavirus outbreak', 13 March, available at https://hongkongfp.com/2020/03/13/chinese-official-zhao-lijian-echoes-conspiracy-theory-us-blame-coronavirus-outbreak/ (access date: 20 February 2021).

Hui Jin (2020) 'The four self-confidences: New horizon of socialism with Chinese characteristics', *Open Journal of Political Science* 10:1, 41–49.

Hu Xijin (2021) 'US hard to dress as a global beacon of democracy again', *Global Times*, 11 January, available at https://www.globaltimes.cn/page/202101/1212496.shtml (access date: 20 February 2021).

Lewis, D. (2014) 'Digital diplomacy', Retrieved from http://www. gatewayhouse.in/digital-diplomacy-2/. (access date: 2 February 2022).

Lowy Interpreter 2015. Does Australia do digital diplomacy? Retrieved from http://www.lowy interpreter.org/ (access date: 2 February 2022).

MERICS (2020) 'Reports about Tibet, muddy Xinjiang propaganda blitz', available at https://merics.org/en/analysis/reports-about-tibet-muddy-xinjiang-propaganda-blitz (access date: 20 February 2021).

Miller, Carl (2022) 'China's digital diplomacy', available at https://crestresearch.ac.uk/comment/chinas-digital-diplomacy/ (access date: 4 September 2022).

Ministry of Foreign Affairs of the People's Republic of China (2021) 'Foreign Ministry Spokesperson Zhao Lijian's Regular Press Conference on 11 January 2021', available at https://www.fmprc.gov.cn/mfa_eng/xwfw_665399/s2510_665401/t1845634.shtml (access date: 20 February 2021).

Olubukola S. Adesina (2017) Foreign policy in an era of digital diplomacy. *Cogent Social Sciences*, 3:1, DOI: 10.1080/23311886.2017.1297175

Ramzy, Austin (2021) 'China's oppression of Muslims in Xinjiang, explained', *The New York Times*, 20 January, available at https://www.nytimes.com/2021/01/20/world/asia/china-genocide-uighurs-explained.html (access date: 20 February 2021).

Repnikova M., Fang K. (2018) Authoritarian Participatory Persuasion 2.0: Netizens as Thought Work Collaborators in China. *Journal of Contemporary China* 27:113, 763–779

Shepherd, Christian (2020) 'The provocateur driving China's 'wolf warrior' pack', *Financial Times*, 7 December https://www.ft.com/content/a1356c94-3c57-46b0-9d49-aa4b2e465287

Shi Jiangtao (2020) 'China wants its diplomats to show more fighting spirit. It may not be intended to win over the rest of the world', *South China Morning Post*, 12 April, available at https://www.scmp.com/news/china/diplomacy/article/3079493/china-wants-its-diplomats-show-more-fighting-spirit-it-may-not (access date: 19 February 2020).

Sullivan, Jonathan, and Weixiang Wang (2022) 'China's "wolf warrior diplomacy": The interaction of formal diplomacy and cyber nationalism', *Journal of Current Chinese Affairs* 52, 1–21.

Swine, Michael (2010) 'Perspectives on Assertive China', *China Leadership Monitor* 32, 1–19.

Tang, Wenfang (2016) *Populist Authoritarianism: Chinese Political Culture and Regime Survival*, Oxford: Oxford University Press.

The Week (2021) 'After US state dept claims COVID emerged from Wuhan lab, China hits back', 19 January, available at https://www.theweek.in/news/world/2021/01/19/after-us-state-dept-claims-covid-emerged-from-wuhan-lab-china-hits-back.html (access date: 19 February 2021).

Tiezzi, Shannon (2021) 'China is already using the storming of the US Capitol for propaganda', *The Diplomat*, 8 January, available at https://thediplomat.com/2021/01/china-is-already-using-the-storming-of-the-us-capitol-for-propaganda/ (access date: 20 February 2021).

US Consulate, Hong Kong (2020) 'On the Chinese Communist Party's obscene propaganda', available at https://hk.usconsulate.gov/n-2020060601/ (access date: 20 February 2021).

US Embassy, Beijing, 'Fact sheet: Activity at the Wuhan Institute of Virology', available at https://ge.usembassy.gov/fact-sheet-activity-at-the-wuhan-institute-of-virology/ (access date: 19 February 2021).

US Mission to the United Nations (2020) 'Joint statement on the human rights situation in Xinjiang and the recent developments in Hong Kong, delivered by Germany on behalf of 39 countries', available at https://usun.usmission.gov/joint-statement-on-the-human-rights-situation-in-xinjiang-and-the-recent-developments-in-hong-kong-delivered-by-germany-on-behalf-of-39-countries/ (access date: 20 February 2021).

Verma, Raj (2020) 'China's diplomacy and changing the COVID-19 narrative', *International Journal* 75:2, 248–258.

Weichieh Wang, Ray (2022) 'China's wolf warrior diplomacy is fading', *The Diplomat*, 27 July https://thediplomat.com/2022/07/chinas-wolf-warrior-diplomacy-is-fading/.

Weiss, Jessica Chen (2013) 'Authoritarian signaling, mass audiences, and nationalist protest in China', *International Organization* 67:1, 1–35.

Weiss, Jessica Chen, and Allan Dafoe (2019) 'Authoritarian audiences, rhetoric, and propaganda in international crises: Evidence from China', *International Studies Quarterly* 63:4, 963–973.

Whiting, Allen S. (1993) 'Assertive Nationalism in Chinese Foreign Policy', *Asian Survey* 23, 913–933.

Xie, Yu, and Yongai Jin (2021) 'Global attitudes toward China: Trends and correlates', *Journal of Contemporary China* 31:133, 1–16.

Xu, Wei (2019) 'Xi calls for fighting spirit in face of risks', *China Daily*, 4 September, available at https://www.chinadaily.com.cn/a/201909/04/WS5d6ed007a310cf3e35569835.html (access date: 19 February 2020).

Zhang, Qingmin (2018) 'China's Contemporary Diplomacy', In Pauline Kerr and Geoffrey Wiseman (eds), *Diplomacy in a Globalizing World: Theories and Practices*, New York: Oxford University Press, 289–307.

Zhao, Suisheng (2017) 'The State as the Mobilizer and De-mobilizer in China's Nationalist Protests', paper presented at International Conference on State Mobilized Contention: The State-Protest Movement Nexus at the University of Hong Kong, Hong Kong, January.

Zhu, Zhiqun (2020) 'Interpreting China's "wolf-warrior diplomacy" What explains the sharper tone of China's overseas conduct recently?' *The Diplomat*, 15 May, available at https://thediplomat.com/2020/05/interpreting-chinas-wolf-warrior-diplomacy/ (access date: 15 February 2020).

CHAPTER 29

DIVERSITIES AND DEVELOPMENTS IN ASIA PACIFIC DIGITAL DIPLOMACY

DAMIEN SPRY

INTRODUCTION—CONDITIONS AND CONTEXTS

DIGITAL diplomacy in the Asia Pacific covers a vast, diverse region: East Asia (Japan, South Korea, Taiwan), Southeast Asia (covered by the Association of Southeast Asian Nations, or ASEAN), and Oceania (Australia, the Pacific Island Nations [PINs]).[1] The region has great disparities in wealth, size, geostrategic heft, demographics, and political systems. The legacies of European colonialism, Cold War conflicts, and Japanese imperialism are still felt; the present is shaped by ongoing great power rivalries, especially that between the United States of America and the People's Republic of China (China henceforth), the omnipresence of global systems of trade and communication, and issues such as climate change and the Covid-19 pandemic. These conditions and contexts are the basis for any discussion of digital diplomacy in this dynamic, complex region.

Asia Pacific digital diplomacy should be approached both on its own terms and comparatively. For good reasons, including the greater resources for—and commitment to—digital diplomacy as a practice, and as a field of scholarly interest, more attention

---

[1] The People's Republic of China and South Asian nations including India are not dealt with directly in this chapter, although their presence is felt. North Korea is excluded: it is diplomatically inactive online in any real sense other than posing a cybersecurity threat. The ASEAN nations are: Brunei Darussalam, Cambodia, Indonesia, Laos, Malaysia, Myanmar, Singapore, Thailand, the Philippines, and Vietnam. Timor Leste is notionally in Southeast Asia but not a member of ASEAN. The Pacific Island countries consist of three regions: Melanesia (including Papua New Guinea and, geographically, the western half of the island of New Guinea), Micronesia, and Polynesia (including New Zealand).

has been given firstly to North American and European digital diplomacy, and more recently to Chinese digital diplomacy as well as conflicts in the digital sphere that have involved some of these major powers. With exceptions (included in the discussion below) research into digital diplomacy has therefore, logically and reasonably, largely hitherto been framed by practices and approaches developed outside the Asia Pacific.

Approaching Asia Pacific digital diplomacy in comparison to what is happening elsewhere risks occluding or underestimating the specific contexts and conditions that shape practice in the region. It is important to incorporate into analysis the specificities of the diverse range of countries, their geostrategic conditions, and their diplomatic relationships. These principles, and the approach that informs this chapter, might usefully be applied also to other regional analyses of digital diplomacy, especially those such as Latin America, Africa, and the Middle East, which have hitherto received less attention.

The Asia Pacific includes some of the world's oldest (Japan, South Korea) and, outside of Africa, youngest (Timor Leste, some PINs, the Philippines) populations; richer nations (Australia, Brunei Darussalam, Japan, South Korea) and poorer (Cambodia, Laos, Timor Leste); large populations (Indonesia, the Philippines) and small (the PINs). The geostrategic (and therefore diplomatic) importance of this vast territory is due to both its size and its position at the crux of the great power contest of our times, between China and the United States. It is home to an immense array of languages and cultures, including the world's oldest continuing cultures in Australia and one of its newest nations in Timor Leste.

Generalizing about the Asia Pacific is therefore not only difficult, it is deceptive. It risks echoing flaws inherent in earlier analyses of development—exemplified by Rostow's (1960) stages of growth hypothesis—in being prescriptively and teleologically normative. These suggest digital media technologies and social media networks offer new and better ways for diplomats to engage with foreign publics, if only they would embrace the potential of new technologies.

The scholarly and professional fields of new public diplomacy and digital diplomacy do offer important and productive insights into transformations in public diplomacy practices and outcomes. New public diplomacy, in brief, places the emphasis on exchange, dialogue, and mutuality, away from 'peddling information to foreigners and keeping the foreign press at bay, towards engaging with foreign audiences' (Melissen, 2005, p. 13). Digital diplomacy can be considered in part as a variant of, or development within, new public diplomacy, including the use of social media for diplomatic purposes (Bjola and Holmes, 2015) as well as—as is outlined in this chapter—other impacts of digitalization broadly that have impacted on diplomacy (Hocking and Melissen, 2015). While scholarship does often engage with the limits, complications, and sometimes problematic aspects of digital diplomacy (Bjola and Pamment, 2019; Manor, 2019), the notion persists that understanding, embracing, and mastering digital diplomacy is a pathway to progress; examples of this from the Asia Pacific are in sections below.

This normative developmental paradigm lacks nuance and skews evaluation but cannot be dismissed entirely—it is a powerful narrative deployed by proponents of digital diplomacy, as is evident in ministerial strategies which direct digital diplomacy practices and public commentary on these practices, as well as in scholarly analysis. Some, extrapolated upon in the sections below, include the orthodox, professional, and institutionalized versions of digital diplomacy—a sub-genre of public diplomacy undertaken by diplomatic missions and ministries of foreign affairs (MFAs) and their equivalents—that are common in analyses of digital diplomacy research.

Understanding digital diplomacy in the Asia Pacific region is therefore more productively attempted using a conceptual framework of digital diplomacy that includes but is not limited to the use of digital means of communication, especially social media platforms, for forms of public diplomacy. Numerous important developments in the field of digital diplomacy have advocated such an expansive approach, to consider, for example: actors and publics other than diplomatic officials (Melissen, 2005); the 'channels, content and conditions' of public diplomacy (Pamment, 2014); the broader impacts of digitalization on diplomacy (Bjola, 2015; Manor, 2019) including with international organizations (Bjola and Zaiotti, 2021) as well as other matters of international relations like aid and regulation (Melissen and de Keulenaar, 2017).

In the discussion below are exemplars of these various approaches to digital diplomacy. Analyses based on the digitalization of (new) public diplomacy include instances from Australia and Japan, who have advanced digital diplomacy programmes, and Indonesia and the Philippines, who have apparent aspirations for them. In other Asia Pacific countries, however, digital diplomacy by MFAs is less developed or it is not a meaningful part of their public diplomacy. This is often due to limited resources for, and attention to, international relations in places where domestic economic and social development is prioritized. However, this observation is incomplete and reflects aforementioned normative and prejudiced notions of 'stages of development' in (new) public (and digital) diplomacy. For these reasons, as well as practical limitations of available data, and the scope of this chapter, a more structured comparative analysis of Asia Pacific digital diplomacy as undertaken by MFAs is not possible here.

A fuller picture of the relationships between the digital and the diplomatic in the Asia Pacific can profitably take a more heterodox approach. Other aspects of digital diplomacy considered in this chapter are therefore, compared to some earlier studies, atypical. These include: the value of social media for diasporic communities; the strategic use of digital fandoms; the pragmatic limitations on cooperation aimed at addressing the digital 'information disorder'; the role of global technology companies; the impacts (positive and negative) of digital culture on nation branding; and the widespread pattern of greater engagement by digital diplomacy publics that are smaller, poorer, and younger (Spry, 2018). From this varied list of features and trends, it is apparent that diversity and development are key, defining aspects of the Asia Pacific region. This is the first and underlying theme of this chapter. The second theme is also evident from this list: digital diplomacy contains more than the actions and plans of the MFAs (although these remain major elements). It includes the digital publics of the region, as well as the global political economy of the social networks and the techno-social system that they form and inhabit. These approaches to digital diplomacy are included here because they are increasingly recognized as crucial for considerations of digital diplomacy, which, as will be outlined, are not entirely digital and not entirely diplomatic. They are also included because in the Asia Pacific, in its vast diversity, are examples of the varied, dynamic, evolving, and polyvalent nature of digital diplomacy.

Along these lines, in this chapter, several related (and overlapping) approaches to digital diplomacy are posited and used to order an account of Asia Pacific practices and policies. The first is the most developed and least adventurous: it engages with the digitalization of (new) public diplomacy and focuses on MFAs and diplomatic missions, especially their use of social media. The second considers digital publics, and their role as active participants in digital diplomacy: forms of 'diplomac(ies) of the public(s)' (Castells, 2008). The third ventures into more adversarial territory, considering 'coercive diplomacy' (Bjola and Kornprobst, 2013), public diplomacy with 'hostile nations' (Wiseman, 2019), foreign interference campaigns, and the roles of, and relationships between, states, publics, and the tech sector vis-à-vis these forms of 'undiplomatic diplomacy'. The fourth looks at the nation more broadly, beyond governments, to consider national political systems and digital cultures as elements of national identities, related to the notion of 'nation branding' and its role in the production and promotion of soft power. The chapter ends with a section on diplomacy *about* the digital—the technologies and infrastructures, the industries, and the publics that form the digital media ecosystem and that are the subject of ongoing international negotiations, agreements, and rivalries.

DIGITAL (NEW) PUBLIC DIPLOMACY

Diplomacy *to* digital publics is what is often and typically thought of when discussing digital diplomacy, and it is most common in practice. As Hedling and Bremberg (2021) note, this thread of digital diplomacy research, associated with terminology including 'strategic communication' and nation branding, is considered under the broader banner of 'new public diplomacy'; it is also popular with practitioners: 'understood as practical knowledge that can easily be transferred and adopted in and through guidelines' (2021: 1597).

In public relations parlance, this is one-way asymmetric communication, or outward-facing publicity (Spry, 2018), akin to broadcast models of communication. An example is a social media post, promoting national activities and interests, aimed at publics and perhaps with a specific goal in mind, such as educational opportunities, or support for international agreements. This type of content may focus on official activities, such as meetings between government representatives. Although often lacking broad appeal (although an exception is when a popular head of state posts such content) these serve as a window into diplomatic affairs and as a journal of record.

Within this category, emergent shifts in diplomatic discourse are evident: more personalized, entertaining, and engaging content are, at times and with varying degrees of competence, posted on social media. This signals an acknowledgement that attention is scarce (see the subsequent section) and the online media space is highly competitive. Empirical studies provide evidence that this approach is as common in Asia Pacific as it is elsewhere (Spry, 2019).

This type of digital diplomacy is most evident in developed economies with established professional diplomatic corps. Some have publicly embedded digital diplomacy formally into their operations: Japan in its annual Blue Book (Japanese Ministry of Foreign Affairs, 2020) and Australia in specific strategy documents (Australian Government, 2106a, 2016b). Singapore and Taiwan also have well-developed social media diplomacy programmes. South Korea does too, although to a lesser extent, and appears to benefit from (and support) the outreach of popular culture successes, including K-Pop and K-Drama, all of which are effective in engaging global digital publics and promoting Korean soft power. The Philippines and Indonesia are strengthening their digital diplomacy—this aligns with both countries' social media cultures as they are among the very highest users (second and tenth) in the world (We Are Social, 2022).

Japanese digital diplomacy is well organized and professional, as is evidenced by the material covered in Blue Book as well as in analyses of its diplomatic social media use. According to some accounts, its diplomatic social media accounts attract the attention of international publics as well as, if not better than, comparable advanced economies (Spry, 2019). Japanese diplomats demonstrate proficiency using social media to address local publics, typically in the language of those publics, to promote their national interests and publicize diplomatic activities and contributions to emergency and relief efforts. Japanese digital diplomacy has also been criticized for being hampered by bureaucracy and overdue for reform (Nagata, 2021).

South Korea, at least when compared (superficially and conservatively) with nations of similar standing, has not displayed the same levels of commitment to digital diplomacy, nor achieved similar levels of attention. South Korean diplomatic missions have fewer social network accounts, and these accounts have lower engagement metrics, than, for example, Japan and Australia. In South Korea's public diplomacy strategy, digital seems absent. Robertson (2018) locates the main source of these (ostensible) deficiencies in the structure and culture of the Ministry of Foreign Affairs (MOFA): the hierarchical, conservative and inward-looking nature of MOFA leaving it 'significantly behind comparable states in the use of digital media' (676). Matters are made more difficult, ironically, due to South Korea's head start on online social networking and the robust success of Korean platforms, especially Kakao, leaving many older diplomats uninterested in internationally popular social media platforms. Hope, for Robertson, lies in generational change. Park, Chung, and Park (2019) offer a more generous evaluation, arguing South Korea's achievements lie in digital 'citizenship diplomacy', which utilizes and supports the deployment of Korean pop cultures, both its stars and its fans, to develop Korean soft power. Digital diplomacy in this context is something which occurs on/through social media, where it can be observed (but not controlled) by MFAs: an example of 'digital listening'.

In Australia, there has been considerable public discussion about digital diplomacy. It was initially regarded with as much caution as enthusiasm by some government officials, who preferred more traditional methods to expand influence (Commonwealth of Australia, 2012) and were characterized as like a 'dinosaur' by think tank commentators who advocated more innovative approaches (Cave, 2015a, 2015b). When Julie Bishop became Foreign Minister, and during the tenure of Prime Minister Malcolm Turnbull, a more positive approach to new opportunities was encouraged. Digital media strategy was produced; a soft power review was commissioned. Bishop's use of social media, especially her creative use of emojis in Tweets, was noted internationally (Twiplomacy, 2016). More recently, a more circumspect outlook is evident. This is probably in part due to changes in political leadership, but also due to a general sense that the prospects for digital mediated public diplomacy are more modest than earlier imagined.

In much of Southeast Asia, support for public diplomacy going digital is evident, especially in Indonesia and the Philippines, and to a lesser extent in Vietnam and Thailand. Indonesian digital diplomacy is shaped by the country's, and its leader's, enthusiasm for digital platforms. The President of Indonesia, Joko Widodo—typically referred to as 'Jokowi'—is a national leader who has adeptly used social media platforms to develop and promote international relations, especially with other foreign leaders. Jokowi is one of the most active and most followed national leaders on Twitter, Facebook, and Instagram. He uses these platforms, often in a warm and informal manner, to communicate with leaders, and to share with the world images of leader-to-leader meetings and conversations (Syaifaru and Qubba, 2017).

The enthusiasm shown by President Widodo is echoed in the actions of the MOFA, which has embraced the use of social media by its diplomats. Indonesia has also since 2018 hosted a series international seminars and conferences on digital diplomacy, including presentations from academia, government, and the tech industry— demonstrating regional leadership and strengthening its image as a digitally progressive nation, an image sustained by the success of numerous Indonesian start up and App-based businesses.

One of the notable aspects of Indonesian digital diplomacy is the development of products and services for Indonesians outside of Indonesia. Like other nations, Indonesia has a 'Safe Travel App' for citizens while travelling (Madu, 2018). More particular to Indonesia is the use made of social media to target and support Indonesian migrant workers and expatriates. Darmastuti et al. (2021) note the various uses of social media by expat communities for cultural diplomacy in the Netherlands, culinary diplomacy in South Africa, and soliciting financial support from the Indonesian diaspora in Australia for disaster relief. Still, commentary on Indonesia's digital diplomacy efforts remains balanced. On one hand, reports acknowledge progress, leadership, and support (Madu, 2018). On the other hand, familiar complaints exist, with familiar recommendations: Indonesia has not yet taken advantage of the opportunities afforded by digital diplomacy—it is evaluated as having reached a 'middle-stage' level (Darmastuti, et al., 2021) and that increased resources and training, and a more explicit strategy, are required (Pohan, et al., 2017).

Like Indonesia, digital diplomacy in the Philippines is supported by senior political leadership: Secretary of Foreign Affairs Teodoro L. Locsin, Jr, popularly referred to as 'Teddyboy' (Amador, 2021) has been described as a 'rock star' for being among the most active Twitter users among world leaders, and the first high ranking government official to mention Covid-19 (then, the 'novel corona virus') in a tweet (MENA Report, 2020). Meanwhile, President Rodrigo Duterte's outspoken and often controversial statements affecting foreign policy are also notable given the significant role social media has played in his campaigning and governing, and the presence of large numbers of online supporters that boost his messages and undermine his opponents.

Training and development programmes seeking to inform and instruct up-and-coming digital diplomats on the use of social media for outreach to Filipino diaspora, for crisis communication, and for community engagement have been able to draw on the experiences of Heads of Mission (MENA Report, 2020). The Public Diplomacy Handbook (2016), while not a formal government policy document, serves as an indicator of an increasingly systematic and formal approach to the development of a digital-first culture within the foreign policy and diplomatic establishment.

Some wariness remains in other MFAs. The Malaysian foreign minister expressed concerns about the limitations of digital diplomacy compared to face-to-face diplomacy (Hazim, 2021). Ironically, he also made use of Twitter to publicly criticize the Cambodia leader for meeting with the leaders of the Myanmar military junta. Elsewhere in the region, digital diplomacy is best characterized as being limited, and not a priority. Many small states are simply otherwise occupied. However, the Asia Pacific media landscape is dominated by social media use, suggesting that the digitalization of international communication is becoming ubiquitous.

Diplomacy *with* Digital Publics

While diplomacy *to* publics characterizes much digital diplomacy, diplomacy *with* publics is aimed at engaging with digital publics as participants in discussions about matters of mutual interest (see, *inter alia*, Melissen, 2006; Cowan and Arsenault, 2008). This moves from one-way to two-way communication (Kampf, Manor, and Segev, 2015). It can include asymmetric modes, with minimal opportunities for feedback such as 'listening' to publics via engagement metrics and comment threads on digital platforms, and more (but not entirely) symmetric modes, includes online question and answer sessions, permitting public posts on social media accounts and bulletin boards, and the like.

Versions of the latter may include invitations to participate via, for example, competitions. These are infrequent in digital diplomacy, including in the Asia Pacific. Rare examples, demonstrating the usefulness of the approach, include the clever invitation to Taiwanese tourists in Australia to post photos of their travels to the Australian office's Facebook account in Taiwan as part of a photo competition, voted on by the public. This resulted in Taiwanese sharing (and promoting, and therefore spreading) positive images of their time in Australia with their fellow Taiwanese. Another is the use of social media by the Indonesian and Philippine consulates in Hong Kong to engage with their sizeable expat communities there, and these pages being sites of communication of important information and coordination of social and cultural events by those communities. Generally, as is discussed below, digital publics are granted very limited impact on diplomatic discourse.

The Asia Pacific is also home to some locales where the publics are far more likely to utilize and engage with diplomatic social media accounts, reflecting a dependence on social media for information and indicating where MFAs should prioritize efforts. Empirical research (Spry, 2018) indicates that—worldwide—most diplomatic Facebook accounts, for example, are followed by less than 1% (and often about 0.1%) of the Facebook population (the total number of people with a Facebook account). Some Asia Pacific countries, like Japan and South Korea, are similar. However, a far greater proportion of the population follows diplomatic Facebook accounts in places like Timor Leste (16%), Papua New Guinea (7%), Cambodia (7%), Fiji (4%), and Myanmar (3%). Overall, it appears Facebook as a medium for digital diplomacy is more useful in countries that are comparatively smaller, poorer, and younger. Moreover, the types of content that appeal are largely those that are useful to those publics, such as information about employment and education opportunities and visa requirements.

One conclusion arising from this research is that publics will decide what is important to them. A related conclusion is that the nature of the media landscape in which these publics exist matters. Where there are larger domestic media markets, these will dominate as sources of information even if this information is distributed via social networks. Conversely, smaller media markets will be less dominated by locally produced content. In an attention economy, where there is an infinite amount of content and a limited amount of attention, what publics pay attention to is more important than what content is posted. (This is doubly so when attention is calculated and has an impact on the algorithms that curate content for social media feeds.) In effect, the diplomacy *to* the public (the posted content) is less impactful than the attention those publics afford it: a type of diplomacy *of* the digital publics.

COERCIVE DIPLOMACY, FOREIGN INTERFERENCE, AND INFORMATION DISORDERS

In the Asia Pacific, three related forms of 'undiplomatic' digital communications are evident: coercive diplomacy, foreign interference, and the information disorder. These are not unique to the region, but Asia Pacific contexts and conditions again shape the modes of action, and strategic intentions of the actors.

In diplomatic theory, the concept of 'coercive diplomacy' (Bjola and Kornprobst, 2013) typically refers to the use (or threat) of military or economic power but includes 'forceful persuasion' (George, 1991: 4). These approaches imply force but avoid, or tactically remain below the threshold of, actual military conflict. Related terms include 'media warfare' (for example, listed one of China's 'three warfares' (Lee, 2014)) and liminal or grey zone conflict. All of these terms refer to practices that straddle and blur the distinctions between diplomacy and conflict.

Since the mid-2010s, a narrative has emerged that frames Internet-based communication, and especially social media, as having ushered in an era of incivility, deception, and malign intent. In the past, optimistic views characterized social media as a facilitator of international connection, communication, and liberalization, even in/with authoritarian states; 'the future could well see the pendulum swing in a pessimistic direction' (Wiseman, 2019: 143). The 'weaponization' of communications, and the 'dark side of digital diplomacy' (Bjola and Pamment, 2019), are at least considerations to contend with and potentially as a form of 'media warfare' to develop and deploy (Hedling and Bremberg, 2021: 1609).

The use of communication for coercive purposes is not new, but it is increasingly problematic for public diplomacy practitioners as at times the lines between propaganda and public diplomacy might appear a bit blurry, especially as a decline in trust, itself a product of deceitful and dishonest communication, may lead to scepticism that affects well-intentioned, legitimate, and benign public diplomacy activities (Bjola and Pamment, 2019).

Diplomatic relations in the Asia Pacific are, not entirely but significantly and increasingly, bound up in the contest for regional influence between the United States and China. In part, this can be conceived territorially: the United States has well-established treaties with and/or bases in a ring around the western edge of the Pacific; China has claims over much of the South China Sea and Taiwan. It should also be considered as a contest of diplomatic styles: the United States representing the more established version, developed over centuries according to largely Western traditions and experiences; the Chinese version presents an alternative approach, which includes more typical (Western) diplomatic forms and norms but also includes more assertive and confrontational communicative modes.

These contrasting approaches are a contextual factor for digital diplomacy in the Asia Pacific. The delicate dance between these great powers affects all, but in different ways: most are entrenched deeply in trade and economic relations with China; some are closely aligned strategically with the United States; others are keen to remain neutral or, in a few cases—or from time to time—deepen political and military ties with China. One result is that, for most nations and most of the time, international communication is characterized by deliberate ambivalence, ambiguity, and imprecision, or by strategic silence, as ways to respond to, manage, or—better still—avoid confrontational, sometimes hostile, elements in international relations. What is notable about this type of hostile digital diplomacy is that it blurs lines between official, semi-official (that is, undertaken by state-sponsored or endorsed institutions like China's *Global Times*), and unofficial proponents. The messaging—by diplomats, by supportive journalists and commentators, and by large numbers of digital nationalists—can appear consistent.

This last group, the online patriots and nationalistic trolls, have emerged as a notable feature of the digital diplomacy landscape in the Asia Pacific. Deep-seated, historical grievances between South Korea and Japan, for example, are popular tropes for on-line nationalistic communities (Sakamoto, 2011). In Indonesia and Malaysia, anxieties exist about cyber skirmishes via nationalistic publics, such as the tit-for-tat hacking of Indonesian and Malaysian websites (Madu, 2018), and a more general concern about the lack of 'civility' online leading to higher levels of harassment, hate speech, and intimida-tion of public figures online (Darmastuti et al., 2021).

A signature event outlining how hostile groups operate across borders to impact politics and international relations is the notorious Dibu Expedition. In January 2016, moderators of the Chinese discussion forum Baidu Dibu urged the over 20 million users to target the Facebook pages of the Taiwanese presidential candidate Tsai Ing-Wen and Taiwan media outlet Apple Daily, and other supporters of Taiwanese independence. The Dibu Expedition trended on Chinese social media platforms such as WeChat, QQ, and Weibo (Lui, 2019). This combination of fandom, nationalism, and digital communi-cation strategies and modalities (including memetic imagery, shared shibboleths and argots, irony, and performative outrage) constitute a form of transnational discourse that impacts on diplomatic relations, and may be incorporated into national strategic discourses.

As Hedling and Bremberg (2021: 1609) note, '[d]igital disinformation and efforts aimed at countering it are now commonly considered practices of digital diplomacy'. These efforts are rendered more complex challenges when the networks of disinfor-mation include—or indeed are largely constituted of—non-state actors, including self-organizing, dynamic networks of digital media users, 'challenging conceptions of diplomatic agency by participating and shaping social exchanges rather than merely acting as audiences of communication' (Hedling and Bremberg, 2021: 1609).

More explicitly state-sponsored or operated digital interference campaigns, the type of which were associated with the 2016 Brexit and American presidential ballots, are present in the Asia Pacific but have not received the same level of attention as elsewhere. In 2016, prior to the US and UK ballots, the election campaign in the Philippines was characterized by social media's role in the rise of an outsider candidate, including the engagement of key digital influencers and their digital fandoms, highly charged partisan online keyboard warriors, use of incendiary language and disputed, misleading, and false content, and the targeting of opponents, including the mainstream press (Sinpeng, Gueorguiev, and Arugay, 2020). Partisan politics, post-election, impacted on public dip-lomacy: keyboard warriors became 'patriotic trolls'; pro-Duterte influencers took roles in the administration and consulted for the Department of Foreign Affairs (Etter, 2017).

Elsewhere, some covert operations including deliberate disinformation campaigns have been detected. A *Graphika* report (Nimmo, Eib, and Ronzaud, 2020) identified an online disinformation network dubbed 'Operation Naval Gazing'. Originating from China, it promoted pro-Jokowi, pro-Duterte, and pro-China content on inauthentic

Facebook accounts. Accusations of American interference in Thai politics arose when photos purporting to show a meeting between a former American diplomat and a student leader were circulated on Facebook by the Land Destroyer Report, an outlet monitoring US influence in Thailand and with association to *New Eastern Outlook*, a Russian state-supported journal (ThaiPBS, 2020). In both cases, the relevant accounts were identified as 'coordinated inauthentic behaviour' and removed by Facebook.

In the Asia Pacific, Australia appears the most openly concerned about foreign interference, including via social media campaigns. Earlier more optimistic views of the international digital environment have evolved: '(f)rom perceiving the internet as a communication platform that allows for listening *to* and dialogue *with* foreign publics, Australian foreign policy is increasingly framing the internet as a strategic infrastructure that requires defending' (Di Martino, 2021: 1). The Australian Parliament (2019) is conducting a multi-year inquiry on the matter. The Australian government has developed a Counter Foreign Interference strategy which seeks to counter foreign interference by: outlining clearly the kinds of activity Australia deems unacceptable; showing actors that their attempts at interference will meet with a 'meaningful response'; convincing actors that the costs of their actions will outweigh the benefits; narrow opportunities for interference in the region through regional awareness, reducing vulnerabilities, and strengthening institutions; and mobilizing international cooperation in support of globally acceptable online behaviour (Department of Foreign Affairs and Trade, 2020). This response implies multilateralism and regional outreach are part of the diplomatic strategy to counter social media interference campaigns.

Digital Cultures, Domestic Politics, and Nation Branding

A final point about the role of digital cultures in formal and (semi-)official diplomacy relates to the national brand of a nation or locale, which can be positively associated with its digital cultures. Japan and South Korea both enjoy boosts to the national image due to their reputations as technologically advanced and culturally interesting digital nations. Taiwan, a more singular case, is lauded for its use of 'digital democracy'—both in the sense that it has used digital means to augment and deepen domestic democratic processes and in comparison with the restrictions and surveillance associated with the digital and political culture of the mainland.

Singapore is a regional leader in terms of its institutions and networks that research, and outreach, into matters concerning digital diplomacy, like the Asia-Europe Foundation, ISEAS Yusof Ishak Institute, and the Singapore International Foundation. However, this is mitigated by concerns about measures against political liberalization and free speech (Carson and Fallon, 2021), demonstrating how digital cultures can impact positively and negatively on international public opinion and therefore on national brands. Similarly, several Southeast Asian nations' governments express concerns about the use of social media by political opponents to destabilize while political activists are fearful that social media might be a site of surveillance by authoritarian regimes and a vector for targeted attacks by these regimes against their opponents. The clash between political freedom and political order is stark. This is compounded by—or deliberately conflated with—public health concerns associated with the Covid-19 information disorder. New laws impacting on political speech include Singapore's 2019 Protection from Online Falsehoods and Manipulation Act (POFMA) and Malaysia's anti-fake news law (Emergency (Essential Powers) (No. 2) Ordinance 2021), aimed at the distribution of Covid-19 fake news. In addition to legislation, governments have adopted a 'securitisation approach' to public speech, including military involvement. The Thai government attempts to dominate the information environment using robust military surveillance and direct censorship of online conversations, online bullying, and creating fake online accounts to generate public opinion, with actors like Thai security forces units, party machinery, and civic groups manipulating the online content (Sombatpoonsiri, 2018).

Vietnam has a combination of punitive laws targeting disinformation and activism; the deployment of 'public opinion shapers'—especially Force 47, a unit run by the Ministry of Public Security to target activists on social media; and the co-opting of Facebook and Google through direct requests to remove and block content or risk punitive measures. Vietnam is a valuable market for both Facebook—it constitutes 30% of the company's profits in Southeast Asia—and Google; these companies' acquiescence to the dictates of local laws has been criticized by human rights groups and members of the US Senate (Amnesty International, 2020).

Myanmar's international reputation is probably worst impacted by recent events, including the use of digital communication, especially social media, in political repression and large-scale violence. Ironically, social media has been identified as both a site where violence is organized and encouraged, and a means for the military (*Tatmadaw*) to monitor dissidents, and a rare online site where opponents to authoritarianism and witnesses to violence can publish and communicate. The role of Facebook in facilitating violence against the Muslim Rohingya minority, including acts that have amounted to genocide, and Facebook's refusal to cooperate with efforts to seek justice via the International Court of Justice (Choudhury, 2020) inspired global condemnation of the global social media platform. (In 2018, this led to attempts at atonement through the removal of content (Facebook, 2018) and through support for government and civil society attempts to address the problem.) The April 2021 Tatmadaw crack-down included shutdowns of mobile data services and nightly curfew-style shutdowns of the Internet. These activities sour the reputation of nations and companies and they have given further impetus to regional movements to hold companies to account, including the Southeast Asian Coalition on Tech Accountability (SEACT)—another notable example of regional cooperation on digital matters and a type of informal diplomacy of the public.

DIPLOMACY *ABOUT* DIGITAL NETWORKS

Finally, the role of digital development in diplomatic relations deserves attention, especially where the fundamental infrastructure for digital communications technology, such as undersea Internet cables, are under-developed. Many Pacific Island Nations are connected via only one cable and are vulnerable to disconnection should their sole connection be damaged, as for example has occurred twice to Tonga: in 2019 due to a ship's anchor and in 2022 due to a volcanic eruption (Aualiitia and Seselja, E, 2022). Disruptions make it more difficult for international partners to respond to accompanying crises (such as the Tsunami that accompanied the 2022 eruption).

The implication is that more cables would increase resilience; the question then turns to the provision of cables, which contains its own diplomatic dimensions. In basic terms, the Pacific cabling system has become a site where competing interests, global in scale, are brought sharply into focus. This came to a head in 2016 when Chinese telecommunications company Huawei was contracted to provide a cable for the Solomon Islands government. This would have connected the capital Honiara to Port Moresby, Papua New Guinea, and Sydney, Australia. The Australian government, concerned about Huawei's involvement (Australia has prevented Huawei from providing domestic 5G and Internet infrastructure due to perceived security risks associated with the company's apparent obligations to provide information to the Chinese government) stepped in and paid for the cable to prevent the connection becoming a security risk, and to address broader concerns about increasing Chinese influence (Doran and Dziedzic, 2018).

Diplomacy *about* digital networks is not confined to technology infrastructure; it also includes technology industries, and the regulatory systems they inhabit and affect. On one hand, the roles of the major powers and the companies they are home to (*inter alia*, Huawei and ByteDance/TikTok in China; Alphabet/Google, Meta/Facebook, and Twitter in the United States) need to be factored into diplomatic relations and international politics. Huawei and TikTok are cited as sources of state surveillance (Hoffman and Attrill, 2021); Facebook and Google as threats to democracy, economic sovereignty, personal privacy, data ownership and transfer, and—in some cases—as facilitating gross human rights violations (*inter alia*, Moore, 2018; Srnick, 2017; Zuboff, 2019). Both the Chinese and American companies present concerns related to digital sovereignty—the capacity for nations to enact laws that protect their citizens and preserve national self-determination (Pohle and Thiel, 2020).

A third area of diplomacy relates to the benefits and concerns of the digital media ecosystem and especially the use of social networks by digital publics in ways that raise issues for, and that have met with coordinated responses by, Asia Pacific governments. In Southeast Asia in particular, the problem of disinformation and misinformation is widely considered as a public health or social cohesion concern, to be addressed through content moderation and media literacy. This has been heightened by the Covid-19 pandemic but concerns pre-date this. ASEAN has highlighted shared concerns through joint statements of the ASEAN ministers responsible for information. These statements establish the basis for cooperation, and information- and skill-sharing, especially tackling how Covid-19 misinformation has hampered efforts to inform people about the pandemic and promote health measures like social distancing and vaccinations; they build upon earlier statements that highlight more general shared concerns about 'fake news' (ASEAN Ministers Responsible for Information, 2020). These anxieties about information disorder may be well founded; they are also, as discussed earlier, useful buttresses for supporting more illiberal controls on public and political speech.

CONCLUSION

This chapter provides an overview of characteristics of Asia Pacific digital diplomacy, and the contexts and conditions in which these emerge. It offers some insights based on key aspects of digital diplomacy as evident in case studies of countries or regional and sub-regional groupings. These insights are not the totality of these case studies—every country and region has more to offer than can be accommodated here—but are used as exemplars of forms and uses of digital diplomacy.

This overview argues the only generalization that can be made is that we should not over-generalize. This is compounded by the relatively limited (to date) research into many of the sub-regions of the Asia Pacific; the risk here is that conclusions based on those countries and practices that have been to some extent subject to scholarly inquiry may be extrapolated beyond the bounds of their applicability. This is a perennial problem, but the relative youth of the field of digital diplomacy, especially in the region, and the aforementioned regional diversity, exacerbate the issue.

This chapter considers digital practices that include diplomacy as well as some practices that affect diplomacy. These are both instructive in terms of how digital diplomacy is consistent, or contrasts, with practice elsewhere, and also—and perhaps more productively—outline how we might think differently and more broadly about the relationship between the digital and the diplomatic by considering, first, digital publics as participants in digital diplomacy and, second, the techno-social and techno-political systems that form the environment in which digital diplomacy is practiced and that shape that practice.

SUGGESTED READING

Chia, S.A. (Ed). 2021. *Winning Hearts and Minds: Public Diplomacy in ASEAN*. Singapore International Foundation. https://pdasia.sif.org.sg/publication

Darmawan, Aristyo Rizka. 2021. 'Do you hear the people tweet? The role of social media in Indonesia's foreign policy'. *AsiaGlobal Online*. Available at https://www.asiaglobalonline.

hku.hk/do-you-hear-people-tweet-role-social-media-indonesias-foreign-policy. Accessed 7 August 2023.

Melissen, J. and Emilie V. de Keulenaar. 2017. 'Critical digital diplomacy as a global challenge: The South Korean experience'. *Global Policy Volume* 8 (3): pp. 294–302.

Robertson, J. 2018. 'Organizational culture and public diplomacy in the digital sphere: The case of South Korea'. *Asia Pacific Policy Studies* 5: pp. 672–682.

Sinpeng, Aim and Ross Tapsell. 2020. *Grassroots Activism to Disinformation: Social Media in Southeast Asia*. Singapore: ISEAS Publishing.

Spry, Damien and Trishia Octaviano (Eds). 2021. *Communicating with Purpose: ASEF Public Diplomacy Handbook 2021*. Singapore: Asia-Europe Foundation.

REFERENCES

Amador, J.S. 2021. 'Public Diplomacy in the Age of Digital Media', in Chia, S.A. (Ed) *Winning Hearts and Minds: Public Diplomacy in ASEAN*. Singapore International Foundation. pp. 88–95. https://pdasia.sif.org.sg/publication

Amnesty International. 2020. '*Let Us Breathe*': *Censorship and Criminalisation of Online Expression in Viet Nam*. AI Index: ASA 41/3243/2020. London: Amnesty International.

Association of Southeast Asian Nations. 2020. *Joint Statement of the ASEAN Ministers Responsible for Information to Minimise the Negative Effects of Coronavirus Disease (COVID-19)*. 7 September. https://asean.org/joint-statement-of-the-asean-ministers-responsible-for-information-to-minimise-the-negative-effects-of-coronavirus-disease-2019-covid-19/

Aualiitia, T. and E. Seselja. 2022. 'Tonga could be cut off from the outside world for more than two weeks, after volcano damages undersea cable' *Australian Broadcasting Commission: Pacific Beat*. 18 January. https://www.abc.net.au/news/2022-01-18/when-will-tongas-under sea-cable-be-repaired-/100760998

Australian Government. 2016a. *Australian Public Diplomacy Strategy 2014–16*. Canberra, Australia: Commonwealth of Australia. https://dfat.gov.au/people-to-people/public-diplomacy/Pages/public-diplomacy-strategy.aspx.

Australian Government. 2016b. *Digital Media Strategy 2016–2018*. Canberra, Australia: Commonwealth of Australia.

Australian Parliament. 2019. *Select Committee on Foreign Interference through Social Media*. https://www.aph.gov.au/Parliamentary_Business/Committees/Senate/Foreign_Interferen ce_through_Social_Media/ForeignInterference/Submissions

Bjola, Corneliu and Markus Kornprobst. 2013. *Understanding International Diplomacy: Theory, Practice and Ethics*. London and New York: Routledge.

Bjola, Corneliu and Markus Holmes. 2015. *Digital Diplomacy: Theory and Practice*. Oxon, UK: Routledge.

Bjola, Corneliu and James Pamment. 2019. *Countering Online Propaganda and Extremism: The Dark Side of Digital Diplomacy*. London: Routledge

Bjola, Corneliu and Ruben Zaiotti. 2021. *Digital Diplomacy and International Organisations: Autonomy, Legitimacy and Contestation*. London: Routledge.

Carson, Andrea and Liam Fallon. 2021. *Fighting Fake News: A Study of Online Misinformation Regulation in the Asia Pacific*. Melbourne: La Trobe University. https://www.latrobe.edu.au/__data/assets/pdf_file/0019/1203553/carson-fake-news.pdf

Castells, Manuel. 2008. 'The new public sphere: global civil society, communication networks, and global governance'. *The ANNALS of the American Academy of Political and Social Science* 616 (1): pp. 78–93.

Cave, D. 2015a. 'Does Australia do digital diplomacy?' *The Lowy Interpreter.* 17 April. https://www.lowyinstitute.org/the-interpreter/does-australia-do-digital-diplomacy

Cave, D. 2015b. 'DFAT and digital diplomacy: In denial and in need of review' *The Lowy Interpreter.* 1 October. https://www.lowyinstitute.org/the-interpreter/dfat-digital-diplomacy-denial-and-need-review

Choudhury, Angshuman. 2020. 'How Facebook is complicit in Myanmar's attacks on minorities'. *The Diplomat.* 25 August. Available at: https://thediplomat.com/2020/08/how-facebook-is-complicit-in-myanmars-attacks-on-minorities/

Commonwealth of Australia, 2012. 'Australia's overseas representation – Punching below our weight?' Inquiry of the Foreign Affairs Sub-Committee, Joint Standing Committee on Foreign Affairs, Defence and Trade. Available at: https://www.aph.gov.au/Parliamentary_Business/Committees/Joint/Completed_Inquiries/jfadt/Overseas_Representation/report

Cowan, Geoffrey and Amelia Arsenault, 2008. 'Moving from monologue to dialogue to collaboration: The three layers of public diplomacy'. *ANNALS of the American Academy of Political and Social Science.* 616 (1): pp. 10–30.

Darmastuti, A., A. Inayah, K. Simbolon, and M. Nizar. 2021. 'Social Media, Public Participation, and Digital Diplomacy' *Advances in Social Science, Education and Humanities Research* 606: pp. 38–47.

Department of Foreign Affairs and Trade, 2020. 'Submission into the Parliamentary Joint Committe on Intelligence and Security Inquiry into National Security Risks Affecting the Australian Higher Education and Research Sector' Available at https://www.aph.gov.au › DocumentStore

Di Martino, L. 2021. 'Fear and empathy in international relations: Diplomacy, cyber engagement and Australian foreign policy'. *Place Branding and Public Diplomacy* https://doi.org/10.1057/s41254-021-00211-9

Doran M. and S. Dziedzic. 2018. 'Deal to be inked for Solomon Islands undersea internet cable Australia stopped China building' *Australian Broadcasting Commission News.* 12 June. https://www.abc.net.au/news/2018-06-13/solomon-islands-undersea-cable-internet-china/9861592

Etter, Lauren. 2017, 'What Happens When the Government Uses Facebook as a Weapon' Bloomberg Businessweek. 7 December. https://www.bloomberg.com/news/ features/2017-12-07/how-rodrigo-duterte-turned-facebook-into-a-weapon-with-a-little-help-from-facebook

Facebook. 2018. 'Removing military officials from Facebook'. *Facebook News.* 26 August. https://about.fb.com/news/2018/08/removing-myanmar-officials/

George, A. 1991. *Forceful Persuasion: Coercive Diplomacy as an Alternative to War.* Washington, DC: United States Institute of Peace Press.

Hazim, Anis. 2021. 'Wisma Putra sees challenges in digital diplomacy' *The Malaysian Reserve.* 17 January.

Hedling, E. and N. Bremberg. 2021. 'Practice approaches to the digital transformations of diplomacy: Toward a new research agenda'. *International Studies Review* 23: pp. 1595–1618.

Hocking, Brian and Jan Melissen. 2015. *Diplomacy in the Digital Age.* Netherlands Institute of International Relations Clingendael.

Hoffman, Samantha and Nathan Attrill, 2021. *Mapping China's Technology Giants: Supply chains and the global data collection ecosystem*, Australian Strategic Policy Institute 8 June, https://www.aspi.org.au/report/mapping-chinas-tech-giants-supply-chains-and-global-data-collection-ecosystem

Japanese Ministry of Foreign Affairs. 2020. *Diplomatic Bluebook 2020: Japanese Diplomacy and International Situation in 2019*. Japanese Ministry of Foreign Affairs. https://www.mofa.go.jp/policy/other/bluebook/2020/html/ index.html.

Kampf, Ronit, Ilan Manor and Elad Segev. 2015. 'Digital diplomacy 2.0? A cross-national comparison of public engagement in Facebook and Twitter'. *The Hague Journal of Diplomacy* 10: pp. 331–362.

Lee, S.K. 2014 'China's "Three Warfares": Origins, Applications, and Organizations'. *The Journal of Strategic Studies* 37 (2): pp. 198–221.

Lui, H. 2019. *From Cyber-nationalism to Fandom Nationalism: The Case of Diba Expedition in China*. London: Routledge.

Madu, Ludiro. 2018. 'Indonesia's digital diplomacy: Problems and challenges'. *Journal Hubugan Internasional* 7 (1): pp. 11–18.

Manor, Ilan. 2019. *The Digitalisation of Public Diplomacy*. London: Palgrave McMillan.

Melissen, J. 2005. *The New Public Diplomacy: Between Theory and Practice*. London: Palgrave Macmillan.

Melissen, J. and Emilie V de Keulenaar. 2017. 'Critical Digital Diplomacy as a Global Challenge: The South Korean Experience' *Global Policy* 8 (3): pp. 294–302.

MENA Report. 2020. Philippines: FSI Completes First Online Course on eDiplomacy. MENA Report. Available from https://www.proquest.com/trade-journals/philippines-fsi-completes-first-online- course-on/docview/2448487396/se-2?accountid=14649. Accessed 11 October 2021.

Moore, Martin. 2018. *Democracy Hacked: Political Turmoil and Information Warfare in the Digital Age*. London: Oneworld Press.

Nagata, Kazuaki. 2021. 'Japan launches Digital Agency to push ahead with long-overdue reforms' *The Japan Times*. 1 September. https://www.japantimes.co.jp/news/2021/09/01/national/politics-diplomacy/digital-agency-launch-japan/

Nimmo, C., Shawn Eib, and Léa Ronzaud. 2020. Operation naval gazing: Facebook takes down inauthentic Chinese network. *Graphika*. Available at https://public-assets.graphika.com/reports/graphika_report_naval_gazing.pdf. Accessed 7 August 2023.

Pamment, J. 2014. 'The mediatisation of diplomacy'. *Hague Journal of Diplomacy* 9: pp. 253–280.

Park, S., D. Chung, and H.W. Park. 2019. 'Analytical framework for evaluating digital diplomacy using network analysis and topic modeling: Comparing South Korea and Japan'. *Information Processing and Management* 56: pp. 1468–1483.

Pohan, S., H. Pohan, and I.N. Savitri. 2017. 'Digital diplomacy: Maximising social media in Indonesia's economic and cultural diplomacy'. *Advances in Social Science, Education and Humanities Research* 81: pp. 372–390.

Pohle, J. and T. Thiel. 2020. 'Digital sovereignty'. *Internet Policy Review* 9 (4). Available at https://doi.org/10.14763/2020.4.1532. Accessed 7 August 2023.

Robertson, J. 2018. 'Organizational culture and public diplomacy in the digital sphere: The case of South Korea'. *Asia Pacific Policy Studies* 5: pp. 672–682.

Rostow, W.W. 1960. *The Stages of Economic Growth: A Non-Communist Manifesto*. Cambridge: Cambridge University Press.

Sakamoto, Rumi. 2011. '"Koreans, Go Home!" Internet nationalism in contemporary Japan as a digitally mediated subculture'. *The Asia Pacific Journal* 9 (10): pp. 1–20.

Sinpeng, Aim and Ross Tapsell. 2020. *Grassroots Activism to Disinformation: Social Media in Southeast Asia*. Singapore: ISEAS Publishing.

Sinpeng, A., D. Gueorguiev, and A. Arugay. A. 2020. 'Strong fans, weak campaigns: Social media and Duterte in the 2016 Philippine election'. *Journal of East Asian Studies*, 20 (3): pp. 353–374.

Sombatpoonsiri, Janjira. 2018. *Manipulating Civic Space: Cyber Trolling in Thailand and the Philippines*. Hamburg: GIGA German Institute of Global and Area Studies. https://nbn-resolving.org/urn:nbn:de:0168-ssoar-57960-4

Spry, Damien. 2018. 'Facebook diplomacy: A data-driven, user-focussed approach to Facebook use by diplomatic missions'. *Media International Australia* 168 (1): pp. 62–80.

Spry, Damien. 2019. 'From Delhi to Dili: Facebook diplomacy by Ministries of Foreign Affairs in the Asia Pacific'. *The Hague Journal of Diplomacy* 15 (1–2): pp. 93–125.

Srnicek, Nick. 2017. *Platform Capitalism*. Cambridge: Polity Press.

Syaifini, S. and N.R. Qubba. 2017. 'Joko Widodo's digital diplomacy: A prospect and challenge for Indonesia's digital diplomacy towards middle power'. *Jurnal Hubungan Internasional* 10 (2): pp. 106–117.

Twiplomacy. 2016. 'Emoji diplomacy – A new diplomatic sign language'. *Twiplomacy Blog*. 8 April. https://twiplomacy.com/blog/emoji-diplomacy-a-new-diplomatic-sign-language/

We are Social, 2022. 'Digital 2022: Another year of bumper growth'. 26 January. https://wearesocial.com/au/blog/2022/01/digital-2022-another-year-of-bumper-growth/

Wiseman, G. 2019. 'Public Diplomacy and Hostile Nations'. *The Hague Journal of Diplomacy* 14: pp. 134–153.

Zuboff, Shoshana. 2019. *The Age of Surveillance Capitalism*. London: Profile Books

CHAPTER 30

DIGITAL DIPLOMACY IN LATIN AMERICA: AMONG EARLY ADOPTERS AND LATECOMERS

DANIEL AGUIRRE AND ALEJANDRO RAMOS

INTRODUCTION

IN Mexican politics during the most part of the twentieth century, there was a saying that went: 'if you move, you won't appear in the picture'.[1] Basically, it meant that those presidential hopefuls who did not show discipline and absolute subordination to the official party and to the president himself were disqualified. Fast-forward to the twenty-first century, and as former Mexican Ambassador to the US (and digital diplomacy pioneer) Arturo Sarukhan reframed it: 'if you don't tweet, you won't appear in the picture' (quoted in Zaharna, 2012).

As authors such as Aguirre and Erlandsen (2018) have pointed out on the subject of digital diplomacy, the Latin American region has generally kept in step with the times, albeit with slight time lags and periods of intense activity during this last decade (2010–2020). It is important to note that the adoption of digital tools by ministries of foreign affairs (MFAs) ushered in an organizational atmosphere of statecraft reinvention epitomized by modernization reforms that incorporated twenty-first century diplomatic approaches toward age-old (and often even unpopular) practices codified in the 'diplomatic paleolithic (i.e., Vienna conventions). The reinvention of diplomatic practice in the region fell within a spectrum of formal and informal changes. An example of the latter was the reorganization (or creation) of departments/areas within the ministry's organizational structures. As for the former (and as exemplified in the Mexican and

---

[1] The authors wish to thank Matthias Lüfkens for kindly providing the data of Latin American leaders and official institutions' Twitter accounts. They would also like to thank Rolla Norrish for her editing suggestions to the text, and Harriette Baxter for her support with the mining of social media data.

Chilean cases), reform meant laws that generally spelled out the details and extent of the modernization of foreign policy and diplomatic practice institutionally.

The digitalization of diplomacy was implemented with degrees of variance until around mid-January to early February 2020, when the Covid-19 global pandemic began to find its way into the Latin American region. Reinvention henceforth came out of the urgency to secure medical supplies and bring home thousands of Latin American citizens stranded elsewhere in the world. Thus, global coordination became imperative while the world was simultaneously fragmenting, with borders closing and flights being cancelled in a process that Manfredi (2021) has characterized as deglobalization. Yet, as 2020 came to an end and 2021 began to unfold, globalization in general terms (and the concrete practices of diplomatic actors in particular) found the majority of the activities occurring digitally and remotely, whether asynchronously or synchronously. The diplomatic world, including Latin America, was seemingly fully online.

This chapter aims to recount some of the most significant trends of Latin American digital diplomacy over the course of a decade of implementation and ongoing practice. From a broader perspective it provides a narrative of digital public diplomacy practice from outsider and insider standpoints (scholar and practitioner). Reflecting on regional experiences, it then situates and contextualizes them into two specific illustrative cases: Chile and Mexico. These provide entry points that analytically offer depth and detail to shed light on the broader picture of the regional approach toward conducting digital diplomacy.

We divide the chapter into three sections. Firstly, we refer to general aspects and common features that offer insights on the digitalization of diplomacy in Latin America, providing a synthesis of practices within a conceptual mosaic that seeks to put into context the variety of approaches by which the different countries adopted digital platforms to achieve foreign policy objectives. The mosaic sets out to capture *sui generis* practices found in the region and potentially provides a useful conceptual lens for future comparative studies on the topic. Secondly, we delve deeper into the specific cases of Mexico and Chile and break down different aspects of their experience, to exemplify how the region has ventured into digital diplomacy in the last decade. Lastly, we provide some closing comments on the phenomenon of a perceived growing consularization of practice, particularly following the Latin American countries' response to the Covid-19 pandemic.

An Overview of the Evolution of Digital Diplomacy in Latin America 2010–2020

When referring to Latin America, as Lowenthal (2012) pointed out, it can seem complicated or even nonsensical to try to generalize for an entire region, given its heterogeneity, based on levels of economic, social, and political development. Nonetheless, as Aguirre (2020) contends, some common features stand out in the way some countries recently implemented public diplomacy broadly and digital diplomacy specifically. For instance, approaches based on intuition more than a systematic, institutional, and conceptually driven strategy are generally the norm. In addition, cultural and legal structures enable presidential prerogatives to guide most actions. Lastly, organizational aversion by MFAs and precarious circumstances force the prioritization of high politics over 'softer' image projections in the region.

It should anyway be noted that, as Aguirre and Erlandsen (2018) mentioned, already by 2018, as many as eleven countries in the region had a digital public policy in place, whether in the form of specific legislation on the matter or as part of the official discourse or practice. This signals a change in attitudes by MFA institutions and diplomacy practitioners towards incorporating several digital diplomacy tools and practices, pointing to a shift towards embracing the digital paradigm to achieve foreign policy objectives. Nowadays, governments of all the countries in the region understand not only the potential that digital platforms offer, but even more importantly, the danger that their absence would entail. Accordingly, albeit with a range of approaches, different Latin American countries have explored the digital field in the last decade, to the extent that currently it seems that in the region the debate on the relevance or otherwise of developing a strong online presence no longer has a foothold.

Over the course of the decade, Twitter serves as the most relevant indicator of digital diplomacy practice given its extensive use across the region. In Figure 30.1,

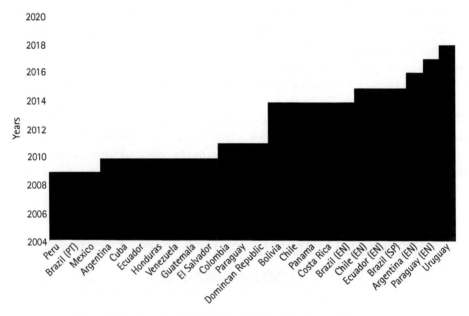

FIGURE 30.1. Years Latin American MFAs joined Twitter (2009-2020)

Notes: Costa Rica and Panama according to Twiplomacy Data (2018), appeared possessing accounts prior to 2014. PT= Portuguese; EN=English; SP=Spanish.

Source: Elaborated by the authors

a thirteen-years-in-use group marks a set of early institutional digital diplomacy adopters (Peru to Dominican Republic). In the eight-years group Bolivia to Costa Rica are part of the second wave of ministries going digital. Simultaneously to the second wave a number of ministries added accounts in English, such as Brazil, Chile, and Ecuador. The implication is that most MFAs are part of this practice and that the sophistication of use is expanding, even beyond Twitter (as will be discussed later in this text).

Nonetheless, as demonstrated elsewhere, these tools and practices are not used to their full potential. Once again, Arturo Sarukhan reminds us of an incomplete use by many, especially by referring to the Mexican case, as follows.

> With the growing access to and use of digital platforms and social networking tools and technology that allow for the projection of those assets, the region should be home to at least three or four major public diplomacy and soft power players. But the persistent problem has been that Mexico, as with others in the region, has been unable to harness those assets. They have failed to implement proper strategies for promotion, nation branding, and public diplomacy (2016).

Furthermore, as Ramos and Espinoza conclude after analysing a series of tweets of several Mexican diplomats and foreign missions during a specific time period, Twitter is mainly used 'as another tool to inform, disseminate and promote the foreign actions and policies of Mexico—with a clear focus on Mexican communities abroad—and not as the powerful and sophisticated instrument of public diplomacy that it could potentially be' (2018: 61). Ramos and Espinoza's conclusions for Mexico do offer a similar assessment of others in the region.

Broadly speaking, a few concepts can help to describe the traits and general parameters of digital practice in the region. Table 30.1 provides some detail on concepts identified from the field. We anticipate that the consularization of practice has notably increased since 2020. Nonetheless, instead of incorporating it into the continuums, we thought better to elaborate further on that matter, with specific reference to the pandemic. This phenomenon is expected to remain predominant for some time, but it might gradually take on a secondary role when Covid-19 is no longer afflicting the globe.

A Mosaic of Approximations towards Digital Diplomacy

Over the last decade the digitalization of diplomacy among Latin American MFAs, while indeed differing in scope and pace, shows some common patterns of adoption and uses which are encapsulated in the notion of practice. As displayed in Table 30.1, what is observable covers—in the authors' view—five continuums that are the most salient and can propose a degree of generalization, even when other contingent factors might contribute to differing plausible explanations. The description of the continuums is as follows.

Table 30.1 A Latin American conceptual mosaic of a decade of digital diplomacy

Conceptualization Continuums	Description
Institutional-Personalized	Existence of behaviours and norms within the national bureaucracy or predominance of presidential and ambassadorial-level use of digital tools.
Centralized-Proliferation (Listening, Advocacy, & Broadcasting)	From Nicholas Cull's main taxonomies, mixed/hybrid types of public diplomacy, intersecting instruments and channels that offer public opinion monitoring and campaign/messaging resources.
Holistic-Specific Implementation	Broad approximation of digital as opposed to a narrowly focused public diplomacy in digital spaces.
Breakdown of Emphases (public diplomacy, cultural diplomacy, and/or place branding)	Idiosyncratic approximations toward global engagement. Content that might refer to Cold War frameworks including Third Worldism and Counterhegemonic approaches, but also economic development of the country.
Official and Non-Official Legitimacy (state and non-state actors)	Refers to the notion of legitimacy of actors conducting digital diplomacy in the real world and leveraging public-private partnerships or even civil society actors in their practice.

Source: Elaborated by the authors.

Institutional vs. personalized digital diplomacy. Firstly, from the field, a pendular swing between personalized and institutionalized forms of digital diplomacy seems evident, but with variations that necessitate appreciating trends of political communication and to an extent electoral/local political cycles and dynamics. Similarly, international events can provide impetus toward one side of the continuum or the other. By means of example, suffice it to say that the use of social media in politics was on the rise during the first decade of the 2000s. Hence, individual politicians, generally as candidates, especially in the global North, went on digital platforms to promote themselves and their electoral campaigns.

Subsequently, this phenomenon was noticeably echoed in Latin America, as presidential hopefuls began incorporating social media (mainly Twitter) into their campaigning efforts for electoral purposes. Once in office, the personal account of the newly elected president would broadcast and at times dominate all aspects of policy messaging, including those of international scope. While this trend was most noticeable among leaders deemed populist (e.g., Nicolás Maduro in Venezuela, Jair Bolsonaro in Brazil, and Nayib Bukele in El Salvador), others often also became the most prominent voice of their country's communication efforts regarding the international arena, as evidenced by follower counts surpassing those of almost non-existent institutional accounts on social media (see Table 30.2). Therefore, as the trend became a norm, digital diplomacy—in an ideal scenario—became less monopolized by the president as a single international voice and instead became one shared amongst ministers, ambassadors, and, in an advanced stage of digitalization, institutional accounts.

Table 30.2 Twitter Follower Count of MFA Institutions vs. President and FA Minister

Country	Institutional (MFA)*	Personalized**	Digital Diplomacy Following
Mexico	1,244,615	10,635,594	11,880,209
Brazil	366,104	7,203,639	7,569,743
Venezuela	459,677	4,171,491	4,631,168
El Salvador	355,366	3,372,395	3,727,761
Colombia	329,190	3,168,229	3,497,419
Chile	108,753	2,866,923	2,975,676

*May have multiple official MFA accounts on Twitter; **President and FA minister Twitter accounts.

Source: Elaborated by the authors with data retrieved using Audiense.com on 1 January 2022 and kindly provided by Matthias Lüfkens.

Exceptions to the rule do exist as some countries created institutional accounts early on or even in the first instance, but dominant/popular leaders overshadowed institutional accounts on many occasions even as latecomers (e.g., Bolivia's former president, Evo Morales). Not surprisingly, however, at an advanced stage of institutionalized digital diplomacy in the region, most of the activity on social media remained driven by public figure accounts instead of MFA ones. This is perhaps explained by the nature of Twitter and social media itself: public figure notoriety and a perceived notion by users that they are truly connected to and can interact directly with the leader in question. However, seen critically, this also speaks to institutional constraints or practitioner reluctance to embrace digital diplomacy for a variety of reasons.

Centralized-Proliferation of channels. This classification provides yet another level of complexity when examining Latin American experiences with digital diplomacy. With this continuum, we refer to levels of message control and strategies (or even lack thereof) in terms of conducting digital diplomacy as a public diplomacy activity within Nicholas Cull's (2019) framework. The modes multiply as certain social media platforms become more popular or decline in interest among users, as can be seen in the recent attention given to opening Instagram accounts. However, figures do continue to demonstrate the long-lasting dominance of Twitter for digital diplomacy, as seen in Figure 30.2.

Judging by the empirical data and personal experiences, we can observe that a country such as Mexico is closer to the centralized end of the continuum, as the Foreign Ministry has for several years preferred to have only one official institutional account across the different social media platforms, with a few exceptions, instead of promoting that each division and department of the MFA possess a separate account. The Mexican practice also offers an interesting case study when it comes to messaging control, since all its embassies, consulates, and multilateral missions abroad are requested to replicate some of the posts crafted at and sent from headquarters. This is in an attempt to both

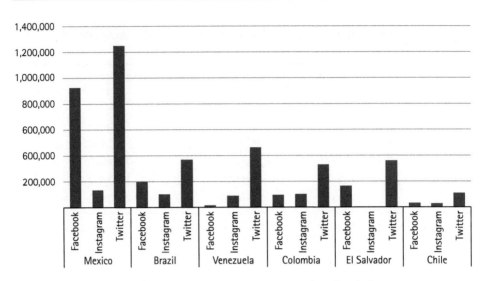

FIGURE 30.2. Ranking of Latin American presence on social media platforms
Source: Elaborated by the authors. Data as of January 2022.

put in place a coordinated strategy and to reach a wider audience on topics deemed important to attain certain foreign policy objectives or in order to garner sympathy towards Mexican positions on relevant international matters. For instance, after suing US gun manufacturers over arms trafficking in 2021, the Mexican MFA has involved its diplomatic and consular networks abroad in an all-encompassing social media messaging strategy to further attract attention to the issue and gain supporters to the cause.

At the other end of the spectrum, proliferation as a strategy is found among those countries that apparently seek to engage and attract support from very diverse target audiences, such as Venezuela, which possesses accounts in multiple languages (Spanish, English, French, Russian, and Chinese). In other aspects, countries such as Argentina, Brazil, and Chile, have created not only English language accounts, but also ad-hoc accounts, i.e., specific to a topic or circumstance, such as the Chilean governmental Twitter account that dealt with the territorial dispute with Bolivia at The International Court of Justice (@ChileanteLaHaya) or accounts for missions to the United Nations. Social media accounts devoted to cultural diplomacy have also flourished, and it goes without saying that embassies, as well as ambassadors, consuls, and diplomats at large have also adopted digital diplomacy in some capacity during this last decade. The uses given to these platforms have differed as some were actively advocating policy positions, and others promoting cultural understanding, while others still were simply informing on day-to-day activities in a broadcast modality.

Holistic-Specific implementation approach. A holistic vs. specific digital diplomacy continuum undoubtedly is one that also requires a detailed, case-by-case analysis, given that it does offer a number of exceptions to a general practice. To consider this continuum, the observation focuses on the divide between public diplomacy as adapted to the digital sphere, and diplomacy and economic policy pursuits vis-à-vis the global technological sector and ecosystems. The growing recognition of the need to pursue the digitalization of the economy and eventually increased levels and sophistication of national markets has proven to give impetus to what has been referred to as tech diplomacy. The holistic approach can be observable when Latin American countries have MFA accounts on social media, but also have representatives connecting on the ground with angel investors and companies from Silicon Valley pitching/advocating for the next 'killer app' developed in Latin America.

With the exception perhaps of the short-lived experience of Dr Mohammed Mostajo-Radji, whom the Bolivian government appointed to both the United Nations and to Silicon Valley in early 2020 as its Extraordinary and Plenipotentiary Ambassador for Science, Technology, and Innovation, it is important to highlight that none of the Latin American countries have as yet sent tech envoys in the same fashion as Denmark did in 2017 by appointing the first ever tech ambassador to Silicon Valley. Nevertheless, as Gual Soler (2021) documented, since the mid-2010s, science diplomacy has been on the rise on the agendas of many countries and some multilateral institutions in the region. For instance, 'Argentina, Brazil, Chile, Costa Rica, Cuba, Mexico, and Panama have started, reinforced and labeled their activities (sic.) the science-foreign policy interface as "science diplomacy" actions, adopting diverse strategies to incorporate science, technology and innovation into their foreign policy structures' (Gual Soler, 2021). Furthermore, over the past few years, countries such as Brazil, Chile, and Mexico have started to appoint scientific attachés to their embassies and consulates.

Breakdown of Emphases. The content emphasis of digital diplomacy is another area that also begs further consideration. Especially when unpacked, the messaging entails most of the *sui generis* aspects of the Latin American perspective on diplomacy and engagement with the world. Cold War legacies tend to provide guidance in understanding approximations as well as views on the current international system's opportunities and threats. In response, the observation covers three discernible areas found in the field: cultural diplomacy, place branding, and public diplomacy. Relative to foreign policy history and views toward place in the Western Hemisphere, it is reasonable to say that cultural diplomacy remains quite a generalized practice in a digital form, particularly from countries that practice defensive messaging or those with considerable cultural resources (Venezuela/Cuba in the first case, and Mexico/Peru/Brazil in the second case). Place branding in most countries is a predominant content emphasis and often the largest if not main component of what is understood as public diplomacy. In this last regard, public diplomacy in the region and as defined in the global North is not followed as closely; instead, a fluid interpretation of it is implemented in digital spaces.

Official and non-official actors engaging in digital diplomacy. The rise of diasporas and Latin American corporations and civil society organizations with global reach also helps to understand digital diplomacy from the region within its diversity as a mosaic. When considering actors engaged in digital diplomacy activities in the region, notably along with official voices (i.e., the foreign ministries, its missions abroad and diplomats), over the last decade the emergence of a variety of other subnational actors in the international arena has contested the nation-state monopoly in diplomatic matters. Some of these include cities and regional/local governments, multinational corporations, civil society organizations, and global diasporas. For instance, as subnational actors, regions and places such as the cities of Buenos Aires (Argentina; @gcba), Lima (Peru; @munlima), and Mexico City (@cdmx_oficial) possess an important following on Instagram: 30,400, 141,000, and 686,000 respectively. While indeed one might think of these accounts serving mostly local communities, the separation between a national and foreign public does seem sufficiently blurred to require considering a flexible definition of the desired reach of digital diplomacy.

Another set of actors becoming increasingly involved, albeit indirectly in digital diplomacy, are what is known as *multilatina* corporations. Essentially via corporate social responsibility efforts, Latin American transnational corporations wield considerable influence within the region as communities can recognize their country of origin and contribution to local economies. By way of example, we could name Latam Airlines (Chile-Brazil), Petrobras (Brazil), Bimbo and Telcel (Mexico), amongst others.

Last, but certainly not least, Latin American civil society via social media platforms has increased its interaction with different actors on the international scene, including with other governments as well as their own. Transnational advocacy networks in line with Keck and Sikkink's (1999) work have only strengthened (and proliferated) via social media. The context of Covid-19 within the region provides a plethora of examples of civil society engaging and organizing to request and provide support and relief during the period of the pandemic. This will be discussed in the final section of this text.

Latin American Experiences with Digital Diplomacy in Focus: The Cases of Mexico and Chile

The experiences of Mexico and Chile offer two valuable case studies that help exemplify how Latin America has ventured into digital diplomacy albeit through slightly different institutional arrangements and with differing outcomes.

The case of Mexico, as previously stated, falls arguably within the institutionalized end of the institutional-personalized digital diplomacy continuum. In 2012, during Peña Nieto's administration, the National Development Plan (a document that sets out the government programme at the beginning of each six-year presidential term) was the first one to include a specific reference to the need for defining goals in matters pertaining to public and cultural diplomacy as a means to promote Mexico's values abroad. Similarly, in 2013 the government presented the first digital action plan, entitled National Digital Strategy, which established a set of actions and policies aimed at incorporating information and communication technologies (ICT) in all aspects of the daily life of the population. Furthermore, as Ramos and Espinoza (2018) recall, in the 2016 edition of the annual Ambassadors and Consuls Meeting—which the MFA has been convening since

1989—there was an unprecedented debate concerning the emergence of new digital platforms and their impact on diplomatic activities. The heads of diplomatic and consular posts who were summoned to Mexico City that year even had the opportunity to listen to a master class in digital diplomacy by Alec Ross, the Obama-era guru on the subject and creator of the concept known as '21st Century Diplomacy Statecraft'.

Thus, the issue of digital public diplomacy and specifically the use of social digital networks as indispensable tools of contemporary diplomacy were included for the first time on the agenda. As a result of this exercise, the Mexican MFA started to recognize the importance of adapting its work and institutional culture to the new digital context, both to achieve a better rapprochement with citizens (in Mexico and abroad) and other international actors, and to showcase Mexico abroad in a more positive fashion. Ever since that 2016 edition, public and digital diplomacy have been amongst the topics discussed in the aforementioned annual Ambassadors and Consuls Meeting.

It is also important to highlight that in 2018, President López Obrador appointed Marcelo Ebrard as foreign minister. Both former mayors of Mexico City, they understand the potential of social media for communication purposes and extensively use their Twitter accounts to communicate with the public. They are respectively the president and the foreign minister in Latin America with the largest number of followers on such a platform. At more than 2.2 million, Ebrard's follower count is greater than the official MFA's account (1.2 million), and those of many presidents of the region. This is illustrated in Table 30.3, below.

In terms of institutional adaptation and reform, in 2018 the Mexican MFA created a new unit for Strategy and Public Diplomacy, which advises the minister in this field. This could be seen as a reflection of the country's commitment to developing a more comprehensive strategy in this area. However, it is worth noting that the Directorate General for Social Communications remained responsible for developing the media and communications strategy of the ministry, managing social media channels, and largely being in charge of coordinating the activity of the diplomatic and consular posts on these matters.

With respect to digital diplomacy infrastructure, as of January of 2022, Mexico had a total of 158 diplomatic and consular posts worldwide, i.e., eighty embassies, sixty-seven consulates, eight multilateral missions, and three representation offices (in Palestine, in Taiwan, and at the Council of Europe in Strasbourg). All the diplomatic and consular posts had Twitter and Facebook accounts, while some multilateral missions did as well. Some other offices had a presence also on Instagram, Twitter, and/or YouTube, and four of them (the Embassy in Canada and the consulates in Houston, Texas, and in Miami and Orlando, Florida, USA) even had TikTok accounts. In fact, Mexico was one of the first countries in Latin America to issue internal guidelines for the use of social media (2013). In said document, it made it mandatory for all its missions abroad to open accounts on both Twitter and Facebook, and all heads of posts also had to open an account on Twitter, while doing so on Facebook was optional. This signalled from an early stage a clear preference for Twitter for digital diplomacy purposes, as well as a recognition of the importance of developing a strong online presence.

Table 30.3 Latin American ranking of the most followed leaders and foreign ministers on Twitter

#	Name / Account	Country	Followers
1	President Andrés Manuel López Obrador (@lopezobrador_)	Mexico	8,405,698
2	President Jair Bolsonaro (@jairbolsonaro)	Brazil	7,225,724
3	President Nicolás Maduro (@NicolasMaduro)	Venezuela	4,019,725
4	President Nayib Bukele (@nayibbukele)	El Salvador	3,318,789
5	President Sebastián Piñera (@SebastianPinera)	Chile	2,501,664
6	President Iván Duque (@IvanDuque)	Colombia	2,384,206
7	Foreign Minister Marcelo Ebrard (@m_ebrard)	Mexico	2,264,662
8	President Alberto Fernández (@alferdez)	Argentina	2,156,339
9	President Luis Abinader (@luisabinader)	Dominican Republic	717,701
10	President Mario Abdo Benítez (@MaritoAbdo)	Paraguay	627,998
11	President Miguel Díaz-Canel Bermúdez (@DiazCanelB)	Cuba	568,335
12	President Juan Orlando Hernández (@JuanOrlandoH)	Honduras	454,551

Source: Elaborated by the authors with data retrieved from the original Twitter accounts on 10 January 2022.

Moreover, given that the MFA has opted for a centralized model of digital diplomacy by concentrating its communication efforts through the accounts it manages on various platforms, in practice this has limited the number of voices authorized to disseminate the country's official position on international issues. While this main guideline applies to central offices, as already noted, all missions abroad and the heads of mission themselves must have their own social media accounts.

With regards to message coordination and content control, this net of roughly 160 missions is requested to systematically repost or reshare messages that are crafted in headquarters in Mexico City, thereby multiplying the impact in terms of agenda setting and permitting the MFA to reach a wider audience. However, after analysing a sample of Twitter accounts of a number of Mexican diplomats and official institutions, using the model developed by Lu and Bjola (2015), Ramos and Espinoza (2018) demonstrated that those accounts that post local content and in two or more languages tend to fare better in the level of engagement with different audiences and in terms of expansion of their digital presence. Moreover, it is worth noting that the authors found that the accounts tweet primarily in Spanish, which arguably shows that the Mexican communities abroad and even the domestic constituencies are the primary addressees of the Mexican MFA's communication efforts.

Finally, regarding the breakdown of emphasis continuum mentioned above, as César Villanueva's (2016) comprehensive study on the international image of Mexico in the period 2006–2015 shows, the country has traditionally concentrated its public diplomacy efforts in portraying the vast cultural heritage and tourist attractions that the country offers. Nevertheless, the key findings of this study point out that the Mexico brand has been 'relegated to economic and tourism affairs, thus failing to take advantage of the potential that public diplomacy could offer in the communication of other social and political issues that the societies of other countries might find interesting'.

Almost conversely, Chile's venture into digital diplomacy teetered within informal and formalized paths of use and institutionalized implementation. While one of the late adopters within the first decade of digital diplomacy, a sustained effort took hold between 2014 and 2016 during President Michelle Bachelet's second term. However, as her time in office was coming to an end in 2017, some of the enthusiasm of that three-year period waned for a number of reasons.

The 2014–2016 digital diplomacy activity by the Chilean MFA was intense and supported by a climate of necessity that justified the hiring of a handful of specialists to manage Chile's foreign policy digital presence beyond simply redesigning or keeping the MFA's official website updated. In a way, creating a small digital diplomacy team of three specialists was a *de facto* means of formalizing within the MFA institution a practice that remained sidelined and criticized by reluctant groups within the non-politically appointed personnel. The foreign affairs minister at the time, Heraldo Muñoz, and many of his ambassadors came into their roles in 2014 with a vision favouring digital engagement and breathed new life into Chilean diplomacy, specifically in digital terms. In effect, as Muñoz was concluding his mission, a modernization bill was approved in congress to implement changes in the Chilean MFA in forthcoming years.

The historically sought-after modernization of Chilean foreign policy now had a roadmap to bring Chile's diplomacy into the twenty-first century. In the following administration of President Sebastián Piñera, efforts toward implementation would take place, arguably marking a second phase of digital transformation at the Chilean MFA through highly institutional means—an approved modernization law. During Piñera's second term (2018–2021), much of the proliferation of social media accounts occurred. Roberto Ampuero, a high-profile, prolific social media figure, was named FA minister. Known mostly as the author of a number of works of fiction and having a place in Latin American literary circles, Ampuero was also already very active on Twitter on his personal account. In addition, during Piñera's first administration, he was ambassador to Mexico and was known for his sometimes controversial opinions expressed on the platform and in traditional media.

At any rate, implementation of digital diplomacy via a modernization law occurred mostly by Ampuero maintaining an active presence on multiple social media platforms, and by incorporating Facebook and Instagram into the MFA's approach. Within the modernization law a reorganization of the Chilean MFA included creating a unit for strategic communication (*Dirección de Comunicación Estratégica*). Its status and scope provided an update and significant upgrade of what had been for years a press division that focused primarily on engaging with journalists/editors and news clipping/monitoring services. Whether the status upgrade repositioned its relevance within the

MFA and Chilean diplomatic practice remains to be seen. Notwithstanding, it was an important step, since previously digital diplomacy was by and large scrutinized and those non-senior level pioneers practicing it were often marginalized and not involved in foreign policy formulation and in important decision-making circles within Chilean diplomacy—with the exception of a few politically appointed high-ranking diplomats.

Of additional relevance to Chile's experience with digital diplomacy is a public-private organization founded in 2009 to cultivate Chile's presence overseas for mostly commerce, tourism, and to an extent foreign direct investment. As Chile sought out international markets for exports, to attract tourism and capital to the country, *Fundación Imagen de Chile* or Foundation Image Chile, became a pioneer in terms of digital approximations designed for world audiences. Over the years its work provides evidence of public diplomacy practice, but overall, its role in branding Chile is the organization's strength, especially as an implementer of programming of its main donor the Undersecretary of Economic Relations of the Chilean MFA, formerly Direcon (General Directorate of International Economic Relations). If the truth be told, during the early years some of the most innovative practices of *Imagen de Chile* were influential to MFA digital practice yet its financially subordinated status, while providing degrees of flexibility to conduct its promotional activities, also sidelined its staff from policy ideas at its origins at the MFA.

While most of the visible digital diplomacy practice of the Chilean MFA and its practitioners refer to the public diplomacy sphere, Chile did also venture into a more policy-centric notion of digital diplomacy, otherwise known as tech diplomacy. Chile's economic success since the end of the Pinochet dictatorship meant increased levels of development within the country, including the recent digitalization of its economy. Higher-than-average Internet penetration rates in the region enabled a technological innovation environment that began expanding as the Chilean government deliberately pursued an ambitious digital agenda during the early years of the Internet. Of relevance to tech diplomacy, Chile leveraged one of its long-standing relationships with California (and the University of California system) to position Chilean innovation in the state and specifically engage with Silicon Valley's tech ecosystem. Interestingly, during 2011–2014 (Sebastián Piñera's first term) a representative to the State of California was charged with making the establishment of ties to tech sectors a reality. While innovative for the region, if not the world, this role was considered unusual and was not fully understood or known among diplomats or those who study Latin American diplomacy and foreign policy.

DIGITAL DIPLOMACY IN TIMES OF CRISES: LESSONS LEARNT FROM THE COVID-19 PANDEMIC AND THE ROAD AHEAD

To state that the Covid-19 pandemic has upended the world order in unimagined ways is undoubtedly a truism. Moreover, any attempt to predict how long the transformations it has brought about will last would be unwise and premature. However, it is a given that it will leave behind a trail of enduring geopolitical, socio-economic, and even cultural effects.

On the one hand, the pandemic laid bare just how much we depend on technology, while on the other dramatically increasing this dependence and accelerating the trend to migrate to digital platforms. It also meant that we had to act fast and become much more creative, innovative and, perhaps paradoxically, more collaborative than in the past, subjected as we were to all sorts of measures that severely curtailed our rights of free movement and assembly. In sum: it made the international community realize that no single country could face the emergency alone and it consequently made us aware of just how much we depend on collective action to accomplish any goal.

As was observed elsewhere, during the initial emergency management phase, foreign ministries attempted to assess the severity of the crisis. In a second immediate phase, it is only natural that the top priority of MFAs and their diplomatic and consular posts abroad then became the providing of assistance to citizens in need. With respect to communication and outreach duties, MFAs had to be highly competent and capable of updating and conveying to their nationals all the information available about Covid-19-related measures, travel restrictions, border closures, repatriation flights, and so on in real time, mainly through social media platforms.

We performed an informal analysis of a sample of tweets from the Mexican and Chilean MFAs' Twitter accounts of April 2020, coming a month after the World Health Organization declared Covid-19 a pandemic (one of the most critical months of that first stage of the emergency). This exercise yielded results that are quite telling and that help to demonstrate how the pandemic was tweeted. Some of the main findings are as follows:

In the Mexican case, almost all—91% of 241 tweets posted in that month—were unsurprisingly related to Covid-19, while more than half of the total—53%—had to do with one of the following three topics: 1) consular assistance matters, 2) information about air routes, frequencies, and repatriation flights, and 3) reporting to the public the general repatriation statistics of Mexican nationals.

As for the Chilean sample, there was a smaller universe of tweets—132—during that month, of which 73.5% of the total was related to Covid-19 (97 tweets). Furthermore, 23.5% (31 tweets) had to do with repatriation efforts of Chilean nationals who were stranded after the pandemic hit, and roughly 20% (27 tweets) referred to the national strategy or policies put in place to address the impact of Covid-19. In addition, whereas only four tweets (i.e., 3%) were about reporting to the public the general repatriation statistics, in the Mexican case, 21 tweets had to do with that topic (almost 9%). These findings coincide with those of Romero Vara et al. (2021), who after conducting a similar analysis of posts on Twitter by seven MFAs in the Americas, in the period between 15 February and 30 April of 2020, concluded that '82.9% of the tweets of the sample were related to some aspect of the pandemic, vs. 17.1% that were not'.

It is also worth mentioning that the communication efforts of both countries' foreign ministries were directed almost exclusively to either their nationals abroad or their domestic constituencies. A good indicator of the former is that almost all of the tweets of the Mexican MFA were in Spanish (236 out of 241), while in fact all of the Chilean tweets were in said language, although as already noted, the Chilean MFA has an account also in English (albeit with far fewer followers). These results should not come as a surprise and only attest to the growing importance and the usefulness of social media during the initial phases of the pandemic as an extraordinary means to reach out and offer a helping hand to the tens of thousands of nationals—whether stranded or otherwise in need—in a foreign land.

To further consider the consularization of diplomacy in this period and beyond, it is worth underscoring what authors such as Melissen (2020) and Fernández Pasarín (2016) observed prior to the outbreak of Covid-19. Melissen for instance refers to some of the expanded and renewed competencies required to engage in digital diplomacy from a consular standpoint, using as examples cases of coordinated digital outreach efforts during recent natural disasters across the globe. Similarly, Fernández-Pasarín refers to the shift of consular affairs towards increased integration with diplomacy as diasporas seek out assistance in newer and increasing ways, such as migration crises. As both studies show, the consularization of diplomacy in the digital realm is indeed highly recognizable during the outbreak of the pandemic. In that same vein, Romero et al. provide empirical backing to the consularization phenomena by comparing interaction levels of some of Latin America's MFA Twitter accounts. Their conclusions provide evidence of a shift, although, beyond the context of Covid-19 (whenever that occurs), it is yet to be seen if the current intensified level of consular practice within digital diplomacy action will persist.

Conclusions

A decade's worth of digital diplomacy in the Latin American region offers a varied yet also unified approximation of its practice. Admittedly, a close reading and an examination of countries draw out particular details that can make generalization difficult. However, just as when observing a mosaic from a distance, common traits and similar implementations start to emerge, which allows for an analysis that brings certain similarities to light. When focusing as we have done specifically on two cases, namely Mexico and Chile, diversity in approximations is noticeable, but outcomes appear to be somewhat similar. By means of five proposed conceptualizations, this chapter discussed how both cases—and the practice of digital diplomacy of the whole region—fit within a conceptual mosaic. Considering that Mexico and Chile are the bookends of early and late adoption of digital practice, countries that fall in between these experiences in our view possess behaviours described within each continuum. For instance, the chapter refers to an institutional vs. personalized continuum, in which Mexico's early institutional implementation of digital diplomacy is evident, including the clear strategies and guidelines that the Mexican MFA laid out early on to manage the use of and content on social media.

Some of Chile's early approximation to digital diplomacy appeared mostly concentrated in the hands of President Piñera and after that, during Bachelet's administrations, in those of the FA minister and high-ranking politically appointed ambassadors. Chile then pursued an institutional approach towards digital diplomacy beginning in 2014 when a team of digital strategists was assembled and around 2017–2018 a modernization law came into force establishing clearer parameters and legitimacy of digital diplomacy practice. Other continuums offer analytical lenses to examine both the region and specific cases, allowing for a diversity of experiences in Latin America. Indeed, while digitalization is a dynamic and ongoing process, as Manor (2019) pointed out, we envision parts of each conceptual continuum as a natural progression toward higher levels of sophistication. For instance, proliferation of modes generally seems to entail mostly advanced uses of digital tools, whereas this is less the case with centralization. A specific or holistic approach or a combination of the two might also signal a better understanding and institutional learning of what digital diplomacy should pursue and in what manner.

Now, to clarify, the two final concepts discussed, namely emphases and legitimacy of actors conducting digital diplomacy, do provide more leeway in terms of gauging sophistication. However, our view is that mixed definitions of diplomacies and branding, and who can influence in public diplomacy terms, do illustrate the richness of the diversity that the Latin American regional experience provides. This seems especially relevant as textbook definitions are challenged by practices guided by foreign policy interests and largely economic development needs. Thus, a *sui generis* Latin American digital diplomacy is one that in its complexity extends alternatives of function and utility of digital and public diplomacy outside of established conventions. To an extent, digital diplomacy in the region challenges a mainstream view of international engagement broadly and specifically in/through cyberspace.

The ongoing Covid-19 pandemic and the way governments in the region have responded to the emergency shed light on the changing landscape in which MFAs communicate with their target audiences, mainly with citizens abroad in need, and accelerate the speed with which they must act to meet the real-time demands of their nationals. Consular dominance, as is also probably the case in other parts of the world, brings to the fore the pressing need to maintain a spirit of innovation and technological adaptation, so as to continue to improve the level of consular assistance and services to national communities abroad, while at the same time underscoring the necessity of incorporating consular diplomacy to a comprehensive digital diplomacy strategy.

Moving beyond the context of the pandemic and judging by a decade of accumulated experience in digital diplomacy in Latin America, there are compelling reasons that lead us to the conclusion that the different countries of the region will continue to be engaged in the race to achieve their respective foreign policy goals through the increasing use of both digital and diverse diplomacy approximations. Similarly, it is foreseeable that they will most probably continue to embrace the digital paradigm in their diplomatic work and further underpin their efforts to develop a strong online presence, given the benefits and opportunities that it can provide, as well as the risk of being left out of the conversation.

SUGGESTED READING

Aguirre, D., Erlandsen, M., and López, M. 2018. *Diplomacia pública digital: el contexto iberoamericano.* https://doi.org/10.34720/atb5-z184 (In Spanish)

Aguirre, D., Manor, I., and Ramos, A. eds. 2018. 'Special Bilingual Issue on Public Diplomacy in the Digital Era'. *Revista Mexicana de Política Exterior,* (113), https://revistadigital.sre.gob.mx/index.php/rmpe/issue/view/14

Bravo, V. and De Moya, M. eds. 2021. *Latin American Diasporas in Public Diplomacy.* Palgrave Macmillan.

Heine, J. and Turcotte, J.F. 2012. 'Tweeting as Statecraft: How, Against All Odds, Twitter is Changing the World's Second Oldest Profession'. *Crossroads: The Macedonian Foreign Policy Journal,* vol. 3 (2): 57–70.

Manfredi-Sánchez, J.-L. 2022. 'Thinking About Latin American Public Diplomacy'. *Latin American Policy,* vol. 13 (35): 1–14. https://doi.org/10.1111/lamp.12242

REFERENCES

Aguirre, Daniel. 2020. 'Public Diplomacy in Latin America, An Emerging Field of Practice'. In *Routledge Handbook of Public Diplomacy,* edited by Snow, Nancy, and N. Cull, 368–378. New York: Routledge.

Aguirre, Daniel and M. Erlandsen. 2018. 'Digital Public Diplomacy in Latin America: Challenges and Opportunities'. *Revista Mexicana de Política Exterior,* (113) (May-August): 119–139 [https://revistadigital.sre.gob.mx/images/stories/numeros/n113/aguirreerlandseni.pdf].

Bjola, Corneliu and Lu Jiang. 2015. 'Social Media and Public Diplomacy. A Comparative Analysis of the Digital Diplomatic Strategies of the EU, US and Japan in China'. In *Digital Diplomacy, Theory and Practice,* edited by Bjola, Corneliu and M. Holmes, 89–108. New York: Routledge.

Cull, Nicholas J. 2019. *Public Diplomacy: Foundations for Global Engagement in The Digital Age.* Cambridge: John Wiley & Sons.

Fernández-Pasarín, Ana Mar. 2016. 'Consulates and Consular Diplomacy'. In *The SAGE Handbook of Diplomacy,* edited by Constantinou, Costa, P. Kerr, and P. Sharp, 161–170. London: SAGE doi: http://dx.doi.org/10.4135/9781473957930.n14.

Gual Soler, Marga. 2021. 'Science Diplomacy in Latin America and the Caribbean: Current Landscape, Challenges, and Future Perspectives'. *Frontiers in Research Metrics and Analytics,* vol. 6, doi: https://doi.org/10.3389/frma.2021.670001.

Keck, Margaret E. and K. Sikkink. 1999. 'Transnational Advocacy Networks in International and Regional Politics'. *International Social Science Journal,* vol. 51 (159): 89–101.

Lowenthal, Abraham F. 2012. 'Un desglose de Latinoamérica: Diferentes trayectorias, grupos emergentes y sus implicaciones'. *Foreign Affairs Latinoamérica,* vol. 12 (1): 47–58.

Manfredi, Juan Luis. 2021. 'Deglobalization and Public Diplomacy'. *International Journal of Communication,* vol. 15: 905–926 [https://ijoc.org/index.php/ijoc/article/view/15379/3357].

Manor, Ilan. 2019. *The Digitalization of Public Diplomacy*. Cham: Palgrave Macmillan.

Melissen, Jan. 2020. 'Consular Diplomacy's First Challenge: Communicating Assistance to Nationals Abroad'. *Asia & the Pacific Policy Studies*, vol. 7 (2) (21 April 2020): 217–228 doi: https://doi.org/10.1002/app5.298.

Ramos, Alejandro, and L.M. Espinoza. 2018. 'La diplomacia en 140 caracteres: El caso de México'. In *Diplomacia Pública Digital: el Contexto Iberoamericano*, edited by Aguirre, Daniel, M. Erlandsen, and M.A. López, 33–70. Heredia, Costa Rica: Universidad Nacional doi: https://doi.org/10.34720/atb5-z184

Romero Vara, Laura, A.C. Alfaro Muirhead, E. Hudson Frías, and D. Aguirre Azócar. 2021. 'La diplomacia digital frente a la COVID-19: una aproximación exploratoria a la interactividad y asistencia consular en Twitter'. *Comunicación y Sociedad*, (118): 1–23 doi: https://doi.org/10.32870/cys.v2021.7960.

Sarukhan, Arturo. 2016. 'I Say Poder Suave, You Say Soft Power'. CPD Blog, 16 June 2016, date accessed 1 June 2022 [https://uscpublicdiplomacy.org/blog/i-say-poder-suave-you-say-soft-power].

Villanueva Rivas, César. 2016. *La imagen de México en el mundo 2006-2015*. Mexico City: Fernández Editores.

Zaharna, R.S. 'The Ironies of Social Media in Public Diplomacy', CPD Blog, 20 May 2012, https://uscpublicdiplomacy.org/blog/ironies-social-media-public-diplomacy

CHAPTER 31

DIPLOMACY IN TIMES OF CRISIS IN THE GCC: THE BLOCKADE AND THE PANDEMIC

BANU AKDENIZLI

THE Gulf Cooperation Council (GCC), established in 1981 in Riyadh, aimed to achieve unity among member states who share similar political and cultural identities. Often described as modern and tribal (Cooke, 2014), GCC countries are home to the world's wealthiest populations. Classified as rentier states, their revenues come from selling natural resources (such as oil and gas) to foreign nations (Beblawi and Luciani, 1987).

The scholarly study of public diplomacy is a growing field in the GCC. This is a welcome change considering the usual focus seemed to be centred around the Western powers' public/digital diplomacy performance towards the Middle East to forge better communication strategies in a post 9/11 world (such as the social media activities of Western embassies in such states to promote and represent the home country in the host country, e.g., Strauss, Kruikemeir, van der Meulen, and Van Noort, 2015; Khatib, Dutton, and Thelwall, 2012). Works on the role of international broadcasting (Powers and Gilboa, 2007; Seib, 2008, 2014); religious diplomacy (El-Nawawy, 2013; Kourgiotis, 2020; Sheikholeslami and Saradar, 2012; Ulrichsen, 2021); branding and rebranding (Allagui and Alnajjar, 2018; Govers, 2012; Hayden, 2009; Williamson, 2022; Zeineddine, 2017); cultural diplomacy (Eggeling, 2017; Erskin-Loftus, Hightower, and Al-Mulla, 2016); and sport diplomacy (Branaggan and Giulianotti, 2015; Côme and Raspaud, 2018; Ginesta and de San Eugenio, 2014) are some examples of the common topics scholars are exploring and writing about the region.

This chapter investigates the digital transformation of diplomacy in the GCC. Digital diplomacy, in the context of this chapter, is defined as the practice of diplomacy and international relations via information and communication technologies. In doing so, the chapter concentrates on the social media use (specifically Twitter) of the ministries of foreign affairs (MFAs) and embassies of the GCC countries during two pivotal periods in recent history: the Blockade 2017–2021 and the Covid-19 pandemic 2019–2021.

Duncombe (2019) notes how Twitter has evolved into a significant platform for states to articulate and develop policy responses. Twitter statements, she claims, have the ability to both represent and elicit strong emotional responses from other users, resulting in large-scale debates that influence offline political outcomes. It is arguable that the role of social media in facilitating emotional expressions such as anger, disgust, sympathy, and empathy raises concerns about the shifting power dynamics between states and their publics, as well as the implications of this communication shift for state responses to political crises. This expansion of a platform on which political contestation and negotiation can occur is a major source of Twitter's power (Duncombe, 2019: 140).

Digital diplomacy entails not only disseminating information to foreign publics, but also effectively managing change within the international system (Holmes, 2015). Both the Blockade and the Covid-19 pandemic are classified as 'exogenous shocks' (Holmes, 2015) within the context of this chapter. Crisis communication and conflict resolution are key ways in which actors deal with these shocks (Kaufmann, 1998; Reynolds, 2007 as cited in Holmes, 2015). These two periods are unique in the history and aspirations of the region, as they are characterized by crisis and management, both regionally and internationally. How MFAs construct frames that enable digital publics to make sense of a crisis (Manor, 2019) is a central aspect of this chapter's analysis. Among the primary research questions addressed in this chapter are: what tactics and strategies did MFAs use to project themselves online during these eras; and what contextual factors influenced their online practice? Bjola, Cassidy, and Manor (2020) state that 'transparency, decentralization, informality, interactivity, and real-time management are essential norms for ensuring the effectiveness of digital activity' (406). This chapter focuses on whether these objectives are realizable within the context of the GCC.

The GCC was formed to achieve unity among its members on the basis of their shared political and cultural identities, which are rooted in Arab and Islamic cultures. The Charter emphasizes cooperation, coordination, and integration among members, as well as the development of closer ties and stronger bonds. The GCC area is also marked by historical rivalries and competition. One of the chapter's primary concerns is how these factors will impact the practice of digital diplomacy in times of crisis. Will digital diplomacy increase or decrease regional rivalry during times of crisis, or will it help to foster relationships?

Internet penetration rates are above the world average in the region. The Gulf states enjoy the highest penetration rates in the Middle East. Bahrain (99.67%), Kuwait (99.1%), Oman (95.23%), Qatar (99.65%), Saudi Arabia (97.86), and the United Arab Emirates (UAE) (100%) enjoy universal access (ITU, 2022). In recent years, the use of social media has skyrocketed in the Arab world, and research indicates that the Arab public is increasingly active (as illustrated by the 'Media Use in the Middle East' reports by Dennis, Martin, and Hassan, 2019).

Countries in the Middle East are frequently reprimanded for restricting and banning access to social networking websites and the Internet and for being societies that have traditionally been closed to the free flow of information. The question of whether Islam and democracy can coexist has long been the subject of political debate. Except for Oman, all GCC countries have ratified the Arab Charter on Human Rights, which guarantees citizens 'the right to information, freedom of opinion and expression, as well as the right to seek, receive, and impart information and ideas through any medium, regardless of geographical boundaries'. Nonetheless, media and Internet freedom reports consistently place these countries at the bottom (Freedom House, 2020; Reporters Without Borders, 2021). A 2016 study on GCC countries by Human Rights Watch (2016) shows how GCC states acquired and used surveillance equipment to track and screen nationals' Internet movements. According to publicly available corporate records and reports from Citizen Lab's independent security researchers, Western and Israeli companies provided software to GCC governments that can be used to violate residents' privacy (Marzcak and Scott-Railton, 2016). In the past, political activists, human rights activists, journalists, attorneys, and bloggers have all been detained in the region (Human Rights Watch, 2016). The 2011 uprisings, which initially inspired a more open and diverse media landscape, have been followed by declines in freedom of expression. In the Middle East, GCC countries are cited as the most successful examples of authoritarian adaptation to digital activism (Lynch, 2021).

The GCC countries have been trying to project themselves as places open for business and investment for at least a decade (Cooper and Momani, 2009). Their openness to global capital, as Shires (2022) states, 'has made GCC countries sites of significant digital expertise in e-government, energy, health, and other critical sectors' (para. 2). Investment in e-technologies, as Zayani (2018) notes, is security-driven. Gulf countries are home to large populations of migrant labour. Most Gulf nationals are a minority in their homeland. Smart IDs are used for identification, authentication, and to enable governments to manage immigrant issues and monitor and track them (Zayani, 2018: 13). The latest E-Government Index by the UN indicates a significant improvement in rendering digital services by these states. UAE tops the list with a rank of twenty-one out of 100 countries, followed by Bahrain (38), Saudia Arabia (43), Kuwait (46), Oman (50), and Qatar (66). According to the ITU Global Cybersecurity Index 2020 (GCI), all GCC countries rank in the top ten of the Arab world on the index, with Saudia Arabia, the UAE, Oman, and Qatar in the lead. Saudia Arabia and the UAE rank in the top five of the global GCI. According to Alkhusaili and AlJazzaf's (2020) study, e-government is crucial for managing and guiding the process of change and reform, as well as enhancing public confidence. Strategies set out by GCC states in achieving their visions (such as Qatar 2030 Vision, Saudi Arabia 2030 Vision, Bahrain Economic Vision 2030, Kuwait 2035 Vision, and Oman Vision 2040) demonstrate the regions' aspirations and objectives for networked societies, electronic governance, and sustainable development. The development of smart city projects (such as Lusail in Qatar, Masdar in the UAE, Riyadh in Saudi Arabia, Smart Clean City in Kuwait) and hosting mega-events (such as Dubai Expo 2020, FIFA World Cup Qatar 2022) show digital transformation in GCC is not accidental, but the result of a deliberate strategy.

The GCC Blockade and the Covid-19 pandemic have demonstrated that crises are a natural part of the world and way of life. They are not discrete events. As Cassidy (2018) explains, crises are increasingly characterized by their complexity, interdependence, and politicization. Crisis communication in the digital age is marked by a need for credibility, authenticity, transparency, and responsiveness (Kara, 2019). Were these practiced in the region? The following two sections of this chapter will look at how digital diplomacy was used in the GCC during these critical times, with a focus on determining whether digital diplomacy had any discernible impact on these crises.

It All Began With a Hack: The Blockade

Tensions in the GCC are not new. The 2011 Arab uprisings alarmed many governments in the region, who saw pro-democracy movements as a threat to their own long-standing autocratic rule. Qatar-owned Al Jazeera provided favourable coverage of the protest, causing Qatar's neighbours to become increasingly concerned. Saudi Arabia, the UAE, Bahrain, and Egypt withdrew their ambassadors from Qatar in March 2014, the most severe cut since the formation of the GCC in 1981 (McDonald, 2021). Qatar's support for the Muslim Brotherhood, as well as its relations with Iran, Saudi Arabia's main regional rival, have long been sources of contention in the region.

The Blockade arguably was the first significant crisis provoked by a computer breach. On 23 May 2017, Qatar's News Agency (QNA) website published quotes attributed to the Emir of Qatar Sheikh Tamim Al Thani, saying Iran was an 'Islamic power that cannot be ignored'. The post also stated that Qatar had tense relations with US President Trump's administration and described Hamas as the legitimate representative of the Palestinian people. A day later on May 24, the Qatari government pointed out that QNA was hacked and launched an investigation. But the damage had been done. The regional media was in uproar. Saudi Arabia and the UAE were the first to block Al Jazeera and other Qatar-based news outlets.

On 5 June 2017, Saudi Arabia, the UAE, Bahrain, and Egypt, collectively known as 'the Quartet', announced severing diplomatic ties with Doha and imposed a land, sea, and air blockade over accusations it 'supports terrorism'. Saudi Arabia, the UAE, and Bahrain gave Qatari visitors and residents two weeks to leave their countries. The Quartet issued a list of demands, to which Qatar responded negatively.

Unlike previous GCC confrontations, which were contained within the closed doors of regional leaders, the Blockade would be played out in the media (Ulrichsen, 2017). An Al Jazeera story of the same day would report that the hashtag translating as 'cutting ties' became the number one trend worldwide with more than one million mentions. Short-term suspension of Al Jazeera Arabic's Twitter account, the UAE becoming the first blockading nation to ban expressions of support for Qatar, and Bahrain's declaration that any form of communication in support of Qatar is punishable by up to five years in prison and a fine indicate the online nature of the commentary, rumours, and backlash on the Blockade (Akdenizli, 2018b). According to Jones (2019), the crisis was one of the first to originate, gain legitimacy, and intensify as a result of a deliberate cyber and social media campaign.

In his examination of conflicting narratives of the opening days of the crisis, Krieg (2019) describes how the 'anti-terror quartet' and subsequently Qatar began to invest heavily and hire PR and lobbying firms in a bid to win the hearts of not only the Gulf people but also the Western public. In the absence of a diplomatic thaw, his analysis demonstrates that indirect communication between Abu Dhabi and Riyadh, on the one hand, and Doha, on the other, was maintained through social media sites, blogs, broadcast media, and the foreign press on both sides (Krieg, 2019).

Several studies demonstrate how the initial days of the Blockade played out on Twitter. Leber and Abrahams's (2019) work illustrated how state actors manipulated discourse on social media through direct intervention and co-optation of existing social media influencers and bot activity. Saud al-Qahtani, former advisor to the Royal Court of Saudia Arabia, one of the most pronounced Saudi officials on Twitter, launched the #TheBlacklist hashtag urging his followers to put any names or accounts that showed sympathy towards Qatar, and tweet about them using said hashtag. UAE's state minister of foreign affairs, Anwar Gargash, was among the first to express support for the blacklist, tweeting, 'Saud al-Qahtani is an important voice... His tweet regarding the "blacklist" is crucial' (Al Jazeera, 2017). Al-Qathani also tweeted that anyone conspiring against Saudi Arabia, the UAE, Egypt, and Bahrain would not be able to escape trial (Al Jazeera, 2017). In September 2019 Twitter suspended his account along with 4,528 accounts operating from the UAE (TRT World, 2019).

Marc Owen Jones's works have demonstrated how online bots are weaponized to accomplish specific political tasks in the region (Jones, 2017, 2019). During the Blockade, there was ample evidence of promoting fake news, manipulation to increase anti-Qatari tweets, and creating the illusion of online grassroots opposition to Qatari leadership (Jones, 2019). Mitchell's (2019) analysis of derogatory hashtags and posts referencing Sheikha Moza bin Nasser, the mother of the Emir, Sheikh Tamim, and the FIFA World Cup point to the historical tensions and competitive strategies in the region. The use of bots and derogatory hashtags point to the dark side of digital diplomacy, which Bjola and Pamment (2019) define as 'the use of digital technologies as disinformation and propaganda tools by government and non-state actors in the pursuit of strategic interests' (2019: 3).

According to research conducted by Akdenizli (2018b) on the usage of Twitter by MFAs in the GCC, countries in the area have been utilizing social media for the past decade. Qatar and Saudi Arabia have separate Arabic and English accounts. Saudi Arabia emerges as the frontrunner among these accounts, with over a million followers at the time of the Blockade, followed by the UAE and Qatar (UAE with a little over 400,000 and Qatar at 25,000). Foreign ministers of the region have many more followers, with UAE in the lead (Akdenizli, 2018b). At the start of the Blockade, the minister of the UAE had close to four million followers, while the ministry had only approximately 400,000 (Akdenizli, 2018b). At the time, all accounts followed only a few accounts. The foreign minister had the most accounts, which totalled 668. The minister of the UAE was at 620. To a certain extent, to follow others on social media demonstrates symmetrical and dialogical contact (Kent and Taylor, 2021). The primary advantage of social media technologies is that they facilitate two-way communication between political institutions and their constituents. If the purpose of utilizing Twitter in digital diplomacy is to develop contacts, stimulate conversation, solicit opinion, and listen, then the numerical imbalance for all of the aforementioned accounts implies that ministers and ministries did not utilize this function to its fullest extent. There were a total of 1,517 tweets analysed (a total of 110 English tweets from the ministers themselves and 1,407 tweets from the four respective MOFA accounts).

Despite having fewer followers, Qatar's foreign minister was the most active in English tweets (based on the number of tweets and re-tweets), followed by the UAE and Bahrain. He was responsible for nearly half (49.5%) of the sample of English-language tweets from the four ministers. The UAE's foreign minister scored second (30.5%), followed by Bahrain's foreign policy chief (20%). The Saudi minister did not tweet in English during the first 100 days of the boycott. Concerning the actual foreign ministries, over half (43%) belonged to the Qatari ministry. UAE (22%) and Bahrain (29%) followed in second and third place, respectively. During this 100-day period, the Saudi MFA tweeted only eighty-five times, or fewer than 1% of all tweets sent (Akdenizli, 2018a).

What did ministers say regarding the Blockade? Of the tweets by the four ministers: 40% dealt with the blockade; 35.2% did not address any particular issue or news story; and 9.5% dealt with official visits and meetings (informing followers about engagements with local or foreign dignitaries either at home or abroad, usually accompanied by a photograph). When all of the tweets about the Blockade were analysed, however, a clear content creator became apparent. Qatar's foreign minister accounted for 83.3% of all crisis-related tweets, followed by his Bahraini counterpart with 9.5% and the UAE's foreign minister with 7.5%.

The reply tweet is a special type of Twitter activity that represents a public exchange between one account and a specific other Twitter user. The practice of 'talking' to one's audience can be viewed as an attempt to build relationships and increase interactional transparency. During the first 100 days of the crisis, the ministries in question and their ministers rarely interacted with their audiences in this manner. Only twice (23 June and 6 August 2017) did a ministry (the Bahraini on both occasions) respond to a member of the public (Akdenizli, 2018a). Twitter was mainly used to broadcast and draw attention to speeches and announcements; to make and respond to statements; to present oneself, acknowledge and recognize others, and create allegiances. Qatar's foreign minister focused extensively on matters related to international dialogue and diplomacy efforts ('deep and positive discussion today with members of @UKHouseofLords on #GCC crisis. #Qatar remains a strong & trusted partner in the region' dated 6 July 2017; 'positive discussion today in #Berlin w/my friend FM @sigmargabriel. We both agree that the unjustified blockade on #Qatar is unacceptable' dated 9 June 2017). Bahrain's foreign minister was more direct, two examples being: 'In one sentence I heard the word "blockade"; "air routes are open over Iran; through Kuwait, Muscat and Turkey"! Make up your mind Qatar', dated 20 June 2017; 'Thank God we are immensely more rich with wonderful creative people than material wealth, and more thankful for not being nouveau riche', dated 6 August 2017. The UAE minister did not tweet at all himself in English on the subject of the Blockade in its first 100 days; instead he re-tweeted Donald Trump's infamous early tweets on Qatar and the Blockade ('During my recent trip to the Middle East I stated that there can no longer be funding of Radical Ideology. Leaders pointed to Qatar- look!', dated 6 June 2017).

The first 100 days of the Blockade's digital diplomacy resembled official diplomacy policy. It was utilized to make public issues more prominent while also contributing to the propagation of the dominant sociocultural actor's discourse (Akdenizli, 2018b). Competing narratives were apparent: Qatar projected an image of resiliency and optimism by emphasizing diplomatic visits and words of solidarity from around the world. On 14 June 2017, for example, the ministry not only tweeted about the Blockade but also issued back-to-back infographics on the 'kind of human rights violations caused by severing diplomatic ties #Qatar'. These abuses covered press, expression, opinion, movement, education, residency, and private property rights. Other tweets reported the minister's daily activities: '#Ugandan President Meets Minister of State for Foreign Affairs' and 'Foreign Minister @MBA AlThani Meets #Turkish Counterpart' (Akdenizli, 2018b: 153).

Bahrain elected to emphasize its brotherly ties with Egypt, whereas the UAE and Bahrain emphasized terrorism in the region and the Taliban's presence in Doha. Saudi Arabia was unequivocal regarding Qatar's alleged funding of terrorism and its relationship with Iran (such as 'Demands on #Qatar to stop funding terrorism are non-negotiable', dated 1 July 2017; '#Iran sponsors terrorism and fuels sectarianism', dated 16 June 2017; and '#Iran's activities in the region are very negative and must stop in order to have genuine dialogue with them', dated 20 July 2017) (Akdenizli, 2018b: 155).

An analysis of the Arabic discourse on Twitter during the first 100 days by the MFAs shows some differences. First, more ministers and ministries tweeted in Arabic. During the first 100 days, a total of 3,532 tweets were sent (Al-Mansouri et al., 2021). Most of the time, the tweets were written in Fusha (formal and traditional Arabic) and addressed the local Khaleeji (Gulf) and Arab followers (Al-Mansouri et al., 2021). The choice of words was also distinct. Saudi Arabia, for instance, never referred to the Blockade as a blockade but chose the term 'severing ties', a hashtag adopted in the opening days of the crisis to denigrate and isolate Qatar. While bot activity and weaponization of social media were attributed in many reports and documented by Jones's works (2017, 2019) to be emanating from the UAE and Saudi Arabia, interestingly, the Saudi ministry in particular was the most active in their official capacity on Twitter during the periods under study with 36% of the Arabic tweets. Qatar would follow at 29.4%, with UAE at 18.8% and Bahrain at 16.7% (Al-Mansouri et al., 2021). Al-Mansouri et al.'s analysis (2021) also demonstrates how traditional media news stories influence online discourse. One of the highest activity days was on 20 July 2017, when the US State Department released its 'Country Reports on Terrorism'. A CNN story on the leaked confidential Riyadh Agreement in July was also heavily tweeted about, each account highlighting news that was favourable to their own countries and negative towards the others. As Nimmo (2018) points out the Gulf powers fought their dispute via Twitter and diplomatic channels alike. Each side utilized a variety of bots operated by both domestic and foreign sources to amplify their competing messages. Clearly, the focus of these Arabic-language hashtags was local and regional rather than international; it was a matter of communicating with the domestic population and Arabic-speaking rivals rather than with the rest of the world (Nimmo, 2018). When they used English, it was primarily to appeal to international audiences and gain their support.

The almost three-and-a-half-year-long Blockade ended on 5 January 2021. The GCC members share security, military, and foreign policy problems, necessitating close regional cooperation. Extremist elements exist in each country, and each has created powerful security mechanisms to monitor and counter potential threats to its stability (Kabbani, 2021). Relationships with migrant workers, economic pressures from declining hydrocarbon reserves and revenues, and the lowering of oil prices during the coronavirus pandemic might have been issues that helped resolve the Blockade (Kabbani, 2021). Like in many parts of the world, the coronavirus pandemic illustrated that for the GCC, regional alliance, cooperation, communication, and integrated health system were vital. Bruno (2020) pointed out individual GCC states would only be able to mitigate the pandemic's social and economic effects through concerted action and cooperation. Would existing rivalries be put aside in the face of a common threat?

Covid Digital Diplomacy: Rivalries Continue

In January 2020, the UAE reported the first instances of Covid-19 in visitors arriving from Wuhan, China. Bahrain, Oman, Qatar, Kuwait, and Saudi Arabia confirmed towards the end of February 2020 that pilgrims returning from Iran were infected with the virus. In a global pandemic, a nation's reputation and image are strongly tied to its response to the crisis. The World Health Organization is the primary intergovernmental platform for discussing international disease control (Davies et al., 2015: 7). According to studies, information provided by health organizations and state governments boosts public confidence, favourably influencing risk perception, behavioural control, and subjective standards (Lee and Li, 2021). According to Davies et al. (2015), governments absorb international rules, and compliance subsequently becomes normal and automatic. In the context of public and digital diplomacy, a country's capacity to project good influence and manage its national brand depends on its response to the issue (Lee and Kim. 2021). When determining how well or poorly a country handles a crisis, response time and the effectiveness of the government's activities are among the most important considerations (Bloom Consulting, 2020). According to Bjola (2021), empathy and comprehension are necessary for responding to unprecedented circumstances. In digital diplomacy, it is essential to make sense, react, choose a course of action, and present one's positions to international and regional partners and audiences (Bjola, 2021). 'A country's reputation for managing a crisis by balancing its national interests and international duties can have a lasting impact on its relations with other nations after the crisis has passed' (Bjola, 2021: 25). Cull posits four communication methods relevant to the Covid-19 pandemic: (1) the self as success, (2) the other as failure, (3) gifting, and (4) partnering. In the context of the GCC, would we then see frames tailored to demonstrate the pandemic response's competence and success? Would deception campaigns and hashtag battles persist? Would emphasis be placed on humanitarian relief and collaboration?

The OECD (2020) report on Covid-19 responses in the MENA region states that a mid-March 2020 WHO survey that ranks countries on a scale of 1 (no capacity) to 5 (sustainable capacity) on preparedness concluded that all GCC countries except for Qatar scored a four or five. Despite accounting for over half of regional cases, GCC governments successfully controlled the outbreak. Regional recovery rates were higher than global averages (OECD, 2020: 5).

As Hedling and Bremberg (2021) note, the Covid-19 epidemic revealed several challenges associated with the use of digital technologies to convert diplomatic procedures that rely on tacit knowledge. Policymakers decided to provide free medical care to all Covid-19 patients. Some of the swift changes made in the GCC countries included the closure of schools and universities, sterilization campaigns, the suspension of flights from and to the countries, lockdowns, curfews, and the establishment of drive-in testing centres. The GCC Committee of Undersecretaries of Ministries of Health agreed to hold weekly online meetings beginning 16 March 2020, to coordinate joint efforts against Covid-19. Governments created dedicated websites that contained all information about the pandemic in their country. The main goal was to provide answers to the most frequently asked questions, control the spread of the virus, and combat misinformation.

Contact tracing apps have been credited with controlling and reducing Covid infections (Colizza et al., 2021; Keeling et al., 2020; Lewis, 2021). The contact tracing apps 'Al Hosn' in UAE, 'Ehteraz' in Qatar, 'Tarassud plus' in Oman, 'Tabaud' in Saudi Arabia, 'Shlonik' in Kuwait, and 'BeAware Bahrain' in Bahrain use Bluetooth and GPS technology to trace an individual's location. A 2021 report by the Boston Consulting Group on digital government in the GCC details how Saudi Arabia, UAE, and Qatar rose to the top quartile globally for digital services offered and their adoption (Boston Consulting Group, 2021).

There is also evidence of how these apps are putting the privacy and security of hundreds of people at risk (Amnesty International, 2020b). Amnesty's Security Lab Report rates Bahrain's and Kuwait's apps as the most dangerous to human rights due to their ability to carry out live or near-live tracking of location, with frequent uploads to the central server. Both apps can pair with a Bluetooth bracelet; this ensures that the user is in the vicinity of the phone (2020b). People who are in quarantine are required to wear the bracelet. Those who do not can face prison charges for at least three months and may be subject to a fine between BD 1,000 (about US $2,700) and BD 10,000 (about US $27,000). Accounts also revealed that Qatar's Ehteraz app showed vulnerability when the app exposed the personal details of more than one million people (Amnesty International, 2020a). Shaheed (2021: 10) correctly detects: 'like Qatar, most governments in the region have not developed COVID tracing apps with a "clear and limited" purpose, with "data protection by design and default".'

Voice over Internet Protocol (VoIP) technology, including WhatsApp and Skype, have been restricted in Oman, Qatar, Saudi Arabia, and the UAE. There are no blocks in Bahrain and Kuwait. Gulf countries are home to significant migrant populations. Most of the migrant workers and foreign national residents were unable to connect and communicate with their families and communities overseas. On 7 April 2020, Human Rights Watch, along with twenty-eight other organizations, issued a statement calling for the unblocking of VoIP platforms and video Internet calls (Human Rights Watch, 2020).

The pandemic has also provided an opportunity for GCC countries to leverage their role in the MENA region through humanitarian diplomacy. News stories and reports were widely disseminated in online media and official Twitter accounts. Saudi Arabia's allocation of $525 million in aid packages to Yemen (Reuters, 2020); Kuwait's donation of $40 million to the World Health Organization to help combat the spread of the virus (Abueish, 2020); Qatar's $50 million in medical aid to nearly seventy-eight countries (International Cooperation Department Qatar, 2020); and reports by the UAE government showing that the UAE sent 2,062 tons of medical aid to 135 countries around the world (UAE Government Portal, 2021) were some of the main examples. The UAE's contributions to the development of a new vaccine by actively participating in vaccine trials in China and Russia (Ali, 2020) also found their way to online news and social media.

Regional rivalries did prevail, albeit to a lesser extent than the Blockade. In the early days of the Pandemic in March 2020, several Bahraini Shia pilgrims were stranded in Iran. The repatriation process started, and Qatari officials stepped in to offer help. On 28 March 2020, Qatar's Communication Office announced on their website that thirty-one Bahrainis were flown to Doha but were not able to proceed to Bahrain because of the Blockade (Qatar Communication Office, 2020). The announcement also stated that Qatar 'hopes that by the end of the two weeks of quarantine, the government of Bahrain will allow their citizens to return home. And if not, that they will continue to provide them with hospitality and care' (2020). Bahrain's foreign minister quickly responded on Twitter, accusing Qatar of interference. His statement read: 'What Qatar has done is reprehensible and requires a clear international stance towards it. It (Qatar) should stop using a humanitarian issue such as the coronavirus pandemic in its plans and ongoing conspiracies against countries and nations' (Khalid, 2020).

Gengler's (2020) analysis of the pandemic's impact on Gulf domestic politics finds several layers of impact: (1) concern over the state's performance in managing the outbreak, (2) economic and social effects of the pandemic, and (3) peer comparison. Peer comparison and rivalry are part of GCC politics. This rivalry once again found its way to social media.

In April 2020, UAE announced that anyone who shares medical information about the virus that contradicts the government's official statements would be subject to a fine of up to 20,0000 dirhams (about $5,500) (AlJazeera, 2020). On 8 April 2020, imprisoned journalist Mahmoud al-Jaziri was moved to solitary confinement by Bahraini officials for a recording that aired on Bahrain Today3. In said clip, al-Jaziri disputes the official reports of measures to secure the well-being of prisoners and to protect them from the spread of the virus (Committee to Protect Journalists, 2020).

Jones' (2020) study on fake news and weaponization of Covid highlights how regional rivals attack neighbours or bolster the legitimacy of their own regimes once again. Multiple accounts disseminated claims that Qatar had handled the crisis carelessly and had transferred Covid-19 to Argentina in March 2020 (Jones, 2020: 2). Viral videos of Qatar Airways being the 'official carrier' of the virus; an Arabic hashtag translating to #Qatar_is_Corona; tweets by journalist Noura Moteari stating that Qatar was capitalizing on the virus to undermine Dubai Expo 2020 and the Saudi Vision 2030, and manufacturing the virus; and trending topic 'Coup in Qatar', a Saudi based disinformation campaign with fake clips were some of the prominent examples of the information war (Tarawna, 2020).

WHAT IS NEXT FOR DIGITAL DIPLOMACY IN THE REGION?

Both the Blockade and the Covid-19 pandemic have shown that regional authorities are well aware of social media's ability to shape an online image and relay messages between GCC countries and around the world. From communicating government policies to disinformation and hashtag wars, these authoritarian regimes demonstrate how to use and weaponize social media platforms to boost their political legitimacy or attack opponents (Jones, 2020).

The spread of e-government services, the development of smart cities, and the widespread use of the Internet by citizens are some signs that these nations desire to be seen as technologically advanced, forward-thinking, and modern. Aware of the future challenges of climate change, GCC countries acknowledge the need to transition from oil dependence to a knowledge-based economy. In particular, Bahrain, Saudi Arabia, and the UAE are trying to position themselves as technology hubs in MENA. However, it is also important to note that this is a region plagued by negative press and stereotypes. As Cooper and Momani (2009) point out, 'positive stories about a booming Gulf region are countered by an ascendant image as aggressive competitors' (2009: 107). This is still the case to this day.

The spread of disinformation in the region is of concern. Most of these campaigns are in Arabic and thus evade the social media platforms' censorship more easily than Anglophone content. Reports on the way in which Twitter's neoliberal tendencies on what to report and not report illustrate how Twitter has shifted from the rights of individual users to those of business and political interest should be considered (Wilson and Hahn, 2021). Not only specific to Twitter, content moderation on social media is also subject to socio-political contexts. Gillespie noted early on how social media companies are concerned about portraying themselves in a positive light to government stakeholders and lobbying for a favourable business environment (2010). Jones's specific claim that Twitter is not only ambivalent about enforcing policies in the Gulf region, but is also a partisan entity serving the interests of dictators through its Dubai office is noteworthy (2020: 4). This identity fluctuation of social media platforms between a liberation tool and a surveillance tool should be one of the major concerns moving forward in the practice of digital diplomacy not only in the region but also globally.

When it comes to the practice of digital diplomacy in the GCC, both the Blockade and Covid-19 pandemic cases demonstrate that social media is an effective tool for communicating messages and framing issues. Competing frames during the early days of the GCC Blockade indicate that digital diplomacy was ineffective for relationship management and trust building. In their tweeting, MFAs were primarily concerned with building and maintaining their own reputations and attempting to influence the discourse for their political purposes. The success of the GCC region in bringing the pandemic under control by swift national policies and humanitarian diplomacy in the form of aid packages and donations are important when it comes to reputation management. The GCC Committee of Undersecretaries of the Ministries of Health online meetings could be viewed as a step towards re-coordination and building relationships. Yet, existing digital restrictions, such as restrictions on VoIP technology; safety and privacy concerns resulting from digital tracking and surveillance; and the weaponization of social media are realities that must be taken into account in the practice of digital diplomacy in the region. Both cases illustrate that digital diplomacy at this point is not a useful practice for relationship management in the GCC. According to Bjola and Jiang (2015), social media can help deliver a powerful message in a highly effective manner, but it cannot replace good strategy planning, relationship building, and crisis management. In times of crisis, it is possible that much of the networked collaboration associated with digital diplomacy (Clarke, 2105) occurs offline through personal diplomacy. This certainly appears to be plausible in the case of the GCC.

The GCC is a unique region. It is the birthplace of Islam. Countries share similarities while not being afraid to emphasize their specific differences depending on the circumstances. This is evident in the Blockade, responses to the Covid-19 pandemic, and the framing and interpretation of these events in the online sphere by both the public and officials. The GCC's digital diplomacy is power-driven and competitive. According to Zaharna (2021), 'public diplomacy must address the gap between global publics' concern for pressing issues affecting humanity and states' concern with individual power'. The Blockade and the GCC's handling of the Covid-19 pandemic show that we are not there yet. Trust in platforms and trust in governments continue to be major concerns. While there has been some deepening of cooperation among GCC members, as noted by Keating and Abott, there is still a great deal of 'mistrust and suspicion' among the leadership (2021). Furthermore, they argue that this mistrust persists despite the states developing a unified identity. Digital diplomacy has the potential to rebuild trust in the region. It cannot, however, create it on its own, as is frequently stressed in the study of digital diplomacy.

SUGGESTED READING

Gunter, B., Elareshi, M., and Al-Jaber, K. (2016). *Social Media in the Arab World: Communication and Public Opinion in the Gulf States*. London: IB Taurus.

Hamdy, N. N. and Auter, Philip (2022). *Mass Communication in the Arab World: Ongoing Agents of Change Following the Arab Spring*. London: Rowman & Littlefield.

Jones, O. M. (2022). *Digital Authoritarianism in the Middle East: Deception, Disinformation and Social Media*. London: Hurst Publishers.

Kamrava, M. (2013). *The Modern Middle East: A Political History since the First World War*, 3rd ed. Berkeley: University of California Press.

Miller, R. (2016). *Desert Kingdom to Global Powers: The Rise of the Arab Gulf*. New Haven: Yale University Press.

Richter, C., Antonakis, A., and Harders, C. (2018). *Digital Media and the Politics of Transformation in the Arab World and Asia*. Wiesbaden: Springer Vs.

Ulrichsen, K. C. (2015). *The Gulf States in International Political Economy*. Abington: Routledge.

Zayani, M. (2018). *Digital Middle East: State and Society on the Information Age*. New York: Oxford University Press.

REFERENCES

Abueish, T. (2020). Kuwait donates $40 million to World Health Organization to combat coronavirus. Al Arabiya English. https://english.alarabiya.net/News/gulf/2020/03/17/Kuwait-donates-40-mln-to-World-Health-Organization-to-combat-coronavirus. Accessed 1 February 2022.

Akdenizli, B. (2018a). Twitter Diplomacy in the GCC: How Foreign Ministers of the Region are Using Social Media. In Kamalipour, Y.R. (ed.) *Global Discourse in Fractured Times: Perspectives on Journalism, Media, Education, and Politics*. pp. 129–144. Cambridge, UK: Cambridge Scholars Publishing.

Akdenizli, B. (2018b). Twitter as an Instrument of Foreign Policy: Qatar and the GCC. In Miller, R. (ed.) *The 2017 Gulf Crisis: The View from Qatar*. pp. 147–156. Doha: Hamad bin Khalifa University Press.

Ali, M. (2020). Vaccine diplomacy: In 2021, the UAE will become the new vaccine hub of the Middle East. https://www.orfonline.org/expert-speak/uae-will-become-new-vaccine-hub-middle-east/. Accessed 1 February 2022.

Allagui, I. and Alnajjar, A. (2018). From women empowerment to nation branding: A case study from the United Arab Emirates. *International Journal of Communication* 12 (February): 68–85.

Alkhusaili, M. M. and AlJazzaf, Z.M. (2020). The evolution of e-government project on GCC countries. In Proceedings of the International Conference on Industrial Engineering & Operations Management (p. 13). http://www.internetsociety.org/detroit2020/papers/445.pdf.

Al-Mansouri, T., Al-Mohannadi, H. and Feroun, M. (2021). Digital diplomacy during the first 100 days: How GCC ministries of foreign affairs and ministers tweeted the Blockade. *Qscience Connect (Special Issue: Thesis)* 2021 (2):1. H http://doi.org/10.5339/connect.2021.spt.1

Al Jazeera (2017). Saudi Twitter users urged to expose Qatar sympathisers. 20 August. https://www.aljazeera.com/news/2017/8/20/saudi-twitter-users-urged-to-expose-qatar-sympathisers. Accessed 5 May 2021.

Al Jazeera (2020). UAE announces $5,500 fine for coronavirus fake news. 18 April. https://www.aljazeera.com/news/2020/4/18/uae-announces-5500-fine-for-coronavirus-fake-news. Accessed 5 May 2021.

Amnesty International (2020a). Qatar: Contact tracing app security flaw exposed sensitive personal details of more than one million. https://www.amnesty.org/en/latest/news/2020/05/qatar-covid19-contact-tracing-app-security-flaw/. Accessed 4 April 2021.

Amnesty International (2020b). Bahrain, Kuwait and Norway contact tracing apps among most dangerous for privacy. https://www.amnesty.org/en/latest/news/2020/06/bahrain-kuwait-norway-contact-tracing-apps-danger-for-privacy/. Accessed 4 April 2021.

Beblawi, H. and Luciani, G. (1987). *The Rentier State*. London: Routledge.

Bjola, C. (2021). Digital diplomacy as world disclosure: The case of the COVID-19 pandemic. *Place Branding and Public Diplomacy* 18: 22–25.

Bjola, C., Cassidy, A., and Manor, I. (2020). Digital Public Diplomacy: Business as Usual or a Paradigm Shift? In Snow, N. and Cull, N. (eds.) *The Routledge Handbook of Public Diplomacy*, 2nd ed.. pp. 405–412. London: Routledge.

Bjola, C. and Pamment, J. (2019). *Countering Online Propaganda and Extremism: The Dark Side of Digital Diplomacy*. Routledge.

Bjola, C. and Jiang, L. (2015). Social Media and Public Diplomacy: A Comparative Analysis of the Digital Diplomatic Strategies of the EU, US, Japan in China. In Bjola, C. and Holmes, M. (eds.) *Digital Diplomacy, Theory and Practice*. pp. 71–88. London: Routledge.

Bloom Consulting Group (2020). COVID-19: The impact on nation brands. Retrieved from https://www.bloom-consulting.com/journal/the-covid-19-study-the-impact-on-nation-brands/.

Boston Consulting Group (2021). Digital government in the GCC: Accelerating citizen trust. Retrieved from https://www.bgc.com/en-us/publications/2021/digital-government-services-help-build-trust-of-gcc-citizens.

Brannagan, P. M. and Giulianotti, R. (2015). Soft power and soft disempowerment: Qatar, global sport and football's 2022 World Cup finals. *Leisure studies* 34 (6): 703–719.

Bruno, A. (2020). The COVID 19 created opportunities for re-engagement within the GCC. https://gulfif.org/the-covid19-created-opportunities-for-re-engagement-within-the-gcc/. Accessed 12 June 2022.

Cassidy, J. (2018). *Digital Diplomatic Crisis Communication: Reconceptualizing Diplomatic Signaling in an age of Real Time Governance*. Working Paper no:3. Oxford Digital Diplomacy Research Group. Available from: http://www.qeh.ox.ac.uk/sites/www.odid.ox.ac.uk/DigDiploROxWP3.pdf.

Clarke, A. (2015). Business as Usual? An Evaluation of British and Canadian Digital Diplomacy as Policy Change. In Bjola, C. and Holmes, M. (eds.) *Digital Diplomacy, Theory and Practice*. pp. 111–126. London: Routledge.

Colizza, V., Grill, E., Mikolajczyk, R., Catutto, C., Kucharski, A., Riley, S. Kendall, M., Lythgoe, K., Bonsall, D., Wymant, C., Abeler-Dorner, L., Ferrett, L., and Fraser, C. (2021) Time to evaluate COVID-19 contact-tracing apps. *Nat Med* 27: 361–362 https://doi.org/10.1038/s41 591-021-01236-6.

Côme, T. and Raspaud, M. (2018). Sports diplomacy: A strategic challenge for Qatar. *Hermès, La Revue* 81: 169–175.

Committee to Protect Journalists (2020). Bahrain puts imprisoned journalist in solitary confinement after reporting on COVID-19 danger. 20 April. https://cpj.org/2020/04/bahrain-puts-imprisoned-journalist-in-solitary-con/. Accessed 5 May 2020.

Cooke, M. (2014). *Tribal Modern: Branding New Nations in the Arab Gulf.* Los Angeles: University of California Press.

Cooper, A. F. and Momani, B. (2009). The challenge of rebranding progressive countries in the Gulf and Middle East: Opportunities through networked engagements versus constraints of embedded negative images. *Place Branding and Public Diplomacy* 5 (2): 102–117.

Davies, S. E., Kamradt-Scott A., Rushton, S. (2015). *Disease Diplomacy: International Norms and Global Health Security.* Baltimore: Johns Hopkins University Press.

Dennis, E., Martin, J., and Hassan, F. (2019). Media in the Middle East 2019. http://www.mideastmedia.org/survey/2019/. Accessed 31 January 2022.

Duncombe, C. (2019). The politics of Twitter: Emotions and the power of social media. *International Political Sociology* 13: 409–429.

El-Nawawy, M. (2013). Muslim's Online Faith Diplomacy. In Seib, P. (ed.) *Religion and Public Diplomacy.* pp. 113–123. New York: Palgrave Macmillan Series in Public Diplomacy.

Eggeling, K.A. (2017). Cultural diplomacy in Qatar: Between 'virtual enlargement', national identity construction and elite legitimation. *International Journal of Cultural Policy* 23 (6): 717–731. DOI: 10.1080/10286632.2017.1308505.

Erskine-Loftus, P., Hightower, V. P., and Al-Mulla, M. A (2016). *Representing the Nation: Heritage, Museums, National Narratives, and Identity in the Arab Gulf States.* London: Routledge.

Freedom House (2020). Freedom on the Net 2020: The pandemic's digital shadow. https://freedomhouse.org/sites/default/files/2020-10/10122020_FOTN2020_Complete_Report_FINAL.pdf.

Gengler, J.J. (2020). Information, peer comparison and social interdependence: Theorizing the impacts of COVID-19 on Gulf domestic politics. *Global Discourse: An Interdisciplinary Journal of Current Affairs* 10 (4): 423–430.

Gillespie, T. (2010). The politics of platforms. *New Media and Society* 12 (3): 347–364.

Ginesta, X. and de San Eugenio, J. (2014). The use of football as a country branding strategy. Case study: Qatar and the Catalan sports press. *Communication & Sport* 2 (3): 225–241. https://doi.org/10.1177/2167479513486886.

Govers, R. (2012). Brand Dubai and its competitors in the Middle East: An image and reputation analysis. *Place Branding and Public Diplomacy Basingstoke* 8 (1): 48–57.

Hayden, C. (2009). Applied public diplomacy: A marketing communications exchange program in Saudi Arabia. *American Behavioral Scientist* 53 (4): 533–548. https://doi.org/10.1177/0002764209347629.

Hedling, E. and Bremberg, N. (2021). Practice Approaches to the digital transformation of diplomacy: Towards a new research agenda. *International Studies Review* 23 (4): 1595–1618. . London: Routledge.

Human Rights Watch (2016). Arab Gulf States: Attempts to silence 140 characters region-wide crackdown on social media activism. https://www.hrw.org/news/2016/11/01/arab-gulf-states-attempts-silence-140-characters. Accessed 27 January 2022.

Human Rights Watch (2020). COVID-19: Unblock voice over IP platforms in Gulf. https://www.hrw.org/news/2020/04/07/covid-19-unblock-voice-over-ip-platforms-gulf. Accessed 5 May 2021.

International Cooperation Department, Qatar (2020). The State of Qatar's Aid to friendly countries to confront the emerging coronavirus 'Covid-19'. August. https://www.ohchr.org/Documents/Events/GoodPracticesCoronavirus/qatar-submission-covid19.pdf. Accessed 1 February 2022.

ITU (2022). ITU Global Security Index 2020. https://www.itu.int/epublications/publication/D-STR-GCI.01-2021-HTM-E/. Accessed 21 February 2022.

Jones, M.O. (2017). Hacking, bots and information wars in the Qatar Spat. *Washington Post.* 7 June 2017. https://www.washingtonpost.com/news/monkey-cage/wp/2017/06/07/hacking-bots-and-information-wars-in-the-qatar-spat/ Accessed 12 July 2020.

Jones, M.O. (2019). Propaganda, fake news and fake trends: The weaponization of Twitter bots in the Gulf Crisis. *International Journal of Communication* 13: 1–26.

Jones, M. O. (2020). Disinformation superspreaders: The weaponization of COVID-19 fake news in the Persian Gulf and beyond. *Global Discourse: An Interdisciplinary Journal of Current Affairs* 10 (4): 431–437.

Kabbani, N. (2021). The Blockade on Qatar helped strengthen its economy, paving the way to stronger regional integration. https://www.brookings.edu/blog/order-from-chaos/2021/01/19/the-blockade-on-qatar-helped-strengthen-its-economy-paving-the-way-to-stronger-regional-integration/. Accessed 21 February 2022.

Kara, A. S. (2019). *Crisis Communication in the Digital Age: Manage or Rampage.* London: Cambridge Scholars Publishing.

Kaufmann, J. (1998). *The Diplomacy of International Relations: Selected Writings.* London: Kluwer Law International.

Keating, V. C. and Abbott, L. M. (2021). Entrusted norms: Security, trust, and betrayal in the Gulf Cooperation Council crisis. *European Journal of International Relations* 27 (4): 1090–1113. https://doi.org/10.1177/13540661211044197.

Keeling, M. J., Hollingsworth, T. D., and Read, J. M. (2020). Efficacy of contact tracing for the containment of the 2019 novel coronavirus (COVID-19). *J Epidemiol Community Health* 74: 861–866.

Kent, M. L., and Taylor, M. (2021). Fostering Dialogic Engagement: Toward an Architecture of Social Media for Social Change. *Social Media + Society* 7 (1). https://doi.org/10.1177/2056305120984462.

Khalid, T. (2020). Coronavirus: Manama says Qatar exploited Bahrainis by transporting 31 from Iran. *Al Arabiya Net.* March. https://english.alarabiya.net/News/gulf/2020/03/30/COVID-19-Manama-says-Qatar-using-Bahrainis-as-ploy-after-Doha-evacuated-31-from-Iran. Accessed 1 February 2022.

Khatib, L., Dutton, W., and Thelwall, M. (2012). Public diplomacy 2.0: A case study of the U.S. digital outreach team. *The Middle East Journal* 66 (3): 453–472.

Kourgiotis, P. (2020). 'Moderate Islam' made in the United Arab Emirates: Public diplomacy and the politics of containment. *Religions* 11 (1): 43. DOI:10.3390/rel11010043.

Krieg, A. (2019). The Weaponization of Narratives Amid the Gulf Crisis. In Krieg, A. (ed.) *Divided Gulf: The Anatomy of Crisis.* pp. 91–108. Contemporary Gulf Studies. Singapore: Palgrave MacMillan.

Leber, A. and Abrahams, A. (2019). A storm of Tweets: Social media manipulation during the Gulf crisis. *Review of Middle East Studies* 53 (2): 241–258.

Lee, S.T. and Kim, S.T. (2021). Nation branding in the COVID-19 era: South Korea's pandemic public diplomacy. *Place Brand Public Diplomacy* 17 (4): 382–396.

Lee, Y. and Li, JYQ. (2021). The role of communication transparency and organizational trust in publics' perceptions, attitudes and social distancing behaviour: A case study of the COVID-19 outbreak. *Journal of Contingencies and Crisis Management* 29 (4): 368–84.

Lewis, D. (2021). Contact-tracing apps help reduce COVID infections, data suggest. https://www.nature.com/articles/d41586-021-00451-y. Accessed 22 February 2021.

Lynch, M. (2021). Digital activism and authoritarian adaptation in the Middle East. *POMEPS Studies* 43: 4–7.

Manor, I. (2019). *Digital Diplomacy in Times of Upheaval: How Foreign Ministries Use Twitter During Crises* [Ph.D. thesis]. University of Oxford.

Marzcak, B. and Scott-Railton, J. (2016). *Keep Calm and (Don't) Enable Macros: A New Threat Actor Targets UAE Dissidents*. https://citizenlab.ca/2016/05/stealth-falcon/. Accessed 1 February 2022.

McDonald, A. (2021). Qatar Blockade: What caused it and why is it coming to an end? *Middle East Eye*, January 5. Retrieved from https://www.middleeasteye.net/news/qatar-blockade-saudi-arabia-lift-cause-end

Mitchell, J. S. (2019). #Blockade: Social media and the Gulf diplomatic crisis. *Review of Middle East Studies* 53 (2): 200–220.

Nimmo, B. (2018). Robot wars: How bots joined battle in the Gulf. *Journal of International Affairs, Columbia University, 19 September 2018*. https://jia.sipa.columbia.edu/robot-wars-how-bots-joined-battle-gulf.

OECD (2020). COVID-19 crisis responses in MENA countries. https://read.oecd-ilibrary.org/view/?ref=129_129919-4li7bq8asv&title=COVID-19-Crisis-Response-in-MENA-Countries. Accessed 20 February 2022.

Powers, A. and Gilboa, E. (2007). The Public Diplomacy of Al Jazeera. In Seib, P. (ed.) *New Media and the New Middle East*. pp. 74–75. New York: Palgrave Macmillan.

Qatar Communications Office (2020). Government Communications Offices statement on Bahraini citizens transiting home. https://www.gco.gov.qa/en/2020/03/28/government-communications-office-statement-on-bahraini-citizens-transiting-home/. Accessed 14 December 2021.

Reporters Without Borders (2021). 2021 World Press Freedom Index. https://rsf.org/en/ranking/2021. Accessed 27 January 2022.

Reuters (2020). Saudi Arabia to give $525 million for Yemen humanitarian, coronavirus response: minister. https://www.reuters.com/article/us-yemen-security-saudi-coronavirus-idUSKCN21Q3C1. Accessed 1 February 2022.

Seib, P. (2008). *The Al Jazeera Effect*. Dulles, VA: Potomac Books.

Seib, P. (2014). New Media and Public Diplomacy in the New Arab World. In Hudson, L., Iskandar, A., and Kirk, M. (eds.) *Media Evolution on the Eve of the Arab Spring*. pp. 181–192. Palgrave Macmillan Series in International Political Communication. New York: Palgrave Macmillan.

Shaheed, A. and Greenacre, B. (2021). Binary threat: How government's cyber laws and practice undermine human rights in the MENA region. *POMEPS Studies* 43: Digital Activism and Authoritarian Adaptation in the Middle East, August 2021, https://pomeps.org/the-web-insecurity-of-mena-civil-society-and-media.

Sheikholeslami, M. H. and Saradar, H. (2012). Religious approach in Saudi Arabia's cultural diplomacy: A case study of Muslim world league. *Quarterly Journal of Political Research in Islamic World* 4 (2): 103–128.

Shires, J. (2022). The implementation of digital surveillance infrastructures in the Gulf https://pomeps.org/the-implementation-of-digital-surveillance-infrastructures-in-the-gulf. Accessed 7 February 2022.

Strauss, N., Krukemeier, S., van der Meulen, H., and van Noort, G. (2015). Digital diplomacy in GCC countries: Strategic communication of Western embassies on Twitter. *Government Information Quarterly* 32: 369–379.

Tarawna, N. (2020). MENA region battles the infodemic: From fake news to hashtag washing in the region's ongoing information wars. https://ifex.org/mena-region-battles-the-infodemic-from-fake-news-to-hashtag-washing-in-the-regions-ongoing-information-wars/. Accessed 29 May 2021.

TRT World (2019). Twitter suspends Saudi royal adviser Qahtani, fake Gulf accounts. 20 September. Retrieved from https://www.trtworld.com/middle-east/twitter-suspends-saudi-royal-adviser-qahtani-fake-gulf-accounts-29969.

UAE Government Portal (2021). The UAE's humanitarian efforts during COVID-19. https://u.ae/en/information-and-services/justice-safety-and-the-law/handling-the-covid-19-outbreak/humanitarian-efforts. Accessed 1 February 2022.

Ulrichsen, K.C. (2021). Cultural and Religious Diplomacy as Soft Power in EU-GCC Relations. In Abdel Ghafar, A. and Colombo, S. (eds.) *The European Union and the Gulf Cooperation Council. Contemporary Gulf Studies.* pp. 57–78. Singapore: Palgrave Macmillan. https://doi-org.turing.library.northwestern.edu/10.1007/978-981-16-0279-5_4.

Ulrichsen, K.C. (2017). What's going on with Qatar? *POMEPS Briefings* 31: 6–8.

Williamson, W.F. (2022). Claiming change and tradition in the United Arab Emirates: Women's empowerment as a public diplomacy strategy. *Place Branding and Public Diplomacy* 18 (3): 335–345 https://doi-org.turing.library.northwestern.edu/10.1057/s41254-021-00256-w.

Wilson, J. and Hahn, A. (2021). Twitter and Turkey: Social media surveillance at the intersection of corporate ethics and international policy. *Journal of Information Policy* 11: 444–477.

Zaharna, R.S. (2021). The pandemic's wake-up call for humanity-centered public diplomacy. *Place Branding and Public Diplomacy.* 18 (1): 4–7 https://doi.org/10.1057/s41254-021-00244-0

Zayani, M. (2018). Mapping the Middle East. In Zayani, M. (ed.) *Digital Middle East: State and Societies in the Information Age.* pp. 1–31. Oxford University Press.

Zeineddine, C. (2017). Employing nation branding in the Middle East – United Arab Emirates (UAE) and Qatar. *Management & Marketing. Challenges for the Knowledge Society* 12 (2): 208–221. DOI: 10.1515/mmcks-2017-0013.

CHAPTER 32

THE NORTH–SOUTH DIVIDE, THE DIGITAL AGENDA, AND DIGITAL DIPLOMACY

JORGE HEINE AND JUAN PABLO PRADO LALLANDE

In the digital age, few issues are as significant as the one of who controls the Internet (de Nardis, 2010). In a world in which more and more activities are moving towards a virtual mode, a trend accelerated by the Covid-19 pandemic, setting the rules of the Internet is crucial. In this, the Global North, and particularly the United States, has enjoyed an extraordinary advantage. As the country where the Internet was invented, under the guise of multistakeholder governance and the pretence that some sort of loose alliance of private companies, academics, and consumers run the World Wide Web, the US government, through the Department of Commerce, has kept its hand firmly on the lever of Internet governance (Winseck, 2017). While this was not much of an issue in the early days of the web, it has become one as the Internet emerges as a dominant force in a world in which half the population of the planet is connected to it (Mansell, 2012). As the running of governments, businesses, and even our daily lives depends on it, the notion that the world's Internet governance should rely on the whims and wishes of the government of one country has become more and more contested.

In turn, the issue of Internet governance goes to the heart of today's North–South divide. While the United States and other Northern countries defend the principle of multistakeholder governance, in the Global South, countries like China and Brazil espouse multilateralism, that is, the traditional approach to handle global issues (Kleinwachter, 2004; Liu, 2012). In fact, some of the most high-profile clashes in the struggle for primacy between the United States and China are being played out on the digital frontier, as in the efforts of the United States to curtail the business activities of Huawei, the Chinese telecom company and the deployment of its 5G technology (Tang, 2020). Yet, as Shaun Riordan (2018: 3) has observed:

Diplomats have largely ignored Cyberspace as a domain for diplomatic activity. They have focused instead on the tools which Cyberspace can offer for carrying out their tasks, whether messenger apps in multinational negotiations or social media platforms for consular work or public diplomacy. They have left Internet governance ... to technicians, communications experts and the military/intelligence services.

In the spirit of Riordan's sharp insight, the purpose of this chapter is to examine the issue of Internet governance (Broeders, 2015) and related digital matters in the North–South agenda from a diplomatic perspective. A first section discusses the impact of the Edward Snowden revelations in 2013 on the extant debate on 'Internet freedom vs. government control'; a second one discusses the international political economy of Internet governance; a third parses the rise of the Global South; a third parses the international political economy of Internet governance; a fourth one discusses the issue of data collection and privacy rights; a fifth one does so with digitalization and the international political economy; a sixth one examines the debate of multistakeholderism versus multilateralism in Internet governance; a seventh one does so with the clashes between China and the United States on Huawei; an eighth one , with the matter of international electronic espionage and Internet governance; and a ninth one, with the case of the Digital Economic Partnership Agreement (DEPA), an initiative of three small countries that has broken new ground, and raised quite a ruckus in doing so; some conclusions round out the chapter.

Mass Surveillance, Internet Freedom, and Government Control of the Web

The rise of the Internet has gone hand in hand with the growth of social media. Platforms like Facebook, Instagram, Twitter, LinkedIn, Snapchat, WhatsApp, and TikTok Telegram have become key communication tools—displacing traditional media and upending established social and political practices. Although they had an immediate impact in many countries around the world, their use was especially visible during the so-called Arab Spring that erupted in 2011, and particularly so in Egypt. Social media turned into a key organizing and scheduling tool, allowing tens of thousands of demonstrators to coordinate their actions in and around Tahrir Square, in the heart of Cairo, and played an important role in the fall of President Hosni Mubarak. Suddenly, Facebook and Twitter were elevated to the status of democratizing tools, key instruments in the struggle to bring greater openness and freedom to the oppressed peoples of the Global South (Pew Research, 2012). Less remarked upon was the fact that much as social media can be used to organize social protests, the very same technology can be used by governments to track down and repress the demonstrators, which is exactly what happened in Egypt and elsewhere in the Arab world at the time, with results known to all.

No matter. By that time, developments in the Arab world had seemed to buttress the argument that the Internet and the social media apps that go with it was a liberating, democratizing force, one that empowered millions and was turning into the bane of dictators and strongmen everywhere. This also played nicely into the fact that the United States was deploying its own digital diplomacy in a highly ambitious US State Department initiative led by none other than Secretary of State Hillary Clinton herself. Technology and ideology merged seamlessly into the cause of 'Internet freedom', which became a rallying cry of United States diplomacy (Clinton, 2010).The Internet would not only fuel the Arab Spring, it was said, but also the 'color revolutions' in Eastern and Central Europe. US digital diplomacy was husbanded for these purposes—in Syria, Iran, Cuba, and wherever adversarial regimes were to be found. Who but these very regimes could question the wisdom of the established governance mechanisms of the Internet, multistakeholder systems that allowed the Internet to flourish, while being spared the bane of multilateral control by a UN bureaucracy, that would only drive it into the ground? Thus the defence of the Internet Corporation for Assigned Names and Numbers (ICANN), the California-based entity that runs the Internet (Mueller, 1999).

Heavy tomes would be published by Clinton's assistants praising the cause of Internet freedom and the alleged benefits it entailed for humanity (Schmidt and Cohen, 2013; Ross, 2016).

And then it happened. Edward Snowden, a National Security Agency (NSA) contractor employed by Booze Allen Hamilton, revealed in 2013 that, in parallel to championing the cause of Internet freedom, the United States government also engaged in mass surveillance practices around the world (*The Guardian*, 2013). This entailed tapping into the communications of billions of people and dozens of world leaders, including tapping the telephones of the leaders of ostensibly friendly countries like Angela Merkel of Germany and Dilma Rousseff of Brazil. Over 1.7 million top secret documents revealed activities led by the US NSA in consortium with the intelligence agencies of the UK, Australia, Canada, and New Zealand (the famous 'Five Eyes'). This mass surveillance operation through programmes like PRISM introduces spyware into Android and other systems and taps into and stores billions of phone calls and financial transactions (Snowden, 2019).

So far, so good. Spying is as old as humankind. What else is new? The problem is that the US government did this hand in hand with leading technology, telecommunication, and Internet companies, often for the price of millions of dollars. Among the companies involved are Apple, Microsoft, Google, Facebook, and Yahoo. Vodafone admitted that as many as six different countries had asked for access to its submarine Internet cables to monitor communications.

This, of course, is very much against the right to privacy citizens are supposed to enjoy. In other words, while preaching Internet freedom, the United States was busily setting up an Orwellian operation destined to exercise mass surveillance of almost every phone call and electronic communication taking place around the world and store it permanently, in crass violation of the right to privacy.

The reaction around the world was swift and unforgiving, particularly so among the BRICS countries. Brazilian President Dilma Rousseff cancelled a scheduled state visit to the United States and did not relent even after a special phone call from President Obama (Heine, 2013). Brazil would later introduce a resolution at the United Nations to curb electronic espionage, a practice Brazil linked to a deficient Internet governance structure that facilitated it (Abdenur and Gama, 2015). We will come back to this later in this chapter.

In any event, the cause of 'Internet freedom' was dead and buried. The coming to light of these mass surveillance practices, however, gave new impetus to the efforts of Global South countries to gain a measure of international control of the Internet, albeit with little success. The Internet came into its own as a widely used tool in the nineties, at the time of the United States' 'unipolar moment', yet its governance has hardly changed in the past thirty years, despite the emergence of a very different, multipolar system. (Carr, 2016). Not surprisingly, some of the strongest clashes between the United States and rising powers have thus taken place on the digital frontier—with Russia on cyber and ransomware issues, with China on the application of 5G technology, and with Brazil on electronic espionage.

THE INTERNATIONAL POLITICAL ECONOMY OF THE INTERNET

But the issue is not limited to the concern of rising powers. All around the world, countries are being forced to choose between different kinds of telecommunications technology and digital connectivity (Stuenkel, 2021). Accordingly, the issue is coming to the forefront in North–South relations, making for some difficult diplomatic compromises. In the nineties, as the Internet first became a global network, the main issue was largely one of access, with control being of little concern. Yet, as time went by, this changed.

After 9/11 and the emergence of the Global War on Terror (GWOT), electronic espionage increased, and the pressure for international regulation of the Internet grew, leading to the World Summit on the Information Society in 2003 and 2005. Yet, efforts to shift control away from ICANN and towards entities like the International Telecommunications Union (ITU) did not succeed. The India-Brazil-South Africa Forum (IBSA) in 2006 supported some sort of multilateral regulation of the Internet, followed up in 2011 (Mueller, 2011), though subsequent differences within the group rendered the initiative moot. Later on, the BRICS group set forth its own initiative on the subject, proposing the development of submarine, fibre optic cables connecting the member states (BRICS, 2014).

As Winseck (2017) has argued, it is obvious that the United States plays a leading role in the Internet, not just because of its control of Internet governance, but also because the main Internet companies are US-based—Apple, Facebook, Google, Microsoft, and Netflix—and thus exercise an inordinate amount of influence in the digital domain. The US thus holds a strong presence in operating systems, search engines, social networks, e-commerce, browsers, and domain names. That said, the same cannot be said about the material infrastructure of the Internet, things like the fibre optic submarine cables that connect the world, content delivery networks (CDNs), autonomous system numbers (ASN), and Internet exchange points (IXPs) (Winseck, 2017). In the latter, countries like China and others play an important role.

The BRICS group, formed of Brazil, Russia, India, China, and South Africa, has been referred to as 'the acronym that defined the decade without a name' (the 2000s), and with good reason. In a decade book-ended in the North by 9/11 and by the financial crisis of 2008–2009, in the BRICS countries, vigorous growth, an ability to weather the effects of the recession, and a willingness to reach out to the rest of the developing world put them in a sweet spot. While the North seemed absorbed by its own problems, the BRICS countries, hailing from four different continents, appeared as forward-looking, future-oriented nations, ready to tackle not just their own but the world's problems. Without carrying the baggage of former colonial powers, they also represented a friendlier face to their Global South partners, as well as a different, more comprehensive conception of what international cooperation is all about.

The second decade of the new century was less friendly to several of the BRICS member countries, and soon the narrative changed. Suddenly, the conventional wisdom became that their time had come and gone. The BRICS countries were as *passé* as yesterday's *baguette*, or so it was said (Council on Foreign Relations, 2012). By mid-2016, eight years after the financial crisis, it was said, it was the 'serious' countries, i.e., the United States and the United Kingdom, that were back in charge of economic global governance.

Well, that was then, this is now. In June 2016, the United Kingdom voted to leave the European Union, and spent the next four years grappling with Brexit. In November 2016, the United States elected Donald Trump as president, and the United States spent the next four years leaving as many international institutions as it could, even considering at some point leaving the International Postal Union (IPU). And although Trump lost the 2020 presidential elections, and was replaced by a president more friendly to multilateral institutions and international cooperation, Trump has announced he will run again in 2024, and the possibility of him, or an equivalent Republican candidate, returning to the White House with a similar isolationist international agenda looms large.

We are now entering a new global order, some would say a post-Western world (Stuenkel, 2016). What are the implications of this for the Global South? And particularly, what are the implications of it in the digital domain?

From Third World to New South

In the sixties and seventies, the new nations of Asia, Africa, and the Caribbean were weak, highly dependent on trade and investment links with the North, and resentful about the legacy of slavery/colonialism (Getachew, 2019). Believing that there was strength in numbers, they gathered in a vast array of entities, led by the Non-Aligned Movement. They practiced 'diplomacy of the *cahiers des doleances*', that is, grievance diplomacy, with proposals like that of the New International Economic Order.

However, in the 2000s, the rise of the Asian giants, as well as that of countries like Brazil, Indonesia, Turkey, South Africa, and Mexico, changed this. Rather than speaking from weakness, these countries spoke from strength. Instead of assembling in large conglomerates, they did so in smaller, informal diplomatic 'clubs' that allowed them to leverage their newly acquired industrial base (Stuenkel, 2013).Trade, rather than aid, was what they demanded. And countering charges of being mere 'talk shops', they allocated budgetary resources to back up their programmes, engaging in what Roberts et al. (2018) have called 'collective financial statecraft'. China set up the Asian Investment and Infrastructure Bank (AIIB) in 2015, headquartered in Beijing, with a capital of US $100 billion. That same year, the BRICS group, in turn, set up the New Development Bank, headquartered in Shanghai, with a capital of $50 billion.

Thus the confluence of geoeconomics and geopolitics. As Asia rises to become the new centre of the world economy, with China at its core, and the North pulls inward in protectionist and isolationist mode, North–South relations take on a different character. The world moves towards a multipolar order, with no single dominant power, marked by the relentless pressures of globalization. The latter have slowed down somewhat (hence the term 'slowbalization'), due to the extraordinary turnaround in the respective positions of the Global North and the Global South on this. The embrace by different political forces in North America and Europe of anti-globalization as an electoral plank and a key element of their political programme has succeeded in slowing down the flow of goods, services, capital, and people that are the hallmark of our age, but may be ultimately destined to fail. On the other hand, the forces of technology and innovation, in IT, telecoms, AI, nanotechnology, and robotics, are pulling the world together, not apart (Heine, 2020).

As this tension between the forces of technological innovation and the forces of protectionism and isolationism plays itself out, much of the future of the international political economy will be decided. A key role here will be played by the digital agenda and the issues related to digital diplomacy, issues to which we now turn.

Data Collection and Privacy Rights

In this context, a not insignificant issue is that of data collection and management. As Riordan (2018) has commented, the attitude towards the Internet in the leading powers has been very much shaped by the time and the setting in which the web 'arrived' in each of them. As the inventor of the Internet, the United States sees it, at least in theory, as a freewheeling mechanism best left alone to the forces of the market, for individuals to enjoy and companies to profit from, with a minimum of governmental interference—except, of course, when it comes to the activities of the security and intelligence agencies. This view is also strongly marked by the fact that the Internet flourished especially in the rugged West—particularly in California's Silicon Valley, hand in hand with its strong individualistic ethos, and risk-taking venture capitalists. There is a reason why Mark Zuckerberg packed up and moved his nascent Facebook company from Cambridge, Massachusetts, to Mountain View, California—that is where the action was (and is) for up-and-coming social media companies. Yet, as Shoshana Zuboff (2020) has pointed out, these companies quickly realized that, as the saying goes, 'data is the new gold', and that it was from the harvesting, managing, and mining of this data for marketing purposes that the road to profitability lay. Thus the rise of 'surveillance capitalism', one in which 'digital connection is now a means in others' commercial ends' and 'instead of labor, surveillance capitalism feeds on every aspect of every human experience' (Zuboff, 2020: 9). That has been very much the case since then, and as the Big Tech companies like Google, Microsoft, Facebook (today's Meta), and Apple have grown into the giants of today, the United States is still grappling with the issue of how to protect the data of individual citizens, and no federal legislation has been passed in that regard.

In Europe, the situation is very different. As the Internet arrived in Europe in the nineties, in the wake of the fall of the Berlin Wall and the end of the Cold War, the trauma caused by legacy of the security states behind the Iron Curtain raised concerns about how the Internet and the new digital tools could be deployed by 'Big Brother', as well as by commercial companies bent on extracting the most profits through them, often to the detriment of citizens and consumers. Thus, an initial Data Protection Directive adopted by the European Union in 1995 put an emphasis on 'protecting personal data as a fundamental right' (Chase, 2019). This was at the very beginning of the Internet, and much transpired in the following two decades, laying the ground for the EU's General Data Protection Regulation (GDPR) that came into effect on 25 May 2018. And whereas the Directive provided broad guidelines for the EU member states, guidelines that needed to be applied via national legislation, the GDPR stands on its own and has a direct effect in all EU member states. The GDPR thus covers almost all 'processing by both government and non-government entities of personally identifiable information (PII),' where PII is expansively defined as 'any information related to an identified or *identifiable* natural person' (including online identifiers like an IP address) and where 'processing' means 'any operation performed on personal data, *whether or not by automated means*' (Chase, 2019).

The GDPR has since become a major issue of contention between the EU and the (mostly US) Big Tech companies, which have been forced to handle the data they collect in a much less cavalier fashion than they used to—though, revealingly, the GDPR exempts the security and intelligence services from its coverage.

China stands in a category of its own. The Internet came late to China, and was initially received with suspicion. Given China's authoritarian political system, one could very well imagine a situation of government resistance to such an intrusive thing as the World Wide Web, and indeed, the first thing that comes to mind to foreigners when thinking about China and the Internet is the 'Great Firewall of China', the huge censorship apparatus that blocks unwanted content from Chinese netizens. Yet, contrary to Western conventional wisdom, China is one of the most connected societies in the world, with over one billion netizens, some 1.6 billion mobile phones, and a highly advanced e-commerce system, of which the Hangzhou-based company Alibaba, China's Amazon, as it were, is Exhibit A. China's advanced digital technology was in fact key to allow the country to control the Covid-19 pandemic, through sophisticated messaging systems connected to individual mobile phones, making it possible to keep mortality rates much lower than elsewhere. Yet, and such are often the unforeseen consequences of technological breakthroughs, the very systems that were so helpful during the pandemic are now being used to exercise control over people's lives. According to some, the tools that made it possible to monitor the whereabouts of patients infected with the corona virus are now being deployed to monitor the whereabouts of those the government considers to be dissidents, hampering their movements and daily lives (*The New York Times*, 2022).

DIGITALIZATION AND THE INTERNATIONAL POLITICAL ECONOMY

The increased use of digital tools and digital products is one of the hallmarks of the current phase of globalization that started circa 1980, driven largely by IT and telecommunication technologies. These tools have brought more economic growth and development, facilitating access to many things not previously available to vast swathes of the world's population, from education to banking to telemedicine. As Rebolledo (2021) has pointed out, there are six factors that are key for the emergence of the digital economy:

a) Business infrastructure
b) E-business
c) E-commerce
d) Broadband Internet infrastructure

e) ICT apps industry

f) Final users

The digital frontier has been at the cutting edge of innovation and the rise of new products, like e-books, videogames, music, movies, and software, that can be conveyed electronically and that are at the core of the New Economy. In terms of international trade, though there has been a slowdown in the growth rate of global trade in goods, that has not been the case in services, and especially so in digital services, which now comprise 50% of the latter.

Thus, the issue of the rules that govern such a crucial sector of the world economy is key. And it is here that the very different approaches of the United States, in broad alliance with other countries from the Global North (especially the 'Five Eyes' group), and that of China, spearheading a loose coalition of countries from the Global South (particularly the BRICS countries), stand in stark contrast.

Multistakeholderism Versus Multilateralism

In this context, the battle lines have been drawn between two very different approaches on how to run the World Wide Web. On the one hand, the United States espouses the current multistakeholder system based on the participation of a variety of players, including business, consumer, and government representatives. This is done in the name of a supposedly neutral, objective mechanism that respects the rights and interests of all (Hofmann, 2016). On the other hand, China champions a shift towards a multilateral regulatory system akin to that of other global issue areas such as trade, which falls under the purview of the World Trade Organization (WTO) (Liu, 2012). Sometimes this is portrayed as a conflict between a liberal versus a state-centred approach to Internet governance. In practice, the issue is murkier. As discussed above, 'multistakeholderism' stands for a key role played in regulating the Internet by the US Department of Commerce, i.e., the US government. In turn, not just China but also Russia and countries like India, who espouse multilateral Internet governance, take an especially heavy-handed approach to Internet control within their own borders, raising doubts about the kind of regulation they have in mind when they advocate for changes in the current system.

This battle is not just being waged at the level of discourse. Much as the United States reaped the early advantages of having conceived and implemented the World Wide Web, things on the ground are changing, this time to the advantage of 'the Rest'. A majority of Internet users are now in the Global South, and it is to them that many of the Big Tech companies cater. The material infrastructure of the Internet, including the all-important submarine fibre optic cables that transmit 99% of Internet traffic, is also increasingly being built by and in the hands of non-Western companies, mostly but not exclusively Chinese, like China Mobile, China Telecom, and China Unicom (Winseck, 2017). Many of them are state-owned, but some of them are private companies (like Tata, the Indian concern), underlining the complex interface between the state and capital that shapes the political economy of the Internet on both sides of the North–South divide.

In turn, many of the new Internet submarine cables are being built in the Asia-Pacific region, whereas no new fibre optic cables have been built across the North Atlantic since 2003. Moreover, much of the technological advantage that the United States enjoyed in the telecommunications field has eroded. In the critical area of 5G (fifth generation telecom technology), a key tool for the Internet of things, for AI, and for a much faster connectivity, the undisputed leader is the Chinese company Huawei, followed by two European companies, Erikson and Nokia, and Korea's Samsung. No US company has 5G technology. This leads us to the emerging global battle royale between the United States and Huawei. The latter epitomizes in many ways the ongoing struggle to shape the world's digital landscape, especially in the Global South.

Huawei, the United States, and the Battle for 5G

The December 2018 arrest in Vancouver airport of Ms Meng Wanzhou, CFO of Huawei, by the Canadian police, in response to a US request for alleged violations of US legal provisions on export controls, took Washington's offensive against the Chinese telecom company to a new level (Tang, 2020). To detain the daughter of Huawei's founder and owner, Ren Zhengfei, had high symbolic value and led to a worldwide drop in stock markets. Although it is perfectly possible that Huawei, which sells telecom equipment to Iran and which utilizes components from US companies like Intel and Qualcomm, might have violated some US laws against such sales, the standard manner to deal with such violations is via fines, and not by going after company executives, something rarely done by US justice. To criminalize international trade matters leads to a dangerous escalation. Moreover, according to the extradition treaty between the US and Canada, for extradition to proceed the crime in question needs to be specified in both countries' legislation. The treaty also states that if the matter at hand is politically motivated, the extradition may be denied.

Yet Meng, although released from custody, was confined to home arrest in Vancouver for three years, wreaking havoc in the Canada–China relationship, and casting a shadow over US–China links for this whole period. Only at the end of 2021 was she finally released and allowed to go home to China. Why did Washington go to such lengths to humiliate Huawei, perhaps China's foremost national champion?

The reason is simple. With a presence in 170 countries and sales of US $123 billion in 2019, Huawei is a behemoth to contend with, operating as a carrier in the enterprise sector and in consumer products. Established in 1987, and headquartered in Shenzhen, it made its reputation initially in the building of telecom infrastructure, before moving into the more glamorous area of consumer products like mobile phones and laptops. Today, however, its largest claim to fame lies in the pioneering role it plays in the development and deployment of 5G telecom technology, the product of its major investments in R&D over the years (its R&D spending was $18.65 billion in 2019), as well as of its early bet on this technology (Tang, 2020).

As mentioned above, 5G is critical for the most cutting-edge economic activities of the present and the future, and Huawei is in pole position to make the most of it. The United States, in turn, is determined to stop it from doing so. Over the years, Huawei faced many obstacles in developing its business activities in the United States, and has prioritized other markets, including Europe, Africa, the Middle East, the Asia-Pacific, and Latin America. It is thus well-positioned to play a key role in the next phase of digitalizing the world economy. To prevent this, Washington has exerted pressure on countries across the world to block Huawei technology. Yet, it has faced pushback in doing so, even from close allies like the United Kingdom, as Washington's request for 'clean' (meaning no Huawei or other Chinese technology) national telecom grids would mean, in many cases, taking out vast amounts of existing equipment and replacing it with more expensive and less reliable versions, hardly an attractive business proposition. And while some rich countries in the Anglosphere (like Australia, Canada, and New Zealand) have given in to US pressure (in the case of Australia, honouring a long-standing foreign policy tradition, it actually *volunteered* to do so), for the overwhelming majority of countries around the world, and especially in those of the Global South, this has not been the case.

Latin America is one area where this offensive against Chinese telecom companies has played itself out with special brio, with Brazil, Chile, and Ecuador being singled out by the United States in a variety of instances. A good example of that is the $3.5 billion loan offered by the International Development Financial Corporation (IDFC), a US government agency, to Ecuador in January 2021. In the initial stages of the pandemic, Ecuador was ground zero of the Covid-19 pandemic in the region, with corpses piling up on the streets of Guayaquil; with the drop in oil prices, the country also faced foreign debt problems. Taking advantage of the situation, the Trump administration took the much-criticized conditionality of Western IFIs to new heights. The loan came with two conditions. The first was that Ecuador would commit to exclude any type of Chinese technology from its telecommunications grid. The second, that the country should privatize public sector assets for an amount equivalent to that of the loan. These assets were to be determined not by the government of Ecuador, but *jointly* by Ecuador and the IDFC. According to Adam Boehler, the outgoing executive director of the IDFC, this would be an 'innovative model' to expel China from Latin America, something that he had discussed with incoming President Biden's transition team, which had considered it to be 'an interesting and innovative approach' (Gallagher and Heine, 2021).

There is much that is wrong with this 'innovative model'. It means sacrificing Latin American development prospects and technological progress to further US policy objectives in its conflict with China. The United States is not even promoting its own 5G technology (which it does not have), or that of its own telecom companies, but simply blocking the access of Chinese companies to the region, and, in so doing, slowing the growth and development of a small Latin American country in trouble. Along the same lines, the main purpose of a visit by Secretary of State Mike Pompeo to Chile in April 2019 was to block the building of an Internet, trans-Pacific cable from Valparaiso to Shanghai, which had been proposed by the Chilean government to China in 2016, on which a bilateral MOU had been signed, and for which a pre-feasibility study had been undertaken (Emol, 2019). Although this would have been the first Internet cable across the South Pacific, and would have made Chile into China's digital gateway into South America, the Piñera government caved in to Washington's pressure and scuttled the project. Yet, a measure of the limits of this US diplomatic offensive against the digitalization of South America can be gleaned from the fact that a similar visit by US authorities, this time in August 2021, to Brazil by National Security Advisor Jake Sullivan, to press Brazil to exclude Huawei from participating in the country's upcoming 5G tender, offering in exchange a vaguely defined associate membership in NATO, failed to achieve its objectives, despite the pro-US stance of President Bolsonaro's government (Reuters, 2021a).

As US–China diplomatic tensions play themselves out on the digital frontier across the Global South, the irony is obvious. For the past few decades, Northern telecom companies largely neglected Asia, Africa, and Latin America, to focus on what were considered to be the more profitable markets of Europe and North America, while companies like Huawei positioned themselves in the developing world. And then, just at the time when 5G technology comes to the fore as a key driver of progress and innovation, and Huawei is poised to play a leading role in furthering it, the United States attempts to bar developing countries from building up their digital infrastructure, adducing all sorts of unfounded claims about supposed 'back-doors' in Chinese equipment that it cannot back up. In the midst of the digital age, as Chinese companies step in to provide the connectivity these countries so badly need, US policy deploys a worldwide offensive to block such endeavours. Brazil's refusal to play along with such attempts (by the most pro-US government in Brazilian history), shows the limits of such a counterintuitive approach to digital development in the Global South. This takes us to Brazil's initiatives for limiting electronic espionage, another salient issue area in the North–South digital agenda.

Regulating Electronic Espionage

As mentioned above, in addition to the uproar caused by the NSA's mass surveillance activities through programmes such as PRISM revealed by Edward Snowden in 2013, few revelations caused as much impact as the ones about the wiretapping of the personal mobile phones of Brazilian President Dilma Rousseff and German Chancellor Angela

Merkel. The notion that, in peacetime, US intelligence agencies would regularly listen in to what the leaders of ostensibly friendly countries had to say struck many as taking intrusiveness and privacy violations to the limit.

Shortly after cancelling a presidential state visit to the US in the wake of these revelations, the Brazilian government led by Dilma Rousseff presented to the United Nations General Assembly (UNGA) an initiative designed to curb electronic espionage (Rousseff, 2013). Rather than submitting it as a discrete, bounded issue, the matter was framed as one related to the failings of the current system of Internet governance. According to the Brazilian proposal, the issue of electronic espionage, far from being strictly limited to the security arena, impinges directly on human rights and development, constituting a serious human rights violation (Abdenur and Gama, 2015).

Brazil's take on the matter reveals in many ways the limitations of international law and of Internet governance on the subject. While electronic spying is strictly regulated by domestic legislation, international law remains silent on it. And while such espionage existed long before the invention of the Internet, the latter has exponentially increased its reach and ambit. Brazil's argument, thus, was that Internet governance reform, i.e. moving away from the current multistakeholder model represented by ICANN to a multilateral model akin to other UN bodies, was the best way to deal with this thorny question. Not surprisingly, the United States strongly opposed any such notion, a matter on which the US Congress had earlier pronounced itself as well (US Senate and Congress, 2011–2012). The same goes for other members of the Anglosphere, like Australia, Canada, New Zealand and the United Kingdom (all part of the 'Five Eyes' intelligence-sharing group), which were part of the exercise in the first place. Still the fact that a leading NATO member like Germany actively cooperated with Brazil on this initiative, and parted ways with Washington on it, shows the degree to which Brasilia's point struck a chord that went beyond the North–South divide, and appealed to a broader constituency.

In many ways, this showed Brazilian diplomacy at its best. Embracing a salient issue with considerable emotional and media appeal; taking it in a timely manner to the world's leading multilateral body; addressing it from the ultimate bully pulpit (the opening speech at that year's UNGA); and following up on it with a proposed UNGA resolution on the subject that was approved without a vote, all reflected diplomatic dexterity and *savoir faire*. On the other hand, such resolutions are non-binding, and ultimately nothing happened. Internet governance continues to be ruled by ICANN, and international electronic espionage remains unfettered, with no prospects of any curbs on it anytime soon. That said, there is no reason to think we have seen the last of such initiatives. Brazil's ability to build widespread support for a UN resolution expressing concern about the current state of Internet governance and its deleterious effects on the right to privacy and human rights more generally indicates how fragile the support for current system is, and how vulnerable it remains to future projects aimed at democratizing Internet governance. The BRICS group, with its significant economic and demographic weight, may hold the key to any future such changes.

Digital Economy Partnership Agreement (DEPA) as the Way Forward?

Yet, there may also be other ways through which progress on the North–South digital agenda may be made, an incrementalist rather than a Big-Bang approach to finding common ground on digital issues. An inkling of that may be provided by the DEPA. The latter is an agreement signed by Chile, New Zealand, and Singapore in 2020, whose purpose is to set rules that promote the digital economy, provide a suitable regulatory framework for it, and facilitate the export of digital services and products (Rebolledo, 2021).

On the face of it, any such agreement signed by three small economies should be of marginal interest. Yet, the fact that DEPA is the first international economic agreement signed exclusively on digital matters gives it a special significance, as does the fact that its members hail from three different regions, Latin America, Australasia, and Asia. It was this very same three countries that established the P-3 in 2002 to give a greater impetus to trans-Pacific free trade, which later, with the incorporation of Brunei Daressalam, gave rise to the P-4, and eventually to the Trans-Pacific Partnership (TPP).

At a time when digital trade is growing in leaps and bounds, and the volume of the digital economy as a share of global GDP varies between 4.5 and 15.5%, with the export of digital services reaching as much as half of all service exports, this is especially significant (Rebolledo, 2021). As a result of the Covid-19 pandemic, digital exchanges have received an additional boost. In the midst of the economic recession caused by the pandemic in 2020, relying on digital tools for educational, health, logistics, and governmental services purposes has become critical. The public policy challenges in terms of digital infrastructure and communications (as mentioned earlier in this chapter); the upgrading of government agencies and their adaptation to the digital age; and the training of personnel to deal with the new technologies, are all key tasks for developing nations, in most of which the digital divide is only too apparent.

New subjects that have come to the fore in this new digital environment include tariffs on digital products; online consumer protection; paperless commerce; non-discriminatory treatment of digital products; electronic authentication and digital signatures; the protection of personal information; and how to deal with spam. DEPA aims to provide a further impetus to digital exchanges and the digital economy more generally by pushing for the non-discriminatory treatment of digital products, against the forced localization of servers and the free trans-border flow of data (International Economy Reports, 2017). It aims to act as a catalyst for other entities to act along the same lines.

DEPA responds very much to the needs and priorities of small, open economies, keen to foster greater trans-Pacific trade flows in the digital realm. Yet, as a measure of the role small powers can play in agenda-setting and in breaking through negotiation logjams, in November 2021, much to everyone's surprise, China formally asked to join DEPA (*South China Morning Post*, 2021). This, in turn, followed an earlier formal request by China to initiate the accession mechanisms to the Comprehensive and Progressive Transpacific Partnership (CPTPP) (Reuters, 2021b). At a time when the United States is reluctant to sign any international trade agreements, digital or otherwise, this gives China a leg up in the economic competition with the US in the Asia-Pacific region, one that had already been bolstered by the US ditching of the TPP in January of 2017, and the signing of the Regional Comprehensive Economic Partnership (RCEP) in November of 2020, a fifteen-member agreement among Asian and Australasian economies, which includes China, and is nowadays the biggest regional trade agreement anywhere.

Many observers opine that China's model of state capitalism would have considerable difficulties in meeting the requirements of DEPA and of the CPTPP. Nonetheless, China's formal request to join these agreements allows China to stand up as a champion of trans-Pacific free trade, as well as of boosting the international digital economy, at a time when protectionism and anti-globalization banners have become common in North America and Europe.

Conclusion

As the global order shifts from the US-led, unipolar moment of the post-Cold War era to a multiplex order (Acharya, 2018) in which power is much more diffuse, a shift that overlaps with the rise of not just a digital economy but a digital society, we are thus faced with a paradox. Although the Internet, the web of webs, is at the very centre of this extraordinary revolution, one to which half of humankind is connected, the Internet is not under any kind of international control, but still in the hands of one country, the United States. So far, attempts, like Brazil's, to democratize Internet governance have failed to make any headway.

That said, the rise of emerging powers, like the BRICS countries, and their growing embrace of the Internet and of digital tools is shifting the balance to a greater role of the Global South in digital connectivity. This is especially apparent in what we might call the 'hardware' of the Internet, including the submarine, fibre optic cables that convey 99% of electronic communications. The role of Chinese companies in the laying of these cables, mostly in the Asia-Pacific but also elsewhere, is particularly noteworthy. A key component of China's signature foreign policy project, the Belt and Road Initiative (BRI), a development proposal to countries in Africa, Asia, and Latin America, is that of digital connectivity, a decisive factor for economic progress in today's world (Hillman, 2021). The fact that the Chinese private company, Huawei, holds the lead in 5G telecommunications technology, and enjoys a long-standing presence across 170 countries, mostly in the developing world, puts it in pole position to contribute to their digitalization. US efforts to thwart this have largely failed.

Yet, the unexpected ways in which the diplomatic digital agenda cuts across the North–South divide is reflected in the signing of the DEPA of three small countries in the Asia-Pacific, Chile, New Zealand, and Singapore. To promote the digital economy and both liberalize and facilitate trade of digital products, they have committed to a variety of ways to make this happen.

As the US–China trade war turns into a tech war, and then into what some have referred to as a Second Cold War, there is little doubt that the battle over who will control the digital frontier will continue to hold sway. In this, there is much at stake for the Global South, and the future of many countries in Africa, Asia, and Latin America will depend on how their foreign policy makers and diplomats navigate these perilous waters.

SUGGESTED READING

Abdenur, A. and Gama, C.F. (2015). "Triggering the norms cascade: Brazil's initiatives for curbing electronic espionage", *Global Governance* 21, 3.

Broeders, D. (2015). *The public Core of the Internet: An International Agenda for Internet Governance*. Amsterdam: Amsterdam University Press.

Riordan, Shaun (2018). "The geopolitics of cyberspace: A diplomatic perspective", *Diplomacy and Foreign Policy* 3:3, 3.

Stuenkel, O. (2016). *Post Western World: How Emerging Powers Are Remaking Global Order*. Cambridge: Polity Press.

Tang, M. (2020). "Huawei versus the United States? The geopolitics of extraterritorial internet infrastructure", *International Journal of Communication* 14, 4556–4577.

REFERENCES

Abdenur, A. and Gama, C.F. (2015). "Triggering the norms cascade: Brazil's initiatives for curbing electronic espionage", *Global Governance* 21, 3.

Acharya, A. (2018). *The End of American World Order*, 2nd ed. New York: Polity Press.

BRICS (2014). "IV Cupula BRICS-Decarasao de Fortaleza". 15 July.

Broeders, D. (2015). *The Public Core of the Internet: An International Agenda for Internet Governance*. Amsterdam: Amsterdam University Press.

Carr, M. (2016). *US Power and the Internet in International Relations*. Basingstoke: Palgrave/Macmillan.

Chase, P.H. (2019). "Perspectives on the General Data Protection Regulation of the European Union", prepared remarks to the Hearing on "Privacy Rights and Data Collection on a Digital Economy", before the Committee on Banking, Housing and Urban Affairs of the United States Senate. Washington D.C., 7 May.

Clinton, H. (2010). "Internet Freedom", a speech delivered at the Newseum, Washington D.C., 21 January. https://foreignpolicy.com/2010/01/21/internet-freedom/

Council on Foreign Relations (2012). "Does the BRICS Group Matter? ", 20 March. https://www.cfr.org/interview/does-brics-group-matter

De Nardis, L. (2010). *The Emerging Field of Internet Governance*. Yale Information Society Project Working Paper Series. Yale Information Society Project, Yale Law School.

Emol (2019). "Mike Pompeo advierte a Chile sobre China y Huawei", 12 April.

Gallagher, K. and Heine, J. (2021) "Biden needs to reverse U.S. economic policy in Ecuador", *The Hill*, 26 January.

Getachew, A. (2019). *Worldmaking After Empire: The Rise and Fall of Self-Determination*. Princeton: Princeton University Press.

Heine, J. (2013). "Beyond the US-Brazil spat", *The Hindu*, 1 October.

Heine, J. (2020). "Crisis del orden internacional: ¿de vuelta al futuro?", *Foreign Affairs Latinoamérica* 20:2, 70–75.

Hillman, J. (2021). *The Digital Silk Road: China's Quest to Wire the World and Win the Future*. New York: Harper Business.

Hofmann, J. (2016) "Multi-stakeholderism in Internet governance: Putting fiction into practice", *Journal of Cyber Policy* 1:1, 29–49.

International Economy Report (2017). chapter 5 "International Trade Agreements and Internet Governance".

Kleinwachter, W. (2004). "Beyond ICANN vs ITU? How WSIS tries to enter the new territory of Internet governance", *Gazette: The International Journal for Communication Studies* 66:3–4, 233–251.

Liu, Y (2012). "The rise of China and global Internet governance", *China Media Research* 8:2, 46–55.

Mansell, Robin, (2012). *Reimagining the Internet*. Oxford: Oxford University Press.

Mueller, M. (1999) "ICANN and Internet governance: Sorting through the debris of self-regulation", *The Journal of Policy, Regulation and Strategy for Telecommunications, Information and Media* 1:6 (December).

Mueller, M. (2011). "India, Brazil and South Africa call for creation of 'new body' to deal with Internet governance", Internet Governance Project, Georgia Tech School of Public Policy, 17 September. https://www.internetgovernance.org/2011/09/17/india-brazil-and-south-africa-call-for-creation-of-new-global-body-to-control-the-internet/

Pew Research (2012). "The Role of Social Media in the Arab Spring", 28 November. https://www.pewresearch.org/journalism/2012/11/28/role-social-media-arab-uprisings/

Rebolledo, A. (2021). *Digital Economy Partnership Agreement (DEPA) y Oportunidades para la Alianza del Pacífico*. Santiago: Fundación Chilena del Pacífico.

Reuters (2021a). "U.S. national security advisor visits Brazil, meets with Bolsonaro", 5 August.

Reuters (2021b). "China applies to join Pacific trade pact to boost economic clout", 17 September.

Riordan, Shaun (2018). "The geopolitics of cyberspace: A diplomatic perspective", *Diplomacy and Foreign Policy* 3:3, 3.

Roberts, C, Armijo, L., and Katada S. (2018). *The BRICS and Collective Financial Statecraft*. Oxford: Oxford University Press.

Ross, Alec (2016). *The Industries of the Future*. New York: Simon and Schuster.

Rousseff, D. (2013). "Statement at the Opening of the General Debate of the 68th Session of the UN General Assembly", 24 September.

Schmidt, E. and Cohen, J. (2013). *The New Digital Age: Reshaping the Future of People, Nations and Businesses*. New York: Vintage.

Snowden, E. (2019). *Permanent Record*. New York: Metropolitan Books.

South China Morning Post (2021). "China's interest in DEPA digital trade pact raises questions about 'domestic reforms' and what could be the next big multilateral deal", 5 November.

Stuenkel, O. (2013). *India-Brazil-South Africa Forum (IBSA): The Rise of the Global South*. Abingdon: Routledge.

Stuenkel, O. (2021). "Latin American governments are caught in the middle of the US-China Tech War", *Foreign Policy*, 21 February.

Tang, M. (2020). "Huawei versus the United States? The geopolitics of extraterritorial Internet infrastructure", *International Journal of Communication* 14, 4556–4577.

The New York Times (2022). "Four takeaways from a Times investigation into China's expanding surveillance state", 21 June. https://www.nytimes.com/2022/06/21/world/asia/china-surveillance-investigation.html

The Guardian (2013). "NSA collecting phone records of millions of Verizon customers daily", 6 June.

UN General Assembly (2014). "The Right to Privacy in the Digital Age", A/RES/68/167, 21 January.

US Senate and Congress, House of Representatives (2012). "Whereas Given the Importance of the Internet to the Global Economy, It Is Essential That the Internet Remain Stable, Secure and Free from Government Control". R. 628 IH, 112th Congress, 2011-2012, 2nd Session. S. CON. RES. 50.

Winseck, D. (2017). "The geopolitical economy of the global Internet infrastructure", *Journal of Information Policy* 7, 228–267.

Zuboff, Shoshana (2020). *The Age of Surveillance Capitalism: The Fight for a Human Future and the New Frontier of Power*. New York: PublicAffairs.

CHAPTER 33

INTERNATIONAL GEOPOLITICS AND DIGITAL GAMES IN THE NATIONALIST AGENDA OF GREAT POWERS

ANTONIO CÉSAR MORENO CANTANO

INTRODUCTION

IN the early 1980s, Electronic Arts published an article in *American Scientific* entitled 'Can a Computer Make You Cry?' The answer was clear: 'an interactive tool that can bring people's thoughts and feelings closer together, perhaps closer than ever before' (Anable, 2018: IX). The potential of moving images, even in their simplest geometric forms, was the subject of an interesting experiment conducted by Austrian psychologists Fritz Heider and Marianne Simmel, to understand the workings of the human mind during the Second World War. In front of an audience of hundreds, they projected a short video showing two triangles of different sizes and a circle moving randomly inside a rectangle with a small opening. One hundred and seventeen subjects commented that it was a story of abuse. They expressed sympathy for the smaller triangle when it seemed to be 'bullied' by the larger triangle. In the end, the observers even showed some relief and joy when the 'bullied' geometric shapes managed to escape the rectangle and the 'attacks' of the larger triangle (Heider and Simmel, 1944). Why do we see a narrative in the random animation of four geometric shapes? Why can we empathize with them? According to a study by Robert Dunbar, we spend 65% of our time talking about social topics. We also consume narratives all the time: news, literature, movies, series, video games. Storytelling is one of the few human traits that seems to be truly universal across media and cultures (Dunbar et. al., 1997).

The discipline of Game Studies has validated many of these theorems and has sparked a rich and complex debate about the prevalence of ludic or narrative elements in them, currently leading to a politicization of their content and purposes (Mitchell, 2018; Gómez-García et al., 2022). For example, in the last three years, especially since the Covid-19 pandemic, some of the titles with most millions of players worldwide, such as *Pokémon Go* (Niantic Lab, 2016), *Animal Crossing: New Horizons* (Nintendo, 2020), or *Fortnite Battle Royale* (Epic Games, 2017), have been modified to incorporate political discourses (Davies, 2020; Pearcy, 2020; Venegas and Moreno, 2021). Similarly, important international civil organizations, such as Reporters Without Borders, have used this medium, in this case through *Minecraft* (Mojang Studios, 2011), to create a virtual space—*The Uncensored Library* (see Figure 33.1)—to denounce the lack of freedoms in certain countries: Saudi Arabia, Russia, Egypt, Vietnam, and Mexico (LaCapria, 2021).

Video games are an important tool for spreading ideas and influencing others through persuasion (Bogost, 2009). This is one of the reasons for the growing interest of different state agencies and international actors in boosting their production and regulating their role in global governance, as they contain diplomatic, propagandistic, and nationalistic elements (Seo, 2020). Through vivid images, symbols, and narratives, video games actively invade the player's own space, appealing to acceptance through empathy (Gómez-García et al., 2021; Bos, 2021). The previous scenario confirms the starting point of this study: the process of ludification of culture, which Joost Raessens defines as an activity that 'also emerges in those areas that in the past were considered its opposite', such as

FIGURE 33.1 The Uncensored Library in *Minecraft*

Source: Reporters Without Borders https://www.uncensoredlibrary.com/en

education, politics, or war (Raessens, 2006: 16). The consolidation of digital games and games studies in the media ecosystem therefore allows us to question their contribution to diplomacy, foreign policy, and, more generally, international relations. Narratives and discourses linked to the state, to power, are assumed in an unconscious and playful way, thanks to these creations, which some authors call 'propagames' (Ming-Tak and Wang, 2021). All this within the framework of a global strategy of digital nationalism (Schneider, 2021).

This paper, therefore, provides an answer to the following research question: to what extent are video games part of digital nationalism campaigns, and project an idealized image of the past and present? This format, within mechanisms of cultural and digital diplomacy, constructs narratives about national perception and positioning in international geopolitical issues: territorial claims, political alliances, or economic positioning. To elucidate these elements, the chapter will be divided into two major blocks. In the first, we will relate video games to the aesthetic and emotional turn in international relations. This relationship stems from the growing importance within visual culture studies, and its links to digital cultural diplomacy and the propaganda strategies of some state actors. Finally, our research will provide examples of these dynamics, which affirm the political nature of video games, in countries such as China, Pakistan, and India. These countries were chosen because the state is involved in the production of certain war video games, such as *Glorious Mission* (China), *Glorious Resolve* (Pakistan), and *FAU-G* (India).

Digital Media and the Politics of Emotions

The image, unlike the text, has an affective component that allows the viewer to empathize and engage with what they are observing. There has been a 'cultural and aesthetic turn' in political science and international relations over the last two decades. This means a new perspective that validates the perception of human feelings and sensations, rather than just the practices of reason and logos that prevail in conventional studies (Dittmer and Bos, 2019), by adding other, more creative and open, but equally important forms of perception, 'cultivating a critical attitude to how we understand and engage with the political world around us' (Bleiker, 2001: 526). Michael J. Shapiro (2013: 16) proposes 'to know the connections we make with the world to which we belong', but from a new prism. To this end, a heterogeneous group of researchers (Bleiker et. al., 2013; Methman, 2014; Kirkpatrick, 2015; Gartner and Gelpi, 2016) do not hesitate to include philosophical or psychological approaches to study how reality is represented. There is a growing, and increasingly intense, relationship between geopolitics and visual culture, in which affectivity, emotion, and memory play an important role (Carter and McCormack, 2010).

This interest in the politics of emotions can be traced back to the works of the journalist Walter Lippman (Van Rythoven, 2021). This trend contrasts with the consideration that privileged the rational, the functional, and spoke of 'misperceptions' to refer to fear, hate, anger, or love. Robert Jervis (1976: 3) argued that it was necessary to remove emotions from the political landscape because they were 'accidents that interfered with political reasoning'. Contrary to this trend, as described above, there is a growing desire to include emotions in the study of international geopolitics. Neta Crawford (2000: 138–139) has produced a detailed review of the literature on emotions in world politics research and provides a meaningful theoretical framework and methodological guidance.

Mercer (2006) and Sasley (2011) went on to reflect on the dichotomy between emotions and rationality, and how the former contributes to the construction of identities, perceptions, and intergroup behaviour. Hutchinson and Bleiker (2014: 492–493) made an important contribution in this regard by asking 'How can the behaviour of states be shaped by emotions?' To find an answer to this complex question, they argued that emotions, shaped by society and culture, are originally individual and private in nature. However, through representation and power, individual experiences and perceptions can be homogenized and reach the whole population. Key to this process are the media, social networks, images, or nationalist rhetoric, which give visibility and a public voice to the most intimate feelings of individuals (Hutchinson and Bleiker, 2014: 505–509).

This field becomes even more interesting when we consider the persuasive power of visual elements. Authors such as MacDonald, Hughes, and Dodds (2010: 2) have emphasized that 'geopolitics and visual culture have become co-constitutive', as there is a growing reliance 'on the visual to comprehend and represent the world around us'. This fact has paved the way for a large body of research showing how photographic and video technologies have been used by state and non-state actors to satisfy the symbolic needs of combatants and their supporters. It is therefore necessary to understand the close links that are currently emerging between visual culture and public politics, particularly through simulations, virtual reality, and computer games. Bekkers and Moody (2015: 61–67) analyse some circumstances in which power manifests and seeks to perpetuate itself through digital technologies. Visual technologies help to create and disseminate images that contribute to classifying certain events as meaningful (McCourt, 2022).

For this reason, the prevalence of the visual medium has encouraged states to actively engage in the production of visual technologies. China's state-owned technology conglomerate Tencent is a powerful example of this trend (Tse, 2015). It is a process of concentration and homogenization of information, which reverses the capacity for decentralization and democratization that the World Wide Web supposedly presents (Castells, 2009). Kaempf (2018: 101–103) explains, under the same prism, that the constitution of this digital ecosystem in the twenty-first century is threatened by several factors, highlighting above all the will of states to control this medium and to regulate its access and the stories that are held there. Of course, the video game industry is also involved in these circumstances. In the multiplayer video game *H1Z1* (Daybreak

Game, 2015), the self-proclaimed Chinese player collective 'Red Army' has a widespread presence, disrupting Asian games when China's name or its identity and national symbols are denigrated. Their tactic is to round up anyone who offends the country's image and force them to pay tribute by chanting 'China No. 1'. Many foreign players, especially Americans and Japanese, try to provoke this ultra-nationalist group by shouting 'Taiwan No. 1' in all their games (see Figure 33.2) (Gabriel, 2021: 297–313). On this occasion, virtual space is used as a battlefield of citizenship to expose the political tensions between the great powers.

Visual culture is relevant to international geopolitical studies for several reasons (Bleiker, 2018). Firstly, images are able to convey emotions of individuals and societies in ways that go beyond words. Photographs, films, and video games have a wider audience and acceptance than a verbal or textual representation. Secondly, the emotional status of images, mobilized through patriotic discourses, is closely linked to their ability to create communities through the demand for the defence of the 'we' and the sacrifice of those who do so (Hansen, 2018: 599). And thirdly, aesthetic politics is at the heart of the visual conflicts that arise over what should be shown in images. The empathetic potential of video games, which can attract followers through their striking images and cinematics sequences, and convey explicit or subliminal messages through their narratives and messages (Sicart, 2014), makes them an ideal and dangerous medium in these contexts.

FIGURE 33.2 An *H1Z1* player waves the Taiwanese flag in protest against the Chinese majority group Red Army

Source: Taiwan News https://twitter.com/tw_nextmedia/status/687280530023256071

It is precisely the importance of narrative strategies that directly links video games to the propaganda policies of international powers.

Information, in this case through the explicit and implicit messages it contains, is a weapon of the first order within the rhetorical and ideological mechanisms of modern conflicts (Colley, 2020: 43). As noted in James J. Forest's collective work Influence Warfare (2009), it is not surprising that these kinds of digital creations themselves form part of the war of ideas being waged between governments and terrorist groups. Many of the best first-person shooter games have been shown to use these tools for moral disinhibition not only contributing to the acceptance of violence but also promoting the ability to disable one's own moral control mechanisms. James Der Derian (2009) has called this 'virtuous warfare', which promotes a bloodless, humane, and hygienic view of war.

Video games could facilitate violent radicalization because personalized avatars allow players to engage, within virtual spaces, in cognitive practices of violent acts, which could increase their perceived self-efficacy in relation to real-world violence (Schlegel, 2020). These experiences, termed possibility spaces by Ian Bogost (2009), enable for certain representations of the ordinary world that make it possible to create a simulated environment where the player can think critically or identify fully with the issue represented. Sybille Lammes (2008) goes even further and relates video games with the concept of the 'magic node', believing that game spaces are not separate from the ordinary world, but that both worlds form nodes in a broad social network that feeds back into each other. These game spaces are, in short, influenced by a broad political context that feeds them and can in turn influence the perceptions that the player experiences virtually (Wheatcroft et al., 2017).

In view of all these conditioning factors, and as some studies have highlighted (Prucha, 2011; Robinson, 2012, 2015; Schulzke, 2014, 2016; Al-Rawi, 2016), there is every reason to study the links established between this multimedia entertainment and the propagandistic and ideological goals promoted by terrorist groups, whether through specific creations or modifications of well-known titles. Schulzke (2013) offers a detailed analysis of how terrorism manifests itself in other multimedia formats (notably the work of Van Veeren, 2009), accentuating the validity of video games from an empirical point of view, appealing to their large audience, which facilitates the propagation of their message and representations. Moreover, through simulation, the player becomes the protagonist of the narratives and not just an observer, as in cinema or television. Under this broad and holistic theoretical framework, we will analyse how different countries use video games as part of their strategies of digital cultural diplomacy (Cull, 2008: 51) and nationalist reaffirmation (Schneider, 2018; Moreno, 2021). This techno-nationalism, with a strong propagandistic and geopolitical component, makes this format an object of study of relevance for a better understanding of social sciences in the twenty-first century.

This upsurge of visual culture studies, in which the new attention given to emotions plays an important role, can be perfectly linked to the study of video games. Their format, with the strong protagonism of interactivity, makes the user an active agent within the narratives and symbolic messages they contain. All these components attract the attention of the propaganda strategies of the major international actors. The video game, through its persuasive and large audience, is an extremely valuable element in the nationalism and digital diplomacy of numerous countries.

Theoretical Framework
and Methodology

The research question of this work is how are video games part of digital nationalism campaigns that project an idealized image of the past and the present? The main hypothesis behind this point is the assertion that video games play a prominent role in propaganda and in nationalist and diplomatic strategies within the geopolitical agenda of major international powers. The reason for this interest is their ability to persuade players through the power of emotions (fear, hate, anger). From the field of psychology, we would like to refer to the Theory of Moral Disengagement of Albert Bandura to explain how video games, especially war games, can become a tool in the service of terrorism / counter-terrorism to promote radicalization processes among their users. According to this model (Osofsky et al., 2005), there are several cognitive mechanisms that can lead an individual to perform a behaviour that contradicts their personal values, beliefs, and attitudes without producing a dissonance, that is, an internal conflict between two opposing and mutually exclusive thoughts or feelings. People can turn off their morality in certain situations, in many cases unconsciously, to the extent that they make certain reinterpretations of reality that ultimately justify or legitimize the commission of 'exceptional' behaviour. Our moral reasoning can be consciously misled or turned off by finding moral justifications for violence, making favourable comparisons (the classic 'but our enemies did worse'), using euphemistic labels (targets are 'neutralized' rather than killed), ignoring or distorting the consequences of violence (in games, for example, by not showing an accurate amount of blood or wounds), or blaming the victims.

Following the methodological guidelines proposed by Hutchison and Bleiker (2014), this macro approach is fleshed out in two relevant micro issues of relevance:

- Which state agencies are the driving force behind this genre of video game production?
- How do they contribute to their nationalist discourses and soft power strategies?

Following Lammes's (2008) 'magic nodes' and Bogost's (2009) 'possibility spaces', we will focus on the emitter behind these cultural artefacts and the links to reality that determine the political nature of their messages and symbols. Sybille Lammes has noted that games should not be understood simply as spaces that exist outside the social world and offer a release from it. Rather, games are 'sociospatial practices'; not magic circles that separate the ludic space from the real world, but magic nodes that are part of a social network.

Like the magic circle, the node demarcates the boundaries of a ludic space that operates according to certain rules, but at the same time, the node connects the subject to a social reality that transcends and surrounds the ludic space (Lammes, 2008: 263). The digital ludic space is essentially and precisely a space governed by a set of rules that defines what can be done in this space; which kind of game can be played and which kind cannot. The relationship between ludic spaces and the socio-political environment within which they exist is different from game to game. In other words, the network that games, as magic nodes, connect to is also characterized by a form of bounded ideological context and the narratives that this context helps explain or gives rise to. From this perspective, it is important to understand the organization of ludic space both in terms of the actual spaces they sometimes resemble and the ideologies that inform the player (Lammes, 2008: 265).

This concept and Bogost's 'possibility spaces' are reinforced by another interesting idea. We refer to the identification of our self with the avatar we handle in video games: *proprioception*. As Fedorova (2015) summarizes, that involves the existence of a boundary between the internal and the external that goes beyond the physical boundaries of the body. In this way, it can be explained why a player can feel what his avatar conveys to him. This is a very important element for our analysis because it allows us to understand why Chinese, Indian, or Pakistani video gamers can assimilate geopolitical and nationalist codes by controlling a soldier in certain videogames. In the case studies, we will analyse some of these virtual elements linked to real political aspects that contribute to propagate and promote the digital nationalism of certain countries.

The production, context, and reception of the images, narratives, game mechanics, and audios that characterize this interactive digital medium are examined (Bleiker, 2020: 274–275), as are the actors, interests, sources, and strategies behind them (Bekkers and Moody, 2015: 105). To tackle this complex task, we will look at promotional videos of some of these war video games, game plays, press reports, official websites, and a specialized bibliography that will allow us to contextualize this large amount of data.

DISCUSSION: CASE STUDIES

These countries have been selected because they are actively involved in the development and distribution of video games of a propagandistic nature. They also represent some of the largest user markets at the national and global levels. They are significant examples that allow us to qualitatively transfer our theoretical framework and research questions to the level of reality, namely the political instrumentalization of video games.

China

The great events of the past are reactivated by the new formats and technological channels of the last decades of the twentieth and early twenty-first centuries, such as the world of video games, leading to what Schneider (2018: 18) has defined as digital nationalism. Chinese society is currently experiencing a double cultural identity confrontation between two paradigms: modernity and tradition (Wu, 2014). This conflict is especially visible in the generation born in the 1980s. Most of these young people are shaped by a global mass consumer culture whose most characteristic features include the Internet and electronics. Their identity and historical vision are closely linked to contemporary media. History is 'liberated' from traditional textbooks and integrated into everyday life through popular media culture: movies, TV dramas, video games (Kang, 2012: 17–19). The proliferation of historical video games or the presence of elements related to the country's cultural and political heritage in these digital creations only responds to this demand and desire to spread the national culture to the world. This context determines the essence of most historical video games set in China, from 2001 (release date of *Three Kingdoms: Fate of the Dragon*, Object Software) until today.

At the same time, a patriotic education campaign was launched in China in the 1990s to combat the 'ideological' neglect that had led the country to the Tiananmen Square events in 1989. Under Jiang Zemin's leadership, all sorts of initiatives were promoted to reflect on the nation's 'glorious past' in order to achieve a unified mindset among citizens and reinforce ideas such as territorial integrity, national sovereignty, and the country's independence. To better convey these ideas, the campaign advocated the use of entertainment as a means of education and utilized a wide range of media, art exhibitions, books, newspapers, television programmes, video and audio products, movies, the Internet, and video games (Wang, 2014). As for the world of video games, the Chinese Heroes project was launched in 2005 in collaboration with Shanda Interactive, the country's largest online game provider, and the General Administration of Press and Publication. The goal was to develop games based on historical events that would 'stir' the conscience of the population, whether it was about the Three Kingdoms era or the fight against Japan during World War II, e.g. *Resistance War Online* (PowerNet Interactive, 2007). It is difficult to distinguish whether these creations are indoctrination or educational, especially when these 'heroes' are transposed to the present day and have to do with the country's armed forces. Army recruiters complain that the new generations are dominated by 'spoiled brats' who are only concerned with their technological devices such as the PlayStation Portable (PSP). This comment reveals the military recruiters' exasperation with the young people's value system (Naftali, 2014: 4). For this reason, the Army's propaganda department has promoted cultural digital creations to improve its image and increase its appeal among this niche population.

The 1994 Education Campaign included a 'Guide for the Implementation of Patriotic Education' to strengthen civil–military unity within Chinese society and raise youth awareness of the importance of 'protecting the territorial integrity, national sovereignty and independence of the homeland' (Naftali, 2014: 6). To better communicate these ideas, the campaign advocates the use of entertainment as an educational medium, and to this end employs 'a broad range of media channels for this purpose, including art exhibitions, books, newspapers, television shows, video and audio products, films, computer games, and the Internet' (Naftali, 2014: 6). Let us look at a very illustrative example. One of the big releases of 2023, inspired by Chinese mythology and its great literary classics, will be *Black Myth: Wukong*. Published in 1590, it tells the true story of Xuanzang, a monk who set out for India during the Tang dynasty in search of the true Buddhist texts. In the novel he is accompanied by three disciples: Zhu Bajie (known as Pig), Sha Wujian (Sand), and, the focus of this video game, Sun Wukong, better known as the Monkey King, who served as a reference for the well-known character Son Goku in the Japanese animated series *Dragon Ball*. On the day the trailer for this title was released, in August 2020, it reached more than five million views on the YouTube channel of the specialized website IGN. Thanks to this promotional video, they received more than 10,000 applications from professionals in the country who wanted to participate in the development and design of this project. The game's producer, Feng Ji, stated in a clear nationalistic statement that this video game aims to return the Monkey King to his real name, Wukong: 'the story is from China, but everyone refers to him as Goku ... we want the world to know that his real name is Wukong'. This defence was in line with the opinion of millions of gamers who were able to watch the staging of the game: 'the pride of China' (Young, 2021).

Another theme is the 'traumatic and humiliating experience in the face of Western and Japanese incursions' (Nie, 2013). Unlike American productions, Chinese films and video games focus their argument on sacrifice for the nation as the supreme reason. A clear example of this is the title *Glorious Mission* (Giant Interactive Group, 2013), in which the player must adopt goals of Chinese international policy, such as control of the islands in the China Sea disputed with Japan, as their own. The true intent of this genre of video games, and in response to the demand of some military authorities, was to increase recruitment and glorify war. On this occasion, the possibility space and the magic node would be all those territories that are at the centre of China's current demands: from the Diaoyu Islands to the Gulf of Aden in Somalia.

Alberto Venegas, in Interactive Past (2020), highlighted the relationship between war video games and the improvement of military reputation among players, crossing the intangible boundary of Lamme's 'magic knot'. This means that any portrayal that does not conform to governmental approaches, whether in the video game industry or any other, quickly encounters the heavy curtain of censorship (Holmes, 2021). One of the most recent examples of this problem can be found in the blocking of the trailer of *Call of Duty: Black Ops Cold War* (Activision, 2020) due to the inclusion of an image of the 1989 Tiananmen Square protests against the communist government. Faced with complaints from China, Activision decided to remove this scene for fear of losing the billions that this Asian market brings in. There's something else crucial: Chinese tech conglomerate Tencent owns 5% of Activision (Batchelor, 2020). This title is very significant for the propaganda power that the world of video games can have, capable of bringing historical events to the forefront and triggering debates about them.

Pakistan and India

Robert Kaplan noted in his book *The Revenge of Geography* (2012) that India suffers from political boundaries that do not correspond to the physical boundaries of the subcontinent, and that, of the states that surround it, Pakistan poses a constant threat. These tensions, whose fundamental—though not only—axis is the territorial claim to Kashmir, have degenerated into several conflicts in the twentieth century: the 1947–1948 war, the 1965 war, the 1971 Bangladesh war of independence, to which must be added the appearance of terrorist groups in this troubled region (McLeod, 2016). All these conflicts have had a tremendous impact on the world of entertainment, with the intention of showing a certain interpretation of the past, promoting nationalism and their own signs of identity, defined—on many occasions—by confronting the other.

In the propaganda strategies of the great powers in the twenty-first century, the communication and marketing departments that are set up around the armed forces are of great importance. One of the most outstanding cases is the Inter Service Public Relations Pakistan (ISPR), which promotes all kinds of multimedia creations to publicize Pakistan's major patriotic milestones, from feature films to songs, such as the one commemorating National Day (March 23). The ISPR acts as a bridge between the armed forces and the public. It monitors the media and detects the contours of enemy psychological campaigns so that it can respond effectively (MazherHussain et al., 2019).

Mobile video games feature prominently among its productions. One title promoted by the agency is *Glorious Resolve* (Rockville Games, 2018), about the counter-terrorism operation in the Swat Valley against the Taliban, which has been downloaded over five million times (ISPR, 2018). The first thing that appears on the screen is the exact location of this place and the dates when these attacks took place (from November 2007 to January 2009). Real images and highly accurate maps are used to justify the Pakistan Army's movements in an area that is repeatedly overlaid with the colours of the national flag. This is followed by C-130 and F-16 aircraft, symbols of the might of the national air force. This short trailer, located in the ISPR itself, is complemented by the Google Play trailer, which highlights the role of Google Play as being responsible for the ISPR. This is followed by a reference to the foreign funding of the terrorist forces, which is always portrayed as an anonymous entity, whose face is usually hidden under a balaclava. Finally, a senior Pakistani military officer looks at the portraits of those illustrious soldiers who died defending his country; a magical junction shaped by geopolitical codes carefully designed and implemented by the ISPR.

India is China's second largest neighbour and shares a land border of about 2,000 km. The two countries are currently in dispute over an area of about 125,000 km², which can be divided into eastern, middle, and western sectors. The disputed area, known as Aksai Chin, although a desolate and virtually uninhabited plateau, is of great strategic value to China as it represents an important passage between Tibet and Xingjian province. Recently, confrontations between the two powers have occurred in these latitudes (2013, 2017, or 2020), resulting in a significant military presence there (Paul, 2018). The peak of this escalation of tensions was reached in June 2020, when twenty Indian soldiers were killed in a clash with Chinese soldiers in the Galwan Valley (Ahmed et al., 2020).

These measures of the Indian Army cannot be understood without taking into account the Hindu nationalism of the Naremdra Modi government, known as *Ek Bharat, Shreshtha Bharat*, which, among other things, places great emphasis on digital creations that help reinforce the myths and territorial aspirations of the country. This grand strategy rests on three pillars. The first is *Made in India*, a major government aid programme to facilitate investment, promote innovation, enhance skill development, and protect intellectual property. It is within the framework of this initiative that the measures against the large Chinese technology conglomerate Tencent should be understood. Between June and September 2020, 177 Chinese mobile apps were banned by the Indian Ministry of Electronics and Information Technology. The government claimed that several apps developed and published in China posed a risk to national security as they collected the data of Indian users and sent it to Chinese servers and the Chinese government: 'they are detrimental to the sovereignty and integrity of the country, defence, state security and law and order'. This allowed the Indian executive to invoke its powers under Section 69A of the Information Technology Act to ban Chinese mobile apps. The restriction affected video games and apps such as *PUBG Mobile, Mobile Legends* (ranked the first and tenth best-selling titles in the first half of 2020), *Clash of Kings, Rise of Kingdoms, Arena of Valor, WeChat, TikTok*, and *Alipay*. Just two days later, Tencent lost $14 billion (NikoPartners, 2020).

The second pillar is *Digital India*, a creation of the Ministry of Finance, Electronics and Information Technology which aims to improve the country's online infrastructure by digitally empowering it and ensuring that all or most citizens can use the Internet. And finally, the third pillar is *Atmanirbhar Bharat*, India's quest for self-sufficiency in various economic, cultural, and digital fields (Hall, 2019). In this way, Modi has called for developing video games that help learn about the national past and culture. Added to this is the defence of patriotic values and territorial claims that 'threaten' the unity of the country (Handrahan, 2020). This effort to reaffirm nationalist discourse and territorial claims at the international level has taken concrete shape in the creations of various Indian studios and programmers, such as Neosphere Interactive's *1971: Indian Naval Front*, which they describe as a 'true tribute to the Indian Navy' in the war against Pakistan that year. Modi's heightened Hindu nationalism has only exacerbated the marginalization of the country's Muslim population, which is seen as subservient to the interests of the hated Pakistan (Moreno, 2020).

During the presentation of the war video game *FAU-G* (nCore Games, 2021), the contribution to this initiative became clear (Balakumar, 2021). This title, which was intended to take the place of *PUBG* after its ban in the country in 2020, focused on the conflict zone of the Galwan Valley, which we have already pointed out. The description on Google Play encouraged players to 'step into the shoes of a patriotic soldier and experience the bravery, brotherhood, and sacrifice of the men who protect the country's borders'. Not surprisingly, therefore, 20% of the profits go to the Home Ministry's organization, *Bharat Ke Veer*, which is associated with the families of Indian soldiers killed in action (The Economic Times, 2020). Launched on 26 January (India's Republic Day) the video game has reached an impressive five million downloads in just a few months, with a special highlight being its presentation video and music, which featured renowned composers linked to the country's film industry. The first few seconds of the trailer (Defense Insight, 2021) show the exact coordinates where China and India rival each other, namely Ladakh, highlighting its cold temperatures (-30 degrees Celsius) and altitude (over 4000 m). This is not a minor point, as it gives the Indian citizen an insight into the exact territory for which his country's soldiers are risking their lives and the harsh conditions in which this confrontation is taking place. Next, a Sikh soldier—clearly identifiable by his turban—is shown beating a Chinese soldier who is wearing the red five-pointed star, the symbol of communism, on his visor. Then a Hindi hymn is heard while another soldier with the Indian flag over his shoulder hoists a tent over a frozen desert. Afterwards, four Indian soldiers, back-to-back, symbolizing the country's unity and strength, fire relentlessly at anyone approaching their position. The climax is reached when the national flag flutters in the icy wind and the Indian troops salute victoriously (see Figure 33.3).

FIGURE 33.3 Screenshot of the video game *FAU-G* celebrating the Indian Army in its fight to defend territorial integrity against China

Source: Screenshot video game FAU-G on Google Play.

Aesthetics and action raise popular sentiment and support for its 'brave and invincible' warriors in the world's most inhospitable places, willing to make any sacrifice to protect their territorial integrity against their rivals, in this case China. This is not a simple performative composition. Possibility space and magic nodes transfer to the virtual plane many of the strategic lines of Modi's India in terms of foreign policy and diplomacy.

Conclusions

Emotions and images have become two relevant concepts to understand the workings of different propagandistic and nationalistic strategies of state actors. By overcoming positivist and realist paradigms, both objects allow us to approach the non-rational aspects of international politics (Dune et al., 2020). A format that perfectly combines both elements is the video game. Their interactive nature, immersion, accessibility, and ability to engage the user make them one of the booming media in the digital age to promote certain narratives related to the territorial aspirations and security issues of some countries (China, India, and Pakistan among many others). In addition, they can also be a very appropriate format to improve a country's cultural image beyond its borders, and to participate in digital cultural diplomacy strategies, as we have shown in this text. Increasingly, different government departments, linked to foreign affairs, technology or culture, promote this type of creation with direct economic aid, or censor all those video games that do not adhere to their interpretation of international geopolitics.

From the relevance of image studies, applied to the emotional turn in international relations, we established a theoretical framework based on two concepts: possibility spaces and magic nodes. The video game, due to its possibilities of interactivity and connections between the real and virtual worlds, enables the dissemination of nationalist geopolitical codes in its narratives, mechanics, and visual symbols. For these reasons, the state—through its various diplomatic, cultural, and political policies— seeks to manipulate the process of creation, access, and dissemination.

The use of attractive and stimulating promotional videos, extolling patriotic values, is an increasingly important and promoted operation, reinforcing the importance of their study and contextualization. Why not identify with the special forces of other nations, apart from the familiar US Marines? Some of the wars of the future will undoubtedly be fought from the screens of our computers and video game consoles.

Further nations and games that follow the examples in this chapter include: Bangladesh and its titles on the 1971 Liberation War against Pakistan (*Heroes of 71* series); the creations of the Islamic Revolutionary Guard Corps attacking the US and extolling its military (*Save the Freedom* and *Resistance Commander: Battle of Amerli*); Turkish war games defending the intervention against the Kurds in northern Syria (*Adalet Namluda 2*); the confrontation between the Sri Lankan government and the Liberation Tigers of Tamil Eelam through a heroic sniper, *Nero* (Arimac, 2021); or the disputes between Armenia and Azerbaijan over Nagorno Karabakh in the trilogy *Under Occupation* (AzDimension, 2015–2017). This diversity and multiplicity of video games promoted by different international state actors proves that this medium is a tool with enormous political potential.

Suggested Reading

Bekkers, V. and Moody, R. (2015). *Visual Culture and Public Policy*. Routledge.

Bogost, I. (2009). *Persuasive Games: The Expressive Power of Videogames*. The MIT Press.

Hutchinson, E. and Bleiker, R. (2014). Theorizing Emotions in World Politics. *International Theory* 6 (3), 491–514. https://doi.org/10.1017/S1752971914000232

Lammes, S. (2008). Spatial Regimes of the Digital Playground: Cultural Functions of Spatial Practices in Computer Games. *Space and Culture* 11 (3), 260–272. https://doi.org/10.1177/1206331208319150

MacDonald, F., Hughes, R., and Dodds, K. (Eds.) (2010). *Observant States. Geopolitics and Visual Culture*. I.B. Tauris.

Schneider, F. (2018). *China's Digital Nationalism*. Oxford University Press.

References

Ahmed, T. et al. (2020). Face-off between India and China in Galwan Valley: An Analysis of Chinese Incursions and Interests. *Electronic Research Journal of Social Sciences and Humanities*, 2 (3), 38–50. http://www.eresearchjournal.com/wp-content/uploads/2020/06/4.-gulwan-valley.pdf

Al-Rawi, A. (2016). Video Games, Terrorism, and ISIS's Jihad 3.0. *Terrorism and Political Violence* 30 (4), 740–760. https://doi.org/10.1080/09546553.2016.1207633

Anable, A. (2018). *Playing with Feelings. Video Games and Affect*. University of Minnesota Press.

Balakumar, K. (2021). FAU-G, Made-in-India war game, crosses 5 million downloads. *Techradar*. 27 January. https://www.techradar.com/in/news/fau-g-made-in-india-war-game-gets-over-a-million-downloads-on-day-one

Batchelor, J. (2020). Call of Duty Black Ops Cold War trailer blocked in China. *Games Industry. biz*. 25 August. https://www.gamesindustry.biz/articles/2020-08-25-call-of-duty-black-ops-cold-war-trailer-blocked-in-china

Bekkers, V. and Moody, R. (2015). *Visual Culture and Public Policy*. Routledge.

Bleiker, R. (2001). The Aesthetic Turn in International Political Theory. *Millennium: Journal of International Studies* 30 (3), 509–533. https://doi.org/10.1177/03058298010300031001

Bleiker, R., Campbell, D., Hutchison, E., and Nicholson, X. (2013). The Visual Dehumanisation of Refugees. *Australian Journal of Political Science* 48 (4), 398–416. https://doi.org/10.1080/10361146.2013.840769

Bleiker, R. (2018). *Visual Global Politics*. Routledge.

Bleiker, R. (2020). The Politics of Images: A Pluralist Methodological Framework. In S. Choi, A. Selmeczi, and E. Strausz (Eds.), *Critical Methods for the Study of World Politics. Creativity and Transformation* (272–288). Routledge.

Bogost, I. (2009). *Persuasive Games: The Expressive Power of Videogames*. The MIT Press.

Bos, D. (2021). Playful Encounters: Games for Geopolitical Change. *Geopolitics* 28 (3), 1–25. https://www.tandfonline.com/doi/full/10.1080/14650045.2021.2002846

Carter, S. and McCormarck, D. (2010). Affectivity and Geopolitical Images. In F. MacDonald, R. Hughes, and K. Dodds (Eds.), *Observant States. Geopolitics and Visual Culture* (103–122). I.B. Tauris.

Castells, M. (2009). *Communication Power*. Oxford University Press.

Colley, T. (2020). Strategic Narratives and War Propaganda. In P. Baines, N. O'Shaughnessy, and N. Snow (Eds.), *The SAGE Handbook of Propaganda* (38–54). SAGE Publications Ltd.

Crawford, N. (2000). The Passion of World Politics: Propositions on Emotion and Emotional Relationships. *International Security* 24 (4). http://www.jstor.org/stable/2539317

Cull, N. (2008). Public Diplomacy: Taxonomies and Histories. *The Annals of the American Academy of Political and Social Science* 616, 31–54. https://www.jstor.org/stable/25097993

Davies, H. (2020). Hong Kong and Insect Rhetoric: The Spatial Politics of Pokémon Go. *DIGRA2020 Proceedings*. https://bit.ly/3G0FbXo

Defense Insight (2021). FAU-G Game Trailer & FAU-G Anthem [Video Archive]. 3 January. YouTube. https://www.youtube.com/watch?v=kCH8tem1DjE

Der Derian, J. (2009). *Virtuous War: Mapping the Military-Industrial-Media-Entertainment Network*. Routledge.

Dittmer, J. and Bos, D. (2019). *Popular Culture, Geopolitics, and Identity*. Rowman & Littlefield.

Dunbar, R., Marriot, A., and Duncan, N. (1997). Human Conversational Behavior. *Human Nature* 8 (3), 231–246. https://doi.org/10.1007/BF02912493

Dune, T., Kurki, M., and Smith, S. (2020). *International Relations Theories*. 5th edition. Oxford University Press.

Fedorova, K. (2015). Augmented Reality Art and Proprioception: Towards a Theoretical Framework. *Proceedings of the 21st International Symposium on Electronic Art (ISEA 2015)*. https://isea2015.org/proceeding/submissions/ISEA2015_submission_281.pdf

Forest, J. (Ed.) (2009). *Influence Warfare. How Terrorists and Governments Fight to Shape Perceptions in a War of Idea*. Praeger Security International.

Gabriel, S. (2021). Hate Speech in Digital Games. Are Online Games a Place of Discrimination and Exclusion. In N. Denk, A. Serada, A. Pfeiffer, and T. Wernbacher (Eds.), *A Ludic Society* (297–313). Donau-Universität Krems.

Gartner, S. and Gelpi, C. (2016). The Affect and Effect of Images of War on Individual Opinion and Emotions. *International Interactions* 42 (1), 172–188. https://doi.org/10.1080/03050629.2015.1051620

Gómez-García, S., Chicharro-Merayo, M., Vicent-Ibañez, M., and Durantez-Stolle, P. (2022). La política a la que jugamos. Cultura, videojuegos y ludoficción política en la Plataforma Steam. *Index-comunicación* 12 (2), 277–303. https://doi.org/10.33732/ixc/12/02Lapoli

Gómez-García, S., Paz-Rebollo, M., and Cabeza-San-Deogracias, J. (2021). Newsgames against Hate Speech in the Refugee Crisis. *Comunicar* 67, 123–133. https://doi.org/10.3916/C67-2021-10

Hall, I. (2019). *Modi and the Reinvention of Indian Foreign Policy*. Bristol University Press.

Handrahan, M (2020). India's prime minister appeals for games based on Indian culture and folk tales. *Gamesindustry.biz*. 26 August. https://www.gamesindustry.biz/articles/2020-08-26-indias-prime-minister-appeals-for-games-based-on-indian-culture-and-folk-tales

Hansen, L. (2018). Images and International Security. In A. Gheciu and W. Wohlforth (Eds.), *The Oxford Handbook of International Security* (593–606). Oxford University Press.

Heider, F. and Simmel, M. (1944). An Experimental Study of Apparent Behavior. *The American Journal of Psychology* 57 (2), 243–259. https://doi.org/1416950

Holmes, O. (2021). No cults, no politics, no ghouls: how China censors the video game world. *The Guardian*. 15 July. https://www.theguardian.com/news/2021/jul/15/china-video-game-censorship-tencent-netease-blizzard

Hutchinson, E. and Bleiker, R. (2014). Theorizing Emotions in World Politics. *International Theory* 6 (3), 491–514. https://doi.org/10.1017/S1752971914000232

ISPR (2018). Glorious Resolve. https://www.ispr.gov.pk/PakDefGames

Jervis, R. (1976). *Perception and Misperception in International Ethics*. Princeton University Press.

Kaempf, S. (2018). Digital Media. In R. Bleiker (Ed.), *Visual Global Politics* (99–103). Routledge.

Kang, L. (2012). Searching for a New Cultural Identity: China's Soft Power and Media Culture Today. *Journal of Contemporary China*, 21 (78), 915–931. http://dx.doi.org/10.1080/10670 564.2012.701032

Kaplan, R. (2012). *The Revenge of Geography: What the Map Tells Us About Coming Conflicts and the Battle Against Fate*. Random House.

Kirkpatrick, E. (2015). Visuality, Photography, and Media in International Relations Theory: A Review. *Media, War & Conflict* 8 (2), 199–212. https://doi.org/10.1177/1750635215584281

LaCapria, K. (2021). Uncensored library in Minecraft. *Truth or Fiction?* 23 August. https://www.truthorfiction.com/uncensored-library-in-minecraft/

Lammes, S. (2008). Spatial Regimes of the Digital Playground: Cultural Functions of Spatial Practices in Computer Games. *Space and Culture* 11 (3), 260–272. https://doi.org/10.1177/1206331208319150

MacDonald, F., Hughes, R., and Dodds, K (Eds.) (2010). *Observant States. Geopolitics and Visual Culture*. I.B. Tauris.

MazherHussain, S., Zahid, M., and Chodhry, S. (2019). ISPR'S Visual Content's Role in Image Building of Pakistan. *Orient Research Journal of Social Sciences* 4 (2), 280–294. https://www.gcwus.edu.pk/wp-content/uploads/2019/12/11.-ISPRS-Visual-Contents-Role-in-Image-Building-of-Pakistan.pdf

McCourt, D. (2022). *The New Constructivism in International Relations Theory*. Bristol University Press.

McLeod, D. (2016). *India and Pakistan. Friends, Rivals or Enemies?* Routledge.

Mercer, J. (2006). Human Nature and the First Image: Emotion in International Politics. *Journal of International Relations and Development* 9, 288–303. https://doi.org/10.1057/palgrave.jird.1800091

Methman, C. (2014). Visualising Climate-Refugees: Race, Vulnerability, and Resilience in Global Liberal Politics. *International Political Sociology* 8 (4), 416–435. https://doi.org/10.1111/ips.12071

Ming-Tak, M. and Wang, Y. (2021). How Propagames Work as a Part of Digital Authoritarianism: An Analysis of a Popular Chinese Propagame. *Media, Culture & Society* 43 (8), 1431–1448. https://doi.org/10.1177/01634437211029846

Mitchell, L. (2018). *Ludopolitics: Videogames Against Control*. John Hunt Publishing.

Moreno, A. (2020). India y el mundo del videojuego. Videojuegos & Política – Vol. II. *Hyperhype*. 20 October. https://www.hyperhype.es/videojuegos-politica-vol-ii-india-y-el-mundo-de-los-videojuegos/

Moreno, A. (2021). Videojuegos & Política – Vol. XIV. Geopolítica a través del tráiler. *Hyperhype*. 18 November. https://www.hyperhype.es/videojuegos-politica-vol-xiv-geopolitica-a-traves-del-trailer-parte-ii/

Moreno, A. (2021). *Tecnonacionalismo, guerra digital y videojuegos en China.* Ediciones UCM.

Naftali, O. (2014). Marketing War and the Military to Children and Youth in China: Little Red Soldiers in the Digital Age. *China Information* 28 (1), 3–25. https://doi.org/10.1177/09202 03X13513101

Nie, H. (2013). Gaming, Nationalism, and Ideological Works in Contemporary China: Online Games based on the War of Resistance against Japan. *Journal of Contemporary China* 22 (81), 499–517. https://doi.org/10.1080/10670564.2012.748968

NikoPartners (2020). Indian's ban of Chinese apps and its impacts to the country's game market. https://nikopartners.com/indias-ban-of-chinese-apps-and-its-impacts-to-the-countrys-game-market/

Osofsky, M, Bandura, A., and Zimbardo, P. (2005). The Role of Moral Disengagement in the Execution Process. *Law and Human Behavior* 29, 371–393. https://doi.org/10.1007/s10 979-005-4930-1

Paul, T. (2018). *The China-India Rivalry in the Globalization Era.* Georgetown University Press.

Pearcy, A. (2020). Animal Crossing Isn't Just a Game – It's a Political Platform. *One Zero.* 28 May. https://onezero.medium.com/animal-crossing-isn-t-just-a-game-it-s-a-political-platf orm-c12a29e7cde

Prucha, N. (2011). Worldwide Online Jihad versus the Gaming Industry. Reloaded-Ventures of the Web. In R. Lohlker (Ed.), *New Approaches to the Analysis of Jihadism* (153–182). V&R Unipress GmbH.

Raessens, J. (2006). Playful Identities, or the Ludification of Culture. *Games and Culture* 1 (1), 52–57. doi.org/10.1177/1555412005281779

Robinson, N. (2012). Videogames, Persuasion and the War on Terror: Escaping or Embedding the Military—Entertainment Complex. *Political Studies* 60, 517–19. https://doi.org/10.1111/j.1467-9248.2011.00923.x

Robinson, N. (2015). Have You Won the War on Terror? Military Videogames and the State of American Exceptionalism. *Millennium: Journal of International Studies* 43, 450–470. https://doi.org/10.1177/0305829814557557

Sasley, B. (2011). Theorizing States Emotions. *International Studies Review* 13 (3), 452–476. https://doi.org/10.1111/j.1468-2486.2011.01049.x

Schlegel, L. (2020). Jumanji Extremism? How Games and Gamification Could Facilitate Radicalization Processes. *Journal for Deradicalization* 23, 1–44. https://journals.sfu.ca/jd/index.php/jd/article/view/359/223

Schneider, F. (2018). *China's Digital Nationalism.* Oxford University Press.

Schneider, F. (2021). Emergent Nationalism in China's Sociotechnical Networks: How Technological Affordance and Complexity Amplify Digital Nationalism. *Nation and Nationalism* 28 (1), 267–285. https://doi.org/10.1111/nana.12779

Schulzke, M. (2014). Simulating Terrorism and Insurgency: Video Games in the War of Ideas. *Cambridge Review of International Affairs* 27 (4), 627–643. https://doi.org/10.1080/09557 571.2014.960508

Schulzke, M. (2016). War by Other Means: Mobile Gaming and the 2014 Israel-Gaza Conflict. *Review of International Studies* 1 (3), 1–22. https://doi.org/10.1017/S0260210515000510

Seo, H. (2020). Visual Propaganda and Social Media. In P. Baines, N. O'Shaughnessy, and N. Snow (Eds.), *The SAGE Handbook of Propaganda* (126–136). SAGE Publications Ltd.

Shapiro, M. (2013). *Studies in Trans-Disciplinary Method.* Routledge.

Sicart, M. (2014). *Play Matters.* The MIT Press.

The Economic Times (2020). India's answer to PUBG? Akshay Kumar announces the launch of action game FAU-G. 8 September. https://economictimes.indiatimes.com/tech/software/indias-answer-to-pubg-akshay-kumar-announces-the-launch-of-action-game-fau-g/articleshow/77931375.cms

Tse, E. (2015). *China's Disruptors. How Alibaba, Xiaomi, Tencent and other companies are changing the rules of business.* Portfolio / Penguin Publishing Group.

Van Rythoven, E. (2021). Walter Lippmann, Emotion, and the History of International Theory. *International Theory* 14 (3), 1–25.https://doi.org/10.1017/S1752971921000178

Van Veeren, E. (2009). Interrogating 24: Making Sense of US Counter-terrorism in the Global War on Terrorism. *New Political Science* 31 (3), 361–384. https://doi.org/10.1080/07393140903105991

Venegas, A. (2020). *Pasado Interactivo. Memoria e historia en el videojuego.* Sans Soleins Ediciones.

Venegas, A. and Moreno, A (2021). *Protestas interactivas. El videojuego como medio de reivindicación política y social.* Shangrila.

Wang, Z. (2014). *Never Forget National Humiliation. Historical Memory in Chinese Politics and Foreign Relations.* Columbia University Press.

Wheatcroft, J., Jump, M., Breckell, A., and Adams-White, J. (2017). Unmanned aerial Systems (UAS) Operators Accuracy and Confidence of Decisions: Professional Pilots or Video Game Players? *Cogent Psychology* 4 (1), 1–23. https://www.tandfonline.com/doi/full/10.1080/23311908.2017.1327628

Wu, Y. (2014). Modern Chinese National-Cultural Identity in the Context of Globalization. *Transtext(e)s Transcultures* 7, 1–12. https://doi.org/10.4000/transtexts.456

Young, C. (2021). Black Myth: Wukong. The world exclusive story behind the breakout Actio RPG. *IGN.* 19 February. https://www.ign.com/articles/black-myth-wukong-making-of-behind-the-scenes-exclusive

Ludography

Adalet Namluda 2 (Rigbak,2021)
Animal Crossing: New Horizons (Nintendo, 2020)
FAU-G (nCore Games, 2021)
Fortnite Battle Royale (Epic Games, 2017)
Glorious Mission (Giant Interactive Group, 2013)
Glorious Resolve (Rockville Games, 2018)
Heroes of 71 (Mindfisher Games Inc,2017)
H1Z1 (Daybreak Game, 2015)
Nero (Arimac, 2021)
Resistance Commander of the resistance: Battle of Amerli (Monadian Media, 2022)
Pokémon Go (Niantic Lab, 2016)
Resistance War Online (PowerNet Interactive, 2007).
Save the Freedom (Iran's Revolutionary Guard Corps, 2021)
Under Occupation (AzDimension, 2015–2017)

CHAPTER 34

DIGITAL DIPLOMACY DURING WARS AND CONFLICTS

MORAN YARCHI

INTRODUCTION

DEVELOPMENTS in the digital sphere have enabled various political actors to communicate with the public—promote their messages, engage with different publics, and try to mobilize individuals to support their cause. Digital communication platforms in general and social media in particular have created many opportunities for the field of diplomacy and public diplomacy, but at the same time brought about many challenges and even threats. That is especially prominent in the realm of conflicts and wars, as the image component has become a significant aspect of today's conflicts, a component that could have real implications for the ability of political actors to achieve their goals. This chapter focuses on digital diplomacy during wars and conflicts, while emphasizing political actors' usage of digital platforms as part of the 'Image War'.

Recent years have seen a significant increase in the usage of digital diplomacy during conflicts, while more political actors—both state and non-state actors—have learned how to take advantage of various social media platforms (taking into consideration the unique characteristics of each platform and its target audience), while realizing its potential to influence perceptions and public opinion. Here too, similar to other fields in which digital diplomacy is being used (Bjola and Holmes, 2015; Copeland, 2013; Manor and Adiku, 2021), we see that countries and ministries of foreign affairs (MFAs) tend to be late adopters of technologies and more reactive to the actions of other political actors, while non-state organizations are more tech-savvy and use the platforms to their benefit much faster (Weimann, 2016). Due to the nature of the digital sphere and the characteristics of social media, we see more individuals engaging in diplomatic efforts in regard to political issues and conflicts, alongside other non-institutionalized initiatives that receive public attention and serve political actors in their attempt to rally international support.

Before we can discuss various examples from recent years, such as the war in Ukraine, various rounds of the Israeli-Palestinian conflict, or the United States' activity in the Middle East, we need to gain a better understanding of the atmosphere of today's conflicts, and the role of the digital sphere as a fighting arena. To this end, the chapter begins with a presentation of the image war.

The Image War and the Battle over Perceptions

Twenty-first-century conflicts differ from past conflicts because they are battles of ideas and not only of military power. Conflicts today are fought simultaneously in a few arenas: the military front, the home front, and the international front. Each of these fighting arenas includes political, legal, and image components. In today's reality, image considerations play a crucial role in political actors' ability to achieve their goals, so the image component has a significant impact on both the political and the legal components (Yarchi and Ayalon, 2023; Ganor, 2012). Alongside the military confrontation, an image war and a fight over perceptions takes place (Rabasa, 2011; Roger, 2013). Each side of the conflict tries to promote its narrative and justify its ideas, beliefs, and actions, in an attempt to gain the empathy and support of the public, as this could help actors achieve their political goals (Ayalon, Popovich, and Yarchi, 2016; van Evera, 2006; Yarchi and Ayalon, 2023). If so, the image war and the competition over the ability to promote the actors' narrative represents an important front in the comprehensive struggle between antagonists in today's conflicts and wars (Archetti, 2010; Betz, 2008; Douglas, 2007). Political actors' understanding regarding the importance of this fighting arena during wars and conflicts has led them to invest time and resources in an attempt to influence public perceptions in their favour, using all available tools and platforms, especially social media (Yarchi, 2022).

The discussion about the image war is wider than visual components, although visual images are important for the creation of public world views, as they make complicated situations seem simplistic and easy to interpret, thus influencing the audience's perceptions. In this chapter, references to the image war refer to the broader image of political actors, which includes the way they present themselves (that is, the story or narrative they try to share), and the way they are perceived by the international arena.

Wars and events that occur as part of conflicts are highly newsworthy, creating dramatic, negative, and personalized stories that fit journalistic norms, and therefore tend to 'glue' the audience to the screens, making them consume more news (Altheide, 1997; Entman, 2003; Knightley, 2004; Wolfsfeld, 2022; Wolfsfeld and Yarchi, 2015). In recent years we have seen similar attention being given to conflicts and war related issues by individual users on social media platforms, in line with the tendency of traditional outlets to extensively cover those stories, further enhancing the news value of this type of event or story. The notion of extensive attention to wars, and its impact on the image of the actors involved in the conflict, is not a new phenomenon, but it has become increasingly prominent in recent years as people consume information around the clock, especially via social media. The reality in which conflicts receive extensive attention, and the understanding regarding its impact on public opinion, has led political actors to view the media as a fighting arena in which they need to present their arguments and share their narratives.

The coverage of conflicts has an emotional impact on the public, since images of victimization, death, and destruction can have powerful effects on both local populations and the international community (Entman, 2003; Knightley, 2004; Wolfsfeld, 1997). This is especially the case when dealing with visual images, as they have a stronger cognitive impact on consumers. Exposure to visual images, such as pictures and videos, tends to have a great impact on people's perceptions regarding the situation, as they perceive the occurrences as reality, since they sensed it with their own senses and did not just hear or read about it (Hoskins and O'Loughlin, 2010; O'Loughlin, 2011). If so, exposure to visual images that fit a political actor's narrative can help that actor gain public support for their cause.

Various revolutions that have taken place simultaneously during the last few decades have changed the political environment, influencing aspects of our reality, including violent conflicts. Some of those revolutions have occurred in the political arena—in which more nations became democracies, mostly following World War II and the collapse of the Soviet Union, which enhanced the power of the public. There have been technological developments (which led to the information age), and globalization—the social revolution of our time (Gilboa, 2000; Yarchi and Ayalon, 2023). Technological developments, together with globalization, have led to a reality in which we are all surrounded by information. Satellite capabilities that enabled people to receive live coverage of events globally, followed by the spread of the Internet and especially social media, have altered the flow of information around the world. In this reality, in which many people are both consumers and producers of information,[1] social networks have further empowered individuals and organizations to present information and communicate their message directly to their target audience, without the mediation of journalists and editors (the gatekeepers of traditional media) and have allowed citizens to take an active part in the image war, as seen in recent conflicts (Cull, 2011; Yarchi, Samuel-Azran, and Bar-David, 2017). Therefore, people are surrounded by extensive media coverage about various occurrences worldwide, which helps them shape their world views on the issues at hand, especially while dealing with foreign affairs, in which most people have less knowledge and experience that is based on sources other than the media (Soroka, 2003).

---

[1] This phenomenon, which is unique to the online realm, is known as 'prosumers', since users can consume information as well as produce and distribute content, especially on social media. For more information, see Kaplan and Haenlein (2010).

The spread of information in general and visual images in particular on social media is salient during conflicts as some of the platforms (Instagram, YouTube, TikTok, etc.) are visual in nature. Alongside the opportunities to promote their messages (enabling them to communicate directly with various target audiences, promoting their messages as they see fit), this interconnected reality creates various challenges and even threats for political actors. In the past, while dealing only with traditional media outlets, institutionalized actors and mostly countries were better able to control the flow of information and the narrative, as they had greater access to journalists and editors (Ayalon, Popovich, and Yarchi, 2016). Social media changed that reality, as anyone with an Internet connection could upload information as they saw fit, with almost no editing or censorship, while using minimal resources (Weimann, 2006). This has enabled us, the public, to be exposed to different voices or world views, but on the other hand has enabled different actors to spread misinformation and disinformation. Therefore, countries and other political actors need to compete over attention and support with other actors—some of whom are much faster and more Internet-savvy than states—and fight against the spread of fake news, which is in many cases more newsworthy and tends to spread faster, reach more people, and generate more engagement (Vosoughi, Roy, and Aral, 2018).

Many of today's conflicts are asymmetrical in nature, with large disparities between the actors involved in the conflict (non-state actors fighting states, or situations in which superpowers are fighting against small states). In those wars especially, the extensive attention affects the behaviour of the actors involved in the conflict. We would logically expect the stronger adversary to be more powerful and achieve victory while using force. However, various restrictions, most of which are related to the actors' image (especially through public opinion and fear of international sanctions), prevent them from using their military capabilities. The vast disparity between the actors in these kinds of conflicts and the extensive media coverage environment creates a 'reverse asymmetry' effect; the weaker adversary uses the media and images as a weapon and, through coverage and public opinion, tries to raise support (and international intervention) and balance the conflict. In this reality, the camera and visual images are weapons (Roger, 2013) and usually serve the weaker adversary. Since the Western media's narrative is now one of compassion, in which people are empathetic towards victims (in line with Judeo-Christian values), in terms of media coverage the weaker side is in fact the stronger side as it usually has a better—newsworthy—story, in a media environment that emphasizes victimization (Ayalon, Popovich, and Yarchi, 2016; Wolfsfeld, 1997; Wolfsfeld, 2022). Especially in those asymmetrical conflicts, the weaker side relies on media attention, while the stronger side would rather not receive any coverage, allowing it to conduct its actions in the conflict as it sees fit, only according to military needs without any image considerations that may restrict its use of force (Yarchi, 2022).

In this reality of information space conflicts—asymmetric conflicts that receive extensive media coverage (Ayalon, Popovich, and Yarchi, 2016)—the geographical borders of the conflict are less important. Since images serve as weapons, the conflict's borders are anywhere that people are exposed to those images and can receive information about the conflict, either through traditional or social media. In the current political environment, public opinion (and, due to its impact on public opinion, the media coverage itself) has an impact on the creation of foreign policies and, ultimately, on the ability of countries to achieve their goals in the international arena (de Vreese, Boomgaarden, and Semetko, 2011; Entman, 2008). The influence on publics and policies is a process; the representation of the conflict and the political actors over time can shape the public world views on the issue and actors (especially since the media's coverage is their main source of information). When the representation of political actors fits a certain narrative, it has a cognitive effect on the audience and can shape their attitudes regarding the actors involved in the war (Yarchi, 2016; Soroka, 2003). As mentioned above, conflicts today are battles of ideas and perceptions, and not just battles of military power. Receiving the empathy of foreign publics is a main goal of political actors, as they understand the power that public opinion has in the current reality, first on people's attitudes and behaviours toward the actors involved in a conflict (their support, consumption patterns, electoral decisions, etc.), and later on their governments' policies, which could have implications for the political actors involved in the conflict (Archetti, 2010; Rabasa, 2011; van Evera, 2006). This reality leads political actors to perceive the image war as a significant fighting arena, and through the usage of public diplomacy on various outlets—these days mostly on digital platforms—seek to gain the support of the international community.

If so, many political actors in today's political environment understand the importance of their international image and its impact on the ability to achieve their goals, especially during conflicts, and invest resources into generating support on social media platforms while using digital diplomacy tactics. A few strategic communication factors can be helpful in the examination of their efforts and success:

a. *The identity of the political actor.* While examining political actors trying to promote their messages on social media platforms, two indicators should be taken into account. First, in line with the reverse asymmetry effect presented above, there is a difference between the stronger adversary's ability to generate support, and that of the weaker adversary—as the latter usually has a better story of victimization that can create empathy and fits the narrative of compassion. Thus, stronger adversaries work harder in their attempt to generate international support on social media (Ayalon, Popovich, and Yarchi, 2016). The second indicator is the type of actor promoting messages—here we see differences between official governmental messages and civic initiatives. As mentioned above, the nature of social media allows individuals and organizations to engage with foreign audiences and be active in digital diplomacy. In many cases, those civic diplomacy initiatives are successful in generating support as they appear more authentic and credible in comparison to governmental messages that could appear as propaganda (Yarchi, Samuel-Azran, and Bar-David, 2017).

b. *Narratives and messages.* Political actors involved in conflicts tend to promote a similar narrative (in line with Entman's 1993 definition of framing): they all present themselves as the victim (that is the problem), place the blame on the other side of the conflict (that is the cause), and offer their solution (Yarchi, 2014). In addition, their messages could be divided into two types: emphasizing their legitimacy or delegitimizing the other side (Samuel-Azran and Yarchi, 2018)—in line with Entman's (2003) claim that political actors are successful when they are able to promote their narrative or prevent the other side from promoting their messages.

c. *Target audiences.* Political actors are communicating with various target audiences on social media. The two most salient audiences during conflicts are the enemy and the international community, as the messages aimed at those two audiences are very different. In their communication to the international community, actors emphasize their side of the conflict story and victimization while placing the blame on the other side, whereas their communication aimed at the enemy focuses on the price they—the enemy—are paying due to the conflict, alongside messages of pride and deterrence (Al-Rawi, 2020; Samuel-Azran and Yarchi, 2018; Yarchi, 2022).

DIGITAL DIPLOMACY AND THE IMAGE WAR

As presented above, the image war is a prominent aspect of conflicts in the digital age, and public diplomacy—the direct communication with foreign peoples, with the aim of affecting their thinking and, ultimately, that of their governments (Malone, 1985)—helps political actors influence publics' perceptions and gain their empathy and support. In the current media environment, many of those efforts by political actors occur in the digital sphere and especially on social media platforms, due to their popularity among users around the world. This section will focus on usages of digital diplomacy as a salient tool for political actors during conflicts, while presenting various case studies from recent conflicts. Three case studies will be presented in an attempt to present political actors' digital usage in promoting their conflict narrative, while taking into account the political actor's identity, its narrative, and its target audience. First, we focus on the United States' activity in the Middle East, which began following the attacks of 11 September 2001; we then look at examples from different rounds of the Israeli-Palestinian conflict, and conclude with the most recent example: the 2022 Russian invasion of Ukraine.

The United States' Activity in the Middle East

The terror attacks of 11 September 2001, and the American invasion of Afghanistan that followed it, led the United States to realize that it was facing a different kind of war. It may have been fighting against Al-Qaida and global Jihad on the military battlefield, but in order to defeat radical Islam it needed to engage in a different fighting arena— the war of ideas. In the battle over the 'hearts and minds' of the Muslim world, the

United States needed to engage with the Muslim public, using public diplomacy as its main tool, and fight against the radical Islam anti-American sentiment, mostly on digital platforms (van Ham, 2003; Krause and van Evera, 2009). Those experiences have led both practitioners and scholars to the understanding that, in the information era, in order to stop extremism, Western democracies must fight against the spread of the terrorist narrative and replace it with a 'better story' (Casebeer and Russell, 2005). While facing the challenges in the Middle East following the September 11 attacks, the United States pioneered the field of digital diplomacy. In 2002, the State Department initiated the Taskforce on eDiplomacy, whose mission was to actively promote the United States' public diplomacy online (Hanson, 2012).

In order to fight against terrorism, especially since terror organizations utilize the digital sphere as part of their fighting strategies (Weimann, 2016; Yarchi, 2019), the United States had to communicate its messages on various platforms, taking into account different target audiences. On top of its general digital diplomacy efforts, targeting mostly other Western democracies and allies, efforts were made to communicate with the Arab and Muslim world—the society of the enemy in the fight against Islamic terrorism. The Department of State's Digital Outreach Team (DOT) was established in 2006 with the aim of linking the United States Department of State with the Arab masses via the Internet, while communicating in various Middle Eastern languages (mainly Arabic) on digital platforms.[2] The DOT's communication had various goals. On one hand, it sought to present American foreign policies as well as cultural aspects of the American society, in an attempt to legitimize the United States. On the other hand, a lot of its activity was centred around countering extremists' ideology, especially those who express animosity against the United States, as part of the efforts to delegitimize terrorists' activities (mostly Al-Qaida and ISIS) (Al-Rawi, 2020; Cottee, 2015; Khatib, Dutton, and Thelwall, 2012; Miller and Higham, 2015). Most of the responses to the DOT's activity on social media platforms were negative, presenting mistrust in the United States and criticizing its policies, as its actions were perceived as American propaganda (Al-Rawi, 2020).

The actions taken by the United States during its withdrawal from Afghanistan in 2021 show that although it had come a long way since its invasion of that country in 2001, there is still a long way to go in the realm of diplomacy and in its understanding of the importance of image considerations. The images of Afghani people trying to hold onto the wheels of the American aircraft leaving the country, sending a message of desperate people who have nothing to lose in light of the Taliban's return to power, resonate with the notion of the narrative of compassion and damage the United States' international image and credibility. Understanding the importance of its international reputation, and the impact of those images, the United States and its diplomats were using the digital sphere in an attempt to prevent an image crisis, as presented in various

---

[2] The DOT team members are American citizens with Middle Eastern origins who have a deep understanding of both the languages and cultures of their target audiences, and attempt to connect with their audience in an authentic manner.

social media publications, mostly on Twitter, as revealed in a qualitative content analysis of thirty social media posts, examining the themes promoted as part of the American digital diplomacy efforts. First, President Biden and Secretary of State Blinken were presenting their country's narrative, claiming that the United States had completed its mission in Afghanistan—focusing on counterterrorism and not nation building. At the same time, they emphasized United States' continuing efforts, alongside its allies (among them the EU and NATO) to build a better future for the people of Afghanistan. Following those official statements, and in line with the understanding regarding the importance of visual images and their cognitive effect, the department of defence had published various pictures promoting a different frame—presenting American humanitarian activity in Afghanistan, in pictures of American troops providing water and food or playing with Afghan children, and taking care of Afghan babies. Those visuals of humanitarian aid were part of an attempt to promote a different narrative than the visuals of the desperate deserted Afghani people in Kabul airport, and to send a message that the United States remains committed to the future of Afghanistan. Only time will tell whether those efforts were successful in reshaping public perceptions, as the images of Kabul airport were very powerful. Considering international image concerns, the United States could have handled the situation at the airport differently and have a better starting point in the competition over the framing of American withdrawal from Afghanistan.[3]

Digital Diplomacy in the Israeli-Palestinian Conflict

The second case study presented here deals with the Israeli-Palestinian conflict. Since social media platforms emerged and became popular outlets of communication, we have witnessed a few rounds of the conflict, mostly with clashes between the terror organization Hamas and the Israeli military (the IDF). The rounds of 2008–09; 2012; 2014; and 2021, among other events occurring in the conflict, have provided us with many opportunities to examine the actors' activities in the realm of the image war and their digital efforts to garner international support.

Israel is considered a pioneer in the field of digital diplomacy in general, and in relation to wars and conflicts in particular (Manor and Crilley, 2020). In addition to the MFA's widespread international digital activity, the IDF's spokesperson also operates accounts on various platforms and in different languages, while trying to communicate with foreign publics. During the 2008–09 round of the conflict, in the initial stages of social media platforms, the digital efforts were minor and focused mostly on YouTube. However, the 2012 round had a very different online presence; first and foremost, the

---

[3] More information about the digital diplomacy efforts during the American withdrawal from Afghanistan can be found in Ilan Manor's blog, at: https://digdipblog.com/2021/08/19/who-won-the-framing-competition-over-afghanistan-a-twitter-analysis/; https://digdipblog.com/2021/08/24/how-the-us-army-visually-narrates-the-fall-of-afghanistan/

military operation was announced on Twitter in publications by official Israeli accounts (Manor and Crilley, 2018). In addition, the various official accounts (MFA, IDF, and other Israeli accounts) on different platforms presented updates and information throughout the war, as they also did in other rounds of the conflict that followed the 2012 round. Interestingly, although the Israeli accounts used digital platforms to promote their narrative, they were less successful at garnering international support than the Palestinian side, while digital technologies have become an increasingly important tool for Palestinians and pro-Palestinian solidarity groups, which use the online realm to generate support for the Palestinian cause (Aouragh, 2016). In line with the characteristics of the image war, the Palestinians, as the weaker side of the conflict, were able to create a reverse asymmetry effect—as their story of victimization is stronger than the Israeli narrative, and compatible with the notion of the narrative of compassion presented above, they were able to create more engagement and receive more international support on social media outlets. The Palestinian digital publications focus mostly on victimization and use emotional images and information (presenting casualties, the suffering of children, and destruction), while the Israeli messages focus more on rational and logic arguments, emphasizing legitimation for their actions (and at the same time delegitimizing Hamas' actions), while trying to counter the Palestinian narrative (Manor and Crilley, 2018; Manor and Crilley, 2020).

Similar to the American DOT initiative presented above, an interesting official Israeli initiative to communicate with Arab audiences can be found in the Facebook account of Avichai Adraee, the IDF Arabic spokesman. This account, which has over two million followers (mainly from Arab and Middle Eastern countries), is very active and seeks to engage with the Arab world, while using Arabic and Arab culture as well as trends in the Arab world (and the online realm) to engage with its target audience (Samuel-Azran and Yarchi, 2018). A quantitative content analysis of 414 posts, focusing on the message strategies used, reveals that the account promotes different messages; some focus on Israel's policies, actions, deterrence, and culture—promoting the legitimization of Israel—while others present a counter-narrative to anti-Israeli publications. Again, similar to the American DOT example, Adraee's account received mostly negative reactions from the followers, who nevertheless chose to continue following the account, enabling the IDF to communicate directly with Arab audiences. In their analysis of Adraee's Facebook page, Samuel-Azran and Yarchi (2018) referred to this trend of negative reactions and high engagement by saying they 'like to hate him'.

As mentioned above, public diplomacy in the digital age is characterized not only by governments' messages, but also by many citizen initiatives, where local citizens who believe in their government's cause disseminate government messages and even create and disseminate their own content on social media and other relevant online platforms to help their governments' policies reach and influence foreign audiences across the world. The Israeli-Palestinian conflict provides us with interesting examples of citizens' initiatives in the realm of digital diplomacy, and some in the field of celebrities' diplomacy. A salient example of a civic digital diplomacy initiative is the civilian Israeli 'Israel Under Fire' initiative, which operated during two rounds of the Palestinian-Israeli conflict (2012, 2014). The citizens' campaign, entitled Israel Under Fire, was designed to explain Israel's actions to the world and specifically to extend the image war to social media platforms. This citizens' diplomacy initiative engaged hundreds of volunteers and exposed over 40 million unique users to its materials and messages across different platforms. Their website was used by people from 117 countries, and their messages were translated into thirty languages. The volunteers created and managed five Facebook pages in five different languages, as well as a Twitter account and an Instagram account, all of which were updated daily during the operations, reaching a total of over 100,000 likes and followers. Yarchi, Samuel-Azran, and Bar-David's (2017) quantitative content analysis of their Facebook publications in English (examining 926 posts) revealed four message strategies (two of which legitimize Israel, and two of which delegitimize Hamas): (1) Israel has the Right (and Duty) to Defend Itself—focusing on justifying Israel's actions in light of attacks by Hamas and other hostile organizations; (2) What Would YOU Do?—encouraging international audiences to identify with Israelis while thinking about how they would have acted similarly under the same circumstances; (3) Exposing Hamas' Propaganda—exposing fake images and information published by Hamas on online platforms; and (4) Free Gaza from Hamas—promoting the idea that Hamas should be held accountable for the suffering of Palestinian civilians, as they have become captives of Hamas as a result of the organization's aggression. An analysis of the engagement the different strategies have generated (in terms of likes, shares, and comments) revealed that the identification-based strategy of 'What Would YOU Do?' was the most successful of the 'Israel Under Fire' civic diplomacy initiative's message strategy (Yarchi, Samuel-Azran, and Bar-David, 2017).

A recent development in the realm of digital diplomacy in relation to conflict is the usage of TikTok as a fighting arena. The platform, which has become very popular in recent years and is mostly used by younger users (many of whom are teenagers), is becoming a salient digital space for political issues in general, and of conflict-related issues in particular (Boxman-Shabtai, 2022; Weimann and Masri, 2023), as seen especially in the 2021 round of the Israel-Palestinian conflict (operation Guardian of the Walls). In line with the nature of the platform, most of the conflict-related content published on TikTok is user-generated content, with only a few posts by official institutions or the political actors involved in the conflict. Initial results of the civic diplomacy content posted by individuals on TikTok during the days of the 2021 war in Gaza, while focusing on two popular hashtags—#gazaunderattack and #israelunderattack—reveal wide usage of TikTok as an image fighting arena, with over 1,400 videos posted only with those two hashtags during the eleven days of the military operation (and many other videos posted under other related hashtags). The initial content analysis (examining 500 videos) reveals that many of those videos were directed at the international community (mainly using English as the communication language), and that, in line with the notion of the image war, each side was trying to present itself as the victim and its actions as justified. Two interesting trends are apparent in the initial results. First, and in line with the other TikTok publications, some of the conflict-related content published is presented as part of a TikTok challenge (similar to other popular challenges appearing on the platform). The Israel side was promoting the '15-second challenge', in which people presented what are they capable of doing in 15 seconds, the warning time Israelis have to run to a shelter each time a rocket is fired from Gaza into Israeli populated areas. This challenge fits other successful messaging strategies used by Israelis to generate support through identification (as presented above and in Yarchi, Samuel-Azran, and Bar-David, 2017). The second TikTok trend seen is an interesting usage of hashtags. In addition to presenting a few hashtags in the same post (in order to increase exposure), users from both sides tend to add hashtags representing the other side's narrative to those of their side (for example, a pro-Palestinian video that uses #israelunderattack in addition to #freegaza and #gazaunderattack), in an attempt to expend the exposure beyond their supporters. Thus, TikTok has recently become another arena for the fight over the image of political actors during conflicts, and its visual nature alongside its young audience is expected to influence perceptions.

The Ukrainian Image Front in the 2022 Russian Invasion to the Ukraine

The important role that digital diplomacy plays in the ability of political actors to achieve their goals was especially prominent during the recent Russian invasion of Ukraine. Most of the information presented below is based on Yarchi's (2022) detailed analysis of the Ukrainian battle over perceptions. Early in the war, the Ukrainian leadership understood that, in the current political environment, it is dealing with a different kind of war that will not be determined on the military battlefield alone. The Ukrainians realized that as the weaker adversary they could not defeat Russia in military battle, as the Russians have significant military superiority, and that the only way they would be able to achieve their goals is through an international intervention. Thus, they needed to garner the support of the international community and mobilize various countries and leaders to assist the Ukrainians in the fight over the future of their nation. Since the beginning of the war, President Zelensky has invested much of his time and efforts in the perceptions arena, using mainly digital diplomacy tools. He published updates and information on various social media outlets, communicating directly with publics and with world leaders seeking their support, and addressed parliaments around the world to mobilize international decision makers to act in favour of the Ukrainian people (while using digital platforms such as Zoom, which became very popular during the Covid-19 pandemic). The qualitative analysis is based on over 120 Ukrainian social media publications on different platforms (mostly in President Zelensky's accounts) and public addresses by President Zelensky.

The Ukrainian narrative fits that of political actors during conflicts—presenting themselves as victims, placing the blame on the other side, and offering their solution— in line with the problem, cause, and solution emphasis of framing (Entman, 1993). The problem: Ukraine presents itself as the victim, emphasizing the suffering of the

Ukrainian people, especially children and women, presenting casualties, destruction, and refugees who had to flee from their homes and lives. Those messages fit the strategy of the image war—presenting a narrative of compassion in an attempt to gain the support and empathy of the public (in line with reporting trends of the Western media). The Ukrainians have also emphasized their steadfastness in light of the challenges the war creates, sharing stories of heroism and presenting themselves as defenders of Europe and of Western values. Especially in their communication to the international community, the Ukrainians emphasize their shared values with the Western society—values of equality and democracy. The cause: blaming and delegitimizing Russia, and especially President Putin, for the invasion of their country, emphasizing their aggression and claiming that Russia is committing war crimes against Ukrainians (presenting examples such as a bombing of a maternity hospital or a theatre that served as a civilian shelter occupied by families and children). Furthermore, Russia and Putin have been presented as a danger to other European countries and as a threat to democratic values. The solution: the Ukrainian leadership emphasize two elements—the need to stop the war and Russian aggression while making sure Ukraine will continue to function as an independent sovereign state. At the same time, they talk about the need to defend Ukraine and the Ukrainian people. The Ukrainians call upon the international community to help them achieve those goals—putting pressure on Russia, providing Ukraine with military and financial aid, and any assistance that would bring the war to an end. As the weaker side in the conflict, and in line with the reverse asymmetry effect, the Ukrainians were successful at raising awareness for their cause, as their stories of victims, destruction, and refugees fit the narrative of compassion.

Interestingly, due to their need to keep receiving the support of the international community in an ongoing conflict, the Ukrainians use different message strategies over time; in the initial stages of the conflict their emphasis was on victimization trying to mobilize empathy. At the second stage their message strategy focused on Ukrainian bravery and steadfastness, and recently they moved to a third strategy promoting crowdfunding of military aid and turning social media users into an actual part of the War. The need to change strategies is unique to the Ukrainian case study, due to the duration of the war and the need to retain public attention in a reality of short media cycles in which social media users are flooded with information and ready to move to the next crisis. By using different message strategies and creating media events (such as Zelensky's public addresses in various events, among them the Grammy awards), the Ukrainians were able to stay on the agenda and keep garnering international support.

Again, we are witnessing an attempt to communicate with the population of the other side of the conflict: the Russian people. Especially during the first stages of the war, knowing that the Russian invasion of Ukraine was not being presented by the Russian media, due to the regime's control over the flow of information (and as part of President Putin's attempt to minimize criticism), the Ukrainians tried to influence the Russian public in a very creative manner, identifying the families of Russian troops fighting in Ukraine as the soft spot. First, they opened a 'hotline' that Russian mothers could call to find out whether their soldier sons had been captured or killed. Later, the Ukrainians started posting videos of Russian soldiers in captivity, calling their mothers, who only then learned that their children were fighting in Ukraine and had been captured (the mothers' reactions in those videos were mostly of anger at the sons who went to participate and fight in the war). The last creative use of this strategy, aimed at Russian soldiers' families, was an official announcement made by the Ukrainian Ministry of Defense that it would release any Russian soldier in captivity as long as his mother would come to pick him up from Ukraine. The Ukrainians repeatedly emphasized the Russian soldiers' families (and especially their mothers) as a tool to influence the Russian people's perceptions, in an attempt to raise awareness of the invasion of Russian troops to Ukraine, while using digital platforms in their communication. In addition, President Zelensky addressed the Russian people directly in some social media videos, speaking Russian and providing them with updates from the battlefield, focusing mostly on Russian casualties and the price Russia is paying in this war.

In addition to the official attempts made by the Ukrainian leadership and government, and due to the opportunities social media had provided to individuals and organizations, in terms of engaging with audiences and promoting their perspectives while trying to influence publics, various Ukrainian civic initiatives promoted their side of the conflict. These include citizens sharing their personal authentic war stories on social media, videos of experiences in shelters during bombings and visions of destruction, representations of the civic resistance to Russian aggression in the streets of Ukrainian cities, distribution of stories of heroism alongside stories of victims of the war, and authentic testimonies of refugees fleeing from conflict zones to save their lives. Another interesting social media trend was the ridiculing of Russian forces, presenting videos of their inability to function as fighting forces, pictures of their military equipment lying on the side of the road unable to move, and online humour about the Russian army, such as the example of selling a Russian tank on eBay. Various attempts to boost the Ukrainian spirit in this complex reality can also be found, such as infographics glorifying President Zelensky's leadership while presenting him as a superhero, TikTok videos of Ukrainian soldiers dancing to Western music, memes and jokes comparing Zelensky's leadership skills with Putin's inability to lead, and comparisons of Ukraine's successes with Russia's failures. The issue of the Russian invasion of Ukraine was a salient topic on social media during the first stages of the war, while many people around the world shared and reacted to the information Ukrainians had published.

The Ukrainian people received unprecedented international support. Social media were flooded with expressions of support for the Ukrainian people and condemnations of Russia (including from celebrities and influencers, such as Arnold Schwarzenegger). Images presenting the Ukrainian people's steadfastness and President Zelensky's heroism on one side, and accusations of President Putin being a war criminal on the other, became viral. Many social media users have added the Ukrainian flag to their profile pictures in support of Ukraine. Various initiatives to assist Ukrainians have started on social media, and many have moved into the physical world, with individuals volunteering to help refugees on the Ukrainian borders or in other countries they had fled to, and collecting and distributing donations of food and supplies. Public buildings around the world were lit up in the colours of the Ukrainian flag, raising awareness of the war and showing support for the Ukrainian people. Politically, alongside many statements supporting Ukraine and the Ukrainian leadership and condemnations of Russia and Putin, we have witnessed military and financial aid being provided to Ukraine, international pressure and sanctions being placed on Russia by countries, as well as by international corporations (Amazon, Netflix, Nike, McDonald's, Coca-Cola, etc.), and international involvement in the negotiations between the sides. It appears that the Ukrainian, and especially Zelensky's, activity in the realm of the image war and the battle over perceptions had worked to Ukraine's benefit and helped it achieve its goals during the 2022 Russian invasion (Yarchi, 2022).

Conclusions

Conflicts of today are different to those of the past; alongside the military confrontation, an image war is taking place, in which each side tries to promote its narrative and garner international support. This battle of ideas and perceptions plays a significant role in the ability of political actors to achieve their goals, and leads countries and other political actors to invest time and resources in an attempt to influence public perceptions in their favour, using all available tools, and in the current technological environment many of those efforts are centred around digital platforms.

As presented above, we are witnessing a wide usage of digital diplomacy in various conflicts around the world. Official diplomatic attempts are made to communicate one side's narrative, using various platforms and message strategies that aim to influence different target audiences. Alongside the official governmental digital diplomacy efforts, we can see civic initiatives, both structured and unstructured, some being well organized and others just diplomatic activism by individuals (and sometimes by celebrities). All of those initiatives fit the characteristics of the digital sphere, and especially of social media, which enables and empowers individuals to engage with others in civic diplomacy. The messages promoted by both governments and individuals are part of the image war and the battle over perceptions in the international arena.

As the examples presented in this chapter have shown, digital diplomacy during conflicts went a long way from the American understanding that they were fighting a 'different' war in the aftermath of the September 11 attacks, to a TikTok battle over perceptions as seen recently in the Israeli-Palestinian conflict. It will be interesting to see what the future holds in this realm, especially as immersive environments are expected to emerge on the Metaverse, and create opportunities alongside many challenges in the image war field. Countries and other political actors will try to rally our support in situations where we may feel we had experienced 'reality' ourselves, and know more about the conflict. As the consumption of information is expected to take place through virtual reality experiences that may be accurate or fake, but are expected to have a cognitive impact on the way we perceive the conflict and the actors involved in it, the ability of countries to present their side of the story and generate support will become more challenging.

SUGGESTED READING

Bjola C. and Holmes M. (2015). *Digital Diplomacy: Theory and Practice.* New York: Routledge.
Entman, R.M. (2003). *Projections of Power: Framing News, Public Opinion, and US Foreign Policy.* Chicago: The University of Chicago Press.
Manor, I. and Crilley, R. (2018). Visually Framing the Gaza War of 2014: The Israel Ministry of Foreign Affairs on Twitter. *Media, War and Conflict,* 11(3), 369–391.
Wolfsfeld, G. (2022). *Making Sense of Media and Politics: Five Principles in Political Communication.* 2nd edition. New York: Routledge.
Yarchi, M. (2014). 'Badtime' Stories: the Frames of Terror Promoted by Political Actors. *Democracy & Security,* 10(1), 22–51.

REFERENCES

Al-Rawi, A. (2020). US Public Diplomacy in the Middle East and the Digital Outreach Team. *Place Branding and Public Diplomacy,* 16(1), 18–24.
Altheide, D. (1997). The News Media, the Problem Frame, and the Production of Fear. *The Sociological Quarterly,* 38(4), 647–658.
Aouragh, M. (2016). Hasbara 2.0: Israel's Public Diplomacy in the Digital Age. *Middle East Critique,* 25(3), 271–297.
Archetti, C. (2010). *Terrorism, Communication, and the War of Ideas: Al-Qaida's Strategic Narrative as a Brand.* Paper presented at the ICA, Singapore, June.
Ayalon, A., Popovich, E., and Yarchi, M. (2016). From Warfare to Imagefare: How States Should Manage Asymmetric Conflicts with Extensive Media Coverage. *Terrorism and Political Violence,* 28(2), 254–273.
Betz, D. (2008). The Virtual dimension of Contemporary Insurgency and Counterinsurgency. *Small Wars & Insurgencies,* 19(4), 510–540.
Bjola, C. and Holmes, M. (2015). *Digital Diplomacy: Theory and Practice.* New York: Routledge.
Boxman-Shabtai, L. (2022). When Arms Speak, Memes Roar: Mimetic Communication during Israel's Guardian of the Walls Offensive. Paper presented at the ICA annual conference, Paris France, May.
Casebeer, W.D. and Russell J.A. (2005). Storytelling and Terrorism: Towards a Comprehensive 'Counter-Narrative Strategy'. *Strategic Insights,* 4(3), 1–17.
Copeland, D. (2013). Taking Diplomacy Public: Science, Technology, and Foreign Ministries in a Heteropolar World. In R.S. Zaharna, A. Arsenault, and A. Fisher (Eds.), *Relational, Networked and Collaborative Approaches to Public Diplomacy* (pp. 70–83). Oxon: Routledge.
Cottee, S. (2015).Why It's So Hard to Stop ISIS Propaganda. *The Atlantic.* Accessed from http://www.theatlantic.com/international/archive/2015/03/why-its-so-hard-to-stop-isis-propaganda/38621 6/.
Cull, N. (2011). WikiLeaks, Public Diplomacy 2.0 and the State of Digital Public Diplomacy. *Place Branding and Public Diplomacy,* 7, 1–8.

de Vreese, C.H., Boomgaarden, H.G., and Semetko, H.A. (2011). (In)direct Framing Effects: The Effects of News Media Framing on Public. *Communication Research*, 38(2), 179–205.

Douglas, S. (2007). Waging the Inchoate War: Defining, Fighting, and Second-Guessing the 'Long War'. *Journal of Strategic Studies*, 30(3), 391–420.

Entman, R.M. (1993). Framing: Towards Clarification of a Fractured Paradigm. *Journal of Communication*, 43(4), 51–58.

Entman, R.M. (2003). *Projections of Power: Framing News, Public Opinion, and US Foreign Policy*. Chicago: The University of Chicago Press.

Entman, R. M. (2008). Theorizing Mediated Public Diplomacy: The U.S. Case. *Press/Politics*, 13, 87–102.

Ganor, B. (2012). The Hybrid Terrorist Organization and Incitement. In A. Baker (Ed.), *The Changing Forms of Incitement to Terror and Violence: The Need for a New International Response* (pp. 13–19). Jerusalem: Jerusalem Center for Public Affairs.

Gilboa, E. (2000). Mass Communication and Diplomacy: A Theoretical Framework. *Communication Theory*, 10(3), 275–309.

Hanson, F. (2012). *Revolution@ State: The Spread of Ediplomacy*. Sydney: Lowy Institute for International Policy.

Hoskins, A. and O'Loughlin, B. (2010). *War and Media*. Cambridge UK: Polity.

Kaplan, A.M. and Haenlein, M. (2010). Users of the World, Unite! The Challenges and Opportunities of Social Media. *Business Horizons*, 53(1), 59–68.

Khatib, L., Dutton, W. and Thelwall, M. (2012). Public Diplomacy 2.0: A Case Study of the US Digital Outreach Team. *The Middle East Journal*, 66(3), 453–472.

Knightley, P. (2004). *The First Casualty: The War Correspondent as Hero and Myth-Maker from the Crimea to Iraq*. Baltimore, MD: John Hopkins Press.

Krause, P.J.P. and Van Evera, S.W. (2009). *Public Diplomacy: Ideas for the War of Ideas*. MIT Open Access.

Malone, G.D. (1985). Managing Public Diplomacy. *Washington Quarterly*, 8(3), 199–213.

Manor, I. and Adiku, G.A. (2021). From 'Traitors' to 'Saviours': A Longitudinal Analysis of Ethiopian, Kenyan and Rwandan Embassies' Practice of Digital Diaspora Diplomacy. *South African Journal of International Affairs*, 28(3), 403–427.

Manor, I. and Crilley, R. (2018). Visually Framing the Gaza War of 2014: The Israel Ministry of Foreign Affairs on Twitter. *Media, War and Conflict*, 11(3), 369–391.

Manor, I. and Crilley, R. (2020). The Mediatisation of MFAs: Diplomacy in the New Media Ecology. *The Hague Journal of Diplomacy*, 15, 66–92.

Miller, G. and Higham, S. (2015). In a Propaganda War Against ISIS, the US Tried to Play by the Enemy's Rules. *Washington Post*. https://doi.org/10.1080/15295036.2017.1393097

O'Loughlin, B. (2011). Images as Weapons of War: Representation, Mediation and Interpretation. *Review of International Studies*, 37, 71–79.

Rabasa, A. (2011). Where Are We in the 'War of Ideas'? In B.M. Jenkins and J.P. Godges (Eds.). *The Long Shadow of 9/11: America's Response to Terrorism* (pp. 61–70). California: RAND Corporation.

Roger, N. (2013). *Image Warfare in the War on Terror*. London: Palgrave Macmillan.

Samuel-Azran, T. and Yarchi, M. (2018). Military Public Diplomacy 2.0: Reception of the Israeli Defence Force Spokesperson's Arabic Facebook Page. *The Hague Journal of Diplomacy*, 13(3), 323–344.

Soroka, S.N. (2003). Media, Public Opinion, and Foreign Policy. *The International Journal of Press/Politics*, 8(1): 27–48.

Van Evera, S.V. (2006). Assessing US Strategy in the War on Terror. *Annals of the American Academy of Political and Social Science*, 607(1), 10–26.

Van Ham, P. (2003). War, Lies, and Videotape: Public Diplomacy and the USA's War on Terrorism. *Security Dialogue*, 34(4), 427–444.

Vosoughi, S., Roy, D. and Aral, S. (2018). The Spread of True and False News Online. *Science*, 359(6380), 1146–1151.

Weimann, G. (2006). *Terror on the Internet: the New Arena, the New Challenges.* Washington DC: US Institute of Peace Press.

Weimann, G. (2016). Terrorist Migration to the Dark Web. *Perspectives on Terrorism*, 10(3), 40–44.

Weimann, G. and Masri, N. (2023). Research Note: Spreading Hate on TikTok. *Studies in Conflict & Terrorism*, 46(5), 752–765.

Wolfsfeld, G. (1997). *Media and Political Conflict: News from the Middle East.* Cambridge, UK: Cambridge University Press.

Wolfsfeld, G. (2022). *Making Sense of Media and Politics: Five Principles in Political Communication.* 2nd edition. New York: Routledge.

Wolfsfeld, G. and Yarchi, M. (2015). Conflict/War. In G. Mazzoleni, K.G. Barnhurst, K. Ikeda, R.C.M. Maia, and H. Wessler (Eds.), *The International Encyclopedia of Political Communication* (199–201). Hoboken, NJ: Wiley.

Yarchi, M. (2014). 'Badtime' Stories: the Frames of Terror Promoted by Political Actors. *Democracy & Security*, 10(1), 22–51.

Yarchi, M. (2016). Does Using 'Imagefare' as a State's Strategy in Asymmetric Conflicts Improve its Foreign Media Coverage? The Case of Israel. *Media, War & Conflict*, 9(3), 290–305.

Yarchi, M., (2019). ISIS's Media's Strategy as Image Warfare: Strategic Messaging over Time and across Platforms. *Communication and the Public*, 4(1), 53–67.

Yarchi, M. (2022). The Image War as a Significant Fighting Arena – Evidence from the Ukrainian Battle Over Perceptions During the 2022 Russian Invasion. *Studies in Conflict & Terrorism.*

Yarchi, M. and Ayalon, A. (2023). Fighting over the Image: the Israeli–Palestinian Conflict in the Gaza Strip 2018–19. *Studies in Conflict & Terrorism*, 46(2), 123–136.

Yarchi, M., Samuel-Azran, T., and Bar-David, L. (2017). Facebook Users' Engagement with Israel's Public Diplomacy Messages During the 2012 and 2014 Military Operations in Gaza. *Place Branding and Public Diplomacy*, 13(4), 360–375.

INDEX

....

For the benefit of digital users, indexed terms that span two pages (e.g., 52–53) may, on occasion, appear on only one of those pages.

Tables and figures are indicated by *t* and *f* following the page number; 'n.' after a page number indicates the footnote number.

#

5G (fifth generation telecom technology) 591
   Huawei 540, 582, 591–93, 596
   US 591, 592–93

A

Abbott, Lucy M. 575–76
Abeywardena, Penny 413
Abrahams, Alexei 568
Access Now 387–88
accountability
   AI and 255
   digital diplomacy 3–4, 160–61
   international bureaucracies 354–55, 358–59
   international development
      cooperation 254–55
   political accountability 18, 354–55
   soft power 67, 68, 72, 74–75
Acuto, Michele 294, 401, 403–4
Adler, Emmanuel 32
Adler-Nissen, Rebecca 13–14, 16, 115, 312,
   319–20, 394–95
Ad Library 81
Adraee, Avichai 627
advertising 80
   micro-targeted advertising 84–85, 88
Afghanistan
   NATO's involvement in 478, 480, 481
   US invasion and withdrawal from 624–26
Aggestam, Karin 339
Aguirre, Daniel 21, 546–48
AI (Artificial Intelligence) 22–23, 243, 422, 432
   accountability and 255

AI artists and curators 208
AI-driven disinformation and
   counter-operations 81
automated weapons systems and 133
China and 515–16
cybersecurity and 133
dual-use technology 432
ethical AI audits 81
international development cooperation
   and 261–62
AIIB (Asian Investment and Infrastructure
   Bank) 587
Ai Weiwei 205–6
@jack (aka Jack Dorsey) 427
Akdenizli, Banu 22, 568–69
Albania 427
algorithms 243, 429–30
   'algorithmic diplomacy' 11–12
   algorithmic gatekeepers 281–82
   algorithmic governance 6, 20–21, 270, 282
   'black' propaganda 80
   computational personalization and 10
   flow of cultural communication and 202–3
   geopolitics/algorithmic geopolitics 270,
      271, 273, 281–82
   influence on choices of digital users 11
Alibaba 257, 589
Aliyev, Ilham 29–30
Al-Jaziri, Mahmoud 574
AlJazzaf, Z.M. 566
Alkhusaili, M. M. 566
Al-Mansouri, T. 570–71
Al-Qahtani, Saud 568

638 INDEX

Amazon 423, 440, 589, 631–32
Amnesty International 275, 387–88
    Security Lab Report 572–73
Ampuero, Roberto 557–58
Anholt, Simon 404, 408–9
ANT (Actor-Network Theory) 293–94n.1,
    294
APEC (Asia-Pacific Economic
    Cooperation) 360–61
Apple 423, 584, 585–86, 588
Applebaum, Anne 65, 68–69, 73, 75–76
Arab Spring (2011) 205, 322, 565–66, 567
    social media and 46–47, 427, 429, 583–84
    Twitter and 427
Arceneaux, Phillip 16
Archetti, Cristina 220–21
Archimedes Global 87
Argentina 552, 553–54
    see also Latin America digital diplomacy
Arundell, Col. Ralph 90–91
ASEAN (Association of Southeast Asian
    Nations) 367, 528n.1, 540–41
    'ASEAN Way' 320–21
    digital diplomacy 235
    multilateral diplomacy's digital
        culture 320–21, 325
    regional diplomatic culture 320–21
    Twitter 235
Ashley, Kavoy Anthony 342
Asian Development Bank 352–53, 354–55
Asia Pacific digital diplomacy 21, 528–31, 541
    coercive diplomacy 531, 535
    Covid-19 information disorder 538–39,
        540–41
    digital (new) public diplomacy 530, 531–34
    digital publics 531, 534–35, 541
    diplomacy *about* the digital 531, 540–41
    disinformation 537–38, 539, 540–41
    diversity within the region 528, 529, 530–31
    Facebook 535, 537–38, 539
    foreign interference 531, 535, 537–38
    hostile digital diplomacy 531, 536–37
    information disorder 530–31, 535, 538–39,
        540–41
    MFAs 530, 531, 535
    misinformation 540–41
    nation branding 531, 538–39

social media 529, 531, 532, 534–35, 538,
    539
social networks, global political economy
    and techno-social system of 530–31, 541
'undiplomatic diplomacy' 531, 535
US/China contest for regional influence
    and 536–37
astroturfing 84–85, 87–88, 89, 214, 390
    definition 84n.7
Atlantic Treaty Organisations 478
AU (African Union) 367
audience
    anonymous engagement 43
    Asia Pacific digital diplomacy and digital
        publics 531, 534–35, 541
    audience engagement 43, 406
    cities and digitalization of diplomacy 402–
        3, 404, 406, 415, 416
    digital diplomacy in wars and
        conflicts 620–21, 624
    digital games, large audience of 605–6
    digital propaganda and 83
    international bureaucracies and audience
        diversity 354–55
    multiple audiences 38–39, 110–11
    performers/audiences interaction 33–34
    projection and retrieval: power of
        the audience and power of the
        performer 34–36, 38–39, 42–43
    'suspend disbelief' 35
    symbolic interactionist framework for 32
    target audience 16, 83, 242, 495, 624, 632
    visual simplicity and 8
Australia 530, 533, 540
    Australian Museum 200–1
    cyber governance 446
    foreign interference 538
    tech ambassadors 428–29
    see also Asia Pacific digital diplomacy
authoritarianism 396, 422, 429
    China: populist authoritarianism 514–16,
        522, 523
    Internet governance: democratic vs
        authoritarian model 127
    propaganda and 220
Aytac, U. 270
Azerbaijan 613–14

B

Bachelet, Michelle 557, 561
Bahrain 565, 566, 573, 574
  censorship 574
  Twitter 569–70, 573
  see also GCC countries's digital diplomacy
Baines, Victoria 17
Bakir, V. 86n.11, 89
Bandura, Albert 606
Bangladesh 613–14
Ban Ki-moon 353–54
Bansky 205
Barber, B. R. 403–4
Bar-David, L. 627–28
Barlow, John Perry 437
Batora, Jozef 319, 320–21
Bauman, Zygmunt 52
Bekkers, V. 603
Bengtsson, Stina 184
Bennett, Naftali 278
Bennett, W. L. 10–11
Benwell, M. 390–91
Berk, M. 83
Bernal, Victoria 388
Berners-Lee, Tim 63–64, 75
Bhuyan, D. 84n.5
Bicchi, Federica 319–20
Biden, Joe 128–29, 625–26
  Biden administration 232, 445, 592
  digital diplomacy 30
  on Russia–Ukraine War 124
  Twitter 29–30
Big Tech 52, 433
  DII and 81, 86–87, 92
  EU General Data Protection Regulation
    and 589
  as foreign and security policy actors 423–
    24, 429
  'libertarian' ideology 449–50
  privacy rights and 429–30
  regulation of 443, 444–47, 451–52, 588
bilateral diplomacy 313–14
  2022 Russia's invasion of Ukraine 315–16
  analogue tendencies in the analogue–digital
    spectrum 315–17
  bilateral diplomacy's digital culture 313,
    314–17, 325

bilateral/multilateral diplomacy
    differences 316
  Cold War 315
  consular services 314, 317
  diplomatic corps 314, 315–16, 317
  as hybrid diplomacy 314–15, 316–17
  public diplomacy and 314, 317
  Russia–Ukraine War 315–16
  social media and 314, 316–17
  Vienna Conventions on Consular
    Relations 314–15
  see also digital diplomatic cultures
Bildt, Carl 17–18, 183, 297, 425–27
Bishop, Julie 533
Bitetti, D. 277
Bjola, Corneliu 4–5n.1, 13, 17, 179–80, 215, 221,
    316, 319–20, 323–24, 424, 484, 495, 565,
    568, 571–72, 575
  *Digital Diplomacy and International
    Organisations* 317
'Black Lives Matter' movement 91, 201–2, 322, 521
Bleiker, R. 602, 603, 606
blended diplomacy 13–14, 104, 261–62, 311–12,
    320
  EU digital diplomacy 114
  see also hybrid diplomacy
Blinken, Antony 177–78, 625–26
blogs 17–18
  domestic digital diplomacy and 48–49
  UK FCO/FCDO and blogs/
    blogosphere 48–49, 426
'Blue Lives Matter' movement 91
Blue Whale Challenge 441–42
Blumenthal, Corinne 15–16
Bobbitt, Philip 70
Boehler, Adam 592
Bogost, Ian 605, 606–7
Boko Haram 39
Bolivia 548–49, 551, 553
  see also Latin America digital diplomacy
Bolsonaro, Jair 316–17, 550, 556t, 592–93
Booze Allen Hamilton 584
botnets 84–85, 84n.5, 121
bots 133, 142–43, 144, 208, 214, 216, 225, 570–71
  chat bots 208, 303–4, 357–58
  Russia and 243
  weaponization of 568

640 INDEX

Bouchard, Caroline 18
Boucher, Philip 45–46
branding 31n.6
  Asia Pacific digital diplomacy: nation
    branding 531, 538–39
  'Brand Norway' 38
  British Museum, nation-branding
    campaign 200–1
  cities and digitalization of diplomacy 411–
    12, 412t
  city branding 19–20, 402–3, 404
  feminist foreign policy and 'branding' (as
    soft power 'resource') 163, 168, 171
  MFAs 20
  nation-branding 31, 37–38, 158, 404
  social media brands 20
  soft power and nation branding 160, 531
  Sweden's nation-branding 183, 184, 235
Brazil 548–49, 550, 552, 553, 592
  on electronic espionage 585, 594
  US/China rivalry and 592–93
  see also BRICS countries; Latin America
    digital diplomacy
Bremberg, Niklas 408–9, 476, 531, 537, 572
Briant, Emma L. 19, 217, 222
BRICS countries (Brazil, Russia, India, China,
    and South Africa) 585, 586, 589, 594, 596
  on electronic espionage 585
  New Development Bank 587
Brinkerhoff, J. M. 386
Brommesson, D. 470
Bruno, A. 571
Bukele, Nayib 278–79
Bull, Hedley 312
Busan High Level Forum of Aid
    Effectiveness 254
Bush, George W. 183–84
ByteDance (China) 423, 540
  Douyin 269–70, 271
  TikTok 269–70, 271, 281–82

C

Cabañes, J. V. A. 85, 86
Cambridge Analytica 73, 85, 88, 420–21
  links to Russia and unethical election
    campaigns 90
Canada 20, 49, 174

NATO Twitter account 38–39
  Victoria, digitalization of diplomacy 402,
    407, 410, 411–12, 413, 414, 415
capitalism
  digital capitalism 214
  state capitalism 596
  surveillance capitalism 87, 588
Carlson, Brownwyn 202
Cassidy, Jennifer A. 18, 565, 566–67
Castells, Manuel 421
celebrities 145, 253–54, 276, 351, 370, 371, 488,
    627–28, 631–32
  NATO and celebrity diplomacy 481,
    482–83
  see also Jolie, Angelina
censorship 75–76, 126–27, 422
  Bahrain 574
  China 75–76, 126–27, 222–23, 444, 518, 589
  content moderation 270, 387–88, 429,
    574–75
  'geo-blocking' 387–88
  Myanmar 539
  Russia 126–27, 444, 630–31
  'sharp power' and 66
  soft power and 73, 75–76
  Thailand 538–39
  UAE 567–68, 574
  Vietnam 387–88, 539
Central Asian countries 492–95, 506–9
  ADD 493
  challenges faced by 492
  Covid-19 pandemic 492–93, 507
  development of digital technologies and
    digital economy 494
  digital diplomacy 492–93, 494–95
  diplomatic priorities 492
  FDD 492–93
  Internet freedom 493–94
  Internet use, social media, and mobile
    connection in 493–94, 493t
  Kazakhstan 491, 493–94, 507
  Kyrgyzstan 491, 493–94
  statecraft 492, 506–7
  Tajikistan 491, 494
  Turkmenistan 491, 494, 507
  Uzbekistan 491, 493–94
  video-conferencing 492–93

Central Asian countries and SMD (social
media diplomacy) 491, 495–506, 507–9
  actors 495–96, 505
  CAC presidents' social media
    accounts 497–99, 498t
  dominant strategy 496, 505, 506, 507
  embassies in Moscow, social media
    accounts 504–5, 504t
  embassies in Washington (DC), social
    media accounts 504, 504t
  Facebook 497–98, 500–1, 501t
  game setting 496, 505–6
  home-oriented social media 508
  Instagram 497–98
  languages used 497–98, 500, 501, 505–6, 507
  MFAs' social media accounts 499–501,
    499t, 500t, 501t, 508
  payoff 497, 506
  permanent missions to the UN, social
    media accounts 501–2, 502t
  permanent representatives to the UN 503,
    503t
  recommendations 508–9
  reputation-building public diplomacy 508
  strategic goal and objectives 496, 506
  Telegram 492–93, 497–98
  troubleshooting (game strategy) 496n.11
  Twitter 497–98, 499–500, 500t, 501–3, 502t,
    503t
  YouTube 497–98
Chen, Titus 72
Chen, X. 269–70
Chernobrov, Dmitry. 217
Chile 547, 553, 557–58, 560–61
  Covid-19 pandemic 559
  Fundación Imagen de Chile (Foundation
    Image Chile) 558
  MFA 557–58, 559–60
  social media 557–58
  tech diplomacy 558
  territorial dispute with Bolivia 552
  Twitter 548–49, 552, 559–60
  US/China rivalry and 592–93
  see also DEPA; Latin America digital
    diplomacy
China (PRC—People's Republic of China)
  1989 Tiananmen Square events 608, 609

  2022 Zhengzhou violence 75–76
  civil society 18, 72
  Covid-19 pandemic 22, 53, 72, 75–76, 589
  global superpower status 222–23
  India/China clashes 610–13
  international development 254
  national sovereignty and territorial
    integrity 511–12, 514, 520–21, 608–9
  neo-totalitarianism 514
  North–South divide and 589, 590
  nuclear diplomacy: US tweets about arms
    control with China 146–47
  nuclear weapons 146
  'sharp power' 66, 220
  state capitalism 596
  US/China rivalry 422, 442–43, 445, 517–18,
    519–20, 528, 536–37, 582, 592–93, 595–96,
    597
  US/China trade war 511, 597
  see also BRICS countries
China: digital technologies
  BRI (Belt and Road Initiative) 596
  censorship 75–76, 126–27, 222–23, 444, 518,
    589
  China's UN permanent mission 338–39
  control of society 18, 75–76
  cyberattacks and threats by 123–24, 125
  cyber governance 443–44, 445, 446,
    448–49
  cybersecurity 126–27, 129, 130
  digital games and nationalist agenda 19–
    20, 607–9
  digital propaganda and public
    diplomacy 222–23
  espionage 130, 134
  Facebook and 282
  Great Firewall 126–27, 444, 589
  Internet governance 589, 590
  public diplomacy 338–39
  social media 22, 75–76, 338–39
  soft power 18, 64–65, 72–73, 75–76, 159–60
  surveillance 72, 75, 126–27, 134, 205, 444,
    540, 589
  Twitter 75–76, 242, 520–21, 523
  as world leader in digital
    communications 72
  see also Douyin; Huawei; TikTok

642 INDEX

China: 'Wolf Warrior' diplomacy 22, 511–12, 523–24
   2016 Dibu Expedition 537
   as aggressive diplomacy 224, 517, 518, 522
   AI 515–16
   analytical framework 515–17, 516*f*, 522–23
   assertive nationalism 513–14, 515–16, 517–18, 522–23
   attack on external actors for involvement in China's national issues 511–12, 514, 520–22
   Covid-19 pandemic 224, 511–12, 517–18, 522
   CPC (Communist Party of China) and 511–12, 513–17, 518, 519–20, 522, 523–24
   cyberspace and 517–18, 519, 520, 522, 523
   digital technologies 316–17, 511–12, 516–17, 522–24
   disinformation campaigns 537–38
   emergence of 512, 513, 514
   emotional component 511
   Global Times 518, 519–20, 536–37
   grassroots cyber nationalism 522–23
   Hong Kong issues 511–12, 514, 519, 520–22
   impact on the West 523
   internal and external goals of 515–17, 523–24
   national sovereignty and territorial integrity 511–12, 514, 520–21
   populism/populist authoritarianism 511–12, 514–16, 522, 523
   propaganda 514, 522–24
   Realism and 511–12
   social media 511–12, 515–18, 520–21
   strategic narratives 511–12, 514, 515–16
   Taiwan issues 242, 243, 511–12, 520–22, 537
   Tibet issues 511–12, 514, 520–22
   US democracy, critiques of (6 January 2021 event) 511–12, 519–20, 522
   Xi Jinping and 22, 513, 514, 516–17, 522–23
   Xinjiang issues 511–12, 514, 520–22
Chung, D. 532
Churchill, Winston 367
cities 401–2, 416
   C40 Cities Climate Leadership Group 403–5
   city branding 19–20, 402–3, 404
   city–country relationship 404–5

   city diplomacy 19–20, 223–24, 263, 401–3, 404–5, 415
   as diplomatic actors 403–4
   international activities of 404–5, 406, 415
   SCI (Sister Cities International) 404–5, 407
   status as 'in-between powers' 402
   UCLG (United Cities and Local Governments) 403–5
cities and digitalization of diplomacy 19–20, 402, 414–16
   Akureyri (Iceland) 402, 407, 410, 412, 413, 414, 415
   audiences 402–3, 404, 406, 415, 416
   case selection 402, 407–8, 407*t*
   case selection: branding activities 411–12, 412*t*
   case selection: diplomatic activities 409–10, 410*t*
   challenges 416
   digitization of international activities 406, 413–15, 413*t*, 414*t*
   digitization of internationalization 405–6
   Izmir (Turkey) 402, 407, 410, 411, 413, 414, 415
   logic of practice 408–9, 408*t*, 415–16
   methodology 407–9, 408*t*, 415
   New York (US) 402, 407, 409–10, 411, 413
   Twitter 413–14, 413*t*
   Victoria (Canada) 402, 407, 410, 411–12, 413, 414, 415
   see also cities
civil society
   China 18, 72
   digital diplomacy and 4, 238
   digital diplomacy in wars and conflicts 621, 623, 625n.2, 631, 632
   disruption from the side and 19
   as indicator of group autonomy within a political culture 64
   Israeli-Palestinian conflict 627–28
   Latin America digital diplomacy and 554
   NATO and 478
   soft power and 66, 67, 72, 75
   US Muslim Ban and 67
   see also CSOs; NGOs; polylateral diplomacy
Clark, J. 110
clickbait 85, 86, 429

climate change 70, 402, 574
  C40 Cities Climate Leadership Group 403–44
  COP26 UN Climate Change Conference 378–79
  COP27 UN Climate Change Conference 262
  denial of global warming 233
  Kiribati 262
  Paris Agreement on Climate Change 462
  Tuvalu 262
  UN and 351, 361–62
Clinton, Bill 87–88, 183–84, 425–26
Clinton, Hillary 17, 123, 184, 426, 584
Cohen, Jared 17
Cold War 367
  bilateral diplomacy and 315
  cultural diplomacy 195–96, 197–98
  'New Cold War' 217–20
  nuclear diplomacy 139–40, 141
  nuclear weapons 139, 141, 146
  public diplomacy and 181–82, 183, 187, 188, 217
Coleridge, Samuel Taylor 35
Collective Security Treaty Organization 352–53
Commonwealth Secretariat 353–54
communication
  communication ethics 239, 243
  computational communication 11
  Cull's communication methods 571–72
  Plato on 239
  'weaponization' of 536
  see also message
conspiracy theories 21, 53, 54, 214
Constantinou, Costas M. 235, 324, 390
Cooper, Andrew F. 22, 212, 574
Coplen, Michaela 316, 319–20
Cornago, Noé 324
Cornut, Jérémie 15–16, 316–17
Costa Rica 548–49, 553
  see also Latin America digital diplomacy
Coughlin, Charles 186–87
Couldry, Nick 195, 197
Council of Europe 131–32, 352–53, 438, 555
Covid-19 pandemic 558–59
  Asia Pacific digital diplomacy and Covid-19 information disorder 538–39, 540–41
  Central Asian countries 492–93, 507
  China 22, 53, 72, 75–76, 589
  China's 'Wolf Warrior' diplomacy and 224, 511–12, 517–18, 522
  conspiracy theories 53
  consularization of diplomacy 560
  contact tracing apps 572–73, 575
  digital diplomacy and 4, 22, 46, 103–4, 325, 343, 421, 433, 572
  digital propaganda and 224
  disinformation 189–90, 224, 276–77
  economy and digital tools 595
  EU digital diplomacy and 108, 110, 112–13, 319, 457
  GCC countries 564–65, 571–74, 575–76
  global humanism and 241
  hybrid diplomacy and 13, 22, 320, 429
  'infodemic' 255, 264
  Latin America digital diplomacy and 547, 549, 558–60, 561
  Malaysia 538–39
  MFAs 20, 49
  misinformation 276, 540–41
  NATO digital diplomacy 484, 487
  origin theories 22, 53, 233, 517
  Russia's Covid-19 vaccine (Sputnik) 54–55
  Singapore 538–39
  state Internet shutdowns 392
  TikTok and 275–77
  UN and 318, 337, 341, 343, 351, 392
  vaccines 54–55, 276–77, 540–41
  video-conferencing 13, 108, 337, 421, 433
  virtual diplomatic summitry and 367–68, 371–72, 375–76, 377–79
  WhatsApp groups and 16
  WHO Organization 53, 54, 276, 559, 572, 573
CPTPP (Comprehensive and Progressive Transpacific Partnership) 595–96
Crawford, Neta 603
Crilley, Rhys 8, 22, 225, 406
crises 4, 36–37, 429, 566–67, 571–72
  digital media and 178–80
  disruption through crises 15, 21–23
  humanitarian crises and digital media 427
  new media technology disruption and global crises (historical perspective) 178, 185–87, 188, 189, 190–91

644 INDEX

crises (*cont.*)
offline diplomacy and 575
propaganda and 187–88, 221–22, 226
refugee crises (Europe) 48–49, 468–69
virtual diplomatic summitry in context of
crises 375
see also Covid-19 pandemic; Russia–
Ukraine War; wars and conflicts
crowdfunding 150–51, 190, 422, 630
crowdsourcing 150–52, 177–78, 206
CSOs (civil society organizations) 390–92
1992 Earth Summit in Rio de Janeiro
and 389
see also civil society; NGOs; TANs
Cuba 342, 441, 450–51, 553, 584
1962 Cuban Missile Crisis 141, 142–43
see also Latin America digital diplomacy
Cull, Nicholas J. 19, 179, 551, 571–72
cultural diplomacy 17, 194–95, 207–8
'Actors' Typology' 195, 198–207, 208
adversarial diplomacy 199, 202, 206
algorithms and flow of cultural
communication 202–3
changes in cultural diplomacy in the digital
age 195–99
Cold War 195–96, 197–98
content: digitizing arts and cultures 195–96
content providers 195, 198–99, 200–2, 207
cross-cultural dialogue: digitalizing
communications 197–99
cultural diplomacy actorness 195, 197, 198–
99, 207, 208
cultural memes 202
definition 194
dependencies among actors 200, 206–8
digital cultural diplomacy 17, 194–95
digital games, nationalist agenda and digital
cultural diplomacy 19–20, 605, 613
environment: digitalizing exchange
infrastructures 196–97
Europeana 203–4
Facebook 202–3
Google Arts and Culture Institute 203, 204
individual influencers 195, 198, 205, 206–7
infrastructure builders 195, 198–99, 202–4,
207
Instagram 202–3, 205

(inter)governmental actors 206
jazz 195–96
Mexico 553
Mona Lisa (Leonardo da Vinci) 196–97
museums 199, 200–1, 202, 203, 205
national cultural heritage
digitization 200–2
national governments and 196–99, 201–2
non-human actors 208
opinion makers 195, 198–99, 200, 205–7
South Korea 204
state actors 195, 200, 207
state/non-state actors dichotomy 195, 199,
200
streaming 196
transnational corporations and 194–95, 197,
199, 203–4, 207
Twitter 202–3, 205–6
UK 200–1
US 196–98, 199, 200–2
culture
definition 312
'diplomatic culture' 312–13
ludification of culture 601–2
'post-truth culture' 213, 214–15, 221
see also cultural diplomacy; digital
diplomatic cultures
Cummings, Dominic 223
Curtis, Simon 294
cyberattacks and threats 121–24, 422, 437
1st generation of 121–22, 123–24
2nd generation of 122–24
3rd generation of 123–24
1988 'Morris worm' 122
2007 Estonia, DDOS attack 121–22
2008 Georgia, DDOS attack 122
2010 'Stuxnet' worm 122–23, 128, 130–31
2012 'Shamoon' wiper virus 122–23
2017 wiper virus 'NotPetya' 124–25
2021 Russian attack on the Colonial pipeline
network 131
China and 123–24, 125
DDOS attacks 89, 121–22, 127, 130
'deepfakes' 133
ransomware 125–26, 437, 585
Russia and 121, 122, 123–24, 125, 127, 128–29,
131, 585

state institutions and democratic processes
as targets 123, 422
war-like features of 124–25
see also cybersecurity; cyberwar; hacking;
information warfare; trolling
cyber crimes 131, 441–42, 450
see also cyberattacks and threats; espionage/
electronic espionage
cyber governance 17, 438, 440, 441, 446, 451
Australia 446
Big Tech, regulation of 443, 444–47, 451–52,
588
China 443–44, 445, 446, 448–49
Cybercrime Conventions (Council of
Europe) 131–32, 438
cyberwarfare, regulation of 261
digital diplomatic practice and 446–48, 450
digital regulation as expression of national
and regional sovereignty 443–46
DII, regulation and policy 85, 88, 92
EU 117, 442, 443, 445–46, 449, 450–51
future prospects 451–52
Germany 444
Group of Governmental Experts 438–39,
450–51
'international internet law' 449
international law and 441–43, 446–48, 450
international law on cyberspace, theoretical
approaches 448–51
Internet governance/cyber governance
distinction 129–30
Microsoft and 131–32, 439–40
multilateral deliberations, multistakeholder
norm shaping 438–40, 448–49, 450
non-state actors 440
private sector 439, 440, 442–43
restriction of access to services and
content 444–45
Russia 438–39, 440, 441–42, 443–44, 446,
448–49, 451
sovereignty and cyberspace 437, 438, 441–
46, 448, 451
Tallinn Manuals 437, 438
UK 444, 446–47, 449–50, 451
UN 438, 450
UN Ad Hoc Committee 439, 440, 441,
442–43, 448, 449

UN Cybercrime Convention 441–43, 447–49
UN OEWG 131–32, 134, 439–40, 449, 450–51
US 444–45, 447–49, 451
see also cyberspace; Internet governance
cybersecurity 20–21, 81, 121, 297–99, 341, 429
AI and 133
challenges 122, 125–26, 133–34
China 126–27, 129, 130
clashing national perspectives 126–29
closed regimes vs open model regimes 126–
27, 129–30
cyber diplomacy, successes and failures
of 129–33
cyber legalism 128–29, 131–32
cyber peace 131
cybersecurity statecraft 121, 122–24, 134
emergence of a problem 121–26
Estonia 297–99
EU, Cybersecurity Strategy 128, 467–68
Facebook 134
fitting punishment with offensive
activity 125–26
geopolitics/cyberspace convergence 124–25
Google 134
'information security' vs vital infrastructure
protection 126–27
international cyber conflict 122, 123
legal interpretation of interstate cyber
conflict 125–26, 127–29, 130–32
LOAC (law of armed conflict) 125–26, 128,
130–31
NATO 128–29, 132
NGOs and cybersecurity risks 391, 392, 396
quantum computing 133–34
regulation, lack of 341
Russia 126–27, 129, 130
space systems and 134
Tallinn Manuals 437, 438
Twitter 134
UK 128, 130
unpeace/technological unpeace 124–25,
126, 130, 131
US 128–29, 130
Western security doctrine and 125–26,
128–29
see also cyberattacks and threats; cyberwar;
information warfare

646 INDEX

cyberspace 583
  China's 'Wolf Warrior' diplomacy and 517–18,
    519, 520, 522, 523
  geopolitics/cyberspace convergence 124–25
  militarization of 438
  responsible behaviour in 438–40, 441, 442,
    443, 449, 450–51
  see also cyber governance; cybersecurity
cyberwar 130–31, 132, 215
  2016 US presidential elections, Russia's
    intervention as 'cyberwar' 215
  regulation of cyberwarfare 261

D
D'Amelio, Charli 141–42, 275
D'Amelio, Dixie 275
Darmastuti, A. 533
data 7
  Big Data 21, 38, 51, 177–78, 216, 256, 307,
    429, 491, 493
  dark analytics market 88, 429
  data collection 164, 588–89
  datafication 86–87, 88, 197, 307
  data mining 32n.9, 73, 588
  data protection regulation 88, 429–30,
    572–73
  digital diplomacy and 30
  EU Data Protection Directive and General
    Data Protection Regulation 88, 588–89
  generation of data by people/real-world
    events 7
  PII (personally identifiable
    information) 588–89
  privacy rights 52, 256, 423, 429–30, 565–66,
    572–73, 584, 588–89, 594
  real, synthetic, unstructured data 7
Davies, S. E. 571–72
Davis, J. H. 242
Dawson, J. 80, 84n.4, 87
DDOS attacks (distributed denial of
  service) 89, 127, 130
  2007 Estonia, DDOS attack 121–22
  2008 Georgia, DDOS attack 122
  see also cyberattacks and threats
deep-fake technology 133, 144–45, 208
De Hoop Scheffer, Jaap 477
DeLanda, Manuel 293–94, 295

Deleuze, Gilles 293–94
democracy
  digital diplomacy and 238, 429
  fight for liberal values and
    democracy 431–32
  Internet governance: democratic vs
    authoritarian model 127
  public diplomacy and liberal
    democracies 220
Denmark
  compact assemblages 302–3, 304, 305, 306,
    307–8
  digital diplomacy 297
  Digital Growth Strategy 297
  digital hybridization of diplomacy 299–300,
    301, 302
  tech ambassadors 297, 428
  see also digital hybridization of diplomacy
DEPA (Digital Economic Partnership
  Agreement) 595–96
Der Derian, James 250–51, 605
development *see* international development
  cooperation
Deverell, Edward 226
dialogic politics 450–51
diaspora organizations and digital
  diplomacy 19–20, 383, 388–89, 395–96
  diaspora diplomacy 384–85, 386
  diaspora organizations as digital diplomacy
    pioneers and innovators 388–91
  'new diplomacy' and 384–88
  see also NGOs and digital diplomacy
diasporas 425
  diaspora diplomacy 384–85, 386
  diaspora forums 426
  digital diasporas, impact on countries of
    origin 19
  disruption from the side and 18–19
  MFAs and 18–19
  remittances 18–19
  states's digital ties with 18–19
digital assemblages
  assemblage theory 292, 293–94, 302, 303,
    306, 307–8
  canvas assemblages 304, 305*t*, 306
  compact assemblages 302, 305*t*, 306–7
  digital hybridization of diplomacy and 17, 292

digital hybridization as assemblage
formation 294–96, 296*f*
'knobs' 293–95, 296
mosaic assemblages 303–4, 305*t*, 306–7
strong assemblages 295–96
weak assemblages 295–96
see also digital hybridization of diplomacy;
digital hybridization of diplomacy:
Nordic/Baltic countries comparison
digital diplomacy
accountability 3–4, 160–61
actors in 194–95
ADD (analytical digital diplomacy) 491n.1,
493, 495
benefits of 3–4, 237, 476, 513
as change management in the international
system 30, 476, 565
definition 3–5, 250–51, 311–12, 320, 564–65
democracy and 238
dialogic communication and 406
Digital Diplomacy 3.0 262
digital technology and 142
digitization of diplomacy/digital diplomacy
distinction 4–5
'diplomacy by digital means' 311–12
FDD (functional or operational digital
diplomacy) 491n.1, 492, 495
fighting with values in winning the global
technological race 431–32
increasing use of 4, 352–53, 421–22
'new diplomacy' and the pluralising
potential of digital diplomacy 384–88
next phase of 430–31, 433
observation, listening, and data
gathering 30
online 'front-stage'/offline diplomatic
'back-stage' relationship 291–92, 307,
393–94, 421–22, 512–13
as practice and strategy 160–61
public, communication with 3–4, 105, 237,
513
'real-time diplomacy' 46–47, 51, 421, 513
transparency 3–4, 46, 160–61, 388, 395
upgrading, augmenting, and rewiring
diplomacy 4–5, 22–23
digital diplomacy: challenges 4, 16, 46, 619
cities and digitalization of diplomacy 416

confidentiality 105–6, 107, 112, 426–27
'dark side' of digital diplomacy 14, 179–80,
214–15, 323–24, 536, 568
digitalization as challenge 105–6, 112–14,
116–17
digital propaganda 4, 214–15, 226
EU digital diplomacy 112–14, 115–16, 458,
466–70
international bureaucracies and 349–50,
356–62
multiple audiences 38–39
NGOs and digital diplomacy 391–92, 394,
396
patience and tact 106, 112, 116–17, 359–60
personalization 343, 360–61
see also disinformation; espionage/
electronic espionage; hacking;
misinformation; propaganda; public
diplomacy: ethical challenges of
digitalization
digital diplomacy: phases 425
1st phase: baby steps 425–26
2nd phase: running wild 426–29
3rd phase: sobering up 429–30
digital diplomacy and disruption 3–4, 112,
177–78, 425
digital disruption, definition 45–46
disruptive role of digital diplomacy as
instrument of foreign policy 5–6, 45
see also digital disruption patterns;
disruption; micro/macro-level
disruptions
digital diplomatic cultures 21, 311–14, 325
analogue–digital spectrum 311–12, 313, 315–
17, 319, 320–21, 322–23, 324, 325
bilateral diplomacy's digital culture 313,
314–17, 325
definition 311–13
'diplomatic culture' 312–13
Internet, reliance on 313
multilateral diplomacy's digital culture 313,
317–21, 325
omnilateral diplomacy's digital culture 313,
323–25
plural diplomatic cultures 313
polylateral diplomacy's digital culture 313,
321–25

648 INDEX

digital diplomatic cultures (*cont.*)
  research problems 313–14, 321
  *un*diplomatic cultures 316–17
  see also bilateral diplomacy; multilateral
    diplomacy; omnilateral diplomacy;
    polylateral diplomacy
digital disruption patterns 6, 15–23
  digital grammar rules and 15, 16
  disruption from above 15, 17–18
  disruption from aside 15, 18–20
  disruption from below 15–17
  disruption through crises 15, 21–23
  disruption through diffusion 15, 20–21
  see also disruption
digital divide 256, 378–79, 595
  access inequality to Internet 391–92
  Internet and gender digital divide 257
  UN: digitalization of permanent missions
    and 331, 340–41, 344
  see also North–South divide
digital games (video games) 600–2
  interactivity 605–6, 613
  large audience 605–6
  persuasion and 601–2, 605–6
  politicization of 600–2, 607
digital games and nationalist agenda 19–20,
    602, 603–4, 613–14
  Activision: *Call of Duty: Black Ops Cold
    War* 609
  Azerbaijan: *Under Occupation* 613–14
  Bangladesh: *Heroes of 71* series 613–14
  China 19–20, 607–9
  China: *Black Myth: Wukong* 608–9
  China: *Glorious Mission* 602, 609
  China: *H1Z1* 603–4, 604*f*
  China: *Three Kingdoms* 607–8
  digital cultural diplomacy and 19–20, 605,
    613
  India 19–20, 610–13
  India: *FAU-G* 602, 611–12, 612*f*, 613
  Iran's Revolutionary Guard Corps:
    Save the Freedom and *Resistance
    Commander* 613–14
  'magic node' 605, 606–7, 613
  Pakistan 19–20, 610–13
  Pakistan: *Glorious Resolve* 602, 610
  'possibility spaces' 605, 606–7, 613

'propagames' 601–2
propaganda 602, 605–6, 607, 609
proprioception 607
radicalization 605, 606
Sri Lanka: *Nero* 613–14
techno-nationalism 19–20, 605
terrorism 605, 606
theoretical framework and
  methodology 606–7, 613
Turkey: *Adalet Namluda 2* 613–14
war video games and improvement of
  military reputation among players 609
digital grammar rules 6, 7–14
  computational personalization 7, 10–12, 12*f*
  constructive/destructive purposes in
    diplomatic relations 14
  digital disruption patterns and 15, 16
  emotional framing 7, 8–10, 10*f*, 20
  engagement hybridization 7, 13
  impact on policy outcomes 6, 15
  visual simplicity 7–8, 9*f*, 20
digital hybridization of diplomacy 17, 291–92,
    307–8
  assemblage theory 292, 293–94, 302, 303,
    306, 307–8
  compact, mosaic, canvas assemblages 292,
    302, 303–4, 305*t*, 306–8
  definition 295, 307–8
  digital assemblages and 17, 292
  digital hybridization, theoretical
    framework 293–96
  digital hybridization as assemblage
    formation 294–96, 296*f*
  methodology 293, 296
  transformation of boundaries
    between diplomacy and digital
    technology 306–7
digital hybridization of diplomacy: Nordic/
    Baltic countries comparison 292, 296,
    307–8
  canvas assemblages 302, 304–5, 305*t*, 306,
    307–8
  compact assemblages 302–3, 305, 305*t*,
    306–8
  Denmark 299–300, 301, 302
  Denmark, compact assemblages 302–3,
    304, 305, 306, 307–8

digital diplomacy 1.0 in Nordic and Baltic
states 297–99, 298*t*
digital hybridization, distribution of the
intensity by country 300–1, 301*t*
digital hybridization in action 306–7
digital hybridization in practice 299–301
digital hybridization themes 299, 299*t*
digital hybridization themes, distribution
by country 299–300, 300*t*
digital hybridization themes and intensity,
distribution by region 301, 302*t*
digital hybridization in theory 302–5
Estonia 300, 301, 302
Estonia, canvas assemblages 302, 304–5,
306, 307–8
Finland 300, 301, 302
Finland, mosaic assemblages 302, 303–4,
305, 306, 307–8
Latvia 300, 301, 302
Latvia, canvas assemblages 302, 304–5, 306,
307–8
Lithuania 299–300, 301, 302
Lithuania, mosaic assemblages 302, 303–4,
305, 306, 307–8
mosaic assemblages 302, 303–4, 305, 305*t*,
306–8
Sweden 299–300, 301, 302
Sweden, compact assemblages 302–3, 304,
305, 306, 307–8
see also digital hybridization of diplomacy
digital influence industry *see* DII
digitalization 420–21
international political economy
and 589–90
national borders and 57
uncertainty 57
digitalization of diplomacy 21, 311–12
as contested issue within international
diplomacy 117
definition 4–5
digitalization of diplomacy/digital
diplomacy distinction 4–5
impact of digitalization 103–7, 108–17
Latin America 547–49
see also cities and digitalization of
diplomacy; UN: digitalization of
permanent missions

digital medium
data and 7
as message 6–14
see also digital grammar rules
digital propaganda 212–13, 226
2016 US presidential elections: Russian
intervention in 215
'attention backbone' and 'propaganda
pipeline' 216
audience and 83
'black' propaganda 80
challenges in analysis of 224–26
China and 222–23
computational propaganda 143, 212–13,
214, 233
Covid-19 pandemic 224
as 'dark side' of digital diplomacy 214–15
digital diplomacy: challenges 4, 214–15, 226
digital games and nationalist agenda 602,
605–6, 607, 609
digital propaganda and digital
diplomacy 212–13, 214–15, 216, 217–22,
224–25, 226
digital propaganda/digital diplomacy
distinction 217–23, 218*t*
disinformation and misinformation 214
grey propaganda 90–91
hybrid media landscapes and 212–13, 216,
223, 225–26
as multimodal practice 212–13
'network propaganda' 215–16
'Niagara of spin' 213
'participatory propaganda' 83–84
Poland: 'LGBT-free zones' 223–24
'post-truth culture' 213, 214–15, 221
'reality effects' 214–15, 221
Russian state-sponsored propaganda 217–
20, 225–26
social media and 83, 213, 215, 216, 225
'strategic lying' 223
surveillance and 83
UK: Brexit referendum 223
see also DII; propaganda
Digital Revolution 22–23, 179, 184, 313–14
DII (digital influence industry) 19, 80, 84–86, 92
actor-centric analysis 83–84, 92
Big Techs and 81, 86–87, 92

650 INDEX

DII (digital influence industry) (*cont.*)
  definition 84, 85, 86
  development of 86–89
  DII cases 89
  DIM (digital influence mercenaries) 86,
    87–88, 92
  distribution of propaganda, deception,
    information advantage 80, 84
  ethical AI audits 81
  Facebook and 90
  governments and politicians/state
    actors 86–87, 89, 90, 92
  grey propaganda goes digital 90–91
  influence actors 81–83, 86
  influence economy 86
  information collection and analysis 80,
    84–85
  international politics and 84, 89–90
  legacy industries and 86–88
  lobbying and 82, 85, 87–88
  NATO's survey 89–90
  priority of surveying the DII 89–90
  regulation and policy 85, 88, 92
  Russia and 89–91
  surveillance and 84–85, 87, 88
  tactics 84
  UK and 90–91
  unethical behaviour 87–88, 89, 90
  US and 87, 90–91
  Western democracies and 90–91
  see also digital propaganda; IO; propaganda
Dijk, J. van 237
Dinnie, Keith 38
diplomacy
  city diplomacy 19–20, 223–24, 263, 401–3,
    404–5, 415
  coercive diplomacy 536
  definition 106, 212, 237, 312
  diplomatic agency 134, 237–38, 292, 390, 537
  diplomatic ethics 238, 239–40, 243
  diplomatic loyalty 239–41
  diplomatic representation, four waves
    of 424
  everyday diplomacy 103–4, 324
  feminist foreign policy and 'diplomacy' (as
    soft power 'resource') 163, 168, 172
  humanity-centred diplomacy 241

open diplomacy 233, 238
  'quantum diplomacy' 250–51, 263
  reciprocal relationship between society and
    diplomacy 59
  transnational diplomacy 384
  undiplomatic diplomacy 316–17, 370–71,
    531, 535
  see also bilateral diplomacy; blended
    diplomacy; cultural diplomacy; digital
    diplomacy; diplomatic negotiations;
    face-to-face diplomacy; hybrid
    diplomacy; multilateral diplomacy;
    nuclear diplomacy; omnilateral
    diplomacy; polylateral diplomacy; public
    diplomacy
diplomatic corps 312, 394, 532
  digital diplomatic cultures and 314, 315–16,
    317
  EEAS (EU) 459–60
  New York City: MOIA (US) 409–10
diplomatic negotiations (digital age) 16, 103–
    4, 116–17
  digitalization as challenge 105–6, 112–14,
    116–17
  digitalization as facilitator 105, 109–11,
    116–17
  digitalization as negotiated 106–7, 114–17
  digitally modified documents 106–7
  EU 104, 107–16
  impact of digitalization 103–7, 108–17
  negotiation as 'blended practice' 104
  smartphones 104, 110
  social media apps 104, 105, 110, 111
  Telegram 105
  video conferencing 104, 105
  WhatsApp 105
  see also EU digital diplomacy
diplomatic summitry 367–68, 369–70
  bilateral/multilateral summits 369–70
  civil society, private sector, media
    representatives, celebrities,
    protesters 370, 371
  definition 369–70
  'EU summits' 370
  multilateral diplomacy and 367, 368, 369–
    70, 372
  propaganda purposes 370–71

Sherpas/sub-Sherpas 370
see also virtual diplomatic summitry
diplomats
  digital tools and 425
  Facebook 52
  future for diplomats in a digital age 433
  information keeping vs information
    sharing 50–51
  as 'interpreters' or 'translators' 238
  as lobbyists and facilitators 47
  omnilateral diplomacy and 323
  power and 237–38, 421
  social media and 426–27
  as societal actors moulding public
    opinion 50
  transparency 425
  use of technology as shaped by personal
    experiences 16
  see also MFAs; tech ambassadors
disinformation 51, 65, 179–80, 422, 537,
    574–75
  China 537–38
  Covid-19 pandemic 189–90, 224, 276–77
  decline in trust and credibility toward
    government and experts 47
  definition 213
  digital nuclear diplomacy and 142–43,
    144–45
  digital propaganda and 214
  GCC countries 574–75
  malinformation/disinformation
    distinction 54
  misinformation/disinformation
    distinction 213
  non-state actors and 537
  nuclear diplomacy and 142–43, 144–45
  Online Disinformation of the European
    Commission 213
  organizational models of 'disinformation
    production' 85
  Russia 189–90, 240, 243
  Russia–Ukraine War 189–90
  social media and 355, 622
  virality of 53
  Wild West 19, 80
disruption
  definition 3

as different from technological
    innovation 45
digital disruption, definition 45–46
new media technology disruption and
    global crises (historical perspective) 178,
    185–87, 188, 189, 190–91
positive/negative connotations of 3
technological disruption 3, 5–6, 45–46, 430
see also digital diplomacy and disruption;
    digital disruption patterns
Dittmer, Jason 294
Dodds, K. 603
Douek, E. 82
Douyin (ByteDance, China) 269–70, 271,
    272–73, 280–81
Drew, Alexi 144
Drezner, Daniel W. 45, 59
Drieschova, Alena 115
Duda, Andrzej 278
Dunbar, Robert 600
Duncombe, Constance 145, 406, 476–77, 564–65
Duterte, Rodrigo 534

E
East Timor 389
Ebrard, Marcelo 555
EBRD (European Bank of Reconstruction and
    Development) 354–55
Ecker-Ehrhardt, Matthias 18
ECOSOC (Economic and Social
    Council) 255–56
Ecuador 548–49, 592
  see also Latin America digital diplomacy
Edenborg, Emil 483–84
Edward VII, King of the United Kingdom and
    the British Dominions 180, 181
EEAS (European External Action Service) 8,
    9f, 107–8, 274–75, 457–58, 463–64, 466–67
  creation of 319, 459–60, 469
  digital diplomacy 459–61, 462, 465, 467,
    468–69
  Digital Diplomacy Task Force 460–61
  digitalization of EU foreign policy 460–61
  social media and 460–61, 463–64, 467–68
  Strategic Communication and Foresight
    unit 460
  see also EU; EU digital diplomacy

652 INDEX

Egeland, Kjølv 145
Eggeling, Kristin Anabel 13–14, 16, 312, 319–20, 394–95
Egypt 583–84
Einstein, Albert 133–34, 141
Ekengren, A. M. 470
Electronic Arts 600
Ellul, Jacques 81, 83
El Salvador 550
  see also Latin America digital diplomacy
embassies
  'algorithmic diplomacy' 11–12
  computational personalization and 11
  Internet and 421
  physical embassies 4
  social media and 30, 291, 297, 421
  TikTok and 273–74
  US embassies 183
  video-conferencing 13
  virtual embassies 5, 17–18, 262, 426
  see also digital hybridization of diplomacy
emotions/emotionality
  China's 'Wolf Warrior' diplomacy and 511
  digital media and politics of emotions 602–6, 613
  emotional contagion 8–9
  emotional framing as digital grammar rule 7, 8–10, 10f, 20
  emotional turn in international relations 602, 613
  social media and 8–9, 20, 178–79, 243, 349
  Twitter 10, 10f, 564–65
Engtoft, Anne Marie 19–20
ENISA (European Network and Information Security Agency) 468–69
Entman, R.M. 623–24
Erlandsen, M. 546–47, 548
Espinoza, L. M. 549, 554–55, 556
espionage/electronic espionage 130, 134, 585
  Brazil on 585, 594
  BRICS countries on 585
  China 130, 134
  EU digital diplomacy and 112
  international law and 594
  Internet governance and 585, 593–94
  spyware 84–85, 86, 88, 584
  see also surveillance

Estonia 121, 179–80, 427
  canvas assemblages 302, 304–5, 306, 307–8
  cybersecurity 297–99
  DDOS attacks 121–22
  digital diplomacy 297–99
  digital hybridization of diplomacy 300, 301, 302
  see also digital hybridization of diplomacy
ethics 233–34
  ambiguity of 234
  communication ethics 239, 243
  diplomatic ethics 238, 239–40, 243
  ethical AI audits 81
  Kant on 234
  Plato on 234, 239
  traditional/digital diplomacy difference 238–39
  see also public diplomacy: ethical challenges of digitalization
EU (European Union)
  2009 Lisbon Treaty 112–13, 461, 466
  2016 *EU Global Strategy* 462–64, 466
  Brussels 107–8
  COREPER (Councils of C6 Permanent Representatives) 107–8, 110
  COREPER I 107–8, 111f, 113
  COREPER II 107–8, 113
  Council of the EU 53
  Council presidency 110–11, 116
  cyber governance 117, 442, 443, 445–46, 449, 450–51
  Cybersecurity Strategy 128
  Data Protection Directive and General Data Protection Regulation 88, 588–89
  EUSRs (Special Representatives) 461n.5
  intergovernmental/supranational cooperation 319
  international development 254, 263
  Online Disinformation of the European Commission 213
  PERMREPs (permanent representations) 107–8
  PSC (Political and Security Committee) 107–8, 110
  as regional diplomatic system 319

'resilience' (foreign policy
  approach) 462–63
Ukrainian entry into 190
see also EEAS
EU digital diplomacy 18, 108, 115, 325, 355,
  457–59, 469–71
2015 Iran Nuclear Deal 18, 465
blended diplomacy 114
capability-expectations digital gap 471
challenges and risks of 112–14, 115–16, 458,
  466–70
confidentiality 114, 116
COREPER 110, 113–14
COREPER I 111*f*
Covid-19 pandemic 108, 110, 112–13, 319,
  457
crises faced by 468–69
cyber governance 117, 442, 443, 445–46,
  449, 450–51
Cybersecurity Strategy 128, 467–68
digitally oriented culture 321
Digital Services Act and Digital Markets
  Act 117, 445–46, 449
espionage and 112
EU ambassadors 15–16, 461
EU civilian and military
  missions 461–62n.7
EU delegations 461–62, 467, 469–70
European Commission's DGs 462, 463–65,
  466
Facebook 112–13
hacking 112
hybrid institutional arrangement
  and 457–58
impact of digitalization 108–9
'Interactio' platform 112–13
leaking 112, 114
legitimacy and reputation 457–58, 459–62,
  467–69
live streaming/*Council Live* 109–10
multilateral diplomacy's digital culture 316,
  319–20, 325
'open data' portal 109–10
origins and evolution of 459–62, 459n.1
'Pexit' platform 112–13
public diplomacy 459–60, 461, 466–67,
  468–69

recommendations for 469–70
Signal 110
social media and 18, 457, 460–61, 463–64,
  465, 467–68, 469, 470
soft power 457–58, 462–63
Telegram 110, 341
transparency 114
Twitter 110–11, 114, 117, 457, 464–65
unmanageable information flows 115–16,
  466–67
video-conferencing 108, 110
virtual meetings as informal meetings (no
  formal decision-making power) 112–13
virtual voting 378
WhatsApp 110, 111, 112–13, 116
see also diplomatic negotiations; EEAS
Extinction Rebellion 322

F

Facebook 5, 6–7, 427, 585–86, 588
6 January 2021 (US) and 91
Asia Pacific digital diplomacy and 535,
  537–38, 539
attribution data and analysis 81
Cambridge Analytica and 73
Central Asian countries 497–98, 500–1,
  501*t*
China 282
cultural diplomacy and 202–3
cybersecurity 134
DII and 90
diplomats 52
EU digital diplomacy and 112–13
international bureaucracies 349–50, 351–53,
  353*f*
Israeli-Palestinian conflict 627–28
mass removal of pro-US fake
  accounts 90–91
NATO 477–78
Nordic/Baltic countries comparison 298*t*
Russia and 91
Russia–Ukraine War 51
surveillance and 73n.2, 584
as threat 540
UN and 338, 342
UN Secretariat 351
see also social media

654 INDEX

face-to-face diplomacy (in-person/analogue/
offline diplomacy) 4, 141, 177–78, 190–91
advantages of 13
compared to virtual interaction 378
hybridity complementing face-to-face
diplomacy 13, 14f, 320
Malaysia 534
offline diplomacy 5, 9–10, 13, 325, 421–22
online 'front-stage'/offline diplomatic
'back-stage' relationship 291–92, 307,
393–94, 421–22, 512–13
'fake news' 69n.1, 73–74, 216, 226
conflict escalation and 143, 144–45
definition 214
diplomacy and 214
GCC countries 568
High Level Expert Group on Fake News 213
UK 88
Farkas, J. 214
Fedorova, K. 607
feedback loop 22, 32, 36–38, 39, 42, 216
Feinberg, R. 370
feminist foreign policy (digital) 18, 157–59, 175
backlash against a state 174
'branding' (soft power 'resource') 163, 168, 171
Canada 174
conceptual framework 161–63
'culture' (soft power 'resource') 162–63,
166–68, 170–71
digital diplomacy and 160–61
'diplomacy' (soft power 'resource') 163, 168,
172
France 174
gender equality, advocacy of 158, 161, 162–
63, 165–66, 167f, 169, 170f, 172–73, 175, 235
methodology 163–65
Mexico 158–59, 161–62, 169, 172–73, 175
Mexico's soft power 'resources' 170–72, 171f
Mexico's Twitter Account @SRE_mx 169–
72, 170f
Mexico/Sweden comparative analysis 169,
171, 172–74, 173f
politics of attraction 158, 159–60, 162–63,
174, 175
soft power and 158–59, 160, 161–62, 175
soft power 'resources' 162–63, 162f, 164, 172,
173f

as strategy for states to express their morals
and values 158, 175
as strategy for states to promote their brand
and image 158, 161, 175
Sweden 158–59, 161–63, 165–66, 172–73, 175,
235, 297
Sweden's soft power 'resources' 166–68,
167f
Sweden's Twitter Account @SweMFA 166–
68, 167f
'tourism' (soft power 'resource') 163, 168, 171
'trade' (soft power 'resource') 163, 168, 172
Twitter as digital diplomacy tool 161, 163–65,
173–74
see also soft power
Feng Ji 608–9
Fernández Pasarín, Ana Mar 314, 560
Finland
Capital of Metal 297–99
digital diplomacy 297–99
digital hybridization of diplomacy 300,
301, 302
mosaic assemblages 302, 303–4, 305, 306,
307–8
national emojis 297–99
see also digital hybridization of diplomacy
Finnemore, Martha 440
Fisher, C. 223
Fjällhed, Alicia 20–21
Fletcher, Tom 16, 19–20, 66
Flew, Terry 65–66
Flockhart, Trine 479
foreign policy as tool of attraction 18, 157–59,
174
Forest, James J. 85, 86, 605
Fox, Vincente 67
France 20, 174
Louvre Museum 236
François, C. 82
Frank, John 439–40
Franz Ferdinand, Archduke 185–86
Fraser, Matthew 65–66
Fraser, Ryan 202
Freelon, D. 213
Friedman, Thomas 68–69
Fuchs, C. 237
Fulbright, William J. 70

G

G7 (Group of Seven) 13, 172–73, 367, 377
G20 (Group of Twenty) 367, 375, 377
Gaber, I. 223
Gagarin, Yuri 54–55
games
 Central Asian countries and SMD: game
  setting 496, 505–6
 Game Studies 600–2, 605
 game theory 431–32, 492, 495, 505
 gaming 177–78
 ludification of culture 601–2
 see also digital games; digital games and
  nationalist agenda
Gaston, Sophia 68
Gates, Melinda 257
GCC/GCC countries (Gulf Cooperation
  Council) 564, 575–76
 2011 Arab uprisings 565–66, 567
 Arab Charter on Human Rights 565–66
 Arab and Islamic cultures 565
 authoritarian adaptation to digital
  activism 565–66
 Charter 565
 climate change challenges 574
 disinformation 574–75
 e-government 566
 Global Cybersecurity Index 566
 migrant populations in 566, 571, 573
 online surveillance 565–66, 575
 public diplomacy 564
 VoIP technology (Voice over Internet
  Protocol), restrictions on 573, 575
GCC countries's digital diplomacy 22, 564–65
 2017–2021 Blockade 564–65, 567–71, 573,
  574, 575–76
 censorship 567–68
 competition and rivalry 22, 565, 573, 574,
  575–76
 Covid-19 pandemic 564–65, 571–74, 575–76
 Covid-19 pandemic: contact tracing
  apps 572–73, 575
 fake news 568
 Internet 565
 MFAs 564–65, 568–71, 575
 social media 564–65, 568–69, 573, 574, 575
 Twitter 564–65, 567–71, 573

GCSC (Global Commission on the Stability of
  Cyberspace) 439
Gehl, R. 83
Gelb, Leslie 65–66
Gengler, J.J. 573
Geng Shuang 511–12
GenZ For Change 273–74
Georgia 122
Germany 56, 444, 594
Ghica, Luciana Alexandra 18
Gilboa, Eytan 69–70, 250–51
Gillard, Julia 273–74
Gillespie, T. 574–75
Glassman, James K. 183–84
global humanism and 240, 241
globalization 68–69, 124, 194, 195, 235, 384,
  589, 621
 anti-globalization 587, 596
 deglobalization 547
 diplomacy and 240–41, 368, 547
 'slowbalization' 587
Goebbels, Josef 186
Goffman, Erving
 dramaturgical symbolic interactionism/
  social theory 31–32, 33–37
 *Presentation of the Self in Everyday Life,
  The* 33
Golan, G. J. 217
Golovchenko, Y. 225–26
Google 423, 451, 539, 584, 585–86
 cybersecurity 134
 global cultural digitization activities
  by 203–4
 Google Arts and Culture Institute 203, 204
 Google Books Project 203–4
 as threat 540
Gorbachev, Mikhail S. 188, 315
governance
 algorithmic governance 6, 20–21, 270, 282
 China and global governance 523
 global governance 348–49, 357–58, 362,
  380, 420–21, 439–40, 601–2
 global governance actors 199, 348–49, 360–
  61, 371, 586
 international bureaucracies and global
  governance 348–49, 350, 351–52, 358–59,
  361–62

656 INDEX

governance (*cont.*)
  IOs and global governance 348–49, 351–52
  social media and global governance 360–61
  see also cyber governance; Internet
    governance
Gray, J. E. 271, 272–73, 281–82
Greenhill, Kelly M. 143
Gregory, Bruce 404
Grincheva, Natalia 17
Griner, Brittney 232, 314–15
Grix, Jonathan 161–62
Grossi, Rafael Mariano 150, 151*f*
Grove, Nicole Sunday 151–52
Gual Soler, Marga 553
Guardian, The 281–82, 342
Guattari, Felix 293–94
Guerrina, Roberta 467–68
Guterres, Antonio (UN Secretary-General) 8,
    9*f*, 353–54, 360–61

H
Habegger, Michael 324
Habermas, J. 35–36, 238, 450
hacking 73, 82, 84–85, 422
  2014 North Korean hacking against Sony
    Pictures Entertainment 122–23, 131
  2016 North Korean hacking against
    Bangladeshi Central Bank 122–23, 131
  2016 US presidential election and Russian
    hacking 123, 125–26, 128–29
  2020 'Solar Winds' hacking, US 131
  2022 Iranian hacking of Albania's
    governmental systems 128
  DII and 84–85
  EU digital diplomacy 112
  of 'Starlink' satellite-based Internet service
    (Elon Musk's) 134
  see also information warfare
Hague, William 482–83
Hai-chi Loo, Jeff 22
Hall, Nina 322
Hamilton, Jack 185–86
Hamilton, K. 384
Hankey, S. 85
Hannan, Patrick 67
Hansen, Abbey 273–74
Hanska, J. 478–79

Hao, K. 82
hard power 65–66, 67–68, 263–64, 462–63
  'hard'/soft power distinction 66
  'hard'/soft power intersection 65, 69–70
  see also power
Hartig, F. 222–23
Haugen, Frances 446–47
Hedling, Elsa 22, 319–20, 408–9, 476, 483–84,
    531, 537, 572
Heider, Fritz 600
Heine, Jorge 21
Heinonen, S. 405
Hershey, John 141
Hersman, Rebecca 144–45
Heusgen, Christoph 273–74
Hindman, M. 91
Hitler, Adolf 186, 187
Ho, E. L. E. 386
Hoffman, Donns L. 294–95
Hofstede, Geert 312
Hollis, D. B. 440
Holmes, Marcus 22, 315
Höne, Katharina E. 342, 343
Hong Kong 511–12, 514, 519, 520–22
Horowitz, I. L. 233
Howard, P. 214
HRC (Human Rights Council, UN) 390–92
Hua Chunying 511–12, 517–18, 519–20
Huang, Zhao Alexandre 16
Huawei 540, 591–92
  5G 540, 582, 591, 596
  US/China clashes on 445, 582, 583, 591–93,
    596
Hughes, R. 603
Human Rights Watch 565–66, 573
humour 12, 20, 46, 47
  nuclear diplomacy and 138, 139, 148
  Ukraine 20, 631
  see also memes
Hurel, L. 440
Hutchinson, E. 603, 606
Hu Xijin 519–20
hybrid diplomacy 5, 46, 261–62, 311–12, 320
  as analogue/digital spectrum 311–12
  bilateral diplomacy as 314–15, 316–17
  as complement to face-to-face
    diplomacy 13, 14*f*, 320

Covid-19 pandemic and 13, 22, 320, 429
definition 13
diplomatic summitry 367–68, 371–72, 377–79
efficacy of 13
engagement hybridization as digital
    grammar rule 7, 13
engagement hybridization and disruption
    from below 15–16
international development cooperation
    and 261–62
see also blended diplomacy; digital
    hybridization of diplomacy

I

IACtHR (InterAmerican Human Rights
    Court) 353–54
IAEA (International Atomic Energy
    Agency) 140, 146, 150–51, 151*f*
IATI (International Aid Transparency
    Initiative) 254
ICAN (International Campaign to Abolish
    Nuclear Weapons) 146, 148–50
Instagram and 148–49, 149*f*
TikTok and 148–49, 274
ICANN (Internet Corporation for Assigned
    Names and Numbers) 439, 584, 585, 594
Iceland 427
Akureyri, digitalization of diplomacy 402,
    407, 410, 412, 413, 414, 415
ICRC (International Committee of the Red
    Cross) 274
ICTs (Information Communications
    Technologies) 70–71
international development cooperation
    and 256–57, 263, 264–65
SDGs and ICT skills 256–57
identity
digital identity 31
projection of 30, 31, 36–38
Ifantis, Kostas 65–66
IFRC (International Federation of Red Cross
    and Red Crescent Societies) 274–75
IIE (Institute of International
    Education) 187–88
Ilden, Tacam 477–78
image war
battle over perceptions and 620–24, 629–32

digital diplomacy and 624–32
digital platforms and 619
visual images 620, 621, 622–23, 625–26,
    630–31
see also wars and conflicts: digital
    diplomacy in
IMF (International Monetary Fund) 252,
    371–72
India 590–91
Atmanirbhar Bharat 611
digital games and nationalist agenda 19–
    20, 610–13
Digital India 611
India/China clashes 610–13
international development 254
Made in India 611
nationalism 611
TikTok and 273, 282
see also BRICS countries
Indonesia 530, 532, 533, 537
social media 533, 534–35
see also Asia Pacific digital diplomacy
influencers 84–85, 141–42
cultural diplomacy and 195, 198, 205, 206–7
NATO and 145
power of 198
TikTok and 273–74, 275–76, 277–78, 281
see also DII
information
information overload 73–74, 144
Information Revolution 63, 105
'prosumers' 621n.1
information warfare 73, 80, 144–45, 213, 221–
    22, 478
'virtuous warfare' 605
see also cyberattacks and threats; cyberwar;
    hacking; trolling
Instagram 6–7, 117, 349
Central Asian countries 497–98
cultural diplomacy and 202–3, 205
ICAN and 148–49, 149*f*
Latin America digital diplomacy
    and 553–54
NATO 477–78
Nordic/Baltic countries comparison 298*t*
UN and 338
see also social media

Institute for Propaganda Analysis 187–88
intelligence
  CIA 51
  data mining 32n.9
  intelligence gathering 30, 51, 106
  MI6 51
  OSINT (Open Source Intelligence) 82, 177–78, 395–96
  social media and 32n.9, 51
Intercept, The 281–82
international bureaucracies and digital diplomacy 18, 348–50, 362
  acceleration 359–60
  accountability 354–55, 358–59
  advocacy 355–56, 361–62
  audience diversity 354–55
  challenges 349–50, 356–62
  digitalization of international bureaucracies 350–53
  EU 355
  Facebook 349–50, 351–53, 353f
  global governance and 348–49, 350, 351–52, 358–59, 361–62
  NATO 352–54, 355
  organized hypocrisy 357–58
  personalization 360–61
  pluralization 358
  polarization 361–62
  reasons for digitalization 353–56
  'secretariats' 348
  selectivity 358–59
  self-legitimation 355, 358–59, 360–61, 362
  social media 349, 350–53, 355–56, 357–59, 360–61
  top-down mode of broadcasting 357–58
  transparency 354–55
  Twitter 349–53, 353f, 359–60
  UN Secretariat 350–51, 353–54, 355–56, 358–62
  see also IOs
international development cooperation 18, 250–51, 264–65
  AI and 261–62
  'blended'/'hybrid' diplomacy 261–62
  Bruntland report 252–53
  CDG (Global Digital Compact) 261
  coherence, effectiveness, and transparency mechanisms 253–55

development 251–55
  digital cooperation agenda 255–61
  digital cooperation agenda: current framework 255–57
  digital cooperation agenda: preparing for the future 257–61
  digital skills and 256–57
  diplomatic work, challenges and trends 261–64
  donors/providers of funding 254, 263
  Global North/South divide 251–52, 254
  ICTs and 256–57, 263, 264–65
  Internet connectivity 261
  ODA 251, 254, 263
  OECD 251, 254
  open-data initiatives 263
  'quantum diplomacy' 250–51, 263
  SDGs 253–54, 256–57
  sustainable development framing, emergence of 252–53
  Tuvalu 262
  UN and 18, 250, 252–53, 256–62, 264–65
  UN *Agenda 2030* 253, 256
  UN *Roadmap for Digital Cooperation* 257, 259t, 261–62
  UN Secretary General 255–56, 257–61
  US, 3D approach (Defence, Diplomacy, and Development) 253
  Web 3.0 technologies 261–62
international law
  cyber governance and 441–43, 446–48, 450
  electronic espionage and 594
  'international internet law' 449
  international law on cyberspace, theoretical approaches 448–51
  see also cyber governance
international relations
  digital diplomacy and disruption 4
  emotional turn in 602, 613
  soft power and international relations discourse 70
  technological innovation and 45
Internet 420–21, 493
  access inequality to 391–92, 540
  Central Asian countries 493–94, 493t
  China 126–27, 444, 589
  digital and broadband divides 257

digital diplomatic cultures and 313
Estonia 121
GCC countries 565
gender digital divide 257
global open Internet 126–27
Internet access as human right 121
Internet cables 540, 584, 585–86, 590–91,
 592–93, 596
Internet connectivity 261
material infrastructure of 585–86, 590, 596
public diplomacy and 183–84
Russia 126–27, 444, 589
Splinternet 127
state Internet shutdowns 392
surveillance and censorship 126–27, 444,
 589
Sweden 183
US 183–84
see also Internet governance
Internet Engineering Task Force 439
Internet governance 21, 396, 450, 582–83
 Brazil 585, 594, 596
 China 589, 590
 democratic vs authoritarian model 127
 electronic espionage, regulation of 585,
  593–94
 Europe 588–89
 Germany 594
 IGF (Internet Governance Forum) 255–56
 India 590–91
 international political economy of 585–86
 Internet freedom vs. government
  control 583–85
 Internet governance/cyber governance
  distinction 129–30
 multilateral approach 582, 585, 590–91, 594
 muti-stakeholder approach 199, 255–56,
  439, 582, 585, 590–91
 reform of 594
 Russia 590
 US 582, 585–86, 588, 590–91, 594, 596
 see also cyber governance; governance;
  ICANN; North–South divide
IO (influence operations) 80, 85, 92
 attribution methods 81, 82
 destabilization operations 89
 hybrid threats/attacks 85–86, 89

non-attribution, rise of 91
 scholarship on 81, 89
 see also DII
IOs (international organizations) 348, 476–77
 'algorithmic diplomacy' 11–12
 definition 348
 digital diplomacy and 3–4
 global governance and 348–49, 351–52
 ICTs and 330
 permanent missions 330–31
 permanent missions, digitalization of 330
 see also international bureaucracies
  and digital diplomacy; NATO; UN:
  digitalization of permanent missions
IP migration 129–30
 IPv4/IPv6 129–30
Iran 48
 2015 Iran Nuclear Deal (JCPOA—Joint
  Comprehensive Plan of Action) 18, 51,
  53, 145, 425, 465
 2022 hacking of Albania's governmental
  systems 128
 Revolutionary Guard Corps: *Save
  the Freedom* and *Resistance
  Commander* 613–14
 soft power 71
 Twitter 10, 10*f*, 71
Israel 626–27
 MFAs 20, 21, 55–56
 nostalgic tropes in diplomacy 55–56
 soft power 179–80
 Twitter 55–56
Israeli-Palestinian conflict 626–29, 632–33
 2008–09 round 626–27
 2012 round 626–27
 2014 Gaza War 406
 2021 Gaza War 628–29
 civil society 627–28
 Facebook 627–28
 Israeli side 626–29
 Palestinian side 626–27, 628–29
 TikTok 628–29, 632–33
 Twitter 626–28
 YouTube 626–27
 see also wars and conflicts: digital
  diplomacy in
Ito, Kenji 140

660   INDEX

ITU (International Telecommunication
    Union) 129–30, 585
  Global Cybersecurity Index 566
  WSIS (World Summit on the Information
    Society) 255–56

J

Jablinski, Danielle 142–43
Jakobsen, P. V. 479
Japan 183
  Blue Book 532
  digital diplomacy 530, 532, 537, 538
  Hiroshima and Nagasaki 139, 141, 149–50
  nation branding 538
  social media 532
  see also Asia Pacific digital diplomacy
Jervis, Robert 603
Jiang, L. 575
Jiang Zemin 608
Johnson, Boris 58, 67, 232
Jolie, Angelina 145, 480, 481, 482–84
Jones, A. 110
Jones, Marc Owen 75–76, 567–68, 570–71,
    574–75
Jowett, G. 215–16

K

Kaempf, S. 603–4
Kant, Immanuel 234, 323, 324
Kaplan, Robert 610
Kappe, Nikolas 273–74
Kaye, D. B. V. 269–70
Kazakhstan *see* Central Asian countries;
    Central Asian countries and SMD
Keating, M. 390
Keating, Vincent Charles 575–76
Keck, Margaret E. 322, 385–86, 554
Keesing, Roger M. 312
Kello, Lucas 20–21
Kennedy, John F. 141, 183
Kenya 420–21, 426
Kerr, Jaclyn 143
Kerry, John 427, 430
Khrushchev, Nikita 141
King, Martin Luther Jr 141
Kitsell, Corinne 447
Kļaviņš, Didzis 17

Kocher, Tiana 275–76
Kornprobst, Markus 4–5n.1
Kosovo 427–28, 475–76
Krieg, A. 568
Kumbleben, Mark 143
Kurbalija, J. 389
Kuwait 565, 566, 573
    see also GCC countries's digital diplomacy
Kuzmanovic, A. 276
Kyrgyzstan *see* Central Asian countries;
    Central Asian countries and SMD
Kyslytsya, Sergiy 10, 10f

L

Laity, Mark 91
Lallande, Juan Pablo Prado 21
Lammes, Sybille 605, 606–7
Lampa, Graham 37–38
Langhorne, R. 384
Lapid, Yair 56, 278
Lasso, Guillermo 278–79
Laswell, Harold 187–88
Latin America
    US/China rivalry and 592–93
Latin America digital diplomacy 21, 529, 546–
    47, 560–62
  breakdown of emphases 553, 556–57, 561
  centralized-proliferation of channels 551–
    52, 556
  civil society 554
  consularization of practice 547, 549, 560, 561
  Covid-19 pandemic 547, 549, 558–60, 561
  digitalization of diplomacy 547–49
  electoral campaigns 550
  holistic-specific implementation
    approach 552–53, 556
  Instagram 553–54
  institutional vs. personalized digital
    diplomacy 550–51, 551t, 554–55, 557–58,
    560–61
  MFAs 546–48, 548f, 551t, 552–53, 559, 560,
    561
  mosaic of approximations towards digital
    diplomacy 547, 549–54, 550t, 560
  multilatina corporations 554
  official and non-official actors engaging in
    digital diplomacy 553–54, 561

populism 550
public diplomacy 549
science diplomacy 553
social media 550, 552f, 552–53
soft power 549
statecraft 546–47
Twitter 548–49, 548f, 550, 551t, 551–52, 556t, 560
see also Chile; Mexico
Latvia
canvas assemblages 302, 304–5, 306, 307–8
digital diplomacy 297
digital hybridization of diplomacy 300, 301, 302
see also digital hybridization of diplomacy
Lavrov, Sergey 41
Lawson, S. 83
League of Nations 187–88, 431
leaking 105–6, 112, 114
Leber, Andrew 568
Lemke, Tobias 324
Lewis, Jeffrey 143
liberalism 450
Lin, Herbert S. 142–43
LinkedIn 334–35, 350–51, 421, 477, 583–84
Lippman, Walter 603
Lithuania
digital diplomacy 297
digital hybridization of diplomacy 299–300, 301, 302
mosaic assemblages 302, 303–4, 305, 306, 307–8
see also digital hybridization of diplomacy
live streaming 19, 276
EU digital diplomacy 109–10
UN Security Council sessions 51, 425
Li Ziqi 236
Lobato, L. 440
lobbying
DII and 82, 85, 87–88
'torturer's lobby' 87–88
Locsin, Jr, Teodoro L. 534
Loehrke, Benjamin 142–43
López Obrador, Andrés Manuel 555
Lowenthal, Abraham F. 547–48
Lüfkens, Matthias 20–21
Lutkenhaus, Roel 196

Lynch, D. 459
Lynch, Jessica 201–2
Lyon, David 52

M
Ma, Jack 257
Ma, W. 271
McCarthy, Joe 187
Machiavelli, Niccolò 3
McClory, Jonathan 160
McConnell, Fiona 19–20, 294, 306–7, 324, 386, 393–94
McDermott, Rose 143
MacDonald, F. 603
McDonald, Sir Simon 68
McFaul, Michael 125–26
McGeever, Brendan 58
McLuhan, Marshall 6–7, 30–31, 184–85, 308, 405
Macron, Emmanuel 278–79
Maduro, Nicolás 550
Mahmud Ali, S. 147
Malaysia 534, 537, 538–39
see also Asia Pacific digital diplomacy
malinformation 54
Malala (Yousafzai) 277
Malala Fund 277
Manafort, Paul 87–88
Manby, Alex 19–20
Manfredi-Sánchez, Juan-Luis 224, 547
Manor, Ilan 13, 15–16, 37–38, 39, 42–43, 57, 71, 72–73, 74–75, 221, 232, 316–17, 319–20, 338, 406, 484, 565
Marconi, Guglielmo 180, 181
Matberg, Lasse 480, 481, 483–84
May, Theresa 69, 232
Mayer, R.C. 242
media
digital communication technologies and 141–42
media disarmament 187–88, 190–91
media ecology 142–43, 144, 181–82, 405, 406
media gatekeepers 141–43, 184–85, 242, 243, 281–82, 621
'media warfare' 536
new media ecology 142–43, 144

662   INDEX

media (*cont.*)
  new media technology disruption and
    global crises (historical perspective) 178,
      185–87, 188, 189, 190–91
  weaponization of 178–79
  see also Internet; newspapers/printing
    press; radio; social media; telegraph;
    telephone; television
'media logic' 470
mediatization 239, 402, 406, 471
Melissen, Jan 159–60, 314–15, 318–19, 529, 560
memes 46, 138–39, 141–42, 184–85, 280–81, 631
  BFR (Blackfulla Revolution) 185
  cultural memes 202
  NAFO 138n.1, 150–51
  nuclear diplomacy and 138–39
  Ukraine and 20, 47, 138, 190
  see also humour
MENA region (Middle East and North
    Africa) 572, 573, 574
Meng Wanzhou 591
Mercer, J. 603
Merkel, Angela 584, 593–94
message
  delivery mechanisms and impact of 30–31
  medium as message 6–14, 30–31, 308, 405
  see also communication
Meta 423
metaverse 22–23, 204, 451, 632–33
  definition 204
  digital diplomacy and 3–4, 262, 451
  Tuvalu 262
methodology and research: key objectives 5–6
'MeToo' movement 10–11, 322
Mexico
  Covid-19 pandemic 559–60
  cultural diplomacy 553
  digital diplomacy 547, 549, 551–52, 553–57,
    560
  digital diplomacy infrastructure 555
  feminist foreign policy 158–59, 161–62,
    169–73, 175
  MFA 551–52, 554–56, 559–60
  National Development Plan 554–55
  National Digital Strategy 554–55
  public diplomacy 549
  social media 555–56, 560

Twitter 546, 549, 555, 556, 559–60
Twitter Account @SRE_mx 169–72, 170f
Twitter Account @SRE_mx: soft power
    'resources' 170–72, 171f
  see also feminist foreign policy; Latin
    America digital diplomacy
MFAs (ministries of foreign affairs) 3–4, 20,
    291–92, 343, 423–24, 425, 426
  'algorithmic diplomacy' 11–12
  Asia Pacific countries 530, 531, 535
  branding 20
  Canada 20, 49
  Chile 557–58, 559–60
  computational personalization 11
  Covid-19 pandemic 20, 49
  digital diplomacy as domestic
    diplomacy 20, 47, 48–50
  early adopters 291, 297, 334, 457–58
  emphasis on consular affairs 20
  France 20
  GCC countries 564–65, 568–71, 575
  Israel 20, 21, 55–56
  Latin America 546–48, 548f, 551t, 552–53,
    559, 560, 561
  Lithuania 21
  Mexico 551–52, 554–56, 559–60
  micro/macro-level disruptions and 49–50, 51
  mimicry among 20
  Poland 20, 49
  risk averse/prone MFAs 49
  sarcasm 10, 20
  smartphone applications 20, 49, 50
  social media 20, 21, 31–32, 38, 51, 52–53, 291,
    307–8, 427
  Sweden 38
  UK 12, 20, 21, 48
  Ukraine 20, 40
  US 20, 48
  see also digital hybridization of diplomacy:
    Nordic/Baltic countries comparison;
    feminist foreign policy
Michael, Paul 161–62
micro/macro-level disruptions 16, 58–59
  Big Tech companies 52
  domestic digital diplomacy 47, 48–50
  increased transparent diplomacy 47, 50–54
  MFAs and 49–50, 51

interaction between micro/macro-level
disruptions 46–47, 49, 50, 51, 52, 57, 58–59
macro-level disruption, definition 46–47
micro-level disruption, definition 46
nostalgic tropes in diplomacy 47, 54–58
social media 52–53
see also digital diplomacy and disruption;
nostalgic tropes in diplomacy;
transparency
Microsoft 451, 584, 585–86
cyber governance and 131–32, 439–40
Microsoft Teams 13, 340
see also video-conferencing
Middle East
access to social networking and
Internet 565–66
digital diplomacy in wars and conflicts: US's
activity in the Middle East 624–26
see also GCC/GCC countries; GCC's digital
diplomacy
military, the
cyberspace, militarization of 438
image war 620
military social media sites 148
NATO as military power 476, 478, 486
nuclear diplomacy: US Strategic
Command's nonsensical tweets 146,
147–48, 148f
misinformation 4, 65, 81
2016 Brexit referendum and Russian spread
of misinformation 123
Covid-19 pandemic 276, 540–41
digital propaganda and 214
League of Nations on 187–88
MFAs's initiatives to counter spread of 21
misinformation/disinformation
distinction 213
Russia 39–40
social media and 21, 467–68, 622
TikTok and 276–77
Miskimmon, Alister 145, 478–79
Mitchell, J. S. 568
Modi, Naremdra 611, 613
Mogherini, Federica 457, 460–61, 465, 468–
69, 471
Momani, B. 574
Moody, R. 603

Moon Jae-in 204
Moore, Richard 51
Morales, Evo 551
Moravcsik, Andrew 333
Moreno Cantano, Antonio César 19–20
Morgenthau, H. J. 448–49
Mostajo-Radji, Mohammed 553
Moteari, Noura 574
Mowlana, H. 235–36
Moza bin Nasser, Sheikha 568
Mullen, Mike, Admiral 67
multilateral diplomacy 313–14, 317, 380
analogue–digital spectrum, tendencies
in 319, 320–21, 325
ASEAN 320–21, 325
bilateral/multilateral diplomacy differences 316
diplomatic summitry and 367, 368, 369–70,
371–72
EU 316, 319–20, 325
ITCs and 330
multilateral diplomacy's digital culture 313,
317–21, 325
NGOs and 388
UN 317–19, 325, 333, 341, 344
see also digital diplomatic cultures
Muñoz, Heraldo 557
Murray, S. 107
Murrow, Edward R. 187, 430
Musk, Elon 134, 423, 442–43
Myanmar 539
see also Asia Pacific digital diplomacy

N

NAFO (North Atlantic Fellas
Organization) 138n.1, 146, 150–51, 152f
crowdsourcing 150–52
memes 138n.1, 150–51
Russian war on Ukraine and 138, 150–51
Nagorno-Karabakh dispute 29–30
Nail, Thomas 293–94
nationalism 523
China's assertive nationalism 513–14, 515–
16, 517–18, 522–23
India 611
nostalgic tropes in diplomacy and 47, 58
techno-nationalism 19–20, 605
see also digital games and nationalist agenda

INDEX

nation-state 19, 58, 401–2, 424, 425, 553–54
  cities and 403–5
  cyberwar 215
  see also states/governments
NATO (North Atlantic Treaty
    Organization) 367
  2008 Bucharest Summit 132
  2009 Strasbourg-Kehl Summit 477
  2016 Warsaw Summit 132
  2021 Brussels Summit 132
  Article 5 130–31, 132, 475–76
  between 'values' and 'realpolitik' 475–76
  CCD-COE (Cooperative Cyber Defense
    Centre of Excellence) 132
  CDMA (Cyber Defense Management
    Authority) 132
  cybersecurity 128–29, 132
  DII: NATO's survey 89–90
  Military Committee 352–53
  as military power 476, 478, 486
  Russia–Ukraine War and 13, 421, 475–77
  Sweden's accession to 475–76
NATO digital diplomacy 18, 353–54, 475,
    476–77, 488
  Afghanistan, NATO's involvement in
    (*Return to Hope*) 478, 480, 481, 482–84
  Angelina Jolie's partnership with
    NATO 480, 481, 482–84
  audience for 479
  challenges 478
  civil society and 478
  Covid-19 pandemic 484, 487
  digital nuclear diplomacy 145
  emerging from the 'stone age' 477–78
  Facebook 477–78
  future directions 487–88
  hybrid diplomacy 13
  identity narrative 475, 479, 481–84, 485–87,
    488
  Instagram 477–78
  Islamic State and 478
  issue narratives 475, 479, 484, 485–86, 487
  LinkedIn 477–78
  Matberg, Lasse as 'face of NATO' 480, 481,
    483–84
  method and approach 480
  public diplomacy 477–78, 481–84, 488

Russian invasion of Crimea 478
Russia–Ukraine War 477, 480, 484–87, 488
social media 143, 145, 352–53, 355, 477–78
StratComm 477–79
strategic narratives 475, 476, 478–80,
    481–88
system-level narratives 475, 477, 479, 484
Telegram 477–78, 488
Twitter 38–39, 477–78, 480, 481, 485,
    486–87
WPS agenda (Women, Peace, and
    Security) 481, 484, 486
YouTube 477–78
Navalny, Alexei 444
Neoliberalism 449, 574–75
Neorealism 240, 449
Netanyahu, Benjamin 278
Netflix 423, 585–86, 631–32
Neumann, Iver B. 374
neuromarketing 87
newspapers/printing press 5, 6–7, 65, 313, 430,
    608–9
  World War I and 185–86
New Zealand 442, 479, 584, 592, 594
  see also DEPA
NGOs (non-governmental organizations) 321
  advocacy NGOs 322, 323
  definition and characteristics 385
  paradiplomacy 390
  'parallel diplomacy' 385
  service NGOs 322, 323
  UN and 385
  see also civil society
NGOs and digital diplomacy 4, 19–20, 383–84
  access inequality to Internet and technical
    support 391–92
  benefits of diplomacy digitalization 386–88
  challenges 391–92, 394, 396
  creativity 383–84, 390–91
  cybersecurity risks 391, 392, 396
  emerging trends 395–96
  flexibility 383–84, 388
  formality of diplomatic exchanges 388
  innovation 383–84, 388–91, 395–96
  multilateral diplomacy 388
  'new diplomacy' and the pluralising
    potential of digital diplomacy 384–88

NGOs as digital diplomacy pioneers and
innovators 383–84, 388–91
NGOs, professionalization as diplomatic
actors 389–90
omnilateral diplomacy 323–24
social media 387–88, 390–91
theorizing: spatial and embodied
performances 383–84, 392–95
see also polylateral diplomacy
Nicolson, Sir Harold 212
non-state actors 384
cyber governance 440
digital diplomacy and 4, 194–95, 384–85
disinformation and 537
state/non-state actors dichotomy 195, 199,
200
transnational actors 384
see also civil society; CSOs; diasporas;
NGOs; NGOs and digital diplomacy;
omnilateral diplomacy; polylateral
diplomacy; TANs
North Korea 122–23, 131, 528n.1
North–South divide 21, 596–97
BRICS countries 585, 586, 587, 589, 590,
594, 596
China 589, 590
data collection and privacy rights 588–89
DEPA 595–96
digitalization and international political
economy 589–90
electronic espionage, regulation of 585,
593–94
Europe 588–89
'Five Eyes' group 584, 590, 594
Global South, rise of 587
grievance diplomacy 587
Huawei, US/China clashes on 583, 591–93, 596
international development
cooperation 251–52, 254
Internet, material infrastructure of 585–86,
590, 596
Internet cables 584, 585–86, 590–91, 596
Internet freedom vs. government
control 583–85
Internet governance 582–83, 585, 596
Internet governance, international political
economy of 585–86

Internet governance, multistakeholderism
vs multilateralism 582, 585, 590–91
Non-Aligned Movement 587
US 582, 584, 585–86, 588, 590, 593, 596
US/China rivalry 592–93, 595–96, 597
see also Internet governance
Norway 38
nostalgic tropes in diplomacy 47, 54–58
Brexit campaign 58
Germany 56
Israel 55–56
Lapid and Scholz's visit to the Wannsee
Villa 56
nationalism 47, 58
reliance on nostalgic tropes 47, 57–58
Russia 54–55
social media and 57
UK 55
see also micro/macro-level disruptions
Notthaft, H. 225–26
Novak, Thomas P. 294–95
nuclear diplomacy 22, 138–39, 152–53
anti-nuclear movement 148–50
'atomic diplomacy' 139–40
case study: US Strategic Command's
nonsensical tweets 146, 147–48, 148f
case study: US tweets about arms control
with China 146–47
Cold War 139–40, 141
communication/communication
technologies and 141
conflict escalation 138–39, 142–43, 144–46,
148, 151–52
crisis stability 139, 142–43, 145–46
critique of 140
deterrence 139–40, 142–43, 148–49
digital communication technologies
and 142–46, 152–53
digital nuclear diplomacy 138–39, 141–46,
152–53
digital nuclear diplomacy, scholarship
on 142–46, 152
disinformation and 142–43, 144–45
history of 139–41
humour and 138, 139, 148
Iran Nuclear Deal 51, 53, 145, 425, 465
media and the press 141

666 INDEX

nuclear diplomacy (*cont.*)
  memes and 138–39
  NATO and 145
  new nuclear age 146, 147, 152
  nuclear alliances/umbrellas 140
  nuclear proliferation 140
  nuclear signalling 138–39, 140
  nuclear war 139, 142–43, 146, 148, 150, 152–53
  populism as threat to nuclear order 145
  as processes and practices occurring at
    broad range of sites 140–41
  Putin's nuclear threats 150–51
  social media and 143, 144, 145–46, 147, 148–
    50, 151–53
  trolling and 138–39, 142–43, 144
  Zaporizhzhya power plant 150, 151*f*
  see also IAEA; ICAN; NAFO; nuclear
    weapons
nuclear weapons
  1962 Cuban Missile Crisis 141, 142–43
  arms control 139–40, 141, 146–47, 152–53
  arms race 146, 431–32
  China 146
  Cold War 139, 141, 146
  development of 140, 146
  disarmament 140, 150, 152–53
  Hiroshima and Nagasaki, Japan 139, 141,
    149–50
  legitimacy of nuclear weapons and social
    media 145
  Manhattan project 431–32
  New START treaty 146–47
  NPT (Non-Proliferation Treaty) 140
  online normalization of 148–49
  Russia 146–47
  Soviet Union 139, 141
  TPNW (Treaty on the Prohibition of
    Nuclear Weapons) 148–49
  US 139–40, 141, 145, 146–47
  see also nuclear diplomacy
Nye, Joseph 66, 67, 69–71, 72, 74–75, 157, 159,
  160

O

Obama, Barak 128–29, 217
  Obama administration 37–38, 39, 42, 48,
    50, 184

Obama, Michelle 39
Occupy protests (2011) 10–11
ODA (Official Development Aid) 251, 254,
  263
O'Donnell, V. 215–16
OECD (Organisation for Economic Cooperation and Development) 251, 254,
  572
offline diplomacy *see* face-to-face diplomacy
Ohnesorge, Hendrick 66
O'Loughlin, Ben 144, 145, 478–79
Oman 565, 566
  see also GCC countries's digital diplomacy
omnilateral diplomacy
  analogue–digital spectrum, tendencies
    in 324
  definition 323
  NGOs 323–24
  omnilateral diplomacy's digital culture 313,
    323–25
  see also digital diplomatic cultures
Ong, J. C. 85, 86
online diplomacy *see* digital diplomacy
Open Secrets 89–90
Oppenheimer, Robert 431–32
Orden, H. 91
Orwell, George 68
O'Shaughnessy, N. J. 224–25
Oxford Internet Institute 89

P

Painter, Christopher 128
Pakistan
  digital games and nationalist agenda 19–
    20, 610–13
  ISPR (Inter Service Public Relations
    Pakistan) 610
  UN permanent mission 339
Pamment, James 16, 81, 82, 91, 179–80, 323–24,
  406, 568
Panama 553
  see also Latin America digital diplomacy
Park, H. W. 532
Park, S. 532
PayPal 423
Pelosi, Nancy 242
Perlroth, Nicole 87

Peru 553–54
  see also Latin America digital diplomacy
Philip, Prince and Duke of Edinburgh 55
Philippines, the 530, 532, 533, 534
  foreign interference 537
  Public Diplomacy Handbook 534
  social media 534–35
  see also Asia Pacific digital diplomacy
phishing 73, 392
Piñera, Sebastián 557, 561, 592–93
Pinkerton, A. 390–91
PINs (Pacific Island Nations) 528n.1, 529, 540
  see also Asia Pacific digital diplomacy
Pirotte, G. 238
platforms
  data security 271
  deplatformization 243
  infrastructural influence of 197, 269–70,
    281–82
  parallel platformization 269–70, 271
  platformization 197, 224–25, 243
  platforms' algorithms 197, 269
  platform society 269–70
  politics of platforms as immersed in
    geopolitical tensions 271
  technical attributes of digital platforms 293
  see also Big Tech; TikTok
Plato 234, 239
Poland 20, 49, 223–24
policymaking
  at the back-stage 52–53
  on misinformation 81
  projection and retrieval and 42–43
politics of attraction 158, 159–60, 162–63, 174,
  175
polylateral diplomacy 395
  advocacy NGOs 322, 323
  analogue–digital spectrum, tendencies
    in 322–23
  civil society 321
  definition 321
  grassroots organizations and social
    movements 322, 323
  polylateral diplomacy's digital culture 313,
    321–25
  service NGOs 322, 323
  see also digital diplomatic cultures

Pompeo, Mike 517–18, 519–20, 592–93
populism 53, 70, 523
  China: populism/populist
    authoritarianism 511–12, 514–16, 522, 523
  Latin America 550
  populist leaders and social media 355
  as threat to nuclear order 145
Postman, N. 405
'post-truth' world 73–74, 76, 142–43, 243,
  361–62
  'post-truth culture' 213, 214–15, 221
  post-truth politics 243
Pottinger, Bell 89
Powell, Colin 183–84
power 596
  balance of power 4, 45, 242, 422
  coercive power 240, 241
  Neorealism 240
  Realism 240
  'sharp power' 66, 73, 220, 242
  see also hard power; soft power
PRC (People's Republic of China) see China
projection 31
  see also projection and retrieval
projection and retrieval 29–32, 42–43
  2014 Russian invasion of Crimea 38–40
  2022 Russian invasion of Ukraine 22, 32,
    39–43
  Canada at NATO 38–39
  counter-projections 39
  digital diplomacy and 30–31, 42–43
  dramaturgical theory of projection and
    retrieval 32, 33–39, 42–43
  feedback loop 22, 32, 36–38, 39, 42, 43
  policymaking and 42–43
  power of the audience and power of the
    performer 34–36, 38–39, 42–43
  projection/retrieval interaction 32, 43
  Russia 39–41
  social media 36–37
  states on a digital stage 36–39, 42
  states and social media 33, 36, 38
  Sweden 38
  Ukraine 39–40, 41–42
  US State Department 37–38, 39–40
  see also Goffman, Erving; projection;
    retrieval

propaganda 22, 65
  authoritarianism and 220
  China's 'Wolf Warrior' diplomacy and 514,
    522–24
  'deception effects', 'disruptive effects',
    'coercive effects' 220
  definition 82, 180, 215–16
  deterministic model of 83
  diplomatic summitry and 370–71
  global crises and 187–88, 221–22, 226
  as persuasion 212, 217–21, 226
  propaganda studies 81, 82, 83, 92, 213
  propaganda technologies 84–85
  as threat 217
  use of personal data for 420–21
  World War I and 187
  see also digital propaganda
public, the
  digital diplomacy and communication with
    the public 3–4, 105, 237, 513
  diplomats and 50
  disillusionment with global leadership 47
  domestic diplomacy 48, 50
public diplomacy 234–35, 404
  2022 Russian invasion of Ukraine
    and 189–90
  agenda for leadership in digital public
    diplomacy 189–91
  bilateral diplomacy and 314, 317
  Central Asian countries 508
  China 338–39
  Cold War 181–82, 183, 187, 188, 217
  core areas: listening, advocacy, cultural
    diplomacy, exchange diplomacy,
    international broadcasting 179, 189,
    234–35
  core objective 235–36
  digitalization of 217, 220, 235–36, 313–14,
    338
  digital media and crisis 178–80
  digital propaganda and digital public
    diplomacy 217–22, 218t, 226
  digital public diplomacy 177–78, 314
  EU digital diplomacy 459–60, 461, 466–67,
    468–69
  horizontal two-way communication 236
  Internet and 183–84

  Latin America digital diplomacy 549
  media disarmament 187–88, 190–91
  mediated public diplomacy 217
  multinational corporations, NGOs, cultural
    institutions 236
  NATO public diplomacy 477–78, 481–84,
    488
  new media technology disruption and
    global crises (historical perspective) 178,
    185–87, 188, 189, 190–91
  new public diplomacy 529, 530, 531–34
  non-state actors 236
  as persuasion 217–21, 226, 240
  propaganda and global crises 187–88, 221–
    22, 226
  'Public Diplomacy 2.0' 183–85, 241, 426
  radio and 180–82
  Russia–Ukraine War and 190
  satellite television and 183
  secret diplomacy/public diplomacy
    distinction 238
  social media and 178–79, 183, 184, 189, 217,
    236, 237, 240–41, 314, 513, 619
  terrestrial television and 182
  Ukraine 190
  UN and 338–39, 350
  US 624–25
  World War I 185–86, 187–88
  World War II 181–82, 186–87, 188
public diplomacy: ethical challenges of
    digitalization 16, 232, 243–44
  building trust vs fermenting chaos 233,
    242–43
  disinformation, computational propaganda,
    misinformation, and fake news 233
  exclusivity vs inclusivity 232, 233
  professionalization of public
    diplomacy 234–37, 243
  secrecy vs transparency 232–33, 237–39
  state vs public interest 232, 233, 239–41
  UK: Nazanin Zaghari-Ratcliffe's case 232
  US: Brittney Griner's case 232
  see also public diplomacy
public diplomacy: pattern for new technology
    introduction 19, 180, 190–91
  1st phase: symbolic use 19, 180, 181, 182,
    183

2nd phase: early application 19, 180, 181,
182, 183
3rd phase: mature application 19, 180, 181–
82, 183
see also public diplomacy
Purayil, M. P. 280–81
Putin, Vladimir 47, 58, 138, 217, 429, 629–32
nuclear threats by 150–51
see also Russia; Russian invasion of Crimea;
Russian invasion of Ukraine; Russia–
Ukraine War

Q

Qatar 565, 566, 567, 573, 574
2017–2021 Blockade 564–65, 567–71, 573
Al Jazeera 567–68
Qatar/Saudi Arabia tensions 567
QNA (Qatar's News Agency) 567
Twitter 568–69, 570
see also GCC countries's digital diplomacy
quantum computing 133–34, 422, 451
Qureshi, Waseem Ahmad 89

R

radio 6–7, 65, 313
public diplomacy and 180–82, 187
World War II and 186–87
Raessens, Joost 601–2
Ramos, Alejandro 21, 549, 554–55, 556
Rasmussen, Anders Fogh 353–54
Rawnsley, Gary D. 18
RCEP (Regional Comprehensive Economic
Partnership) 595–96
Reagan, Ronald 188, 315
Realism 238–39, 240, 372, 448, 450–51, 511–12
Rebolledo, A. 589
reflexive control 91, 215
refugee crises (Europe) 48–49
Regmi, B. 277
Rentetzi, Maria 140
Ren Zhengfei 591
Reporters Without Borders: *Minecraft* 600–1,
601f
retrieval 31–32
see also projection and retrieval
right-wing politics 58, 214
Ringsmose, J. 479

Rinkēvičs, Edgars 297
Riordan, Shaun 507, 582–83, 588
Roberts, C. 587
Robertson, Jeffrey 316–17, 532
Rodrigo, Olivia 273–74
Romero Vara, Laura 559, 560
Roosevelt, Franklin D. 186–87
Roosevelt, Theodore 180
Rosamond, Annika Bergman 482–83
Roselle, Laura 478–79
Ross, Alec 17, 426, 554–55
Rousseff, Dilma 584, 585, 593–94
Rumsfeld, Donald 65–66
Ruotsalainen, J. 405
Russia
2016 US elections, Russian intervention
in 21, 91, 123, 125–26, 128–29, 215, 319–20,
537
2016 Brexit referendum and 123, 319–20,
429, 537
2018 Skripal affair 189–90
2020 US elections, Russian intervention
in 85
2022 Russian invasion of Ukraine:
projection and retrieval 39–41
'black market' for campaign management
and technology 90
Bucha massacre 240
Cambridge Analytica and 90
censorship 126–27, 444, 630–31
Covid-19 vaccine (Sputnik) 54–55
cyberattacks and threats by 121, 122, 123–24,
125, 127, 128–29, 131, 585
cyber governance 438–39, 440, 441–42,
443–44, 446, 448–49, 451
cybersecurity 126–27, 129, 130
DDOS attacks by 121, 122, 127
DII 89–91
disinformation 189–90, 240, 243
Facebook 91
hacking by 123, 125–26, 128–29, 134
Internet governance 590
IRA (Internet Research Agency) 82, 89–90,
217–20
misinformation 39–40
nostalgic tropes in diplomacy 54–55
nuclear weapons 146–47

Russia (*cont.*)
   RT (state-funded international
      broadcaster) 150
   'sharp power' 66, 220
   state-sponsored digital propaganda 217–
      20, 225–26
   surveillance 125, 126–27, 444
   transparency performance 54
   Twitter 40–41
   tying Ukraine to Nazism 40, 58
   victimhood image 40–41
   Western liberal democracies/Russia
      rivalry 221–22
   see also BRICS countries; Soviet Union
Russian invasion of Crimea (2014) 48–49,
      189–90, 429
   NATO digital diplomacy on 478
   projection and retrieval 38–40
Russian invasion of Ukraine (2022) 22,
      189–90
   bilateral diplomacy and 315–16
   projection and retrieval 22, 32, 39–43
   Twitter 10, 10*f*, 40–42
Russia–Ukraine War (2022–present) 124
   bilateral diplomacy and 315–16
   condemnations of Russia and Putin 631–32
   data-driven influence arms race 89
   disinformation 189–90
   Facebook 51
   G7 leaders, virtual diplomatic summitry 13
   hybrid diplomacy 13
   information war 69–70
   international support for Ukraine 631–32
   memes on 47, 138n.1, 150–51
   NAFO on 138, 150–51
   NATO and 13, 421, 475–77
   NATO digital diplomacy on 477, 480, 484–
      87, 488
   public diplomacy and 190
   Russian national interests 240
   sanctions on Russia 51, 125, 423, 631–32
   social media and 150, 630–32
   soft power 69–70
   tech companies and 423
   transparency of diplomacy 51
   Twitter 12, 12*f*, 51, 150, 151*f*
   Ukrainian digital innovations 21–22

   Ukrainian digital struggle against
      Russia 10, 10*f*, 11–12, 12*f*, 422
   Ukrainian image front in 629–32
   video-conferencing 421
   Zaporizhzhya power plant 150, 151*f*
   see also NAFO; Russian invasion of Ukraine;
      wars and conflicts: digital diplomacy in

S

Saavedra, Pablo 353–54
Samuel-Azran, T. 627–28
Sandre, Andreas 20–21
Sanger, David 69n.1
Sarukhan, Arturo 546, 549
Sasley, B. 603
Satow, E. 106
Saudi Arabia 565, 566, 568, 573, 574
   Qatar/Saudi Arabia tensions 567
   Twitter 568–69, 570
   see also GCC countries's digital diplomacy
Schade, Daniel 319–20
Schelling, Thomas 495, 496n.10
Schneider, Cynthia 196, 197–98
Schneider, F. 607–8
Scholz, Olaf 56
School Strike for Climate 322
Schoorman, F. D. 242
Schou, J. 214
Schulzke, M. 605
Schwarzenegger, Arnold 8, 9*f*, 631–32
SCL (Strategic Communication
      Laboratories) 85, 87
Scotland, Patricia 353–54
SCOT theory (social construction of
      technology) 15
SDGs (Sustainable Development Goals) 253–
      54, 256–57, 462
SEACT (Southeast Asian Coalition on Tech
      Accountability) 539
Segerberg, A. 10–11
Segev, Elad 37–38, 74–75
selfies 52, 278–79, 370–71
   'national selfie' 74–75
Selimi, Petrit 427
Sevin, Efe 19–20, 316–17
Shanghai Cooperation Organization 127
Shapiro, Michael J. 602

Shires, J. 566
Sikkink, Kathryn 322, 386, 554
Silicon Valley 179–80, 271, 323, 429, 588
   Russia–Ukraine War and 423
   tech ambassadors to 297, 428
Simmel, Marianne 600
Singapore 532, 538–39
   see also Asia Pacific digital diplomacy;
      DEPA
Singularity (Ukrainian company) 89–90
Skype 337, 341, 573
Slovic, Paul 143
smartphones 51, 71, 73–74
   diplomatic negotiations and 104, 110
   smartphone applications 18–19, 20, 49, 50,
      427
SMD (social media diplomacy) 491–92,
      495–97
   as game of strategy 495, 496
   game theory and 492, 495, 505
   see also Central Asian countries and SMD
Smith, Courtney B. 330–31, 332–33, 336, 337
Smith, V. 82
Snow, Nancy 221–22
Snowden, Edward 583, 584, 593–94
Social Constructivism 450
social media
   2011 Arab Spring and 46–47, 427, 429,
      583–84
   Asia Pacific digital diplomacy and 529, 531,
      532, 534–35, 538, 539
   bilateral diplomacy and 314, 316–17
   China and 22, 75–76, 338–39
   China's 'Wolf Warrior' diplomacy and 511–
      12, 515–18, 520–21
   conflict escalation and 144, 476–77
   digital diplomacy 3–4, 5, 29–30, 421, 426,
      513, 619
   digital diplomacy in wars and conflicts 151–
      52, 619, 620–22, 623, 625, 630–32
   digital propaganda and 83, 213, 215, 216, 225
   diplomats and 426–27
   disinformation 355, 622
   disruption 189–90
   EEAS and 460–61, 463–64, 467–68
   embassies and 30, 291, 297, 421
   emotionality 8–9, 20, 243, 349, 564–65

   EU digital diplomacy and 18, 457, 460–61,
      463–64, 465, 467–68, 469, 470
   fake social media accounts 21, 429
   GCC countries and 564–65, 568–69, 573,
      574, 575
   global governance 360–61
   falsehoods 225
   international bureaucracies and 349, 350–
      53, 355–56, 357–59, 360–61
   Latin America digital diplomacy and 550,
      552–53, 552*f*
   leaking 105–6
   'likes' 52
   'masspersonal social engineering' 83, 91
   MFAs and 20, 21, 31–32, 38, 51, 52–53, 291,
      307–8, 427
   micro/macro-level disruptions 52–53
   misinformation 21, 467–68, 622
   NATO and 143, 145, 352–53, 355, 477–78
   NGOs and 387–88, 390–91
   nuclear diplomacy and 143, 144, 145–46,
      147, 148–50, 151–53
   performers/audiences interaction 33–34, 36
   populism 355
   projection and retrieval 36–37
   public diplomacy and 178–79, 183, 184, 189,
      217, 236, 237, 240–41, 314, 513, 619
   Russia–Ukraine War and 150, 630–32
   social media brands 20
   soft power 69–70, 72
   states and 33, 36, 38, 583–84
   as tool of political contestation 467–68,
      564–65, 583–84
   transparency 52
   UN and 350–51
   UN permanent missions and 334–35, 338–
      39, 343
   US State Department and 17, 36–37
   viral content 8, 349
   visual representation 20, 406
   see also Central Asian countries and SMD;
      Facebook; Instagram; projection and
      retrieval; SMD; Telegram; TikTok;
      Twitter; WhatsApp
soft power 75–76
   accountability 67, 68, 72, 74–75
   Berners-Lee, Tim 63–64, 75

672   INDEX

soft power (*cont.*)
  China 18, 64–65, 72–73, 75–76, 159–60
  civil society and 66, 67, 72, 75
  creation of soft power as long-term
    process 70
  credibility and 67, 73–75
  'credibility gap' between words and
    actions 74–75
  definition 65–70, 157, 159–60, 178–79
  digital space and 64, 65, 70–75, 76, 157–58,
    160, 263–64
  EU digital diplomacy 457–58, 462–63
  free flow of information/ideas 67, 71, 72,
    73, 75
  government interference 71
  'hard'/soft power distinction 66
  'hard'/soft power intersection 65, 69–70
  international relations discourse and 70
  Iran 71
  Israel 179–80
  Latin America 549
  limitations of soft power in the digital
    space 75–76
  markers of 67–68, 72, 160
  narratives 69–70, 73
  nation branding 160, 531
  Norway 38
  offline/online spaces interaction 64–65, 71,
    72–73, 76
  Russia–Ukraine War 69–70
  'smart power' 66
  social media and 69–70, 72
  soft power capacity 67, 72, 73, 74, 75–76
  South Korea 532
  states and 70, 157–58, 159–60, 236
  states and governments: digital space and
    soft power 64–65, 72–73
  surveillance 65, 72–73, 75
  transparency 67, 68, 72, 74–75
  UK 67, 68–69
  US 63, 64, 67, 68, 71, 74–75, 179–80
  Zewail, Ahmed 63, 64, 71, 75
  see also feminist foreign policy
South Korea 204, 532, 537
  digital 'citizenship diplomacy' 532
  MOFA (Ministry of Foreign Affairs) 532
  nation branding 538

  soft power 532
  see also Asia Pacific digital diplomacy
Soviet Union 139, 141, 181, 195–96
  see also Russia
Spector, J. Brooks 69
Spry, Damien 21
Sri Lanka 613–14
Standage, Tom 65
Starbird, Kate 83–84, 143
statecraft 18, 30, 430
  Central Asian countries 492, 506–7
  'collective financial statecraft' 587
  cybersecurity statecraft 121, 122–24, 134
  Latin America 546–47
  see also intelligence
states/governments
  cultural diplomacy and national
    governments 196–99, 201–2
  cultural diplomacy and state actors 195,
    200, 207
  digital space and soft power 64–65, 72–73
  DII and state actors 86–87, 89, 90, 92
  Internet shutdowns 392
  nation-branding 31, 37–38, 158, 404
  public diplomacy: state vs public
    interest 232, 233, 239–41
  social media and 33, 36, 38, 583–84
  soft power 70, 157–58, 159–60, 236
  sovereignty and cyberspace 437, 438, 441–
    46, 448, 451
  state capitalism 596
  states on a digital stage 36–39, 42
  see also nation-state
Stavridis, James, Admiral 122
Stengel, Richard 37–38
Stephenson, Neal 204
Stoltenberg, Jens 128–29, 353–54
Stopford, Michael 478
Strand, Sanna 483–84
STS (Science and Technology Studies) 115
Sullivan, Jake 592–93
Sun Tzu 240
Surowiec-Capell, Paweł 22, 221
surveillance 83, 387–88, 392, 422, 574–75
  China 72, 75, 126–27, 134, 205, 444,
    540, 589
  DII and 84–85, 87, 88

Facebook 73n.2, 584
GCC countries 565–66, 575
Huawei 540
mass surveillance 84–85, 584–85, 593–94
Russia 125, 126–27, 444
soft power and 65, 72–73, 75
surveillance capitalism 87, 588
targeted surveillance 65
Thailand 538–39
TikTok 540
US 584, 593–94
see also espionage/electronic espionage
Sweden
compact assemblages 302–3, 304, 305, 306, 307–8
digital diplomacy 183, 297, 425–26
digital hybridization of diplomacy 299–300, 301, 302
feminist foreign policy 158–59, 161–63, 165–68, 172–73, 175, 235, 339
nation-branding 183, 184, 235
NATO, accession to 475–76
projection and retrieval 38
soft power 'resources' 166–68, 167*f*
Sweden's UN permanent mission 339
Twitter Account @SweMFA 166–68, 167*f*
virtual embassy 17–18, 184
see also digital hybridization of diplomacy; feminist foreign policy
symbolic interactionism 31–32
see also Goffman, Erving
Syria 392
Syrian Civil War 48–49, 51
Szilard, Leo 141
Szostek, J. 221–22

T
Taiwan 254, 603–4, 604*f*
2016 Dibu Expedition 537
China's 'Wolf Warrior' diplomacy and 242, 243, 511–12, 520–22, 537
'digital democracy' 538
digital diplomacy 532, 534–35
see also Asia Pacific digital diplomacy
Tajikistan *see* Central Asian countries; Central Asian countries and SMD
Tallberg, Jonas 352n.6

Tamim Al Thani, Sheikh and Emir of Qatar 567, 568
Tang, Wenfang 514–15
TANs (transnational advocacy networks)
benefits of diplomacy digitalization 386–88
definition and characteristics 385–86
digital diplomacy and 19–20, 383–84
emerging trends 395–96
'new diplomacy' and 384–88
professionalization as diplomatic actors 389–90
TANs as digital diplomacy pioneers and innovators 388–91
see also NGOs; NGOs and digital diplomacy
tech ambassadors 5, 423–24, 428
Australia 428–29
CTR (Cyber and Tech Retreat) 428–29
Denmark 297, 428
fourth wave of diplomacy and 424
Global Network of Cyber and Tech Ambassadors 428–29
Silicon Valley, tech ambassadors to 297, 428
tech companies and 424
see also diplomats
technology
digital diplomacy: fighting with values in winning the global technological race 431–32
digital technology, dual nature of 422–23
digital technology, resistance to 13–14
as foreign and security policy 422–23
impact on society 420–22
technological disruption 3, 5–6, 45–46, 430
technological innovation 45, 420
technology companies as foreign and security policy actors 423–24
technology design 15
techno-nationalism 19–20, 605
unpeace/technological unpeace 124–25, 126, 130, 131
see also Big Tech; ICTs; tech ambassadors
Telegram
Central Asian countries 492–93, 497–98
diplomatic negotiations and 105
EU digital diplomacy 110, 341
NATO 477–78, 488

674 INDEX

telegraph/telegram 55, 65, 114–15, 180, 181, 421, 425–26
telephone 65, 184–85, 430, 584
television 5, 6–7, 65, 313, 370–71, 475, 605, 608–9
    China 159–60
    Cold War 187
    satellite television 183
    terrestrial television 182
Temple, John Henry (Lord Palmerston) 114–15
Tencent 423, 460–61, 603–4, 609, 611
terrorism 21, 402, 422
    9/11 attacks 183–84, 221–22, 624–25
    counter-terrorism 87, 222, 606, 610, 625–26
    digital games and 605, 606
    Global War on Terror 585
    multimedia formats and 605
    UK 48
    US war on terror 39, 74–75, 222, 624–25
Thailand 533, 537–39
    see also Asia Pacific digital diplomacy
Thomas, T. 215
Thunberg, Greta 371
Tibet 511–12, 514, 520–22
TikTok 20–21, 271–73, 281–82
    algorithmic governance 270, 282
    Amnesty International and 275
    ban of 273, 282
    ByteDance 269–70, 271, 281–82
    China as country of origin 270, 271, 272–73, 281–82
    China's use of TikTok for digital diplomacy 280–81
    Covid-19 pandemic and 275–77
    data security 271
    digital diplomacy and 270, 281–82
    diplomatic institutions on 273–78
    EEAS and 274–75
    election campaigns and 278
    embassies and 273–74
    geopolitics/algorithmic geopolitics 270, 271, 273, 281–82
    ICAN and 148–49, 274
    ICRC and 274
    IFRC and 274–75
    India and 273, 282

    influencers/creators and 273–74, 275–76, 277–78, 281
    infrastructural influence of the platform 269–70, 281–82
    Israeli-Palestinian conflict 628–29, 632–33
    KOL (Key Opinion Leaders) 274
    Malala Fund 277
    misinformation 276–77
    Musical.ly and 271–72
    parallel platformization 269–70, 271
    platform' algorithms 271
    published journal articles on 272–73
    security concerns 271, 272–73, 274, 281
    surveillance 540
    TikTok For Good 274–75, 277–78
    UN and 274, 275, 282, 338, 341
    UNHCR 277–78
    UNICEF and 274–75, 276
    US and 273, 282
    videos/TikToks 271, 274, 279–80, 281–82
    WHO and 276
    world leaders on 270, 278–81
    young user base 271–72, 274, 279–80
    see also social media
time and space
    digital technologies and 312, 394, 421
    virtual diplomatic summitry 368–69, 374–77, 379–80
    see also virtual diplomatic summitry
Topbas, Kadir 403–4
Towns, Ann 172–73
TPP (Trans-Pacific Partnership) 595–96
transnational corporations 423
    digital cultural diplomacy and 194–95, 197, 199, 203–4, 207
    multilatina corporations 554
transparency 19
    2014 Geneva 2 conference 51
    2015 Iran Deal 51
    actual transparency vs transparency performance 53–54, 114
    digital diplomacy and 3–4, 46, 160–61, 388, 395
    diplomats and 425
    EU digital diplomacy 114
    international bureaucracies and 354–55

international development cooperation
and 254
public diplomacy: secrecy vs
transparency 232–33, 237–39
Russia 54
sharing society and 51–53
soft power and 67, 68, 72, 74–75
strategic use of 47
suspicion and lack of diplomatic
transparency 53
transparency/truth distinction 54
virtual diplomatic summitry and 376–77
as virtue 52
see also micro/macro-level disruptions
Trinkunas, Harold 142–43, 144
trolling 138, 214
nuclear diplomacy and 138–39, 142–43, 144
'patriotic trolls' 537
troll farms 84–85, 84n.6, 429
Truman, Harry S. 139–40
Trump, Donald 10, 58, 128–29, 316–17, 377, 586
2016 election campaign 87–88
2020 election campaign 83–84, 85
China and 519–20
denial of global warming 233
Muslim Ban 67
'participatory propaganda' 83–84
racism 67
soft power and 67, 74–75
transparency performance 53–54
Twitter 29–30, 53–54, 143, 429
undiplomatic ways of 370–71
trust 242
disinformation and 47
public diplomacy: building trust vs
fermenting chaos 233, 242–43
Turkey 613–14
Izmir, digitalization of diplomacy 401, 402,
407, 410, 411, 413, 415
Twitter 46–47
Turkmenistan *see* Central Asian countries;
Central Asian countries and SMD
Turnbull, Malcolm 533
Tuvalu 262
Twitter (X) 5, 6–7, 349, 427, 625–26
2011 Arab Spring 427
2014 Russian invasion of Crimea 40

2022 Russian invasion of Ukraine 10, 10*f*,
40–42
Ai Weiwei 205–6
Aliyev, Ilham 29–30
ASEAN 235
Biden, Joe 29–30
broadcasting of summits, negotiations, and
deliberations 19
Canada 38–39
Central Asian countries 497–98, 499–500,
500*t*, 501–3, 502*t*, 503*t*
China 75–76, 242, 520–21, 523
CIA 51
cities and digitalization of diplomacy 413–
14, 413*t*
conflict escalation and 143
cultural diplomacy and 202–3, 205–6
cybersecurity 134
as digital diplomacy tool 161, 163–65, 173–
74, 427, 564–65
disruption from below and 16
domestic diplomacy and 48
emotional framing in 10, 10*f*, 564–65
EU digital diplomacy and 110–11, 114, 117,
457, 464–65
Fletcher, Tom 16
GCC countries 564–65, 567–71, 573
Germany 56
'human-centric' approach 163
IAEA 150, 151*f*
Iceland 427
international bureaucracies and 349–53,
353*f*, 359–60
Iran 10, 10*f*, 71
Israel 55–56
Israeli-Palestinian conflict 626–28
Kosovo 427
Latin America 548–49, 548*f*, 550, 551–52,
551*t*, 556*t*, 560
'likes' and 're-tweets' 52
mass removal of pro-US fake
accounts 90–91
MI6 51
NATO 38–39, 477–78, 480, 481, 485,
486–87
neoliberal tendencies 574–75
Nordic/Baltic countries comparison 298*t*

676 INDEX

Twitter (X) (*cont.*)
  nuclear diplomacy: US Strategic
    Command's nonsensical tweets 146,
    147–48, 148*f*
  nuclear diplomacy: US tweets about arms
    control with China 146–47
  Obama, Michelle 39
  Obama administration 48
  politwoops 31n.8
  Russia 40–41
  Russia–Ukraine War 12, 12*f*, 51, 150, 151*f*
  Trump, Donald 29–30, 53–54, 143, 429
  Turkey 46–47
  UK 16, 55
  UK FCO/FCDO 16, 48
  Ukraine 10, 10*f*, 11–12, 12*f*, 40, 41–42, 138
  UN 338, 342
  UN Secretariat 350–51
  US 145
  visual simplicity in 8, 9*f*
  see also feminist foreign policy; NAFO;
    social media

U

UAE (United Arab Emirates) 565, 566, 573,
  574
  censorship 567–68, 574
  Covid-19 pandemic 571–72
  Twitter 568–70, 574–75
  see also GCC countries's digital diplomacy
UK (United Kingdom)
  2012 London Olympics 63–64
  Arts and Humanities Research
    Council 201
  British diplomats and social media 16
  British Museum, digital nation-branding
    campaign 200–1
  cultural diplomacy 200–1
  cyber governance 444, 446–47, 449–50, 451
  cybersecurity 128, 130
  digital diplomacy 334
  DII and 90–91
  fake news 88
  MFAs 12, 20, 21, 48
  MI6 51, 123
  nostalgic tropes in diplomacy 55
  Online Safety Bill 444, 446–47, 450

soft power 67, 68–69
  Twitter 16, 55
UK: Brexit 55, 58, 319
  2016 Brexit referendum 68–69, 80, 223,
    420–21, 586
  2016 Brexit referendum and Russian
    intervention 123, 319–20, 429, 537
  as disaster/negative effects 64, 68–69, 586
  a 'political farce' 68–69
  UK as 'banana republic' 69
UK FCO/FCDO (Foreign and
  Commonwealth Office/Foreign,
  Commonwealth and Development
  Office) 20, 21, 48, 50, 68
  2018 Skripal affair 189–90
  blogs/blogosphere 48–49, 426
  Digital Strategy 334
  Twitter 16, 48
Ukraine
  2022 Russian invasion: projection and
    retrieval 39–40, 41–42
  'Brave Ukraine' 21–22
  EU, Ukrainian entry into 190
  hybrid-warfare against 179–80
  memes 20, 47, 138, 190
  MFAs 20, 40
  public diplomacy 190
  Twitter 10, 10*f*, 11–12, 12*f*, 40, 41–42, 138
  video-conferencing 190
  see also Russian invasion of Ukraine;
    Russia–Ukraine War; Zelenskyy,
    Volodymyr
Ulyanov, Mikhail 447–48
UN (United Nations) 182, 317–18
  Agenda 2030 253, 256, 462
  'bloc-diplomacy' 336
  climate change 351, 361–62
  COP26 UN Climate Change
    Conference 378–79
  COP27 UN Climate Change
    Conference 262
  Covid-19 pandemic 318, 337, 341, 343, 351,
    392
  decision making 332, 336
  Facebook 338, 342
  'first, second, third UN' 332, 334–35, 338,
    340

headquarters 332–33
Instagram 338
international development cooperation
    and 18, 250, 252–53, 256–62, 264–65
multilateral diplomacy 333, 341, 344
multilateral diplomacy's digital
    culture 317–19, 325
permanent missions 332–33, 343
polylateralism 321
public diplomacy 338–39, 350
social media and 350–51
TFM (Technology Facilitation
    Mechanism) 256
TikTok 274, 275, 282, 338, 341
Twitter 338, 342
UN 2.0 261
UN as personality-driven
    environment 343
UN reform 261
video-conferencing 335, 337, 340, 342, 343,
    392
WhatsApp 110, 336, 340, 341, 342, 425
Zoom 337, 340, 342, 392
see also cyber governance
UN: digitalization of permanent missions 18,
    330–31, 343–44
AI tools 343
challenges 331, 339–41
challenges experienced by diplomats 340–
    41, 343
China's permanent mission 338–39
confidentiality 341
consequences linked to digitalization 339,
    341–42
digital divide 331, 340–41, 344
digital ICTs in permanent missions'
    activities 333, 334, 335–39
gaining internal and external support in the
    digital sphere 337–39
Global South 339, 341
in-person meetings 340
marginalization of some missions 342, 343
messaging applications 335–37, 338, 342, 343
multilevel approach 331, 333–35, 343
Pakistan's permanent mission 339
socialization process 334
social media 334–35, 338–39, 343

New York permanent missions 330–31,
    332–33
Sweden's permanent mission 339
UN decision making and digital
    tools 335–37
UN Social Media Day 334–35
see also UN
UN Charter 127–29, 317–18, 350
    Chapter VII 318
UN CSD (UN Commission on Sustainable
    Development) 253
UNCTAD (UN Conference on Trade and
    Development) 255–56
UNESCO (UN Educational, Scientific and
    Cultural Organization) 188, 261
    ICOM (International Commission of
    Museums) 206
UN General Assembly 351, 360–61, 594
    formal regional groupings 336n.2
    hybrid diplomacy 318, 319
UNGGE (UN Group of Governmental
    Experts) 127–28, 131–32, 134
UN Global Pulse 256
UNHCR (UN High Commissioner for
    Refugees) 277–78
UN HLPF (UN High-Level Political
    Forum) 253, 256
UNICEF (UN International Children's
    Emergency Fund) 274–75, 276, 410, 415
UN IGF (Internet Governance Forum) 255–
    56, 439
UN OEWG (Open-Ended Working
    Group) 131–32, 134, 439–40, 449, 450–51
UN Secretariat 256, 274, 318–19, 332, 334–35,
    350
    Department of Global
    Communications 318–19, 350–51
    digital diplomacy 350–51, 353–54, 355–56,
    358–62
    Facebook 351
    Goodwill Ambassadors
    programmes 318–19
    Messenger of Peace programmes 318–19
    Social Media Team 350–51, 355–56, 358–59
    Twitter 350–51
    see also international bureaucracies and
    digital diplomacy

678 INDEX

UN Secretary General 255–56, 257–61, 350, 487
  HLP DC (High-level Panel on Digital
    Cooperation) 257
  Our Common Agenda 257–61
  Roadmap for Digital Cooperation 257, 259t,
    261–62
UN Security Council 319
  2015 Iran Nuclear Deal 465
  confidentiality 318
  in-person meetings 318
  Mexico's non-permanent seat 169, 172–73
  Resolution 1325 318, 481
  Resolution 2250 on Youth, Peace, and
    Security 318
  sessions in YouTube 51, 425
  Sweden's non-permanent seat 169, 172–73
  voting system 51
upgrading diplomacy 4–5, 22–23, 301, 304–5,
  469, 595
US (United States)
  3D approach (Defence, Diplomacy, and
    Development) 253
  5G 591, 592–93
  6 January 2021 91, 519–20, 522
  1996 Communications Decency Act 444–
    45, 449
  2016 elections 80, 420–21
  2016 elections and Russian intervention 21,
    91, 123, 125–26, 128–29, 215, 319–20, 537
  2020 elections 85, 91
  China/US rivalry 422, 442–43, 445, 517–18,
    519–20, 528, 536–37, 582, 592–93, 595–96,
    597
  China/US trade war 511, 597
  cultural diplomacy 196–98, 199, 200–2
  cyber governance 444–45, 447–49, 451
  cybersecurity 128–29, 130
  DARPA (Defense Advanced Research
    Projects Agency) 87
  Department of Commerce 582, 590
  digital diplomacy 334, 584
  digital diplomacy in wars and conflicts: US's
    activity in the Middle East 624–26
  DII and 87, 90–91
  Guggenheim Museum 200–1
  IDFC (International Development
    Financial Corporation) 592

  international development 254, 263
  Internet governance 582, 585–86, 588, 590–
    91, 594, 596
  MFAs 20, 48
  New York, digitalization of diplomacy 402,
    407, 409–10, 411, 413
  New York, MOIA (Mayor's Office of
    International Affairs) 407–8, 409–10,
    416
  North–South divide and 582, 584, 585–86,
    588, 590, 593, 596
  NSA (National Security Agency) 584,
    593–94
  nuclear weapons 139–40, 141, 145, 146–47
  public diplomacy 624–25
  soft power 63, 64, 67, 68, 71, 74–75, 179–80
  surveillance 584, 593–94
  TikTok and 273, 282
  Twitter 145
  war on terror 39, 74–75, 222, 624–25
US State Department 183–84
  'Country Reports on Terrorism' 570–71
  digital technologies and 17, 20, 425, 584
  DOT (Digital Outreach Team) 625
  projection and retrieval 37–38, 39–40
  social media 17, 36–37
  Taskforce on eDiplomacy 624–25
Uzbekistan *see* Central Asian countries;
    Central Asian countries and SMD

V

Van Dijck, Jose 203
Van Rij, Armida L.M. 68
Ven Bruusgaard, Kristin 143
Venegas, Alberto 609
Venezuela 550, 552, 553
  see also Latin America digital diplomacy
Vériter, S. L. 224
video-conferencing
  Central Asian countries 492–93
  Covid-19 pandemic 13, 108, 337, 421, 433
  digital ICT 330, 335, 337
  diplomatic negotiations 104, 105
  embassies 13
  EU digital diplomacy 108, 110
  IOs 330
  Russia–Ukraine War 421

Ukraine 190
UN and 335, 337, 340, 342, 343, 392
virtual diplomatic summitry and 368, 374, 377
Zelensky, Volodymyr 190, 318
see also Microsoft Teams; Skype; Webex; Zoom
video games *see* digital games
Vietnam 387–88, 533, 539
see also Asia Pacific digital diplomacy
Villanueva, César 556–57
Virdee, Satnam 58
virtual diplomatic summitry 22, 51, 367–69, 379–80
advantages 371, 375, 378–80
challenges 371, 373, 375, 376, 378
in context of crises 375
Covid-19 pandemic and 367–68, 371–72, 375–76, 377–79
definition 368, 376
difference between face-to-face and virtual interaction 378
diplomatic entanglements and 377–79
diplomatic summitry: from institutionalization to digitalization 369–72
G7 summits 13, 377
G20 summits 375, 377
hybrid meetings 367–68, 371–72, 377–79
impact of 103–4, 375, 376–77
interactionist perspective on 373
multilateral diplomacy and 368, 371–72
rationalist perspective on 373
realist perspective on 372
relational perspective on 368–69, 374–77, 379–80
role of 372–73
'sited diplomacy' 374
transparency and 376–77
Zelensky, Volodymyr and 376
video-conferencing and 368, 374, 377
see also diplomatic summitry
viruses (computer viruses) 73
2012 'Shamoon' wiper virus 122–23
2017 wiper virus 'NotPetya' 124–25
visual culture/the visual 479–80
digital media and politics of emotions 602–6

geopolitics and visual culture 602, 603, 604–5
image war and visual images 620, 621, 622–23, 625–26, 630–31
social media and visual representation 20, 406
visual culture studies 602, 605–6
visual simplicity as digital grammar rule 7–8, 9f, 20
see also digital games; digital games and nationalist agenda
Vodafone 584
Von Neumann, John 431–32

W
Walker, Christopher 66, 73
Wallström, Margot 235
Waltz, K. N. 449
Wang, Yin 72
Wanless, A. 81, 82, 83
wars and conflicts 22
1998 Desert Fox bombings of Iraq 185
Afghanistan war 37–38
Anglo-Boer War 185
Gulf War 185
hybrid-warfare 179–80
Iraq war 37–38
Korean War 187
Nagorno-Karabakh dispute 29–30
nuclear war 139, 142–43, 146, 148, 150, 152–53
Spanish American wars 185
Syrian Civil War 48–49, 51
World War I 185–86, 187–88, 431–32
World War II 181–82, 186–87, 188, 243, 431–32, 600
see also Cold War; cyberattacks and threats; cyberwar; Israeli-Palestinian conflict; Russian invasion of Crimea; Russian invasion of Ukraine; Russia–Ukraine War; wars and conflicts: digital diplomacy in
wars and conflicts: digital diplomacy in 619–20, 632–33
asymmetrical conflicts 622–23
audience/target audiences 620–21, 624
civil society 621, 623, 625n.2, 631, 632

680 INDEX

wars and conflicts: digital diplomacy in (*cont.*)
coverage of war and conflicts 621, 622
crowdsourcing in war 150–52
disruption through crises 21–22
identity of the political actor 623
image war 620–24, 629–32
image war and digital diplomacy 624–32
Israeli-Palestinian conflict 626–29, 632–33
narratives and messages 623–24, 629–30
non-state actors 619
public opinion 622–23
'reverse asymmetry' effect 622, 623
social media 151–52, 619, 620–22, 623, 625, 630–32
technological unpeace 124
Twitter 625–26
Ukrainian image front in 2022 Russian invasion 629–32
US's activity in the Middle East 624–26
see also image war; Israeli-Palestinian conflict; Russian invasion of Ukraine; Russia–Ukraine War
Warsi, Sayeeda 68
WCED (World Commission on Environment and Development) 252–53
Webex 112–13, 337, 342
Weibo 72, 236, 280–81, 301, 318–19, 348–49, 350–51, 517–18, 537
Sina Weibo and Tencent Weibo 460–61
Weil-Dubuc, P.-L. 233
Weiss, Thomas G. 332
Wekesa, Bob 341
Welles, Orson 186–87
Wells, Ch. 213
Wells, David A. 312
Weng, L. 8
Westphalia Peace (1648) 317, 424, 431
WhatsApp
Covid-19 pandemic and 16
diplomatic negotiations 105
disruption from below 15–16
EU digital diplomacy 110, 111, 112–13, 116
improvisation and collective struggle to define new protocols 13–14
UN and 110, 336, 340, 341, 342, 425
WhatsApp diplomacy 336
see also social media

Wheeler, Nicholas J. 315
whistleblowing 81, 82, 85, 90, 420–21, 446–47
Whiting, Allen S. 513–14
WHO (World Health Organization) 49, 355, 571–72
Covid-19 pandemic 53, 54, 276, 559, 572, 573
TikTok and 276
Wibben, Annick T. R. 482
Widodo, Joko 533
Wikileaks revelations 107, 123
Wild West 19, 80, 444
Wilkinson, Cai 484–85
Williams, Heather 144
Wilson, Woodrow 233
Winseck, D. 585–86
Wiseman, Geoffrey 21, 313, 323, 536
Wooley, Samuel C. 143, 214
World Bank 252, 352–53, 371–72
Wright, Katharine A. M. 18, 145, 467–68, 482–83
WSIS (World Summit on the Information Society) 255–56
WTO (World Trade Organization) 590

X
Xi Jinping 22, 513, 514, 516–17, 522–23
Xinjiang 511–12, 514, 520–22

Y
Yahoo 584
Yarchi, Moran 22, 627–28, 629
YouTube
Central Asian countries 497–98
Israeli-Palestinian conflict 626–27
Li Ziqi 236
NATO 477–78
UN Security Council sessions in 51, 425

Z
Zaghari-Ratcliffe, Nazanin 232
Zaharna, R.S. 217–20, 241, 575–76
Zaiotti, Ruben 18
Digital Diplomacy and International Organisations 317
Zakaria, Fareed 69
Zarif, Javad 10, 10f, 71
Zayani, M. 566

Zelensky, Volodymyr 47, 150, 629, 630, 631–32
  video-conferencing 190, 318
  virtual diplomatic summitry and 376
Zeng, J. 269–70
Zewail, Ahmed 63, 64, 71, 75
Zhao Lijian 511–12, 517–18, 519–21
Zoom
  hybrid diplomacy and 13
  non-state actors and 394
  UN and 337, 340, 342, 392
'Zoom fatigue' 13
'Zoom Plus' 451
  see also video-conferencing
Zuboff, Shoshana 87, 588
Zuckerberg, Mark 428–29, 588